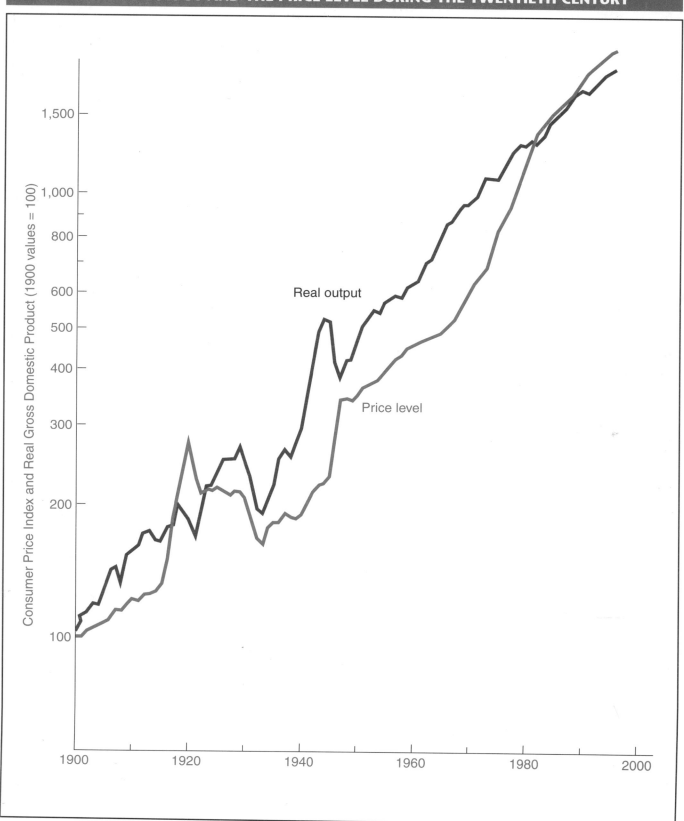

ECONOMICS

ECONOMICS

SIXTEENTH EDITION

PAUL A. SAMUELSON
Institute Professor Emeritus
Massachusetts Institute of Technology

WILLIAM D. NORDHAUS
A. Whitney Griswold Professor of Economics
Yale University

Irwin
McGraw-Hill

Boston   Burr Ridge, IL   Dubuque, IA   Madison, WI   New York   San Francisco   St. Louis
Bangkok   Bogotá   Caracas   Lisbon   London   Madrid
Mexico City   Milan   New Delhi   Seoul   Singapore   Sydney   Taipei   Toronto

Irwin/McGraw-Hill

A Division of The **McGraw·Hill** Companies

This book is printed on acid-free paper.

domestic   2 3 4 5 6 7 8 9 0   VNH VNH   9 0 0 9 8
international   2 3 4 5 6 7 8 9 0   VNH VNH   9 0 0 9 8

ISBN 0-07-057947-4

VP/Editorial Director: Michael Junior
Publisher: Gary Burke
Sponsoring editor: Lucille Sutton
Developmental editor: Kezia Pearlman
Marketing manager: Nelson Black
Project manager: Terri Edwards
Production supervisor: Tanya Nigh
Cover and interior designer: Suzanne Montazer
Compositor: York Graphic Services, Inc.
Typeface: New Baskerville
Printer: Von Hoffmann Press, Inc.

Library of Congress Cataloging-in-Publication Data
Samuelson, Paul Anthony. 1915–
    Economics / Paul A. Samuelson, William D. Nordhaus. — 16th ed.
      p.   cm.
    Also issued in two separate volumes under titles: Macroeconomics, sixteenth ed. and Microeconomics, sixteenth ed.
    Includes index.
    ISBN 0-07-057947-4 (acid-free paper)
    1. Economics.   I. Nordhaus, William D. II. Samuelson, Paul Anthony, 1915– Macroeconomics. III. Samuelson, Paul Anthony, 1915– Macroeconomics. IV. Title.
HB171.5.S25   1998   97-38915
330—dc21   CIP

When ordering this title, use ISBN 0-07-115542-2.

http://www.mhhe.com

ABOUT THE AUTHORS

PAUL A. SAMUELSON, founder of the renowned MIT graduate department of economics, was trained at the University of Chicago and Harvard. His many scientific writings brought him world fame at a young age, and in 1970 he was the first American to receive a Nobel Prize in economics. One of those rare scientists who can communicate with the lay public, Professor Samuelson wrote an economics column for *Newsweek* for many years and was economic adviser to President John F. Kennedy. He testifies often before Congress and serves as academic consultant to the Federal Reserve, the U.S. Treasury, and various private, nonprofit organizations. Professor Samuelson, between researches at MIT and tennis games, is a visiting professor at New York University. His six children (including three triplet boys) have contributed 15 grandchildren.

WILLIAM D. NORDHAUS is one of America's eminent economists. Born in Albuquerque, New Mexico, he was an undergraduate at Yale, received his Ph.D. in economics at MIT, and is now the A. Whitney Griswold Professor of Economics at Yale University and on the staff of the Cowles Foundation for Research in Economics. His economic research has spanned a wide variety of topics—including the environment, price measurement, energy, technological change, economic growth, and trends in profits and productivity. In addition, Professor Nordhaus takes a keen interest in economic policy. He served as a member of President Carter's Council of Economic Advisers from 1977 to 1979, was Provost of Yale University from 1986 to 1988, and writes occasionally for the *New York Times* and other periodicals. He regularly teaches the Principles of Economics course at Yale. Professor Nordhaus and his family live the urban life in New Haven, Connecticut, and share an enthusiasm for music, hiking, and skiing.

To

Our

Children

and

Students

CONTENTS IN BRIEF

Second exam 8, 9, 10, 12
20, 21, 25, 26
M   T   W

CONTENTS

PART THREE
FACTOR MARKETS: LAND, LABOR, CAPITAL, AND INCOME DISTRIBUTION
207

PART FOUR
GOVERNMENT'S ROLE IN THE ECONOMY
279

PART FIVE

MACROECONOMICS: THE STUDY OF GROWTH AND BUSINESS CYCLES
369

A NOTE FROM THE PUBLISHER

This is the fiftieth year that it has been our privilege and our pleasure at McGraw-Hill to publish Paul Samuelson's and, later, Samuelson and William Nordhaus's *Economics*. In that time, Professor Samuelson defined the field of economics in this remarkable book. Millions of students have been taught how economics can unravel the mysteries and problems of modern societies, problems that go to the heart of how, and how well, we live.

As William Nordhaus joined Professor Samuelson at the helm, this book continued to introduce later generations to the power of economic science. And as the ideas of monetarism, rational expectations, and supply-side economics captured the headlines, this book calmly included them in its presentation without crowding out the basic truths of the Keynesian and classical models. Today's students learn that economics can also shine a bright light on environmental problems, on dilemmas of health care, and on how to reckon the opportunity cost of a college education.

Keynes wryly observed, "In the long run, we are all dead." Now, sixteen editions later, I'm not so sure. We seem to have quite a pulse rate.

Gary Burke
Publisher

A GOLDEN BIRTHDAY

At its fiftieth birthday, this *Economics* has witnessed an exciting half-century of progress in economics. Our subject has come a long way. But there is so much farther to go before this, or any social science, can make pretense to be anywhere near an exact science. Economics will always be as much an art as a science, but still there's a world of difference between informed economics and just plain bad economics.

Today the number of jobs for economists has exploded. Statistical databases—inside government, in private industry, and within academia—are many times more comprehensive than they were in the late 1940s. Now information gets reported sooner, and computers give us access to statistical facts and knowledge with the speed of light. No branch of production has benefited more from the advance of computer hardware and technology than research in political economy itself. And that includes economic theory and applied economics.

And yet the fundamentals remain broadly intact. History—at least economic history—has taught the world certain basic economic principles that have been learned and tested the hard way. Repeated recessions and inflationary booms have been the economists' substitute for the chemists' controlled laboratory experiments. The tragic comedies of Russian and Chinese communistic organization of production and distribution have robbed three generations of the potential fruits of rising standards of material life. At the same time, the completely free market mechanism has not been able to bring all of humankind measurable near-equality of opportunity and outcome.

Because of "the poor we have always with us," the modern democratic state has evolved everywhere into a "mixed economy"—neither pure laissez-faire market mechanism nor Robin Hood utopia. Alas, only by their study of the rudiments of economics can the citizenry understand and decide about where should lie the *golden mean* between the selfishness of individual initiative and the regulatory, stabilizing, and redistributive functions of government. The mixed economy must, perforce, be the "limited mixed economy."

A Time to Look Back

A fiftieth birthday is a good time to look back. What is the story that emerges from this history of a trend-setting bestseller? How did this textbook come to be? Gaze back to 1945. Germany and Japan were defeated and American colleges were nearly overflowing with people returning from World War II. At the same time, the science of economics was entering a golden age. The Great Depression of 1929–1935 had finally been licked by forceful programs that threw out the window the old orthodoxies of do-nothing monetary and fiscal policies. Britain and America had later mobilized their economies for war in a way that Hitler, Mussolini, and Hirohito had never dreamed of. And, though we could not know it in 1945, the Marshall Plan and American occupation of Japan were about to set the stage for miraculous decades of postwar economic growth.

College students deserved to understand all this. But, as teachers of my generation knew to our sorrow, the best-selling economics textbooks were seriously out-of-date. No wonder beginners were bored. My students at Harvard and MIT often had that glassy-eyed look.

In 1948, when *Economics* was first published, the word "macroeconomics"—the study of what determines a society's unemployment, its price level and inflation rate, and its rate of overall real GNP growth—was not even in the dictionary! But had *Economics* not brought guns-and-butter choices into elementary microeconomics, someone, somewhere, would soon have done so. The time was ripe for a revolutionary approach to introductory economics. The real question is: Why me?

I was back from the MIT Radiation Laboratory, where I had worked at the mathematical job of designing automatic servomechanisms to ward off enemy bombers, and I "thirsted" for a return to economic research and teaching. And I was 30 years old, a good age to write a text or innovate a treatise. By chance, my advanced work, *Foundations of Economic Analysis,* which was to win me a Nobel Prize in economics 25 years later, was already in press.

However, in those days, a promising scholar was not supposed to write textbooks—certainly not basic texts for freshmen and sophomores. Only hacks were supposed to do that. But because I had already published so many research articles, it seemed that my reputation and prospects for lifetime tenure could allow me the elbowroom to respond positively to the request for a new textbook by my department head at MIT. Being cocky, even brash, in those good old days, I had only myself to please. And I agreed it was high time that we got some of the leaders in economic research back in the trenches of general education.

The Long Grind of Creation

Starting a project is easy. Bringing it to full term involves enormous labor and great travail. As soon as each chapter was written, the mimeograph machine ground it out for testing on our MIT students. I

found it demanding but pleasant work. But what I naively thought might be a year's job turned into three years of writing and rewriting. And my tennis suffered, as weekends and summer vacation had to be devoted to the task of reducing to plain and understandable prose the fundamental complexities of economic science. Even the traditional diagrams of economics, I discovered, needed redesigning if the "dismal science of economics" was to become the exciting subject it really is.

The Moment of Truth

In the autumn of 1948 the first edition of *Economics* rolled off the presses. No matter how hard the advance work or how optimistic the dreams, one can of course never be sure how the future will turn out. Fortunately, from the word go, this novel approach to economics seemed to have hit a responsive chord. Colleges big and small opted for the new book, and as each fresh printing was sold out, *Economics* was back again for new press runs.

When a Guggenheim fellowship took me to Europe, I checked each main bookstore in major cities for the availability of translations into French, German, Italian, Spanish, and Swedish. And in addition to experiencing the natural vanity of an author, I was pleased as an educator to see that the citizenry, who would be deciding global policies, was being exposed to the pros and cons of up-to-date mainstream economics.

Reviews of the book speeded up the bandwagon. The first came from the pen of John Kenneth Galbraith, then an editor of the conservative business magazine *Fortune.* He predicted that the next generation would learn its economics from Samuelson's *Economics.* And although praise is sweet to an author's ears, I confess that the durability of the book's dominance did surprise me. Galbraith turned out to be more prescient than I, and *Economics* did set a new and lasting pattern. Most of its successful rivals have been written in its general evolving mode, and it is heartwarming that much of the competition has come from the pens of personal friends.

Rough Pebbles along the Way

Not always has it been fun and games. In the reactionary days of Senator Joseph McCarthy, when accusations of radicalism were being launched from the pulpit and in the classroom, my book got its share of condemnation. A conservative alumnus of MIT warned university president Karl Compton that Paul Samuelson would jeopardize his scholarly reputation if he were allowed to publish his apologetics for the "mixed economy." Dr. Compton replied that the day his faculty was subjected to censorship would be the day of his resignation from office. It all seems slightly comical four decades later, but it was no joke to be a teacher at a public university when many of the fashionable textbooks of the time were being denounced as subversive. (One excellent text, which came out a year before mine, was killed in its infancy by vicious charges of Marxism that were false from the beginning.) Actually, when your cheek is smacked from the Right, the pain may be assuaged in part by a slap from the Left. *Anti-Samuelson,* a two-volume critique authored in the 1960s when student activism was boiling over on campuses here and abroad, portrayed me as an apologist for the laissez-faire world of markets where dog eats dog, a veritable running jackal of capitalism.

Each cold wind imparts a useful lesson, and I learned to write with special care wherever controversial matters were concerned. It was certainly not that I was perfect in all things. Rather, it was that I could only gain by leaning over backward to state fairly the arguments against the positions popular in mainstream economics.

And by dealing carefully and fully with the contending schools within the mainstream, the work kept its representative status as a reference source book. Even Soviet Russia had felt a translation was mandatory, and within a month the entire supply of translated copies had been exhausted. (Experts tell me that in Stalin's day my book was kept on the special reserve shelf in the library, along with books on sex, forbidden to all but the specially licensed readers.) In the post–Cold War era, new translations have been authorized in Hungary, the Czech Republic, Croatia, Bosnia, Serbia, Romania, and other Eastern European countries as well as in China, Japan, Vietnam, and two-score other countries.

The Ever-Young Child

Just as a child takes on an individual identity distinct from a parent's, so it was with the *Economics.* At first I was in command of it; later it took over in its own right and came to be in charge of me. As the years passed, my hair turned from blond to brown and then to gray. But like the portrait of Dorian Gray, which never grew old, *Economics* remained forever 21. Its cover turned from green to blue and from brown to black; and now it turns to gold. Aided by hundreds of letters and suggestions to the author from students and teachers, the economics inside the covers evolved and developed. A historian of mainstream economic doctrines, like a paleontologist who studies the bones and fossils in different layers of the earth, could date the ebb and flow of ideas by analyzing how Edition 1 was revised to Edition 2 and, eventually, to Edition 16.

And so it went. Hard, hard work—but ever so rewarding. Finally came the day when the call of tennis was too strong to be denied. To McGraw-Hill I said: "I've paid my dues. Let others carry on as I enjoy the good life of an emeritus professor, cultivating the researches that interest me most." McGraw-Hill had a ready answer: "Let us find you a coauthor. We'll make a list of congenial economists whose competence and views you admire." And so the search for the perfect William Nordhaus began.

Yale is only 150 miles from MIT, and it was there that the real Nordhaus was to be found. It only helped that Bill had earned his Ph.D. at MIT. And in the days since then he has won his spurs serving on the President's Council of Economic Advisers and doing tours of duty in Cambridge (England), Delhi, and Vienna. Like Gilbert and Sullivan or Rogers and Hart, we turned out to be a most congenial team.

And so, as in the classic tales, we have lived happily ever after. What matters is that the book stays young, pointing to where the mainstream of economics will be flowing.

Science or Art?

Why has economics become in most colleges one of the largest elective courses? The reasons are many. Economics deals with the real life around us. On the job. At the store. When inflation comes, it hits us all. When recession strikes, the tide goes out for all the boats. And the early bird that seeks the worm needs to know about supply and demand. The same goes for the senior citizen constrained to live on a limited pension and for the young idealist determined to improve and reform society.

Good sense economics is not all obvious. The common sense you bring with you from home to college will not let you understand why a rich country and a poor country can both gain great benefit from free international trade at the same time. (And your senator won't understand the point either without taking a good course in *comparative advantage*.) On the other hand, *after* you have mastered instruction in so-called microeconomics and macroeconomics, there will remain no mysteries. If it doesn't make good sense, it isn't good economics.

A first course in economics will not make you a master of all its intricate and esoteric topics. But this I can tell you, based upon students' experience everywhere: your best course in economics will be your introductory course. After you have stepped into this new strange garden of ideas, the world will never be quite the same. And when, years from now, you look back on the experience, even what you didn't quite understand at the time will have perceptibly ripened.

Enjoy!

Paul A. Samuelson
Massachusetts Institute of Technology
Cambridge, Massachusetts
1998

PREFACE

1998 marks the fiftieth anniversary of this textbook. Over the last half-century, the economic world has changed enormously. In 1948, most people were living in piles of rubble from World War II, international financial markets were in a state of shock, and much of Eurasia was entering the long despotic night of socialist central planning.

Fifty Years of Economics

Economics at midcentury also lived in a different world. It was contending with the increasing virulence of business cycles, trying to explain depressions and hyperinflations and stock-market crashes, and debating the superiority of socialism and market capitalism.

At century's end, the economic world, and the world of economics, have evolved tremendously. America's total output has quadrupled in the last five decades, and the average real income has doubled during this period. Outside the United States, the changes are even more dramatic. Dozens of countries have rejected the socialist experiment and adopted market systems, and strong economic growth has been experienced in countries as diverse as Ireland, Botswana, and the Philippines. At no time in recorded history have so many enjoyed such a sustained period of economic growth as they have during the Great Peace of 1948–1998.

You might think that prosperity would lead to a declining interest in economic affairs. Paradoxically,

an understanding of the enduring truths of economics has become even more vital in the affairs of people and nations. The United States has grappled with slow growth in living standards and large government budget deficits, even as structural changes in American industries have shaken managers, workers, and entire communities. The world has become increasingly interconnected as computers and communications create an ever-more-competitive global marketplace. Countries like Russia or Poland, which are making the transition from central planning, need a firm understanding of the institutions of a market economy if they are to make a successful transition. At the same time, there is growing concern about international environmental problems and the need to forge agreements to preserve our precious natural heritage. All these fascinating changes are part of the modern drama that we call economics.

Fifty Years of *Economics*

For half a century, this book has served as the standard-bearer for the teaching of elementary economics in classrooms in America and throughout the world. Each new edition has distilled the best thinking of economists about how markets function and about what society can do to improve people's living standards.

But economics has changed profoundly since the first edition of this text appeared in 1948. Economics is above all a living and evolving organism. The need to keep *Economics* at the frontier in the rapidly evolving world economy affords the authors an exciting opportunity to present the latest thinking of modern economists and to show how the subject can contribute to a more prosperous world.

Our task in these pages is straightforward: to present a clear, accurate, and interesting introduction to the principles of modern economics and to the institutions of the American and world economy. Our primary goal is to survey economics. In doing this we emphasize the basic economic principle that will endure beyond today's headlines.

THE SIXTEENTH EDITION

Economics is a dynamic science—changing to reflect the shifting trends in economic affairs, in the environment, in the world economy, and in society at large. As economics and the world around it evolve, so does this book. Ten features differentiate this edition from earlier ones:

1. The Core Truths of Economics. Often, economics appears to be an endless procession of new puzzles, problems, and difficult dilemmas. But as experienced teachers have learned, there are a few basic concepts that underpin all of economics. Once these basic concepts have been mastered, learning is much quicker and more enjoyable. We have therefore chosen to focus on the central core of economics—on those enduring truths which will be just as important in the twenty-first century as they were in the twentieth. Microeconomic concepts such as scarcity, efficiency, the gains from trade, and the principle of comparative advantage will never lose their central role in economics as long as scarcity itself exists. The use of marginal analysis revolutionizes decision making. Students of macroeconomics must receive a firm grounding in the concepts of aggregate supply and demand and must understand the role of national and international monies. Students will learn the widely accepted theory of economic growth, but they should also understand controversial theories of the business cycle.

2. Innovation in the Economy. One of the striking features of the modern economy is the rapidity of innovations in virtually every sector. We

are accustomed to the dizzying speed of invention in computers, where new products and software appear monthly. Nowhere in recorded history do we find such a raid rate of improvement as has been seen for computers over the last three decades. But other sectors are also witnessing rapid innovation. The pulse of change is rapid virtually everywhere in the modern economy—we run in athletic equipment made of miraculous new materials and relax while listening to crystal-clear audio equipment. Our understanding of economic trends and policies must reflect this rapid change in our societies.

Economics is increasingly attentive to rapid innovation. In macroeconomics, new economic growth theories emphasize the importance of technology, invention, and human capital in the growth process. In microeconomics, we have included a new section on the economics of information, showing how externalities in the production of information and new technologies lead to market failures. A case study of the economics of the Internet explores the dilemmas of pricing information.

3. Innovation in Economics. In addition, we emphasize innovations in economics itself. Economists are innovators, and economic ideas can produce tidal waves when they are applied to real-world problems. Among the important innovations studied here is the application of economics to our environmental problems through "emissions trading" plans. Other important economic innovations discussed are improved regulatory mechanisms and radical ideas such as European monetary unification. One of the most influential economic innovations of the last few years involves the measurement of consumer prices. Economists have persuasively argued that better techniques for measuring prices show much more rapid improvement in the quality of goods and services; the striking implication of these analyses is that we may have dramatically underestimated the growth in living standards in recent years.

4. Small Is Beautiful. Economics has increased its scope greatly over the last half-century. The flag of economics flies over its traditional territory of the marketplace but also covers the environment, legal studies, statistical and historical methods, art, gender and racial discrimination, and even family life. But at its core, economics is the science of choice. And this means that we, as the authors, have to choose the most important and enduring issues for this text. In a survey as in a meal, small is beautiful because it is digestible.

Choosing the subjects for this text required many hard choices. To select these topics, we surveyed teachers and leading scholars to determine which ones were most crucial for an informed citizenry and a new generation of economists. We drew up a list of key ideas and said sad farewell to many appendices and sections. At every stage, we asked whether the material was, as best as we could predict, necessary for a student's understanding of the economics of the twenty-first century. Only when a subject passed this test was it included. The result of this campaign is a book that has lost more than one-quarter of its weight in the last two editions. Farming, labor unions, and Marxian economics have been trimmed to make room for environmental economics, information economics, and real business cycles.

5. Policy Issues at Century's End. Each generation of economists finds new challenges to contend with in the attempt to understand the evolving economic policy problems. Three areas that have been at the forefront of economics in the last decade have received expanded treatment in the sixteenth edition. As human societies grow, they begin to overwhelm the environment and ecosystems of the natural world around us. *Environmental economics,* presented in Chapter 18, helps students understand the externalities associated with economic activity and analyzes different approaches to making human economies compatible with natural systems. A second area of growing importance has been *health-care economics.* As humans become more affluent, they naturally pay more attention to their own health and longevity, and the result is a rapidly growing share of national output devoted to health care. But health care poses fundamental economic dilemmas as the principles of equality and universal coverage collide with the fact of scarcity. Chapter 19 analyzes these questions and presents some innovative ideas about how to resolve these dilemmas. A third growing area is international economics. A new Chapter 31 is devoted to *open-economy macroeconomics,* which studies the behavior of our economy when it is part of a larger world economy. Our treatment of international economics has been expanded and integrated

into every section of the text. In addition, we have reorganized the last part of the book to emphasize the major issues in the international arena.

6. The Incredible Shrinking Globe. A century ago, the leading military strategist of the age, Captain A. T. Mahan, declared in his important book *The Influence of Sea Power on History:* "Whether they will or no, Americans must now begin to look outward." President Bill Clinton echoed these words when he wrote about economic affairs, "There is simply no way to close our borders and return to the insular days. To try to do so would be an exercise in futility, doomed not only to fail but to lower living standards in the process." Americans are learning that no nation is an island. Immigration and international trade have profound effects on the goods that are available, the prices we pay, and the wages we earn. Labor economists have found that the surge of uneducated immigrants over the last two decades has been an important contributor to the declining real wages of unskilled workers. Development economists have found striking results regarding the impact of economic openness on economic growth. No complete understanding of modern economics is possible without a thorough grounding in the world economy. The sixteenth edition continues to increase the material devoted to international economics and the interaction between international trade and domestic economic events.

7. Advances in Modern Macroeconomics. One of the major obstacles to understanding modern economics is the proliferation of contesting schools of macroeconomics. Teachers often wonder how students can understand the subject when macroeconomists themselves are so divided. While many fret about the divisiveness of modern macroeconomics, we think it is a sign of health and prefer lively debate to complacent consensus.

The sixteenth edition analyzes all major schools of modern macroeconomics within the clear organizing synthesis of aggregate supply and demand. We show how macroeconomics of the Keynesian, old and new classical, supply-side, and monetarist varieties can be understood as emphasizing different aspects of expectations, market clearing, and aggregate demand. Each school is clearly presented and compared with its competitors in a balanced and evenhanded way. For each, the empirical evidence is presented and evaluated. The major schools are presented in Chapter 32, "The Warring Schools of Macroeconomics." But we also emphasize the importance of the *policy implications* of the different approaches. These questions are addressed in a completely reorganized Chapter 33 called "Policies for Growth and Stability," which examines the role of budget deficits and considers such issues as rules versus discretion.

Although much macroeconomic combat is devoted to arguing about the sources of the business cycle, one of the major recent developments in economics has been the resurgence of attention to the forces underlying long-run economic growth. Economists are increasingly examining the determinants of long-run economic growth, the sources of the slowdown in productivity growth, and the generation of innovation and new technological knowledge. Putting economic growth front and center is necessary if students are to understand modern debates about the role of government debt and deficits. The sixteenth edition reflects this revival by synthesizing growth theories and findings into the central section on macroeconomics. We include growth theory as an integral part of aggregate supply and potential output and have revised and moved the chapter on economic development to follow the material on economic-growth theory.

8. Triumph of the Market.

One leitmotif in this edition is what we call "rediscovery of the market." All around the world, nations are discovering the power of the market as a tool for allocating resources. The most dramatic examples were the fall of communism in the former Soviet Union and Eastern Europe and the breakdown of Chairman Mao's one-party bureaucracy in China. Nation after nation rejected the command economy and began to move to the market. In 1990, Poland embarked on a grand experiment of undergoing "shock therapy" by introducing markets into much of its economy. Russia started down the road by liberalizing prices in 1991 but seemed to take one step backwards for every two steps forward. Nowhere was the transition painless. Virtually every country found that the road to the market was filled with obstacles such as raging inflation, high unemployment, and sharp declines in real wages and output. But by 1997, signs of recovery were found in those transition economies that had moved decisively.

The market was rediscovered in market economies as well. Many countries deregulated industries or privatized industries that had been in the public sectors. The results were generally favorable as productivity rose and prices fell in those sectors. Countries were applying market principles to novel areas, for example, by allowing pollution permits to be bought and sold or auctioning off the radio spectrum. These topics are part of the sixteenth edition's analysis of how market economies promote efficiency but also of the need for limited public controls.

9. Emphasis on History and Policy.

Students study economics to understand the rapidly changing world around them. For this reason, economics is at its core an empirical science. It first aims to explain the world around us and then helps us devise economic policies, based on sound economic principles, that can enhance the living standards of people at home and abroad.

Drawing upon history, economic chronicles, and the experience of the authors, the sixteenth edition continues to emphasize the use of case studies and empirical evidence to illustrate economic theories. The rediscovery of the market is made vivid when we examine how central planning failed or the way the East Asian economies have grown so rapidly. The dilemmas involved in combating poverty become real when we understand the 1996 welfare reforms or the problems of the current health-care system. Our appreciation of macroeconomic analysis increases when we see how government deficits in the 1980s lowered national saving and slowed capital accumulation in the United States or when we examine the promises and pitfalls of the European Monetary Union.

The microeconomic chapters draw upon case studies, economic history, business decisions, and real-world experience to illustrate the fundamental principles. Examples such as the economics of addictive substances, the health-care crisis, the threat of greenhouse warming, the minimum-wage debate, performance regulation, trading pollution permits, and the history of stock markets help bring the theorems of microeconomics to life. Game theory becomes serious—and has striking implications—

when applied to pollution or winner-take-all games. Established ideas such as the negative income tax can be used in innovative ways to resolve seemingly impossible policy dilemmas such as providing universal and affordable health care.

This "hands-on" approach to economics allows students to understand better the relevance of economic analysis to real-world problems. The abstract notion of scarcity becomes concrete when we see its implications for whether we have a good job, a healthy environment, adequate health care, and a secure nest egg for our retirement.

10. Clarity. Although there are many new features in the sixteenth edition, the pole star for our pilgrimage in preparing this edition has been to present economics in a clear and student-friendly way. Students enter the classroom with a wide range of backgrounds and with many preconceptions about the way the world works. Our role is not to change their values. Rather, we want students first to understand the enduring economic principles and then to be able to apply them to make the world a better place for them, their families, and their communities. Nothing aids understanding better than a clear and simple exposition. We have labored over every page to improve this survey of introductory economics. We have received thousands of comments and suggestions from teachers and students and have incorporated their counsel in the sixteenth edition.

Optional Matter

Economics courses range from one-quarter surveys to year-long intensive honors courses. This textbook has been carefully designed to meet all situations. The more advanced materials have been put in separate appendices or specially designated sections. These will appeal to curious students and to students in demanding courses that survey the entire discipline thoroughly. We have included advanced questions for discussion to test the mettle of the most dedicated student.

If yours is a fast-paced course, you will appreciate the careful layering of the more advanced material. Hard-pressed courses can skip the advanced sections, covering the core of economic analysis without losing the thread of the economic reasoning. This book will challenge the most advanced young scholar. Indeed, many of today's leading economists have written to say they've relied upon *Economics* all along their pilgrimage to the Ph.D.

Format

The sixteenth edition employs a set of in-text logos and material to help illustrate the central topics. You will find three distinctive logos: warnings for the fledgling economist, examples of economics in action, and biographical material on the great economists of the past and present. But these central topics are not sitting off by themselves in unattached boxes. Rather, they are integrated right into the chapter so that students can read them without breaking their train of thought. Keep these logos in mind as you read through the text:

is a warning that students should pause to ensure that they understand a difficult or subtle point.

is an interesting example or application of the analysis, and often it represents one of the major innovations of modern economics.

presents biographies of important economic figures. Sometimes these are famous economists like Adam Smith, while at other times they are people who introduced economics into public policy.

New features in this edition include fresh end-of-chapter questions, with a special accent upon short problems that reinforce the major concepts surveyed in the chapter. Terms printed in bold type in the text mark the first occurrence and definition of the most important words that constitute the language of economics.

But these many changes have not altered one bit the central stylistic beacon that has guided *Economics* since the first edition: to use simple sentences, clear explanations, and concise tables and graphs.

For Those Who Prefer Macro First

Although, like the previous edition, this new edition has been designed to cover microeconomics first, many teachers continue to prefer beginning with macroeconomics. They may think that the beginning student finds macro more approachable and will more quickly develop a keen interest in economics when the issues of macroeconomics are encountered first. We have taught economics in both sequences and find both work well.

Whatever your philosophy, this text has been carefully designed for it. Instructors who deal with microeconomics first can move straight through the chapters. Those who wish to tackle macroeconomics first should skip from Part One directly to Part Five, knowing that the exposition and cross-references have been tailored with their needs in mind.

In addition, for those courses that do not cover the entire subject, the sixteenth edition is available in two paperback volumes, *Microeconomics* (Chapters 1 to 19 and 34 to 36 of the text) and *Macroeconomics* (Chapters 1 to 3 and 20 to 36 of the text).

Auxiliary Teaching and Study Aids

Students of this edition will benefit greatly from the *Study Guide.* This carefully designed aid has been prepared by Laurence Miners and Kathryn Nantz of Fairfield University who worked in close collaboration with us in our revision. Both when used alongside classroom discussions and when employed independently for self-study, the *Study Guide* has proved to be an impressive success. There is a full-text *Study Guide,* as well as micro and macro versions.

In addition, instructors will find the *Instructor's Resource Manual and Test Bank* useful for planning their courses and preparing multiple sets of test questions in both print and computerized formats. Moreover, Irwin/McGraw-Hill has designed a beautiful set of two-color overhead transparencies for presenting the tabular and graphical material in the classroom. The graphs and figures in this edition can also be viewed electronically as Powerpoint slides. The slides can be downloaded from our website (http://www.mhhe.com). These items can all be obtained by contacting your local Irwin/McGraw-Hill sales representative.

Economics in the Computer Age

The electronic age has revolutionized the way that scholars and students can access information. In economics, the information revolution allows us quick access to economic statistics and research. One of the new features of the sixteenth edition is the section "Economics and the Internet," which appears just before Chapter 1. This little section provides a road map for the state of economics on the Information Superhighway.

Two new interactive tutorials are available with this edition: *The Microeconomics and Macroeconomics Interactive CD-ROM* and *WinEcon.*

Developed by Charles Link and Jeffrey Miller at the University of Delaware, *The Microeconomics and Macroeconomics Interactive CD-ROM* offers students a rich, easy-to-use menu covering the six core topics in introductory economics. Both tutorials have a real-world focus: newspaper and magazine articles highlight economic concepts and interactive videos allow students to "interview" business leaders.

WinEcon is an interactive software package offering over 75 hours of tutorial material. It includes self-assessment questions and exams, economic databases, and an economic glossary and references to leading economic texts. It is the first computer-based learning package to cover the entire first-year economics syllabus. *WinEcon* combines two products in one: teaching software and student tools, and *WinEcon* Lecturer with tests, exam, course management, and customization program. *WinEcon* was developed at the University of Bristol with the help of the Teaching and Learning Technology Programme Economics Consortium (TLTP), a group of eight UK university economics departments.

Students can also purchase *The Power of Macroeconomics* and *The Power of Microeconomics,* which contain lessons directly tied to this text. *The Power of Macroeconomics* and *The Power of Microeconomics* are lively combinations of Powerpoint and audio designed to reinforce economics concepts. *The Power of Macroeconomics* and *The Power of Microeconomics* were developed by Peter Navarro at the University of California at Irvine, Graduate School of Management.

Acknowledgments

This book has two authors but a multitude of collaborators. We are profoundly grateful to colleagues, reviewers, students, and McGraw-Hill's staff for contributing to the timely completion of the sixteenth edition of *Economics*.

Colleagues at MIT, Yale, and elsewhere who graciously contributed their comments and suggestions include William C. Brainard, William Buiter, E. Cary Brown, John Geanakoplos, Robert J. Gordon, Lyle Gramely, Paul Joskow, Alfred Kahn, Richard Levin, Robert Litan, Barry Nalebuff, Merton J. Peck, Gustav Ranis, Paul Craig Roberts, Herbert Scarf, Robert M. Solow, James Tobin, Janet Yellen, and Gary Yohe.

In addition, we have benefited from the tireless devotion of those whose experience in teaching elementary economics is embodied in this edition. We are particularly grateful to the reviewers of the sixteenth edition. They include

Nik Mustapha Raja Abdullah, *University of Pertanian—Malaysia*

Marion Beaumont, *California State University—Long Beach*

Tom Beveridge, *The University of North Carolina—Greenville*

Erwin A. Blackstone, *Temple University*

Parantop Busu, *Fordham University*

Kevin Carey, *University of Miami*

Anthony Chen, *Woodbury University*

Jen-Chi Cheng, *Wichita State University*

Evangelos Djimopoulos, *Fairleigh Dickinson University*

George Euskirchen, *Thomas Moore College*

Gary Galles, *Pepperdine University*

Erwin Kelly, *California State University—Sacramento*

James F. McCarley, *Albion College*

Myra Moore, *Texas Christian University*

Ibrahim M. Oweiss, *Georgetown University*

Walter Park, *American University*

J. Hanns Pichler, *Economic Theory Institute*

Thomas Shea, *Springfield College*

Bo Shippen, *Macon University*

David Sisk, *San Francisco State University*

Sebastian Thomas, *St. Francis College*

Lawrence Weiser, *University of Wisconsin—Stevens Point*

George Zestos, *Christopher Newport University*

Students at MIT, Yale, and other colleges and universities have served as an "invisible college." They constantly challenge and test us, helping to make this edition less imperfect than its predecessor. Although they are too numerous to enumerate, their influence is woven through every chapter. The statistical and historical material was prepared and double-checked by Joseph Boyer and Andrew Pearlman. Nancy King and Glena Ames provided help in word processing. Marnie Wiss coordinated the editorial process at the authors' end.

This project would have been impossible without the skilled team from McGraw-Hill who nurtured the book at every stage. We particularly would like to thank, in chronological order to their appearance on the scene, Economics Editor Lucille Sutton, Developmental Editor Kezia Pearlman, Project Managers Sharla Volkersz and Terri Edwards, Production Manager Tanya Nigh, and Marketing Manager Nelson Black. This group of skilled professionals turned a pile of diskettes and a mountain of paper into a finely polished work of art.

A WORD TO THE SOVEREIGN STUDENT

You have read in the history books of waves of revolutions that shake civilizations to their roots—religious conflicts, wars for political liberation, struggles against colonialism and imperialism. Over the last decade, economic revolutions in Eastern Europe, in the former Soviet Union, in China, and elsewhere have wrenched those societies. Young people battered down walls, overthrew established authority, and agitated for democracy and a market economy because of discontent with their centralized socialist governments. Students like yourselves are marching, and even going to jail, to win the right to study radical ideas and learn from Western textbooks like this one in hopes that they may enjoy the freedom and economic prosperity of democratic market economies.

The Intellectual Marketplace

Just what is the market that Russian and Chinese students are agitating for? In the pages that follow, you will learn about the markets for stocks and bonds, French francs and Russian rubles, unskilled labor and highly trained neurosurgeons. You have probably read in the newspaper about the gross domestic product, the consumer price index, the stock market, and the unemployment rate. After you have completed a thorough study of the chapters in this textbook, you will know precisely what these words mean. Even more important, you will also understand the economic forces that influence and determine them.

There is also a marketplace of ideas, where contending schools of economists fashion their theories and try to persuade their scientific peers. You will find in the chapters that follow a fair and impartial review of the thinking of the intellectual giants of our profession—from the early economists like Adam Smith, David Ricardo, and Karl Marx to modern-day titans like John Maynard Keynes, Milton Friedman, and Robert Solow.

Skoal!

As you begin your journey into the land of markets, it would be understandable if you are somewhat anxious. But take heart. The fact is that we envy you, the beginning student, as you set out to explore the exciting world of economics for the first time. This is a thrill that, alas, you can experience only once in a lifetime. So, as you embark, we wish you bon voyage!

Paul A. Samuelson
William D. Nordhaus

ECONOMICS AND THE INTERNET

The electronic age has revolutionized our lives in many ways. The impact on scholars and students has been particularly profound because it allows inexpensive and rapid access to vast quantities of information. The Internet—which is a huge and growing public network of linked computers and information—is changing the way we shop, do business, share our culture, and communicate with our friends and family.

In economics, the information revolution allows us quick access to economic statistics and research. With just a few clicks of a mouse, we can find out about the most recent unemployment rate, track down information on poverty and incomes, or delve into the intricacies of our banking system. A few years ago, it might take weeks to dig out the data necessary to analyze an economic problem. Today, with a computer and a little practice, that same task can be done in a few minutes.

This book is not a manual for driving on the Information Superhighway. That skill can be learned in classes on the subject or from informal tutorials. Rather, we want to provide a road map which shows the locations of economic data and research. With this map and rudimentary skills at navigating the Web, you can explore the various sites and find a rich array of data, information, studies, and chat rooms.

Data and Institutions. The Internet is an indispensable source of useful data and other information. Since most economic data are provided by governments, the first place to look is the Web pages of government agencies and international organizations. A neat starting point for the government's economic statistics is *The White House Briefing Room* found on the Web at ***http://www.whitehouse.government/fsbr/esbr.html.*** This site will take you to the major statistical agencies of the federal government. Another place to find general data is the Department of Commerce, which encompasses the Bureau of Economic Analysis (BEA) (***http://www.bea.doc.gov***) and Census Bureau (***http://www.census.gov***). The BEA site includes all data and articles published in the *Survey of Current Business,* including the national income and product accounts, international trade and investment flows, output by industry, economic growth, personal income and labor series, and regional data.

The Census site goes well beyond a nose count of the population. It also includes the economic census as well as information on housing, income and poverty, government finance, agriculture, foreign trade, construction, manufacturing, transportation, and retail and wholesale trade. In addition to making Census publications available, the Census site allows users to create custom extracts of popular microdata sources including the Survey of Income and Program Participation, Consumer Expenditure Survey, Current Population Survey, American Housing Survey, and, of course, the most recent census.

The Bureau of Labor Statistics (*http://stats.bls.gov*) allows easy access to commonly requested labor data, including employment and unemployment, prices and living conditions, compensation, productivity, and technology. Also available are labor-force data from the Current Population Survey and payroll statistics from the Current Employment Statistics Survey.

A useful source for financial data is Federal Reserve Economic Data (*http://www.stls.frb.org/fred*). This site, hosted by the St. Louis branch of the Fed, provides historical U.S. economic and financial data, including daily interest rates, monetary and business indicators, exchange rates, balance-of-payments data, and price indices. In addition, the Office of Management and Budget (*http://www.access.gpo. gov/su_docs/budget/index.html*) makes available the federal budget and related documents.

Two other sites are useful entry points for U.S. government statistics. FedStats (*http://www.fedstats. gov*) provides links to over 70 government agencies that produce statistical information. Sources are organized by subject or by agency, and the contents are fully searchable. The Commerce Department operates a huge database at *http://www.stat-usa.gov,* but use of parts of this database requires a subscription (which may be available at your college or university).

International statistics are often harder to find. The World Bank (*http://www.worldbank.org*) has information on its programs and publications at its site, as does the International Monetary Fund, or IMF (*http://www.imf.org*). The United Nations website has links to most international institutions and their databases (*http://www.unsystem.org*). For many international comparisons, the Penn-World Tables are available at the National Bureau of Economic Research (*http://www.nber.org/pwt56.html*) as well as many other sites. Another good source of information about high-income countries is the Organisation for Economic Cooperation and Development, or OECD (*http:// www.oecd.org*). The OECD's website contains an array of data on economics, education, health, science and technology, agriculture, energy, public management, and other topics. Additionally, the CIA world factbook (*www.odci.gov/cia/publications/nsolo/wfb-all.html*) has a wide range of unspooky economic and other information about any country in the world.

Economic Research and Journalism. The Internet is rapidly becoming the world's library.

Newspapers, magazines, and scholarly publications are increasingly posting their writing in electronic form. Most of these present what is already available in the paper publications. Some interesting sources can be found at the *Economist* (*http://economist.com*), the *Wall Street Journal* (*http://www.wsj.com*), and the on-line-only *Slate* magazine (*http://www.slate.com*). Current policy issues are discussed at *http://www. policy.com,* and you can play budget games with the "National Budget Simulator" at (*http://socrates.berke-ley.edu:3333/budget/budget.html*).

For scholarly writings, many journals are making their contents available on-line. WebEc (*http://netec. wustl.edu/%7eadnetec/WebEc/journals.html*) offers a comprehensive list of links to economics journals. For working papers, the National Bureau of Economic Research (NBER) website (*http://www.nber.org*) contains current economic research. The NBER site also contains general resources, including links to data sources and the official U.S. business-cycle dates. More generally, Washington University maintains an archive of working papers from myriad sources, usefully organized by topic.

Two excellent general purpose websites for economics are Bill Goffe's *Resources for Economists on the Internet* (*http://econwpa.wustl.edu/EconFAQ/EconFAQ. html*) and WebEc (*http://netec.wustl.edu*).

Did someone tell you that economics is the dismal science? You can chuckle over economist jokes (mostly at the expense of economists) at *http://netec.wustl.edu/JokEc.html.*

A Word of Warning. Note that, because of rapid technological change, this list will soon be out of date. New sites with valuable information and data are appearing every day... and others are disappearing almost as rapidly.

Before you set off into the wonderful world of the Web, we would pass on to you some wisdom from experts. Remember the old adage, you only get what you pay for:

Warning: Be careful to determine that your sources and data are reliable. The Internet and other electronic media are notorious: easy to use and equally easy to abuse.

The Web costs you nothing, and that price may sometimes overstate its value. But there are many diamonds buried in the mountains of bits.

ECONOMICS

PART ONE
BASIC CONCEPTS

CHAPTER 1
THE FUNDAMENTALS OF ECONOMICS

It is not from the benevolence of the butcher, the brewer, or the baker that we expect our dinner, but from their regard to their own interest.

Adam Smith, The Wealth of Nations *(1776)*

A. INTRODUCTION

Pause for a moment to consider the paradoxical words above, penned in 1776 by Adam Smith, the founder of modern economics. That same year was also marked by the American Declaration of Independence. It is no coincidence that both ideas appeared at the same time. Just as the American revolutionaries were proclaiming freedom from tyranny, Adam Smith was preaching a revolutionary doctrine emancipating trade and industry from the shackles of a feudal aristocracy.

In the last two centuries, most of the world has experienced an era of unimagined prosperity. In the United States and other high-income countries, most people today can afford to buy far more than the bare necessities of food, clothing, and shelter. Superfast personal computers, high-tech home entertainment centers, and fast air transportation to any part of the globe are examples of an astonishing range of goods and services that have become part of everyday life. Developing countries have also seen their standards of living rise rapidly in recent years.

But widespread prosperity has not brought economic security. In an average year, 10 million Americans lose their jobs and almost 100,000 businesses go bankrupt. About 14 percent of households are designated as poor, and the number is almost 50 percent among households headed by black females. Many families worry about the catastrophic financial consequence of illness because they have no health insurance. The affluent society is an anxious society.

For most of human history, people who experienced economic misfortunes lived on the mercy of their families or friends. Starting about a century ago, governments introduced the "welfare state," which provided social insurance and income support to needy people. Gradually, poor people in rich countries got access to minimal levels of income, food, and health care. But rising taxes and growing government spending on health care and public pensions have produced a revolt of the middle class, which is the taxed class. In 1996, the United States removed its guarantee of income support for poor families. Everywhere, countries are rethinking the boundaries between state and market, trying to balance the growing need for providing public services with the increasing clamor for cutting taxes and shrinking government.

This is the age of the global marketplace. Today, money, goods, and information cross national borders more readily than ever before. In earlier times,

3

we did business with people down the street or in the next town, and we bought mainly local goods. Today, we ride in the "world car." Look at this world car or at a fast computer. It incorporates materials, labor, capital, and innovations from around the world. The rise of the global marketplace raises new challenges. Who can best adapt to increased foreign competition? Who can quickly adapt to the information age? The stakes are high. To the winners go the profits, while the losers lag behind.

For Whom the Bell Tolls

As you begin your studies, you are probably wondering, Why study economics? Understanding the role of government and the challenges of the global marketplace are only two reasons why people study economics today.

Some people study economics because they hope to make money. Others worry that they will be illiterate if they cannot understand the laws of supply and demand. Many people are interested in learning about how we can improve our environment or why inequality in the distribution of income in the United States has risen so sharply in recent years.

All these reasons, and many more, make good sense. Still, we have come to realize, there is one overriding reason for learning the basic lessons of economics: All your life—from cradle to grave and beyond—you will run up against the brutal truths of economics. As a voter, you will make decisions on issues—on the government deficit, on taxes, on free trade, on inflation and unemployment—that cannot be understood until you have mastered the rudiments of this subject.

Choosing your life's occupation is the most important economic decision you will make. Your future depends not only on your own abilities but also on how economic forces beyond your control affect your wages. Also, economics may help you invest the nest egg you save from your earnings. Of course, studying economics cannot make you a genius. But without economics the dice of life are loaded against you.

There is no need to belabor the point. We hope you will find that, in addition to being useful, economics is a fascinating field in its own right. Generations of students, often to their surprise, have discovered how stimulating economics can be.

SCARCITY AND EFFICIENCY: THE TWIN THEMES OF ECONOMICS

What, then, is economics? Over the last 30 years the study of economics has expanded to include a vast range of topics. What are the major definitions of this growing subject? The important ones are that economics[1]

- studies how the prices of labor, capital, and land are set in the economy, and how these prices are used to allocate resources.
- explores the behavior of the financial markets, and analyzes how they allocate capital to the rest of the economy.
- examines the distribution of income, and suggests ways that the poor can be helped without harming the performance of the economy.
- looks at the impact of government spending, taxes, and budget deficits on growth.
- studies the swings in unemployment and production that make up the business cycle, and develops government policies for improving economic growth.
- examines the patterns of trade among nations, and analyzes the impact of trade barriers.
- looks at growth in developing countries, and proposes ways to encourage the efficient use of resources.

This list is a good one, yet you could extend it many times over. But if we boil down all these definitions, we find one common theme:

Economics is the study of how societies use scarce resources to produce valuable commodities and distribute them among different people.

Behind this definition are two key ideas in economics: that goods are scarce and that society must use its resources efficiently. Indeed, economics is an important subject because of the fact of scarcity and the desire for efficiency.

Take **scarcity** first. If infinite quantities of every good could be produced or if human desires were

---

[1] This list contains several specialized terms from economics, and to master the subject, you will need to understand its vocabulary. If you are not familiar with a particular word or phrase, you should consult the Glossary at the back of this book. The Glossary contains most of the major technical economic terms used in this book. All terms printed in boldface are defined in the Glossary.

fully satisfied, what would be the consequences? People would not worry about stretching out their limited incomes, because they could have everything they wanted; businesses would not need to fret over the cost of labor or health care; governments would not need to struggle over taxes or spending, because nobody would care. Moreover, since all of us could have as much as we pleased, no one would be concerned about the distribution of incomes among different people or classes.

In such an Eden of affluence, there would be no **economic goods,** that is, goods that are scarce or limited in supply. All goods would be free, like sand in the desert or seawater at the beach. Prices and markets would be irrelevant. Indeed, economics would no longer be a useful subject.

But no society has reached a utopia of limitless possibilities. Goods are limited, while wants seem limitless. Even after two centuries of rapid economic growth, production in the United States is simply not high enough to meet everyone's desires. If you add up all the wants, you quickly find that there are simply not enough goods and services to satisfy even a small fraction of everyone's consumption desires. Our national output would have to be many times larger before the average American could live at the level of the average doctor or lawyer. And outside the United States, particularly in Africa and Asia, hundreds of millions of people suffer from hunger and material deprivation.

Given unlimited wants, it is important that an economy make the best use of its limited resources. That brings us to the critical notion of **efficiency**. Efficiency denotes the most effective use of a society's resources in satisfying people's wants and needs.

More specifically, the economy is producing efficiently when it cannot increase the economic welfare of anyone without making someone else worse off.

The essence of economics is to acknowledge the reality of scarcity and then figure out how to organize society in a way which produces the most efficient use of resources. That is where economics makes its unique contribution.

Microeconomics and Macroeconomics

Adam Smith is usually considered the founder of the field of **microeconomics,** the branch of economics which today is concerned with the behavior of individual entities such as markets, firms, and households. In *The Wealth of Nations*, Smith considered how individual prices are set, studied the determination of prices of land, labor, and capital, and inquired into the strengths and weaknesses of the market mechanism. Most important, he identified the remarkable efficiency properties of markets and saw that economic benefit comes from the self-interested actions of individuals. All these are still important issues today, and while the study of microeconomics has surely advanced greatly since Smith's day, he is still cited by politicians and economists alike.

The other major branch of our subject is **macroeconomics,** which is concerned with the overall performance of the economy. Macroeconomics did not even exist in its modern form until 1935, when John Maynard Keynes published his revolutionary *General Theory of Employment, Interest and Money*. At the time, England and the United States were still stuck in the Great Depression of the 1930s, and over one-quarter of the American labor force was unemployed. In his new theory Keynes developed an analysis of what causes unemployment and economic downturns, how investment and consumption are determined, how central banks manage money and interest rates, and why some nations thrive while others stagnate. Keynes also argued that governments had an important role in smoothing out the ups and downs of business cycles. Although macroeconomics has progressed far since his first insights, the issues addressed by Keynes still define the study of macroeconomics today.

The two branches—microeconomics and macroeconomics—converge to form modern economics. At one time the boundary between the two areas was quite distinct; more recently, the two subdisciplines have merged as economists have applied the tools of microeconomics to such topics as unemployment and inflation.

THE LOGIC OF ECONOMICS

Economic life is an enormously complicated hive of activity, with people buying, selling, bargaining, investing, persuading, and threatening. The ultimate purpose of economic science and of this text is to understand this complex undertaking. How do economists go about their task?

Economists use the *scientific approach* to understand economic life. This involves observing economic affairs and drawing upon statistics and the historical record. For complex phenomena like the impacts of budget deficits or the causes of inflation, historical research has provided a rich mine of insights. Often, economics relies upon analyses and theories. Theoretical approaches allow economists to make broad generalizations, such as those concerning the advantages of international trade and specialization or the disadvantages of tariffs and quotas.

A final approach is the use of statistical analyses. Economists have developed a specialized technique known as **econometrics,** which applies the tools of statistics to economic problems. Using econometrics, economists can sift through mountains of data to extract simple relationships. For example, in recent years people have argued about the impact of a higher minimum wage on employment. From dozens of studies, economists have concluded that it is *likely* that raising the minimum wage will reduce employment of low-wage workers. This knowledge is essential to policymakers who are struggling with the question of how high to set the minimum wage.

Budding economists must also be alert to common fallacies in economic reasoning. Because economic relationships are often complex, involving many different variables, it is easy to become confused about the exact reason behind events or the impact of policies on the economy. The following are some of the common fallacies encountered in economic reasoning:

- *The post hoc fallacy.* The first fallacy involves the inference of causality. *The post hoc fallacy occurs when we assume that, because one event occurred before another event, the first event caused the second event.*[2] An example of this syndrome occurred in the Great Depression of the 1930s in the United States. Some people had observed that periods of business expansions were preceded or accompanied by rising prices. From this, they concluded that the appropriate remedy for depression was to raise wages and prices. This idea led to a host of legislation and regulations to prop up wages and prices in an inefficient manner. Did these measures promote economic recovery? Almost surely not. Indeed, they probably slowed recovery, which did not occur until total spending began to rise as the government increased military spending in preparation for World War II.

- *Failure to hold other things constant.* A second pitfall is failure to hold other things constant when thinking about an issue. For example, we might want to know whether raising tax rates will raise or lower tax revenues. Some people have put forth the seductive argument that we can eat our cake and have it too. They argue that cutting tax rates will at the same time raise government revenues and lower the budget deficit. They point to the Kennedy-Johnson tax cuts of 1964, which lowered tax rates sharply and were followed by an increase in government revenues in 1965. Ergo, they argue, lower tax rates produce higher revenues.

What is wrong with this reasoning? This argument overlooks the fact that the economy grew from 1964 to 1965. Because people's incomes grew during that period, government revenues also grew, even though tax rates were lower. Careful studies indicate that revenues would have been even higher in 1965 had tax rates not been lowered in 1964. Hence, this analysis fails to hold other things (namely, total incomes) constant.

Remember to hold other things constant when you are analyzing the impact of a variable on the economic system.

- *The fallacy of composition.* Sometimes we assume that what holds true for part of a system also holds true for the whole. In economics, however, we often find that the whole is different from the sum of the parts. *When you assume that what is true for the part is also true for the whole, you are committing the fallacy of composition.*

Here are some true statements that might surprise you if you ignore the fallacy of composition: (1) If one farmer has a bumper crop, she has a higher income; if all farmers produce a record crop, farm incomes will fall. (2) If one

---

[2] Post hoc is shorthand for *post hoc, ergo propter hoc.* Translated from the Latin, the full expression means "after this, therefore necessarily because of this."

person receives a great deal more money, that person will be better off; if everyone receives a great deal more money, the society is likely to be worse off. (3) If a high tariff is put on the product of a particular industry, the producers in that industry are likely to profit; if high tariffs are put on all industries, most producers and consumers will be worse off. (4) When teachers grade on a curve, grades are a "zero-sum game": if one student performs well, he will raise his grade; if all students perform well, the average grade is unchanged.

These examples contain no tricks or magic. Rather, they are the results of systems of interacting individuals. When individuals interact, often the behavior of the aggregate looks very different from the behavior of individual people.

We mention these fallacies only briefly in this introduction. Later, as we introduce the tools of economics, we will reinforce this discussion and provide examples of how inattention to the logic of economics can lead you to false and sometimes costly errors. When you reach the end of this book, you can look back to see why each of these paradoxical examples is true.

COOL HEADS AT THE SERVICE OF WARM HEARTS

Since the time of Adam Smith, economics has grown from a tiny acorn into a mighty oak. Under its spreading branches we find explanations of the gains from international trade, advice on how to reduce unemployment and inflation, formulas for investing your retirement funds, and even proposals for selling the rights to pollute. Throughout the world, economists are laboring to collect data and improve our understanding of economic trends.

You might well ask, What is the purpose of this army of economists measuring, analyzing, and calculating? The ultimate goal of economic science is to improve the living conditions of people in their everyday lives. Increasing the gross domestic product is not just a numbers game. Higher incomes mean good food, warm houses, and hot water. They mean safe drinking water and inoculations against the perennial plagues of humanity.

They mean even more. Higher incomes allow governments to build schools so that young people can learn to read and develop the skills necessary to operate complex technologies. As incomes rise further, nations can afford deep scientific inquiries into biology and discover yet other vaccines against yet other diseases. With the resources freed up by economic growth, talented artists have the opportunity to write poetry and compose music, while others have the leisure time to read, to listen, and to perform. Although there is no single pattern of economic development, and the evolution of culture will differ around the world, freedom from hunger, disease, and the elements is a universal human aspiration.

But centuries of human history also show that warm hearts alone will not feed the hungry or heal the sick. Determining the best route to economic progress requires cool heads, ones that objectively weigh the costs and benefits of different approaches, trying as hard as humanly possible to keep the analysis free from the taint of wishful thinking. Sometimes, economic progress will require shutting down an outmoded factory. Sometimes, as when the formerly socialist countries adopted market principles, things get worse before they get better. Choices are particularly difficult in the field of health care, where limited resources literally involve life and death.

You may have heard the saying, "From each according to his ability, to each according to his need." Governments have learned that no society can long operate solely on this utopian principle. To maintain a healthy economy, governments must preserve incentives for people to work and to save. Societies can shelter for a while those who become unemployed, but if social insurance becomes too generous, people come to depend upon the government. If they begin to believe that the government owes them a living, this may dull the sharp edge of enterprise. Just because government programs derive from lofty purposes does not mean that they should be pursued without care and efficiency.

Society must find the right balance between the discipline of the market and the generosity of the welfare state. By using cool heads to inform our warm hearts, economic science can do its part in ensuring a prosperous and just society.

B. THE THREE PROBLEMS OF ECONOMIC ORGANIZATION

Every human society—whether it is an advanced industrial nation, a centrally planned economy, or an isolated tribal nation—must confront and resolve three fundamental economic problems. Every society must have a way of determining *what* commodities are produced, *how* these goods are made, and *for whom* they are produced.

Indeed, these three fundamental questions of economic organization—*what, how,* and *for whom*—are as crucial today as they were at the dawn of human civilization. Let's look more closely at them:

- *What* commodities are produced and in what quantities? A society must determine how much of each of the many possible goods and services it will make, and when they will be produced. Will we produce pizzas or shirts today? A few high-quality shirts or many cheap shirts? Will we use scarce resources to produce many consumption goods (like pizzas)? Or will we produce fewer consumption goods and more investment goods (like pizza-making machines), which will boost production and consumption tomorrow.
- *How* are goods produced? A society must determine who will do the production, with what resources, and what production techniques they will use. Who farms and who teaches? Is electricity generated from oil, from coal, or from the sun? With much air pollution or with little?
- *For whom* are goods produced? Who gets to eat the fruit of economic activity? Or, to put it formally, how is the national product divided among different households? Are many people poor and a few rich? Do high incomes go to managers or athletes or workers or landlords? Will society provide minimal consumption to the poor, or must they work if they are to survive?

Warning: In thinking about economic questions, we must distinguish questions of fact from questions of fairness. Positive economics describes the facts of an economy, while normative economics involves value judgments.

Positive economics deals with questions such as: Why do doctors earn more than janitors? Does free trade raise or lower wages for most Americans? What is the economic impact of raising taxes? Although these are difficult questions to answer, they can all be resolved by reference to analysis and empirical evidence. That puts them in the realm of positive economics.

Normative economics involves ethical precepts and norms of fairness. Should poor people be required to work if they are to get government assistance? Should unemployment be raised to ensure that price inflation does not become too rapid? Should the United States penalize China because it is pirating U. S. books and CDs? There are no right or wrong answers to these questions because they involve ethics and values rather than facts. They can be resolved only by political debate and decisions, not by economic analysis alone.

MARKET, COMMAND, AND MIXED ECONOMIES

What are the different ways that a society can answer the questions of *what, how,* and *for whom?* Different societies are organized through *alternative economic systems,* and economics studies the various mechanisms that a society can use to allocate its scarce resources.

We generally distinguish two fundamentally different ways of organizing an economy. At one extreme, government makes most economic decisions, with those on top of the hierarchy giving economic commands to those further down the ladder. At the other extreme, decisions are made in markets, where individuals or enterprises voluntarily agree to exchange goods and services, usually through payments of money. Let's briefly examine each of these two forms of economic organization.

In the United States and most democratic countries, most economic questions are solved by the market. Hence their economic systems are called market economies. A **market economy** is one in which individuals and private firms make the major decisions about production and consumption. A system of prices, of markets, of profits and losses, of incentives and rewards determines *what, how,* and *for whom.* Firms produce the commodities that yield the highest profits (the *what*) by the techniques of production that are least costly (the *how*). Consumption is determined by individuals' decisions about how to spend the wages and property incomes generated by their labor and property ownership (the *for whom*). The extreme case of a market economy, in which the government keeps its hands off economic decisions, is called a **laissez-faire** economy.

By contrast, a **command economy** is one in which the government makes all important decisions about production and distribution. In a command economy, such as the one which operated in the Soviet Union during most of this century, the government owns most of the means of production (land and capital); it also owns and directs the operations of enterprises in most industries; it is the employer of most workers and tells them how to do their jobs; and it decides how the output of the society is to be divided among different goods and services. In short, in a command economy, the government answers the major economic questions through its ownership of resources and its power to enforce decisions.

No contemporary society falls completely into either of these polar categories. Rather, all societies are **mixed economies,** with elements of market and command. There has never been a 100 percent market economy (although nineteenth-century England came close).

Today most decisions in the United States are made in the marketplace. But the government plays an important role in overseeing the functioning of the market; governments pass laws that regulate economic life, produce educational and police services, and control pollution. Most societies today operate mixed economies.

C. SOCIETY'S TECHNOLOGICAL POSSIBILITIES

Every gun that is made, every warship launched, every rocket fired signifies, in the final sense, a theft from those who hunger and are not fed.

President Dwight D. Eisenhower

Each economy has a stock of limited resources—labor, technical knowledge, factories and tools, land, energy. In deciding *what* and *how* things should be produced, the economy is in reality deciding how to allocate its resources among the thousands of different possible commodities and services. How much land will go into growing wheat? Or into housing the population? How many factories will produce computers? How many will make pizzas? How many children will grow up to play professional sports or to be professional economists or to program computers?

Faced with the undeniable fact that goods are scarce relative to wants, an economy must decide how to cope with limited resources. It must choose among different potential bundles of goods (the *what*), select from different techniques of production (the *how*), and decide in the end who will consume the goods (the *for whom*).

INPUTS AND OUTPUTS

To answer these three questions, every society must make choices about the economy's inputs and outputs. **Inputs** are commodities or services that are used to produce goods and services. An economy uses its existing *technology* to combine inputs to produce outputs. **Outputs** are the various useful goods or services that result from the production process and are either consumed or employed in further production. Consider the "production" of pizza. We say that the eggs, flour, heat, pizza oven, and chef's skilled labor are the inputs. The tasty pizza is the output. In education, the inputs are the time of the faculty, the laboratories and classrooms, the textbooks, and so on, while the outputs are educated and informed citizens.

Another term for inputs is **factors of production.** These can be classified into three broad categories: land, labor, and capital.

- *Land*—or, more generally, natural resources—represents the gift of nature to our productive processes. It consists of the land used for farming or for underpinning houses, factories, and roads; the energy resources that fuel our cars and heat our homes; and the nonenergy resources like copper and iron ore and sand. In today's congested world, we must broaden the scope of natural resources to include our environmental resources, such as clean air and drinkable water.
- *Labor* consists of the human time spent in production—working in automobile factories, tilling the land, teaching school, or baking pizzas. Thousands of occupations and tasks, at all skill levels, are performed by labor. It is at once the most familiar and the most crucial input for an advanced industrial economy.
- *Capital* resources form the durable goods of an economy, produced in order to produce yet other goods. Capital goods include machines, roads, computers, hammers, trucks, steel mills, automobiles, washing machines, and buildings. As we will later see, the accumulation of specialized capital goods is essential to the task of economic development.

Restating the three economic problems in terms of inputs and outputs, a society must decide (1) *what* outputs to produce, and in what quantity; (2) *how* to produce them—that is, by what techniques inputs should be combined to produce the desired outputs; and (3) *for whom* the outputs should be produced and distributed.

THE PRODUCTION-POSSIBILITY FRONTIER

Societies cannot have everything they want. They are limited by the resources and the technology available to them. Take defense spending as an example.

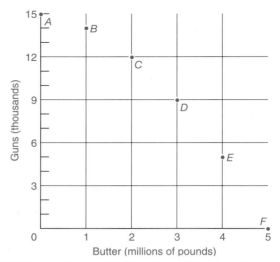

FIGURE 1-1. The Production Possibilities in a Graph

This figure displays the alternative combinations of production pairs from Table 1-1.

Alternative Production Possibilities

Possibilities	Butter (millions of pounds)	Guns (thousands)
A	0	15
B	1	14
C	2	12
D	3	9
E	4	5
F	5	0

TABLE 1-1. Limitation of Scarce Resources Implies the Guns-Butter Tradeoff

Scarce inputs and technology imply that the production of guns and butter is limited. As we go from A to B . . . to F, we are transferring labor, machines, and land from the gun industry to butter and can thereby increase butter production.

Countries are always being forced to decide how much of their limited resources goes to their military and how much goes into other activities (such as new factories or education). Some countries, like Japan, allocate about 1 percent of their national output to their military. The United States spends 5 percent of its national output on defense, while a fortress economy like North Korea spends up to 20 percent of its national output on the military. The more output that goes for defense, the less there is available for consumption and investment.

Let us dramatize this choice by considering an economy which produces only two economic goods, guns and butter. The guns, of course, represent military spending, and the butter stands for civilian spending. Suppose that our economy decides to throw all its energy into producing the civilian good, butter. There is a maximum amount of butter that can be produced per year. The maximal amount of butter depends on the quantity and quality of the economy's resources and the productive efficiency with which they are used. Suppose 5 million pounds of butter is the maximum amount that can be produced with the existing technology and resources.

At the other extreme, imagine that all resources are instead devoted to the production of guns. Again, because of resource limitations, the economy can produce only a limited quantity of guns. For this example, assume that the economy can produce 15,000 guns of a certain kind if no butter is produced.

These are two extreme possibilities. In between are many others. If we are willing to give up some butter, we can have some guns. If we are willing to give up still more butter, we can have still more guns.

A schedule of possibilities is given in Table 1-1. Combination F shows the extreme where all butter and no guns are produced, while A depicts the opposite extreme where all resources go into guns. In between—at E, D, C, and B—increasing amounts of butter are given up in return for more guns.

How, you might well ask, can a nation turn butter into guns? Butter is transformed into guns not physically but by the alchemy of diverting the economy's resources from one use to the other.

We can represent our economy's production possibilities more vividly in the diagram shown in Figure 1-1. This diagram measures butter along the horizontal axis and guns along the vertical one. (If you are unsure about the different kinds of graphs or about how to turn a table into a graph, consult the appendix to this chapter.) We plot point F in Figure 1-1 from the data in Table 1-1 by counting over 5 butter units to the right on the horizontal axis and going up 0 gun units on the vertical axis; similarly, E is obtained by going 4 butter units to the right and going up 5 gun units; and finally, we get A by going over 0 butter units and up 15 gun units.

If we fill in all intermediate positions with new rust-colored points representing all the different combinations of guns and butter, we have the con-

tinuous rust curve shown as the *production-possibility frontier,* or *PPF,* in Figure 1-2.

The **production-possibility frontier** (or *PPF*) shows the maximum amounts of production that can be obtained by an economy, given its technological knowledge and quantity of inputs available. The *PPF* represents the menu of goods and services available to society.

Putting the *PPF* to Work

The *PPF* in Figure 1-2 was drawn for guns and butter, but the same analysis applies to any choice of goods. Thus the more resources the government uses to build public goods like highways, the less will be left to produce private goods like houses; the more we choose to consume of food, the less we can consume of clothing; the more society decides to consume today, the less can be its production of capital goods to turn out more consumption goods in the future.

FIGURE 1-2. A Smooth Curve Connects the Plotted Points of the Numerical Production Possibilities

This frontier shows the schedule along which society can choose to substitute guns for butter. It assumes a given state of technology and a given quantity of inputs. Points outside the frontier (such as point *I*) are infeasible or unattainable. Any point inside the curve, such as *U,* indicates that the economy has not attained productive efficiency, as occurs when unemployment is high during severe business cycles.

The Production-Possibility Frontier

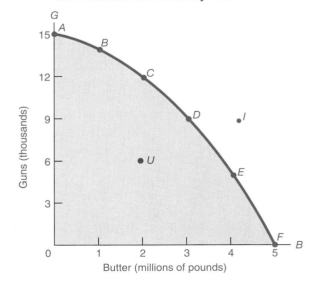

The graphs of Figures 1-3 to 1-5 present some important applications of *PPF*s. Figure 1-3 shows the effect of economic growth on a country's production possibilities. An increase in inputs, or improved technological knowledge, enables a country to produce more of all goods and services, thus shifting out the *PPF*. The figure also illustrates that poor countries must devote most of their resources to food production while rich countries can afford more luxuries as productive potential increases.

Figure 1-4 depicts the electorate's choice between private goods (bought at a price) and public goods (paid for by taxes). Poor countries can afford little of public goods like public health and scientific research. But with economic growth, public goods as well as environmental quality take a larger share of output.

Figure 1-5 portrays an economy's choice between (*a*) current-consumption goods and (*b*) investment or capital goods (machines, factories, etc.). By sacrificing current consumption and producing more capital goods, a nation's economy can grow more

rapidly, making possible more of *both* goods (consumption and capital) in the future.

The production-possibility frontier can also show the crucial economic notion of tradeoffs. To take one important case, time is scarce. People have limited time available to pursue different activities. For example, as a student, you might have 10 hours to study for upcoming tests in economics and history. If you study only history, you will get a high grade there and do poorly in economics, and vice versa. Treating the grades on the two tests as the "output" of your studying, sketch out the *PPF* for grades, given your limited time resources. Alternatively, if the two student commodities are "grades" and "fun," how would you draw this *PPF*? Where are you on this frontier? Where are your lazy friends?

Opportunity Costs

Life is full of choices. Because resources are scarce, we must always consider how to spend our limited incomes or time. When you decide whether

FIGURE 1-3. Economic Growth Shifts the *PPF* Outward

(a) Before development, the nation is poor. It must devote almost all its resources to food and enjoys few comforts. (b) Growth of inputs and technological change shift out the *PPF*. With economic growth, a nation moves from *A* to *B*, expanding its food consumption little compared with its increased consumption of luxuries. It can increase its consumption of both goods if it desires.

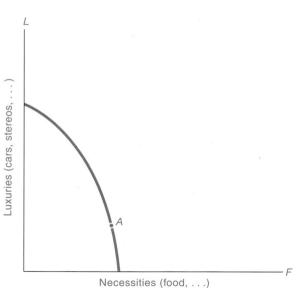

(a) Poor Nation

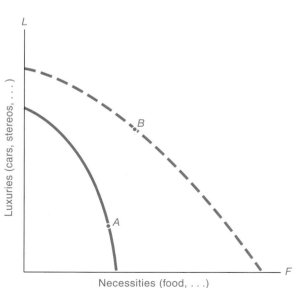

(b) High-Income Nation

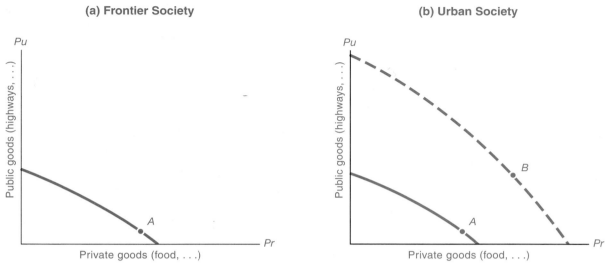

FIGURE 1-4. Economies Must Choose Between Public Goods and Private Goods

(**a**) A poor frontier society lives from hand to mouth, with little left over for public goods like superhighways or public health. (**b**) A modern urbanized economy is more prosperous and chooses to spend more of its higher income on public goods and government services (roads, environmental protection, and education).

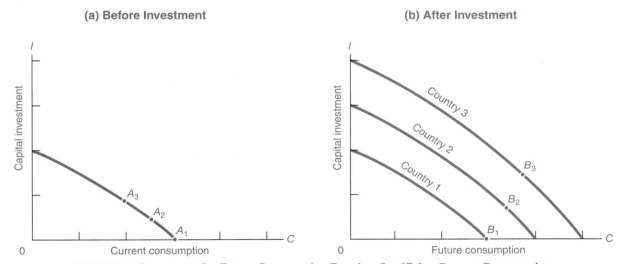

FIGURE 1-5. Investment for Future Consumption Requires Sacrificing Current Consumption

A nation can produce either current-consumption goods (pizzas and concerts) or investment goods (pizza ovens and concert halls). (**a**) Three countries start out even. They have the same *PPF,* shown in the panel on the left, but they have different investment rates. Country 1 does no investment for the future and remains at A_1 (merely replacing machines). Country 2 abstains modestly from consumption and invests at A_2. Country 3 sacrifices a great deal of current consumption and invests heavily. (**b**) In the following years, countries that invest more heavily forge ahead. Thus thrifty Country 3 has shifted its *PPF* far out, while Country 1's *PPF* has not moved at all. Countries that invest heavily have higher investment *and* consumption in the future.

to study economics, buy a car, or go to college, in each case you must consider how much the decision will cost in terms of forgone opportunities. The cost of the forgone alternative is the *opportunity cost* of the decision.

The concept of opportunity cost can be illustrated using the *PPF*. Examine the frontier in Figure 1-2, which shows the tradeoff between guns and butter. Suppose the country decides to increase its gun purchases from 9000 guns at *D* to 12,000 units at *C*. What is the opportunity cost of this decision? You might calculate the cost in dollar terms. But in economics we always need to "pierce the veil" of money to examine the *real* impacts of alternative decisions. On the most fundamental level, the opportunity cost of moving from *D* to *C* is the butter that must be given up to produce the extra guns. In this example, the opportunity cost of the 3000 extra guns is 1 million pounds of butter forgone.

Or consider the real-world example of the cost of opening a gold mine near Yellowstone National Park. The developer argues that the mine will have but a small cost because the fees for Yellowstone will hardly be affected. But an economist would answer that the dollar receipts are too narrow a measure of cost. We should ask whether the unique and precious qualities of Yellowstone might be degraded if a gold mine were to operate, with the accompanying noise, water and air pollution, and degradation of amenity value for visitors. While the dollar cost might be small, the opportunity cost in lost wilderness values might be large indeed.

In a world of scarcity, choosing one thing means giving up something else. The **opportunity cost** of a decision is the value of the good or service forgone.

Efficiency

All of our explanations up to now have implicitly assumed that the economy is producing efficiently— that is, it is on, rather than inside, the production-possibility frontier. Remember that efficiency means that the economy's resources are being used as effectively as possible to satisfy people's needs and desires. One important aspect of overall economic efficiency is *productive efficiency*. Productive efficiency occurs when an economy cannot produce more of one good without producing less of another good; this implies that the economy is on its production-possibility frontier.

Let's see why productive efficiency requires being on the *PPF*. Start in the situation shown by point *D* in Figure 1-2. Say the market calls for another million pounds of butter. If we ignored the constraint shown by the *PPF*, we might think it possible to produce more butter without reducing gun production, say, by moving to point *I*, to the right of point *D*. But point *I* is outside the frontier, in the "infeasible" region. Starting from *D*, we cannot get more butter without giving up some guns. Hence point *D* displays productive efficiency, while point *I* is infeasible.

Productive efficiency occurs when society cannot increase the output of one good without cutting back on another good. Productive efficiency means that an economy is on its production-possibility frontier.

One further point about productive efficiency can be illustrated using the *PPF*: Being on the *PPF* means that producing more of one good inevitably requires sacrificing other goods. When we produce more guns, we are substituting guns for butter. Substitution is the law of life in a full-employment economy, and the production-possibility frontier depicts the menu of society's choices.

Unemployed Resources and Inefficiency.
Even casual observers of modern life know that society has unemployed resources in the form of idle workers, idle factories, and idled land. When there are unemployed resources, the economy is not on its production-possibility frontier at all but, rather, somewhere *inside* it. In Figure 1-2, point *U* represents a point inside the *PPF;* at *U*, society is producing only 2 units of butter and 6 units of guns. Some resources are unemployed, and by putting them to work, we can increase our output of all goods; the economy can move from *U* to *D*, producing more butter and more guns and improving the economy's efficiency. We can have our guns and eat more butter too.

One source of inefficiency occurs during business cycles. From 1929 to 1933, in the Great Depression, the total output produced in the United States declined by almost 25 percent. This occurred not because the *PPF* shifted in but because various shocks reduced spending and pushed the economy inside its *PPF*. Then the buildup for World War II expanded demand, and output grew rapidly as the economy pushed back to the *PPF*. Similar forces were at work in much of the industrial world between 1990 and 1996 as macroeconomic factors pushed Europe and Japan inside their *PPF*s.

Business-cycle depressions are not the only reason why an economy might be inside its *PPF*. An economy might suffer from inefficiency or dislocations because of strikes, political changes, or revolution. Such a case occurred during the early 1990s in countries that threw off their socialist planning systems and adopted free markets. Because of the disruptive changes, output fell and unemployment rose as firms responded to changing markets and the new rules of capitalism. No period of history saw such sustained declines in output as the economies in transition experienced after 1990.

However, economists expect that this "real business cycle" will be but a temporary setback. Already, those economies that have made the most thorough reforms—such as Poland or the Czech Republic—have turned the corner and are beginning to recover. Their *PPF*s are once again shifting outward, and their incomes are likely to surpass the incomes of countries like Ukraine or Belarus, which have been reluctant reformers.

As we close this introductory chapter, let us return briefly to our opening theme, Why study economics? Perhaps the best answer to the question is a famous one given by Keynes in the final lines of *The General Theory of Employment, Interest and Money*:

> The ideas of economists and political philosophers, both when they are right and when they are wrong, are more powerful than is commonly understood. Indeed the world is ruled by little else. Practical men, who believe themselves to be quite exempt from any intellectual influences, are usually the slaves of some defunct economist. Madmen in authority, who hear voices in the air, are distilling their frenzy from some academic scribbler of a few years back. I am sure that the power of vested interests is vastly exaggerated compared with the gradual encroachment of ideas. Not, indeed, immediately, but after a certain interval; for in the field of economic and political philosophy there are not many who are influenced by new theories after they are twenty-five or thirty years of age, so that the ideas which civil servants and politicians and even agitators apply to current events are not likely to be the newest. But, soon or late, it is ideas, not vested interests, which are dangerous for good or evil.

To understand how the powerful ideas of economics apply to the central issues of human societies—ultimately, this is why we study economics.

SUMMARY

A. Introduction

1. What is economics? Economics is the study of how societies choose to use scarce productive resources that have alternative uses, to produce commodities of various kinds, and to distribute them among different groups. We study economics to understand not only the world we live in but also the many potential worlds that reformers are constantly proposing to us.

2. Goods are scarce because people desire much more than the economy can produce. Economic goods are scarce, not free, and society must choose among the limited goods that can be produced with its available resources.

3. Microeconomics is concerned with the behavior of individual entities such as markets, firms, and households. Macroeconomics views the performance of the economy as a whole. Through all economics, beware of the fallacy of composition and the post hoc fallacy, and remember to keep other things constant.

B. The Three Problems of Economic Organization

4. Every society must answer three fundamental questions: *what, how,* and *for whom? What* kinds and quantities are produced among the wide range of all possible goods and services? *How* are resources used in producing these goods? And *for whom* are the goods produced (that is, what is the distribution of income and consumption among different individuals and classes)?

5. Societies answer these questions in different ways. The most important forms of economic organization today are *command* and *market*. The command economy is directed by centralized government control; a market economy is guided by an informal system of prices and profits in which most decisions are made by private individuals and firms. All societies have different combinations of command and market; all societies are mixed economies.

C. Society's Technological Possibilities

6. With given resources and technology, the production choices between two goods such as butter and guns can be summarized in the *production-possibility frontier* (*PPF*). The *PPF* shows how the production of one good (such as guns) is traded off against the production of another good (such as butter). In a world of scarcity, choosing one thing means giving up something else. The value of the good or service forgone is its opportunity cost.

7. Productive efficiency occurs when production of one good cannot be increased without curtailing production of another good. This is illustrated by the *PPF*. When an economy is on its *PPF*, it can produce more of one good only by producing less of another good.

8. Production-possibility frontiers illustrate many basic economic processes: how economic growth pushes out the frontier, how a nation chooses relatively less food and other necessities as it develops, how a country chooses between private goods and public goods, and how societies choose between consumption goods and capital goods that enhance future consumption.

9. Societies are sometimes inside their production-possibility frontier. When unemployment is high or when revolution or inefficient government regulations hamper economic activity, the economy is inefficient and operates inside its *PPF*.

CONCEPTS FOR REVIEW

Fundamental Concepts

scarcity and efficiency
free goods vs. economic goods
macroeconomics and microeconomics
normative vs. positive economics
fallacy of composition, post hoc fallacy
"keep other things constant"
cool heads, warm hearts

Key Problems of Economic Organization

what, how, and *for whom*
alternative economic systems:
    command vs. market
laissez-faire
mixed economies

Choice Among Production Possibilities

inputs and outputs
production-possibility frontier (*PPF*)
productive efficiency and inefficiency
opportunity cost

QUESTIONS FOR DISCUSSION

1. The great English economist Alfred Marshall (1842–1924) invented many of the tools of modern economics, but he was most concerned with the application of these tools to the problems of society. In his inaugural lecture, Marshall wrote:

   It will be my most cherished ambition to increase the numbers who Cambridge University sends out into the world with cool heads but warm hearts, willing to give some of their best powers to grappling with the social suffering around them; resolved not to rest content till they have opened up to all the material means of a refined and noble life. (*Memorials of Alfred Marshall*, A. C. Pigou, ed. (MacMillan and Co., London, 1925), p. 174 with minor edits.)

   Explain how the cool head might provide the essential positive economic analysis to implement the normative value judgments of the warm heart. Do you agree with Marshall's view of the role of the teacher? Do you accept his challenge?

2. The late George Stigler, an eminent conservative Chicago economist, wrote as follows:

   No thoroughly egalitarian society has ever been able to construct or maintain an efficient and progressive economic system. It has been universal experience that some system of differential rewards is necessary to stimulate workers. [*The Theory of Price*, 3d ed. (Macmillan, New York, 1966), p. 19.]

   Are these statements positive or normative economics? Discuss Stigler's view in light of Alfred Marshall's quote in Question 1. Is there a conflict?

3. Define each of the following terms carefully and give examples: *PPF*, scarcity, productive efficiency, inputs, outputs.

4. In deciding how to use your scarce time and income, determine what the opportunity cost would be for you of going to a movie before your economics exam. What is the opportunity cost of buying a car?

5. Assume that Econoland produces haircuts and shirts with inputs of labor. Econoland has 1000 hours of labor available. A haircut requires ½ hour of labor, while a shirt requires 5 hours of labor. Construct Econoland's production-possibility frontier.

6. Assume that scientific inventions have doubled the productivity of society's resources in butter production without altering the productivity of gun manufacture. Redraw society's production-possibility frontier in Figure 1-2 to illustrate the new trade-off.

7. Many scientists believe that we are rapidly depleting our natural resources. Assume that there are only two inputs (labor and natural resources) producing two goods (concerts and gasoline) with no improvement in society's technology over time. Show what would happen to the *PPF* over time as natural resources are exhausted. How would invention and technological improvement modify your answer? On the basis of this example, explain why it is said that "economic growth is a race between depletion and invention."

8. Say that Diligent has 10 hours to study for upcoming tests in economics and history. Draw a *PPF* for grades, given Diligent's limited time resources. If Diligent studies inefficiently by listening to loud music and chatting with friends, where will Diligent's grade "output" be relative to the *PPF*? What will happen to the grade *PPF* if Diligent increases study inputs from 10 hours to 15 hours?

APPENDIX 1
HOW TO READ GRAPHS

A picture is worth a thousand words.

Chinese Proverb

Before you can master economics, you must have a working knowledge of graphs. They are as indispensable to the economist as a hammer is to a carpenter. So if you are not familiar with the use of diagrams, invest some time in learning how to read them—it will be time well spent.

What is a *graph*? It is a diagram showing how two or more sets of data or variables are related to one another. Graphs are essential in economics because, among other reasons, they allow us to analyze economic concepts and examine historical trends.

You will encounter many different kinds of graphs in this book. Some graphs show how variables change over time (see, for example, the inside of the front cover); other graphs show the relationship between different variables (such as the example we will turn to in a moment). Each graph in the book will help you understand an important economic law or trend.

THE PRODUCTION-POSSIBILITY FRONTIER

The first graph that you encountered in this text was the production-possibility frontier. As we showed in the body of this chapter, the production-possibility frontier, or *PPF*, represents the maximum amounts of a pair of goods or services that can both be produced with an economy's given resources assuming that all resources are fully employed.

Let's follow up an important application, that of choosing between food and machines. The essential data for the *PPF* are shown in Table 1A-1, which is very much like the example in Table 1-1. Recall that each of the possibilities gives one level of food production and one level of machine production. As the quantity of food produced increases, the production of machines falls. Thus, if the economy produced 10 units of food, it could produce a maximum of 140 machines, but when the output of food is 20 units, only 120 machines can be manufactured.

Production-Possibility Graph

The data shown in Table 1A-1 can also be presented as a graph. To construct the graph, we represent each of the table's pairs of data by a single point on a two-dimensional plane. Figure 1A-1 displays in a graph the relationship between the food and machines outputs shown in Table 1A-1. Each pair of numbers is represented by a single point in the graph. Thus the row labeled "A" in Table 1A-1 is graphed as point *A* in Figure 1A-1, and similarly for points *B*, *C*, and so on.

In Figure 1A-1, the vertical line at left and the horizontal line at bottom correspond to the two variables—food and machines. A **variable** is an item of interest that can be defined and measured and that takes on different values at different times or places. Important variables studied in economics are prices,

Alternative Production Possibilities		
Possibilities	Food	Machines
A	0	150
B	10	140
C	20	120
D	30	90
E	40	50
F	50	0

TABLE 1A-1. The Pairs of Possible Outputs of Food and Machines
The table shows six potential pairs of outputs that can be produced with the given resources of a country. The country can choose one of the six possible combinations.

quantities, hours of work, acres of land, dollars of income, and so forth.

The horizontal line on a graph is referred to as the *horizontal axis*, or sometimes the *X axis*. In Figure 1A-1, food output is measured on the black horizontal axis. The vertical line is known as the *vertical axis*, or *Y axis*. In Figure 1A-1, it measures the number of machines produced. Point *A* on the vertical axis stands for 150 machines. The lower left-hand corner where the two axes meet is called the *origin*. It signifies 0 food and 0 machines in Figure 1A-1.

FIGURE 1A-1. Six Possible Pairs of Food-Machines Production Levels

This figure shows the data of Table 1A-1 in graphical form. The data are exactly the same, but the visual display presents the data more vividly.

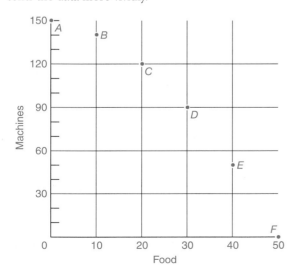

A Smooth Curve. In most economic relationships, variables can change by small amounts as well as by the large increments shown in Figure 1A-1. We therefore generally draw economic relationships as continuous curves. Figure 1A-2 shows the *PPF* as a smooth curve in which the points from *A* to *F* have been connected.

By comparing Table 1A-1 and Figure 1A-2, we can see why graphs are so often used in economics. The smooth *PPF* reflects the menu of choice for the economy. It is a visual device for showing what types of goods are available in what quantities. Your eye can see at a glance the relationship between machine and food production.

Slopes and Lines

Figure 1A-2 depicts the relationship between maximum food and machine production. One important way to describe the relationship between two variables is by the slope of the graph line.

The **slope** of a line represents the change in one variable that occurs when another variable changes. More precisely, it is the change in the variable *Y* on the vertical axis per unit change in the variable *X* on the horizontal axis. For example, in Figure 1A-2,

FIGURE 1A-2.

A smooth curve fills in between the plotted pairs of points, creating the production-possibility frontier.

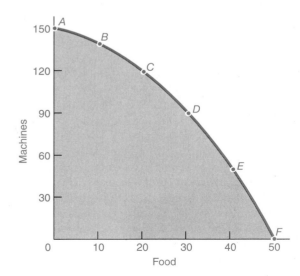

The Production-Possibility Frontier

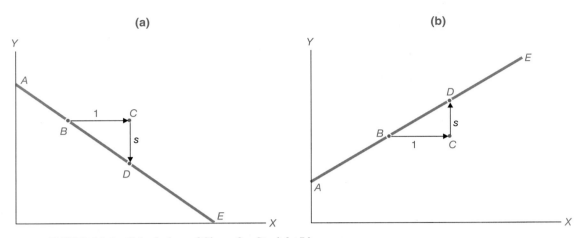

FIGURE 1A-3. Calculation of Slope for Straight Lines

It is easy to calculate slopes for straight lines as "rise over run." Thus in both (**a**) and (**b**), the numerical value of the slope is rise/run = $CD/BC = s/1 = s$. Note that in (**a**), CD is negative, indicating a negative slope, or an inverse relationship between X and Y.

say that food production rose from 25 to 26 units. The slope of the curve in Figure 1A-2 tells us the precise change in machinery production that would take place. *Slope is an exact numerical measure of the relationship between the change in* Y *and the change in* X.

We can use Figure 1A-3 to show how to measure the slope of a straight line, say, the slope of the line between points B and D. Think of the movement from B to D as occurring in two stages. First comes a horizontal movement from B to C indicating a 1-unit increase in the X value (with no change in Y). Second comes a compensating vertical movement up or down, shown as s in Figure 1A-3. (The movement of 1 horizontal unit is purely for convenience. The formula holds for movements of any size.) The two-step movement brings us from one point to another on the straight line.

Because the BC movement is a 1-unit increase in X, the length of CD (shown as s in Figure 1A-3) indicates the change in Y per unit change in X. On a graph, this change is called the *slope* of the line $ABDE$.

Often slope is defined as "the rise over the run." The *rise* is the vertical distance; in Figure 1A-3, the rise is the distance from C to D. The *run* is the horizontal distance; it is BC in Figure 1A-3. The rise over the run in this instance would be CD over BC. Thus the slope of BD is CD/BC.

The key points to understand about slopes are the following:

1. The slope can be expressed as a number. It measures the change in Y per unit change in X, or "the rise over the run."
2. If the line is straight, its slope is constant everywhere.
3. The slope of the line indicates whether the relationship between X and Y is direct or inverse. *Direct relationships* occur when variables move in the same direction (that is, they increase or decrease together); *inverse relationships* occur when the variables move in opposite directions (that is, one increases as the other decreases).

Thus a negative slope indicates the X-Y relation is inverse, as it is in Figure 1A-3(*a*). Why? Because an increase in X calls for a decrease in Y.

People sometimes confuse slope with the appearance of steepness. This conclusion is often valid—but not always. The steepness depends on the scale of the graph. Panels (*a*) and (*b*) in Figure 1A-4 both portray exactly the same relationship. But in (*b*), the horizontal scale has been stretched out compared with (*a*). If you calculate carefully, you will see that the slopes are exactly the same (and are equal to ½).

FIGURE 1A-4. Steepness Is Not the Same as Slope Note that even though (**a**) looks steeper than (**b**), they display the same relationship. Both have slope of ½, but the X axis has been stretched out in (**b**).

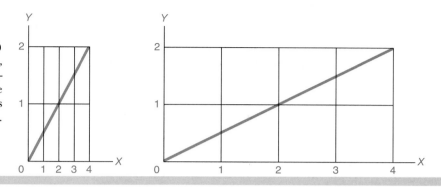

Slope of a Curved Line. A curved or non-linear line is one whose slope changes. Sometimes we want to know the slope *at a given point*, such as point *B* in Figure 1A-5. We see that the slope at point *B* is positive, but it is not obvious exactly how to calculate the slope.

To find the slope of a smooth curved line at a point, we calculate the slope of the straight line that just touches, but does not cross, the curved line at the point in question. Such a straight line is called a *tangent* to the curved line. Put differently, the slope of a curved line at a point is given by the slope of the

straight line that is tangent to the curve at the given point. Once we draw the tangent line, we find the slope of the tangent line with the usual right-angle measuring technique discussed earlier.

To find the slope at point *B* in Figure 1A-5, we simply construct straight line *FBJ* as a tangent to the curved line at point *B*. We then calculate the slope of the tangent as *NJ/MN*. Similarly, the tangent line *GH* gives the slope of the curved line at point *D*.

Another example of the slope of a nonlinear line is shown in Figure 1A-6. This shows a typical micro-economics curve, which is dome shaped and has a

FIGURE 1A-5. Tangent as Slope of Curved Line
By constructing a tangent line, we can calculate the slope of a curved line at a given point. Thus the line *FBMJ* is tangent to smooth curve *ABDE* at point *B*. The slope at *B* is calculated as the slope of the tangent line, i.e., as *NJ/MN*.

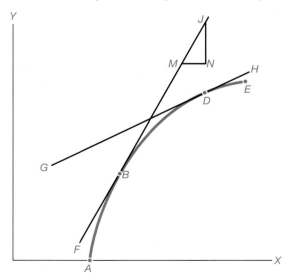

FIGURE 1A-6. Different Slopes of Nonlinear Curves
Many curves in economics first rise, then reach a maximum, then fall. In the rising region from *A* to *C* the slope is positive (see point *B*). In the falling region from *C* to *E* the slope is negative (see point *D*). At the curve's maximum, point *C,* the slope is zero. (What about a U-shaped curve? What is the slope at its minimum?)

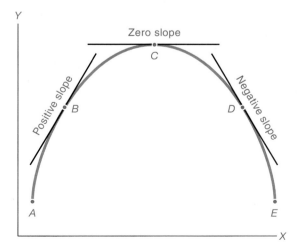

maximum at point *C.* We can use our method of slopes-as-tangents to see that the slope of the curve is always positive in the region where the curve is rising and negative in the falling region. At the peak or maximum of the curve, the slope is exactly zero. A zero slope signifies that a tiny movement in the *X* variable around the maximum has no effect on the value of the *Y* variable.[1]

Shifts of and Movement Along Curves

An important distinction in economics is that between shifts of curves and movement along curves. We can examine this distinction in Figure 1A-7. The inner production-possibility frontier reproduces the *PPF* in Figure 1A-2. At point *D* society chooses to produce 30 units of food and 90 units of machines. If society decides to consume more food with a given *PPF,* then it can *move along* the *PPF* to point *E.* This movement along the curve represents choosing more food and fewer machines.

Suppose that the inner *PPF* represents society's production possibilities for 1990. If we return to the same country in 2000, we see that the *PPF* has *shifted* from the inner 1990 curve to the outer 2000 curve. (This shift would occur because of technological change or because of an increase in labor or capital available.) In the later year, society might choose to be at point *G,* with more food and machines than at either *D* or *E.*

The point of this example is that in the first case (moving from *D* to *E*) we see movement along the curve, while in the second case (from *D* to *G*) we see a shift of the curve.

Some Special Graphs

The *PPF* is one of the most important graphs of economics, one depicting the relationship between two economic variables (such as food and machines or guns and butter). You will encounter other types of graphs in the pages that follow.

---

[1] For those who enjoy algebra, the slope of a line can be remembered as follows: A straight line (or linear relationship) is written as $Y = a + bX$. For this line, the slope of the curve is *b,* which measures the change in *Y* per unit change in *X.*

A curved line or nonlinear relationship is one involving terms other than constants and the *X* term. An example of a nonlinear relationship is the quadratic equation $Y = (X - 2)^2$. You can easily verify that the slope of this equation is negative for $X < 2$ and positive for $X > 2$. What is its slope for $X = 2$?

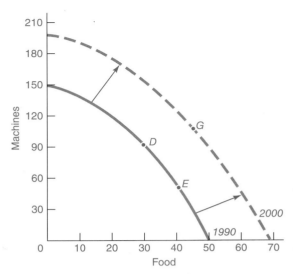

FIGURE 1A-7. Shift of Curves Versus Movement Along Curves

In using graphs, it is essential to distinguish *movement along* a curve (such as from high-investment *D* to low-investment *E*) from a *shift of* a curve (as from *D* in an early year to *G* in a later year).

Time Series. Some graphs show how a particular variable has changed over time. Look, for example, at the graphs on the inside front cover of this text. The left-hand graph shows a time series, since the American Revolution, of a significant macroeconomic variable, the ratio of the federal government debt to total gross domestic product, or *GDP*—this ratio is the *debt-GDP ratio.* Time-series graphs have time on the horizontal axis and variables of interest (in this case, the debt-GDP ratio) on the vertical axis. This graph shows that the debt-GDP ratio has risen sharply during every major war.

Scatter Diagrams. Sometimes individual pairs of points will be plotted, as in Figure 1A-1. Often, combinations of variables for different years will be plotted. An important example of a scatter diagram from macroeconomics is the *consumption function,* shown in Figure 1A-8. This scatter diagram shows the nation's total disposable income on the horizontal axis and total consumption (spending by households on goods like food, clothing, and housing) on the vertical axis. Note that consumption is very closely linked to income, a vital clue for understanding changes in national income and output.

FIGURE 1A-8. Scatter Diagram of Consumption Function Shows Important Macroeconomic Law Observed points of consumption spending fall near the *CC* line, which displays average behavior over time. Thus, the rust-colored point for 1990 is so near the *CC* line that it could have been quite accurately predicted from that line even before the year was over. Scatter diagrams allow us to see how close the relationship is between two variables.

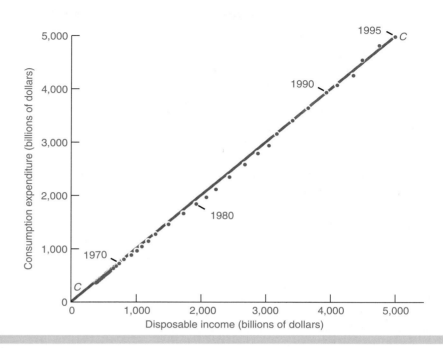

Diagrams with More Than One Curve. Often it is useful to put two curves in the same graph, thus obtaining a "multicurve diagram." The most important example is the *supply-and-demand diagram,* shown in Chapter 3 (see page 52). Such graphs can show two different relationships simultaneously, such as how consumer purchases respond to price (demand) and how business production responds to price (supply). By graphing the two relationships together, we can determine the price and quantity that will hold in a market.

This concludes our brief excursion into graphs. Once you have mastered these basic principles, the graphs in this book, and in other areas, can be both fun and instructive.

SUMMARY TO APPENDIX

1. Graphs are an essential tool of modern economics. They provide a convenient presentation of data or of the relationships among variables.
2. The important points to understand about a graph are: What is on each of two axes (horizontal and vertical)? What are the units on each axis? What kind of relationship is depicted in the curve or curves shown in the graph?
3. The relationship between the two variables in a curve is given by its slope. The slope is defined as "the rise over the run," or the increase in *Y* per unit increase in *X*. If it is upward- (or positively) sloping, the two variables are directly related; they move upward or downward together. If the curve has a downward (or negative) slope, the two variables are inversely related.
4. In addition, we sometimes see special types of graphs: time series, which show how a particular variable moves over time; scatter diagrams, which show observations on a pair of variables; and multicurve diagrams, which show two or more relationships in a single graph.

CONCEPTS FOR REVIEW

Elements of Graphs

horizontal, or X, axis
vertical, or Y, axis

slope as "rise over run"
slope (negative, positive, zero)
tangent as slope of curved line

Examples of Graphs

time-series graphs
scatter diagrams
multicurve graphs

QUESTIONS FOR DISCUSSION

1. Consider the following problem: After your 8 hours a day of sleep, you have 16 hours a day to divide between leisure and study. Let leisure hours be the X variable and study hours be the Y variable. Plot the straight-line relationship between all combinations of X and Y on a blank piece of graph paper. Be careful to label the axes and mark the origin.

2. In question 1, what is the slope of the line showing the relationship between study and leisure hours? Is it a straight line?

3. Let us say that you absolutely need 6 hours of leisure per day, no more, no less. On the graph, mark the point that corresponds to 6 hours of leisure. Now consider a *movement along the curve*: Assume that you decide that you need only 4 hours of leisure a day. Plot the new point.

4. Next show a *shift of the curve*: You find that you need less sleep, so you have 18 hours a day to devote to leisure and study. Draw the new (shifted) curve.

5. Keep a record of your leisure and study for a week. Plot a time-series graph of the hours of leisure and study each day. Next plot a scatter diagram of hours of leisure and hours of study. Do you see any relationship between the two variables?

CHAPTER 2
THE SHIFTING BOUNDARY
BETWEEN MARKETS AND GOVERNMENT

The important thing for Government is not to do things which individuals are doing already, and to do them a little better or a little worse; but to do those things which at present are not done at all.

John Maynard Keynes, "The End of Laissez Faire" (1926)

One of the principal problems of political economy —emphasized by the opening quote from Keynes— is deciding on the appropriate boundary between state and market. We can better understand the issues if we examine how the boundaries evolved to their present point. In medieval times, the aristocracy and town guilds directed much of the economic activity in Europe and Asia. However, about two centuries ago, governments began to exercise less and less power over prices and production methods. Gradually, the restraints of feudalism were replaced by what we call the "market mechanism" or "competitive capitalism."

In most of Europe and North America, the nineteenth century became the age of **laissez-faire**. This doctrine, which translates as "leave us alone," holds that government should interfere as little as possible in economic affairs and leave economic decisions to the interplay of supply and demand in the marketplace. Many governments espoused this economic philosophy in the middle of the nineteenth century.

Nevertheless, by the end of the century, the unbridled excesses of capitalism led the United States and the industrialized countries of Western Europe to retreat from full laissez-faire. Governments assumed a steadily expanding economic role, regulating monopolies, collecting income taxes, and taking on such tasks as providing support for the elderly (social security). This new system, called the **welfare state**, is one in which markets direct the detailed activities of day-to-day economic life while governments regulate social conditions and provide pensions, health care, and other aspects of the social safety net.

Under the guiding hand of government, the market economies of Western Europe and North America flourished in the three decades after World War II. Those years witnessed an unprecedented period of sustained economic growth and prosperity. Then, around 1980, the tides shifted again, as conservative governments in many countries began to reduce taxes and deregulate government's control over the economy. Particularly influential was the "Reagan revolution," which changed public attitudes about taxes and government and reversed the trends in U.S. federal spending on civilian programs.

The most dramatic turn toward the market came in Russia and the socialist countries of Eastern Europe. After decades of extolling the advantages of central planning and a government-run command economy, these countries started to make the difficult transition to a decentralized, market economy. China, while still run by the dictatorship of the Communist party, has enjoyed an economic boom in the late 1980s and early 1990s by allowing markets to operate within its borders. Developing countries like Taiwan, Thailand, and Chile have enjoyed rapid income growth by embracing capitalism and reducing the role of government in their economies.

This capsule history of the shifting balance between state and market will naturally raise many questions. What exactly is a market economy, and what makes it so powerful? What is the "capital" in "capitalism"? What government controls are needed to help markets? The time has come to understand the principles that lie behind the market economy and to review government's role in economic life.

A. WHAT IS A MARKET?

Not Chaos, but Economic Order

We usually take for granted the smooth running of the economy. When you go to the supermarket, the items you want—bread, cereal, and bananas—are usually on the shelf. You pay your bill, pop the food in your mouth, and have a juicy meal. What could be simpler?

If you pause for a moment and look more closely, you may begin to appreciate the complexity of the economic system that provides your daily bread. The food may have passed through five or ten links before getting to you, traveling for days or months from every state and every corner of the globe as it moved along the chain of farmers, food processors, packagers, truckers, wholesalers, and retailers. It seems almost a miracle that food is produced in suitable amounts, gets transported to the right place, and arrives in a palatable form at the dinner table.

But the true miracle is that this entire system works without coercion or centralized direction by anybody. Literally millions of businesses and consumers engage in voluntary trade, and their actions and purposes are invisibly coordinated by a system of prices and markets. Nobody decides how many chickens will be produced, where the trucks will drive, and when the supermarkets will open. Still, in the end, the food is in the store when you want it.

Markets perform similar miracles around us all the time, as can easily be seen if only we observe our economy carefully. Thousands of commodities are produced by millions of people, willingly, without central direction or master plan. Indeed, with a few important exceptions (like the military, police, and schools) most of our economic life proceeds without government intervention, and that's the true wonder of the social world.

The Market Mechanism

A market economy is an elaborate mechanism for coordinating people, activities, and businesses through a system of prices and markets. It is a communication device for pooling the knowledge and actions of billions of diverse individuals. Without central intelligence or computation, it solves problems of production and distribution involving billions of unknown variables and relations, problems that are far beyond the reach of even today's fastest supercomputer. Nobody designed the market, yet it functions remarkably well. *In a market economy, no single individual or organization is responsible for production, consumption, distribution, and pricing.*

How do markets determine prices, wages, and outputs? Originally, a market was an actual place where buyers and sellers could engage in face-to-face bargaining. The *marketplace*—filled with slabs of butter, pyramids of cheese, layers of wet fish, and heaps of vegetables—used to be a familiar sight in many villages and towns, where farmers brought their goods to sell. In the United States today there are still important markets where many traders gather together to do business. For example, wheat and corn are traded at the Chicago Board of Trade, oil and platinum are traded at the New York Mercantile Exchange, and gems are traded at the Diamond District in New York City.

More generally, a market should be thought of as a mechanism by which buyers and sellers can determine prices and exchange goods and services. There are markets for almost everything, from art to pollution. A market may be centralized, like the stock market. It may be decentralized, as in the case of houses or labor. Or it may exist only electronically, as in the case of many financial assets and services, which are traded by computer. The crucial characteristic of a market is that it brings buyers and sellers together to set prices and quantities.

A **market** is a mechanism by which buyers and sellers interact to determine the price and quantity of a good or service.

In a market system, everything has a **price**, which is the value of the good in terms of money (the role of money will be discussed in Section B of this chapter). Prices represent the terms on which people and firms voluntarily exchange different commodities. When I agree to buy a used Ford from a dealer for $4050, this agreement indicates that the Ford is worth more than $4050 to me and that the $4050 is worth more than the Ford to the dealer. The used-car market has determined the price of a used Ford and, through voluntary trading, has allocated this good to the person for whom it has the highest value.

In addition, prices serve as *signals* to producers and consumers. If consumers want more of any good, the price will rise, sending a signal to producers that more supply is needed. For example, every summer, as families set out on their vacations, the demand for gasoline rises, and so does the price. The higher price encourages oil companies to increase gasoline production and, at the same time, discourages travelers from lengthening their trips.

On the other hand, if a commodity such as cars becomes overstocked, dealers and automobile companies will lower their prices in order to reduce their inventory. At the lower price, more consumers will want cars, and producers will want to make fewer cars. As a result, a balance, or equilibrium, between buyers and sellers will be restored.

What is true of the markets for consumer goods is also true of markets for factors of production, such as land or labor. If computer programmers rather than textile workers are needed, job opportunities will be more favorable in the computing field. The price of computer programmers (their hourly wage) will tend to rise, and that of textile workers will tend to fall, as they did during the 1980s. The shift in relative wages will attract workers into the growing occupation.

The nursing crisis of the 1980s shows the labor market at work. During that decade the growth in the health-care sector led to an enormous expansion of nursing jobs with far too few trained nurses to fill them. Hospitals offered all sorts of fringe benefits to attract nurses, including subsidized apartments, low-cost on-site child care, and signing bonuses as high as $10,000. One hospital even ran a lottery for nurses, with the prize being a gift certificate at a nearby department store. But what really attracted people into the nursing profession was rising wages. Between 1983 and 1992, the pay for registered nurses rose almost 70 percent, so they were making about as much money as the average accountant or architect. The rising pay drew so many people into nursing that by 1992 the nursing shortage had disappeared in most parts of the country.

Prices coordinate the decisions of producers and consumers in a market. Higher prices tend to reduce consumer purchases and encourage production. Lower prices encourage consumption and discourage production. Prices are the balance wheel of the market mechanism.

Market Equilibrium. At every moment, some people are buying while others are selling; firms are inventing new products while governments are passing laws to regulate old ones; foreign companies are opening plants in America while American firms are selling their products abroad. Yet in the midst of all this turmoil, markets are constantly solving the *what, how,* and *for whom.* As they balance all the forces operating on the economy, markets are finding a **market equilibrium of supply and demand.**

A market equilibrium represents a balance among all the different buyers and sellers. Depending upon the price, households and firms all want to buy or sell different quantities. The market finds the equilibrium price that simultaneously meets the desires of buyers and sellers. Too high a price would mean a glut of goods with too much output; too low a price would produce long lines in stores and a deficiency of goods. Those prices for which buyers desire to buy exactly the quantity that sellers desire to sell yield an equilibrium of supply and demand.

How Markets Solve the Three Economic Problems

We have just described how prices help balance consumption and production (or demand and supply) in an individual market. What happens when we put all the different markets together—gasoline, cars, land, labor, capital, and everything else? These markets work simultaneously to determine a *general equilibrium* of prices and production.

By matching sellers and buyers (supply and demand) in each market, a market economy simultaneously solves the three problems of *what, how,* and *for whom.* Here is an outline of a market equilibrium:

1. *What* goods and services will be produced is determined by the dollar votes of consumers—not every 2 or 4 years at the polls, but in their daily purchase decisions. The money that they pay into businesses' cash registers ultimately provides the payrolls, rents, and dividends that consumers, as employees, receive as income.

   Firms, in turn, are motivated by the desire to maximize profits. **Profits** are net revenues, or the difference between total sales and total costs. Firms abandon areas where they are losing profits; by the same token, firms are lured by high profits into production of goods in high demand. A familiar example is Hollywood. If one film makes huge profits—say, a film about a cute dinosaur and an evil scientist—other studios will rush to produce imitations.

2. *How* things are produced is determined by the competition among different producers. The best way for producers to meet price competition and maximize profits is to keep costs at a minimum by adopting the most efficient methods of production. Sometimes change is incremental and consists of little more than tinkering with the machinery or adjusting the input mix to gain a cost advantage, which can be very important in a competitive market. At other times there are drastic shifts in technology, as with steam engines displacing horses because steam was cheaper per unit of useful work, or airplanes replacing railroads as the most efficient mode for long-distance travel. Right now we are in the midst of just such a transition to a radically different technology, with computers replacing typewriters, paper, and many white-collar workers.

3. *For whom* things are produced—who is consuming, and how much—depends, in large part, on the supply and demand in the markets for factors of production. Factor markets (i.e., markets for factors of production) determine wage rates, land rents, interest rates, and profits. Such prices are called *factor prices.* The same person may

receive wages from a job, dividends from stocks, interest from a certificate of deposit, and rent from a piece of property. By adding up all the revenues from factors, we can calculate the person's market income. The distribution of income among the population is thus determined by the amounts of factors (person-hours, acres, etc.) owned and the prices of the factors (wage rates, land rents, etc.).

Be warned, however, that incomes reflect much more than the rewards for sweaty labor or abstemious saving. High incomes come also from large inheritances, good luck, favorable location, and skills highly prized in the marketplace. Those with low incomes are often pictured as lazy, but the truth is that low incomes are generally the result of poor education, discrimination, or living where jobs are few and wages are low. When we see someone on the unemployment line, we might say, "There, but for the grace of supply and demand, go I."

Monarchs of the Marketplace

Who rules a market economy? Do giant companies like General Electric and AT&T call the tune? Or perhaps Congress and the President? Or the advertising moguls from Madison Avenue? If we examine the structure of a market economy carefully, we see a dual monarchy shared by *consumers and technology.* Consumers direct by their innate and acquired tastes—as expressed by their dollar votes—the ultimate uses to which society's resources are channeled. They pick the point on the production-possibility frontier (*PPF*).

But consumers alone cannot dictate *what* goods will be produced. The available resources and technology place a fundamental constraint on their choices. The economy cannot go outside its *PPF.* You can fly to Hong Kong, but there are no flights to Mars. An economy's resources, along with the available science and technology, limit the candidates for the dollar votes of consumers. Consumer demand has to dovetail with business supply of goods. So business cost and supply decisions, along with consumer demand, help determine what is produced.

Not every technology, however, will find a use. From the Stanley Steamer—a car that ran on steam—to the Premiere smokeless cigarette, which was smokeless but also tasteless, history is full of products that found no markets. How do useless products die off? Is there a government agency that pronounces upon the value of new products? No such agency is necessary. Rather, it is profits which serve as the rewards and penalties for businesses and guide the market mechanism.

Like a farmer using a carrot and a stick to coax a donkey forward, the market system deals out profits and losses to induce firms to produce desired goods efficiently.

A Picture of Prices and Markets

We can picture the circular flow of economic life in Figure 2-1 on page 30. The diagram provides an overview of how consumers and producers interact to determine prices and quantities for both inputs and outputs. Note the two different kinds of markets in the circular flow. At the top are the product markets, or the flow of outputs like pizza and shoes; at the bottom are the markets for inputs or factors of production like land and labor. Further, see how decisions are made by two different entities, households and businesses.

Households buy goods and sell factors of production; businesses sell goods and buy factors of production. Households use their income from sale of labor and other inputs to buy goods from businesses; businesses base their prices of goods on the costs of labor and property. Prices in goods markets are set to balance consumer demand with business supply; prices in factor markets are set to balance household supply with business demand.

All this sounds complicated. But it is simply the total picture of the intricate web of interdependent supplies and demands, interconnected through a market mechanism to solve the economic problems of *what*, *how*, and *for whom*. Look at Figure 2-1 carefully. A few minutes spent studying it will surely help you understand the workings of a market economy.

The Invisible Hand and "Perfect Competition"

The orderliness of the market system was first recognized by Adam Smith, whose classic work *The Wealth of Nations* (1776) is still read today. Smith proclaimed the principle of the **"invisible hand."** This principle holds that, in selfishly pursuing only his or her personal good, every individual is led, as if by an invisible hand, to achieve the best good for all. Smith held that in this best of all possible worlds, government interference with market competition is almost certain to be injurious. In one of the most famous passages in all of economics, Smith saw harmony between private interest and public interest:

> Every individual endeavors to employ his capital so that its produce may be of greatest value. He generally neither intends to promote the public interest, nor knows how much he is promoting it. He intends only his own security, only his own gain. And he is in this led by an invisible hand to promote an end which was no part of his intention. By pursuing his own interest he frequently promotes that of society more effectually than when he really intends to promote it.[1]

Smith's insight about the functioning of the market mechanism has inspired modern economists—both the admirers and the critics of capitalism. Economic theorists have proved that under restrictive conditions a perfectly competitive economy is efficient (remember that an economy is producing efficiently when it cannot increase the economic welfare of anyone without making someone else worse off).

After two centuries of experience and thought, however, we recognize the scope and realistic limitations of this doctrine. We know that there are "market failures" and that markets do not always lead to the most efficient outcome. One set of market failures concerns monopolies and other forms of imperfect competition. A second failure of the invisible hand comes when there are spillovers or externalities outside the marketplace—positive externalities such as scientific discoveries and negative spillovers such as pollution. A final reservation comes when the income distribution is politically or ethically unacceptable. When any of these elements occur, Adam Smith's invisible-hand doctrine breaks down and government may want to step in to mend the flawed invisible hand.

In summary:

Adam Smith discovered a remarkable property of a competitive market economy. Under perfect competition and with no market failures, markets will squeeze as many useful goods and services out of the available resources as is possible. But where monopolies or pollution or similar market failures become pervasive, the remarkable efficiency properties of the invisible hand may be destroyed.

---

[1] Adam Smith, *The Wealth of Nations*, 1776.

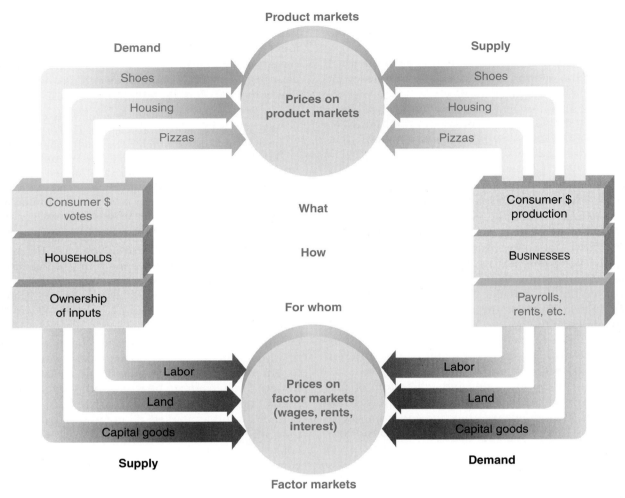

FIGURE 2-1. The Market System Relies on Supply and Demand to Solve the Trio of Economic Problems

We see here the circular flow of a market economy. Dollar votes of households interact with business supply in the product markets at top, helping to determine *what* is produced. Further, business demand for inputs meets the public's supply of labor and other inputs in the factor markets below to help determine wage, rent, and interest payments; incomes thus influence *for whom* goods are delivered. Business competition to buy factor inputs and sell goods most cheaply determines *how* goods are produced.

Adam Smith: Founding father of economics. "For what purpose is all the toil and bustle of this world? What is the end of avarice and ambition, of the pursuit of wealth, of power, and preeminence?" Thus wrote Adam Smith (1723–1790), of Scotland, who glimpsed for the social world of economics

what Isaac Newton recognized for the physical world of the heavens. Smith answered his questions in *The Wealth of Nations* (1776), where he explained the self-regulating natural order by which the oil of self-interest lubricates the economic machinery in an almost miraculous fashion. Smith believed that the toil and bustle had the effect of improving the lot of the common man and woman. "Consumption is the sole end and purpose of all production."

Smith was the first apostle of economic growth. At the dawn of the Industrial Revolution, he pointed to the great strides in productivity brought about by specialization and the division of labor. In a famous example, he described the specialized manufacturing of a pin factory in which "one man draws out the wire, another straightens it, a third cuts it," and so it goes. This operation allowed 10 people to make 48,000 pins in a day, whereas if "all wrought separately, they could not each of them make twenty, perhaps not one pin a day." Smith saw the result of this division of labor as "universal opulence which extends itself to the lowest ranks of the people." Imagine what he would think if he returned today to see what two more centuries of economic growth have produced!

Smith wrote hundreds of pages railing against countless cases of government folly and interference. Consider the seventeenth-century guild master who was attempt-

ing to improve his weaving. The town guild decided, "If a cloth weaver intends to process a piece according to his own invention, he should obtain permission from the judges of the town to employ the number and length of threads that he desires after the question has been considered by four of the oldest merchants and four of the oldest weavers of the guild." Smith argued that such restrictions—whether imposed by government or by monopolies, whether on production or on foreign trade—limit the proper workings of the market system and ultimately hurt both workers and consumers.

None of this should suggest that Smith was an apologist for the establishment. He had a distrust of all entrenched power, private monopolies as much as public monarchies. He was for the common people. But, like many of the great economists, he had learned from his research that the road to waste is paved with good intentions.

Above all, it is Adam Smith's vision of the self-regulating "invisible hand" that is his enduring contribution to modern economics.[2]

B. TRADE, MONEY, AND CAPITAL

Since the time of Adam Smith, market economies have evolved enormously. Advanced capitalist economies, such as the United States, Western Europe, and Japan, have three distinguishing features: trade and specialization, money, and capital.

- An advanced economy is characterized by an elaborate network of *trade,* among individuals and countries, that depends on great *specialization* and an intricate division of labor.
- The economy today makes extensive use of *money,* or the means of payment. The flow of money is the lifeblood of our system. Money provides the yardstick for measuring the economic value of things and for financing trade.
- Modern industrial technologies rest on the use of vast amounts of *capital:* precision machinery,

large-scale factories, and stocks of inventories. Capital goods leverage human labor power into a much more efficient factor of production and allow productivity many times greater than that possible in an earlier age.

TRADE, SPECIALIZATION, AND DIVISION OF LABOR

Compared to the economies of the 1700s, today's economies depend on the specialization of individuals and firms, connected by an extensive network

---

[2] An eloquent introduction to the lives of the great economists can be found in Robert L. Heilbroner, *The Worldly Philosophers* (Simon and Schuster, New York, 1980).

of trade. Western economies have enjoyed rapid economic growth as increasing specialization has allowed workers to become highly productive in particular occupations and to trade their output for the commodities they need.

Specialization occurs when people and countries concentrate their efforts on a particular set of tasks—it permits each person and country to use to best advantage its specific skills and resources. One of the facts of economic life is that, rather than have everyone do everything in a mediocre way, it is better to establish a *division of labor*—dividing production into a number of small specialized steps or tasks. A division of labor permits tall people to become basketball players, numerate people to teach, and persuasive people to sell cars.

In our economic system, it sometimes takes many years to receive the training for particular careers—it takes 14 years to become a certified neurosurgeon. Capital and land are also highly specialized. Land can be specialized, as in the vineyard lands of California and France, which it has taken decades to cultivate. The computer program that went along with the labor to write this textbook took over a decade to be developed, but it is useless at managing an oil refinery or solving large numerical problems. One of the most impressive examples of specialization is the computer chip that manages automobiles and increases their efficiency.

The enormous efficiency of specialization allows the intricate network of trade among people and nations that we see today. Very few of us produce a single finished good; we make but the tiniest fraction of what we consume. We might teach a small part of one college's curriculum, or empty coins from parking meters, or separate the genetic material of fruit flies. In exchange for this specialized labor, we will receive an income adequate to buy goods from all over the world.

The idea of *gains from trade* forms one of the central insights of economics. Different people or countries tend to specialize in certain areas and then to engage in the voluntary exchange of what they produce for what they need. Japan has grown enormously productive by specializing in manufacturing goods such as automobiles and consumer electronics; it exports much of its manufacturing output to pay for imports of raw materials. By contrast, countries which have tried the strategy of becoming self-sufficient, attempting to produce most of what they

consume, have discovered that this is the road to stagnation. Trade can enrich all nations and increase *everyone's* living standards.

To summarize:

Advanced economies engage in specialization and division of labor, which increase the productivity of their resources. Individuals and countries then voluntarily trade goods in which they specialize for others' products, vastly increasing the range and quantity of consumption and having the potential to raise everyone's living standards.

MONEY: THE LUBRICANT OF EXCHANGE

If specialization permits people to concentrate on particular tasks, money then allows people to trade their specialized outputs for the vast array of goods and services produced by others. What is money? **Money** is the means of payment or exchange—that is, the currency and checks that we use when we buy things. But more than that, money is a lubricant that facilitates exchange. When everyone trusts and accepts money as payment for goods and debts, trade is facilitated. Just imagine how complicated economic life would be if you had to barter goods for goods every time you wanted to buy a pizza or go to a concert. What services could you offer Sal's Pizza? And what about your education—what could you barter with your college for tuition that it needs? Because everyone accepts money as the medium of exchange, the need to match supplies and demands is enormously simplified.

Governments control the money supply through their central banks. But like other lubricants, money can get gummed up. It can grow out of control and cause a hyperinflation, in which prices increase very sharply. When that happens, people concentrate on spending their money quickly, before it loses its value, rather than investing it for the future. That's what happened to several Latin American countries in the 1980s, and many former socialist economies in the 1990s, when they had inflation rates exceeding 1000 percent or even 10,000 percent per year. Imagine getting your paycheck and having it lose 20 percent of its value by the end of the week!

Proper management of the money supply is one of the major issues for government macroeconomic policy in all countries.

CAPITAL

An advanced industrial economy like the United States uses an enormous amount of buildings, machinery, computers, and so on. These are the factors of production called **capital**, a produced factor of production, a durable input which is itself an output of the economy.

Most of us do not realize how much our daily activities rely, directly or indirectly, on capital, including our houses, the highways we drive on, and the wires that bring electricity and cable TV to our homes. The total net amount of capital stock in the economy is almost $18.5 trillion—including government-owned, business, and residential capital. On average, this is more than $70,000 per person.

As we have seen, capital is one of the three major factors of production. The other two, land and labor, are often called *primary factors of production*. That means their supply is mostly determined by non-economic factors, such as the fertility rate and the country's geography. Capital, by contrast, has to be produced before you can use it. For example, some companies build textile machinery, which is then used to make shirts; some companies build farm tractors, which are then used to help produce corn.

Note that capital inherently involves time-consuming, roundabout methods of production. In fact, people learned long ago that indirect and roundabout production techniques often are more efficient than direct methods of production. For example, the most direct method of catching fish is to wade into a stream and grab fish with your hands, but this yields more frustration than fish. By using a fishing rod (which is capital equipment), fishing time becomes more productive in terms of fish caught per day. By using even more capital, in the form of nets and fishing boats, fishing becomes productive enough to feed many people and provide a good living to those who operate the specialized nets and equipment.

Growth from the Sacrifice of Current Consumption. If people are willing to save—to abstain from present consumption and wait for future consumption—society can devote resources to new capital goods. A larger stock of capital helps the economy grow faster by pushing out the *PPF*. Look back at Figure 1-5 to see how forgoing current consumption in favor of investment adds to future production possibilities. High rates of saving and investment help explain how Japan, Korea, and other Asian countries have grown so fast. By comparison, many economists believe that the U.S. economy is lagging behind other countries in the growth race because it saves and invests too little.

Is there no limit to the amount of useful capital? Should we continue to boost productivity by adding more capital, by replacing all direct processes with more productive, roundabout ones and all roundabout processes with still more roundabout processes. While this seems sensible, it has a high cost because too much roundabout investment would cause too great a reduction in today's consumption. Investing resources to give every worker an advanced degree, to remove 99.9 percent of pollution, and to build a dense subway system under every city would certainly increase productivity. But the payoff would not be worth the enormous cost in consumption.

We summarize as follows:

Much of economic activity involves forgoing current consumption to increase our capital. Every time we invest—building a new factory or road, increasing the years or quality of education, or increasing the stock of useful technical knowledge—we are enhancing the future productivity of our economy and increasing future consumption.

Capital and Private Property

In a market economy, capital typically is privately owned, and the income from capital goes to individuals. Every patch of land has a deed, or title of ownership; almost every machine and building belongs to an individual or corporation. *Property rights* bestow on their owners the ability to use, exchange, paint, dig, drill, or exploit their capital goods. These capital goods also have market values, and people can buy and sell the capital goods for whatever price the goods will fetch. *The ability of individuals to own and profit from capital is what gives capitalism its name.*

However, while our society is one built on private property, property rights are limited. Society determines how much of "your" property you may bequeath to your heirs and how much must go in inheritance and estate taxes to the government. Society determines how much your factory can pollute and where you can park your car. Even your home is not your castle: you must obey zoning laws and, if necessary, make way for a road.

Interestingly enough, the most valuable economic resource, labor, cannot be turned into a commodity that is bought and sold as private property. Since the abolition of slavery, it has been against the law to treat human earning power like other capital assets. You are not free to sell yourself; you must rent yourself at a wage.

 Property rights for capital and pollution: Property rights define the ability of individuals or firms to own, buy, sell, and use the capital goods and other property in a market economy. These rights are enforced through the legal framework, which constitutes the set of laws within which an economy operates. An efficient and acceptable legal framework for a market economy includes the definition of property rights, the laws of contract, and a system for adjudicating disputes. As the ex-communist countries are discovering, it is very difficult to have a market economy when there are no laws enforcing contracts or guaranteeing that a company can keep its own profits. And when the legal framework breaks down, as in the former Yugoslavia or sometimes even in impoverished urban areas of America, people begin to fear for their lives and have little time or inclination to make long-term investments for the future. Production falls and the quality of life deteriorates. Indeed, many of the most horrifying African famines were caused by civil war and the breakdown in the legal order, not by bad weather.

The environment is another example where poorly designed property rights harm the economy. Water and air are generally common property, meaning that no one owns and controls them. As the saying goes, everyone's business is nobody's business. As a result, people do not weigh all the costs of their actions. Someone might throw trash into the water or emit smoke into the air because the costs of dirty water or foul air are borne by other people. By contrast, people are less likely to throw trash on their own lawn or burn coal in their own living room because they themselves will bear the costs. In recent years, economists have proposed extending property rights to environmental commodities by selling or auctioning permits to pollute and allowing them to be traded on markets. Preliminary evidence suggests that this extension of property rights has given much more powerful incentives to reduce pollution efficiently.

Specialization, trade, money, and capital form the key to the productiveness of an advanced economy. But note as well that they are closely interrelated. Specialization creates enormous efficiencies, while increased production makes trade possible. Use of money allows trade to take place quickly and efficiently. Without the facility for trade and exchange that money provides, an elaborate division of labor would not be possible. Money and capital are related because the funds for buying capital goods are funneled through financial markets, where people's savings can be transformed into other people's capital.

C. THE ECONOMIC ROLE OF GOVERNMENT

An ideal market economy is one in which all goods and services are voluntarily exchanged for money at market prices. Such a system squeezes the maximum benefits out of a society's available resources without government intervention. In the real world, however, no economy actually conforms totally to the idealized world of the smoothly functioning invisible hand. Rather, every market economy suffers from imperfections which lead to such ills as excessive pollution, unemployment, and extremes of wealth and poverty.

For that reason, no government anywhere in the world, no matter how conservative, keeps its hands off the economy. In modern economies governments take on many tasks in response to the flaws in the market mechanism. The military, the police, the national weather service, and highway construction are all typical areas of government activity. Socially useful ventures such as space exploration and scientific research benefit from government funding. Governments may regulate some businesses (such as banking and garbage collection) while subsidizing others (such as education and health care). And governments tax their citizens and redistribute some of the proceeds to the elderly and needy.

But for all the wide range of possible activities, governments have three main economic functions in a market economy. These functions are increasing efficiency, promoting equity, and fostering macroeconomic stability and growth.

1. Governments increase *efficiency* by promoting competition, curbing externalities like pollution, and providing public goods.
2. Governments promote *equity* by using tax and expenditure programs to redistribute income toward particular groups.
3. Governments foster *macroeconomic stability and growth*—reducing unemployment and inflation while encouraging economic growth—through fiscal policy and monetary regulation.

We will examine briefly each function.

EFFICIENCY

Adam Smith recognized that the virtues of the market mechanism are fully realized only when the checks and balances of perfect competition are present. What is meant by **perfect competition**? It means that all goods and services have a price and are traded on markets. It also means that no firm or consumer is large enough to affect the market price. For example, the wheat market is perfectly competitive because the largest wheat farm, producing only a minuscule fraction of the world's wheat, can have no appreciable effect upon the price of wheat.

The invisible-hand doctrine applies to economies in which all the markets are perfectly competitive. In such a circumstance, markets will produce an efficient allocation of resources, so the economy is on its production-possibility frontier. When all industries are subject to the checks and balances of perfect competition, as we will see later in this book, markets will produce the efficient bundle of outputs using the most efficient techniques and the minimum amount of inputs.

Alas, there are many ways that markets can fall short of perfect competition. The three most important involve imperfect competition, such as monopolies; externalities, such as pollution; and public goods, such as national defense and highways. In each case, market failure leads to inefficient production or consumption, and government can play a useful role in curing the disease.

Imperfect Competition

One serious deviation from an efficient market comes from *imperfect competition* or *monopoly* elements. Whereas under perfect competition no firm or consumer can affect prices, **imperfect competition** occurs when a buyer or seller can affect a good's price. For example, if the telephone company or a labor union is large enough to influence the price of phone service or labor, respectively, some degree of imperfect competition has set in. When imperfect competition arises, society may move inside its *PPF*. This would occur, for example, if a single seller (a monopolist) raised the price of a good sky-high to earn extra profits. The output of that good would be reduced below the most efficient level, and the efficiency of the economy would thereby suffer. In such a situation, the invisible-hand property of markets may be violated.

What is the effect of imperfect competition, which is the ability of a large firm to affect the price in a given market? Imperfect competition leads to prices that rise above cost and to consumer purchases that are reduced below efficient levels. The pattern of too high price and too low output is the hallmark of the inefficiencies associated with imperfect competition.

In reality, almost all industries possess some measure of imperfect competition. Airlines, for example, may have no competition on some of their routes but face several rivals on others. The extreme case of imperfect competition is the *monopolist*—a single supplier who alone determines the price of a particular good or service.

Over the last century, most governments have taken steps to curb the most extreme forms of imperfect competition. Governments sometimes regulate the prices and profits of monopolies such as local water, telephone, and electric utilities. In addition, government antitrust laws prohibit actions such as price fixing or agreeing to divide up markets. The most important check to imperfect competition, however, is the opening of markets to competitors, whether they be domestic or foreign. Few monopolies can long withstand the attack of competitors unless governments protect them through tariffs or regulations.

Externalities

A second type of inefficiency arises when there are spillovers or externalities, which involve involuntary imposition of costs or benefits. Market transactions involve voluntary exchange in which people exchange goods or services for money. When a firm buys a chicken to make frozen drumsticks, it buys the chicken from its owner in the chicken market, and the seller receives the full value of the hen. When you buy a haircut, the barber receives the full value for time, skills, and rent.

But many interactions take place outside markets. While airports produce a lot of noise, they generally do not compensate the people living around the airport for disturbing their peace. On the other hand, some companies which spend heavily on research and development have positive spillover effects for the rest of society. For example, researchers at AT&T invented the transistor and launched the electronic revolution, but AT&T's profits increased by only a small fraction of the global social gains. In each case, an activity has helped or hurt people outside the market transaction; that is, there was an economic transaction without an economic payment.

Externalities (or spillover effects) occur when firms or people impose costs or benefits on others outside the marketplace.

Governments are today often more concerned with negative externalities than positive ones. As our society has become more densely populated and as the production of energy, chemicals, and other materials increases, negative externalities or spillover effects have grown from little nuisances into major threats. This is where governments come in. Government *regulations* are designed to control externalities like air and water pollution, damage from strip mining, hazardous wastes, unsafe drugs and foods, and radioactive materials.

In many ways, governments are like parents, always saying no: Thou shalt not expose thy workers to dangerous conditions. Thou shalt not pour out poisonous smoke from thy factory chimney. Thou shalt not sell dangerous drugs. Thou shalt not drive without wearing thy seat belt. And so forth. Finding the exactly correct regulations is a difficult task, requiring complex science and economics, and subject to heavy political pressure, but few today would argue for returning to the unregulated economic jungle where firms can dump plutonium wherever they want.

Public Goods

While negative externalities like pollution or global warming command most of the headlines, positive externalities may well be economically more significant. Important examples of positive externalities are construction of a highway network, operation of a national weather service, support of basic science, and provision of measures to enhance public health. These are not goods which can be bought and sold in markets. Adequate private production of these public goods will not occur because the benefits are so widely dispersed across the population that no single firm or consumer has an economic incentive to provide the service and capture the returns.

The extreme example of a positive externality is a public good. **Public goods** are commodities for which the cost of extending the service to an additional person is zero and which it is impossible to exclude individuals from enjoying.[3] The best example of a public good is national defense. When a nation protects its freedoms and way of life, it does so for all its inhabitants, whether they want the protection or not and whether they pay for it or not.

Because private provision of public goods is generally insufficient, government must step in to encourage the production of public goods. In buying public goods like national defense or lighthouses, government is behaving exactly like any other large spender. By casting sufficient dollar votes in certain directions, it causes resources to flow there. Once

---

[3] Lighthouses are an interesting example of a public good provided by government. They save lives and cargos. Lighthouse signals are a "public good" because it costs no more to warn 100 ships than to warn a single ship of the rocks and shoals. In an earlier age, lighthouses were sometimes privately owned, and lighthouse owners attempted to collect fees from ships in port. But private provision encounters a "free-rider" problem that can lead to underprovision and underfinancing of such socially desirable goods. We have here a positive externality, a divergence between private and social benefit, which is efficiently provided free of charge.

the dollar votes are cast, the market mechanism then takes over and channels resources to firms so that the lighthouses or tanks get produced.

Taxes. Government must find the revenues to pay for its public goods and for income-redistribution programs. Such revenues come from taxes levied on personal and corporate incomes, on wages, on sales of consumer goods, and on other items. All levels of government—city, state, and federal—collect taxes to pay for their spending.

Taxes sound like another "price"—in this case the price we pay for public goods. But taxes differ from prices in one crucial respect: taxes are not voluntary. Everyone is subject to the tax laws; we are all obligated to pay for our share of the cost of public goods. Of course, through our democratic process, we as citizens choose both the public goods and the taxes to pay for them. However, the close connection between spending and consumption that we see for private goods does not hold for taxes and public goods. I pay for a hamburger only if I want one, but I must pay my share of the taxes used to finance defense and public education even if I don't care a bit for these activities.

EQUITY

Our discussion of market failures like monopoly or externalities focused on defects in the allocative role of markets—imperfections that can be corrected by judicious intervention. But assume for the moment that the economy functioned with complete efficiency—always on the production-possibility frontier and never inside it, always choosing the right amount of public versus private goods, and so forth. Even if the market system worked perfectly, it might still lead to a flawed outcome.

Markets do not necessarily produce a fair distribution of income. A market economy may produce unacceptably high levels of inequality of income and consumption.

Why might the market mechanism produce an unacceptable solution to the question of *for whom?* The reason is that incomes are determined by a wide variety of factors, including effort, education, inheritance, factor prices, and luck. The resulting income distribution may not correspond to a fair outcome. Moreover, recall that goods follow dollar votes and not the greatest need. A rich man's cat may drink the milk that a poor boy needs to remain healthy. Does this happen because the market is failing? Not at all, for the market mechanism is doing its job—putting goods in the hands of those who have the dollar votes. If a country spends more fertilizing its lawns than feeding poor children, that is a defect of income distribution, not of the market. Even the most efficient market system may generate great inequality.

Often the income distribution in a market system is the result of accidents of birth. Every year *Forbes* magazine lists the 400 richest Americans, and it's impressive how many of them either received their wealth by inheritance or used inherited wealth as a springboard to even greater wealth. Would everyone regard that as necessarily right or ideal? Probably not. Should someone be allowed to become a billionaire simply by inheriting 5000 square miles of rangeland or the family's holding of oil wells? That is the way the cookie crumbles under laissez-faire capitalism.

For most of American history, economic growth was a rising tide that lifted all boats, raising the incomes of the poor as well as those of the rich. But over the last two decades, changes in family structure and declining wages of the less skilled and less educated have reversed the trend. With a return to greater emphasis on the market has come greater homelessness, more children living in poverty, and deterioration of many of America's central cities.

Income inequalities may be politically or ethically unacceptable. A nation does not need to accept the outcome of competitive markets as predetermined and immutable; people may examine the distribution of income and decide it is unfair. If a democratic society does not like the distribution of dollar votes under a laissez-faire market system, it can take steps to change the distribution of income.

Let's say that voters decide to reduce income inequality. What tools could the government use? First, it can engage in *progressive taxation*, taxing large incomes at a higher rate than small incomes. It might impose heavy taxes on wealth or on large inheritances to break the chain of privilege. The federal income and inheritance taxes are examples of such redistributive progressive taxation.

Second, because low tax rates cannot help those who have no income at all, governments can make *transfer payments,* which are money payments to people. Such transfers today include aid for the elderly, blind, and disabled and for those with dependent children, as well as unemployment insurance for the jobless. This system of transfer payments provides a "safety net" to protect the unfortunate from privation. And, finally, governments sometimes subsidize consumption of low-income groups by providing food stamps, subsidized medical care, and low-cost housing—though in the United States, such spending comprises a relatively small share of total spending.

These programs have become increasingly unpopular in the last two decades. As the real wages of the middle class have stagnated, people naturally ask why they should support the homeless or able-bodied people who do not work. What can economics contribute to debates about equality? Economics as a science cannot answer such normative questions as how much of our market incomes—if any—should be transferred to poor families. This is a political question that can be answered only at the ballot box.

Economics can analyze the costs or benefits of different redistributive systems. Economists have devoted much time to analyzing whether different income-redistribution devices (such as taxes and food stamps) lead to social waste (e.g., people work less or buy drugs rather than food). They have also studied whether giving poor people cash rather than goods is likely to be a more efficient way of reducing poverty. Economics cannot answer questions of how much poverty is acceptable and fair, but it can help design more effective programs to increase the incomes of the poor.

MACROECONOMIC GROWTH AND STABILITY

Since its origins, capitalism has been plagued by periodic bouts of inflation (rising prices) and recession (high unemployment). Since World War II, for example, there have been nine recessions in the United States, some putting millions of people out of work.

Today, thanks to the intellectual contribution of John Maynard Keynes and his followers, we know how to control the worst excesses of the business cycle. By careful use of fiscal and monetary policies, governments can affect output, employment, and inflation. The *fiscal policies* of government are the power to tax and the power to spend. *Monetary policy*

involves determining the supply of money and interest rates; these affect investment in capital goods and other interest-rate-sensitive spending. Using these two fundamental tools of macroeconomic policy, governments can influence the level of total spending, the rate of growth and level of output, the levels of employment and unemployment, and the price level and rate of inflation in an economy.

Governments in advanced industrial countries successfully applied the lessons of the Keynesian revolution over the last half-century. Spurred on by active monetary and fiscal policies, the market economies witnessed a period of unprecedented economic growth in the three decades after World War II.

In the 1980s, governments became more concerned with also designing macroeconomic policies to promote long-term objectives, such as economic growth and productivity. (*Economic growth* denotes the growth in a nation's total output, while *productivity* represents the output per unit input or the efficiency with which resources are used.) For example, tax rates were lowered in most industrial countries in order to improve incentives for saving and production. Many economists emphasized the importance of public saving through smaller budget deficits as a way to increase national saving and investment.

Macroeconomic policies for stabilization and economic growth include fiscal policies (of taxing and spending) along with monetary policies (which affect interest rates and credit conditions). Since the development of macroeconomics in the 1930s, governments have succeeded in curbing the worst excesses of inflation and unemployment.

Table 2-1 summarizes the economic role played by government today. It shows the important governmental functions of promoting efficiency, achieving a fairer distribution of income, and pursuing the macroeconomic objectives of economic growth and stability. In all advanced industrial societies we find a mixed economy in which the market determines output and prices in most individual sectors while government steers the overall economy with programs of taxation, spending, and monetary regulation.

TWILIGHT OF THE WELFARE STATE?

In 1942, the great Austrian-born Harvard economist Joseph Schumpeter argued that the United States

Failure of market economy	Government intervention	Current examples of government policy
Inefficiency:		
Monopoly	Encourage competition	Antitrust laws, deregulation
Externalities	Intervene in markets	Antipollution laws, antismoking ordinances
Public goods	Encourage beneficial activities	Build lighthouses, subsidize scientific research
Inequality:		
Unacceptable inequalities of income and wealth	Redistribute income	Progressive taxation of income and wealth; Income-support programs (e.g., food stamps)
Macroeconomic problems:		
Business cycles (high inflation and unemployment)	Stabilize through macroeconomic policies	Monetary policies (e.g., changes in money supply and interest rates); Fiscal policies (e.g., taxes and spending programs)
Slow economic growth	Stimulate growth	Invest in education; Raise national savings rate by reducing budget deficit

TABLE 2-1. Government Can Remedy the Shortcomings of the Market

was "capitalism living in an oxygen tent" on its march to socialism. Capitalism's success would breed alienation and self-doubt, sapping its efficiency and innovation. The next quarter-century saw sustained growth in government's involvement in the economies of North America and Western Europe *along with the most impressive economic performance ever recorded.*

The return to more-normal growth rates in the last two decades has been accompanied by increased skepticism about government's role. Critics of government say that the state is overly intrusive; governments create monopoly; government failures are just as pervasive as market failures; high taxes distort the allocation of resources; social security reduces saving; environmental regulation dulls the spirit of enterprise; government attempts to stabilize the economy must fail at best and increase inflation at

worst; and inflation chokes off investment. In short, for some, government is the problem rather than the solution.[4]

These views remind us how easy it is to take the achievements of the last century for granted. They remind us of the tendency to credit ourselves for successes while blaming others—particularly the government—for failures. In economics as in life, success has many parents, while failure is an orphan. Diatribes against government forget the many successes of collective action over the last century. We have reduced malnutrition and conquered many terrible diseases like smallpox. Government programs have increased literacy and life expectancy. Macro-

---

[4] For an eloquent account of economic controversies over the last three decades, see Paul Krugman, *Peddling Prosperity* (Norton, New York, 1994).

economic successes have reduced the sting of inflation and unemployment, while government transfer programs have brought health care to the poor and improved the quality of life for the aged. State-supported science has penetrated the atom, discovered the DNA molecule, and explored outer space.

Of course, these successes did not belong to governments alone. Governments harnessed private ingenuity through the market mechanism to help achieve these social aims. And, in some cases, governments were like orators who didn't know when enough was enough. Government's successes and failures remind us that drawing the right boundary between market and government is an enduring problem. The tools of economics are indispensable to help societies find the *golden mean* between *laissez faire* market mechanisms and democratic rules of the road: the good Mixed Economy is, perforce, the Limited Mixed Economy. But those who would reduce government to the constable plus a few lighthouses are living in the last century. An efficient and humane society requires both halves of the mixed system—market and government. Operating a modern economy without both is like trying to clap with one hand.

SUMMARY

A. What Is a Market?

1. In an economy like the United States, most economic decisions are made in markets, which serve as mechanisms by which buyers and sellers meet to trade and to determine prices and quantities for commodities. Adam Smith proclaimed that the *invisible hand* of markets would lead to the optimal economic outcome as individuals pursue their own self-interest. And while markets are far from perfect, they have proved remarkably effective at solving the problems of *how*, *what*, and *for whom*.

2. The market mechanism works as follows to determine the what and the how: The dollar votes of people affect prices of goods; these prices serve as guides for the amounts of the different goods to be produced. When people demand more of a good, businesses can profit by expanding production of that good. Under perfect competition, a business must find the cheapest method of production, efficiently using labor, land, and other factors; otherwise, it will incur losses and be eliminated from the market.

3. At the same time that the *what* and *how* problems are being resolved by prices, so is the problem of *for whom*. The distribution of income is determined by the ownership of factors of production (land, labor, and capital) and by factor prices. People possessing fertile land or the ability to hit home runs will earn many dollar votes to buy consumer goods. Those without property and with skills, color, or sex that the market does not value will receive low incomes.

B. Trade, Money, and Capital

4. As economies develop, they become more specialized. Division of labor allows a task to be broken into a number of smaller chores that can each be mastered and performed more quickly by a single worker. Specialization arises from the increasing tendency to use roundabout methods of production that require many specialized skills. As individuals and countries become increasingly specialized, they tend to concentrate on particular commodities and trade their surplus output for goods produced by others. Voluntary trade, based on specialization, benefits all.

5. Trade in specialized goods and services today relies on money to lubricate the wheels of trade. Money is the universally acceptable medium of exchange—currency and checks. It is used to pay for everything from apple tarts to zebra skins. By accepting money, people and nations can specialize in producing a few goods and trade them for others; without money, we would waste much time constantly bartering one good for another.

6. Capital goods—produced inputs such as machinery, structures, and inventories of goods in process—permit roundabout methods of production that add much to a nation's output. These roundabout methods take time and resources to get started and therefore require a temporary sacrifice of present consumption in order to increase future consumption. The rules that define how capital and other assets can be bought, sold, and used are the system of property rights. In no economic system are private-property rights unlimited.

C. The Economic Role of Government

7. Although the market mechanism is an admirable way of producing and allocating goods, sometimes market failures lead to deficiencies in the economic outcomes. Government may step in to correct these failures. Government's role in a modern economy is to ensure efficiency, to correct an unfair distribution of income, and to promote economic growth and stability.

8. Markets fail to provide an efficient allocation of resources in the presence of imperfect competition or externalities. Imperfect competition, such as monopoly, produces high prices and low levels of output. To combat these conditions, governments regulate businesses or put legal antitrust constraints on business behavior. Externalities arise when activities impose costs or bestow benefits that are not paid for in the marketplace. Governments may decide to step in and regulate these spillovers (as it does with air pollution) or provide for *public goods* (as in the case of public health).

9. Markets do not necessarily produce a fair distribution of income; they may spin off unacceptably high inequality of income and consumption. In response, governments can alter the pattern of incomes (the *for whom*) generated by market wages, rents, interest, and dividends. Modern governments use taxation to raise revenues for transfers or income-support programs that place a financial safety net under the needy.

10. Since the development of macroeconomics in the 1930s, government has undertaken a third role: using fiscal powers (of taxing and spending) and monetary policy (affecting credit and interest rates) to promote long-run economic growth and productivity and to tame the business cycle's excesses of inflation and unemployment. Since 1980, the blend of the mixed economy called the welfare state has been on the defensive in the enduring struggle over the boundary between state and market.

CONCEPTS FOR REVIEW

The Market Mechanism

market, market mechanism
markets for goods and for factors of
    production
prices as signals
market equilibrium
perfect and imperfect competition
Adam Smith's invisible-hand doctrine

Features of a Modern Economy

specialization and division of labor
money
factors of production (land, labor,
    capital)
capital, private property, and property
    rights

Government's Economic Role

efficiency, equity, stability
inefficiencies: monopoly and exter-
    nalities
inequity of incomes under markets
macroeconomic policies:
    fiscal and monetary policies
    stabilization and growth

QUESTIONS FOR DISCUSSION

1. What determines the composition of national output? In some cases, we say that there is "consumer sovereignty," meaning that consumers decide how to spend their incomes on the basis of their tastes and market prices. In other cases, decisions are made by political choices of legislatures. Consider the following examples: transportation, education, police, energy efficiency of appliances, health-care coverage, television advertising. For each, describe whether the allocation is by consumer sovereignty or by political decision. Would you change the method of allocation for any of these goods?

2. Consider the following cases of government intervention in the economy: regulations to limit air pollution, research on an AIDS vaccine, income supplements to the elderly, price regulation of a local water monopoly, a monetary-policy step to curb inflation. What role of government is being pursued in each case?

3. When a good is limited, some means must be found to ration the scarce commodity. Some examples of rationing devices are auctions, ration coupons, and first-come, first-served systems. What are the strengths and weaknesses of each? Explain carefully in what sense a market mechanism "rations" scarce goods and services.

4. The circular flow of goods and inputs illustrated in Figure 2-1 has a corresponding flow of dollar incomes and spending. Draw a circular-flow diagram for the dollar flows in the economy, and compare it with the circular flow of goods and inputs. What is the role of money in the dollar circular flow?

5. This chapter discusses many "market failures," areas in which the invisible hand guides the economy poorly, and describes the role of government. Is it possible that there are, as well, "government failures," government attempts to curb market failures that are worse

than the original market failures? Think of some examples of government failures. Give some examples in which government failures are so bad that it is better to live with the market failures than to try to correct them.

6. Give three examples of specialization and division of labor. In what areas are you and your friends thinking of specializing? What might be the perils of *over* specialization?

7. "Lincoln freed the slaves. With one pen stroke he destroyed much of the capital the South had accumulated over the years." Comment.

8. The table to the right shows some of the major expenditures of the federal government. Explain how each one relates to the economic role of government.

Major Expenditure Categories for Federal Government	
Budget category	Federal spending, 1998 ($, billion)
Social security	384
National defense	259
Income security	247
Interest on public debt	250
Natural resources and environment	22
Administration of justice	24
Science and technology	16

Source: Office of Management and Budget, *Budget of the United States Government,* Fiscal Year 1998.

CHAPTER 3
BASIC ELEMENTS OF SUPPLY AND DEMAND

The level of the sea is not more surely kept, than is the equilibrium of value in society, by the demand and supply: the artifice or legislation punishes itself, by reactions, gluts, and bankruptcies.

Ralph Waldo Emerson (1860)

VOLATILE MARKETS

Markets are akin to the weather. They are always changing, dynamic, unpredictable, subject to frequent periods of storm and calm, complex, and fascinating. As with the weather, careful study of markets also shows certain forces and patterns underneath the daily and apparently random movements. The essential tool for understanding the movement of prices and outputs in individual markets is called the analysis of supply and demand.

Take the example of gasoline prices, illustrated in Figure 3-1 on the next page. (This shows the "real gasoline price," or the price corrected for movements in the general price level.) Demand for gasoline and other oil products rose sharply after World War II as people fell in love with the automobile and moved increasingly to the suburbs. Next, in the 1970s, supply restrictions, wars among producers, and revolutions reduced production, with the consequent price spikes seen after 1973 and 1979. Then, as a result of energy conservation, smaller cars, and price wars, the real price of gasoline fell sharply, from about $2.50 per gallon in 1980 to around $1.40 in 1996.

What lay behind these dramatic shifts? Econom-

ics has a very powerful tool for explaining these and many other changes in the economic environment. It is called the *theory of supply and demand*. This theory shows how consumer preferences determine consumer demand for commodities, while business costs are the foundation of the supply of commodities. The increases in the price of gasoline occurred either because the demand for gasoline had gone up or because the supply of oil had decreased. The same is true for every market, from computers to diamonds to land: changes in supply and demand drive changes in output and prices. If you understand how supply and demand work, you have gone a long way toward understanding a market economy.

This chapter introduces the notions of supply and demand, and it shows how they operate in competitive markets for *individual commodities*. We begin with demand curves and then discuss supply curves. Using these basic tools, we will see how the market price is determined (or reaches its competitive equilibrium) where these two curves intersect—where the forces of demand and supply are just in balance. It is the movement of prices, the price mechanism, which brings supply and demand into balance or equilibrium. This chapter closes with some examples of how supply-and-demand analysis can be applied.

43

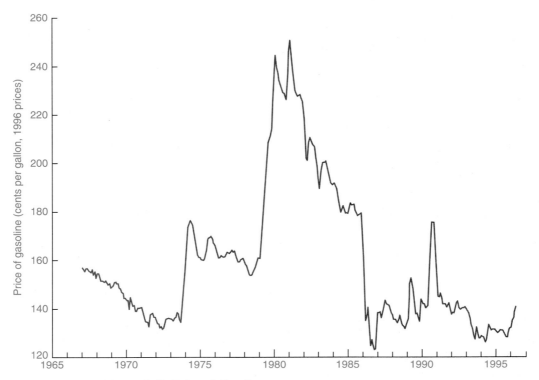

FIGURE 3-1. The Volatile Price of Gasoline

Gasoline prices have fluctuated widely over the last three decades. The little wiggle at the end
—the price run-up before the 1996 U.S. presidential election—led to widespread charges of
profiteering and a call for a reduction of the federal gasoline tax. You can easily understand
the social unrest provoked by the enormous price increases in the 1970s. Supply and
demand are crucial for understanding these trends. (Source: U.S. Departments of Energy
and Labor. The price of gasoline has been converted into 1996 prices using the consumer
price index.)

A. THE DEMAND SCHEDULE

Both common sense and careful scientific observation show that the amount of a commodity people
buy depends on its price. The higher the price of an
article, other things being constant,[1] the fewer units

consumers are willing to buy. The lower its market
price, the more units of it are bought.

There exists a definite relationship between the
market price of a good and the quantity demanded
of that good, other things held constant. This relationship between price and quantity bought is called
the **demand schedule,** or the **demand curve.**

Let's look at a simple example. Table 3-1 presents
a hypothetical demand schedule for cornflakes. At

---

[1] Later in this chapter we discuss the other factors that influence demand, including income and tastes. The term "other
things held constant" simply means we are varying the price
without changing any of these other determinants of
demand.

Demand Schedule for Cornflakes		
	(1)	(2)
	Price ($ per box) *P*	Quantity demanded (millions of boxes per year) *Q*
A	5	9
B	4	10
C	3	12
D	2	15
E	1	20

TABLE 3-1. The Demand Schedule Relates Quantity Demanded to Price

At each market price, consumers will want to buy a certain quantity of cornflakes. As the price of cornflakes falls, the quantity of cornflakes demanded will rise.

each price, we can determine the quantity of cornflakes that consumers purchase. For example, at $5 per box, consumers will buy 9 million boxes per year.

At a lower price, more cornflakes are bought. Thus, at a cornflakes price of $4, the quantity bought is 10 million boxes. At yet a lower price (*P*) equal to $3, the quantity demanded (*Q*) is still greater, at 12 million. And so forth. We can determine the quantity demanded at each listed price in Table 3-1.

THE DEMAND CURVE

The graphical representation of the demand schedule is the *demand curve*. We show the demand curve in Figure 3-2, which graphs the quantity of cornflakes demanded on the horizontal axis and the price of cornflakes on the vertical axis. Note that quantity and price are inversely related, *Q* going up when *P* goes down. The curve slopes downward, going from northwest to southeast. This important property is called the *law of downward-sloping demand*. It is based on common sense as well as economic theory and has been empirically tested and verified for practically all commodities—cornflakes, gasoline, college education, and illegal drugs being a few examples.

Law of downward-sloping demand: When the price of a commodity is raised (and other things are held constant), buyers tend to buy less of the commodity. Similarly, when the price is lowered, other things being constant, quantity demanded increases.

Why does quantity demanded tend to fall as price rises? For two reasons. First is the **substitution effect.** When the price of a good rises, I will substitute other similar goods for it (as the price of beef rises, I eat more chicken). A second reason for the depressing effect of price increases on purchases is the **income effect.** This comes into play because when a price goes up, I find myself somewhat poorer than I was before. If gasoline prices double, I have in effect less real income, so I will naturally curb my consumption of gasoline and other goods.

Market Demand

Our discussion of demand has so far referred to "the" demand curve. But whose demand is it? Mine? Yours? Everybody's? The fundamental building block for demand is individual tastes and needs. However, in this chapter we will always focus on the *market demand,* which represents the sum total of all

FIGURE 3-2. A Downward-Sloping Demand Curve Relates Quantity Demanded to Price

In the demand curve for cornflakes, prices (*P*) are measured on the vertical axis while quantity demanded (*Q*) is measured on the horizontal axis. Each pair of (*P,Q*) numbers from Table 3-1 is plotted as a point and then a smooth curve is passed through the points to give us a demand curve, *DD*. The negative slope of the demand curve illustrates the law of downward-sloping demand.

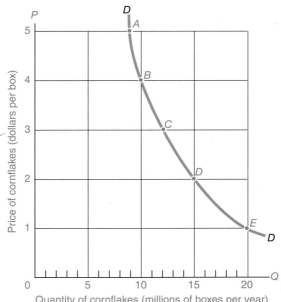

individual demands. The market demand curve is found by adding together the quantities demanded by all individuals at each price. The market demand is what is observable in the real world.

Does the market demand curve obey the law of downward-sloping demand? It certainly does. If prices drop, for example, the lower prices attract new customers, through the substitution effect. In addition, a price reduction will induce extra purchases of goods by existing consumers, through both the income and substitution effects. Conversely, a rise in the price of a good will cause some of us to buy less.

We can illustrate the law of downward-sloping demand for the case of personal computers (PCs). In the early 1980s, the price of PCs was astronomical, and they were found in few businesses and even fewer homes. People used typewriters or pens to write papers and did calculations by hand.

But the prices of PCs fell sharply in the last decade, and the lower prices enticed new buyers. As more and more people could afford them, PCs came to be widely used for work, for school, and for fun. Even today, the computer revolution is unfinished. As prices for personal computers drop further, even more people will find it worthwhile to buy their first PC or to buy an extra one.

Behind the Demand Curve

What determines the market demand curve for cornflakes or gasoline or computers? A whole array of factors influences how much will be demanded at a given price: average levels of income, the size of the population, the prices and availability of related goods, individual and social tastes, and special influences.

- The *average income* of consumers is a key determinant of demand. As people's incomes rise, individuals tend to buy more of almost everything, even if prices don't change. Automobile purchases tend to rise sharply with higher levels of income.
- The *size of the market*—measured, say, by the population—clearly affects the market demand curve. California's 32 million people tend to buy 32 times more apples and cars than do Rhode Island's 1 million people.

- The prices and availability of *related goods* influence the demand for a commodity. A particularly important connection exists among substitute goods—ones that tend to perform the same function, such as cornflakes and oatmeal, pens and pencils, small cars and large cars, or oil and natural gas. Demand for good A tends to be low if the price of substitute product B is low. (For example, if the price of beef rises, will that increase or decrease the demand for chicken?)
- In addition to these objective elements, there is a set of subjective elements called *tastes* or *preferences*. Tastes represent a variety of cultural and historical influences. They may reflect genuine psychological or physiological needs (for liquids, love, or excitement). And they may include artificially contrived cravings (for cigarettes, drugs, or fancy sports cars). They may contain a large element of tradition or religion (eating beef is popular in America but taboo in India, while curried jellyfish is a delicacy in Japan but would make many Americans gag).
- Finally, *special influences* will affect the demand for particular goods. The demand for umbrellas is high in rainy Seattle but low in sunny Phoenix; the demand for air conditioners will rise in hot weather; the demand for automobiles will be low in New York, where public transport is plentiful and parking is a nightmare. In addition, expectations about future economic conditions, particularly prices, may have an important impact on demand.

The determinants of demand are summarized in Table 3-2, which uses automobiles as an example.

A Change in Demand

As economic life evolves, demand changes incessantly. Demand curves sit still only in textbooks.

Why does the demand curve shift? Because the influences other than the good's price change. For example, there are many possible reasons why the American demand for cars grew sharply from 1950 to 1997: the average real income of Americans almost doubled; the adult population rose by more than half; and there was a decline in the availability of alternative forms of local transportation (bus,

Factors affecting the demand curve	Example for automobiles
1. **Average income**	As incomes rise, people increase car purchases.
2. **Population**	A growth in population increases car purchases.
3. **Prices of related goods**	Lower gasoline prices raise the demand for cars.
4. **Tastes**	Having a new car becomes a status symbol.
5. **Special influences**	Special influences include availability of alternative forms of transportation, safety of automobiles, expectations of future price increases, etc.

TABLE 3-2. Many Factors Affect the Demand Curve

trolley, and rail). The result of all these changes was a rightward shift in the demand curve for cars.

The net effect of the changes in underlying influences is what we call an *increase in demand*. An increase in the demand for automobiles is illustrated in Figure 3-3 as a rightward shift in the demand curve. Note that the shift means that more cars will be bought at every price.

FIGURE 3-3. Increase in Demand for Automobiles

As elements underlying demand change, the demand for automobiles is affected. Here we see the effect of rising average income, increased population, and lower gasoline prices on the demand for automobiles. We call this shift in the demand curve an increase in demand.

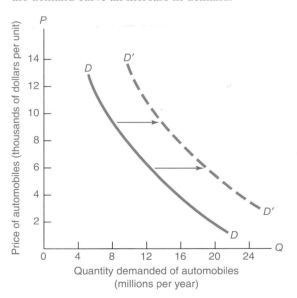

You can test yourself by answering the following questions: Will a warm winter shift the demand curve for heating oil leftward or rightward? Why? What will happen to the demand for baseball tickets if young people lose interest in baseball and watch basketball instead? What will a sharp fall in the price of personal computers do to the demand for typewriters? What happens to the demand for a college education if wages are falling for blue-collar jobs which don't require a college degree?

Do not confuse movement along curves with shift of curves. Great care must be taken not to confuse a change in demand (which denotes a shift of the demand curve) with a change in the quantity demanded (which means moving to a different point on the same demand curve after a price change).

A change in demand occurs when one of the elements underlying the demand curve shifts. Take the case of pizzas. As incomes increase, consumers will want to buy more pizzas even if pizza prices do not change. In other words, higher incomes will increase demand and shift the demand curve for pizzas out and to the right. This is a shift in the demand for pizzas.

Distinguish this from a change in quantity demanded that occurs because consumers tend to buy more pizzas as pizza prices fall, all other things remaining constant. Here, the increased purchases result not from an increase in demand but from the price decrease. This change represents *a movement along* the demand curve, not a *shift of* the demand curve. A movement along the demand curve means that other things were held constant when price changed.

B. THE SUPPLY SCHEDULE

Let us now turn from demand to supply. The supply side of a market typically involves the terms on which businesses produce and sell their products. The supply of tomatoes tells us the quantity of tomatoes that will be sold at each tomato price. More precisely, the supply schedule relates the quantity supplied of a good to its market price, other things constant. In considering supply, the other things that are held constant include costs of production, prices of related goods, and government policies.

The **supply schedule** (or **supply curve**) for a commodity shows the relationship between its market price and the amount of that commodity that producers are willing to produce and sell, other things held constant.

THE SUPPLY CURVE

Table 3-3 shows a hypothetical supply schedule for cornflakes, and Figure 3-4 plots the data from the table in the form of a supply curve. These data show that at a cornflakes price of $1 per box, no cornflakes at all will be produced. At such a low price, breakfast cereal manufacturers might want to devote their factories to producing other types of cereal, like bran flakes, that earn them more profit than

cornflakes. As the price of cornflakes increases, ever more cornflakes will be produced. At ever-higher cornflakes prices, cereal makers will find it profitable to add more workers and to buy more automated cornflakes-stuffing machines and even more cornflakes factories. All these will increase the output of cornflakes at the higher market prices.

Figure 3-4 shows the typical case of an upward-sloping supply curve for an individual commodity. One important reason for the upward slope is "the law of diminishing returns" (a concept we will learn more about later). Wine will illustrate this important law. If society wants more wine, then additional labor will have to be added to the limited land sites suitable for producing wine grapes. Each new worker will be adding less and less extra product. The price needed to coax out additional wine output is there-

FIGURE 3-4. Supply Curve Relates Quantity Supplied to Price
The supply curve plots the price and quantity pairs from Table 3-3. A smooth curve is passed through these points to give the upward-sloping supply curve, *SS*.

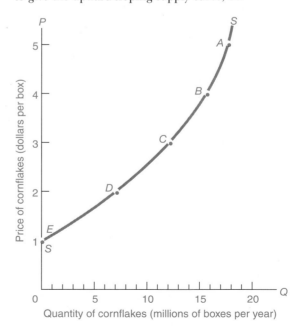

	Supply Schedule for Cornflakes	
	(1) Price ($ per box) P	(2) Quantity supplied (millions of boxes per year) Q
A	5	18
B	4	16
C	3	12
D	2	7
E	1	0

TABLE 3-3. Supply Schedule Relates Quantity Supplied to Price
The table shows, for each price, the quantity of cornflakes that cornflakes makers want to produce and sell. Note the positive relation between price and quantity supplied.

fore higher. By raising the price of wine, society can persuade wine producers to produce and sell more wine; the supply curve for wine is therefore upward-sloping. Similar reasoning applies to many other goods as well.

Behind the Supply Curve

In examining the forces determining the supply curve, the fundamental point to grasp is that producers supply commodities for profit and not for fun or charity. For example, a cereal maker will supply more cornflakes at higher prices because it is profitable to do so; conversely, when the price of cornflakes falls below the cost of production, cereal makers will switch to other lines of business.

One major element underlying the supply curve is the *cost of production.* When production costs for a good are low relative to the market price, it is profitable for producers to supply a great deal. When production costs are high relative to price, firms produce little, switch to the production of other products, or may simply go out of business.

Production costs are primarily determined by the *prices of inputs* and *technological advances.* The prices of inputs such as labor, energy, or machinery obviously have a very important influence on the cost of producing a given level of output. For example, when oil prices rose sharply in the 1970s, the increase raised the price of energy for manufacturers, increased their production costs, and lowered their supply. As computer prices fell over the last three decades, businesses increasingly substituted computerized for manual technologies, as in payroll or accounting operations.

An equally important determinant of production costs is *technological advances,* which consist of changes that lower the amount of inputs needed to produce the same quantity of output. Such advances include everything from actual scientific breakthroughs to better application of existing technology or simply reorganization of the flow of work. For example, manufacturers have become much more efficient over the last decade or so. It takes far fewer hours of labor to produce an automobile today than it did just 10 years ago. This advance enables car makers to produce more automobiles at the same cost. Or, to give another example, if a computer program allows a new customer to open a checking account with a few quick entries

on a computer screen, that, too, lowers the cost of production.

But production costs are not the only ingredient that goes into the supply curve. Firms are always alert to alternative opportunities to use their productive assets. So supply is also influenced by the *prices of related goods,* particularly goods that can be readily substituted for one another as outputs of the production process. If the price of one production substitute rises, the supply of another substitute will decrease. For example, auto companies typically make several different car models in the same factory. If there's more demand for one model, and its price rises, they will switch more of their assembly lines to making that model, and the supply of the other models will fall. Or if the demand and price for trucks rise, the entire factory can be converted to making trucks, and the supply of cars will fall.

Government policy also has an important impact on the supply curve. Environmental and health considerations determine what technologies can be used, while taxes and minimum-wage laws can significantly raise input prices. In the local electricity market, government regulations influence both the number of firms that can compete and the prices they charge. And government trade policies have a major impact upon supply. For instance, when a free-trade agreement opens up the U.S. market to Mexican goods, the supply of Mexican goods increases.

Finally, *special influences* affect the supply curve. The weather exerts an important influence on farming and on the ski industry. The computer industry has been marked by a keen spirit of innovation, which has led to a continuous flow of new products. Market structure will affect supply, and expectations about future prices often have an important impact upon supply decisions.

Table 3-4 on page 50 highlights the important determinants of supply, using automobiles as an example.

Shifts in Supply

Businesses are constantly changing the mix of products and services they provide. What lies behind these changes in supply behavior?

Supply changes when any influences other than the commodity's own price change. In terms of a supply curve, we say that supply increases (or decreases) when the amount supplied increases (or decreases) at each market price.

Factors affecting the supply curve	Example for automobiles
1. **Technology**	Computerized manufacturing lowers production costs and increases supply.
2. **Input prices**	A reduction in the wage paid to autoworkers lowers production costs and increases supply.
3. **Prices of related goods**	If truck prices fall, supply of cars rises.
4. **Government policy**	Removing quotas and tariffs on imported automobiles increases automobile supply.
5. **Special influences**	If the government lowers standards on pollution-control equipment, supply of cars may increase.

TABLE 3-4. Supply Is Affected by Production Costs and Other Factors

When automobile prices change, producers change their production and quantity supplied, but the supply and the supply curve do not shift. By contrast, when other influences affecting supply change, supply changes and the supply curve shifts.

We can illustrate a shift in supply for the automobile market. Supply would increase if the introduction of cost-saving computerized design and manufacturing reduced the labor required to produce cars, if autoworkers took a pay cut, if Japanese automakers were allowed to export more cars to the United States, or if the government removed some of the regulatory requirements on the industry. Any of these elements would increase the supply of automobiles in the United States at each price. Figure 3-5 illustrates an increase in supply of automobiles.

To test your understanding of supply shifts, think about the following: What would happen to the world supply curve for oil if a revolution in Saudi Arabia led to declining oil production? What would happen to the supply curve for tomatoes in the United States if quotas on Mexican tomatoes were imposed to pander to Florida tomato growers in an election year? What happens to the supply curve for computers if Intel introduces a new Sextium chip that dramatically increases computing speeds?

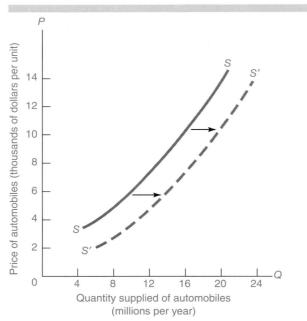

FIGURE 3-5. Increased Supply of Automobiles
As production costs fall or Japanese competition increases, the supply of automobiles increases. At each price, domestic and foreign producers will supply more automobiles, and the supply curve therefore shifts to the right. (What would happen to the supply curve if Congress put a restrictive quota on automobile imports?)

⊙ **Reminder on shifts of curves vs. movements along curves:** As you answer the questions above, make sure to keep in mind the difference between moving along a curve and a shift of the curve. Look back at the gasoline-price curve in Figure 3-1 on page 44. When the price of oil rose and the production of oil declined because of political disturbances in the 1970s, these changes resulted from an inward shift in the supply curve. When sales of gasoline declined in response to the higher price, that was a movement along the demand curve. How would you describe a rise in chicken production that was induced by a rise in chicken prices? What about the case of a rise in chicken production because of a fall in the price of chicken feed?

C. EQUILIBRIUM OF SUPPLY AND DEMAND

Up to this point we have been considering demand and supply in isolation. We know the amounts that are willingly bought and sold at each price. We have seen that consumers demand different amounts of cornflakes, cars, and computers as a function of these goods' prices. Similarly, producers willingly supply different amounts of these and other goods depending on their prices. But how can we put both sides of the market together?

The answer is that supply and demand interact to produce an equilibrium price and quantity, or a market equilibrium. The **market equilibrium** comes at that price and quantity where the forces of supply and demand are in balance. At the equilibrium price, the amount that buyers want to buy is just equal to the amount that sellers want to sell. The reason we call this an equilibrium is that, when the forces of supply and demand are in balance, there is no reason for price to rise or fall, as long as other things remain unchanged.

Let us work through the cornflakes example in Table 3-5 to see how supply and demand determine a market equilibrium; the numbers in this table come from Tables 3-1 and 3-3. To find the market price and quantity, we find a price at which the amounts desired to be bought and sold just match. If we try a price of $5 per box, will it prevail for long? Clearly not. As row A in Table 3-5 shows, at $5 pro-

ducers would like to sell 18 million boxes per year while demanders want to buy only 9. The amount supplied at $5 exceeds the amount demanded, and stocks of cornflakes pile up in supermarkets. Because too few consumers are chasing too many cornflakes, the price of cornflakes will tend to fall, as shown in column (5) of Table 3-5.

Say we try $2. Does that price clear the market? A quick look at row D shows that at $2 consumption exceeds production. Cornflakes begin to disappear from the stores at that price. As people scramble around to find their desired cornflakes, they will tend to bid up the price of cornflakes, as shown in column (5) of Table 3-5.

We could try other prices, but we can easily see that the equilibrium price is $3, or row C in Table 3-5. At $3, consumers' desired demand exactly equals producers' desired production, each of which is 12 units. Only at $3 will consumers and suppliers both be making consistent decisions.

✓ A market equilibrium comes at the price at which quantity demanded equals quantity supplied. At that equilibrium, there is no tendency for the price to rise or fall. The equilibrium price is also called the *market-clearing price*. This denotes that all supply and demand orders are filled, the books are "cleared" of orders, and demanders and suppliers are satisfied.

TABLE 3-5. Equilibrium Price Comes Where Quantity Demanded Equals Quantity Supplied

The table shows the quantities supplied and demanded at different prices. Only at the equilibrium price of $3 per box does amount supplied equal amount demanded. At too low a price there is a shortage and price tends to rise. Too high a price produces a surplus, which will depress price.

Combining Demand and Supply for Cornflakes				
(1)	(2)	(3)	(4)	(5)
Possible price ($ per box)	Quantity demanded (millions of boxes per year)	Quantity supplied (millions of boxes per year)	State of market	Pressure on price
A 5	9	18	Surplus	↓Downward
B 4	10	16	Surplus	↓Downward
C 3	12	12	Equilibrium	Neutral
D 2	15	7	Shortage	↑Upward
E 1	20	0	Shortage	↑Upward

EQUILIBRIUM WITH SUPPLY AND DEMAND CURVES

We often show the market equilibrium through a supply-and-demand diagram like the one in Figure 3-6; this figure combines the supply curve from Figure 3-4 with the demand curve from Figure 3-2. Combining the two graphs is possible because they are drawn with exactly the same units on each axis.

We find the market equilibrium by looking for the price at which quantity demanded equals quantity supplied. *The equilibrium price comes at the intersection of the supply and demand curves, at point C.*

How do we know that the intersection of the supply and demand curves is the market equilibrium? Let us repeat our earlier experiment. Start with the initial high price of $5 per box, shown at the top of the price axis in Figure 3-6. At that price, suppliers want to sell more than demanders want to buy. The result is a *surplus,* or excess of quantity supplied over quantity demanded, shown in the figure by the black line labeled "Surplus." The arrows along the curves show the direction that price tends to move when a market is in surplus.

At a low price of $2 per box, the market shows a *shortage,* or excess of quantity demanded over quantity supplied, here shown by the black line labeled "Shortage." Under conditions of shortage, the competition among buyers for limited goods causes the price to rise, as shown in the figure by the arrows pointing upward.

We now see that the balance or equilibrium of supply and demand comes at point *C, where the supply and demand curves intersect.* At point *C,* where the price is $3 per box and the quantity is 12 units, the quantities demanded and supplied are equal: there are no shortages or surpluses; there is no tendency for price to rise or fall. At point *C* and only at point *C,* the forces of supply and demand are in balance and the price has settled at a sustainable level.

✓ The equilibrium price and quantity come at that level where the amount willingly supplied equals the amount willingly demanded. In a competitive market, this equilibrium is found at the intersection of the supply and demand curves. There are no shortages or surpluses at the equilibrium price.

Effect of a Shift in Supply or Demand

The analysis of the supply-and-demand apparatus can do much more than tell us about the equi-

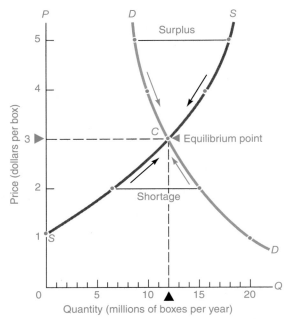

FIGURE 3-6. Market Equilibrium Comes at the Intersection of Supply and Demand Curves

The market equilibrium price and quantity come at the intersection of the supply and demand curves. At a price of $3, at point *C,* firms willingly supply what consumers willingly demand. When price is too low (say, at $2), quantity demanded exceeds quantity supplied, shortages occur, and the price is driven up to equilibrium. What occurs at a price of $4?

librium price and quantity. It can also be used to predict the impact of changes in economic conditions on prices and quantities. Let's change our example to the staff of life, bread. Suppose that a spell of bad weather raises the price of wheat, a key ingredient of bread. That shifts the supply curve for bread to the left. This is illustrated in Figure 3-7(*a*), where the bread supply curve has shifted from *SS* to *S′S′.* In contrast, the demand curve has not shifted; people have the same desire for their daily sandwich whether the harvest is good or bad.

What happens in the bread market? The bad harvest causes bakers to produce less bread at the old price, so quantity demanded exceeds quantity supplied. The price of bread therefore rises, encouraging

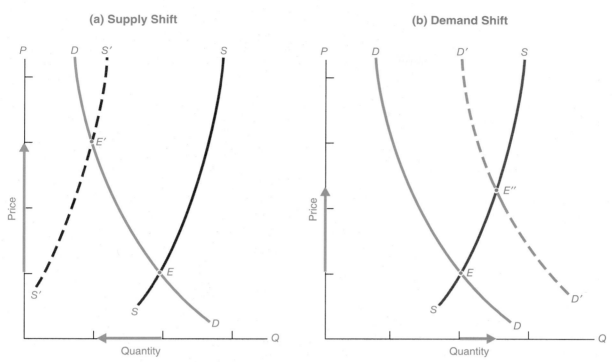

FIGURE 3-7. Shifts in Supply or Demand Change Equilibrium Price and Quantity
(**a**) If supply shifts leftward, a shortage will develop at the original price. Price will be bid up until quantities willingly bought and sold are equal, at new equilibrium E'. (**b**) A shift in the demand curve leads to excess demand. Price will be bid up as equilibrium price and quantity move upward to E''.

production and thereby raising quantity supplied, while simultaneously discouraging consumption and lowering quantity demanded. The price continues to rise until, at the new equilibrium price, the amounts demanded and supplied are once again equal.

As Figure 3-7(a) shows, the new equilibrium is found at E', the intersection of the new supply curve $S'S'$ and the original demand curve. Thus a bad harvest (or any leftward shift of the supply curve) raises prices and, by the law of downward-sloping demand, lowers quantity demanded.

Suppose that new baking technologies lower costs and therefore increase supply. That means the supply curve shifts down and to the right. Draw in a new $S''S''$ curve, along with the new equilibrium E'''. Why is the equilibrium price lower? Why is the equilibrium quantity higher?

We can also use our supply-and-demand apparatus to examine how changes in demand affect the market equilibrium. Suppose that there is a sharp increase in family incomes, so everyone wants to eat more bread. This is represented in Figure 3-7(b) as a "demand shift" in which, at every price, consumers demand a higher quantity of bread. The demand curve thus shifts *rightward* from DD to $D'D'$.

The demand shift produces a shortage of bread at the old price. A scramble for bread ensues, with long lines in the bakeries. Prices are bid upward until supply and demand come back into balance at a higher price. Graphically, the increase in demand has changed the market equilibrium from E to E'' in Figure 3-7(b).

For both examples of shifts—a shift in supply and a shift in demand—a variable underlying the

	Demand and supply shifts	Effect on price and quantity
If demand rises . . .	The demand curve shifts to the right, and . . .	Price ↑ Quantity ↑
If demand falls . . .	The demand curve shifts to the left, and . . .	Price ↓ Quantity ↓
If supply rises . . .	The supply curve shifts to the right, and . . .	Price ↓ Quantity ↑
If supply falls . . .	The supply curve shifts to the left, and . . .	Price ↑ Quantity ↓

TABLE 3-6. The Effect on Price and Quantity of Different Demand and Supply Shifts

demand or supply curve has changed. In the case of supply, there might have been a change in technology or input prices. For the demand shift, one of the influences affecting consumer demand—incomes, population, the prices of related goods, or tastes—changed and thereby shifted the demand schedule (see Table 3-6).

When the elements underlying demand or supply change, this leads to shifts in demand or supply and to changes in the market equilibrium of price and quantity.

Interpreting Changes in Price and Quantity

Let's go back to our bread example. Suppose that you go to the store and see that the price of bread has doubled. Does the increase in price mean that the demand for bread has risen, or does it mean that bread has become more expensive to produce? The correct answer is that without more information, you don't know—it could be either one, or even both. Let's look at another example. If fewer airline tickets are sold, is the cause that airline fares have gone up or that demand for air travel has gone down? Airlines will be most interested in the answer to this question.

Economists deal with these sorts of questions all the time: When prices or quantities change in a market, does the situation reflect a change on the supply side or the demand side? Sometimes, in simple situations, looking at price and quantity simultaneously gives you a clue about whether it's the supply curve that's shifted or the demand curve. For example, a

rise in the price of bread accompanied by a *decrease* in quantity suggests that the supply curve has shifted to the left (a decrease in supply). A rise in price accompanied by an *increase* in quantity indicates that the demand curve for bread has probably shifted to the right (an increase in demand).

This point is illustrated in Figure 3-8. In both panel (*a*) and panel (*b*), quantity goes up. But in (*a*) the price rises, and in (*b*) the price falls. Figure 3-8(*a*) shows the case of an increase in demand, or a shift in the demand curve. As a result of the shift, the equilibrium quantity demanded increases from 10 to 15 units. The case of a movement along the demand curve is shown in Figure 3-8(*b*). In this case, a supply shift changes the market equilibrium from point E to point E''. As a result, the quantity demanded changes from 10 to 15 units. But demand does not change in this case; rather, quantity demanded increases as consumers move along their demand curve from E to E'' in response to a price change.

The elusive concept of equilibrium: The notion of equilibrium is one of the most elusive concepts of economics. We are familiar with equilibrium in our everyday lives from seeing, for example, an orange resting at the bottom of a bowl or a pendulum at rest. In economics, equilibrium means that the different forces operating on a market are in balance, so the resulting price and quantity align the desires of purchasers and suppliers. Too low a price means that the forces are *not* in balance—that the forces attracting demand are greater than the forces attracting supply, so there is excess

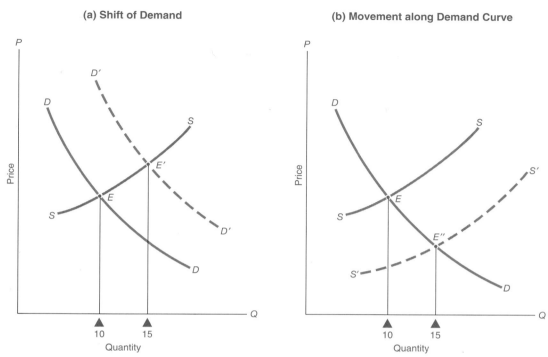

(a) Shift of Demand

(b) Movement along Demand Curve

FIGURE 3-8. Shifts of and Movements along Curves
Start out with initial equilibrium at E and a quantity of 10 units. In (**a**), an increase in demand (i.e., a shift of the demand curve) produces a new equilibrium of 15 units at E'. In (**b**), a shift in supply results in a movement along the demand curve from E to E''.

demand or a shortage. We also know that a competitive market is a mechanism for producing equilibrium. If price is too low, demanders will bid up the price to the equilibrium level.

The notion of equilibrium is tricky, however, as is seen by the statement of a leading pundit: "Don't lecture me about supply and demand equilibrium. The supply of oil is always equal to the demand for oil. You simply can't tell the difference." The pundit is right in an accounting sense. Clearly the oil sales recorded by the oil producers should be exactly equal to the oil purchases recorded by the oil consumers. But this bit of arithmetic cannot repeal the laws of supply and demand. More important, if we fail to understand the nature of economic equilibrium, we cannot hope to understand the way that different forces affect the marketplace.

In economics, we are interested in knowing the quantity of sales that will clear the market, that is, the equilibrium quantity. We also want to know the price at which

consumers willingly buy what producers willingly sell. Only at this price will both buyers and sellers be satisfied with their decisions. Only at this price and quantity will there be no tendency for price and quantity to change. Only by looking at the equilibrium of supply and demand can we hope to understand such paradoxes as the fact that immigration may not lower wages in the affected cities, that land taxes do not raise rents, and that bad harvests raise (yes, raise!) the incomes of farmers.

Supply, Demand, and Immigration

A fascinating and important example of supply and demand, full of complexities, is the role of immigration in determining wages. If you ask people, they are likely to tell you that immigration into California or Florida surely lowers the wages of people in those regions. It's just supply and demand. They might point to Figure 3-9(a), which shows a

(a) Immigration Alone

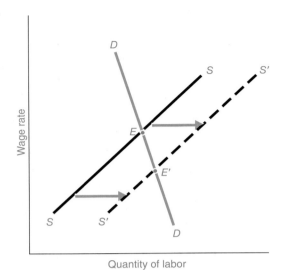

(b) Immigration to Growing Cities

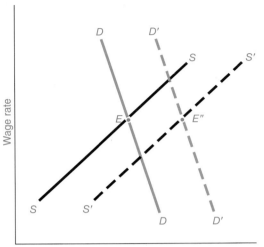

FIGURE 3-9. **Analysis of Supply and Demand Must Hold All Other Things Constant**
In (**a**), new immigrants cause the supply curve for labor to shift from SS to $S'S'$, lowering equilibrium wages. What if immigrants go only to cities with growing labor markets? Then, as shown in (**b**), the wage may not fall if demand shifts right to $D'D'$ at the same time as supply shifts.

supply-and-demand analysis of immigration. According to this analysis, immigration into a region shifts the supply curve for labor to the right and pushes down wages.

Careful economic studies cast doubt on this simple proposition, however. A recent survey of the evidence concludes:

> [The] effect of immigration on the labor market outcomes of natives is small. There is no evidence of economically significant reductions in native employment. Most empirical analysis ... finds that a 10 percent increase in the fraction of immigrants in the population reduces native wages by at most 1 percent.[2]

How can we explain the small impact of immigration on wages? The main mistake is to forget how mobile the American population is and that the

impact of immigration will quickly spread around the entire country. For example, immigrants may move to cities where they can get jobs—that is, people move to those cities where the demand for labor is already rising because of a strong local economy.

This possibility is illustrated in Figure 3-9(*b*), where a shift in labor supply to S' is associated with a higher demand curve, D'. The new equilibrium wage at E'' is the same as the original wage at E. Another possibility is that native-born residents move out (or do not move in) when immigrants move in, so total supply of labor is unchanged. This would leave the supply curve for labor in its original position and leave the wage unchanged.

How do economists sort out the possible reasons for the puzzling finding that immigration is not associated with depressed city wages? The key step in isolating the impact of a single variable is to hold other things constant. This means that all other variables must be held constant while the variable under consideration is changed. If we want to measure the

[2] Rachel M. Friedberg and Jennifer Hunt, "The Impact of Immigrants on Host Country Wages, Employment, and Growth," *Journal of Economic Perspectives* (Spring 1995), pp. 23–44.

impact of immigration on wages, we must examine the effect of new immigrants when the strength of the local economy and the number of native-born residents in a city are unchanged—that is, when these "other things" are held constant. Unless you exclude the effects of other changing variables, you cannot accurately gauge the impact of immigration.

The same principle holds in doing a supply-and-demand analysis of any market. As much as possible, when you are examining the impact of a supply or demand shift, you must try to keep all other things constant.

RATIONING BY PRICES

Let us now take stock of what the market mechanism accomplishes. By determining the equilibrium prices and quantities of all inputs and outputs, the market allocates or rations out the scarce goods of the society among the possible uses. Who does the rationing? A planning board? Congress or the President? No. The marketplace, through the interaction of supply and demand, does the rationing. This is *rationing by the purse.*

What goods are produced? This is answered by the signals of the market prices. High oil prices stim-

ulate oil production, whereas low food prices drive resources out of agriculture. Those who have the most dollar votes have the greatest influence on what goods are produced.

For whom are goods produced? The power of the purse dictates the distribution of income and consumption. Those with higher incomes end up with larger houses, more clothing, and longer vacations. When backed up by cash, the most urgently felt needs get fulfilled through the demand curve.

Even the *how* question is decided by supply and demand. When corn prices are low, it is not profitable for farmers to use expensive tractors and irrigation systems, and only the best land is cultivated. When oil prices are high, oil companies drill in deep offshore waters and employ novel seismic techniques to find oil.

With this introduction to supply and demand, we begin to see how desires for goods, as expressed through demands, interact with costs of goods, as reflected in supplies. Further study will deepen our understanding of these concepts and will show how this tool can be applied to other important areas. But even this first survey will serve as an indispensable tool for interpreting the economic world in which we live.

SUMMARY

1. The analysis of supply and demand shows how a market mechanism solves the three problems of *what, how,* and *for whom.* It shows how dollar votes decide the prices and quantities of different goods and services. A market blends together demands, coming from consumers who are spreading their incomes among available goods and services, with supplies, such as those provided by businesses interested in maximizing their profits.

A. The Demand Schedule

2. A demand schedule shows the relationship between the quantity demanded and the price of a commodity, other things held constant. Such a demand schedule, depicted graphically by a demand curve, holds constant other things like family incomes, tastes, and the prices of other goods. Almost all commodities obey the *law of downward-sloping demand,* which holds that quantity demanded falls as a good's price rises. This law is represented by a downward-sloping demand curve.

3. Many influences lie behind the demand schedule for the market as a whole: average family incomes, population, the prices of related goods, tastes, and special influences. When these influences change, the demand curve will shift.

B. The Supply Schedule

4. The supply schedule (or supply curve) gives the relationship between the quantity of a good that producers desire to sell—other things constant—and that good's price. Quantity supplied generally responds positively to price, so the supply curve rises upward and to the right.

5. Elements other than the good's price affect its supply. The most important influence is the commodity's production cost, determined by the state of technology and by input prices. Other elements in supply include the prices of related goods, government policies, and special influences.

C. Equilibrium of Supply and Demand

6. The equilibrium of supply and demand in a competitive market is attained at a price at which the forces of supply and demand are in balance. The equilibrium price is the price at which the quantity demanded just equals the quantity supplied. Graphically, we find the equilibrium as the intersection of the supply and demand curves. At a price above the equilibrium, producers want to supply more than consumers want to buy, which results in a surplus of goods and exerts downward pressure on price. Similarly, too low a price generates a shortage, and buyers will therefore tend to bid price upward to the equilibrium.

7. Shifts in the supply and demand curves change the equilibrium price and quantity. An increase in demand, which shifts the demand curve to the right, will increase both equilibrium price and quantity. An increase in supply, which shifts the supply curve to the right, will decrease price and increase quantity demanded.

8. To use supply-and-demand analysis correctly, we must (a) distinguish a change in demand or supply (which produces a shift in a curve) from a change in the quantity demanded or supplied (which represents a movement along a curve); (b) hold other things constant, which requires distinguishing the impact of a change in a commodity's price from the impact of changes in other influences; and (c) look always for the supply-and-demand equilibrium, which comes at the point where forces acting on price and quantity are in balance.

9. Competitively determined prices ration the limited supply of goods among those with the demands.

CONCEPTS FOR REVIEW

supply-and-demand analysis	supply schedule or curve, *SS*	shifts in supply and demand curves
demand schedule or curve, *DD*	influences affecting supply curve	all other things held constant
law of downward-sloping demand	equilibrium price and quantity	rationing by prices
influences affecting demand curve		

QUESTIONS FOR DISCUSSION

1. a. Define carefully what is meant by a demand schedule or curve. State the law of downward-sloping demand. Illustrate the law of downward-sloping demand with two cases from your own experience.
   b. Define the concept of a supply schedule or curve. Show that an increase in supply means a rightward and downward shift of the supply curve. Contrast this with the rightward and upward shift in the demand curve implied by an increase in demand.

2. What might increase the demand for hamburgers? What would increase the supply? What would inexpensive frozen pizzas do to the market equilibrium for hamburgers? To the wages of teenagers who work at McDonald's?

3. Explain why the price in competitive markets settles down at the equilibrium intersection of supply and demand. Explain what happens if the market price starts out too high or too low.

4. Explain why each of the following is *false*:
   a. A freeze in Brazil's coffee-growing region will lower the price of coffee.
   b. "Protecting" American tomato producers from Mexican tomato imports will lower tomato prices in the United States.
   c. The rapid increase in college tuitions will lower the demand for college.
   d. The war against drugs, with increased interdiction of imported cocaine, will lower the price of domestically produced marijuana.

5. The four laws of supply and demand are the following:
   a. An increase in demand generally raises price and raises quantity demanded.
   b. A decrease in demand generally _____ price and _____ quantity demanded.
   c. An increase in supply generally lowers price and raises quantity demanded.
   d. A decrease in supply generally _____ price and _____ quantity demanded.
   Fill in the blanks. Demonstrate each law with a supply-and-demand diagram.

6. For each of the following, explain whether quantity demanded changes because of a demand shift or a price change, and draw a diagram to illustrate your answer:
   a. As a result of decreased military spending, the price of Army boots falls.
   b. Fish prices fall after the pope allows Catholics to eat meat on Friday.

c. An increase in gasoline taxes lowers the consumption of gasoline.

d. After the Black Death struck Europe in the fourteenth century, wages rose.

7. Examine the graph for the price of gasoline in Figure 3-1, page 44. Then, using a supply-and-demand diagram, illustrate the impact of each of the following on price and quantity demanded:

a. Improvements in transportation lower the costs of importing oil into the United States in the 1960s.

b. After the 1973 war, oil producers cut oil production sharply.

c. After 1980, smaller automobiles get more miles per gallon.

d. A record-breaking cold winter in 1995–1996 unexpectedly raises the demand for heating oil.

8. From the following data, plot the supply and demand curves and determine the equilibrium price and quantity:

Supply and Demand for Pizzas		
Price ($ per pizza)	Quantity demanded (pizzas per semester)	Quantity supplied (pizzas per semester)
10	0	40
8	10	30
6	20	20
4	30	10
2	40	0
0	125	0

What would happen if the demand for pizzas tripled at each price? What would occur if the price were initially set at $4 per pizza?

PART TWO

MICROECONOMICS: SUPPLY, DEMAND, AND PRODUCT MARKETS

CHAPTER 4
APPLICATIONS OF SUPPLY AND DEMAND

The Age of Chivalry is gone; that of sophisters, economists, and calculators has succeeded.

Edmund Burke

Having completed our introductory survey, we begin our study of microeconomics, which is concerned with the behavior of the individual markets that make up the economy. Individual markets contain most of the grand sweep and drama of economic history and the controversies of economic policy. Within the confines of microeconomics we will study the reasons for the vast disparities in earnings between neurosurgeons and textile workers. Microeconomics is crucial to understanding why computer prices have fallen so dramatically and why the use of computers has expanded exponentially. We cannot hope to understand the bitter debates about health care or the minimum wage without applying the tools of supply and demand to these sectors. Even topics such as illegal drugs or crime and punishment are usefully illuminated by considering the way the demand for addictive substances differs from that for other commodities.

Our survey of microeconomics will proceed in three parts. In this part, we focus on the behavior of *product markets,* the markets for all the goods and services that firms produce. We will examine where consumer demand comes from, how businesses make decisions, and how prices and profits efficiently coordinate the allocation of scarce economic resources

in a perfectly competitive market. We will also examine the market failures that arise when monopolies or other forms of imperfect competitors dominate industry.

Then in Part Three we turn to the study of *factor markets,* which are the markets for factors of production such as labor, capital, and land. These critical markets affect us all, because the prices of these factors—wages, interest, and rent—help determine what income workers, investors, and landowners will receive. We will see how prices in these markets are set and how they affect the distribution of income in a market economy.

Looking further down the road, in Part Four we examine the critical role of government in the modern market economy. We will see how the government must balance *efficiency* and *fairness* in its taxation and spending policies. We will also study how government regulation can both help and hurt the workings of the economy and how government policies can help alleviate the poverty and hardship resulting from the market distribution of income. Finally, we will turn our attention to environmental economics, which proposes ways to halt environmental degradation without harming economic growth.

A. ELASTICITY OF DEMAND AND SUPPLY

Here we start our study of product markets. We have already seen in Chapter 3 how supply and demand can be combined to produce market equilibrium. The theory of supply and demand can be used to answer a wide range of important and interesting questions. For example, when a new tax is put on gasoline, do drivers bear the burden of the tax or does it fall on the oil companies? Does raising the minimum wage help workers or hurt them? Should the airlines raise ticket prices to increase their profits, or will lower ticket prices increase the number of passengers so much that profits actually rise?

In order to turn supply and demand curves into truly useful tools, we need to know *how much* supply and demand respond to changes in price. Some purchases, like those for vacation travel, are very sensitive to price changes. Others, like food or electricity, are necessities for which consumer purchases respond very little to price changes. These issues are analyzed using the crucial concept of elasticity, which is a way of quantifying how responsive quantities supplied and demanded are to changes in prices. The payoff will come in the second half of the chapter, when we use this new tool to examine the microeconomic impacts of taxes and other types of government intervention.

PRICE ELASTICITY OF DEMAND

Let's look first at the response of consumer demand to price changes:

The **price elasticity of demand** (sometimes simply called **price elasticity**) measures how much the quantity demanded of a good changes when its price changes. The precise definition of price elasticity is the percentage change in quantity demanded divided by the percentage change in price.

Goods vary enormously in their price elasticity, or sensitivity to price changes. When the price elasticity of a good is high, we say that the good has "elastic" demand, which means that its quantity demanded responds greatly to price changes. When the price elasticity of a good is low, it is "inelastic" and its quantity demanded responds little to price changes.

For necessities like food, fuel, shoes, and prescription drugs demand tends to be inelastic. Such items are the staff of life and cannot easily be forgone when their prices rise. By contrast, you can substitute other goods when luxuries like European holidays, 17-year-old Scotch whiskey, and Italian designer clothing rise in price.

In addition, goods that have ready substitutes tend to have more elastic demand than those that have no substitutes. If all food or footwear prices were to rise 20 percent tomorrow, you would hardly expect people to stop eating or to go around barefoot, so food and footwear demands are price-inelastic. On the other hand, if mad-cow disease drives up the price of British beef, people can turn to beef from other countries or to lamb or poultry for their meat needs. Therefore, British beef shows a high price elasticity.

The length of time that people have to respond to price changes also plays a role. A good example is that of gasoline. Suppose you are driving across the country when the price of gasoline suddenly increases. Is it likely that you will sell your car and abandon your vacation? Not really. So in the short run, the demand for gasoline may be very inelastic.

In the long run, however, you can adjust your behavior to the higher price of gasoline. You can buy a smaller and more fuel-efficient car, ride a bicycle, take the train, move closer to work, or carpool with other people. For many goods, the ability to adjust consumption patterns implies that demand elasticities are higher in the long run than in the short run.

Economic factors determine the size of price elasticities for individual goods: elasticities tend to be higher when the goods are luxuries, when substitutes are available, and when consumers have more time to adjust their behavior.

Calculating Elasticities

If we can observe how much quantity demanded changes when price changes, we can calculate the elasticity. The precise definition of price elasticity, E_D, is the percentage change in quantity demanded divided by the percentage change in price.

We can calculate the coefficient of price elasticity numerically according to the following formula:

Price elasticity of demand = E_D

$$= \frac{\text{percentage change in quantity demanded}}{\text{percentage change in price}}$$

Now we can be more precise about the different categories of price elasticity:

- When a 1 percent change in price calls forth more than a 1 percent change in quantity demanded, the good has **price-elastic demand.** For example, if a 1 percent increase in price yields a 5 percent decrease in quantity demanded, the commodity has a highly price-elastic demand.
- When a 1 percent change in price evokes less than a 1 percent change in quantity demanded, the good has **price-inelastic demand.** This case occurs, for instance, when a 1 percent increase in price yields only a 0.2 percent decrease in demand.
- One important special case is **unit-elastic demand,** which occurs when the percentage change in quantity is exactly the same as the percentage change in price. In this case, a 1 percent increase in price yields a 1 percent decrease in demand. We will see later that this condition implies that total expenditures on the commodity (which equal $P \times Q$) stay the same even when the price changes.

To illustrate the calculation of elasticities, let us examine the simple case of the response to a price increase which is shown in Figure 4-1. In the original situation, price was 90 and quantity demanded was 240 units. A price increase to 110 led consumers to reduce their purchases to 160 units. In Figure 4-1, consumers were originally at point A but moved along their demand schedule to point B when the price rose.

Table 4-1 shows how we calculate price elasticity. The price increase is 20 percent, with the resulting

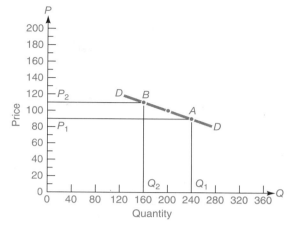

FIGURE 4-1. Elastic Demand Shows Large-Quantity Response to Price Change

Market equilibrium is originally at point A. In response to a 20 percent price increase, quantity demanded declines 40 percent, to point B. Price elasticity is $E_D = 40/20 = 2$. Demand is therefore elastic in the region from A to B.

quantity decrease being 40 percent. The price elasticity of demand is evidently $E_D = 40/20 = 2$. The price elasticity is greater than 1, and this good therefore displays price-elastic demand in the region from A to B.

In practice, calculating elasticities is somewhat tricky, and we emphasize three key steps where you have to be especially careful. First, note that we drop the minus signs from the numbers by treating all percentage changes as positive. That means all elasticities are positive, even though prices and quantities

TABLE 4-1. Example of Good with Elastic Demand

Consider the situation where price is raised from 90 to 110. According to the demand curve, quantity demanded falls from 240 to 160. Price elasticity is the ratio of percentage change in quantity divided by percentage change in price. We drop the minus sign from the numbers so that all elasticities are positive.

Case A: Price = 90 and quantity = 240

Case B: Price = 110 and quantity = 160

Percentage price change = $\Delta P/P$ = 20/100 = 20%

Percentage quantity change = $\Delta Q/Q$ = ⁻80/200 = ⁻40%

Price elasticity = E_D = 40/20 = 2

demanded move in opposite directions because of the law of downward-sloping demand.

Second, note that the definition of elasticity uses percentage changes in price and demand rather than actual changes. That means that a change in the units of measurement does not affect the elasticity. So whether we measure price in pennies or dollars, the price elasticity stays the same.

A third point concerns the exact procedure for calculating percentage changes in price and quantity. The formula for a percentage change is $\Delta P/P$. The value of ΔP in Table 4-1 is clearly $20 = 110 - 90$. But it's not immediately clear what value we should use for P in the denominator. Is it the original value of 90, the final value of 110, or something in between?

For very small percentage changes, such as from 100 to 99, it doesn't much matter whether we use 99 or 100 as the denominator. But for larger changes, the difference is significant. To avoid ambiguity, we always take the average price to be the base price for calculating price changes. In Table 4-1, we used the average of the two prices $[P = (90 + 110)/2 = 100]$ as the base or denominator in the elasticity formula. Similarly, we used the average quantity $[Q = (160 + 240)/2 = 200]$ as the base for measuring the percentage change in quantity. The exact formula for calculating elasticity is therefore

$$E_D = \frac{\Delta Q}{(Q_1 + Q_2)/2} \div \frac{\Delta P}{(P_1 + P_2)/2}$$

where P_1 and Q_1 represent the original price and quantity and P_2 and Q_2 stand for the new price and quantity.

Price Elasticity in Diagrams

It's possible to determine price elasticities in diagrams as well. Figure 4-2 illustrates the three cases of elasticities. In each case, price is cut in half and consumers change their quantity demanded from A to B.

In Figure 4-2(a), a halving of price has tripled quantity demanded. Like the example in Figure 4-1, this case shows price-elastic demand. In Figure 4-2(c), cutting price in half led to only a 50 percent increase in quantity demanded, so this is the case of price-inelastic demand. The borderline case of unit-elastic demand is shown in Figure 4-2(b); in this example, the doubling of quantity demanded exactly matches the halving of price.

Figure 4-3 displays the important polar extremes where the price elasticities are infinite and zero, or completely elastic and completely inelastic. Completely inelastic demands, or ones with zero elasticity, are ones where the quantity demanded responds not at all to price changes; such demand is seen to be a vertical demand curve. By contrast, when demand is infinitely elastic, a tiny change in price will lead to an indefinitely large change in quantity demanded, as in the horizontal demand curve in Figure 4-3.

FIGURE 4-2. Price Elasticity of Demand Falls into Three Categories

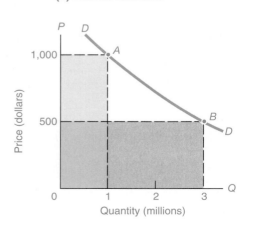

(a) Elastic Demand

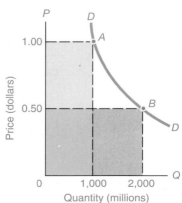

(b) Unit-Elastic Demand

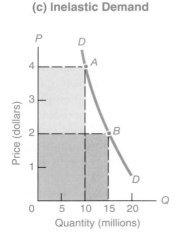

(c) Inelastic Demand

				Numerical Calculation of Elasticity Coefficient		
Q	ΔQ	P	ΔP	$\dfrac{Q_1 + Q_2}{2}$	$\dfrac{P_1 + P_2}{2}$	$E_D = \dfrac{\Delta Q}{(Q_1 + Q_2)/2} \div \dfrac{\Delta P}{(P_1 + P_2)/2}$
0		6				
	10		2	5	5	$\dfrac{10}{5} \div \dfrac{2}{5} = 5 > 1$
10		4				
	10		2	15	3	$\dfrac{10}{15} \div \dfrac{2}{3} = 1$
20		2				
	10		2	25	1	$\dfrac{10}{25} \div \dfrac{2}{1} = 0.2 < 1$
30		0				

TABLE 4-2. Calculation of Price Elasticity along a Linear Demand Curve

ΔP denotes the change in price, i.e., $\Delta P = P_2 - P_1$, while $\Delta Q = Q_2 - Q_1$. To calculate numerical elasticity, percentage change of price equals price change ΔP divided by average price; the percentage change in output is calculated as $\Delta Q/Q$, where Q is given by the average Q. Treating all figures as positive numbers, the resulting ratio gives numerical price elasticity of demand, E_D. Note that for a straight line, elasticity is high at the top, low at the bottom, and exactly 1 in the middle.

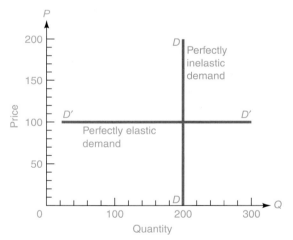

FIGURE 4-3. Perfectly Elastic and Inelastic Demands

Polar extremes of demand are vertical demand curves, which represent perfectly inelastic demand ($E_D = 0$), and horizontal demand curves, which show perfectly elastic demand ($E_{D'} = \infty$).

Warning: Elasticity is not the same as slope.

We must always remember not to confuse the elasticity of a curve with its slope. This distinction is easily seen when we examine the straight-line demand curves that are often found in illustrative examples. We often depict demand curves as linear or straight lines because they are easy to draw. So it's only natural to ask, What is the price elasticity of a straight-line demand curve?

That question turns out to have a surprising answer. Along a straight-line demand curve, the price elasticity varies from zero to infinity! Table 4-2 gives a detailed set of elasticity calculations using the same technique as that in Table 4-1. This table shows that linear demand curves start out with high price elasticity, where price is high and quantity is low, and end up with low elasticity, where price is low and quantity high.

This illustrates an important point. When you see a demand curve in a diagram, it is in general not true that a steep slope for the demand curve means inelastic demand and a flat slope signifies elastic demand. The slope is not the same as the elasticity because the demand curve's slope depends upon the changes in P and Q, whereas the elasticity depends upon the percentage changes in P and Q. The only exceptions are the polar cases of completely elastic and inelastic demands.

One way to see this point is to examine Figure 4-2(b). This demand curve is clearly not a straight line with constant slope. Yet it has a constant demand elasticity of $E_D = 1$ because the percentage change in price is everywhere equal to the percentage change in quantity. So remember: Elasticity is definitely different from slope.

Figure 4-4 illustrates the pitfall of confusing slope and elasticity. This figure plots a linear or straight-line demand curve. Because it is linear, it has the same slope everywhere. But the top of the line, near *A*, has a very small percentage price change and a very large percentage quantity change, and elasticity is extremely large. Therefore, price elasticity is relatively large when we are high on the linear *DD* curve. Conversely, when we are in the bottom part of the linear demand curve, the price elasticity is less than unity. Near the horizontal axis, price elasticity is close to zero.

More generally, above the midpoint *M* of any straight line, demand is elastic, with $E_D > 1$. At the midpoint, demand is unit-elastic, with $E_D = 1$. Below the midpoint, demand is inelastic, with $E_D < 1$.

In summary, while the extreme cases of completely elastic and completely inelastic demand can be determined from the slopes of the demand curves alone, for the in-between cases, which correspond to virtually all goods, elasticities cannot be inferred by slope alone (see Figure 4-5 for one way to calculate elasticity from a diagram).[1]

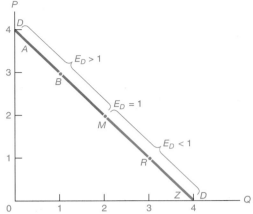

Elasticity of Straight Line

FIGURE 4-4. Slope and Elasticity Are Not the Same Thing
All points on the straight-line demand curve have the same slope. But above the midpoint, demand is elastic; below it, demand is inelastic; at the midpoint, demand is unit-elastic. Only in the case of vertical or horizontal curves, shown in Fig. 4-3, can you infer the price elasticity from slope alone.

ELASTICITY AND REVENUE

One important application of elasticity is to help clarify whether a price increase will raise or lower revenue. This is a key question for many businesses, ranging from airlines to restaurants to magazines, which must decide whether it is worthwhile to raise prices and whether the higher prices make up for lower demand. Let's look at the relationship between price elasticity and total revenue.

Total revenue is by definition equal to price times quantity (or $P \times Q$). If consumers buy 5 units at \$3 each, total revenue is \$15. If you know the price elasticity of demand, you know what will happen to total revenue when price changes:

1. When demand is price-inelastic, a price decrease reduces total revenue.
2. When demand is price-elastic, a price decrease increases total revenue.
3. In the borderline case of unit-elastic demand, a price decrease leads to no change in total revenue.

For example, business travelers have an inelastic demand for air travel, so an increase in business

---

[1] A simple trick will allow you to calculate the price elasticity of a demand curve: *The elasticity of a straight line at a point is given by the ratio of the length of the line segment below the point to the length of the line segment above the point.*

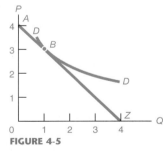

FIGURE 4-5

To see this, first examine Fig. 4-4. Note that at the midpoint *M* the length of the segment above (*AM*) and that of the segment below (*MZ*) are exactly equal; hence the elasticity is *MZ/AM* = 1. At point *B*, this formula yields $E_D = BZ/AB = 3/1 = 3$; at *R*, $E_D = 1/3$.

Knowing how to calculate E_D for a straight line enables you to calculate it for any point along a curved demand curve, as shown in Fig. 4-5. (1) Draw the straight line tangent to the curve at your point (e.g., at *B* in Fig. 4-5), and then (2) calculate E_D for the straight line at that point (e.g., E_D at *B* = 3). The result will be the correct elasticity for the curve at point *B*.

fares tends to raise revenue. By contrast, leisure travelers have a much more elastic demand for air travel, because they have a far greater choice about where and when they are traveling. As a result, raising leisure fares tends to decrease revenue.

Fly the financial skies of "Elasticity Air." Understanding the demand elasticities of their passengers' travel is worth billions of dollars each year to U.S. airlines. Ideally, airlines would like to charge the highest price they can to business travelers, while charging leisure passengers a low-enough price to fill up all their empty seats. That is how they would raise revenues and maximize profits.

But if they charge low-elasticity business travelers one price and high-elasticity leisure passengers a lower price, the airlines have a big problem—keeping the two classes of passengers separate. How can they stop the low-elasticity business travelers from buying up the cheap tickets meant for the leisure travelers and not let high-elasticity leisure flyers take up seats that business passengers would have been willing to buy? The airlines have solved their problem by engaging in "price discrimination" among their different customers in a way that exploits different price elasticities. (*Price discrimination* is the practice of charging different prices for the same service to different customers.) Airlines offer discount fares for travelers who plan ahead and who tend to choose times when prices are low. At the same time, airlines might require a stay over Saturday night to get the discount fare, a rule that discourages business travelers who would like to get home for the weekend. Also, discounts are often unavailable at the last minute because many business trips are unplanned expeditions to handle an unforeseen crisis—another case of price-inelastic demand. Airlines have devised extremely sophisticated computer programs to manage their seat availability as a way of ensuring that their low-elasticity passengers cannot benefit from discount fares. As a result, their profits have continued to be healthy while they fill their planes with budget travelers.

The Paradox of the Bumper Harvest

We can use elasticities to illustrate one of the most famous paradoxes of all economics: the paradox of the bumper harvest. Imagine that in a particular year nature smiles on farming. A cold winter kills off the pests; spring comes early for planting; there are no killing frosts; rains nurture the growing shoots; and a sunny October allows a record crop to come to market. At the end of the year, family Jones happily settles down to calculate its income for the year. The Joneses are in for a major surprise: *The good weather and bumper crop have lowered their and other farmers' incomes.*

How can this be? The answer lies in the elasticity of demand for foodstuffs. The demands for basic food products such as wheat and corn tend to be inelastic; for these necessities, consumption changes very little in response to price. But this means farmers as a whole receive less total revenue when the harvest is good than when it is bad. The increase in supply arising from an abundant harvest tends to lower the price. But the lower price doesn't increase quantity demanded very much. The implication is that a low price elasticity of food means that large harvests (high Q) tend to be associated with low revenue (low $P \times Q$).

These ideas can be illustrated by referring back to Figure 4-2. We begin by showing how to measure revenue in the diagram itself. Total revenue is the product of price times quantity, $P \times Q$. Further, the area of a rectangle is always equal to the product of its base times its height. Therefore, total revenue at any point on a demand curve can be found by examining the area of the rectangle determined by the P and Q at that point.

Next, we can check the relationship between elasticity and revenue for the unit-elastic case in Figure 4-2(b). Note that the shaded revenue region ($P \times Q$) is $1000 million for both points A and B. The shaded areas representing total revenue are the same because of offsetting changes in the Q base and the P height. This is what we would expect for the borderline case of unit-elastic demand.

We can also see that Figure 4-2(a) corresponds to elastic demand. In this figure, the revenue rectangle expands from $1000 million to $1500 million when price is halved. Since total revenue goes up when price is cut, demand is elastic.

In Figure 4-2(c) the revenue rectangle falls from $40 million to $30 million when price is halved, so demand is inelastic.

Which diagram illustrates the case of agriculture, where a bumper harvest means lower total revenues for farmers? Clearly it is Figure 4-2(c).

Value of demand elasticity	Description	Definition	Impact on revenues
Greater than one ($E_D > 1$)	Elastic demand	Percentage change in quantity demanded *greater* than percentage change in price	Revenues *increase* when price decreases
Equal to one ($E_D = 1$)	Unit-elastic demand	Percentage change in quantity demanded *equal* to percentage change in price	Revenues *unchanged* when price decreases
Less than one ($E_D < 1$)	Inelastic demand	Percentage change in quantity demanded *less* than percentage change in price	Revenues *decrease* when price decreases

TABLE 4-3. Elasticities: Summary of Crucial Concepts

Which represents the case of vacation travel, where a lower price could mean higher revenues? Surely Figure 4-2(*a*).

Table 4-3 shows the major points to remember about price elasticities.

PRICE ELASTICITY OF SUPPLY

Of course, consumption is not the only thing that changes when prices go up or down. Businesses also respond to price in their decisions about how much to produce. Economists define the price elasticity of supply as the responsiveness of the quantity supplied of a good to its market price.

More precisely, the **price elasticity of supply** is the percentage change in quantity supplied divided by the percentage change in price.

Suppose the amount supplied is completely fixed, as in the case of perishable fish brought to market to be sold at whatever price they will fetch. This is the limiting case of zero elasticity, or completely inelastic supply, which is a vertical supply curve.

At the other extreme, say that a tiny cut in price will cause the amount supplied to fall to zero, while the slightest rise in price will coax out an indefinitely large supply. Here, the ratio of the percentage change in quantity supplied to percentage change in price is extremely large and gives rise to a horizontal supply curve. This is the polar case of infinitely elastic supply.

Between these extremes, we call supply elastic or inelastic depending upon whether the percentage

change in quantity is larger or smaller than the percentage change in price. In the borderline unit-elastic case, where price elasticity of supply equals 1, the percentage increase of quantity supplied is exactly equal to the percentage increase in price.

You can readily see that the definitions of price elasticities of supply are exactly the same as those for price elasticities of demand. The only difference is that for supply the quantity response to price is positive, while for demand the response is negative.

The exact definition of the price elasticity of supply, E_S, is as follows:

$$E_S = \frac{\text{percentage change in quantity supplied}}{\text{percentage change in price}}$$

Figure 4-6 displays three important cases of supply elasticity: (a), the vertical supply curve, showing completely inelastic supply; (c), the horizontal supply curve, displaying completely elastic supply; and (b), an intermediate case of a straight line, going through the origin, illustrating the borderline case of unit elasticity.[2]

What factors determine supply elasticity? The major factor influencing supply elasticity is the ease with which production in the industry can be increased. If all inputs can be readily found at going market prices, as is the case for the textile industry,

---

[2] You can determine the elasticity of a supply curve that is not a straight line in the fashion described for the demand curve in footnote 1 on page 68 by drawing the straight line that lies tangent to the curve at a point and measuring the elasticity of the tangential straight line.

then output can be greatly increased with little increase in price. This would indicate that supply elasticity is relatively large. On the other hand, if production capacity is severely limited, as is the case for the mining of South African gold, then even sharp increases in the price of gold will call forth but a small response in production of South African gold; this would be inelastic supply.

Another important factor in supply elasticities is the time period under consideration. A given change in price tends to have a larger effect on amount supplied as the time for suppliers to respond increases. For very brief periods after a price increase, firms may be unable to increase their inputs of labor, materials, and capital, so supply may be very price-inelastic. However, as time passes and businesses can hire more labor, build new factories, and expand capacity, supply elasticities will become larger.

We can use Figure 4-6 to illustrate how supply may change over time for the fishing case. Supply curve (a) might hold for fish on the day it is brought to market, where it is simply auctioned off for whatever it will bring. Curve (b) might hold for the intermediate run of a year or so, with the given stock of fishing boats and before new labor is attracted to the industry. Over the very long run, as new fishing boats are built, new labor is attracted, and new fish farms

are constructed, the supply of fish might be very price-elastic, as in case (c) in Figure 4-6.

Supply Elasticities

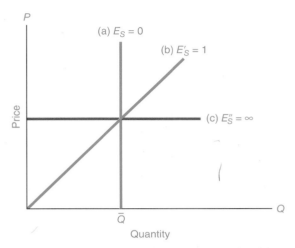

FIGURE 4-6. Supply Elasticity Depends upon Producer Response to Price

When supply is fixed, supply elasticity is zero, as in curve (a). Curve (c) displays an indefinitely large quantity response to price changes. Intermediate case (b) arises when the percentage quantity and price changes are equal.

B. APPLICATIONS TO CURRENT ECONOMIC ISSUES

Having laid the groundwork with our study of elasticities, we show how the tools can assist our understanding of many of the basic economic trends and policy issues. We begin with one of the major transformations since the Industrial Revolution, the decline of agriculture. Next, we examine the implications of taxes on an industry, using the example of a gasoline tax. We then analyze the consequences of various types of government intervention in markets.

THE ECONOMICS OF AGRICULTURE

Our first application of supply-and-demand analysis comes from agriculture. The first part of this section

lays out some of the economic fundamentals of the farm sector. Then we will use the theory of supply and demand to study the effects of government intervention in agricultural markets.

Long-Run Relative Decline of Farming

Farming was once our largest single industry. A hundred years ago, half the American population lived and worked on farms, but that number has declined to less than 3 percent of the work force today. At the same time, prices for farm products have fallen relative to incomes and other prices in the economy. As Table 4-4 shows, over the last half-century, median family income has more than doubled. By contrast, farm incomes have stagnated. Farm-state senators fret about the decline of the family farm.

A single diagram can explain the cause of the sagging trend in farm prices better than libraries of books and editorials. Figure 4-7 shows an initial equilibrium with high prices at point *E*. Observe what happens to agriculture as the years go by. Demand for food increased slowly because most foods are necessities; the demand shift is consequently modest in comparison to growing average incomes.

What about supply? Although many people mistakenly think that farming is a backward business, statistical studies show that productivity (output per unit of input) has grown more rapidly in agriculture than in most other industries. Important advances include mechanization through tractors, combines, and cotton pickers; fertilization and irrigation; selective breeding; and development of new seeds. All these innovations have vastly increased the productivity of agricultural inputs. Rapid productivity growth has increased supply greatly, as shown by the supply curve's shift from *SS* to *S′S′* in Figure 4-7.

What must happen at the new competitive equilibrium? Sharp increases in supply outpaced modest increases in demand, producing a downward trend in farm prices relative to other prices in the economy. And this is precisely what has happened in recent decades, as is seen in Table 4-4.

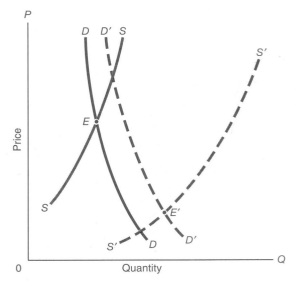

FIGURE 4-7. Agricultural Distress Results from Expanding Supply and Price-Inelastic Demand

Equilibrium at *E* represents conditions in the farm sector decades ago. Demand for farm products tends to grow more slowly than the impressive increase in supply generated by technological progress. Hence competitive farm prices tend to fall. Moreover, with price-inelastic demand, farm incomes decline with increases in supply.

TABLE 4-4. Farm Prices Have Declined and Farm Incomes Have Lagged

Since World War II, productivity in farming has increased sharply, resulting in a dramatic drop in the relative prices of farm products. Farm prices today are but 34 percent of their 1947 level. The stagnation of farm incomes is explained by a correct supply-and-demand analysis. (Source: U.S. Bureau of the Census and U.S. Department of Labor.)

Item	1994 level* (1947 = 100)
Real median family income	210
Real farm incomes	95
Real farm prices	34

*"Real" levels are the dollar values corrected by the change in the general price level as measured by the consumer price index.

Crop Restrictions. In response to falling incomes, farmers have often lobbied the federal government for economic assistance. Over the years, governments at home and abroad have taken many steps to help farmers. They have raised prices through price supports; they have curbed imports through tariffs and quotas; and they sometimes simply sent checks to farmers who agreed *not* to produce on their land.

The paradox of the bumper harvest has an interesting application here. *Many governments attempt to help farmers by reducing their production.* How could this be in the interests of farmers? Figure 4-8 shows the economics of this policy. If the Department of Agriculture requires every farmer to reduce the amount of production, the effect is a shifting of the supply curve up and to the left. Because food demands are inelastic, crop restrictions not only raise the price of crops but also tend to raise farmers' total revenues

FIGURE 4-8. Crop-Restriction Programs Raise Both Price and Farm Income

Before the crop restriction, the competitive market produces an equilibrium with low price at E. When government restricts production, the supply curve is shifted leftward to $S'S'$, moving the equilibrium to E' and raising price to B. With inelastic demand, confirm that new revenue rectangle $0BE'S'$ is larger than original revenue rectangle $0AEX$.

and earnings. Just as bumper harvests hurt farmers, crop restrictions tend to raise farm incomes. Of course, consumers are hurt by the crop restrictions and higher prices—just as they would be if a flood or drought created a scarcity of food.

Production restrictions are typical of government market interferences that raise the incomes of one group at the expense of others. We will see in later chapters that this kind of policy is inefficient: The gain to farmers is actually less than the harm to consumers.

IMPACT OF A TAX ON PRICE AND QUANTITY

Governments levy taxes on a wide variety of commodities—on cigarettes and alcohol, on payrolls and profits. Supply-and-demand analysis can help us predict who will bear the true burden of a tax and how a tax will affect output.

As an example, we will look at the case of a gasoline tax to illustrate the way that taxes affect market output and price. Although American politicians periodically make a fuss about them, gasoline taxes are far lower in the United States than in most European countries, where gas taxes are $2 to $5 per gallon—as compared to around 50 cents on average in the United States. Many economists and environmentalists advocate much higher gasoline taxes for the United States. They point out that higher taxes would curb consumption, and thereby reduce pollution and our dependence on insecure foreign sources of oil.

For concreteness, say that the government decided to raise the tax by $1 per gallon. Prudent legislators would of course be reluctant to raise gas taxes so sharply without a firm understanding of the consequences of such a move. They would want to know the incidence of the tax. *By* **incidence** *we mean the ultimate economic impact or burden of a tax.* Just because businesses write a check for the taxes does not mean that the taxes in fact reduce their profits. By using supply and demand, we can analyze who actually bears the burden, or what the incidence is, of the tax.

It could be that the burden of the tax is shifted forward to the consumers, if the retail price of gasoline goes up by the full $1 of the tax. Or perhaps consumers cut back so sharply on gasoline purchases that the burden of the tax is shifted back completely onto the oil companies. Where the actual impact lies between these extremes can be determined only from supply-and-demand analysis.

Figure 4-9 on page 74 provides the answer. It shows the original pretax equilibrium at E, the intersection of the original SS and DD curves, at a gasoline price of $1 a gallon and total consumption of 100 billion gallons per year. We portray the imposition of a $1 tax in the retail market for gasoline as an upward shift of the supply curve, with the demand curve remaining unchanged. The demand curve does not shift because the quantity demanded at each retail price is unchanged after the gasoline-tax increase. Note that the demand curve for gasoline is relatively inelastic.

By contrast, the supply curve definitely does shift upward by $1. The reason is that producers are willing to sell a given quantity (say, 100 billion gallons) only if they receive the same *net* price as before. That

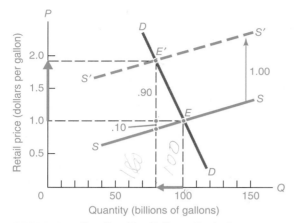

FIGURE 4-9. Gasoline Tax Falls on Both Consumer and Producer

What is the incidence of a tax? A $1 tax on gasoline shifts the supply curve up $1 everywhere, giving a new supply curve, $S'S'$, parallel to the original supply curve, SS. This new supply curve intersects DD in the new equilibrium at E', where price to consumers has risen 90 cents and producers' price has fallen 10 cents. The rust arrows show changes in P and Q.

is, at each quantity supplied, the market price must rise by exactly the amount of the tax. If producers had originally been willing to sell 80 billion gallons at $0.90 per gallon, they would still be willing to sell the same amount at a retail price of $1.90 (which, after subtracting the tax, yields the producers the same $0.90 per gallon).

What will be the new equilibrium price? The answer is found at the intersection of the new supply and demand curves, or at E', where $S'S'$ and DD meet. Because of the supply shift, the price is higher. Also, the quantity supplied and demanded is reduced. If we read the graph carefully, we find that the new equilibrium price has risen from $1 to about $1.90. The new equilibrium output, at which supply and demand are in equilibrium, has fallen from 100 billion to about 80 billion gallons.

Who ultimately pays the tax? What is its incidence? Clearly the oil industry pays a small fraction, for it receives only 90 cents ($1.90 less the $1 tax) rather than $1. But the consumer bears most of the burden, with the retail price rising 90 cents, because supply is relatively price-elastic whereas demand is relatively price-inelastic.

Subsidies. If taxes are used to discourage consumption of a commodity, subsidies are used to encourage production. One pervasive example of subsidies comes in agriculture. You can examine the impact of a subsidy in a market by shifting *down* the supply curve. The general rules for subsidies are exactly parallel to those for taxes.

General Rules on Tax Shifting. Gasoline is just a single example of how to analyze tax shifting. Using this apparatus we can understand how cigarette taxes affect both the prices and consumption of cigarettes; how taxes or tariffs on imports affect foreign trade; and how property taxes, social security taxes, and corporate-profit taxes affect land prices, wages, and interest rates.

The key issue in determining the incidence of a tax is the relative elasticities of supply and demand. If demand is inelastic relative to supply, as in the case of gasoline, most of the cost is shifted to consumers. By contrast, if supply is inelastic relative to demand, as is the case for land, then most of the tax is shifted to supply. Here is the general rule for determining the incidence of a tax:

The incidence of a tax is determined by the effect on prices and quantities in supply-and-demand equilibrium. In general, the burden or incidence depends upon the relative elasticities of demand and supply. A tax is shifted forward to consumers if the demand is inelastic relative to supply; a tax is shifted backward to producers if supply is relatively more inelastic than demand.

MINIMUM FLOORS AND MAXIMUM CEILINGS

Sometimes, rather than taxing or subsidizing a commodity, the government legislates maximum or minimum prices. History is full of examples. From biblical days, governments have limited the interest rates that lenders can charge (so-called usury laws). In wartime, governments often impose wage and price controls to prevent spiraling inflation. During the energy crisis of the 1970s, there were controls on gasoline prices. Today, there are increasingly stringent limitations on the prices that doctors or hospitals can charge, and many large cities, including New

York, have rent controls on apartments. Proposals to increase the minimum wage are among the most controversial issues of economic policy.

These kinds of interferences with the laws of supply and demand are genuinely different from those in which the government imposes a tax and then lets the market act through supply and demand. Although political pressures always exist to keep prices down and wages up, experience has taught that sector-by-sector price and wage controls tend to create major economic distortions. Nevertheless, as Adam Smith well knew when he protested against mercantilist policies of an earlier age, most economic systems are plagued by inefficiencies stemming from well-meaning but inexpert interferences with the mechanisms of supply and demand. Setting maximum or minimum prices in a market tends to produce surprising and sometimes perverse economic effects. Let's see why.

Two important examples of government intervention are the minimum wage and price controls on gasoline. These will illustrate the surprising side effects that can arise when governments interfere with market determination of price and quantity.

The Minimum-Wage Controversy

The minimum wage sets a minimum on what employers are allowed to pay workers. In the United States, the federal minimum wage began in 1938 when the government required that covered workers in covered industries be paid at least 25 cents an hour. At that time, the minimum wage was about 40 percent of the average manufacturing wage. The minimum wage was raised occasionally, and by 1996 it had reached $4.25 per hour, which was only 33 percent of the average manufacturing wage rate. Because the minimum wage had declined relative to average earnings, President Clinton proposed and Congress passed a minimum-wage increase to $5.15 per hour in 1997.

This is an issue that divides even the most eminent economists. For example, Nobel laureate Gary Becker stated flatly, "Hike the minimum wage, and you put people out of work." Another group of Nobel Prize winners countered, "We believe that the federal minimum wage can be increased by a moderate amount without significantly jeopardizing employment opportunities." Yet another leading economist, Alan Blinder of Princeton and former economic adviser to President Clinton, wrote as follows:

> The folks who earn the lowest wages have been suffering for years. They need all the help they can get, and they need it in a hurry. About 40 percent of all minimum-wage employees are the sole wage earner in their households, and about two-thirds of the teenagers earning the minimum wage live in households with below-average incomes. Frankly, I do not know whether a modest minimum-wage increase would decrease employment or not. If it does, the effect will likely be very small. (*New York Times*, May 23, 1996.)

How can nonspecialists sort through the issues when the experts are so divided? How can we resolve these apparently contradictory statements? To begin with, we should recognize that statements on the desirability of raising the minimum wage contain personal value judgments. Such statements might be informed by the best positive economics and still make different recommendations on important policy issues.

A cool-headed analysis indicates that the minimum-wage debate centers primarily on issues of interpretation rather than fundamental disagreements on empirical findings. Begin by looking at Figure 4-10 on page 76, which depicts the market for unskilled workers. The figure shows how a minimum wage rate sets a floor for most jobs. As the minimum wage rises above the market-clearing equilibrium at *M*, the total number of jobs moves up the demand curve to *E*, so employment falls. The gap between labor supplied and labor demanded is shown as *U*. This represents the amount of unemployment.

Using supply and demand, we see that there is likely to be a rise in unemployment and a decrease in employment of low-skilled workers. But how large will these magnitudes be? And what will be the impact on the wage income of low-income workers? On these questions, we can look at the empirical evidence.

Most studies indicate that a 10 percent increase in the minimum wage would reduce employment of teenagers by between 1 and 3 percent. The impact on adult employment is even smaller. Some recent studies put the employment effects very close to zero, and one set of studies suggests that employment might even increase. So a careful reading of the quotations from the eminent economists indicates that some economists consider small to be "insignificant" while others emphasize the existence of at least some

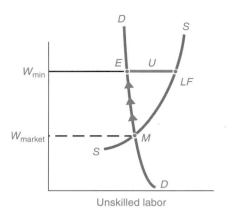

FIGURE 4-10. Effects of a Minimum Wage

Setting the minimum-wage floor at W_{min}, high above the free-market equilibrium rate at W_{market}, results in forced equilibrium at E. Employment is reduced, as the arrows show, from M to E. Additionally, unemployment is U, which is the difference between labor supplied at LF and employment at E. If the demand curve is inelastic, increasing the minimum wage will increase the income of low-wage workers. To see this, pencil in the rectangle of total wages before and after the minimum-wage increase.

job losses. Our example in Figure 4-10 shows a case where the *employment* decline is very small while the *unemployment* increase is quite large.

Another factor in the debate relates to the impact of the minimum wage on incomes. Virtually every study concludes that the demand for low-wage workers is price-inelastic. The results we just cited indicate that the price elasticity is between 0.1 and 0.3. This implies that raising the minimum wage would increase the incomes of low-income workers as a whole. Roughly speaking, a 10 percent increase in the minimum wage will increase the incomes of the affected groups by 7 to 9 percent.

The impact on incomes is yet another reason why people may disagree about the minimum wage. Those who are particularly concerned about the welfare of low-income groups may feel that modest inefficiencies are a small price to pay for higher incomes. Others—who worry more about the cumulative costs of market interferences or about the impact of higher costs upon prices, profits, and international competitiveness—may hold that the inefficiencies are too high a price. Yet another

group might believe that the minimum wage is an inefficient way to transfer buying power to low-income groups; this third group would prefer using direct income transfers or government wage subsidies rather than gumming up the wage system. How important are each of these three concerns to *you*? Depending upon your priorities, you might reach quite different conclusions on the advisability of increasing the minimum wage.

Energy Price Controls

Another example of government interference comes when the government legislates a maximum price ceiling. This occurred in the United States in the 1970s, and the results were sobering. We return to our analysis of the gasoline market to see how price ceilings function.

Let's set the scene. Suppose there is suddenly a crisis in the oil industry. This has happened time and again because of political disturbances in the Middle East due to war and revolution. We saw in Figure 3-1 the results of the 1973 and 1979 disturbances on the price of gasoline.

Politicians, seeing the sudden jump in prices, rise to denounce the situation. They claim that consumers are being "gouged" by profiteering oil companies. They worry that the rising prices threaten to ignite an inflationary spiral in the cost of living. They fret about the impact of rising prices on the poor and elderly. They call upon the government to "do something." In the face of rising prices, the U.S. government might be inclined to listen to these arguments and place a ceiling on oil prices, as it did from 1973 to 1981.

What are the effects of such a ceiling? Suppose the initial price of gasoline is $1 a gallon. Then, because of a drastic cut in oil supply, the market price of gasoline rises to $2 a gallon. Now consider the gasoline market after the supply shock. In Figure 4-11, the post-shock equilibrium is given at point E. Enter the government, which passes a law setting the maximum price for gasoline at the old level of $1 a gallon. We can picture this legal maximum price as the ceiling-price line *CJK* in Figure 4-11.

At the legal ceiling price, quantities supplied and demanded do not match. Consumers want more gasoline than producers are willing to supply at the controlled price. This is shown by the gap between *J* and *K*. This gap is so large that before long the pumps run dry. Somebody will have to go without the desired gasoline. If the free market were allowed to operate, the market would clear with a price of $2 or more; consumers would grumble but would willingly pay the higher price rather than go without fuel.

But the market cannot clear because it is against the law for producers to charge a higher price. There follows a period of frustration and shortage— a game of musical cars in which somebody is left without gasoline when the pump runs dry. The inadequate supply of gasoline must somehow be rationed. Initially, this may be done through a "first come, first served" approach, with or without limiting sales to each customer. Lines form, and much time has to be spent foraging for fuel.

Eventually, some kind of nonprice rationing mechanism evolves. For gasoline and other storable goods, the shortage is often managed by making people wait in line—rationing by the queue. Sometimes people who have privileged access to the good engage in black-market sales, which are illegal transactions above the regulated price. There is great waste as people spend valuable time trying to secure their needs. Sometimes, governments design a more efficient system of nonprice rationing based on formal allocation or coupon rationing.

Under coupon rationing, each customer must have a coupon as well as money to buy the goods— in effect, there are two kinds of money. When rationing is adopted and coupons are meted out according to "need," shortages disappear because demand is limited by the allocation of the coupons. Just how do ration coupons change the supply-and-demand picture? Clearly, the government must issue just enough of them to lower the demand curve to *D'D'* in Figure 4-11, where supply and the new demand balance at the ceiling price.

Price controls on goods like energy, with or without formal rationing, have fallen out of favor in most market economies. The only area where they are significant today is medical care. History has shown

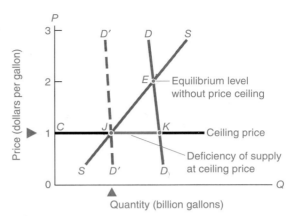

FIGURE 4-11. Price Controls Produce Shortages
Without a legal price ceiling, price would rise to *E*. At the ceiling price of $1, supply and demand do not balance, and shortages break out. Some method of rationing, formal or informal, is needed to allocate the short supply and bring the actual demand down to *D'D'*.

that legal and illegal evasions of price controls grow over time, and the inefficiencies eventually overwhelm whatever favorable impacts the controls might have on consumers. Particularly when there is room for ample substitution (i.e., when elasticities of supply or demand are high), price controls are costly and difficult to administer.

But there is a deeper lesson here: Goods are always scarce. Society can never fulfill everyone's wishes. In normal times, price itself rations the scarce supplies. When governments step in to interfere with supply and demand, prices no longer fill the role of rationers. Waste, inefficiency, and aggravation are certain companions of such interferences.

This concludes our survey of supply-and-demand analysis. In the next few chapters we investigate the foundations of demand and supply in consumer choice and business costs. These chapters will help to explain patterns of pricing in competitive and monopolistic markets and to show why competitive markets lead to an efficient (although possibly inequitable) allocation of resources.

SUMMARY

A. Elasticity of Demand and Supply

1. Price elasticity of demand measures the quantitative response of demand to a change in price. Price elasticity of demand (E_D) is defined as the percentage change in quantity demanded divided by the percentage change in price. That is,

   Price elasticity of demand $= E_D$

   $$= \frac{\text{percentage change in quantity demanded}}{\text{percentage change in price}}$$

   In this calculation, the sign is taken to be positive, and P and Q are averages of old and new values.

2. We divide price elasticities into three categories: (*a*) Demand is elastic when the percentage change in quantity demanded exceeds the percentage change in price; that is, $E_D > 1$. (*b*) Demand is inelastic when the percentage change in quantity demanded is less than the percentage change in price; here, $E_D < 1$. (*c*) When the percentage change in quantity demanded exactly equals the percentage change in price, we have the borderline case of unit-elastic demand, where $E_D = 1$.

3. Price elasticity is a pure number, involving percentages; it should not be confused with slope.

4. The demand elasticity tells us about the impact of a price change on total revenue. Demand is elastic if a price reduction increases total revenue; demand is inelastic if a price reduction decreases total revenue; in the unit-elastic case, a price change has no effect on total revenue.

5. Price elasticity of demand tends to be low for necessities like food and shelter and high for luxuries like snowmobiles and air travel. Other factors affecting price elasticity are the extent to which a good has ready substitutes, the length of time that consumers have to adjust to price changes, and the fraction of the consumer budget spent on the commodity.

6. Price elasticity of supply measures the percentage change of output supplied by producers when the market price changes by a given percentage.

B. Applications to Current Economic Issues

7. One of the most fruitful arenas for application of supply-and-demand analysis is agriculture. Improvements in agricultural technology mean that supply increases greatly, while demand for food rises less than proportionately with income. Hence free-market prices for foodstuffs tend to fall. No wonder governments have adopted a variety of programs, like crop restrictions, to prop up farm incomes.

8. A commodity tax shifts the supply-and-demand equilibrium. The tax's burden (or incidence) will fall more heavily on consumers than on producers to the degree that the demand is inelastic relative to supply.

9. Governments occasionally interfere with the workings of competitive markets by setting maximum ceilings or minimum floors on prices. In such situations, quantity supplied need no longer equal quantity demanded; ceilings lead to excess demand, while floors lead to excess supply. Sometimes, the interference may raise the incomes of a particular group, as in the case of farmers or low-skilled workers. Often, distortions and inefficiencies result.

CONCEPTS FOR REVIEW

Elasticity Concepts

price elasticity of demand, supply
elastic, inelastic, unit-elastic demand
$E_D = \%$ change in $Q / \%$ change in P
determinants of elasticity

total revenue $= P \times Q$
relationship of elasticity and revenue
   change

Applications of Supply and Demand

incidence of a tax
rationing by price
distortions from price controls
rationing by prices vs. coupons

QUESTIONS FOR DISCUSSION

1. "A good harvest will generally lower the income of farmers." Illustrate this proposition using a supply-and-demand diagram.

2. For each pair of commodities, state which you think is the more price-elastic and give your reasons: perfume and salt; penicillin and ice cream; automobiles and automobile tires; ice cream and chocolate ice cream.

3. "The price drops by 1 percent, causing the quantity demanded to rise by 2 percent. Demand is therefore elastic, with $E_D > 1$." If you change 2 to 1/2 in the first

sentence, what two other changes will be required in the quotation?

4. Consider a competitive market for apartments. What would be the effect on the equilibrium output and price after the following changes (other things held equal)? In each case, explain your answer using supply and demand.
   a. A rise in the income of consumers
   b. A $10-per-month tax on apartment rentals
   c. A government edict saying apartments could not rent for more than $200 per month
   d. A new construction technique allowing apartments to be built at half the cost
   e. A 20 percent increase in the wages of construction workers

5. Explain and show graphically how the 1990–1991 embargo of Iraqi oil exports affected oil supply and demand and thereby the equilibrium oil price and quantity.

6. A conservative critic of government programs has written, "Governments know how to do one thing well. They know how to create shortages and surpluses." Explain this quotation using examples like the minimum wage or interest-rate ceilings. Show graphically that if the demand for unskilled workers is price-elastic, a minimum wage will decrease the total earnings (wage times quantity demanded of labor) of unskilled workers.

7. Consider what would happen if a tariff of $2000 were imposed on imported automobiles. Show the impact of this tariff on the supply and the demand, and on the equilibrium price and quantity, of American automobiles. Explain why American auto companies and autoworkers often support import restraints on automobiles.

8. Elasticity problems:
   a. The world demand for crude oil is estimated to have a short-run price elasticity of 0.05. If the initial price of oil were $3 per barrel, what would be the effect on oil price and quantity of an embargo that curbed world oil supply by 5 percent? (For this problem, assume that the oil-supply curve is completely inelastic.)
   b. To show that elasticities are independent of units, refer to Table 3-1. Calculate the elasticities between each demand pair. Change the price units from dollars to pennies; change the quantity units from millions of boxes to tons, using the conversion of 10,000 boxes equals 1 ton. Then recalculate the elasticities in the first two rows. Explain why you get the same answer.
   c. Demand studies find that the price elasticity of demand for crack is 0.1. Suppose that half the crack users in New York City support their habit by criminal activities. Using supply-and-demand analysis, show the impact on crime in New York City of a tough law-enforcement program that decreases the supply of crack into the New York market by 50 percent. What would be the effect on criminal activities and on drug use of legalizing crack if this lowered the price of crack by 90 percent? Discuss the impact on price and addiction of a program that successfully rehabilitated half of the crack users.
   d. Can you explain why farmers during a depression might approve of a government program requiring that pigs be killed and buried under the ground?

CHAPTER 5
DEMAND AND CONSUMER BEHAVIOR

What is a cynic? A man who knows the price of everything and the value of nothing.

Oscar Wilde

Each day we make countless decisions about how to allocate our scarce money and time. Should we eat breakfast or sleep late? Spend our evenings reading or visit with friends? Buy a new car or fix our old one? Spend our income today or save for the future? As we balance competing demands and desires, we make the choices that define our lives.

The results of these individual choices are what underlie the demand curves and price elasticities that we saw in earlier chapters. In this chapter we extend our survey of demand by looking at the basic principles of consumer choice and behavior. We shall see how the process of individuals' pursuing their most preferred bundle of consumption goods explains observed patterns of market demand, and we will learn how to measure the benefits that each of us receives from participating in a market economy.

CHOICE AND UTILITY THEORY

In explaining consumer behavior, *economics relies on the fundamental premise that people tend to choose those goods and services they value most highly.* To describe the way consumers choose among different consumption possibilities, economists a century ago developed the notion of *utility*. From the notion of utility, they were able to derive the demand curve and explain its properties.

What do we mean by "utility"? In a word, **utility** denotes satisfaction. More precisely, it refers to how consumers rank different goods and services. If basket A has higher utility than basket B for Smith, this ranking indicates that Smith prefers A over B. Often, it is convenient to think of utility as the subjective pleasure or usefulness that a person derives from consuming a good or service. But you should definitely resist the idea that utility is a psychological function or feeling that can be observed or measured. Rather, utility is a scientific construct that economists use to understand how rational consumers divide their limited resources among the commodities that provide them with satisfaction. *In the theory of demand, we say that people maximize their utility, which means that they choose the bundle of consumption goods that they most prefer.*

Marginal Utility and the Law of Diminishing Marginal Utility

How does utility apply to the theory of demand? Say that consuming the first unit of ice cream gives you a certain level of satisfaction or utility. Now imagine consuming a second unit. Your total utility goes up because the second unit of the good gives you some additional utility. What about adding a third and fourth unit of the same good? Eventually, if you eat enough ice cream, instead of adding to your satisfaction or utility, it makes you sick!

This leads us to the fundamental economic concept of marginal utility. When you eat an additional unit of ice cream, you will get some additional satisfaction or utility. The increment to your utility is called **marginal utility.**

The expression "marginal" is a key term in economics and always means "extra." Marginal utility denotes the additional utility arising from consumption of an additional unit of a commodity.

A century ago, when economists thought about utility, they enunciated the **law of diminishing marginal utility.** This law states that the amount of extra or marginal utility declines as a person consumes more and more of a good.

What is the reason for this law? Utility tends to increase as you consume more of a good. However, according to the law of diminishing marginal utility, as you consume more and more, your total utility will grow at a slower and slower rate. Growth in total utility slows because your marginal utility (the extra utility added by the last unit consumed of a good) diminishes as more of the good is consumed. The diminishing marginal utility results from the fact that your enjoyment of the good drops off as more and more of it is consumed.

The law of diminishing marginal utility states that, as the amount of a good consumed increases, the marginal utility of that good tends to diminish.

A Numerical Example

We can illustrate utility numerically as in Table 5-1. The table shows in column (2) that total utility (U) enjoyed increases as consumption (Q) grows, but it increases at a decreasing rate. Column (3) measures marginal utility as the extra utility gained when 1 extra unit of the good is consumed. Thus as the individual consumes 2 units, the marginal utility is $7 - 4 = 3$ units of utility (call these units "utils").

Focus next on column (3). The fact that marginal utility declines with higher consumption illustrates the law of diminishing marginal utility.

Figure 5-1 on page 82 shows graphically the data on total utility and marginal utility from Table 5-1. In part (a), the gray blocks add up to the total utility at each level of consumption. In addition, the smooth gray curve shows the smoothed utility level for fractional units of consumption. It shows utility

(1) Quantity of a good consumed Q	(2) Total utility U	(3) Marginal utility MU
0	0	
		4
1	4	
		3
2	7	
		2
3	9	
		1
4	10	
		0
5	10	

TABLE 5-1. Utility Rises with Consumption

As we consume more of a good or service like pizza or concerts, total utility increases. The increment of utility from one unit to the next is the "marginal utility"—the extra utility added by the last extra unit consumed. By the law of diminishing marginal utility, the marginal utility falls with increasing levels of consumption.

increasing, but at a decreasing rate. Figure 5-1(b) depicts marginal utilities. Each of the gray blocks of marginal utility is the same size as the corresponding block of total utility in (a). The straight black line in (b) is the smoothed curve of marginal utility.

The law of diminishing marginal utility implies that the marginal utility (MU) curve in Figure 5-1(b) must slope downward. This is exactly equivalent to saying that the total utility curve in Figure 5-1(a) must look concave, like a dome.

Relationship of Total and Marginal Utility. Using Figure 5-1, we can easily see that the total utility of consuming a certain amount is equal to the sum of the marginal utilities up to that point. For example, assume that 3 units are consumed. Column (2) of Table 5-1 shows that the total utility is 9 units. In column (3) we see that the sum of the marginal utilities of the first 3 units is also $4 + 3 + 2 = 9$ units.

Examining Figure 5-1(b), we see that the total area under the marginal utility curve at a particular level of consumption—as measured either by blocks or by the area under the smooth MU curve—must equal the height of the total utility curve shown for the same number of units in Figure 5-1(a).

(a) Total Utility

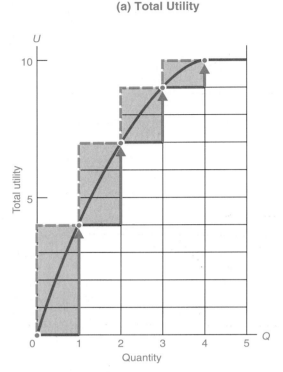

(b) Marginal Utility

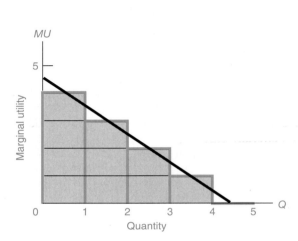

FIGURE 5-1. The Law of Diminishing Marginal Utility

Total utility in (**a**) rises with consumption, but it rises at a decreasing rate, showing diminishing marginal utility. This observation led early economists to formulate the law of downward-sloping demand.

The gray blocks show the extra utility added by each new unit. The fact that total utility increases at a decreasing rate is shown in (**b**) by the declining steps of marginal utility. If we make our units smaller, the steps in total utility are smoothed out and total utility becomes the smooth gray curve in (**a**). Moreover, smoothed marginal utility, shown in (**b**) by the black downward-sloping smooth curve, becomes indistinguishable from the slope of the smooth curve in (**a**).

Whether we examine this relationship using tables or graphs, we see that total utility is the sum of all the marginal utilities that were added from the beginning.

History of Utility Theory

Modern utility theory has its source in *utilitarianism*, which has been one of the major currents of Western intellectual thought for the last two centuries. The notion of utility arose soon after 1700, as the basic ideas of mathematical probability were being developed. Thus Daniel Bernoulli, a member of a brilliant Swiss family of mathematicians, observed in 1738 that people act as if the dollar they

stand to gain in a fair bet is worth less to them than the dollar they stand to lose. This means that they are averse to risk and that successive new dollars of wealth bring them smaller and smaller increments of true utility.[1]

An early introduction of the utility notion into the social sciences was accomplished by the English philosopher Jeremy Bentham (1748–1831). After studying legal theory, and under the influence of Adam Smith's doctrines, Bentham turned to the study of the principles necessary for drawing up

---

[1] The economics of risk, uncertainty, and gambling are examined in Chapter 11.

social legislation. He proposed that society should be organized on the "principle of utility," which he defined as the "property in any object . . . to produce pleasure, good or happiness or to prevent . . . pain, evil or unhappiness."[2] All legislation, according to Bentham, should be designed on utilitarian principles, to promote "the greatest happiness of the greatest number." Among his other legislative proposals were quite modern-sounding ideas about crime and punishment in which he suggested that raising the "pain" to the criminal by harsh punishments would deter crimes.

Bentham's views about utility seem elementary to many people today. But they were revolutionary 200 years ago because they emphasized that social and economic policies should be designed to achieve certain practical results, whereas earlier justifications were generally based upon tradition, the will of the monarch, or religious doctrines. Today, many political thinkers defend their legislative proposals with utilitarian notions of what will make the largest number of people best off.

The next step in the development of utility theory came when the neoclassical economists—such as William Stanley Jevons (1835–1882)—extended Bentham's utility concept to explain consumer behavior. Jevons thought economic theory was a "calculus of pleasure and pain," and he showed that rational people would base their consumption decisions on the extra or marginal utility of each good. Many utilitarians of the nineteenth century believed that utility was a psychic reality—directly and cardinally measurable, like length or temperature. They looked to their own sentiments for affirmation of the law of diminishing marginal utility.

Ordinal Utility. Economists today generally reject the notion of a cardinal, measurable utility that is attached to consumption of ordinary goods like shoes or pasta. Instead, we can easily derive demand curves without ever mentioning the notion of utility. What counts for modern demand theory is the principle of **ordinal utility.** Under this approach, we examine only the preference ranking of bundles of commodities. Ordinal utility asks, "Is A preferred to B?" Using such preference rankings,

we can establish firmly the general properties of market demand curves described in this chapter and in its appendix.[3]

EQUIMARGINAL PRINCIPLE: EQUAL MARGINAL UTILITIES PER DOLLAR FOR EVERY GOOD

We now want to use utility theory to explain consumer demand and to understand the nature of demand curves. For this purpose, we need to know the condition under which I, as a consumer, am most satisfied with my market basket of consumption goods. We say that a consumer attempts to maximize his or her utility, which means that the consumer chooses the most preferred bundle of goods from what is available.

Can we see what a rule for such an optimal decision would be? Certainly I would not expect that the last egg I am buying brings exactly the same marginal utility as the last pair of shoes I am buying, for shoes cost much more per unit than eggs. A more sensible rule would be: If good A costs twice as much as good B, then buy good A only when its marginal utility is at least twice as great as good B's marginal utility.

This leads to the *equimarginal principle* that I should arrange my consumption so that every single good is bringing me the same marginal utility per dollar of expenditure. In such a situation, I am attaining maximum satisfaction or utility from my purchases.

Equimarginal principle: The fundamental condition of maximum satisfaction or utility is the equimarginal principle. It states that a consumer having a fixed income and facing given market prices of goods

---

[2] *An Introduction to the Principles of Morals* (1789). Note that the term "utility" was used by Bentham in quite a different way from today's usage, in which utility is something that is useful.

[3] A statement such as "Situation A is preferred to situation B"—which does not require that we know how much A is preferred to B—is called *ordinal*, or dimensionless. Ordinal variables are ones that we can rank in order, but for which there is no measure of the quantitative difference between the situations. We might rank pictures in an exhibition by order of beauty without having a quantitative measure of beauty.

For certain special situations the concept of *cardinal*, or dimensional, utility is useful. An example of a cardinal measure comes when we say that a substance at 100 K (kelvin) is twice as hot as one at 50 K. People's behavior under conditions of uncertainty is today often analyzed using a cardinal concept of utility. This topic will be examined further in Chapter 11.

will achieve maximum satisfaction or utility when the marginal utility of the last dollar spent on each good is exactly the same as the marginal utility of the last dollar spent on any other good.

Why must this condition hold? If any one good gave more marginal utility per dollar, I would increase my utility by taking money away from other goods and spending more on that good—until the law of diminishing marginal utility drove its marginal utility per dollar down to equality with that of other goods. If any good gave less marginal utility per dollar than the common level, I would buy less of it until the marginal utility of the last dollar spent on it had risen back to the common level.[4] The common marginal utility per dollar of all commodities in consumer equilibrium is called the *marginal utility of income.* It measures the additional utility that would be gained if the consumer could enjoy an extra dollar's worth of consumption.

This fundamental condition of consumer equilibrium can be written in terms of the marginal utilities (*MU*s) and prices (*P*s) of the different goods in the following compact way:[5]

$$\frac{MU_{\text{good 1}}}{P_1} = \frac{MU_{\text{good 2}}}{P_2}$$

$$= \frac{MU_{\text{good 3}}}{P_3} = \cdots$$

$$= MU \text{ per \$ of income}$$

---

[4] At a few places in economics the indivisibility of units is important and cannot be glossed over. Thus, Cadillacs cannot be divided into arbitrarily small portions the way juice can. Suppose I buy one Cadillac, but definitely not two. Then the marginal utility of the first car is enough larger than the marginal utility of the same number of dollars spent elsewhere to induce me to buy this first unit. The marginal utility that the second Cadillac would bring is enough less to ensure I do not buy it. When indivisibility matters, our equality rule for equilibrium can be restated as an inequality rule.

[5] The discerning reader will wonder whether the following mathematical condition seems to imply cardinal, or dimensional, utility (see footnote 3). In fact it does not. An ordinal utility measure is one that we can stretch while always maintaining the same greater-than or less-than relationship (like measuring with a rubber band). If the utility scale is stretched (say, by doubling or multiplying times 3.1415), then you can see that all the numerators in the condition are changed by the same amount, so the consumer equilibrium condition still holds. This is shown in the appendix to this chapter by the use of indifference curves.

Why Demand Curves Slope Downward

Using the fundamental rule for consumer behavior, we can easily see why demand curves slope downward. For simplicity, hold the common marginal utility per dollar of income constant. Then increase the price of good 1. With no change in quantity consumed, the first ratio (i.e., $MU_{\text{good 1}}/P_1$) will be below the *MU* per dollar of all other goods. The consumer will therefore have to readjust the consumption of good 1. The consumer will do this by (*a*) lowering the consumption of good 1, (*b*) thereby raising the *MU* of good 1, until (*c*) at the new, reduced level of consumption of good 1, the new marginal utility per dollar spent on good 1 is again equal to the *MU* per dollar spent on other goods.

Therefore, a higher price for a good reduces the consumer's desired consumption of that commodity; this shows why demand curves slope downward.

Leisure and the Optimal Allocation of Time

A Spanish toast to a friend wishes "health, wealth, and the time to enjoy them." This saying aptly captures the idea that we must allocate our time budgets in much the same way as we do our dollar budgets. Indeed, our time budget is even more constrained than our dollar budget because we have only 24 hours a day whether we are rich or poor in dollars. Let's see how our earlier analysis of allocating scarce dollars applies to time.

Consider leisure, often defined as "time which one can spend as one pleases." Leisure brings out our personal eccentricities. The seventeenth-century philosopher Francis Bacon held that the purest of human pleasures was gardening. The modern British statesman Winston Churchill wrote of his holiday: "I have had a delightful month building a cottage and dictating a book: 200 bricks and 2000 words a day."

Whatever *your* tastes, the principles of utility theory can apply well. Suppose that, after satisfying all your obligations, you have 3 hours a day of free time and can devote it to gardening, laying bricks, or writing history. What is the best way to allocate your time? Let's ignore the possibility that time spent on some of these activities might be an investment that will enhance your earning power in the future. Rather, assume that these are all pure consumption or utility-yielding pursuits. The principles of consumer choice suggest that you will make the best use of your time when you equalize the marginal utilities of the last minute spent on each activity.

To take another example, suppose you want to maximize your knowledge in your courses but you have only a limited amount of time available. Should you study each subject for the same amount of time? Surely not. You may find that an equal study time for economics, history, and chemistry will not yield the same amount of knowledge in the last minute. If the last minute produces a greater marginal knowledge in chemistry than in history, you would raise your total knowledge by shifting additional minutes from history to chemistry, and so on, until the last minute yields the same incremental knowledge in each subject.

The same rule of maximum utility per hour can be applied to many different areas of life, including charitable activities, improving the environment, or losing weight. It is not merely a law of economics. It is a law of rational choice.

Consumers as wizards? A word of caution is in order about how we view consumers. We do not expect consumers to be wizards. They may make most decisions in a routine and unthinking way. What is assumed is that consumers are fairly consistent in their tastes and actions—that they do not flail around in unpredictable ways, making themselves miserable by persistent errors of judgment or arithmetic. If enough people act consistently, avoiding erratic changes in buying behavior and generally choosing their most preferred commodities, our scientific theory will provide a reasonably good approximation to the facts.

AN ALTERNATIVE APPROACH: SUBSTITUTION EFFECT AND INCOME EFFECT

The concept of marginal utility has helped explain the fundamental law of downward-sloping demand. But over the last few decades, economists have developed an alternative approach to analysis of demand—one that makes no mention of marginal utility. This alternative approach uses "indifference curves," which are explained in the appendix to this chapter, to rigorously and consistently produce the major propositions about consumer behavior. This approach also helps explain the factors that tend to make the responsiveness of quantity demanded to price—the price elasticity of demand—large or small.

Indifference analysis asks about the substitution effect and the income effect of a change in price. By looking at these, we can see why the quantity demanded of a good declines as its price rises.

Substitution Effect

The first factor explaining downward-sloping demand curves—the substitution effect—is obvious. If the price of coffee goes up while other prices do not, then coffee has become relatively more expensive.

When coffee becomes a more expensive beverage, less coffee and more tea or cola will be bought. Similarly, because sending electronic mail is cheaper and quicker than sending letters through the regular mail, people are increasingly relying on electronic mail for correspondence. More generally, the **substitution effect** says that when the price of a good rises, consumers will tend to substitute other goods for the more expensive good in order to satisfy their desires more inexpensively.

Consumers, then, behave the way businesses do when the rise in price of an input causes firms to substitute low-priced inputs for high-priced inputs. By this process of substitution, businesses can produce a given amount of output at the least total cost. Similarly, when consumers substitute toward less expensive goods, they are buying a given amount of satisfaction at less cost.

Income Effect

In addition, when your money income is fixed, a price increase is just like a reduction in your "real income," which signifies the actual amount of goods and services that your money income can buy. When a price rises and money incomes are fixed, consumers' real incomes fall and they are likely to buy less of almost all goods (including the good whose price has risen). This produces the **income effect**, which denotes the impact of a price change on a good's quantity demanded that results from the effect of the price change on consumers' real incomes. Because a lower real income generally leads to lower consumption, the income effect will normally reinforce the substitution effect in making the demand curve downward-sloping.

To obtain a quantitative measure of the income effect, we examine a good's **income elasticity.** This term denotes the percentage change in quantity demanded divided by the percentage change in income, holding other things, such as prices, constant. High income elasticities, such as are found for airline travel or yachts, indicate that the demand for these goods rises rapidly as income increases. Low income elasticities, such as for food or cigarettes, denote a weak response of demand as income rises.

Income and substitution effects combine to determine the major characteristics of different commodities. Under some circumstances the resulting demand curve is very price-elastic, as where the consumer has been spending a good deal on the commodity and ready substitutes are available. In this case both the income and the substitution effects are strong and the quantity demanded responds strongly to a price increase.

But consider a commodity like salt, which requires only a small fraction of the consumer's budget. Salt is not easily replaceable by other items and is needed in small amounts to complement more important items. For salt, both income and substitution effects are small, and demand will tend to be price-inelastic.

FROM INDIVIDUAL TO MARKET DEMAND

Having analyzed the principles underlying a single individual's demand for coffee or electronic mail, we next examine how the entire market demand derives from the individual demand. *The demand curve for a good for the entire market is obtained by summing up the quantities demanded by all the consumers.* Each consumer has a demand curve along which the quantity demanded can be plotted against the price; it generally slopes downward and to the right. If all consumers were exactly alike in their demands and if there were 1 million consumers, we could think of the market demand curve as a million-fold enlargement of each consumer's demand curve.

But people are not all exactly alike. Some have high incomes, some low. Some greatly desire coffee; others prefer cola. To obtain the total market curve, all we have to do is calculate the sum total of what all the different consumers will consume at any given price. We then plot that total amount as a point on the market demand curve. Or, if we like, we might construct a numerical demand table by summing the quantities demanded for all individuals at each market price.[6]

The market demand curve is the sum of individual demands at each price. Figure 5-2 shows how to add individual *dd* demand curves horizontally to get the market *DD* demand curve.

Demand Shifts

We know that changes in the price of coffee affect the quantity of coffee demanded. We know this from budget studies, from historical experience, and from examining our own behavior. We discussed briefly in Chapter 3 some of the important nonprice determinants of demand. We now review the earlier discussion in light of our analysis of consumer behavior.

An increase in income tends to increase the amount we are willing to buy of most goods. Necessities tend to be less responsive than most goods to income changes, while luxuries tend to be more responsive to income. And there are a few anomalous goods, known as inferior goods, for which purchases may shrink as incomes increase because people can afford to replace them with other, more desirable goods. Soup bones, intercity bus travel, and used TVs are examples of inferior goods for many Americans today.

What does all this mean in terms of the demand curve? The demand curve shows how the quantity of a good demanded responds to a change in its own price. But the demand is also affected by the prices of other goods, by consumer incomes, and by special influences. The demand curve was drawn on the assumption that these other things were held constant. But what if these other things change? Then the whole demand curve will shift to the right or to the left.

Figure 5-3 illustrates changes in factors affecting demand. Given people's incomes and the prices for other goods, we can draw the demand curve for coffee as *DD*. Assume that price and quantity are at point *A*. Suppose that incomes rise while the prices of coffee and other goods are unchanged. Because coffee is a normal good with a positive income elasticity, people will increase their purchases of coffee. Hence the demand curve for coffee will shift to the

---

[6] Here and in other chapters, we label *individual* demand and supply curves with lowercase letters (*dd* and *ss*), while using uppercase letters (*DD* and *SS*) for the *market* demand and supply curves.

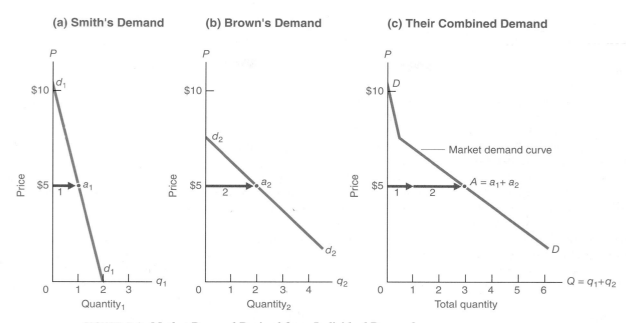

FIGURE 5-2. Market Demand Derived from Individual Demands
We add all individual consumers' demand curves to get the market demand curve. At each price, such as $5, we add quantities demanded by each person to get the market quantity demanded. The figure shows how, at a price of $5, we add horizontally Smith's 1 unit demanded to Brown's 2 units to get the market demand of 3 units.

right, say, to $D'D'$, with A' indicating the new quantity demanded of coffee. If incomes should fall, then we would expect a reduction in demand and in quantity bought. This downward shift we illustrate by $D''D''$ and by A''.

Substitutes and Complements

Everyone knows that raising the price of beef will decrease the amount of beef demanded. We have seen that it will also affect the demand for other commodities. For example, a higher price for beef will increase the demand for substitutes like chicken. A higher beef price may lower the demand for goods like hamburger buns and ketchup that are used along with beef hamburgers. It will probably have little effect on the demand for economics textbooks.

We say, therefore, that beef and chicken are substitute products. Goods A and B are **substitutes** if an increase in the price of good A will increase the demand for substitute good B. Hamburgers and hamburger buns, or cars and gasoline, on the other hand, are complementary products; they are called **complements** because an increase in the price of good A causes a decrease in the demand for its complementary good B. In between are **independent**

FIGURE 5-3. Demand Curve Shifts with Changes in Income or in Other Goods' Prices
As incomes increase, consumers generally want more of a good, thus increasing demand or shifting demand outward (explain why higher incomes shift DD to $D'D'$). Similarly, a rise in the price of a substitute good increases or shifts out the demand curve (e.g., from DD to $D'D'$). Explain why a decrease in income would generally shift demand to $D''D''$. Why would a decrease in chicken prices shift hamburger demand to $D''D''$?

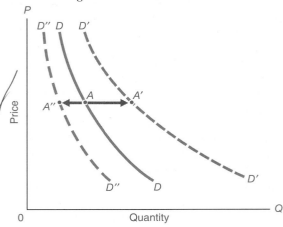

goods, such as beef and textbooks, for which a price change for one good has no effect on the demand for the other. Try classifying the pairs turkey and cranberry sauce, oil and coal, college and textbooks, shoes and shoelaces, salt and shoelaces.

Say Figure 5-3 represented the demand for beef. A fall in the price of chickens may well cause consumers to buy less beef; the beef demand curve would therefore shift to the left, say, to $D''D''$. But what if the price of hamburger buns were to fall? The resulting change on DD, if there is one, will be in the direction of increased beef purchases, a rightward shift of the demand curve. Why do we see this difference in response? Because chicken is a rival or substitute product for beef, while hamburger buns are complements to beef.

Review of key concepts:

- The substitution effect occurs when a higher price leads to substitution of other goods for the good whose price has risen.
- The income effect is the change in the quantity demanded of a good because the change in its price has the effect of changing a consumer's real income.
- Income elasticity is the percentage change in quantity demanded of a good divided by the percentage change in income.
- Goods are substitutes if an increase in the price of one increases the demand for the other.
- Goods are complements if an increase in the price of one decreases the demand for the other.
- Goods are independent if a price change for one has no effect on the demand for the other.

Empirical Estimates of Price and Income Elasticities

For many economic applications, it is essential to have numerical estimates of price elasticities. For example, an automobile manufacturer will want to know the impact on sales of the higher car prices that result from installation of costly pollution-control equipment; a college needs to know the impact of higher tuition rates on student applications; and a publisher will calculate the impact of higher textbook prices on its sales. All these applications require a numerical estimate of price elasticity.

Commodity	Price elasticity
Tomatoes	4.60
Green peas	2.80
Legal gambling	1.90
Taxi service	1.20
Furniture	1.00
Movies	0.87
Shoes	0.70
Legal services	0.61
Medical insurance	0.31
Bus travel	0.20
Residential electricity	0.13

TABLE 5-2. Selected Estimates of Price Elasticities of Demand

Estimates of price elasticities of demand show a wide range of variation. Elasticities are generally high for goods for which ready substitutes are available, like tomatoes or peas. Low price elasticities exist for those goods like electricity which are essential to daily life and which have no close substitutes. [Source: Heinz Kohler, *Intermediate Microeconomics: Theory and Applications*, 2d ed. (Scott Foresman, New York, 1986).]

Similar decisions depend on income elasticities. A government planning its road or rail network will estimate the impact of rising incomes on automobile travel; the federal government must calculate the effect of higher incomes on energy consumption in designing policies for air pollution or global warming; in determining the necessary investments for generating capacity, electrical utilities require income elasticities for estimating electricity consumption.

Economists have developed useful statistical techniques for estimating price and income elasticities. The quantitative estimates are derived from market data on quantities demanded, prices, incomes, and other variables. Tables 5-2 and 5-3 show selected estimates of elasticities.

THE ECONOMICS OF ADDICTION

In a free-market economy, government generally lets people decide what to buy with their money. If some individuals want to eat ice cream rather than pizza, we assume that they know what is best for them and that in the interests of personal freedom the government should respect their preferences. In some cases, but sparingly and with great hesitation, the government decides to overrule private adult decisions. These are cases of *merit goods*, whose consumption is thought intrinsically worthwhile (to be contrasted with *demerit goods*, whose consumption is deemed harmful). For these goods, we recognize that some consumption activities have such serious effects that overriding private decisions may be desirable. Today, most societies provide for free public education and emergency health care; on the other hand, society also penalizes or forbids consumption of such harmful substances as cigarettes, alcohol, and heroin.

One of the most controversial cases of demerit goods concerns addiction. An addictive substance is one for which the desire to consume depends significantly on past consumption. The hooked smoker, the addicted crack user, may regret bitterly the acquired habit; but, such is the nature of addiction, one cannot resist the habit after it has become established. A regular user of cigarettes or heroin is much more likely to desire these substances than is a nonuser. Moreover, for highly addictive goods, demand is likely to be quite price-inelastic. By contrast, for conventional goods, demands today are not likely to depend so directly on consumption patterns yesterday.

TABLE 5-3. Income Elasticities for Selected Products
Income elasticities are high for luxuries, whose consumption grows rapidly relative to income. Negative income elasticities are found for *inferior goods*, whose demand falls as income rises. Demand for many staple commodities, like clothing, grows proportionally with income. [Source: Heinz Kohler, *Intermediate Microeconomics: Theory and Applications*, 2d ed. (Scott Foresman, New York, 1986).]

Commodity	Income elasticity
Automobiles	2.50
Owner-occupied housing	1.50
Furniture	1.50
Books	1.40
Restaurant meals	1.00
Clothing	1.00
Physicians' services	0.75
Tobacco	0.64
Eggs	0.37
Margarine	−0.20
Pig products	−0.20
Flour	−0.36

The markets for addictive substances are big business. Annual cigarette expenditures today are around $50 billion, while those on alcohol are about $30 billion. Numbers for illegal drugs are obviously conjectural, but estimates of total spending range from $20 to $50 billion annually. Consumption of these substances raises major public policy issues because addictive substances may harm the users and often impose costs and harms on society. The harms to users include early mortality and a wide range of medical problems in the case of cigarettes; 10,000 highway fatalities a year attributed to alcohol; binges and psychosis in the use of crack cocaine; and failures in school, job, and family, along with high levels of AIDS, from intravenous heroin use. Harms to society include the predatory crime that addicts of high-priced drugs engage in, the costs of providing medical care to unhealthy drug users, and the rapid spread of communicable disease, especially AIDS and pneumonia.

One policy approach, often followed in the United States, is to prohibit the sale and use of addictive substances and to enforce prohibition with criminal sanctions. Economically, prohibition can be interpreted as a sharp upward shift in the supply curve. After the upward shift, the price of the addictive substance is much higher. During Prohibition (1920–1933), alcohol prices were approximately 3 times higher than before. Estimates are that cocaine currently sells for at least 20 times its free-market price.

But what has happened to quantity demanded, to the use, of addictive substances? And how does the prohibition affect the injuries to self and to society? To answer these questions, we need to consider the nature of the demand for addictive substances. The evidence indicates that casual consumers of illegal drugs have cheap substitutes like alcohol and tobacco and thus will have relatively high price elasticity of demand. By contrast, hard-core users are often addicted to particular substances and have price-inelastic demands.

One possible outcome is shown in Figure 5-4. This illustrates the impact of moving from legalized drugs to drug prohibition by tightening supply from *SS* to *S'S'* for the hard-core users of a highly addictive substance like heroin. In this case, demand is highly price-inelastic. As a result of the shift in supply and rise in price, total spending on drugs increases sharply. For such drugs, the outlays may be so great

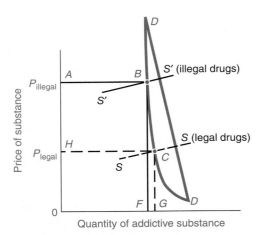

FIGURE 5-4. Demand for Addictive Substances by Hard-Core Users

Demand for addictive substances is very price-inelastic for hard-core users of drugs like heroin. As a result, if the street price rises after prohibition shifts supply from *SS* to *S'S'*, total spending on drugs will rise from 0*HCG* to 0*ABF*. For drugs that are highly price-inelastic, this implies that spending on drugs will rise sharply when supply is restrained. What will happen to criminal activity after prohibition if a substantial fraction of the income of addicts is obtained by theft and prostitution? Can you see why some people would argue for reduced drug enforcement or even legalization in this case?

that the user engages in predatory crime. The results, in the view of two economists who have studied the subject, are that "the market in illegal drugs promotes crime, destroys inner cities, spreads AIDS, corrupts law enforcement officials and politicians, produces and exacerbates poverty, and erodes the moral fabric of society."[7]

Others argue that drug use is highly price-sensitive, especially for casual users, as is shown in Figure 5-5. For example, a teenager might experiment with an addictive substance if it is affordable, while a high price (accompanied by low availability) would be unlikely to tempt that person down the road to addiction. In this case, supply restraints are likely to both lower use sharply and reduce spending on addictive substances.

---

[7] The quote is from Jeffrey A. Miron and Jeffrey Zwiebel, "The Economic Case against Drug Prohibition," *Journal of Economic Perspectives* (Fall 1995), pp. 175–192, which is an excellent nontechnical survey of the economics of drug prohibition.

One of the major difficulties with regulating addictive substances comes because of the patterns of substitution. Many drugs appear to be close substitutes. As a result, experts caution, raising the price of one substance mainly serves to drive users to other harmful substances. For example, states that have criminal penalties for marijuana use tend to have higher teenage consumption of alcohol and tobacco.

Clearly, social policy toward addictive substances raises extremely complex issues. But the economic theory of demand provides some important insights into the impacts of alternative approaches. First, it suggests that raising the prices of harmful addictive substances can reduce the number of casual users who will be attracted into the market. Second, it cautions us that many of the negative consequences of illegal drugs result from the prohibition of addictive substances rather than from their consumption. Many thoughtful observers conclude with the paradoxical observation that the overall costs of addictive substances—to users, to other people, and to the ravaged inner cities in which the drug trade thrives—would be lower if government prohibition were relaxed and the resources currently devoted to supply restrictions were instead put into treatment and counseling.

THE PARADOX OF VALUE

More than two centuries ago, in *The Wealth of Nations*, Adam Smith posed the paradox of value:

> Nothing is more useful than water; but it will scarce purchase anything. A diamond, on the contrary, has scarce any value in use; but a very great quantity of other goods may frequently be had in exchange for it.

In other words, how is it that water, which is essential to life, has little value, while diamonds, which are generally used for conspicuous consumption, command an exalted price?

Although it troubled Adam Smith 200 years ago, we can today resolve this paradox as follows: "The supply and demand curves for water intersect at a very low price, while supply and demand for diamonds are such that their equilibrium price is very high." Having said that, we would naturally go on to ask, "But why do supply and demand for water intersect at such a low price?" The answer is that diamonds are very scarce and the cost of getting extra

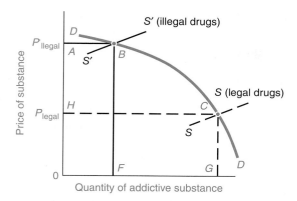

FIGURE 5-5. Demand for Addictive Substances by Casual Users

Demand may be quite elastic for casual users (those who are not addicted or for whom substitute products are readily available). In this case, restrictions or price increases will have significant impact on use. Moreover, because demand is price-elastic, total spending on drugs falls from 0*HCG* to 0*ABF* with restrictions. This depicts the argument of those who would severely limit the availability of addictive substances.

ones is high, while water is relatively abundant and costs little in many areas of the world.

Yet this answer still does not reconcile the cost information with the equally valid fact that the world's water is vastly more critical than the world's supply of diamonds. We need to add a second truth: The total utility from water consumption does not determine its price or demand. Rather, water's price is determined by its marginal utility, by the usefulness of the last glass of water. Because there is so much water, the last glass sells for very little. Even though the first few drops are worth life itself, the last few are needed only for watering the lawn or washing the car. *We thus find that an immensely valuable commodity like water sells for next to nothing because its last drop is worth next to nothing.*

As one student put the matter: The theory of economic value is easy to understand if you just remember that in economics the tail wags the dog. It is the tail of marginal utility that wags the dog of prices and quantities.

We can resolve the paradox of value as follows: The more there is of a commodity, the less is the relative desirability of its last little unit. It is therefore clear why water has a low price and why an absolute necessity like air could become a free good. In both cases, it is the large quantities that pull the marginal utilities so far down and thus reduce the prices of these vital commodities.

CONSUMER SURPLUS

The paradox of value emphasizes that the recorded money value of a good (measured by price times quantity) may be very misleading as an indicator of the total economic value of that good. The measured economic value of the air we breathe is zero, yet air's contribution to welfare is immeasurably large.

The gap between the total utility of a good and its total market value is called **consumer surplus.** The surplus arises because we "receive more than we pay for" as a result of the law of diminishing marginal utility.

We have consumer surplus basically because we pay the same amount for each unit of a commodity that we buy, from the first to the last. We pay the same price for each egg or glass of water. Thus we pay for *each* unit what the *last* unit is worth. But by our fundamental law of diminishing marginal utility, the earlier units are worth more to us than the last. Thus, we enjoy a surplus of utility on each of these earlier units.

Figure 5-6 illustrates the concept of consumer surplus in the case where money provides a firm measuring rod for utility. Here, an individual consumes water, which has a price of $1 per gallon. This is shown by the horizontal rust line at $1 in Figure 5-6. The consumer considers how many gallon jugs to buy at that price. The first gallon is highly valuable, slaking extreme thirst, and the consumer is willing to pay $9 for it. But this first gallon costs only the market price of $1, so the consumer has gained a surplus of $8.

Consider the second gallon. This is worth $8 to the consumer, but again costs only $1, so the surplus is $7. And so on down to the ninth gallon, which is worth only 50 cents to the consumer, and so it is not bought. The consumer equilibrium comes at point *E*, where 8 gallons of water are bought at a price of $1 each.

But here we make an important discovery: Even though the consumer has paid only $8, the total value of the water is $44. This is obtained by adding up each of the marginal utility columns (= $9 + $8 + · · · + $2). Thus the consumer has gained a surplus of $36 over the amount paid.

Consumer Surplus for an Individual

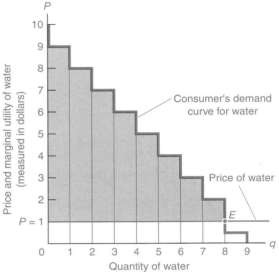

FIGURE 5-6. Because of Diminishing Marginal Utility, Consumer's Satisfaction Exceeds What Is Paid

The downward-sloping demand for water reflects the diminishing marginal utility of water. Note how much excess or surplus satisfaction occurs from the earlier units. Adding up all the gray surpluses ($8 of surplus on unit 1 + $7 of surplus on unit 2 + · · · + $1 of surplus on unit 8), we obtain the total consumer surplus of $36 on water purchases.

In the simplified case seen here, the area between the demand curve and the price line is the total consumer surplus.

Figure 5-6 examines the case of a single consumer purchasing water. We can also apply the concept of consumer surplus to a market as a whole. The market demand curve in Figure 5-7 is the horizontal summation of the individual demand curves. The logic of the individual consumer surplus carries over to the market as a whole. The area of the market demand curve above the price line, shown as *NER* in Figure 5-7, represents the total consumer surplus.

Because consumers pay the price of the last unit for all units consumed, they enjoy a surplus of utility over cost. Consumer surplus measures the extra utility that consumers receive over what they pay for a commodity.

Applications of Consumer Surplus

The concept of consumer surplus is useful in helping evaluate many government decisions. For example, how can the government decide on the value of building a new highway or of preserving a recreation site? Suppose a new highway has been proposed. Being free to all, it will bring in no revenue. The value to users will be found in time saved or in safer trips and can be measured by the individual consumer surplus. To avoid difficult issues of interpersonal utility comparisons, we assume that there are 10,000 users, all identical in every respect.

By careful experimentation, we determine that each individual's consumer surplus is $350 for the highway. The highway will raise consumer economic welfare if its total cost is less than $3.5 million (10,000 × $350). Economists use consumer surplus when they are performing a *cost-benefit analysis*, which attempts to determine the costs and benefits of a

FIGURE 5-7. Total Consumer Surplus Is the Area under the Demand Curve and above the Price Line

The demand curve measures the amount consumers would pay for each unit consumed. Thus the total area under the demand curve (*0REM*) shows the total utility attached to the consumption of water. By subtracting the market cost of water to consumers (equal to *0NEM*), we obtain the consumer surplus from water consumption as the gray triangle *NER*. This device is useful for measuring the benefits of public goods and the losses from monopolies and import tariffs.

Consumer Surplus for a Market

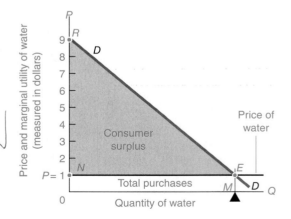

government program. Generally, an economist would recommend that a free road should be built if its total consumer surplus exceeds its costs. Similar analyses have been used for environmental questions such as whether to preserve wilderness areas for recreation or whether to require new pollution-abatement equipment.

The concept of consumer surplus also points to the enormous privilege enjoyed by citizens of modern societies. Each of us enjoys a vast array of enormously valuable goods that can be bought at low prices. This is a humbling thought. If you know someone who is bragging about *his* economic productivity, or explaining how high *her* real wages are, suggest a moment of reflection. If they were transported with their specialized skills to an uninhabited desert island, how much would their wages buy? Indeed, without capital machinery, without the cooperation of others, and without the technological knowledge which each generation inherits from the past, how much could any of us produce? It is only too clear that all of us reap the benefits of an eco-

nomic world we never made. As the great British sociologist L. T. Hobhouse said:

> The organizer of industry who thinks that he has "made" himself and his business has found a whole social system ready to his hand in skilled workers, machinery, a market, peace and order—a vast apparatus and a pervasive atmosphere, the joint creation of millions of men and scores of generations. Take away the whole social factor and we [are] but . . . savages living on roots, berries, and vermin.

We have now completed our survey of how consumer preferences interact with prices and incomes to determine the demand for goods and services. But what of business? What of the production and supply of the goods that consumers demand? The next two chapters turn to this other partner in supply and demand. Once our survey of business decisions is complete, we will have a fuller understanding of the forces that lie behind the two curves that dance through the pages of textbooks and indeed through economic life itself.

SUMMARY

1. Market demands or demand curves are explained as stemming from the process of individuals' choosing their most preferred bundle of consumption goods and services.

2. Economists explain consumer demand by the concept of utility, which denotes the relative satisfaction that a consumer obtains from using different commodities. The additional satisfaction obtained from consuming an additional unit of a good is given the name *marginal utility*, where "marginal" means the extra or incremental utility. The law of diminishing marginal utility states that as the amount of a commodity consumed increases, the marginal utility of the last unit consumed tends to decrease.

3. Economists assume that consumers allocate their limited incomes so as to obtain the greatest satisfaction or utility. To maximize utility, a consumer must satisfy the *equimarginal principle* that the marginal utilities of the last dollar spent on each and every good must be equal.

Only when the marginal utility per dollar is equal for apples, bacon, coffee, and everything else will the consumer attain the greatest satisfaction from a limited dollar income. But be careful to note that the marginal utility of a $50-per-ounce bottle of perfume is not equal to the marginal utility of a 50-cent glass of cola. Rather, their marginal utilities divided by price per unit are all equal in the consumer's optimal allocation. That is, their marginal utilities per last dollar, *MU/P*, are equalized.

4. Equal marginal utility per unit of resource is a fundamental rule of choice that transcends demand theory and dollars. If you want to allocate any limited resource among competing uses, you can benefit by transferring from the low marginal advantage per unit of resource to the high marginal advantage until a final equilib-

rium is reached at which all marginal advantages per unit of resource have become equal. An important application of this rule is the use of time.

5. The market demand curve for all consumers is derived by adding horizontally the separate demand curves of each consumer. A demand curve can shift for many reasons. For example, a rise in income will normally shift *DD* rightward, thus increasing demand; a rise in the price of a substitute good (e.g., chicken for beef) will also create a similar upward shift in demand; a rise in the price of a complementary good (e.g., hamburger buns for beef) will in turn cause the *DD* curve to shift downward and leftward. Still other factors—changing tastes, population, or expectations—can affect demand.

6. We can gain added insight into the factors that cause downward-sloping demand by separating the effect of a price rise into substitution and income effects. (*a*) The substitution effect occurs when a higher price leads to substitution of other goods to meet satisfactions; (*b*) the income effect means that a price increase lowers real income and thereby reduces the desired consumption of most commodities. For most goods, substitution and income effects of a price in-

crease reinforce one another and lead to the law of downward-sloping demand. We measure the quantitative responsiveness of demand to income by the income elasticity, which measures the percentage change in quantity demanded divided by the percentage change in income.

7. Remember that it is the tail of marginal utility that wags the market dog of prices and quantities. This point is emphasized by the concept of *consumer surplus*. We pay the same price for the last quart of milk as for the first. But, because of the law of diminishing marginal utility, marginal utilities of earlier units are greater than that of the last unit. This means that we would have been willing to pay more than the market price for each of the earlier units. The excess of total value over market value is called consumer surplus. Consumer surplus reflects the benefit we gain from being able to buy all units at the same low price. In simplified cases, we can measure consumer surplus as the area between the demand curve and the price line. It is a concept relevant for many public decisions—such as deciding when the community should incur the heavy expenses of a road or bridge or set aside land for a wilderness area.

CONCEPTS FOR REVIEW

utility, marginal utility
utilitarianism
law of diminishing marginal utility
demand shifts from income and
    other sources
ordinal utility

equimarginal principle of equal *MU*
    of last dollar spent on each good:
    $MU_1/P_1 = MU_2/P_2 = \cdots$
    $= MU$ per $ of income
market demand vs. individual
    demand

income elasticity
substitutes, complements, independent goods
substitution effect and income effect
merit goods, demerit goods
paradox of value
consumer surplus

QUESTIONS FOR DISCUSSION

1. Explain the meaning of utility. What is the difference between total utility and marginal utility? Explain the law of diminishing marginal utility and give a numerical example.

2. Each week, Tom Wu buys two hamburgers at $2 each, eight cokes at $0.50 each, and eight slices of pizza at $1 each, but he buys no hot dogs at $1.50 each. What can you deduce about Tom's marginal utility for each of the four goods?

3. Which pairs of the following goods would you classify as complementary, substitute, or independent goods:

beef, ketchup, lamb, cigarettes, gum, pork, radio, television, air travel, bus travel, taxis, and paperbacks? Illustrate the resulting shift in the demand curve for one good when the price of another good goes up. How would a change in income affect the demand curve for air travel? The demand curve for bus travel?

4. Why is it wrong to say, "Utility is maximized when the marginal utilities of all goods are exactly equal"? Correct the statement and explain.

5. How much would you be willing to pay each year rather than give up *all* movies? How much do you

spend on movies? Estimate roughly your consumer surplus.

6. Consider the following table showing the utility of different numbers of days skied each year:

Number of days skied	Total utility ($)
0	0
1	30
2	55
3	73
4	88
5	98
6	98

Construct a table showing the marginal utility for each day of skiing. Assuming that there are 1 million people with preferences shown in the table, draw the market demand curve for ski days. If lift tickets cost $20 per day, what are the equilibrium price and quantity of days skied?

7. For each of the commodities in Table 5-2, calculate the impact of a doubling of price on quantity demanded. Similarly, for the goods in Table 5-3, what would be the impact of a 50 percent increase in consumer incomes?

8. As you add together the identical demand curves of more and more people (in a way similar to the procedure in Figure 5-2), the market demand curve becomes flatter and flatter on the same scale. Does this fact indicate that the elasticity of demand is becoming larger and larger? Explain your answer carefully.

9. An interesting application of supply and demand to addictive substances compares alternative techniques for supply restriction. For this problem, assume that the demand for addictive substances is inelastic.

   a. One approach (used today for heroin and cocaine and for alcohol during Prohibition) is to reduce supply at the nation's borders. Show how this raises price and increases the total income of the suppliers in the drug industry.

   b. An alternative approach (followed today for tobacco and alcohol) is to tax the goods heavily. Using the tax apparatus developed in Chapter 4, show how this reduces the total income of the suppliers in the drug industry.

   c. Comment on the difference between the two approaches.

10. Suppose you are very rich and very fat. Your doctor has advised you to limit your food intake to 2000 calories per day. What is your consumer equilibrium for food consumption?

APPENDIX 5
GEOMETRICAL ANALYSIS
OF CONSUMER EQUILIBRIUM

A century ago, the economist Vilfredo Pareto (1848–1923) discovered that all the important elements of demand theory could be analyzed without the utility concept. Pareto developed what are today called indifference curves. This appendix presents the modern theory of indifference analysis and then derives the major conclusions of consumer behavior with that new tool.

THE INDIFFERENCE CURVE

Start by assuming that you are a consumer who buys different combinations of two commodities, say, food and clothing, at a given set of prices. For each combination of the two goods, assume that you prefer one to the other or are indifferent between the pair. For example, when asked to choose between combination A of 1 unit of food and 6 units of clothing and combination B of 2 units of food and 3 of clothing, you might (1) prefer A to B, (2) prefer B to A, or (3) be indifferent between A and B.

Now suppose that A and B are equally good in your eyes—that you are indifferent as to which of them you receive. Let us consider some other combinations of goods about which you are likewise indifferent, as listed in the table for Figure 5A-1.

Figure 5A-1 shows these combinations diagrammatically. We measure units of clothing on one axis and units of food on the other. Each of our four combinations of goods is represented by its point, A,

B, C, D. But these four are by no means the only combinations among which you are indifferent. Another batch, such as 1½ units of food and 4 of clothing, might be ranked as equal to A, B, C, or D, and there are many others not shown. The curved contour of Figure 5A-1, linking up the four points, is an **indifference curve.** The points on the curve represent consumption bundles among which the consumer is indifferent; all are equally desirable.

Law of Substitution

Indifference curves are drawn as bowl-shaped, or convex to the origin. Hence, as you move downward and to the right along the curve—a movement that implies increasing the quantity of food and reducing the units of clothing—the curve becomes flatter. The curve is drawn in this way to illustrate a property that seems most often to hold true in reality and which we call the law of substitution:

The scarcer a good, the greater its relative substitution value; its marginal utility rises relative to the marginal utility of the good that has become plentiful.

Thus, in going from *A* to *B* in Figure 5A-1, you would swap 3 of your 6 clothing units for 1 extra food unit. But from *B* to C, you would sacrifice only 1 unit of your remaining clothing supply to obtain a third food unit—a 1-for-1 swap. For a fourth unit of food, you would sacrifice only ½ unit from your dwindling supply of clothing.

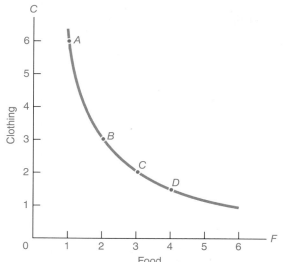

A Consumer's Indifference Curve

Indifference Combinations

	Food	Clothing
A	1	6
B	2	3
C	3	2
D	4	1½

FIGURE 5A-1. Indifference Curves for a Pair of Goods

Getting more of one good compensates for giving up some of the other. The consumer likes situation *A* exactly as much as *B*, *C*, or *D*. The food-clothing combinations that yield equal satisfaction are plotted as a smooth indifference curve. This is convex from below in accord with the law of substitution, which says that as you get more of a good, its substitution ratio, or the indifference-curve's slope, diminishes.

If we join the points *A* and *B* of Figure 5A-1, we find that the slope of the resulting line (neglecting its negative sign) has a value of 3. Join *B* and *C*, and the slope is 1; join *C* and *D*, and the slope is ½. These figures—3, 1, ½—are the *substitution ratios* (sometimes called the *marginal rates of substitution*) between the two goods. As the size of the movement along the curve becomes very small, the closer the substitution ratio comes to the actual slope of the indifference curve.

The slope of the indifference curve is the measure of the goods' relative marginal utilities, or of the substitution terms on which—for very small changes—the consumer would be willing to exchange a little less of one good in return for a little more of the other.

An indifference curve that is convex in the manner of Figure 5A-1 conforms to the law of substitution. As the amount of food you consume goes up—and the clothing goes down—food must become relatively cheaper and cheaper in order for you to be persuaded to take a little extra food in exchange for a little sacrifice of clothing. The precise shape and

slope of an indifference curve will, of course, vary from one consumer to the next, but the typical shape will take the form shown in Figures 5A-1 and 5A-2.

The Indifference Map

The table in Figure 5A-1 is one of an infinite number of possible tables. We could start with a more preferred consumption situation and list some of the different combinations that would bring the consumer this higher level of satisfaction. One such table might have begun with 2 food units and 7 clothing units; another with 3 food units, 8 clothing units. Each table could be portrayed graphically; each has a corresponding indifference curve.

Figure 5A-2 shows four such curves; the curve from Figure 5A-1 is labeled U_3. This diagram is analogous to a geographical contour map. A person who walks along the path indicated by a particular height contour on such a map is neither climbing nor descending; similarly, the consumer who moves from one position to another along a single indifference curve enjoys neither increasing nor decreasing satisfaction from the change in consumption. Only a few

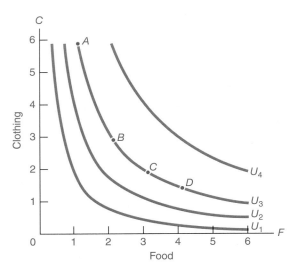

FIGURE 5A-2. A Family of Indifference Curves
The curves labeled U_1, U_2, U_3, and U_4 represent indifference curves. Which indifference curve is most preferred by the consumer?

of the possible indifference curves are shown in Figure 5A-2.

Note that as we increase both goods and thus move in a northeasterly direction across this map, we are crossing successive indifference curves; hence, we are reaching higher and higher levels of satisfaction (assuming that the consumer gets greater satisfaction from receiving increased quantities of both goods). Curve U_3 stands for a higher level of satisfaction than U_2; U_4, for a higher level of satisfaction than U_3; and so forth.

BUDGET LINE OR BUDGET CONSTRAINT

Now let us set a particular consumer's indifference map aside for a moment and give the consumer a fixed income. He has, say, $6 per day to spend, and he is confronted with fixed prices for each food and clothing unit—$1.50 for food, $1 for clothing. It is clear that he could spend his money on any one of a variety of alternative combinations of food and clothing. At one extreme, he could buy 4 food units and no clothing; at the other, 6 clothing units and no food. The table with Figure 5A-3 illustrates some of the possible ways in which he could allocate his $6.

Figure 5A-3 plots these five possibilities. Note that all the points lie on a straight line, labeled NM. Moreover, any other attainable point, such as $3\frac{1}{3}$ food units and 1 clothing unit, lies on NM. The straight budget line NM sums up all the possible combinations of the two goods that would just exhaust the consumer's income.[1] The slope of NM (neglecting its sign) is $\frac{3}{2}$, which is the ratio of the food price to the clothing price. The meaning of the slope is that, given these prices, every time our consumer gives up 3 clothing units (thereby dropping down 3 vertical units on the diagram), he can gain 2 units of food (i.e., move right 2 horizontal units).

We call NM the consumer's *budget line* or *budget constraint*.

THE EQUILIBRIUM POSITION OF TANGENCY

Now we are ready to put our two parts together. The axes of Figure 5A-3 are the same as those of Figures 5A-1 and 5A-2. We can superimpose the gray budget line NM upon this rust consumer indifference map, as shown in Figure 5A-4 on page 100. The consumer is free to move anywhere along NM. Positions to the right and above NM are not allowed because they require more than $6 of income; positions to the left and below NM are irrelevant because the consumer is assumed to spend the full $6.

Where will the consumer move? Obviously, to that point which yields the greatest satisfaction—that is, to the highest possible indifference curve—which in this case must be at the rust point B. At B, the budget line just touches, but does not cross, the indifference curve U_3. At this point of tangency, where the budget line just kisses but does not cross an indifference contour, is found the highest utility contour the consumer can reach.

Geometrically, the consumer is at equilibrium where the slope of the budget line (which is equal to

---

[1] This is so because, if we designate quantities of food and clothing bought as F and C, respectively, total expenditure on food must be $1.50F$ and total expenditure on clothing, $1C$. If daily income and expenditure are $6, the following equation must hold: $6 = 1.50F + 1C$. This is a linear equation, the equation of the budget line NM. Note:

Arithmetic slope of NM = $1.50 \div 1

= price of food $\div$ price of clothing

A Consumer's Budget Line

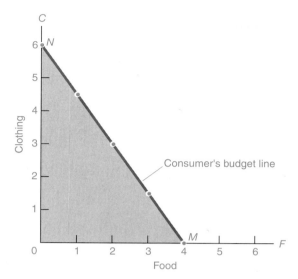

Alternative Consumption Possibilities

	Food	Clothing
M	4	0
	3	1$\frac{1}{2}$
	2	3
	1	4$\frac{1}{2}$
N	0	6

FIGURE 5A-3. Income Constrains Consumer Spending
The budget limit on expenditures can be seen in a numerical table. The total cost of each budget (reckoned as $1.50F + $1C$) adds up to exactly $6 of income. We can plot the budget constraint as a straight line whose absolute slope equals the P_F/P_C ratio. NM is the consumer's budget line. When income is $6, with food and clothing prices $1.50 and $1, the consumer can choose any point on this budget line. (Why is its slope $1.50/$1 = $\frac{3}{2}$?)

the ratio of food to clothing prices) is exactly equal to the slope of the indifference curve (which is equal to the ratio of the marginal utilities of the two goods).

Consumer equilibrium is attained at the point where the budget line is tangent to the highest indifference curve. At that point, the consumer's substitution ratio is just equal to the slope of the budget line.

Put differently, the substitution ratio, or the slope of the indifference curve, is the ratio of the marginal utility of food to the marginal utility of clothing. So our tangency condition is just another way of stating that the ratio of prices must be equal to the ratio of marginal utilities; in equilibrium, the consumer is getting the same marginal utility from the last penny spent on food as from the last penny spent on clothing. Therefore, we can derive the following equilibrium condition:

$$\frac{P_F}{P_C} = \text{substitution ratio} = \frac{MU_F}{MU_C}$$

This is exactly the same condition as we derived for utility theory in the main part of this chapter.

CHANGES IN INCOME AND PRICE

Two important applications of indifference curves are frequently used to consider the effects of (*a*) a change in money income and (*b*) a change in the price of one of the two goods.

Income Change

Assume, first, that the consumer's daily income is halved while the two prices remain unchanged. We could prepare another table, similar to the table for Figure 5A-3, showing the new consumption possibilities. Plotting these points on a diagram such as Figure 5A-5, we should find that the new budget line occupies the position $N'M'$ in Figure 5A-5. The line has made a parallel shift inward.[2] The consumer is

---

[2] The equation of the new $N'M'$ budget line is now $3 = $1.50F + $1C$.

Consumer's Equilibrium

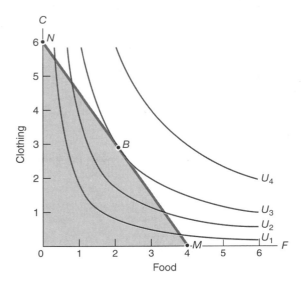

FIGURE 5A-4. Consumer's Most Preferred and Feasible Consumption Bundle Is Attained at *B*

We now combine the budget line and indifference contours on one diagram. The consumer reaches the highest indifference curve attainable with fixed income at point *B*, which is the tangency of the budget line with highest indifference curve. At tangency point *B*, substitution ratio equals price ratio P_F/P_C. This means that all goods' marginal utilities are proportional to their prices, with the marginal utility of the last dollar spent on every good being equalized.

now free to move only along this new (and lower) budget line; to maximize satisfaction, he will move to the highest attainable indifference curve, or to point *B'*. A tangency condition for consumer equilibrium applies here as before.

Single Price Change

Now return our consumer to his previous daily income of $6, but assume that the price of food rises from $1.50 to $3 while the price of clothing is unchanged. Again we must examine the change in the budget line. This time we find that it has pivoted on point *N* and is now *NM''*, as illustrated in Figure 5A-6.[3]

The common sense of such a shift is clear. Since the price of clothing is unchanged, point *N* is just as

---
[3] The budget equation of *NM''* is now $6 = $3F + $1C.

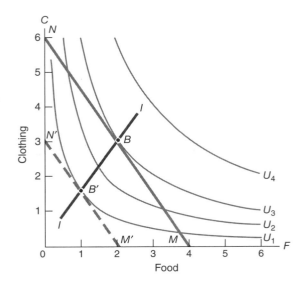

FIGURE 5A-5. Effect of Income Change on Equilibrium

An income change shifts the budget line in a parallel way. Thus, halving income to $3 shifts *NM* to *N'M'*, moving equilibrium to *B'*. (Show what raising income to $8 would do to equilibrium. Estimate where the new tangency point would come.)

available as it was before. But since the price of food has risen, point *M* (which represents 4 food units) is no longer attainable. With food costing $3 per unit, only 2 units can now be bought with a daily income of $6. So the new budget line still passes through *N*, but it must pivot at *N* and pass through *M''*, which is to the left of *M*.

Equilibrium is now at *B''*, and we have a new tangency situation. Higher food price has definitely reduced food consumption, but clothing consumption may move in either direction. To clinch your understanding, work out the cases of an increase in income and a fall in the price of clothing or food.

DERIVING THE DEMAND CURVE

We are now in a position to derive the demand curve. Look carefully at Figure 5A-6. Note that as we increased the price of food from $1.50 per unit to $3 per unit, we kept other things constant. Tastes as represented by the indifference curves did not change, and money income and the price

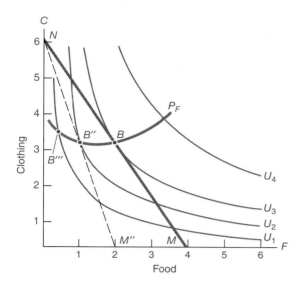

FIGURE 5A-6. Effect of Price Change on Equilibrium
A rise in the price of food makes the budget line pivot on *N*, rotating from *NM* to *NM"*. The new tangency equilibrium is at *B"*, with less food but either more or less clothing.

of clothing stayed constant. Therefore, we are in the ideal position to trace the demand curve for food. At a price of $1.50, the consumer buys 2 units of food, shown as equilibrium point *B*. When the price rises to $3 per unit, the food purchased is 1 unit, at equilibrium point *B"*. If you draw in the budget line corresponding to a price of $6 per unit of food, the equilibrium occurs at point *B'''*, and food purchases are 0.45 units.

Now plot the price of food against the purchases of food, again holding other things constant. You will have derived a neat downward-sloping demand curve from indifference curves. Note that we have done this without ever needing to mention the term "utility"—basing the derivation solely on measurable indifference curves.

SUMMARY TO APPENDIX

1. An indifference curve depicts the points of equally desirable consumption bundles. The indifference contour is usually drawn convex (or bowl-shaped) in accordance with the law of diminishing relative marginal utilities.

2. When a consumer has a fixed money income, all of which she spends, and is confronted with market prices of two goods, she is constrained to move along a straight line called the budget line or budget constraint. The line's slope will depend on the ratio of the two market prices; how far out it lies will depend on the size of her income.

3. The consumer will move along this budget line until reaching the highest attainable indifference curve. At this point, the budget line will touch, but not cross, an indifference curve. Hence, equilibrium is at the point

of tangency, where the slope of the budget line (the ratio of the prices) exactly equals the slope of the indifference curve (the substitution ratio or the ratio of the marginal utilities of the two goods). This gives additional proof that, in equilibrium, marginal utilities are proportional to prices.

4. A fall in income will move the budget line inward in a parallel fashion, usually causing less of both goods to be bought. A change in the price of one good alone will, other things being constant, cause the budget line to pivot so as to change its slope. After a price or income change, the consumer will again attain a new tangency point of highest satisfaction. At every point of tangency, the marginal utility per dollar is equal in every use. By comparing the new and old equilibrium points, we trace the usual downward-sloping demand curve.

CONCEPTS FOR REVIEW

indifference curves
slope or substitution ratio
budget line or budget constraint

convexity of indifference curves and
   law of diminishing relative marginal utilities

optimal tangency condition: $P_F/P_C =$ substitution ratio $= MU_F/MU_C$

CHAPTER 6
PRODUCTION AND BUSINESS ORGANIZATION

The business of America is business.

Calvin Coolidge

Before we can eat our daily bread, someone must bake it. The productive capacity of a country—the number of loaves of bread, barrels of oil, kilowatt-hours of electricity, and so forth—is the measure of a country's economic potential. Productive capacity is determined by the size and quality of the labor force, by the quantity and quality of the capital stock, by the nation's technical knowledge along with the ability to use that knowledge, and by the nature of public and private institutions. Why are living standards high in North America? Low in tropical Africa? For answers, we should look to how well the machine of production is running.

Our goal is to understand how market forces determine the supply of goods and services. Over the next three chapters we will lay out the essential con-cepts of production, cost, and supply and show how they are linked. First we explore the fundamentals of production theory, showing how firms transform inputs into desirable outputs. Production theory also helps us understand why productivity and living standards have risen over time and how firms manage their internal activities.

Building on our knowledge of production, Chapter 7 then develops the essential concepts of business cost. Businesses decide what inputs to employ in production on the basis of the costs and productivities of various inputs. Finally, we use the theory of production and cost to show how businesses decide how much output to produce. This is the basis for the supply curve we first saw in our basic analysis of supply and demand.

A. THEORY OF PRODUCTION AND MARGINAL PRODUCTS

BASIC CONCEPTS

Productive activities are as diverse as life itself. A farm takes fertilizer, seed, land, and labor and turns them into wheat or corn. Modern factories take inputs such as energy, raw materials, computerized machinery, and labor and use them to produce trac-tors, TVs, or tubes of toothpaste. An airline takes air-planes, fuel, labor, and computerized reservation systems and provides passengers with the ability to travel quickly from one end of the country to the other. An accounting firm takes pencils, computers, paper, office space, and labor and produces audits or tax returns for its clients.

102

Our discussion assumes that the farm, factory, airline, and accounting firm always strive to produce efficiently, or at lowest cost. That is, they always attempt to produce the maximum level of output for a given dose of inputs, avoiding waste whenever possible. Later on, in deciding what goods or services to produce and sell, firms are assumed to maximize economic profits as well.

The Production Function

We have spoken of inputs like land and labor and outputs like wheat and toothpaste. But if you have a fixed amount of inputs, how much output can you get? In practice, the answer depends on the state of technology and engineering knowledge. On any day, given the available technical knowledge, land, machinery, and so on, only a certain quantity of tractors or toothpaste can be obtained from a given amount of labor. The relationship between the amount of input required and the amount of output that can be obtained is called the *production function*.

The **production function** specifies the maximum output that can be produced with a given quantity of inputs. It is defined for a given state of engineering and technical knowledge.

For example, we can imagine a book of technical specifications that shows the production function for generating electricity. On one page there are specifications for different-size gas turbines, showing their inputs (initial capital cost, fuel consumption, and the amount of labor needed to run the turbine) and their outputs (amount of electricity generated). The next page includes descriptions of several sizes of coal-fired generating plants, showing inputs and outputs. Yet other pages describe nuclear power plants, solar power stations, and so forth. Together they constitute the production function for electricity generation.

Or consider the humble task of ditchdigging. Outside our windows in America, we see a large and expensive tractor, driven by one person with another to supervise. This team can easily dig a trench 5 feet deep and 50 feet long in 2 hours. When we visit China, we see 50 laborers armed only with picks. The same trench might take an entire day. These two techniques—one very capital-intensive and the other highly labor-intensive—represent the production function for ditchdigging.

There are literally millions of different production functions—one for each and every product or

service. Most of them are not written down anywhere. In areas of the economy where technology is changing rapidly, like telecommunications and biotechnology, production functions may become obsolete soon after they are used. And some, like the blueprints of a medical laboratory or cliff house, are specially designed for a specific location and purpose and would be useless anywhere else. Nevertheless, economists have found that production functions are a useful way of describing the productive capabilities of a firm.

Total, Average, and Marginal Product

Starting with a firm's production function, we can calculate three important production concepts: total, average, and marginal product. We begin by computing the total physical product, or **total product**, which designates the total amount of output produced, in physical units such as bushels of wheat or number of telephone calls produced. Figure 6-1(*a*) and column (2) of Table 6-1 illustrate the concept of total product. For this example, they show how total product responds as the amount of labor applied is increased. The total product starts at zero for zero labor and then increases as additional units of labor are applied, reaching a maximum of 3900 units when 5 units of labor are used.[1]

Once we know the total product, it is easy to derive an equally important concept, the marginal product. Recall that the term "marginal" means "extra."

The **marginal product** of an input is the extra product or output added by 1 extra unit of that input while other inputs are held constant.

For example, assume that we are holding land, machinery, and all other inputs constant. Then labor's marginal product is the extra output obtained by adding 1 unit of labor. The third column of Table 6-1 calculates the marginal product. The marginal product of labor starts at 2000 for the first unit of labor and then falls to only 100 units for the

---

[1] In this chapter we talk of "units of labor" as being one input into the production process. How are units of labor measured? It is customary to measure labor in terms of hours of work (person-hours) to reflect the fact that people work different numbers of hours per week. For simplicity, however, we simply refer to numbers of workers and assume that each person works the same number of hours.

(1) Units of labor	(2) Total product	(3) Marginal product	(4) Average product
0	0		
		2,000	
1	2,000		2,000
		1,000	
2	3,000		1,500
		500	
3	3,500		1,167
		300	
4	3,800		950
		100	
5	3,900		780

TABLE 6-1. Total, Marginal, and Average Product

The table shows the total product that can be produced for different inputs of labor when other inputs (capital, land, etc.) and the state of technical knowledge are unchanged. From total product, we can derive important concepts of marginal and average products.

fifth unit. Marginal product calculations such as this are crucial for understanding how wages and other factor prices are determined.

The final concept is the **average product**, which equals total output divided by total units of input. The fourth column of Table 6-1 shows the average product of labor as 2000 units per worker with one worker, 1500 units per worker with two workers, and so forth. In this example, average product falls through the entire range of increasing labor input.

Figure 6-1 plots the total and marginal products from Table 6-1. Study this figure to make sure you understand that the blocks of marginal products in (b) are related to the changes in the total product curve in (a).

The Law of Diminishing Returns

Using production functions, we can understand one of the most famous laws in all economics, the law of diminishing returns:

The **law of diminishing returns** holds that we will get less and less extra output when we add additional doses of an input while holding other inputs fixed. In other words, the marginal product of each unit of input will decline as the amount of that input increases, holding all other inputs constant.

The law of diminishing returns expresses a very basic relationship. As more of an input such as labor is added to a fixed amount of land, machinery, and other inputs, the labor has less and less of the other factors to work with. The land gets more crowded, the machinery is overworked, and the marginal product of labor declines.

The law of diminishing returns can be fleshed out by putting ourselves in the boots of a farmer performing an agricultural experiment illustrated by Table 6-1. Given a fixed amount of land and other inputs, assume that we use no labor inputs at all. With zero labor input there is no corn output. Hence, Table 6-1 records zero product when labor is zero.

Now add 1 unit of labor to the same fixed amount of land. We observe that 2000 bushels of corn are produced. In the next stage in our controlled experiment, we continue to hold other inputs fixed and go from 1 unit of labor to 2 units of labor. What is the impact of the added labor on production? The second unit of labor adds only 1000 bushels of additional output, which is less than what the first unit of labor added. The third unit of labor has an even lower marginal product than does the second, and the fourth unit adds yet a bit less. The hypothetical experiment reported in Table 6-1 thus illustrates the law of diminishing returns.

Figure 6-1 also illustrates the law of diminishing returns for labor, holding land and other inputs constant. Here we see that the marginal product curve declines as labor inputs increase, which is the precise meaning of diminishing returns. In Figure 6-1(a), diminishing returns are seen as a concave or dome-shaped total product curve.

What is true for labor is also true for land and any other input. We can interchange land and labor, now holding labor constant and varying land. Land's marginal product is the change in total output that results from 1 additional unit of land, with all other inputs held constant. We can calculate the marginal product of each input (labor, land, machinery, water, fertilizer, etc.), and the marginal product would apply to any output (wheat, corn, steel, soybeans, and so forth). We would find that other inputs also tend to show the law of diminishing returns.

Economics at work: Diminishing returns. The law of diminishing returns makes good economic sense. In the case of farming, output will

(a) Total Product

(b) Marginal Product

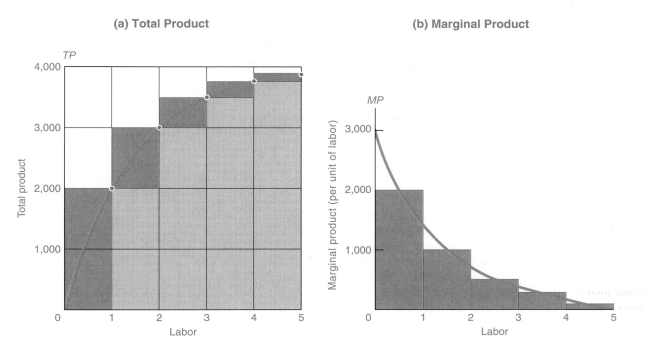

FIGURE 6-1. Marginal Product Is Derived from Total Product

Diagram (**a**) shows the total product curve rising as additional inputs of labor are added, holding other things constant. However, total product rises by smaller and smaller increments as additional units of labor are added (compare the increments of the first and the fifth worker). By smoothing between points, we get the rust-colored total product curve.

Diagram (**b**) shows the declining steps of marginal product. Make sure you understand why each dark rectangle in (**b**) is equal to the equivalent dark rectangle in (**a**). The area in (**b**) under the rust-colored marginal product curve (or the sum of the dark rectangles) adds up to the total product in (**a**).

increase sharply as we add labor—the fields will be more thoroughly seeded and weeded, irrigation ditches will be neater, and scarecrows better oiled. At some point, however, the additional labor becomes less and less productive. The third hoeing of the day or the fourth oiling of the machinery adds little to output. Eventually, output grows very little as more people crowd onto the farm; too many tillers spoil the crop.

Diminishing returns are a key factor in explaining why many countries in Asia are so poor. Living standards in crowded China and India are low because there are so many workers per acre of land and not because farmers are ignorant or fail to respond to economic incentives.

We can also use the example of studying to illustrate the law of diminishing returns. You might find that the first hour of studying economics on a given day was productive—you learned new laws and facts, insights and history. The second hour might find your attention wandering a bit, with less learned. The third hour might show that diminishing returns had set in with a vengeance—so that by the next day you could remember nothing of what you had read during the third hour. Does the law of diminishing returns suggest why the hours devoted to studying should be spread out rather than crammed into the day before exams?

The law of diminishing returns is a widely observed empirical regularity rather than a universal truth like the law of gravity. It has been found in numerous empirical studies, but exceptions have also been uncovered. Moreover, diminishing returns might not hold for all levels of production. The very first inputs of labor might actually show increasing marginal products, since a minimum amount of labor may be needed just to walk to the field and pick up a shovel. Notwithstanding these reservations, diminishing returns will prevail in most situations.

RETURNS TO SCALE

Diminishing returns and marginal products refer to the response of output to an increase of a *single* input when all other inputs are held constant. We saw that increasing labor while holding land constant would increase food output by ever-smaller increments.

But sometimes we are interested in the effect of increasing *all* inputs. For example, what would happen to wheat production if land, labor, water, and other inputs were increased by the same proportion? Or what would happen to production of tractors if the quantities of labor, computers, robots, steel, and factory space were all doubled? These questions refer to the *returns to scale*, or the effects of scale increases of inputs on the quantity produced. Put differently, the returns to scale reflect the responsiveness of total product when *all* the inputs are increased proportionately. Three important cases should be distinguished:

- **Constant returns to scale** denote a case where a change in all inputs leads to a proportional change in output. For example, if labor, land, capital, and other inputs are doubled, then under constant returns to scale output would also double. Many handicraft industries (such as haircutting in America or handloom operation in a developing country) show constant returns.
- **Increasing returns to scale** arise when an increase in all inputs leads to a more-than-proportional increase in the level of output. For example, an engineer planning a small-scale chemical plant would generally find that increasing the inputs of labor, capital, and materials by 10 percent will increase the total output by more than 10 percent. Engineering studies have determined that many manufacturing processes enjoy

modestly increasing returns to scale for plants up to the largest size used today.
- **Decreasing returns to scale** occur when a balanced increase of all inputs leads to a less-than-proportional increase in total output. In many processes, scaling up may eventually reach a point beyond which inefficiencies set in. These might arise because the costs of management or control become large. One case has occurred in electricity generation, where firms found that when plants grew too large, risks of plant failure grew too large. Many productive activities involving natural resources, such as growing wine grapes or providing clean drinking water to a city, show decreasing returns to scale.

Production shows increasing, decreasing, or constant returns to scale when a balanced increase in all inputs leads to a more-than-proportional, less-than-proportional, or just-proportional increase in output.

One of the common findings of engineers is that modern mass-production techniques require that factories be a certain minimum size. Chapter 2 showed that as output increases, firms may divide production into smaller steps, taking advantage of specialization and division of labor. In addition, large-scale production allows intensive use of specialized capital equipment, automation, and computerized design and manufacturing to perform simple and repetitive tasks quickly.

What kind of returns prevail in production today? Economists often think that most production activities should be able to attain constant returns to scale. They reason that if production can be adjusted by simply replicating existing plants over and over again, the producer would simply be multiplying both inputs and output by the same number. In such a case, you would observe constant returns to scale for any level of output.

Productivity. Economies of scale and mass production have fueled much of the economic growth of nations over the last century. Most production processes are many times larger than they were during the nineteenth century. A large ship in the mid-nineteenth century could carry 2000 tons of goods, while the largest supertankers today carry over 1 million tons of oil.

What would be the effect of a general increase in the scale of economic activity? If increasing returns prevailed, the larger scale of inputs and production would lead to greater productivity—where **productivity** is a concept measuring the ratio of total output to a weighted average of inputs. Suppose that the typical firm's inputs increased by 1 percent and that because of economies of scale output increased by 3 percent. We then calculate that productivity (output per unit of input) rose by 2 (= 3 − 1) percent. This example suggests that increases in a nation's per capita output and living standards may result in part from exploiting increasing returns to scale in production.

While increasing returns to scale are potentially large in many sectors, at some point decreasing returns to scale may take hold. As firms become larger and larger, the problems of management and coordination become increasingly difficult. In relentless pursuit of greater profits, a firm may find itself expanding into more geographic markets or product lines than it can effectively manage. A firm can have only one chief executive officer, one chief financial officer, one board of directors. With less time to study each market and spend on each decision, top managers may become insulated from day-to-day production and begin to make mistakes.

Like empires that have been stretched too thin, such firms find themselves exposed to invasion by smaller and more agile rivals. Those who study management report that the world's largest automobile manufacturer, General Motors, became increasingly isolated from the outside world and from competitive pressures. As a result, it was slow to respond to changes in the automobile market when oil prices rose in the 1970s, and it lost much market share to smaller and nimbler firms. Hence, while technology might ideally allow constant or increasing returns to scale, the need for management and supervision may eventually lead to decreasing returns to scale in giant firms.

SHORT RUN AND LONG RUN

Production requires not only labor and land but also time. Pipelines cannot be built overnight, and once built they last for decades. Farmers cannot change crops in midseason. It often takes a decade to plan, construct, test, and commission a large power plant. Moreover, once capital equipment has been put in the concrete form of a power plant on the Ten-

nessee River or a giant petrochemical factory in Mexico, the capital cannot be economically dismantled and moved to another location or transferred to another use.

To account for the role of time in production and costs, we distinguish two different time periods. We define the **short run** as a period in which firms can adjust production by changing variable factors such as materials and labor but cannot change fixed factors such as capital. The **long run** is a period sufficiently long so that all factors including capital can be adjusted.

To understand these concepts more clearly, consider the way the production of steel might respond to changes in demand. Say that Nippon Steel is operating its furnaces at 70 percent of capacity when an unexpected increase in the demand for steel occurs because of the need to rebuild from an earthquake in Japan or California. To adjust to the higher demand for steel, the firm can increase production by increasing worker overtime, hiring more workers, and operating its plants and machinery more intensively. The factors which are increased in the short run are called *variable* factors. We define the short run as the period in which production can be changed by changing variable inputs.

Suppose that the increase in steel demand persisted for an extended period of time, say, several years. Nippon Steel would examine its capital needs and decide that it should increase its productive capacity. More generally, it might examine all its *fixed* factors, those that cannot be changed in the short run because of physical conditions or legal contracts. The period of time over which all inputs, fixed and variable, can be adjusted is called the long run. In the long run, Nippon might add new and more efficient production processes, install a rail link or new computerized control system, or build a plant in Mexico. When all factors can be adjusted, the total amount of steel will be higher and the level of efficiency can increase.

Efficient production requires time as well as conventional inputs like labor. We therefore distinguish two different time periods in production and cost analysis. The short run is the period of time in which only some inputs, the variable inputs, can be adjusted. In the short run, fixed factors, such as plant and equipment, cannot be fully modified or adjusted. The long run is the period in which all factors employed by the firm can be changed, including capital.

TECHNOLOGICAL CHANGE

Economic history records that total output in the United States has grown more than tenfold since the turn of the century. Part of that gain has come from increased inputs, such as labor and machinery. But much of the increase in output has come from technological change, which improves productivity and raises living standards.

Technological change refers to improvements in the processes for producing goods and services, changes in old products, or introduction of new products. Some examples of technological change are dramatic: wide-body jets that increased the number of passenger-miles per unit of input by almost 50 percent; fiber optics that have lowered cost and improved reliability in telecommunications; and improvements in computer technologies that have increased computational power by more than 1000 times in three decades. Other forms of technological change are more subtle, as is the case when a firm adjusts its production process to reduce waste and increase output.

We distinguish *process innovation*, which occurs when new engineering knowledge improves production techniques for existing products, from *product innovation*, whereby new or improved products are introduced in the marketplace. For example, a process innovation allows firms to produce more output with the same inputs or to produce the same output with fewer inputs. In other words, a process innovation is equivalent to a shift in the production function.

Figure 6-2 illustrates how technological change, in the form of a process innovation, would shift the total product curve. The lower line represents the feasible output, or production function, for a particular industry in the year 1995. Suppose that productivity, or output per unit of input, in this industry is rising at 4 percent per year. If we return to the same industry a decade later, we would likely see that changes in technical and engineering knowledge have led to an almost 50 percent improvement in output per unit of input [$(1.04)^{10} = 1.48$].

Now let's consider technological change which leads to new products. Product innovations are

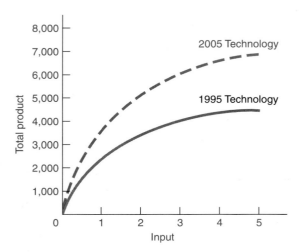

FIGURE 6-2. Technological Change Shifts Production Function Upward

The solid line represents maximum producible output for each level of inputs given the state of technical knowledge in 1995. As a result of improvements in technology and management practices, technological change shifts the production function upward, here allowing 50 percent greater output to be produced in 2005 for each level of input.

much harder to quantify than process innovations, but they are probably even more important in raising living standards over the long run. Today's array of goods and services is clearly far different from what prevailed just 50 years ago. In producing this textbook, the authors used computer software, microprocessors, color monitors, and Internet databases that were not available when the last edition was written. Medicine, communications, and entertainment are other areas where product innovations have been critical. The very notion of cellular telephones would have been unimaginable just 20 years ago. For fun, and to see this point, try to find any commodity or production process that has not changed since your grandparents were your age!

Figure 6-2 shows the happy case of a technological advance. Is the opposite case—technological regress—possible? For a well-functioning market economy, the answer is no. Indeed, that is one of the key advantages of a market economy over an economy ruled by government dictates or tradition. Inferior technologies tend to be discarded in a market economy, while superior technologies—ones with higher productivity—are introduced because they will increase the profits of the innovating firms. If, for example, someone invented a new type of photocopying machine that cost twice as much as existing varieties, no sensible profit-oriented firm would produce such a machine, and if a wrongheaded firm were to produce it, no sensible person would purchase it.

When there are market failures, however, technological regress might occur even in a market economy. An unregulated company might introduce a socially wasteful process, say, one dumping toxic wastes into a stream, because the wasteful process was cheaper to operate. But the economic advantage arises only because the social costs of pollution are not included in the firm's calculations of costs of production. If pollution costs were included in a firm's decisions, say, by strict liability rules or pollution taxes, the retrogressive process would no longer be profitable. In competitive markets, inferior products follow the Neanderthal man into extinction.

THE AGGREGATE PRODUCTION FUNCTION FOR THE UNITED STATES

Now that we have examined the principles of production theory, we can apply these theories to measure how well the whole U.S. economy has been performing. To do this, we need to look at what's happened to total output, to the quantity of inputs (like labor, capital, and land), and to total productivity. Because they involve serious problems of measurement, all such magnitudes must be calculated with great care. Yet they are useful in giving a broad description of an economy's overall behavior.

Empirical studies of the aggregate production function date back to the 1920s, when Paul Douglas (a professor at the University of Chicago and later a U.S. senator) analyzed data for manufacturing. Over the last 30 years some of the best minds of economics have examined this subject, including John Kendrick, Edward Denison, Robert Solow (a winner of the Nobel Prize in economics for his work in this area), and Dale Jorgenson. The goal of these studies was to understand how economic growth depends upon capital, labor, and productivity growth. Recall

from our earlier discussion that productivity measures the total quantity of output per unit of input. Productivity growth denotes the rate of growth of the level of productivity. For example, if output per worker is 100 units in 1996 and it grows to 102.5 units in 1997, we say that productivity growth was 2.5 percent per year.

In measuring productivity, we denote _labor productivity_ as the amount of output per unit of labor; _capital productivity_ as output per unit of capital; and _total factor productivity_ as output per unit of total inputs of capital and labor.

**Empirical Findings.** What have economic studies found? Here are a few of the important results:

- Total factor productivity has been increasing throughout this century because of technological progress and higher levels of worker education and skill. The average rate of total productivity growth has been slightly under $1\frac{1}{2}$ percent per year during the twentieth century. Average real output per worker has grown slightly faster than the rate of growth of total factor productivity.
- The capital stock has been growing faster than the number of worker-hours. As a result, labor has a growing quantity of capital goods to work with; hence labor productivity and wages have tended to rise even faster than the $1\frac{1}{2}$ percent per year attributable to productivity growth alone.
- The rate of return on capital (the rate of profit) might have been expected to encounter diminishing returns because each capital unit now has less labor to cooperate with it. In fact, capital's rate of return has remained about the same.
- In the last two decades, all measures of productivity have shown a marked growth slowdown. From 1973 to 1996, total factor productivity grew only $\frac{3}{4}$ percent per year. Because of slow growth in productivity, real wages and living standards have grown slowly in the United States since the early 1970s.

A final encouraging word: Although measured productivity growth has been slow in the last few years, recent empirical studies suggest that we have seriously underestimated productivity growth. Studies of medical care, capital-goods pricing, computer software, and lighting indicate that our measuring rod for productivity may be badly flawed. One particularly important shortcoming is the failure to account for the economic value of new products. For example, when compact discs replace records, our measures of productivity do not include the improvement in durability and sound quality. One study found that productivity in treatment of heart attacks was 5 percent per year more rapid than the conventional measure. If further studies confirm these tentative conclusions, we may find that productivity growth over the last quarter-century was significantly faster—maybe even double—the meager ¾ percent per year reported in the official statistics.

B. BUSINESS ORGANIZATIONS

THE NATURE OF THE FIRM

So far we have talked about production functions as if they were machines that could be operated by anyone: put a pig in one end and get sausage out the other. In reality, almost all production is done by specialized organizations—the small, medium, and large businesses that dominate the landscape of modern economies. Why does production generally take place in firms rather than in our basements?

Firms or business enterprises exist for many reasons, but the most important are to exploit economies of mass production, to raise funds, and to organize the production process. The most compelling factor leading to the organization of production in firms arises from *economies of mass production.* Efficient production requires specialized machinery and factories, assembly lines, and the division of labor into many small operations. Studies indicate that efficient production of automobiles requires production rates of at least 300,000 units per year.

We could hardly expect that workers would spontaneously gather to perform each task correctly and in the right sequence. Instead, we need firms to coordinate the production process, purchasing or renting land, capital, labor, and materials. If there were no need for specialization and division of labor, we could each produce our own electricity, digital watch, and compact disc in our own backyard. We obviously cannot perform such feats, so

  efficiency generally requires large-scale production in businesses.

A related function of firms is *raising resources* for large-scale production. Developing a new commercial aircraft costs well over $1 billion; the research and development expenses for a new computer microprocessor, like Intel's Pentium chip, are just as high. Where are such funds to come from? In the nineteenth century, businesses could often be financed by wealthy risk-taking individuals. But the days of such fabulously wealthy captains of industry are past. Today, in a private-enterprise economy, most funds for production must come from company profits or from money borrowed in financial markets. Indeed, efficient production by private enterprise would be virtually unthinkable if corporations could not raise billions of dollars each year for new projects.

A third reason for the existence of firms is to *manage the production process.* The manager is the person who organizes production, introduces new ideas or products or processes, makes the business decisions, and is held accountable for success or failure. Production cannot, after all, organize itself. Someone has to supervise the construction of a new factory, negotiate with labor unions, and purchase materials and supplies.

If you were to purchase the franchise for an AA baseball team, you would have to rent a stadium, hire baseball players, negotiate with people for concessions, hire ushers, deal with unions, and sell tickets.

Once all these factors of production are engaged, someone has to monitor their daily activities to ensure that the job is being done effectively and honestly.

Production is organized in firms because efficiency generally requires large-scale production, the raising of significant financial resources, and careful management and monitoring of ongoing activities.

BIG, SMALL, AND INFINITESIMAL BUSINESSES

Production in a market economy takes place in a wide variety of business organizations—from the tiniest individual proprietorships to the giant corporations that dominate economic life in a capitalist economy. There are currently more than 18 million different businesses in America. The majority of these are tiny units owned by a single person—the individual proprietorship. Others are partnerships, owned by two or perhaps two hundred partners. The largest businesses tend to be corporations.

Tiny businesses predominate in numbers. But in sales and assets, in political and economic power, and in size of payroll and employment, the few hundred largest corporations dominate the economy.

The Individual Proprietorship

At one end of the spectrum are the individual proprietorships, the classic small businesses often called "mom-and-pop" stores. A small store might do a few hundred dollars of business per day and barely provide a minimum wage for the owners' efforts.

These businesses are large in number but small in total sales. For most small businesses, a tremendous amount of personal effort is required. The self-employed often work 50 or 60 hours per week and take no vacations, yet the average lifetime of a small business is only a year. Still, some people will always want to start out on their own. Theirs may be the successful venture that gets bought out for millions of dollars.

The Partnership

Often a business requires a combination of talents—say, lawyers or doctors specializing in different areas. Any two or more people can get together and form a partnership. Each agrees to provide some fraction of the work and capital, to share some percentage of the profits, and of course to share the losses or debts.

Today, partnerships account for only a small fraction of total economic activity. The reason is that partnerships pose certain disadvantages that make them impractical for large businesses. The major disadvantage is *unlimited liability*. General partners are liable without limit for all debts contracted by the partnership. If you own 1 percent of the partnership and the business fails, you will be called upon to pay 1 percent of the bills and the other partners will be assessed their 99 percent. But if your partners cannot pay, you may be called upon to pay all the debts even if you must sell off your prize possessions to do so.

The peril of unlimited liability and the difficulty of raising funds explain why partnerships tend to be confined to small, personal enterprises such as agriculture and retail trade. Partnerships are simply too risky for most situations.

The Corporation

The bulk of economic activity in an advanced market economy takes place in private corporations. Centuries ago, corporate charters were awarded by special acts of the monarch or legislature. The British East India Company was a privileged corporation and as such it practically ruled India for more than a century. In the nineteenth century, railroads often had to spend as much money on getting a charter through the legislature as on preparing their roadbeds. Over the past century, laws have been passed that allow almost anyone the privilege of forming a corporation for almost any purpose.

Today, a **corporation** is a form of business organization, chartered in one of the fifty states or abroad and owned by a number of individual stockholders. The corporation has a separate legal identity, and indeed is a legal "person" that may on its own behalf buy, sell, borrow money, produce goods and services, and enter into contracts. In addition, the corporation enjoys the right of *limited liability*, whereby each owner's investment in the corporation is strictly limited to a specified amount.

The central features of a modern corporation are the following:

- The ownership of a corporation is determined by the ownership of the company's common stock. If you own 10 percent of a corporation's shares, you have 10 percent of the ownership. Publicly owned corporations are valued on stock exchanges, like the New York Stock Exchange. It is in such stock markets that the titles to the largest corporations are traded and that much of the nation's risk capital is invested.
- In principle, the shareholders control the companies they own. They collect dividends in proportion to the fraction of the shares they own, and they elect directors and vote on many important issues. But don't think that the shareholders have a significant role in running giant corporations. In practice, shareholders of giant corporations exercise virtually no control because they are too dispersed to overrule the entrenched managers.
- The corporation's managers and directors have the legal power to make decisions for the corporation. They decide what to produce and how to produce it. They negotiate with labor unions and decide whether to sell the firm if another firm wishes to take it over. When the newspaper announces that a firm has laid off 20,000 workers, this decision was made by the managers. The shareholders own the corporation, but the managers run it.

> *Advantages and Disadvantages of Corporations.* Why are corporations so predominant in a market economy? Simply because it is an extremely efficient way to engage in business. A corporation is a legal person that can conduct business. Also, the corporation may have perpetual succession or existence, regardless of how many times the shares of stock change hands. Corporations are hardly little democracies, so their managers can make decisions quickly, and often ruthlessly, which is in stark contrast to the way economic decisions are made by legislatures.

In addition, corporate stockholders enjoy limited liability, which protects them from incurring the debts or losses of the corporation beyond their initial contribution. If we buy $1000 of stock, we cannot lose more than our original investment.

Corporations face one major disadvantage: There is an extra tax on corporate profits. For an unincorporated business, any income after expenses is taxed as ordinary personal income. The corporation is treated differently in that corporate income is doubly taxed—first as corporate profits and then as individual income on dividends. The double taxation of corporations has been severely criticized by some economists in recent years, although most countries continue to find corporate income a convenient source of tax revenues.

Because efficient production often requires large-scale enterprises, with billions of dollars of capital, investors need a way to pool their funds. Corporations, with limited liability and a convenient management structure, can attract large supplies of private capital, produce a variety of related products, and pool risks.

THE ECONOMICS OF ORGANIZATIONS

This overview of the organizations of modern capitalism can provide only the barest hint of the richness of the *economics of organizations*. The last few years have seen a concerted effort by economists to understand why organizations take the particular form they do and why decisions are made in the controlled hierarchy of firms rather than by the arm's-length contracts of markets. Economists like Ronald Coase, Kenneth Arrow, Herbert Simon, and Oliver Williamson point to the importance of transaction costs in determining the boundaries between firm and market.

Those who study economic history point to the vital importance of organizational efficiency and innovation in increasing productivity. Railroads not only brought wheat from farm to market but also introduced time zones. Indeed the very notion of being "on time" first became crucial when being off schedule produced train wrecks. History shows how crucial organizations are for the achievement of human goals. As the sad story of centrally planned economies so clearly shows, without the organizational genius of the modern private-enterprise firm, all the land, labor, and capital would work for naught.

SUMMARY

A. Basic Concepts

1. The relationship between the quantity of output (such as wheat, steel, or automobiles) and the quantities of inputs (of labor, land, and capital) is called the production function. Total product is the total output produced. Average product equals total output divided by the total quantity of inputs. We can calculate the marginal product of a factor as the extra output added for each additional unit of input while holding all other inputs constant.

2. According to the law of diminishing returns, the marginal product of each input will generally decline as the amount of that input increases, when all other inputs are held constant.

3. The returns to scale reflect the impact on output of a balanced increase in all inputs. A technology in which doubling all inputs leads to an exact doubling of outputs displays constant returns to scale. When doubling inputs leads to less than double (more than double) the quantity of output, the situation is one of decreasing (increasing) returns to scale.

4. Because decisions take time to implement, and because capital and other factors are often very long-lived, the reaction of production may change over different time periods. The short run is a period in which variable factors, such as labor or material inputs, can be easily changed. In the long run, the capital stock (a firm's machinery and factories) can depreciate and be replaced. In the long run, all inputs, fixed and variable, can be adjusted.

5. Technological change refers to a change in the underlying techniques of production, as occurs when a new product or process of production is invented or an old product or process is improved. In such situations, the same output is produced with fewer inputs or more output is produced with the same inputs. Technological change shifts the production function upward.

6. Attempts to measure an aggregate production function for the American economy tend to corroborate theories of production and marginal products. In this century, technological change has increased the productivity of both labor and capital. Total factor productivity (measuring the ratio of total output to total inputs) has grown at around $1\frac{1}{2}$ percent per year over the twentieth century, although since 1970 the rate of productivity growth has slowed markedly and real wages have stopped growing. But underestimating the importance of new and improved products may lead to a significant underestimate of productivity growth.

B. Business Organizations

7. In a market economy, production is organized in firms—with some economic activity in tiny one-person proprietorships, some in partnerships, and the bulk in corporations.

8. Each kind of enterprise has advantages and disadvantages. Small businesses are flexible, can market new products, and can disappear quickly. But they suffer from the fundamental disadvantage of being unable to accumulate large amounts of capital from a dispersed group of investors. Today's large corporation, granted limited liability by the state, is able to amass billions of dollars of capital by borrowing from banks, bondholders, and stock markets.

9. In a modern economy, firms produce most goods and services because economies of mass production necessitate that output be produced at high volumes, the technology of production requires much more capital than a single individual would willingly put at risk, and efficient production requires careful management and coordination of the tasks by a centrally directed entity.

CONCEPTS FOR REVIEW

inputs, outputs, production function
total, average, and marginal product
diminishing marginal product and the law of diminishing returns
constant, increasing, and decreasing returns to scale

short run vs. long run
technological change: process innovation, product innovation
productivity
aggregate production function

reasons for firms: scale economies, financial needs, management
major business forms: individual proprietorship, partnership, corporation
unlimited and limited liability

QUESTIONS FOR DISCUSSION

1. Explain the concept of a production function. Describe the production function for hamburgers, concerts, haircuts, and a college education.

2. In the following table, which describes the actual production function for oil pipelines, fill in the missing values for marginal products and average products:

(1) Pumping horsepower	(2) 18-inch pipe Total product (barrels per day)	(3) 18-inch pipe Marginal product (barrels per day per hp)	(4) 18-inch pipe Average product (barrels per day per hp)
10,000	86,000		
20,000	114,000		
30,000	134,000		
40,000	150,000		
50,000	164,000		

3. Using the data in question 2, plot the production function of output against horsepower. On the same graph, plot the curves for average product and marginal product.

4. Suppose you are running the food concession at the athletic events for your college. You sell hot dogs, colas, and potato chips. What are your inputs of capital, labor, and materials? If the demand for the hot dogs declines, what steps could you take to reduce output in the short run? In the long run?

5. An important distinction in economics is between shifts in the production function and movements along the production function. For the food concession in question 4, give an example of both a shift of and a movement along the hot-dog production function. Illustrate each with a graph of the relation between hot-dog production and labor employed.

6. Substitution occurs when firms replace one input for another, as when a farmer uses tractors rather than labor when wages rise. Consider the following changes in a firm's behavior. Which represent substitution of one factor for another with an unchanged technology, and which represent technological change? Illustrate each with a graphical production function.
   a. When the price of oil increases, a firm replaces an oil-fired plant with a gas-fired plant.
   b. A chemical company decides to replace its old coal-fired electrical generation equipment with a newly invented gas turbine, reducing costs by 20 percent.
   c. Over the period 1970–1995, a typesetting firm decreases its employment of typesetters by 200 workers and increases its employment of computer operators by 100 workers.
   d. After a successful unionization drive for clerical workers, a college buys personal computers for its faculty and reduces its secretarial work force.

7. Consider a firm that produces wheat with land and labor inputs. Define and contrast diminishing returns and decreasing returns to scale. Explain why it is possible to have diminishing returns for one input and constant returns to scale for both inputs.

8. Show that if the marginal product is always decreasing, the average product is always above the marginal product.

9. List 5 products that are important to you today. For each, describe how product, process, or organizational inventions have affected the product over the last century.

CHAPTER 7

ANALYSIS OF COSTS

Costs merely register competing attractions.

Frank Knight, **Risk, Uncertainty, and Profit** (*1921*)

Everywhere that production goes, costs follow close behind like a shadow. In a world of scarcity, firms have to pay for their inputs: steel, screws, solvents, engineers, secretaries, computers, telephones, lights, and pencils. Profitable businesses are acutely aware of this simple fact as they set their production strategies, since every dollar of unnecessary costs reduces the firm's profits by that same dollar. Indeed, too much production can be as dangerous as too little; history shows that overexpansion can often drive a fast-growing company into bankruptcy, by pushing up costs far faster than revenues.

But the role of costs goes far beyond influencing the level of production. Smart businesses also pay close attention to their costs when they are making their operating decisions. Is it cheaper to hire a new worker or to pay overtime? To open a new factory or expand an old one? To invest in new machinery at home or relocate production abroad? Businesses want to choose that method of production which is efficient, which produces the most at the lowest costs.

This chapter is devoted to a thorough analysis of cost. First we consider the full array of economic costs, including the all-important notion of marginal costs. Then we examine how business accountants measure cost in practice. Finally, we look at the notion of opportunity cost, a broad concept that can be applied to a wide range of decisions. This comprehensive study of cost will lay the foundation for understanding the supply decisions of business firms.

A. ECONOMIC ANALYSIS OF COSTS

TOTAL COST: FIXED AND VARIABLE

Consider a firm that produces a quantity of output (denoted by q) using inputs of capital, labor, and materials. The firm buys these inputs in the factor markets. A profit-minded firm will keep an eagle eye on its costs to maintain profitability. The firm's accountants have the task of calculating the total dollar costs incurred at each level of q.

Table 7-1 on page 116 shows the total cost (TC) for each different level of output q. Looking at columns (1) and (4), we see that TC goes up as q

(1) Quantity q	(2) Fixed cost FC ($)	(3) Variable cost VC ($)	(4) Total cost TC ($)
0	55	0	55
1	55	30	85
2	55	55	110
3	55	75	130
4	55	105	160
5	55	155	210
6	55	225	280

TABLE 7-1. Fixed, Variable, and Total Costs

The major elements of a firm's costs are its fixed costs (which do not vary at all when output changes) and variable costs (which increase as output increases). Total costs are equal to fixed plus variable costs: $TC = FC + VC$.

goes up. This makes sense because it takes more labor and other inputs to produce more of a good; extra factors involve an extra money cost. It costs $110 in all to produce 2 units, $130 to produce 3 units, and so forth. In our discussion, we assume that the firm always produces output at the lowest possible cost.

Fixed Cost

Columns (2) and (3) of Table 7-1 break total cost into two components: total fixed cost (FC) and total variable cost (VC).

What are a firm's **fixed costs**? Sometimes called "overhead" or "sunk costs," they consist of items such as rent for factory or office space, contractual payments for equipment, interest payments on debts, salaries of tenured faculty, and so forth. These must be paid even if the firm produces no output, and they will not change if output changes. For example, a law firm might have an office lease which runs 10 years and remains an obligation even if the firm shrinks to half its previous size. Because FC is the amount that must be paid regardless of the level of output, it remains constant at $55 in column (2).

Variable Cost

Column (3) of Table 7-1 shows variable cost (VC). **Variable costs** are those which vary as output changes. Examples include materials required to produce output (such as steel to produce automobiles), production workers to staff the assembly lines, power to operate factories, and so on. In a super-

market, checkout clerks are a variable cost, since managers can easily adjust the clerks' hours worked to match the number of shoppers coming through the store.

By definition, VC begins at zero when q is zero. It is the part of TC that grows with output; indeed, the jump in TC between any two outputs is the same as the jump in VC. Why? Because FC stays constant at $55 throughout and cancels out in the comparison of costs between different output levels.

Let us summarize these cost concepts:

Total cost represents the lowest total dollar expense needed to produce each level of output q. TC rises as q rises.

Fixed cost represents the total dollar expense that is paid out even when no output is produced; fixed cost is unaffected by any variation in the quantity of output.

Variable cost represents expenses that vary with the level of output—such as raw materials, wages, and fuel—and includes all costs that are not fixed.

Always, by definition,

$$TC = FC + VC$$

 Minimum attainable costs. Anyone who has managed a business knows that when we write down a cost schedule like the one in Table 7-1, we make the firm's job look altogether too simple. Why so? Because much hard work lies behind Table 7-1. To attain the lowest level of costs, the firm's managers have to make sure that they are paying the least possible amount for necessary materials such as energy, that the lowest-cost engineering techniques are incorporated into the factory layout, that employees are being honest, and that countless other decisions are made in the most economical fashion. As a result of such managerial effort, the fixed and variable costs shown in Table 7-1 are the minimum costs necessary for the firm to produce that level of output.

DEFINITION OF MARGINAL COST

Marginal cost is one of the key concepts of economics. **Marginal cost** (MC) denotes the extra or additional cost of producing 1 extra unit of output. Say a firm is producing 1000 compact discs for a total cost of $10,000. If the total cost of producing 1001 discs is $10,006, the marginal cost of production is $6 for the 1001st disc.

Sometimes, the marginal cost of producing an extra unit of output can be quite low. For an airline flying planes with empty seats, the added cost of another passenger is simply the cost of the peanuts and snack; no additional capital (planes) or labor (pilots and flight attendants) is necessary. In other cases, the marginal cost of another unit of output can be quite high. Consider an electric utility. Under normal circumstances, it can generate enough power using only its lowest-cost, most efficient plants. But on a hot summer day, when everyone's air conditioners are running and electric demand is high, the utility may be forced to turn on its old, high-cost, inefficient generators. This added electric power comes at a high marginal cost to the utility.

Table 7-2 uses the data from Table 7-1 to illustrate how we calculate marginal costs. The rust-colored

(1) Output q	(2) Total cost TC ($)	(3) Marginal cost MC ($)
0	55	
		30
1	85	
		25
2	110	
		20
3	130	
		30
4	160	
		50
5	210	

TABLE 7-2. Calculation of Marginal Cost

Once we know total cost, it is easy to calculate marginal cost. To calculate the MC of the fifth unit, we subtract the total cost of the four units from the total cost of the five units, i.e., $MC = \$210 - \$160 = \$50$. Fill in the blank for the marginal cost of the fourth unit.

FIGURE 7-1. The Relationship between Total Cost and Marginal Cost

This figure graphs the data from Table 7-2. Marginal cost in (**b**) is found by calculating the extra cost added in (**a**) for each unit increase in output. Thus to find the MC of producing the fifth unit, we subtract $160 from $210 to get MC of $50. A smooth black curve has been drawn through the points of TC in (**a**), and the smooth black MC curve in (**b**) links the discrete steps of MC.

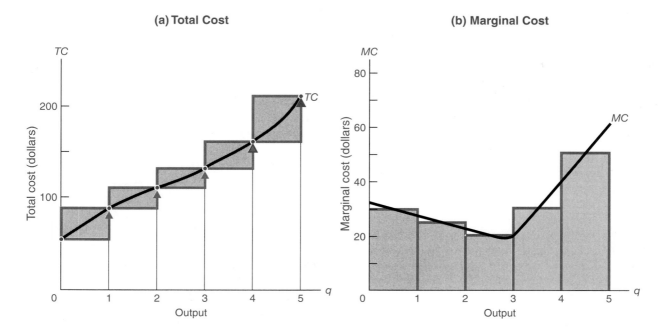

(a) Total Cost (b) Marginal Cost

MC numbers in column (3) of Table 7-2 come from subtracting the *TC* in column (2) from the *TC* of the subsequent quantity. Thus the *MC* of the first unit is $30 (= $85 − $55). The marginal cost of the second unit is $25 (= $110 − $85). And so on.

Instead of getting *MC* from the *TC* column, we could get the *MC* figures by subtracting each *VC* number of column (3) of Table 7-1 from the *VC* in the row below it. Why? Because variable cost always grows exactly like total cost, the only difference being that *VC* must—by definition—start out from 0 rather than from the constant *FC* level. (Check that 30 − 0 = 85 − 55, and 55 − 30 = 110 − 85, and so on.)

The marginal cost of production is the additional cost incurred in producing 1 extra unit of output.

Marginal Cost in Diagrams. Figure 7-1 illustrates total cost and marginal cost. It shows that

TC is related to *MC* in the same way that total product is related to marginal product or that total utility is related to marginal utility.

What kind of shape would we expect actual *MC* curves to have? Empirical studies have found that for most production activities in the short run (i.e., when the capital stock is fixed), marginal cost curves are U-shaped like the one shown in Figure 7-1(*b*). This U-shaped curve falls in the initial phase, reaches a minimum point, and finally begins to rise.

AVERAGE COST

We complete our catalog of the cost concepts important in economics and business with a discussion of different kinds of average or unit cost. Table 7-3 expands the data of Tables 7-1 and 7-2 to include three new measures: average cost, average fixed cost, and average variable cost.

TABLE 7-3. All Cost Concepts Derive from Total Cost Schedule

We can derive all the different cost concepts from the *TC* in column (4). Columns (5) and (6) are the important ones to concentrate on: incremental or marginal cost is calculated by subtraction of adjacent rows of *TC* and is shown in the rust color. The lighter numbers of smoothed *MC* come from Fig. 7-2(*b*). In column (6) note the point of minimum cost of $40 on the U-shaped *AC* curve in Fig. 7-2(*b*). (Can you see why the starred *MC* equals the starred *AC* at the minimum? Also, calculate and fill in all the missing numbers.)

(1)	(2)	(3)	(4)	(5)	(6)	(7)	(8)
	Fixed cost	Variable cost	Total cost	Marginal cost per unit	Average cost per unit	Average fixed cost per unit	Average variable cost per unit
Quantity	*FC*	*VC*	*TC = FC + VC*	*MC*	$AC = \dfrac{TC}{q}$	$AFC = \dfrac{FC}{q}$	$AVC = \dfrac{VC}{q}$
q	($)	($)	($)	($)	($)	($)	($)
0	55	0	55	33	Infinity	Infinity	Undefined
				30			
1	55	30	85	27	85	55	30
				25			
2	55	55	110	22	55	27½	27½
				20			
3	55	75	130	21	43⅓	18⅓	25
				30			
4*	55	105	160	40*	40*	13¾	26¼
				50			
5	55	155	210	60	42	11	___
				70			
6	55	225	280	80	46⅔	9⅙	37½
				90			
7	55	___	370	100	52⁶⁄₇	7⁶⁄₇	45
				110			
8	55	___	480	120	60	6⅞	53⅛

*Minimum level of average cost.

Average or Unit Cost

Like marginal cost, average cost (*AC*) is a concept widely used in business; by comparing average cost with price or average revenue, businesses can determine whether or not they are making a profit. **Average cost** is the total cost divided by the total number of units produced, as shown in column (6) of Table 7-3. That is,

$$\text{Average cost} = \frac{\text{total cost}}{\text{output}} = \frac{TC}{q} = AC$$

In column (6), when only 1 unit is produced, average cost has to be the same as total cost, or $85/1 = $85. But for $q = 2$, $AC = TC/2 = $110/2 = 55, as shown. Note that average cost, at first, falls lower and lower. (We shall see why in a moment.) *AC* reaches a minimum of $40 at $q = 4$, and then slowly rises.

Figure 7-2 plots the cost data shown in Table 7-3. Figure 7-2(*a*) depicts the total, fixed, and variable costs at different levels of output. Figure 7-2(*b*) shows the different average cost concepts, along with a smoothed marginal cost curve. Graph (*a*) shows how total cost moves with variable cost while fixed cost remains unchanged.

Now turn to graph (*b*). This plots the U-shaped *AC* curve and aligns *AC* right below the *TC* curve from which it is derived.

Finally, Figure 7-3 shows how marginal cost is related to the slope of the total cost curve.

Average Fixed and Variable Cost

Just as we separated total cost into fixed and variable cost, we can also break average cost into fixed and variable components. **Average fixed cost** (*AFC*) is defined as *FC/q*. Since total fixed cost is a constant, dividing it by an increasing output gives a steadily falling average fixed cost curve [see column (7) of Table 7-3]. In other words, as a firm sells more output, it can spread its overhead cost over more and more units. For example, a software firm may have a large staff of programmers to develop a new graphics program. The number of copies sold does not

---

FIGURE 7-2. All Cost Curves Can Be Derived from the Total Cost Curve

(**a**) Total cost is made up of fixed cost and variable cost. (**b**) The rust-colored curve of marginal cost falls and then rises, as indicated by the lighter *MC* figures given in column (5) of Table 7-3. The three average cost curves in (**b**) are calculated by dividing total, fixed, and variable cost by total output:

$$AC = TC/q \quad AVC = VC/q \quad AFC = FC/q$$

Also, $$AC = AVC + AFC$$

Note that *MC* intersects *AC* at its minimum.

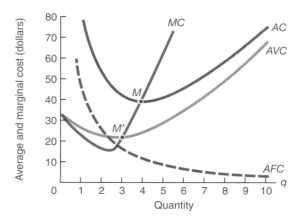

(a) Total, Fixed, and Variable Cost

(b) Average Cost, Marginal Cost

Relation between Slope and Marginal Cost

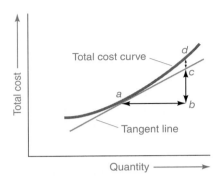

FIGURE 7-3. Relation of Slope and Marginal Cost

Focus a microscope on the total cost curve, examining the cost of going from an output of 3999 to 4000. The figure clarifies the distinction between (1) *MC* as incremental cost for a finite-step change in output and (2) *MC* as the cost for an infinitesimal change in output measured by the tangent. The distance from *a* to *b* represents 1 extra unit of output. The *b* to *d* distance represents the resulting increase in total cost. Hence $MC = (d - b)/(b - a)$, which is the first and simplest definition of marginal cost.

The second definition of marginal cost is as the slope of the total cost curve. The slope of the curve at point *a* is given by the slope of the tangent at point *a*, which is given by the distance from *b* to *c* divided by the distance from *a* to *b*. In the limit for a smooth curve, as the size of the output increment becomes smaller and smaller and we recalculate the ratios in the new, smaller triangle, the discrepancy between the two definitions becomes negligible. That is, *bd/bc* approaches 1 as *b* approaches *a*.

directly affect how many programmers are necessary, making them a fixed cost. So if the program is a best-seller, the *AFC* of the programmers is low; if the program is a failure, their *AFC* is high.

The dashed gray *AFC* curve in Figure 7-2(*b*) is a hyperbola, approaching both axes: it drops lower and lower, approaching the horizontal axis as the constant *FC* gets spread over more and more units. If we allow fractional units of *q*, *AFC* starts infinitely high as finite *FC* is spread over ever-tinier *q*.

Average variable cost (*AVC*) equals variable cost divided by output, or $AVC = VC/q$. As you can see in both Table 7-3 and Figure 7-2(*b*), for this example *AVC* first falls and then rises.

Minimum Average Cost

Do not confuse average cost with marginal cost—it's an easy mistake to make. Indeed, average cost can be much higher or lower than marginal cost, as Figure 7-2(*b*) shows.

But Figure 7-2(*b*) also shows that there is an important link between *MC* and *AC:* When the *MC* of an added unit of output is below its *AC*, its *AC* is declining. And when *MC* is above *AC*, *AC* is increasing. At the point where *MC* equals *AC*, the *AC* curve is flat. For the typical U-shaped *AC* curve, the point where *MC* equals *AC* is also the point where *AC* hits its minimum level. Check this for yourself on the graph.

To summarize:

When marginal cost is below average cost, it is pulling average cost down; when *MC* just equals *AC*, *AC* is neither rising nor falling and is at its minimum; when *MC* is above *AC*, it is pulling *AC* up. Hence, at the bottom of a U-shaped *AC*, *MC* = *AC* = minimum *AC*.

This is a critical relationship. It means that a firm searching for the lowest average cost of production should look for the level of output at which marginal costs equal average costs.

Why is this so? If *MC* is below *AC*, the last unit produced costs less than the average cost of all the previous units produced. If the last unit costs less than the previous ones, the new *AC* (i.e., the *AC* including the last unit) must be less than the old *AC*, so *AC* must be falling. By contrast, if *MC* is above *AC*, the last unit costs more than the average cost of the previous units. Hence the new average cost (the *AC* including the last unit) must be higher than the old *AC*. Finally, when *MC* is just equal to *AC*, the last unit costs exactly the same as the average cost of all previous units. Hence the new *AC*, the one including the last unit, is equal to the old *AC;* the *AC* curve is flat when *AC* equals *MC*.

To better understand the relationship between *MC* and *AC*, study the curves in Figure 7-2(*b*) and the numbers in Table 7-3. Note that for the first 3 units, *MC* is below *AC*, and *AC* is therefore declining. At exactly 4 units, *AC* equals *MC*. Over 4 units, *MC* is above *AC* and pulling *AC* up steadily. Graphically, that means the rising *MC* curve will intersect the *AC* curve precisely at the point where it turns upward: *the AC curve is always pierced at its minimum point by the rising MC curve.* In terms of our cost curves, if the *MC* curve is below the AC curve, the AC curve must be falling.

Marginals, averages, and grades: We can illustrate the MC and AC relationship using college grade averages. Let AG be your average grade (or cumulative grade average up to now) and MG be your grade average for this year, which we will call the "marginal grade average" because it is the last one. When MG is below AG, it will pull the new AG down. Thus, if your AG for the first 2 years is 3 and your MG for your junior year is 2, the new AG (at the end of your junior year) is $2\frac{2}{3}$. Similarly, if your MG in your third year is higher than your AG up till then, your new AG will be pulled up. Where MG equals AG, AG will be flat over time, or unchanged. The same relation holds for average cost and marginal cost.

THE LINK BETWEEN PRODUCTION AND COSTS

What determines a firm's cost curve? Clearly the prices of inputs like labor and land are important factors influencing costs. Higher rents and wages mean higher costs, as any business manager will tell you.

But the cost curve for a firm also depends very closely on the firm's production function. To see this, note that if technological improvements allow the firm to produce the same output with fewer inputs, the firm's costs will fall, and the cost curve will shift down.

Indeed, if you know factor prices and the production function, you can calculate the cost curve. Suppose a firm is aiming to produce a particular level of output. The production function (plus factor prices) will tell us what is the least costly combination of inputs the firm can select that can yield that output. Calculate the total cost of the least-cost bundle of inputs. When we do that for every possible level of output, we have the total cost shown in Tables 7-1 through 7-3.

We can see the derivation of cost from production data in the simple numerical example shown in Table 7-4. Suppose Farmer Smith rents 10 acres of land and can hire farm labor to produce wheat. Per period, land costs $5.5 per acre and labor costs $5 per worker. Using up-to-date farming methods, Smith can produce according to the production function shown in the first three columns of Table 7-4. In this example, land is a fixed cost (because Farmer Smith operates under a 10-year lease), while labor is a variable cost (because farmworkers, unlike faculty members, can easily be hired and fired).

TABLE 7-4. Costs Are Derived from Production Data and Input Costs

Farmer Smith rents 10 acres of wheatland and employs variable labor. According to the farming production function, careful use of labor and land allows the inputs and yields shown in columns (1) to (3) of the table. At input prices of $5.5 per acre and $5 per worker, we obtain Smith's cost of production shown in column (6). All other cost concepts (such as those shown in Table 7-3) can be calculated from the total cost data.

(1) Output (tons of wheat)	(2) Land inputs (acres)	(3) Labor inputs (workers)	(4) Land rent ($ per acre)	(5) Labor wage ($ per worker)	(6) Total cost ($)
0	10	0	5.5	5	55
1	10	6	5.5	5	85
2	10	11	5.5	5	110
3	10	15	5.5	5	130
4	10	21	5.5	5	160
5	10	31	5.5	5	210
6	10	45	5.5	5	280
7	10	63	5.5	5	370
8	10	85	5.5	5	480

Using the production data and the input-cost data, for each level of output we calculate the total cost of production shown in column (6) of Table 7-4. As an example, consider the total cost of production for 3 tons of wheat. Using the given production function, Smith can produce this quantity with 10 acres of land and 15 farmhands. The total cost of producing 3 tons of wheat is (10 acres × $5.5 per acre) + (15 workers × $5 per worker) = $130. Similar calculations will give all the other total cost figures in column (6) of Table 7-4.

Note that these total costs are identical to the ones shown in Tables 7-1 through 7-3, so the other cost concepts shown in the tables (i.e., *MC, FC, VC, AC, AFC,* and *AVC*) are also applicable to the production-cost example of Farmer Smith.

Diminishing Returns and U-Shaped Cost Curves

The relationship between cost and production helps us explain why average cost curves tend to be U-shaped. Recall that Chapter 6's analysis of production distinguished two different time periods, the short run and the long run. The same concepts can be applied to costs as well:

- The *short run* is the period of time that is long enough to adjust variable inputs, such as materials and production labor, but too short to allow all inputs to be changed. In the short run, fixed or overhead factors such as plant and equipment cannot be fully modified or adjusted. Therefore, in the short run, typically labor and materials costs are variable costs, while capital costs are fixed.

- In the *long run,* all inputs can be adjusted— including labor, materials, and capital. Hence, in the long run, all costs are variable and none are fixed.[1]

Note that whether a particular cost is fixed or variable depends on the length of time we are considering. In the short run, for example, the number of planes that an airline owns is a fixed cost. But over the longer run, the airline can clearly control the size of its fleet by buying or selling planes. Indeed, there is an active market in used planes, making it relatively easy to dispose of unwanted planes. Typi-

cally, in the short run, we will consider capital to be the fixed cost and labor to be the variable cost. That is not always true (think of your college's tenured faculty), but generally labor inputs can be adjusted more easily than can capital.

Why is the cost curve U-shaped? Consider the short run in which capital is fixed but labor is variable. In such a situation, there are diminishing returns to the variable factor (labor) because each additional unit of labor has less capital to work with. As a result, the marginal cost of output will rise because the extra output produced by each extra labor unit is going down. In other words, diminishing returns to the variable factor will imply an increasing short-run marginal cost. This shows why diminishing returns lead to rising marginal costs after some point.

Figure 7-4, which contains exactly the same data as Table 7-4, illustrates the point. It shows that the region of increasing marginal product corresponds to falling marginal costs, while the region of diminishing returns implies rising marginal costs.

We can summarize the relationship between the productivity laws and the cost curves as follows:

In the short run, when factors such as capital are fixed, variable factors tend to show an initial phase of increasing returns followed by diminishing returns. The corresponding cost curves show an initial phase of declining marginal costs followed by increasing *MC* after diminishing returns have set in.

CHOICE OF INPUTS BY THE FIRM

Marginal Products and the Least-Cost Rule

Every firm must decide *how* to produce its output. Should electricity be produced with oil or coal? Should cars be assembled in the United States or Mexico? Should classes be taught by faculty or graduate students? We now complete the link between production and cost by using the marginal product concept to illustrate how firms select the least-cost combinations of inputs.

In our analysis, we will rely on the fundamental assumption that *firms minimize their costs of production.* This cost-minimization assumption actually makes good sense not only for perfectly competitive firms but for monopolists or even nonprofit organizations like colleges or hospitals. It simply states that the

---

[1] For a more complete discussion of the long and short runs, see Chapter 6.

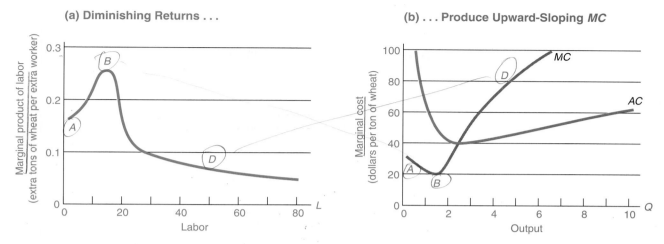

(a) Diminishing Returns . . .

(b) . . . Produce Upward-Sloping MC

FIGURE 7-4. Diminishing Returns and U-Shaped Cost Curves

The U-shaped marginal cost curve in (**b**) arises from the shape of the marginal product curve in (**a**). With fixed land and variable labor, the marginal product of labor in (**a**) first rises to the left of B, peaks at B, and then falls at D as diminishing returns to labor set in.

The marginal cost curve derives from production data. In the region to the left of B in (**b**)—such as at point A—rising marginal product means that marginal cost is falling; at B, peak marginal product occurs at minimum marginal cost; in the region to the right of B, say, at D, as the marginal product of labor falls, the marginal cost of producing output increases.

Overall, increasing and then diminishing marginal product to the variable factor produces a U-shaped marginal cost curve.

firm should strive to produce its output at the lowest possible cost and thereby have the maximum amount of revenue left over for profits or for other objectives.

A simple example will illustrate how a firm might decide between different input combinations. Say a firm's engineers have calculated that the desired output level of 9 units could be produced with two possible options. In both cases, energy (E) costs \$2 per unit while labor (L) costs \$5 per hour. Under option 1, the input mix is $E = 10$ and $L = 2$. Option 2 has $E = 4$ and $L = 5$. Which is the preferred option? At the market prices for inputs, total production costs for option 1 are (\$2 × 10) + (\$5 × 2) = \$30, while total costs for option 2 are (\$2 × 4) + (\$5 × 5) = \$33. Therefore, option 1 would be the preferred least-cost combination of inputs.

More generally, there are usually many possible input combinations, not just two. But we don't have to calculate the cost of every different combination of inputs in order to find the one which costs the least. Here's a simple way to find the least-cost combination: Start by calculating the marginal product of each input, as we did in Chapter 6. Then divide the

marginal product of each input by its factor price. *This gives you the marginal product per dollar of input.* The cost-minimizing combination of inputs comes when the marginal product per dollar of input is equal for all inputs. That is, the marginal contribution to output of each dollar's worth of labor, of land, of oil, and so forth, must be just the same.

Following this reasoning, a firm will minimize its total cost of production when the marginal product per dollar of input is equalized for each factor of production. This is called the least-cost rule.

Least-cost rule: To produce a given level of output at least cost, a firm should buy inputs until it has equalized the marginal product per dollar spent on each input. This implies that

$$\frac{\text{Marginal product of } L}{\text{Price of } L}$$

$$= \frac{\text{marginal product of } A}{\text{price of } A} = \cdots$$

This rule for firms is exactly analogous to what consumers do when they maximize utilities, as we saw in Chapter 5. In analyzing consumer choice, we saw that to maximize utility, consumers should buy goods so that the marginal utility per dollar spent on each consumer good is equalized for all commodities.

What is the rationale for the least-cost rule? Let's say that land costs $800 an acre and labor costs $8 per hour. No one of sound mind would expect to achieve least cost if land and labor were chosen so that their marginal *physical* products were equal. If the marginal products of land and labor were both $100 worth of wheat, equal marginal products would mean that $800 of extra land would produce $100 of wheat while $8 of extra labor would also produce $100 of wheat. Clearly this is inefficient, and the firm would want to decrease inputs of land and increase inputs of labor. Examine the situation of $800 of extra land producing $1200 of wheat while $8 of extra labor produces $12 of extra wheat. This is clearly the efficient input mix because the marginal products per dollar of land and labor are equal, so the firm is minimizing its costs of production.

Another way of understanding the least-cost rule is the following: Break each factor into units worth $1 each. (In our earlier energy-labor example, $1 of labor would be one-fifth of an hour, while $1 of energy would be $\frac{1}{2}$ unit.) Then the least-cost rule states that the marginal product of each dollar-unit of input must be equalized.

A corollary of the least-cost rule is the substitution rule.

Substitution Rule: If the price of one factor falls while all other factor prices remain the same, firms will profit by substituting the now-cheaper factor for all the other factors.

Let's take the case of labor (L). A fall in the price of labor will raise the ratio MP_L/P_L above the MP/P ratio for other inputs. Raising the employment of L lowers MP_L by the law of diminishing returns and therefore lowers MP_L/P_L. Lower price and MP of labor then bring the marginal product per dollar for labor back into equality with that ratio for other factors.

B. ECONOMIC COSTS AND BUSINESS ACCOUNTING

From General Motors down to the corner deli, businesses use more or less elaborate systems to keep track of their costs. Many of the cost categories in business accounting look very similar to the concepts of economic cost we learned above. But there are some important differences between how businesses measure costs and how economists would do it. In this section we will lay out the rudiments of business accounting and point out the differences and similarity with economic costs.

THE INCOME STATEMENT, OR STATEMENT OF PROFIT AND LOSS

Let us start with a small company, called Hot Dog Ventures, Inc. As the name suggests, this company sells gourmet frankfurters in a small store. The operation consists of buying the materials (hot dogs, top-flight buns, expensive mustard, espresso coffee beans) and hiring people to prepare and sell the food. In addition, the company has taken out a loan of $100,000 for its cooking equipment and other restaurant furnishings, and it must pay rent on its store. The founders of Hot Dog Ventures have big aspirations, so they incorporated the business and issued common stock (see Chapter 6 on forms of business organization).

To determine whether Hot Dog Ventures is earning a profit, we must turn to the **income statement**, or—as many companies prefer to call it—the statement of profit and loss, shown in Table 7-5. This statement reports the following: (1) Hot Dog Venture's revenues from sales in 1997, (2) the expenses to be charged against those sales, and (3) the net income, or profits remaining after expenses have been deducted. This gives the fundamental identity of the income statement:

 Net income (or profit) =

total revenue − total expenses

	**Income Statement of Hot Dog Ventures, Inc.** **(July 1, 1997, to December 31, 1997)**		
(1)	Net sales (after all discounts and rebates)		$250,000
	Less cost of goods sold:		
(2)	Materials	$ 50,000	
(3)	Labor cost	90,000	
(4)	Miscellaneous operating costs (utilities, etc.)	10,000	
(5)	Less overhead costs:		
(6)	Selling and administrative costs	15,000	
(7)	Rent for building	5,000	
(8)	Depreciation	15,000	
(9)	Operating expenses	$185,000	185,000
(10)	Net operating income		$ 65,000
	Less:		
(11)	Interest charges on equipment loan		6,000
(12)	State and local taxes		4,000
(13)	Net income (or profit) before income taxes		$ 55,000
(14)	Less: Corporation income taxes		18,000
(15)	**Net income (or profit) after taxes**		$ 37,000
(16)	Less: Dividends paid on common stock		15,000
(17)	Addition to retained earnings		$ 22,000

TABLE 7-5. The Income Statement Shows Total Sales and Expenses for a Period of Time

This definition gives the famous "bottom line" of profits that firms want to maximize. And in many ways, business profits are close to an economist's definition of economic profits. Let's next examine the profit-and-loss statement in more detail, starting from the top. The first line gives the revenues, which were $250,000. Lines 2 through 9 represent the cost of different inputs into the production process. For example, the labor cost is the annual cost of employing labor, while rent is the annual cost of using the building. The selling and administrative costs include the cost of advertising the store and running the back office, while miscellaneous operating costs include the cost of electricity.

The first three cost categories—materials, labor cost, and miscellaneous operating costs—basically correspond to the variable cost of the firm, or its *cost of goods sold*. The next three categories, lines 6 through 8, correspond to the firm's fixed costs, since in the short run they cannot be changed.

Line 8 shows a term we haven't seen before, *depreciation*, which relates to the cost of capital goods.

Firms can either rent capital or own their capital goods. In the case of the building, which Hot Dog Ventures rented, we deducted the rent in item (7) of the income statement.

When the firm owns the capital good, the treatment is more complicated. Suppose the cooking equipment has an estimated useful lifetime of 10 years, at the end of which it is useless and worthless. In effect, some portion of the cooking equipment is "used up" in the productive process each year. We call the amount used up "depreciation," and calculate that amount as the cost of the capital input for that year. **Depreciation** measures the annual cost of a capital input that a company actually owns itself.

The same reasoning would apply to any capital goods that a company owns. Trucks wear out, computers become obsolete, and buildings eventually begin to fall apart. For each of these, the company would take a depreciation charge. There are a number of different formulas for calculating each year's depreciation, but each follows two major principles: (*a*) The total amount of depreciation over the asset's lifetime must equal the capital good's historical cost or purchase price; (*b*) the depreciation is taken in annual accounting charges over the asset's accounting lifetime, which is usually related to the actual economic lifetime of the asset.

We can now understand how depreciation would be charged for Hot Dog Ventures. The equipment is depreciated according to a 10-year lifetime, so the $150,000 of equipment has a depreciation charge of $15,000 per year (using the simplest "straight-line" method of depreciation). If Hot Dog Ventures owned its store, it would have to take a depreciation charge for the building as well.

Adding up all the costs so far gives us the operating expenses (line 9). The net operating income is net revenues minus operating expenses (line 1 minus line 9). Have we accounted for all the costs of production yet? Not quite. Line 11 includes the annual cost of interest on the $100,000 loan. This should be thought of as the cost of borrowing the financial capital. While this is a fixed cost, it is typically kept separate from the other fixed costs. State and local taxes, such as property taxes, are treated as another expense. Deducting lines 11 and 12 gives a total of $55,000 in profits before income taxes. How are these profits divided? Approximately $18,000 goes to the federal government in the form of corporate income taxes. That leaves a profit of $37,000 after taxes. Dividends of $15,000 on the common stock are paid, leaving $22,000 to be plowed back as retained earnings in the business. Again, note that profits are a residual of sales minus costs.

THE BALANCE SHEET

Business accounting is concerned with more than the profits and losses that are the economic driving force. Business accounts also include the **balance sheet**, which is a picture of financial conditions on a given date. This statement records what a firm, person, or nation is worth at a given point in time. On one side of the balance sheet are the **assets** (valuable properties or rights owned by the firm). On the other side are two items, the **liabilities** (money or obligations owed by the firm) and **net worth** (or net value, equal to total assets minus total liabilities).

One important distinction between the income statement and the balance sheet is that between stocks and flows. A **stock** represents the level of a variable, such as the amount of water in a lake or, in this case, the dollar value of a firm. A **flow** variable represents the change per unit of time, like the flow of water in a river or the flow of revenue and expenses into and out of a firm. *The income statement measures the flows into and out of the firm, while the balance sheet measures the stocks of assets and liabilities at the end of the accounting year.*

The fundamental identity or balancing relationship of the balance sheet is that total assets are balanced by total liabilities plus the net worth of the firm to its owners:

$$\text{Total assets} = \text{total liabilities} + \text{net worth}$$

We can rearrange this relationship to find

$$\text{Net worth} = \text{assets} - \text{liabilities}$$

Let us illustrate this by considering Table 7-6, which shows a simple balance sheet for Hot Dog Ventures, Inc. On the left are assets, and on the right are liabilities and net worth. A blank space has been deliberately left next to the net worth entry because the only correct entry compatible with our fundamental balance sheet identity is $200,000. *A balance sheet must always balance because net worth is a residual defined as assets minus liabilities.*

To illustrate how net worth always balances, suppose that hot dogs valued at $40,000 have spoiled. Your accountant reports to you: "Total assets are down $40,000; liabilities remain unchanged. This means total net worth has decreased by $40,000, and I have no choice but to write net worth down from the previous $200,000 to only $160,000." That's how accountants keep score.

Accounting Conventions

In examining the balance sheet in Table 7-6 you might well ask, How are the values of the different items measured? How do the accountants know that the buildings are worth $100,000?

The answer is that accountants use a set of agreed-upon rules or accounting conventions to answer most questions. The most important assumption used in a balance sheet is that the value placed on almost every item reflects its *historical costs*. This differs from the economist's concept of "value," as we will see in the next section. For example, the inventory of hot-dog buns is valued at the price that was paid for them. A newly purchased fixed asset—a piece of equipment or

Balance Sheet of Hot Dog Ventures, Inc. (December 31, 1997)			
Assets		**Liabilities and net worth**	
		Liabilities	
Current assets:		Current liabilities:	
Cash	$ 20,000	Accounts payable	$ 20,000
Inventory	80,000	Notes payable	30,000
Fixed assets:		Long-term liabilities:	
Equipment	150,000	Bonds payable	100,000
Buildings	100,000		
		Net worth	
		Stockholders' equity:	
		Common stock	200,000
Total	$350,000	Total	$350,000

TABLE 7-6. The Balance Sheet Records the Stock of Assets and Liabilities, plus Net Worth, of a Firm at a Given Point in Time

a building—is valued at its purchase price (this being the historical cost convention). Older capital is valued at its purchase price minus accumulated depreciation, thus measuring the gradual decline in usefulness of capital goods. Accountants use historical cost because it reflects an objective evaluation and is easily verified.

In Table 7-6 current assets are convertible into cash within a year, while fixed assets represent capital goods and land. Most of the specific items listed are self-explanatory. Cash consists of coins, currency, and money on deposit in the bank. Cash is the only asset whose value is exact rather than an estimate.

On the liabilities side, accounts payable and notes payable are sums owed to others for goods bought or for borrowed funds. Bonds payable are long-term loans floated in the market. The last item

on the balance sheet is net worth, or stockholders' equity. This is the net value of the firm's assets less liabilities, when valued at historical cost. The net worth must equal $200,000.

We summarize our analysis of accounting concepts as follows:

1. The income statement shows the flow of sales, cost, and revenue over the year or accounting period. It measures the flow of dollars into and out of the firm over a specified period of time.
2. The balance sheet indicates an instantaneous financial picture or snapshot. It is like a measure of the stock of water in a lake. The major items are assets, liabilities, and net worth.

C. OPPORTUNITY COSTS

In this section we look at costs from yet another angle. Remember that one of the cardinal tenets of economics is that resources are scarce. That means every time we choose to use a resource one way,

we've given up the opportunity to utilize it another way. That's easy to see in our own lives, where we must constantly decide what to do with our limited time and income. Should we go to a movie or study for next week's test? Should we travel in Mexico or buy a car? Should we get postgraduate or professional training or begin work right after college?

In each of these cases, making a choice in effect costs us the opportunity to do something else. The alternative forgone is called the opportunity cost, which we met briefly in Chapter 1 and develop more thoroughly here. The immediate dollar cost of going to a movie instead of studying is the price of a ticket, but the opportunity cost also includes the possibility of getting a higher grade on the exam. The opportunity costs of a decision include all its consequences, whether they reflect monetary transactions or not.

Decisions have opportunity costs because choosing one thing in a world of scarcity means giving up something else. The **opportunity cost** is the value of the good or service forgone.

One important example of opportunity cost is the cost of going to college. If you went to a public university, you might calculate the total costs of tuition, books, and travel to be approximately $14,000 in 1996. Does this mean that $14,000 is your opportunity cost of going to school? Definitely not! You must include as well the opportunity cost of the *time* spent studying and going to classes. A full-time job for a 19-year-old high school graduate would on average pay around $16,000 in 1996. If we add up both the actual expenses and the earnings forgone, we would find that the opportunity cost of college is $30,000 (equal to $14,000 + $16,000) rather than $14,000 per year.

Business decisions have opportunity costs, too. Do all opportunity costs show up on the profit-and-loss statement? Not necessarily. In general, business accounts include only transactions in which money actually changes hands. By contrast, the economist always tries to "pierce the veil of money" to uncover the real consequences that lie behind the dollar flows and to measure the true *resource costs* of an activity. Economists therefore include all costs—whether they reflect monetary transactions or not.

There are several important opportunity costs that do not show up on income statements. For example, in many small businesses, the family may put in many unpaid hours, which are not included as accounting costs. Nor do business accounts include a capital charge for the owner's financial contributions. Nor do they include the cost of the environ-

mental damage that occurs when a business dumps toxic wastes into a stream. But from an economic point of view, each of these is a genuine cost to the economy.

Let's illustrate the concept of opportunity cost by considering the owner of Hot Dog Ventures. The owner puts in 60 hours a week but earns no "wages." At the end of the year, as Table 7-5 showed, the firm earns a profit of $22,000—pretty good for a neophyte firm.

Or is it? The economist would insist that we should consider the value of a factor of production regardless of how the factor happens to be owned. We should count the owner's own labor as a cost even though the owner does not get paid directly but instead receives compensation in the form of profits. Because the owner has alternative opportunities for work, we must value the owner's labor in terms of the lost opportunities.

A careful examination might show that Hot Dog's owner could find a similar and equally interesting job working for someone else and earning $45,000. This represents the opportunity cost or earnings forgone because the owner decided to become the unpaid owner of a small business rather than the paid employee of another firm.

Therefore, the economist continues, let us calculate the true economic profits of the hot-dog firm. If we take the measured profits of $22,000 and subtract the $45,000 opportunity cost of the owner's labor, we find a net *loss* of $23,000. Hence, although the accountant might conclude that Hot Dog Ventures is economically viable, the economist would pronounce that the firm is an unprofitable loser.

OPPORTUNITY COST AND MARKETS

At this point, however, you might well say: "Now I'm totally confused. First I learned that price is a good measure of true social cost in the marketplace. Now you tell me that opportunity cost is the right concept. Can't you economists make up your minds?"

Actually, there is a simple explanation: *In well-functioning markets price equals opportunity cost.* Assume that a commodity like coal is bought and sold in a competitive market. If I bring my ton of coal to market, I will receive a number of bids from prospective buyers: $25.02, $24.98, $25.01. These represent the values of my coal to, say, three electric utilities. I pick the highest—$25.02. The opportunity cost of this sale is the value of the best available alternative— that is, the second-highest bid at $25.01—which is almost identical to the price that is accepted. As the market approaches perfect competition, the bids get closer and closer until in the limit the second-highest bid (which is our definition of opportunity cost) exactly equals the highest bid (which is the price). In competitive markets, numerous buyers compete for resources to the point where price is bid up to the best available alternative and is therefore equal to the opportunity cost.

Opportunity Costs outside Markets. The concept of opportunity cost is particularly crucial when you are analyzing transactions that take place outside markets. How do you measure the value of a road or a park? Of a health or safety regulation? Even the allocation of student time can be explained using opportunity cost.

- The notion of opportunity cost explains why students watch more TV the week after exams than the week before exams. Watching TV right before an exam has a high opportunity cost, for the alternative use of time (studying) would have high value in improving grade performance. After exams, time has a lower opportunity cost.
- Say the federal government wants to drill for oil off the California coast. A storm of complaints is heard. A defender of the program states, "What's all the ruckus about? There's valuable oil out there, and there is plenty of seawater to go around. This is very low-cost oil for the nation." In fact, the opportunity cost might be very high. If drilling leads to oil spills that spoil the beaches, it might reduce the recreational value of the ocean. That opportunity cost might not be easily measured, but it's every bit as real as the value of oil under the waters.

The Road Not Traveled. Opportunity cost, then, is a measure of what has been given up when we make a decision. Consider what Robert Frost had in mind when he wrote:

> Two roads diverged in a wood, and I—
> I took the one less traveled by,
> And that has made all the difference.

What other road did Frost have in mind? An urban life? An avocation where he would not be able to write of roads and walls and birches? Imagine the immeasurable opportunity cost to all of us if Robert Frost had taken the road more traveled by.

But let us return from the poetic to practical concepts of cost. The crucial point to grasp is this: *Economic costs include, in addition to explicit money outlays, those opportunity costs incurred because resources can be used in alternative ways.*

SUMMARY

A. Economic Analysis of Costs

1. Total cost (*TC*) can be broken down into fixed cost (*FC*) and variable cost (*VC*). Fixed costs are unaffected by any production decisions, while variable costs are incurred on items like labor or materials which increase as production levels rise.

2. Marginal cost (*MC*) is the extra total cost resulting from 1 extra unit of output. Average total cost (*AC*) is the sum of ever-declining average fixed cost (*AFC*) and average variable cost (*AVC*). Short-run average cost is generally represented by a U-shaped curve that is always intersected at its minimum point by the rising *MC* curve.

3. Useful rules to remember are

$$TC = FC + VC \quad AC = \frac{TC}{q} \quad AC = AFC + AVC$$

At the bottom of U-shaped *AC*, *MC* = *AC* = minimum *AC*.

4. Costs and productivity are like mirror images. When the law of diminishing returns holds, the marginal product falls and the *MC* curve rises. When there is an initial stage of increasing returns, *MC* initially falls.

5. We can apply cost and production concepts to understand a firm's choice of the best combination of factors of production. Firms that desire to maximize profits will want to minimize the cost of producing a given level of output. In this case, the firm will follow the least-cost

rule: different factors will be chosen so that the marginal product per dollar of input is equalized for all inputs. This implies that $MP_L/P_L = MP_A/P_A = \cdots$.

B. Economic Costs and Business Accounting

6. To understand accounting, the most important relationships are:
   a. The character of the income statement (or profit-and-loss statement); the residual nature of profits; depreciation on fixed assets
   b. The fundamental balance sheet relationship between assets, liabilities, and net worth; the breakdown of each of these into financial and fixed assets; and the residual nature of net worth

C. Opportunity Costs

7. The economist's definition of costs is broader than the accountant's. Economic cost includes not only the obvious out-of-pocket purchases or monetary transactions but also more subtle opportunity costs, such as the return to labor supplied by the owner of a firm. These opportunity costs are tightly constrained by the bids and offers in competitive markets, so price is close to opportunity cost for marketed goods and services.
8. The most important application of opportunity cost arises for nonmarket goods—those like clean air or health or recreation—whose services may be highly valuable even though they are not bought and sold in markets.

CONCEPTS FOR REVIEW

Analysis of Costs

total costs: fixed and variable
marginal cost
least-cost rule:

$$\frac{MP_L}{P_L} = \frac{MP_A}{P_A} = \frac{MP_{\text{any factor}}}{P_{\text{any factor}}}$$

$TC = FC + VC$
$AC = TC/q = AFC + AVC$

Accounting Concepts

income statement: sales, cost, profits
fundamental balance sheet identity

assets, liabilities, and net worth
stocks vs. flows
opportunity cost
cost concepts in economics and accounting

QUESTIONS FOR DISCUSSION

1. Explain the difference between marginal cost and average cost. Why should *AVC* always look much like *MC*? Why is *MC* the same when computed from *VC* as from *TC*?
2. To the $55 of fixed cost in Table 7-3, add $90 of additional *FC*. Now calculate a whole new table, with the same *VC* as before but new *FC* = $145. What happens to *MC, AVC*? To *TC, AC, AFC*? Can you verify that minimum *AC* is now at $q^* = 5$ with $AC = \$60 = MC$?
3. Explain why *MC* cuts *AC* and *AVC* at the bottom of their U's.
4. "Compulsory military service allows the government to fool itself and the people about the true cost of a big army." Compare the budget cost and the opportunity cost of a voluntary army (where army pay is high) and compulsory service (where pay is low). What does the concept of opportunity cost contribute to analyzing the quotation?
5. Consider the data in Table 7-7, which contains a situation similar to that in Table 7-4.
   a. Calculate the *TC, VC, FC, AC, AVC,* and *MC*. On a piece of graph paper, plot the *AC* and *MC* curves.
   b. Assume that the price of labor doubles. Calculate a new *AC* and *MC*. Plot the new curves and compare them with those in **a**.
   c. Now assume that total factor productivity doubles (i.e., that the level of output doubles for each input combination). Repeat the exercise in **b**. Can you see two major factors that tend to affect a firm's cost curves?
6. Explain the fallacies in each of the following:
   a. Average costs are minimized when marginal costs are at their lowest point.
   b. Because fixed costs never change, average fixed cost is a constant for each level of output.
   c. Average cost is rising whenever marginal cost is rising.
   d. The opportunity cost of drilling for oil in Yosemite Park is zero because no firm produces anything there.
   e. A firm minimizes costs when it spends the same amount on each input.

(1) Output (tons of wheat	(2) Land inputs (acres)	(3) Labor inputs (workers)	(4) Land rent ($ per acre)	(5) Labor wage ($ per worker)
0	15	0	12	5
1	15	6	12	5
2	15	11	12	5
3	15	15	12	5
4	15	21	12	5
5	15	31	12	5
6	15	45	12	5
7	15	63	12	5

TABLE 7-7.

7. In 1997 a company has $10 million of net sales and $9 million of costs of all kinds (including taxes, rentals, etc.) and rents its equipment and plant. Its inventory doesn't change in the year. It pays no dividends. Draw up its simplified 1997 income statement.

8. At the end of 1996, the company in question 7 owes no money, having been completely financed by common stock. Fill in the year-end balance sheet for 1996 using the data provided in Table 7-8. Then, using the data and income statement from question 7, complete the balance sheet for 1997 in Table 7-8.

TABLE 7-8.

	Assets (end of year)			Liabilities and net worth (end of year)	
	1996	1997		1996	1997
			Liabilities	0	0
			Net worth	....	
Total	$50 million	....	Total	....	....

APPENDIX 7
PRODUCTION, COST THEORY, AND DECISIONS OF THE FIRM

The production theory described in Chapter 6 and the cost analysis of this chapter are among the fundamental building blocks of microeconomics. A thorough understanding of production and cost is necessary for an appreciation of how economic scarcity gets translated into prices in the marketplace. This appendix develops these concepts further and introduces the concept of an equal-product curve, or isoquant.

A NUMERICAL PRODUCTION FUNCTION

Production and cost analysis have their roots in the concept of a production function, which shows the maximum amount of output that can be produced with various combinations of inputs. Table 7A-1 starts with a numerical example of a constant-returns-to-scale production function, showing the amount of inputs along the axes and the amount of output at the grid points of the table.

Along the left-hand side are listed the varying amounts of land, going from 1 unit to 6 units. Along the bottom are listed amounts of labor, which also go from 1 to 6. Output corresponding to each land row and labor column is listed inside the table.

If we are interested in knowing exactly how much output there will be when 3 units of land and

2 units of labor are available, we count up 3 units of land and then go over 2 units of labor. The answer is seen to be 346 units of product. (Can you identify

TABLE 7A-1. A Tabular Picture of a Production Function Relating Amount of Output to Varying Combinations of Labor and Land Inputs

When you have 3 land units and 2 labor units available, the engineer tells you the maximum obtainable output is 346 units. Note the different ways to produce 346. Do the same for 490. (The production function shown in the table is a special case of the Cobb-Douglas production function, one given by the formula $Q = 100\sqrt{2LA}$.)

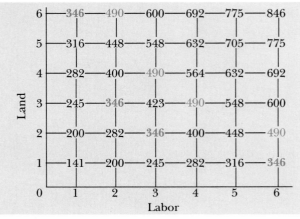

some other input combinations to produce $q =$ 346?) Similarly, we find that 3 units of land and 6 of labor produce 600 units of q. Remember that the <u>production function shows the maximum output available given engineering skills and technical knowledge available at a given time.</u>

THE LAW OF DIMINISHING MARGINAL PRODUCT

Table 7A-1 can nicely illustrate the law of diminishing returns. First recall that the marginal product of labor is the extra production resulting from 1 additional unit of labor when land and other inputs are held constant. At any point in Table 7A-1, we can find the marginal product of labor by subtracting the output from the number on its right in the same row. Thus, when there are 2 units of land and 4 units of labor, the marginal product of an additional laborer would be 48, or 448 minus 400 in the second row.

By the "marginal product of land" we mean, of course, the extra product resulting from 1 additional unit of land when labor is held constant. It is calculated by comparing adjacent items in a given column. Thus, when there are 2 units of land and 4 units of labor, the marginal product of land is shown in the fourth column as $490 - 400$, or 90.

We can easily find the marginal product of each of our two factors by comparing adjacent entries in the vertical columns or horizontal rows of Table 7A-1.

Having defined the concept of marginal product of an input, we now can easily define the law of diminishing returns: The law of diminishing returns states that as we increase one input and hold other inputs constant, the marginal product of the varying input will, at least after some point, decline.

To illustrate this, hold land constant in Table 7A-1 by sticking to a given row—say, the row corresponding to land equal to 2 units. Now let labor increase from 1 to 2 units, from 2 to 3 units, and so forth. What happens to q at each step?

As labor goes from 1 to 2 units, the level of output increases from 200 to 282 units, or by 82 units. But the next dose of labor adds only 64 units, or $346 - 282$. Diminishing returns have set in. Still further additions of a single unit of labor give us, respectively, only 54 extra units of output, 48 units, and finally 42 units. You can easily verify that the law holds for other

rows and that the law holds when land is varied and labor held constant.

We can use this example to verify our intuitive justification of the law of diminishing returns—the assertion that <u>the law holds because the fixed factor decreases relative to the variable factor.</u> According to this explanation, each unit of the variable factor has less and less of the fixed factor to work with. So it is natural that extra product should drop off.

If this explanation is to hold water, output should increase proportionately when both factors are increased together. When labor increases from 1 to 2 and land simultaneously increases from 1 to 2, we should get the same increase in product as when both increase *simultaneously* from 2 to 3. This can be verified in Table 7A-1. In the first move we go from 141 to 282, and in the second move the product increases from 282 to 423, an equal jump of 141 units.

LEAST-COST FACTOR COMBINATION FOR A GIVEN OUTPUT

The numerical production function shows us the different ways to produce a given level of output. But

TABLE 7A-2. Inputs and Costs of Producing a Given Level of Output

Assume that the firm has chosen 346 units of output. Then it can use any of the four choices of input combinations shown as A, B, C, and D. As the firm moves down the list, production becomes more labor-intensive and less land-intensive. Fill in the missing numbers.

The firm's choice among the different techniques will depend on input prices. When $P_L = \$2$ and $P_A = \$3$, verify that the cost-minimizing combination is C. Show that lowering the price of land from \$3 to \$1 leads the firm to a more land-intensive combination at B.

	(1) Input Combinations		(3) Total cost when $P_L = \$2$ $P_A = \$3$ ($)	(4) Total cost when $P_L = \$2$ $P_A = \$1$ ($)
	Labor L	Land A		
A	1	6	20	*8*
B	2	3	13	7
C	3	2	12	*8*
D	6	1	15	*13*

which of the many possibilities should the firm use? If the desired level of output is $q = 346$, there are no less than four different combinations of land and labor, shown as A, B, C, and D in Table 7A-2.

As far as the engineer is concerned, each of these combinations is equally good at producing an output of 346 units. But the manager, interested in minimizing cost, wants to find the combination that costs least.

Let us suppose that the price of labor is $2 and the price of land $3. The total costs when input prices are at this level are shown in the third column of Table 7A-2. For combination A, the total labor and land cost will be $20, equal to $(1 \times \$2) + (6 \times \$3)$. Costs at B, C, and D will be, respectively, $13, $12, and $15. At the assumed input prices, C is the least costly way to produce the given output.

If either of the input prices changes, the equilibrium proportion of the inputs will also change so as to use less of the input that has gone up most in price. (This is just like the substitution effect of Chapter 5's discussion of consumer demand.) As soon as input prices are known, the least-cost method of production can be found by calculating the costs of different input combinations.

Equal-Product Curves

The commonsense numerical analysis of the way in which a firm will combine inputs to minimize costs can be made more vivid by the use of diagrams. We will take the diagrammatic approach by putting together two new curves, the equal-product curve and the equal-cost line.

Let's turn Table 7A-1 into a continuous curve by drawing a smooth curve through all the points that yield $q = 346$. This smooth curve, shown in Figure 7A-1, indicates all the different combinations of labor and land that yield an output of 346 units. This is called an **equal-product curve** or **isoquant** and is analogous to the consumer's indifference curve discussed in the appendix to Chapter 5. You should be able to draw on Figure 7A-1 the corresponding equal-product curve for output equal to 490 by getting the data from Table 7A-1. Indeed, an infinite number of such equal-product contour lines could be drawn in.

Equal-Cost Lines

Given the price of labor and land, the firm can evaluate the total cost for points A, B, C, and D or for

---

FIGURE 7A-1. Equal-Product Curve

All the points on the equal-product curve represent the different combinations of land and labor that can be used to produce the same 346 units of output.

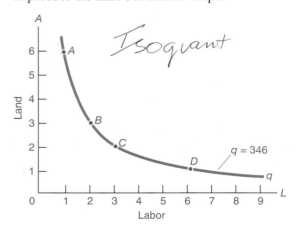

FIGURE 7A-2. Equal-Cost Lines

Every point on a given equal-cost line represents the same total cost. The lines are straight because factor prices are constant, and they all have a negative slope equal to the ratio of labor price to land price, $2/$3, and hence are parallel.

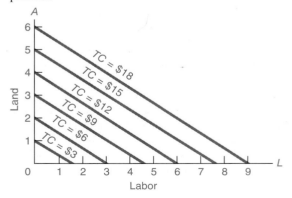

Substituting Inputs to Minimize Cost of Production

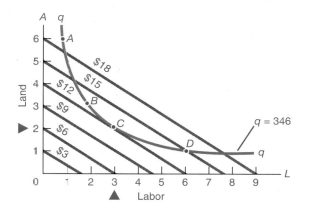

FIGURE 7A-3. Least-Cost Input Combination Comes at *C*

The firm desires to minimize its costs of producing a given output of 346. It thus seeks out the least expensive input combination along its rust-colored equal-product curve. It looks for the input combination that is on the lowest of the equal-cost lines. Where the equal-product curve touches (but does not cross) the lowest equal-cost line is the least-cost position. This tangency means that factor prices and marginal products are proportional, with equalized marginal products per dollar.

any other point on the equal-product curve. The firm will minimize its costs when it selects that point on its equal-product curve that has the lowest total cost.

An easy technique for finding the least-cost method of production is to construct **equal-cost lines**. This is done in Figure 7A-2, where the family of parallel straight lines represents a number of equal-cost curves when the price of labor is $2 and the price of land $3.

To find the total cost for any point, we simply read off the number appended to the equal-cost line going through that point. The lines are all straight and parallel because the firm is assumed to be able to buy all it wishes of either input at constant prices. The lines are somewhat flatter than 45° because the price of labor P_L is somewhat less than the price of land P_A. More precisely, we can always say that the arithmetic value of the slope of each equal-cost line must equal the ratio of the price of labor to that of land—in this case $P_L/P_A = \frac{2}{3}$.

Equal-Product and Equal-Cost Contours: Least-Cost Tangency

Combining the equal-product and equal-cost lines, we can determine the optimal, or cost-minimizing, position of the firm. Recall that the optimal input combination comes at that point where the given output of $q = 346$ can be produced at least cost. To find such a point, simply superimpose the single rust-colored equal-product curve upon the family of gray equal-cost lines, as shown in Figure 7A-3. The firm will always keep moving along the rust-colored convex curve of Figure 7A-3 as long as it is able to cross over to lower cost lines. Its equilibrium will therefore be at *C*, where the equal-product curve touches (but does not cross) the lowest equal-cost line. This is a point of tangency, where the slope of the equal-product curve just matches the slope of an equal-cost line and the curves are just kissing.

We already know that the slope of the equal-cost curves is P_L/P_A. But what is the slope of the equal-product curve? Recall from Chapter 1's appendix that the slope at a point of a curved line is the slope of the straight line tangent to the curve at the point in question. For the equal-product curve, this slope is a "substitution ratio" between the two factors. It depends upon the relative marginal products of the two factors of production, namely, MP_L/MP_A—just as the rate of substitution between two goods along a consumer's indifference curve was earlier shown to equal the ratio of the marginal utilities of the two goods (see the appendix to Chapter 5).

Least-Cost Conditions

Using our graphical apparatus, we have therefore derived the conditions under which a firm will minimize its costs of production:

1. The ratio of marginal products of any two inputs must equal the ratio of their factor prices:

Substitution ratio

$$= \frac{\text{marginal product of labor}}{\text{marginal product of land}}$$

$$= \begin{array}{c} \text{slope of} \\ \text{equal-product} \\ \text{curve} \end{array} = \frac{\text{price of labor}}{\text{price of land}}$$

2. We can also rewrite condition 1 in a different and illuminating way. From the last equation it follows that the marginal product per dollar received from the (last) dollar of expenditure must be the same for every productive factor:

$$\frac{\text{Marginal product of } L}{\text{Price of } L}$$

$$= \frac{\text{marginal product of } A}{\text{price of } A} = \cdots$$

But you should not be satisfied with abstract explanations. Always remember the commonsense economic explanation which shows how a firm will distribute its expenditure among inputs to equalize the marginal product per dollar of spending.

SUMMARY TO APPENDIX

1. A production-function table lists the output that can be produced for each labor column and each land row. Diminishing returns to one variable factor, when other factors are held fixed or constant, can be shown by calculating the decline of marginal products in any row or column.

2. An equal-product curve or isoquant depicts the alternative input combinations that produce the same level of output. The slope, or substitution ratio, along such an equal-product curve equals relative marginal products (e.g., MP_L/MP_A). Curves of equal total cost are parallel lines with slopes equal to factor-price ratios (P_L/P_A). Least-cost equilibrium comes at the tangency point, where an equal-product curve touches but does not cross the lowest TC curve. In least-cost equilibrium, marginal products are proportional to factor prices, with equalized marginal product per dollar spent on all factors (i.e., equalized MP_i/P_i).

CONCEPTS FOR REVIEW

equal-product curves
parallel lines of equal TC
substitution ratio $= MP_L/MP_A$

P_L/P_A as the slope of parallel equal-
TC lines

least-cost tangency condition:
$MP_L/MP_A = P_L/P_A$ or MP_L/P_L
$= MP_A/P_A$

QUESTIONS FOR DISCUSSION

1. Show that raising labor's wage while holding land's rent constant will steepen the gray equal-cost lines and move tangency point C in Figure 7A-3 northwest toward B with the now-cheaper input substituted for the input which is now more expensive. If we substitute capital for labor, restate the result. Should union leaders recognize this relationship?

2. What is the least-cost combination of inputs if the production function is given by Table 7A-1 and input prices are as shown in Figure 7A-3, where $q = 346$? What would be the least-cost ratio for the same input prices if output doubled to $q = 692$? What has happened to the "factor intensity," or land-labor ratio? Can you see why this result would hold for any output change under constant returns to scale?

CHAPTER 8
THE BEHAVIOR OF PERFECTLY COMPETITIVE MARKETS

Cost of production would have no effect on competitive price if it could have none on supply.

John Stuart Mill

We now come to one of the most important topics in economics: how firms respond to the price signals that the market sends them. Common sense tells us that an astute business will increase production if the price of its product goes up. For example, if the price of oil rises, we would expect that oil companies will drill deeper and in more remote locations.

But armed with our knowledge of production and costs, we can achieve a much sharper understanding of the supply behavior of competitive firms and industries. In this chapter we will establish three key propositions. First, we see that the supply decisions of a firm depend upon its marginal cost of production. Second, we show that in the long run firms will enter or exit an industry until the profits in that industry are driven to zero. Finally, we show that a perfectly competitive industry will be efficient, meaning that there is no reorganization of production that can make everybody better off.

A. SUPPLY BEHAVIOR OF THE COMPETITIVE FIRM

Business enterprises are crucial to an efficient market economy. High-income nations are populated by businesses that produce efficiently and generate new products rapidly. But how exactly does a business enterprise behave? How much should a perfectly competitive firm produce?

BEHAVIOR OF A COMPETITIVE FIRM

How much wheat should Farmer Smith produce if wheat sells at $3 per bushel? How many pairs of shoes should tiny Fabiola's Fabulous Formfitters pro-

duce and sell if the market price of shoes is $40? These questions concern the supply behavior of perfectly competitive firms. In this chapter, we will assume that our competitive firm *maximizes profits*, which are equal to total revenues minus total costs. Profit maximization requires that the firm manage its internal operations efficiently (prevent waste, encourage worker morale, choose efficient production processes, and so forth) and make sound decisions in the marketplace (buy the correct quantity of inputs at least cost and choose the optimal level of output).

Why would a firm want to maximize profits? Profits are like the net earnings or take-home pay of a corporation. They represent the amount a firm can pay in dividends to the owners, reinvest in new plant and equipment, or employ to make financial investments. All these activities increase the value of the firm to its owners.

 Reminder on key terms: Because profits involve both costs and revenues, the firm must have a good grasp of its cost structure. Turn back to Table 7-2 in the last chapter to make sure you are clear on the important concepts of total cost, average cost, and marginal cost. Recall as well that the world of perfect competition is the world of price-takers. A perfectly competitive firm is so small relative to its market that it cannot affect the market price; it simply takes the price as given. When Farmer Smith sells a homogeneous product like wheat, she sells to a large pool of buyers who are willing to pay the market price of $3 per bushel. Just as most households must accept the prices that are charged by grocery stores or movie theaters, so must competitive firms accept the market prices of the wheat or oil or shoes that they produce.

We can depict a price-taking perfect competitor by examining the way the market looks to a competitive firm. Figure 8-1 shows the contrast between the industry demand curve (the *DD* curve) and the demand curve facing a single competitive firm (the *dd* curve). Because a competitive industry is populated by firms that are small relative to the market, the firm's segment of the demand curve is but a tiny segment of the industry's curve. Graphically, the competitive firm's portion of the demand curve is so small that, to the lilliputian eye of the perfect competitor, the firm's *dd* demand curve looks completely horizontal or infinitely elastic. Figure 8-1 illustrates how the elasticity of demand for a single competitor appears very much greater than that for the entire market.

Because competitive firms cannot affect the price, the price for each unit sold is the extra revenue that the firm will earn. For example, at a market price of $40 per unit, the competitive firm can sell all it wants at $40. If it decides to sell 101 units rather than 100 units, its revenue goes up by exactly $40.

Recall these key points:

1. Under perfect competition, there are many small firms, each producing an identical product and each too small to affect the market price.
2. The perfect competitor faces a completely horizontal demand (or *dd*) curve.
3. The extra revenue gained from each extra unit sold is therefore the market price.

Competitive Supply Where Marginal Cost Equals Price

Given its costs, demand, and desire to maximize profits, how does a competitive firm decide on the amount that it will supply? Clearly, the amount of output supplied will depend upon the costs of production. Take the supply of bicycles as an example. No sane firm would supply bicycles at a dollar a dozen, for that price would not even cover the cost of the seats. On the other hand, if bicycles were selling at $10 million apiece, everyone would rush in to open up new bicycle firms. Under normal circumstances, a firm's output decision is not so obvious and will involve the marginal cost of producing output. Let's see how.

Say *you* are managing Fabiola's Fabulous Formfitters and deciding on the profit-maximizing output. The data in Table 8-1 can help us understand the determinants of the supply decisions of a competitive

FIGURE 8-1. Demand Curve Looks Horizontal to a Perfect Competitor

The industry demand curve is on the left, showing inelastic demand at competitive equilibrium at *A*. However, the perfect competitor on the right has such a tiny part of the market that demand looks completely horizontal (i.e., perfectly elastic). The perfect competitor can sell all it wants at the market price.

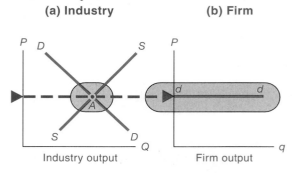

		Supply Decision of Competitive Firm				
(1)	(2)	(3)	(4)	(5)	(6)	(7)
	Total cost	Marginal cost per unit	Average cost	Price	Total revenue	Profit
Quantity q	TC ($)	MC ($)	AC ($)	P ($)	TR ($)	π ($)
0	55,000					
1,000	85,000	27	85	40	40,000	−45,000
2,000	110,000	22	55	40	80,000	−30,000
3,000	130,000	21	43.33	40	120,000	−10,000
3,999	159,960.01	38.98	40.000+	40	159,960	−0.01
		39.99				
4,000	160,000	40	**40**	**40**	**160,000**	**0**
		40.01				
4,001	160,040.01	40.02	40.000+	40	160,040	−0.01
5,000	210,000	60	42	40	200,000	−10,000

TABLE 8-1. Profit Is Maximized at Production Level Where Marginal Cost Equals Price
This table uses the same cost data as that analyzed in the previous chapter (see Table 7-3).
We made a tiny adjustment in output to find the cost levels around the point of minimum
average cost at 4000 units. The dark rust-colored marginal cost figures in column (3) are the
numbers that are read off the smoothed *MC* curve. The light rust-colored *MC* numbers in
column (3) between the rows are the exact *MC* calculated between output levels in column (1).

firm like Fabiola's. (Note that this table contains the
same cost data in thousands as Table 7-3 in the previous
chapter.) For this example, assume that the market price
for shoes is $40 per unit. Say Fabiola's starts out by sell-
ing 3000 pairs. This yields total revenue of $40 × 3000 =
$120,000 with total cost of $130,000, so the firm incurs a
loss of $10,000.

Now you look at your operations and see that if you
sell more shoes, the revenue from each unit is $40 while
the marginal cost is only $21. Additional units bring in
more than they cost. So you raise production to 4000
pairs. At this output, the firm has revenues of $40 × 4000 =
$160,000 and costs of $160,000, so profits are zero.

Flush with your success, you decide to boost output
some more, to 5000 pairs. At this output, the firm has
revenues of $40 × 5000 = $200,000 and costs of
$210,000. Now you're losing $10,000 again. What went
wrong?

When you go back to your books, you see that at the
output level of 5000, the marginal cost is $60, which is

more than the price of $40, so you are losing $20
(equal to price minus *MC*) on the last unit produced. Now you and your accountant see the light:

The maximum-profit output comes at that output where marginal cost equals price.

The reason underlying this proposition is that the
competitive firm can always make additional profit as
long as the price is greater than the marginal cost of
the last unit. Total profit reaches its peak—is maximized—when there is no longer any extra profit to
be earned by selling extra output. At the maximum-
profit point, the last unit produced brings in an
amount of revenue exactly equal to that unit's cost.
What is that extra revenue? It is the price per unit.
What is that extra cost? It is the marginal cost.

Let's test this rule by looking at Table 8-1. Starting at the maximum-profit output of 4000 units, if
Fabiola's sells 1 more unit, that unit would bring a
price of $40 while the marginal cost of that unit is
$40.01. So the firm would lose money on the 4001st

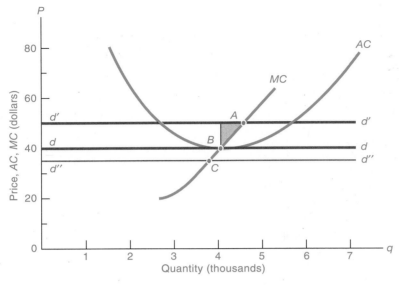

Firm's Supply and Marginal Cost

FIGURE 8-2. Firm's Supply Curve Is Its Rising Marginal Cost Curve
For a profit-maximizing competitive firm, the upward-sloping marginal cost (*MC*) curve is the firm's supply curve. For market price at *d'd'*, the firm will supply output at intersection point at *A*. Explain why intersection points at *B* and *C* represent equilibria for prices at *d* and *d''* respectively.

unit. Similarly, the firm would lose $0.01 if it produced 1 less unit. This shows that the firm's maximum-profit output comes at exactly $q = 4000$, where price equals marginal cost.

Rule for a firm's supply under perfect competition: A firm will maximize profits when it produces at that level where marginal cost equals price:

$$\text{Marginal cost} = \text{price} \quad \text{or} \quad MC = P$$

Figure 8-2 illustrates a firm's supply decision diagrammatically. When the market price of output is $40, the firm consults its cost data in Table 8-1 and finds that the production level corresponding to a marginal cost of $40 is 4000 units. Hence, at a market price of $40, the firm will wish to produce and sell 4000 units. We can find that profit-maximizing amount in Figure 8-2 at the intersection of the price line at $40 and the *MC* curve at point *B*.

In general, then, the firm's marginal cost curve can be used to find its optimal production schedule: the profit-maximizing output will come where the price intersects the marginal cost curve.

We choose the example so that at the profit-maximizing output the firm has zero profits, with total revenues equal to total costs. (Recall that these are economic profits and include all opportunity costs, including the owner's labor and capital.) Point *B* is the **zero-profit point**, the production level at which the firm makes zero profits; at the zero-profit point, price equals average cost, so revenues just cover costs.

What if the firm chooses the wrong output? If the market price were $50, the firm should choose output at intersection point *A* in Figure 8-2. We can calculate the loss of profit if the firm mistakenly produces at *B* when price is at $50 by the shaded gray triangle in Figure 8-2. This depicts the surplus of price over *MC* for production between *B* and *A*. Draw in a similar shaded triangle above *A* to show the loss from producing too much.

The general rule then is:

A profit-maximizing firm will set its output at that level where marginal cost equals price. Diagrammatically, this means that a firm's marginal cost curve is also its supply curve.

Total Cost and the Shutdown Condition

Our general rule for firm supply leaves open one possibility—that the price will be so low that the firm will want to shut down. Isn't it possible that at the $P = MC$ equilibrium, Fabiola's may be losing a truckful of money and want to shut down? In general, a firm will want to shut down in the short run when it can no longer cover its variable costs.

For example, suppose the firm were faced with a market price of $35, shown by the horizontal $d''d''$ line in Figure 8-2. At that price, MC equals price at point C, a point at which the price is actually less than the average cost of production. Would the firm want to keep producing even though it was incurring a loss?

Surprisingly, the correct answer is yes. The firm should *minimize its losses*, which is the same thing as maximizing profits. Because the firm's fixed costs are $55,000, producing at point C would result in a loss of only $20,000. Hence, continuing to operate would mean losing $20,000, whereas shutting down would involve losing $55,000. The firm should therefore continue to produce.

To understand this point, remember that a firm must still cover its contractual commitments even when it produces nothing. In the short run, the firm must pay fixed costs such as interest to the bank, rentals on the shoe factory, patent royalties to Fabiola, and directors' salaries. The balance of the firm's costs are variable costs, such as those for materials, production workers, and fuel. It will be advantageous to continue operations, with $P = MC$, as long as revenue minus variable costs covers some part of these fixed costs.

The critically low market price at which revenues just equal variable costs (or, equivalently, at which losses exactly equal fixed costs) is called the **shutdown point.** For prices above the shutdown point, the firm will produce along its marginal cost curve because, even though the firm might be losing money, it would lose more money by shutting down. For prices below the shutdown point, the firm will produce nothing at all because by shutting down the firm will lose only its fixed costs. This gives the shutdown rule:

Shutdown rule: The shutdown point comes where revenues just cover variable costs or where losses are equal to fixed costs. When the price falls below the level where revenues are equal to variable costs, the firm will minimize its losses by shutting down.

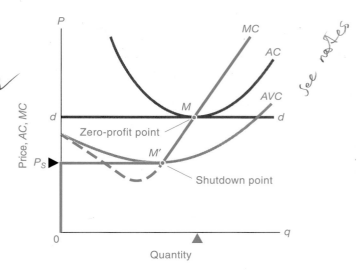

Zero-Profit and Shutdown Prices

FIGURE 8-3. Firm's Supply Curve Travels Down the MC Curve to the Shutdown Point

The firm's supply curve corresponds to its MC curve as long as revenues exceed variable costs. Once price falls below P_S, the shutdown point, losses are greater than fixed costs, and the firm shuts down. Hence the solid rust-colored curve is the firm's supply curve.

Explain why the firm has positive, zero, and negative profits for price above, at, and below the price of the dd curve.

Figure 8-3 shows the shutdown and zero-profit points for a firm. The zero-profit point comes where price is equal to AC, while the shutdown level of output comes where price is equal to AVC. Therefore, the firm's supply curve is the solid rust line in Figure 8-3. It goes up the vertical axis to the price corresponding to the shutdown point; jumps to the shutdown point at M', where P equals the level of AVC; and then continues up the MC curve for prices above the shutdown price.

The analysis of shutdown conditions leads to the surprising conclusion that profit-maximizing firms may in the short run continue to operate even though they are losing money. This condition will hold particularly for firms that are heavily indebted and therefore have high fixed costs (the airlines being a good example). For these firms, as long as losses are less than fixed costs, profits are maximized and losses are minimized when they pay the fixed costs and still continue to operate.

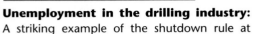

Unemployment in the drilling industry: A striking example of the shutdown rule at work is seen in the oil industry. In 1985, when the price of crude oil was $27 a barrel, there were about 35,000 oil wells drilled in the United States. But by the next year, the number of wells being drilled had fallen to less than 19,000, a drop of almost half. Had the oil fields run dry?

Hardly. Rather, what happened was that the average price of oil fell dramatically, to only $14 a barrel. It was the profits, not the wells, that dried up. As a result, the companies just shut the drilling rigs down. This works in reverse, as well. During the Persian Gulf war in 1990, the price of oil skyrocketed and drilling activity increased as drilling became more profitable.

B. SUPPLY BEHAVIOR IN COMPETITIVE INDUSTRIES

Our discussion up to now has concerned only the individual firm. But a competitive market comprises many firms, and we are interested in the behavior of all firms together, not just a single firm. How can we move from the one to the many? From Fabiola's to the entire shoe industry?

SUMMING ALL FIRMS' SUPPLY CURVES TO GET MARKET SUPPLY

Suppose we are dealing with a competitive market for shoes. At a given price, firm A will bring so many shoes to market, firm B will bring another quantity, and so on for firms C, D, etc. In each case, the quantity supplied will be determined by each firm's marginal costs. The *total* quantity brought to market at a given price will be the *sum* of the individual quantities that firms supply at that price.[1]

This reasoning leads to the following relationship between individual and market supplies:

To get the market supply curve for a good, we must add horizontally the supply curves of all the individual producers of that good.

Figure 8-4 illustrates this for two firms. To get the industry's supply curve SS, add horizontally, at the same price, all firms' supply curves ss. At a price of $40, firm A will supply 4000 units while firm B will supply 11,000 units. Therefore, the industry supply curve, shown in Figure 8-4(*c*), adds the two supplies together and finds total industry supply of 15,000 units at a price of $40. If there are 2 million rather than 2 firms, we would still derive industry output by adding all the 2 million individual-firm quantities at the going price. Horizontal addition of output at each price gives us the industry supply curve.

SHORT-RUN AND LONG-RUN EQUILIBRIUM

At the turn of the century, Cambridge University's great economist Alfred Marshall helped forge the supply-and-demand tools we use today. He noticed that in the short run, demand shifts produce greater price adjustments and smaller quantity adjustments than they do in the long run. We can understand this observation by distinguishing two time periods for market equilibrium that correspond to different cost categories: (1) *short-run* equilibrium, when any increase or decrease in output must use the same fixed amount of plant and equipment, and (2) *long-run* equilibrium, when all factors are variable, so firms can abandon old plants or build new ones and firms can enter or exit the industry.

Let's illustrate this distinction with an example. Consider the market for fresh fish, supplied by a local fishing fleet. Suppose the demand for fish increases; this case is shown in Figure 8-5(*a*) on page 144 as a shift from DD to D'D'. With higher prices, fishing captains will want to increase their catch. In the short run, they cannot build new boats, but they can hire extra

---

[1] Recall that the DD market demand curve is similarly obtained by horizontal summation of individual dd demand curves.

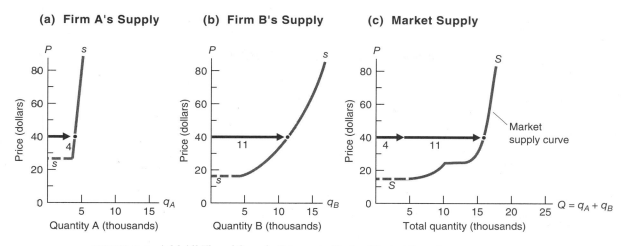

FIGURE 8-4. Add All Firms' Supply Curves to Derive Market Supply
The diagrams show how the market supply curve (*SS*) is composed of two individual supply curves (*ss*). We horizontally add quantities supplied by each firm at \$40 to get total market supply at \$40. This applies at each price and to any number of firms. If there are 1000 firms identical to firm A, the market supply curve would look like firm A's supply curve with a thousandfold change of horizontal scale.

crews and work longer hours. Increased inputs of variable factors will produce a greater quantity of fish along the *short-run supply curve* S_SS_S, shown in Figure 8-5(*a*). The short-run supply curve intersects the new demand curve at *E'*, the point of short-run equilibrium.

In the long run, the higher prices coax out more shipbuilding, attract more sailors into the industry, and induce new firms to enter the industry. This gives us the *long-run supply curve* S_LS_L in Figure 8-5(*b*) and the long-run equilibrium at *E"*. The intersection of the long-run supply curve with the new demand curve yields the long-run equilibrium attained when all economic conditions (including the number of ships, shipyards, and firms) have adjusted to the new level of demand.

The Long Run
for a Competitive Industry

Our analysis of zero-profit conditions showed that firms might stay in business for a time even though they are unprofitable. This situation is possible particularly for firms with high fixed capital costs. With this analysis we can understand why in business

downturns many of America's largest companies, such as General Motors, stayed in business even though they were losing billions of dollars.

Such losses raise a troubling question: Is it possible that capitalism is heading toward "euthanasia of the capitalists," a situation where increased competition produces chronic losses? For this question, we need to analyze the long-run shutdown conditions. We showed that firms shut down when they can no longer cover their variable costs. But in the long run, *all* costs are variable. A firm that is losing money can pay off its bonds, release its managers, and let its leases expire. In the long run, all commitments are once again options. Hence, in the long run firms will produce only when price is at or above the zero-profit condition where price equals average cost.

There is, then, a critical zero-profit point below which long-run price cannot remain if firms are to stay in business. In other words, long-run price must cover out-of-pocket costs such as labor, materials, equipment, taxes, and other expenses, along with opportunity costs such as competitive return on the owner's invested capital. That means long-run price must be equal to or above total long-run average cost.

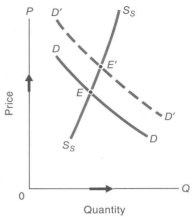
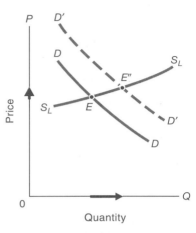

FIGURE 8-5. Effect of Increase in Demand on Price Varies in Different Time Periods
We distinguish between periods in which firms have time to make (**a**) adjustments of labor and variable factors (short-run equilibrium) and (**b**) full adjustment of all factors, fixed as well as varying (long-run equilibrium). The longer the time for adjustments, the greater the elasticity of supply response and the less the rise in price.

What happens if the long-run price falls below this critical zero-profit level? Firms, not making a profit, will start leaving the industry. The market supply curve will shift to the left, and the price will rise (draw the graph for yourself). Eventually, the price will rise enough so that the industry is no longer unprofitable.

But the process works in the other direction, as well. Suppose that the long-run price is above total long-run average cost, so firms are making positive economic profits. Now suppose entry into the industry is absolutely free in the long run, so any number of identical firms can come into the industry and produce at exactly the same costs as those firms already in the industry. In this situation, new firms will be attracted by prospective profits, the supply curve shifts to the right, and price falls. Eventually it falls to the zero-profit level, so it is no longer profitable for other firms to enter the industry.

The conclusion is that in the long run, the price in an industry will tend toward the critical point where identical firms just cover their full competitive costs. Below this critical long-run price, firms would leave the industry until price returns to long-run average cost. Above this long-run price, new firms would enter the industry, thereby forcing market

price back down to the long-run equilibrium price where all competitive costs are just covered.

Zero-profit long-run equilibrium: When an industry is supplied by competitive firms with identical cost curves, and when firms can enter and leave the industry freely, the long-run equilibrium condition is that price equals marginal cost equals the minimum long-run average cost for each identical firm:

$P = MC =$ minimum long-run $AC =$ zero-profit price

This is the long-run *zero-economic-profit* condition.

Long-Run Industry Supply. What is the shape of the long-run supply curve for an industry? Suppose that an industry has free entry of identical firms. If the identical firms use general inputs, such as unskilled labor, that can be attracted from the vast ocean of other uses without affecting the prices of those general inputs, we get the case of constant costs shown by the horizontal $S_L S_L$ supply curve in Figure 8-6.

By contrast, suppose some of the inputs used in the industry are in relatively short supply—for example, fertile vineyard land for the wine industry or scarce beachfront properties for summer vacations. Then the supply curve for the wine or vacation industry must be upward-sloping, as shown by $S_L S_L'$ in Figure 8-6.

Why must the long-run supply curve of industries using scarce factors be rising? We must invoke the law of diminishing returns. For the case of the rare vineyard land, when firms apply increasing inputs of labor to fixed land, they receive smaller and smaller increments of wine-grape output; but each dose of labor costs the same in wages, so the MC of wine rises. This long-run rising MC means that the long-run supply curve must be rising.

What can we conclude about the long-run profitability of competitive capitalism? We have found that the forces of competition tend to push firms and industries toward a zero-profit long-run state. Those industries that are profitable tend to attract entry of new firms, thereby driving down prices and reducing profits toward zero. By contrast, those industries that are suffering losses tend to drive firms out as they seek industries with better profit opportunities. Prices and profits then tend to rise. *The long-run equilibrium in a competitive industry is therefore one with no economic profits.*

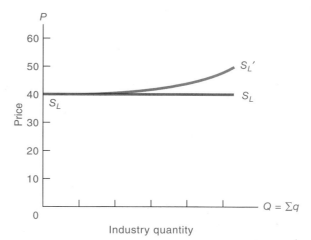

FIGURE 8-6. Long-Run Industry Supply Depends on Cost Conditions
With entry and exit free and any number of firms able to produce on identical, unchanged cost curves, the long-run $S_L S_L$ curve will be horizontal at each firm's minimum average cost or zero-profit price. If the industry uses a specific factor, such as scarce beachfront property, the long-run supply curve must slope upward like $S_L S_L'$ as higher production employs less well-suited inputs.

C. SPECIAL CASES OF COMPETITIVE MARKETS

We have now developed the basic apparatus of supply and demand. This section probes more deeply into supply-and-demand analysis. We first consider certain general propositions about competitive markets and then continue with some special cases.

GENERAL RULES

We analyzed above the impact of demand and supply shifts in competitive markets. These findings apply to virtually any competitive market, whether it is for codfish, brown coal, Douglas fir, Japanese yen, IBM stock, or petroleum. Are there any general rules? The propositions that follow investigate the impact of shifts in supply or demand upon the price and quantity bought and sold. Remember always that by a shift in demand or supply we mean a shift in the demand or supply curve or schedule, not a movement along the curve.

Demand rule: (*a*) Generally, an increase in demand for a commodity (the supply curve being unchanged) will raise the price of the commodity. (*b*) For most commodities, an increase in demand will also increase the quantity demanded. A decrease in demand will have the opposite effects.

Supply rule: An increase in supply of a commodity (the demand curve being constant) will generally lower the price and increase the quantity bought and sold. A decrease in supply has the opposite effect.

These two rules of supply and demand summarize the qualitative effects of shifts in supply and demand. But the quantitative effects on price and quantity depend upon the exact shapes of the supply and demand curves. In the cases that follow, we will see the response for a number of important cost and supply situations.

Constant Cost

Production of many manufacturing items, such as textiles, can be expanded by merely duplicating factories, machinery, and labor. Producing 200,000 shirts per day simply requires that we do the same thing as we did when we were manufacturing 100,000 per day, but on a doubled scale. In addition, assume that the textile industry uses land, labor, and other inputs in the same proportions as the rest of the economy.

In this case the long-run supply curve SS in Figure 8-7 is a horizontal line at the constant level of unit costs. A rise in demand from DD to $D'D'$ will shift the new intersection point to E', raising Q but leaving P the same.

Increasing Costs and Diminishing Returns

We noted in the last section cases where a product uses an input in limited supply, such as wine grapes that require a certain kind of soil and climate. Such sites are limited in number. The annual output of wine can be increased to some extent by adding more labor and fertilizer to each acre of land. But as we saw in Chapter 6, the law of diminishing returns will eventually operate if variable factors of production, such as labor and fertilizer, are added to fixed amounts of a factor such as land.

As a result of diminishing returns, the marginal cost of producing wine increases as wine production rises. Figure 8-8 shows the rising supply curve SS. How will price be affected by an increase in demand? The figure shows that higher demand will increase the price of this good even in the long run with identical firms and free entry and exit.

Fixed Supply and Economic Rent

Some goods or productive factors are completely fixed in amount, regardless of price. There is only one *Mona Lisa* by da Vinci. Nature's original endowment of land can be taken as fixed in amount. Raising the price offered for land cannot create an additional corner at 57th Street and Fifth Avenue in New York City. Raising the pay of star athletes is unlikely to change their effort. When the quantity supplied is constant at every price, the payment for the use of such a factor of production is called **rent** or **pure economic rent.**

When supply is independent of price, the supply curve is vertical in the relevant region. Land will continue to contribute to production no matter what its price. Figure 8-9 shows the case of land, for which a higher price cannot coax out any increase in output.

An increase in the demand for a fixed factor will affect only the price. Quantity supplied is

FIGURE 8-7. Constant-Cost Case

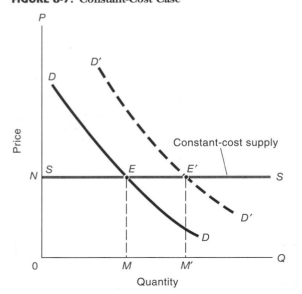

FIGURE 8-8. Increasing-Cost Case

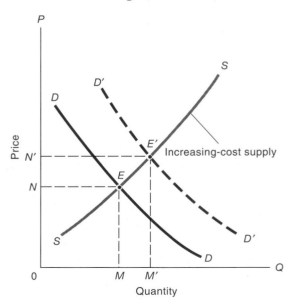

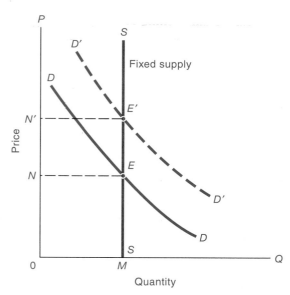

FIGURE 8-9. Factors with Fixed Supply Earn Rent

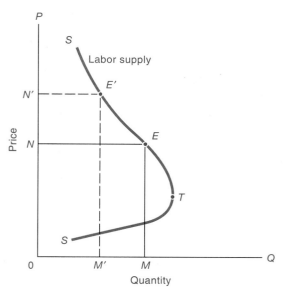

FIGURE 8-10. Backward-Bending Supply Curve

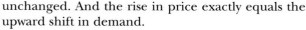

unchanged. And the rise in price exactly equals the upward shift in demand.

When a tax is placed upon the fixed commodity, the effect is that the price received by the supplier is reduced by exactly the amount of the tax. The tax is completely paid by (or "shifted" back to) the supplier (say, the landowner). The supplier absorbs the entire tax out of economic rent. The consumer buys exactly as much of the good or service as before and at no higher price.

Backward-Bending Supply Curve

Firms in poor countries noted that when they raised wages, the local workers often worked fewer hours. When the wage was doubled, instead of continuing to work 6 days a week, the workers might work 3 days and go fishing for the other 3 days. The same has been observed in high-income countries. As improved technology raises real wages, people feel that they want to take part of their higher earnings in the form of more leisure and early retirement. Chapter 5 described income and substitution effects, which explain why a supply curve might *bend backward*.

Figure 8-10 shows what a supply curve for labor might look like. At first the labor supplied rises as higher wages coax out more labor. But beyond point *T*, higher wages lead people to work fewer hours and to take more leisure. An increase in demand raises

the price of labor, as was stated in the demand rule at the beginning of this section. But note why we were cautious to add "for most commodities" to demand rule (*b*), for now the increase in demand decreases the quantity of labor supplied.

Verification of backward-bending supply can be found in many areas. One of the most interesting examples came when oil-rich countries curbed their production of oil after the price of oil quadrupled in the early 1970s.

Shifts in Supply

All the above discussions dealt with a shift in demand and no shift in supply. To analyze the supply rule, we must now shift supply, keeping demand constant. If the law of downward-sloping demand is valid, increased supply must decrease price and increase quantity demanded. You should draw your own supply and demand curves and verify the following quantitative corollaries of the supply rule:

(*c*) An increased supply will decrease *P* most when demand is inelastic.

(*d*) An increased supply will increase *Q* least when demand is inelastic.

What are commonsense reasons for these rules? Illustrate with cases of elastic demand for autos and of inelastic demand for electricity.

D. EFFICIENCY AND EQUITY OF COMPETITIVE MARKETS

EVALUATING THE MARKET MECHANISM

One of the remarkable features of the last decade has been the "rediscovery of the market." Many countries have abandoned the heavy-handed interventionism of government command and regulation for the subtle coordination of the invisible hand. Having reviewed the basic operation of competitive markets, let's ask how well they perform. Do they deserve high grades for satisfying people's economic needs? Is society getting many guns and much butter for a given amount of inputs? Or does the butter melt on the way to the store, while the guns have crooked barrels? We will give a preliminary answer to these questions at this point; a full answer must be postponed to Chapter 15, after we have analyzed factor markets.

The Concept of Efficiency

The answer to these questions lies in the concept of **allocative efficiency** (or **efficiency**, for short). An economy is efficient when it provides its consumers with the most desired set of goods and services, given the resources and technology of the economy.

Allocative efficiency (or **efficiency**) occurs when no possible reorganization of production can make anyone better off without making someone else worse off. Under conditions of allocative efficiency, one person's satisfaction or utility can be increased only by lowering someone else's utility.

We can think of the concept of efficiency intuitively in terms of the production-possibility frontier. An economy is clearly inefficient if it is inside the *PPF*. If we move out to the *PPF*, no one need suffer a decline in utility. At a minimum, an efficient economy is on its *PPF*. But efficiency goes further and requires not only that the right mix of goods be produced but also that these goods be allocated among consumers to maximize consumer satisfactions.

Efficiency of Competitive Equilibrium

One of the major results in all economics is that the allocation of resources by ideal competitive markets is efficient. This important result assumes that

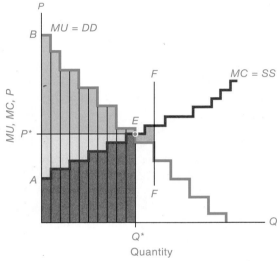

FIGURE 8-11. At Competitive Equilibrium Point E, the Marginal Costs and Utilities of Food Are Exactly Balanced
Many identical farmer-consumers bring their food to market. The upward-stepping $MC = SS$ curve adds together the marginal cost curves, while the downward-stepping $MU = DD$ curve represents the consumer valuation of food. At competitive market equilibrium E, the marginal gain from the last unit of food is exactly equal to the marginal labor cost required to produce the last unit of food at E.

The cost of producing food (the disutility of sweaty labor) is shown by the dark gray slices. Vertical rust-color slices under MU and above MC are the net economic gain from the competitive equilibrium at E. Note that no reorganization of production can attain a larger net gain of the rust-color area as compared to a competitive market. For example, the light gray area to the right of E shows the economic loss from producing too much food at FF.

all markets are perfectly competitive and that there are no externalities like pollution. However, even if the economy is efficient, this says nothing about the fairness of the distribution of income in competitive markets. In this section, we use a simplified example to illustrate the general principles underlying the efficiency of competitive markets.

Consider an idealized situation where all individuals are identical. Further assume: (*a*) Each person works at growing food. As people increase their work, and leisure hours are therefore curtailed, each additional hour of work becomes increasingly tiresome. (*b*) Each extra unit of food consumed brings diminished marginal utility (*MU*). (*c*) Because food production takes place on fixed plots of land, by the law of diminishing returns, each extra minute of work brings less and less extra food.

Figure 8-11 shows supply and demand for our simplified competitive economy. When we sum horizontally the identical supply curves of our identical farmers, we get the upward-stepping *MC* curve. As we saw earlier in this chapter, the *MC* curve is also the industry's supply curve, so the figure shows $MC = SS$. Also, the demand curve is the horizontal summation of the identical individuals' marginal utility (or demand-for-food) curves; it is represented by the downward-stepping $MU = DD$ curve for food in Figure 8-11.

The intersection of the *SS* and *DD* curves shows the competitive equilibrium for food. At point *E*, farmers supply exactly what consumers want to purchase at the equilibrium market price. Each person will be working up to the critical point where the declining marginal-utility-of-consuming-food curve intersects the rising marginal-cost-of-growing-food curve.

A careful analysis of this competitive equilibrium will show that it is efficient. At the competitive equilibrium at point *E* in Figure 8-11, the representative consumer will have higher utility than with any other feasible allocation of resources. This is so because at competitive equilibrium *E*, the marginal utility of the consumed good (*MU*) equals the price (*P*), which in turn equals the marginal cost of producing the good (*MC*). As the following three-step process shows, if $MU = P = MC$, then the allocation is efficient.

1. $P = MU$. Consumers choose food purchases up to the amount where $P = MU$. As a result, every person is gaining *P* utils of satisfaction from the last unit of food consumed.

2. $P = MC$. As producers, each person is supplying food up to the point where the price of food exactly equals the *MC* of the last unit of food supplied (the *MC* here being the cost in terms of the disutility of the sweaty labor needed to produce the last unit of food). The price then is the utils of satisfaction lost by working that last bit of time

needed to grow that last unit of food.

3. Putting these two equations together, we see that $MU = MC$. This means that the utils gained from the last unit of food consumed exactly equal the utils lost from the sweaty labor required to produce that last unit of food. *It is exactly this condition—that the marginal gain to society from the last unit consumed equals the marginal cost to society of that last unit produced—which guarantees that a competitive equilibrium is efficient.*

Equilibrium with Many Consumers and Markets

Let us now turn from our simple parable about identical farmer-consumers to an economy populated by millions of different firms, hundreds of millions of people, and countless commodities. Can a perfectly competitive economy still be efficient in this more complex world?

The answer is "yes," or better yet, "yes, if . . ." Efficiency requires some stringent conditions that are addressed in later chapters. These include having reasonably well-informed consumers, perfectly competitive producers, and no externalities like pollution or improved knowledge. For such economies, a system of perfectly competitive markets will earn the economist's gold star of allocational efficiency.

Figure 8-12 illustrates how a competitive system brings out a balance between utility and cost for a single commodity with nonidentical firms and consumers. On the left, we add horizontally the demand curves for all consumers to get the market curve *DD* in the middle. On the right, we add all the separate firms' *MC* curves to get the industry *SS* curve in the middle.

At the competitive equilibrium at point *E*, consumers on the left get the quantity they are willing to purchase of the good at the price reflecting efficient social *MC*. On the right, the equilibrium market price also allocates production efficiently among firms. The gray area under *SS* in the middle represents the minimized sum of gray cost areas on the right. Each firm is setting its output so that $MC = P$. Production efficiency is achieved because there is no reorganization of production that would allow the same level of industry output to be produced at lower cost.

Many Goods. Our economy produces not only food but also clothing, movies, vacations, and many other commodities. How does our analysis apply when consumers must choose among many products?

The principles are exactly the same, but now we recall one further condition: Utility-maximizing consumers spread their dollars among different goods until the marginal utility of the last dollar is equalized for each good consumed. In this case, as long as the ideal conditions are met, a competitive economy is efficient with a multitude of goods and factors of production.

In other words, a perfectly competitive economy is efficient when private and social costs and utilities coincide. Each industry must balance MC and MU. For example, if movies have 2 times the MC of hamburgers, the P and the MU of movies must also be twice those of hamburgers. Only then will the MUs, which are equal to the Ps, be equal to the MCs. By equating price and marginal cost, competition guarantees that an economy can attain allocative efficiency.

The perfectly competitive market is a device for synthesizing (*a*) the willingness of people possessing dollar votes to pay for goods as represented by demand with (*b*) the marginal costs of those goods as represented by firms' supply. Under certain conditions, competition guarantees efficiency, in which no consumer's utility can be raised without lowering another consumer's utility. This is true even in a world of many factors and products.

The Central Role of Marginal-Cost Pricing

This chapter has stressed the importance of competition and marginal cost in attaining an efficient allocation of resources. But the importance of marginal cost extends far beyond perfect competition. Using marginal cost to achieve production efficiency holds for any society or organization trying to make the most effective use of its resources—whether that entity is a capitalist or socialist economy, a profit-maximizing or nonprofit organization, a university or a church, or even a family.

FIGURE 8-12. Competitive Market Integrates Consumers' Demands and Producers' Costs

(**a**) Individual demands are shown on the left. We add the consumers' *dd* curves horizontally to obtain the market demand *DD* curve in the middle.

(**b**) The market brings together all consumer demands and firm supplies to reach market equilibrium at *E*. The horizontal price-of-food line shows where each consumer on the left and each producer on the right reach equilibrium. At *P**, see how each consumer's *MU* is equated to each firm's *MC*, leading to allocative efficiency.

(**c**) For each competitive firm, profits are maximized when the supply curve is given by the rising *MC* curve. The gray area depicts each firm's cost of producing the amount at *E*. At prices equal to marginal cost, the industry produces output at the least total cost.

(a) Consumers' Demands   **(b) Industry Output**   **(c) Firms' Supplies**

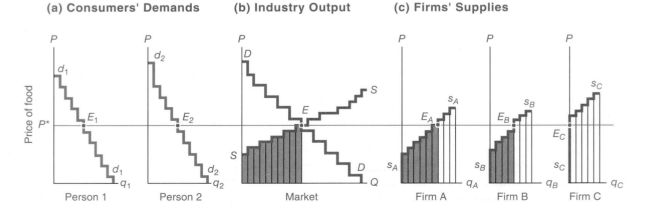

The essential role of marginal cost in a market economy is this: Only when prices are equal to marginal costs is the economy squeezing the maximum output and satisfaction from its scarce resources of land, labor, and capital.

Only when each firm has its own marginal cost equal to each other firm's *MC*—as will be the case when each *MC* has been set equal to a common price—will the industry be producing its total output at minimum total cost. Only when price is equal to marginal cost for all firms will society be on its production-possibility frontier.

The use of marginal cost as a benchmark for efficient resource allocation is applicable to all economic problems and not just to profit-maximizing firms. Say that you are convinced that "market socialism" should replace central planning in China. Your socialist firms will surely want to produce wheat efficiently. Efficiency requires that the marginal cost of wheat and all other goods be set by equating some kind of price with the marginal cost of production for each and every farm and firm.

Or suppose that you have been charged with solving a critical environmental problem, such as global warming or acid rain. You will soon find that marginal cost will be crucial to attaining your environmental objectives most efficiently. By ensuring that the marginal costs of reducing emissions or of cleaning the environment are equalized in every sector, you can guarantee that your environmental objectives are being reached at the lowest possible costs. Even noble goals should be efficiently attained in a world of scarcity.

Two Cheers for the Market, but Not Three

We have seen that markets have remarkable efficiency properties. But we cannot say that laissez-faire capitalism produces the greatest happiness of the greatest numbers. Nor does it necessarily result in the fairest possible use of resources. Why not? Because people are not equally endowed with purchasing power. Some are very poor through no fault of their own, while others are very rich through no virtue of their own. So the weighting of dollar votes, which lie behind the individual demand curves, may look unfair.

A system of prices and markets may be one in which a few people have most of the income and wealth. They may have inherited the society's scarce land or may own valuable patents and oil fields. The economy might be highly efficient, squeezing a great amount of guns and butter from its resources, but the rich few are eating the butter or feeding it to their poodles, while the guns are merely protecting the butter of the rich.

A society does not live on efficiency alone. Philosophers and the populace ask, Efficiency for what? And for whom? A society may choose to change a laissez-faire equilibrium to improve the equity or fairness of the distribution of income and wealth. The society may decide to sacrifice efficiency to improve equity. Is society satisfied with outcomes where the maximal amount of bread is produced? Or will modern democracies take loaves from the wealthy and pass them out to the poor?

There are no correct answers here. These are normative questions that are answered in the political arena by democratic voters or autocratic planners. Positive economics cannot say what steps governments should take to improve equity. But economics can offer some insights into the efficiency of different government policies that affect the distribution of income and consumption.

SUMMARY

A. Supply Behavior of the Competitive Firm

1. A perfectly competitive firm is one that can sell all the output it wants at the going market price. Competitive firms are assumed to maximize their profits. To maximize profits, the competitive firm will choose that output level at which price equals the marginal cost of production, i.e., $P = MC$. Diagrammatically, the competitive firm's equilibrium will come where the rising MC curve intersects its horizontal demand curve.

2. Variable costs must be taken into consideration in determining a firm's short-run shutdown point. Below the shutdown point, the firm loses more than its fixed

costs. It will therefore shut down and produce nothing when price falls below the shutdown price.

3. A competitive industry's long-run supply curve, $S_L S_L$, must take into account the entry of new firms and exodus of old ones. In the long run, all of a firm's commitments expire. It will stay in business only if price is at least as high as long-run average costs. These costs include out-of-pocket payments to labor, lenders, material suppliers, or landlords and opportunity costs, such as returns on the property assets owned by the firm.

B. Supply Behavior in Competitive Industries

4. Each firm's rising MC curve is its supply curve. To obtain the supply curve of a group of competitive firms, we add horizontally their separate supply curves. The supply curve of the industry hence represents the marginal cost curve for the competitive industry as a whole.

5. Because firms can adjust production over time, we distinguish two different time periods: (a) short-run equilibrium, when variable factors like labor change but fixed factors like capital and the number of firms do not change, and (b) long-run equilibrium, when the numbers of firms and plants, and all other conditions, adjust completely to the new demand conditions.

6. In the long run, when firms are free to enter and leave the industry, and where no one firm has any particular advantage of skill or location, competition will eliminate any excess profits earned by existing firms in the industry. So, just as free exit means price cannot fall below the zero-profit point, free entry means price cannot exceed long-run average cost in long-run equilibrium.

7. When an industry can expand by replication without pushing up the prices of its factors of production, the resulting long-run supply curve will be horizontal. When an industry uses factors specific to it, its long-run supply curve will slope upward.

C. Special Cases of Competitive Markets

8. Recall the general rules that apply to competitive supply and demand: Under the demand rule, an increase in the demand for a commodity (the supply curve being unchanged) will generally raise the price of the commodity and also increase the quantity demanded. A decrease in demand will have the opposite effects.

Under the supply rule, an increase in the supply of a commodity (the demand curve being constant) will generally lower the price and increase the quantity sold. A decrease in supply has the opposite effects.

9. Important special cases include constant and increasing costs, completely inelastic supply (which produces economic rents), and backward-bending supply. These special cases will explain many important phenomena found in markets.

D. Efficiency and Equity of Competitive Markets

10. The analysis of competitive markets sheds light on the efficient organization of a society. Allocative efficiency occurs when there is no way of reorganizing production and distribution such that everyone's satisfaction can be improved. Put differently, an economy is efficient when no individual can be made better off without making another individual worse off.

11. Under ideal conditions, a competitive economy attains allocative efficiency. Efficiency requires that all firms are perfect competitors and that there are no externalities like pollution or improved information. Efficiency comes because (a) when consumers maximize satisfaction, the marginal utility just equals the price; (b) when competitive producers supply goods, they choose output so that marginal cost just equals price; (c) Since $MU = P$ and $MC = P$, it follows that $MU = MC$. Thus the marginal social cost of producing a good under perfect competition just equals its marginal utility valuation.

12. The outcome of competitive markets, even when efficient, may not be socially desirable. Competitive markets by themselves will not necessarily ensure outcomes that correspond to the society's ideals about the fair distribution of income and consumption. Societies may modify the laissez-faire equilibrium to change the income distribution to correct for a perceived unfairness of dollar votes of demand.

CONCEPTS FOR REVIEW

Competitive Supply

$P = MC$ as maximum-profit condition
firm's ss supply curve and its MC curve
zero-profit condition, where
    $P = MC = AC$

shutdown point, where
    $P = MC = AVC$
summing individual ss curves to get
    industry SS
short-run and long-run equilibrium
long-run zero-profit condition

Efficiency and Equity

allocative efficiency
conditions for allocative efficiency:
    $MU = P = MC$
efficiency of competitive markets
efficiency vs. equity

QUESTIONS FOR DISCUSSION

1. Explain why each of the following statements about profit-maximizing competitive firms is incorrect. Restate each one correctly.
   a. A competitive firm will produce output up to the point where price equals average variable cost.
   b. A firm's shutdown point comes where price is less than minimum average cost.
   c. A firm's supply curve depends only on its marginal cost. Any other cost concept is irrelevant for supply decisions.
   d. The $P = MC$ rule for competitive industries holds for upward-sloping, horizontal, and downward-sloping MC curves.
   e. The competitive firm sets price equal to marginal cost.

2. Explain why a firm might supply goods at a loss.

3. One of the most important rules of economics, business, and life is the *sunk-cost principle*, "Let bygones be bygones." This means that sunk costs (which are bygone in the sense that they are unrecoverably lost) should be ignored when decisions are being made. Only future costs, involving marginal and variable costs, should count in making rational decisions.

   To see this, consider the following: We can calculate fixed costs in Table 8-1 as the cost level when output is 0. What are fixed costs? What is the profit-maximizing level of output for the firm in Table 8-1 if price is $40 while fixed costs are $0? $55,000? $100,000? $1,000,000,000? Minus $30,000? Explain the implication for a firm trying to decide whether to shut down.

4. Examine the cost data shown in Table 8-1. Calculate the supply decision of a profit-maximizing competitive firm when price is $21, $40, and $60. What would the level of total profit be for each of the three prices? What would happen to the exit or entry of identical firms in the long run at each of the three prices?

5. Using the cost data shown in Table 8-1, calculate the price elasticity of supply between $P = 40$ and $P = 40.02$ for the individual firm. Assume that there are 2000 identical firms, and construct a table showing the industry supply schedule. What is the industry price elasticity of supply between $P = 40$ and $P = 40.02$?

6. Examine Figure 8-12 to see that competitive firm C is not producing at all. Explain the reason why the profit-maximizing output level for firm C is at $q_C = 0$. What would happen to total industry cost of production if firm C produced 1 unit while firm B produced 1 less unit than the competitive output level?

   Say that firm C is a mom-and-pop grocery store. Why would chain grocery stores A and B drive C out of business? How do you feel about keeping C in business? What would be the economic impact of legislation that divided the market in three equal parts between the mom-and-pop store and chain stores A and B?

7. Often, consumer demand for a commodity will depend upon the use of durable goods, such as housing or transportation. In such a case, demand will show a time-varying pattern of response similar to that of supply. A good example is gasoline. In the short run the stock of automobiles is fixed, while in the long run consumers can buy new automobiles or bicycles.

   What is the relationship between the time period and the price elasticity of demand for gasoline? Sketch the short-run and long-run demand curves for gasoline. Show the impact of a decline in the supply of gasoline in both periods. Describe the impact of an oil shortage on the price of gasoline and the quantity demanded in both the long run and the short run. State two new rules of demand, (c) and (d), parallel to the rules of supply (c) and (d), that relate the impact of a shift in supply on price and quantity in the long run and the short run.

8. Interpret this dialogue:
   A: "How can competitive profits be zero in the long run? Who will work for nothing?"
   B: "It is only *excess* profits that are wiped out by competition. Managers get paid for their work; owners get a normal return on capital in competitive long-run equilibrium—no more, no less."

9. Consider three firms which are emitting sulfur into the California air. We will call supply the units of pollution control or reduction. Each firm has a cost-of-reduction schedule, and we will say that these schedules are given by the MC curves of firms A, B, and C in Figure 8-12.
   a. Interpret the "market" supply or MC schedule for reducing sulfur emissions, shown in the middle of Figure 8-12.
   b. Say that the pollution-control authority decides to seek 10 units of pollution control. What is the efficient allocation of pollution control across the three firms?
   c. Say that the pollution-control authority decides to have the first two firms produce 5 units each of pollution control. What is the additional cost?
   d. Say that the pollution authority decides upon a "pollution charge" to reduce pollution to 10 units. Can you identify what the appropriate charge would be using Figure 8-12? Can you say how each firm would respond? Would the pollution reduction be efficient?
   e. Explain the importance of marginal cost in the efficient reduction of pollution in this case.

CHAPTER 9
IMPERFECT COMPETITION AND
ITS POLAR CASE OF MONOPOLY

*The monopolists, by keeping the market constantly understocked,
. . . sell their commodities much above the natural price, and raise
their emoluments, whether they consist in wages or profit.*

Adam Smith, **The Wealth of Nations**

Perfectly competitive markets are the ideal in today's economy: much looked for, seldom found. When you buy your car from Ford or Toyota, your hamburgers from McDonald's or Wendy's, or your computer from IBM or Apple, you are dealing with firms large enough to affect the market price. Indeed, most markets in the economy are dominated by a handful of large firms, often only two or three. Welcome to the world you live in, the world of imperfect competition.

A. PATTERNS OF IMPERFECT COMPETITION

In this chapter and the next one we study the major kinds of imperfect competition—monopoly, oligopoly, and monopolistic competition. We shall see that for a given technology, prices are higher and outputs are lower under imperfect competition than under perfect competition. But imperfect competitors have virtues along with these vices, however. Large firms exploit economies of large-scale production and are responsible for much of the innovation that propels long-term economic growth. If you understand how imperfectly competitive markets work, you will have a much deeper understanding of modern industrial economies.

Reminder on the meaning of perfect competition: Recall that a perfectly competitive market is one in which every firm is too small to affect the market price. That means no matter how much a firm produces, it can sell its entire production at the going market price. A perfect competitor therefore has no reason to undercut the market price. Moreover, it will not raise its price above the market price, because then the firm will sell nothing—consumers would rather buy from its lower-priced competitors.

By the strict definition, few markets in the U.S. economy are perfectly competitive. Think of the following: aircraft, aluminum, automobiles, batteries, breakfast cereals, chewing gum, cigarettes, electricity, refrigerators, and wheat. How many of these are sold in perfectly competitive markets? Certainly not aircraft, aluminum, or automobiles. Until World War II there was only one aluminum company, Alcoa. Even today, the four largest U.S. firms produce three-quarters of U.S. aluminum output. The world commercial aircraft market is dominated by only two firms, Boeing and Airbus. In the automotive industry, too, the top five automakers (including Toyota and Honda) have almost 80 percent of the U.S. car and light-truck market.

What about batteries, breakfast cereals, chewing gum, cigarettes, and refrigerators? These markets are dominated even more completely by a relatively small number of companies. Nor does the market in electricity meet the definition of perfect competition. In most towns, a single company generates and markets all the electricity used by the populace. Very few of us will find it economical to own our own generator or windmill!

Looking at the list above, you will find that only wheat falls within our strict definition of perfect competition. All the other goods, from autos to cigarettes, fail the competitive test for a simple reason: Some of the firms in the industry can affect the market price by changing the quantity they sell. To put it another way, they have some control over the price of their output.

Definition of Imperfect Competition

If a firm can appreciably affect the market price of its output, the firm is classified as an "imperfect competitor."

Imperfect competition prevails in an industry whenever individual sellers have some measure of control over the price of their output.

Imperfect competition does not imply that a firm has absolute control over the price of its product. Take the cola market, where Coca-Cola and Pepsi together have the major share of the market, and imperfect competition clearly prevails. If the average price of other producers' sodas in the market is 75 cents, Pepsi may be able to set the price of a can at 70 or 80 cents and still remain a viable firm. The firm could hardly set the price at $40 or 5 cents a can

because at those prices it would go out of business. We see, then, that an imperfect competitor has some but not complete discretion over its prices.

Moreover, the amount of discretion over price will differ from industry to industry. In some imperfectly competitive industries, the degree of monopoly power is very small. In the retail computer business, for example, more than a few percent difference in price will usually have a significant effect upon a firm's sales. In the monopolistic electricity distribution business, on the other hand, changes of 10 percent or more in the price of electricity will have only a small effect on a firm's sales in the short run.

It is important to recognize that imperfect competition does not preclude intense rivalry in the marketplace. Imperfect competitors often struggle vigorously to increase their market shares. Still, intense rivalry should be distinguished from perfect competition. Rivalry encompasses a wide variety of behavior, from advertising that attempts to shift out the demand curve to improving product quality. Perfect competition says nothing about rivalry but simply denotes that no single firm in the industry can affect the market price.

Graphical Depiction. Figure 9-1 on page 156, shows graphically the difference between perfect and imperfect competition. Figure 9-1(*a*) reminds us that a perfect competitor faces a horizontal demand curve, indicating that it can sell all it wants at the going market price. An imperfect competitor, in contrast, faces a downward-sloping demand curve. Figure 9-1(*b*) shows that if an imperfectly competitive firm increases its sales, it will definitely depress the market price of its output as it moves down its *dd* demand curve.

We can also see the difference between perfect and imperfect competition in terms of price elasticity. *For a perfect competitor, demand is perfectly elastic; for an imperfect competitor, demand has a finite elasticity.* A careful measurement will show that the price elasticity is around 2 at point *B* in Figure 9-1(*b*).

VARIETIES OF IMPERFECT COMPETITORS

A modern industrial economy like the United States is a jungle populated with many species of imperfect

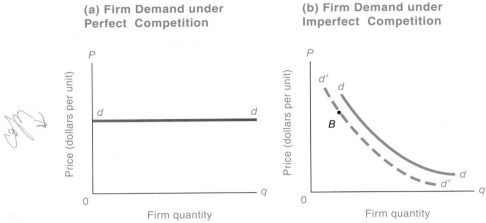

FIGURE 9-1. Acid Test for Imperfect Competition Is Downward Tilt of Firm's Demand Curve

(**a**) The perfectly competitive firm can sell all it wants along its horizontal *dd* curve without depressing the market price. (**b**) But the imperfect competitor will find that its demand curve slopes downward as higher price drives sales down. And unless it is a sheltered monopolist, a cut in its rivals' prices will appreciably shift its own demand curve leftward to *d'd'*.

competition. The dynamics of the personal computer industry, driven by rapid improvements in technology, are different from the patterns of competition in the not-so-lively funeral industry. Nevertheless, much can be learned about an industry by paying careful attention to its market structure, particularly the number and size of sellers and how much of the market the largest sellers control. Economists classify imperfectly competitive markets into three different market structures.

Monopoly

How imperfect can imperfect competition get? The most extreme case is **monopoly:** a single seller with complete control over an industry. (It is called a "monopolist," from the Greek words *mono* for "one" and *polist* for "seller.") It is the only firm producing in its industry, and there is no industry producing a close substitute.

True monopolies are rare today. Indeed, they typically exist only with some form of government protection. For example, a pharmaceutical company which discovers a new wonder drug will be granted a patent, which gives it monopoly control over that drug for a number of years. Another important

example of monopoly is a franchised local utility, such as a firm that provides your electricity or water. In such cases there is truly a single seller of a service with no close substitutes. But in today's highly competitive economy, even protected monopolists must reckon with competition. The pharmaceutical company will find that a rival will produce a similar drug; telephone companies that were monopolists a decade ago now must reckon with cellular telephones. *In the long run, no monopolist is completely secure from attack by competitors.*

Oligopoly

The term **oligopoly** means "few sellers." Few, in this context, can be a number as small as 2 or as large as 10 or 15 firms. The important feature of oligopoly is that each individual firm can affect the market price. In the airline industry, the decision of a single airline to lower fares can set off a price war which brings down the fares charged by all its competitors.

Oligopolistic industries are relatively common in the U.S. economy, especially in the manufacturing, transportation, and communications sectors. For example, there are only a few car makers, even though the automobile industry sells many different models. The same is true in the market for house-hold appliances: stores are filled with many different models of refrigerators and dishwashers, all made by a handful of companies. You might be surprised to know that the breakfast cereal industry is an oligopoly dominated by a few firms even though there seem to be endless varieties of cereals.

Competition vs. rivalry: When studying oligopolies, it is important to remember that imperfect competition is not the same as no competition. In many oligopolistic industries, competition is very brisk. Indeed, some of the most vigorous rivalries in the economy are in markets where there are but a few rival firms. Just look at the cutthroat competition in the airline industry, where often only two or three airlines will fly a particular route, but they still engage in periodic fare wars.

Monopolistic Competition

The last category of imperfect competition is **monopolistic competition;** this occurs when a large number of sellers produce differentiated products. This market structure resembles perfect competition in that there are many sellers, none of whom have a large share of the market. It differs from perfect competition in that the products sold by different firms are not identical. **Differentiated products** are ones whose important characteristics vary; for example, for automobiles, important characteristics include size, performance, fuel economy, and safety. Because companies sell slightly different products, they can sell at slightly different prices.

The classic case of monopolistic competition is the retail gasoline market. You may go to the local Exxon station, even though it charges slightly more, because it is on your way to work. But if the price at Exxon rises more than a few pennies above the competition, you might switch to the Mobil station a short distance away.

Indeed, this example illustrates that one important source of product differentiation comes from location. It takes time to go to the bank or the grocery store, and the amount of time needed to reach different stores will affect our shopping choices. In economic language, the total opportunity cost of goods (including the cost of time) will depend upon how far we live from a store. Because the opportunity cost of local shops is lower, people generally tend to shop in nearby locations. This consideration also explains why large shopping complexes are so popular: they allow people to buy a wide variety of goods while economizing on shopping time. The product differentiation that comes from different locations is an important reason why these tend to be monopolistically competitive markets.

Product quality is an increasingly important part of product differentiation today. Goods differ in their characteristics as well as their prices. Most IBM-compatible personal computers these days can all run the same software, and there are many manufacturers. Yet the personal computer industry is a monopolistically competitive industry, because computers differ in speed, size, memory, repair services, and ancillaries like CD-ROMs, internal modems, and sound systems. Indeed, a whole batch of monopolistically competitive computer magazines is devoted to explaining the differences between the computers produced by the monopolistically competitive computer manufacturers!

Table 9-1 on page 158 gives a picture of the various possible categories of imperfect and perfect competition. This table is an important summary of the different kinds of market structure and warrants careful study.

Joan Robinson of Cambridge: Anyone who believes that economists are a dull lot never met Joan Robinson (1903–1983), who, along with Edward Chamberlin (1867–1967) of Harvard University, developed the theory of imperfect competition in the 1930s. Robinson, of Cambridge University, England, was justly renowned for taking controversial positions. She made her first mark in 1933 with the publication of *The Economics of Imperfect Competition*. This landmark book questioned the assumption of perfect competition that had dominated the economics profession and started economics down the road toward analysis of more realistic market structures.

Later, as one of the earliest and most visible proponents of Keynesian macroeconomics, Robinson engaged in heated disputes with several prominent American economists on the meaning of capital and the viability of capitalism. Toward the end of her career she increasingly worried about the instability of the capitalist system, the distribution of income, and the social value of capitalists. "Owning capital is not a productive activity," she wrote, adding: "It is clear enough that income from property is not the reward of waiting but the reward of employing a good stock broker." Did her iconoclastic views prevent her from being the first woman to win a Nobel Prize? Some believe so, but notwithstanding this slight she stands as one of the intellectual giants of twentieth-century economics.

SOURCES OF MARKET IMPERFECTIONS

Why do certain industries display near-perfect competition while others are dominated by a handful of large firms? Most cases of imperfect competition can be traced to two principal causes. First, industries tend to have fewer sellers when there are significant economies of large-scale production and decreasing costs. Under these conditions, large firms can simply produce more cheaply and then undersell small firms, which cannot survive.

Second, markets tend toward imperfect competition when there are "barriers to entry" that make it difficult for new competitors to enter an industry. In some cases, the barriers may arise from government laws or regulations which limit the number of competitors. In other cases, there may be reasons why it is simply too expensive for a new competitor to break into a market. We will examine both sources of imperfect competition.

Costs and Market Imperfection

The technology and cost structure of an industry help determine how many firms that industry can support and how big they will be. The key is whether there are economies of scale in an industry. If there are economies of scale, a firm can decrease its average costs by expanding its output, at least up to a point. That means bigger firms will have a cost advantage over smaller firms.

TABLE 9-1. Alternative Market Structures

Most industries are imperfectly competitive. Here are the major features of different market structures.

	Types of Market Structures			
Structure	Number of producers and degree of product differentiation	Part of economy where prevalent	Firm's degree of control over price	Methods of marketing
Perfect competition	Many producers; identical products	Financial markets and agricultural products	None	Market exchange or auction
Imperfect competition				
Monopolistic competition (many differentiated sellers)	Many producers; many real or perceived differences in product	Retail trade (pizzas, beer, . . .)	Some	Advertising and quality rivalry; administered prices
Oligopoly	Few producers; little or no difference in product	Steel, chemicals, . . .		
	Few producers; products are differentiated	Cars, cereals, . . .		
Monopoly	Single producer; product without close substitutes	Local electricity and water utilities ("natural monopolies")	Considerable, but usually regulated	Advertising and service promotion

Industry	(1) Share of U.S. output needed by a single firm to exploit economies of scale (%)	(2) Actual average market share of top three firms (%)	(3) Main reason for economies of large-scale operations
Beer brewing	10–14	13	Need to create a national brand image and to coordinate investment
Cigarettes	6–12	23	Advertising and image differentiation
Glass bottles	4–6	22	Need for central engineering and design staff
Cement	2	7	Need to spread risk and raise capital
Refrigerators	14–20	21	Marketing requirements and length of production runs
Petroleum	4–6	8	Spread risk on crude-oil ventures and coordinate investment

TABLE 9-2. Industrial Competition Is Based on Cost Conditions
A classic study examined different products to determine if cost conditions could lie behind existing concentration patterns. Column (1) shows the estimate of the point where the long-run average cost curve begins to turn up, as a share of industry output. Compare this with the average market share of each of the top three firms in column (2). [Source: F. M. Scherer, Alan Beckenstein, Erich Kaufer, and R. D. Murphy, *The Economics of Multi-Plant Operation: An International Comparisons Study* (Harvard University Press, Cambridge, Mass., 1975).]

What is the result? When economies of scale prevail, one or a few firms will expand their outputs to the point where they produce a significant part of the industry's total output. The industry then becomes imperfectly competitive. Perhaps a single monopolist will dominate the industry; a more likely outcome is that a few large sellers will control most of the industry's output; or there might be a large number of firms, each with slightly different products. Whatever the outcome, we must inevitably find some kind of imperfect competition instead of the atomistic perfect competition of price-taking firms.

Many industries enjoy increasing returns to scale. Numerous detailed econometric and engineering studies confirm that many nonagricultural industries show declining average long-run costs. For example, Table 9-2 shows the results of one study of six U.S. industries. It suggests that in many industries the point of minimum average cost occurs at a large fraction of industry output—10 or 20 or even 50 percent. These industries will tend to be oligopolistic, since they can support only a few large producers.

To understand further how costs may determine market structure, let's look at a case which is favorable for perfect competition. Figure 9-2(c) on page 160 shows an industry where the point of minimum average cost is reached at a relatively low level of output. Any firm which tries to expand its output beyond this point will find its costs rapidly rising. As a result, this industry can support the large number of efficiently operating firms that are needed for perfect competition. Figure 9-2(c) illustrates the cost curves in the perfectly competitive farm industry.

Now consider Figure 9-2(b), which shows an industry where firms enjoy increasing returns to scale up to a point, above which the scale economies are exhausted and average costs begin to increase. However, the *AC* curve does not turn up soon enough to avoid the breakdown of perfect competition: the industry total demand curve *DD* is only big enough to enable a relatively small number of firms to coexist at the point of minimum average cost. Such a cost structure will tend to lead to oligopoly. Most manufacturing industries in the United States—including steel, automobiles, cement, and oil—have a demand and cost structure similar to the one in Figure 9-2(b).

Finally, look at Figure 9-2(a), which illustrates the extreme case of *natural monopoly*. In Figure 9-2(a), the firm is shown to have average and marginal

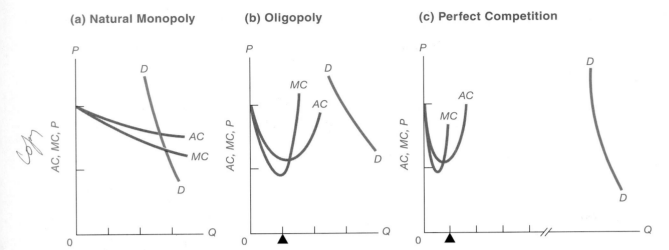

FIGURE 9-2. Market Structure Depends on Relative Cost and Demand Factors

Cost and demand conditions affect market structures. In perfectly competitive (**c**), total industry demand *DD* is so vast relative to the efficient scale of a single seller that the market allows viable coexistence of numerous perfect competitors. In (**b**), costs turn up at a higher level of output relative to total industry demand *DD*. Coexistence of numerous perfect competitors is impossible, and oligopoly will emerge. When costs fall rapidly and indefinitely, as in the case of natural monopoly in (**a**), one firm can expand to monopolize the industry.

costs that fall forever. It displays perpetual increasing returns to scale. As output grows, the firm can charge lower and lower prices and still make a profit, since its average cost is falling. So peaceful competitive coexistence of thousands of perfect competitors will be quite impossible because one large firm is so much more efficient than small firms.

A few years ago, economists believed that many industries were natural monopolies. Utilities such as telephone, electricity, water, and natural gas were regarded as natural monopolies because they have high fixed costs and a relatively low cost of providing an additional phone call or an additional kilowatt-hour of electricity. Recent technological advances, however, weaken the argument that these industries are natural monopolies. Most of the U.S. population is now served by two cellular telephone networks, which use radio waves instead of wires. Similar trends in other industries are breaking down the impediment to entry in these industries.

Barriers to Entry

Although cost differences are the most important factor behind market structures, barriers to entry can also increase concentration. **Barriers to** entry are factors that make it hard for new firms to enter an industry. When barriers are high, an industry may have few firms and limited pressure to compete. Economies of scale act as one common type of barrier to entry, but there are others, including legal restrictions, high cost of entry, advertising, and product differentiation.

Legal Restrictions. Governments sometimes restrict competition in certain industries. Important legal restrictions include patents, entry restrictions, and foreign-trade tariffs and quotas. A *patent* is granted to an inventor to allow temporary exclusive use (or monopoly) of the product or process that is patented. For example, pharmaceutical companies are often granted valuable patents on new drugs in which they have invested hundreds of millions of dollars. Governments grant patent monopolies to encourage inventive activity. Without the prospect of patent protection, a company or a sole inventor might be unwilling to devote time and resources to research and development.

Governments also impose *entry restrictions* on many industries. Typically, utilities, such as telephone, electricity, and water, are given *franchise monopolies* to serve an area. In these cases, the firm gets an exclusive right to provide a service, and in return the firm agrees to limit its profits and provide universal service in the area even when some customers might be unprofitable.

Finally, governments can impose *import restrictions*, which have the effect of keeping out foreign competitors. It could very well be that a single country's market for a product is only big enough to support two or three firms in an industry, while the world market is big enough to support a large number of firms. Then a protectionist policy might change the industry structure from Figure 9-2(*c*) to (*b*) or even to (*a*). When markets are broadened by abolishing tariffs in a large free-trade area, vigorous and effective competition is encouraged and monopolies tend to lose their power. One of the most dramatic examples of increased competition has come in the European Union, which has lowered tariffs among member countries steadily over the last three decades and has benefited from larger markets for firms and lower concentration of industry.

High Cost of Entry. In addition to legally imposed barriers to entry, there are economic barriers as well. In some industries the price of entry simply may be very high. Take the commercial aircraft industry, for example. The high cost of designing and testing new airplanes serves to discourage potential entrants into the market. It is likely that only two companies—Boeing and Airbus—can afford the $10 to $15 billion that the next generation of aircraft will cost to develop.

In addition, companies build up intangible forms of investment, and such investments might be very expensive for any potential new entrant to match. Consider the software industry. Once a spreadsheet program (like Lotus 1-2-3) or a word-processing program (like Microsoft Word) has achieved wide acceptability, potential competitors find it difficult to make inroads into the market. Users, having learned one program, are reluctant to switch to another. Consequently, in order to get people to try a new program, any potential entrant will need to run a big promotional campaign, which is expensive and may still result in the failure to produce a profitable product.

Advertising and Product Differentiation. Sometimes it is possible for companies to create barriers to entry for potential rivals by using advertising and product differentiation. Advertising can create product awareness and loyalty to well-known brands. For example, Pepsi and Coca-Cola spend together hundreds of millions of dollars per year advertising their brands, which makes it very expensive for any potential rivals to enter the cola market.

In addition, product differentiation can impose a barrier to entry and increase the market power of producers. In many industries—such as breakfast cereals, automobiles, household appliances, and cigarettes—it is common for a small number of manufacturers to produce a vast array of different brands, models, and products. In part, the variety appeals to the widest range of consumers. But the enormous number of differentiated products also serves to discourage potential competitors. The demands for each of the individual differentiated products will be so small that they will not be able to support a large number of firms operating at the bottom of their U-shaped cost curves. The result is that perfect competition's *DD* curve in Figure 9-2(*c*) contracts so far to the left that it becomes like the demand curves of monopoly and oligopoly shown in Figure 9-2(*a*) and (*b*). Hence, *differentiation, like tariffs, produces greater concentration and more imperfect competition.*

B. MARGINAL REVENUE AND MONOPOLY

In this section we will consider the most extreme form of imperfect competition, monopoly. Our analysis will illustrate the major drawbacks of imperfect competition, which are that it restricts output and raises prices. As an essential part of this analysis, we will define a new concept, marginal revenue,

		Total and Marginal Revenue	
(1) Quantity q	(2) Price $P = AR = TR/q$ ($)	(3) Total revenue $TR = P \times q$ ($)	(4) Marginal revenue MR ($)
0	200	0	+200
			+180
1	180	180	+160
			+140
2	160	320	+120
			+100
3	140	420	+80
			+60
4	120	480	+40
			+20
5	100	500	0
			−20
6	80	480	−40
			−60
7	60	420	−80
			−100
8	40	320	−120
			−140
9	20	180	−160
			−180
10	0	0	

TABLE 9-3. Marginal Revenue Is Derived from Demand Schedule
Total revenue (TR) in column (3) comes from multiplying P by q. To get marginal revenue (MR), we increase q by a unit and calculate the change in total revenue. MR is less than P because of the lost revenue from lowering the price on previous units to sell another unit of q. Note that MR is at first positive when demand is elastic. But after demand turns inelastic, MR becomes negative even though price is still positive.

which will turn out to have important applications for oligopolists and perfect competitors as well.

THE CONCEPT OF MARGINAL REVENUE

Price, Quantity, and Total Revenue

Suppose that a firm finds itself in possession of a complete monopoly in its industry. The firm might be the fortunate owner of a patent for a new anticancer drug, or it might have an exclusive franchise to sell electricity in a region. If the monopolist wishes to maximize its profits, <u>what price should it charge and what output level should it produce?</u>

To answer these questions, we need a new concept, marginal revenue (or MR). From the firm's demand curve, we know the relationship between price (P) and quantity sold (q). These are shown in columns (1) and (2) of Table 9-3 and as the black demand curve (dd) for the monopolist in Figure 9-3(a).

We next calculate the total revenue at each sales level by multiplying price times quantity. Column (3) of Table 9-3 shows how to calculate the **total revenue** (TR), which is simply P times q. Thus 0 units bring in TR of 0; 1 unit brings in $TR = \$180 \times 1 = \$180$; 2 units bring in $\$160 \times 2 = \$320$; and so forth.

In this example of a straight-line or linear demand curve, total revenue at first rises with output, since the reduction in P needed to sell the extra q is moderate in this upper, elastic range of the demand curve. But when we reach the midpoint of the straight-line demand curve, TR reaches its maximum. This comes at $q = 5$, $P = \$100$, with $TR = \$500$. Increasing q beyond this point brings the firm into the inelastic demand region. For inelastic demand, a 1 percent price cut produces less than a 1 percent sales increase, so total revenue falls as price is cut. Figure 9-3(*b*) shows TR to be dome-shaped, rising from zero at a very high price to a maximum of $500 and then falling to zero as price approaches zero.

How could you find <u>the price at which revenues are maximized?</u> You would see in Table 9-3 that TR is maximized when $q = 5$ and $P = 100$. <u>This is the point where the demand elasticity is exactly 1.</u>

Note that the price per unit can be called average revenue (AR) to distinguish it from total revenue. Hence, we get $P = AR$ by dividing TR by q (just as we earlier got AC by dividing TC by q). Verify that if column (3) had been written down before column (2), we could have filled in column (2) by division.

Marginal Revenue and Price

The final new concept is marginal revenue.

<u>Marginal revenue</u> (MR) is the change in revenue that is generated by an additional unit of sales. MR can be either positive or negative.

Table 9-3 shows marginal revenue in column (4). MR is calculated by subtracting the total revenues of adjacent outputs. When we subtract the TR we get by selling q units from the TR we get by selling $q + 1$ units, the difference is extra revenue or MR. Thus, from $q = 0$ to $q = 1$, we get $MR = \$180 - \$0$. From $q = 1$ to $q = 2$, MR is $\$320 - \$180 = \$140$.

FIGURE 9-3. Marginal Revenue Curve Comes from Demand Curve

(**a**) The rust-colored steps show the increments of total revenue from each extra unit of output. MR falls below P from the beginning. MR becomes negative when dd turns inelastic. Smoothing the incremental steps of MR gives the smooth, thin rust-colored MR curve, which in the case of straight-line dd will always have twice as steep a slope as dd. (**b**) Total revenue is dome-shaped—rising from zero where $q = 0$, to a maximum (where dd has unitary elasticity) and then falling back to zero where $P = 0$. TR's slope gives smoothed MR just as jumps in TR give steps of incremental MR. (Source: Table 9-3.)

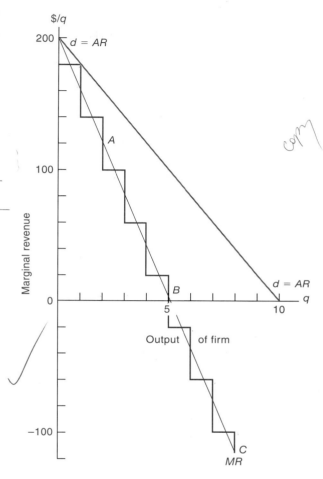

(a) Marginal Revenue

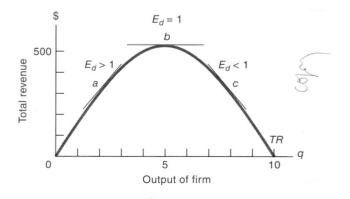

(b) Total Revenue

MR is positive until we arrive at $q = 5$ and negative from then on. What does the strange notion of negative marginal revenue mean? That the firm is paying people to take its goods? Not at all. *Negative MR means that in order to sell additional units, the firm must decrease its price on earlier units so much that its total revenues decline.*

For example, when the firm sells 5 units, it gets

TR (5 units) = 5 × $100 = $500

Now say the firm wishes to sell an additional unit of output. Because it is an imperfect competitor, it can increase sales only by lowering price. So to sell 6 units, it lowers the price from $100 to $80. It gets $80 of revenue from the sixth unit, but it gets only 5 × $80 on the first 5 units, yielding:

$$TR \text{ (6 units)} = 5 \times \$80 + 1 \times \$80$$
$$= \$400 + \$80 = \$480$$

Marginal revenue between 5 and 6 units is $480 − $500 = −$20. The necessary price reduction on the first 5 units was so large that, even after adding in the sale of the sixth unit, total revenue fell. This is what happens when *MR* is negative. To test your understanding, fill in the blanks in columns (2) to (4).

Note that even though *MR* is negative, *AR* or price is still positive. Do not confuse marginal revenue with average revenue or price. Table 9-3 shows that they are different. In addition, Figure 9-3(*a*) plots the demand (*AR*) curve and the marginal revenue (*MR*) curve. Scrutinize Figure 9-3(*a*) to see that the plotted rust-colored steps of *MR* definitely lie below the black *dd* curve of *AR*. In fact, *MR* turns negative when *AR* is halfway down toward zero.

To summarize:

With demand sloping downward,

$P > MR$ (= P − reduced revenue on all previous q)

Elasticity and Marginal Revenue.

What is the relationship between the price elasticity of demand and marginal revenue?

Marginal revenue is positive when demand is elastic, zero when demand is unit-elastic, and negative when demand is inelastic.

This result is really a different way of stating the definition of elasticity that we used in Chapter 4. Recall that demand is elastic when a price decrease leads to a revenue increase. In such a situation, a price decrease raises output demanded so much that

revenues rise, so marginal revenue is positive. For example, in Table 9-3, as price falls in the elastic region from $P = \$180$ to $P = \$160$, output demanded rises sufficiently to raise total revenue, and marginal revenue is positive.

What happens when demand is unit-elastic? A price cut then just matches an increase in output, and marginal revenue is therefore zero. Can you see why marginal revenue is always negative in the inelastic range? Why is the marginal revenue for the perfect competitor's infinitely elastic demand curve always positive?

PROFIT-MAXIMIZING CONDITIONS

We are now ready to find the maximum-profit equilibrium of the monopolist. If a monopolist faces a given demand curve and wishes to maximize total profit (*TP*), what should it do? By definition, total profit equals total revenue minus total costs; in symbols, $TP = TR - TC = (P \times q) - TC$.

To maximize its profits, the firm must find the equilibrium price and quantity, P^* and q^*, that give the largest profit, or the largest difference between *TR* and *TC*. An important result is that *maximum profit will occur when output is at that level where the firm's marginal revenue is equal to its marginal cost.*

One way to determine this maximum-profit condition is by using a table of costs and revenues, such as Table 9-4. To find the profit-maximizing quantity and price, compute total profit in column (5). This column tells us that the monopolist's best quantity, which is 4 units, requires a price of $120 per unit. This produces a total revenue of $480, and, after subtracting total costs of $250, we calculate total profit to be $230. A glance shows that no other price-output combination has as high a level of total profit.

A second and equivalent way of arriving at the same answer is to compare marginal revenue, column (6), and marginal cost, column (7). As long as each additional unit of output provides more revenue than it costs—that is to say, as long as *MR* is greater than *MC*—the firm's profit will increase. So the firm should continue to increase its output as long as *MR* is greater than *MC*. By contrast, suppose that at a given level of output *MR* is less than *MC*. This means that increasing output would lead to a lower level of profits, so the profit-maximizing firm should at that point cut back on output. Clearly, the

Summary of Firm's Maximum Profit							
(1) Quantity q	(2) Price P ($)	(3) Total revenue TR ($)	(4) Total cost TC ($)	(5) Total profit TP ($)	(6) Marginal revenue MR ($)	(7) Marginal cost MC ($)	
0	200	0	145	−145	+200	34	
					+180	30	*MR > MC*
1	180	180	175	+5	+160	27	
					+140	25	
2	160	320	200	+120	+120	22	
					+100	20	
3	140	420	220	+200	+80	21	
					+60	30	
4*	120	480	250	+230	+40	40	*MR = MC*
					+20	50	
5	100	500	300	+200	0	60	
					−20	70	
6	80	480	370	+110	−40	80	
					−60	90	
7	60	420	460	−40	−80	100	
					−100	110	*MR < MC*
8	40	320	570	−250			

*Maximum-profit equilibrium.

TABLE 9-4. Equating Marginal Cost to Marginal Revenue Gives Firm's Maximum-Profit q and P
Total and marginal costs of production are now brought together with total and marginal revenues. The maximum-profit condition is where $MR = MC$, with $q^* = 4$, $P^* = \$120$, and maximum $TP = \$230 = (\$120 \times 4) - \$250$. (For convenience, the light MR and MC numbers are put in to give the smoothed values at each q point.)

best-profit point comes at the point where marginal revenue exactly equals marginal cost, as is shown by the data in Table 9-4. The rule for finding maximum profit is therefore:

The maximum-profit price and quantity of a monopolist come where the firm's marginal revenue equals its marginal cost:

$MR = MC$, at the maximum-profit P^* and q^*

These examples show the logic of the $MC = MR$ rule for maximizing profits, but we always want to understand the intuition behind the rules. Look for a moment at Table 9-4 and suppose that the monopolist is producing $q = 2$. At that point, its MR for producing 1 full additional unit is +$100, while its MC is $20. Thus, if it produced 1 additional unit, the firm would make additional profits of $MR - MC = \$100 - \$20 = \$80$. Indeed, column (5) of Table 9-4 shows that the extra profit gained by moving from 2 to 3 units is exactly $80.

Thus, when MR exceeds MC, additional profits can be made by increasing output; when MC exceeds MR, additional profits can be made by decreasing q. Only when $MR = MC$ can the firm maximize profits, because there are no additional profits to be made by changing its output level.

Monopoly Equilibrium in Graphs
Figure 9-4 on page 166 shows the monopoly equilibrium. Part (*a*) combines the firm's cost and revenue curves. The maximum-profit point comes at that output where MC equals MR, which is given at their intersection at E. The monopoly equilibrium, or maximum-profit point, is at an output of $q^* = 4$. To find the profit-maximizing price, we run vertically up from E to the DD curve at G, where $P = \$120$. The fact that average revenue at G lies above average cost at F guarantees a positive profit. The actual amount of profit is given by the rust shaded area in Figure 9-4(*a*).

(a) Profit Maximization

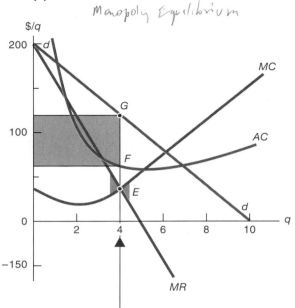

(b) Total Cost, Revenue, and Profit

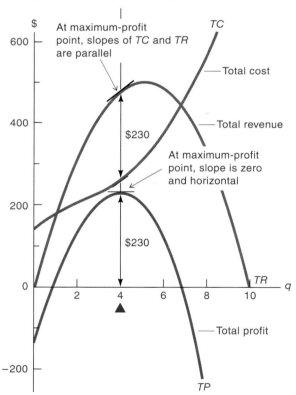

The same story is told in part (*b*) with curves of total revenue, cost, and profit. Total revenue is dome-shaped. Total cost is ever rising. The vertical difference between them is total profit, which begins negative and ends negative. In between, *TP* is positive, reaching its maximum of $230 at $q^* = 4$. At the maximum-profit output, the black slopes of *TR* and *TC* (which are *MR* and *MC* at those points) are parallel and therefore equal. If the slopes were pointing outward in a nonparallel fashion (as at $q = 2$), the firm would gain extra profit by expanding *q*. At $q^* = 4$, marginal cost and marginal revenue are balanced. At that point total profit (*TP*) reaches its maximum, as an additional unit adds exactly equal amounts to costs and revenues.

A monopolist will maximize its profits by setting output at the level where $MC = MR$. Because the monopolist has a downward-sloping demand curve, this means that $P > MR$. Because price is above marginal cost for a profit-maximizing monopolist, the monopolist reduces output below the level that would be found in a perfectly competitive industry.

Perfect Competition as a Polar Case of Imperfect Competition

Although we have applied the *MC* and *MR* rule to monopolists who desire to maximize profits, this rule is actually applicable far beyond the present analysis. A little thought shows that the $MC = MR$ rule applies with equal validity to a profit-maximizing perfect competitor. We can see this in two steps:

FIGURE 9-4. **Profit-Maximizing Equilibrium Can Be Shown Using Either Total or Marginal Curves**

(**a**) At *E*, where *MC* intersects *MR*, the equilibrium position of maximum profit is found. Any move from *E* will lose some profit. Price is at *G*, above *E*; and since *P* is above *AC*, the maximized profit is a positive profit. (Can you explain why the rust-colored shaded rectangle measures total profit? And why the gray triangles of shading on either side of *E* show the reduction in total profit that would come from a departure from $MR = MC$?) Panel (**b**) tells the same story of maximizing profit as does (**a**), but it uses total concepts rather than marginal concepts. Total profit (*TP*) is given by the vertical distance from *TC* up to *TR*. *TP* is at a maximum where its thin black slope is zero. At the maximum-profit point, the total revenue and total cost curves have equal and parallel slopes, $MR = MC$.

1. MR *for a perfect competitor.* The first question is, What is *MR* for a perfect competitor? For a perfect competitor, the sale of extra units will never depress price, and the "lost revenue on all previous *q*" is therefore equal to zero. Price and marginal revenue are identical for perfect competitors.

   Under perfect competition, price equals average revenue equals marginal revenue ($P = MR = AR$). A perfect competitor's *dd* curve and its *MR* curve coincide as horizontal lines.

2. $MR = P = MC$ *for a perfect competitor.* In addition, we can see that the logic of profit maximization for monopolists applies equally well to perfect competitors, but the result is a little different. Economic logic requires that profits are maximized at that output level where *MC* equals *MR*. But by step 1 above, for a perfect competitor, *MR* equals *P*. *Therefore,* the $MR = MC$ profit-maximization condition becomes the special case of $P = MC$ that we derived above for a perfect competitor:

   Because a perfect competitor can sell all it wants at the market price, $MR = P = MC$ at the maximum-profit level of output.

You can see this result visually by redrawing Figure 9-4(*a*). If the graph applied to a perfect competitor, the *DD* curve would be horizontal at the market price, and it would coincide with the *MR* curve. The profit-maximizing $MR = MC$ intersection would also come at $P = MC$. We see then how the general rule for profit maximization applies to perfect as well as imperfect competitors.

THE MARGINAL PRINCIPLE: LET BYGONES BE BYGONES

We close this chapter with a more general point about the use of marginal analysis in economics. While economic theory will not necessarily make you fabulously wealthy, it does introduce you to some new ways of thinking about costs and benefits. *One of the most important lessons of economics is that you should look at the marginal costs and marginal benefits of decisions and ignore past or sunk costs.* We might put this as follows:

Let bygones be bygones. Don't look backward. Don't cry over spilt milk or moan about yesterday's losses.

Make a hard-headed calculation of the extra costs you'll incur by any decision, and weigh these against its extra advantages. Make a decision based on marginal costs and marginal benefits.

This is the **marginal principle**, which means that people will maximize their incomes or profits or satisfactions by counting only the marginal costs and marginal benefits of a decision. There are countless situations in which the marginal principle applies. We have just seen that the marginal principle of equating marginal cost and marginal revenue is the rule for profit maximization by firms. Another example is investment decisions. When deciding about whether to invest in a company or sell a house, forget about past gains or losses and decide only on the basis of marginal returns and costs. The marginal principle is one of the central lessons of economics.

MONOPOLISTS OF THE GILDED AGE

Because abstract concepts like marginal cost and deadweight loss hide the human drama of monopoly, we close this section by recounting one of the most colorful periods of American business history. Because of changing laws and customs, monopolies in today's America bear little resemblance to the brilliant, inventive, unscrupulous, and often dishonest robber barons of the Gilded Age (1870–1914). Legendary figures like Rockefeller, Gould, Vanderbilt, Frick, Carnegie, Rothschild, and Morgan were driven by visions that created entire industries like railroads, oil, and steel, provided their finance, developed the western frontier, destroyed their competitors, and passed on fabulous fortunes to their heirs.

The robber barons of the last century were sometimes ingenious tricksters. Daniel Drew was a cattle rustler, horse trader, and railroader who mastered the trick of "watering the stock." This practice involved depriving his cattle of water until they reached the slaughterhouse; he then induced a great thirst with salt and allowed the beasts to engorge themselves on water just before being weighed. Later, tycoons would "water their stock" by inflating the value of their securities.

The railroaders of the American frontier west were among the most unscrupulous entrepreneurs on record. The transcontinental railroads were funded with vast federal land grants, aided by bribes and stock gifts to numerous members of Congress and the cabinet. Shortly after the Civil War, the wily railroader Jay Gould attempted to corner the entire gold supply of the United States, and with it the nation's money supply. Gould later promoted his railroad by describing the route of his northern railroad—snowbound much of the year—as a tropical paradise, filled with orange groves, banana plantations, and monkeys. By century's end, all the bribes, land grants, watered stock, and fantastic promises had led to the greatest rail system in the world.

The story of John D. Rockefeller epitomizes the nineteenth-century monopolist. Rockefeller saw visions of riches in the fledgling oil industry and began to organize oil refineries. He was a meticulous manager and sought to bring "order" to the quarrelsome wildcatters. He bought up competitors and consolidated his hold on the industry by persuading the railroads to give him deep and secret rebates and supply information about his competitors. When competitors stepped out of line, Rockefeller refused to ship their oil and even spilled it on the ground. By 1878, John D. controlled 95 percent of the pipelines and oil refineries in the United States. Prices were raised and stabilized, ruinous competition was ended, and monopoly was achieved.

Rockefeller devised an ingenious new device to ensure control over his alliance. This was the "trust," in which the stockholders turned their shares over to "trustees" who would then manage the industry to maximize its profits. Other industries imitated the Standard Oil Trust, and soon trusts were set up in kerosene, sugar, whiskey, lead, salt, and steel. This practice so upset agrarians and populists that the nation soon passed antitrust laws (see Chapter 17). Indeed, in 1910, the Standard Oil Corporation was dissolved in the first great victory by the Progressives against "Big Business."

Great monopolies produced great wealth. Whereas the United States had three millionaires in 1861, there were 4000 of them by 1900 ($1 million at the turn of the century was equivalent to about $100 million in today's dollars).

Great wealth in turn begot conspicuous consumption (a term introduced into economics by Thorstein Veblen in *The Theory of the Leisure Class,* 1899). Like European popes and aristocrats of an earlier era, American tycoons wanted to turn their fortunes into lasting monuments. The wealth was spent in constructing princely palaces such as the "Marble House," which can still be seen in Newport, Rhode Island; in buying vast art collections, which form the core of the great American museums like New York's Metropolitan Museum of Art; and in launching foundations and universities such as those named after Stanford, Carnegie, Mellon, and Rockefeller. Long after their private monopolies were broken up by the government or overtaken by competitors, and long after their wealth was largely dissipated by heirs and overshadowed by later generations of entrepreneurs, the philanthropic legacy of the robber barons continues to shape American arts, science, and education.

SUMMARY

A. Patterns of Imperfect Competition

1. Most market structures today fall somewhere on a spectrum between perfect competition and pure monopoly. Under imperfect competition, a firm has some control over its price, a fact seen as a downward-sloping demand curve for the firm's output.

2. Important kinds of market structure are (*a*) monopoly, where a single firm produces all the output in a given industry; (*b*) oligopoly, where a few sellers of a similar or differentiated product supply the industry; (*c*) monopolistic competition, where a large number of small firms supply related but somewhat differentiated products; and (*d*) perfect competition, where a large number of small firms supply an identical prod-

uct. In the first three cases, firms in the industry face downward-sloping demand curves.

3. Economies of scale, or decreasing average costs, are the major source of imperfect competition. When firms can lower costs by expanding their output, the situation tends to destroy perfect competition because a few companies can produce the industry's output most efficiently. When the minimum efficient size of plant is large relative to the national or regional market, cost conditions produce imperfect competition.

4. In addition to declining costs, other forces leading to imperfections are barriers to entry in the form of legal restrictions (such as patents or government regulation), high entry costs, advertising, and product differentiation.

B. Marginal Revenue and Monopoly

5. We can easily derive a firm's total revenue curve from its demand curve. From the schedule or curve of total revenue, we can then derive marginal revenue, which denotes the change in revenue resulting from an additional unit of sales. For the imperfect competitor, marginal revenue is less than price because of the lost revenue on all previous units of output that will result when the firm is forced to drop its price in order to sell an extra unit of output. That is, with demand sloping downward,

$$P = AR > MR = P - \text{lost revenue on all previous } q.$$

6. A monopolist will find its maximum-profit position where $MR = MC$, that is, where the last unit it sells brings in extra revenue just equal to its extra cost. This same $MR = MC$ result can be shown graphically by the intersection of the MR and MC curves or by the equality of the slopes of the total revenue and total cost curves. In any case, *marginal revenue = marginal cost* must always hold at the equilibrium position of maximum profit.

7. For perfect competitors, marginal revenue equals price. Therefore, the profit-maximizing output for a competitor comes where $MC = P$.

8. Economic reasoning leads to the important *marginal principle*. In making decisions, count marginal future advantages and disadvantages, and disregard sunk costs that have already been paid.

CONCEPTS FOR REVIEW

Patterns of Imperfect Competition

perfect vs. imperfect competition
monopoly, oligopoly, monopolistic
 competition
product differentiation

barriers to entry (government and
 economic)

Marginal Revenue and Monopoly

marginal (or extra) revenue, MR

$MR = MC$ as the condition for maximizing profits
$MR = P$, $P = MC$, for perfect competitor
natural monopoly
the marginal principle

QUESTIONS FOR DISCUSSION

1. List the distinguishing features of perfect and imperfect competition. What are the main varieties of imperfect competition? In which category would you place General Motors? Your local water company? Sears? Farmer Sam? Your college or university?

2. Explain why each of the following statements is false. For each, write the correct statement.
   a. A monopolist maximizes profits when $MC = P$.
   b. The higher the price elasticity, the higher is a monopolist's price above its MC.
   c. Monopolists ignore the marginal principle.
   d. Monopolists will maximize sales. They will therefore produce more than perfect competitors and their price will be lower.

3. What is MR's numerical value when dd has unitary elasticity? Explain.

4. Figure 9-4 shows the maximum-profit equilibrium position. Explain in detail how it really shows two different ways of describing exactly the same fact: namely, that a firm will stop expanding its production where the extra cost of further output just balances its extra revenue.

5. Redraw Figure 9-4(*a*) for a perfect competitor. Why is dd horizontal? Explain why the horizontal dd curve coincides with MR. Then proceed to find the profit-maximizing MR and MC intersection. Why does this yield the competitive condition $MC = P$? Now redraw Figure 9-4(*b*) for a perfect competitor. Show that the slopes of TR and TC must still match at the maximum-profit equilibrium point for a perfect competitor.

6. Banana Computer Company has fixed costs of production of $100,000, while each unit costs $600 of labor and $400 of materials and fuel. At a price of $3000, consumers would buy no Banana computers, but for each $10 reduction in price, sales of Banana computers increase by 1000 units. Calculate marginal cost and marginal revenue for Banana Computer, and determine its monopoly price and quantity.

7. Show that a profit-maximizing monopolist will never operate in the price-inelastic region of its demand curve.

8. Explain the error in the following statement: "A firm out to maximize its profits will always charge the highest price that the traffic will bear." State the correct result, and use the concept of marginal revenue to explain the difference between the correct and the erroneous statement.

CHAPTER 10
OLIGOPOLY AND MONOPOLISTIC COMPETITION

Putnam (Braniff): **Do you have a suggestion for me?**
Crandall (American): **Yes. I have a suggestion for you. Raise your [expletive deleted] fares 20% and I'll raise mine the next morning.**
Putnam: **Robert, we . . .**
Crandall: **You'll make more money and I will too.**
Putnam: **We can't talk about pricing.**
Crandall: **Oh [expletive deleted], Howard. We can talk about any [expletive deleted] thing we want to talk about.**

A tape-recorded conversation between Howard Putnam, head of Braniff Airlines, and Robert Crandall, head of American Airlines

Earlier chapters analyzed the market structures of perfect competition and complete monopoly. If you look out the window at the American economy, however, you'll find that such polar cases are rare; you are more likely to see varieties of imperfect competition between these two extremes. Most industries are populated by a small number of firms competing with each other.

What are the key features of these intermediate types of imperfect competitors? How do they set their prices? And why do their practices lead to inefficiencies? To answer these questions, this chapter begins with a close look at what happens under oligopoly and monopolistic competition, paying special attention to the role of concentration and strategic interaction. The next section then focuses on large corporations, since these are the predominant form of economic organization in the modern capitalist economy. We end the chapter with a comparison of the economic costs and benefits of imperfect competition.

A. BEHAVIOR OF IMPERFECT COMPETITORS

Look back at Table 9-1, which shows the following kinds of market structures: (1) *Perfect competition* is found when a large number of firms produce an identical product—so many firms, indeed, that none of them can affect the market price. This market structure thrives mainly on farms and in financial markets such as the market for foreign currencies or bonds. (2) *Monopolistic competition* occurs when a large number of firms produce slightly differentiated products, while (3) *oligopoly* is an intermediate form

of imperfect competition in which an industry is dominated by a few firms. The most concentrated market structure is (4) *monopoly*, in which a single firm produces the entire output of an industry.

In many situations—such as deciding whether government should intervene in a market or whether a firm has abused its monopoly position—economists need a quantitative measure of the extent of market power. **Market power** signifies the degree of control that a single firm or a small number of firms has over the price and production decisions in an industry. The most common measure of market power is the *concentration ratio* for an industry, illustrated in Figure 10-1 on page 172. The **four-firm concentration ratio** is defined as the percent of total industry output (or shipments) that is accounted for by the largest four firms. Similarly, the eight-firm concentration ratio is the percent of output shipped by the top eight firms. In a pure monopoly, the four- or eight-firm concentration ratio would be 100 percent, while for perfect competition, both ratios would be close to zero.

How concentrated is American manufacturing? For 1992, data show that 19 percent of manufacturing output takes place in highly concentrated industries (those with four-firm concentration ratios above 60 percent), while 16 percent resides in unconcentrated industries (those with four-firm concentration ratios less than 20 percent). Historical studies indicate that the measured degree of concentration has been decreasing in recent years.

Warning on concentration measures: Although traditional concentration measures are still widely used in economics and in law, they are becoming obsolete because of international competition and structural change. Conventional concentration measures include only domestic production and exclude imports. Because imports and import competition have risen sharply over the last two decades, the actual concentration or market power probably declined even more sharply than is indicated by these measures. As a result, in those industries that are exposed to international competition, concentration ratios will overstate the extent of market power. For example, the conventional concentration measure shown in Figure 10-1 indicates that the top four automotive firms had 84 percent of the market. But if imports are included in sales, these same four firms had only 67 percent of the market.

In addition, these concentration measures also ignore the growing impact of competition from other industries. For example, concentration ratios are typically calculated for a narrow industry definition, such as paired-wire telephone services. Sometimes, however, strong competition can come from other quarters. Cellular telephones provide a major threat to conventional paired-wire local telephone service even though the two are in different industries. Care must always be taken to interpret quantitative indexes of market power appropriately.

THE NATURE OF IMPERFECT COMPETITION

In analyzing the determinants of concentration, economists have found that three major factors are present in imperfectly competitive markets. These factors are costs, barriers to entry, and strategic interaction:

- *Costs.* When the minimum efficient size of operation for a firm occurs at a sizable fraction of industry output, only a few firms can profitably survive and oligopoly is likely to result.
- *Barriers to competition.* When there are large economies of scale or government restrictions to entry, they will limit the number of competitors in an industry.
- *Strategic interaction.* When only a few firms operate in a market, they will soon recognize their interdependence. **Strategic interaction**, which is a genuinely new feature of oligopoly that has inspired the field of game theory, occurs when each firm's business plans depend upon the behavior of its rivals.

Why are economists particularly concerned about industries characterized by imperfect competition? The answer is that such industries behave in certain ways that are inimical to the public interest. For example, imperfect competition generally leads to prices that are above marginal costs; this results in an inefficient allocation of resources.

As a result of high prices, oligopolistic industries often (but not always) have supernormal profits. The profitability of the highly concentrated tobacco and pharmaceutical industries has been the target of political attacks on numerous occasions. Careful studies show, however, that concentrated industries tend to have only slightly higher rates of profit than unconcentrated ones. This is a surprising finding, and it has especially perplexed critics of big business, who expected to find the biggest companies earning enormous profits.

Concentration Measured by Value of Shipments in Manufacturing Industries, 1992

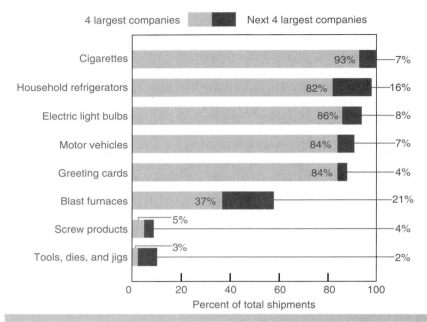

FIGURE 10-1. Concentration Ratios Are Quantitative Measures of Market Power

For refrigerators, motor vehicles, and many other industries, a few firms produce most of the domestic output. Compare this with the ideal of perfect competition, in which each firm is too small to affect the market price. (Source: U.S. Bureau of the Census, 1992 data.)

Another point concerns research and development (R&D). Industries with high levels of concentration sometimes have high levels of R&D spending per dollar of sales as they try to get a technological edge over their rivals. By contrast, there's no sense in a small farmer or tiny bakery setting up a scientific laboratory. The high levels of R&D are generally regarded favorably by economists, and this is seen as one of the major mitigating features of imperfect competition.

THEORIES OF IMPERFECT COMPETITION

While the concentration of an industry is important, it does not tell the whole story. Indeed, to explain the behavior of imperfect competitors, economists have developed a field called *industrial organization*. We cannot cover this vast area here. Instead, we will focus on three of the most important cases of imperfect competition—collusive oligopoly, monopolistic competition, and small-number oligopoly.

Collusive Oligopoly

The degree of imperfect competition in a market is influenced not just by the number and size of firms but by how they behave. When only a few firms operate in a market, they see what their rivals are doing and react. For example, if there are two airlines operating along the same route and one raises its fare, the other must decide whether to match the increase or to stay with the lower fare, undercutting its rival. *Strategic interaction* is a term that describes how each firm's business strategy depends upon its rivals' business behavior.

When there are only a small number of firms in a market, they have a choice between *cooperative* and *noncooperative* behavior. Firms act noncooperatively when they act on their own without any explicit or implicit agreement with other firms. That's what produces price wars. Firms operate in a cooperative mode when they try to minimize competition between themselves. When firms in an oligopoly actively cooperate with each other, they engage in **collusion**. This term denotes a situation in which two or more firms jointly set their prices or outputs, divide the market among themselves, or make other business decisions jointly.

During the early years of American capitalism, before the passage of effective antitrust laws, oligopolists often merged or formed a trust or cartel (recall Chapter 9's discussion of the Golden Age, pages 167–68). A **cartel** is an organization of independent firms, producing similar products, that work together to raise prices and restrict output. Today, with only a few exceptions, it is strictly illegal in the United States and most other market economies for companies to collude by jointly setting prices or dividing markets. (The antitrust laws pertaining to such behavior are discussed in Chapter 17.)

Nonetheless, firms are often tempted to engage in tacit collusion, which occurs when they refrain from competition without explicit agreements. When firms tacitly collude, they often quote identical (high) prices, pushing up profits and decreasing the risk of doing business. A recent examination found that about 9 percent of major corporations have admitted to or been convicted of illegal price fixing. In recent years, makers of infant formula, scouring pads, and kosher Passover products have been investigated for price fixing, while universities, art dealers, the airlines, and the telephone industry have been accused of collusive behavior.

The rewards of successful collusion can be great. Imagine a four-firm industry—call the firms A, B, C, and D—where all the rivals have tired of ruinous price wars. They tacitly agree to charge the same price and not undercut each other. In such a situation, firms may seek the **collusive oligopoly** equilibrium by finding the price which maximizes their joint profits. Figure 10-2 illustrates oligopolist A's situation. A's demand curve, $D_A D_A$, is drawn assuming that the other firms all follow firm A's lead in raising and lowering prices. Thus the firm's demand curve has the same elasticity as the industry's DD curve. Firm A will get one-fourth of the shared market as long as all firms charge the same price.

The maximum-profit equilibrium for the collusive oligopolist is shown in Figure 10-2 at point E, the intersection of the firm's MC and MR curves. Here, the appropriate demand curve is $D_A D_A$, which recognizes that the other firms will charge the same price as A. The optimal price for the collusive oligopolist

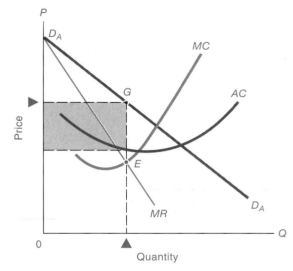

FIGURE 10-2. Collusive Oligopoly Looks Much Like Monopoly
After experience with disastrous price wars, firms will surely recognize that each price cut is canceled by competitors' price cuts. So oligopolist A may estimate its demand curve $D_A D_A$ by assuming that others will be charging similar prices. When firms collude to set a jointly profit-maximizing price, the price will be very close to that of a single monopolist. Can you see why profits are equal to the gray rectangle?

is shown at point G on $D_A D_A$, just above point E. This price is identical to the monopoly price: it is well above marginal cost and earns the colluding oligopolists a handsome monopoly profit.

When oligopolists can collude to maximize their joint profits, taking into account their mutual interdependence, they will produce the monopoly output and price and earn the monopoly profit.

Although many oligopolists would be delighted to earn such high profits, in reality many obstacles hinder effective collusion. First, collusion is illegal. Second, firms may "cheat" on the agreement by cutting their price to selected customers, thereby increasing their market share. Secret price cutting is particularly likely in markets where prices are secret, where goods are differentiated, where there is more than a handful of firms, or where the technology is changing rapidly. Third, the growth of international trade means that many companies face intensive competition from foreign firms as well as domestic companies.

Indeed, experience shows that it's hard to put together a successful cartel which lasts very long today, whether it's explicit or tacit.

Two notable failures at collusion can be cited. Since 1973, the Organization of Petroleum Exporting Countries (OPEC) has attempted to set up an oil cartel. That strategy worked from 1973 to 1975, when prices skyrocketed. But a successful cartel requires that members curtail their production to keep prices high. Sometimes OPEC succeeds, but every few years price competition breaks out, as one or more OPEC countries exceed their quota for production. This happened in a spectacular way in 1986, when Saudi Arabia drove oil prices from $28 per barrel down to below $10. It is particularly hard to enforce a cartel agreement among parties that hate each other or even—as with Iraq, Iran, and Kuwait—are fighting real wars as well as price wars.

The airline industry is another example of a market with a history of repeated—and failed—attempts at collusion. It would seem a natural candidate for collusion. There are only a few major airlines, and on many routes there are only one or two rivals. But just look at the quote at the beginning of the chapter, an apparent attempt at collusion. Since then, Braniff has gone bankrupt twice, and American Airlines and other airlines, while successful in the mid-1980s, lost more than $10 billion between 1990 and 1993. If collusion exists, it clearly has not raised profits. Indeed, the evidence shows that the only time an airline can boost fares is when it has a near-monopoly on all flights to a city.

Monopolistic Competition

At the other end of the spectrum from collusive oligopolies is **monopolistic competition**. Monopolistic competition resembles perfect competition in three ways: there are many buyers and sellers, entry and exit are easy, and firms take other firms' prices as given. The distinction is that products are identical under perfect competition, while products are differentiated under monopolistic competition.

Monopolistic competition is very common—just scan the shelves at any supermarket, and you'll see a dizzying array of different brands of breakfast cereals, shampoos, and frozen foods. Within each product group, products or services are different, but close enough to compete with each other. Here are some other examples of monopolistic competition: There may be several grocery stores in a neighborhood, each carrying the same goods but at different locations. Gas stations, too, all sell the same product, but they compete on the basis of location and brand name. The several hundred magazines on a newsstand rack are monopolistic competitors, as are the fifty or so competing brands of personal computers. The list is endless.

For our analysis, the important point is that product differentiation means each seller has some freedom to raise or lower prices, more so than in a perfectly competitive market. *Product differentiation leads to a downward slope in each seller's demand curve.* Figure 10-3 might represent a monopolistically competitive fishing magazine which is in short-run equilibrium at *G*. The firm's *dd* demand curve shows the

---

FIGURE 10-3. Monopolistic Competitors Produce Many Similar Goods

Under monopolistic competition, numerous small firms sell differentiated products and therefore have downward-sloping demand. Each firm takes its competitors' prices as given. Equilibrium has *MR* = *MC* at *E*, and price is at *G*. Because price is above *AC*, the firm is earning a profit, area *ABGC*.

Monopolistic Competition Before Entry

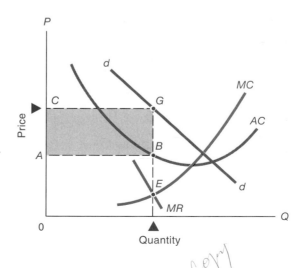

relationship between sales and its price when other magazine prices are unchanged; its demand curve slopes downward since this magazine is a little different from everyone else's because of its special focus. The profit-maximizing price is at *G*. Because price at *G* is above average cost, the firm is making a handsome profit represented by area *ABGC*.

But our magazine has no monopoly on writers or newsprint or insights on fishing. Firms can enter the industry by hiring an editor, having a bright new idea and logo, locating a printer, and hiring workers. Since the fishing magazine industry is profitable, entrepreneurs bring new fishing magazines into the market. With their introduction, the demand curve for the products of existing monopolistically competitive fishing magazines shifts leftward as the new magazines nibble away at our magazine's market.

The ultimate outcome is that fishing magazines will continue to enter the market until all economic

---

FIGURE 10-4. Free Entry of Numerous Monopolistic Competitors Wipes Out Profit

The typical seller's original profitable *dd* curve in Fig. 10-3 will be shifted downward and leftward to *d'd'* by the entry of new rivals. Entry ceases only when each seller has been forced into a long-run, no-profit tangency such as at *G'*. At long-run equilibrium, price remains above *MC*, and each producer is on the left-hand declining branch of its long-run *AC* curve.

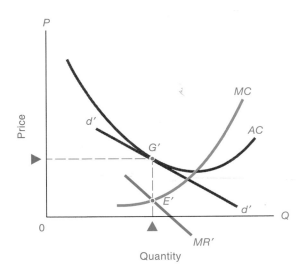

Monopolistic Competition After Entry

profits (including the appropriate opportunity costs for owners' time, talent, and contributed capital) have been beaten down to zero. Figure 10-4 shows the final long-run equilibrium for the typical seller. In equilibrium, the demand is reduced or shifted to the left until the new *d'd'* demand curve just touches (but never goes above) the firm's *AC* curve. Point *G'* is a long-run equilibrium for the industry because profits are zero and no one is tempted to enter or forced to exit the industry.

This analysis is well illustrated by the personal computer industry. Originally, such computer manufacturers as Apple and Compaq made big profits. But the personal computer industry turned out to have low barriers to entry, and numerous small firms entered the market. Today, there are dozens of firms, each with a small share of the computer market but no economic profits to show for its efforts.

The monopolistic competition model provides an important insight into American capitalism: The rate of profit will in the long run be zero in this kind of imperfectly competitive industry as firms enter with new differentiated products.

In the long-run equilibrium for monopolistic competition, prices are above marginal costs but economic profits have been driven down to zero.

Some critics believe that monopolistic competition is inherently inefficient, even though profits are zero in the long run. They argue that monopolistic competition breeds an excessive number of new products and that eliminating unnecessary product differentiation could really cut costs and lower prices. To understand their reasoning, look back at the long-run equilibrium price at *G'* in Figure 10-4. At that point, price is above marginal cost; hence, output is reduced below the ideal competitive level.

This argument against monopolistic competition has considerable appeal. It takes real ingenuity to demonstrate the gains to human welfare from adding Apple Cinnamon Cheerios to Honey Nut Cheerios and Whole Grain Cheerios. It is sometimes hard to see the reason for gasoline stations on every corner of an intersection. But there is strong logic to the incredible variety we find in the American economy. Reducing the number of monopolistic competitors, while cutting costs, might well end up lowering consumer welfare because it would reduce the diversity of available goods and services. Centrally planned socialist countries tried to standardize output on a small number of varieties, and this left their consumers highly dissatisfied. People will pay a great deal to be free to choose.

Rivalry Among the Few

For our third example of imperfect competition, we turn back to markets in which only a few firms compete. This time, instead of focusing on collusion, we consider the fascinating case where firms have a strategic interaction with each other. Strategic interaction is found in any market which has relatively few competitors. Like a tennis player trying to outguess her opponent, each business must ask how its rivals will react to changes in key business decisions. If Wrigley, which controls 50 percent of the chewing-gum markets, cuts its prices, how will its competitors react? If GE introduces a new model of refrigerator, what will Whirlpool, its principal rival, do? If American Airlines lowers its transcontinental fares, how will United react?

Consider as an example the market for air shuttle services between New York and Washington, currently served by Delta and USAir. This market is called a *duopoly* because it is served by two firms. Suppose that Delta has determined that if it cuts fares 10 percent, its profits will rise as long as USAir does not match its cut, but its profits will fall if USAir does match its price cut. If they cannot collude, Delta must make an educated guess as to how USAir will respond to its price moves. Its best approach would be to estimate how USAir would react to each of its actions and then to maximize profits *with strategic interaction recognized*. This analysis is the province of game theory, to which we turn shortly.

Similar strategic interactions are found in many large industries: in television, in automobiles, even in economics textbooks. Unlike the simple approaches of monopoly and perfect competition, it turns out that there is no simple theory to explain how oligopolists behave. Different cost and demand structures, different industries, even different temperaments on the part of the firms' managers will lead to different strategic interactions and to different pricing strategies. Sometimes, the best behavior is to introduce some randomness into the response simply to keep the opposition off balance.

Competition among the few introduces a completely new feature into economic life: It forces firms to take into account competitors' reactions to price and output deviations and brings strategic considerations into their markets.

Game Theory

To analyze the outcome of strategic interactions, economists rely upon a fascinating area of economic theory known as *game theory*. This is the analysis of situations involving two or more decision makers who have conflicting objectives. Game theory was originated in the 1940s by John von Neumann and Oskar Morgenstern in their pathbreaking work, *The Theory of Games and Economic Behavior*.[1] Game theory has been used by economists to study the interaction of duopolists, union-management disputes, countries' trade policies, international environmental agreements, reputations, and a host of other situations. In the area of imperfect competition, some of the important results are the following:

- As the number of noncooperative or competing oligopolists becomes large, industry price and quantity tend toward the output of the perfectly competitive market.
- If firms decide to collude rather than compete, the market price and quantity will be close to those generated by a monopoly. But experiments suggest that as the number of firms increases, collusive agreements are more difficult to police, and the frequency of cheating and noncooperative behavior increases.
- In many situations, there is no stable equilibrium for oligopoly. Strategic interplay may lead to unstable outcomes as firms threaten, bluff, start price wars, capitulate to stronger firms, punish weak opponents, signal their intentions, or simply exit from the market.

Game theory offers insights for politics, warfare, and everyday life as well. For example, it suggests that in some circumstances a carefully chosen random pattern of behavior may be the best strategy. A security guard should make rounds at random, not in a set routine. And you should occasionally bluff at poker, not simply to win a pot with a weak hand but also to ensure that other players do not drop out when you bet high on a good hand. The next chapter explores the theory of games in greater depth.

---

[1] 3d ed. (Princeton University Press, Princeton, N.J., 1953).

B. CONTROL, INNOVATION, AND INFORMATION

The world of imperfect competition contains many different species, from huge corporations to tiny vendors on the information superhighway. The largest corporations like GE and IBM are qualitatively different from competitive firms. They possess enormous resources, and they operate globally in many markets simultaneously. Their survival depends not just on pricing but also on developing new commodities, new technologies, and new markets that can pay off for years to come.

In this section we examine two of the crucial features of imperfect competition. We begin by analyzing the structure of large firms. We will see that there is a divergence of interest between owners and managers that suggests that big firms may have other objectives besides maximizing profits. We then examine the issues raised by the increasing importance of information as an economic commodity. We look at the significant role of large firms in the innovation of new products and processes—an argument first made by Joseph Schumpeter—and then discuss the novel issues raised by the Internet and the growing problem of intellectual property rights.

DIVORCE OF OWNERSHIP AND CONTROL IN THE LARGE CORPORATION

The first step in understanding the behavior of large corporations is to realize that they are mostly "publicly owned." Corporate shares can be bought by anyone, and ownership is spread among many investors. Take a company like AT&T. In 1996, more than 2.3 million people owned its shares, which were worth almost $100 billion. But no single person owned as much as 1 percent of the total. Such dispersed ownership is typical of our large publicly owned corporations. While pension funds and mutual funds hold growing blocks of shares in many companies, each one still owns only a small share of the total.

Because the stock of large companies is so widely dispersed, ownership is typically divorced from control. Individual owners cannot easily affect the actions of large corporations. And while the stockholders of a company elect its board of directors—a group of insiders and knowledgeable outsiders—most often it is the salaried management that makes the major decisions about corporate strategy and day-to-day operations. The managers have acquired special training and management skills, and they are much more intimately acquainted with the details of the company.

In most situations, there is no clash of goals between the management and stockholders. Higher profits benefit everyone. But there are three important potential conflicts of interest between managers and stockholders. First, insiders may vote themselves large salaries, expense accounts, bonuses, and generous retirement pensions at the stockholders' expense. Nobody is arguing that managers should work for the minimum wage, but in recent years some top executives at poorly performing companies have received salaries and bonuses totaling $50 million or more.

A second conflict of interest may arise in connection with paying out dividends. The managers of a company have an understandable tendency to hold on to profits and use them to expand the size of the company instead of paying them out as dividends. But there may be situations where the profits that are plowed back into a company could be more profitably invested outside the company. In some cases, shareholders would benefit if the company would agree to be taken over by another corporation or to simply liquidate itself and pay out the proceeds. But few are the occasions when management gladly votes itself out of jobs and the firm out of business.

The third conflict of interest comes about because managers are often primarily interested in maintaining the smooth operation of the organization rather than running major risks and making revolutionary changes. If firms avoid worthwhile but risky investments because their managers fear the possibility of large losses, the pace of invention and innovation could be slowed. On an economywide basis, excessive managerial aversion to risk could retard productivity growth and thereby hurt a nation's living standard. Some economists believe that this is an important reason why the U.S. economy has fared poorly in recent years.

These conflicts of interest all grow worse the bigger the company is. As soon as a firm gains some market power, it begins to have the ability to seek objectives beyond pure profit maximization. A monopolist can divert profits to uneconomic purposes without going bankrupt. The eminent British economist J. R. Hicks wrote, "The best of all monopoly profits is the quiet life." This saying captures the notion that market power allows managers to pursue alternative goals which may not maximize profits.

However, the decisions of managers cannot diverge too far from profit maximization. If a firm is reckless in making its cost, revenue, and profit decisions, market forces will eventually eliminate that firm, or its managers, from the scene. That has been especially true in recent years, as more and more companies face true competition from foreign rivals. Hence, to survive, a firm must pay some attention to the profitability of its actions. Perhaps firms do not always make optimal, profit-maximizing decisions, but they cannot cast around randomly either.

Rationality and rules of thumb: Economists often write of optimizing behavior in which consumers maximize utility and firms maximize profits. But in the real world, people have limited resources and information and are therefore forced to make decisions based on incomplete information or analysis. Searching for the absolute maximum of profits or utility would take too much time. Consumers cannot spend all day looking for the lowest-priced head of lettuce; a firm cannot spend millions of dollars hiring econometricians to study the price elasticity for each one of its thousand products. Instead, as Nobel Prize–winning economist Herbert Simon has emphasized, firms or consumers often exhibit *bounded rationality*. This means that they usually strive to make a good decision, rather than waste resources hunting for the best decision.

In some situations the use of a "rule of thumb"—or simplified decision rule—is an economical way of making choices. For example, it is common practice for companies—especially ones in imperfectly competitive markets—to set prices on a "cost-plus-markup" basis. This is how it works: Instead of setting prices by an *MR* and *MC*

comparison, companies take the calculated average cost of a product and mark it up by adding a fixed percentage—say, 20 percent of the average cost. This cost-plus-markup figure then becomes the selling price. Note that if all goes as planned, the price will cover all direct and overhead costs and earn the firm a solid profit.

Does markup pricing indicate that firms do not maximize profits? To some extent, yes. But a better explanation would be that markup pricing is a useful rule of thumb that economizes on scarce managerial resources in a world of bounded rationality. Managers have many tasks other than setting prices. So while markup pricing does not maximize profits to the last decimal point, it comes reasonably close to maximum profits given the other demands on management time.

INFORMATION, INNOVATION, AND SCHUMPETERIAN ECONOMICS

Economic theory tends to glorify perfect competition as the most efficient market structure. Imperfect competitors, by contrast, set prices too high, earn supernormal profits, and neglect product quality. This dismal view of monopoly was challenged by one of the great economists of this century, Joseph Schumpeter. He argued that the essence of economic development is innovation and that monopolists in fact are the wellsprings of innovation in a capitalist economy.

Joseph Schumpeter: Economist as romantic. Born in the Austrian Empire, Joseph Schumpeter (1883–1950) was a legendary scholar who ranged widely in the social sciences and led a flamboyant private life. His three ambitions were to be the world's greatest economist, Austria's greatest horseman, and Vienna's greatest lover—although he is reported to have said that there were too many fine horsemen in Austria for him to succeed in all his aspirations.

He began studying law, economics, and politics at the University of Vienna—then one of the world centers of economics and home of the "Austrian School" that today reveres laissez-faire capitalism. He became the youngest professor in the Austrian Empire and was both the bane and the champion of his students. Six months into his teaching career at the University of Czernowitz (on the

Russian border of the waning Austrian Empire), he charged into the library and scolded the librarian for not allowing his students to have free use of the books. After trading insults, the librarian challenged Schumpeter to a duel which, thanks to his aristocratic training, Schumpeter won by nicking the librarian on the shoulder. After that, his students had unlimited access to the needed books.

Between duels, insulting the stodgy faculty by showing up at faculty meetings in riding pants, and carousing, Schumpeter devoted himself to introducing economic theory on the European continent, founding the Econometric Society, and traveling to England and America. At the end of World War I, he had a disastrously short career as Austrian state secretary of finance. Because he was a monarchist believer in free-enterprise capitalism, Schumpeter ran into trouble when he undermined the left-wing government's program of socializing industry. He was soon thrown out of the government when he challenged the program of union (*Anschluss*) with Germany. He later moved to Harvard, where he eventually became embittered as the theories of his great rival, John Maynard Keynes, swept the profession and his students and the war ravaged his homeland.

Schumpeter's writings covered much of economics, sociology, and history, but his first love was economic theory. His magisterial *History of Economic Analysis* (published posthumously in 1954) has never been surpassed as a survey of the emergence of modern economics. His "popular" book, *Capitalism, Socialism, and Democracy* (1942), laid out the *Schumpeterian hypothesis* on the technological superiority of monopoly and developed the theory of competitive democracy which later grew into public-choice theory. He ominously predicted that capitalism would wither away because of disenchantment among the elites. While this prophesy has not been borne out, he might well join in the conservative complaint today that the welfare state drains the economic vitality of the market economy.[2]

Schumpeter's early classic, *The Theory of Economic Development* (1911), broke with the traditional static analysis of that time by emphasizing the importance of the entrepreneur or innovator, the person who introduces "new combinations," in the form of new products or methods of organization. Innovations result in temporary supernormal innovational profits, which are eventually eroded away by imitators. Ever the romantic, Schumpeter saw in the entrepreneur the hero of capitalism, the person of "superior qualities of intellect and will," motivated by the will to conquer and the joy of creation.

This vision of capitalism as a dynamic process has inspired a new generation of growth theorists, such as Stanford's Paul Romer, who have developed a Schumpeterian theory of induced innovation to supplement the more traditional neoclassical growth theory. Modern interpretations of the Schumpeterian vision emphasize the special economic problems involved in the **economics of information.** Information is a fundamentally different commodity from normal goods. *Because information is costly to produce but cheap to reproduce, markets in information are subject to severe market failures.*

Consider the production of a software program, such as Windows 95. This program took several years and cost Microsoft about $1 billion to develop. Yet you can buy a legal copy for about $100 or even purchase a pirated copy in Beijing for $5. The same phenomenon is at work in publishing, pharmaceuticals, entertainment, and other areas where goods have high information content. In each of these areas, the actual conception and development of the product may be a laborious process that takes years or even a lifetime. But once the work is recorded on paper, in a computer, on a tape or compact disc—at that point, it can be reproduced and used by a second person with virtually no resource cost.

The inability of firms to capture the full monetary value of their inventions is called **inappropriability.** Case studies by Edwin Mansfield and others have found that the social return to invention (that is, the value of inventions to all consumers and producers) is around 3 times the appropriable private return to the inventor (that is, the monetary value of the invention to the inventor).

To the extent that the rewards to invention are inappropriable, we would expect private research and development to be underfunded, with the most significant underinvestment in basic research. The inappropriability and high social returns on research lead most governments to subsidize basic research in health and science and to promise special incentives for creative activities.

---

2 Of the many biographies of Schumpeter, one by a former student captures the drama of his life particularly effectively. See Robert Loring Allen, *Opening Doors: The Life and Work of Joseph Schumpeter* (Transaction, New Brunswick, N.J., 1991).

Intellectual Property Rights and the Dilemma of the Internet. Because the rewards to producing valuable information like inventions are reduced by imitation, governments take steps to create **intellectual property rights**. These are special laws governing patents, copyrights, trade secrets, and, most recently, electronic media. The purpose of intellectual property rights is to give the owner special protection against the material being copied and used by others without compensation to the owner or original creator.[3]

One of the earliest forms of intellectual property rights was the **patent**, which is a monopoly over the use of an invention conveyed by a government for a limited period of time, currently 20 years. Why would governments actually *create* monopolies? By allowing the creators monopolies on intellectual property, the government increases the degree of appropriability and thereby increases the incentives for people to invent useful new products, write books, compose songs, and write computer software. Examples of successful patents include those on the telephone, the Xerox machine, and the Polaroid camera. Patent protection is particularly valuable in the creation of new drugs.

The growth of electronic storage, access, and transmission of information highlights the dilemma of providing incentives for creating new information. With the low and decreasing cost of electronic information systems like the Internet, it is technologically possible to make most information available to everyone, everywhere, at essentially zero resource cost.

This prospect raises the conflict between efficiency and incentives. On the one hand, all information might be provided free—databases, economics textbooks, movies, performances. This would appear to be economically efficient because the price would be set at the marginal cost of zero. On the other hand, this regime of zero returns on intellectual property would reduce or destroy the profit incentives to produce new data, books, performances, or other information because creators would reap no reward from their creative activity.

Society has struggled with this dilemma in the past. But with reproduction costs so much cheaper for electronic information than for traditional information—ever more expensive to produce and ever cheaper to reproduce—finding sensible public policies and enforcing intellectual property rights is becoming ever more difficult.

Experts emphasize that intellectual property rights are imperfect. Recently, the United States got into a trade dispute with China because that country was condoning the illegal copying of American movies, recordings, and software. Appropriability is increased by strengthening intellectual property rights. It is also increased when the innovating firm has a large share of the product market. If Microsoft sells 90 percent of the operating systems for personal computers, it will naturally benefit substantially from research in that area. By contrast, small firms have less ability to appropriate the value of their inventions, particularly if intellectual property rights are weak. If I invent a new programming language and cannot protect it with a patent or other means, I have such a small share of the computer market that I will probably not benefit at all.

It was just this view that led Joseph Schumpeter to advance his bold hypothesis:

> The modern standard of life of the masses evolved during the period of relatively unfettered "big business." If we list the items that enter the modern workman's budget and, from 1899 on, observe the course of their prices, . . . we cannot fail to be struck by the rate of the advance which, considering the spectacular improvement in qualities, seems to have been greater and not smaller than it ever was before. . . .
>
> Nor is this all. As soon as we . . . inquire into the individual items in which progress was most conspicuous, the trail leads not to the doors of those firms that work under conditions of comparatively free competition but precisely to the doors of the large concerns—which, as in the case of agricultural machinery, also account for much of the progress in the competitive sector—and a shocking suspicion dawns upon us that big business may have had more to do with creating that standard of life than keeping it down.[4]

How well has the bold Schumpeterian hypothesis survived a half-century of scrutiny? The facts are

---

[3] For an entry point into economics on the web, you can go to the excellent source by Bill Goffe of the University of Southern Mississippi, "Resources for Economists on the Internet," which is found at http://econwpa.wustl.edu:80/EconFAQ. Starting there, you can find a wide variety of different sources of data and information.

[4] J. A. Schumpeter, *Capitalism, Socialism and Democracy* (Harper, New York, 1942), p. 81.

Industrial R&D Performance by Size of Company			
Size of company (number of employees)	R&D-sales ratio (percent)		Total company R&D (billions of dollars)
	1983	1993	1993
Fewer than 500	2.2	3.6	13.9
500 to 999	na	2.7	3.0
1,000 to 4,999	2.0	2.4	12.2
5,000 to 9,999	1.3	2.7	8.3
10,000 to 24,999	2.3	2.5	12.6
25,000 or more	3.4	3.6	45.7

TABLE 10-1. Research and Development by Size of Firm
Large firms do most of the research and development (R&D). In the last decade, however, small firms have forged ahead in the invention business and now have larger R&D-sales ratios than all but the largest industrial corporations. (Source: National Science Foundation, *Science and Engineering Indicators: 1996.*)

much more complex than this simple hypothesis would suggest. To begin with, this view might have had greater validity a century ago, when large firms were tiny by today's standards and most firms had great difficulty raising capital to promote their innovations. Moreover, it is surely true that our corner grocery store today does little R&D.

But careful studies indicate that individuals and small firms play a vital role in the inventive process. Table 10-1 shows the amount of R&D performed by different firm classes as well as the ratio of R&D to sales for each. In earlier years, most R&D was indeed undertaken by large firms. But in the last decade, particularly with the cottage-industry approach of the computer industry, research in small firms has grown rapidly and they now finance more than one-fifth of all R&D.

Moreover, studies indicate that small firms are responsible for a disproportionate share of major inventions and innovations. When John Jewkes and

his colleagues traced the history of the most important inventions of this century, they found that less than half came from the laboratories of large corporations. The importance of small inventors has been confirmed in recent years as major new products seem to arise from nowhere—every day we seem to receive an advertisement for a new software package developed by some unheard-of start-up firm.

The relationship between innovation and market power is complex. Because large firms have made a major contribution to research and innovation, we should be cautious about claims that bigness is unmitigated badness. At the same time, we must recognize that small businesses and individuals have made some of the most revolutionary technological breakthroughs and are performing an ever-larger share of industry-financed R&D. To promote rapid innovation, a nation must preserve a variety of approaches and organizations.

C. A BALANCE SHEET ON IMPERFECT COMPETITION

Politicians like to extol "small business" and the "family farm" while disparaging "big businesses" with their "obscene profits." Does economic analysis justify this romantic picture? In this section we assess the economic impact of imperfect competition on today's economy. We begin by showing how imper-

fect competition distorts resource allocation. Then we provide quantitative estimates of the waste due to imperfect competition. We conclude by examining the policy measures that governments can use to control the damage from imperfect competition.

ECONOMIC COSTS OF IMPERFECT COMPETITION

The Cost of Inflated Prices and Insufficient Output

Our analysis has shown how imperfect competitors reduce output and raise price, thereby producing less than would be forthcoming in a perfectly competitive industry. This can be seen most clearly for monopoly, which is the most extreme version of imperfect competition. To see how and why monopoly keeps output too low, imagine that all dollar votes are distributed properly and that all industries other than one are perfectly competitive, with MC equal to P and no externalities. In this world, price is the correct economic standard or measure of scarcity: price measures both the marginal utility of consumption to households and the marginal cost of producing goods by firms.

Now Monopoly Inc. enters the picture. A monopolist is not a wicked firm—it doesn't rob people or force its goods down consumers' throats. Rather, Monopoly Inc. exploits the fact that it is the sole seller of a good or service. By keeping its output a little scarce, Monopoly Inc. raises its price above marginal cost. Hence society does not get as much of the monopolist's output as it wants in terms of the good's marginal cost and marginal value to consumers. The same is true for oligopoly and monopolistic competition, as long as companies can hold prices above marginal cost.

Measuring the Waste from Imperfect Competition

We can depict the efficiency losses from imperfect competition by using a simplified version of our monopoly diagram, here shown in Figure 10-5. If the industry could be competitive, then the equilibrium would be reached at the point where $MC = P$, at point E. Under universal perfect competition, this industry's quantity would be 6 with a price of 100.

Now consider the impact of monopoly—perhaps one gained by a tariff, perhaps by a foreign-trade quota, or perhaps because government prevented entry by regulation or allowed a labor union to monopolize the labor in the industry. Whatever the source, the monopolist would set its MC equal to MR (not to industry P), displacing the equilibrium

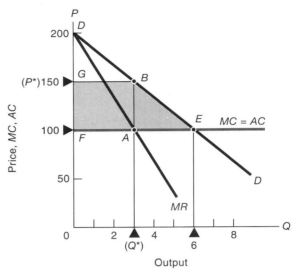

FIGURE 10-5. Monopolists Cause Economic Waste by Restricting Output

Monopolists make their output scarce and thereby drive up price and increase profits. If industry were competitive, equilibrium would be at point E, where social MC equals social MU and welfare is maximized.

At the monopolist's output at point B (with $Q = 3$ and $P = 150$), social MU is above social MC, and consumer surplus is lost. Adding together all the consumer-surplus losses between $Q = 3$ and $Q = 6$ leads to economic waste from monopoly equal to the gray shaded area ABE. In addition, the monopolist has monopoly profits given by the rust-colored shaded region $GBAF$.

to $Q = 3$ and $P = 150$ in Figure 10-5. The rust-colored area $GBAF$ is the monopolist's profit, which compares with a zero-profit competitive equilibrium.

We can measure the inefficiency from monopoly by using the tools of consumer surplus (see Chapter 5). Economists measure the economic harm from inefficiency in terms of the **deadweight loss**; this term signifies the loss in real income that arises because of monopoly, tariffs and quotas, taxes, or other distortions. Recall that for each unit of output reduction below E, the efficiency loss is the vertical distance between the demand curve and the MC curve. The total deadweight loss from the monopolist's output restriction is the sum of all such losses, represented by the gray triangle ABE in Figure 10-5.

To see this, recall that the DD curve represents the good's marginal value to consumers at each level of output, while the *MC* curve represents the opportunity cost of devoting production to this good rather than to other industries. For example, at $Q = 3$, the vertical difference between *B* and *A* represents the difference between the value and the cost of a small increase in the output of *Q*. Adding up all these differences from $Q = 3$ to $Q = 6$ gives the shaded region *ABE*.

The technique of measuring the costs of market imperfections by "little triangles" of deadweight loss, such as the one in Figure 10-5, can be extended to other areas. Similar analysis applies to foreign-trade tariffs and quotas, taxes and subsidies, and externalities.

EMPIRICAL STUDIES OF COSTS OF MONOPOLY

Economists have applied the analysis of deadweight loss to measure the overall costs of imperfect competition in the United States. In essence, these studies estimate the deadweight loss of consumer surplus in *ABE* of Figure 10-5 for all industries. Early studies set the total deadweight loss from monopoly at less than 0.1 percent of GDP. In today's economy, it would total only about $7 billion. One economist quipped that economists might make a larger social contribution fighting fires and eradicating termites than attempting to curb monopolies.

More recent studies have calculated that the deadweight welfare loss attributable to monopolistic resource misallocation in the United States lies somewhere between 0.5 and 2 percent of gross national product.[5] Some critics believe that the efficiency losses may be compounded as the higher prices pile on top of each other as goods cascade from one stage of production to the other.

The most important reservation about this approach is that it ignores the impact of market structure upon technological advance or "dynamic efficiency." The deadweight loss measured in Figure 10-5 assumes that the cost curves are the same for perfect competitors and for imperfect competitors. But some economists point out that according to the Schumpeterian hypothesis, discussed in the previous section, imperfect competition actually pro-

---

[5] F. M. Scherer and David Ross, *Industrial Market Structure and Economic Performance*, 3d ed. (Houghton Mifflin, Boston, 1990), p. 667.

motes invention and technological change and reduces costs. This suggests that the gains from invention may offset the efficiency losses from too high prices.

But not everyone accepts this argument. Some skeptical economists retort that monopolists mainly promote the quiet life, poor quality, and uncivil service. Indeed, a common complaint about companies with a dominant market position is that they pay little attention to quality of product. When AT&T had a monopoly on telephone equipment, consumers had to be satisfied with plain black phones for many years. Once competitors entered, there was a sharp increase in the variety of colors, styles, and ancillary equipment (such as answering machines). In the automobile industry as well, foreign competition forced U.S. automakers to produce more reliable and safer cars.

INTERVENTION STRATEGIES

In discussing the problem of imperfect competition, Milton Friedman, a Nobel Prize winner and perhaps the leading conservative economist of the modern age, wrote: "There is only a choice among three evils: private unregulated monopoly, private monopoly regulated by the state, and government operation." In this final subsection, we examine the six major approaches that governments in market economies can use to deal with imperfect competition. The first three policy measures form the core of modern policies toward big business. The next three have been tried but are seldom used in modern market economies like the United States.

1. The major method for combating market power is the use of *antitrust policy*. Antitrust policies are laws that prohibit certain kinds of behavior (such as firms' joining together to fix prices) or curb certain market structures (such as pure monopolies and highly concentrated oligopolies). This important policy approach will be explored in detail in Chapter 17.

2. More generally, anticompetitive abuses can be avoided by *encouraging competition* whenever possible. There are many government policies that can promote vigorous rivalry even among large firms. It is particularly crucial to reduce barriers to entry into all lines of business. That means

encouraging small businesses and not walling off domestic markets from foreign competition.

3. Over the last 100 years, American government has evolved a new tool for government control of industry: _regulation._ Economic regulation allows specialized regulatory agencies to oversee the prices, outputs, entry, and exit of firms in regulated industries such as public utilities and transportation. Unlike antitrust policies, which tell businesses what _not_ to do, regulation tells businesses what to do and how to price products. It is, in effect, government control without government ownership. This important tool for containing monopoly is used particularly for local natural monopolies. It will be discussed in detail in Chapter 17 in our survey of government's role in curtailing market power.

4. _Government ownership_ of monopolies has been an approach widely used outside the United States. For some natural monopolies such as water, gas, and electricity distribution, it is thought that efficient production requires a single seller. In such cases, the real dilemma is whether to impose government ownership or government regulation on such firms. Most market economies have chosen the regulatory route, and in recent years many governments have "privatized" industries that were in former times public enterprises.

5. _Price controls_ on most goods and services have been used in wartime, partly as a way of containing inflation, partly as a way of keeping down prices in concentrated industries. Studies indicate that these controls are a very blunt instrument: they lead to numerous distortions and subterfuges that undermine the economy's efficiency. During the most recent experience with price controls in the United States, in the 1970s, there were long lines for gasoline when its price was set too low, and shortages also cropped up for beef, natural gas, and even toilet paper. Placing the entire economy under price controls to curtail a few monopolists is like poisoning the entire garden to kill a few chinch bugs.

6. _Taxes_ have sometimes been used to alleviate the income-distribution effects. By taxing monopolies, a government can reduce monopoly profits, thereby softening some of the socially unacceptable effects of monopoly. But if taxation over-

comes the objections to monopoly based on equity, it does little to reduce the distortion of output. A nondistorting tax drains profits but has no effect on output. If the tax increases marginal cost, it is likely to push the monopolist even further from the efficient level of output—raising price and lowering output even more.

**The Bottom Line.** What is the bottom line on the advantages and disadvantages of imperfect competition? To begin with, the question of "monopoly vs. competition" is too simple to be useful—it is much like asking whether big animals are more beautiful or more efficient than small animals. As the survey above emphasizes, there is a vast array of species of imperfect competition. Most have evolved to handle the special characteristics of the market they deal with—automobile firms are large publicly owned companies because they need to raise capital to gain the efficiencies of mass production; lawyers are organized in partnerships because of the need to pool skills and enhance trust among clients; colleges are nonprofit organizations because profits and teaching are hard to mix; farms are operated by families because of the need to perform a wide variety of activities in sparsely populated regions.

In virtually all cases, as Milton Friedman states in his quote on page 183, governments are choosing among different evils when they curb excessive market power. After two centuries of observing different market structures, many economists have concluded that _promoting vigorous competition among unregulated firms is almost always the least of these evils._ Removing barriers to entry and exit and ensuring strong prohibitions against collusion are the surest formula for preventing monopoly pricing and encouraging rapid innovation. The keys to this strategy might be summarized in the following rules:

Remove government constraints to competition.
Remember that "the tariff is the mother of monopoly."
Promote vigorous competition from foreign firms.
Use auctions and competitive bidding whenever possible.
Don't try to second-guess future technological trends.
Encourage small businesses to challenge established firms.

SUMMARY

A. Behavior of Imperfect Competitors

1. Recall the four major market structures: (*a*) *Perfect competition* is found when no firm is large enough to affect the market price. (*b*) *Monopolistic competition* occurs when a large number of firms produce slightly differentiated products. (*c*) *Oligopoly* is an intermediate form of imperfect competition in which an industry is dominated by a few firms. (*d*) *Monopoly* comes when a single firm produces the entire output of an industry.

2. Measures of concentration are designed to indicate the degree of market power in an imperfectly competitive industry. Industries which are more concentrated tend to have higher levels of R&D expenditures, but their profitability is not higher on average.

3. High barriers to entry and complete collusion can lead to collusive oligopoly. This market structure produces a price and quantity relation similar to that under monopoly.

4. Another common structure is the monopolistic competition that characterizes many retail industries. Here we see many small firms, with slight differences in the quality of products (such as different kinds of gasoline or groceries). The existence of product differentiation leads each firm to face a downward-sloping *dd* demand curve. In the long run, free entry extinguishes profits as these industries show an equilibrium in which firms' *AC* curves are tangent to their *dd* demand curves. In this tangency equilibrium, prices are above marginal costs but the industry exhibits greater diversity of quality and service than under perfect competition.

5. A final situation recognizes the strategic interplay when an industry has but a handful of firms. Where a small number of firms compete in a market, they must recognize their strategic interactions. Competition among the few introduces a completely new feature into economic life: It forces firms to take into account competitors' reactions to price and output deviations and brings strategic considerations into these markets. Game theory explores the way firms choose strategies that try to anticipate the reactions of their opponents.

B. Control, Innovation, and Information

6. As public corporations grow, and their owners become numerous and dispersed, we see the phenomenon of the separation of ownership from control. Such a trend can introduce conflicts of interest between shareholders and managers—such as when managers shun risk or pay themselves overly generous compensation.

7. A careful study of the actual behavior of oligopolists shows certain kinds of behavior at variance with standard economic assumptions about profit maximization. One limit on profit maximization is bounded rationality. This principle recognizes that it is costly to make decisions, so managers may make less-than-perfect decisions, often employing rules of thumb, to economize on search and decision time. An important example of rule-of-thumb behavior is markup pricing—where prices are set by adding a percentage increase on top of costs of production.

8. Schumpeter emphasized the importance of the innovator, who introduces "new combinations" in the form of new products or methods of organization and is rewarded by temporary entrepreneurial profits. The Schumpeterian hypothesis holds that traditional monopoly theory ignores the dynamics of technological change. According to this view, monopolies and oligopolies are the chief source of innovation and growth in living standards—to turn large firms into perfect competitors would risk raising prices in the long run as the fragmentation of industry slows technological progress.

9. Today, the economics of information emphasizes the difficulties involved in efficient production and distribution of new and improved knowledge. Information is different from normal goods because it is expensive to produce but cheap to reproduce. The inability of firms to capture the full monetary value of their inventions is called inappropriability. To increase appropriability, governments create intellectual property rights governing patents, copyrights, trade secrets, and electronic media. The rise of electronic information systems like the Internet raises, in heightened form, the dilemma of the efficient pricing of information services.

C. A Balance Sheet on Imperfect Competition

10. Exercise of monopoly power leads to economic inefficiency when price rises above marginal cost, and deterioration in quality may also occur. Empirical studies indicate that the deadweight or efficiency losses from imperfect competition are small relative to national output.

11. To curb the abuses of imperfect competition, governments in an earlier age sometimes used taxation, price controls, and nationalization. These are little used

today in most market economies. The three major tools in American industrial policy today are regulation, antitrust laws, and the encouragement of competition. Of these, the most important is to ensure vigorous rivalry by lowering the barriers to competition whenever possible.

CONCEPTS FOR REVIEW

Models of Imperfect Competition

concentration
market power
strategic interaction
tacit and explicit collusion
imperfect competition:
  collusive oligopoly
  monopolistic competition
  small-number oligopoly
no-profit equilibrium in monopolistic
  competition
inefficiency of $P > MC$

Aspects of Imperfect Competition

separation of ownership from control
limits on profit maximization:
  bounded rationality
  markup pricing
Schumpeterian hypothesis
economics of information:
  inappropriability
  protection of intellectual property rights
  dilemma of efficient production of knowledge

deadweight losses
older approaches:
  taxation
  price controls
  nationalization
current approaches:
  regulation
  antitrust policy
  pro-competitive policies

QUESTIONS FOR DISCUSSION

1. Review the first two theories of imperfect competition analyzed in the first section of this chapter. Draw up a table that compares perfect competition, monopoly, and the two theories with respect to the following characteristics: (*a*) number of firms; (*b*) extent of collusion; (*c*) price vs. marginal cost; (*d*) price vs. long-run average cost; (*e*) efficiency.

2. The market shares in the U.S. airline industry for 1995 are shown in Table 10-2. Calculate the four-firm and six-firm concentration ratios. What would be the change in these indexes if Delta merged with United?

3. "The tragedy of most industries characterized by monopolistic competition is not at all excessive profits. Rather, there are no profits, and prices are excessive as resources are frittered away in low levels of production." Explain what this writer might mean in terms of the long-run equilibrium shown in Figure 10-4. Defend monopolistic competition by showing how it might lead to greater diversity of products.

4. "It is naive to try to break up monopolies into even a few effectively competing units, because the basic cause of monopoly is the law of decreasing cost with mass production. Moreover, if there are even a few firms, the price is likely to be close to marginal cost." Discuss both parts of this statement.

5. A recent interesting study of the Internet by two economists states, "Traditional pricing schemes are not appropriate [for information services]. If you buy a table we like, we generally have to go to the manufacturer to buy one for ourselves; we can't simply copy yours. With information goods, the pricing-by-replication breaks down. Once the sunk costs of software are invested, replication costs are essentially zero. This is a much greater problem [with electronic information] than that which publishers face from unauthorized photocopying, since the cost of replication is essentially zero."[6]

Analyze this quotation in terms of the issues concerning the economics of information. Explain why appropriability is an issue for a book or page on the Internet but not for a chair or gallon of gasoline. Why might high charges for photocopying material or access to the Internet impede efficiency? Relate this question to the Schumpeterian hypothesis.

TABLE 10-2.
(Source: U.S. Department of Transportation, *Air Carrier Financial Statistics Quarterly*, 1995.)

Firm	Market share (%)	Firm	Market share (%)
American	13	USAir	8
Delta	13	Continental	5
United	12	Southwest	4
Northwest	11	America West	2

[6] This is slightly condensed from Jeffrey K. MacKie-Mason and Hal Varian, "Economic FAQs about the Internet," *Journal of Economic Perspectives* (Summer 1994), p. 92. Further information can be obtained on the Internet under the heading "intellectual property" or at the authors' home pages.

6. Explain the following statements:
   a. In the retail drugstore business, each store has a little market power but fails to earn any economic profit on its activities.
   b. According to the theory of bounded rationality, it is truly efficient for GE not to adjust the price of its refrigerators so that $MC = MR$ each and every day.
7. The government decides to tax a monopolist at a constant rate of $\$x$ per unit. Show the impact upon output and price. Is the posttax equilibrium closer to or further from the ideal equilibrium of $P = MC$?
8. Firms often lobby for tariffs or quotas to provide relief from import competition.
   a. Suppose that the monopolist shown in Figure 10-5 has a foreign competitor that will supply output perfectly elastically at a price slightly above the monopolist's $AC = MC$. Show the impact of the foreign competitor's entry into the market.
   b. What would be the effect on the price and quantity if a prohibitive tariff were levied on the foreign good? (A prohibitive tariff is one that is so high as to effectively wall out all imports.) What would be the effect of a small tariff? Use your analysis to explain the statement, "The tariff is the mother of monopoly."
9. Explain in words and with the use of diagrams why a monopolistic equilibrium leads to economic inefficiency relative to a perfect competitor. Why is the condition $MC = P = MU$ of Chapter 8 critical for this analysis?

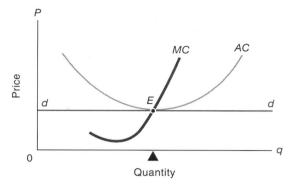

FIGURE 10-6. Perfect Competition

10. In long-run equilibrium, both perfectly competitive and monopolistically competitive markets achieve a tangency between the firm's *dd* demand curve and its *AC* average cost curve. Figure 10-4 shows the tangency for a monopolistic competitor, while Figure 10-6 displays the tangency for the perfect competitor. Discuss the similarities or differences in the two situations with respect to:
    a. The elasticity of the demand curve for the firm's product
    b. The extent of divergence between price and marginal cost
    c. Profits
    d. Economic efficiency

CHAPTER 11
UNCERTAINTY AND GAME THEORY

Risk varies inversely with knowledge.

Irving Fisher, **The Theory of Interest** *(1930)*

Life is full of uncertainty and strategic behavior. A capsule history of exploring for oil in Russia will illustrate this point. During the turmoil of the early 1990s, oil production in Russia declined sharply, and Russia fell from being the world's largest oil producer to number three. Western oil companies were invited to participate in investing in and modernizing the Russian oil fields.

Suppose that you are in charge of a Texaco joint venture in Siberia. What obstacles would you face? You would of course face the normal risks that plague oil producers everywhere—the risks of a price plunge, of embargoes, or of an attack on your tankers by some hostile regime. Added to these are the uncertainties of operating in a new area: you are unfamiliar with the geological formations, with the terrain for getting the oil to the market, with the success rate on drilling wells, and with the skills of the work force.

In addition to these uncertainties is a set of political risks involved in dealing with a divided central government in Moscow, with autonomous regions, with localities, and with the Russian "mafia" in a country where property rights, bribes, and taxation are subject to haggling and the rule of bureaucracy rather than the rule of law.

The dilemmas of the Texaco joint venture show that economic activity often raises complexities that are not captured in our elementary theories. One complication arises because of the vast uncertainties involved in economic life. Our oil company must deal with the uncertainties of drilling, of costs, of prices, and of marketing. Households must contend with uncertainty about future wages or employment and about the return on their investments in education or in financial assets. Occasionally, people suffer from misfortunes such as devastating hurricanes or the mighty Mississippi overrunning its banks. Firms must also contend with uncertainties about the prices of their products and inputs, political turmoil when they produce abroad, taxes and interest rates, the course of technological change in their industry, and the strength of rivalry from domestic and foreign competitors. The study of this first area is called the *economics of uncertainty.*

A second complication arises because much of economic life involves haggling, bargaining, and strategizing. In perfectly competitive markets, all parties take prices as given and need not worry about others' reactions to their actions. In a wide variety of circumstances, however, strategic considerations are of the essence. Our oil company must worry about whether a big oil find will simply be expropriated by the Russians. Closer to home, in an oligopolistic industry, each firm must worry about how other firms will react to price or output decisions. Will a price cut lead to a price war? Will the price war lead to bankruptcy? Most large firms engage in collective bargaining with a union to determine wages and conditions of work. Will too tough a position lead to a crippling strike?

We often see elements of bargaining in economic policy-making. When governments make decisions about taxes and expenditures, these often result from intricate bargaining between political parties, or between the President and Congress, or among the many power brokers in Congress. The struggle between President Clinton and the Republicans after the big Republican congressional victory in 1994 involved an intricate series of bargains and threats over shutting down the government, and at one point the Republicans threatened to cause a default on the national debt. Even family life involves subtle elements of strategy and bargaining about the allocation of chores or the division of the family's income. No sphere of the economy is exempt from strategizing about *what, how,* and *for whom.*

The study of the economic games people, firms, and nations play is known as *game theory*. No study of the realities of economic life is complete without a thorough study of the fascinating interplay of uncertainty and strategy.

A. ECONOMICS OF RISK AND UNCERTAINTY

Our analysis of markets presumed that costs and demands were known for certain and that each firm could foresee how other firms would behave. In reality, business life is teeming with risk and uncertainty. Let's return briefly to our Russian oil investment and examine how risk clouds the picture. Let's say that you have decided to drill a well. To begin with, you might plan on costs of $100 million for the well, but this is just a guess because you don't know how deep you need to drill to find oil, or whether your equipment will break down and need to be replaced, or how long your crew will need to be on the job. In addition, you cannot know about the revenues from the well because of price and output uncertainty. Price uncertainty comes because oil prices fluctuate widely—they have been as low as $10 a barrel and as high as $38 a barrel over the last 15 years. Output uncertainty is undoubtedly the major worry, for your well may be dry, or it may yield too little to be worth operating, or it may be a lucrative gusher.

These problems are not confined to the oil business. Virtually all firms find that output prices will fluctuate from month to month; input prices of labor, land, machines, and fuel are often highly volatile; the behavior of competitors cannot be forecast in advance. The essence of business is to invest now in order to make profits in the future, in effect putting fortunes up as hostage to future uncertainties. Economic life is a risky business.

Modern economics has developed useful tools to incorporate uncertainty into the analysis of business and household behavior. This section examines the role of markets in spreading risks over space and time, presents the theory of individual behavior under uncertainty, and provides the essential theory underlying insurance markets. These topics are but a brief glimpse into the fascinating world of risk and economic life.

SPECULATION: SHIPPING GOODS ACROSS SPACE AND TIME

We begin by considering the role of speculative markets. **Speculation** is the activity which involves making profits from the fluctuations in prices. Generally, a speculator buys a commodity with an eye to selling it later for a profit when the price has risen. The commodity might be grain, oil, eggs, or foreign currencies. Speculators are not interested in using the product or making something with it. Rather, they want to buy low and sell high. The last thing they want is to see the egg truck roll up to their door!

Why might speculation be beneficial to society? The economic function of speculators is to "move" goods from periods of abundance to periods of scarcity—where the "move" will be across space, time, or uncertain states of nature. Even though speculators never once see a barrel of oil or a truckload of eggs, they may help even out the price differences of these commodities among regions or over time. They do this by buying at a time or place when goods are abundant and prices are low and selling when goods are scarce and prices are high.

Arbitrage and Geographical Price Patterns

The simplest case is one in which speculative activity reduces or eliminates regional price differences by buying and selling the same commodity. This activity is called **arbitrage**, which is the purchase of a good or asset in one market for immediate resale in another market in order to profit from a price discrepancy.

Let's say that the price of wheat is 50 cents per bushel higher in Chicago than in Kansas City. Further, suppose that the costs of insurance and transportation are 10 cents per bushel. Then an *arbitrager* (someone engaged in arbitrage) can purchase wheat in Kansas City, ship it to Chicago, and make a profit of 40 cents per bushel. As a result of market arbitrage, the differential must be reduced so that the price differential between Chicago and Kansas City can never exceed 10 cents per bushel. *More generally, as a result of arbitrage, the price difference between markets will generally be less than the cost of moving the good from one market to the other.*

The frenzied activities of arbitragers—talking on the phone simultaneously to several brokers in several markets, searching out price differentials, trying to eke out a tiny profit every time they can buy low and sell high—tend to align the prices of identical products in different markets. Once again, we see the invisible hand at work—the lure of profit acts to smooth out price differentials across markets and make markets function more efficiently.

Speculation and Price Behavior Over Time

Forces of speculation will tend to establish definite patterns of prices over time as well as over space. But the difficulties of predicting the future make this pattern less perfect: We have an equilibrium that is constantly being disturbed but is always in the process of re-forming itself—rather like a lake's surface under the play of the winds.

Consider the simplest case of a crop like corn that is harvested once a year and can be stored for

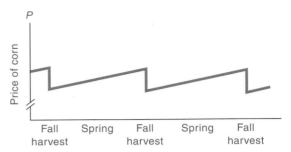

FIGURE 11-1. Speculators Even Out the Price of a Commodity over Time
When a good is stored, the expected price rise must match holding costs. In equilibrium, price is lowest at harvest time, rising gently with accumulated storage, insurance, and interest costs until the next harvest. This flexible pattern tends to even out consumption over the seasons. Otherwise, a harvest glut would cause very low autumn price and sky-high spring price.

future use. To avoid shortages, the crop must last for the entire year. Since no one passes a law regulating the storage of corn, how does the market bring about an efficient pattern of pricing and use over the year? The equilibrium is set by the activities of speculators trying to make a profit.

A well-informed corn speculator realizes that if all the corn is thrown on the market after the autumn harvest, it will fetch a very low price because there will be a glut on the market. Several months later, when corn is running short, the price will tend to skyrocket. In this case, speculators can make a profit by (1) purchasing some of the autumn crop while it is cheap, (2) putting it into storage, and (3) selling it later when the price has risen.

As a result of the speculative activities, the autumn price increases, the spring supply of corn increases, and the spring price declines. The process of speculative buying and selling tends to even out the supply and therefore the price over the year.

Moreover, if there is brisk competition among well-informed speculators, none of them will make excess profits. The returns to speculators will include the interest on invested capital, the appropriate earnings for their time, plus a risk premium to compensate them for whatever risks they incur with their funds. The speculators will probably never touch a kernel of corn, nor need they know anything about the technology of storage or delivery. They merely buy and sell pieces of paper.

There is one and only one monthly price pattern that will result in zero profits for competitive speculators. A little thought will show that it will not be a pattern of constant prices. Rather, the competitive speculative price pattern will produce the lowest prices after the autumn harvest, followed by a gradual price rise until the peak is reached just before the new corn is harvested. The price would normally rise from month to month to compensate for the storage and interest costs of carrying the crop. Figure 11-1 shows the behavior of prices over an idealized yearly cycle.

Speculation reveals the invisible-hand principle at work. By leveling out supplies and prices, speculation actually increases economic efficiency. By moving goods over time from periods of abundance to periods of scarcity, the speculator is buying where the price and marginal utility of the good are low and selling where the price and marginal utility are high. By pursuing their private interests (profits), speculators are at the same time increasing the public interest (total utility).

Shedding Risks through Hedging

One important function of speculative markets is to allow people to shed risks through hedging. **Hedging** consists of reducing the risk involved in owning a commodity by making a counteracting sale of that commodity. Let's see how it works. Consider someone who owns a corn warehouse. She buys 2 million bushels of Kansas corn in the fall, stores it for six months, and sells it in the spring. She makes her living by storing corn, charging 10 cents per bushel of storage. With a full warehouse, she would earn $200,000 before expenses, which is sufficient to cover all costs.

The problem is that corn prices tend to fluctuate. If the price of corn rises, she makes a large windfall gain. But if the price falls sharply, the decrease could completely wipe out her storage profits or even drive her into bankruptcy. The warehouse owner wants to earn her living by storing corn and wants to avoid speculating on the price of corn. What can she do to accomplish this?

The answer is that she can avoid all the corn-price risk by hedging her investments. The owner hedges by selling the corn the moment it is bought

from the farmers rather than waiting until it is shipped 6 months later. Upon buying 2 million bushels of corn in September, she sells the corn immediately for delivery in the future at an agreed-upon price that will just yield a 10-cents-per-bushel storage charge. She thereby protects herself against all corn-price risk. *Hedging by making the counterpart sale allows businesses to insulate themselves from the risk of price changes.*

The Economic Impacts of Speculation

But who buys the corn, and why? Here is where the speculator and the speculative market enter: The speculator agrees to buy the warehouse owner's corn now for future delivery. This moves the risks from the original owner to the speculator. You might wonder exactly why the speculator agreed to take on the corn-price risk. Perhaps the speculator believed that corn prices were rising and that he would make a supernormal return on the investment; perhaps he sold the futures contract to buyers (possibly a bakery chain which desired to reduce the risk of input prices for its bread) who wished to lock in the price of corn before it rose; perhaps he sold it to investors who put a small corn position in their portfolios. The point is that someone, somewhere, had an economic incentive to take on the risk of corn-price fluctuations.

Speculative markets serve to improve the price and allocation patterns across space and time as well as to help transfer risks. These tasks are performed by speculators who, spurred on by the desire to profit from price changes, in fact show the invisible hand at work, reallocating goods from times of feast (when prices are low) to times of famine (when prices are high).

Our discussion has suggested that ideal speculative markets can increase economic efficiency. Let's see how. Say that identical consumers have utility schedules in which satisfaction in one year is independent of that in every other year. Now suppose that in the first of 2 years there is a big crop—say, 3 units per person—while the second year has a small crop of only 1 unit per person. If this crop deficiency could be foreseen perfectly, how should the consumption of the 2-year, 4-unit total be spread over the 2 years? Neglecting storage, interest, and insurance costs, *total utility and economic efficiency for the 2 years together will be maximized only when consumption is equal in each year.*

(a) Without Carryover   **(b) With Carryover**

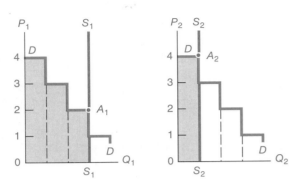 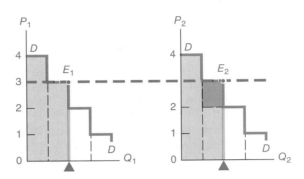

FIGURE 11-2. Speculative Storage Can Improve Efficiency

The gray areas measure total utility enjoyed each year. Carrying 1 unit to the second year equalizes Q and also P and MU and increases total utility by the amount of the dark rust block. This diagram will apply equally well to a number of situations.

It could be labeled "(**a**) Without Arbitrage across Regional Markets" and "(**b**) With Arbitrage across Markets." We can also use this diagram to illustrate risk aversion if we label it "(**a**) With a Risky Gamble" and "(**b**) Without a Risky Gamble." Insurance then serves to move people from (**a**) to (**b**) by spreading the risks across many independent potential gambles.

Why is uniform consumption better than any other division of the available total? Because of the law of diminishing marginal utility. This is how we might reason: "Suppose I consume more in the first year than in the second. My marginal utility (MU) in the first year will be low, while it will be high in the second year. So if I carry some crop over from the first to the second year, I will be moving consumption from low-MU times to high-MU times. When consumption levels are equalized, MUs will be equal and I will be maximizing my total utility."

A graph can illuminate this argument. If utility could be measured in dollars, with each dollar always denoting the same marginal utility, the demand curves for the risky commodity would look just like the marginal utility schedule of Figure 5-1 on page 82. The two curves of Figure 11-2(a) show what would happen if there were no carryover—with price determined first at A_1, where S_1S_1 intersects DD, and second at A_2, where the lower supply S_2S_2 intersects DD. Total utility of the gray shaded areas would add up to only $(4 + 3 + 2) + 4$, or \$13.

But with optimal carryover of 1 unit to the second year, as shown in Figure 11-2(b), Ps and Qs will be equalized at E_1 and E_2, and the total utility of the

shaded areas will add up to $(4 + 3) + (4 + 3)$, or \$14 per head. A little analysis can show that the gain in utility of \$1 is measured by Figure 11-2(b)'s dark rust block, which represents the excess of the second unit's marginal utility over that of the third. This shows why the equality of marginal utilities, which is achieved by ideal speculation, is optimal.

Ideal speculation serves the important function of reducing the variation in consumption. In a world with individuals who display diminishing marginal utility, speculation can increase total utility and allocational efficiency.

RISK AND UNCERTAINTY

Why do people try to shed economic risks? What institutions in a market economy help individuals pool risks or spread them to the broader community? Why do markets fail to provide insurance in some circumstances? We turn now to these issues.

Whenever you drive a car, own a house, store corn, make an investment, or work on a risky job, you are risking life, limb, or fortune. How do people behave in the face of risks? We generally find that people want to avoid uncertainties about their income and consumption. When we desire to avoid risk and uncertainty, we are "risk-averse."

A person is **risk-averse** when the displeasure from losing a given amount of income is greater than the pleasure from gaining the same amount of income.

For example, suppose that we are offered a risky coin flip in which we will win $1000 if the coin comes up heads and lose $1000 if the coin comes up tails. This bet has an *expected value* of 0 (equal to a probability of $\frac{1}{2}$ times $1000 and a probability of $\frac{1}{2}$ times $-$1000); a bet which has a zero expected value is called a fair bet. If we turn down all fair bets, we are risk-averse.

In terms of the utility concept that we analyzed in Chapter 5, risk aversion is the same as *diminishing marginal utility of income.* Being risk-averse implies that the gain in utility achieved by getting an extra amount of income is less than the loss in utility from losing the same amount of income. For a fair bet (such as flipping a coin for $1000), the expected dollar value is zero. But in terms of utility, the expected utility value is negative because the satisfaction you stand to win is less than the satisfaction you stand to lose.

We can use Figure 11-2 to illustrate the concept of risk aversion. Say that situation (*b*) is the initial position, in which you have equal amounts of consumption in states 1 and 2, consuming 2 units in both states. A "risk lover" comes to you and says, "Let's flip a coin for 1 unit." The risk lover is in effect offering you the chance to move to situation (*a*), where you would have 3 units of consumption if the coin came up heads and 1 unit if tails. By careful calculation, you see that if you refuse the bet and stay in situation (*b*), the expected value of utility is 7 utils (= $\frac{1}{2}$ × 7 utils + $\frac{1}{2}$ × 7 utils), whereas if you accept the bet, the expected value of utility is $6\frac{1}{2}$ utils (= $\frac{1}{2}$ × 9 utils + $\frac{1}{2}$ × 4 utils). This example shows that if you are risk-averse, with diminishing marginal utility, you will avoid actions that increase uncertainty without some expectation of gain.

Say that I am a corn farmer. While I clearly must contend with the natural hazards of farming, I do not also want to bear corn-price risks. Suppose that the expected value of the corn price is $4 per bushel, where this expectation arises from two equally likely outcomes with prices of $3 and $5 per bushel. Unless

I can shed the price risk, I am forced into a lottery where I must sell my 10,000-bushel crop for either $30,000 or $50,000 depending upon the flip of the corn-price coin.

But by the principle of risk aversion and diminishing marginal utility, I would prefer a sure thing. That is, I would prefer to hedge my price risk by selling my corn for the expected-value price of $4, yielding a total of $40,000. Why? Because the prospect of losing $10,000 is more painful than the prospect of gaining $10,000 is pleasant. If my income is cut to $30,000, I will have to cut back on important spending, such as college tuition or a roof repair. On the other hand, the extra $10,000 might be less critical, yielding only some jewelry or a new 100-horsepower, eight-speed, air-conditioned lawn mower.

People are generally risk-averse, preferring a sure thing to uncertain levels of consumption—that is, people prefer outcomes with less uncertainty and the same average values. For this reason, activities that reduce the uncertainties of consumption lead to improvements in economic welfare.

INSURANCE AND RISK SPREADING

Risk-averse individuals want to avoid risks. But risks cannot simply be buried. When a house burns down, when someone is killed in an automobile accident, or when a hurricane tears through Florida—someone, somewhere, must bear the cost.

Markets handle risks by **risk spreading**. This process takes risks that would be large for one person and spreads them around so that they are but small risks for a large number of people. The major form of risk spreading is **insurance**, which is a kind of gambling in reverse.

For example, in buying fire insurance on a house, homeowners seem to be betting with the insurance company that the house will burn down. If it does not, the owners forfeit the small premium charge. If it does burn down, the company must reimburse the owners for the loss at an agreed-upon rate. What is true of fire insurance is equally true of life, accident, automobile, or any other kind of insurance.

The insurance company is spreading risks by pooling many different risks: it may insure millions of houses or lives or cars. The advantage for the insurance company is that what is unpredictable for an individual is highly predictable for a population. Say that the Inland Fire Insurance Company insures 1 million homes, each worth $100,000. The chance that a house will burn down is 1 in 1000 per year. The expected value of losses to Inland is then .001 × $100,000 = $100 per house per year. It charges each homeowner $100 plus another $100 for administration and for reserves.

Each homeowner is faced with the choice between the *certain* loss of $200 for each year or the *possible* 1-in-1000 catastrophic loss of $100,000. Because of risk aversion, the household will choose to buy insurance that costs more than the expected value of the household's loss in order to avoid the small chance of a catastrophic loss. Insurance companies can set a premium that will earn the company a profit and at the same time produce a gain in expected utility of individuals. Where does the economic gain come from? It arises from the law of diminishing marginal utility.

We see therefore how insurance, which appears to be just another form of gambling, actually has exactly the opposite effect. Whereas nature deals us risks, insurance helps to lessen and spread risks.

Capital Markets and Risk Sharing

Another form of risk sharing takes place in the capital markets because the *financial* ownership of *physical* capital can be spread among many owners through the vehicle of corporate ownership.

Take the example of investment to develop a new commercial aircraft. A completely new design, including research and development, might require $2 billion of investment spread over 10 years. Yet there is no guarantee that the plane will find a large enough commercial market to repay the invested funds. Few people have the wealth or inclination to undertake such a risky venture.

Market economies accomplish this task through publicly owned corporations. A company like Boeing is owned by millions of people, none of whom owns a major portion of the shares. In a hypothetical case, divide Boeing's ownership equally among 10 million individuals. Then the $2 billion investment becomes $200 per person, which is a risk that many would be willing to bear if the returns on Boeing stock appear attractive.

The principle of risk spreading extends into the international dimension as well. The risks of large-scale investment and production are shared with investors from Japan, Britain, Germany, and other countries when they buy shares of American corporations. And, just as an insurance company reduces its risks by insuring houses in different cities, so investors can reduce the riskiness of their portfolios by holding shares in companies operating around the world.

By spreading the ownership of capital or of individual risky investments among a multitude of owners, capital markets can spread risks and allow much larger investments and risks than would be tolerable for individual owners.

The Troubling Rise in Gambling

Speculation must be distinguished from gambling, which has spread rapidly in recent years. While ideal speculative activity increases economic welfare, gambling raises serious economic issues. To begin with, aside from recreational value, gambling does not create goods and services. In the language of game theory described in the second half of this chapter, it is a "zero-sum game" for society. Indeed, in lotteries and professionally run casinos, it is a "negative-sum game" in which the customers are (almost) sure to lose in the long run. In addition, by its very nature, gambling increases income inequality. People who sit down to the gambling table with the same amount of money go away with widely different amounts. A gambler's family must expect to be on top of the world one week only to be living on crumbs and remorse when luck changes.

Given the substantial economic case against gambling, how can we understand the recent trend to legalize gambling and operate lotteries? One reason is that when states are starved for tax revenues, they look under every tree for new sources; they rationalize lotteries and casinos as a way to channel private vices to the public interest by skimming off some of the revenues. In addition, by bringing gambling above ground, legal gambling may drive out illegal numbers rackets and take some of the profitability out of organized crime. Notwithstanding these rationales, many observers raise questions about an activity in which the state profits by promoting irrational behavior among those who can least afford it.

MARKET FAILURES IN INFORMATION

Our analysis up to now has assumed that investors and consumers are well informed about the risks they face and that speculative and insurance markets function efficiently. In reality, markets involving risk and uncertainty are plagued by market failures. Two of the major failures are adverse selection and moral hazard. When these are present, markets may give the wrong signals, incentives may get distorted, and sometimes markets may simply not exist. In such cases, governments may decide to step in and offer social insurance.

Moral Hazard and Adverse Selection

While insurance is undoubtedly a useful device for spreading risks across the population, the fact is that we cannot buy insurance for all the risks of life, and sometimes the price of insurance makes it too unattractive to buy. The reason behind the incompleteness of insurance markets is that these markets can thrive only under limited conditions.

What are the conditions for the functioning of efficient insurance markets? First, there must be a large number of events. Only then will companies be able to pool different events and spread the risks so that what is a large risk to an individual will become a small risk to many people. Moreover, the events must be relatively independent. No prudent insurance company would sell all its fire-insurance policies in the same building or sell only earthquake insurance in San Francisco. Rather, insurance companies strive to spread their coverage around to different and independent risks. Additionally, there must be sufficient experience regarding such events so that insurance companies can reliably estimate the losses. Finally, the insurance must be relatively free of moral hazard. **Moral hazard** is at work when insurance reduces a person's incentive to avoid or prevent the risky event and thereby changes the probability of loss.

When these ideal conditions are met—when there are many risks, all more or less independent, and the probabilities can be accurately gauged and are not contaminated by individual gain—private insurance markets can function efficiently.

In many situations moral hazard is unimportant. Few people will tempt fate simply because they have a generous life-insurance policy—partly because life is precious and additionally because you can't take the proceeds with you into the grave. In other areas, moral hazard is severe. Studies indicate that the presence of full medical insurance has a major impact upon the amount of cosmetic surgery and the utilization of long-term care such as nursing homes, and most medical-insurance policies consequently exclude these services.

As another example, say that students tried to buy "grade insurance." This would compensate them for the income loss from poor grades. Can you see why no sane insurance company would offer such coverage? The reason is that grades depend so much on individual effort. We would say that the presence of moral hazard in cosmetic surgery and student grades leads to incomplete or missing markets in the sense that supply and demand intersect at zero or very low levels of insurance.

In addition, sometimes private insurance is unavailable or is priced at unfavorable terms because of adverse selection. **Adverse selection** arises when the people with the highest risk are the most likely ones to buy the insurance. Let's take the case where the population is equally divided between two kinds of people—healthy people and the terminally ill. The healthy families average $2000 of medical care each year; the terminally ill—faced with a terrible illness and long hospitalization—have costs averaging $8000. If both kinds of people were included, the average cost would be $5000 per year.

Say that Blue Cross set a uniform price for all insured. This might be the case because government required *nondiscrimination* among insured people. Or it might occur because of *asymmetric information*, where people know about their health status but the insurance company does not. In any case, the ill would gladly buy the Blue Cross policy; by contrast, on looking at that price, a healthy family might decide to run the risk of remaining uninsured rather than to pay the high premiums. The insurance company is therefore left with only the high-cost people, and the price must rise to $8000 to cover the costs. Indeed, in New York, a family of four pays over $8000 for Blue Cross coverage in part because of adverse selection.

We see here that uniform and voluntary pricing of medical insurance has led to adverse selection, raising the price, limiting the coverage, and producing an incomplete market. Similar market failures are important factors in automobile insurance, in disability insurance, and in long-term-care insurance.

Social Insurance

When market failures are so severe that the private market cannot provide adequate coverage, there may be a role for **social insurance**, which is mandatory insurance provided by the government. In these circumstances, the government may choose to step in and provide broad and universal coverage. The taxing and regulatory powers of government, plus the ability to avoid adverse selection through universal coverage, can make government insurance a welfare-improving measure.

One important example of social insurance is unemployment insurance. This is an example of a private market that cannot function because so many of the requirements for private insurance are violated. Insurance companies do not provide unemployment insurance because the moral hazard is so high (people may decide to become unemployed if benefits are generous), because of severe adverse

selection (those who often lose jobs are more likely to participate), and because spells of unemployment are not independent (they tend to occur together during business-cycle recessions). At the same time, countries feel that people should have a safety net under them should they lose their job. As a result, governments often step in to provide unemployment insurance. The government cannot remove the problem of moral hazard, but adverse selection is avoided by universal coverage.

Another important example of cases where governments step in is health insurance for the elderly. We noted above the problems of adverse selection that arise when healthy people decline coverage and leave insurers to cover only high-cost individuals. Adverse selection is particularly serious for the aged because medical costs in the last year of life are almost 20 percent of all health-care costs. Today, to avoid adverse selection, the U.S. government offers universal health coverage for the elderly, Medicare, paid for through premiums and through taxes on active workers.

B. GAME THEORY

> **Strategic thinking is the art of outdoing an adversary, knowing that the adversary is trying to do the same to you.**
>
> *Avinash Dixit and Barry Nalebuff,* **Thinking Strategically** *(1991)*

Economic life is full of situations in which people or firms or countries jockey for dominance. The oligopolies that we analyzed in the last chapter sometimes break out into economic warfare. Such rivalry was seen in the last century when Vanderbilt and Drew cut and recut shipping rates on their parallel railroads. In recent years, Continental Airlines tried to lure customers from its bigger rivals by offering fares far under prevailing levels. When larger airlines such as American and United were deciding how to react, they also had to take into account how Continental would react when they reacted, and so forth. These situations typify an area of economic analysis known as "game theory."

Game theory analyzes the way that two or more players or parties choose actions or strategies that jointly affect each participant. This theory, which may sound frivolous in its terminology, is in fact fraught with significance and was largely developed by John von Neumann (1903–1957), a Hungarian-born mathematical genius. We will sketch the major concepts involved in game theory and discuss some important economic applications.[1]

---

[1] A witty and readable introduction to game theory, filled with examples from economics and daily life, is contained in Avinash Dixit and Barry Nalebuff, *Thinking Strategically* (Norton, New York, 1991).

Let's begin by analyzing the dynamics of price cutting. You are the head of Berney, a New York–based department store, whose motto is "We will not be undersold." Your arch-rival, Sax Fifth Avenue, runs an advertisement, "We sell for 10 percent less." Figure 11-3 shows the dynamics. The vertical rust arrows show Sax's price cuts; the horizontal rust arrows show Berney's responding strategy of matching each price cut.

By tracing through the pattern of reaction and counterreaction, you can see that this kind of rivalry will end in mutual ruin at a zero price. Why? Because the only price compatible with both strategies is a price of zero: 90 percent of zero is zero.

Sax finally realizes that when it cuts its price, Berney will match the price cuts. Only if you are shortsighted will you think you can undercut your rival for long. You will then start to ask what Sax will do if you charge price A, price B, and so forth. *Once you begin to consider how others will react to your actions, you have entered the realm of game theory.*

BASIC CONCEPTS

We will illustrate the basic concepts of game theory by analyzing a **duopoly price war.** This is a situation

where the market is supplied by two firms that are deciding whether to engage in economic warfare of ruinously low prices. For simplicity, we assume that each firm has the same cost and demand structure. Further, each firm can choose whether to charge its normal price or lower its price below marginal costs and try to drive its rival into bankruptcy. The novel element in the duopoly game is that the firm's profits will depend on its rival's strategy as well as on its own.

A useful tool for representing the interaction between two firms or people is a two-way **payoff table**. A payoff table is a means of showing the strategies and the payoffs of a game between two players. Figure 11-4 on page 198 shows the payoffs in the duopoly price game for our two stores. In the payoff table, a firm can choose between the strategies listed in its rows or columns. For example, Sax can choose between its two columns and Berney can choose between its two rows. In this example, each firm decides whether to charge its normal price or to start a price war by choosing a low price.

Combining the two decisions of each duopolist gives four possible outcomes, which are shown in the four cells of the table. Cell A, at the upper left, shows the outcome when both firms choose the normal price; D is the outcome when both choose a price war; and B and C result when one firm has a normal price and one a war price.

The numbers inside the cells show the **payoffs** of the two firms; that is, these are the profits earned by each firm for each of the four outcomes. The rust number in the lower left shows the payoff to the player on the left (Berney); the black entry in the upper right shows the payoff to the player at the top (Sax). Because the firms are identical, the payoffs are mirror images.

Alternative Strategies

Now that we have seen the basic structure of a game, consider how you should behave as a player in the duopoly or any other game. In economics, we assume that firms maximize profits and consumers maximize utility. The new element in game theory is to think through the goals and actions of your opponent and to make your decisions based on your opponent's goals and actions. But you must always remember that your opponent will also be trying to outwit you.

FIGURE 11-3. What Happens When Two Firms Insist on Undercutting Each Other?
Trace through the steps by which dynamic price cutting leads to ever-lower prices for two rivals.

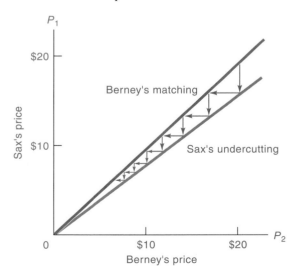

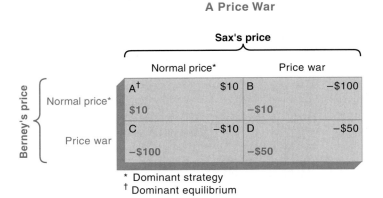

A Price War

* Dominant strategy
† Dominant equilibrium

FIGURE 11-4. A Payoff Table for a Price War
The payoff table shows the payoffs associated with different strategies. Berney has a choice between two strategies, shown as its two rows. Sax can choose between its two strategies, shown as two columns. The entries in the cells show the profits for the two players. For example, in cell C, Berney plays "price war" and Sax plays "normal price." The result is that Berney has rust profit of −$100 while Sax has black profit of −$10. Thinking through the best strategies for each player leads to the dominant equilibrium in cell A.

The guiding philosophy in game theory is the following: Pick your strategy by asking what makes most sense for you assuming that your opponent is analyzing your strategy and acting in his or her best interest.

Let's apply this maxim to the duopoly example. First, note that our two firms have the highest joint profits in outcome A. Each firm earns $10 when both follow a normal-price strategy. At the other extreme is the price war, where each cuts prices and runs a big loss.

In between are two interesting strategies where only one firm engages in the price war. In outcome C, for example, Sax follows a normal-price strategy while Berney engages in a price war. Berney takes most of the market but loses a great deal of money because it is selling below cost. Sax is actually better off selling at normal prices rather than responding.

Dominant Strategy. In considering possible strategies, the simplest case is that of a **dominant strategy**. This situation arises when one player has a best strategy *no matter what strategy the other player follows.*

In our price-war game, for example, consider the options open to Berney. If Sax conducts business as usual with a normal price, Berney will get $10 of

profit if it plays the normal price and will lose $100 if it declares economic war. On the other hand, if Sax starts a war, Berney will lose $10 if it follows the normal price but will lose even more if it also engages in economic warfare. You can see that the same reasoning holds for Sax. Therefore, no matter what strategy the other firm follows, each firm's best strategy is to have the normal price. *Charging the normal price is a dominant strategy for both firms in the price-war game.*

When both (or all) players have a dominant strategy, we say that the outcome is a **dominant equilibrium**. We can see that in Figure 11-4, outcome A is a dominant equilibrium because it arises from a situation where both firms are playing their dominant strategies.

Nash Equilibrium. Most interesting situations do not have a dominant equilibrium, and we must therefore look further. We can use our duopoly example to explore this case. In this example, which we call the *rivalry game*, each firm considers whether to have its normal price or to raise its price toward the monopoly price and try to earn monopoly profits.

The rivalry game is shown in Figure 11-5. The firms can stay at their normal-price equilibrium, which we found in the price-war game. Or they can raise their price in the hopes of earning monopoly

The Rivalry Game

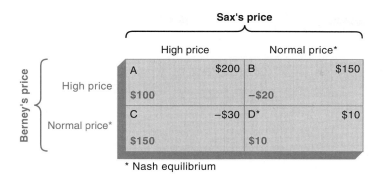

Sax's price

		High price	Normal price*
Berney's price	**High price**	A $200 $100	B $150 −$20
	Normal price*	C −$30 $150	D* $10 $10

* Nash equilibrium

FIGURE 11-5. Should a Duopolist Try the Monopoly Price?
In the rivalry game, each firm can earn $10 by staying at its normal price. If both raise price to the high monopoly level, their joint profits will be maximized. However, each firm's temptation to "cheat" and raise its profits ensures that the normal-price Nash equilibrium will prevail in the absence of collusion.

profits. It is interesting that our two firms have the highest *joint* profits in cell A, where they earn a total of $300 when each follows a high-price strategy. Situation A would surely come about if the firms could collude and set the monopoly price. At the other extreme is the competitive-style strategy of the normal price, where each rival has profits of $10.

In between are two interesting strategies where one firm chooses a normal-price and one a high-price strategy. In cell C, for example, Sax follows a high-price strategy but Berney undercuts. Berney takes most of the market and has the highest profit of any situation, while Sax actually loses money. In cell B, Berney gambles on high price, but Sax's normal price means a loss for Berney.

In this example of the rivalry game, Berney has a dominant strategy; it will profit more by choosing a normal price no matter what Sax does. On the other hand, Sax does not have a dominant strategy, because Sax would want to play normal if Berney plays normal and would want to play high if Berney plays high.

Sax has an interesting dilemma. Should it play high and hope that Berney will follow suit? Or play safe by playing normal? By thinking through the payoffs, it becomes clear that Sax should play normal price. The reason is simple. Sax should start by putting itself in Berney's shoes. You can see that Berney will play normal price no matter what Sax

does because that is Berney's dominant strategy. Therefore, Sax should find its best action by assuming that Berney will follow Berney's best strategy, which immediately leads to Sax's playing normal. This illustrates the basic rule of game theory: you should set your strategy on the assumption that your opponent will act in his or her best interest.

The solution that we have discovered is actually a very general one which is called the **Nash equilibrium** after mathematician John Nash, who won the Nobel Prize in economics for his contributions to game theory. *A Nash equilibrium is one in which no player can improve his or her payoff given the other player's strategy.* That is, given player A's strategy, player B can do no better, and given B's strategy, A can do no better. Each strategy is a best response against the other player's strategy.[2]

The Nash equilibrium is also sometimes called the **noncooperative equilibrium**, because each party chooses that strategy which is best for itself—without collusion or cooperation and without regard for the welfare of society or any other party.

---

[2] More precisely, suppose that firm A picks strategy S_A while firm B picks strategy S_B. The pair of strategies (S_A^*, S_B^*) is a Nash equilibrium if neither player can find a better strategy to play under the assumption that the other player sticks to his or her original strategy. That is, as long as A plays strategy S_A^*, B cannot do better than to play strategy S_B^*, and the analogous rule holds for A.

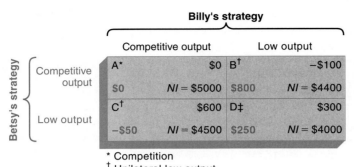

The Invisible-Hand Game

* Competition
† Unilateral low output
‡ Monopolistic collusion

FIGURE 11-6. Under Perfect Competition, Private Profit Seeking Leads to Social Efficiency
Under perfect competition, each competitor can decide on its competitive output (where
$MC = P$) or lower its output to secure some monopoly profits. Consider two out of many
competitors, Billy and Betsy. If either lowers output, his or her own profits go down from the
zero-profit level. The table also shows in the lower right of each cell the total national income
(NI), which is a measure of total social utility. National income declines if competitors depart
from the efficient Nash equilibrium. This demonstrates the invisible-hand principle that,
under perfect competition, social utility is maximized when each firm behaves in a noncooperative or Nash manner to maximize its own profits.

     If all the Billies and Betsies successfully collude, they might move to the monopolistic col-
lusion equilibrium in the lower right cell. Note that their joint profits are maximized and that
national income declines under monopoly. What prevents collusive monopoly in most circumstances is that each competitor has a powerful incentive to defect and behave in a noncooperative manner, moving the market back to the competition in the upper left cell.

We can verify that the starred strategies in Figure
11-5 are Nash equilibria. That is, neither Sax nor
Berney can improve its payoffs from the (normal,
normal) equilibrium as long as the other doesn't
change its strategy. If Berney moves to its high-price
strategy, its profits go from $10 to −$20, while if Sax
raises its price from the normal-price Nash equilibrium, its profits go from $10 to −$30. (Verify that the
dominant equilibrium shown in Figure 11-4 is also a
Nash equilibrium.)

SOME IMPORTANT EXAMPLES OF GAME THEORY

The Invisible-Hand Game

     We can use game theory to illustrate some of the
important principles of microeconomics. Begin with
the *invisible-hand game* shown in Figure 11-6. We have
shown two perfect competitors, Billy and Betsy. They
are just two of many competitors in the auction mar-

ket for identical computer chips. Consider Billy's
strategy. He might follow the textbook rule for a competitor and produce up to the point where marginal
cost equals price. This is the competitive strategy.

     Then a poor strategist comes to Billy and says,
"Why don't you lower your output to get a little
monopoly going?" Billy decides to try the low-output
strategy, lowering output in the hope that his competitors will do the same, thereby raising the market
price. Billy knows that if the competitors do not
lower their output, his profits will fall from 0 to
minus $100. Nonetheless, he gives it a try.

     Alas, this strategy is foolish and doomed, as Billy
would have seen if he had looked at the payoff table
in Figure 11-6. The reason is that Betsy's dominant
strategy is to follow the competitive-output rule.
Whether Billy has competitive or low output, Betsy
will still do best by setting output at the level where
$MC = P$. The profit incentives in a perfectly competitive market will lead firms to the efficient noncoop-

erative equilibrium; the competitive equilibrium is a Nash or noncooperative equilibrium.

Note also that total social utility is maximized when each firm behaves noncooperatively. This point recalls Adam Smith's doctrine of the invisible hand: "By pursuing [an individual's] own interest, he frequently promotes that of society more effectually than when he really intends to promote it." The paradox of the invisible hand is that, even though each person is behaving in a noncooperative manner, the economic outcome is socially efficient. Moreover, the competitive equilibrium is a Nash equilibrium in the sense that no individual would be better off by changing strategies if all other individuals hold firm to their strategies.

In an ideal, perfectly competitive economy, noncooperative behavior produces the socially desirable state of economic efficiency.

The Collusion Game

Why don't the firms collude to raise their profits? Remember Adam Smith's maxim: "People of the same trade seldom meet together . . . but the conversation ends . . . in some contrivance to raise prices." They might form a cartel or persuade the government to limit entry into the industry.

Figure 11-6 shows what happens if the firms collude or behave in a cooperative manner. A **cooperative equilibrium** comes when the players act in unison to find strategies that will maximize their joint payoffs. The cooperative equilibrium comes at the collusive monopoly prices in the lower right cell of Figure 11-6, where both Billy and Betsy have low outputs. Although joint profits are maximized at the cooperative equilibrium, total social utility is definitely lower than it would be at the competitive equilibrium.

What are the impediments to the cooperative monopoly solution? To begin with, cartels and collusion in restraint of trade are illegal in most market economies. But the highest hurdle is self-interest. As is illustrated in Figure 11-6, each firm has a powerful incentive to cheat on the agreement and move toward the noncooperative equilibrium. If Billy defects, his profits go up from $300 to $600. Soon after Billy defects, Betsy would notice that her profits had declined sharply from $250 to −$50. She would reassess her strategy, probably conclude that the cartel had come unglued, and return to a competitive

strategy. If the cooperative equilibrium was not enforceable, the firms would probably gravitate to the noncooperative or Nash equilibrium in the upper left cell of Figure 11-6.

To summarize:

In a perfectly competitive economy, noncooperative behavior of many independent firms produces an efficient allocation of resources. Cooperation and collusion on low outputs and high prices lead to economic losses to consumers. This suggests why governments want to enforce antitrust laws that contain harsh penalties for those who collude to fix prices or divide up the markets.

The Pollution Game

You definitely should not conclude from the invisible-hand game, however, that all attempts at cooperation are antisocial. In many circumstances, noncooperative behavior leads to economic inefficiency or social misery. One important economic example is the *pollution game* shown in Figure 11-7 on page 202. Consider an economy with externalities such as pollution. In this world of unregulated firms, each profit-maximizing firm would prefer to pollute rather than install expensive pollution-control equipment. Moreover, any firm which behaves altruistically and cleans up its wastes will have higher production costs, higher prices, and fewer customers. If its costs are high enough, the firm may even go bankrupt. The pressures of Darwinian competition will drive all firms to the starred Nash equilibrium in cell D in Figure 11-7; here neither firm can improve its profits by lowering pollution.

The pollution game is an example of a situation in which the invisible-hand mechanism of efficient perfect competition breaks down. *This is a situation in which the noncooperative or Nash equilibrium is inefficient.* When markets or decentralized equilibria become dangerously inefficient, governments may step in. By setting efficient regulations or emissions charges, government can induce firms to move to outcome A, the "low-pollute, low-pollute" world. In that equilibrium, the firms make the same profit as in the high-pollution world, and the earth is a healthier place to live in.

Deadly Arms Races

Game theory has wide applications in political science, military strategy, and evolutionary biology. A

The Pollution Game

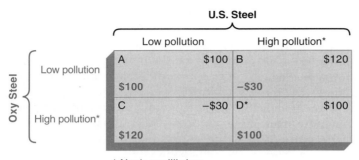

* Nash equilibrium

FIGURE 11-7. *Noncooperative Behavior Leads to More Pollution*
In the deadly pollution game, each unregulated profit-maximizing steel firm emits pollution into streams and air. If a single firm tries to clean up its production, it raises prices, loses business, and suffers a decline in profits. The noncooperative Nash equilibrium in D leads to the high-pollution solution at bottom right. Government can overcome this by enforcing the cooperative equilibrium in A, where profits are the same and the environment has been cleaned up.

particularly dangerous game with an inefficient noncooperative equilibrium is the *arms race*. Say you are superpower A facing hostile superpower R. You want to make sure that you have sufficient nuclear weapons to deter aggression. Since you are not sure about your opponent's intentions, you play it safe by having a modest weapons superiority over your opponent. This is, your generals tell you, just prudent policy.

Now put yourself in the shoes of R, which is watching you engage in a military buildup. R does not know *your* intentions. Its generals also counsel a strategy of prudent superiority. So A wants 10 percent more bombs than R, and R wants 10 percent more bombs than A. This triggers an explosive arms race. Nor is this a fanciful example. The noncooperative arms race between the United States and the Soviet Union over the 1945–1991 period led to massive military spending and an arsenal of almost 100,000 nuclear warheads, many of which are still floating around the remnants of the Soviet empire.

Some people fear that easy availability of guns in America may lead to a domestic arms race as people arm themselves out of fear of other people's guns.

These situations call for cooperative solutions in which the parties get together to reduce the armaments. Arms-control agreements move the outcome

from an inefficient noncooperative equilibrium to a less inefficient cooperative outcome. In doing so, they can increase the security and welfare of all participants.

Winner-Take-All Society?

Is it possible that economic life is increasingly becoming a giant tournament—the civilian equivalent of an arms race?

Ask yourself what all of the following have in common: best-sellers, patents, Olympic swimmers, supermodels, victorious lawsuits, and the President of the United States. These are all outcomes of **winner-take-all games,** situations in which the payoffs are determined primarily by relative merit rather than absolute merit. There is only one gold medalist in the 400-meter dash, only one winner to a lawsuit, and only one book at the top of the best-seller list. Compare such situations with factory workers, whose earnings are determined by absolute marginal productivity rather than relative marginal productivity.

A second feature of such contests is that the rewards are heavily concentrated at the very top. A top fashion model like Claudia Schiffer might be paid $25,000 for a fashion show, while most models make nothing. Best-selling authors like Stephen King

The Winner-Take-All Game

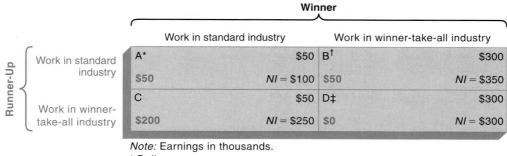

	Work in standard industry	Work in winner-take-all industry
Work in standard industry	A* $50 $50 *NI* = $100	B† $300 $50 *NI* = $350
Work in winner-take-all industry	C $50 $200 *NI* = $250	D‡ $300 $0 *NI* = $300

Note: Earnings in thousands.
* Dull
† Efficient
‡ Overcrowded

FIGURE 11-8. When Too Many People Enter Contests, National Income Can Fall
In the winner-take-all game, Winner at top prevails in professional sports or best-selling books. Runner-Up at left is lured into the winner-take-all market by the possibility of a large gain. Like too many fishing boats chasing the same fish, winner-take-all markets are overcrowded with people ultimately getting low earnings. Total incomes would rise if Runner-Up stayed in a standard, absolute-reward industry.

or Danielle Steel are paid up to $60 million for the rights to their books, while surveys indicate that the average writer makes not much more than the minimum wage. A few movie superstars like Mel Gibson or Kevin Costner get millions of dollars per film. By contrast, in a recent year, only one-tenth of the members of the actors' guild were actually paid for appearing in films, while hopefuls kept the wolf from the door with activities such as driving taxis and waiting on tables.

Figure 11-8 shows the winner-take-all game. Lucky or talented Winner has a powerful incentive to participate in the winner-take-all tournament; she ultimately prevails and gets income of $300,000. Runner-Up has the choice of working in an absolute-return industry like manufacturing or joining the tournament in entertainment, athletics, or law. If Runner-Up thinks he has an even chance of prevailing, he enters the race because he estimates that his expected earnings are $100,000 in winner-take-all industries and $50,000 in conventional occupations.

The equilibrium comes in the "overcrowded" equilibrium at the lower right, where both people enter the tournament. National income is higher here than in the dull equilibrium, where there are no exciting contests, but lower than in the efficient outcome, where Runner-Up does not enter the contest. An inefficient winner-take-all equilibrium generates the highest inequality of earnings of all.

A fascinating study by Robert Frank and Philip Cook explores the consequences of what they call a "winner-take-all society." The following quote suggests how game theory has illuminated this important part of economic life:

> Whereas free marketeers maintain that market incentives lead to socially efficient results, our claim is that winner-take-all markets attract too many contestants, result in inefficient patterns of consumption and investment, and often degrade our culture. . . . The explosion of top salaries has stemmed largely from the growing prevalence of winner-take-all markets.[3]

Frank and Cook argue the need for "positional arms control" (such as reforming the legal system) and progressive taxes on consumption as a way of reducing the waste from excessive competition for large prizes in entertainment, athletics, and business.

Games, Games, Everywhere . . .
The insights of game theory pervade economics, the social sciences, business, and everyday life. In

---

[3] Robert H. Frank and Philip J. Cook, *The Winner-Take-All Society* (Free Press, New York, 1995), pp. 6, 19. Many examples in this section are drawn from their study.

economics, for example, game theory can explain trade wars as well as price wars (some illuminating examples are provided in the questions at the end of this chapter).

Game theory can also suggest why foreign competition may lead to greater price competition. What happens when Japanese firms enter a U.S. market where firms had tacitly colluded on a price strategy that led to a high oligopolistic price? The foreign firms may "refuse to play the game." They did not agree to the rules, so they may cut prices to gain market shares. Collusion may break down.

A key feature in many games is the attempt of players to build *credibility*. You are credible if you are expected to keep your promises and carry out your threats. But you cannot gain credibility with simple promises. Credibility must be consistent with the incentives of the game.

How can you get credibility? Here are some examples: Central banks earn reputations for being tough on inflation by adopting politically unpopular policies. Even greater credibility comes when the central bank's rules are written into law or the nation's constitution. Businesses make credible promises by writing contracts that inflict penalties if they do not perform as promised. A more paradoxical approach is for an army to burn its bridges behind it. Because there is no retreat, the threat to fight to the death is a credible one.

These few examples provide a small tasting from the vast harvest produced by game theorists over the last half-century. This area has been enormously useful in helping economists and other social scientists think about situations where small numbers of people are well informed and try to outwit each other in markets, politics, or military affairs.

SUMMARY

A. Economics of Risk and Uncertainty

1. Economic life is full of uncertainty. Consumers face uncertain incomes and employment patterns as well as the threat of catastrophic losses; businesses have uncertain costs and their revenues contain uncertainties about price and production.

2. In well-functioning markets, arbitrage, speculation, and insurance help smooth out the unavoidable risks. Speculators are people who buy and sell commodities with an eye to making profits on price differentials across markets. They move goods across regions from low-price to high-price markets, across time from periods of abundance to periods of scarcity, and even across uncertain states of nature to periods when chance makes goods scarce.

3. The profit-seeking action of speculators and arbitragers tends to create certain equilibrium patterns of price over space and time. These market equilibria are zero-profit outcomes where the marginal costs and marginal utilities in different regions, times, or uncertain states of nature are in balance. To the extent that speculators moderate price and consumption instability, they are part of the invisible-hand mechanism that performs the socially useful function of reallocating goods from fat times (when prices are low) to lean times (when prices are high).

4. Speculative markets allow individuals to hedge against unwelcome risks. The economic principle of risk aver-

sion, which derives from diminishing marginal utility, implies that individuals will not accept risky situations with zero expected value. Risk aversion implies that people will buy insurance to reduce the disastrous declines in utility from fire, death, or other calamities.

5. Insurance and risk spreading tend to stabilize consumption in different states of nature. Insurance takes large individual risks and spreads them so broadly that they become acceptable to a large number of individuals. Insurance is beneficial because, by helping to equalize consumption across different uncertain states, it raises the expected level of utility.

6. The conditions for operation of efficient insurance markets are stringent: there must be large numbers of independent events, with little chance of moral hazard or adverse selection. When market failures arise, prices can become distorted or markets may simply not exist. If private insurance markets fail, the government may step in to provide social insurance. Even in the most laissez-faire of advanced market economies today, governments insure against unemployment and health risks in old age.

B. Game Theory

7. Economic life contains many situations of strategic interaction among firms, households, governments, or others. Game theory analyzes the way that two or more parties, who interact in an arena such as a market,

choose actions or strategies that jointly affect each participant.

8. The basic structure of a game includes the players, who have different actions or strategies, and the payoffs, which describe the profits or other benefits that the players obtain in each outcome. The key new concept is the payoff table of a game, which shows the strategies and the payoffs or profits of the different players.

9. The key to choosing strategies in game theory is for players to think through both their own and their opponent's goals, never forgetting that the other side is doing the same. When playing a game in economics or any other field, assume that your opponent will choose his or her best option. Then pick your strategy so as to maximize your benefit, always assuming that your opponent is similarly analyzing your options.

10. Sometimes a dominant strategy is available, one that is best no matter what the opposition does. More often,

we find the Nash equilibrium (or noncooperative equilibrium) most useful. A Nash equilibrium is one in which no player can improve his or her payoff given the other player's strategy. Sometimes, parties can collude or cooperate, which produces the cooperative equilibrium.

11. A Nash equilibrium produces an efficient outcome in Adam Smith's invisible-hand game. Here, noncollusive firms produce at prices equal to marginal costs, and the noncooperative equilibrium is efficient. In such situations, cooperation leads to inefficient production.

12. Sometimes, however, noncooperative behavior leads to social ruin, as when competitors pollute the planet or engage in dangerous arms races. Winner-take-all games, such as lawsuits or athletic contests, can induce the entry of too many contestants and increase the inequality of incomes. In these cases, regulation or taxation may enhance economic efficiency by harnessing private competition to the public interest.

CONCEPTS FOR REVIEW

Risk and Uncertainty

spatial P equality
ideal seasonal price pattern
speculation, arbitrage, hedging
risk aversion and diminishing marginal utility
consumption stability vs. instability
insurance and risk spreading

market failure in information
moral hazard, adverse selection
social insurance

Game Theory

players, strategies, payoffs
payoff table
dominant strategy and equilibrium

Nash or noncooperative equilibrium
cooperative or collusive equilibrium
important games:
   invisible hand
   collusion
   pollution
   winner-take-all
credibility

QUESTIONS FOR DISCUSSION

1. Suppose an honest friend offers to flip a fair coin, with you paying your friend $100 if it comes up heads and your friend paying you $100 if it comes up tails. Explain why the expected dollar value is $0. Then explain why the expected utility value is negative if you are risk-averse. Can you see why your friend must be a risk lover (someone with increasing marginal utility of income)?

2. Consider the example of grade insurance (see page 195). Suppose that under grade insurance, students would be compensated $5000 a year for each point that their grade point average fell below the top grade (this figure might be an estimate of the impact of grades on future earnings). Explain why the presence of grade insurance would produce moral hazard and adverse selection. Why would moral hazard and adverse selection make insurance companies reluctant

to sell grade insurance? Are you surprised that you cannot buy grade insurance?

3. List some important differences between private and social insurance. Explain why it might be sensible for social insurance to provide universal health care for the elderly or unemployment insurance for workers but not fire insurance for homeowners.

4. In the early nineteenth century, little of the nation's agricultural output was sold in markets, and transportation costs were very high. What would you expect to have been the degree of variation of prices across regions compared with today?

5. Assume that a firm is making a risky investment (say, spending $1 billion developing a new commercial aircraft). Can you see how the widely diversified ownership of this firm could allow near-perfect risk spreading on the aircraft investment?

Free Trade vs. Protection

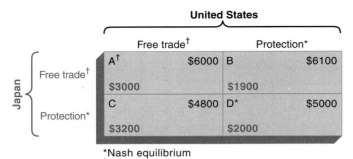

*Nash equilibrium
†Cooperative equilibrium

FIGURE 11-9. Countries Gain from Trade but Lose from Trade War

Japan and the United States can agree to the cooperative equilibrium at A in which they reduce all tariffs and quotas and enjoy the benefits of free trade. Each would, however, be tempted to "cheat" by putting trade restrictions on imports, thus gaining income at home while hurting total world income, moving to B or C. Retaliation would lead to the worst of all worlds, at D.

6. In the late 1980s, "arbs" (arbitragers) who became rich upon the illegal use of inside information gave a bad name to speculation and arbitrage. Suppose that speculation and arbitrage are made a criminal offense (as was the case until recently in Russia). Explain the economic damage that could result.

7. Explain the logic behind the invisible-hand game. Explain why a Nash or noncooperative equilibrium is efficient in the invisible-hand game and inefficient in the pollution game.

8. "In a world with no spillovers or externalities, collusion harms the public interest. In a world full of pollution, arms races, and winner-take-all markets, cooperation is essential." Interpret this statement in light of your understanding of game theory.

9. Consider the dilemma of maintaining free trade shown in the payoff table in Figure 11-9, which gives total real national incomes (in billions) for two countries as a function of foreign-trade policies. Each country can have a policy of either free trade with no tariffs or quotas or protectionism with tight quotas on imported goods and services. The payoffs are the real incomes in each country.
   a. List the four outcomes, and calculate each region's national income and world income.
   b. Show how countries acting noncooperatively (without agreements and in their own selfish national interest) will be led to a trade war at the Nash equilibrium in cell D. What is the effect of the trade war on total world income?

   c. What is the impact on incomes of a trade agreement that abolishes all trade restrictions and produces free trade?
   d. Is there an incentive for each country to "cheat" on the trade agreement? What happens if the cheating leads to retaliation and to the high-tariff outcome?

10. **Advanced problem:** We can modify Figure 11-2 to show the gains from insurance. Redraw Figure 11-2 by labeling the left-hand pair in (*a*) "Individual Does Not Buy Insurance," while the right-hand set in (*b*) can be titled "Individual Buys Insurance." Then, from left to right, label the four states of the world as "No fire and no insurance," "Fire and no insurance," "No fire with insurance less premiums," and "Fire with insurance reimbursement."

   By purchasing insurance, people can remove the risks of fire and thereby equalize the amount of consumption in each state of nature. In new panel (*a*), note that the no-fire state of nature has very high consumption while the fire state of nature has low consumption. In new panel (*b*), by paying insurance premiums, the individual lowers consumption a little if no fire occurs but gains greatly if a fire strikes. Because of diminishing marginal utility, people gain greatly by paying a fair insurance premium to ensure the same level of housing (or cars or health) no matter how the dice of life turn up.

PART THREE

FACTOR MARKETS: LAND, LABOR, CAPITAL, AND INCOME DISTRIBUTION

CHAPTER 12
HOW MARKETS DETERMINE INCOMES

You know, Ernest, the rich are different from us.

F. Scott Fitzgerald

Yes, I know. They have more money than we do.

Ernest Hemingway

Earlier chapters examined product markets: the way that markets determine *what* should be produced under different market structures like perfect competition and monopoly. We are also vitally concerned with the *for whom* question of the incomes that people earn from their labor and other sources of income. In Part Three, we turn to the functioning of factor markets along with the **theory of income distribution,** which examines the determination of income in a society. This chapter lays out the basic principles, while the next two chapters apply these principles to the markets for labor, land, and capital.

A. INCOME AND WEALTH

America is a land of extremes of income and wealth. If you are one of the 400 richest Americans, you are a 63-year-old white male with a degree from an Ivy League school and a net worth of $750 million. You probably made your fortune in manufacturing or real estate. Your voyage to the top was as much the product of birth as of brains, for your family is likely to have given you a nice head start with at least a few million dollars in the family business. You might also have succeeded by blazing new trails in computer software or discount stores for small towns.

At the other extreme are forgotten people who never make the cover of *Forbes* or *People* magazine. Listen to the story of Robert Clark, homeless and unemployed. A roofer and Vietnam veteran, he came to Miami from Detroit looking for work in 1992. He slept on the city streets on a piece of cardboard covered by a stolen sheet. Every day he and other homeless men crept out of the culverts into the daylight to work for temporary employment firms. These firms charged clients $8 to $10 an hour, paid the men the minimum wage, and then took most of the money back for transportation and tools. Clark's pay stub showed earnings of $31.28 for 31 hours of work.

How can we understand these extremes of income and wealth? Why are some people paid $1 million a year, while others net only $1 an hour? Why

Type of income	Amount ($, billion)	Share of total (%)	Examples
Labor income:			
Wages and salaries	3,634	58.1	Autoworker's wages; teacher's salary
Benefits and other labor income	793	12.7	Company contribution to pension fund
Property income:			
Proprietors' income	520	8.3	Proceeds from owner-run business; lawyer's share of partnership earnings
Net rent	146	2.3	Landlord's rental from apartments, after expenses and depreciation
Corporate profits	736	11.8	Microsoft's profits
Net interest	425	6.8	Interest paid on savings account
Total	**6,254**	**100.0**	

TABLE 12-1. Division of National Income, 1996
National income includes all the incomes paid to factors of production. Three-quarters consists of wages and other kinds of compensation of labor, while the rest is divided among rents, corporate profits, and the incomes of proprietors. (Source: U.S. Department of Commerce, *Survey of Current Business.*)

is real estate in Tokyo or Manhattan worth thousands of dollars a square foot, while land in the desert may sell for but a few dollars an acre? And what is the source of the billions of dollars of profits earned by giant enterprises like Exxon or Toyota?

The questions about the distribution of income are among the most controversial in all economics. Some people argue that high incomes are the unfair result of past inheritance and luck while poverty stems from discrimination and lack of opportunity. Others believe that people get what they deserve and that interfering with the market distribution of income would injure an economy's efficiency and make almost everyone worse off. In the broad middle are those who believe that the government should ensure that a social "safety net" catches those who fall below some minimum standard of living.

INCOME

In measuring the economic status of a person or a nation, the two yardsticks most often used are income and wealth. **Income** refers to the total receipts or cash earned by a person or household during a given time period (usually a year). The aggregate of all incomes is *national income*, the com-

ponents of which are shown in Table 12-1. The biggest share of national income goes to labor, either as wages or salaries or as fringe benefits. The remainder goes to the different types of *property income*: rent, net interest, corporate profits, and proprietors' income. This last category basically includes the returns to the owners of small businesses.

The proceeds from a market economy are distributed to the owners of the economy's factors of production in the form of wages, profits, rent, and interest.

About three-quarters of national income goes to labor, while the rest is distributed as some form of returns to capital. The last quarter-century has been a turbulent one. What has been the impact of oil-price shocks, the computer revolution, globalization, and corporate downsizing on labor's share of the total income pie? Looking at Figure 12-1, we can see that the share of national income going to labor has changed very little in recent decades. This is one of the remarkable features of the income distribution in the United States.

Role of Government

How does government fit into this picture? Federal, state, and local governments are the major

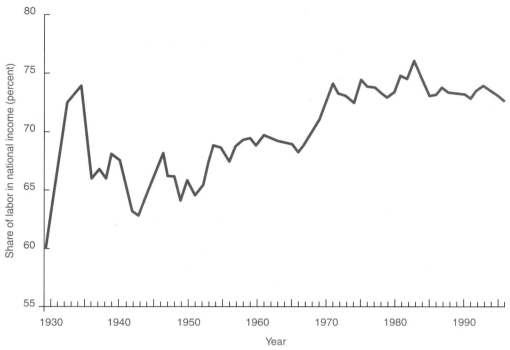

FIGURE 12.1. The Share of Labor in National Income

The share of labor income increased gradually from 1929 to 1970. Since then, it has been remarkably stable at around 75 percent of national income. The remainder of income is distributed among rents, interest, corporate profits, and proprietors' income. The share of property-type income is 100 minus the labor share. (Source: U.S. Department of Commerce.)

source of income for millions of people. They employ about 16 percent of the work force, paying about $641 billion in wages and salaries annually. In 1996, governments paid almost $189 billion in interest to holders of government bonds and other debt. Moreover, governments rent millions of square feet of office space and are responsible, directly and indirectly, for billions in profits to corporations which do business with them. All these direct payments to factors of production are reflected in Table 12-1.

Yet government also has a direct role in incomes that does not show up in Table 12-1. To begin with, the government collects a sizable share of national income through taxation and other levies. In 1996 about 32 percent of gross domestic product was collected by federal, state, and local governments as various types of taxes, including personal income taxes, corporate-profit taxes, and social security taxes.

But what the government taketh, it also giveth away. Governments at all levels provide incomes in the form of **transfer payments,** which are direct dollar payments from government to individuals that are not made in return for current goods or services. The biggest single category of transfer payments is social security for older Americans, but transfer payments also include veterans' benefits, farm subsidies, and welfare payments. Whereas Americans derived almost none of their incomes from governments in 1929, fully 17 percent of personal incomes in 1996 came from government transfer payments.

Personal income equals market income plus transfer payments. Most market income comes from wages and salaries; a small, prosperous minority derives its market income from earnings on property. The major component of government transfers is social security payments to the elderly.

Factor Incomes vs. Personal Incomes

It is important to understand the distinction between factor incomes and personal incomes.

What American Households Own, 1989		
Type of asset	Amount of assets ($, billion)	Percentage held by richest 1% of households
Tangible:		
Own home	6,415	8.4
Other real estate	2,907	43.0
Motor vehicle	773	7.6
Business investment	3,719	67.7
Other tangible assets	815	39.2
Financial:		
Checking, savings, and money market accounts	2,630	19.9
Stocks and bonds	2,056	54.5
Other financial assets (such as life insurance)	772	35.0
Total	**20,092**	**32.8**
Average dollar value of assets per household, 1989	216,043	

TABLE 12-2. Tangible and Financial Assets of Households

Households own tangible assets (such as houses and cars) as well as financial assets (such as savings accounts and stocks). Even though the average assets per household totaled more than $216,000, much of this was concentrated in a few hands. (Source: Arthur Kennickell and R. Louise Woodburn, "Estimation of Household Net Worth," April 1992.)

Table 12-1 reports the distribution of factor income—how much is paid in wages, in profits, and so on. But the same person may own many different factors of production. For example, someone might receive a salary, earn interest on money in a savings account, get dividends from shares in a mutual fund, and collect rent on a real-estate investment. In economic language, we observe that a person's market income is simply the quantities of factors of production sold by that person times the earnings of each factor. In addition, many people, particularly retirees on social security, receive transfer payments from the government.

WEALTH

We see that some income comes from interest or dividends on holdings of bonds or stocks. This brings us to the second important economic concept: **Wealth** consists of the net dollar value of assets owned at a given point in time. Note that wealth is a *stock* (like

the volume of a lake) while income is a *flow* per unit of time (like the flow of a stream). A household's wealth includes its tangible items (houses, cars and other consumer durable goods, and land) and its financial holdings (such as cash, savings accounts, bonds, and stocks). All items that are of value are called *assets,* while those that are owed are called *liabilities.* The difference between total assets and total liabilities is called wealth or *net worth.*

Table 12-2 presents a breakdown of the asset holdings of Americans. The single most important asset of the majority of households is the family home: 64 percent of families own houses, as compared with 55 percent a generation ago. Most households own a modest amount of financial wealth in savings accounts and corporate stocks. But it turns out that a large proportion of the nation's financial wealth is concentrated in the hands of a small fraction of the population. About one-third of all wealth is owned by the richest 1 percent of American households.

B. INPUT PRICING BY MARGINAL PRODUCTIVITY

Why do different people have such different incomes? We begin by observing that the theory of income distribution is a special case of the theory of prices. When we look for the price of labor, we look for wages; similarly, the price for using land is land rent. The prices of factors of production are set by the interaction between supply and demand for different factors—just as the prices of goods are determined by the supply and demand for goods.

But pointing to supply and demand is just the first step on the road to economic understanding. It leaves unanswered important questions: Why are Americans paid 5 times as much as Mexicans? Why are women paid only two-thirds of the average wage of men? What determines the profit rate on capital? Why are land prices so much higher in the city than in the desert?

The key to these questions is the marginal-productivity theory of incomes. By applying the production theory of earlier chapters, we will see that the demands for factors of production can be expressed in terms of the revenues earned on their marginal products. This key finding on demand, combined with supplies of factors, will determine the prices and quantities of factors and thereby market incomes.

THE NATURE OF FACTOR DEMANDS

The demand for factors differs from that for consumption goods in two important respects: (1) Factor demands <u>are derived</u> demands, and (2) factor demands are <u>interdependent</u> demands.

Demands for Factors Are Derived Demands

Let's consider the demand for office space by a firm which produces computer software. A software company will rent office space for its programmers, customer service representatives, and other workers. Similarly, other companies like pizza shops or banks will need space for their activities. In each region, there will be a downward-sloping demand curve for office space linking the rental being charged by landlords to the amount of office space desired by companies—the lower the price, the more space companies will want to rent.

But there is an essential difference between ordinary demands by consumers and the demand by firms for inputs. Consumers demand final goods like computer games or pizzas because of the direct enjoyment or utility these consumption goods provide. By contrast, a business does not pay for inputs like office space because they yield direct satisfaction. Rather, it buys inputs because of the production and revenue that it can gain from employment of those factors.

Satisfactions are in the picture for inputs—but at one stage removed. The satisfaction that consumers get from playing computer games determines how many games the software company can sell, how many order takers it needs, and how much office space it must rent. The more successful its software, the more the demand curve for office space shifts to the right. An accurate analysis of the demand for inputs must, therefore, recognize that <u>consumer demands do *ultimately* determine business demands</u> for office space.

This analysis is not limited to office space. Consumer demands determine the demand for all inputs, including farmland, oil, pizza ovens, and even college professors!

The firm's demand for inputs is derived indirectly from the consumer demand for its final product.

Economists therefore speak of the demand for productive factors as a **derived demand.** This means that when firms demand an input, they do so because that input permits them to produce a good which consumers desire now or in the future. Figure 12-2 on page 214 shows how the demand for a given input, such as fertile cornland, must be regarded as derived from the consumer demand curve for corn. In the same way, the demand for office space is derived from the consumer demand for software and all the other products and services provided by the companies that rent office space.

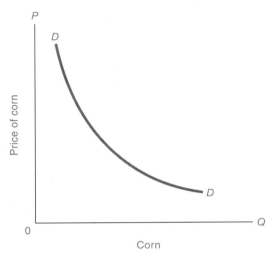

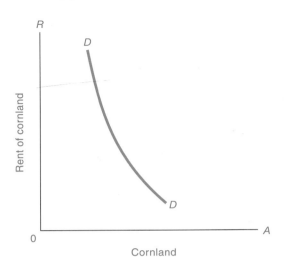

FIGURE 12-2. Demand for Factors Is Derived from Demand for Goods They Produce
The rust curve of derived demand for cornland comes from the black curve of commodity demand for corn. Shift the black curve out, and out goes the rust curve. If the black commodity curve becomes more inelastic, the same tends to happen to the rust input demand curve.

Demands for Factors Are Interdependent

Production is a team effort. A chain saw by itself is useless to me if I want to cut down a tree. A worker with empty hands is equally worthless. Together, the worker and the saw can cut the tree very nicely. In other words, the productivity of one factor, such as labor, depends upon the amount of other factors available to work with.

That means it is generally impossible to say how much output has been created by a single input taken by itself. The different inputs interact with one another. Sir William Petty put the matter in this striking way: Labor is the father of product and land the mother. We cannot say which is more essential in producing a baby—a mother or a father. So, too, it is generally impossible to say how much output has been created by any one of the different inputs taken by itself.

It is this *interdependence* of productivities of land, labor, and capital goods that makes the distribution of income a complex topic. Suppose we had to distribute at one time the entire output of a nation. If land had by itself produced so much, and labor had alone produced so much, and machinery had by

itself produced the rest, distribution might be easy. Under supply and demand, if each factor produced a certain amount by itself, it could enjoy the undivided fruits of its own work.

But reread the above paragraph and underline such words as "by itself produced" and "had alone produced." They refer to a fantasy world of independent productivities which simply does not exist in reality. When an omelette is produced by chef's labor and chicken's eggs and cow's butter and land's natural gas, how can you unscramble the separate contributions of each input?

To find the answer, we must look to the interaction of marginal productivities (which affect demand) and factor supplies—both of which determine the competitive price and quantity.

REVIEW OF PRODUCTION THEORY

The fundamental point to understand is that *the demands for the various factors of production are derived from the revenues that each factor yields on its marginal product.* Before showing this result, we will review the essentials of Chapter 6's production theory.

		Marginal Revenue Product		
(1) Units of labor (workers)	(2) Total product (bushels)	(3) Marginal product of labor (bushels per worker)	(4) Price of output ($ per bushel)	(5) Marginal revenue product of labor ($ per worker)
0	0			
		20,000	3	60,000
1	20,000			
		10,000	3	30,000
2	30,000			
		5,000	3	15,000
3	35,000			
		3,000	3	9,000
4	38,000			
		1,000	3	3,000
5	39,000			

TABLE 12-3. Calculation of Marginal Revenue Product for Perfectly Competitive Firm
The marginal product of labor is shown in column (3). Marginal revenue product of labor shows how much additional revenue the firm receives when an additional unit of labor is employed. It equals the marginal product in column (3) times the competitive output price in column (4).

The theory of production begins with the notion of the production function. The *production function* indicates the maximum amount of output that can be produced, with a given state of technical knowledge, for each combination of factor inputs. The production-function concept provides a rigorous definition of marginal product. Recall that the *marginal product* of an input is the extra product or output added by 1 extra unit of that input while other inputs are held constant.[1] The first three columns of Table 12-3 provide a review of the way marginal products are calculated.

As a final element of review, recall the *law of diminishing returns.* Column (3) of Table 12-3 shows that each successive unit of labor has a declining marginal product. "Declining marginal product" is another name for diminishing returns. Moreover, we can interchange land for labor, varying the amount of land while holding constant labor and other inputs, and we would generally observe the law of diminishing returns at work for land as well as for labor.

Marginal Revenue Product

We can use the tools of production theory to devise a key concept in distribution theory, *marginal revenue product (MRP).* Suppose we are operating a giant shirt factory. We know how many shirts each additional worker produces. But the firm wants to maximize profits measured in dollars, for it pays salaries and dividends with money, not with shirts. We therefore need a concept that measures the additional *dollars* each additional unit of input produces. Economists give the name "marginal revenue product" to the money value of the additional output generated by an extra unit of input.

The **marginal revenue product** of input A is the additional revenue produced by an additional unit of input A.

Competitive Case. It is easy to calculate marginal revenue product when product markets are perfectly competitive. In this case, each unit of the worker's marginal product (MP_L) can be sold at the competitive output price (P). Moreover, since we are considering perfect competition, the output price is unaffected by the firm's output, and price therefore equals marginal revenue (MR). If we have an MP_L of 10,000 bushels and a price and MR of $3, the dollar value of the output produced by the last worker—the marginal revenue product of labor

---

[1] Note that the marginal product of a factor is expressed in *physical* units of product per unit of additional input. So economists sometimes use the term "marginal physical product" rather than "marginal product," particularly when they want to avoid any possible confusion with a concept we will soon encounter called "marginal revenue product." For brevity, we will skip the word "physical" and abbreviate marginal product as *MP.*

(MRP_L)—is \$30,000 (equal to 10,000 × \$3). This is shown in column (5) of Table 12-3. Hence, under perfect competition, each worker is worth to the firm the dollar value of the last worker's marginal product; the value of each acre of land is the marginal product of land times the output price; and so forth for each factor.

Imperfect Competition. What happens in the case of imperfect competition, where the individual firm's demand curve is downward-sloping? Here, the marginal revenue received from each extra unit of output sold is less than the price because the firm must lower its price on previous units to sell an additional unit. Each unit of marginal product will be worth $MR < P$ to the firm.

To continue our previous example, say that the MR is \$2 while the price is \$3. Then the MRP of the second worker in Table 12-3 would be \$20,000 (equal to the MP_L of 10,000 × the MR of \$2), rather than the \$30,000 of the competitive case.

To summarize, the additional revenue gained by a firm from an additional unit of input is called the marginal revenue product. It is measured in dollar terms by the marginal revenue multiplied by the marginal product of the input.

Marginal revenue product represents the additional revenue a firm earns from employment of an additional unit of an input, with other inputs held constant. It is defined as the marginal product of the input multiplied by the marginal revenue obtained from selling an extra unit of output. This holds for labor (L), land (A), and other inputs:

$$\text{Marginal revenue product of labor}$$
$$(MRP_L) = MR \times MP_L$$

$$\text{Marginal revenue product of land}$$
$$(MRP_A) = MR \times MP_A$$

and so forth.

Under conditions of perfect competition, because $P = MR$:

$$\text{Marginal revenue product}$$
$$(MRP_i) = P \times MP_i$$

for each input.

THE DEMAND FOR FACTORS OF PRODUCTION

Having analyzed the underlying concepts, we now turn to the determinants of the demand for inputs.

We then show how profit-maximizing firms decide upon the optimal combination of inputs, which allows us to derive the demand for inputs.

Factor Demands for Profit-Maximizing Firms

Where did the demand for cornland shown in Figure 12-2 come from? For that matter, what determines the demand for any factor of production? To understand these issues, we must analyze how a profit-oriented firm chooses its optimal combination of inputs.

Imagine that you are a profit-maximizing farmer. In your area, you can hire all the farmhands you want at \$20,000 per year. Your accountant hands you a spreadsheet with the data in Table 12-3. How would you proceed?

You could try out different possibilities. If you hire one worker, the additional revenue (the MRP) is \$60,000 while the marginal cost of the worker is \$20,000, so your extra profit is \$40,000. A second worker gives you an MRP of \$30,000 for an additional profit of \$10,000. The third worker produces extra output yielding revenue of only \$15,000 but costs \$20,000; hence, it is not profitable to hire the third worker. Table 12-3 shows that the maximum profit is earned by hiring two workers. We have by trial and error found an interesting rule:

A firm will maximize profits by hiring a factor of production as long as the MRP of that input exceeds the extra cost of that input.

By using this reasoning, we can derive the rule for choosing the optimal combination of inputs: To maximize profits, inputs should be added as long as the marginal revenue product of the input exceeds the marginal cost or price of the input.

For perfectly competitive factor markets, the rule is even simpler. Recall that under competition the marginal revenue product equals price times marginal product ($MRP = P \times MP$).

The profit-maximizing combination of inputs for a perfectly competitive firm comes when the marginal product times the output price equals the price of the input:

$$\text{Marginal product of labor} \times \text{output price}$$
$$= \text{price of labor} = \text{wage rate}$$
$$\text{Marginal product of land} \times \text{output price}$$
$$= \text{price of land} = \text{rent}$$

and so forth.

We can understand this rule by the following reasoning: Say that inputs into corn production (or any competitive industry) are bundled into $1 units—$1 units of labor, $1 units of land, and so forth. The firm will want to hire that quantity of $1 units of each input which will cause the revenue earned on the last unit to also be just $1. The incremental revenue is the corn *MP* of the input times the corn price, *P*. When inputs have been added so that the $MP \times P$ just reaches $1, the $1 of additional input cost just equals the $1 of additional revenue.

Least-Cost Rule. We can restate the condition much more generally in a way that applies to both perfect and imperfect competition in product markets (as long as factor markets are competitive). Reorganizing the basic conditions shown above, we have

$$\frac{\text{Marginal product of labor}}{\text{Price of labor}} = \frac{\text{marginal product of land}}{\text{price of land}} = \cdots$$

$$= \frac{1}{\text{marginal revenue}}$$

Suppose that you own a cable television monopoly in Denver. If you want to maximize profits, you will want to choose the best combination of workers, land easements for your cables, trucks, and testing equipment to minimize costs. If a month's truck rental costs $8000 while monthly labor costs per worker are $800, costs are minimized when the marginal products *per dollar of input* are the same. Since trucks cost 10 times as much as labor, truck *MP* must be 10 times labor *MP*.

Least-cost rule: Costs are minimized when the marginal product per dollar of input is equalized for each input. This holds for both perfect and imperfect competitors in product markets.

Marginal Revenue Product and the Demand for Factors

Having derived the *MRP* for different factors, we can now understand the demand for factors of production. We just saw that a profit-maximizing firm would choose input quantities such that the price of each input equaled the *MRP* of that input. This means that from the *MRP* schedule for an input, we can immediately determine the relationship

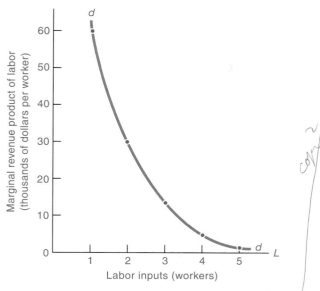

FIGURE 12-3. Demand for Inputs Derived through Marginal Revenue Products

The demand for labor is derived from the marginal revenue product of labor. This figure uses the data for the competitive firm displayed in Table 12-3.

between the price of the input and the quantity demanded of that input. This relationship is what we call the demand curve.

Glance back at Table 12-3 on p. 215. This table shows in the last column the *MRP* of labor for our corn farm. By the profit-maximizing condition, we know that at a wage of $60,000 the firm would choose 1 unit of labor; at a $30,000 wage, 2 units of labor would be sought; and so forth.

The *MRP* schedule for each input gives the demand schedule of the firm for that input.

We have used this result in Figure 12-3 to draw a labor demand curve for our corn farm using the data shown in Table 12-3. We have in addition drawn a smooth curve through the individual points to show how the demand curve would appear if fractional units of labor could be purchased.

Substitution Rule. A corollary of the least-cost rule is the **substitution rule:** If the price of one factor rises while other factor prices remain fixed, the firm will profit from substituting more of the other inputs for the more expensive factor. A rise in labor's price, P_L, will reduce MP_L/P_L. Firms will respond by reducing employment and increasing land use until equality of marginal products per dollar of input is restored—thus lowering the amount of needed L and increasing the demand for land acres. A rise in land's price, P_A, alone will, by the same logic, cause labor to be substituted for more expensive land. Like the least-cost rule, the substitution rule and the derived demand for factors apply to both perfect and imperfect competition in product markets.

SUPPLY OF FACTORS OF PRODUCTION

A complete analysis of the determination of factor prices and of incomes must combine both the demand for inputs just described and the supplies of different factors. The general principles of supply vary from input to input, and this topic will be explored in depth in the next two chapters. At this point we provide a few introductory comments.

In a market economy, most factors of production are privately owned. People "own" their labor in the sense that they control its use; but this crucial "human capital" can today only be rented, not sold. Capital and land are generally privately owned by households and by businesses.

Decisions about *labor* supply are determined by many economic and noneconomic factors. The important determinants of labor supply are the price of labor (i.e., the wage rate) and demographic factors, such as age, gender, education, and family structure. The quantity of *land* and other natural resources is determined by geology and cannot be significantly changed, although the quality of land is affected by conservation, settlement patterns, and improvements. The supply of *capital* depends upon past investments made by businesses, households, and governments. In the short run, the stock of capital is fixed like land, but in the long run the supply of capital is sensitive to economic factors such as risks and rates of return.

Can we say anything about the elasticity of supply of inputs? Actually, the supply curve may slope positively or be vertical and might even have a negative slope. For most factors, we would expect that the supply responds positively to the factor's price in the long run; in this case, the supply curve would slope upward and to the right. The supply of land is usually thought to be unaffected by price, and in this case the supply of land will be perfectly inelastic, with a vertical supply curve. In some special cases, when the return to the factor increases, owners may supply less of the factor to the market. For example, if people feel they can afford to work fewer hours when wages rise, the supply curve for labor might bend backward at high wage rates, rather than slope upward.

The different possible elasticities for the supply of factors are illustrated by the *SS* supply curve shown in Figure 12-4.

DETERMINATION OF FACTOR PRICES BY SUPPLY AND DEMAND

A full analysis of the distribution of income must combine the supply and demand for factors of production. Earlier parts of this section provided the underpinnings for analysis of demand and gave a brief description of supply. We showed that, for given factor prices, profit-maximizing firms would choose input combinations according to their marginal revenue products. As the price of land falls, each farmer would substitute land for other inputs such as labor, machinery, and fertilizer. Each farmer therefore would show a demand for cornland inputs like that in Figure 12-2(*b*).

How do we obtain the *market demand* for inputs (whether cornland, unskilled labor, or computers)? We add together the individual demands of each of the firms. Thus at a given price of land, we add together all the demands for land of all the firms at that price; and we do the same at every price of land. In other words, *we add horizontally all the demand curves for land of the individual firms to obtain the market demand curve for land.* We follow the same procedure for any input, summing up all the derived demands of all the businesses to get the market demand for each input. And in each case, the derived demand for the input is based on the marginal revenue product of the input under consideration.[2] Figure 12-5 shows a general demand curve for a factor of production as the *DD* curve.

How do we find the overall market equilibrium? *The equilibrium price of the input in a competitive market*

---

[2] Note that this process of adding factor demand curves horizontally is exactly the same procedure that we followed in obtaining market demand curves for consumers in Chapter 5.

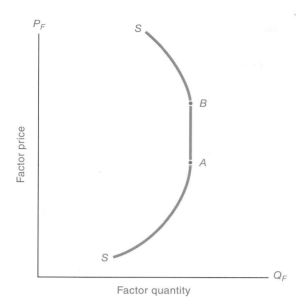

FIGURE 12-4. Supply Curve for Factors of Production
Supplies of factors of production depend upon character-istics of the factors and the preferences of their owners. Generally, supplies will respond positively to price, as in the region below *A*. For factors that are fixed in supply, like land, the supply curve will be perfectly inelastic, as from *A* to *B*. In special cases where a higher price of the factor increases the income of its owner greatly, such as for labor or oil, the supply curve may bend backward, as in the region above *B*.

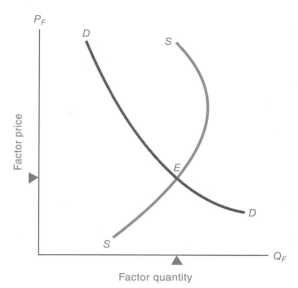

FIGURE 12-5. Factor Supply and Derived Demand Inter-act to Determine Factor Prices and Income Distribution
Factor prices are determined by the interaction of factor supply and demand. If the demand for an inelastically sup-plied factor such as land rises, that factor's total income will rise. Similarly, supplies and demands for trucks or computer programmers or office buildings will affect their prices and quantities sold. At what point will an increase in demand decrease both quantity supplied and total income of this factor?

comes at that level where the quantities supplied and demanded are equal. This is illustrated in Figure 12-5, where the derived demand curve for a factor inter-sects its supply curve at point *E*. Only at that price will the amount that owners of the factor willingly supply just balance the amount that the buyers will-ingly purchase.

Of Slicers and Flippers.
We can apply these concepts to two factor markets to see why disparities in incomes are so high. Figure 12-6 on page 220 shows the markets for two kinds of labor—surgeons and fast-food workers. The supply of surgeons is severely limited by the need for medical licensing and the length and cost of education and training; as a result, there are but 50,000 practicing surgeons in the United States. Demand for surgery is growing rapidly along with other health-care services. The

result is that surgeons earn $245,000 a year on average. Moreover, an increase in demand will result in a sharp increase in earnings with little increase in output.

At the other end of the earnings scale are fast-food workers. These jobs have no skill or educational requirements and are open to virtually everyone. The supply is highly elastic, and employment has grown from 1.5 million workers in 1970 to 2.5 mil-lion workers in 1993. Wages are close to the mini-mum wage because of the ease of entry into this mar-ket, and the average full-time employee makes $12,000 a year. What is the reason for the vast differ-ence in earning power of surgeons and hamburger flippers? It is mainly the quality of labor, not the quantity of hours.

The Rich and the Rest.
If you are one of the richest Americans, you might have $50 million of

interest, dividends, and other property income, while the median household earns less than $1000 a year on its financial wealth. Figure 12-7 explains this difference. The rate of return on stocks or bonds is not that much higher for the richest than for the middle class. Rather, the rich have a much bigger wealth base to earn on. The shaded rectangles in Figure 12-7 show the capital earnings of the two groups. Make sure you understand that it is the amount of wealth rather than the rate of return that makes the rectangle of the top wealth holders so large.

These two examples show that factor prices and people's incomes are not determined solely by chance. Rather, the forces of supply and demand operate to create high returns to factors that have either limited supply or high demand as reflected in high marginal revenue product. If a factor such as surgeons becomes scarcer, say, because training requirements are tightened, the price of this factor will rise and surgeons will enjoy higher incomes. However, if demand decreases in some field like psy-

chiatry—perhaps because insurance companies decide to cut back on psychiatric coverage, or close substitutes like social workers and psychologists lure away patients, or people stop wanting so much counseling—psychiatrists' incomes will fall. Competition giveth, and competition taketh away.

THE DISTRIBUTION OF NATIONAL INCOME

With our new understanding of marginal-productivity theory, we can now come back to the question raised at the beginning of the chapter. In a world of intense competition, how do markets allocate national output among two or more factors of production?

A simplified theory of factor-income distribution was first proposed around the turn of the century by John Bates Clark, a distinguished economist at Columbia University. It can be applied to competitive markets for any number of final products and

FIGURE 12-6. The Markets for Surgeons and Fast-Food Workers

In (**a**), we see the impact of a limited supply of surgeons: small output and high earnings per surgeon. What would be the effect on total earnings of surgeons and on the price of an operation if a rising share of elderly led to increases in the demand for surgeons?

In (**b**), open entry and low skill requirements imply a highly elastic supply of fast-food workers. Wages are beaten down and employment is high. What would be the effect on wages and employment if more teenagers look for jobs?

(a) Market for Surgeons

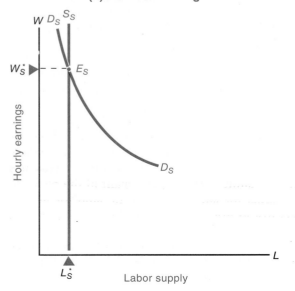

(b) Market for Fast-Food Workers

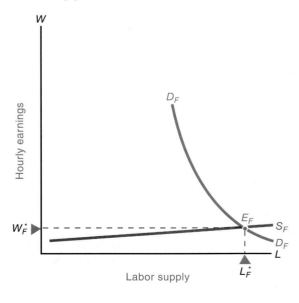

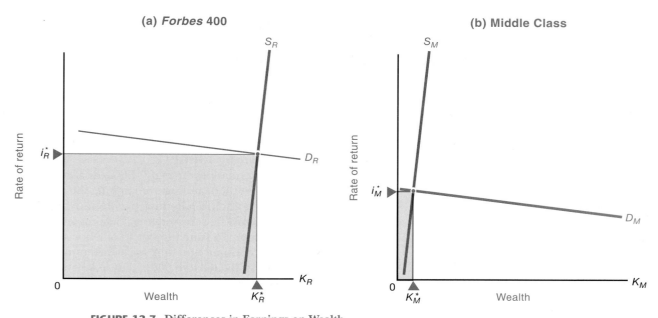

FIGURE 12-7. Differences in Earnings on Wealth

The top wealth holders in (**a**) bring vastly more wealth to the market. Because they invest in riskier areas, their investments have slightly higher returns than those of the middle class. Shaded rectangles are the product of wealth and rate of return and give annual property income.

    The middle class in (**b**) has little property and invests it conservatively. Total property income is modest in comparison with (**a**).

factor inputs. But it is most easily grasped if we consider a simplified world with only one product in which all accounts are kept in real terms. The product could be corn or a basket of goods, but we will call it Q. Moreover, by setting the price equal to 1, we can conduct the entire discussion in real terms, with the value of output being Q and with the wage rate being the real wage in terms of goods or Q. In this situation, a production function tells how much Q is produced for each quantity of labor-hours, L, and for each quantity of acres of homogeneous land, A. Note that because $P = 1$, under perfect competition $MRP = MP \times P = MP \times 1 = MP$ and the wage $= MP_L$.

    Clark reasoned as follows: A first worker has a large marginal product because there is so much land to work with. Worker 2 has a slightly smaller marginal product. But the two workers are alike, so they must get exactly the same wage. The puzzle is, which wage? The MP of worker 1, or of worker 2, or the average of the two?

Under perfect competition, the answer is clear: Landlords will not hire a worker if the market wage exceeds that worker's marginal product. So the demand curve for labor will ensure that *all* the workers receive a wage rate equal to the marginal product of the last worker.

    But now there is a surplus of total output over the wage bill because earlier workers had higher MPs than the last worker. What happens to the excess MPs produced by all the earlier workers? The excess stays with the landlords as their residual earnings, which we will later call *rent*. Why, you might ask, do the landlords, who may be sipping their martinis thousands of miles away, earn anything on the land? The reason is that each landowner is a participant in the competitive market for land and rents the land for its best price. Just as worker competes with worker for jobs, landowner competes with landowner for workers. There are no conspiracies, no employer associations, and no unions in Clark's competitive world—just the operation of supply and demand.

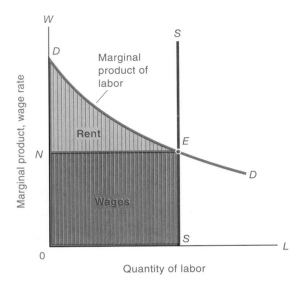

FIGURE 12-8. Marginal Product Principles Determine
Factor Distribution of Income

Each vertical slice represents the marginal product of that
unit of labor. Total national output $0DES$ is found by
adding all the vertical slices of MP up to the total supply of
labor at S.

The distribution of output is determined by marginal
product principles. Total wages are the lower rectangle
(equal to the wage rate $0N$ times the quantity of labor $0S$).
Land rents get the residual upper triangle NDE.

We have therefore determined the total wages
paid to labor. Figure 12-8 shows that the marginal
product curve of labor gives the demand curve of all
employers in terms of real wages. Labor-supply factors determine the supply of labor (shown as SS).
The equilibrium wage comes at E. The total wages
paid to labor are given by $W \times L$ (for example, if W
= 5 and L = 1 million, total wages = 5 million); this
is shown by the dark area of the rectangle, $0SEN$.

Surprisingly, we can also calculate the rent
income of land. The light rust rent triangle NDE in
Figure 12-8 measures all the surplus output which
was produced but was not paid out in wages. The
size of the rent triangle is determined by how much
the MP of labor declines as additional labor is
added—that is, by the extent of diminishing
returns. If there are a few high-quality plots, additional units of labor will show sharp diminishing
returns and rent's share will be large. If, by contrast,
there is a great deal of homogeneous frontier land

just waiting to be cleared, there may be little tendency to diminishing returns and land's rent triangle will be very small.

We have drawn Figure 12-8 so that labor's wages
are about 3 times larger than property's rents. This 3-
to-1 relationship reflects the fact that labor earnings
constitute about three-quarters of national income.

Marginal-Productivity Theory with Many Inputs

The marginal-productivity theory is a great step
forward in understanding the pricing of different
inputs. Note additionally that the positions of land
and labor could be reversed to get a complete theory
of distribution. To switch the roles of labor and land,
hold labor constant and add successive units of variable land to fixed labor. Calculate each successive
acre's marginal product.

Then draw a demand curve showing how many
acres labor owners will demand of land at each rent
rate. In the new version of Figure 12-8 that you draw,
find a new E' point of equilibrium. Identify land's
rectangle of rent as determined by rent $\times$ quantity of
land. Identify labor's residual wage triangle. Finally,
note the complete symmetry of the factors. This new
graph shows that we should think of the distributive
shares of each and every factor of production as
being simultaneously determined by their interdependent marginal products.

That is not all. Instead of labor and land, suppose the only two factors were labor and some versa-
tile capital goods. Suppose a smooth production
function relates Q to labor and capital with the same
general properties as in Figure 12-8. In this case, you
can redraw Figure 12-8 and get an identical picture
of income distribution between labor and capital.
Indeed, we can perform the same operation for
three, four, or any number of factors.

In competitive markets, the demand for inputs is
determined by the marginal products of factors. In
the simplified case where factors are paid in terms of
the single output, we get

Wage = marginal product of labor
Rent = marginal product of land

and so forth for any factor. This distributes 100 percent of output, no more and no less, among all the
factors of production.

We see, then, that the aggregate theory of the distribution of income is compatible with the competitive pricing of any number of goods produced by any number of factors. This simple but powerful theory shows how the distribution of income is related to productivity in a competitive market economy.

Now that we are armed with the general principles underlying the pricing of factors of production and the determination of the distribution of income, we can turn to a detailed discussion of the special features in the three major factor markets—land, labor, and capital.

SUMMARY

A. Income and Wealth

1. Distribution theory is concerned with the basic question of *for whom* economic goods are to be produced. In examining how the different factors of production—land, labor, and capital—get priced in the market, distribution theory considers how supplies and demands for these factors are linked and how they determine all kinds of wages, rents, interest rates, and profits.

2. Income refers to the total receipts or cash earned by a person or household during a given time period (usually a year). Income consists of labor earnings, property income, and government transfer payments.

3. National income consists of the labor earnings and property income generated by the economy in a year. Government takes a share of that national income in the form of taxes and gives back part of what it collects as transfer payments. The posttax personal income of an individual includes the returns on all the factors of production—labor and property—that the individual owns, plus transfer payments from the government, less taxes.

B. Input Pricing by Marignal Productivity

4. To understand the demand for factors of production, we must analyze the theory of production and the derived demand for factors. The demand for inputs is a derived demand: We demand pizza ovens and wheatland not for their own sake but for the pizzas and bread that they can produce for consumers. Factor demand curves are derived from commodity demand curves. An upward shift in the final demand curve causes a similar upward shift in the derived factor demand curve; greater inelasticity in commodity demand produces greater inelasticity of derived factor demand.

5. We met in earlier chapters the concepts of the production function and marginal products. The demand for a factor is drawn from its marginal revenue product (MRP), which is defined as the extra revenue earned from employing an extra unit of a factor. In any market, MRP equals the marginal revenue earned by the sale of an additional unit of the product times the marginal product of an input ($MRP = MR \times MP$). For competitive firms, because price equals marginal revenue, this simplifies to $MRP = P \times MP$.

6. A firm maximizes profits (and minimizes costs) when it sets the MRP of each factor equal to that factor's marginal cost, which is the factor's price. This can be stated equivalently as a condition in which the MRP per dollar of input is equalized for each input. This must hold in equilibrium because a profit-maximizing employer will hire any factor up to the point where the factor's marginal product will return in dollars of marginal revenue just what the factor costs.

7. To obtain the market demand for a factor, we add horizontally all firms' demand curves. This, along with the particular factor's own supply curve, determines the supply-and-demand equilibrium. At the market price for the factor of production, the amounts demanded and supplied will be exactly equal—only at equilibrium will the factor price have no tendency to change.

8. The marginal-productivity theory of income distribution analyzes the way total national income gets distributed among the different factors. Competition of numerous landowners and laborers drives factor prices to equal their marginal products. That process will allocate exactly 100 percent of the product. Any factor, not just labor alone, can be the varying factor. Because each unit of the factor gets paid only the MP of the last unit hired, there is a residual surplus of output left over from the MPs of early inputs. This residual is exactly equal to the incomes of the other factors under marginal productivity pricing. Hence, the marginal-productivity theory of distribution, though simplified, is a logically complete picture of the distribution of income under perfect competition.

CONCEPTS FOR REVIEW

income distribution
income, wealth
national income
transfer payments
personal income
marginal product, marginal revenue
    product, derived demand

marginal revenue product of input i
    $= MRP_i = MR \times MP_i = P \times MP_i$
    for competitive firm
aggregate distribution theory
MP rectangle, residual rent triangle

factor demands under competition:
    $MP_i \times P = $ factor price$_i$, which
    gives least-cost rule:

$$\frac{MP_L}{P_L} = \frac{MP_A}{P_A} = \cdots$$

$$= \frac{1}{\text{marginal revenue}}$$

QUESTIONS FOR DISCUSSION

1. Over the last century, hours of work per lifetime have declined about 50 percent while real wages have increased about 8 times. Assuming that the main change was an increase in the marginal-productivity-of-labor schedule, draw supply-and-demand diagrams for labor in 1895 and 1995 that will explain this trend. In your diagrams, put the number of hours worked per lifetime on the horizontal axis and the real wage rate on the vertical axis. What key factor about the supply of labor must you invoke to explain this historical trend?

2. For each of the following factors, name the final output for which the item is a derived demand: wheatland, gasoline, barber, machine tool for basketballs, wine press, economics textbook.

3. Study Figure 12-6. Assume that as the population ages, demand moves away from hamburgers and toward medical care. Draw the new demand curves and the new equilibria. Describe the outcome in terms of the wages, employment, and total income of surgeons and fast-food workers.

4. Why is each of the following incorrect? State the correct proposition.
   a. Marginal revenue product is calculated as total revenue earned per worker.
   b. Distribution theory is simple. You simply figure out how much each factor produces and then give the factor its share of output.
   c. Under competition, workers get paid the total output produced minus the costs of raw materials.

5. Figure 12-1 shows that the share of labor in national income changed little from 1935 to 1996 even though total national output rose by 700 percent. Draw a set of economywide curves like those in Figure 12-8 which can explain these two facts.

6. Labor leaders used to say, "Without any labor there is no product. Hence labor deserves *all* the product." Apologists for capital would reply, "Take away all capital goods, and labor scratches a bare pittance from the earth; practically all the product belongs to capital."

   Analyze the flaws in these arguments. If you were to accept the arguments, show that they would allocate 200 or 300 percent of output to two or three factors, whereas only 100 percent can be allocated. How does Clark's marginal-productivity theory resolve this dispute?

7. Draw the supply and demand curves for the oil market. Now suppose that a workable electric car shifts demand away from oil. Draw the new demand curve and the new equilibrium. Describe the outcome in terms of the price of oil, the quantity consumed, and the total income of the oil producers.

8. Consider the marginal product distribution theory in Figure 12-8. If immigration increases labor supply, the economy moves down the labor demand curve. Will labor's wage fall? (Show that the answer is yes.) Will the residual earnings of land, capital, and other factors rise? (Again, show that the answer is yes.) Can you tell what will happen to the absolute total of labor's rectangle as well as the share of labor income in the total? (Show that the answers are both no.)

9. In the marginal-productivity theory shown in Figure 12-8, let land rather than labor be the varying input. Draw a new figure and explain the theory with this new diagram. What is the residual factor?

CHAPTER 13
THE LABOR MARKET

Work is the curse of the drinking class.

Oscar Wilde

Workers are more than abstract factors of production. The economy, after all, is a method for organizing society whose purpose is to serve people both as consumers and as workers. It is for that reason that we worry about the quality and quantity of jobs, that the unemployment rate is a central social concern, and that the labor market is a constant source of controversy, social strife, and political ferment. The last century has witnessed pitched battles between labor and capital over wages, working conditions, and the right to organize; today, women and minorities struggle for good jobs and pay equity.

This chapter explores how wages are set in a market economy. Section A reviews the supply of labor and the determination of wages under competitive conditions. This is followed by a survey of labor unions, which are one means by which workers can collectively control their labor supply. We close with a review of the thorny problem of racial and gender discrimination in labor markets.

A. FUNDAMENTALS OF WAGE DETERMINATION

THE GENERAL WAGE LEVEL

In analyzing labor earnings, economists tend to look at the average **real wage**, which represents the purchasing power of an hour's work, or the money wages divided by the cost of living.[1] By that measure, American workers today are far better off than they

were 100 years ago. Figure 13-1 on page 226 shows the average hourly wage, adjusted for inflation, along with the average length of workweek.

The same powerful gains for workers are found in every industrial country. Across Western Europe, Japan, and the rapidly industrializing countries of East Asia, there has definitely been a steady, long-term improvement in the average worker's ability to buy food, clothing, and housing, as well as in the health and longevity of the population. In Europe and the United States, these gains began in earnest

---

[1] In this chapter, we will generally use the term "wages" as a shorthand expression for "wages, salaries, and other forms of compensation."

FIGURE 13-1. Wages Have Improved as Hours of Work Have Declined
With advancing technology and improved capital goods, American workers enjoy higher
wages while working shorter hours. Slower growth in productivity in the last two decades has
led to slower growth in real wages.

in the early 1800s, with the advent of the technological and social changes associated with the Industrial
Revolution. By comparison, before that time real
wages meandered up and down, with few long-term
gains.

That is not to say that the Industrial Revolution
was an unmitigated benefit to workers, especially in
the laissez-faire days of the 1800s. In point of fact, a
Dickens novel could hardly do justice to the dismal
conditions of child labor, workplace dangers, and
poor sanitation in early-nineteenth-century factories.
A workweek of 84 hours was the prevailing rule, with
time out for breakfast and sometimes supper. A good
deal of work could be squeezed out of a 6-year-old
child, and if a woman lost two fingers in a loom, she
still had eight left.

Was it a mistake for people to leave the farms for
the rigors of the factory? Probably not. Modern historians emphasize that even with the demanding
conditions in the factories, living standards were nevertheless greatly improved over those in the earlier
centuries of agrarian feudalism. The Industrial Revolution was a giant step forward for the working
class, not a step back. The idyllic picture of the
healthful, jolly countryside peopled by stout yeomen
and happy peasantry is a historical myth unsup-
ported by statistical research.

DEMAND FOR LABOR

We begin our examination of the general wage level
by examining the factors underlying the demand for
labor. The basic tools were provided in the last chapter, where we saw that the demand for a factor of production reflects the marginal productivity of that
input.

Figure 13-2 illustrates the marginal-productivity
theory. At a given time and with a given state of tech-

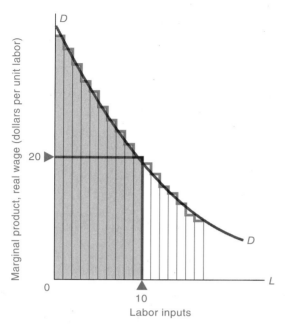

FIGURE 13-2. Demand for Labor Reflects Marginal Productivity

The demand for labor is determined by its marginal productivity in producing national output. The light gray vertical slices represent the extra output produced by the first, second, . . . unit of labor. The competitively determined general wage level at 10 units of labor is $20 per unit, equal to the marginal productivity of the tenth unit. The labor demand curve shifts up and out over time with capital accumulation, technological advance, and improvements in labor quality.

nology, there exists a relationship between the quantity of labor inputs and the amount of output. By the law of diminishing returns, each additional unit of labor input will add a smaller and smaller slab of output. In the example shown in Figure 13-2, at 10 units of labor, the competitively determined general wage level will be $20 per unit.

But probe deeper and ask what lies behind the marginal product. To begin with, the marginal productivity of labor will rise if workers have more or better capital goods to work with. Compare the productivity of a ditchdigger using a bulldozer with that of a similar digger using a hand shovel, or the copying capabilities of the medieval scribes with those of modern secretaries. Second, marginal productivity

of better-trained or better-educated workers will generally be higher than that of workers with less "human capital."

These reasons explain much of why wages and living standards have risen so much over the last century. Wages are high in the United States and other advanced countries because these nations have accumulated substantial capital stocks: dense networks of roads, rails, and communications; substantial amounts of plant and equipment for each worker; and adequate inventories of spare parts. Even more important are the vast improvements in technologies compared to those of an earlier era. Over the last century we have seen light bulbs replace oil lamps, airplanes replace horses, xerography replace quill and ink, and computers replace abacuses. Just imagine how productive the average American would be today with the technologies of 1897.

The quality of labor inputs is another factor determining the general wage level. By any measure—literacy, education, or training—the U.S. labor force of 1997 is vastly superior to the one of 1897. Years of education are necessary to produce an engineer capable of designing precision equipment. A decade of training must precede the ability to perform successful brain surgery. Overall, the proportion of adults who have completed college rose from 6 percent in 1950 to 22 percent in 1995. Such accumulations of human capital provide a substantial boost to the productivity of labor.

International Comparisons

The same reasoning explains why wage levels differ so dramatically across the world. Look at Table 13-1 on page 228, which gives the average wages plus benefits in manufacturing industries for eight countries. Wages are more than 10 times higher in the United States than in Mexico, 4 times higher in Japan than in South Korea, and almost 20 times higher in Great Britain than in India. We also see that compensation levels in Germany and Japan have pushed ahead of those in North America.

What accounts for the enormous differences? It's not that governments in India and Mexico are suppressing wage increases, though government policies do have some impact on the minimum wage and other aspects of the labor market. Rather, real

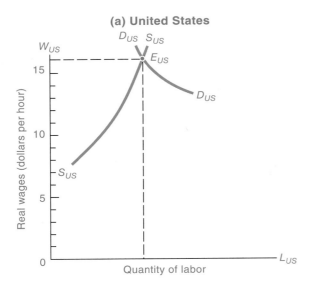

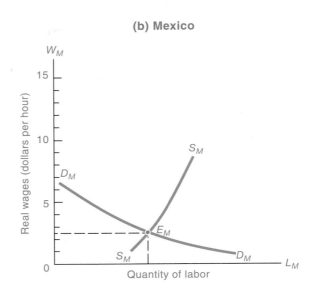

FIGURE 13-3. Favorable Resources, Skills, Management, Capital, and Technology Explain High U.S. Wages
Supply and demand determine a higher competitive wage in the United States than in Mexico. The major forces leading to high U.S. wages are a better-educated and more skilled work force, a larger stock of capital per worker, and modern technologies.

wages differ among countries primarily because of the operation of the supply and demand for labor. Look at Figure 13-3. Suppose that Figure 13-3(*a*) represents the state of affairs in the United States while Figure 13-3(*b*) describes Mexico. In Figure 13-3(*a*), the supply of U.S. workers is shown by the supply curve, $S_{US}S_{US}$, while the demand for workers is represented by $D_{US}D_{US}$. The equilibrium wage will settle at the level shown at E_{US}. If the wage were lower than E_{US}, shortages of labor would occur and employers would bid up wages to E_{US}, restoring the equilibrium. Similar forces determine E_M, the Mexican wage.

We see that the Mexican wage is lower than the U.S. wage principally because the Mexican demand curve for labor is far lower as a result of the low marginal productivity of labor in Mexico. Compared to the United States, a country like Mexico has much less capital to work with: many of the roads are unpaved, few computers and fax machines are in use, and much of the equipment is old or poorly maintained. In addition, the average educational levels in Mexico fall far short of the American standard, with a substantial fraction of the population still illiterate. All these factors make labor's marginal productivity low.

TABLE 13-1. General Wage Levels Vary Enormously across Countries
Western European nations, Japan, and the United States are high-wage countries, while Indian hourly wages are a tiny fraction of American levels. General wage levels are determined by supply and demand, but behind supply and demand lies the relative abundance of labor, capital, and resources, along with levels of skill and technology. (Source: U.S. Bureau of Labor Statistics *Monthly Labor Review*, 1996.)

Region	Wages and fringe benefits in manufacturing ($ per hour, 1995)
Western Germany	31.88
Japan	23.66
United States	17.20
Italy	16.48
Great Britain	13.77
South Korea	5.25
Mexico	1.51
India	0.71

This analysis can also help explain why wages are rising rapidly in East Asian countries like Hong Kong, South Korea, and Thailand. These countries are devoting a sizable share of their outputs to educating their population, investing in new capital goods, and importing the latest productive technologies. As a result, real wages in these countries have doubled over the last 20 years, while wages have stagnated in countries whose investments and economic policies are less well designed.

THE SUPPLY OF LABOR

Determinants of Supply

So far we have focused on the demand side of the labor market. Now we turn to the supply side of the labor market. *Labor supply* refers to the number of hours that the population desires to work in gainful activities. The three key elements for labor supply are hours per worker, labor-force participation, and immigration.

Hours Worked. While some people have jobs with flexible hours, most Americans work between 35 and 40 hours a week, without much leeway to increase or cut back their weekly hours. However, most people have a lot of control over how many hours they work over the course of their lifetimes. The decisions to go to college, to retire early, and to work part-time rather than full-time—all of these can reduce the number of total lifetime hours worked. On the other hand, the decision to moonlight and take on a second job will increase the lifetime hours worked.

Suppose that wages rise. Will that increase or decrease the lifetime hours of work? Look at the supply curve of labor in Figure 13-4. Note how the supply curve rises at first in a northeasterly direction; then at the critical point *C*, it begins to bend back in a northwesterly direction. How can we explain why higher wages may first increase and then decrease the quantity of labor supplied?

Put yourself in the shoes of a worker who has just been offered higher hourly rates and is free to choose the number of hours to be worked. You are tugged in two different directions. On the one hand, you are affected by the *substitution effect*, which tempts you to work longer hours because each hour of work is now better paid. Each hour of leisure has

FIGURE 13-4. As Wages Rise, Workers May Work Fewer Hours

Above the critical point *C*, raising the wage rate reduces the amount of labor supplied as the income effect outweighs the substitution effect. Why? Because at higher wages workers can afford more leisure even though each extra hour of leisure costs more in wages forgone.

become more expensive, and you have an incentive to substitute extra work for leisure.

But acting against the substitution effect is the *income effect.*[2] With the higher wage, your income is higher. With a higher income, you will want to buy more goods and services, and, in addition, you will want more leisure time. You can afford to take a week's vacation in the winter or an extra week in the summer or to retire earlier than you otherwise would.

Which will be more powerful, the substitution effect or the income effect? There is no single correct answer; it depends upon the individual. In the case shown in Figure 13-4, for all wage rates up to point *C*, labor supplied increases with a higher wage: the substitution effect outweighs the income effect. But from point *C* upward, the income effect outweighs the substitution effect, and labor supplied declines as wage rates climb higher.

---

[2] See Chapter 5 for a discussion of substitution and income effects in connection with consumption.

Labor-Force Participation. One of the most dramatic developments in recent decades has been the sharp influx of women into the work force. The labor-force participation rate of women (i.e., the fraction of women over 15 employed or actively looking for jobs) has jumped from 34 percent in 1950 to 60 percent today. In part this can be explained by rising real wages, which have made working more attractive for women. However, a change of this magnitude cannot be explained by economic factors alone. To understand such a significant alteration in working patterns, one must look outside economics to changing social attitudes toward the role of women as mothers, homemakers, and workers.

At the same time that more women have entered the labor force, the participation rate of older men has fallen sharply, especially for men over 65. The most important reason for this change is probably the increased generosity of federal health and retirement benefits, which has made it possible for many people to retire rather than keep working.

Immigration. The role of immigration in the labor-force supply has always been important in the United States. Whereas only 5 percent of the U.S. population was foreign-born in 1970, by 1990 the number had risen to almost 10 percent.

The flow of legal immigrants is controlled by an intricate quota system which favors skilled workers and their families, as well as close relatives of U.S. citizens and permanent residents. In addition, there are special quotas for political refugees. In recent years, the biggest groups of legal immigrants have come from places like Mexico, the Philippines, Vietnam, and some of the Central American and Caribbean countries.

The major change in immigration in recent decades has been a change in the characteristics of immigrants. In the 1950s, Germany and Canada were the major sources, while in the 1980s Mexico and the Philippines were the dominant sources. As a result, recent immigrants have been relatively much less skilled and educated than those of an earlier age.

From the point of view of labor supply, the overall effect of recent immigration has been an increase in the supply of low-skilled workers in the United States relative to high-skilled workers. Studies have estimated that this change in supply has contributed to a sharp decline in the wages of less-educated groups relative to the college-educated.

TABLE 13-2. Empirical Estimates of Labor-Supply Responses
Economists have devoted careful study to the response of labor supply to real wages. For males, the supply curve looks firmly backward-bending, while teenagers and adult females generally respond positively to wages. For the economy as a whole, the labor supply curve is close to completely inelastic or vertical. [Source: U.S. Department of Labor, *Employment and Earnings* (May 1997).]

Labor-Supply Patterns			
	Labor-force participation rate (% of population)		
Group of workers	1960	1997	Response of labor supply to increase in real wages
Adult males	86	77	Supply curve found to be backward-bending in most studies. Thus income effect dominates substitution effect. Supply elasticity is relatively small, in the order of -0.1 to -0.2; this implies that a 10% increase in real wages would lead to a 1% to 2% reduction in labor supplied.
Adult females	38	60	Most studies find positive effect of labor supplied in response to higher real wages.
Teenagers	46	52	Highly variable response.
Entire population 16 years and over	59	67	Elasticity of total labor supply is close to zero, with income effects just balancing out substitution effects. Estimated labor-supply elasticity for entire population is in the range from 0 to 0.2.

Empirical Findings

Theory does not tell us whether the labor supply of a group will react positively or negatively to a wage change. Will an income-tax increase on high-income workers—which reduces their after-tax wages—cause them to reduce their work effort? Will subsidizing the wages of the working poor reduce or increase their hours worked? These vital questions must be considered by the President and legislators as they weigh issues of equity and efficiency. We often need to know the exact shape or elasticity of the labor supply curve.

Table 13-2 presents a summary of numerous studies of the subject. This survey shows that the labor supply curve for adult males appears to be slightly backward-bending, while the response of other demographic groups looks more like a conventional upward-sloping supply curve. For the population as a whole, labor supply appears to respond very little to a change in real wages.

WAGE DIFFERENTIALS

While analysis of the general wage level is important for comparing different countries and times, we often want to understand *wage differentials*. In practice, wage rates differ enormously. The average wage is as hard to define as the average person. An auto executive may earn $4 million a year at the same time that a clerk earns $15,000 and a farmhand $12,000. A doctor may earn 15 or 20 times more than a lifeguard even though both are saving lives. In the same factory, a skilled machinist may earn $500 a week, while an unskilled janitor gets $200. Women may be paid $300 a week at the same time that equally qualified men earn $400.

In addition, there is a wide range of wage rates among broad industry groups. Table 13-3 shows that smaller, nonunionized sectors such as farming or retail trade tend to pay low wages, while the larger firms in manufacturing pay twice as much. But within major sectors there are large variations that depend on worker skills and market conditions—

fast-food workers make much less than doctors even though they all provide services.

How can we explain these wage differentials? Let's consider first a *perfectly competitive labor market*, one in which there are large numbers of workers and employers, none of which has the power to affect wage rates appreciably.[3] If all jobs and all people are identical in a perfectly competitive labor market, competition will cause the hourly wage rates to be exactly equal. No employer would pay more for the work of one person than for that person's identical twin or for another person who possessed identical skills.

This means that to explain the pervasive wage differences across industries or individuals, we must look to either differences in jobs, differences in people, or imperfect competition in labor markets.

Differences in Jobs: Compensating Wage Differentials

Some of the tremendous wage differentials observed in everyday life arise because of differences in the quality of jobs. Jobs differ in their attractive-

TABLE 13-3. Wages in Different Sectors
Average annual wages and salaries by broad industry groups range from a high of $44,200 in mining to a low of $17,500 in farming. Among industry groups, we see that average hourly earnings vary by a factor of 4 between computer programmers and fast-food workers. [Source: U.S. Department of Labor, *Employment and Earnings* (May 1997); U.S. Bureau of Economic Analysis.]

Compensation by Industry		
Industry	Average wages per full-time employee, 1996 ($ per year)	Average hourly earnings, January 1997 ($ per hour)
Farming	18,709	—
Mining	48,329	16.05
Manufacturing	37,165	13.02
Retail trade	18,821	8.23
Eating and drinking places	—	5.93
Services	29,935	12.25
Computer programming	—	22.74
Financial and real estate	44,629	13.16
Government	35,300	—

---

[3] Few labor markets are perfectly competitive in reality, but some (such as a large city's market for inexperienced teenagers or clerical workers) approach the competitive concept reasonably closely.

ness; hence wages may have to be raised to coax people into the less attractive jobs.

Wage differentials that serve to compensate for the relative attractiveness, or nonmonetary differences, among jobs are called **compensating differentials.**

Window washers must be paid more than janitors because of the risks of climbing skyscrapers. Workers often receive 5 percent extra pay on the 4 P.M. to 12 P.M. "swing shift" and 10 percent extra pay for the 12 midnight to 8 A.M. "graveyard shift." For hours beyond 40 per week or for holiday and weekend work, $1\frac{1}{2}$ to 2 times the base hourly pay is customary. Jobs that involve hard physical labor, tedium, low social prestige, irregular employment, seasonal layoff, or physical risk all tend to be less attractive. No wonder, then, that companies must pay $50,000 to $80,000 a year to recruit people to work at dangerous and lonely jobs on offshore oil platforms or in northern Alaska. Similarly, for jobs that are especially pleasant or psychologically rewarding, such as those of park rangers and the clergy, pay levels tend to be modest.

To test whether a given difference in pay between two jobs is a compensating differential, ask people who are well qualified for both jobs: "Would you take the higher-paying job in preference to the lower?" If they are not eager to take the higher-paying job, the pay difference is probably a compensating differential that reflects the nonmonetary differences between the jobs.

Differences in People: Labor Quality

We have just seen that some wage differentials serve to compensate for the differing degrees of attractiveness of different jobs. But look around you. Garbage collectors make much less than lawyers, yet surely the legal life has higher prestige and much more pleasant working conditions. We see countless examples of high-paying jobs that are more pleasant rather than less pleasant than low-paying work. We must look to factors beyond compensating differentials to explain the reason for most wage differences.

One key to wage disparities lies in the tremendous qualitative differences among people, differences traceable to differences in innate mental and

FIGURE 13-5. Earnings Benefit from Education and Experience
Earnings profiles of men show that earnings rise with both education and years of experience. [Adapted from Kevin M. Murphy and Finis Welch, "The Structure of Wages," *Quarterly Journal of Economics* (February 1992).]

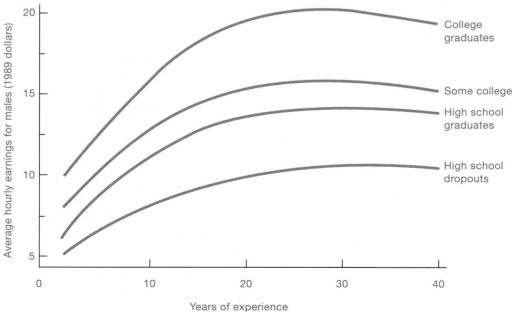

physical abilities, upbringing, education and training, and experience. A biologist might classify all of us as members of the species *homo sapiens,* but a personnel officer would insist that people differ enormously in their abilities to contribute to a firm's output.

While many of the differences in labor quality are determined by noneconomic factors, the decision to accumulate human capital can be evaluated economically. The term **human capital** refers to the stock of useful and valuable skills and knowledge accumulated by people in the process of their education and training. Doctors, lawyers, and engineers invest many years in their formal education and on-the-job training. They spend large sums on tuition and wages forgone, investing $100,000 to $200,000 in college and graduate training, and often work long hours. Part of the high salaries of these professionals should be viewed as a return on their investment in human capital—a return on the education that makes these highly trained workers a very special kind of labor.

Economic studies of incomes and education show that human capital is a good investment on average. Figure 13-5 shows the income profiles for different groups as a function of their education and experience. Groups with higher education start out with higher incomes and enjoy more rapid growth in incomes than do less educated groups.

Figure 13-6 shows the ratio of the hourly earnings of college graduates to those of high school graduates. Relative earnings rose sharply during the 1980s as the "price of skill" rose. Studies by labor economists have shown that individuals who have high quantitative abilities or computer skills have an economic advantage in today's labor market.

The return to investments in human capital: What is an investment in human capital? When a student goes to college, each year he or she might pay $10,000 in tuition and $15,000 in oppor-

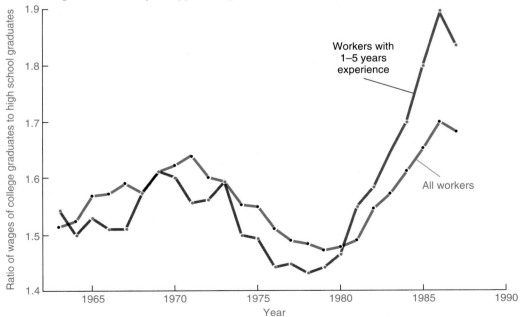

FIGURE 13-6. Relative Income Gains Have Been Dramatic for College Graduates
Income profiles changed dramatically during the turbulent 1980s. Incomes of college graduates rose sharply relative to those of high school graduates, and the largest gains were among the young. [Adapted from Lawrence F. Katz and Kevin M. Murphy, "Changes in Relative Wages: 1963–87," *Quarterly Journal of Economics* (February 1992).]

tunity costs of earnings forgone. That would mean a 4-year outlay of $100,000.

Does college actually pay off? The evidence suggests that it does. In return for this substantial investment, the earnings of the college graduate might exceed those of a high school graduate by $10,000 or more per year. Moreover, the returns to a college education have soared dramatically over the last 15 years. Whereas a college graduate earned 45 percent more than a high school graduate with the same background in the late 1970s, a decade later the earnings differential had widened to 85 percent (see Figure 13-6). More and more, in today's service economy, companies are processing information rather than raw materials. In the information economy, the skills learned in college are a prerequisite for a high-paying job. A high school dropout is generally at a severe disadvantage in the job market.

Even if you have to borrow for your education, put off years of gainful employment, live away from home, and pay for food and books, your lifetime earnings in the occupations that are open only to college graduates will probably more than compensate you for the costs. Recent data show that an 18-year-old male who graduates from college will earn about $4.5 million (at 1996 price and income levels) before the age of 65. A member of the same generation who graduates only from high school will earn about $2.7 million. Someone who does not finish high school will earn an average of only $1.8 million.

Often, people point to the role of luck in determining economic circumstances. But, as Louis Pasteur remarked, "Chance favors the prepared mind." In a world of rapidly changing technologies, education prepares people to understand and profit from new circumstances.

Differences in People: The "Rents" of Unique Individuals

For the lucky few, fame has lifted incomes to astronomical levels. Entertainers like Bill Cosby, basketball stars like Michael Jordan, singers like Whitney Houston, and even academic scribblers who served as advisers to presidents earn fabulous sums for their services.

These extremely talented people have a particular skill that is highly valued in today's economy. Outside their special field, they might earn but a small fraction of their high incomes. Moreover, their labor supply is unlikely to respond perceptibly to wages that are 20 or even 50 percent higher or lower. Econ-

omists refer to the excess of these wages above those of the next-best available occupation as a *pure economic rent*; these earnings are logically equivalent to the rents earned by fixed land.

Some economists have suggested that technological changes are making it easier for a small number of top individuals to serve a larger share of the market (recall our discussion of "winner-take-all markets" in Chapter 11). Top entertainers or athletes can now give a single performance that reaches a billion people via television and recordings—something that was not possible just a few years ago. If this trend continues, and labor rents rise further, the income gap between the winners and the runners-up may widen even further in the years ahead.

Segmented Markets and Noncompeting Groups

Even in a perfectly competitive world where people could move easily from one occupation to another, substantial wage differentials would appear. These differences would be necessary to reflect differences in the costs of education and training or in the unattractiveness of certain occupations or to indicate rewards for unique talents.

But even after taking into account all these reasons for wage differentials, we still find a large disparity in wage rates. The major reason for the difference is that labor markets are segmented into *noncompeting groups.*

A moment's thought will suggest that, instead of being a single factor of production, labor is many different, but closely related, factors of production. Doctors and mathematicians, for example, are noncompeting groups because it is difficult and costly for a member of one profession to enter into the other. Just as there are many different kinds of houses, each commanding a different price, so are there many different occupations and skills that compete only in a general way. Once we recognize the existence of many different submarkets of the labor market, we can see why wages may differ greatly among groups.

Why is the labor market divided into so many noncompeting groups? The major reason is that, for professions and skilled trades, it takes a large investment of time and money to become proficient. If coal mining declines because of environmental restrictions, the miners can hardly hope to land jobs

Summary of Competitive Wage Determination	
Labor situation	**Wage result**
1. People are all alike—jobs are all alike.	No wage differentials.
2. People are all alike—jobs differ in attractiveness.	Compensating wage differentials.
3. People differ, but each type of labor is in unchangeable supply (noncompeting groups).	Wage differentials that reflect supply and demand for segmented markets.
4. People differ, but there is some mobility among groups (partially competing groups).	General-equilibrium pattern of wage differentials as determined by general demand and supply (includes 1 through 3 as special cases).

TABLE 13-4. Market Wage Structure Shows Great Variety of Patterns under Competition

teaching environmental economics overnight. Once people specialize in a particular occupation, they become part of a particular labor submarket. They are thereby subject to the supply and demand for that skill and will find that their own labor earnings rise and fall depending upon events in that occupation and industry. Because of this segmentation, the wages for one occupation can diverge substantially from the wages in other areas.

The job choice of new immigrants is a classic case of noncompeting groups. Rather than go into the open job market, new immigrants from a particular country tend to cluster in certain occupations. For example, in many cities, such as Los Angeles and New York, a large number of grocery stores tend to be owned by Koreans. The reason is that the Koreans can get advice and support from friends and relatives who also own grocery stores. As immigrants get more experience and education in the United States and become more fluent in English, their job choice widens and they become part of the overall labor supply.

In addition, the theory of noncompeting groups helps us understand labor market discrimination. We will see in the next section of this chapter that much discrimination arises because workers are separated by gender, race, or ethnic background into noncompeting groups as a result of custom, law, or prejudice.

While the theory of noncompeting groups highlights an important aspect of labor markets, we must recognize that in the longer run entry and exit will reduce differentials. It is true that copper miners are unlikely to become computer programmers when computers and fiber optics displace rotary dials and copper wires. Consequently, we may see wage differentials arise between the two kinds of labor. But in the longer run, as more young people study computer science rather than work in copper mines, competition will tend to reduce some of the differentials of these noncompeting groups.

Table 13-4 summarizes the different forces at work in determining wage rates in competitive conditions.

B. THE AMERICAN LABOR MOVEMENT

So far we have looked at competitive labor markets. But for the 16 million Americans who belong to labor unions, some of the labor-supply decisions are made collectively. Unions negotiate collective bargaining agreements which often specify who can fill different jobs, what they will be paid, and what the

work rules are. And unions can decide to go on strike—withdraw their labor supply completely—in order to win a better deal from the employer.

The study of unions is an important part of understanding the dynamics of the U.S. labor market. For one thing, about one-seventh of the work force still belongs to unions, although that percentage reflects a significant decrease during recent years. Furthermore, in negotiating collective bargaining contracts, unions raise issues which are important to all workers, such as pensions, health-care benefits, and working hours.

HISTORY AND PRACTICE OF LABOR UNIONS

How did American labor unions begin? Although the first stirrings of American labor unions predate the Civil War, it was not until the last third of the nineteenth century that labor began to revolt against big business. In 1881, the present-day labor movement began to take shape with the founding of the American Federation of Labor (AFL). For almost half a century, until his death in 1924, Samuel Gompers dominated this organization and gave the movement its characteristic pattern.

Gompers' strategy was simple: Because he believed that no movement opposed to capitalism would flourish on American soil, he insisted on *business unionism*. Under this principle, American unions were engaged primarily in improving the economic status of workers—the struggle for higher wages, shorter hours, more vacations, better working conditions, and improved fringe benefits. American unions were the opposite of the labor movements in many European countries; abroad, unions have sometimes dominated major political parties and waged a class struggle to alter the form of government or to promote socialism.

At the beginning, labor was organized as *craft unions*, in which workers were grouped on the basis of a particular skill, such as carpentry or bricklaying. This strategy prevented the organization of huge mass-production industries into a single union. By the 1930s, astute union advocates began to see the handwriting on the wall: *industrial unions* (those organizing an entire industry, such as steel or coal) were the wave of the future. Industrial unions were introduced in 1935 with the formation of the Congress of Industrial Organizations (CIO). Today, American labor unions are organized into the AFL-CIO, which is the major national labor organization in the United States.

The wages and fringe benefits of unionized workers are determined by **collective bargaining.** This is the process of negotiation between representatives of firms and of workers for the purpose of establishing mutually agreeable conditions of employment. We have all heard of the last-minute, all-night sessions before a labor agreement is reached. What is actually in this agreement? The central part, of course, is the *economic package*. This includes the basic wage rates for different job categories, along with the rules for holidays and coffee breaks. In addition, the agreement will contain provisions for fringe benefits such as a pension plan, coverage for health care, and similar items. During periods of high inflation the agreement will generally contain a cost-of-living-adjustment (COLA) clause, which adjusts wages upward when consumer prices rise rapidly.

A second important and often controversial subject is *work rules*. These concern work assignments and tasks, job security, and workloads. Particularly in declining industries, the staffing requirements are a major issue because the demand for labor is falling. In the railroad industry, for example, there were decades of disputes about the number of people needed to run a train.

Collective bargaining is a complicated business, a matter of give-and-take. Much effort is spent negotiating purely economic issues, dividing the pie between wages and profits. Sometimes agreements get hung up on issues of management prerogatives, such as the ability to reassign workers or change work rules. In the end, both workers and management have a large stake in ensuring that workers are satisfied and productive on their jobs.

Government and Collective Bargaining

The history of labor unions reminds us that the legal framework is an important determinant of economic organization. Two hundred years ago, when labor first tried to organize in England and America, common-law doctrines against "conspiracy in restraint of trade" were used against union members. Well into this century, unions and their members were convicted by courts, fined, jailed, and harassed by various injunctive procedures. The Supreme Court repeatedly struck down acts designed to improve working conditions for women and children and other reform legislation on hours and wages.

It was only after the pendulum swung toward support of unions and collective bargaining that the explosive growth of unions began. A major landmark was the Clayton Act (1914), hailed as "labor's Magna Carta" and designed to remove labor from antitrust prosecution. The Fair Labor Standards Act (1938) barred child labor, called for time-and-a-half pay for weekly hours over 40, and set a federal minimum wage for most nonfarm workers.

The most important labor legislation of all was the National Labor Relations (or Wagner) Act of 1935. This law stated: "Employees shall have the right to . . . join . . . labor organizations, to bargain collectively . . . , and to engage in concerted activities." Spurred by pro-labor legislation, union membership rose from under one-tenth of the labor force in the 1920s to one-quarter of the work force by the end of World War II. Since the early 1970s, with deregulation of many industries and increasing international competition, union monopolies have been undermined, and the fraction of the labor force belonging to unions in the United States has steadily declined.

HOW UNIONS RAISE WAGES

How can labor unions raise the wages and improve the working conditions of their members? *Unions gain market power by obtaining a legal monopoly on the provision of labor services to a particular firm or industry.* Using this monopoly, they compel firms to provide wages, benefits, and working conditions that are above the competitive wage. For example, if nonunion plumbers earn $15 per hour in Alabama, a union might bargain with a large construction firm to set the wage at $25 per hour for that firm's plumbers.

Such an agreement is, however, valuable to the union only if the firm's access to alternative labor supplies can be restricted. Hence, under a typical collective bargaining agreement, firms agree not to hire nonunion plumbers, not to contract out plumbing services, and not to subcontract to nonunion firms. Each of these provisions helps prevent erosion of the union's monopoly lock on the supply of plumbers to the firm. In some industries, like steel and autos, unions will even try to unionize the entire industry so that firm A's unionized workers need not compete with firm B's nonunion workers. All these steps are necessary to protect high union wage rates.

Figure 13-7 shows the impact of agreed-upon high standard wages, where the union forces

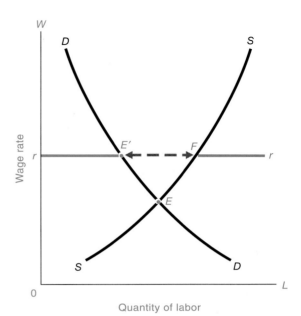

FIGURE 13-7. Unions Set High Standard Wage and Limit Employment

Raising the standard wage to rr increases wages and decreases the employment in the unionized labor market. Because of supply and demand imbalance, workers from E' to F cannot find employment in this market.

If unions push real wages too high for an entire economy, firms will demand E', while workers will supply F. Thus the black arrow from E' to F represents the amount of classical unemployment. This source of unemployment is particularly important when a country cannot affect its price level or exchange rate, and it differs from the unemployment caused by insufficient aggregate demand.

employers to pay wages at the standard rate shown by the horizontal line rr. The equilibrium is at E', where rr intersects the employers' demand curve. Note that the union has not directly reduced supply when it sets high standard wage rates. How does the market operate when wages are set above the market-clearing level? At the high wage rates, employment is limited by the firms' demand for labor. The number of workers who seek employment exceeds the demand by the segment $E'F$. These excess workers might be unemployed and waiting for vacancies in the high-paying union sector, or they might become discouraged and look for jobs in other sectors. The workers from E' to F are as effectively excluded from jobs as they would be if the union had directly limited entry.

The need to prevent nonunion competition also explains many of the political goals of the national labor movement. It explains why unions want to limit immigration; why unions support protectionist legislation to limit imports of foreign goods, which are goods made by workers who are not members of American unions; why quasi unions like medical associations fight to restrict the practice of medicine by other groups; and why unions sometimes oppose deregulation in industries such as trucking, communications, and airlines.

Theoretical Indeterminacy of Collective Bargaining.

In most collective bargaining negotiations, the workers press for higher wages while management holds out for lower compensation costs. This is a situation known as *bilateral monopoly*—where there is but one buyer and one seller. The outcome of bilateral monopoly cannot be predicted by economic forces of costs and demands alone; it depends as well on psychology, politics, and countless other intangible factors.[4]

EFFECTS ON WAGES AND EMPLOYMENT

The advocates of labor unions claim that unions have raised real wages and have benefited workers. Critics argue that the result of raising wages is high unemployment, inflation, and distorted resource allocation. What are the facts?

Has Unionization Raised Wages?

Let's start by reviewing the effects of unions on relative wages. Economists have estimated the economic impacts of unions by examining wages in unionized and nonunionized industries. On the basis of these analyses, economists have concluded

that union workers receive on average a 10 to 15 percent wage differential over nonunion workers. The differential ranges from a negligible amount for hotel workers and barbers to 25 to 30 percent higher earnings for skilled construction workers or coal miners. The pattern of results suggests that where unions can effectively monopolize labor supply and control entry, they will be most effective in raising wages.

Another approach examines the wages of individual workers, correcting for worker characteristics and taking into account whether the worker is in a union or nonunion job. Orley Ashenfelter of Princeton University examined a panel of workers over the period of 1967 to 1975. Correcting for the influence of each worker's sex, race, education, and other personal characteristics, he found that the workers who belonged to unions had wages 16 percent above those of nonunion workers. In addition, Ashenfelter found that black males who belonged to unions obtained even higher wage differentials than other groups: 23 percent higher wages as compared to 16 percent for white males. Since 1975, there has been relatively little change in the wages of union members relative to nonunionized workers, but the overall share of union workers in the labor force has declined.

Overall Impacts. Granted that unions raise the wages of union members, we might ask whether unions bootstrap the entire economy to a higher real wage. Most economists now believe that unions redistribute income not from capital to labor but from nonunion labor to union labor. Put differently, if unions succeed in raising their wages above competitive levels, their gains come at the expense of the wages of nonunion workers.

This analysis is supported by empirical evidence showing that the share of national income going to labor has changed little over the last six decades. Once cyclical influences on labor's share are removed, we can see no appreciable impact of unionization on the share of wages in the United States (see Figure 12-1 on page 211). The evidence from heavily unionized European countries suggests that when unions succeed in raising money wage rates, they sometimes trigger an inflationary wage-price spiral with little or no permanent effect upon real wages.

---

[4] Situations like labor-management bargains are the subject of game theory, analyzed in Chapter 11. The theoretical indeterminacy of collective bargaining stems from the following result from game theory: A two-person noncooperative game does not generally have a unique outcome. Rather, as with wars or strikes, the outcome depends on many factors, such as bargaining power, prestige, bluffing ability, and even each side's perception of the strength of its opponent.

Effects on Employment

If unions do not affect overall real wage levels, this suggests that their impact lies primarily upon *relative* wages. That is, wages in unionized industries would rise relative to those in nonunionized industries. Moreover, employment would tend to be reduced in unionized and expanded in nonunionized industries.

When powerful unions raise real wages to artificially high levels, the result is an excess supply of labor and what is called *classical unemployment.* This case is also illustrated by Figure 13-7. Assume that unions raise wages above the market-clearing wage at E to a higher real wage at rr. Then, if the supply and demand for labor in general are unchanged, the arrow between E' and F will represent the number of workers who want to work at wage rr but cannot find work. This is called *classical unemployment* because it results from too high real wages.

Economists often contrast classical unemployment with the unemployment that occurs in business cycles, often called Keynesian unemployment, which results from insufficient aggregate demand. The effects of too high real wages were seen after the economic unification of Germany in 1990. The economic union fixed East German wages at a level estimated to be at least twice as high as could be justified by labor's marginal revenue product. The result was a sharp decline in employment in eastern Germany after unification.

This analysis suggests that when a country or region gets locked into real wages that are too high, high levels of unemployment may result. The unemployment will not respond to the traditional macroeconomic policy of increasing aggregate spending but, rather, will require remedies that lower real wages.

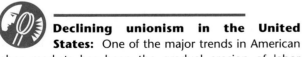 **Declining unionism in the United States:** One of the major trends in American labor markets has been the gradual erosion of labor unions since World War II. Whereas unions had organized one-quarter of the labor force in 1955, the fraction has fallen sharply since 1980. The share of workers in manufacturing has shrunk dramatically in the last two decades; only in the public sector are unions still a powerful force.

One of the reasons for the decline in unions is the waning power of the strike, which is the ultimate threat in collective bargaining. In the 1970s U.S. labor unions used that weapon regularly, averaging almost 300 strikes per year. More recently, though, strikes have become relatively uncommon; in fact, they have virtually disappeared from the American labor market. The reason for the decline is that strikes have often backfired on workers. In 1981, the striking air-traffic controllers were all fired by President Reagan. When the professional football players went on strike in 1987, they were forced back to work when the football owners put on the games with replacement players. In 1992, workers striking Caterpillar Inc., a huge maker of heavy equipment, had to end their 6-month strike when Caterpillar threatened to fill their jobs with permanent replacements. The inability to hurt firms through strikes has led to a significant weakening in the overall power of labor unions in the last two decades.

You might wonder if the declining power of unions would reduce labor compensation. Economists generally hold that a decline in union power will lower the relative wages of union workers rather than lower the overall share of labor. Look back at Figure 12-1 to examine the share of labor in national income. Can you determine any effect of the declining power of unions after 1980 on labor's share? Most economists believe not.

The Lump-of-Labor Fallacy

We close our analysis of wage theory by examining an important fallacy that often motivates labor market policies. Whenever unemployment is high, people often think that the solution lies in spreading existing work more evenly among the labor force. For example, Europe in the 1990s suffered extremely high unemployment, and many labor leaders and politicians suggested that the solution was to reduce the workweek so that the same number of hours would be worked by all the workers. This view—that the amount of work to be done is fixed—is called the **lump-of-labor fallacy.**

To begin with, we note the grain of truth in this viewpoint. For a particular group of workers, with special skills and stuck in one region, a reduction in the demand for labor may indeed pose a threat to their incomes. If wages adjust slowly, these workers may face prolonged spells of unemployment. The lump-of-labor fallacy may look quite real to these workers.

But from the point of view of the economy as a whole, the lump-of-labor argument implies that there is only so much remunerative work to be done, and this is indeed a fallacy. A careful examination of economic history in different countries shows that an increase in labor supply can be accommodated by higher employment, although that increase may require lower real wages. Similarly, a decrease in the demand for a particular kind of labor because of technological shifts in an industry can be adapted to—lower relative wages and migration of labor and capital will eventually provide new jobs for the displaced workers.

Work is not a lump that must be shared among the potential workers. Labor market adjustments can adapt to shifts in the supply and demand for labor through changes in the real wage and through migration of labor and capital. Moreover, in the short run, when wages and prices are sticky, the adjustment process can be lubricated by appropriate macroeconomic policies.

C. DISCRIMINATION BY RACE AND GENDER

Some earnings differentials arise from differences in education, work experience, and other factors; earnings disparities are inevitable in a market economy. But even after correction for such differences, a gap remains between the wages of white males and those of other groups. African-American and Hispanic citizens in the United States have long experienced a measurably lower level of income and wealth than other groups. And a woman will typically end up earning 20 percent less than a man with the same amount of schooling, the same test scores, and the same social background. In this section, we see how discrimination affects labor markets and incomes.

THE ECONOMICS OF DISCRIMINATION

When differences in earnings arise simply because of an irrelevant personal characteristic, such as race, gender, sexual orientation, or religion, we call this **discrimination.**

The history of black Americans illustrates how social processes depressed their wages and social status. After slavery was abolished, the black population of the American south fell into a caste system of peonage under "Jim Crow" legislation. Even though legally free and subject to the laws of supply and demand, black workers had earnings far below those of whites. Why? Because they had inferior schooling and were excluded from the best jobs by trade unions, local laws, and customs. They were consequently shunted into menial, low-skilled occupations that were effectively noncompeting groups.

Supply and demand can illustrate how exclusion lowers the incomes of groups that are targets of discrimination. Under discrimination, certain jobs are reserved for the privileged group, as is depicted in Figure 13-8(a). In this labor market, the supply of privileged workers is shown by $S_p S_p$, while the demand for such labor is depicted as $D_p D_p$. Equilibrium wages occur at the high level shown at E_p.

Meanwhile, Figure 13-8(b) shows what is happening for low-paid unskilled jobs. Minority workers live in areas with poor schools and cannot afford private education, so they do not receive training for the high-paying jobs. With low levels of skills, they have low marginal revenue products in the low-skilled jobs, so their wages are depressed to the low-wage equilibrium at E_m.

Note the differential between the two markets. Because minorities are excluded from good jobs, market forces have decreed that they earn much lower wages than the privileged workers. Someone might even argue that minorities "deserve" lower wages because their competitive marginal revenue products are lower. But this rationalization overlooks the root of the wage differentials, which is that wage differences arose because certain groups were excluded from the good jobs by their inability to obtain education and training and by the force of custom, law, or collusion.

Statistical Discrimination

Discrimination is particularly harmful when it distorts incentives for visible groups to work hard and invest in human capital. This occurs under sta-

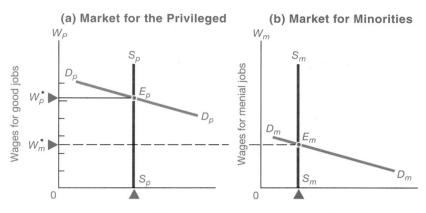

FIGURE 13-8. Discrimination by Exclusion Lowers the Wage Rates of Excluded Minorities
Discrimination is often enforced by excluding certain groups from privileged jobs. If minorities are excluded from good jobs in market (**a**), they must work in inferior jobs in (**b**). The privileged group enjoys high wage rates at E_p, while minorities earn low wage rates at E_m in market (**b**).

tistical discrimination, in which individuals are treated on the basis of the average behavior of members of the group to which they belong.

One common example arises when an employer screens employees on the basis of their college. Experience has shown that people who graduate from better schools are *on average* more productive; in addition, grade point averages are often difficult to evaluate because of differences in grading standards at schools. Employers therefore often hire people on the basis of their college rather than on their grades. A more careful screening process would show that there are many highly qualified workers from the less well-known schools. We see here a common form of statistical discrimination on the basis of average quality of schooling.

Statistical discrimination becomes pernicious because it reinforces stereotypes and reduces the incentives of individual members of a group to develop skills and experience. Consider someone who goes to a less well known school. She knows that she will be largely judged by the quality of her schooling credentials. The grade point average, the difficulty of the courses taken, the actual learning, and on-the-job experience may be ignored. The result is that, when subject to statistical discrimination, individuals have greatly reduced incentives to invest in activities that will improve skills and make better workers.

Statistical discrimination is seen in many areas of society. Life insurance and automobile insurance generally average the risks of people who are careful with those who live dangerously; this tends to reduce the incentive to behave cautiously and leads to a decrease in the average amount of caution in the population. Women were traditionally excluded from quantitatively oriented professions like engineering; as a result, women were more likely to choose humanities and social sciences, thereby reinforcing the stereotype that women were uninterested in engineering.

Statistical discrimination not only stereotypes individuals on the basis of group characteristics; it also reduces the incentives of individuals to make investments in education and training and thereby tends to reinforce the original stereotype.

Gary Becker: Economics as a tool for understanding social issues. The economics of discrimination was pioneered by Gary Becker of the University of Chicago in his doctoral dissertation. He pointed out that even if some employers are biased against a group of workers, their bias is not sufficient to reduce that group's incomes. Suppose that a group of firms in a competitive market decides to pay blue-eyed workers more than equally productive brown-eyed workers. Nondiscriminating firms could enter the market, undercut the costs and prices of the discriminating firms by hiring mainly brown-eyed workers, and drive the discriminating firms out of business. This theory does not deny the existence of economic discrimination; rather, it points to the importance of nonmarket forces like exclusion, educational barriers, and caste systems as important factors in maintaining discrimination.

Becker, who won the Nobel Prize in economics in 1992, has been a leading advocate of the idea that economic reasoning applies to a wide range of social issues. Becker was a pioneer in the theory of human capital, arguing that utility-maximizing people make educational decisions as investments—just as a profit-maximizing company selects its best combination of plant and equipment. He also studied the economics of crime and punishment and the way that economic forces influence the choice of family size, marriage, and divorce.

ECONOMIC DISCRIMINATION AGAINST WOMEN

The largest group to suffer from economic discrimination is women. Even year-round, full-time female workers on average earn only 80 percent as much as men of comparable education and background.

The pattern of earnings is clear. Female college graduates earn about the same amount as male high school graduates. Although white males generally receive increases in annual earnings as they grow older, income profiles show that women in their late twenties earn as much on average as do older women.

What lies behind the income differentials between men and women? The causes are complex, grounded in social customs and expectations, statistical discrimination, and economic factors such as education and work experience. In general, women are not paid less than men for the same job. Rather, the lower pay of women arose because women were excluded from certain high-paying professions, such as engineering, construction, and coal mining. In addition, women tended to interrupt their careers to have children and perform household duties. Also, economic inequality of the sexes was maintained because, until recently, few women were elected to the boards of directors of large corporations, to senior partnerships in major law firms, or to tenured professorships in top universities.

Like minority groups, then, women are often found in low-paying noncompeting groups. The extent of labor market segmentation is detailed in Table 13-5, which shows the fraction of women in selected high-paying and low-paying occupations. To understand discrimination, we should avoid simple explanations like the idea that employers simply beat down the wage demands of women or African-Americans or Hispanics. Rather, discrimination involves subtle exclusionary processes that prevent certain groups from participating fully in all occupations, as well as the stubborn persistence of stereotypes and perverse incentives due to statistical discrimination.

Empirical Evidence

Having analyzed the mechanisms by which the political process and the market economy enforce discrimination against women and minority groups, let's examine the size of earnings differentials. Table 13-6 shows the ratio of total annual earnings of males and females of different minority groups relative to those of white males. On average, earnings differentials are substantial for women and for minorities. Note that women are generally penalized in the labor market only once; many minority women show earnings close to those of white women.

TABLE 13-5. Many High-Paid Occupations Are Reserved for Men
Discrimination today seldom occurs because women get lower wages for the same job. Rather, women have been limited to lower-paying occupations. Overall, for full-time workers, the median weekly earnings are only 75 percent of those of men. (Source: U.S. Department of Labor, Bureau of Labor Statistics.)

Labor Market Segmentation, 1996	
Occupation	Percentage female
High-paid occupations:	
Engineers	8.5
Physicians	26.4
Lawyers	29.5
Low-paid occupations:	
Child-care workers	97.1
Secretaries	98.6
Nurses' aides	88.4

Earnings Differentials, 1990		
	Earnings of group (as % of earnings of white males of European ancestry)	
Group	Males	Females
White		
European (except Spain)	100	67
Hispanic	73	57
Asian	94	71
Black	73	56
Native American	71	53

TABLE 13-6. Minorities and Women Earn Substantially Less Than White Males

How do different ethnic groups and sexes fare in the marketplace? Data were examined on the total annual earnings of full-time, year-round workers in different groups in the United States. These data do not correct for education, labor-force status, or previous work experience. The most disadvantaged minority-group males earn only 71 percent of white male earnings. Females earn even less. (Source: 1990 Census. Compiled by Ann Green of the Yale Stat Lab using the Explorer program of the 1990 Public Use Sample, available on the Internet.)

Economists have found that earnings differentials among different groups are not entirely due to discrimination. The first section of this chapter noted that there are differences in quality of labor. African-American workers have historically received less education than have whites; women customarily spend more time out of the labor force than do men. Since both education and continuing work experience are linked to higher pay, it is not surprising that some earnings differentials exist.

Economists in recent years have conducted numerous empirical studies that attempt to separate the earnings differentials due to measurable characteristics (such as education, labor market experience, absenteeism, and long-term career plans) from those due to discrimination and other factors. Studies indicate that one-half to three-quarters of the male-female wage gap can be explained by differences in education and job experience. This leaves one-quarter to one-half to be explained by discrimination and other nonmeasured sources.

REDUCING LABOR MARKET DISCRIMINATION

Over the last 25 years, governments have taken numerous steps to end discriminatory practices. But even today, the United States has been unable to eradicate discrimination based on race, gender, and other characteristics.

What approaches are available to combat discrimination? The major steps were legal landmarks, such as the Civil Rights Act of 1964 (which outlaws discrimination in hiring, firing, and employment) and the Equal Pay Act of 1963 (which requires employers to pay men and women equally for the same work).

Such laws helped dismantle the most blatant discriminatory practices, but more subtle barriers remain. To counter them, more aggressive and controversial policies have been introduced, including measures such as *affirmative action*. This requires employers to show that they are taking extra steps to locate and hire underrepresented groups. Studies indicate that this approach, labeled by critics as "reverse discrimination," has had a modest positive effect on the hiring and wages of women and minorities.

Often, discrimination can be combated by encouraging employers to pay more attention to personal performance. If statistical discrimination tends to harm women and minority groups and reduce incentives to invest in human capital, discrimination will be reduced if employers look at measures of personal skills such as school grades as well as teacher and employer recommendations. It is instructive to note that in those industries where individual performances are more easily measured—such as athletics and entertainment—women and minorities are relatively more highly paid than in those sectors where skills and marginal products are harder to measure and there is consequently more room for statistical and personal discrimination.

Uneven Progress

Discrimination is a complex social and economic process. It is rooted in social customs and was enforced by laws that denied disadvantaged groups a decent education and good jobs. Even after equality was established by law, separation of races and sexes perpetuated social and economic stratification.

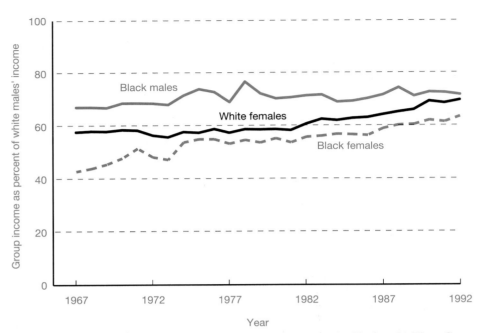

FIGURE 13-9. Minorities and Females Show Uneven Progress in Closing the Wage Gap
The wage gap between white males and other groups closed significantly in the last half-century. Black females have gained parity with white females, but females and black males earn significantly less than white males. [Source: G. D. Jaynes and R. M. Williams Jr., eds., *A Common Destiny: Blacks and American Society* (National Academy Press, Washington, 1989), p. 295, updated by authors.]

Progress is being made, but the results are uneven. In recent years, members of disadvantaged groups have entered the best educational institutions and the highest-paying professions in large numbers. For example, among those under 35 years of age, women now constitute 41 percent of mathematicians and computer scientists, 29 percent of lawyers and judges, and half of managerial and professional workers. Figure 13-9 shows the slow progress toward closing the earnings gap between nonwhite and white members of the population.

But substantial differences in incomes, wealth, and jobs persist. The deteriorating social order in central cities, the disintegration of the traditional nuclear family, cuts in government social programs, a backlash against many antidiscrimination programs, and the declining relative wages of the unskilled have led to declining living standards for many minority groups. Women and minorities have succeeded at the ballot box, but they continue to have lagging incomes in the marketplace.

SUMMARY

A. Fundamentals of Wage Determination

1. The demand for labor, as for any factor of production, is determined by labor's marginal product. A country's general wage level tends to be higher when its workers are better trained and educated, when it has more and better capital to work with, and when it uses more advanced production techniques.

2. For a given population, the supply of labor depends on three key factors: population size, average number of hours worked, and labor-force participation. For the United States, immigration has been a major source of new workers in recent years, increasing the proportion of relatively unskilled workers.

3. As wages rise, there are two opposite effects on the supply of labor. The substitution effect tempts each worker to work longer because of the higher pay for each hour of work. The income effect operates in the opposite direction because higher wages mean that workers can now afford more leisure time along with other good things of life. At some critical wage, the supply curve may bend backward. The labor supply of very gifted, unique people is quite inelastic: their wages are largely pure economic rent.

4. Under perfect competition, if all people and jobs were exactly alike, there would be no wage differentials. The equilibrium wage rates determined by supply and demand would all be equal. But once we drop unrealistic assumptions concerning the uniformity of people and jobs, we find substantial wage differentials even in a perfectly competitive labor market. Compensating wage differentials, which compensate for nonmonetary differences in the quality of jobs, explain some of the differentials. Differences in the quality of labor explain many of the other differentials. In addition, the labor market is made up of innumerable categories of noncompeting and partially competing groups.

B. The American Labor Movement

5. Labor unions occupy an important but diminishing role in the American economy, in terms of both membership and influence. Management and labor representatives meet together in collective bargaining to negotiate a contract. Such agreements typically contain provisions for wages, fringe benefits, and work rules. Unions affect wages by bargaining for standard rates. However, in order to raise real wages above prevailing market-determined levels, unions generally must prevent entry or competition from nonunion workers.

6. According to economic theory, there is no unique outcome of a collective bargaining session. Bilateral monopoly or management-union bargaining (like war or two-person games) has a theoretically indetermi-

nate solution. Empirical studies find that unions have raised the wages of union members relative to those of nonunionized workers. Studies estimate that, on average, union workers have earned wages 10 to 30 percent higher than nonunion workers with the same characteristics. This union differential may have eroded in the last decade's period of competition from nonunion and foreign labor.

7. While unions may raise the wages of their members, they probably do not increase a country's real wages or labor's share of national income. They are likely to increase unemployment among union members who would prefer to wait for recall from layoff of their high-paid jobs rather than move or take low-paying jobs in other industries. And in a nation with inflexible prices, real wages that are too high may induce classical unemployment.

C. Discrimination by Race and Gender

8. By an accident of history, a tiny minority of white males in the world has enjoyed the greatest affluence. Even a century after the abolition of slavery, inequality of opportunity and economic, racial, and gender discrimination can be shown, by the tools of competitive supply and demand, to lead to loss of income by underprivileged groups.

9. There are many sources of discrimination. An important mechanism is the establishment and maintenance of noncompeting groups. By segmenting labor markets, reserving managerial and professional positions for white men while relegating women and minorities to menial, dead-end jobs, an economy can allow inequality of earnings to persist for decades. In addition, statistical discrimination occurs when individuals are treated on the basis of the average behavior of members of the group to which they belong. This subtle form of discrimination stereotypes individuals on the basis of group characteristics, reduces the incentives of individuals to engage in self-improvement, and thereby reinforces the original stereotype.

10. Steps to reduce labor market discrimination have been taken in many directions. Early approaches focused on outlawing discriminatory practices, while later steps mandated policies such as affirmative action.

CONCEPTS FOR REVIEW

Wage Determination under Perfect Competition

elements in demand for labor:

labor quality
technology
quality of other inputs

elements in supply of labor:
   hours
   labor-force participation

immigration
income effect vs. substitution effect
compensating differentials in wages
rent element in wages
segmented markets and noncompet-
    ing groups

Impact of Unions

collective bargaining
unions as monopolies
control of entry by unions
effect of unions on real wages
classical unemployment

Discrimination in Labor Markets

discrimination
earnings differentials: quality differ-
    ences vs. discrimination
statistical discrimination
antidiscrimination policies

QUESTIONS FOR DISCUSSION

1. What steps could be taken to break down the seg-mented markets shown in Table 13-5?
2. Explain, both in words and with a supply-and-demand diagram, the impact of each of the following upon the wages and employment in the affected labor market:
    a. *Upon union bricklayers:* The bricklayers' union negotiated a lower standard work rule, from 26 bricks per hour to 20 bricks per hour.
    b. *Upon airline pilots:* After the deregulation of the airlines, nonunion airlines like Continental increased their market share by 20 percent.
    c. *Upon M.D.s:* Many states begin to allow nurses to be given more of the physicians' responsibilities.
    d. *Upon American autoworkers:* Japan agreed to limit its exports of automobiles to the United States.
3. Explain what would happen to wage differentials as a result of each of the following:
    a. An increase in the cost of going to college
    b. Free migration among the nations of Europe
    c. Introduction of free public education into a country where education had previously been private and expensive
    d. Through technological change, a large increase in the number of people reached by popular sports and entertainment programs.
4. Discrimination occurs when disadvantaged groups like women or African-Americans are segmented into low-wage markets. Explain how each of the following practices, which prevailed in some cases until recently, helped perpetuate discriminatory labor market segmentation:
    a. Many state schools would not allow women to major in engineering.
    b. Many top colleges would not admit women.
    c. Nonwhites and whites received schooling in separate school systems.

    d. Elite social clubs would not admit women, African-Americans, or Catholics.
    e. Employers refused to hire workers who had attended inner-city schools because the average productivities of workers from there were low.
5. Recent immigration has increased the number of low-skilled workers with little impact upon the supply of highly trained workers. A recent study by George Borjas, Richard Freeman, and Lawrence Katz estimated that the wages of high school dropouts declined by 4 percent relative to the wages of college graduates in the 1980s as a result of immigration and trade. This problem shows how to understand the reasons.
    a. To see the impact of *immigration,* turn back to Figure 12-6 in the last chapter. Redraw these diagrams, labeling part (*a*) "Market for Skilled Workers" and part (*b*) "Market for Unskilled Workers." Then let immigration increase the supply of unskilled labor down and to the right while leaving the supply of skilled workers unchanged. What would happen to the relative wages of the skilled and unskilled and to the relative levels of employment as a result of immigration?
    b. Next analyze the impact of *international trade* on wages and employment. Suppose that lower trade barriers increased the demand for skilled workers in (*a*) while reducing the demand for domestic unskilled workers in (*b*). Show that this would tend to increase the inequality between skilled and unskilled workers.
6. In periods of high unemployment, people often think that a solution lies in spreading the existing amount of work more evenly. In Europe during the 1990s, for example, many governments proposed that the work-week be reduced to spread the declining employment among more workers—this being the lump-of-labor

fallacy. Use diagrams to explain the impact of a reduced workweek in a competitive market as well as in a market with classical unemployment.

7. People often worry that high tax rates would reduce the supply of labor. Consider the impact of higher taxes with a backward-bending supply curve as follows: Define the before-tax wage as W, the posttax wage as W_p, and the tax rate as t. Explain the relationship $W_p = (1 - t) W$. Draw up a table showing the before-tax and posttax wages when the before-tax wage is \$20 per hour for tax rates of 0, 15, 25, and 40 percent. Next add a supply-and-demand diagram to Figure 13-4. For the regions above and below point C, show the impact of a lower tax rate upon labor supplied. In your table, show the relationship between the tax rate and the government's tax revenues.

CHAPTER 14
LAND AND CAPITAL

> In the first stone which [a person] flings at the wild animal he pursues, in the first stick that he seizes to strike down the fruit which hangs above his reach, we . . . discover the origin of capital.
>
> *Robert Torrens*, An Essay on the Production of Wealth *(1821)*

The United States is a "capitalist" economy. By this, we mean that capital, land, and assets are largely privately owned. In 1995, the net stock of capital in the United States was $70,000 per capita, of which 68 percent was owned by private corporations, 14 percent by private persons, and 19 percent by governments. Moreover, the ownership of the nation's wealth was highly concentrated in the portfolios of the richest Americans.

By contrast, in socialist countries, like Russia before 1991 or China today, most of the land and capital is owned by government, and there are no super-rich families like the du Ponts or the Gettys. Under capitalism, individuals and private firms do most of the saving, own most of the wealth, and get most of the profits on these investments.

The difference between poor and rich countries comes in large measure from the ability to generate large flows of savings and invest those savings in high-return capital. But a nation's nonhuman assets include much beyond its plant and equipment. We would also want to count its land, natural resources like oil and minerals, and environmental assets like clean air and healthy drinking water.

In this chapter we will study the workings of the factor markets for the major nonlabor inputs, land and capital. Both are durable assets that are privately owned, can be bought and sold in markets, and can be "rented" out for a period of time. We will start by looking at the market for land, which is a nonproduced factor. Then we will turn to the crucial questions of the supply and demand for capital, which is an output of the economy as well as an input. This will give us a much deeper understanding of some key features of a market economy.

A. LAND AND RENT

Rent as Return to Fixed Factors

Unless you are planning to run your company from a balloon, land is an essential factor of production for any business. The essential feature of land is that its quantity is fixed and completely unresponsive to price.[1] Will Rogers put this nicely when he

---

[1] Sometimes natural resources are included along with land. We postpone our analysis of the economics of natural resources until Chapter 18.

quipped, "Land is a good investment: they ain't making it no more."

The price of using a piece of land for a period of time is called its **rent** or, sometimes, **pure economic rent.** Rent is calculated as dollars per unit of time. The notion of paying rent applies not only to land but to any factor that is fixed in supply. For example, da Vinci's portrait *Mona Lisa* is unique; if you could get it for an exhibition, you would be paying rent for its temporary use.

Rent is the payment for the use of factors of production that are fixed in supply.

Market Equilibrium. The supply curve for land is completely inelastic—that is, vertical—because the supply of land is fixed. In Figure 14-1, the demand and supply curves intersect at the equilibrium point *E*. It is toward this factor price that the rent of land must tend. Why?

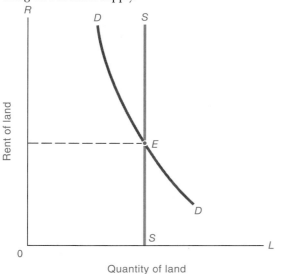

FIGURE 14-1. **Fixed Land Must Work for Whatever It Can Earn**

Perfectly inelastic supply characterizes the case of rent, sometimes also called pure economic rent. We run up the *SS* curve to the factor demand curve to determine rent. Aside from land, we can apply rent considerations to rich oil and gold properties, 7-foot basketball players, and anything else in fixed supply.

If rent were above the equilibrium price, the amount of land demanded by all firms would be less than the existing amount that would be supplied. Some property owners would be unable to rent their land at all; they would have to offer their land for less and thus bid down its rent. By similar reasoning, the rent could not remain below the equilibrium intersection for long. If it did, the bidding of unsatisfied firms would force the factor price back up toward the equilibrium level. Only at a competitive price where the total amount of land demanded exactly equals the fixed supply will the market be in equilibrium.

Suppose the land can be used only to grow corn. If the demand for corn rises, the demand curve for cornland will shift up and to the right, and the rent will rise. This leads to an important point about land: The price of land is high because the price of corn is high. This is a fine example of the fact that the demand for factors is a derived demand—derived from the demand for the product produced by the factor.

Because the supply of land is inelastic, land will always work for whatever competition gives it. Thus the value of the land derives entirely from the value of the product, and not vice versa.

Taxing Land

The fact that the supply of land is fixed has a very important consequence. Consider the land market in Figure 14-2 on page 250. Suppose the government introduces a 50 percent tax on all land rents, taking care to ensure that there is no tax on buildings or improvements, because that certainly would affect the volume of construction activity. All that is being taxed is the income or rent on the fixed supply of agricultural and urban land sites.

After the tax, the total demand for the land's services will not have changed. At a price (*including* tax) of $200 in Figure 14-2, people will continue to demand the entire fixed supply of land. Hence, with land fixed in supply, the market rent on land services (including the tax) will be unchanged and must be at the original market equilibrium at point *E*.

What will happen to the rent received by the landowners? Demand and quantity supplied are unchanged, so the market price will be unaffected by the tax. Therefore, the tax must have been completely paid out of the landowner's income.

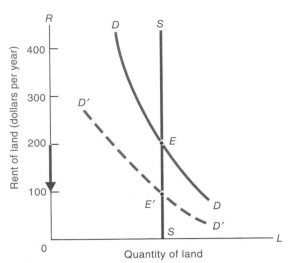

FIGURE 14-2. Tax on Fixed Land Is Shifted Back to Landowners, with Government Skimming Off Pure Economic Rent

A tax on fixed land leaves prices paid by users unchanged at E but reduces rent retained by landowners to E'. What can the landowners do but accept a lower return? This provides the rationale for Henry George's single-tax movement, which aimed to capture for society the increased land values that result from urbanization.

The situation can be visualized in Figure 14-2. What the farmer pays and what the landlord receives are now two quite different things. As far as the landlords are concerned, once the government steps in to take its 50 percent share, the effect is just the same as it would be if the net demand to the owners had shifted down from DD to $D'D'$. Landowners' equilibrium return after taxes is now only E', or only half as much as E. *The whole of the tax has been shifted backward onto the owners of the factor in inelastic supply.*

Landowners will surely complain. But under perfect competition there is nothing they can do about it, since they cannot alter the total supply and the land must work for whatever it can get. Half a loaf is better than none.

You might at this point wonder about the effects of such a tax on economic efficiency. The striking result is that *a tax on rent will lead to no distortions or economic inefficiencies.* Why not? Because a tax on pure economic rent does not change anyone's economic

behavior. Demanders are unaffected because their price is unchanged. The behavior of suppliers is unaffected because the supply of land is fixed and cannot react. Hence, the economy operates after the tax exactly as it did before the tax—with no distortions or inefficiencies arising as a result of the land tax.

A tax on pure economic rent will lead to no distortions or inefficiencies.

Henry George's single-tax movement: The theory of pure economic rent was the basis for the single-tax movement of the late 1800s. At the time, America's population was expanding rapidly as people migrated here from all over the world. With the growth in population and the expansion of railroads into the American west, land rents soared, creating handsome profits for those who were lucky or farsighted enough to buy land early.

Why, some people asked, should lucky landowners be permitted to receive these "unearned land increments"? Henry George (1839–1897), a journalist who thought a great deal about economics, crystallized these sentiments in his best-selling book *Poverty and Progress* (1879). His book called for financing government principally through property taxes on land, while cutting or eliminating all other taxes on capital, labor, and the improvements on the land. George believed that such a tax could improve the distribution of income without harming the productivity of the economy.

While the U.S. economy obviously never went very far toward the single-tax ideal, many of George's ideas were picked up by subsequent generations of economists. In the 1920s, the English economist Frank Ramsey asked the natural sequel to George's exploration: What are the most efficient kinds of taxes? This led to the development of efficient or Ramsey tax theory. This analysis shows that taxes are least distortionary if levied on sectors whose supplies or demands are highly price-inelastic.

The reasoning behind Ramsey taxes is essentially the same as that shown in Figure 14-2: If a commodity is highly inelastic in supply or demand, a tax on that sector will have very little impact on production and consumption, and the distortion will be relatively small.

B. CAPITAL AND INTEREST

You can have your cake and eat it too: Lend it out at interest.

Anonymous

BASIC CONCEPTS

Economic analysis traditionally divides factors of production into three categories: land, labor, and capital. The first two of these are called *primary* or *original factors* of production, whose supplies are determined largely outside the marketplace. To them we add a *produced factor* of production, capital.

Capital (or capital goods) consists of those durable produced goods that are in turn used as productive inputs for further production. Some capital goods might last a few years, while others might last for a century or more. But the essential property of a capital good is that it is both an input and an output.

There are three major categories of capital goods: structures (such as factories and homes), equipment (consumer durable goods like automobiles and producer durable equipment like machine tools and computers), and inventories of inputs and outputs (such as cars in dealers' lots).

Prices and Rentals on Capital Goods

Capital goods are bought and sold in capital-goods markets. For example, IBM sells computers to businesses; these computers are used by firms to help improve the efficiency of their payroll systems or production management. When sales occur, we observe the *prices of capital goods.*

Most capital goods are owned by the firm that uses them. Some capital goods, however, are rented out by their owners. Payments for the temporary use of capital goods are called *rentals*. An apartment that is owned by Ms. Landlord might be rented out for a year to a student—the monthly payment of $400 constitutes a rental. We distinguish rent on fixed factors like land from rentals on durable factors like capital.

Rate of Return on Capital Goods

One of the most important tasks of any economy, business, or household is to allocate its capital across different possible investments. Should a country devote its investment resources to heavy manufacturing like steel or to information technologies like the Internet? Should Intel build a $4 billion factory to produce the next generation of microprocessors? Should Farmer Jones, hoping to improve his record keeping, buy a customized accounting program or go with one of the popular varieties available for around $100? All these questions involve costly investments—laying out money today to obtain a return in the future.

In deciding upon the best investment, we need a measure for that yield or return on capital. One important measure is the **rate of return on capital,** which denotes the net dollar return per year for every dollar of invested capital.

Let's consider the example of a rental car company. Ugly Duckling Rental Company buys a used Ford for $10,000 and rents it out for $2500 per year. After calculating all expenses (maintenance, insurance, depreciation,[2] etc.), and ignoring any change in car prices, Ugly Duckling earns a net rental of $1200 each year. We say, then, that the rate of return on the Ford is 12 percent per year (= $1200 ÷ $10,000). Note also that the rate of return is a pure number per unit of time. That is, it has the dimensions of (dollars per period)/(dollars) and is usually calculated as percent per year.

---

[2] *Depreciation* is an estimate of the loss in dollar value of a capital good due to obsolescence or wear and tear during a period of time.

You might be considering different investments: rental cars, oil wells, apartments, education, and so forth. Your financial advisers tell you that you do not have sufficient cash to invest in everything, so how can you decide which investments to make?

One useful approach is to compare the rates of return on capital of the different investments. For each one, you first calculate the dollar cost of the capital good. Then estimate the net annual dollar receipts or rentals yielded by the asset. The ratio of the annual net rental to the dollar cost is the rate of return on capital: It tells you the amount of money you get back for every dollar invested, measured as dollars per year per dollar of investment.

The rate of return on capital is the annual net return (rentals less expenses) per dollar of invested capital. It is a pure number—percent per year.

Of Wine, Trees, and Drills. Here are some examples of rates of return on investments:

- I buy grape juice for $10 and sell it a year later as wine for $11. If there are no other expenses, the rate of return on this investment is $1/$10, or 10 percent per year.
- I plant a pine tree with labor cost of $100. At the end of 25 years the grown tree sells for $430. The rate of return on this capital project is then 330 percent per quarter-century, which, a calculator will show, is equivalent to a return of 6 percent per year. That is, $100 \times (1.06)^{25} = 429.2$.
- I buy a $20,000 piece of oil-drilling equipment. For 10 years it earns annual rentals of $30,000, but I incur annual expenses of $26,000 for fuel, insurance, and maintenance. The $4000 net return covers interest and repays the principal of $20,000 over 10 years. What is the rate of return on the drill? Amortization tables show that the rate of return is 15 percent per year.

Financial Assets and Interest Rates

We have spoken so far of capital goods like computers. But where do the resources needed to produce capital come from? Someone must be saving, or abstaining from current consumption, to provide real resources for buying the capital goods. In a modern market economy like the United States, households and firms channel funds into capital goods by saving money in various financial assets. People buy bonds and stocks; they put money in savings accounts; they put dollars away for retirement in their pension funds. All these are vehicles that carry funds from savers to the investors who actually buy capital goods.

When people save, they expect a return. This is the **interest rate,** or the financial return on funds, or the annual return on borrowed funds. The yield you get when you put your money in a time deposit at a commercial bank is an example of an interest rate. Say that the interest rate for 1998 is 5 percent per year. If you deposit $1000 on January 1, 1998, you will end up with $1050 on January 1, 1999.

You will usually see interest rates quoted as x percent per year. This is the interest that would be paid if the sum were borrowed for an entire year; for shorter or longer periods, the interest payment is adjusted proportionately.

There are many varieties of interest rates. There are long-term and short-term interest rates, depending on the duration of the loan or the bond; there are fixed-interest-rate loans and variable-interest-rate loans; there are interest rates on super-safe bonds (like U.S. government securities); and there are interest rates on highly risky "junk bonds."

To summarize:

Households and other savers provide financial resources or funds to those who want to purchase physical capital goods. The rate of interest represents the price that a bank or other financial intermediary pays a lender for the use of the money for a period of time; interest rates are quoted as a certain percent yield per year.

Real vs. Nominal Interest Rates

The interest rates just discussed are measured in dollar or *nominal* terms and not in terms of trees or wine or cars. Interest is the yield on an investment measured in dollars per year per dollar of investment. But dollars can become distorted yardsticks. The prices of fish, trees, wine, and other goods change from year to year as the general price level rises due to inflation.[3] We therefore need to find a

---

[3] The *rate of inflation* is defined as the rate of change of prices from one period to the next. If the general price level is 100 in 1997 and 103.5 in 1998, the rate of inflation is 3.5 percent per year.

real return on capital, one that measures the quantity of goods we get tomorrow for goods forgone today.

As an example, say that you invested 1000 pesos in a Mexican bond in 1995. Because you were offered a 70 percent interest rate, you might have looked forward to getting a hefty return, ending up with 1700 pesos at the end of the year. But when you later took your money out to buy some consumer goods, you found that prices had risen 65 percent during 1995. In terms of the real quantity of goods, you could actually buy only 3 percent more (1.030 = 1.70/1.65) than you could have bought at the start of the year. In other words, if you were to lend 1000 market baskets of goods at the beginning of 1995, you could obtain only 1030 market baskets of goods the following year. The difference between real and nominal interest rates is particularly dramatic during periods of high inflation.

We call the real yield on funds the **real interest rate,** as opposed to the **nominal interest rate,** which is the dollar return on dollars invested. For low rates of interest and inflation, the real interest rate is very close to the nominal interest rate minus the rate of inflation.[4]

The real interest rate is the return on funds in terms of goods and services; we generally calculate the real interest rate as the nominal interest rate minus the rate of inflation.

Table 14-1 shows nominal interest rates on different instruments over the last three decades. (Using the formula, you can obtain real interest rates by taking into account that inflation averaged 4 percent per year over this period.)

PRESENT VALUE OF ASSETS

Capital goods are durable assets that produce a stream of rentals or receipts over time. If you own an apartment building, you will collect rental payments over the life of the building, much as the owner of a fruit orchard will pick fruit from the trees each season.

Suppose you become weary of tending the building and decide to sell it. To set a fair price for the

U.S. financial instrument	Nominal rate of return, 1967–1996 (% per year)
State and local bonds:	
High grade, tax free	3.5
Federal government bonds:	
Short term	4.1
Long term	5.2
Corporate bonds:	
Safe (Aaa)	4.5
Risky (< Baa)	6.0
Consumer loans:	
Mortgages	4.8
Credit cards	10.8
New-car loans	15.8

TABLE 14-1. Interest Rates on Selected Financial Instruments

Nominal interest rates depend upon risk, inflation, and tax treatment. The lowest interest rates are on tax-free and safe state and local securities, followed by taxable federal government obligations. New-car loans carry high interest rates because of default risks. Foreign debt from risky countries with high sovereign risk and high inflation can be many times higher. (Source: Federal Reserve Board.)

building, you would need to determine the value today of the entire stream of future income. The value of that stream is called the present value of the capital asset.

The **present value** is the dollar value today of a stream of income over time. It is measured by calculating how much money invested today would be needed, at the going interest rate, to generate the asset's future stream of receipts.

Let's start with a very simple example. Let's say somebody offers to sell you a bottle of wine that matures in exactly 1 year and can then be sold for exactly $11. Assuming the market interest rate is 10 percent per year, what is the present value of the wine—that is, how much should you pay for the wine today? Pay exactly $10, because $10 invested today at the market interest rate of 10 percent will be worth $11 in 1 year. So the present value of next year's $11 wine is today $10.

Present Value for Perpetuities

We present the first way of calculating present value by examining the case of a *perpetuity*, which is an asset like land that lasts forever and pays $N each

---

[4] In other words, let π be the inflation rate, i the nominal interest rate, and r the real interest rate. The exact calculation of the real interest rate is $1 + r = (1 + i)/(1 + \pi)$. For small values of i and π, however, $r = i - \pi$.

year from now to eternity. We are seeking the present value (V) if the interest rate is i percent per year, where the present value is the amount of money invested today that would yield exactly $\$N$ each year. This is simply

$$V = \frac{\$N}{i}$$

where V = present value of the land ($\$$)
 $\$N$ = permanent annual receipts ($\$$ per year)
 i = interest rate in decimal terms (e.g., 0.05, or $^5/_{100}$ per year)

This says that if the interest rate is always 5 percent per year, an asset yielding a constant stream of income will sell for exactly 20 (= $1 \div ^5/_{100}$) times its annual income. In this case, what would be the present value of a perpetuity yielding $\$100$ every year? At a 5 percent interest rate its present value would be $\$2000$ (= $\$100 \div 0.05$).

General Formula for Present Value

Having seen the simple case of the perpetuity, we move to the general case of the present value of an asset with an income stream that varies over time. The main thing to remember about present value is that future payments are worth less than current payments and they are therefore *discounted* relative to the present. Future payments are worth less than current payments just as distant objects look smaller than nearby ones. The interest rate produces a similar shrinking of time perspective.

Let's take a fantastic example. Say that someone proposes to pay $\$100$ billion to your heirs in 999 years. How much should you pay for this today? According to the general rule for present value, to figure out the value today of $\$P$ payable t years from now, ask yourself how much must be invested today to grow into $\$P$ at the end of t years. Say the interest rate is 6 percent per annum. Applying this each year to the growing amount, a principal amount of $\$P$ grows in t years proportionally to $P \times \$(1 + 0.06)^t$. Hence, we need only invert this expression to find present value: the present value of $\$P$ payable t years from now is only $\$P/(1 + 0.06)^t$. Using this formula, we determine that the present value of $\$100$ billion paid in 999 years is $\$0.0000000000000052$.[5]

---

[5] Question 9 at the end of this chapter asks about the present value of the real estate of Manhattan when it was purchased by the Dutch.

In most cases, there are several terms in an asset's stream of income. In present-value calculations, each dollar must stand on its own feet. Evaluate the present value of each part of the stream of future receipts, giving due allowance for the discounting required by its payment date. Then simply add together all these separate present values. This summation will give you the asset's present value.

The exact formula for present value is the following:

$$V = \frac{N_1}{1 + i} + \frac{N_2}{(1 + i)^2} + \cdots + \frac{N_t}{(1 + i)^t} + \cdots$$

In this equation, i is the one-period market interest rate (assumed constant). Further, N_1 is the net receipts (positive or negative) in period 1, N_2 the net receipts in period 2, N_t the net receipts in period t, and so forth. Then the stream of payments (N_1, N_2, ..., N_t, ...) will have the present value, V, given by the formula.

For example, assume that the interest rate is 10 percent per year and that I am to receive $\$1100$ next year and $\$2662$ in 3 years. The present value of this stream is

$$V = \frac{1100}{(1.10)^1} + \frac{2662}{(1.10)^3} = 3000$$

Figure 14-3 shows graphically the calculation of present value for a machine that earns steady net annual rentals of $\$100$ over a 20-year period and has no scrap value at the end. Its present value is not $\$2000$ but only $\$1157$. Note how much the later dol-

FIGURE 14-3. Present Value of an Asset
The lower rust area shows the present value of a machine giving net annual rentals of $\$100$ for 20 years with an interest rate of 6 percent per year. The upper gray area has been discounted away. Explain why raising the interest rate increases the gray area and therefore depresses the market price of an asset.

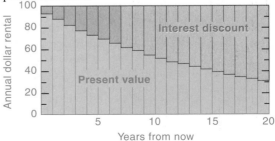

lar earnings are scaled down or discounted because of our time perspective. The total area remaining after discounting (the rust shaded area) represents the machine's total present value—the value today of the stream of all future incomes.

Acting to Maximize Present Value

The present-value formula tells us how to calculate the value of any asset once we know the earnings. But note that an asset's future receipts usually depend on business decisions: Shall we use a truck 8 or 9 years? Overhaul it once a month or once a year? Replace it with a cheap, nondurable truck or an expensive, durable one?

There is one rule that gives correct answers to all investment decisions: Calculate the present value resulting from each possible decision. Then always act so as to maximize present value. In this way you will have more wealth to spend whenever and however you like.

PROFITS

In addition to wages, interest, and rent, economists often talk about a fourth category of income called *profits*. What are profits? How do they differ from interest and the returns on capital more generally?

Reported Profit Statistics

Accountants define **profits** as the difference between total revenues and total costs. To calculate profits, start with total revenues from sales. Subtract all expenses (wages, salaries, rents, materials, interest, excise taxes, and the rest). What is left over is the residual called profits.[6]

Determinants of Profits

What determines the rate of corporate profits in a market economy? Profits are in fact a combination

of different elements, including the implicit returns on owners' capital, reward for risk bearing, and innovational profits.

Profits as Implicit Returns. To the economist, business profits are a hodgepodge of different elements. Much of reported business profits is primarily the return to the owners of the firm for the capital and labor provided by the owners, that is, for factors of production supplied by them.

For example, some profits are the return on the personal work provided by the owners of the firm—such as the doctor or lawyer who works in a small professional corporation. Part is the rent return on self-owned natural resources. In large corporations, most profits are the opportunity costs of invested capital. These returns are called *implicit returns*, which is the name given to the opportunity costs of factors owned by firms.

Thus some of what is ordinarily called profit is really nothing but rentals, rents, and wages under a different name. "Implicit rentals," "implicit rent," and "implicit wages" are the names economists give to the earnings on factors that the firm itself owns.

Profits as Reward for Risk Bearing. Profits also include an element of reward for risk bearing. In analyzing the reward for risk bearing, however, we would not want to include default risk or insurable risk. A provision for *default risk* would cover the possibility that a loan or investment could not be paid, say, because the borrower went bankrupt. *Insurable risks*, such as those analyzed in Chapter 11, would include fires or hurricanes, which could be covered through purchase of insurance. Default and insurable risks are the normal costs of doing business and should be counted as costs.

A kind of risk that must be considered in profit calculations is the *uninsurable* or *systematic risk of investments*. A company may have a high degree of sensitivity to business cycles, which means that its earnings fluctuate a great deal when aggregate output goes up or down. Because investors are averse to risky situations, they require a risk premium on this uncertain investment to compensate for their risk aversion. Developing countries are subject to *sovereign risk*, which occurs when the government defaults on its obligations and (because the government is "sovereign" and exercises ultimate legal authority) there is no recourse in the legal system.

---

[6] In analyzing profits, it is important to distinguish *business profits* from *economic profits*. Business profits are the residual income, equal to sales less costs, measured by accountants. Business profits include an implicit return on the capital owned by firms. Economic profits are the earnings after all costs—both money and implicit or opportunity costs—are subtracted. In large corporations, therefore, economic profits would equal business profits less an implicit return on the capital owned by the firm along with any other costs (such as unpaid management time) not fully compensated at market prices.

Corporate profits are a risky component of national income, so corporate capital must contain a significant risk premium to attract investors. Empirical studies that we will review later in this chapter (see Table 14-2 on page 260) suggest that between 3 and 6 percentage points of the annual return on corporate stocks is the risk premium necessary to attract people to hold this risky investment.

Profits as Reward for Innovation. A third kind of profits consists of the returns to innovation and invention. A modern economy is constantly producing new products—from software programs to exotic materials to jet skis. These new products are the result of research, development, and marketing. We call the person who brings a new product or process to market an *innovator* or *entrepreneur*.

What do we mean by "innovators"? Innovators are people who have the vision, originality, and daring to introduce new ideas in business. History has seen great inventors like Alexander Graham Bell (the telephone), Thomas Edison (the light bulb), and Chester Carlson (xerography). Some inventors amass great fortunes from their entrepreneurship. The modern age has seen Steven Jobs launch Apple Computers, while Bill Gates' Microsoft dominates the software business with innovative operating systems and software.

Every successful innovation creates a temporary pool of monopoly. We can identify *innovational profits* (sometimes called *Schumpeterian profits*) as the temporary excess return to innovators or entrepreneurs. For a short time, innovational profits are earned. These profit earnings are temporary and are soon competed away by rivals and imitators. But just as one source of innovational profits is disappearing, another is being born. Innovational profits will continue to exist as long as the economy produces technological change.

Review

Let's review the terms we have learned before turning to apply them:

- A modern industrial economy has accumulated large stocks of *capital,* or capital goods. These are the machines, buildings, and inventories that are so vital to an economy's productivity.

- The annual dollar earnings on capital are called *rentals.* When we divide the net earnings (rentals less costs) by the dollar value of the capital generating the rentals, we obtain the *rate of return on capital* (measured in percent per year).
- Capital is financed by savers who lend funds and hold financial assets. The dollar yield on these financial assets is the *interest rate*, measured in percent per year.
- Capital goods and financial assets generate a stream of income over time. This stream can be converted into a *present value*, i.e., the value that the stream of income would be worth today. This conversion is made by asking what quantity of dollars today would be just sufficient to generate the asset's stream of income at going market interest rates.
- *Profits* are a residual income item, equal to total revenues minus total costs. Profits contain elements of implicit costs (such as return on owners' capital), return for risk bearing, and innovational profits.

THE THEORY OF CAPITAL AND INTEREST

Now that we have surveyed the major concepts, we turn to an analysis of the *classical theory of capital*. This approach was developed independently by the Austrian E. V. Bohm-Bawerk, the Swede Knut Wicksell, and Yale's Irving Fisher in the United States.

Roundaboutness

In Chapter 2, we noted that investment in capital goods involves indirect or *roundabout* production. Instead of catching fish with our hands, we find it ultimately more worthwhile first to build boats and make nets—and then to use the boats and nets to catch many more fish than we could by hand.

Put differently, investment in capital goods involves forgoing present consumption to increase future consumption. Consuming less today frees labor for making nets to catch many more fish tomorrow. In the most general sense, capital is productive because by forgoing consumption today we get more consumption in the future.

To see this, imagine two islands that are exactly alike. Each has the same amount of labor and natural

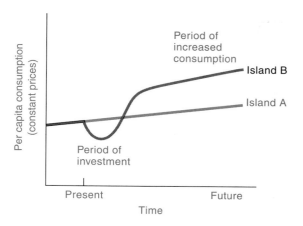

FIGURE 14-4. Investments Today Yield Consumption Tomorrow

Two islands begin with equal endowments of labor and natural resources. Spendthrift Island A invests nothing and shows a modest growth in per capita consumption. Thrifty Island B devotes an initial period to investment, forgoing consumption, and then enjoys the harvest of much higher consumption in the future.

resources. Island A uses these primary factors directly to produce consumption goods like food and clothing; it uses no produced capital goods at all. By contrast, thrifty Island B sacrifices current consumption and uses its resources and labor to produce capital goods, such as plows, shovels, and looms. After this temporary sacrifice of current consumption, B ends up with a large stock of capital goods.

Figure 14-4 shows the way that Island B forges ahead of A. For each island, measure the amount of consumption per person that can be enjoyed while maintaining the existing capital stock. Because of its thrift, Island B, using roundabout, capital-intensive methods of production, will enjoy more future consumption than Island A. B gets more than 100 units of future-consumption goods for its initial sacrifice of 100 units of present consumption.

By sacrificing current consumption and building capital goods today, societies can increase their consumption in the future.

Diminishing Returns and the Demand for Capital

What happens when a nation sacrifices more and more of its consumption for capital accumulation as production becomes more and more roundabout or

indirect? We would expect the law of diminishing returns to set in. Let's take the example of computers. The first computers were expensive and used intensively. Three decades ago, scientists would eke every last hour of time from an expensive mainframe computer that had less power than today's personal computer. By the late 1990s, the nation's stock of computers had millions of times more computational and storage capacity. But the marginal product of computer power—the value of the last calculation or the last byte of storage—had diminished greatly as computer inputs increased relative to labor, land, and other capital. More generally, as capital accumulates, diminishing returns set in and the rate of return on the investments tends to fall.

Unless offset by technological change, the diminishing returns from rapid investment will drive down the rate of return on investment. Surprisingly, the rate of return on capital has not fallen markedly over the course of the last 150 years, even though our capital stocks have grown manyfold. Rates of return have remained high because innovation and technological change have created profitable new opportunities as rapidly as past investment has annihilated them. Even though computers are thousands of times more powerful than they were three decades ago, new applications in every corner of society from electronic mail to medical diagnostics continue to make investments in computers profitable.

Determination of Interest and the Return on Capital

We can use the classical theory of capital to understand the determination of the rate of interest. Households *supply* funds for investment by abstaining from consumption and accumulating saving over time. At the same time, businesses *demand* capital goods to combine with labor, land, and other inputs. In the end, a firm's demand for capital is driven by its desire to make profits by producing goods.

Or as Irving Fisher put the matter at the beginning of this century:

> The quantity of capital and the rate of return on capital are determined by the interaction between (1) people's *impatience* to consume now rather than accumulate more capital goods for future consumption (perhaps for old-age retirement or for that proverbial rainy day); and (2) *investment opportunities* that yield higher or lower returns to such accumulated capital.

To understand interest rates and the return on capital, consider an idealized case of a closed economy with perfect competition and without risk or inflation. In deciding whether to invest, a profit-maximizing firm will always compare its cost of funds with the rate of return on capital. If the rate of return is higher than the market interest rate at which the firm can borrow funds, it will undertake the investment. If the interest rate is higher than the rate of return on investment, the firm will not invest.

Where will this process end? Eventually, firms will undertake all investments whose rates of return are higher than the market interest rate. Equilibrium is then reached when competition among firms beats down the return on investment to the level of the market interest rate.

In a competitive economy without risk or inflation, the competitive rate of return on capital would be equal to the market interest rate. The market interest rate serves two functions: It rations out society's scarce supply of capital goods for the uses that have the highest rates of return, and it induces people to sacrifice current consumption in order to increase the stock of capital.

Graphical Analysis of the Return on Capital

We can illustrate capital theory by concentrating on a simple case in which all physical capital goods are alike. In addition, assume that the economy is in a steady state with no population growth or technological change.

In Figure 14-5, *DD* shows the demand curve for the stock of capital; it plots the relationship between the quantity of capital demanded and the rate of return on capital. Recall from Chapter 12 that the demand for a factor like capital is a "derived demand"—the demand comes from the *marginal product of capital*, which is the extra output yielded by additions to the capital stock.

The law of diminishing returns can be seen in the fact that the demand-for-capital curve in Figure 14-5 is downward-sloping. When capital is very scarce, the most profitable roundabout projects have a very high rate of return. Gradually, as the community exploits all the high-yield projects by accumulating capital, with total labor and land fixed, diminishing returns to capital set in. The community must

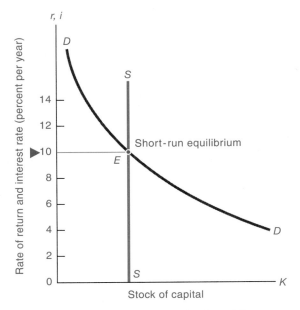

FIGURE 14-5. Short-Run Determination of Interest and Returns

In the short run, the economy has inherited a given stock of capital from the past, shown as the vertical *SS* supply-of-capital schedule. Intersection of the short-run supply curve with the demand-for-capital schedule determines the short-run return on capital, and the short-run real interest rate, at 10 percent per year.

then invest in lower-yield projects as it moves down the demand-for-capital curve.

     Short-Run Equilibrium. We can now see how supply and demand interact. In Figure 14-5, past investments have produced a given stock of capital, shown as the vertical short-run supply curve, *SS*. Firms will demand capital goods in a manner shown by the downward-sloping demand curve, *DD*.

At the intersection of supply and demand, at point *E*, the amount of capital is just rationed out to the demanding firms. At this short-run equilibrium, firms are willing to pay 10 percent a year to borrow funds to buy capital goods. At that point, the lenders of funds are satisfied to receive exactly 10 percent a year on their supplies of capital.

Thus, in our simple, riskless world, the rate of return on capital exactly equals the market interest rate. Any higher interest rate would find firms unwilling to borrow for their investments; any lower

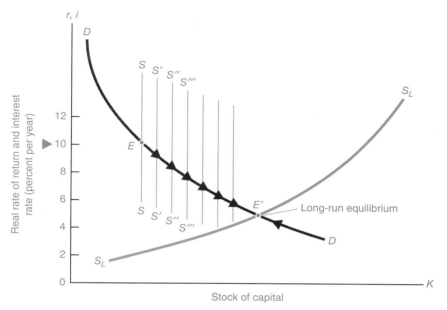

FIGURE 14-6. Long-Run Equilibration of the Supply and Demand for Capital

In the long run, society accumulates capital, so the supply curve is no longer vertical. As pictured here, the supply of wealth is responsive to higher interest rates. At the original short-run equilibrium at E there is net investment, so the economy moves down the DD demand curve as shown by the black arrows. Long-run equilibrium comes at E', where net saving ceases.

interest rate would find firms clamoring for the too scarce capital. Only at the equilibrium interest rate of 10 percent are supply and demand equilibrated. (Recall that these are *real* interest rates because there is no inflation.)

But the equilibrium at E is sustained only for the short run: At this high interest rate, people will want to go on saving. At the short-run equilibrium, people desire to accumulate more capital, i.e., to continue saving. This means that the capital stock increases. However, because of the law of diminishing returns, the rate of return and the interest rate move downward. As capital increases—while other things such as labor, land, and technical knowledge remain unchanged—the rate of return on the increased stock of capital goods falls to ever-lower levels.

This process is shown graphically in Figure 14-6. Note that capital formation is taking place at point E. So each year, the capital stock is a little higher as net investment occurs. As time passes, the community moves slowly down the DD curve as shown by the black arrows in Figure 14-6. You can actually see a

series of very thin short-run supply-of-capital curves in the figure—S, S', S'', S''', ... These curves show how the short-run supply of capital increases with capital accumulation.

Long-Run Equilibrium. Where does long-run equilibrium occur? It comes at E' in Figure 14-6; this is where the long-run supply of capital (shown as $S_L S_L$) intersects with the demand for capital. The long-run equilibrium is attained when the interest rate has fallen to the point where the capital stock held by firms has expanded so as to match the amount of wealth that people desire to supply. At the long-run equilibrium, net saving stops, net capital accumulation is zero, and the capital stock is no longer growing.

The long-run equilibrium stock of capital comes at that real interest rate and rate of return on capital where the value of assets that people want to hold exactly matches the amount of capital that firms want for production.

APPLICATIONS OF CLASSICAL CAPITAL THEORY

We have completed our survey of the classical theory of interest and capital. But capital theory needs some amplifications and qualifications to account for important realistic features of economic life.

Taxes and Inflation

Investors always keep a sharp eye out for inflation and taxes. Recall that inflation tends to reduce the quantity of goods you can buy with your dollars. Therefore, we want to calculate the real interest rate or the real return to our investments, removing the effect of the changing yardstick of money. Another important feature is taxes. Part of our incomes go to the government to pay for public goods and other government programs. Therefore, investors will want to focus on the posttax return on investments.

Technological Disturbances

A deeper complexity involves technological change. Historical studies show that inventions and discoveries raise the return on capital and thereby affect equilibrium interest rates. Indeed, the tendency toward falling interest rates via diminishing returns has been just about canceled out by inventions and technological progress.

Some economists (such as Joseph Schumpeter) have likened the investment process to a plucked violin string: In a world of unchanging technology, the string gradually comes to rest as capital accumulation drives down returns on capital. But before the economy has settled into a steady state, an outside event or invention comes along to pluck the string and set the forces of investment in motion again.

Uncertainty and Expectations

The final qualification concerns the risks that exist in investment decisions. In real life no one has a crystal ball to read the future. All investments, resting as they do on estimates of future earnings, must necessarily be guesses about future costs and payoffs. Our discussion assumed that there were no risks. But in fact almost any loan or investment has an element of risk. Machines break down; an oil well may turn out to be a dry hole; your favorite computer company may go belly up. Investments differ in their degree of risk, but no investment is completely risk-free.

Investors are generally averse to holding risky assets. They would rather hold an asset that is sure to yield them 10 percent than an asset that is equally likely to yield 0 or 20 percent. Investors must therefore receive an extra return, or *risk premium*, to induce them to hold investments with high systematic or uninsurable risk.

EMPIRICAL FINDINGS

Returns on Different Assets

What are the actual real returns on investments in different forms? Table 14-2 shows a summary of recent studies on the return to capital in different fields. The rates of return on assets like corporate capital, farmland, and real estate have averaged around 6 percent over the last three decades. Because these assets can be packaged and sold as stocks and bonds, they tend to have lower returns

TABLE 14-2. Real Rates of Return on Different Assets
The real returns to tangible capital, land, and human capital vary widely depending upon country and risk. Because consumers cannot pool risks on their investments and often are liquidity-constrained, consumer investments have the highest returns. [Source: Tabulation by the authors from a variety of sources, including Roger G. Ibbotson and Gary P. Brinson, *Investment Markets* (McGraw-Hill, New York, 1987); United Nations Development Program; World Bank; and scholarly studies.]

Asset class	Period	Real rate of return (% per year)
Corporate capital (U.S.):		
Posttax return	1959–1996	5.4
Pretax return	1959–1996	9.3
Real estate	1960–1984	5.5
Farmland	1947–1984	5.5
Human capital:		
United States	1980s	6–12
Developing countries	1970s–1980s	13–26
Consumer durables	1970s–1980s	48
Energy conservation	1970s–1980s	19
Nonresidential capital stock (7 major industrial countries)	1975–1990	15

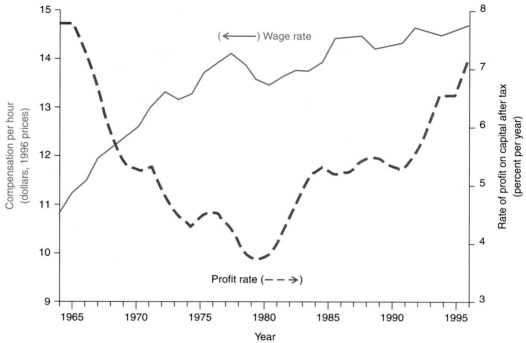

Figure 14-7. Trends in Wages and Profits in the United States
How have the returns to labor and capital varied in recent years? Real wages (including fringe benefits) grew sharply in the period after World War II and then slowed after the 1970s. After falling in the turbulent 1970s, the post-tax rate of profit on American business capital doubled since 1980. Explanations of the reversal of fortunes include the trend toward deregulation, greater openness to trade, and the information revolution. (Source: U.S. Departments of Commerce and Labor with profit data from James Poterba, "Recent Developments in Corporate Profitability: Patterns and Explanations," March 1997.)

than riskier, nondiversified assets like human capital, venture capital, consumer durables, and developing-country capital. These riskier investments have returns ranging from around 10 percent upward.

Returns to Labor and Capital

A final comparison, shown in Figure 14-7, shows the trends in labor and capital returns in the United States over the last 35 years. We see that labor's earnings grew sharply but then stagnated after the early 1970s. The rate of profit on capital, by contrast, has skyrocketed in recent years, with a near-doubling of the after-tax rate of return to nonfinancial corporate capital since 1980. This trend led one commentator to the conclusion that this is a good time to be a capitalist in the United States.

What were the forces that lay behind the sharp reversal of fortunes of workers and capitalists over

the last two decades? While economists are just beginning to sort out the reasons, the following are among the leading possibilities:

• Since the 1980s, the conservative and pro-market political movement has led to a deregulation of many industries, allowing capital to pursue fields of highest profitability. This trend is seen most dramatically for electric utilities, where the capital intensity of production has declined sharply as former monopolies have faced increasing competition in the electricity market.

• A sharp increase in trade with developing countries means that U.S. workers—particularly unskilled workers—must compete with the vast army of workers in the rest of the world. By contrast, domestic management and capital are scarce factors in the world, and we would expect to see their return rise with the opening of markets at home and abroad.

- One intriguing possibility is that technological change in the last decade has become "capital-saving" as compared with the "labor-saving" technological change that characterized most of the period since the Industrial Revolution. In an earlier era, new technologies used power looms to replace textile workers. Today, computers and other informational capital form an ever-larger share of investment. Informational capital can be capital-saving because it helps airlines schedule aircraft and passengers, allows oil companies to run refineries and find oil rather than just drill blindly, and helps all companies keep their inventories down.

People will be watching wage and profit trends carefully to see if the divergent trends continue.

VALEDICTORY THOUGHTS ON FACTOR PRICES, EFFICIENCY, AND DISTRIBUTION

The recent reversal of fortune of labor and capital—with capital earnings rising rapidly over the last two decades as wages stagnated—raises questions about the fairness as well as the efficiency of the distribution of income in a market economy. Economists emphasize that a free market in capital and land will promote high rates of saving and investment, rapid economic growth, and healthy productivity growth. In the political arena, people worry that this same free market will lead the rich to become richer while the poor are falling behind. We would offer three final thoughts on these debates:

1. People's market incomes are determined by rents, interest, and wages. We may or may not like the competitive distribution of income, but we must recognize that competitive pricing helps solve the question of *how* goods are to be produced in an efficient manner. Getting the prices right is crucial to ensuring efficient selection of inputs in the production process.

    Consider, for example, how different relative proportions of land and labor are reflected in different countries. Compare America, with plentiful land and scarce labor, with Hong Kong,

where land is precious and labor abundant. As a result of supply and demand, wages are high relative to rents in America while the opposite is true in Hong Kong. Because these relative scarcities are transmitted by factor prices, markets help ensure that the efficient land-labor combinations are used. Americans have huge farms and use labor sparingly, while land in Hong Kong is reserved for industry and housing rather than for land-intensive agriculture.

2. The debates about profits tend to obscure the basic point about the role of capital in a market economy. The accumulation of capital and its return are driven by two fundamental forces. On the one hand, the demand for capital results from the fact that indirect or roundabout production processes are productive; by abstaining from consumption today, society can raise consumption in the future. On the other hand, people must be willing to abstain from consumption in order to accumulate financial assets, lending funds to firms that will make the productive investments in roundabout productive processes. These two forces of technology and impatience are brought into balance by the interest rate, which ensures that society's accumulation of capital just matches the amount that people are willing to hold back from consumption in the form of saving.

3. Finally, we must remember that the factor prices of wages, rents, interest, and profits are not carved in granite. They are subject to government policies. As Henry George's approach emphasizes, if society dislikes the inequality brought about by high land rents or fabulous wages of unique individuals, taxes on these factors can reduce inequality without inducing great inefficiencies. Well-designed taxes on high incomes and inheritance, efficient wage subsidies to low-wage workers, and transfer programs to help the truly needy can reduce the worst inequalities of a market economy without impairing the ability of factor prices to guide markets to efficient allocations or unduly reducing saving, investment, and economic growth.

With well-designed tax and transfer programs, a country can have its cake of growing productivity and share the cake more fairly among its citizens.

SUMMARY

A. Land and Rent

1. The return to fixed factors like land is called pure economic rent, or rent for short. Since the supply curve for land is vertical and totally inelastic, the rent will be price-determined rather than price-determining.

2. A factor like land that is inelastically supplied will continue to work the same amount even though its factor reward is reduced. For this reason, Henry George pointed out that rent is in the nature of a surplus rather than a reward necessary to coax out the factor's effort. This provides the basis for his single-tax proposal to tax the unearned increment of land value, without shifting the tax forward to consumers or distorting production. Modern tax theory extends this proposition by showing that inefficiencies are minimized by taxing goods that are relatively inelastic in supply or demand.

B. Capital and Interest

3. A third factor of production is capital, a produced durable good that is used in further production. In the most general sense, investing in capital represents deferred consumption. By postponing consumption today and producing buildings or equipment, society increases consumption in the future. It is a technological fact that roundabout production yields a positive rate of return.

4. Recall the definitions:
   Capital goods: durable produced goods used for further production
   Rentals: net annual dollar returns on capital goods
   Rate of return on capital: net annual receipts on capital divided by dollar value of capital (measured as percent per year)
   Interest rate: yield on funds, measured as percent per year
   Real interest rate: yield on funds corrected for inflation, also measured as percent per year
   Present value: value today of a stream of future returns generated by an asset
   Profits: a residual income item equal to revenues minus costs

5. Assets generate streams of income in future periods. By calculating the present value, we can convert the stream of returns into a single value today. This is done by asking what amount of dollars today will generate the stream of future returns when invested at the market interest rate.

6. The exact present-value formula is as follows: Each dollar payable t years from now is a present value (V) of $\$1/(1 + i)^t$. So for any net receipt stream (N_1, N_2, . . . , N_t, . . .) where N_t is the dollar value of receipts t years in the future, we have

$$V = \frac{N_1}{1 + i} + \frac{N_2}{(1 + i)^2} + \cdots + \frac{N_t}{(1 + i)^t} + \cdots$$

7. Interest is a device that serves two functions in the economy. As a motivating device, it provides an incentive for people to save and accumulate wealth. As a rationing device, interest allows society to select only those investment projects with the highest rates of return. However, as more and more capital is accumulated, and as the law of diminishing returns sets in, the rate of return on capital and the interest rate will be beaten down by competition. Falling interest rates are a signal to society to adopt more capital-intensive projects with lower rates of return.

8. Saving and investment involve waiting for future consumption rather than consuming today. Such thrift interacts with the net productivity of capital to determine interest rates, the rate of return on capital, and the capital stock. The funds or financial assets needed to purchase capital are provided by households that are willing to sacrifice consumption today in return for larger consumption tomorrow. The demand for capital comes from firms that have a variety of roundabout investment projects. In long-run equilibrium, the interest rate is thus determined by the interaction between the net productivity of capital and the willingness of households to sacrifice consumption today for consumption tomorrow.

9. Important qualifications of classical capital theory include the following: Technological change shifts the productivity of capital; imperfect foresight means that capital's return is highly volatile; and investors must consider the impact of taxes and inflation.

10. Profits are revenues less costs. Reported business profits are chiefly corporate earnings. Economically, we distinguish three categories of profits. (*a*) An important source is profits as implicit returns. Firms generally own many of their own nonlabor factors of production—capital, natural resources, and patents. In these cases, the implicit return on unpaid or owned inputs is part of profits. (*b*) Another source of profits is uninsurable risk, particularly that associated with the business cycle or sovereign risk. (*c*) Finally, innovational profits will be earned by entrepreneurs who introduce new products or innovations.

***

CONCEPTS FOR REVIEW

***

Land

rent
inelastic supply of land
taxation of fixed factors

Capital and interest

capital, capital goods

rentals, rate of return on capital,
  interest rate, profits
investment as abstaining from consumption
real vs. nominal interest rate
present value

twin elements in interest determination: returns to roundaboutness
  and impatience
source of profits:
  implicit returns
  uninsurable risks
  innovation

***

QUESTIONS FOR DISCUSSION

***

1. Define "pure economic rent."
   a. Show that an increase in supply of the rent-earn-
      ing factor will depress its rent and lower the prices
      of goods that use much of it.
   b. Explain the following statement from rent theory:
      "It is not true that the price of corn is high because
      the price of land is high. Rather, the reverse is
      closer to the truth: The price of cornland is high
      because the price of corn is high." Illustrate with a
      diagram.
   c. Consider the quotation in (**b**). Why is this correct
      for the market as a whole but incorrect for the
      individual farmer? Explain the fallacy of composi-
      tion that is at work here.
2. Reread the section on "winner-take-all markets" in
   Chapter 11. Some observers have suggested that taxing the highest incomes would reduce income
   inequality. What would you expect to be the result of
   such a tax on the work efforts of top rock stars or basketball players?
3. Calculate the real interest rates for each financial
   instrument in Table 14-1 if the inflation rate was 4 percent during the 1967–1996 period.
4. Contrast the following four returns on durable assets:
   (*a*) rent on land, (*b*) rental of a capital good, (*c*) rate
   of return on a capital good, and (*d*) real interest rate.
   Give an example of each.
5. Using the supply-and-demand analysis of interest,
   explain how each of the following would affect interest
   rates in capital theory:
   a. An innovation that increased the marginal prod-
      uct of capital at each level of capital
   b. A decrease in the desired wealth holdings of
      households
   c. A 50 percent tax on the return on capital (in the
      short run and the long run)
6. Looking back to Figures 14-5 and 14-6, review how the
   economy moved from the short-run equilibrium inter-

est rate at 10 percent per year to the long-run equilibrium. Now explain what would occur in both the long
run and the short run if innovations shift up the
demand-for-capital curve. What would happen if the
government debt became very large and a large part of
people's supply of capital was siphoned off to holdings
of government debt?

7. Explain the rule for calculating the present discounted value of a perpetual income stream. At 5 percent, what is the worth of a perpetuity paying $100 per
   year? Paying $200 per year? Paying $*N* per year? At 10
   or 8 percent, what is the worth of a perpetuity paying
   $100 per year? What does doubling the interest rate do
   to the capitalized value of a perpetuity—say, a perpetual bond?
8. Recall the algebraic formula for a convergent geometric progression:

$$1 + K + K^2 + \cdots = \frac{1}{1 - K}$$

   for any fraction K less than 1. If you set $K = 1/(1 + i)$,
   can you verify the present-value formula for a permanent income stream, $V = \$N/i$? Provide an alternative
   proof using common sense. What would be the value
   of a lottery that paid you and your heirs $5000 per year
   forever at an interest rate of 6 percent per year?
9. The value of land in Manhattan was in 1997 around
   $60 billion. Imagine that it is 1626 and you are the eco-
   nomic adviser to the Dutch when they are considering
   whether to buy Manhattan. Further, assume that the
   relevant interest rate for calculating the present value
   is 4 percent per year. Would you advise the Dutch that
   a purchase price of $24 is a good deal or not? How
   would your answer change if the interest rate were 6
   percent? 8 percent? (*Hint:* For each interest rate, calculate the present value in 1626 of the land value as of
   1997. Then compare that with the purchase price in
   1626.)

CHAPTER 15
MARKETS AND ECONOMIC EFFICIENCY

> A market economy . . . is the only natural economy, the only kind that makes sense, the only one that can lead to prosperity, because it is the only one that reflects the nature of life itself. The essence of life is infinitely and mysteriously multiform, and therefore it cannot be contained or planned for, in its fullness and variability, by any central intelligence.
>
> *Václav Havel*, **Summer Meditations** *(1993)*

By the end of the 1980s, socialist Eastern Europe and the Soviet empire were in ruins, with long lines for bread and other necessities in the stores, low and declining living standards, outdated technologies, and deteriorating environmental conditions. This large and once-prosperous region had been laid low, not by war or pestilence, but by an ambitious social experiment called *socialist central planning*, devised by Vladimir Lenin and his communist followers. When the communists were thrown out of office in 1989–1991, the new leaders of the affected countries, people like the playwright-turned-president Václav Havel of Czechoslovakia, decided without hesitation that introducing a market economy was the first step toward regaining economic health.

Why did the leaders of these centrally planned economies turn to the market? As Havel's quotation at the beginning of this chapter states, they were convinced that a market economy, based on principles of decentralized supply and demand, was the surest route to economic health. They had seen West Germany become the powerhouse of Europe while East Germany stagnated; they lived in a Czechoslovakia poisoned by toxic wastes, while southern neighbor Austria, with its mixed capitalist system, was a rural idyll. They were reading the lessons of history.

How well does the market perform, and what are its shortcomings? Our analysis of the basic properties of a market economy—of both product and factor markets—concludes in this chapter with an explanation of the remarkable efficiency properties of competitive capitalism. The chapter then identifies some market failures, those areas where the market fails to provide the proper signals and leads to inefficiencies.

A. THE EFFICIENCY OF PERFECT COMPETITION

Two centuries ago, Adam Smith proclaimed that, through the workings of the invisible hand, those who pursue their own self-interest in a competitive economy would most effectively promote the public interest. This concept—that the rough-and-tumble of market competition is a potent force for raising output and living standards—is one of the most profound and powerful ideas in history.

One of the great achievements of modern economics has been understanding the exact meaning of Adam Smith's argument. Over the last two centuries, economists have refined the notion of "public interest" and today understand its logic and limitations. Efficiency, as economists define it, is a process by which society squeezes the maximum amount of consumer satisfaction out of the available resources. More precisely, **allocative efficiency** (sometimes called **Pareto efficiency,**[1] or just *efficiency* for short) occurs when there is no way to reorganize production or consumption so that it will increase the satisfaction of one person without reducing the satisfaction of another person. Or, to put it another way, an efficient situation is one where no one can be made better off without making someone else worse off.

Today, we know the following:

Under limited conditions, including perfect competition, a market economy will display allocative efficiency, In such a system, the economy as a whole is efficient, and no one can be made better off without making someone else worse off.

This is truly an astounding statement about the power of competition to produce beneficial results. It means that, given the resources and technology of the society, even the most skilled planner cannot come along with a computer or an ingenious reorganization scheme and find a solution superior to the competitive marketplace; no reorganization can make everyone better off. And this result is true whether the economy has one or two or two million competitive markets for goods and factors.

A GENERAL EQUILIBRIUM OF ALL MARKETS

Having stated the fundamental proposition about competitive markets, we will explore the reasons behind this remarkable result. Let's review first what we have learned in earlier chapters about the behavior of individual markets:

1. Competitive supply and demand operate to determine prices and quantities in individual markets.
2. Market demand curves are derived from the marginal utilities of different goods.

3. The marginal costs of different commodities lie behind their competitive supply curves.
4. Firms calculate marginal costs of products and marginal revenue products of factors and then choose inputs and outputs so as to maximize profits.
5. These marginal revenue products, summed for all firms, provide the derived demands for the factors of production.
6. These derived demands for land, labor, or capital goods interact with their market supplies to determine factor prices such as rent, wages, and interest rates.
7. The factor prices and quantities determine incomes, which then close the circle back to steps 1 and 2 by helping to determine the demand for different commodities.

All these statements are the result of **partial-equilibrium analysis,** which involves the behavior of a single market, household, or firm, taking the behavior of all other markets and the rest of the economy as given. In this chapter, we are concerned with **general-equilibrium analysis,** which examines how (and how successfully) all the households, firms, and markets interact simultaneously to solve the questions of *how, what,* and *for whom.*

Interaction of All Markets in General Equilibrium

It is the interconnectedness of economic life that makes it so intricate and complex. How was it that a revolution in Iran in 1979 led to a worldwide oil-price increase, lowering the demand for automobiles and causing thousands of steelworkers to lose their jobs? How did the reunification of Germany in 1990 lead to higher interest rates in Germany, thereby producing stagnation in the rest of Europe, and then to a currency crisis and a breakdown of the European Monetary System? These and countless other economic impacts take place through the general-equilibrium interactions of the seven steps outlined above.

Notice how our list of steps follows a logical progression from step to step. The textbook chapters follow in almost the same order. But in real life, which comes first? Is there an orderly sequence that determines prices in single markets on Monday, evaluates consumer preferences on Tuesday, and reckons

---

[1] It is so-called after Vilfredo Pareto (1848–1923), the Italian economist who first proposed the concept.

business costs on Wednesday and marginal products on Thursday? Obviously not. *All these partial-equilibrium processes are going on simultaneously.*

That is not all. These different activities do not go on independently, each in its own little groove, careful not to get in the way of the others. All the processes of supply and demand, of cost and preference, of factor productivity and demand are really different aspects of one vast, simultaneous, interdependent process.

A Circular Flow. Like an invisible web, the markets for inputs and outputs are connected in an interdependent system that we call a general equilibrium. Figure 15-1 depicts the general structure of a general equilibrium. The outer loops show the

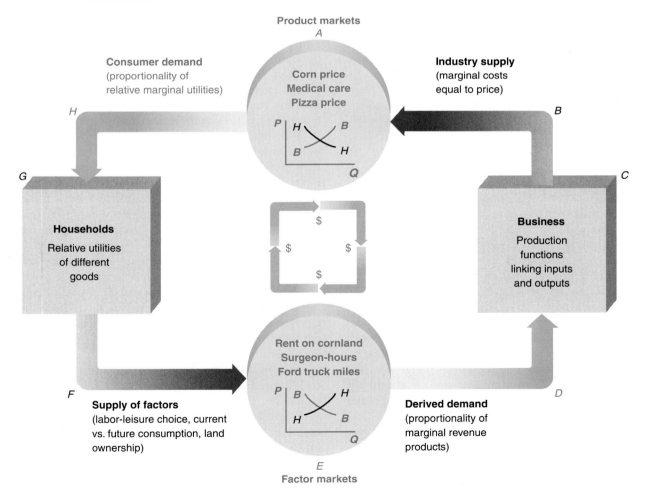

FIGURE 15-1. Inputs, Production, Outputs, and Consumption Form the Circular Flow of Economic Life

The general equilibrium of an economy links together the supplies and demands of a vast number of factors and products. Observe how profit-maximizing firms and utility-maximizing households interact in product markets at *A* and in factor markets at *E*. Also, note that the flow of money inside the circular flow moves in the opposite direction from the flow of goods and factors.

demands and supplies of all goods and factors. We speak here not of a single good or factor but of *all* different products (corn, medical care, pizzas, etc.), which are made by a vast array of factors of production (cornland, surgeons, trucks, etc.).

Each good or factor is exchanged in a market, and the equilibrium of supply and demand determines the price and quantity of the item. That marriage of supply and demand is occurring millions of times every day, for all kinds of commodities from abacuses to zwieback. Note in Figure 15-1 that the upper loop carries the supplies and demands for products, while the lower loop matches it with the supplies and demands for factors of production. See how consumers demand products and supply factors; indeed, households buy their consumption goods with the incomes they earn from the factors they supply. Similarly, businesses buy factors and supply products, paying out factor incomes and profits with the revenues from the products that they sell.

Thus we see a logical structure behind the millions of markets determining prices and outputs: (1) Households, which want to maximize their satisfactions, supply factors and buy products while (2) firms, guided by the lure of profits, transform factors bought from households into products sold to households. The logical structure of a general-equilibrium system is complete.

Properties of a Competitive General Equilibrium

Not surprisingly, analyzing a general-equilibrium system is more complicated than using partial-equilibrium analysis, which deals with only a single market. A general-equilibrium system represents a whole economy, rather than just part of one. It may contain many different kinds of labor, machines, and land, all of which are serving as inputs to produce dozens of different kinds of computers, hundreds of different specifications of automobiles, thousands of different items of clothing, and so on. It contains services like cellular connections, college courses, and vacations to Disneyland, as well as goods like heavy construction equipment, pizzas, and cellular telephones.

How can we possibly know that a competitive market economy is efficient? In answering this question, we proceed as follows: We first describe the assumptions of our general economic equilibrium.

We then describe in a summary fashion the properties of a general equilibrium. Next, in a more technical discussion, we sketch the properties of a general equilibrium in more detail. Finally, we show why a perfectly competitive general equilibrium will be efficient.

The Basic Principles. What assumptions do we make in analyzing a competitive economy? We assume that all markets are perfectly competitive—that is, they are subject to the relentless competition of many buyers and sellers. Each price, whether for an input or an output, moves flexibly enough to equilibrate supply and demand at all times. Firms maximize profits, while consumers choose their most preferred market baskets of goods. Each good is produced under conditions of constant or decreasing returns to scale. No pollution, externalities, entry-limiting regulations, or monopolistic labor unions mar the competitive landscape. Consumers and producers are well informed about prices and economic opportunities. These conditions are obviously an idealized situation. But were such an economy to exist, it would be one in which Adam Smith's invisible hand could rule without any impediment from externalities or imperfect competition.

For this economy, we can describe consumer behavior and producer behavior and then show how they dovetail to produce an overall equilibrium. First, consumers will allocate their incomes across different goods in order to maximize their satisfactions. They choose goods such that the marginal utilities per dollar of expenditure are equal for the last unit of each commodity.

What are the conditions for the profit maximization of producers? In product markets, each firm will set its output level so that the marginal cost of production equals the price of the good. Since this is the case for every good and every firm, it follows that the competitive market price of each good reflects society's marginal cost of that good.

Putting together these two statements yields the conditions for a competitive equilibrium. For each consumer, the marginal utility of consumption for each good is proportional to that good's marginal cost. Hence, the marginal utility per last dollar spent on each good is equalized for every good.

An example will clarify this result. Say that we have two individuals, Ms. Smith and Mr. Ricardo, and two kinds of goods, pizza and clothing. Set the utility scale so that 1 util equals $1.[2] In the consumer equilibrium, Ms. Smith buys pizza and clothing until her *MU* per dollar of each good is 1 (Smith) util. Similarly, Mr. Ricardo distributes his income so that he gets 1 (Ricardo) util per dollar of spending. The pizza and clothing producers set their output levels such that price equals marginal cost, so a dollar-bundle of pizza will have a marginal cost of production of $1 for each producer, as will a dollar-bundle of clothing. If society were to produce one more dollar-bundle of pizza, the cost to society would be exactly 1 dollar's worth of a bundle of scarce labor, land, and capital resources.

Putting these conditions together, we see that each extra dollar of consumption, by either Smith or Ricardo, yields exactly 1 extra util of subjective satisfaction, whether that extra spending is on clothing or on food. Similarly, each extra unit of spending will have a marginal or additional cost to society of 1 extra dollar of resources, and this is so whether that extra dollar is spent by Smith or Ricardo or on food or clothing. *The general equilibrium of markets therefore determines prices and outputs so that the marginal utility of each good to consumers equals the marginal cost of each good to society.*

Detailed Analysis of General Equilibrium[3]

Let us look more closely at the *conditions of a competitive general equilibrium.* These conditions fall naturally into two categories; the first, relating to consumers, corresponds to the upper loop of Figure 15-1 on page 267, while the second, concerning production, corresponds to the lower loop.

1. Consumer Equilibrium. Our analysis of consumer behavior in Chapter 5 showed that, when choosing among goods, consumers would maximize their utility by equalizing the marginal utility per dollar of spending. This rule implies the following condition:

$$\frac{MU_1}{MU_2} = \frac{P_1}{P_2}$$

In words, the ratio of the marginal utilities of two goods is equal to the ratio of their prices. This condition must hold for any individual consumer who buys the two goods in question.

2. Producer Equilibrium. The behavior of profit-maximizing firms leads to an analogous but somewhat more complex set of conditions, covered in Chapters 6 through 8. In those chapters we found that competitive firms choose input and output levels as follows:

a. The *output condition* for producers is that the level of output is set so that the price of each good equals the marginal cost of that good. By rearranging terms in this equation, we then find:

$$\frac{MC_1}{MC_2} = \frac{P_1}{P_2}$$

This equation says that, in a competitive economy, the ratio of the marginal costs of two final products is equal to their price ratio. The equality holds for all goods that are produced and for all firms that produce these goods. We can also interpret the ratio of marginal costs as the slope of the production-possibility frontier, which gives the rate at which society can transform one good into another. If a pizza's *MC* is $1 and a haircut's *MC* is $10, then, by transferring resources from barbers to farmers, society can transform one haircut into 10 units of pizza.

The fundamental point to understand about a competitive economy is that the competitive prices reflect social costs or scarcities. We just noted that the ratio of marginal costs tells us the rate at which society can transform one good into another. But because the ratio of marginal costs equals the price ratio, it follows that relative prices reflect the rate at which society can transform one good into another. It is just this essential result—that competitive prices provide an accurate signal of the relative scarcity of different goods—that shows how perfectly competitive markets contribute to allocative efficiency.

---

[2] To simplify the analysis, we have adopted a "money metric" for utility. This means that we adjust our utility yardstick so that the marginal utility of an additional hour of leisure is always constant and has a value of $1. We can then express all prices in these dollar-units of leisure, so a "util" is a unit of utility in this money metric.

[3] This section is relatively technical and can be skipped in short courses.

b. Competition also leads to certain *input conditions* for producers. We have seen that profit-maximizing firms choose the amount of each input so that the value of its marginal product is equal to its price. Hence:

Marginal product of land in good 1
× price of good 1 = rent on land

Marginal product of land in good 2
× price of good 2 = rent on land

Marginal product of labor in good 1
× price of good 1 = wage of labor

and so forth.

These relationships have several important implications. First, because each firm in a given industry faces the same prices for inputs and outputs, the marginal product of input A is the same for each firm in that industry.

By rearranging the terms in the above equations, we can see that the ratio of marginal revenue products of inputs is equal to the ratio of their prices:

$$\frac{\text{Marginal revenue product of land in good 1}}{\text{Marginal revenue product of labor in good 1}} = \frac{\text{price of land}}{\text{price of labor}}$$

In addition, this relationship holds for all firms that use land and labor to produce good 1. Moreover, it holds for all factors of production (capital, oil, unskilled labor, etc.) and for all produced goods.

The input conditions are important because they imply that the ratios of marginal products of factors are the same for all inputs and all firms in all uses. If labor is scarce relative to land in the American southwest, land rents will be low relative to labor wages. The low rent-wage ratio will signal farms to spread their labor thinly across large farms and will lead to large houses, wide roads, and shorter commuting times. In Manhattan, with much higher ratios of land prices to labor wages, we see more high-rise apartments and longer commuting times, and farms are found only in the dreams of rural life.

To summarize:

In competitive general equilibrium, with utility-maximizing consumers and profit-maximizing firms:

- The ratios of marginal utilities of goods for all consumers are equal to the relative prices of those goods.
- The ratios of marginal costs of goods produced by firms are equal to the relative prices of those goods.
- The relative marginal revenue products of all inputs are equal for all firms and all goods and are equal to those inputs' relative prices.

THE EFFICIENCY OF COMPETITIVE MARKETS

Now that we have seen the way a competitive economy allocates resources, we can understand why a competitive economy is efficient.

A general-equilibrium market system will display allocative efficiency when there is perfect competition, with well-informed producers and consumers and no external effects. In such a system, each good's price is equal to its marginal costs and each factor's price is equal to the value of its marginal product. When each producer maximizes profits and each consumer maximizes utility, the economy as a whole is efficient. No one can be made better off without making someone else worse off.

What is the reason for this surprising coincidence between public welfare and private interest? We can easily see the logic by using an example. Suppose some economic wizard comes forth and says, "I have found a way of reorganizing the perfectly competitive economy to make everyone better off. We are producing too few pizzas. Simply give everyone more pizzas and fewer shirts and everyone will be better off."

But the self-proclaimed wizard is mistaken. Suppose the current price of shirts is $15, while the price of pizzas is $5. On the consumer's side, each individual has allocated his or her budget so that the marginal utility of the last pizza is just one-third of the marginal utility of the last shirt. So consumers would certainly not want to have more pizzas and fewer shirts unless they could get more than three pizzas for each shirt given up.

Can the economy squeeze out more than three pizzas for each forgone shirt? Not if it is competitively organized. Under perfect competition, the ratio of the price of shirts to the price of pizzas is the ratio of the marginal costs of the two goods. Hence, if their price ratio is \$15/\$5 = 3, producers can squeeze out only three more pizzas for each shirt not produced. Indeed, if the production-possibility frontier is bowed out, producers will actually get somewhat less than three pizzas for every shirt forgone.

So we see why our wizard is wrong. Consumers are willing to eat more pizzas and have fewer shirts only if they can improve their satisfactions, which means that they must get more than three pizzas for every shirt forgone. But this is not possible because profit-maximizing producers cannot get more than three pizzas by producing one less shirt. Therefore the proposed reorganization will not improve everybody's economic satisfaction.

The reasoning, of course, extends far beyond pizzas and shirts. With a little thought, you can see that it works as well for all consumer goods. With a little more work, you can even see how it will extend to include reorganizations of inputs and production across firms. And it is easy to see that it would apply to trade among nations as well as trade within a nation.

The basic point to see is that, because prices serve as signals of economic scarcity for producers and social utility for consumers, a competitive price mechanism allows the best mix of goods and services to be produced from a society's resources and technology.

A Graphic Demonstration

These points can be shown neatly using a device known as the *utility-possibility frontier* (or the *UPF*). This curve shows the outer limit of utilities or satisfactions that an economy can attain. Such a concept is very similar in spirit to the production-possibility frontier. The major difference is that the *UPF* places utilities or levels of satisfaction on the two axes, as is shown in Figure 15-2. The *UPF* slopes downward to indicate that, on the frontier, as one person's satisfaction increases, the other person's must decrease.

Note that the *UPF* is drawn somewhat wavy. This shape indicates that the scale of the individual util-

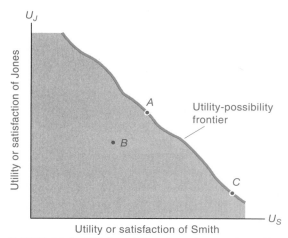

FIGURE 15-2. Efficient Allocations Are on the Utility-Possibility Frontier

Economic efficiency occurs when no one's satisfaction can be improved without hurting someone else. This means that efficient outcomes are on society's utility-possibility frontier (*UPF*). Moving from outcome *A* to outcome *C* improves Smith's welfare only by hurting Jones; both are efficient allocations. Point *B* is inside the *UPF* and is inefficient because Jones, Smith, or both can be made better off without hurting anyone else.

ity measure is arbitrary; however, the inability to measure and compare individual utilities is completely unimportant for analyzing efficiency. All that matters here is that a person's level of satisfaction rises as the utility index increases. Because of this positive relation between utility and desired levels of consumption, we are guaranteed that each person will want to move out as far as possible on his or her utility axis.

Now comes the important point: An efficient economy is one that is on the frontier of its utility-possibility curve. One such efficient (or Pareto-efficient) point is shown at *A* in Figure 15-2. Why is point *A* Pareto-efficient? Because there is no feasible economic reorganization that makes anyone better off without making someone else worse off. We can, of course, move to point *C*. Such a move would certainly delight Smith, whose consumption and satisfaction are increased. But Smith's gain comes only at Jones' expense. When all possible gains to Smith must come at Jones' expense, the economy is on its *UPF* and is operating efficiently.[4]

An economy is efficient when it is on the utility-possibility frontier.

Efficient International Trade

The general principles laid out here can be used to illustrate one of the most important propositions of all economics: the efficiency of free international trade and the harms from tariffs and other trade barriers. A free-trade system is one in which there are no tariffs, quotas, or other barriers to imports and exports. In a free-trade regime, the costs of importing foreign goods would involve only the true marginal costs and not artificial costs imposed by governments to "protect" domestic firms and workers.

International trade is no different from trade within a nation, which means that *in a free-trade situation the world would be on its utility-possibility frontier.* The efficiency of free trade is illustrated in Figure 15-3. We have divided the world into two countries, America and Japan, and have shown the satisfactions of the consumers of the two countries on the two axes. Point *A* represents an efficient, perfectly competitive, free-trade equilibrium.

Now suppose that an American politician enters and says, "We need to protect our automobile and computer workers from unfair competition. Let's limit imports of cars and computer chips." These measures would distort prices and push the economy inside the world *UPF.* If the trade barriers were well crafted, America might improve the economic position of its consumers, say, by moving to point *B* in Figure 15-3. This is clearly a "beggar-thy-neighbor" policy in which America wins at the expense of Japan.

---

[4] The text discussion has analyzed the first theorem of competitive systems. In addition, a second theorem is the converse of the first theorem. Consider an economy in which preferences and technology are "regular"—that is, one with diminishing marginal utilities of consumption and no increasing returns in production. Under these and a few other conditions, any efficient allocation of resources can be reached by some perfectly competitive equilibrium. Put differently, if the government wishes to reach some particular efficient outcome, such as point *A* in Fig. 15-2, in principle it can do so by redistributing initial incomes (say, by ideal lump-sum taxes and transfers) and then allowing the invisible hand to guide the economy to the desired point. In such regular economies, a combination of efficient income redistribution plus competition is enough to reach any efficient allocation of resources on the *UPF.*

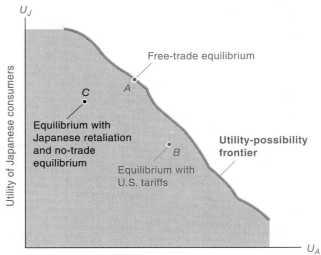

FIGURE 15-3. Free Trade vs. Managed Trade

Free and open international trade among perfectly competitive economies secures the efficient equilibrium at point *A*. If America manages trade through tariffs or other trade barriers, it might move the equilibrium to *B*, which improves America's position at the expense of Japanese consumers. If Japan retaliates or restricts its exports, however, both countries may lose as restrictions on trade raise prices and lower real incomes everywhere at point *C*.

The diagram can also show the gains from trade. Countries with no trade might start at point *C*. After opening economy to free trade, the utilities of both countries must improve, as illustrated by the free-trade point at *A*.

More likely is that the measures will end up hurting both countries. A Japanese bureaucrat might respond by saying, "If you feel threatened by our automobile industry, let us ration out the exports among our firms." The result would be that Japan would in effect exercise market power, raise the prices of its exports, and lower the welfare of American consumers. Another possibility is that Japan might retaliate by putting tariffs on American imports. Such dismal outcomes would be illustrated by point *C*, where interferences with free trade have ended up hurting both countries.

We can also use this discussion to illustrate the gains from trade. The basic idea is that isolated communities or nations can improve their consumption possibilities by engaging in trade with others. Without trade, each group can consume only what it produces.

Free international trade allows each country to improve its living standards. The potential improvement in income and consumption from allowing free and open interchange is called the **gains from trade.**

The reason why countries gain from trade is a simple corollary of the efficiency of competitive markets. Boundaries are irrelevant for the invisible-hand principle. In the idealized conditions, competitive markets are efficient in Houston, in Texas, in the United States, in North America, and in the world. The maximum consumption possibilities are attained when there are no interferences with the free flow of products. This point is easily seen in Figure 15-3. Say that point C is the utilities of the two countries without trade. Then borders are opened to free trade. We know that in a competitive economy, the equilibrium must move to the northeast, such as to point A. The difference between points A and C represents the gains from trade.

To summarize:

Under free trade, the world economy can attain its highest consumption and utility levels. The increase in consumption from opening borders to trade is the gains from trade. Interferences with the free international flow of goods push the economy inside its *UPF* and lowers potential consumption.

Searching for the truth in the invisible-hand doctrine: A careful reader might now ask: "Are you sure that the supply-and-demand equations will lead to a complete and consistent set of supply-and-demand equilibria for all inputs and outputs?" A further question is, "Do we know that a competitive market is efficient?" Although Adam Smith understood the essence of competitive markets more than two centuries ago, it required some of the most powerful minds of mathematics and economics to provide a rigorous answer to these issues.

Economists have pondered these profound questions for almost a century. Léon Walras, a French economist of the nineteenth century, is usually credited with discovery of the theory and equations of general equilibrium. He was, however, unable to provide a rigorous proof that there is an equilibrium of the competitive system. Only in the middle third of the twentieth century was a complete proof of the existence of a competitive equilibrium given, using high-powered mathematical tools such as topology and set theory, by mathematical genius John von Neumann and American Nobel Prize–winning economists Kenneth Arrow and Gerard Debreu. This revolutionary discovery showed that under certain limited conditions there will always exist at least one set of prices that will exactly balance the supplies and demands for all inputs and outputs—even if there are millions of inputs and outputs, in many different regions, and even if goods are produced and sold at different times.

A giant step into the computer age occurred when Herbert Scarf developed the first method of actually calculating a general economic equilibrium—thus giving rise to the new field of computable general-equilibrium models.

The idea of efficiency of a competitive equilibrium was understood in an intuitive way by the physiocrats and Adam Smith. The decisive breakthrough in actually proving the efficiency of competitive economies came first with the introduction of the concept of efficiency by Vilfredo Pareto and then with a rigorous proof of efficiency by Arrow and Debreu. Today, economists tend to emphasize the dynamic advantages of competition—that competition breaks the bread of custom and spurs innovation and the adoption of best-practice technologies. Historical studies point to rapidly growing East Asian countries as examples of how competition not only "gets the prices right" but also leads to robust investment and rapid technological change.

B. QUALIFICATIONS

This chapter has spoken of the remarkable efficiency properties of competitive markets. But be warned: Economies do not live on markets alone. The United

States has a mixed economy, which combines private markets with elements of government intervention. Why do market-oriented countries still rely on government interventions? There are two reasons. First, efficiency may be hard to achieve in many real-world situations when pollution or other externalities are present or when there is imperfect competition. Second, the outcomes of competitive markets, even when they are efficient, may not be socially desirable or acceptable.

Let's review, then, the two major qualifications of efficiency of markets: market failures and unacceptable income distribution.

MARKET FAILURES

A number of market failures spoil the idyllic picture assumed in our discussion of efficient markets: imperfect competition, externalities, and imperfect information. We have explored these issues in earlier chapters and will return to them in our analysis of government's role in economic life.

Imperfect Competition. When a firm has market power in a particular market (say it has a monopoly because of a patented drug or a local electricity franchise), the firm can raise the price of its product above its marginal cost. Consumers buy less of such goods than they would under competition, and consumer satisfaction is reduced. This kind of reduction of consumer satisfaction is typical of the inefficiencies created by imperfect competition.

Externalities. A second market failure is externalities. Recall that externalities arise when some of the side effects of production or consumption are not included in market prices. For example, a utility might pump sulfurous fumes into the air, causing damage to neighboring homes and to people's health. If the utility does not pay for these impacts, pollution will be inefficiently high and consumer welfare will suffer.

Not all externalities are harmful. Some are beneficial, such as the externalities that come from knowledge-generating activities. For example, when Chester Carlson invented xerography, he became a millionaire; but he still received only a tiny fraction of the benefits when the world's secretaries and students were relieved of billions of hours of drudgery. Another positive externality arises from public-health programs, such as inoculation against smallpox, cholera, or typhoid; an inoculation protects not only the inoculated person but also others whom that person might infect.

Imperfect Information. A third important market failure is imperfect information. The invisible-hand theory assumes that buyers and sellers have full information about the goods and services they buy and sell. Firms are assumed to know about all the blueprints for operating in their industry. Consumers are presumed to know about the quality and prices of goods—such as which cars are lemons or the safety and efficacy of pharmaceuticals and angioplasty.

Clearly, reality is far from this idealized world. The critical question is, How damaging are departures from perfect information? In some cases, the loss of efficiency is slight. I will hardly be greatly disadvantaged if I buy a chocolate ice cream that is slightly too sweet or if I don't know the exact temperature of the beer that flows from the tap. In other cases, the loss is severe. Take the case of steel mogul Eben Byers, who early in this century took Radithor, sold as an aphrodisiac and cure-all, to relieve his ailments. Later analysis showed that Radithor was actually distilled water laced with radium. Byers died a hideous death when his jaw and other bones disintegrated. This kind of invisible hand we don't need.

Luckily, few products are as poorly understood as Radithor. One of the important tasks of the government is to identify those areas where informational deficiencies are significant and then to find appropriate remedies.

Economics in a Vacuum?

We have already encountered many examples of market failure or the breakdown of competition. We have seen that wages are often rigid in contrast to the minute-to-minute flexibility of competitive auction prices seeking their equilibria. We have seen that two equally skilled people may work for different wage rates at similar jobs. We have seen how oligopolies and monopolies can restrain quantities to raise prices and profits. In later chapters, we will examine environmental problems like the greenhouse effect and informational deficiencies that muddy the market for medical care.

After reading this list of qualifications, you may wonder about the relevancy of the competitive theory. Taken literally, no one could believe that a perfect and absolutely efficient competitive mechanism has ever existed. But the insights of the competitive theory still retain a great deal of validity.

The perfectly competitive world of the economist is like the frictionless vacuum of the physicist. Even though engineers know that they can never create a perfect vacuum, they still find the analysis of behavior in a vacuum extremely valuable for illuminating many complex problems. So it is with our competitive model. In the long run, many imperfections turn out to be transient as monopolies are eroded by competing technologies. While oversimplified, the competitive model points to many important hypotheses about economic behavior, and these hypotheses appear especially valid in the long run.

Suppose, for example, that a revolution in the Middle East greatly reduces the supply of oil to world markets. Competitive analysis says that the price of oil will rise and that the quantity demanded will fall. Sophisticated analysts of n-person game theory will quarrel with that conclusion, arguing that the world oil market is not perfectly competitive and that no hard-and-fast conclusions can be drawn. But put your money with the competitive model, betting that oil prices will rise in the short run but eventually fall as supply responds, and you will probably end up wealthier than the sophisticated skeptics.

THE DISTRIBUTION OF INCOME

Let us for the moment close our eyes to the many market failures. What do ideal competitive markets mean for the distribution of income? Is there an invisible hand in the marketplace that ensures that the most deserving people will obtain their just rewards? Or that those who toil long hours will receive a decent standard of living? No. In fact, competitive markets do not guarantee that income and consumption will necessarily go to the neediest or most deserving. Rather, the distribution of income and consumption in a market economy reflects initial endowments of inherited talents and wealth along with a variety of factors such as race, gender, location, effort, health, and luck.

Laissez-faire competition might lead to massive inequality, to malnourished children who grow up to produce more malnourished children, and to the perpetuation of inequality of incomes and wealth for generation after generation. Those who

tout the wonders of the market point to the major gains in efficiency that have come with the deregulation, privatization, reduced trade barriers, and decline in unions over the last two decades. *But the movement toward greater market competition has been accompanied by greater inequality of incomes in countries as different as the United States, Sweden, and Russia.* In many "winner-take-all" markets, the rewards have gone predominantly to a tiny group of superstars who won lawsuits, elections, or athletic races by a hair's breadth.

In short, Adam Smith was not wholly justified in asserting that an invisible hand successfully channels individuals who selfishly seek their own interests into promoting the "public interest"—if the public interest includes a fair distribution of income and property. Smith proved nothing of this kind, nor has any economist since 1776.

MARKETS AND ECONOMIC POLICY

We have now concluded our basic analysis of the functioning of markets. In Part Four, we will be confronting some of the major ethical and political issues of modern society. We will consider whether government should impose expensive controls to curb pollution, whether the tax system should redistribute income from rich to poor, and whether the government should override the market in the health-care industry. In examining these issues, we will continue to use the supply-and-demand framework along with the refined analyses of contemporary economists.

But economics cannot have the final word on these controversial problems. For underlying all these issues are normative assumptions and value judgments about what is good and right and just. What an economist does, therefore, is try very hard to keep positive science cleanly separated from normative judgments—to keep a distance between the economic calculations of the head and the human feelings of the heart.

But keeping description separate from prescription does not mean that the professional economist must turn into a bloodless robot. Economists are as divided in their political philosophies as is the rest of the population. Conservative economists argue strenuously for reducing the scope of government and ending programs to redistribute income. Liberal economists are often passionate advocates for extending health coverage to the uninsured or using macroeconomic policies to combat unemployment.

Economic science cannot in the end tell us which political point of view is right or wrong. But it can arm us for the great debate.

SUMMARY

A. The Efficiency of Perfect Competition

1. Under certain conditions, including perfect competition, a market economy will display allocative efficiency. Allocative efficiency (sometimes called Pareto efficiency) signifies that no one person can be made better off without someone else being made worse off.

2. This surprising result can be shown by analyzing the *general equilibrium* of all markets. The general equilibrium of all markets is interrelated in a circular flow by a web of price connections. Households supply factors of production and demand final goods; businesses buy factors of production and transform and sell them as final goods.

3. The central result of general-equilibrium analysis is this: Because prices serve as signals of economic scarcity for producers and social utility for consumers, a competitive price mechanism allows the maximum output and satisfaction to be produced from a society's resources and technology. Under idealized perfect competition, the economy is on both its production-possibility frontier and its utility-possibility frontier.

4. The efficiency of competitive markets can be fruitfully applied to international trade. Free trade allows the world economy to attain the highest consumption and utility levels. The increases in consumption from opening borders to trade are called the gains from trade. Interferences with the free international flow of goods create inefficiency and lower potential consumption.

B. Qualifications

5. There are exacting limits on the conditions under which an efficient competitive equilibrium can be attained: There can be no externalities and no imperfect competition; and consumers and producers must have complete information. The presence of imperfections leads to a breakdown of the *price ratio = marginal cost ratio = marginal utility ratio* conditions, and hence to inefficiency.

6. Even if the ideal conditions for efficient perfect competition were to hold, one major reservation about the outcome of competitive laissez-faire would remain. We have no reason to think that income under laissez-faire will be fairly distributed. The outcome might be one with enormous disparities in income and wealth that persist for generations. In most market economies, governments act to reduce the sting of poverty.

CONCEPTS FOR REVIEW

partial equilibrium vs. general equilibrium
allocative (or Pareto) efficiency
utility-possibility frontier (*UPF*)
invisible-hand theory: in Adam Smith's doctrine and in today's general-equilibrium theory

key conditions in efficient general equilibrium:
MUs proportional to Ps
MCs proportional to Ps
$\therefore$ MUs proportional to input MCs
two theorems about competitive economies

gains from international trade
qualifications to the invisible-hand doctrine:
market failures (imperfect competition, externalities, imperfect information)
arbitrary distribution of income

QUESTIONS FOR DISCUSSION

1. Summarize how a competitive pricing system solves the three fundamental economic problems.

2. List the qualifications to the invisible-hand theory. Illustrate each qualification with an example from your own experience or reading.

3. List the conditions for competitive general equilibrium described in the text under "Detailed Analysis of General Equilibrium." State each condition in a sentence or two. Explain why monopoly or a pollution externality would lead to a failure of one of these conditions.

4. State carefully the two theorems about competitive economies. How would they apply to the following quotations?

   a. "Perfect competition affords the ideal condition for the distribution of wealth." (Francis Walker, 1892)

   b. "The invisible hand, if it is to be found anywhere, is likely to be found picking the pockets of the poor." (Edward Nell, 1982)

   c. Adam Smith's quotation on the invisible hand (see Chapter 2, page 29).

   d. "Pareto . . . suggested that competition brought about a state in comparison to which no consumer's satisfaction can be made higher, within the limitations of available resources and technological know-how, without at the same time lowering at least one other consumer's satisfaction level." (Tjalling Koopmans, 1957)

   e. "Perfect competition can achieve anything that can be obtained under socialism."

5. The analysis of the efficiency of competitive economies assumes that there is no technological advance. Recall the Schumpeterian hypothesis from Chapter 10. How does this elaboration qualify the view of economic efficiency of the competitive mechanism? What kind of market failure is exemplified by invention? In a world of rapid potential technological advance, use production-possibility curves to illustrate how in the long run an innovative economy with imperfect competition might produce higher consumption than an efficient but technologically stagnant competitive economy.

6. **Advanced problem:** "The second theorem about competitive economies (page 272, footnote 4) means that all the debates about socialism versus capitalism are vacuous. Anything that can be done by ideal, centrally planned socialism can, by the second theorem, be done by competitive markets plus the proper dose of redistributive taxation." Comment on the logic behind this statement. State whether you agree or not, and defend your position.

PART FOUR
GOVERNMENT'S ROLE IN THE ECONOMY

CHAPTER 16
GOVERNMENT TAXATION AND EXPENDITURE

The spirit of a people, its cultural level, its social structure, the deeds its policy may prepare, all this and more is written in its fiscal history. . . . He who knows how to listen to its messenger here discerns the thunder of world history more clearly than anywhere else.

Joseph Schumpeter

The scope of government control over the economy has been a political battleground for centuries. Today, liberals want government to correct flaws in the market mechanism and alleviate social problems for the poor and disadvantaged. Conservatives demand that governments "get off our backs" so that markets can work their miracles in raising everybody's living standards. What are the flaws and social problems that liberals worry about, and is it true that governments can improve things? How can a government of the people, by the people, and for the people be on the backs of the people? These are some of the questions that economic analysis must soberly address in the continuing examination of the government's role in economic life.

Markets have over the last two centuries proved to be a mighty engine for powering the economies of industrial countries. Nonetheless, about a century ago, governments in virtually all countries of Europe and North America began to intervene in economic activity to correct the perceived market failures and imbalances of economic power. The increase of government involvement has brought a vast increase in the influence of the state over economic life, both in the share of national income devoted to transfers and income-support payments and in the legal and regulatory controls over economic activity.

Government encroachment on the private sector has not been continuous; rather, following the cycle of politics, market economies take two steps forward, then one step backward, on the road to greater government involvement. Not too long ago, we witnessed the *reemergence of the market* in both capitalist and socialist countries. The crusade for reduced government involvement, launched during the Reagan and Bush administrations in the United States during 1981–1992, was joined by governments in many other countries. Then, starting in 1993 the Clinton administration attempted to find the "vital center" in which vital government programs were retained while the size of government and the budget deficit were reduced. Throughout, the electorate has remained divided on the proper role of government. Some people want to continue expanding the scope of government; others take up the banner of the conservative revolution and strive to cut taxes and reduce government's role.

As economists, we want to go beyond the partisan debates and analyze the functions of government—government's comparative advantage in the mixed economy. In some countries, such as the former socialist countries that are adopting market systems, government has been withdrawing from much of the economy. At the same time, the major industrialized countries have still been funneling one-third to one-half of their national output into government spending. All countries across the world are grappling to find the appropriate balance between state and market.

The chapters in Part Four, then, are devoted to many of the key issues of our age. The first chapter examines the role of government in an advanced industrialized economy. What are the appropriate goals for economic policy in a market economy, and what instruments are available to carry them out? The chapter then takes a close look at government taxation and spending.

The next chapter investigates the tools that government has to promote vigorous competition: antitrust policies and regulation. Chapter 18 examines the emerging issue of protecting the environment. Finally, Chapter 19 addresses one of the most divisive economic issues where the realities of the market butt heads squarely with the forces of compassion. The unfettered market creates extremes of poverty and deprivation that a humane society wants to cushion. Yet attempts to redistribute income from the rich to the poor reduce some of the incentives that make a market economy thrive. This dilemma lies at the heart of the effort in the United States and other countries to redefine the welfare state.

A. GOVERNMENT CONTROL OF THE ECONOMY

Debates about the role of government often take place on bumper stickers such as "No new taxes" or "Balance the budget." These simplistic phrases cannot capture the serious business of government economic policy. Say the populace decides that it wants to devote more resources to improving public health or reducing famine; or that the country needs to mobilize when the armies of a foreign dictator overrun a friendly country and attack our ships; or that protecting our precious environment for future generations is a key national priority; or that more resources should be devoted to educating the young; or that the rich are getting too large a slice of the national pie and more resources should flow to the poor; or that unemployment in a deep recession should be reduced. The market cannot automatically solve these problems. Each of these objectives can be met if and only if the government changes its taxes, spending, or regulations. The thunder of world history is heard in fiscal policy because taxing and spending are such powerful instruments for social change.

THE TOOLS OF GOVERNMENT POLICY

In a modern industrial economy, no sphere of economic life is untouched by the government. We can identify three major instruments or tools that government uses to influence private economic activity. These are

1. *Taxes* on incomes and goods and services. These reduce private income, thereby reducing private expenditures (on automobiles or restaurant food) and providing resources for public expenditure (on tanks and school lunches). The tax system also serves to discourage certain activities which are taxed more heavily (such as smoking cigarettes) while encouraging lightly taxed sectors (such as owner-occupied housing).

2. *Expenditures* on certain goods or services (such as tanks, education, or police protection), along with *transfer payments* (like social security and health-care subsidies) that provide resources to individuals.

3. *Regulations* or controls that direct people to perform or refrain from certain economic activities. Examples include rules that limit the amount firms can pollute, or that divide up the radio spectrum, or that mandate testing the safety of new drugs.

Fiscal History

When Schumpeter wrote of the thunder of fiscal history, he referred to the drama over government budgets and their impacts on the economy. For more than a century, national income and production have been rising in all industrial economies. At the same time, in most countries, government expenditures have been rising even faster. Each period of emergency—depression, war, or concern over social problems such as poverty or pollution—expanded the activity of government. After the crisis passed, government controls and spending never returned to their previous levels.

Before World War I, the combined federal, state, and local government expenditures or taxation amounted to little more than one-tenth of our entire national income. The war effort during World War II compelled government to consume about half the nation's greatly expanded total output. In the mid-1990s, expenditures of all levels of government in the United States ran around 35 percent of GDP.

Figure 16-1 shows the trend in taxes and expenditures for all levels of government in the United States. The rising curves indicate that the shares of government taxes and spending have grown steadily upward over the course of this century.

Government's expansion has not occurred without opposition; each new spending and tax program provoked a fierce reaction. For example, when social security was first introduced in 1935, opponents denounced it as an ominous sign of socialism. But with the passage of time, political attitudes evolve. The "socialistic" social security system was defended by conservative President Ronald Reagan in the 1980s as part of the "safety net." The radical doctrines of one era become accepted gospel of the next.

Figure 16-2 on page 284 shows how government spending as a percent of GDP varies among countries. High-income countries tend to tax and spend a larger fraction of GDP than do poor countries. Can we discern a pattern among wealthy countries? Within the high-income countries, no simple law relating tax burdens and the citizenry's well-being

FIGURE 16-1. Government's Share of the Economy Has Grown Sharply in This Century

Government expenditures include spending on goods, services, and transfers at the federal, state, and local levels. Note how spending grew rapidly during wartime but did not return to prewar levels afterward. The difference between spending and taxes is the government deficit or surplus. (Source: U.S. Department of Commerce.)

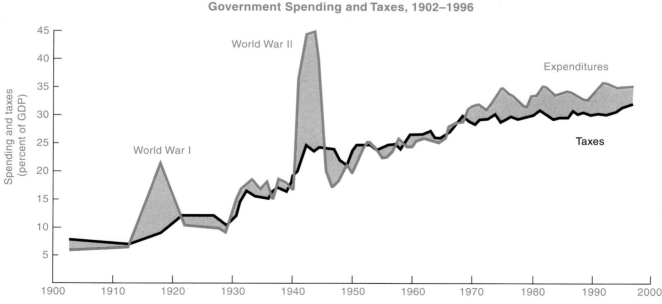

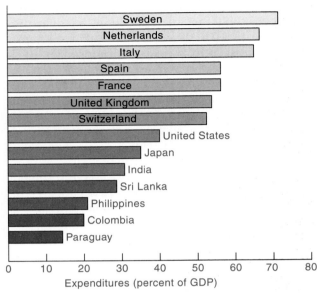

FIGURE 16-2. Government Spending Is Highest in High-Income Lands

Governments of poor countries tax and spend relatively little of national income. With affluence come greater demands for public goods and redistributive taxation to aid low-income families. (Source: International Monetary Fund.)

can do justice to the true diversity of the fiscal facts of nations.[1] For example, financing for the education and health-care systems, two of the largest components of government spending, is organized very differently across countries.

The Growth of Government Controls and Regulation

The increase in collective expenditures is only part of the story. In addition to the rapid growth in spending and taxing, there has also been a vast

---

[1] Figs. 16-1 and 16-2 show the total expenditures of governments. Such expenditures include purchases of goods and services (like missiles and teachers) as well as transfer payments (like social security payments and interest on the government debt). Purchases of goods and services are called "exhaustive" because they make a direct claim upon the production of a country; transfer payments, by contrast, increase people's income and allow individuals to purchase goods and services but do not directly reduce the quantity of goods and services available for private consumption and investment.

expansion in the laws and regulations governing economic affairs.

Nineteenth-century America came as close as any economy has come to being a pure laissez-faire society—the system that the British historian Thomas Carlyle labeled "anarchy plus the constable." This philosophy permitted people great personal freedom to pursue their economic ambitions and produced a century of rapid material progress. But critics saw many flaws in this laissez-faire idyll. Historians record periodic business crises, extremes of poverty and inequality, deep-seated racial discrimination, and poisoning of water, land, and air by pollution. Muckrakers and progressives called for a bridle on capitalism so that the people could steer this wayward beast in more humane directions.

Beginning in the 1890s, the United States gradually turned away from the belief that "government governs best which governs least." Presidents Theodore Roosevelt, Woodrow Wilson, Franklin Roosevelt, and Lyndon Johnson—in the face of strenuous opposition—pushed out the boundaries of federal control over the economy, devising new regulatory and fiscal tools to combat the ailments of the day.

Constitutional powers of government were interpreted broadly and used to "secure the public interest" and to "police" the economic system. In 1887, the federal Interstate Commerce Commission (ICC) was established to regulate rail traffic across state boundaries. Soon afterward, the Sherman Antitrust Act and other laws were aimed against monopolistic combinations in "restraint of trade."

During the 1930s, a whole set of industries came under *economic regulation*, in which government sets the prices, conditions of exit and entry, and safety standards. Regulated industries since that time have included the airlines, trucking, and barge and water traffic; electric, gas, and telephone utilities; financial markets; and oil and natural gas, as well as pipelines.

In addition to regulating the prices and standards of business, the nation attempted to protect health and safety through increasingly stringent *social regulation*. Following the revelations of the muckraking era of the early 1900s, pure food and drug acts were passed. During the 1960s and 1970s, Congress passed a series of acts that regulated mine safety and then worker safety more generally; regulated air and water pollution; authorized safety standards for automobiles and consumer products; and regulated strip mining, nuclear power, and toxic wastes. More recent legislation was aimed at reducing the threats to the international environment from ozone-depleting chemicals.

Over the last two decades, the tide of government economic regulation has ebbed. Economists argued persuasively that many economic regulations were impeding competition and keeping prices up rather than down. Indeed, the first major federal regulatory agency, the Interstate Commerce Commission, was abolished shortly after its hundredth birthday. In the area of social regulations, economists have emphasized the need to ensure that the benefits of regulations outweigh their costs.

Still, there is no likelihood of a return to the laissez-faire era. When conservative Republicans captured Congress in 1994, they attempted to roll back the welfare state and many environmental laws. They did succeed in ending the entitlement to welfare benefits by poor families. In other areas, such as the attempt to dismantle environmental laws, they retreated after a storm of popular protest. Government constraints have changed the very nature of capitalism. Private property is less and less wholly private. Free enterprise has become progressively less free. Irreversible evolution is part of history.

THE FUNCTIONS OF GOVERNMENT

We are beginning to get a picture of how government directs and interacts with the economy. What are the appropriate economic goals for government action in a modern mixed economy? Let's examine the four major functions:

1. Improving economic efficiency
2. Improving the distribution of income
3. Stabilizing the economy through macroeconomic policies
4. Conducting international economic policy

Improving Economic Efficiency

A central economic purpose of government is to assist in the socially desirable allocation of resources. This is the *microeconomic* side of government policy; it concentrates on the *what* and *how* of economic life. Microeconomic policies differ among countries according to customs and political philosophies. Some countries emphasize a hands-

off, laissez-faire approach, leaving most decisions to the market. Other countries lean toward heavy government regulation, or even ownership of businesses, in which production decisions are made by government planners.

The United States is fundamentally a market economy. On any microeconomic issue, most people presume that the market will solve the economic problem at hand. But sometimes there is good reason for government to override the allocational decisions of market supply and demand.

The Limits of the Invisible Hand. Chapter 15 explained how the invisible hand of perfect competition would lead to an efficient allocation of resources. But this invisible-hand result holds only under very limited conditions. All goods must be produced efficiently by perfectly competitive firms. All goods must be private goods like loaves of bread, the total of which can be cut up into separate slices of consumption for different individuals, so that the more I consume out of the total, the less you consume. There can be no externalities like air pollution. Consumers and firms must be fully informed about the prices and characteristics of the goods they buy and sell.

If all these idealized conditions were met, the invisible hand could provide perfectly efficient production and distribution of national output, and there would be no need for government intervention to promote efficiency.

Yet even in this case, if there were to be a division of labor among people and regions, and if a price mechanism were to work, government would have an important role. Courts and police forces would be needed to ensure fulfillment of contracts, nonfraudulent and nonviolent behavior, freedom from theft and external aggression, and the legislated rights of property.

Inescapable Interdependencies. Laissez-faire with minimal government intervention might be a good system if the idealized conditions listed above were truly present. In reality, each and every one of the idealized conditions enumerated above is violated to some extent in all human societies. Most production takes place in units too large for truly perfect competition. Unregulated factories do tend to pollute the air, water, and land. Often, contagious diseases break out and private markets have little incentive to develop effective public-health programs. Consumers are sometimes poorly informed about the characteristics of the goods they buy. The market is not ideal. There are market failures.

In other words, government often deploys its weapons to correct important market failures, of which the most important are the following:

- *The breakdown of perfect competition.* When monopolies or oligopolies collude to reduce rivalry or drive firms out of business, government may apply antitrust policies or regulation.
- *Externalities and public goods.* The unregulated market may produce too much air pollution and too little investment in public health or knowledge. As we will see in Chapter 18, government may use its influence to control harmful externalities or to fund programs in science and public health. Government can levy taxes on activities which impose external public costs (such as cigarette smoking), or it can subsidize activities which are socially beneficial (such as education or prenatal health care).
- *Imperfect information.* Unregulated markets tend to provide too little information for consumers to make well-informed decisions. In an earlier era, hucksters hawked snake oil remedies that would just as easily kill you as cure you. This led to food and drug regulations that require pharmaceutical companies to provide extensive data on the safety and efficacy of new drugs before they can be sold. Because of inadequate information, the government requires companies to provide information on energy efficiency of major household appliances like refrigerators and water heaters. In addition, government may use its spending power to collect and provide needed information itself, as it does with automobile crash-and-safety data.

Clearly, there is much on the agenda of possible allocational problems for government to handle.

Improving the Distribution of Income

Even when the invisible hand works and is marvelously efficient, it may at the same time produce a very unequal distribution of income. Under laissez-faire, people end up rich or poor depending on their inherited wealth, on their talents and efforts,

on their luck in finding oil or owning land in the right place, and on their gender or the color of their skin. To some people, the distribution of income arising from unregulated competition looks as arbitrary as the Darwinian distribution of food and plunder among animals in the jungle.

In the poorest societies, there is little excess income to take from the better-off and provide to the unfortunate. But as societies become more affluent, they can devote more resources to providing services for poor people; this activity—income redistribution—is the second major economic function of government. The welfare states of North America and Western Europe now devote a significant share of their revenues to maintaining minimum standards of health, nutrition, and income.

Income redistribution is usually accomplished through taxation and spending policies, though regulation sometimes plays a role as well. Most advanced countries now rule that children shall not go hungry because of the economic circumstances of their parents; that the poor shall not die because of insufficient money for needed medical care; that the young shall receive free public education; and that the old shall be able to live out their years with a minimum level of income. In the United States, these government activities are provided primarily by transfer programs, such as food stamps, Medicaid, and social security.

But attitudes about redistribution evolve as well. With rising tax burdens and government budget deficits, along with rising costs of income-support programs, taxpayers increasingly resist redistributive programs and progressive taxation. Sweden, which took the welfare state to its extreme and collects 70 percent of national income as taxes, is today struggling to trim spending while maintaining the most important redistributive programs.

Stabilizing the Economy Through Macroeconomic Policies

Early capitalism was prone to financial panics and bouts of inflation and depression, and the traumatic memory of the Great Depression of the 1930s is still vivid among older Americans. Today government has the responsibility of preventing such calamitous business depressions by the proper use of monetary and fiscal policy, as well as close regulation of the financial system. In addition, government tries to smooth out the ups and downs of the business cycle, in order to avoid either large-scale unemployment at the bottom of the cycle or raging price inflation at the top of the cycle. More recently, government has become concerned with finding economic policies which boost long-term economic growth. These questions are considered at length in the branch of economics called macroeconomics.

Conducting International Economic Policy

In recent years, international trade and finance have become far more important to the United States than they were in the past. Government now plays a critical role representing the interests of the nation on the international stage and negotiating beneficial agreements with other countries on a wide range of issues. We can group the international issues of economic policy into four main areas:

- *Reducing trade barriers.* An important part of economic policy involves harmonizing laws and reducing trade barriers so as to encourage fruitful international specialization and division of labor. In recent years, nations have negotiated a series of trade agreements to lower tariffs and other trade barriers on agricultural products, manufactured goods, and services (recall from Chapter 15 how competitive free trade puts countries on the world utility-possibility frontier).

  Such agreements are often contentious. They sometimes harm certain groups, as when removing textile tariffs reduces employment in that industry. In addition, international agreements may require giving up national sovereignty as the price of raising incomes. Suppose that one country's laws protect intellectual property rights, such as patents and copyrights, while another country's laws allow free copying of books, videos, and software. Whose laws shall prevail?

- *Conducting assistance programs.* Rich nations have numerous programs designed to improve the lot of the poor in other countries. These involve direct foreign aid, disaster and technical assistance, the establishment of institutions like the World Bank to give low-interest-rate loans to poor countries, and concessionary terms on exports to poor nations.

- *Coordinating macroeconomic policies.* Nations have found that their increased economic interdependence means that macroeconomic policies must be coordinated to combat inflation and unemployment. Exchange rates (which are the relative prices of the currencies of different nations) do not manage themselves; establishing a smoothly functioning exchange-rate system is a prerequisite for efficient international trade. Nations have seen that fiscal and monetary policies of other nations can affect domestic economic conditions. When the United States raised interest rates to fight inflation in 1979, the tight money led to a world recession and an international debt crisis in the 1980s. Particularly in tightly integrated regions, like Western Europe, countries work to coordinate their fiscal, monetary, and exchange-rate policies, or even adopt a common currency, so that inflation or unemployment in one country does not spill over to hurt the entire area.

- *Protecting the global environment.* The most recent facet of international economic policy is to work with other nations to protect the global environment in cases where several countries contribute to or are affected by spillovers. The most active areas historically have been protecting fisheries and water quality in rivers. More recently, as scientists have raised concerns about ozone depletion, deforestation, global warming, and species extinction, nations have begun to consider ways to protect our global resources. Clearly, international environmental problems can be resolved only through the cooperation of many nations.

Even the staunchest conservatives agree that government has a major role to play in representing the national interest in the anarchy of nations.

PUBLIC-CHOICE THEORY

For the most part, our analysis has concentrated on the *normative* theory of government—on the appropriate policies that the government *should follow* to increase the welfare of the population. But economists are not starry-eyed about the government any more than they are about the market. Governments can make bad decisions or carry out good ideas badly. Indeed, just as there are market failures such as monopoly and pollution, so are there "government failures" in which government interventions lead to waste or redistribute income in an undesirable fashion.

These issues are the domain of **public-choice theory,** which is the branch of economics and political science that studies the way that governments make decisions. Public-choice theory examines the way different voting mechanisms can function and shows that there are no ideal mechanisms to sum up individual preferences into social choices. This approach also analyzes government failures, which arise when state actions fail to improve economic efficiency or when the government redistributes income unfairly. Public-choice theory points to issues such as short time horizons of elected representatives, the lack of a hard budget constraint, and the role of money in financing elections as sources of government failures. A careful study of government failures is crucial for understanding the limitations of government and ensuring that government programs are not excessively intrusive or wasteful.

The economics of politics: Since the time of Adam Smith, economists have focused most of their energy on understanding the workings of the marketplace. But serious thinkers have also pondered the government's role in society. Joseph Schumpeter pioneered public-choice theory in *Capitalism, Socialism, and Democracy* (1942), and Kenneth Arrow's Nobel Prize–winning study on social choice brought mathematical rigor to this field. The landmark study by Anthony Downs, *An Economic Theory of Democracy* (1957), sketched a powerful new theory which held that politicians set economic policies in order to be reelected. Downs showed how parties tend to move toward the center of the political spectrum, and he posed the "voting paradox," which holds that it is irrational for people to vote given the small likelihood of any individual's affecting the outcome.

Further studies by James Buchanan and Gordon Tullock in *The Calculus of Consent* (1959) defended checks and balances and advocated the use of unanimity in political decisions—arguing that unanimous decisions do not coerce anyone and therefore impose no costs. For this and other works, Buchanan received the Nobel Prize in 1986. Public-choice economics received careful study by conservative politicians during the early 1980s. It was applied to such areas as farm policy, regulation, and the courts, and it formed the theoretical basis for a proposed constitutional amendment to balance the budget.

B. GOVERNMENT EXPENDITURES

Nowhere can the changes in government's role be seen more clearly than in the area of government spending. Look back at Figure 16-1 on page 283. It shows the share of national output going for government spending, which includes things like purchases of goods, salaries of government workers, social security and other transfers, and interest on the government debt. You can see that government's share has been steadily rising for the last 60 years, with temporary bulges during wartime.

FISCAL FEDERALISM

While we have been referring to government as if it were a single entity, in fact Americans face three levels of government: federal, state, and local. This reflects a division of fiscal responsibilities among the different levels of government—a system known as *fiscal federalism.* The boundaries are not always clear-cut, but in general the federal government directs activities that concern the entire nation—paying for defense, space, and foreign affairs. Local governments educate children, police streets, and remove garbage. States build highways, run university systems, and administer welfare programs.

The amounts of spending by the different government levels are shown in Table 16-1. The dominance of the federal role is a comparatively recent phenomenon. Before the twentieth century, local government was by far the most important of the three levels. The federal government did little more than support the military, pay interest on the national debt, and finance a few public works. Most of its tax collection came from liquor and

Level of government	Total spending, 1994* ($, billion)
Federal	1,412
State	550
Local (including counties)	710

*Outlays exclude transfers to lower levels.

TABLE 16-1. Government Spending at Different Levels

In the early days of the Republic, most spending was at the state and local levels. Today, more than half of total government outlays are federal. (Source: Bureau of the Census.)

tobacco excises and import tariffs. But the combination of two hot world wars and one cold war—along with the rise of transfer programs such as social security and Medicare—boosted spending, while the advent of the national income tax in 1913 provided a source of funds that no state or locality could match.

To understand fiscal federalism, economists emphasize that spending decisions should be allocated among the levels of government according to the spillovers from government programs. In general, localities are responsible for *local public goods,* activities whose benefits are largely confined to local

residents. Since libraries are used by townspeople and streetlights illuminate city roads, decisions about these goods are appropriately made by local residents. Many federal functions are *national public goods,* which provide benefits to all the nation's citizens. For example, an AIDS vaccine would benefit people from every state, not just those living near the laboratory where it is discovered; similarly, when the U.S. Army waged war in the Persian Gulf, oil supplies were protected for the entire country. What about global public goods like protecting the ozone layer or slowing global warming? These are *international public goods* because they transcend the boundaries of individual countries.

An efficient system of fiscal federalism takes into account the way the benefits of public programs spill over political boundaries. The most efficient arrangement is to locate the tax and spending decisions so that the beneficiaries of programs pay the taxes and can weigh the tradeoffs.

Federal Expenditures

Let's look now at the different levels of government. The U.S. government is the world's biggest enterprise. It buys more automobiles and steel, meets a bigger payroll, and handles more money

TABLE 16-2. Federal Spending Is Dominated by Defense and Entitlement Programs

About one-third of federal spending is for defense and interest or pensions due to past wars. More than half today is for rapidly growing entitlement programs—income security, social security, and health. Note how small is item 10's traditional cost of government. (Source: Office of Management and Budget, *Budget of the U.S. Government, Fiscal Year 1998.*)

Federal Expenditures, Fiscal Year 1998	Budget ($, billion)	Percentage of total
1. Social security	384.3	22.8
2. National defense, veterans, and international affairs	315.3	18.7
3. Health and Medicare	345.3	20.5
4. Income security	247.5	14.7
5. Interest on government debt	249.9	14.8
6. Education, training, employment, and social service	56.2	3.3
7. Transportation, commerce, and housing	42.6	2.5
8. Energy, natural resources, and environment	24.6	1.5
9. Science, space, and technology	16.5	1.0
10. General government	12.9	0.8
11. Agriculture	12.3	0.7
12. Miscellaneous and offsetting receipts	−19.9	−1.2
Total	**1,687.5**	**100.0**

than any other organization anywhere. The numbers involved in federal finance are astronomical—in the billions and trillions of dollars. The federal budget for 1998 is projected to be in the neighborhood of $1.7 trillion; this enormous number amounts to roughly $6300 for each American or approximately 2.5 months of total national output (gross domestic product, or GDP).

Table 16-2 on page 289 lists the major categories of federal expenditure for fiscal year 1998. (The federal fiscal year 1998 covers October 1, 1997, through September 30, 1998.)

The most rapidly expanding items in the last two decades have been *entitlement programs*, which provide benefits or payments to any persons who meet certain eligibility requirements set down by law. The major entitlements are social security (old-age, survivors, and disability insurance), health programs (including Medicare for those over 65 and Medicaid for indigent families), and income security programs (including subsidies for food and unemployment insurance). In fact, virtually the entire growth in federal spending in recent years can be accounted for by entitlement programs, which increased from 28 percent of the budget in 1960 to 59 percent in 1994.

State and Local Expenditures

Although the battles over the federal budget command the headlines, state and local units provide many of the essential functions in today's economy. Figure 16-3 illustrates the way states and localities spend their money. By far the largest item is education because most of the nation's children are educated in schools financed primarily by local governments. By attempting to equalize the educational resources available to every child, public education helps level out the otherwise great disparities in economic opportunity.

In recent years, the fastest-growing categories of spending for states and localities have been health care and prisons. In the 1980s the number of prisoners in state prisons tripled, as the United States fought a war on crime partly by using longer prison sentences, especially for drug offenders. At the same time, state and local governments were forced to absorb their share of rising health-care costs.

CULTURAL AND TECHNOLOGICAL IMPACTS

Government programs have subtle impacts on the country beyond the dollar spending. The federal government has changed the landscape through the interstate highway system. By making automotive travel much faster, this vast network lowered transportation costs, displaced the railroads, and brought goods to every corner of the country. It also helped accelerate urban sprawl and the growth of the suburban culture. Similarly, the social security system, by raising the income of senior citizens, gave older Americans the financial ability to pick up roots and move. Thus were created retirement havens in Florida and Arizona.

The government has put the United States on the map in many areas of science and technology. Government support gave a powerful running start to the budding U.S. electronics industries. The development of the transistor by Bell Labs, for example, was partially funded by the U.S. military, anxious for better radar and communications. And accord-

FIGURE 16-3. State and Local Governments Concentrate on Local Public Goods

State and local programs include providing education, financing hospitals, and maintaining the streets. In the division of labor among governments, cities pave their streets and states construct highways between cities, while the federal government pays for 90 percent of interstate highways. Do you see a pattern of fiscal federalism here? (Source: U.S. Bureau of the Census, *Government Finances in 1989–1990.*)

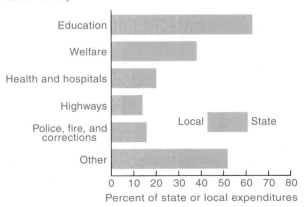

ing to some economists, the government's role went much further:

> It was not just R&D grants that greased the electronics industries' wheels, but the prospect of ensured government markets. *All* of the early semiconductor production of Western Electric, Bell's manufacturing affiliate, went to military shipments. From 1956 to 1964, the Pentagon consumed over 70 percent of the industry's output, particularly in the Minuteman missile program.[2]

Today's healthy computer and airplane industries were boosted in their early years by strong government support.

Because of the weight of its spending power, the government has an enormous voice in the development of science and technology. Throughout the 1980s and early 1990s, federal funds have continued to support about half of all research and development. In recent years, federal funding for health-care research has more than doubled, helping spawn the booming biotechnology industry. Often, if you follow a successful invention upstream to its source, you will find that government subsidized the education, supported basic university research in biology or physics, and purchased prototype versions for defense. Economic studies indicate that these funds were well spent, moreover, for the rates of return to education and research are estimated to compare favorably with those in other areas.

C. ECONOMIC ASPECTS OF TAXATION

Taxes are what we pay for a civilized society.

Justice Oliver Wendell Holmes

Governments must pay for their programs. The funds come mainly from taxes, and any shortfall is a deficit that is borrowed from the public.

But in economics we always need to pierce the veil of monetary flows to understand the flow of real resources. Behind the dollar flows of taxes, what the government really needs is the economy's scarce land, labor, and capital. When the nation fights a war in the desert, it appears to tax and borrow to pay for the war; but what really happens is that people are diverted from their civilian jobs, airplanes transport troops rather than tourists, and oil goes to tanks rather than cars. When the government gives out a grant for biotechnology research, its decision really means that a piece of land that might have been used for an office building is now being used for a laboratory.

In taxing, government is in reality deciding how to draw the required resources from the nation's households and businesses for public purposes. The money raised through taxation is the vehicle by which real resources are transferred from private goods to collective goods.

PRINCIPLES OF TAXATION

Benefit vs. Ability-to-Pay Principles

Once the government has decided to collect some amount of taxes, it has a bewildering array of possible taxes available to it. It can tax income, tax profits, or tax sales. It can tax the rich or tax the poor, tax the old or tax the young. Are there any guidelines that can help construct a fair and efficient tax system?

Indeed there are. Economists and political philosophers have proposed two major principles for organizing a tax system:

* The **benefit principle,** which holds that different individuals should be taxed in proportion to the benefit they receive from government programs. Just as people pay private dollars in proportion to their consumption of private bread, a person's

---

[2] Ann Markusen and Joel Yudken, *Dismantling the Cold War Economy* (Basic, New York, 1992), p. 48.

taxes should be related to his or her use of collective goods like public roads or parks.

- The **ability-to-pay principle,** which states that the amount of taxes people pay should relate to their income or wealth. The higher the wealth or income, the higher the taxes. Usually tax systems organized along the ability-to-pay principle are also *redistributive*, meaning that they raise funds from higher-income people to increase the incomes and consumption of poorer groups.

For instance, if the construction of a new bridge is funded by tolls on the bridge, that's a reflection of the benefit principle, since you pay for the bridge only if you use it. But if the bridge is funded out of income-tax collections, that would be an example of the ability-to-pay principle.

Horizontal and Vertical Equity

Whether they are organized along benefit or ability-to-pay lines, most modern tax systems also attempt to incorporate modern views about fairness or equity. One important principle is that of **horizontal equity,** which states that those who are essentially equal should be taxed equally.

The notion of equal treatment of equals has deep roots in Western political philosophy. If you and I are alike in every way except the color of our eyes, all principles of taxation would hold that we should pay equal taxes. In the case of benefit taxation, if we receive exactly the same services from the highways or parks, the principle of horizontal equity states that we should therefore pay equal taxes. Or if a tax system follows the ability-to-pay approach, horizontal equity dictates that people who have equal incomes should pay the same taxes.

A more controversial principle is **vertical equity,** which concerns the tax treatment of people with different levels of income. Abstract philosophical principles provide little guidance in resolving the issues of fairness here. Imagine that A and B are alike in every respect except that B has 10 times the property and income of A. Does that mean that B should pay the same absolute tax dollars as A for government services such as police protection? Or that B should pay the same percentage of income in taxes? Or, since the police spend more time protecting the property of well-to-do B, is it perhaps fair for B to pay a larger fraction of income in taxes?

Be warned that general and abstract principles cannot determine the tax structure for a nation. When Ronald Reagan campaigned for lower taxes, he did so because he thought high taxes were unfair to those who had worked hard and saved for the future. A decade later, Bill Clinton said, "We now have real fairness in the tax code with over 80 percent of the new tax burden being borne by those who make over $200,000 a year." What looks fair to the goose seems foul to the gander.

Pragmatic Compromises in Taxation

How have societies resolved these thorny philosophical questions? Governments have generally adopted pragmatic solutions that are only partially based on benefit and ability-to-pay approaches. Political representatives know that taxes are highly unpopular. After all, the cry of "taxation without representation" helped launch the American Revolution. Modern tax systems are an uneasy compromise between lofty principles and political pragmatism. As the canny French finance minister Colbert wrote three centuries ago, "Raising taxes is like plucking a goose: you want to get the maximum number of feathers with the minimum amount of hiss."

FIGURE 16-4. Progressive, Proportional, and Regressive Taxes

Taxes are progressive if they take a larger fraction of income as income rises; proportional if they are a constant fraction of income; and regressive if they place a larger relative burden on low-income families than on high-income families.

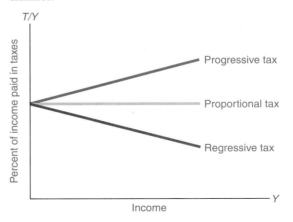

What practices have emerged? Often, public services primarily benefit recognizable groups, and those groups have no claim for special treatment by virtue of their average incomes or other characteristics. In such cases, modern governments generally rely on benefit taxes.

Thus, local roads are usually paid for by local residents. "User fees" are charged for water and sewage treatment, which are treated like private goods. Taxes collected on gasoline may be devoted (or "earmarked") to roads.

Progressive and Regressive Taxes. Benefit taxes are a declining fraction of government revenues. Today, advanced countries rely heavily on **progressive income taxes.** With progressive taxes, a family with $50,000 of income is taxed more than one with $20,000 of income. Not only does the higher-income family pay a larger income tax, but it in fact pays a higher fraction of its income.

This progressive tax is in contrast to a strictly **proportional tax,** in which all taxpayers pay exactly the same proportion of income. A **regressive tax** takes a larger fraction of income in taxes from poor families than it does from rich families.

A tax is called *proportional, progressive,* or *regressive* depending on whether it takes from high-income people the same fraction of income, a larger fraction of income, or a smaller fraction of income than it takes from low-income people.[3]

The different kinds of taxes are illustrated in Figure 16-4. What are some examples? A personal income tax that is graduated to take more and more out of each extra dollar of income is progressive. A cigarette tax is regressive because spending on cigarettes takes a larger fraction of income from low-income groups.

Direct and Indirect Taxes. Taxes are classified as direct or indirect. **Indirect taxes** are ones that are levied on goods and services and thus only "indirectly" on individuals. Examples are excise and sales taxes, cigarette and gasoline taxes, tariff duties on imports, and property taxes. By contrast, **direct taxes** are levied directly upon individuals or firms. Examples of direct taxes are personal income taxes, social security or other payroll taxes, and inheritance and gift taxes. Direct taxes have the advantage of being easier to tailor to fit personal circumstances, such as size of family, income, age, and more generally the ability to pay. By contrast, indirect taxes have the advantage of being cheaper and easier to collect, since they can be taxed at the retail or wholesale level.

FEDERAL TAXATION

Let us now try to understand the principles by which the federal system of taxation is organized. Table 16-3 provides an overview of the major taxes collected by the federal government and shows whether they are progressive, proportional, or regressive.

The Individual Income Tax

Our discussion will concentrate on the individual income tax, which is the most complex and controversial part of the tax system. The income tax is a direct tax, and it is the tax which most clearly reflects the ability-to-pay principle.

The individual income tax arrived late in our nation's history. The Constitution forbade any direct

TABLE 16-3. Income and Payroll Taxes Are the Main Federal Revenue Sources

Progressive taxes are still the leading source of federal revenues, but proportional payroll taxes are closing fast. (Source: Office of Management and Budget, *Budget of the U.S. Government, Fiscal Year 1998.*)

Federal Tax Receipts, Fiscal Year 1998	
	Receipts (% of total)
Progressive:	
Individual income taxes	44.1
Death and gift taxes	1.2
Corporate income taxes	12.1
Proportional:	
Payroll taxes	35.6
Regressive:	
Excise taxes	3.9
Other taxes and receipts	3.1
Total	**100.0**

---

[3] It should be noted that the words "progressive" and "regressive" are technical economic terms relating to the proportions that taxes bear to different incomes.

tax that was not apportioned among the states according to population. This was changed in 1913, when the Sixteenth Amendment to the Constitution provided that "Congress shall have power to lay and collect taxes on income, from whatever source derived."

How does the federal income tax work? The principle is simple, although the forms are complicated. You start by calculating your income; you next subtract certain expenses, deductions, and exemptions, to obtain taxable income. You then calculate your taxes on the basis of your taxable income.

Table 16-4 shows a calculation of individual taxes for a family of four at different levels of income. Column (1) shows different levels of *adjusted gross income*—that is, wages, interest, dividends, and other income earned by the household. Assuming that our household has four people and takes certain deductions, column (2) shows the tax due. Note that the tax is negative for those with wage incomes of $5000, $10,000, and $20,000 because of the *earned-income tax credit*; in this income range, the government is actually transferring income to low-income families.

Column (3) shows the **effective** or **average tax rate,** which is equal to total taxes divided by total

income. From this calculation, we see just how progressive the personal-income-tax code really is. A $50,000-a-year family is made to bear a relatively heavier burden than a $20,000-a-year family—the former pays 9 percent of income in taxes, while the latter has a negative rate of minus 2 percent. Someone earning $1 million each year is made to bear a still heavier relative burden.

Column (4) introduces a new and significant concept. The **marginal tax rate** is the extra tax that is paid per dollar of additional income. We have met the term "marginal" before, and it always means "extra." If you must pay $30 of additional taxes for every $100 of extra income, your marginal tax rate is 30 percent. Under current law, the marginal tax rate is minus 34 percent for poor families and rises to 15 percent for those just entering the positive tax system.

For incomes above $250,000, the marginal tax rate from the federal income tax is about 41 percent. If you live in New York City, you would add 8 percent for New York state and city taxes and 2.5 percent of health insurance for a total marginal tax rate on labor earnings of close to 50 percent. This may seem like a high rate, but the top rate today is far below the top rate of 94 percent during World

TABLE 16-4. Federal Income Tax for a Family of Four, 1996

The table shows incomes, taxes, and tax rates for a representative family of four in 1996. Because of the earned-income tax credit, low-income workers get a tax rebate—this is a "negative income tax" on wages. Marginal tax rates are initially negative, are zero at around $10,000 of income, then rise to 41 percent of income for top taxpayers. Average or effective rates are always less than marginal rates because the income tax is progressive. (Source: Derived from *TurboTax* computerized tax program. Table assumes that deductions are the greater of the standard deduction or 20 percent of income.)

(1) Adjusted gross income (before exemptions and deductions) ($)	(2) Individual income tax ($)	(3) Average tax rate (%) (3) = [(2) ÷ (1)] × 100	(4) Marginal tax rate (= tax on extra dollar) (%)	(5) Disposable income ($) (5) = (1) − (2)
5,000	−1,709	−34	−34	6,709
10,000	−2,152	−22	0	12,152
20,000	−338	−2	31	20,338
50,000	4,474	9	15	45,526
100,000	14,338	14	28	85,662
150,000	27,300	18	33	122,700
250,000	60,900	24	35	189,100
1,000,000	302,279	30	41	697,721
10,000,000	3,260,399	33	41	6,739,601

War II. Figure 16-5 shows the history of the highest marginal tax rate in the United States.

The notion of marginal tax rates is extremely important in modern economics. Remember the "marginal principle": People should be concerned only with the extra costs or benefits that occur; they should "let bygones be bygones." Under this principle, the major effect of any tax on incentives comes from the marginal tax rate. This notion has formed the intellectual core of supply-side economics.

Column (5) shows the amount of *disposable income after taxes*. Note that it always pays to get more income: Even when a rock star makes another million dollars, she still has $590,000 of disposable income left over [= $1,000,000 − (41% × $1,000,000)].

Social Insurance Taxes

Virtually all industries now come under the Social Security Act. Workers receive retirement benefits that depend on their earnings history and past social security taxes. The social insurance program also funds a disability program and health insurance for the poor and elderly.

To pay for these benefits, employees and employers are charged a *payroll tax*. In 1996, this consisted of a total of 15.4 percent of all wage income below a ceiling of about $57,600 a year per person, with an additional 2.9 percent of annual wage income between $57,600 and $135,000. The tax is split between employer and employee.

Table 16-3 shows the payroll tax as a proportional tax because it taxes a fixed fraction of employment earnings. It does have some regressive features, however, because it exempts property income and is higher on low wages than on high wages.

The payroll tax is the fastest-growing source of federal revenues, rising from zero in 1929, to 18 percent of revenues in 1960, to 37 percent in 1996.

Other Taxes

The Federal government collects a wide variety of other taxes, some of which are shown in Table 16-3. The *corporate income tax* is a tax on the profits of corporations. The top federal corporation tax rate in 1996 was set at 35 percent of corporate profits. The corporation income tax is heavily criticized among economists. Some oppose this tax, arguing that the corporation is but a legal fiction and should not be

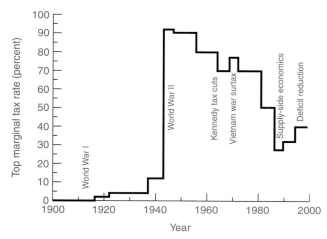

FIGURE 16-5. History of Top Marginal Tax Rate in the United States

The marginal tax rate is the extra tax that is paid per dollar of additional income. The top marginal tax rate on individual incomes reached 94 percent during World War II, was reduced in steps to a low of 28 percent during the Reagan years, and was raised to 40 percent in the 1993 Clinton economic package. (Source: U.S. Department of the Treasury.)

taxed. By taxing first corporate profits and then the dividends paid by corporations and received by individuals, the government subjects corporations to double taxation. Because of double taxation, corporate production is the most heavily taxed sector of the economy, a fact that may discourage investment in this dynamic sector.

The United States has no national sales tax, although there are a number of *federal excise taxes* on specific commodities such as cigarettes, alcohol, and gasoline. Sales and excise taxes are generally regressive, because consumption in general, and purchase of these items in particular, takes a larger fraction of income from a poor family than from a rich one.

Many economists and political leaders have argued that the United States should rely more heavily on sales or consumption taxes than it has up till now. One proposal, widely used outside the United States, is the *value-added tax*, or VAT. The VAT is like a sales tax, but it collects taxes at each stage of production. Thus, if a VAT were levied on bread, it would be collected from the farmer for wheat production, from the miller for flour production, from the baker at the dough stage, and from the grocer at the delivered-loaf stage.

Sales taxes and VATs are part of a more general class of *consumption taxes*. Their advocates argue that the country is currently saving and investing less than is necessary for future needs and that by substituting consumption taxes for income taxes, the national savings rate would increase. Critics of consumption taxes respond that such a change is undesirable because sales taxes are more regressive than today's income tax. One recent tax-reform proposal is the *flat tax*, which is a highly simplified system of personal consumption taxation. This approach would set all marginal tax rates at a uniform low rate (around 20 percent) and eliminate most deductions and tax-exempt fringe benefits, such as for health care and mortgage interest (see Question for Discussion 9). After a flurry of enthusiasm for flat taxes, the administration and Congress instead chose the "Christmas-tree" approach in the 1997 Taxpayer Relief Act. This bill introduced much greater complexity into the tax code by giving tax breaks to property income earned as capital gains, promoting a number of complicated new devices to encourage retirement saving, and helping students and their families through education tax credits and deductibility of interest on student loans. While the total annual impact on revenues will be small—about 0.3 percent of GDP—the increased complexity will make tax-related decisions more difficult and provide full employment for tax specialists for a long time to come.

STATE AND LOCAL TAXES

Under the U.S. system of fiscal federalism, state and local governments rely on a very different set of taxes than does the federal government. Figure 16-6 illustrates the main sources of funds that finance state and local expenditures.

Property Tax

The *property tax* is levied primarily on real estate—land and buildings. Each locality sets an annual tax rate which is levied on the assessed value of the land and structures. In many localities, the assessed value may be much smaller than the true market value. The property tax accounts for about 30 percent of the total revenues of state and local finance. Figure 16-6 shows that localities are the main recipient of property taxes.

Because about one-fourth of property values are from land, the property tax has elements of a capital tax and elements of a Henry George–type land tax. Economists believe that the land component of the property tax has little distortion, while the capital component will drive investment from high-tax central cities out to the low-taxed suburbs.

Whatever the views of economists, the property tax became controversial during the housing boom of the 1970s, when housing valuations and taxes skyrocketed. Across the country, taxpayers revolted. In Massachusetts, voters passed "Proposition $2\frac{1}{2}$," limiting tax payments to $2\frac{1}{2}$ percent of market value. Today, almost half the states have limitations on property or other taxes; these limits prevent state and local taxes from rising as rapidly as they did in the 1970s. During recessions, the tax limits sometimes push cities and states into fiscal crises as the governments run out of tax funds and are forced to cut services.

Other Taxes

Most other state taxes are closely related to the analogous federal taxes. States get most of their rev-

FIGURE 16-6. Property and Sales Taxes Dominate at State and Local Levels

Cities rely heavily on property taxes because houses and land cannot easily flee to the next town to avoid a city's tax. (Source: U.S. Bureau of the Census, *Government Finances in 1989–1990*.)

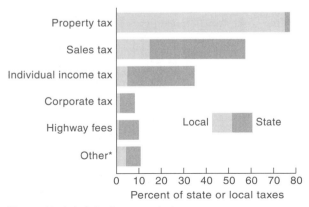

*Does not include federal revenue sharing.

enues from *general sales taxes* on goods and services. Each purchase at the department store or restaurant incurs a percentage tax (food and other necessities are exempt in some states). States tax the net income of corporations. Forty-five states imitate the federal government, on a much smaller scale, by taxing individuals according to the size of their incomes.

There are other miscellaneous revenues. Many states levy "highway user taxes" on gasoline. A growing source of revenue is lotteries and legalized gambling, in which the states benefit from encouraging people to impoverish themselves.

TAXES AND EFFICIENCY

Taxes affect both economic efficiency and the distribution of income. In recent years, the impacts on efficiency have become a principal concern of tax policy as economists and policymakers study the effect of incentives upon individual and business behavior. In tax policy, this involves primarily the question of how people respond to different levels of marginal tax rates.

An important political movement was the rise of *supply-side economics* in the 1980s. This program, championed by Republican President Ronald Reagan, pursued a macroeconomic policy directed toward long-run economic growth rather than business-cycle management; followed a budget policy that bolstered defense, cut civilian programs, and gave little weight to fiscal deficits; launched a regulatory program to reduce the burden of federal regulations, especially those pertaining to health, safety, and the environment; and, most important, lowered tax rates and tax burdens.

The major legacy of this period was the tax reforms of 1981 and 1986. These acts lowered marginal tax rates dramatically, broadened the tax base, and completely overhauled the individual income tax. The fiscal programs of these periods also led to a major increase in the federal budget deficit and to a government debt that grew sharply relative to national output.

How do high tax rates affect economic behavior? In the area of labor supply, the impacts are mixed. As we saw in Chapter 13, the impact of tax rates on hours worked is unclear because the income and substitution effects of wage changes work in opposite directions. As a result of progressive taxes, some

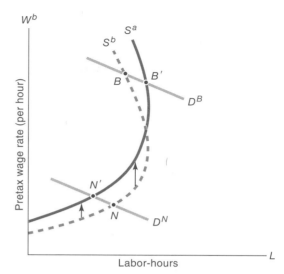

FIGURE 16-7. Response of Work to Taxes Depends on Shape of Supply Curve

Supply and demand plots labor supplied against pretax wage. Before-tax supply curve of labor (S^b) shifts vertically upward to after-tax supply (S^a) after imposition of a 25 percent income tax on labor earnings. If demand for labor intersects supply in the normal region at bottom, we see an expected decline in labor supplied from N to N'. If the labor supply is backward-bending, as at top, the labor supplied actually rises with the tax increase, going from B to B'.

people may choose more leisure over more work. Other people may work harder in order to make their millions. Many high-income doctors, artists, celebrities, and business executives, who enjoy their jobs and the sense of power or accomplishment that they bring, will work as hard for $800,000 after tax as for $1,000,000 after tax. Moreover, high taxes on winner-take-all activities may reduce the supply of talent to those overcrowded areas. Figure 16-7 shows how an increase in the tax rate on labor will affect labor supply; note the paradox that work effort may actually decline after a tax-rate cut if the labor supply curve is backward-bending.

In the area of saving and investment, taxes clearly have major impacts upon economic activity. When taxes are high in one sector, resources will flow into more lightly taxed areas. For example, because corporate capital is double-taxed, people's savings will flow out of the corporate sector and into lightly taxed sectors like oil and gas or into vacation homes financed by tax-deductible interest payments. If risky investments are taxed unfavorably, investors may prefer safer investments. The inefficiency comes as much from the divergence of taxes across sectors as from the existence of high taxes.[4]

Efficiency vs. Fairness

Economists have long been concerned with the impact of taxes on economic efficiency. Recall from Chapter 14 that Henry George argued that a tax on land will have little impact on efficiency because the supply of land is completely inelastic. The modern theory of efficient taxation puts forth the *Ramsey tax rule*, which states that the government should levy the heaviest taxes on those inputs and outputs that are most price-inelastic in supply or demand.[5] The rationale for the Ramsey tax rule is that if a commodity is very price-inelastic in supply or demand, a tax on the commodity will have little impact upon consumption and production. In some circumstances, Ramsey taxes may constitute a way of raising revenues with a minimum loss of economic efficiency.

But economies and politics do not run on efficiency alone. While stiff taxation of land rents or food might be efficient, many would think them unfair. A sober reminder of the dilemma was the proposal to introduce a poll tax in Britain in 1990. A *poll tax* is a *lump-sum tax*, or a fixed tax per person. The advantage of this tax is that, like a land tax, it would induce no inefficiencies. After all, people are unlikely to decamp to Russia or commit harikari to avoid the tax, so the economic distortions would arguably be minimal.

Alas, the British government underestimated the extent to which the populace felt this tax to be unfair. The poll tax is highly regressive because it places a much higher proportional burden on low-income people than on high-income people. Criticism of the poll tax played a key role in bringing down the Thatcher government after 11 years in power. This illustrates clearly the difficult choice between efficiency and fairness in taxes and other areas of economic policy.

---

[4] One interesting example of the interaction of efficiency and taxes is the Laffer curve, which is discussed in question 8 at the end of this chapter.

[5] Recall Chapter 14's discussion of Henry George's single tax and the extension to efficient or Ramsey taxes.

Taxing "Bads" Rather Than "Goods": Green Taxes

While poll taxes have been little advocated by economists, economists have favored an approach wherein the tax system would weigh more heavily on "bads" than on "goods." The main source of inefficiency is that taxes generally tax "goods"—economic activities like working, investing in capital, saving, or risk taking—and thereby discourage these activities. An alternative approach is to tax "bads." Traditional taxes on bads include "sin taxes": taxes on alcohol, cigarettes, and other substances that have harmful health effects.

A new approach to taxation is to tax pollution and other undesirable externalities; such taxes are called *green taxes* because they are designed to help the environment as well as to raise revenues. Say that the nation decides to help slow global warming by levying a "carbon tax," which is a tax on carbon-dioxide emissions from power plants and other sources. By standard economic reasoning we know that the tax will lead firms to lower their carbon-dioxide emissions, thereby improving the environment. In addition, of course, this green tax will provide revenues, which the government can use either to finance its activities or to reduce tax rates on beneficial activities like working or saving. So green taxes are doubly effective: The state gets revenue, and the environment is improved because the taxes discourage harmful externalities.

THE THORNY PROBLEM OF TAX INCIDENCE

Who actually ends up paying all these taxes that governments levy? We should not assume that the people or firms that send the tax revenues to the government will end up paying that tax. Just because the oil company sends the gasoline-tax receipts to the Treasury does not mean that the taxes come out of the profits of the oil company. Businesses may be able to shift the tax "forward" onto their customers by raising their price by the amount of the tax. Or they may shift the tax "backward" onto their suppliers (owners of labor, land, and other factors), who find themselves with lower wages, rents, and other factor prices than they would have enjoyed had there been no tax.

The question of shifting of taxes concerns **tax incidence.** This concept involves the way the tax burden ultimately is borne and its total effects on prices, quantities, and the composition of production and consumption.

Tax-incidence questions include these: Did the 4.3-cent-a-gallon tax on fuels passed in 1993 raise the price at the pump by 4.3 cents so that the incidence was on the consumer? Or did it lower the price of crude oil so that the incidence was on the oil producers? Or was the incidence somewhere in between? Did it change coal prices? And did the tax kill off oil production, so it had incidence effects beyond those which show up in money prices and wages and even beyond the burdens that you can allocate among the different citizens?

Microeconomics provides some important tools for analyzing tax incidence. In earlier chapters, we saw the incidence of a gasoline tax. In such simple cases, involving only supply of and demand for a single commodity, incidence analysis is straightforward. In other cases, the effects cascade through the economy, making analysis extremely complex and sometimes requiring general-equilibrium approaches.

We might want to know the *fiscal incidence* of the government tax and transfer system as a whole. Fiscal incidence examines the impact of both tax and expenditure programs on the incomes of the population. Fiscal incidence concerns the overall degree of progressivity or regressivity of government programs. It is estimated by allocating all taxes and transfer payments to different groups. Such a study is only approximate, since no one is sure how much the corporation tax or the property tax gets shifted.

The conceptual experiment we want to make is

- to measure incomes without taxes and transfers,
- then to measure incomes with taxes and transfers,
- and finally to measure *incidence* as the difference between these two situations.

Of course, economists are not magicians who can make such controlled experiments, but they take careful measurements and use good judgment to estimate the effects of taxes and spending.

Incidence of Federal Taxes and Transfers

Figure 16-8 shows the results of a recent study of the incidence of all U.S. taxes and cash transfers; in

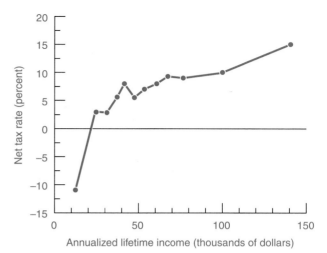

FIGURE 16-8. Who Pays the Taxes and Who Benefits from Transfers?

How does the modern welfare state affect the income of its citizens over their entire life cycle? Fullerton and Rogers estimate the impact on a household's lifetime income of all federal, state, and local taxes and cash transfers that were in place in 1984. The tax and transfer system is progressive at almost every income category. Note that the system actually transfers income to the lowest group while the highest group has a net tax rate of 15 percent. [Source: Don Fullerton and Diane Lim Rogers, *Who Bears the Lifetime Tax Burden?* (Brookings Institution, Washington, D.C., 1993), p. 123. The data have been updated to 1993 incomes, and the lifetime incomes were converted into annualized incomes using a 5 percent real interest rate.]

this figure, transfers are treated as negative taxes and are measured in the negative direction. The interesting contribution of this approach is that it examines *lifetime income and taxes* rather than looking at only a single year. Thus it takes into account important changes that occur over a lifetime (e.g., people go in and out of the labor market, and they pay social security taxes when young and then receive the taxes as benefits when retired). The study also takes into account the incredible complexity of our tax system, as described above.

The results indicate that the tax system is generally progressive from the top to the bottom, with the lowest group receiving net transfers while the top group has the highest average tax rate. A closer look at the structure of the tax and transfer system indicates that its progressive structure, particularly at the bottom, comes primarily from transfers rather than from taxes.

This pattern of net fiscal impact is similar to that found in most advanced market economies today. As one survey of fiscal incidence in high-income countries concluded:

> The evidence for almost all countries suggests that the tax system overall has almost no effect on income distribution. . . . This results from the progressive impact of income taxes being offset by regressive taxes, notably employers' social security contributions and indirect taxes. . . . When tax, transfer, and expenditure programs are viewed together, it is apparent that public expenditure programs, particularly the provision of cash transfers, have been almost totally responsible for the changes in income distribution which governments have brought about.[6]

FINAL WORD

Our introductory survey of government's role in the economy is a sobering reminder of the responsibilities and shortcomings of collective action. On the one hand, governments must defend their borders, stabilize their economies, protect the public health, and regulate pollution. On the other hand, many policies designed to benefit the public interest suffer from inefficiencies and inconsistencies.

Does this mean we should abandon the visible hand of government for the invisible hand of markets? Economics cannot answer such deep political questions; all it can do is examine the strengths and weaknesses of both collective and market choices, and point to mechanisms (such as green taxes or subsidies to research and development) by which a mended invisible hand may be more efficient than the extremes of either pure laissez-faire or unbridled bureaucratic rule making.

SUMMARY

A. Government Control of the Economy

1. The economic role of government has increased sharply over the last century. The government influences and controls private economic activity by using taxes, expenditures, and direct regulation.

2. A modern welfare state performs four economic functions: (*a*) It remedies market failures; (*b*) it redistributes income and resources; (*c*) it establishes macroeconomic stabilization policy to stabilize the business cycle and promote long-term economic growth; and (*d*) it manages international economic affairs.

3. Public-choice theory analyzes how governments actually behave. Just as the invisible hand can break down, so there are government failures, in which government interventions lead to waste or redistribute income in an undesirable fashion.

B. Government Expenditures

4. The American system of public finance is one of fiscal federalism. The federal government concentrates its spending on issues of national concern—on national public goods like defense and space exploration.

States and localities generally focus on local public goods—those whose benefits are largely confined within state or city boundaries.

5. Government spending and taxation today take approximately one-third of total national output. Of this total, 70 percent is spent at the federal level, and the balance is divided between state and local governments. Only a tiny fraction of government outlays is devoted to traditional functions like police and the courts.

C. Economic Aspects of Taxation

6. Notions of "benefits" and "ability to pay" are two principal theories of taxation. A tax is progressive, proportional, or regressive as it takes a larger, equal, or smaller fraction of income from rich families than it does from poor families. Direct and progressive taxes on incomes are in contrast to indirect and regressive sales and excise taxes.

7. More than half of federal revenues come from personal and corporation income taxes. The rest comes from taxes on payrolls or consumption goods. Local governments raise most of their revenue from property taxes, while sales taxes are most important for states.

8. The individual income tax is levied on "income from whatever source derived," less certain exemptions and

---

[6] Peter Saunders, "Evidence on Income Redistribution by Governments," OECD, Economics and Statistics Department, Working Papers, no. 11 (January 1984).

deductions. The marginal tax rate, denoting the fraction paid in taxes for every dollar of additional income, is key to determining the impact of taxes on incentives to work and save. Marginal tax rates were lowered sharply during the 1980s, but top rates were then raised in President Clinton's fiscal package of 1993.

9. The fastest-growing federal tax is the payroll tax, used to finance social security. This is an "earmarked" levy, with funds going to provide public pensions and health and disability benefits. Because there are visible benefits at the end of the stream of payments, the payroll tax has elements of a benefit tax.

10. Economists point to the Ramsey tax rule, which emphasizes that efficiency will be promoted when

taxes are levied more heavily on those activities that are relatively price-inelastic. A new approach is green taxes, which levy fees on environmental externalities, reducing harmful activities while raising revenues that would otherwise be levied on goods or productive inputs. But in all taxes, equity and political acceptability are severe constraints.

11. The incidence of a tax refers to its ultimate economic burden and to its total effect on prices, outputs, and other economic magnitudes. Those who pay a tax can often pass its burden forward to consumers or backward to factors of production. The current U.S. tax and transfer system is moderately progressive.

CONCEPTS FOR REVIEW

Functions of Government

three tools of government economic control:
  taxes
  expenditures
  regulation
market failures vs. government failures
public-choice theory

four functions of government:
  efficiency
  distribution
  stabilization
  international representation

Government Expenditures and Fiscal Incidence

fiscal federalism and local vs. national public goods

economic impact of government spending
benefit and ability-to-pay principles
horizontal and vertical equity
direct and indirect taxes
progressive, proportional, and regressive taxes
tax and transfer incidence and shifting
Ramsey and green taxes

QUESTIONS FOR DISCUSSION

1. Recall Justice Oliver Wendell Holmes' statement, "Taxes are what we pay for a civilized society." Interpret this statement, remembering that in economics we always need to pierce the veil of monetary flows to understand the flow of real resources.

2. In considering whether you want a pure laissez-faire economy or government regulation, discuss whether there should be government controls over prostitution, addictive drugs, heart transplants, assault weapons, and alcohol. Discuss the relative advantages of high taxes and prohibition for such goods (recall the discussion of drug prohibition in Chapter 5).

3. Critics of the U.S. tax system argue that it harms incentives to work, save, and innovate and therefore reduces long-run economic growth. Can you see why "green taxes" might promote economic efficiency and economic growth? Consider, for example, taxes on sulfur or carbon-dioxide emissions or on leaky oil tankers. Construct a list of taxes that you think would increase

efficiency, and compare their effects with the effects of taxes on labor or capital income.

4. Tax economists often speak of lump-sum taxes, which are levied on individuals without regard to their economic activity. Lump-sum taxes like poll taxes have no distortion or inefficiencies because they have no effect on incentives; in other words, they impose zero marginal tax rates on all inputs and outputs. Assume that the government imposes a lump-sum tax of $200 on each individual. Show in a supply-and-demand diagram why this will have no effect on either wages or labor supplied. (Recall Henry George's analysis of land taxes.)

   In a lifetime framework, we could think of the dynamic equivalent of the lump-sum tax as an "endowment tax," which would tax individuals on the basis of their potential labor incomes. Fullerton and Rogers (op. cit., page 299) find that a perfectly efficient proportional endowment tax would increase average lifetime incomes by 1.3 percent. Would you favor such a change? Describe some of the difficulties in implementing an endowment tax.

5. Make a list of different federal taxes in order of their progressiveness. If the federal government were to trade in income taxes for consumption or sales taxes, what would be the effect in terms of overall progressiveness of the tax system?

6. Some public goods are local, spilling out to residents of small areas; others are national, benefiting an entire nation; some are global, affecting all nations. A private good is one whose spillover is negligible. Give some examples of purely private goods and of local, national, and global public goods or externalities. For each, indicate the level of government that could design policies most efficiently, and suggest one or two appropriate government actions that could solve the externality.

7. Some incidence questions that can be answered using supply and demand:

    a. In the 1993 Budget Act, Congress raised federal gasoline taxes by 4.3 cents a gallon. Assuming the wholesale price of gasoline is determined in world markets, what is the relative impact of the tax on American producers and consumers?

    b. Social insurance taxes are generally levied on labor earnings. What is their incidence if labor supply is perfectly inelastic? If labor supply is backward-bending?

    c. If firms must earn a posttax rate of return on investment determined in world capital markets, what is the incidence of a tax on corporate income in a small open economy?

8. An interesting question involves the *Laffer curve,* named for California economist and sometime senatorial candidate Arthur Laffer. In Figure 16-9, the Laffer curve shows how revenues rise as *tax rates* are increased, reach a maximum at point *L,* and then decline to zero at a 100 percent tax rate as activity is completely discouraged. The exact shape of the Laffer curve for different taxes is highly controversial.

    A common mistake in discussing taxes is the post hoc fallacy (see Chapter 1's discussion of this). Proponents of lower taxes often invoke the Laffer curve in their arguments. They point to tax cuts of the 1960s to suggest that the economy is to the right of the peak of Mt. Laffer, say at *B.* They say, in effect, "After the Kennedy-Johnson tax cuts of 1964, federal revenues actually rose from $110 billion in 1963 to $133 billion in 1966. Therefore, cutting taxes raises revenues." Explain why this does not prove that the economy was to the right of *L.* Further explain why this is an example of the *post hoc* fallacy. Give a correct analysis.

9. A popular tax reform proposal of the 1990s was the "flat tax," developed by economists Robert Hall and Alvin Rabushka of Stanford University. The idea of the flat tax is to tax all personal and corporate income only once at a low constant rate. Table 16-5 shows how such a flat tax might work. Compare the average and marginal tax rates of the flat tax with the tax schedule shown in Table 16-4 in the text. List advantages and disadvantages of both. Which is more progressive?

FIGURE 16-9. The Laffer Curve

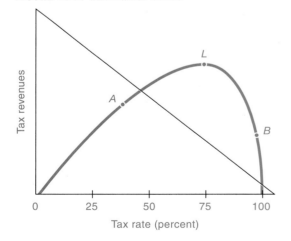

TABLE 16-5.

(1) Adjusted gross income ($)	(2) Deductions and exemptions ($)	(3) Taxable income ($)	(4) Individual income tax ($)
5,000	20,000	0	0
10,000	20,000	0	0
20,000	20,000	0	0
50,000	20,000	30,000	6,000
100,000	20,000	80,000	16,000
1,000,000	20,000	980,000	196,000

CHAPTER 17
CURBING MARKET POWER

> Both theoretical and empirical research question the extent to which regulation can achieve the goals for which it has been promulgated.
>
> *Stephen Breyer and Paul MacAvoy,*
> **Regulation and Deregulation (1987)**

Before studying economics, many people think that the government needs to be a watchdog to prevent monopolistic abuses and price gouging. A little learning might easily lead students to reverse this view, for the invisible-hand theory teaches that the forces of profit seeking themselves serve as guarantees against excess profits. If a firm enjoys profits above the normal rate of return, these profits will lure in new competitors, raise output, and lower prices and profits. For the most part, then, governments in market economies rely on the force of rivalry and competition—the carrot of profits and the stick of bankruptcy—to stimulate the private sector to behave efficiently.

But the forces of competition cannot work effectively when competitors are absent or feeble. When businesses have market power, they can raise prices above the competitive level for a long time. When there is excessive market power, government can take steps to promote competition.

Moreover, the government steps in to help ameliorate a whole range of perceived market failures.

Sometimes people may not have the information or the capability to protect themselves. So the government requires drug companies to demonstrate the safety and efficacy of new drugs or monitors the safety performance of airlines. The government also regulates industries like banking and electricity, tries to protect consumers from false advertising and financial misrepresentation, and engages in zoning decisions which control the economic use of land.

How can governments deal with market failures and the excesses of monopoly power without obstructing the powerful efficiency gains of unfettered market competition and rivalry? This has proved to be a mighty dilemma. Sometimes, the public interest compels regulation in a limited domain; at other times, economic regulation creates more problems than it solves, and governments are advised to deregulate a sector. Governments also attempt to promote competition and prevent monopoly abuses by banning certain kinds of anticompetitive practices; this area of government activity, antitrust policy, is the subject of the second half of this chapter.

A. BUSINESS REGULATION: THEORY AND PRACTICE

Federal regulation of American industry goes back more than a century to the founding of the Interstate Commerce Commission (ICC) in 1887. The ICC was designed as much to prevent price wars and to guarantee service to small towns as it was to control monopoly. Later, federal regulation spread to banks in 1913, to electric power in 1920, and to communications, securities markets, labor, trucking, and air travel during the 1930s. In recent years, as we will see, the federal government has changed its course by deregulating many industries.

In attempting to control economic activity, governments can use commands or market incentives. Historically the main form of regulation has been a direct approach, where governments issue *command-and-control orders*. In this approach, governments command people to undertake or desist from certain activities through government regulation. For example, the government might require that businesses locate only in commercial areas or that they do not pour chemicals in the river. Government commands today cover a wide variety of areas, including not only pollution and zoning but also informational reporting, labor standards on wages and hours, and many regulations specific to particular industries such as those using pesticides, producing new drugs, or engaged in international trade.

Recently, economists have been instrumental in convincing government to try a brand-new form of regulation: relying on *market incentives*. The best example of market incentives is the 1990 Clean Air Act, discussed in the next chapter. This bill set up markets for buying and selling "tradeable emissions permits"—in essence, licenses to pollute. Such harnessing of market forces has the possibility of achieving regulatory goals much more efficiently than command-and-control methods.

Regulation consists of government rules or market incentives designed to control the price, sale, or production decisions of firms.

TWO BRANDS OF REGULATION

It is customary to distinguish between two forms of regulation. **Economic regulation** involves the control of prices, entry and exit conditions, and standards of service in a particular industry. Prominent examples are regulation of public utilities (telephone, electricity, natural gas, and water) as well as regulations in other industries (transportation, radio, and TV). The financial industry has been heavily regulated since the 1930s, with strict rules specifying what banks, brokerage firms, and insurance companies can and cannot do.

In addition, there is a newer form of regulation, known as **social regulation**, which is used to protect the environment along with the health and safety of workers and consumers. Its rules are aimed at correcting a wide variety of side effects or externalities that result from economic activity. Programs to clean our air and water or to ensure the safety of nuclear power or drugs or cars are the most prominent examples of social regulation. Because of its importance, we will study environmental regulation in detail in the next chapter.

WHY REGULATE INDUSTRY?

Regulation restrains the unfettered market power of firms. What are the legitimate reasons why governments might choose to override the decisions made in free markets? There are three major *public-interest justifications* of regulation. The first is to regulate firm behavior to prevent abuses of market power by monopolies or oligopolies. A second major reason is to correct negative externalities like pollution—this is the subject of social regulation, studied in the next chapter. A third reason is to remedy informational failures, such as occur when consumers have inadequate information about the characteristics of important products like drugs or energy-using appliances.

Containing Market Power

The traditional public-interest view of economic regulation is normative: that regulatory measures should be taken to reduce excessive market power. More specifically, government should regulate industries where there are too few firms to ensure vigorous rivalry. Government should regulate industries particularly in the extreme case of natural monopoly, especially where the monopoly occurs for necessities that have a low price elasticity of demand.

An important example of a natural monopoly is local water distribution. The cost of gathering water, building a water-distribution system, and piping water into every home is sufficiently great that it would not pay to have more than one firm provide local water service, so this is a natural monopoly. Sometimes water service is provided by the government; more often, it is provided by a regulated privately owned water company.

Another type of natural monopoly can occur when an industry has *economies of scope*, which arise when a number of different products can be produced more efficiently together than by separate firms. For example, transport-equipment firms show economies of scope—a firm producing cars and trucks has a cost advantage in producing buses and tanks. Why? Because specialized knowledge and machinery are shared across the different products. These firms have economies of scope in production of ground-based transport systems.

We know from our discussion of declining costs in Chapter 7 that pervasive economies of scale are inconsistent with perfect competition; we will see oligopoly or monopoly in such cases. But the point here is even more extreme: *When there are such powerful economies of scale or scope that only one firm can survive, we have a natural monopoly.*

Why do governments regulate natural monopolies? They do so because a natural monopolist, enjoying a large cost advantage over its potential competitors and facing price-inelastic demand, can jack up its price sharply, obtain enormous monopoly profits, and create major economic inefficiencies. In recent years, cable television companies have exploited their local monopolies in providing multiple channels with high-quality pictures by raising prices sharply. This provoked Congress and several states to enact legislation regulating the prices set by companies. Studies indicated that this price regulation was ineffective and may actually have raised prices in some categories. Consequently, in the 1995 Communications Act, Congress changed its mind and lifted price and entry controls with the idea that greater competition would be more beneficial for consumers than price controls.

In earlier times, regulation was justified on the dubious grounds that it was needed to prevent cutthroat or destructive competition. This was one argument for continued control over railroads, trucks, airlines, and buses, as well as for regulation of the level of agricultural production. Economists today have little sympathy for this argument. After all, competition with increased efficiency and low prices is exactly what an efficient market system is designed to ensure.

Remedying Information Failures
Another reason for regulation is that consumers have inadequate information about products. For example, testing pharmaceutical drugs is expensive and scientifically complex. The government regulates drugs by allowing the sale of only those drugs which are proved "safe and efficacious." Government also prohibits false and misleading advertising. In both cases, the government is attempting to correct for the market's failure to provide information efficiently.

Much of the regulation of the financial industry serves the purpose of increasing the quantity and quality of information so that markets can work better. For example, when a company sells stocks or bonds in the United States, it is required to issue copious documentation of its current financial condition and future prospects. This helps protect investors from fraudulent claims about the value of the company's securities. Government requirements are sometimes reinforced by the private sector: companies which list on the New York Stock Exchange must comply with an even tougher set of accounting regulations. Financial regulations are less stringent in other countries, with the consequence that investors often find themselves bilked when companies inflate profits or hide damaging information. Paradoxically, tough reporting standards are beneficial to financial markets because they reduce informational asymmetries between buyers and sellers.

Safety regulation in the workplace, too, helps cure informational deficiencies. Remember from Chapter 13 that the theory of compensating differentials says that more hazardous jobs should entail premium wages. The problem is that many hazards may not be obvious, and companies clearly have an interest in not publicizing problems in their workplaces. For this reason it may be efficient for the government to set minimum standards for worker safety, so that an individual worker does not have to undertake a costly investigation of the safety record of every company where he or she is applying for a job.

Dealing with Externalities

Government regulation can also be justified when there are externalities. The classic example of regulation of this type, which we analyze in the next chapter, is antipollution measures. But there are other interesting cases. One pervasive example is local zoning regulation, which limits how landowners can use their land. Most zoning regulations specify whether a plot of land can be used for residences, stores, or industry and how big the buildings can be.

What is the justification for zoning regulation? Allowing a junkyard in a quiet residential area, for instance, would generate externalities that might harm everyone in the neighborhood. Similarly, a 50-story office building in a neighborhood of 2-story homes might overwhelm the local transportation system and other neighborhood services.

The economic impact of zoning can be huge. Being able to build a 50-story building on a plot of land, as opposed to a 2-story one, can dramatically affect the value of the land. That's why zoning is perhaps the most important type of regulation done at the local level of government.

Interest-Group Theories of Regulation

So far we have been looking at the normative public-interest justifications for government regulation. We should recognize, however, that regulation redistributes income and thereby creates interest groups that have vested interests in the regulatory outcomes. Sometimes, because of the interaction between regulation and politics, regulation has the perverse result of restricting entry into the regulated industry, which actually *raises prices and profits* for established companies.[1] Hence, a regulated industry may actually lobby in favor of continued regulation, in order to keep out competitors and keep profits high.

Economists who emphasize the anticompetitive aspect of regulation argue, "You say that regulation is in the interest of consumers and workers. Don't believe it. Rather, regulation is designed to boost the incomes of producers by limiting entry and preventing competition in the regulated industry. Any gains to consumers or workers are purely incidental."

The historical record shows that there is much truth to this view. For example, numerous economic studies of regulation have shown that regulation often keeps prices *high*. For many years, trucking companies and airlines had to get permission before lowering prices or entering new markets. Other types of regulation also have the effect of limiting competition. For example, high standards for new drugs means that the process of getting regulatory approval is lengthy and expensive. That keeps out many smaller companies which cannot afford the years of testing that a new drug requires.

The most recent example of a regulatory program benefiting the industry at the expense of taxpayers came in the savings and loan industry. The federal program of deposit insurance was established in the 1930s to help restore confidence and

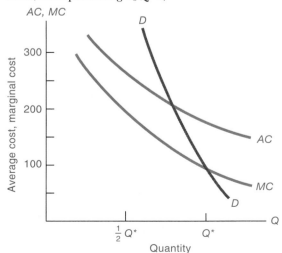

FIGURE 17-1. Cost Curves for a Natural Monopolist
For a natural monopolist, the *AC* curve is still falling at the point where it cuts the industry's *DD* curve. Thus efficient production requires output to be concentrated in a single firm. (Can you estimate from the diagram how much more expensive it would be if Q^* were to be produced by two firms, each producing $\frac{1}{2} Q^*$?)

---

[1] The germinal work in this area was by George Stigler of the University of Chicago, who won a Nobel Prize for this and other contributions. The Chicago School has been highly influential in its view that government intervention in the economy often does more harm than good.

prevent bank panics. By the early 1980s, however, it became clear that the program was poorly designed. It provided a government guarantee on bank deposits without ensuring that banks behaved prudently with the insured deposits. As a result, many banks could pay high interest rates to attract deposits and then use the money to make risky loans and investments and to pay high salaries to their executives. When the banks began going bankrupt, the government had to pick up the tab; losses mounted to the hundreds of billions of dollars. Because of intense lobbying and generous campaign contributions, appropriate government action to stop the wasteful practices was delayed for years until Congress acted to curb the worst abuses in 1989. Who were the major beneficiaries of the corrupt regulatory regime in the banking industry? Primarily

bankers, banks, and bank stockholders. Who were the losers? The taxpayers.

PUBLIC-UTILITY REGULATION OF NATURAL MONOPOLY

A traditional economic argument for regulation is to prevent monopoly pricing by natural monopolists. Let us see exactly how regulators control excessive price increases of monopolists. Recall that a natural monopoly is an industry in which the most efficient way of organizing production is through a single firm. Figure 17-1 shows the way the *AC*, *MC*, and industry demand curve might look for a natural monopoly. Note that the industry demand curve (*DD*) intersects the firm's *MC* curve where *AC* is falling. If two similar firms were to produce the

FIGURE 17-2. Ideal and Practical Regulation of Monopolists

Maximum-profit equilibrium for the unregulated monopolist is at *M*, directly above the intersection of *MR* and long-run *MC*, with price above *MC*.

Public-utility commissions customarily require prices to be equal to average cost at *R*, where the demand curve intersects the long-run average cost curve. This wipes out excess profit and brings price down closer to marginal cost. Ideally, price should be forced all the way down to *I*, where price = *MC* and hence marginal social costs and marginal benefits are appropriately balanced. At point *I*, there is no efficiency loss from price being above marginal cost.

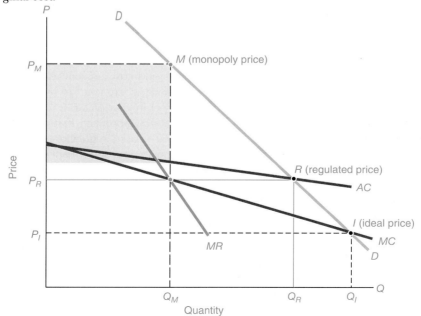

industry output, the average cost for the two firms would be well above that of a single firm.

Suppose that the legislature decides to impose *public-utility regulation* on a particular industry. How would it proceed? It would first set up a public-utility commission to oversee prices, service, and entry into and exit from the industry. The most important decision would be to determine the pricing of the monopoly firm.

Traditionally, regulation imposes *average cost pricing* on regulated firms. For example, an electric utility would take all its costs (fixed as well as variable) and distribute them to each product sold (say, electricity and steam). Then each class of customer would be charged the *fully distributed average cost* of that type of service.

Figure 17-2 illustrates public-utility regulation. Point M (associated with output Q_M) is the unregulated profit-maximizing output of the monopolist we examined in Chapter 9. Here we find high price, reduced quantity, and handsome profits (as shown by the shaded region in Figure 17-2).

In traditional regulation, the monopolist is allowed to charge a price only high enough to cover average cost. In this case, the firm will set its price where the demand curve DD intersects the AC curve. Hence, the equilibrium is at point R, with output Q_R.

How good is the solution? Economically speaking, it might represent an improvement over unregulated monopoly. First, the owners of the monopoly are presumably no more deserving than the consumers. So there is no reason to allow them to extract monopoly profits from consumers.

Second, in making the monopolist cut its price from P_M to P_R, the regulators have reduced the discrepancy between price and marginal cost. This change improves economic efficiency because the additional output is worth more to consumers in marginal utility than it costs society in terms of the marginal cost. Only when price is equal to marginal cost in all sectors is society using its resources most efficiently.

Ideally Regulated Pricing. If $P = MC$ is such a good thing, why shouldn't the regulators force the monopolist to lower price until it equals marginal cost at the intersection point of the DD and MC curves (at I)?

Actually, *marginal-cost pricing* where $P = MC$ is the ideal target for economic efficiency. But it presents a

serious practical obstacle: if a firm with declining average cost sets price equal to marginal cost, it will incur a chronic loss. The reason is that if AC is falling, then $MC < AC$, so setting $P = MC$ implies having $P < AC$. When price (or average revenue) is less than average cost, the firm is losing money. To see this point visually, examine the ideal regulatory solution at point I in Figure 17-2. At that point, price equals marginal cost, but MC is less than average cost. When average cost is greater than price, the firm is losing money. Since firms will not operate at a loss for long, and governments are reluctant to subsidize monopolists, the ideal regulatory solution is rarely pursued.

In an alternative approach, pricing is based on *two-part tariffs*. The firm charges a fixed fee (say, a few dollars a month) to cover the overhead costs and then adds a variable cost (per phone call, unit of electricity, or whatever the commodity is) to cover the marginal cost. This approach can come even closer to the ideal marginal-cost pricing than does traditional average cost pricing.

 Economic innovations: price-cap regulation. As we saw above, under traditional rate-of-return regulation, prices are determined as the cost of production plus an authorized rate of return on invested capital. This approach has very weak incentives to economize and is biased toward capital-intensive production techniques. The incentives are actually perverse because if price equals average cost, firms can actually increase profits by raising costs. As one economist noted, this is the only market where you can profit by putting a fancy Oriental carpet in your office!

A radical new approach that can improve incentives is performance-based regulation. Under this approach, firms are regulated on performance rather than on inputs, usually by use of a *price cap*. One formula is that regulated prices should move with "inflation minus X." Under this approach, the maximum price would be raised each year by an amount equal to the inflation rate ("inflation") less a normative annual efficiency improvement ("X"). The attractiveness of this approach is that it mimics a competitive market. Firms become price-takers, and any cost reduction flows directly into profits. The perverse incentives of conventional regulation are removed. Well-designed price-cap regulation encourages utilities to reduce costs, allows the introduction of competition, and reduces uneconomical cross subsidization.

This novel technique has been employed in several industries over the last decade. One of the early examples occurred with the deregulation of the electricity industry in Britain (discussed below). While price caps provide superior incentives for efficiency, they are not without flaws. The major disadvantage of this approach is uncertainty about the appropriate X rate. X should represent the target rate of cost reduction relative to the economy as a whole. When British electricity regulators set X, they were extremely conservative and chose $X = 0$, implicitly assuming that there would be no differential productivity improvement in the electricity industry. If X is set incorrectly for too long, the system will either degenerate into a state of chronic losses or earn large windfall monopoly profits. In setting $X = 0$, the British appear to have been more averse to losses than to excess profits. Economists and regulators are monitoring the experience with performance-based regulation closely to see whether it lives up to its promise.

THE COSTS OF REGULATION

Economists have studied the impact of regulation to weigh its costs and benefits. The results of a recent survey are shown in Table 17-1 on page 310. The effects of regulation include both efficiency gains or losses (such as those that come when inefficiently high levels of pollution are curbed) and income redistribution (as occurs when high trucking prices redistribute income from consumers to truckers). Most studies suggest that the main effects of economic regulation are losses in efficiency and large amounts of income redistribution. The record of social regulation is mixed, with some cases showing significant benefits and others having large costs with few benefits. The costs of both social and economic regulation (including the restrictions on international trade) are estimated to have been around 3.3 percent of net domestic product as of 1988.

Decline of Economic Regulation

For the last two decades, many economists have argued that most economic regulation was actually creating monopoly power rather than curbing it. This idea is partially based on the interest-group view of regulation analyzed above. In addition, observers

noted that economic regulation had spread far beyond the local natural monopolies. By the mid-1970s, regulators were issuing their orders to railroads and trucks, airlines and buses, radio and TV broadcasting, oil and natural gas, pecans and milk, and virtually all financial markets. Many of these regulated industries were closer to the pole of perfect competition than to natural monopoly, as Figure 17-3 on page 311 suggests.

Pioneering Deregulation in the Airline Industry

Since 1975, the federal government has partially or totally deregulated many industries, including petroleum, airlines, trucking, railroad, stockbroking, long-distance telephone service, banking, communications, and natural gas. Each of these industries has structural characteristics that are favorable to competition because their markets are large relative to the efficient size of individual firms.

The airline industry provides a dramatic example of the dilemmas of deregulation. Since its creation in the 1930s, the Civil Aeronautics Board (CAB) viewed its role as deterring competition. No major new air carriers were allowed to enter the interstate market from 1938 to 1978. When innovative low-cost and no-frills airfares were proposed, the CAB slapped these proposals down. The CAB was (as the interest-group view of regulation predicted) devoted to keeping airfares up, not down.

In 1977, President Carter appointed Alfred Kahn chairman of the CAB. A distinguished economist and critic of regulation, Kahn set out to allow more competition through entry and fare flexibility. Shortly thereafter, Congress passed legislation allowing free entry and exit on all domestic air routes. Airlines were free to set whatever fares the traffic would bear.

Many people worried that there would be massive layoffs and loss of service without regulation. However, after almost two decades of experience with deregulation, the airline industry employs 65 percent more people and logs 70 percent more domestic passenger-miles. Studies indicate that (after correcting for inflation) average fares fell sharply over the years after deregulation; that utilization of aircraft has increased; and that airlines have become extraordinarily innovative in their pricing strategies. The competition has been so intense

The Impact of Regulation, U.S., 1988*				
	Efficiency gains or losses			Income redistribution ($, billion)
	Benefits ($, billion)	Costs ($, billion)	Net benefits ($, billion)	
Economic regulation:				
Telecommunications	0.0	14.1	−14.1	42.3
Agriculture	0.0	6.7	−6.7	18.4
Airline	0.0	3.8	−3.8	7.7
Rail	0.0	2.3	−2.3	6.8
Milk	0.0	0.7	−0.7	2.2
Natural gas	0.0	0.3	−0.3	5.0
Credit	0.0	0.3	−0.3	0.8
Barge	0.0	0.3	−0.3	0.8
Davis-Bacon Act	0.0	0.2	−0.2	0.5
Ocean	0.0	0.1	−0.1	0.2
Postal rates	0.0	na	0.0	8.0
Social regulation:				
Environment	58.4	66.5	−8.1	na
Nuclear power	na	6.5	na	na
Occupational safety	0.0	8.8	−8.8	na
Highway safety	35.6	7.7	27.9	na
Pharmaceuticals	na	2.3	na	na
Equal opportunity	na	0.9	na	na
Consumer products	na	0.03	na	na
Other:				
International trade	0.0	17.3	−17.3	98.1
Total, all regulations and trade:†				
Billions of dollars	**94**	**139**	**−35**	**191**
As percent of gross domestic product	**2.1**	**3.2**	**−0.8**	**4.4**

*All estimates are in 1988 dollars; na = not available.

† Note that the na's are set at zero. This is likely to understate benefits slightly and to underestimate the total amount of redistribution.

TABLE 17-1. Regulation Affects Efficiency and Redistributes Income

Studies of the impact of economic and social regulation show that economic regulations have few benefits, cause substantial efficiency losses, and redistribute much income. Social regulations have benefits, although they are often extremely difficult to measure. (Source: Robert W. Hahn and John A. Hird, "The Costs and Benefits of Regulation: Review and Synthesis," *Yale Journal on Regulation*, vol. 8, 1991, pp. 233–287. Where a range of estimates is given, the midpoint is taken.)

that the airline industry has shown very low profitability over the last decade, and bankruptcies are quite common. New airlines like Southwest Airlines have started up to replace bankrupt old ones. By most measures, the industry has operated more efficiently since deregulation.

The success of airline deregulation encouraged economists and noneconomists around the world to trust an unregulated market to make allocational decisions even in industries where firms have the potential for significant market power.

Deregulating the Electricity Industry

The most recent battleground for deregulation has been the electricity industry. Electricity has traditionally been one of the most heavily regulated industries. Many countries have regulated electricity through government ownership of major facilities,

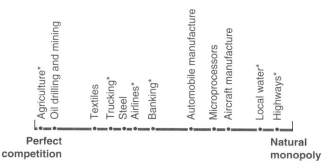

FIGURE 17-3. Degree of Natural Monopoly in Different Industries

This figure displays several regulated and unregulated industries by their degree of natural monopoly or of perfect competition. In perfectly competitive industries, the efficient level of output is tiny relative to the market, while the average cost for a natural monopoly continues to decline even when the firm produces total industry output. Agriculture and mining are inherently quite competitive, while highways and local network utilities such as for water are close to polar natural monopolies. The asterisk (*) indicates industries that have historically been heavily regulated or even operated by governments.

while others have used traditional rate-of-return public-utility regulation to control the prices and markets of electric utilities. The electricity industry in the United States is populated predominantly by vertically integrated local monopolies supplying relatively large areas.

Electricity has been heavily regulated because it was typically cast as a natural monopoly. It is useful to divide the electricity industry into three parts: generation, transmission, and distribution. Until recently, it was commonly assumed that because of the high transmission costs and significant economies of scale in generation, the entire industry should be treated as a local natural monopoly. In the last decade, this view has been challenged, and only the transmission and small-customer distribution networks are now commonly viewed as having major elements of natural monopoly. The shift in viewpoint has come partly because of the successful breakup of vertically and horizontally integrated telecommunications networks and partly because of the exhaustion of the economies of scale in generation. Most independent specialists today hold that, while the generation segment is technically complex, the optimal scale of plant is sufficiently small so that reasonably competitive markets can emerge among alternative generators.

These theoretical presumptions have been strengthened by experience around the world in the actual deregulation of electricity markets—particu-

larly the British case. Before deregulation, the British system consisted of two vertically integrated state-owned segments—one for generation and one for transmission. The British government decided to break up and privatize the industry. The generation segment was divided into two private companies. The transmission segment was to remain a regulated monopoly, National Grid.

One of the most radical features of the British reforms was the establishment of a "spot market" to coordinate generation. Many systems coordinate electricity generation by a centralized "pool" system whereby a central dispatcher brings power stations on line in increasing order of their marginal production costs. Under the British spot market, each generator must declare its offers of quantities and prices of supply for each half-hour of the following day. The National Grid Company ranks these offers on the basis of costs, and, together with estimates of demand, sets up a plan for least-cost operations for the coming day. This also generates a series of spot (or short-term) prices, which have proved highly variable (as is appropriate for an industry in which the marginal cost varies so greatly depending upon the load).

No conclusive evaluation of the British reforms is possible at this time, but a few tentative conclusions can be reached on the basis of evidence to date. First, the system as a whole appears to have been a major success and to be functioning relatively smoothly. Second, by opening up the generation market and separating generation from transmission, the British reforms have induced significant new entry. Third, the use of inflation-minus-X or price-cap regulation has been a technical success, although there have been no noticeable price benefits of deregulation to consumers.

The United States is currently considering similar deregulation proposals, emphasizing the deregulation of electricity generation. There continue to be major vested interests opposing full deregulation, however. An important issue concerns the fate of $100 billion worth of "stranded assets." These are electricity-generation plants, built under the inefficient cost-plus pricing system, whose production costs are so high that they would lose money under deregulation. The fairness issues rasied by these stranded assets have been a major roadblock to electricity deregulation in the United States.

A Cautionary Word

As regulation loosens its grip on industries like the airlines, electricity, and banking, it is important to remember the broader role of government in economic life. Just because price regulation has often been poorly designed does not imply that all government programs are wasteful. In the banking industry, economists worry that inadequate regulation will lead to bank failures and potential macroeconomic disturbances. In the airlines, people became concerned that intense competition was leading airlines to cut corners on maintenance. A similar concern was raised as increased competition in the electricity industry induced some nuclear power plants to curtail their safety investments. These incidents were a sober reminder that regulation is not an either/or situation—that government oversight includes much more than telling firms what to produce and at what price.

B. ANTITRUST POLICY

Now we will examine in detail one of the oldest and most important forms of government oversight of business, antitrust policy. This branch of microeconomic policy is designed to promote vigorous competition and rivalry in markets and to prevent monopolistic abuses.

Review of Imperfect Competition

Chapters 9 and 10 discussed the way that imperfect competitors set their prices and quantities. Let's begin by reviewing the major elements of the economic theory that relate to government antimonopoly policies:

- Imperfect competitors are inefficient because they set prices above marginal cost. The consumers in the monopolistic or oligopolistic industry are consuming less of its goods than would be the case if the goods were efficiently supplied.
- Many industries have technologies that exhibit significant economies of scale. It would be unrealistic to try to produce the output of such industries with perfectly competitive firms, for that would require that firms be inefficiently small. In

rare cases, the technology in an industry can be efficiently produced only by a single firm; we call this a "natural monopoly."

- In the long run, most economic progress comes from technological change. According to the Schumpeterian hypothesis, large firms with considerable market power are responsible for much invention and technological change. Government policies should be especially careful not to harm the incentives for innovation.
- The major abuses in markets—either too high a price or poor product quality—come when an industry is effectively monopolized. A good rule of thumb is that an industry behaves like a monopolist when a single firm or colluding group of firms produces more than three-quarters of the output in an industry.
- The government has taken on the responsibility of preventing monopolization from occurring and of regulating monopolies when they are inevitable. Antitrust policies attempt to prevent monopolization or anticompetitive abuses; economic regulation is used to control the exercise of monopoly power in natural monopolies.

With the decline of economic regulation as a major tool for preventing monopolistic abuses, governments increasingly focus on promoting competition and on applying antitrust policy as the major weapons for encouraging economic efficiency in markets. In this section we discuss antitrust policies, which attack anticompetitive abuses in two different ways. First, they prohibit certain kinds of *business conduct*, such as price fixing, that restrain competitive forces. Second, they restrict some market structures, such as monopolies, that are thought most likely to restrict commerce and abuse their economic power in other ways.

The framework for antitrust policy was set by a few key legislative statutes and by a century of court decisions. In recent years, under the prodding of economists, antitrust policy has been evolving away from the "big is bad" philosophy and toward the *economic approach to antitrust*. Emphasizing the intrinsic rivalry of oligopolists, the economic approach holds that the most powerful incentives for large business to reduce prices and improve product quality occur in a deregulated world in which barriers to entry are low and markets are open to domestic and foreign competition. In this view, antitrust policy should be reserved for the worst abuses of market power.

THE FRAMEWORK STATUTES

Antitrust law is like a huge forest that has grown from a handful of seeds. The statutes on which the law is based are so concise and straightforward that they can be quoted in Table 17-2; it is astounding how much law has grown from so few words.

Sherman Act (1890)

Monopolies had long been illegal under the common law, based on custom and past judicial deci-

TABLE 17-2. American Antitrust Law Is Based on a Handful of Statutes

The Sherman, Clayton, and Federal Trade Commission acts laid the foundation for American antitrust law. Interpretation of these acts has fleshed out modern antitrust doctrines.

The Antitrust Laws
Sherman Antitrust Act (1890, as amended)
§1. Every contract, combination in the form of trust or otherwise, or conspiracy, in restraint of trade or commerce among the several States, or with foreign nations, is declared to be illegal.
§2. Every person who shall monopolize, or attempt to monopolize, or combine or conspire with any other person or persons, to monopolize any part of the trade or commerce among the several States, or with foreign nations, shall be deemed guilty of a felony. . . .
Clayton Antitrust Act (1914, as amended)
§2. It shall be unlawful . . . to discriminate in price between different purchasers of commodities of like grade and quality . . . where the effect of such discrimination may be substantially to lessen competition or tend to create a monopoly in any line of commerce. . . . *Provided,* That nothing herein contained shall prevent differentials which make only due allowance for differences in the cost. . . .
§3. That it shall be unlawful for any person . . . to lease or make a sale or contract . . . on the condition, agreement, or understanding that the lessee or purchaser thereof shall not use or deal in the . . . commodities of a competitor . . . where the effect . . . may be to substantially lessen competition or tend to create a monopoly in any line of commerce.
§7. No [corporation] . . . shall acquire . . . the whole or any part . . . of another [corporation] . . . where . . . the effect of such an acquisition may be substantially to lessen competition, or to tend to create a monopoly.
Federal Trade Commission Act (1914, as amended)
§5. Unfair methods of competition . . . and unfair or deceptive acts or practices . . . are declared unlawful.

sions. But the body of laws proved ineffective against the mergers and trusts[2] that began to grow in the 1880s. Populist sentiments then led to passage of the Sherman Act in 1890.

The Sherman Act made it illegal to "monopolize trade" and outlawed any "combination or conspiracy in restraint of trade." But beyond an antipathy toward "monopolizing" there is no evidence that anyone had clear notions about which actions were to be regarded as legal or illegal.

Clayton Act (1914)

The Clayton Act was passed to clarify and strengthen the Sherman Act. It outlawed *tying contracts* (in which a customer is forced to buy product B if she wants product A); it ruled *price discrimination* and exclusive dealings illegal; it banned *interlocking directorates* (in which some people would be directors of more than one firm in the same industry) and *mergers* formed by acquiring common stock of competitors. These practices were not illegal per se (meaning "in themselves") but only when they might substantially lessen competition. The Clayton Act emphasized prevention as well as punishment.

Another important element of the Clayton Act was that it specifically provided antitrust immunity to labor unions.

Federal Trade Commission

In 1914 the Federal Trade Commission (FTC) was established to prohibit "unfair methods of competition" and to warn against anticompetitive mergers. In 1938, the FTC was also empowered to ban false and deceptive advertising. To enforce its powers, the FTC can investigate, hold hearings, and issue cease-and-desist orders.

BASIC ISSUES IN ANTITRUST: CONDUCT AND STRUCTURE

While the basic antitrust statutes are straightforward, it is not easy in practice to decide how to apply them to specific situations of market structure or conduct. Actual law has evolved through an interaction of economic theory and actual case law.

---

[2] A *trust* is a group of firms, usually in the same industry, that combine together by a legal agreement to regulate production, prices, or other industrial conditions.

Illegal Conduct

Some of the earliest antitrust decisions concerned illegal behavior. The courts have ruled that certain kinds of collusive behavior are illegal per se; there is simply no defense that will justify these actions. The offenders cannot defend themselves by pointing to some worthy objective (such as product quality) or mitigating circumstance (such as low profits).

The most important class of per se illegal conduct is agreements among competing firms to fix prices, restrict output, or divide markets. Such actions have the effect of raising prices and lowering output. Even the severest critics of antitrust policy can find no redeeming virtue in price fixing.

Other forms of conduct are also limited by antitrust laws. These include:

- *Predatory pricing,* in which a firm sells its goods for less than production costs (usually interpreted as marginal cost or average variable cost). The argument against predatory pricing is that a big company can use its financial resources to cut prices and drive smaller rivals out of business, and then it can jack up prices. In recent years, some giant discount chains have been accused of predatory pricing by smaller local competitors.
- *Tying contracts* or arrangements, whereby a firm will sell product A only if the purchaser buys product B.
- *Price discrimination,* in which a firm sells the same product to different customers at different prices for reasons not related to cost or meeting competition.

Note that the practices on this list relate to a firm's *conduct.* It is the acts themselves that are illegal, not the structure of the industry in which the acts take place. Perhaps the most celebrated example is the great electric-equipment conspiracy. In 1961, the electric-equipment industry was found guilty of collusive price agreements. Executives of the largest companies—such as GE and Westinghouse—conspired to raise prices and covered their tracks like characters in a spy novel by meeting in hunting lodges, using code names, and making telephone calls from phone booths. Although the top executives in these companies were apparently unaware of what the vice presidents just below them were doing, they had put much pressure on their vice presidents for increased sales. The companies agreed to pay extensive damages to their customers for overcharges, and some executives were jailed for their antitrust violations.

Recent Price-Fixing Cases. Recent cases involve some interesting features of law and economics. One case involved Archer Daniels Midland (ADM), a large food-processing company. The company engaged in price fixing of lysine, an additive that makes pigs grow properly. In 1996, the company was fined $100 million—the largest antitrust fine in history—indicating that price fixing not only is illegal but also is not a profitable business practice. In addition, the government relied on game theory by using a "prisoner's dilemma" strategy on ADM executives. Each was told that if he confessed to price fixing, he would have a reduced sentence, while if he did not, he would be treated harshly. One unanticipated side effect of this strategy was that one executive actually manufactured evidence against his own employer!

An interesting academic case involved an investigation by the Justice Department of the way that colleges and universities set tuition and scholarship aid. The government claimed that a small group of educational institutions conspired to reduce scholarship competition for top students by agreeing to award scholarships only on the basis of financial need and by comparing prospective aid awards to commonly admitted applicants. One of the defendants, the Massachusetts Institute of Technology (MIT), fought the government in the courts, arguing that nonprofit institutions should meet a different standard than profit-maximizing businesses. MIT prevailed on appeal in court, but this case raised novel issues about the manner in which antitrust law and regulations will be applied to activities of educational and other nonprofit institutions.

Structure: Is Bigness Badness?

While price fixing and other illegal activities are important, the most visible antitrust cases concern the structure of industries rather than the conduct of companies. They consist of attempts to *break up* large firms as well as preventive *antimerger* proceedings against proposed mergers of large firms.

The first surge of antitrust activity under the Sherman Act focused on dismantling existing

monopolies. In 1911, the Supreme Court ordered that the American Tobacco Company and Standard Oil be broken up into many separate companies. In condemning these flagrant monopolies, the Supreme Court enunciated the important "rule of reason": Only *unreasonable* restraints of trade (mergers, agreements, and the like) came within the scope of the Sherman Act and were considered illegal.

The rule-of-reason doctrine virtually nullified the antitrust laws' attack on monopolistic mergers, as shown by the U.S. Steel case (1920). J. P. Morgan had put this giant together by merger, and at its peak it controlled 60 percent of the market. But the Supreme Court held that size alone was no offense. In that period, as today, courts focused more on anticompetitive *conduct* than on pure monopoly *structure*.

The high-water mark of antitrust activity against bigness was the Alcoa case in 1945. Alcoa had gained a 90 percent market share in aluminum, by means that were not in themselves illegal. It had installed capacity in anticipation of the growth of demand and kept prices low to prevent potential competition. It had attempted to maintain its large market share by keeping entry unprofitable rather than by engaging in anticompetitive acts. The Court nonetheless found that Alcoa had violated the Sherman Act, holding that monopoly power, even if lawfully acquired, could constitute an economic evil and should be condemned. During this period, the courts came to emphasize market structure along with market conduct: *Monopoly power, even without otherwise illegal conduct, was declared illegal.*

Recent Developments. The most important antitrust cases of recent years involved three giant firms in two vitally important industries—telecommunications and computers. A review of the three cases reveals the flavor of modern thinking about antitrust policy.

The AT&T case. Until 1983 AT&T had a virtual monopoly on the telecommunications market. It handled more than 95 percent of all long-distance calls, provided 85 percent of all local lines, and sold most of the nation's telephone equipment. The complex of companies owned by AT&T—often called the Bell System—included Bell Telephone Labs, Western Electric Company, and 23 Bell operating companies.

In 1974, the Department of Justice filed a far-reaching suit. It contended that AT&T had (1) prevented competing long-distance carriers (like MCI) from connecting to local exchanges and (2) obstructed other equipment manufacturers from selling telecommunications equipment to subscribers or to Bell operating companies. The government's central legal and economic argument was that Bell had used its regulated natural monopoly in the local telephone market to create monopoly power in the long-distance and telephone-equipment markets.

Bell took two lines of defense. First, it denied many factual charges or rebutted their relevance. Second, it claimed that the U.S. telephone system was the best in the world precisely *because* Bell owned and operated most of that system. In a line of argument similar to the Schumpeterian hypothesis (see Chapter 10), AT&T argued that the size and scope of the Bell System promoted rapid technological change and made its monopoly a reasonable and efficient way to conduct the telephone business.

The bizarre ending of the case astonished everyone. Fearful that the case might end unfavorably, Bell's management settled with the government in a consent decree that met every point of the government's proposed remedy. Bell's local telephone operating companies were divested (or legally separated) from AT&T and, in 1984, were regrouped into seven large regional telephone holding companies. AT&T retained its long-distance operations as well as Bell Labs (the research organization) and Western Electric (the equipment manufacturer). The net effect was an 80 percent reduction in the size and sales of the Bell System.

The dismantling of the Bell System set off a breathtaking revolution in the telecommunications industry. This revolution was completed when Congress passed the 1995 Communications Act, which essentially took the gloves off all the players—including AT&T. Today, telephone companies are free to buy equipment from anyone and are entering joint ventures in cellular telephone, cable television, data services, and Internet provision, as well as traditional telephone service.

More significant is the explosion of new technologies that are invading the traditional communications markets. Cellular phone systems are breaking the natural monopoly of Alexander Graham Bell's twisted copper wires; telephone companies are joining forces to bring television signals into homes; fiber-optic lines are beginning to function as data superhighways, carrying massive amounts of data around the country and the world. The Internet is linking people and places together in ways that were unimagined a decade ago. No one can say whether these technologies would have come as far and as fast had the Bell System not been broken up, but it is clear that monopoly is not necessary for rapid technological change.

The IBM case. A second set of antitrust cases in recent years involved computer companies. The first case was an attempt by the government to dismember IBM. Filed in 1969, the suit charged that IBM "has attempted to monopolize and has monopolized . . . general purpose digital computers." The government charged that IBM had a dominant market share, with 76 percent of the market in 1967. Moreover, the government claimed that IBM had used many devices to prevent others from competing; the alleged anticompetitive steps included tie-in pricing, excessively low prices to discourage entry, and introduction of new products that tended to reduce the attractiveness of the products of other companies.

IBM contested the government case with tenacity and vigor. IBM's major defense was that the government was penalizing success rather than anticompetitive behavior. The fundamental dilemma in such cases had been crisply stated in the Alcoa case: "The successful competitor having been urged to compete must not be turned on when he wins." IBM claimed that the government was punishing the firm that had accurately foreseen the enormous potential in the computer revolution and had dominated the industry through its "superior skill, foresight, and industry."

The case dragged along inconclusively until the Reagan administration's antitrust chief, William Baxter, decided in 1982 to dismiss the case as "without merit." The government's reasoning was that, unlike the telecommunications industry, the computer industry was unregulated and subject to the full force of market competition. Baxter held that this industry was intrinsically competitive and that government attempts to restructure the computer market were more likely to harm than promote economic efficiency.

The Microsoft case. The most recent major cases of market structure have involved government investigation of the giant software company Microsoft. In the early 1990s, the government investigated claims that Microsoft was monopolizing the market for operating systems. In that period, more than 80 percent of the world's computers were running on Microsoft operating systems like MS-DOS and Windows. The government made a number of complaints about Microsoft's behavior. Most involved the possibility that Microsoft would project its market power in operating systems into the market for applications. This could occur because Microsoft would bundle its applications or network services with its operating system. Another concern was that Microsoft was engaging in predatory pricing of its operating systems by charging computer companies for Windows even when they didn't install it. Microsoft defended itself vigorously. In 1994, the government and Microsoft agreed on a consent decree in which Microsoft agreed to change its pricing practices but would continue to be able to develop applications. But the government has continued to monitor Microsoft's activities closely, including criticizing Microsoft's attempt to purchase another large software firm. The latest concern has been that Microsoft might displace Netscape as the leading web browser. Too much commercial success is apparently a mixed blessing.

Lessons from the Structural Cases.

What lessons have economists drawn from the large structural cases we have reviewed? It is ironical that breaking up large companies appears to have benefited not only consumers but even the companies themselves. The remnants of the Bell System have in fact prospered, while the once-mighty IBM has fallen sharply in terms of both market share and market value. Since 1983, IBM share prices have fallen more than 20 percent, while the total value of all the parts of the former Bell System has risen over 200 percent. Some industrial-organization specialists hold that the forced dismantling of the Bell System may have been just what the doctor ordered, bringing more vitality and competition to that industry as the information revolution picked up speed.

By contrast, leaving IBM intact allowed the company to make a series of blunders that left it a weakened and discouraged organization. What brought IBM down? IBM was unable to capitalize on the revolution in personal computers and watched that technology gradually displace the mainframe computers that IBM dominated. According to one critic, it was "IBM's fear of risk, its civil-service mentality, its brainwashing of employees, its failure to make innovative products that anticipate customers' desires, its inability to adapt its work force quickly enough."[3] IBM survived the antitrust wars only to be humbled because it could not adapt to a changing marketplace. Many industrial-organization economists are wondering how the government's scrutiny of Microsoft will affect that company's innovative vigor.

Mergers: Law and Practice

Companies can gain market power through growth (plowing back earnings and building new plants). But a much easier way to gain market share, or simply to get bigger, is to merge with another company. The 1980s saw a tremendous growth in merger activity.

Horizontal mergers—in which companies in the same industry combine—are forbidden under the Clayton Act when the merger is likely to reduce competition in the industry substantially. Case law and the Department of Justice's 1982, 1984, and 1992 merger guidelines clarified the meaning of the vague statutory language. Under these guidelines, industries are divided into three groups: unconcentrated, moderately concentrated, and highly concentrated. Mergers in the latter two types of industries will be challenged even in cases where the firms involved have small market shares. For example, in a highly concentrated industry, if a firm with a market share of 10 percent acquires one with a share of 2.5 percent or more, the Department of Justice is likely to challenge the merger.

Vertical mergers occur when two firms at different stages of the production process come together. In recent years, the courts took a hard line toward vertical mergers. They worried about the potential restriction of competition through exclusive dealings if two independent firms merged. Courts tended to pay relatively little heed to the potential efficiencies of joint operations in vertical mergers.

---

[3] Paul Carroll, *Big Blues: The Unmaking of IBM* (Crown, New York, 1993).

As part of its campaign to reduce government intervention, the Reagan administration changed the guidelines on mergers. The new guidelines greatly relaxed enforcement with respect to both vertical and horizontal mergers. Many economists believe that these changes brought on the great wave of mergers and acquisitions of the 1980s.

A third kind of combination, called **conglomerate mergers**, joins together unrelated businesses. In a conglomerate merger, a chemical or steel company might buy an oil company. The critics of conglomerates make two points. First, they note that the absolute size of the largest corporations is awesome. The largest 200 corporations control almost $2.5 trillion of assets. The largest corporations therefore have great economic and political power. Increasingly, many observers worry more about the way that large organizations can buy favors in the political process than about how they abuse their market power.

The second point made by the critics of conglomerates is that many of these combinations serve no economic purpose. They are, it is argued, simply a brand of "boardroom poker" to entertain managers bored with supervising their tiresome steel or chemical operations. And, indeed, there is a point here: What does the airplane business have in common with meat-packing? Or typewriters with birth-control pills? Or computer leasing with passenger-bus operations?

Conglomerates are not without defenders. Some economists argue that these mergers bring good modern management to backward firms and that takeovers, like bankruptcy, represent the economy's way of eliminating deadwood in the economic struggle for survival. But there is no consensus on the merits or demerits of conglomerate mergers. No study has found major gains or costs, so perhaps the best policy is to keep a watchful eye.

ANTITRUST LAWS AND EFFICIENCY

Economic and legal views toward regulation and antitrust have changed dramatically over the last two decades. During the period, industries were deregulated, and antitrust law abandoned its mission "to put an end to great aggregations of capital because of the helplessness of the individual before them" (to quote from the 1945 Alcoa decision). Increasingly, both these instruments were directed toward the goal of improving economic efficiency. If big is efficient, big shall reign.

What has prompted the changing attitude toward antitrust policy? First, it grew out of technical developments in economic research. Economists found that performance was not always closely associated with structure. Some large firms (Intel, Microsoft, and Boeing, for example) and some highly concentrated markets (microprocessors, telecommunications, and aircraft manufacture) proved to be among the industries with the highest performance with respect to innovation and productivity growth. Whereas economic theory held that monopoly keeps prices high, historical experience indicated that highly concentrated industries often had rapidly declining prices relative to less concentrated industries. At the same time, some unconcentrated industries, such as agriculture and financial services, exhibited outstanding performance. No iron law has been found to link structure and performance.

How can we explain this paradox? Some economists invoke the Schumpeterian hypothesis. Firms in concentrated industries collect monopoly profits, to be sure. But the size of the market also means that large firms can appropriate much of the return on research and development (R&D) investments, and this explains the high levels of R&D and the rapid technological change in concentrated industries. If, as Schumpeter claimed, technological change originates in large firms, it would be foolish to slay these giant geese who lay such golden eggs. This view has been well expressed by Lester Thurow, former dean of the MIT Sloan School of Management: "The millions spent on the IBM [antitrust] case would have been better spent if they had been plowed back into research and development on keeping America No. 1 in computers."

A second thrust of the new approach to regulation and antitrust arose from revised views of the nature of competition. Considering both experimental evidence and observation, many economists have come to believe that intense rivalry will spring up even in oligopolistic markets as long as collusion is strictly prohibited. Indeed, in the words of Richard Posner, formerly a law professor and currently a federal judge:

> The only truly unilateral acts by which firms can get or keep monopoly power are practices like commit-

ting fraud on the Patent Office or blowing up a competitor's plant, and fraud and force are in general adequately punished under other statutes.[4]

In this view, the only valid purpose of the antitrust laws should be to replace existing statutes with a simple prohibition against *agreements*—explicit or tacit—that unreasonably restrict competition.

Third, the swing of the pendulum against strict antitrust enforcement came from the increasing emphasis on market forces and market-based incentives. This position was inspired by proponents of the Chicago School, which held that most monopoly power derives from government interventions. According to this view, the major pools of monopoly power lie in areas protected by government fiat. Important examples include economic regulations and rules (see Table 17-1) in such diverse areas as foreign trade, the exemption of labor unions from antitrust laws, monopoly protection conveyed by the patent laws, barriers to entry into the professions, and restrictions in medical care. Advocates of the

laissez-faire view argue that reducing government regulation would enhance competition.

A final reason for the reduced activism in antitrust has been the increase in import competition. As more foreign firms gain a foothold in the American economy, they tend to compete vigorously for market share and often upset established sales patterns and pricing practices. As the sales of Japanese automakers increased, the cozy coexistence of the Big Three American auto firms dissolved. Many economists believe that the threat of foreign competition is a much more powerful tool for enforcing market discipline than are antitrust laws.

What is the future of antitrust? No one can predict the direction of future attitudes toward big business. Nonetheless, the views supporting the efficiency-oriented approach are shared by economists and lawyers across the political spectrum, and the intensity of foreign competition is unlikely to change, so a return to the trust-busting fervor of earlier years appears unlikely in the near future.

SUMMARY

A. Business Regulation: Theory and Practice

1. Regulation consists of government rules commanding firms to alter their business conduct. Economic regulation involves the control of prices, production, entry and exit conditions, and standards of service in a particular industry; social regulation consists of rules aimed at correcting information failures and externalities, particularly those that impinge on health and safety and the environment.

2. The normative view of regulation is that government intervention is appropriate when there are major market failures. These include excess market power in an industry, inadequate supply of information to consumers and workers, and externalities such as pollution. Economists have developed a positive theory of regulation in which regulation often serves the purpose of actually benefiting regulated firms, whose

interests are furthered by exclusion of potential rivals.

3. The strongest case for economic regulation comes in regard to natural monopolies. Natural monopoly occurs when average costs are falling for every level of output, so the most efficient organization of the industry requires production by a single firm. Few industries come close to this condition today—perhaps only local utilities like water and electricity.

4. In conditions of natural monopoly, governments regulate the price and service of private companies. Traditionally, government regulation of monopoly has required that price be set at the average cost of production. The ideal regulation would require price to be set equal to marginal cost, but this approach is impractical because it requires that government subsidize the monopolist. A new approach is performance-based regulation, such as price caps, which provide superior incentives to regulated firms to reduce costs and improve productivity.

5. Given the strength of competitive forces, particularly from the global marketplace, the case for economic regulation holds for few industries today. The deregu-

[4] Richard A. Posner, *Antitrust Law: An Economic Prospectus* (University of Chicago Press, Chicago, 1976), p. 212. The writings of Posner—along with those of Robert Bork, William Baxter, and William Landes—have been highly influential in determining the new climate of antitrust thinking.

lation movement of the 1970s reduced the extent of economic regulation markedly, producing gains in industries such as the airlines.

B. Antitrust Policy

6. Antitrust policy, prohibiting anticompetitive conduct and preventing monopolistic structures, is the primary way that public policy limits abuses of market power by large firms. This policy grew out of legislation like the Sherman Act (1890) and the Clayton Act (1914). The primary purposes of antitrust are (*a*) to prohibit anti-competitive activities (which include agreements to fix prices or divide up territories, price discrimination, and tie-in agreements) and (*b*) to break up monopoly structures. In today's legal theory, such structures are those that have excessive market power (a large share of the market) and also engage in anticompetitive acts.

7. In addition to limiting the behavior of existing firms, antitrust law prevents mergers that would lessen competition. Today, horizontal mergers (between firms in the same industry) are the main source of concern, while vertical and conglomerate mergers tend to be tolerated.

8. Antitrust policy has been significantly influenced by economic thinking during the last two decades. As a result, antitrust policy now focuses almost exclusively on improving efficiency, while it ignores earlier populist concerns with bigness itself. Moreover, in today's economy—with intense competition from foreign producers and deregulated rivals—many believe that antitrust policy should concentrate primarily on preventing collusive agreements like price fixing.

CONCEPTS FOR REVIEW

Regulation

two kinds of regulation:
   economic vs. social regulation
old-style (command-and-control) vs.
   new (economic-incentive)
   regulation
natural monopoly

reasons for regulation:
   market power
   externalities
   information failures

Antitrust Policy

Sherman, Clayton, and FTC acts

per se prohibitions vs. the "rule of
   reason"
mergers:
   vertical
   horizontal
   conglomerate
efficiency-oriented antitrust policy

QUESTIONS FOR DISCUSSION

1. What are the major weapons that government has to restrain monopoly power? Describe the strengths and weaknesses of each policy.
2. Review the three pricing outcomes in Figure 17-2. Can you think of the difficulties of implementing the ideal regulated price? (*Hint:* Where does the country get the revenues? Is *MC* easy to measure?) Similarly, can you think of reasons why many economists would prefer the unregulated to the regulated outcome? (*Hint:* What if P_M is not much above P_R? What if you worried about the interest-group theory of regulation?)
3. Explain why price-cap or inflation-minus-*X* price regulation has better incentives than average cost price regulation. Explain why the latter is better able to prevent monopoly profits.
4. "Microsoft, the large software company, is not bad just because it is big." Discuss, particularly with reference to the application of antitrust laws to large companies.
5. Examine the cost and demand curves in Figure 17-1. Using those curves, draw in the monopoly price and output. Compare these with the ideal regulated output and price. Describe the difference.
6. Two important approaches to antitrust are *structure* and *conduct*. The former looks only at the structure of the industry (such as the concentration of firms); the latter, at firm conduct (e.g., price fixing).
   a. Review the various statutes and cases to see which are related to conduct and which to structure. What about the merger guidelines of the 1980s?
   b. What are the advantages and disadvantages of each approach?
7. Make a list of the industries that you feel are candidates for the title "natural monopoly." Then review the different strategies for intervention to prevent exercise of monopoly power. What would you do about each industry on your list?

8. Show that a profit-maximizing, unregulated monopolist will never operate in the price-inelastic region of its demand curve. Show how regulation can force the monopolist onto the inelastic portion of its demand curve. What will be the impact of an increase in the regulated price of a monopolist upon revenues and profits when it is operating on (*a*) the elastic portion of the demand curve, (*b*) the inelastic portion of the demand curve, and (*c*) the unit-elastic portion of the demand curve?

CHAPTER 18
PROTECTING THE ENVIRONMENT

Growth for the sake of growth is the ideology of the cancer cell.

Edward Abbey

Clean air, clean water, unspoiled land—all of us would agree that these are desirable goals. But how much are we willing to pay to achieve them? And what is the threat to humanity if we do not respect the limits of our natural environment?

At one pole is an environmentalist philosophy of confines and perils. In this view, human activities threaten to disrupt the intricate web of natural ecosystems, unintended consequences threaten to overwhelm human ingenuity, and we must be ever vigilant lest the dikes break and we are inundated by the angry seas. The environmentalist point of view is well expressed in the bleak warning from the distinguished Harvard biologist E. O. Wilson:

> Environmentalism . . . sees humanity as a biological species tightly dependent on the natural world. . . . Many of Earth's vital resources are about to be exhausted, its atmospheric chemistry is deteriorating, and human populations have already grown dangerously large. Natural ecosystems, the wellsprings of a healthful environment, are being irreversibly degraded. . . . I am radical enough to take seriously the question heard with increasing frequency: Is humanity suicidal?[1]

Believers in this dismal picture argue that humans must practice "sustainable" economic growth and

learn to live with the limitations of our scarce natural resources or we will suffer dire and irreparable consequences.

At the other pole are "cornucopians," who believe that we are far from exhausting either natural resources or the capabilities of technology. In this optimistic view, we can look forward to limitless economic growth and rising living standards, with human ingenuity well able to cope with any environmental problems. If oil runs out, there is plenty of coal and uranium. If those don't pan out, then new technologies will be induced by rising prices. In this view, technology, economic growth, and market forces are the saviors, not the villains.

In fact, humans have been encroaching on the environment for ages. Historically, the major interventions occurred when humans moved into settlements, converted forests into farms, and began to breed domestic plants and animals. But this qualitative transformation pales beside today's massive bioengineering, deforestation, and extraction of mineral and plant resources from the earth.

All these points raise the fundamental concerns voiced by Wilson and others. Generally, economists tend to lie between the environmentalist and the cornucopian extremes, pointing to the importance of a wise combination of market forces and government intervention as key to both environmental survival and continued improvements in living standards.

---

[1] Edward O. Wilson, "Is Humanity Suicidal?" *New York Times Magazine*, May 30, 1993, p. 27.

322

A. POPULATION AND RESOURCE LIMITATIONS

MALTHUS AND THE DISMAL SCIENCE

Fear of the voracious appetite of a fast-growing human population lies at the heart of many worries about the environment, as the quotation from Wilson at the start of this chapter suggests. Consider the following editorial from the world's leading scientific journal:

> First of all, it is important to identify the main villain as overpopulation. In the good old days, . . . in truth there were famine, starvation, horses and buggies that contributed to pollution, fireplaces that spewed forth soot from burning soft coal, and water contaminated with microorganisms. The humans were so few, and the land so vast, that these insults to nature could be absorbed without serious consequences. This is no longer true.[2]

Half of this proposition concerns the sources of pollution and other environmental problems, a topic which is taken up in Section C. The other half concerns the behavior of human populations, which we take up here.

Economic analysis of population dates back to the Reverend T. R. Malthus. He first developed his views while arguing at breakfast against his father's perfectionist opinion that the human race was always improving. Finally the son became so agitated that he wrote *An Essay on the Principle of Population* (1798). This was an instantaneous best-seller and since then has influenced the thinking of people all over the world about population and economic growth.

Malthus began with the observation of Benjamin Franklin that in the American colonies, where resources were abundant, population tended to double every 25 years or so. He then postulated a universal tendency for population—unless checked by limited food supply—to grow exponentially, or by a geometric progression. Eventually, a population which doubles every generation—1, 2, 4, 8, 16, 32, 64, 128, 256, 512, 1024, . . . —becomes so large that there is not enough space in the world for all the people to stand.

Economics at work: Compound interest and exponential growth. Exponential growth and compound interest are important tools in economics. Exponential (or geometric) growth occurs when a variable increases at a constant proportional rate from period to period. Thus, if a population of 200 is growing at 3 percent per year, it would equal 200 in year 0, 200×1.03 in year 1, $200 \times 1.03 \times 1.03$ in year 2, $200 \times (1.03)^3$ in year 3, . . . , $200 \times (1.03)^{10}$ in year 10, and so on.

When money is invested continuously, it earns compound interest, meaning that interest is earned on past interest. Money earning compound interest grows geometrically. An intriguing calculation is to determine how much the $24 received by the Indians for Manhattan Island would, if deposited at compound interest, be worth today. Say that this fund was placed in an endowment that earned 6 percent each year from 1626. It would be worth $60 billion in 1997.

A useful rule about compound interest is the **rule of 70**, which states that a magnitude growing at a rate of r per year will double in $(70/r)$ years. For example, a human population growing at 2 percent a year will double in 35 years, whereas if you invest your funds at 7 percent per year, the funds will double in value every 10 years.

After invoking compound interest, Malthus had one further card to play. At this point he unleashed the devil of diminishing returns. He argued that because land is fixed while labor inputs keep growing, food would tend to grow by an arithmetic progression and not by a geometric progression. (Compare 1, 2, 3, 4, . . . , with 1, 2, 4, 8, ...) Malthus concluded gloomily:

> As population doubles and redoubles, it is as if the globe were halving and halving again in size—until finally it has shrunk so much that the supply of food falls below the level necessary for life.

When the law of diminishing returns is applied to a fixed supply of land, food production tends not to keep up with a population's geometric-progression rate of growth.

---

[2] *Science*, Sept. 10, 1993, p.1371.

Now, Malthus did not say that population necessarily would increase at a geometric rate. This was only its tendency if unchecked. He described the checks that operate, in all times and places, to hold population down. In his first edition, he stressed the "positive" checks that increase the death rate: pestilence, famine, and war. Later, he backed down from this gloomy doctrine, holding out hope that population growth could be slowed by "moral restraint" such as abstinence and postponed marriages.

This important application of diminishing returns illustrates the profound effects a simple theory can have. Malthus' ideas had wide repercussions. His book was used to support a stern revision of the English poor laws. Under the influence of Malthus' writings, people argued that poverty should be made as uncomfortable as possible. His opinions also bolstered the argument that trade unions could not improve the welfare of workers—since any increase in their wages would allegedly only cause workers to reproduce until all were reduced to a bare subsistence.

Even today, the ghost of Malthus reappears in "doomsday" economics, such as a famous computer study called *The Limits to Growth* and its 1992 sequel *Beyond the Limits*.[3] The predictions of this modern-day Malthusianism were even more dismal than the original gospel:

> If present growth trends in world population, industrialization, pollution, food problems, and resource depletion continue unchanged, the limits to growth on this planet will be reached within the next one hundred years. The most probable results will be a rather sudden and uncontrollable decline in both population and industrial capacity.[4]

Flawed Prophecies of Malthus. Despite Malthus' careful statistical studies, demographers today think that his views were oversimplified. In his discussion of diminishing returns, Malthus never fully anticipated the technological miracle of the Industrial Revolution. Nor did he foresee that after 1870 population growth in most Western nations would begin to decline just as living standards and real wages grew most rapidly.

In the century following Malthus, technological advance shifted out the production-possibility frontiers of countries in Europe and North America. Indeed, technological change occurred so quickly that output far outpaced population, resulting in a rapid rise in real wages. Nevertheless, the germs of truth in Malthus' doctrines are still important for understanding the population behavior of India, Ethiopia, Nigeria, and other parts of the globe where the race between population and food supply continues today.

POPULATION, POLLUTION, AND LIVING STANDARDS

There is no doubt that growing human populations are not healthy for the trees, wolves, and marsh weeds that are pushed aside to make way for cities and other forms of human settlement. But is it also true, as modern-day Malthusians suggest, that those areas that are most heavily populated are also the most miserable? Are economic growth and industrialization the road to environmental ruin?

No such simple conclusion can be read from the historical record. Figure 18-1 shows population density and per capita income along with the line that best fits the data for 72 major countries. In fact, those areas with higher population density tend to have higher, not lower, living standards.

What about population and human health? On the whole, studies by the World Bank clearly indicate that human health is highly correlated with per capita income and, moreover, that the most important indicators of environmental degradation, such as poor sanitation and unsafe drinking water, are found in the poorest countries. One of the most thoughtful students of the relationship between population, economic development, and pollution is Oxford's Wilfred Beckerman, who summarized his findings as follows:

> The important environmental problems for the 75% of the world's population that live in developing countries are local problems of access to safe drinking water or decent sanitation, and urban degradation. Furthermore, there is clear evidence that . . . in the end the best—and probably the only—way to attain a decent environment in most countries is to become rich.[5]

---

[3] Donella H. Meadows, Dennis L. Meadows, and Jørgen Randers, *The Limits to Growth* (Potomac, Wash., 1972) and *Beyond the Limits* (Chelsea Green Publishing, Post Mills, Vt., 1992).

[4] *The Limits to Growth*, p. 23.

---

[5] Wilfred Beckerman, "Economic Growth and the Environment," *World Development*, vol. 20, no. 4, 1992, p. 482.

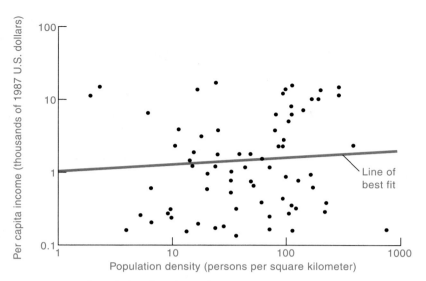

FIGURE 18-1. Population Density and Incomes

Is it true that living standards decline as population increases? Since the golden age of Athens, per capita incomes have generally been weakly but positively associated with population density. This scatter diagram shows the relation in 72 major countries for 1987. (Source: World Bank.)

What about the environment and alternative economic systems? You might think that a centrally planned economy would avoid the problems of a market economy by incorporating the externalities of population and environment into decisions. Experience reveals, ironically, that the socialist economies of Eastern Europe and the Soviet Union left a legacy of filth and far worse environmental problems than exist in the market economies. Under communism, for example, much of East Germany's power was provided by highly polluting brown coal, which poisoned the air with soot and sulfur dioxide. For East Germans, the switch to a market economy promises not only a boost in living standards but also an improved environment.

B. NATURAL-RESOURCE ECONOMICS

RESOURCE CATEGORIES

What are the important natural resources? They include land, water, and the atmosphere. This trio produces a variety of useful goods and services. The land gives us food and wine from fertile soils, as well as oil and other minerals from the earth's mantle. Our waters give us fish, recreation, and a remarkably efficient medium for transportation. The precious atmosphere yields breathable air, beautiful sunsets, and space for airplanes to fly in. Natural resources and the environment are in one sense just another set of factors of production, like labor and capital. They serve humans because we derive output or satisfaction from the services of natural resources.

Appropriable vs. Inappropriable Resources

In analyzing natural resources, economists make two key distinctions. The most important is whether the resources are appropriable or inappropriable. Recall that a commodity is called **appropriable** when firms or consumers can capture its full economic value. Appropriable natural resources include land (whose fertility can be captured by the farmer who sells wheat or wine produced on the land), mineral resources like oil and gas (where the owner can sell the value of the mineral deposit on markets), and trees (where the owner can sell the land or the trees to the highest bidder). In a well-functioning competitive market, we would expect that appropriable natural resources would be efficiently priced and allocated.

But we must be careful not to push these results too far. A second class of natural resources, known as **inappropriable** resources, can definitely cause economic problems. An inappropriable resource is one whose use is free to the individual but costly to society. In other words, inappropriable resources are ones involving externalities. Recall that *externalities* are those situations in which production or consumption imposes uncompensated costs or benefits on other parties.

Goods with externalities can be compared with normal economic goods. Market transactions involve voluntary exchange in which people exchange goods for money. When a firm uses a scarce appropriable resource like land, oil, or trees, it buys the good from its owner, who is fully compensated for the incremental costs of production of the good. But many interactions take place outside markets. Firm A dumps a toxic chemical into a stream and fouls the water for people who fish or swim downstream. Firm A has used the scarce, clean water without paying people whose water is fouled and has generated an external diseconomy.

Examples of inappropriable resources are found in every corner of the globe. Take the example of fish. A school of tuna not only provides food for the dinner table but also stock for breeding future generations of tuna. Yet this breeding potential is not captured or appropriated by markets; no one buys or sells the mating behavior of dog-toothed tuna. Consequently, when a fishing boat pulls out a tuna, it does not compensate society for the depletion of future breeding potential. Therefore, when unregulated, fisheries tend to be overfished.

This leads to the fundamental result of the economics of resources and the environment:

When resources are inappropriable, showing externalities, markets provide incorrect signals. Generally, markets produce too much of goods that generate external diseconomies and too little of goods that produce external economies.

Renewable vs. Nonrenewable Resources

Techniques for managing resources depend on whether the resources are renewable or nonrenewable. A **nonrenewable resource** is one whose services are essentially fixed in supply and which is not regenerated quickly enough to be economically relevant. Important examples are the fossil fuels, which were laid down millions of years ago and can be treated as fixed for human civilizations, and nonfuel mineral resources, such as copper, silver, gold, stone, and sand.

A second category is **renewable resources**, whose services are replenished regularly and which, if properly managed, can yield useful services indefinitely. Solar energy, agricultural land, river water, forests,

TABLE 18-1. Resource Classification

Resources are classified as inappropriable or appropriable according to whether there are significant externalities involved in their production or consumption. In addition, for nonrenewable resources, like oil and natural gas, the economic question is how to allocate the finite resource over space and time. For renewable resources, like timber or fisheries, the key issue is prudent management so that the yield maximizes the value of the resource.

	Renewable	Nonrenewable
Appropriable	Timber, agricultural land, solar energy	Oil, natural gas, copper
Inappropriable	Fisheries, air quality, mountain views	Climate, radioactive wastes

Sector	Value added, 1987* ($, billions)	Percent of gross domestic product, 1987
Renewable-resource industries:		**1.8**
Farming	59.8	
Forestry, timber cut	1.5	
Fisheries	3.7	
Hydroelectric-power generation	15.1	
Nonrenewable-resource industries:		**2.2**
Oil and natural gas	71.8	
Coal	13.3	
Other nonfuel minerals:		
Geologically scarce+	3.7	
Geologically superabundant‡	1.9	
Stone, clay, sand, etc.	7.8	

*Total sales less puchases of materials; includes profit, wages, interest, rent, depreciation, and taxes.

+ Includes 17 minerals such as copper, gold, silver, and vanadium.

‡Includes minerals such as iron and aluminum.

TABLE 18-2. Production from Different Resources, 1987
A wide variety of products are based on natural resources of both the renewable and non-renewable variety. Estimates of total output or sales include not only the economic value of the natural resource but also the returns to capital and labor. [Source: "Annual Input-Output Accounts of the U.S. Economy: 1987," *Survey of Current Business* (April 1992), pp. 55–71; Robert Gordon et al., *Toward a New Iron Age?* (Yale University Press, New Haven, 1989).]

and fisheries are among the most important categories of renewable resources.

The principles of efficient management of these two classes of resources present quite different challenges, as we will see below. Efficient use of a non-renewable resource entails the distribution of a finite quantity of the resource over time: Should we use our low-cost natural gas for this generation or save it for the future? By contrast, prudent use of renewable resources involves ensuring that the flow of services is efficiently maintained, say, through appropriate forest management, protection of breeding grounds of fish, or regulation of pollution into rivers and lakes.

Table 18-1 shows this fundamental division of resources along with major examples of each.

ALLOCATION OF APPROPRIABLE NATURAL RESOURCES

We begin our survey with appropriable resources—those for which the underlying resource is privately owned or managed and where the major costs and benefits of production and consumption are captured in the marketplace. What are the most important natural-resource industries? Table 18-2 shows the value added in each of the major industries as measured in the national income and product accounts. The total of all marketed natural-resource industries constituted 4 percent of total output in 1987; two industries, farming and oil and gas, accounted for three-quarters of the economic output of the marketed natural resources.

Even though the share of resources in total income is low, it would be foolish to be complacent and assume that resources are unimportant for economic growth. Might we not someday exhaust some essential natural resource, like energy, and find ourselves devoting much effort to finding replacement power? Nothing would plunge a modern industrial economy into chaos and poverty more quickly than exhausting the fuel for energy-using factors like the internal combustion engine, central heating and cooling, electric motors, and electronics. This is worrisome because 90 percent of American energy consumption today comes from finite, nonrenewable sources like oil, gas, and coal. Should we be taking steps to limit the use of these most precious stocks of society's capital so that they will still be available for our grandchildren?

Economists answer this question in two ways. First, they point out that fossil fuels like oil and gas are finite but not "essential." An *essential* resource is one, like oxygen, for which there are no substitutes. Substitutes exist for all the energy resources. We can substitute coal for oil and gas in most uses; we can liquefy or gasify coal where liquid or gas fuels are needed; when coal runs out, we can use higher-cost solar energy, nuclear fission, and perhaps someday even nuclear fusion. These last three are superabundant in the sense that when we run out of solar energy, the earth will already be uninhabitable.

A second point concerns the relative productivity of different assets. Many environmentalists argue that energy and other natural resources like wilderness areas and old-growth forests are very special kinds of capital that need to be preserved so that we can maintain "sustainable" economic growth. Economists tend to disagree. They look at natural resources as yet another capital asset that society possesses—along with fast computers, human capital in an educated work force, and technological knowledge in its patents, scientists, and engineers. Both economists and environmentalists agree that this generation should leave an adequate stock of capital assets for future generations; but economists worry less about the exact form of capital than about its productivity. Economists ask, Would future generations benefit more from larger stocks of natural capital such as oil, gas, and coal or from more produced capital such as additional scientists, better laboratories, and libraries linked together by information superhighways?

The substitutability of natural capital and other kinds of capital is shown by the production indifference curve or "isoquant" in Figure 18-2. We show there the amounts of the two kinds of capital that would be required to attain a certain level of output in the future (Q^*), holding other inputs constant. That output can be produced at point C with a conservationist policy that emphasizes reducing energy use today, leaving much oil and gas and relatively little human capital for the future. Or it might be produced with a low-energy-price and high-education strategy at B. Either of these is feasible, and the more desirable one would be the one that has a higher consumption both now and in the future.

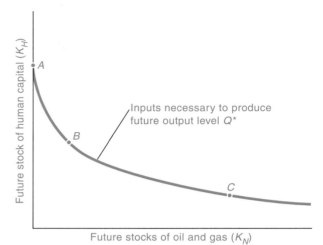

FIGURE 18-2. Natural Capital and Produced Capital Are Substitutes in Production

Output can be produced with either natural capital (K_N) or human capital (K_H). This equal-product curve shows the combination of inputs that will yield a given amount of output in the future (Q^*). Environmentalists urge conserving natural capital so that future stocks are large, as at C. Economists emphasize the need to ensure that scarce capital goes to sectors with the highest yield. If natural capital is abundant, it would be more efficient to go to point B by consuming stocks of natural capital today while building up stocks of human capital and improving technology through research and development.

Note as well that the isoquant hits the vertical axis at point A, indicating that we can produce future output level Q^* *with no oil and gas*. How is this possible? With the greater scientific and technical knowledge represented by point A, society can develop and introduce substitute technologies like clean coal or solar energy to replace the exhausted oil and gas. The curve hits the axis to indicate that in the long run, oil and gas are not essential.

Resource Price Trends

In 1973, following a war and an embargo in the Mideast, the price of oil skyrocketed, and many other resource prices also moved sharply upward. Many people feared that the world was on the verge of running out of its key nonrenewable resources.

Twenty-five years later, the price of oil was in fact only $20 per barrel. Adjusting for overall inflation, that means the price of oil is barely higher now than it was when the oil-price shocks of the 1970s occurred. Surprisingly, the same is true for almost

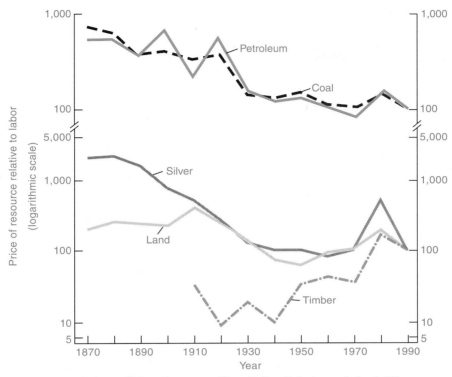

FIGURE 18-3. Prices of Most Resources Have Fallen Relative to Labor's Wage

For most natural resources, productivity and new discoveries have offset depletion, so their market prices have fallen relative to wage rates. The only major exception to this rule is timber. (Source: W. D. Nordhaus, "Lethal Model II: The Limits to Growth Revisited," *Brookings Papers on Economic Activity*, no. 2, 1992, pp. 24, 26.)

every natural resource—prices have been dropping rather than rising in the long run. Figure 18-3 shows the price trends of a number of resources compared to the price of labor. For all major appropriable natural resources except timber, the real price has fallen over the last century.

Looking at this issue from another vantage point, if the resource pessimists were correct, we might expect more and more of our national output to be devoted to resource sectors. Actually, the share of resource industries in the total economy has been declining. Figure 18-4 on page 330 shows the percentage of total national output in agriculture, forestry, fisheries, mining, and resource utilities. These industries formed about 14 percent of the economy in the late 1940s but declined to 6 percent of the economy by the early 1990s. Most of the decline came in agriculture, for reasons that we described in Chapter 4. The impact of the oil crises

of the 1970s is shown as bumps in Figure 18-4, as oil and gas prices and their share of the national economy spiked upward.

What lies behind these trends? The answer parallels our discussion of Malthus, above. In reality, the price-reducing influence of technological change and new discoveries has offset the price-increasing effect of depletion. For example, copper telephone wires are being replaced by fiber-optic cables, which use much cheaper and more plentiful raw materials. This same effect is happening in most of the natural-resource sectors.

The resource wager: In 1980 Julian Simon, an economist and a leading advocate of the cornucopian school, issued a challenge to the environmental pessimists. Offering to let them pick any natural resources they wanted, Simon, who believed that tech-

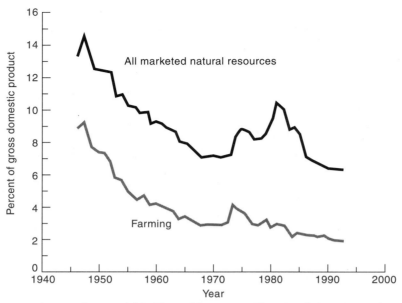

FIGURE 18-4. Appropriable Natural Resources Have Declining Share of Economy

Over the last half-century, agriculture has shrunk while other marketed natural resources have kept their share of national economy. (Source: "All" includes gross domestic product originating in agriculture, forestry, fisheries, mining, and water, gas, and electric utilities from U.S. Commerce Department.)

nology could find substitutes for any depleted resources, was willing to bet that the prices of the chosen resources would fall, and not rise.

Simon's challenge was taken up by Paul Ehrlich, a noted biologist and environmentalist. Ehrlich first came to fame in 1968 as author of *The Population Bomb,* in which he predicted imminent famines across the world. In a later book, he forecast shortages of key raw materials by 1985. Not surprisingly, Ehrlich found Simon's offer irre-

sistible. Ehrlich bet $1000 that the prices of five metals—chrome, copper, nickel, tin, and tungsten—-would rise by 1990, after adjustment for inflation.

Simon won hands down. After adjusting for inflation, the prices of all five metals dropped sharply over the decade (see Figure 18-3 for the general trend). Ehrlich not only overlooked the long-term relative trend in resource prices but had the bad fortune to pick a decade in which the business cycle reinforced longer-term forces.

C. CURBING EXTERNALITIES: ENVIRONMENTAL ECONOMICS

The task of saving the Earth's environment must and will become the central organizing principle of the post-cold-war world.

Albert J. Gore Jr., vice president of the United States (1993–)

During the 1992 presidential campaign, vice-presidential candidate Albert Gore spoke of the need to recognize the potentially catastrophic implications

of unchecked economic growth, pointing to present problems such as the Antarctic ozone hole as well as future problems like global warming. President

George Bush derided Gore, saying, "You know why I call him Ozone Man? This guy is so far off in the environmental extreme, we'll be up to our necks in owls and out of work for every American."

This political debate mirrors a deep division between those who see injury piled on top of damage as nations neglect their pressing environmental problems and others who believe that environmental problems can be easily handled with modern technology and pale beside the serious problems of war, joblessness, pestilence, drugs, and poverty. In this section we explore the nature of environmental externalities, describe why they produce economic inefficiencies, and analyze potential remedies.

In the first section of this chapter, we divided natural resources into appropriable and inappropriable resources, where an inappropriable resource is one which has externalities. An externality occurs when production or consumption inflicts involuntary costs or benefits on others. More precisely, an externality is an effect of one economic agent's behavior on another's well-being where that effect is not reflected in market transactions.

Externalities come in many guises. Some are positive (external economies), while others are negative (external diseconomies). Thus when I dump a barrel of acid into a stream, it kills fish and plants. Because I don't pay anyone for this damage, an external diseconomy occurs. When you discover a better way to clean up oil spills, the benefit will extend to many people who do not pay you for it. This is an external economy.

Some externalities are pervasive, while others have only small spillover components. When a carrier of bubonic plague entered a town during the Middle Ages, the entire population could be felled by the Black Death. On the other hand, when you chew an onion at a football stadium on a windy day, the external impacts are hardly noticeable.

Public vs. Private Goods

To illustrate the concept of external effects, consider the extreme example of a *public good*, which is a commodity that can be provided to everyone as easily as it can be provided to one person.

The case par excellence of a public good is national defense. Nothing is more vital to a society than its security. But national defense, as an economic good, differs completely from a private good

like bread. Ten loaves of bread can be divided up in many ways among individuals, and what I eat cannot be eaten by others. But national defense, once provided, affects everyone equally. It matters not at all whether you are hawk or dove, pacifist or militarist, old or young, ignorant or learned—you will receive the same amount of national security from the Army as does every other resident of the country.

Note therefore the stark contrast: The decision to provide a certain level of a public good like national defense will lead to a number of submarines, cruise missiles, and tanks to protect each of us. By contrast, the decision to consume a private good like bread is an individual act. You can eat four slices, or two, or a whole loaf; the decision is purely your own and does not commit anyone else to a particular amount of bread consumption.

The example of national defense is a dramatic and extreme case of a public good. But when you think of a smallpox vaccine, a park concert, a dam upstream on a river that prevents flood damage downstream, or many similar government projects, you generally find elements of public goods involved. In summary:

Public goods are ones whose benefits are indivisibly spread among the entire community, whether or not individuals desire to purchase the public good. **Private goods**, by contrast, are ones that can be divided up and provided separately to different individuals, with no external benefits or costs to others. Efficient provision of public goods often requires government action, while private goods can be efficiently allocated by markets.

In addition to public goods, we often see public "bads," which are public goods that impose costs uniformly across a group. These are unintended by-products of consumption or production activities. Later in this chapter, we will review the debate about the greenhouse effect, in which combustion of fossil fuels threatens global climate change. Other examples include the air and water pollution that results from chemical production, energy production, and use of automobiles; acid rain, which comes from long-distance transportation of sulfur emissions from power plants; radioactive exposure from atmospheric tests of nuclear weapons or from accidents like that at the Ukrainian plant in Chernobyl; and depletion of the ozone layer from buildup of chloro-fluorocarbons. Note that in all these cases, those who caused the external effect did not desire to hurt anyone. The externalities were the unintentional but harmful side effects of economic activity.

MARKET INEFFICIENCY WITH EXTERNALITIES

Abraham Lincoln said that government is "to do for the people what needs to be done, but which they cannot, by individual effort, do at all, or do so well, for themselves." Pollution control satisfies this guideline since the market mechanism does not provide an adequate check on polluters. Firms will not voluntarily restrict emissions of noxious chemicals, nor will they always abstain from dumping toxic wastes in landfills. Pollution control is therefore generally held to be a legitimate government function.

Analysis of Inefficiency

Why do external diseconomies like pollution lead to economic inefficiency? Take a hypothetical coal-burning electric utility. Dirty Light & Power generates an external diseconomy by spewing out tons of noxious sulfur dioxide fumes. Some of the sulfur harms the utility, requiring more frequent repainting and raising the firm's medical bills. But most of the damage is "external" to the firm, settling throughout the region, harming vegetation and buildings, and causing various kinds of respiratory ailments and even premature death in people.

Being a sound profit-maximizing enterprise, Dirty Light & Power must decide how much pollution it should emit. With no pollution cleanup, its workers and plant will suffer. Cleaning up every molecule, on the other hand, will require heavy expenses for low-sulfur, cleaner fuels, recycling systems, scrubbing equipment, and so forth. A complete cleanup would cost so much that Dirty Light & Power could not hope to survive in the marketplace.

The managers therefore decide to clean up just to the point where the benefits to the firm from additional *abatement* or pollution removal (marginal private benefits) are equal to the extra cost of cleanup (marginal cost of abatement). The firm's accountants estimate that the marginal private benefits are $10 per ton of sulfur dioxide. Further, the firm's engineers tell management that removing 50 of the 400 tons normally emitted will have a marginal cost of $10 per ton. The firm has found its private optimal level of pollution abatement of 50 tons, at which the marginal private benefit to the firm just equals the marginal private cost of abatement. Put differently, when Dirty Light & Power produces electricity in a least-cost manner, weighing only private costs and benefits, it will set its pollution at 350 tons and remove 50 tons.

Suppose, however, that a team of environmental scientists and economists is asked to examine the overall impacts on society rather than the impacts affecting only Dirty Light & Power. In examining the total impacts, the auditors find that the marginal *social* benefits of pollution control—including improved health and increased property values in neighboring regions—are 10 times the marginal private benefits. The impact from each extra ton on Dirty Light & Power is $10, but the rest of society suffers an additional impact of $90 per ton of *external costs*. Why doesn't Dirty Light & Power include the $90 of additional social benefits in its calculations? The $90 is excluded because these benefits are external to the firm and have no effect on its profits.

We now see how pollution and other externalities lead to inefficient economic outcomes: In an unregulated environment, firms will determine their most profitable pollution levels by equating the marginal private benefit from abatement with the marginal private cost of abatement. When the pollution spillovers are significant, the private equilibrium will produce inefficiently high levels of pollution and too little cleanup activity.

Socially Efficient Pollution. Given that private decisions on pollution control are inefficient, is there a way of finding a better solution? Should pollution be completely prohibited? Should we require the damaged parties to negotiate with the polluters or allow them to sue for damages? Is there an engineering solution?

In general, economists look to determine the socially efficient level of pollution by balancing social costs and benefits. More precisely, *efficiency requires that the marginal social benefits from abatement equal the marginal social costs of abatement.* This equality occurs when the marginal benefits to the nation's health and property of reducing pollution by 1 unit just equal the marginal costs of that reduction.

How might an efficient level of pollution be determined? Economists recommend an approach known as *cost-benefit analysis,* in which efficient standards are set by balancing the marginal costs of an action against the marginal benefits of that action. In the case of Dirty Light & Power, suppose that experts study the cost data for abatement and environmental damage. They determine that marginal social costs and marginal social benefits are equalized when the amount of abatement is increased from 50 tons to 250 tons. At the efficient pollution rate, they find that the marginal cost of abatement is $40 per ton, while the marginal social benefits from the last unit removed are also $40 per ton.

Why is it efficient for the firm to emit 150 tons rather than 400 tons? Because at this emissions rate the net social value of production is maximized. If Dirty Light & Power were to emit more than 150 tons of pollution, the extra environmental damage would outweigh the cost savings from lower abatement. On the other hand, if pollution were to be cut below 150 tons, the marginal cost of pollution cleanup would be greater than the marginal benefit from cleaner air. Here again, as in many areas, we find the most efficient outcome by equating marginal cost and marginal benefit of an activity.

Cost-benefit analysis will show why extreme "no-risk" or "zero-discharge" policies are generally wasteful. Reducing pollution to zero would generally impose astronomically high cleanup costs, while the marginal benefits of reducing the last few grams of pollution may be quite modest. In some cases, it may even be impossible to continue to produce with zero emissions, so a no-risk philosophy might require closing down the computer industry or banning all vehicular traffic. Generally, economic efficiency calls for a compromise, balancing the extra value of the industry's output against the extra damage from pollution.

An unregulated market economy will generate levels of pollution (or other externalities) at which the marginal *private* benefit of abatement equals the marginal private costs of abatement. Efficiency requires that marginal *social* benefit equals marginal social abatement cost. In an unregulated economy, there will be too little abatement and too much pollution.

Valuing Damages

One of the major problems in conducting economic studies of the environment arises because many of the benefits are not priced in the market. Reaching the efficient level of regulation generally requires that regulators be able to put a dollar value on the externality. For example, if emissions fees are set to equate marginal social costs with marginal benefits, we clearly must be able to calculate social damages from pollution. In cases where the impacts are on marketed goods and services, the measurement is relatively straightforward. If a warmer climate reduces wheat yields, we can measure the damage by the net value of the wheat. Or if a new road requires tearing down someone's house, we can calculate the market value of a replacement dwelling.

But many types of environmental damage, particularly in nonmarket sectors, are much harder to value. For example, in the late 1980s and the early 1990s environmentalists called for a halt to logging across a wide swathe of the northwest in order to preserve the habitat of the spotted owl. That would cost thousands of logging jobs. How would we value the continued existence of the spotted owl? Or to take another example, the *Exxon Valdez* oil spill in Prince William Sound, Alaska, damaged beaches and killed wildlife. How much is the life of a sea otter worth? Even more controversial is the value of a human life. How much should society pay to reduce illness or life-shortening effects of air pollution?

Economists have developed several approaches for estimating damages which do not show up directly in market prices. Valuation is easiest in those cases in which environmental problems directly harm users. A polluted river or lake will discourage fishing and swimming, and the value of the lost recreational opportunities can be estimated by looking at its opportunity cost—how much people would pay for an equivalent form of recreation.

But what about the value of a spotted owl? Most people will never see a spotted owl, just as they will never see a whooping crane or actually visit Prince William Sound. But they may place a value on these natural resources nevertheless. Some environmental economists use a technique called *contingent valuation*, which involves asking people how much they would be willing to pay in a hypothetical situation, say, to keep some natural resource undamaged. In the case of the *Exxon Valdez* spill, people from around the country were surveyed to help find out how people who had never visited Prince William Sound valued preserving and restoring its pristine environment. The study placed a value of $3 billion on the cost of the accident.

The contingent-valuation methodology has stirred a bitter controversy. Its critics argue that the answers are not believable because people are being asked to value something they don't understand and have never experienced, like asking people how much they would pay to eat green cheese produced on the moon. Critics add that since people never actually have to pay the money, and because they feel good when they offer to pony up lots of hypothetical dollars for a worthy cause, their estimates will be unrealistically high and should be ignored.

Few would doubt that an unspoiled environment has a significant value to many Americans, but valuing the nonmarket components is an elusive business.

Graphical Analysis of Pollution

We can illustrate these points with the help of Figure 18-5. The upward-sloping market *MC* is the marginal cost of abatement. The downward-sloping curves are the marginal benefits of reducing pollution, with the upper solid *MSB* line being the marginal social benefit from less pollution while the lower *MPB* line is the marginal private benefit of abatement to the polluter.

Warning on graphing pollution: In analyzing pollution, it is useful to think of pollution control or abatement as a "good." In the graphs, we therefore measure marginal costs and benefits on the vertical axis and the abatement or pollution removed on the horizontal axis. The trick here is to remember that because pollution removal is a good, it is measured positively on the horizontal axis. You can also think of pollution as measured negatively from the far-right point of 400. So abatement of zero is pollution of 400, while abatement of 400 means zero pollution.

The unregulated market solution comes at point *I*, where the marginal private costs and benefits are equated. At this point, only 50 tons are removed, and the marginal private costs and benefits are $10 per ton. But the unregulated market solution is inefficient. We can see this by performing an experiment that increases abatement by 10 tons; this is represented by the thin slice to the right of point *I*. For this additional removal, the marginal benefits are given by the total area of the slice under the *MSB*

curve, while the marginal costs are given by the area under the *MC* curve. The net benefits are that part of the slice shown by the shaded area between the two curves.

The efficient level of pollution comes at point *E*, where marginal social benefits are equated to marginal cost of abatement. At that point, both *MSB* and *MC* are equal to $40 per ton. Also, because *MSB* and *MC* are equal, the experiment of increasing abatement by a tiny amount will find that there is no difference between the curves, so there is no net benefit from additional pollution control. We can also measure the net benefits of the efficient solution relative to the unregulated market by taking all the little slices of net benefits from the shaded slice to point *E* of Figure 18-5. This calculation shows that the area *ISE* represents the gains from efficient removal of pollutants.

As a final experiment, consider the impact of a rule which said that every bit of pollution had to be removed; this could be called a zero-risk philosophy and would require 400 units of pollution removal. For this action, the marginal social benefits are zero while the marginal costs are at point *Z*, so there are large excess costs of removal. By adding up all the little slices to the right of the efficient point, we can see that the net costs of a zero-risk approach are given by the area *EZB*.

POLICIES TO CORRECT EXTERNALITIES

What are the weapons that can be used to combat inefficiencies arising from externalities? The most visible activities are government antipollution programs that use either direct controls or financial incentives to induce firms to correct externalities. More subtle approaches use enhanced property rights to give the private sector the instruments for negotiating efficient solutions. We survey these approaches in this section.

Government Programs

Direct Controls. For almost all pollution, as well as other health and safety externalities, governments rely on direct regulatory controls; these are often called *social regulations* (see Chapter 17). For example, the 1970 Clean Air Act reduced allowable emissions of three major pollutants by 90 percent. In

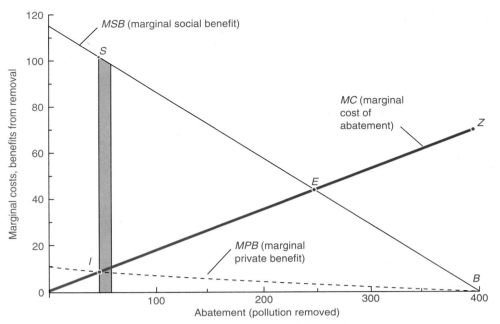

FIGURE 18-5. Inefficiency from Externalities

When marginal social benefit (*MSB*) diverges from marginal private benefit (*MPB*), markets will generate unregulated equilibrium at *I*, with too little abatement or pollution cleanup. Efficient cleanup comes at *E*, where *MSB* equals *MC*.

1977, utilities were told to reduce sulfur emissions at new plants by 90 percent. In a series of regulations over the last decades, firms were told they must phase out ozone-depleting chemicals. And so it goes with regulation.

How does the government enforce a pollution regulation? To continue our example of Dirty Light & Power, the state Department of Environmental Protection might tell Dirty Light & Power to increase its abatement to 250 tons of particulate matter. Under *command-and-control regulations*, the regulator would simply order the firm to comply, giving detailed instructions on what pollution-control technology to use and where to apply it. There would be little scope for novel approaches or tradeoffs within the firm or across firms. *If* standards are appropriately set—a very big "if"—the outcome might approach the efficient pollution level described in the previous part of this section.

While it is possible that the regulator might choose pollution-control edicts in a way that guarantees economic efficiency, in practice that is not very

likely. Indeed, much pollution control suffers from extensive government failures. For example, pollution regulations are often set without comparisons of marginal costs and marginal benefits, and without such comparisons there is no way to determine the most efficient level of pollution control. Indeed, for some regulatory programs, the law specifically prohibits cost-benefit comparison as a way of setting standards.

In addition, standards are inherently a very blunt tool. Efficient pollution reduction requires that the marginal cost of pollution be equalized across all sources of pollution. Command-and-control regulations generally do not allow differentiation across firms, regions, or industries. Hence, regulations are usually the same for large firms and small firms, for cities and rural areas, and for high-polluting and low-polluting industries. Even though firm A might be able to reduce a ton of pollution at a tiny fraction of the cost to firm B, both firms will be required to meet the same standard; nor will there be any incentives for the low-cost firm to reduce pollution more than the standard even though it would be economical to do just that. Study after study has confirmed that our environmental goals have proved unnecessarily costly because we have used command-and-control regulation.

Market Solution: Emissions Fees. In order to avoid some of the pitfalls of direct controls, many economists have suggested that environmental policy rely more on economic incentives than on government commands. One approach is the use of *emissions fees*, which would require that firms pay a tax on their pollution equal to the amount of external damage. If Dirty Light & Power were imposing external marginal costs of $35 per ton on the surrounding community, the appropriate emissions charge would be $35 per ton. This is in effect *internalizing* the externality by making the firm face the social costs of its activities. In calculating its private costs, Dirty Light & Power would find that, at point *E*, an additional ton of pollution would cost it $5 of internal costs to the firm plus $35 in emissions fees, for an overall marginal cost of $40 per ton of pollution. By equating the new marginal *private* benefit (private benefit plus emissions fee) with the marginal abatement cost, the firm would curb its pollution back to the efficient level. *If* the emissions fee were correctly calculated—another big "if"—profit-minded firms would be led as if by a mended invisible hand to the efficient point where marginal social costs and marginal social benefits of pollution are equal.

The alternative approaches are shown graphically in Figure 18-6, which is similar to Figure 18-5 except we have simplified it by removing the marginal private benefit curve. With the direct-control approach, the government simply instructs the firm to remove 250 tons of pollutants (or to emit no more than 150 tons). This would in effect place the standard at the heavy vertical line. If the standard were set at the right level, the firm would undertake the socially efficient level of abatement. Hence, with efficient regulation, the firm will choose point *E*, with *MSB* equal to *MC*.

What about the case of emissions fees? Say that the government charges the firm $35 per ton. In effect, this means that the marginal private benefit of abatement would go from $5 to $40 per ton. Faced with this incentive, the firm would again choose efficient point *E* in Figure 18-6.

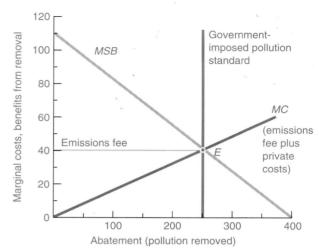

FIGURE 18-6. Pollution Standards and Emissions Fees

When government sets the pollution limitation at 150, or requires removal of 250, this standard will lead to efficient pollution at point *E*. The same result can be achieved with pollution fees of $35 per ton: at $35 per ton fee plus $5 per ton of marginal private damage, the sum will equal marginal cost and lead to efficient abatement at point *E*.

Market Solution: Tradeable Emissions Permits. A new approach that does not require the government to legislate taxes is the use of tradeable emissions permits. With this approach, instead of telling firms that they must pay $*x* per unit of pollution and then allowing firms to choose the level of pollution, the government chooses the level of pollution and allocates the appropriate number of permits. The price of permits, which represents the level of the emissions fee, is then set by supply and demand in the market for permits. Assuming the cost schedule is known, the tradeable permits approach has the same outcome as the emissions fee approach. One major difference between the two approaches is that the government often allocates emissions permits to firms to win their political support. This means that industry gets the revenues from the permits while the government gets the revenues from emissions fees.

Economic innovations: Trading pollution permits. Most environmental regulations use a command-and-control approach that limits the emissions from individual sources, such as power plants or automobiles. This approach cannot cap overall emissions. More importantly, it virtually guarantees that the overall program is extremely inefficient because it does not satisfy the condition that emissions from all sources must have equal marginal costs of abatement.

In 1990, the United States introduced a radical new approach to environmental control in its program on control of sulfur dioxide, which is one of the most harmful environmental pollutants. Under the 1990 Clean Air Act amendments, the government issues a certain number of permits to emit sulfur dioxide each year for the entire country. By the end of the decade, emissions are scheduled to be reduced by 50 percent relative to 1990 levels. The innovative aspect of the plan is that the permits will be freely tradeable. Electric utilities receive pollution permits and are allowed to buy and sell them with each other just like pork bellies or wheat. Those firms which can reduce their sulfur emissions most cheaply do so and sell their permits; other firms which need additional permits for new plants or have no leeway to reduce emissions find it economical to buy permits rather than install expensive antipollution equipment or shut down.

Environmental economists believe that the enhanced incentives allow the ambitious targets to be met at a much lower cost than would be paid under traditional command-and-control regulation. Studies by economist Tom Tietenberg of Colby College in Maine have determined that the traditional approaches cost 2 to 10 times as much as would cost-effective regulations like emissions trading.

The behavior of this market has produced a big surprise. Originally, the government projected that permits in the early years would sell for around $300 per ton of sulfur dioxide. By 1997, however, the market price had fallen to between $60 and $80 per ton. One reason for the success was that the program gave strong incentives for firms to innovate, and firms found that low-sulfur coal could be used much more easily and cheaply than had earlier been anticipated. This important experiment has given powerful support to economists who argue for market-based approaches to environmental policy.

Private Approaches

Not all solutions involve direct government action. Two private approaches may provide a moderately efficient outcome: private negotiations and liability rules.

Negotiation and the Coase Theorem. Let's say that the government decides not to intervene. A startling analysis by Chicago's Ronald Coase suggested that voluntary negotiations among the affected parties would in some circumstances lead to the efficient outcome.

The conditions under which this might occur arise when there are well-defined property rights and the costs of negotiations are low. Suppose, for example, that I am spilling chemicals upstream from your fish ponds and killing many of your fish. Further, say that you can sue me for damage to your fish. In such a case, Coase argued, the two of us would have a powerful incentive to get together and agree on the efficient level of dumping. And this incentive would exist without any government antipollution program.

Some have tried to take Coase's suggestion even further, arguing that efficient bargains *will* occur. But this conclusion is surely too optimistic. Saying that there is room for an efficient, cost-saving bargain does not mean that a deal will always be struck—as the history of war, labor-management disputes, and the theory of games amply demonstrate.[6]

Nevertheless, Coase's analysis does point to certain cases where private bargains may help alleviate externalities—namely, where property rights are well defined and where there are only a few affected parties who can get together and negotiate an efficient solution.

Liability Rules. A second approach relies on the legal framework of liability laws or the tort system rather than upon direct government regulations. Here, the generator of externalities is legally liable for any damages caused to other persons.

---

[6] Those who have studied Chapter 11 will recognize that the theory of games can be fruitfully applied to the bargaining situations involved in this kind of an externality. What lessons emerge? Often, games can end up with an equilibrium that displays a distinctly inefficient outcome. Chapter 11 described the case of the "pollution game," in which polluters' private interests lead them to high levels of soot and waste. This occurred when firms pursued the competitive or noncooperative approach (this outcome is called a Nash equilibrium). Game theorists have found no theorem proving that an invisible hand will lead two or more bargainers to the Pareto-efficient level of pollution. Coase never proved such a result, nor has anyone else.

In some areas, this doctrine is well established. Thus, in most states, if you are injured by a negligent driver, you can sue for damages. Or if you are injured or become ill from a defective product, the company can be sued for product liability.

Returning to our example, how would a perfect liability system contain the externality? If Dirty Light & Power caused $35 of external damages per ton of pollution, the victims would recover these damages through the courts. Thus the liability faced by the firm would be $35 per ton just as if there were a $35-per-ton emissions fee; such costs would give firms strong incentives to reduce pollution back toward the efficient level.

Liability rules are in principle an attractive means of internalizing the nonmarket costs of production. In practice, liability rules are quite limited in their applicability. They usually involve high litigation costs, which adds an additional cost to the original externality. In addition, many harms cannot be litigated because of incomplete property rights (such as those involving clean air) or because of the large number of companies who contribute to the externality (as in the case of chemicals flowing into a stream).

CLIMATE CHANGE: TO SLOW OR NOT TO SLOW

Of all the environmental issues, none is so worrisome to scientists as the threat of global warming from the greenhouse effect. Climatologists and other scientists warn that the accumulation of gases like carbon dioxide (CO_2), largely produced by the combustion of fossil fuels, is likely to lead to global warming and other significant climatic changes over the next century. On the basis of climate models, scientists project that if current trends continue, the earth may warm 4 to 8° Fahrenheit over the next century. This would take the earth's climate out of the range experienced during the entire period of human civilization.

The greenhouse effect is the granddaddy of public-good problems; actions today will affect the climate for all people in all countries for centuries to come. The costs of reducing CO_2 emissions come in the near term as countries cut back their use of fossil fuels by conserving energy and using alternative energy sources (solar energy or perhaps nuclear

power), plant trees, and take other measures. In the short run, that means we will have to accept more expensive energy, lower living standards, and lower consumption levels. The benefits of emissions reductions will come many years in the future, when lower emissions reduce future climate-induced damages—with less disruption to agriculture, seacoasts, and ecosystems.

Economists have begun to study the economic impacts of climate change in order to understand how nations might undertake sensible strategies. To begin with, economists point out that in the long march of economic development, technology has increasingly insulated humans and economic activity from the vagaries of climate. Today, thanks to modern technology, humans live and thrive in virtually every climate on earth. For the bulk of economic activity, variables like wages, unionization, labor-force skills, and political factors swamp climatic considerations.

In general, those sectors of the economy that depend heavily on unmanaged ecosystems—that is, on naturally occurring rainfall, runoff, or temperatures—will be most sensitive to climate change. Agriculture, forestry, outdoor recreation, and coastal activities fall into this category. Countries like Japan and the United States are relatively insulated from climate change, while developing countries like India and Brazil are more vulnerable. Economic studies suggest that the total cost of climate change in the United States by the end of the next century is likely to be at most a few percent of total output. Outside the United States, it might be beneficial for countries like Russia with cold climates, but it could easily be catastrophic for low-lying island countries.

An efficient strategy for containing climate change requires weighing the marginal costs of reducing CO_2 emissions against the marginal benefits. Figure 18-7 shows schematically the marginal cost of reductions as *MC* and the marginal social benefit as *MSB*. The vertical axis measures costs and benefits in dollars, while the horizontal axis measures emissions reductions in percent reduction of carbon dioxide. Point *E* in the graph represents the efficient point at which marginal abatement costs equal marginal benefits from slowing climate change. This is the point which maximizes the present value of future human consumption. By contrast, the pure-market solution comes with emissions

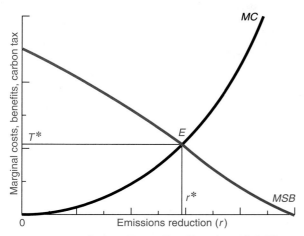

FIGURE 18-7. Carbon Taxes Can Slow Harmful Climate Change

Slowing climate change efficiently requires setting "carbon taxes" on harmful carbon dioxide emissions to balance marginal cost of reductions with marginal benefits of reducing damages from sea-level rise and other impacts of climate change.

reductions at 0, where *MSB* is far above the zero *MC*. An extreme environmentalist solution, which attempts to avoid any disruption to natural ecosystems, comes at the right-hand edge of the graph, where *MC* far exceeds *MSB*.

How can point *E*, the efficient level of CO_2 reduction, be achieved? Since CO_2 emissions come from burning carbon-containing fuels, some have suggested a "carbon tax" on the carbon content of fuels. Fuels which contain more carbon, like coal, would be taxed more heavily than low-carbon fuels like natural gas. Economists have calculated that the efficient carbon tax would be in the range of $5 to $10 per ton of carbon and would rise gradually over the next hundred years. At the higher level, a carbon tax would raise electricity bills by only 2 percent and gasoline prices by only 2 cents per gallon. This level of carbon tax would still allow considerable climate change. Therefore, environmentalists have proposed a much higher carbon tax—on the order of $100 per ton—which would have a larger impact on humans, in order to prevent significant future climate change.

Still, economists and environmentalists may not be as far apart as this analysis makes them seem. Cli-

mate change poses great difficulties for policymakers because its effects are so uncertain and stretch so far into the future. What are some of the major uncertainties? Scientists raise the specter of shifting currents turning Europe's climate into that of Alaska, of continental drying transforming grain belts into deserts, of great rivers drying up as snow packs disappear, of severe storms wiping out whole populations of low-lying regions, of northward migration of old or new tropical pests and diseases decimating the temperate regions, and of environmentally induced migration leading people to overrun borders in search of livable land.

Faced with this dilemma, economists rely upon the techniques of utility theory under uncertainty, surveyed in Chapter 11, to analyze different strategies. In this approach, a reasoned decision process involves listing the events that may occur, estimating the consequences of the events, judging the probability of the occurrence of each event, weighing the expected value of the consequences against the expected costs under different courses of action, and choosing the action that maximizes the expected value or utility of the outcome.

Preliminary studies suggest that because the uncertainties are so one-sided, with a small probability of very substantial damages, it might be rational to pay a "risk premium" in terms of taking additional steps today to slow climate change. Just as individuals find it rational to sacrifice a little income today to buy fire detectors to lower the chance of a catastrophic fire, so might societies find it prudent to sacrifice some of their national incomes today to reduce the chance of catastrophic global warming in the centuries to come.

We began this chapter with gloomy questions about the future of humanity. Having surveyed the field, how should we conclude? Depending on one's perspective, it is easy to become either optimistic or pessimistic about our ability to understand and cope with threats to our global environment. On the one hand, it is true that we are moving into uncharted waters, depleting many resources while altering others in an irreversible manner, and gambling with our universe in more ways than we know. Humans seem just as quarrelsome as they were at the dawn of recorded history, and they have devised weapons that are awesomely effective at avenging their quarrels. At the same time, our powers of observation and analysis are also orders of magnitude more formidable. The combination of monitoring, measuring, analyzing, and computing is growing even faster than our ability to emit wastes, cut trees, and produce yet more people.

What will prevail in this race between our tendency to quarrel and pollute and our power to rea-son and compute? Are there enough resources to allow the poor to enjoy the consumption standards of today's high-income countries, or will today's rich pull the ladder up behind them? There are no final answers to these deep questions, but many economists believe that if we manage our environmental resources wisely, *homo sapiens* can not only survive but also thrive for a long time to come.

SUMMARY

A. Population and Resource Limitations

1. Malthus' theory of population rests on the law of diminishing returns. He contended that population, if unchecked, would tend to grow at a geometric (or exponential) rate, doubling every generation or so. But each member of the growing population would have less land and natural resources to work with. Because of diminishing returns, income could grow at an arithmetic rate at best; output per person would tend to fall so low as to stabilize population at a subsistence level of near-starvation.

2. Over the last century and a half, Malthus and his followers have been criticized on several grounds. Among the major criticisms are that Malthusians ignored the possibility of technological advance and overlooked the significance of birth control as a force in lowering population growth.

3. Studies of the relationship between pollution, population, and income have determined that the demand for environmental quality rises rapidly with per capita income, so for most indicators environmental quality improves rather than deteriorates as per capita income rises.

B. Natural-Resource Economics

4. Natural resources are nonrenewable when they are essentially fixed in supply and cannot regenerate quickly. Renewable resources are ones whose services are replenished regularly and which, if properly managed, can yield useful services indefinitely.

5. From an economic point of view, the crucial distinction is between appropriable and inappropriable resources. Natural resources are appropriable when firms or consumers can capture the full benefits of their services; examples include vineyards or oil fields.

Natural resources are inappropriable when their costs or benefits do not accrue to the owners; in other words, they involve externalities. Examples include air quality and climate, which have externalities that are affected by such activities as the burning of fossil fuels.

6. Important examples of appropriable, nonrenewable natural resources are fossil fuels such as oil, gas, and coal. Economists argue that because private markets can efficiently price and allocate their services, such natural resources should be treated the same as any other capital asset.

C. Curbing Externalities: Environmental Economics

7. A major market failure that is increasing in importance is externalities. These occur when the costs (or benefits) of an activity spill over to other people, without those other people being paid (or paying) for the costs (or benefits) incurred (or received).

8. The most clear-cut example of an externality is the case of public goods, like defense, where all consumers in a group share equally in the consumption and cannot be excluded. Less obvious examples like public health, inventions, parks, and dams also possess public-good properties. These contrast with private goods, like bread, which can be divided and provided to a single individual.

9. Environmental problems arise because of externalities that stem from production or consumption. An unregulated market economy will produce too much pollution and too little pollution abatement. Unregulated firms decide on abatement (and other public goods) by comparing the marginal private benefits with the marginal private costs. Efficiency requires that marginal social benefits equal marginal social abatement costs.

10. There are numerous steps by which governments can internalize or correct the inefficiencies arising from externalities. Alternatives include decentralized solutions (such as negotiations or legal liability rules) and government-imposed approaches (such as pollution-emission standards or emissions taxes). Experience indicates that no approach is ideal in all circumstances, but many economists believe that greater use of marketlike systems would improve the efficiency of regulatory systems.

CONCEPTS FOR REVIEW

Population and Natural Resources

Malthusian population theory
renewable vs. nonrenewable
  resources
appropriable vs. inappropriable
  resources

Environmental Economics

externalities and public goods
private vs. public goods
inefficiency of externalities
internal vs. external costs, social vs.
  private costs

remedies for externalities:
  bargaining
  liability
  standards
  taxes
tradeable emissions permits

QUESTIONS FOR DISCUSSION

1. What is the difference between renewable and nonrenewable resources? Give examples of each.

2. What is meant by an inappropriable natural resource? Provide an example, and explain why the market allocation of this resource is inefficient. What would be your preferred way to improve the market outcome?

3. Many economists believe that the state should not interfere in a market where there are no important externalities—this being the "libertarian" or laissez-faire tradition. Are there externalities in population growth that would lead to positive or negative spillovers? Consider such items as education, national defense, roads, pollution, and the creation of geniuses like Mozart or Einstein.

4. A *geometric progression* is a sequence of terms $(g_1, g_2, \ldots, g_t, g_{t+1}, \ldots)$ in which each term is the same multiple of its predecessor: $g_2/g_1 = g_3/g_2 = \cdots = g_{t+1}/g_t = \beta$. If $\beta = 1 + i > 1$, the terms grow exponentially like compound interest. An arithmetic progression is a sequence $(a_1, a_2, a_3, \ldots, a_t, a_{t+1}, \ldots)$ in which the difference between each term and its predecessor is the same constant: $a_2 - a_1 = a_3 - a_2 \cdots = a_{t+1} - a_t = \cdots$. Give examples of each. Satisfy yourself that any geometric progression with $\beta > 1$ must eventually surpass any arithmetic progression. Relate this to Malthus' theory.

5. Recall that Malthus asserted that unchecked population would grow geometrically, while food supply—constrained by diminishing returns—would grow only arithmetically. Use a numerical example to show why per capita food production must decline if population is unchecked while diminishing returns lead food production to grow more slowly than labor inputs.

6. "Local public goods" are ones that mainly benefit the residents of a town or state—such as beaches or schools open only to town residents. Is there any reason to think that towns might act competitively to provide the correct amount of local public goods to their residents? If so, does this suggest an economic theory of "fiscal federalism" whereby local public goods should be locally supplied?

7. Decide whether each of the following externalities is serious enough to warrant collective action. If so, which of the four remedies considered in the chapter would be most efficient?

    a. Steel mills emitting sulfur oxides into the Birmingham air

    b. Smoking by people in restaurants

    c. Smoking by students without roommates in their own rooms

    d. Driving by persons under the influence of alcohol, involving 25,000 fatalities per year

    e. Driving by persons under 21 under the influence of alcohol

8. Get your classmates together to do a contingent-valuation analysis on the value of the following: Keeping Prince William Sound pristine; preventing the extinction of spotted owls for another 10,000 years; ensuring that there are at least 1 million spotted owls in existence for another 10,000 years; reducing the chance of dying in an automobile accident from 1 in 1000 to 1 in 2000 each year. How reliable do you think this technique is for gathering information about people's preferences?

9. **Advanced problem:** Global public goods pose special problems because no single nation can capture the benefits of its pollution-control efforts. To see this, redraw Figure 18-7, labeling it "Emissions Reduction for the United States." Label all the curves with "US" to indicate that they refer to costs and benefits for the United States alone. Next, draw a new *MSB* curve

which is everywhere 3 times higher than the MSB_{US} to indicate that the benefits to the world are 3 times those to the United States. Consider the "nationalistic" equilibrium at E in which the United States maximizes its own net benefits. Can you see why this is inefficient from the point of view of the entire globe? (*Hint:* The reasoning is exactly analogous to Figure 18-5.)

Consider this issue from the point of view of game theory. The Nash equilibrium would occur when each country chose the nationalistic equilibrium you have just analyzed. Describe why this is exactly analogous to the inefficient Nash equilibrium in the pollution game of Chapter 11—only here the players are nations rather than firms. Now consider the cooperative game where nations get together to find the efficient equilibrium. Describe the efficient equilibrium in terms of global MC and MSB curves. Can you see why the efficient equilibrium would require a uniform carbon tax in each country?

CHAPTER 19

EFFICIENCY VS. EQUALITY: THE BIG TRADEOFF

[The conflict] between equality and efficiency [is] our biggest socioeconomic tradeoff, and it plagues us in dozens of dimensions of social policy. We can't have our cake of market efficiency and share it equally.

Arthur Okun (1975)

About a century ago, many Western governments introduced a wide variety of transfer programs, known as the "welfare state," as a bulwark against socialist pressures. In the industrial democracies of Europe and North America, governments now generally finance retirement and health care for the aged, provide food, health care, and housing assistance for the indigent, replace lost income for the unemployed and disabled, and channel incomes and wage subsidies to the poor. These programs have removed the sting of abject poverty.

But reducing poverty has not come without cost or controversy. A large and growing share of government budgets goes to income-support programs. Taxes have risen steadily over the last half-century. Attempts to equalize incomes can cause adverse effects on incentives and efficiency. Today, people ask: How much of the economic pie must be sacrificed in order to divide it more equally? How should we redesign income-support programs to retain the objective of reducing want and inequality without bankrupting the nation?

The purpose of this chapter is to examine the distribution of income along with the dilemmas of policies to reduce inequality. These issues are among the most controversial economic questions of today. It is here that cool-headed economic analysis of facts and trends in poverty, as well as of the strengths and weaknesses of different programs, will have a large payoff in promoting both a sense of fairness and continued rapid growth of the mixed economy.

A. THE SOURCES OF INEQUALITY

To measure the inequality of control over economic resources, we need to concern ourselves with both income and wealth differences. Recall that by **personal income** we mean the total receipts or cash earned by a person or household during a given time period (usually a year). The major components of personal income are labor earnings, property income (such as rents, interest, and dividends), and government transfer payments. **Disposable personal income** consists of personal income less any taxes

(1)	(2)	(3)	(4)
Income class of households	Income range	Percentage of all households in this class	Percentage of total income received by households in this class
Lowest fifth	Under $14,399	20.0	3.7
Second fifth	$14,400–$26,899	20.0	9.1
Third fifth	$26,900–$41,999	20.0	15.2
Fourth fifth	$42,000–$65,099	20.0	23.3
Highest fifth	$65,100 and over	20.0	48.7
Top 5 percent	$113,000 and over	5.0	21.0

TABLE 19-1. Distribution of Money Incomes of American Households, 1995

How was total income distributed among households in 1995? We group households into the fifth (or quintile) with the lowest income, the fifth with the second-lowest income, and so on. (Source: U.S. Bureau of the Census, *Money Income of Households, Families, and Persons in the United States: 1995*, Current Population Report, Series P-60, No. 184, September 1996.)

paid. **Wealth** or "net worth" consists of the dollar value of financial and tangible assets, minus the amount of money owed to banks and other creditors. You can refresh your memory about the major sources of income and wealth by reviewing Tables 12-1 and 12-2 (pages 210 and 212).

THE DISTRIBUTION OF INCOME AND WEALTH

Statistics show that in 1995 the median income of American families was $30,786—this means that half of all families received less than this figure while half received more. This number concerns the *distribution of income*, which shows the variability or dispersion of incomes. To understand the income distribution, consider the following experiment: Suppose one person from each household writes down the yearly income of his or her household on an index card. We can then sort these cards into *income classes*. Some of the cards will go into the lowest 20 percent, the group with under $14,400 of income. Some go into the next class. A few go into the top 5 percent of households, those with incomes of $113,00 and above.

The actual income distribution of American households in 1995 is shown in Table 19-1. Column (1) shows the different income-class fifths, or *quintiles*, plus the top 5 percent of households. Column (2) shows the range of household incomes in each income class. Column (3) shows the percentage of the households in each income class, while column

(4) shows the percentage of total national income that goes to the households in an income class.

Table 19-1 enables us to see at a glance the wide spread of incomes in the U.S. economy. The poorest fifth of U.S. households have incomes less than $14,400, while households in the top fifth have incomes of $65,100 or more. About 5 percent of households have incomes over $113,000. Some people earn much more than that, but as you move further up the income pyramid, the numbers get smaller and smaller. If we made an income pyramid out of building blocks, with each layer portraying $500 of income, the peak would be far higher than Mount Everest, but most people would be within a few feet of the ground.

How to Measure Inequality Among Income Classes

How can we measure the degree of income inequality? At one pole, if incomes were absolutely equally distributed, there would be no difference between the lowest 20 percent and the highest 20 percent of the population: Each would receive exactly 20 percent of the total income. That's what absolute equality means.

The reality is far different. The lowest fifth, with 20 percent of the households, garners less than 4 percent of the total income. Meanwhile the situation is almost reversed for the top 5 percent of households, who get more than 20 percent of the income.

We can show the degree of inequality in a diagram known as the **Lorenz curve**, a widely used

(1)	(2) Percentage of total income received by households in this class	(3) Percentage of households in this class and lower ones	(4) (5) (6) Percentage of income received by this class and lower ones		
Income class of households			Absolute equality	Absolute inequality	Actual distribution
		0	0	0	0.0
Lowest fifth	3.7	20	20	0	3.7
Second fifth	9.1	40	40	0	12.8
Third fifth	15.2	60	60	0	28.0
Fourth fifth	23.3	80	80	0	51.3
Highest fifth	48.7	100	100	100	100.0

TABLE 19-2. Actual and Polar Cases of Inequality

By cumulating the income shares of each quintile shown in column (2), we can compare in column (6) the actual distribution with polar extremes of complete inequality and equality. (Source: U.S. Bureau of the Census, *Money Income of Households, Families, and Persons in the United States: 1995,* Current Population Report, Series P-60, No. 184, September 1996.)

device for analyzing income and wealth inequality. Figure 19-1 is a Lorenz curve showing the amount of inequality listed in the columns of Table 19-2; that is, it contrasts the patterns of (1) absolute equality, (2) absolute inequality, and (3) actual 1995 American inequality.

Absolute equality is depicted by the gray column of numbers in column (4) of Table 19-2. When they are plotted, these become the diagonal dashed rust-colored line of Figure 19-1's Lorenz diagram.

At the other extreme, we have the hypothetical case of absolute inequality, where one person has all the income. Absolute inequality is shown in column (5) of Table 19-2 and by the lowest curve on the Lorenz diagram—the dashed, right-angled black line.

Any actual income distribution, such as that for 1995, will fall between the extremes of absolute equality and absolute inequality. The rust-colored column in Table 19-2 presents the data derived from the first two columns in a form suitable for plotting as an actual Lorenz curve. This actual Lorenz curve appears in Figure 19-1 as the solid rust-colored intermediate curve. The shaded area indicates the deviation from absolute equality, hence giving us a measure of the degree of inequality of income distribution. A quantitative measure of inequality that is often used is the *Gini coefficient*, which is 2 times the shaded area.

Distribution of Wealth

One source of the inequality of income is inequality of ownership of *wealth*, which is the net ownership of financial claims and tangible property. Those who are fabulously wealthy—whether because of inheritance, skill, or luck—enjoy incomes far above the amount earned by the average household. Those without wealth begin with an income handicap.

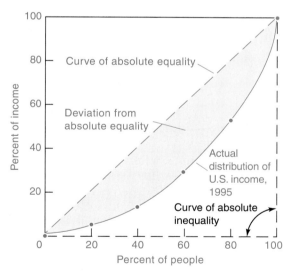

FIGURE 19-1. Lorenz Curve Shows Income Inequality

By plotting the figures from Table 19-2's column (6), we see that the solid rust-colored actual distribution-of-income curve lies between the two extremes of absolute equality and absolute inequality. The shaded area of this Lorenz curve (as a percentage of the triangle's area) measures relative inequality of income. (How would the curve have looked back in the roaring 1920s when inequality was greater? In a Utopia where all have equal inheritances and opportunities?)

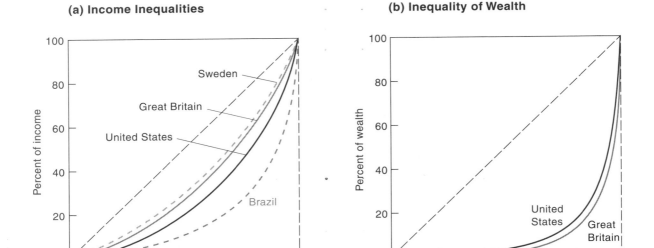

FIGURE 19-2. Inequality Differs in Different Societies and Is Greater for Wealth than for Income

(a) Advanced economies show less inequality of income distribution than do middle-income economies. Contrary to predictions of many socialists that the rich get richer and the poor get poorer under capitalism, the mixed economy shows increasing equality over time.
(b) Holdings of wealth tend to be more concentrated than do annual incomes. The United States and Great Britain have similar income distributions, but British wealth is somewhat more concentrated than America's. Socialist countries like China show much less concentration of private wealth. [Source: Federal Reserve Board, *Survey of Consumer Finances,* Washington, D.C., 1989; A. B. Atkinson and A. J. Harrison, "Trends in the Distribution of Wealth in Britain," in A. B. Atkinson (ed.), *Wealth, Income and Inequality* (Oxford University Press, London, 1980); *World Development Report 1993.*]

In market economies, wealth is much more unequally distributed than is income, as Figure 19-2(*b*) shows. In the United States, 1 percent of the households own almost 40 percent of all assets. Studies by New York University's Edward Wolff show that the distribution of wealth has become much more unequal. Because of the booming stock market, the share of wealth held by the top 1 percent of people has doubled over the last two decades. Given the sharp and growing increases in wealth inequality, Wolff, along with legal scholars Bruce Ackerman and Anne Alstott, have proposed that the United States consider instituting a progressive wealth tax to go along with its progressive income tax.

The vast disparities in ownership of wealth have spurred radicals over the ages to propose heavy taxation of property income, wealth, or inheritance. Revolutionaries have agitated for expropriation by the state of great accumulations of property. In recent years, a more conservative political trend has muted the call for redistribution of wealth. Economists recognize that excessive taxation of property income and wealth dulls the incentives for saving and may reduce a nation's capital formation. Particularly in a world of open borders, countries with high tax rates on wealth may find that the wealth has fled across the borders to tax havens or Swiss bank accounts.

Inequality Across Countries

Countries show quite different income distributions depending upon their economic and social

Country	Average income of poorest fifth as percent of top fifth
Brazil	3
Bolivia	5
Honduras	7
United Kingdom	11
United States	14
Sweden	22
Japan	23
Czech Republic	28

TABLE 19-3. Inequality in Different Countries, 1993

Inequality measured as the ratio of incomes of the bottom quintile to those of the top quintile is highest in middle-income countries with wealthy landowning and industrial elites. North America shows moderate levels of inequality. Greatest equality comes in countries with low immigration, homogeneous populations, and heavy welfare-state spending on redistributive policies. [Source: United Nations Development Program, *From Plan to Market: Human Development Report 1996* (Oxford University Press, Oxford, 1996).]

structure. Lorenz curves of four countries are shown in Figure 19-2(*a*). We see that Sweden has less income inequality than does the United States. The reason for this lies partly in the high levels of redistributive taxation in the European countries. In addition, the United States has growing numbers of single-parent families, who tend to have relatively low incomes. Among advanced market economies, the greatest income equality is found in Japan and Sweden; the most unequal income distributions come in the United States and Canada.

The experience of developing countries shows an interesting relationship. Inequality begins to rise as countries begin to industrialize, after which inequality then declines. The greatest extremes of inequality—with conspicuous opulence appearing alongside the most abject poverty—occur in middle-income countries, particularly Latin American countries like Peru, Brazil, and Venezuela.

Table 19-3 shows the ratio of the income of the bottom fifth of the population to that of the top fifth. Three groups of countries can be seen there: high-income countries with low inequality (such as Sweden or Japan), high-income countries with high inequality (such as the United States), and middle-income countries with the highest inequality of all (such as Brazil).

INEQUALITY IN LABOR INCOME

What are the sources of inequality? The first place we would look for an answer is labor incomes, which account for about 75 percent of factor incomes. Even if property incomes were distributed equally, much inequality would remain. The forces that produce inequalities in earnings are differences in abilities and skills of labor, in intensities of work, in occupations, and in other factors.

Abilities and Skills

People vary enormously in their abilities—in physical, mental, and temperamental dimensions. However, these personal differences are of little help in explaining the puzzle of income dispersion. Physical traits (such as strength or height or girth) and measured mental traits (such as intelligence quotient or tone perception) explain relatively little of the difference among the earnings of people.

This is not to say that individual abilities matter little. The ability to hit a home run or charm an audience greatly enhances a person's earning potential. But the skills valued in the marketplace are varied and often difficult to measure. Markets tend to reward willingness to take risks, ambition, luck, strokes of engineering genius, good judgment, and hard work—none of which is easily measured in standardized tests. As Mark Twain might have said, "You don't have to be smart to make money. But you *do* have to know how to make money."

Intensities of Work

The intensity of work varies enormously among individuals. The workaholic may log 70 hours a week on the job, never take a vacation, and postpone retirement indefinitely. An ascetic might work just enough to pay for life's necessities. Differences in income might be great simply because of differences in work effort, yet no one would say that economic opportunity was therefore genuinely unequal.

Occupations

One important source of income inequality is people's occupations. At the low end of the scale we find domestic servants, fast-food personnel, and unskilled service workers. A full-time, year-round employee at McDonald's or at a car wash might earn $10,000 a year today.

At the other extreme are the high-earning professionals. What single profession seems to make the most money? In recent years it has without question been medical doctors. Physicians had average earnings of $156,000 in 1993, up almost 40 percent since 1986.

What is the source of such vast differences among occupations? Part of the disparity comes from the years of training needed to become a doctor. Abilities also play a role, for example, in limiting engineering jobs to those who have some quantitative skills. Some jobs pay more because they are dangerous or unpleasant. And when the supply of labor is limited in an occupation, say, because of union restrictions or professional licensing rules, the supply restrictions drive up the wages and salaries of that occupation.

In recent years the trend has been for pay in white-collar jobs to rise much faster than pay in blue-collar jobs. According to the Bureau of Labor Statistics, after adjusting for inflation, wages and salaries for white-collar jobs rose by 6.6 percent from 1981 to 1993, while pay in blue-collar jobs dropped by 4.1 percent over the same period. This has tended to increase the amount of income inequality in American society.

Other Factors

In addition to ability, intensity of work, and occupation, other factors affect the inequality of wage earnings. We saw in Chapter 13 that discrimination and exclusion from certain occupations have played an important role in keeping down the incomes of women and many minority groups.

In addition, the home life and community experience of children have a major impact on later earnings. Children of the affluent probably don't start life ahead of the poor, but they benefit from their environment at every stage. A child of poverty often experiences crowding, poor nutrition, run-down schools, and overworked teachers. The scales are tipped against many inner-city children before they are 10 years old.

Some economists believe that changing technology, immigration, international trade, and the increasing prevalence of winner-take-all markets are creating greater inequality. To take the first of these, recall Chapter 11's discussion of how technology is leveraging individual performance so that it reaches many more people. As a result, while talented athletes made little more than the average factory worker three decades ago, signing bonuses for basketball's free agents today are approaching $100 million. Similar trends are seen in other sports, in entertainment, and in salaries of corporate officers.

INEQUALITY IN PROPERTY INCOME

The greatest disparities in income arise from differences in inherited and acquired wealth. With few exceptions, the people at the very top of the income pyramid derive most of their money from property income. By contrast, the poor own few material goods and therefore earn no income on their nonexistent wealth. Let's examine the sources of differences in wealth—saving, entrepreneurship, and inheritance—and thus of inequalities in property income.

Sources of Wealth

While most people scrimp and save to put away a few dollars for their retirement, such thrift is probably not the major source of wealth in the United States. A study by Laurence Kotlikoff and Lawrence Summers suggests that only a small fraction of personal wealth, perhaps 20 percent, can be explained by life-cycle savings.

The difficulty of accumulating a large fortune by saving out of normal labor earnings can be illustrated using a realistic example. Suppose that the average middle-class family saved about $2000 annually (5 percent of its income) for 20 years. Further suppose that it was wise and managed to obtain a real return after tax of 5 percent each year. At the end of the period, total accumulated wealth would be $73,200—a sum equal to only one-quarter of average family net worth.

Entrepreneurship

Compared to thrift, entrepreneurship is a much more important road to riches. Table 19-4 displays the experience of the top 100 wealth holders in 1996. These data suggest that most of the richest people in America got that way by taking risks and creating profitable new businesses, such as computer software companies, television networks, and retail

America's 100 Richest People			
		Amount of net worth	
Source of wealth	Number of persons	Billions of dollars	Percent
Inheritance:	**24**	**58.0**	**22**
Oil	7	15.9	6
Retail	14	37.7	14
Other	3	4.4	2
Finance	**11**	**38.7**	**14**
Entrepreneurship:	**65**	**176.0**	**64**
Computers	10	51.7	19
Entertainment/communication	17	53.1	19
Oil	2	4.0	1
Real estate	5	8.8	3
Retailing	14	31.9	12
Other	17	26.5	10
Total	**100**	**272.7**	**100**

TABLE 19-4. How Did the Richest Americans Reach the Summit?

In 1996, 100 Americans had net worth of at least $1.1 billion, according to *Forbes* magazine. Most gained their wealth by entrepreneurship. Just under one-quarter are the beneficiaries of *earlier* entrepreneurship (like the Rockefellers). A small fraction gained wealth by shrewd financial investments. (Source: *Forbes,* Oct. 14, 1996.)

chains. The people who invented new products or services or organized the companies that brought them to market got rich on the "Schumpeterian profits" from these innovations. This group of wealthy individuals includes folk heroes like Bill Gates, who built software giant Microsoft, or Sam Walton, who founded Wal-Mart.

Inheritance

What about inheritance? About one-quarter of the 100 wealthiest individuals in 1996 got there by inheriting wealth rather than creating it, but that number may understate the importance of inheritance in determining the distribution of income. According to surveys, two-thirds of the top 1 percent of wealth holders in America inherited a substantial fraction of their property. It is this concentration of inherited wealth in a small number of hands which draws the most strenuous objections from people who are worried about the unequal distribution of wealth.

POVERTY IN AMERICA

Societies tend to define and concentrate on particular groups or problems. In the 1960s, the United States declared "war on poverty" and launched ambitious health and nutrition programs to eradicate economic privation. Before we can analyze antipoverty programs, we must examine the definition of poverty, a surprisingly elusive concept.

What Is Poverty?

The word "poverty" means different things to different people. Clearly poverty is a condition in which people have inadequate incomes, but it is hard to draw an exact line between the poor and the nonpoor. Economists have therefore devised certain techniques which provide the official definition of poverty.

Poverty was officially defined in the 1960s in the United States as an income not adequate to maintain a subsistence level of consumption. This was calculated from family budgets and double-checked by examining the fraction of incomes that was spent on food. Since that time, the budget has been updated by the government's consumer price index to reflect changes in the cost of living. According to the standard definition, the subsistence cost of living for a family of four was $15,569 in 1995. This figure represents the "poverty line" or demarcation between

Poverty in Major Groups, 1995	
Population group	Percent of group in poverty
Total population	13.8
By racial and ethnic group:	
White	11.2
Black	29.3
Hispanic	30.3
By age:	
Under 18 years	20.8
18 to 64 years	11.4
65 years and over	10.5
By type of family:	
Married couple	6.8
Female-headed household,	
no spouse present	36.5
Unrelated subfamilies	46.4

TABLE 19-5. Incidence of Poverty in Different Groups
Whites, married couples, and the elderly have lower-than-average poverty rates. Blacks, Hispanics, and female-headed households have above-average poverty rates. (Source: U.S. Bureau of the Census, *Poverty in the United States: 1995*, Current Population Report, Series P-60, No. 194, September 1996.)

poor and nonpoor families. The poverty line also varies by family size.

While an exact figure for measuring poverty is helpful, scholars recognize that "poverty" is a relative term. The notion of a subsistence budget includes subjective questions of taste and social convention. Housing that is today considered substandard often includes household appliances and plumbing that were unavailable to the millionaires and robber barons of an earlier age. With these concerns in mind, a panel of experts of the National Academy of Sciences recommended in 1995 that the definition of poverty be changed to reflect *relative income status*. The panel recommended that a family be considered poor if its consumption is less than 50 percent of the median family's consumption of food, clothing, and housing. Poverty in the relative-income sense would decline when inequality decreased; poverty would be unchanged if the economy prospered with no change in the distribution of income and consumption. In this new world, a rising tide would lift all boats but not change the fraction of the population considered

poor. This radical new approach is being weighed carefully by the government.

Who Are the Poor?

Poverty hits some groups harder than others. Table 19-5 shows the incidence of poverty in different groups for 1995. While close to 14 percent of the total population was counted as falling below the 1995 poverty line, the rate among black families was almost 3 times that of whites.

Perhaps the most ominous trend is that single-parent families headed by women are an increasingly large share of the poor population. In 1959, about 18 percent of poor families were headed by women raising children alone. By 1995, the poverty rate of that group was 37 percent. Social scientists worry that the children in these families will receive inadequate nutrition and education and will find it difficult to escape from poverty when they are adults.

No discussion of poverty would be accurate without an analysis of the position of minorities. Almost one-third of African-American, Hispanic, and Native American families have below-standard incomes.

Why are so many female-headed and minority families poor? What is the role of discrimination?[1] Experienced observers insist that blatant racial or gender discrimination in which firms simply pay minorities or women less is vanishing today. Yet the relative poverty of women and blacks is increasing. How can we reconcile these two apparently contradictory trends? The major factor at work is the increasing gap between earnings of highly educated and skilled workers and those of unskilled and less educated workers. Over the last 25 years, the wage differential between these two groups has grown sharply, as we will see in the next section. The growing wage gap has hit minority groups particularly hard.

Trends in Inequality

The history of inequality in the United States is shown in Figure 19-3. This shows the ratio of the incomes received by the top fifth of families to those received by the bottom fifth. We can see three distinct periods: falling inequality until World War II,

---

[1] The economics of discrimination in the workplace is analyzed in Chapter 13.

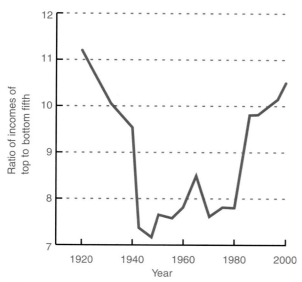

FIGURE 19-3. Trends in Inequality in the United States, 1929–1994

Another measure of inequality is the ratio of the incomes of the top fifth of the population to those of the bottom fifth. The share of top incomes declined after 1929 with the stock market collapse of the 1930s, the low unemployment and reduced barriers to women and minorities during World War II, and the migration from the farm to the city. Since about 1970, income inequality has grown sharply with higher immigration and decline of wages of the unskilled. (Source: U.S. Bureau of the Census, with historical series spliced together by authors.)

stable shares until 1970, then rising inequality over the last two decades. Since 1975, the ratio of upper- to lower-group incomes has increased by almost 50 percent.

Diminishing Inequality: 1929–1975. By any measure, in this period the poor enjoyed the fruits of economic growth along with more affluent groups. According to historical studies, the real income of the bottom fifth of the population rose steadily from the 1920s to the mid-1970s, growing slightly faster than the overall U.S. economy. As a result, the share of total income going to the poorest fifth of families rose from 3.8 percent to about 5 percent between 1929 and 1975. Over the same stretch, the poverty rate dropped so far that some people hoped that poverty could be eliminated completely.

Why did inequality narrow over this period?

Inequality declined in part because of the narrowing of wage inequality. With increasing education of poorer groups and unionization of the work force, the gap declined. Government policies like social security made a big difference for the elderly population, while programs like cash assistance and food stamps for the indigent and unemployment insurance boosted the incomes of other groups. Moreover, our progressive income-tax system, which taxed high incomes more heavily than low incomes, tended to reduce the degree of inequality.

Widening Gaps: 1975–1996. In the last two decades, several of these trends have reversed themselves. The share of total income going to the bottom quintile declined sharply in the 1980s, sinking from 5.4 percent in 1975 to 4.1 percent in 1995. Average real incomes for families in the bottom fifth are well below their peak. And the poverty rate is back up to 13.8 percent, in spite of the long boom that the U.S. economy enjoyed in the 1990s.

At the same time that the poor were falling further behind, the share of income going to the richest Americans soared. From 1979 to 1989, the share of total income going to the top 5 percent of households rose from 16.9 to 18.9 percent. Indeed, a recent study of high-income households indicates that most of the gains at the top were actually at the tip of the income pyramid, going to the top 0.1 percent of taxpayers.

Why did inequality suddenly start to rise again, after falling for so long? After intensely debating this question for years, economists have identified several causes of rising inequality. For one, government policies changed in the early 1980s: Welfare programs for the poor were cut, while the richest groups were helped by the supply-side tax cuts of the 1980s. But government actions are only part of the story. The last two decades saw sharp increases in the compensation of top executives and professionals, while the rising share of births going to single mothers sharply increased the number of female-headed households, which tend to have much higher rates of poverty.

Perhaps the most important cause of rising inequality is the fact that well-educated workers fared far better in the 1980s than their less educated counterparts. Economists have closely studied the *college–high school wage premium,* which is the pay differential between a worker with a college degree and a similar worker with only a high school diploma. Over the last decade the college–high school wage premium has grown sharply. According to the 1994 *Economic Report of the President,* in 1981 college graduates earned about 45 percent more than high school graduates. But by 1992, this difference had widened to almost 65 percent. Since college-educated workers were already paid more, the bigger pay differential had the effect of widening the gap between the top and bottom of the income distribution.

Why did the 1980s see increasing returns to education? One reason was a surge of immigration and competition from foreign imports. Both of these trends tend to hit hardest at less educated workers, who in earlier decades had been able to earn a good living working in factories making automobiles, steel, and other goods. In the 1980s these high-paying manufacturing jobs for workers without college educations began to dry up. In addition, the increasing deregulation and foreign competition tended to erode the market power of labor unions, lowering the relative wages of highly paid union workers. At the same time, many of the new jobs that were being created called for relatively high levels of skills and education. The increasing prevalence of computers in the workplace places a high premium on literacy and analytical skills. All together, these trends have produced the sharp increase of inequality in the United States and most high-income countries.

We can point to at least one factor that did *not* lead to greater inequality: There was no decline in labor's share of national income. The fraction of total incomes coming from wages, salaries, and supplements in 1996 was virtually identical to what it had been a quarter-century earlier. This dog, at least, did not bite.

This concludes our description of the measurement and sources of inequality. In the next section, we turn to an analysis of government programs to combat poverty and reduce inequality. High-income democracies everywhere are rethinking these programs as they redefine the role of the state.

B. ANTIPOVERTY POLICIES

All societies take steps to provide for their poor citizens. But what is given to the poor must come from other groups, and that is undoubtedly the major point of resistance to redistributive programs. In addition, economists worry about the impact of redistribution upon the efficiency and morale of a country. These issues assume greater importance as budget deficits have increased and resistance to tax increases has stiffened. In this section, we review the rise of the welfare state, consider the costs of income redistribution, and survey the current system of income maintenance.

The Rise of the Welfare State

The early classical economists believed the distribution of income was unalterable. They argued that attempts to alleviate poverty by government interventions in the economy were foolish endeavors that would simply end up reducing total national income. This view was contested by the English economist and philosopher John Stuart Mill. While cautioning against interferences with the market mechanism, he argued eloquently that government policies could reduce inequality.

A half-century later, at the end of the nineteenth century, political leaders in Western Europe took steps that marked a historic turning point in the economic role of government. Bismarck in Germany, Gladstone and Disraeli in Britain, followed by Franklin Roosevelt in the United States introduced a new concept of government responsibility for the welfare of the populace.

This marked the rise of the **welfare state,** in which government overrides market forces to protect individuals against specified contingencies and to guarantee people a minimum standard of living.

Important welfare-state policies include public pensions, accident and sickness insurance, unemployment insurance, health insurance, food and housing programs, family allowances, and income supplements for certain groups of people. These policies were introduced gradually from 1880 through to the modern era. The welfare state came late to the United States, being introduced in the New Deal of the 1930s with unemployment insurance and social security. Medical care for the aged and the poor was added in the 1960s. Many attempts to introduce universal health coverage in the United States failed however, with the latest being that of the Clinton administration in 1993–1994 (see Section C below).

THE COSTS OF REDISTRIBUTION

The basic purpose of the modern welfare state is to provide a safety net for those who are temporarily or permanently unable to provide adequate incomes for themselves. One reason for these policies is to promote greater equality.

What are the different concepts of equality? To begin with, democratic societies affirm the principle of equality of *political rights*—generally including the right to vote, trial by jury, and free speech and association. In the 1960s, liberal philosophers espoused the view that people should also have equal *economic opportunity*. In other words, all people should play by the same rules on a level playing field. All should have equal access to the best schools, training, and jobs. Then discrimination on the basis of race or gender or religion would disappear. Many steps were taken to promote greater equality, but inequalities of opportunity have proved very stubborn, and even America of the 1990s falls far short of the goal of equal economic opportunity.

A third, and the most far-reaching, ideal is equality of *economic outcome*. In this idealistic dream, people would have the same consumption whether they were smart or dull, eager or lazy, lucky or unfortunate. Wages would be the same for doctor and nurse, lawyer and secretary. "From each according to his abilities, to each according to his needs" was Karl Marx's formulation of this philosophy.

Today, even the most radical socialist recognizes that some differences in economic outcome are necessary if the economy is to function efficiently. With-

out some differential reward for different kinds of work, how can we ensure that people will do the unpleasant as well as the pleasant work, that they will work on dangerous offshore oil derricks as well as in pleasant parks? Insisting on equality of outcomes would severely hamper the functioning of the economy.

Equality vs. Efficiency

In taking steps to redistribute income from the rich to the poor, governments may harm economic efficiency and reduce the amount of national income available to distribute. On the other hand, if equality is a social good, it is one worth paying for.

The question of how much we are willing to pay in reduced efficiency for greater equity was addressed by Arthur Okun in his "leaky bucket" experiment. He noted that if we value equality, we would approve when a dollar is taken in a bucket from the very rich and given to the very poor. But suppose the bucket of redistribution has a leak in it. Suppose only a fraction—maybe one-half—of each dollar in taxes paid by the rich actually reaches the poor. Then redistribution in the name of equity has been at the expense of economic efficiency.[2]

Okun presented a fundamental dilemma. Redistributional measures like the progressive income tax, analyzed in Chapter 16, will probably reduce real output by reducing incentives to work and save. As a nation considers its income-distribution policies, it will want to weigh the benefit of greater equality against the impact of these policies on total national income.

Redistribution Costs in Diagrams. We can illustrate Okun's point by using the income-possibility curve of Figure 19-4. This graph shows the incomes available to different groups when government programs redistribute income.

We begin by dividing the population in half; the real income of the low-income group is measured on the vertical axis of Figure 19-4, while the income of the upper half is measured on the horizontal axis. At point *A*, which is the pre-redistribution point, no taxes are levied and no transfers are given, so people simply live with their market incomes. In a competi-

---

[2] Arthur M. Okun, *Equality and Efficiency: The Big Tradeoff* (Brookings Institution, Washington, D.C., 1975).

tive economy, point *A* will be efficient and the no-redistribution policy maximizes total national income.

Unfortunately, at laissez-faire point *A*, the upper-income group receives substantially more income than the lower half. People might strive for greater equality by tax and transfer programs, hoping to move toward the point of equal incomes at *E*. If such steps could be taken without reducing national output, the economy would move along the black line from *A* toward *E*. The slope of the *AE* line is −45°, reflecting the assumption about efficiency that the redistributive bucket has no leaks, so every dollar taken from the upper half increases the income of the lower half by exactly $1. Along the −45° line, total national income is constant, indicating that redistributional programs have no impact upon the total national income.

Most redistributive programs do affect efficiency. If a country redistributes income by imposing high tax rates on the wealthiest people, their saving and work effort may be reduced or misdirected, with a resulting lower total national output. They may spend more money on tax lawyers, save less for retirement, or invest less in high yielding but risky innovations. Also, if society puts a guaranteed floor beneath the incomes of the poor, the sting of poverty will be reduced and the poor may work less. All these reactions to redistributive programs reduce the total size of real national income.

In terms of Okun's experiment, we might find that for every $100 of taxation on the rich, the income of the poor increased by only $50, with the rest dissipated because of reduced effort or administrative costs. The bucket of redistribution has developed a large leak. Costly redistribution is shown by the *ABZ* curve in Figure 19-4. Here, the hypothetical frontier of real incomes bends away from the −45° line because taxes and transfers produce inefficiencies.

The experience of socialist countries exemplifies how attempts to equalize incomes by expropriating property from the rich can end up hurting everyone. By prohibiting private ownership of businesses, socialist governments reduced the inequalities that arise from large property incomes. But the reduced incentives for work, investment, and innovation crippled this radical experiment of "to each according to his needs" and impoverished entire countries. By

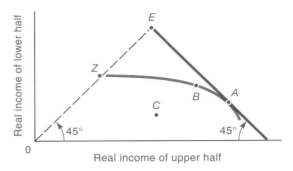

FIGURE 19-4. Redistributing Income May Harm Economic Efficiency

Point *A* marks the most efficient outcome, with maximal national output. If society could redistribute with no loss of efficiency, the economy would move toward point *E*. Because redistributive programs generally create distortions and efficiency losses, the path of redistribution might move along the rust-colored line *ABZ*. Society must decide how much efficiency to sacrifice to gain greater equality. Why would everyone want to avoid inefficient redistributional programs that take the economy to point *C*?

1990, comparisons of living standards in East and West had convinced many socialist countries that private ownership of business would benefit the living standards of workers as well as capitalists.

How Big Are the Leaks?

Okun characterized our redistributive system of taxes and transfers as a leaky bucket. But just how big are the leaks in the American economy? Is the country closer to Figure 19-4's point *A*, where the leaks are negligible? Or to *B*, where they are substantial? Or to *Z*, where the redistributive bucket is in fact a sieve? To find the answer, we must examine the major inefficiencies induced by high tax rates and by generous income-support programs: administrative costs, damage to work and savings incentives, and socioeconomic costs.

- The government must hire tax collectors to raise revenues and social security accountants to disburse them. These are clear inefficiencies or regrettable necessities, but they are small: the Internal Revenue Service spends only half a penny on administrative costs for each dollar of collected revenues.

- As the tax collector's bite grows larger and larger, might I not become discouraged and end up working less? Tax rates might conceivably be so high that total revenues are actually lower than they would be at more modest tax rates. Empirical evidence, however, suggests that the damage of taxes on work effort is limited. For a few groups, the labor supply curve may actually be backward-bending, indicating that a tax on wages might increase rather than decrease work effort. Most studies find a small impact of taxes on labor effort for middle-income and high-income workers. However, there may well be substantial impacts of the tax and transfer system on the behavior of poor people, a controversial topic to which we will turn shortly.

- Perhaps the most important potential leakage from the revenue bucket is the savings component. Some believe that current government programs discourage saving and investment. They worry that the nation's savings rate has declined sharply because of generous social programs—especially social security and Medicare—that reduce the need for people to save for old age and health contingencies. These economists point to the declining national savings rate over the last two decades as evidence of the impact of government programs. For most of the postwar period, the national savings rate averaged around 8 percent of total national product. That number has declined to around 3 percent in the last 5 years. Even economists who do not agree that government redistributive programs are the cause of the declining national savings rate today study how the government can take steps to reverse this trend.

- Some claim that the leaks cannot be found in the cost statistics of the economist; instead, the costs of equality are seen in attitudes rather than in dollars. Is the business ethic downplayed? Are young people so turned off by the prospect of high taxes that they turn on to drugs and idleness? Is the welfare system leading to a permanent underclass, a society of people who are trapped in a culture of dependency?

- Some people criticize the entire notion of costly redistribution, arguing as follows: Poverty is rooted in malnourishment in the early years, broken families, illiteracy at home, poor education, and lack of job training. Poverty begets poverty; the vicious cycle of malnutrition, poor education, drug dependency, low productivity, and low incomes leads to yet another generation of poor families. Programs providing health care and adequate food for poor families will increase productivity and efficiency rather than decrease output. By breaking the vicious cycle of poverty today, we will be raising the skills, human capital, and productivity of the children of poverty tomorrow. Programs to break the cycle of poverty are investments that require resources today to increase productivity tomorrow.

Adding Up the Leaks

When all the leaks are added up, how big are they? Okun argued that the leaks are small, particularly when funds for redistributive programs are drawn from the tap of a broad-based income tax. Others disagree strenuously, pointing to high marginal tax rates or overly generous transfer programs as confusing and destructive of economic efficiency.

What is the reality? While much research has been undertaken on the cost of redistribution, the truth has proved elusive. A cautious verdict is that there are but modest losses to economic efficiency from redistributional programs of the kind used in the United States today. The efficiency costs of redistribution appear small as compared to the economic costs of poverty in malnutrition, poor health, lost job skills, and human misery. But countries whose welfare-state policies have gone far beyond those in the United States see major inefficiencies. Egalitarian countries like Sweden or the Netherlands, which provide cradle-to-grave protection for their citizens, find declining labor-force participation, growing unemployment, and rising budget deficits.

Countries need to design their policies carefully to avoid the extremes of unacceptable inequality or great inefficiency.

ANTIPOVERTY POLICIES: PROGRAMS AND CRITICISMS

All societies provide for their aged, their young, and their sick. Sometimes, the support comes from families or religious organizations. Over the last century, nations have increasingly moved the source of

Federal Programs for the Poor, 1996		
Program	Amount ($, billion)	Percent of total federal spending
All income-security programs	**826.3**	**53.0**
General programs:	**592.7**	**38.0**
Social security	350.2	22.4
Medicare	174.2	11.2
Other (veterans, other retirement)	43.4	2.8
Unemployment compensation	24.9	1.6
Programs for the poor:	**233.6**	**15.0**
Medicaid	82.1	5.3
Other income security	64.3	4.1
Food and nutrition	40.4	2.6
Earned-income tax credit	24.3	1.6
Housing assistance	16.4	1.1
International development and aid	6.1	0.4

TABLE 19-6. Most Federal Income-Security Dollars Go for General Programs Like Social Security

Federal programs for income security are largely concentrated on the population as a whole, rather than the poor. Note as well the high cost of health programs for both the poor and the nonpoor. (Source: *Budget of the United States Government, 1998*. Earned-income tax credit figure includes both outlays and reduced tax revenues.)

income support for the needy to central governments. Yet, as governments have assumed larger responsibilities for more people, the fiscal burdens of transfer programs have grown steadily. Today, most high-income countries face the prospect of rising tax burdens to finance public health and retirement programs as well as income-support programs for poor families. This rising tax burden has provoked a sharp backlash against "welfare programs," particularly in the United States. Let's review the major antipoverty programs and recent reforms.

Income-Security Programs

What are the major income-security programs today? Let's look briefly at a few of the programs that have been established in the United States.

Most income-security programs are targeted at the elderly rather than the poor, as is shown in Table 19-6. The major programs are social security, which is a contributory federal retirement program, and Medicare, which is a subsidized health program for those over 65 years old. These two programs are the largest transfer programs in the United States and in

most other high-income countries, and they are projected to be a source of continued spending growth over the coming decades.

Programs specifically targeted to poor households are a patchwork quilt of federal, state, and local programs. Some of these are cash assistance; some subsidize particular spending (such as the food-stamps program, which provides poor families with coupons that allow them to purchase food at a small fraction of its market cost); and others are transfers "in kind," such as Medicaid, which provides poor families with free health care. Most of the programs targeted to poor families have shrunk sharply over the last two decades.

The most controversial program was cash assistance to poor parents with small children. This program was drastically reformed in 1996, and we will discuss the reform below.

How much do all federal programs add up to in terms of budget expenditures? Table 19-6 shows the level of federal spending for income-security programs for both the general population and poor households. All federal poverty programs today amount to 15 percent of the total federal budget.

Incentive Problems of the Poor

One of the major obstacles faced by poor families is that the rules in most welfare programs severely reduce the incentives of low-income adults to seek work. If a poor person on welfare gets a job, the government will trim back food stamps, income-support payments, and rent subsidies, and the person might even lose medical benefits. We might say that poor people face high marginal "tax rates" (or, more accurately, "benefit-reduction rates") because welfare benefits are sharply reduced as earnings rise.

The following calculation for a family of three (mother and two children) living in Pennsylvania in the 1990s illustrates the problem. We choose the example of Pennsylvania because benefits in that state are close to the national average. If the mother did not have a job, the family would receive welfare benefits of $4584 and food stamps worth $1549, for a total disposable income of $6133. Suppose the parent takes a full-time job, earning $8000 a year. She would lose all the welfare benefits, but would retain $1306 worth of food stamps. After child-care and work-related expenses of $2400, disposable income would equal $6906.

The net gain from taking this $8000 job would be a gain in disposable income of $773 a year; the increase in disposable income is only 9.7 percent of the increase in earnings. If we consider benefit reductions as a kind of "tax," the tax rates on the working poor can easily reach 90 percent—far above the rate faced by the richest Americans and surely a major disincentive to the avid pursuit of work.

The Earned-Income Tax Credit

One popular and rapidly growing program for low-income workers is the *earned-income tax credit.* This credit applies to labor incomes and is in effect a wage supplement. In 1996, it amounted to a supplement to earned income of as much as 40 percent up to a maximum of $3556, and it was then phased out for incomes over $11,650. It is known as a "refundable" credit because it is actually paid to a taxpayer when the taxpayer owes no taxes.

Table 19-7 shows the impact of the earned-income tax credit for a family at different income levels. This example shows that the government can simultaneously support the poorest families and maintain an incentive for people to seek gainful employment.

Current Structure of Earned-Income Tax Credit, 1996		
Market earnings ($)	Algebraic tax (+ if tax; − if benefits received) ($)	Income after tax and credit ($)
0	0	0
4,000	−1,610	5,610
8,000	−3,210	11,210
12,000	−3,469	15,469
24,000	−941	24,941
28,000	−99	28,099

TABLE 19-7. Earned-Income Tax Credit Increases Reward for Work but Does Not Touch the Very Poorest

Under the current earned-income tax credit, labor earnings are increased by a supplement of up to 40 percent up to a maximum of $3,556, then phased out. This provides "negative taxes" for the very low-income wage earners. (Assumes two children.) (Source: U.S. Department of the Treasury.)

Compare this approach with that of the existing welfare system, examined above, to see how the current system destroys incentives while the negative income tax would motivate people to look for work.

THE BATTLE OVER WELFARE REFORM

The current welfare system has few defenders. Some want to dismantle it; others, to strengthen it. Some wish to devolve responsibility for income support to states, localities, or families; others, to strengthen the federal role. These disparate approaches reflect disparate views of poverty and lead to strikingly different policy proposals.

Two Views of Poverty

Social scientists put forth a wide variety of proposals to cure or alleviate poverty. The different approaches often reflect differing views of the roots of poverty. Proponents of strong government action see poverty as the result of social and economic conditions over which the poor have little control. They stress malnutrition, poor schools, broken families, discrimination, lack of job opportunities, and a dangerous environment as central determinants of the fate of the poor. If you hold this view, you might well believe that government bears a responsibility to alleviate poverty—either by providing income to the poor or by correcting the conditions that produce poverty.

A second view holds that poverty grows out of maladaptive individual behavior—behavior that is the responsibility of individuals and is properly cured by the poor themselves. In earlier centuries, laissez-faire apologists held that the poor were shiftless, lazy, or drunk; as a charity worker wrote almost a century ago, "Want of employment . . . is, as often as not, [caused by] drink." Sometimes the government itself is blamed for breeding dependency upon a patchwork of government programs that squelch individual initiative. Critics who hold these views advocate that the government should cut back on welfare programs so that people will develop their own resources.

The poverty debate was succinctly summarized by the eminent social scientist William Wilson:

> Liberals have traditionally emphasized how the plight of disadvantaged groups can be related to the problems of the broader society, including problems of discrimination and social class subordination. . . . Conservatives, in contrast, have traditionally stressed the importance of different group values and competitive resources in accounting for the experiences of the disadvantaged.[3]

Much of today's debate can be better understood if these two views and their implications are factored into the political equation.

Expanding the Federal Role: The Negative Income Tax

Contemplating the perverse effects of the current welfare system on economic efficiency and the social structure of the country, economists of varied political persuasions have concluded that the welfare system needs a fundamental reform. One important approach—proposed by conservatives like Milton Friedman of Chicago and liberals like James Tobin of Yale—is to consolidate all income-support programs into a single unified federal program of cash assistance.

This ambitious reform proposal is called the **negative income tax**. The basic notion is simple. When I

---

[3] William Julius Wilson, "Cycles of Deprivation and the Underclass Debate," *Social Service Review* (December 1985), pp. 541–559.

make $50,000 a year, I pay positive income taxes (as seen in Table 16-4). When I earn an extra thousand dollars, I pay extra taxes of $160, leaving me $840 of additional disposable income. Thus the incentive to earn more is preserved.

Next consider a poor family earning, say, $8000 in 1996. We might decide that such a family deserves an income above $8000, especially if it has earned its $8000 by work and if the family has small children to support. The government wants to provide further income support. Put differently, the family should not pay taxes on its income but should receive a *negative* income tax in the form of an income supplement.

The problem is how to continue to provide government income support without hurting the family's incentives to work. The way to do this is to provide a basic allowance and then permit the family to keep a significant portion of any earnings. A family might receive a basic allowance of $8000 and then get taxed 50 percent of any income. Just as people with high incomes can keep most of their earnings if they earn more money, similarly a poor family could keep much of its additional earnings if a family member gets a job.

In analyzing different systems for supplementing the incomes of the poor, the basic dilemma is whether to increase incentives for work or to increase the living standards of the very poor. The earned-income tax credit is one extreme, which gives nothing to those who do not work and supplements the earnings of those who do work. At the other pole is the current welfare system, which gives a generous allowance to poor families and then "taxes" back the earnings at a high rate. As noted above, such plans often have marginal tax rates on earnings near or even beyond 100 percent. The negative income tax lies between these two poles, retaining an incentive to work yet continuing to provide income to poor, nonworking families.

U.S. Welfare Reform: 1996 Style

In the battle over reforming welfare, the latest step came in 1996 with a radical reform of federal cash assistance. First enacted in the 1930s, the major cash assistance to poor families was Aid to Families with Dependent Children. This was a federal-state *entitlement program*, meaning that anyone who met certain qualifications could receive the benefits as a matter of law.

In 1996, an unusual alliance of a Democratic President who ran on the platform of "reforming welfare as we know it" and a sharply conservative Republican Congress completely changed the rules for cash assistance. The old program was replaced by the Temporary Assistance for Needy Families (TANF) Act of 1996. This act removed the federal entitlement to cash benefits and turned the program over to the 50 states.

The major provisions of the new program are the following:

- A "block grant," a fixed amount of federal funding, is given to the states to fund the federal part of cash benefits. This replaced an earlier system in which the federal government picked up 50 percent or more of state spending.
- The entitlement for federal cash assistance under TANF is removed.
- Each family is subject to a lifetime limit of 5 years of benefits under the federally supported program. After 5 years, TANF funds can no longer be used to support the family, even if it moves to a new state or has been off the welfare rolls for a number of years.
- Adults in the program must engage in work activities after 2 years of benefits.
- Legal immigrants may be excluded from TANF benefits.
- Other major low-income–support programs are largely unchanged.

Most economists agree that the 1996 welfare reform was a radical experiment in social policy that will have many unforeseen consequences in the years to come. The provisions will be implemented gradually over the next few years, and many features are at present poorly understood by both the government and welfare recipients. To the extent that the loss of benefits forces people to seek work, this will increase the supply of relatively uneducated and unskilled labor. This large increase in supply will tend to lower wages of the lowest paid workers and increase income inequality (much the same way that the recent sharp increase in immigration has contributed to lowering of wages of the unskilled in the last two decades). If equilibrium wages of some workers are driven down below the minimum wage, this may also lead to an increase in the unemployment rate of these groups.

One important feature of the new law is the *devolution* of responsibility for cash assistance to the states. This provision is one of the sharpest contrasts with the philosophy behind centralized income-support programs such as the negative income tax. Many economists believe that giving states "block grants" or lump-sum amounts and placing decision-making responsibility in the states for benefits of a mobile population will give strong incentives for states to trim welfare benefits to reduce the costs and the burden of the low-income population. This has been called a "race to the bottom" in which the equilibrium is for states to have the lowest possible benefits. It is unclear whether such an outcome was the intention of the 1996 welfare reform program, but it is likely to be a major force in welfare politics in the coming years.

C. HEALTH CARE: THE PROBLEM THAT WON'T GO AWAY

Each generation has its battleground for warring views of the welfare state. Earlier decades saw debates over the income tax, pensions for the elderly, and redistributive taxation. In the early 1990s, Americans engaged in a protracted struggle over the way that health care should be organized and financed. The Clinton administration bet its political fortunes in 1993 on passing uniform and comprehensive national health insurance. It lost the bet and was humiliated in the 1994 congressional elections, in which Republicans introduced *A Contract with America,* which argued for smaller government and private-sector health care.

Even as this debate took place, the health-care market was being transformed by a trend known as "managed competition." Under managed competition, people were increasingly joining health maintenance organizations, or HMOs, that exercised greater vigilance over costs and access to services and began to turn medical care into a profit-oriented business enterprise.

This final section surveys the economics of health care. This is an important sector of the economy as well as a fascinating area in itself. In addition, the analysis of health care will provide us with a laboratory for understanding the conflict between efficiency and equity and the importance of externalities and market failures such as inadequate information. We see here many of the issues that arise in deciding how far to extend government's role in the economy and how to redesign the welfare state.

GENESIS OF THE HEALTH-CARE DEBATE

What is the background of the debate about health care? In the United States, the health-care system is a partnership between the market system and the government. In recent years, this system has produced some remarkable accomplishments. Many terrible diseases, such as smallpox and polio, have been eradicated. Life expectancy, one of the key indexes of health, has improved in developing countries more from 1950 to 1990 than during the entire span of recorded history. Advances in medical technology, from arthroscopic knee surgery to sophisticated anti-cancer drugs, have enabled more people to live pain-free and productive lives.

Even with these great achievements, major health problems remained unsolved in the United States in the early 1990s. Infant mortality was higher than in many countries with lower incomes; 15 percent of Americans were without insurance coverage; great disparities in care existed between rich and poor; and communicable diseases like AIDS and tuberculosis were spreading.

The issue that most concerned the public, business community, and political leaders, however, was the exploding costs of health care. Health care rose from 4 percent of national output (GDP) in 1940 to 7 percent in 1970 and reached 14 percent in 1993. Virtually everyone agreed that the U.S. health system had contributed greatly to the nation's health, but many worried that it was becoming unaffordable.

Special Economic Features of Health Care

Good health is a crucial ingredient in economic welfare and one that tends to become more important to people as their incomes rise. The health-care system in the United States has three characteristics that have contributed to the rapid growth in that sector in recent years: a high income elasticity, rapid technological advance, and increasing insulation of consumers from prices.

Health care shows a high income elasticity, indicating that ensuring a long and fit life becomes increasingly important as people are able to pay for other essential needs. Goods with high income elasticities, other things constant, tend to take a growing share of consumer spending.

Coupled with a high income elasticity are the rapid developments in medical technology that have occurred during this century. Advances in fundamental biomedical knowledge, discovery and use of a wide variety of vaccines and pharmaceuticals, progress in understanding the spread of communicable diseases, and increasing public awareness of the role of individual behavior in areas such as smoking, drinking, and driving—all these have contributed to the remarkable improvement in the health status of Americans.

These advances have had the unusual consequence of stimulating spending in the health-care sector. The reason is that the new technologies have often been product inventions, that is, inventions that create new or improved products and therefore open up new markets. For example, when the antibiotic drug penicillin was discovered, it created a whole new market and stimulated spending in the health-care sector.

A third feature of the health-care industry that has stimulated rapid spending growth is the increasing insulation of the consumer from the prices of health care. Health-care coverage in the United

States is largely provided by employers as a tax-free fringe benefit.[4] Tax-free status is in effect a government subsidy. In 1960, most health-care expenses were paid directly by consumers; by 1990, only 23 percent of expenses were paid directly by consumers. Indeed, for hospital care, third parties like HMOs or the government pay 95 percent of costs, while the consumer pays only about 5 percent of the cost. This phenomenon is sometimes called the "third-party payment syndrome" to indicate that when a third party pays the bill, the consumer is often inattentive to the cost.

All these forces (high income elasticity, development of new technologies, and increasing scope of third-party payments) plus others (such as the aging of the population) contribute to the rapid growth of expenditures on medical care.

THE ROLE OF GOVERNMENT IN HEALTH CARE

A growing level of spending on health care is not sufficient to justify heavy government regulation, for it may simply indicate the economic vitality of the industry (as in computers). What are the reasons for government intervention in the health industry? In fact, both efficiency and equity considerations motivate government policy.

One set of concerns lies in the fact that control of communicable diseases and development of basic science are public goods that the market will not efficiently provide. Recall that *public goods* are ones whose benefits are indivisibly spread among the entire community, whether or not individuals choose to purchase the public good. *Private goods,* by contrast, are ones with no external costs or benefits. Eradication of smallpox benefited billions of potential victims, yet no firm could collect even a small fraction of the benefits. When one person stops smoking because of knowledge of its dangers, or when another person uses condoms on learning of the way AIDS is transmitted, these steps do not make such

activities less valuable to others. In such situations, government research and public-health programs can offset the market failures that arise when significant externalities and public goods are present.

A second set of market failures arises because of uncertainty and failure of insurance markets. One significant problem is the presence of *asymmetric information* among patients, doctors, and insurance companies. Medical conditions are often isolated occurrences for patients, so patients may be completely dependent upon doctors' recommendations regarding the appropriate level of health care. Sometimes, as when patients are wheeled into the operating room, they may be incapacitated and unable to choose treatment strategies for themselves, so demand depends upon the recommendations of suppliers. Special protection must be given to ensure that consumers do not unwittingly purchase unnecessary, poor-quality, or high-cost services.[5]

Another inefficiency arises because of informational asymmetries between the patient and the third-party payer, say, an insurance company. Insurance is usually priced on the basis of the average cost of service rather than the marginal cost. This leads to inefficiency because people generally know more about their medical condition than do insurance companies. Faced with average-cost premiums, the low-risk individual may choose not to buy insurance. This leads to *adverse selection*, increasing the average riskiness and the cost for those who participate. It is not surprising that healthy people in their twenties are the group most likely to be uninsured.

An additional complication for insurance arises because of *moral hazard*, which occurs when insurance reduces the incentives for individuals to avoid risk and expense through prudent behavior. A recent economic experiment measured the extent of moral hazard by providing one randomly selected

---

[4] The origin of the employer-provided system is instructive: During and after World War II, nonwage benefits were exempt from federal price and wage controls. This gave businesses the incentive to expand such benefits, and employer-provided medical coverage developed. This is a good example of "the law of unintended consequences," whereby a policy designed for one purpose has long-lasting and surprising consequences in other areas.

[5] Society has devised numerous mechanisms for dealing with situations where there are great informational asymmetries between buyer and seller. One mechanism is the brand name. When you buy relatively simple commodities like cars or soft drinks from Toyota or Coca-Cola, you are paying a premium for the quality control provided by those organizations. For more complicated areas like medical care or legal advice, there is no standard commodity or obvious remedy for informational asymmetries, and society relies on "the professional" to bridge the knowledge gap. By law and custom, professionals are put in positions of trust to provide appropriate services. Compare the amounts of confidence consumers put in the recommendations of doctors and used-car dealers.

Problem area	Current approach	Alternatives		
		Pure-market solution	Nationalized health service	Fedicare
Public goods (contagious diseases, basic science, and consumer information)	Through public-health expenditures where covered.	Does not provide public good.	Through public-health expenditures.	Through public-health expenditures.
Market failures:				
Moral hazard (third-party payment syndrome)	Major source of cost escalation and waste because of weak controls over costs.	None because consumer pays for service.	Very serious because all covered services are free. Can be alleviated through rationing and long waits for service.	Potentially serious if no charges for services. Can be alleviated if copayments and deductibles are on plans.
Adverse selection	Serious for uncovered population.	None because consumer pays for service.	Not a problem because of universal coverage.	Not a problem because of universal coverage.
Maldistribution of medical services	Uneven problem: employed, poor, and aged are covered; working poor and unemployed are vulnerable.	Very unequal: market-determined distribution of health care.	Universal and uniform.	Universal and uniform.

TABLE 19-8. Alternative Solutions for Health-Care Market Failures

The current system of health care in the United States experiences high cost because of large subsidies without a budget constraint yet fails to provide coverage for large numbers of people. Alternatives must find a path that rations health care efficiently and equitably while continuing to provide incentives for technological advance.

group of families full insurance and another group a plan with high levels of *coinsurance* (which denotes that the individual shares the costs with the insurer). The fully insured families used 30 percent more medical services, yet follow-up studies could determine no difference in the health status of the two groups after a 3- to 5-year period. The fact that a lower price increased quantity demanded is, of course, hardly surprising to economists; it simply reflects the law of downward-sloping demand.

A third concern of government policy is *equity*: to provide a minimum standard of medical care for the poor. In part, good health for all is increasingly viewed as a basic human right in wealthy countries. But good health for poor people is also a good social investment. Inadequate health care is particularly harmful for poor people not only because they tend to be sicker than wealthier individuals but also because their incomes are almost entirely derived from their labor. A healthier population is a more productive population because healthy people have higher earnings and require less medical care. But nowhere is inadequate care more costly than with children. The medical condition of poor and minority children in the United States has in some dimensions actually worsened in recent years. Sick children are handicapped at the start: They are less likely to attend school, perform more poorly when they do attend, are more likely to drop out, and are less likely to get good jobs at high pay when they grow up. No country can prosper when a significant fraction of its children have inadequate medical care.

Alternative Approaches to Health-Care Reform

The combination of rising costs, a growing number of uninsured, and lagging health status has led to widespread calls for fundamental health-care reform in the United States. What are the major alternatives? At one extreme is the *pure-market* solution. With this approach, which was traditional in most countries until this century, each family pays 100 percent of its medical expenses and there are no government programs providing for public goods or shouldering the burden of medical care for the poor. As Table 19-8 indicates, the pure-market solution solves the market failures of adverse selection and moral hazard, but it does so at great cost to individuals with high medical expenses; more worrisome, a pure-market solution does not provide for public goods like basic science and prevention of communicable diseases. Given the adverse consequences of the pure-market model, it is not surprising that few economists or political figures endorse it.

At the other extreme is a *nationalized health service*, in which health care is publicly provided to all on an equal basis. This approach, used in the Medicare system for the elderly in the United States, solves many of the major market failures. Because health care is universal, there is no adverse selection, and government can provide the public goods of information and prevention. However, critics of nationalized health service point to a number of unattractive features. First, health care would be paid for in taxes or mandatory fees, increasing tax rates, raising business costs, and harming incentives to work and save. Second, since health care is free under this plan, moral hazard would be severe because consumers would have few incentives to limit their use of services; medical costs would grow ever more rapidly.

Nationalized systems have another problem as well, which arises because they limit costs by capping the fees and incomes of doctors and restricting the range of eligible services. The combination of price ceilings and subsidized service leads to chronic excess demand in many medical markets. By preventing market forces from operating in the medical market, shortages crop up, and demand must somehow be choked off. This phenomenon is known as nonprice rationing. *Nonprice rationing* usually takes the form of simply waiting for services. In other cases, the health provider rations the service by deciding which patient is most deserving. Examples of supplier rationing are seen in the British and Canadian national health services, in which there are generally long waits for elective surgery; similarly, because central-city emergency rooms in the United States provide much free care to low-income households, they are often crowded with patients who are there for routine care, even though few are in grave condition.[6] What is at work here? Because price is not allowed to rise to balance supply and demand, some other mechanism must be found to "clear the market."

Figure 19-5 on page 364 illustrates nonprice rationing in the medical market. There are only Q_0 units of medical care available. The market-clearing price would come at C, where quantities supplied and demanded are equal. However, the government pays 80 percent of all medical costs. Because the consumer pays only 20 percent of costs, the quantity demanded is Q_1. The segment from A to B is unsatisfied demand, which is subject to nonprice rationing; the greater the subsidy, the more nonprice rationing must be used.

Fedicare: Harnessing the Market

Virtually everyone agrees that the current system is wasteful and expensive—but few can agree on the appropriate reform. Rather than presenting a smorgasbord of different proposals, we focus here on a single plan which we call *Fedicare*. This is essentially a medical negative income tax, very similar to the neg-

---

[6] An interesting example of rationing comes in wartime, when medics employ *triage*. This practice derives from the French procedure in World War I of dividing the wounded into three categories: (1) those who would be helped by medical treatment, (2) those who would survive without attention, and (3) those who were likely to die no matter how much attention they received. Only the first category received most medical services. Can you see why this hard-headed strategy is "cost-effective" in that it maximizes the number of lives saved? Such a strategy has been proposed by the World Bank in its 1993 *World Development Report*. The World Bank recommends that countries focus on those medical treatments that show the greatest increase in the number of "disability-adjusted life years" per dollar of expenditure. This approach is similar to that of consumers maximizing utility or firms maximizing profits. Some states in the United States have proposed rationing medical care on a similar principle.

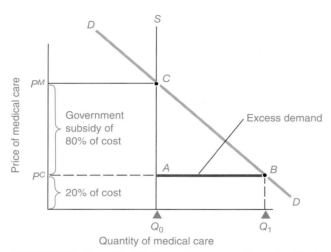

FIGURE 19-5. Free Health Care Guarantees Nonprice Rationing

When governments provide free or subsidized access to medical care, some way must be found to ration out the limited services. In the example of a government subsidy, when quantity demanded exceeds quantity supplied, excess demand *AB* is choked off by some mechanism other than price. Most often, people must wait for nonemergency services, sometimes for hours, sometimes for months.

ative income tax sketched in the last section except that it applies only to health care and not to all incomes.[7]

The basic idea under Fedicare is that the federal government ensures universal health care by providing subsidized medical insurance to all Americans. An important feature of the plan is to disconnect health insurance from employment, thus ending an accidental provision which has led to increasing numbers of uninsured people with the rise of casual and part-time employment. Under the Fedicare plan, the government defines a minimum package of medical benefits (hospital, physicians services, mental health, and so on). The plan could be relatively modest or quite generous depending upon the amount of the budget the country desired to allocate to subsidized medical care. For example, the standard package might cost $2000 per person annually.

The lowest-income family would pay nothing for its Fedicare insurance. However, as income rose, a family would pay an increasing fraction of the cost of the plan. For example, a family of four might start paying for Fedicare when its income reached $10,000, with a "tax rate" of 20 percent. Hence, Fedicare would cost this family nothing at $10,000 of income, $1400 at $17,000 of income, $2000 at an income of $20,000, and so on. Under this plan, payment for health care would come from the government and individuals rather than out of wages.

Such a program would solve some of the problems of the current system without many of the disadvantages of either nationalized health care or a pure laissez-faire system. It would remove the problems of adverse selection and maldistribution of health services through universal coverage. If there were copayments and deductibles on health services, it would alleviate the third-party payment syndrome. And by continuing to encourage the private provision of medical care, it would promote the rapid technological advance that has been enjoyed over recent decades.

Depending upon the plan design, it might initially increase government health-care spending. The prospect, however, is that by explicitly limiting medical benefits and tax deductibility, the long-run costs might well be less than the cost of the current system.

---

[7] The proposal sketched here is similar to that proposed by the Bush administration in 1992 and was developed by Michael Graetz and James Tobin of Yale University.

In summary:

Health care is fundamentally no different from other goods and services in the economy. Physicians, nursing care, hospitalization, psychiatric care, and other services are limited in supply. The demands of the populace—summing up the critical, the reasonable, the marginal, and the ridiculous—far outstrip the available resources. But the resources must be somehow rationed out. Rationing according to the dollar votes of consumers is unacceptable because it does too much damage to the public health, leaves too many crucial demands unmet, and impoverishes too many. What should be the scope of the market, and what nonmarket mechanism should be used where the market is supplanted? These questions are the crux of the great debate about medical care.

REDEFINING GOVERNMENT'S ROLE AT CENTURY'S END

The last four chapters have reviewed the major debates about government's role in the mixed econ-omy. We have seen that a modern mixed economy performs four economic functions: It combats market failures, redistributes income, stabilizes the economy, promotes long-term economic growth, and conducts international economic policy. Each of these is essential. No serious person today proposes to allow nuclear dumping, to let poor orphans starve in the streets, to sell off the central bank, and to shut down all foreign embassies.

As the mixed economy marks its centenary, how should its mission be redefined? The central lesson we read from America and Europe is the following: The critical role of the government also lends a special responsibility for government to operate efficiently. Every public dollar spent on wasteful programs could be used for promoting scientific research or alleviating hunger. Every private dollar wasted because of inefficient taxation reduces people's opportunity to improve their housing or go to college. The central premise of economics is that resources are scarce—and this applies equally to private funds and to government funds, which must be pried out of taxpayers.

SUMMARY

A. The Sources of Inequality

1. In the last century, the classical economists believed that inequality was a universal constant, unchangeable by public policy. This view does not stand up to scrutiny. Poverty made a glacial retreat over the early part of this century, and absolute incomes for those in the bottom part of the income distribution rose sharply. Since the early 1970s, this trend has reversed, and inequality has increased.

2. The Lorenz curve is a convenient device for measuring the spreads or inequalities of income distribution. It shows what percentage of total income goes to the poorest 1 percent of the population, to the poorest 10 percent, to the poorest 95 percent, and so forth.

3. Poverty is essentially a relative notion. In the United States, poverty was defined in terms of the adequacy of incomes in the early 1960s. By this standard of measured income, little progress has been made in the last decade.

4. The distribution of American income today appears to be less unequal than in the early part of this century or than in less developed countries now. But it still shows a considerable measure of inequality and increasing inequality over the last two decades. Wealth is even more unequally distributed than is income, both in the United States and in other capitalist economies.

5. To explain the inequality in income distribution, we can look separately at labor income and property income. Labor earnings vary because of differences in abilities and in intensities of work (both hours and effort) and because occupational earnings differ, due to divergent amounts of human capital, among other factors.

6. Property incomes are more unevenly distributed than labor earnings, largely because of the great disparities in wealth. Inheritance helps the children of the wealthy begin ahead of the average person; only a small fraction of America's wealth can be accounted for by life-cycle savings.

B. Antipoverty Policies

7. Political philosophers write of three types of equality: (*a*) equality of political rights, such as the right to vote; (*b*) equality of opportunity, providing equal access to

jobs, education, and other social systems; and (*c*) equality of outcome, whereby people are guaranteed equal incomes or consumptions. Whereas the first two types of equality are increasingly accepted in most advanced democracies like the United States, equality of outcome is generally rejected as impractical and too harmful to economic efficiency.

8. Equality has costs as well as benefits; the costs show up as drains from Okun's "leaky bucket." That is, attempts to reduce income inequality by progressive taxation or welfare payments may harm economic incentives to work or save and may thereby reduce the size of national output. Potential leakages are administrative costs and reduced hours of work or savings rates.

9. Major programs to alleviate poverty are welfare payments, food stamps, Medicaid, and a group of smaller or less targeted programs. As a whole, these programs are criticized because they impose high benefit-reduction rates (or marginal "tax" rates) on low-income families when families begin to earn wages or other income.

10. People are divided on how to improve the current income-support system. One proposal, called the negative income tax, would consolidate current programs into a unified federal cash income supplement. The supplement would be reduced (that is, income would be "taxed") at a moderate rate (say, one-third or one-half), so that low-income families would have a significant incentive to seek market employment. The United States has adopted a variant known as the earned-income tax credit, which provides a wage supplement to families with low earnings.

11. A second approach is reflected in the 1996 U.S. Temporary Assistance for Needy Families (TANF) program. This approach attempts to reduce long-term welfare dependency by putting time limits on benefits and devolving decisions to the states. Some believe this will result in a "race to the bottom" in which states compete to make themselves unattractive to potential beneficiaries by lowering benefits.

C. Health Care: The Problem That Won't Go Away

12. Health care is one of the largest and most rapidly growing sectors of the economy. It is characterized by multiple market failures that lead governments to intervene heavily. Health systems have major externalities, which include preventing communicable diseases and discovering new biomedical knowledge. In addition, there are market failures such as the asymmetric information between doctors and patients and between patients and insurance companies. These asymmetries lead to adverse selection in the purchase of insurance and to moral hazard (or the third-party payment syndrome) in excessive consumption of medical services. Finally, because health is so important to human welfare and to labor productivity, governments strive to provide a minimum standard of health care to the population.

13. The current health-care system in the United States has been criticized because of rising costs, a growing number of uninsured, and lagging health status, particularly of poor and minority groups. Few advocate returning to a pure-market system because of adverse effects on public health and on the generation of new biomedical knowledge. A nationalized system would provide universal coverage but ration health care by long waits for services. A promising new approach is Fedicare, or a medical negative income tax, which would provide a standard package of benefits. The price of the package would be zero for low-income families and would rise on a percentage basis with family income.

CONCEPTS FOR REVIEW

Inequality and Antipoverty Programs
trends of income distribution
Lorenz curve of income and wealth
labor and property income
relative roles of luck, life-cycle savings, risk taking, inheritance
college–high school wage premium
poverty
welfare state
Okun's "leaky bucket"

equality:
  political
  of opportunity
  of outcome
equality vs. efficiency
income-support programs
income-possibility curve: ideal and realistic cases
earned-income tax credit, negative income tax
1996 welfare reform (TANF)

Health-Care Economics
public goods of discovering new knowledge, preventing communicable diseases
insurance failures of moral hazard and adverse selection
alternative approaches to reform:
  pure market
  nationalized system
  medical negative income tax (Fedicare)

QUESTIONS FOR DISCUSSION

1. Let each member of the class anonymously write down on a card an estimate of his or her family's annual income. From these, draw up a frequency table showing the distribution of incomes. What is the median income? The mean income?

2. What effect would the following have on the Lorenz curve of after-tax incomes? (Assume that the taxes are spent by the government on a representative slice of GDP.)
   a. A proportional income tax (i.e., one taxing all incomes at the same rate)
   b. A progressive income tax (i.e., one taxing high incomes more heavily than low incomes)
   c. A sharp increase in taxes on cigarettes and food
   Draw four Lorenz curves to illustrate the original income distribution and the income distribution after each action, **a** to **c**.

3. Discuss the three different kinds of equality. Why might equality of opportunity not lead to equality of outcome? Should persons of different abilities be given the same access to jobs and education? What might be done to ensure equality of outcome? How might such steps lead to economic inefficiencies?

4. Consider two ways of supplementing the income of the poor: (*a*) cash assistance (say, $500 per month) and (*b*) categorical benefits such as subsidized food or medical care. List the pros and cons of using each strategy. Can you explain why the United States tends to use mainly strategy (*b*)? Do you agree?

5. Instead of using the Lorenz curve to measure inequality, calculate the area between the actual curve of inequality and the curve of equal incomes (i.e., the gray shaded region in Figure 19-1). Two times this ratio is called the Gini coefficient.
   What is the Gini coefficient for a society with absolute equality of income? For one in which one person gets all the income? Estimate the Gini coefficients for the different Lorenz curves in Figure 19-2.

6. In a country called Econoland, there are 10 people. Their incomes (in thousands) are $3, $6, $2, $8, $4, $9, $1, $5, $7, and $5. Construct a table of income quintiles like Table 19-2. Plot a Lorenz curve. Calculate the Gini coefficient defined in question 5.

7. Many people continue to argue about what form assistance for the poor should take. One school says, "Give people money and let them buy health services and the foods they need." The other school says, "If you give money to the poor, they may spend it on beer and drugs. Your dollar goes further in alleviating malnourishment and disease if you provide the services in kind. The dollar that you earn may be yours to spend, but society's income-support dollar is a dollar that society has the right to channel directly to its targets."
   The argument of the first school might rest on demand theory: Let each household decide how to maximize its utility on a limited budget. Chapter 5 shows why this argument might be right. But what if the parents' utility includes mainly beer and lottery tickets and no milk or clothing for the children? Might you agree with the second view? From your own personal experience and reading, which of these two arguments would you endorse? Explain your reasoning.

8. Long-term care for the elderly involves helping individuals with activities (such as bathing, dressing, and toileting) that they cannot perform for themselves. How were these needs taken care of a century ago? Explain why moral hazard and adverse selection make long-term-care insurance so expensive today that few people choose to buy it.

9. Table 19-9 shows illustrative calculations for a Fedicare system. Fill in the missing numbers. Compare this system with both a laissez-faire system and nationalized health care financed by a sales tax. What is the effect on the marginal tax rate at different income levels?

TABLE 19-9. Subsidized Premiums Can Provide Universal Health Coverage

Under an illustrative subsidized health-care system, a family of four would pay 20 cents for each dollar of income over $10,000. The maximum premium would be the insurance cost, assumed to be $8,000. Fill in the missing numbers.

Income ($)	Premiums for medical care package ($)	Income less premiums ($)
0	0	0
10,000	0	____
20,000	2,000	____
30,000	____	26,000
40,000	____	____
100,000	8,000	____

10. A policy is called "cost-effective" if it produces a given level of output at least cost or maximizes the level of output for a given amount of inputs. Assume there is a wartime situation with inadequate medical supplies. There are 100 units of health care (say, medication) and 400 patients equally divided into eight groups of 50. Table 19-10 gives the probabilities of survival with and without 1 unit of medical care.

You are charged with performing triage on the wounded. Your objective is to maximize the expected number of survivors (equal to the sum of the probability of survival times the number of patients, $p_1N_1 + \cdots + p_8N_8$, where p_i is the probability of survival with the medical treatment received and N_i is the number of patients).

a. Devise a triage rule based on the description in footnote 6 (page 363). Which two groups of patients fall into the triage category that receives treatment?

b. Calculate the expected number of surviving patients under your rule. Can you see why this strategy is cost-effective in the sense of maximizing the expected number of surviving patients?

c. Consider a rule that says treatment should go to the worst-off patients (the ones with the lowest probability of survival without care). Why is this not cost-effective?

d. Say that the number of units of medical care increased to 200. Why is your triage rule no longer appropriate? Can you determine the general rule for this example?

TABLE 19-10.

Patient group	Probability of Survival	
	With care	Without care
Tank and truck accidents:		
1. Broken legs	.99	.98
2. Severe burns	.41	.39
Shrapnel wounds:		
3. To limbs	.90	.30
4. To head	.05	.02
Bullet wounds:		
5. To limbs	.88	.85
6. To head	.10	.08
Infection:`		
7. Bacteriological	.98	.30
8. Unknown origin	.60	.59

PART FIVE

MACROECONOMICS: THE STUDY OF GROWTH AND BUSINESS CYCLES

CHAPTER 20
OVERVIEW OF MACROECONOMICS

> The whole purpose of the economy is production of goods or services for consumption now or in the future. I think the burden of proof should always be on those who would produce less rather than more, on those who would leave idle people or machines or land that could be used. It is amazing how many reasons can be found to justify such waste: fear of inflation, balance-of-payments deficits, unbalanced budgets, excessive national debt, loss of confidence in the dollar.
>
> *James Tobin*, National Economic Policy

We now turn to the issues of macroeconomics, which involves the overall performance of an economy. Macroeconomics examines the reasons behind the economic growth and decline of nations—why some nations prosper with high and growing standards of living while others experience high unemployment, rampant inflation, low wages, or large trade deficits. We will focus on the two major elements of performance: the short-term fluctuations in output, employment, and prices that are called the business cycle; and the longer-term trends in output and living standards that we call economic growth. An understanding of the forces behind growth and cycles is crucial for an understanding of the science of macroeconomics.

Before we launch into our survey, recall that **macroeconomics** is the study of the behavior of the economy as a whole. It examines the overall level of a nation's output, employment, and prices. By contrast, **microeconomics** studies individual prices, quantities, and markets.

Macroeconomic issues have dominated the political and economic agenda for much of the twentieth century. In the 1930s, when production, employment, and prices collapsed in the United States and across much of the industrial world, economists and political leaders wrestled with the calamity of the Great Depression. During World War II, and again during the Vietnam war in the 1960s, the problem was one of managing a sustained boom and containing high inflation. In the 1970s the burning issue was "stagflation," a combination of slow growth and rising prices that left Americans feeling miserable.

The last decade has seen an interesting contrast between the United States and Europe. In the United States, output and employment grew healthily, and unemployment over the last few years stayed near the level that economists regard as the lowest sustainable rate. In Europe, by contrast, unemployment has risen steadily, youth unemployment has soared, and governments are seeking new mechanisms to break the cycle of joblessness. In all high-income countries, policymakers face the daunting questions of the slow growth in productivity and real wages along with the need to balance the threat of inflation against the need to ensure jobs for all who desire them.

Sometimes, macroeconomic failures are life-and-death questions for countries and even for ideologies. The communist leaders of the former Soviet Union proclaimed that they would soon overtake the West economically. History proved that to be a hollow macroeconomic promise, as Russia, a country teeming with natural resources and military might, was unable to produce adequate butter for its citizens along with guns for its imperial armies. Eventually, macroeconomic failures brought down the communist regimes and convinced people of the economic superiority of private markets as the best approach to encouraging rapid economic growth.

One of the major breakthroughs of twentieth-century economics has been the development of macroeconomics. This led to a much better understanding of how to combat periodic economic crises and how to stimulate long-term economic growth. In response to the Great Depression, John Maynard Keynes developed his revolutionary theory, which helped explain the forces producing economic fluctuations and suggested an approach for controlling the worst excesses of business cycles. In the last 30 years, economists have devoted their attention to understanding the mechanics of long-term growth. Thanks to Keynes, his critics, and his modern successors, we know that in its choice of macroeconomic policies—those affecting the money supply, taxes, and government spending—a nation can speed or slow its economic growth, trim the excesses of price inflation or unemployment from business cycles, or curb large foreign trade surpluses or deficits.

Nevertheless, macroeconomics is still an area of great controversy among economists and politicians alike. Every American presidential campaign in recent years has focused on the economy. Sometimes—as in 1976, 1980, and 1992—unemployment was rising and the economy was in recession, and the incumbents were attacked as bad for the economy's health. In other years, such as 1972, 1984, and 1996, unemployment was low and the incumbent President argued that he was the key to continued prosperity. In even-numbered years, it seems crucial that taxes be cut, while in odd-numbered years, curbing the federal deficit looms as the central economic issue.

Macroeconomics is today in great ferment. In some areas, such as the basic elements that influence long-term economic growth, economists are largely in agreement about the forces and trends. In others, particularly those involving business cycles, the warring schools of macroeconomics battle over both explanations of cycles and the appropriate policies to avoid unemployment and inflation.

This chapter will serve as an introduction to macroeconomics. It presents the major concepts and theories and shows how they apply to many of the key historical and policy questions of recent years. But this introduction is only a first course to whet the appetite. Not until you have mastered all the chapters in Parts Five and Six can you fully enjoy the rich macroeconomic banquet that has been a source of both inspiration for economic policy and continued controversy among macroeconomists.

A. KEY CONCEPTS OF MACROECONOMICS

THE BIRTH OF MACROECONOMICS

The 1930s marked the first stirrings of the science of macroeconomics, founded by John Maynard Keynes as he tried to understand the economic mechanism that produced the Great Depression. After World War II, reflecting both the increasing influence of Keynesian views and the fear of another depression, the U.S. Congress formally proclaimed federal responsibility for macroeconomic performance. It enacted the landmark Employment Act of 1946, which stated:

> The Congress hereby declares that it is the continuing policy and responsibility of the federal government to use all practicable means consistent with its needs and obligations . . . to promote maximum employment, production, and purchasing power.

For the first time, Congress affirmed the government's role in promoting output growth, promoting employment, and maintaining price stability.

Since the 1946 Employment Act, the nation's priorities among these three goals have shifted; but in the United States, as in all market economies, these goals still frame the central macroeconomic questions:

1. *Why do output and employment sometimes fall, and how can unemployment be reduced?* All market

economies show patterns of expansion and contraction known as *business cycles*. The last major business-cycle downturn in the United States came in 1990–1991, when production of goods and services fell and millions of people lost their jobs. For much of the postwar period, one key goal of macroeconomic policy has been to use monetary and fiscal policy to reduce the severity of business-cycle downturns and unemployment.

From time to time countries experience high unemployment that persists for long periods, sometimes as long as a decade. Such a period occurred in the United States during the Great Depression, which began in 1929. In the next few years, unemployment rose to almost one-quarter of the work force, while industrial production fell by one-half. European countries in the 1990s had a mild depression, with persistent unemployment of over 10 percent in many countries. Macroeconomics examines the sources of such persistent and painful unemployment. Having considered the possible diagnoses, economics can also suggest possible remedies, such as adopting stimulative demand policies or reforming labor market institutions by reducing the incentives not to work or increasing wage flexibility. The lives and fortunes of millions of people depend upon whether macroeconomists can find the right answers to these questions.

2. *What are the sources of price inflation, and how can it be kept under control?* Economists have learned that high rates of price inflation have a corrosive effect on market economies. A market economy uses prices as a yardstick to measure economic values and as a way to conduct business. During periods of rapidly rising prices, the yardstick loses its value: People become confused, make mistakes, and spend much of their time worrying about inflation eating away at their incomes. Rapid price changes lead to economic inefficiency.

As a result, macroeconomic policy has increasingly emphasized price stability as a key goal. In the United States the overall rate of inflation has fallen from more than 10 percent per year in the late 1970s to less than 3 percent per year in the mid- and later 1990s. Some countries today have not succeeded in containing inflation, however, and we see prices rising by 1000 percent per year or more in formerly socialist countries like Russia

or Ukraine and, until recently, in some Latin American countries. Why was the United States able to put the inflationary tiger in the cage, while Russia failed to do so? Macroeconomics can suggest the proper role of monetary and fiscal policies, of exchange-rate systems, and of an independent central bank in containing inflation.

3. *How can a nation increase its rate of economic growth?* Above all, macroeconomics is concerned with the long-run prosperity of a country. Over a period of decades and more, the growth of a nation's productive potential is the central factor in determining the growth in its real wages and living standards. During the last 25 years, rapid economic growth in Asian countries such as Japan, South Korea, and Taiwan produced dramatic gains in living standards for their peoples. A few countries, particularly those of sub-Saharan Africa, have suffered declining per capita output and living standards over the last two decades. Nations want to know the ingredients in a successful growth recipe. They want to understand why high rates of investment and saving usually have a big payoff in promoting economic growth. They want to understand the role of budget deficits and industrial policies in promoting growing living standards. They ask about the role of investment in research and development and in human capital.

A final complication in considering the three central issues is that there are inevitable tradeoffs among these goals. Increasing the rate of growth of output over the long run may require greater investment in knowledge and capital; to increase investment requires lower current consumption of items like food, clothing, and recreation.

Of all the macroeconomic dilemmas, the most agonizing is the tradeoff between unemployment and inflation. High unemployment and high inflation produce economic distress and political unrest. But when output rises too rapidly and unemployment falls, the situation tends to drive up prices and wages. Policymakers are forced to rein in the economy through macroeconomic policies when it grows too fast, or when unemployment falls too low, in order to prevent rising inflation.

There are no simple formulas for resolving these dilemmas, and macroeconomists differ greatly on

Objectives	Instruments
Output: High level and rapid growth GDP	**Monetary policy:** Control of money supply affecting interest rates
Employment: High level of employment with low involuntary unemployment	**Fiscal policy:** Government expenditure Taxation
Price-level stability CPI	

TABLE 20-1. **Goals and Instruments of Macroeconomic Policy**

The left-hand column displays the major goals of macroeconomic policy. The right-hand column contains the major instruments or policy measures available to modern economies. These are the ways that policymakers can affect the pace and direction of economic activity.

the proper approach to take when confronted with high inflation, rising unemployment, or stagnant growth. But with sound macroeconomic understanding, the inevitable pain that comes from choosing the best route can be minimized.

 The patron saint of macroeconomics: Every discussion of macroeconomic policy must begin with John Maynard Keynes. Keynes (1883–1946) was a many-sided genius who won eminence in the fields of mathematics, philosophy, and literature. In addition, he found time to run a large insurance company, advise the British treasury, help govern the Bank of England, edit a world-famous economics journal, collect modern art and rare books, start a repertory theater, and marry a leading Russian ballerina. He was also an investor who knew how to make money by shrewd speculation, both for himself and for his college, King's College, Cambridge.

His principal contribution, however, was his invention of a new way of looking at macroeconomics and macroeconomic policy. Before Keynes, most economists and policymakers accepted the highs and lows of business cycles as being as inevitable as the tides. These long-held views left them helpless in the face of the Great Depression of the 1930s. But Keynes took an enormous intellectual leap in his 1936 book, *The General Theory of Employment, Interest and Money.* Keynes made a twofold argument: First, he argued that it is possible for high unemployment and underutilized capacity to persist in market economies. In addition, he argued that government fiscal and monetary policies can affect output and thereby reduce unemployment and shorten economic downturns.

These propositions had an explosive impact when Keynes first introduced them, engendering much contro-

versy and dispute. In the postwar period, Keynesian economics came to dominate macroeconomics and government policy. During the 1960s, virtually every analysis of macroeconomic policy was grounded in the Keynesian view of the world. Since then, new developments incorporating supply factors, expectations, and alternative views of wage and price dynamics have undermined the earlier Keynesian consensus. While few economists now believe that government action can eliminate business cycles, as Keynesian economics once seemed to promise, neither economics nor economic policy has been the same since Keynes' great discovery.

OBJECTIVES AND INSTRUMENTS OF MACROECONOMICS

Having surveyed the principal issues of macroeconomics, we now turn to a discussion of the major goals and instruments of macroeconomic policy. How do economists evaluate the success of an economy's overall performance? What are the tools that governments can use to pursue their economic goals? Table 20-1 lists the major objectives and instruments of macroeconomic policy.

Measuring Economic Success

In general, economists judge macroeconomic performance by looking at a few key variables—the most important being gross domestic product (GDP), the unemployment rate, and inflation. Let's start by looking at gross domestic product, or national output.

Output. The ultimate objective of economic activity is to provide the goods and services that the

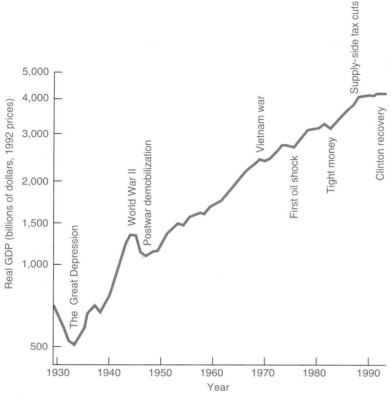

FIGURE 20-1. U.S. Real Gross Domestic Product, 1929–1996

Real GDP is the most comprehensive measure of an economy's output. Note how sharply output fell in the Great Depression of the 1930s. After World War II, GDP growth was very steady until the economy was hit by numerous shocks in the 1970s and 1980s. (Source: U.S. Department of Commerce.)

population desires. What could be more important for an economy than to produce ample shelter, food, education, and recreation for its people?

The most comprehensive measure of the total output in an economy is the **gross domestic product** (GDP). GDP is the measure of the market value of all final goods and services—oatmeal, beer, cars, rock concerts, airplane rides, health care, and so on—produced in a country during a year. There are two ways to measure GDP. *Nominal GDP* is measured in actual market prices. *Real GDP* is calculated in constant or invariant prices (say, prices for the year 1992).

Movements in real GDP are the best widely available measure of the level and growth of output; they serve as the carefully monitored pulse of a nation's economy. Figure 20-1 shows the history of real GDP in the United States since 1929. Note the economic

decline during the Great Depression of the 1930s, the boom during World War II, the recessions in 1975 and 1982, and the steady growth in the long expansion from 1992 to 1996.

Despite the short-term fluctuations in GDP seen in business cycles, advanced economies generally exhibit a steady long-term growth in real GDP and an improvement in living standards; this process is known as *economic growth*. The American economy has proved itself a powerful engine of progress over a period of more than a century, as shown by the growth in potential output.

Potential GDP represents the maximum amount the economy can produce while maintaining reasonable price stability. Potential output is also sometimes called the *high-employment level of output*. When an economy is operating at its potential, unemployment is low and production is high.

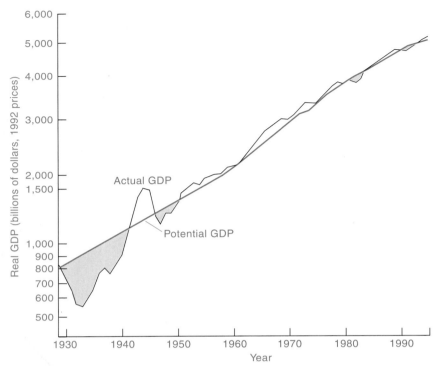

FIGURE 20-2. Actual and Potential GDP

Business cycles occur when actual output departs from its potential. The smooth rust-colored line shows potential or trend output over the period 1930–1996. Potential output has grown about 3 percent annually over the last half-century but has slowed to about $2\frac{1}{2}$ percent annually in the last two decades. Note the large gap between actual and potential output during the Great Depression of the 1930s. (Source: U.S. Department of Commerce and authors' estimates.)

Potential output is determined by the economy's productive capacity, which depends upon the inputs available (capital, labor, land, etc.) and the economy's technological efficiency. Potential GDP tends to grow slowly and steadily because inputs like labor and capital and the level of technology change quite slowly over time. By contrast, actual GDP is subject to large business-cycle swings if spending patterns change sharply. Economic policies (like monetary and fiscal policy) can affect actual output quickly, but the impact of policies on potential output trends operates slowly over a number of years.

During business cycles, actual GDP departs from its potential. In 1982, for example, the U.S. economy produced almost $300 billion less than potential output. This represented $5000 lost per family during a single year. Economic downturns are called *recessions* when real output declines for a year or two and the gap between actual and potential output is small; they are called *depressions* when the output decline is protracted with a large gap between actual and potential output.

Figure 20-2 shows the estimated potential and actual output for the period 1930–1996. Note how large the gap between actual and potential output was during the Great Depression of the 1930s.

High Employment, Low Unemployment. Of all the macroeconomic indicators, employment and unemployment are most directly felt by individuals. People want to be able to find high-paying jobs without searching or waiting too long, and they want to have job security and good benefits when they are working. In macroeconomic terms, these are the

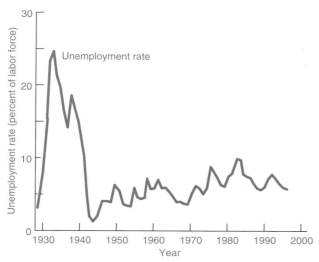

FIGURE 20-3. Unemployment Rises in Recessions, Falls during Expansions

The unemployment rate measures the fraction of the labor force that is looking for but cannot find work. Unemployment reached tragic proportions during the 1930s, peaking at 25 percent in 1933. Unemployment rises in business-cycle downturns and falls during expansions. (Source: U.S. Department of Labor.)

objectives of *high employment,* which is the counterpart of *low unemployment.* Figure 20-3 shows trends in unemployment over the last six decades. The **unemployment rate** on the vertical axis is the percentage of the labor force that is unemployed. The labor force includes all employed persons and those unemployed individuals who are seeking jobs. It excludes those without work who are not looking for jobs.

The unemployment rate tends to reflect the state of the business cycle: When output is falling, the demand for labor falls and the unemployment rate rises. Unemployment reached epidemic proportions in the Great Depression of the 1930s, when as much as one-quarter of the work force was idled. Since World War II, unemployment in the United States has fluctuated but has avoided the high rates associated with depressions and the low levels that would trigger great inflations.

Stable Prices. The third macroeconomic objective is to maintain *stable prices.* To understand this goal, we need some background on measuring overall price trends. The most common measure of the overall price level is the **consumer price index,** known as the CPI. The CPI measures the cost of a fixed basket of goods (including items such as food,

shelter, clothing, and medical care) bought by the average urban consumer. The overall price level is often denoted by the letter *P.*

We call changes in the level of prices the **rate of inflation,** which denotes the rate of growth or decline of the price level from one year to the next.[1] Figure 20-4 on the next page illustrates the rate of inflation for the CPI from 1930 to 1996. Over this entire period, inflation averaged 3.4 percent per year. Note that price changes fluctuated greatly over the years, varying from *minus* 10 percent in 1932 to 14 percent in 1947.

A *deflation* occurs when prices decline (which means that the rate of inflation is negative). At the other extreme is a *hyperinflation,* a rise in the price level of a thousand or a million percent a year. In such situations, as in Weimar Germany in the 1920s, Brazil in the 1980s, or Russia in the 1990s, prices are virtually meaningless and the price system breaks down.

The advantage of price stability is more subtle than is the case with the other objectives. History has

---

[1] More precisely, the rate of inflation of the CPI is

$$\text{Rate of inflation of consumer prices (in percent)} = \frac{\text{CPI (this year)} - \text{CPI (last year)}}{\text{CPI (last year)}} \times 100$$

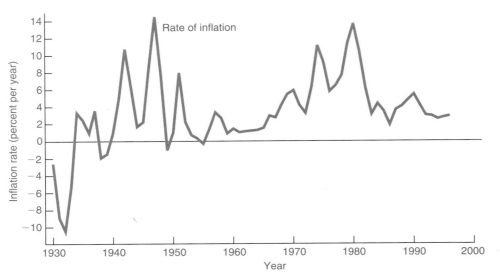

FIGURE 20-4. Consumer Price Inflation, 1929–1996

The rate of inflation measures the rate of change of prices from one year to the next; here we see the rate of inflation as measured by the consumer price index (CPI). Since World War II, prices have mainly moved upward, particularly after the oil shocks of 1973 and 1979. Since 1984, the United States has enjoyed low inflation. (Source: U.S. Department of Labor.)

shown that rapid price changes distort the economic decisions of companies and individuals. With high inflation, taxes become highly variable, the real values of people's pensions are eroded, and people spend real resources to avoid holding depreciating currency. At the same time, slowing inflation generally requires contracting economic activity and raising unemployment. Most nations therefore seek a golden mean between completely stable prices and high inflation, allowing a gentle upward creep of prices as the best way of allowing the price system to function efficiently.

To summarize:
The goals of macroeconomic policy are:

1. A high and growing level of national output (i.e., of real GDP)
2. High employment with low unemployment
3. A stable or gently rising price level

The Tools of Macroeconomic Policy

Put yourself in the shoes of the leader of the United States or another market economy. Unemployment is rising and GDP is falling. Or perhaps productivity growth has declined, and you wish to

increase potential output growth. Or your country has a balance-of-payments crisis, with high imports and lagging exports. What can your government do to improve economic performance? What policy tools can you put your hands on to reduce inflation or unemployment, to speed economic growth, or to correct a trade imbalance?

Governments have certain instruments that they can use to affect macroeconomic activity. A *policy instrument* is an economic variable under the control of government that can affect one or more of the macroeconomic goals. That is, by changing monetary, fiscal, and other policies, governments can avoid the worst excesses of the business cycle and can increase the growth rate of potential output. The two major instruments of macroeconomic policy are listed on the right side of Table 20-1 (page 374).

Fiscal Policy. Begin with **fiscal policy,** which denotes the use of taxes and government expenditures. *Government expenditures* come in two distinct forms. First there are government purchases. These comprise spending on goods and services—purchases of tanks, construction of roads, salaries for judges, and so forth. In addition, there are government transfer payments, which boost the incomes of targeted groups such as the elderly or the unemployed. Government spending determines the relative size of the public and private sectors, that is, how much of our GDP is consumed collectively rather than privately. From a macroeconomic perspective, government expenditures also affect the overall level of spending in the economy and thereby influence the level of GDP.

The other part of fiscal policy, *taxation,* affects the overall economy in two ways. To begin with, taxes affect people's incomes. By leaving households with more or less disposable or spendable income, taxes tend to affect the amount people spend on goods and services as well as the amount of private saving. Private consumption and saving have important effects on output and investment in the short and long run.

In addition, taxes affect the prices of goods and factors of production and thereby affect incentives and behavior. For example, the more heavily business profits are taxed, the more businesses are discouraged from investing in new capital goods. From 1962 until 1986, the United States employed an investment tax credit, which was a rebate to businesses that buy capital goods, as a way of stimulating investment and boosting economic growth. Many provisions of the tax code have an important effect on economic activity through their effect on the incentives to work and to save.

Monetary Policy. The second major instrument of macroeconomic policy is **monetary policy,** which government conducts through the management of the nation's money, credit, and banking system. You may have read how our central bank, the Federal Reserve System, operates to regulate the money supply. But what exactly is the money supply? **Money** consists of the means of exchange or method of payment. Today, people use currency and checking accounts to pay their bills. By engaging in central-bank operations, the Federal Reserve can regulate the amount of money available to the economy.

How does such a minor thing as the money supply have such a large impact on macroeconomic activity? By changing the money supply, the Federal Reserve can influence many financial and economic variables, such as interest rates, stock prices, housing prices, and foreign exchange rates. Restricting the money supply leads to higher interest rates and reduced investment, which, in turn, causes a decline in GDP and lower inflation. If the central bank is faced with a business downturn, it can increase the money supply and lower interest rates to stimulate economic activity.

The exact nature of monetary policy—the way in which the central bank controls the money supply and the relationships among money, output, and inflation—is one of the most fascinating, important, and controversial areas of macroeconomics. A policy of tight money in the United States—lowering the rate of growth of the money supply—raised interest rates, slowed economic growth, and raised unemployment in the period 1979–1982. Then, from 1982 until 1997, careful monetary management by the Federal Reserve supported the longest economic expansion in American history. Over the last decade, monetary policy has become the major weapon used by the U.S. government to fight the business cycle. Exactly how a central bank can control economic activity will be thoroughly analyzed in the chapters on monetary policy.

Other times, other policies: Countries often seek novel ways to solve old economic problems. One experimental approach is called *incomes policies* and involves direct control over prices and wages. This approach is widely applied during wartime and sometimes in peacetime emergencies. The standard approach to slowing inflation, as we will see, has been for governments to take monetary and fiscal steps to reduce output and raise unemployment. Because this is such unpleasant medicine, governments have often searched for other methods of containing inflation. Incomes policies have ranged from wage and price controls (used primarily in wartime) to less drastic measures like voluntary wage and price guidelines used in peacetime.

A generation ago, many economists thought incomes policies might be an inexpensive way to reduce inflation. Evidence on the impact of incomes policies, along with a more conservative attitude toward government intervention, has led to a general disenchantment with direct wage-price policies. Many economists now believe that incomes policies are simply ineffective. Others think they are worse than useless—that they interfere with free markets, gum up relative price movements, and fail to reduce inflation. Most high-income countries no longer use incomes policies, but they are often employed by developing countries and countries making the transition to a market economy.

A nation has a wide variety of policy instruments that can be used to pursue its macroeconomic goals. The major ones are these:

1. Fiscal policy consists of government expenditure and taxation. Government expenditure influences the relative size of collective as opposed to private consumption. Taxation subtracts from incomes, reduces private spending, and affects private saving. In addition, it affects investment and potential output. Fiscal policy is primarily employed today to affect long-term economic growth through its impact on national saving and on incentives to work and save.

2. Monetary policy, conducted by the central bank, determines the money supply. Changes in the money supply move interest rates up or down and affect spending in sectors such as business investment, housing, and net exports. Monetary policy has an important effect on both actual GDP and potential GDP.

THE FOREIGN CONNECTION

No nation is an island unto itself. All nations participate in the world economy and are linked together through trade and finance. The trade linkages of imports and exports of goods and services are seen when the United States imports cars from Japan or exports computers to Mexico. Financial linkages come when the United States borrows from Japan to finance its budget deficit or when American pension funds diversify their portfolios by investing in emerging markets in Asia or Latin America.

Nations keep a close watch on their foreign-trade flows. One particularly important index is **net exports,** which is the numerical difference between the value of exports and the value of imports. When exports exceed imports, the difference is a surplus, while a negative net-export balance is a deficit. Hence when its exports totaled $855 billion in 1996 while imports were $954 billion, the United States had a foreign-trade deficit of $99 billion.

The goal of expanding international trade has become increasingly important as the nations of the globe have seen that foreign trade spurs efficiency and promotes economic growth. As the costs of transportation and communication have declined, international linkages have become tighter than they were a generation ago. International trade has replaced empire building and military conquest as the surest road to national wealth and influence. Some economies today trade over half their output.

One of the major developments of the 1980s was the changing pattern of U.S. international trade. For most of this century, the United States had a surplus in its foreign trade, exporting more than it imported. But in the 1980s, net exports reached a deficit of almost $150 billion, or about 3 percent of GDP. As the deficits piled up, the United States by 1996 owed almost $800 billion to foreigners. Many Americans are concerned about the future impact of a large foreign debt.

As economies become more closely linked, policymakers devote increasing attention to international economic policy. International trade is not an end in itself. Rather, nations are properly concerned about international trade because trade serves the ultimate goal of improving living standards. The major areas of concern are trade policies and international financial management.

Trade policies consist of tariffs, quotas, and other regulations that restrict or encourage imports and exports. Most trade policies have little effect on macroeconomic performance, but from time to time, as was the case in the 1930s, restrictions on international trade are so severe that they cause major economic dislocations, inflations, or recessions.

A second set of policies specifically aimed at the foreign sector is *international financial management.* A country's international trade is influenced by its foreign exchange rate, which represents the price of its own currency in terms of the currencies of other nations. As part of their monetary policies, nations adopt different systems to regulate their foreign exchange markets. Some systems allow exchange rates to be determined purely by supply and demand; others set a fixed exchange rate against other currencies. The United States today is in the first category, generally allowing the dollar's exchange rates to be determined by market forces.

The international economy is an intricate web of trading and financial connections among countries. When the international economic system runs smoothly, it contributes to rapid economic growth; when trading systems break down, production and incomes suffer throughout the world. Countries therefore must monitor their international economic linkages through trade policies and international financial management.

B. AGGREGATE SUPPLY AND DEMAND

The economic history of nations can be seen in their macroeconomic performance. Over the twentieth century, the United States saw periods of wartime boom, stagnation as inflation combined with high unemployment, tight money as the central banks battled against inflation, and then a long expansion under favorable macroeconomic conditions. Through the changing cyclical conditions, the U.S. economy grew steadily, and by 1997 national output was almost 20 times its level a century earlier.

Economists have developed aggregate supply-and-demand analysis to help explain the major trends in output and prices. We begin by explaining this important tool of macroeconomics and then use it to understand some important historical events.

INSIDE THE MACROECONOMY: AGGREGATE SUPPLY AND DEMAND

Definitions of Aggregate Supply and Demand

How do different forces interact to determine overall economic activity? Figure 20-5 on page 382 shows the relationships among the different variables inside the macroeconomy. It separates variables into two categories: those affecting aggregate supply and those affecting aggregate demand. Dividing variables into these two categories helps us understand what determines the levels of output, prices, and unemployment.

 Terminology for economic variables: We begin with some economic terminology about different forces or variables affecting the economy. Some important determinants come from outside the economy. These include the instruments or policy variables discussed in the last section: taxes, monetary policy, and so forth. In addition, there are **exogenous variables** (sometimes called *external variables*), which influence economic activity but are unaffected by the economy. These variables include wars and revolutions, foreign economic conditions, population growth, and many other factors.

The policy instruments and exogenous variables interact to affect the variables determined inside the macroeconomic system. That is, they determine the **induced variables** (sometimes called *endogenous variables*) such as national output, employment and unemployment, and the price level.

The lower part of Figure 20-5 shows the forces affecting aggregate supply. **Aggregate supply** refers to the total quantity of goods and services that the nation's businesses are willing to produce and sell in a given period. Aggregate supply (often written *AS*) depends upon the price level, the productive capacity of the economy, and the level of costs.

In general, businesses would like to sell everything they can produce at high prices. Under some circumstances, prices and spending levels may be depressed, so businesses might find they have excess capacity. Under other conditions, such as during a wartime boom, factories may be operating at capacity as businesses scramble to produce enough to meet all their orders.

We see, then, that aggregate supply depends on the price level that businesses can charge as well as on the economy's capacity or potential output. Potential output in turn is determined by the availability of productive inputs (labor and capital being the most important) and the managerial and technical efficiency with which those inputs are combined.

National output and the overall price level are determined by the twin blades of the scissors of aggregate supply and demand. The second blade is **aggregate demand,** which refers to the total amount that different sectors in the economy willingly spend in a given period. Aggregate demand (often written *AD*) is the sum of spending by consumers, businesses, and governments, and it depends on the level of prices, as well as on monetary policy, fiscal policy, and other factors.

The components of aggregate demand include the cars, food, and other consumption goods bought by consumers; the factories and equipment bought by businesses; the missiles and computers bought by

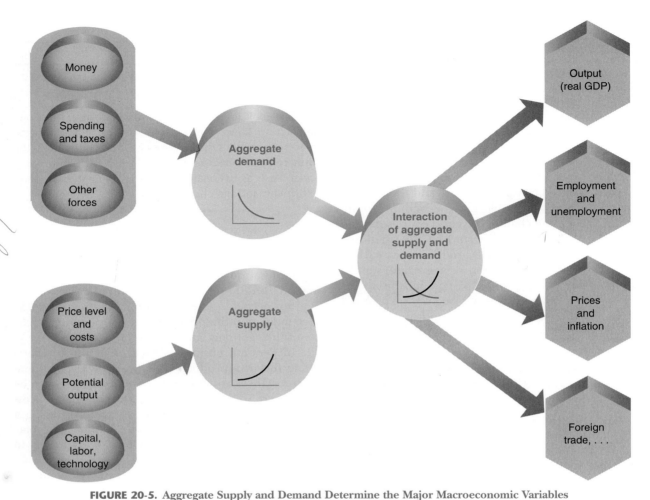

FIGURE 20-5. Aggregate Supply and Demand Determine the Major Macroeconomic Variables

This key diagram shows the major factors affecting overall economic activity. On the left are the major variables determining aggregate supply and demand; these include policy variables, like monetary and fiscal policies, along with stocks of capital and labor. In the center, aggregate supply and demand interact as the level of demand beats upon the available resources. The chief outcomes are shown on the right in hexagons: output, employment, the price level, and foreign trade.

government; and net exports. The total purchases are affected by the prices at which the goods are offered, by exogenous forces like wars and weather, and by government policies.

Using both blades of the scissors of aggregate supply and demand, we achieve the resulting equilibrium, as is shown in the right-hand circle of Figure 20-5. National output and the price level settle at that level where demanders willingly buy what busi-

nesses willingly sell. The resulting output and price level determine employment, unemployment, and foreign trade.

Aggregate Supply and Demand Curves

Aggregate supply and demand curves are often used to help analyze macroeconomic conditions. Recall that in Chapter 3 we used market supply and demand curves to analyze the prices and quantities of individual products. An analogous graphical apparatus can also help us understand how monetary policy or technological change acts through aggregate supply and demand to determine national output and the price level. With the *AS-AD* apparatus, we can see how a monetary expansion leads to rising prices and higher output. We can also see why increases in efficiency may lead to higher output and to a *lower* overall price level.

Figure 20-6 shows the aggregate supply and demand schedules for the output of an entire economy. On the horizontal, or quantity, axis is the total output (real GDP) of the economy. On the vertical axis is the overall price level (say, as measured by the consumer price index). We use the symbol *Q* for output and *P* for the price level.

The downward-sloping curve is the **aggregate demand schedule,** or *AD* curve. It represents what everyone in the economy—consumers, businesses, foreigners, and governments—would buy at different aggregate price levels (with other factors affecting aggregate demand held constant). From the curve, we see that at an overall price level of 150, total spending would be $3000 billion (per year). If the price level rises to 200, total spending would fall to $2300 billion.

The upward-sloping curve is the **aggregate supply schedule,** or *AS* curve. This curve represents the quantity of goods and services that businesses are willing to produce and sell at each price level (with other determinants of aggregate supply held constant). According to the curve, businesses will want to sell $3000 billion at a price level of 150; they will want to sell a higher quantity, $3300 billion, if prices rise to 200. As the level of total output demanded rises, businesses will want to sell more goods and services at a higher price level.

Warning on *AS* and *AD* curves: Before proceeding, here is one important word of caution: Do not confuse the macroeconomic *AD* and *AS* curves with the microeconomic *DD* and *SS* curves. The microeconomic supply and demand curves show the quantities and prices of individual commodities, with such things as national income and other goods' prices held as given. By contrast, the aggregate supply and demand curves show the determination of total output

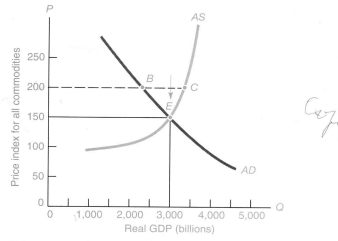

FIGURE 20-6. Aggregate Price and Output Are Determined by the Interaction of Aggregate Supply and Demand

The *AD* curve represents the quantity of total spending at different price levels, with other factors held constant. The *AS* curve shows what firms will produce and sell at different price levels, other things equal.

National output and the overall price level are determined at the intersection of the aggregate demand and supply curves, at point *E*. This equilibrium occurs at an overall price level where firms willingly produce and sell what consumers and other demanders willingly buy.

and the overall price level, with such things as the money supply, fiscal policy, and the capital stock held constant. Aggregate supply and demand explain how taxes affect national output and the movement of all prices; microeconomic supply and demand might consider the way increases in gasoline taxes affect purchases of automobiles. The two sets of curves have a superficial resemblance, but they explain very different phenomena.

Macroeconomic Equilibrium. Let's put the *AS* and *AD* concepts to work to see how *equilibrium values of price and quantity* are determined. What this means in plain English is that we want to find the real GDP and the aggregate price level that would satisfy both buyers and sellers. For the *AS* and *AD* curves shown in Figure 20-6, the overall economy is in equilibrium at point *E*. Only at that point, where the level of output is $Q = 3000$ and $P = 150$, are spenders and sellers satisfied. Only at point E are demanders willing to buy exactly the amount that businesses are willing to produce and sell.

How does the economy reach its equilibrium? Indeed, what do we mean by equilibrium? A **macroeconomic equilibrium** is a combination of overall price and quantity at which neither buyers nor sellers wish to change their purchases, sales, or prices. Figure 20-6 illustrates the concept. If the price level were higher than equilibrium, say, at $P = 200$, businesses would want to sell more than purchasers would want to buy; businesses would desire to sell quantity C, while buyers would want to purchase only amount B. Goods would pile up on the shelves as firms produced more than consumers bought. Eventually, firms would cut production and begin to shave their prices. As the price level declined from its original too high level of 200, the gap between desired spending and desired sales would narrow until the equilibrium at $P = 150$ and $Q = 3000$ was reached. Once the equilibrium is reached, neither buyers nor sellers wish to change their quantities demanded or supplied, and there is no pressure on the price level to change.

MACROECONOMIC HISTORY: 1900–1996

We can use the aggregate supply-and-demand apparatus to analyze some of the major macroeconomic events of twentieth-century American history. We focus on the economic expansion during the Vietnam war, the stagflation caused by the supply shocks of the 1970s, the deep recession caused by the monetary contraction of the early 1980s, and the phenomenal record of economic growth for this century.

Wartime Boom. The American economy entered the 1960s having experienced numerous recessions. John Kennedy took over the presidency hoping to resuscitate the economy. This was the era when the "New Economics," as the Keynesian approach was called, came to Washington. Economic advisers to Presidents Kennedy and Johnson recommended expansionary policies, and Congress enacted measures to stimulate the economy, including sharp cuts in personal and corporate taxes in 1963 and 1964. GDP grew 4 percent annually during the early 1960s, unemployment declined, and prices were stable. By 1965, the economy was at its potential output.

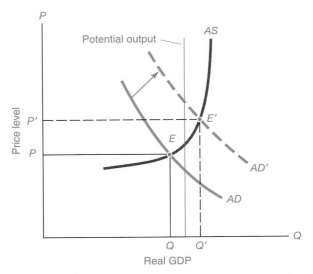

FIGURE 20-7. Wartime Boom Is Propelled by Increasing Aggregate Demand

During wartime, increased defense spending increases aggregate spending, moving aggregate demand from AD to AD', with equilibrium output increasing from E to E'. When output rises far above potential output, the price level moves up sharply from P to P', and wartime inflation ensues.

Unfortunately, the government underestimated the magnitude of the buildup for the Vietnam war; defense spending grew by 55 percent from 1965 to 1968. Even when it became clear that a major inflationary boom was under way, President Johnson postponed painful fiscal steps to slow the economy. Tax increases and civilian expenditure cuts came only in 1968, which was too late to prevent inflationary pressures from overheating the economy. The Federal Reserve accommodated the expansion with rapid money growth and low interest rates. As a result, for much of the period 1966–1970, the economy operated far above its potential output. Under the pressure of low unemployment and high factory utilization, inflation began to rise, inaugurating the "age of inflation" that lasted from 1966 through 1981.

Figure 20-7 illustrates the events of this period. The tax cuts and defense expenditures increased aggregate demand, shifting the aggregate demand curve to the right from AD to AD', with the equilibrium shifting from E to E'. Output and employment rose sharply, and prices began to accelerate as output exceeded capacity limits. Economists learned that it was easier to stimulate the economy than to persuade policymakers to raise taxes to slow the economy when inflation threatened. This lesson led many to question the wisdom of using fiscal policies to stabilize the economy.

Supply Shocks and Stagflation. During the 1970s, the industrial world was struck by a new macroeconomic malady, supply shocks. A **supply shock** is a sudden change in conditions of cost or productivity that shifts aggregate supply sharply. Supply shocks occurred with particular virulence in 1973. Called the "year of the seven plagues," 1973 was marked by crop failures, shifting ocean currents, massive speculation on world commodity markets, turmoil in foreign exchange markets, and a Mideast war that led to quadrupling of the world price of crude oil.

This jolt to crude-material and fuel supplies raised wholesale prices dramatically. The prices of crude materials and fuels rose more from 1972 to 1973 than they had in the entire period from the end of World War II to 1972. Shortly after the supply shock, inflation mounted sharply, and real output fell as the United States experienced a period of stagflation.

How can we understand the combination of falling output and rising prices? This large, unexpected rise in the cost of raw materials constituted a supply shock, which we portray as an upward shift in the aggregate supply curve. An upward shift in *AS* indicates that businesses will supply the same level of output only at substantially higher prices. Figure 20-8 illustrates a supply shift.

Supply shocks produce higher prices, followed by a decline in output and an increase in unemployment. Supply shocks thus lead to a deterioration of all the major goals of macroeconomic policy.

Tight Money, 1979–1982. By 1979 the economy had recovered from the 1973 supply shock. Output had returned to its potential. But unrest in the Middle East led to another oil shock as the Iranian revolution produced a jump in oil prices from $14 per barrel in early 1978 to $34 per barrel in 1979. Inflation increased dramatically—averaging 12 percent per year from 1978 to 1980.

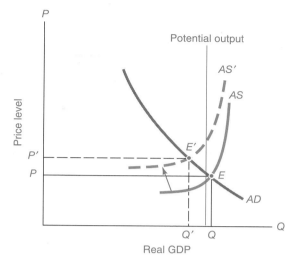

FIGURE 20-8. Effects of Supply Shocks

Sharply higher oil, commodity, or labor costs increase the costs of doing business. This leads to stagflation—stagnation combined with inflation. In the *AS-AD* framework, the higher costs shift the *AS* curve up from *AS* to *AS'*, and the equilibrium shifts from *E* to *E'*. Output declines from *Q* to *Q'*, while prices rise. The economy thus suffers a double whammy—lower output and higher prices.

Double-digit inflation was unacceptable. In response, the Federal Reserve, under the leadership of economist Paul Volcker, prescribed the strong medicine of tight money to slow the inflation. Interest rates rose sharply in 1979 and 1980, the stock market fell, and credit was hard to find. The Fed's tight-money policy slowed spending by consumers and businesses. Particularly hard-hit were interest-sensitive components of aggregate demand. After 1979, housing construction, automobile purchases, business investment, and net exports declined sharply.

We can picture how tight money raised interest rates and reduced aggregate demand in Figure 20-7 simply by reversing the arrow. That is, tight monetary policy reduced spending and produced a leftward and downward shift of the aggregate demand curve—exactly the opposite of the effect of the defense buildup during the 1960s. The decrease in aggregate demand reduced output almost 10 percent below its potential by the end of 1982, and the unemployment rate rose from below 6 percent in 1979 to more than 10 percent at the end of 1982.

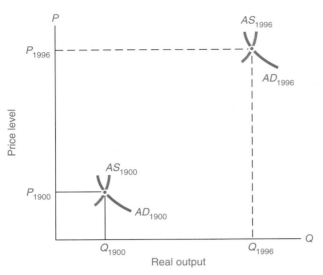

FIGURE 20-9. Growth in Potential Output Determines Long-Run Economic Performance

Over this century, increases in labor, capital, and efficiency have led to a vast increase in the economy's productive potential, shifting aggregate supply far to the right. In the long run, aggregate supply is the primary determinant of output growth.

The reward for these austere measures was a dramatic decline in inflation, from an average of 12 percent per year in the 1978–1980 period to 4 percent during the period from 1983 to 1988. Tight monetary policies succeeded in bringing to an end the age of inflation, but the nation paid for this achievement through higher unemployment and lower output during the period of tight money.

The resolute monetary policies of the early 1980s set the stage for the long economic expansion from 1982 through 1997. This period, marked by only one mild recession in 1990–1991, proved to be the period of the greatest macroeconomic stability in American history. Real GDP grew at an average rate of 3 percent annually, with price inflation averaging slightly above 3 percent. By the late 1990s, many workers had never experienced a severe business cycle or inflationary episode, and some were proclaiming naively that the business cycle was abolished in this "brave-new-world economy."

The Growth Century. The final act in our macroeconomic drama concerns the growth of output and prices over the entire period since 1900. As shown by the graph inside the front cover of this book, output has grown by a factor of more than 16

since the turn of the century. How can we explain this long-term pattern?

A careful look at American economic growth reveals that the growth rate during this century has averaged 3.1 percent per year. Part of this growth was due to growth in the scale of production as inputs of capital, labor, and even land grew sharply over this period. Just as important were improvements in efficiency due to new products (such as automobiles) and new processes (such as electronic computing). Other, less visible factors also contributed to economic growth, such as improved management techniques and improved services (including such innovations as the assembly line and overnight delivery). Many economists believe that the measured growth understates true growth because our measurements tend to miss the contribution to living standards from new products and improvements in product quality. For example, when Thomas Crapper invented the indoor toilet, millions of people no longer had to struggle through the winter snows to relieve themselves in outhouses, yet this increased comfort never showed up in measured gross domestic product.

How can we picture the tremendous rise in output in our *AS-AD* apparatus? Figure 20-9 shows the way. The increase in inputs and improvements in efficiency led to a massive rightward shift of the *AS* curve from AS_{1900} to AS_{1996}. There was also a sharp increase in the cost of production, as average hourly earnings rose from $0.10 per hour to $11.82 per hour, so the *AS* curve also shifted upward. The overall effect, then, was the increase in both output and prices shown in Figure 20-9.

The Role of Economic Policy

How does macroeconomic policy fit into the picture? The major task of macroeconomic policy today is to diagnose the condition of the economy and to prescribe the right medicine. As an example, consider the economic issues discussed during the 1996 presidential debates. Unemployment and inflation were both low, as the economy had avoided both recession and high inflation for several years. However, most observers were concerned about the stagnation in the rate of growth of productivity (or output per worker) and real wages (dollar wages corrected for inflation).

As the incumbent, President Clinton argued that the appropriate approach was to continue to reduce the budget deficit while improving human skills. He and his economic advisers reasoned that reducing the government deficit would increase national saving, increase national investment, and thereby increase the growth of potential output. This would, in effect, shift the *AS* curve out faster for the future versions of Figure 20-9.

The Republican challenger Robert Dole preferred to rely upon supply-side economics, cutting taxes and expenditures and reducing regulatory burdens. The idea behind this approach was that lower taxes would stimulate saving, investment, and innovation. Skeptics argued that the tax cuts would raise the government deficit and crowd out private investment. The supply siders responded that the enhanced incentives would lead to much more rapid output growth, with growth revenues largely offsetting the lower tax rates.

How can macroeconomics contribute to resolving this debate? Part of the difference rests on questions such as those about the size of government and the wisdom of using economic policies to attack social problems. Economists can provide no scientifically correct answer to such questions, for they involve *normative* issues of social and political values. But macroeconomists can analyze questions of *positive* macroeconomics. Macroeconomists estimate the impact of cutting tax rates on tax revenues and the budget deficit; they attempt to determine the extent to which higher saving and investment will increase output growth; and they help weigh the relative advantages of investing in people or technology versus building factories. While answers to these macroeconomic questions cannot resolve the issues of national economic policy, study of macroeconomics arms us for the great debate.

SUMMARY

A. Key Concepts of Macroeconomics

1. Macroeconomics is the study of the behavior of the entire economy: it analyzes long-run growth as well as the cyclical movements in total output, unemployment and inflation, the money supply and the budget deficit, and international trade and finance. This contrasts with microeconomics, which studies the behavior of individual markets, prices, and outputs.

2. The United States proclaimed its macroeconomic goals in the Employment Act of 1946, which declared that federal policy was "to promote maximum employment, production, and purchasing power." Since then, the nation's priorities among these three goals have shifted. But all market economies still face three central macroeconomic questions: (*a*) Why do output and employment sometimes fall, and how can unemploy-

ment be reduced? (*b*) What are the sources of price inflation, and how can it be kept under control? (*c*) How can a nation increase its rate of economic growth?

3. In addition to these perplexing questions is the hard fact that there are inevitable conflicts or tradeoffs among these goals: Rapid growth in future living standards may mean reducing consumption today, and curbing inflation may involve a temporary period of high unemployment.

4. Economists evaluate the success of an economy's overall performance by how well it attains these objectives: (*a*) high levels and rapid growth of output and consumption [output is usually measured by the gross domestic product (GDP), which is the total value of all final goods and services produced in a given year; also,

GDP should be high relative to potential GDP, the maximum sustainable or high-employment level of output]; (*b*) low unemployment rate and high employment, with an ample supply of good jobs; (*c*) price-level stability (or low inflation).

5. Before the science of macroeconomics was developed, countries tended to drift around in the shifting macroeconomic currents without a rudder. Today, there are numerous instruments with which governments can steer the economy: (*a*) Fiscal policy (government spending and taxation) helps determine the allocation of resources between private and collective goods, affects people's incomes and consumption, and provides incentives for investment and other economic decisions. (*b*) Monetary policy (particularly central-bank regulation of the money supply to influence interest rates and credit conditions) affects sectors in the economy that are interest-sensitive. The most affected sectors are housing, business investment, and net exports.

6. The nation is but a small part of an increasingly integrated global economy in which countries are linked together through trade of goods and services and through financial flows. A smoothly running international economic system contributes to rapid economic growth, but the international economy can throw sand in the engine of growth when trade flows are interrupted or the international financial mechanism breaks down. Dealing with international trade and finance is high on the agenda of all countries.

B. Aggregate Supply and Demand

7. The central concepts for understanding the determination of national output and the price level are aggregate supply (*AS*) and aggregate demand (*AD*). Aggregate demand consists of the total spending in an economy by households, businesses, governments, and foreigners. It represents the total output that would be willingly bought at each price level, given the monetary and fiscal policies and other factors affecting demand. Aggregate supply describes how much output businesses would willingly produce and sell given prices, costs, and market conditions.

8. *AS* and *AD* curves have the same shapes as the familiar supply and demand curves analyzed in microeconomics. The downward-sloping *AD* curve shows the amount that consumers, firms, and other purchasers would buy at each level of prices, with other factors held constant. The *AS* curve depicts the amount that businesses would willingly produce and sell at each price level, other things held constant. (But beware of potential confusions of microeconomic and aggregate supply and demand.)

9. The overall macroeconomic equilibrium, determining both aggregate price and output, comes where the *AS* and *AD* curves intersect. At the equilibrium price level, purchasers willingly buy what businesses willingly sell. Equilibrium output can depart from full employment or potential output.

10. Recent American history shows an irregular cycle of aggregate demand and supply shocks and policy reactions. In the mid-1960s, war-bloated deficits plus easy money led to a rapid increase in aggregate demand. The result was a sharp upturn in prices and inflation. In 1973 and again in 1979, adverse supply shocks led to an upward shift in aggregate supply. This led to stagflation, with a simultaneous rise in unemployment and inflation. At the end of the 1970s, economic policymakers reacted to the rising inflation by tightening monetary policy and raising interest rates. The result lowered spending on interest-sensitive demands such as housing, investment, and net exports. The period of austerity lowered inflation and ushered in a long period of macroeconomic stability.

11. Over the long run of the entire century, the growth of potential output has increased aggregate supply enormously and led to continual growth in output and living standards.

CONCEPTS FOR REVIEW

Major Macroeconomic Concepts

macroeconomics vs. microeconomics
gross domestic product (GDP), actual
    and potential
employment, unemployment, unem-
    ployment rate
inflation, deflation

consumer price index (CPI)
net exports
fiscal policy (government expendi-
    tures, taxation)
money, monetary policy

Aggregate Supply and Demand

aggregate supply, aggregate demand

AS curve, *AD* curve
equilibrium of *AS* and *AD*
three macroeconomic shocks:
    wartime boom
    supply shock
    tight money
sources of long-run economic growth

QUESTIONS FOR DISCUSSION

1. What are the major objectives of macroeconomics? Write a brief definition of each of these objectives. Explain carefully why each objective is important.

2. If the CPI were 300 in 1996 and 315 in 1997, what would the inflation rate be for 1997?

3. What would be the effect of each of the following on aggregate demand or on aggregate supply, as indicated?
   a. A large oil-price increase (on *AS*)
   b. An arms-reduction agreement reducing defense spending (on *AD*)
   c. An increase in potential output (on *AS*)
   d. A monetary loosening that lowers interest rates (on *AD*)

4. For each of the events listed in question 3, use the *AS-AD* apparatus to show the effect on output and on the overall price level.

5. Put yourself in the shoes of an economic policymaker. The economy is in equilibrium with $P = 100$ and $Q = 3000$ = potential GDP. You refuse to "accommodate" inflation; i.e., you want to keep prices absolutely stable at $P = 100$, no matter what happens to output. You can use monetary and fiscal policies to affect aggregate demand, but you cannot affect aggregate supply in the short run. How would you respond to:
   a. A surprise increase in investment spending
   b. A sharp food-price increase following catastrophic floods of the Mississippi River
   c. A productivity decline that reduces potential output
   d. A sharp decrease in net exports that followed a deep depression in Europe

6. In 1981–1983, the Reagan administration implemented a fiscal policy that reduced taxes and increased government spending.
   a. Explain why this policy would tend to increase aggregate demand. Show the impact on output and prices assuming only an *AD* shift.
   b. The supply-side school holds that tax cuts would affect aggregate supply mainly by increasing potential output. Assuming that the Reagan fiscal measures affected *AS* as well as *AD*, show the impact on output and the price level. Explain why the impact of the Reagan fiscal policies on output is unambiguous while the impact on prices is unclear.

7. The Clinton economic package as passed by Congress in 1993 had the effect of tightening fiscal policy by raising taxes and lowering spending. Show the effect of this policy (*a*) assuming that there is no counteracting monetary policy and (*b*) assuming that monetary policy completely neutralized the impact on GDP and that the lower deficit leads to higher investment and higher growth of potential output.

8. Consider the data on real GDP and the price level in Table 20-2.
   a. For the years 1981 to 1985, calculate the rate of growth of real GDP and the rate of inflation. Can you guess in which year there was a steep business downturn or recession?
   b. In an *AS-AD* diagram like Figure 20-6 (page 383), draw a set of *AS* and *AD* curves that trace out the price and output equilibria shown in the table. How would you explain the recession that you have identified?

TABLE 20-2. Source: *Economic Report of the President*, 1997.

Year	Real GDP ($, billion, 1992 prices)	Price level* (1992 = 100)
1980	3,776	71.7
1981	3,843	78.9
1982	3,760	83.8
1983	3,907	87.2
1984	4,149	91.0
1985	4,280	94.4

* Note that the price index shown is the price index for GDP, which measures the price trend for all components of GDP.

CHAPTER 21
MEASURING ECONOMIC ACTIVITY

When you can measure what you are speaking about, and express it in numbers, you know something about it; when you cannot measure it, when you cannot express it in numbers, your knowledge is of a meager and unsatisfactory kind; it may be the beginning of knowledge, but you have scarcely, in your thoughts, advanced to the stage of science.

Lord Kelvin

Of all the concepts in macroeconomics, the most important single measure is the gross domestic product (GDP), which measures the total value of goods and services produced in a country. GDP statistics enable the President, Congress, and the Federal Reserve to judge whether the economy is contracting or expanding, whether it needs a boost or should be reined in a bit, and whether a severe recession or inflation threatens. When economists want to determine the level of economic development of a country, they look at its GDP per capita. Data from the national income accounts are like beacons that help policymakers steer the economy toward the key economic objectives. Without measures of national economic aggregates like GDP, policymakers would be adrift in a sea of unorganized data.

While the GDP and the rest of the national income accounts may seem to be arcane concepts, they are truly among the great inventions of the twentieth century. Much as a satellite in space can survey the weather across an entire continent, so can the GDP give an overall picture of the state of the economy. In addition, advances in macroeconomic theory would be impossible without GDP, measures of prices called price indexes, and other measures of national income. These measures enable us to tackle the central issues of macroeconomics, including economic growth, the business cycle, the relationship between economic activity and unemployment, and the measurement and determinants of inflation.

In this chapter, we explain how economists measure GDP and other major macroeconomic concepts.

GROSS DOMESTIC PRODUCT: THE YARDSTICK OF AN ECONOMY'S PERFORMANCE

What is the **gross domestic product**? GDP is the name we give to the total dollar value of the final goods and services produced within a nation during a given year. It is the figure you get when you apply the measuring rod of money to the diverse goods and services—from apples to zithers—that a country produces with its land, labor, and capital resources. GDP equals the sum of the money values of all consumption and investment goods, government purchases, and net exports to other lands.

The gross domestic product (or GDP) is the most comprehensive measure of a nation's total output of goods and services. It is the sum of the dollar values of consumption, gross investment, government purchases of goods and services, and net exports produced within a nation during a given year.

GDP is used for many purposes, but the most important one is to measure the overall performance of an economy. If you ask an economic histo-

Circular Flow of Macroeconomic Activity

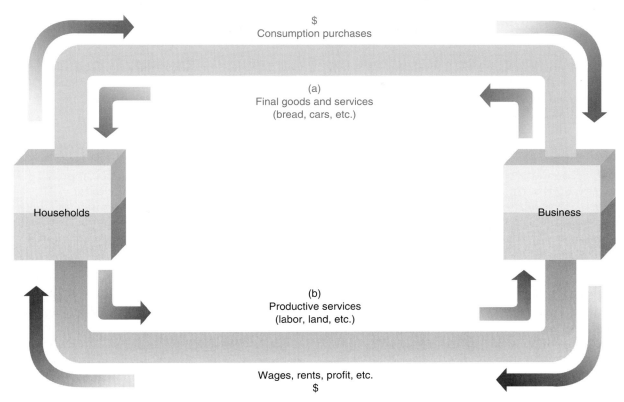

FIGURE 21-1. Gross Domestic Product Can Be Measured Either as (*a*) a Flow of Final Products or, Equivalently, as (*b*) a Flow of Costs

In the upper loop, people spend their money on final goods. The total dollar flow of their spending each year is one measure of gross domestic product. The lower loop measures the annual flow of costs of output: the earnings that businesses pay out in wages, rent, interest, dividends, and profits.

The two measures of GDP must always be identical. Note that this figure is the *macroeconomic* counterpart of Fig. 2-1, which presented the circular flow of supply and demand.

rian what happened during the Great Depression, the best short answer would be:

> Between 1929 and 1933, GDP fell from $104 billion to $56 billion. This sharp decline in the dollar value of goods and services produced by the American economy caused hardship, bankruptcies, bank failures, riots, and political turmoil.

We now discuss the elements of the national income and product accounts. We start by showing different ways of measuring GDP and distinguishing real from nominal GDP. We then analyze the major

components of GDP. We conclude with a discussion of the measurement of the general price level and the rate of inflation.

Two Measures of National Product: Goods Flow and Earnings Flow

How do economists actually measure GDP? One of the major surprises is that we can measure GDP in two entirely independent ways. As Figure 21-1 shows, GDP can be measured either as a flow of products or as a sum of earnings.

To demonstrate the different ways of measuring GDP, we begin by considering an oversimplified world in which there is no government, foreign trade, or investment. For the moment, our little economy produces only *consumption goods,* which are items that are purchased by households to satisfy their wants. (Important note: Our first example is oversimplified to show the basic ideas. In the realistic examples that follow, we will add investment, government, and the foreign sector.)

Flow-of-Product Approach.

Flow-of-Product Approach. Each year the public consumes a wide variety of final goods and services: goods such as apples, oranges, and bread; services such as health care and haircuts. We include only *final goods*—goods ultimately bought and used by consumers. Households spend their incomes for these consumer goods, as is shown in the upper loop of Figure 21-1. Add together all the consumption dollars spent on these final goods, and you will arrive at this simplified economy's total GDP.

Thus, in our simple economy, you can easily calculate national income or product as the sum of the annual flow of *final* goods and services: (price of oranges × number of oranges) plus (price of apples × number of apples) and so forth for all other final goods. The gross domestic product is defined as the total money value of the flow of final products produced by the nation.

Note that we use market prices as weights in valuing different commodities. Why use market prices rather than mass, volume, or the labor-hours used in production? Market prices are used as measuring rods because they reflect the relative economic value of diverse goods and services. That is, the relative prices of different goods reflect how much consumers value their last (or marginal) units of consumption of these goods. Thus the choice of market prices as weights for different goods is not arbitrary; in a well-functioning market economy prices reflect the relative satisfactions that consumers receive from each good.

Earnings or Cost Approach.

Earnings or Cost Approach. The second and equivalent way to calculate GDP is the earnings or cost approach. Go to the lower loop in Figure 21-1. Through it flow all the costs of doing business; these costs include the wages paid to labor, the rents paid to land, the profits paid to capital, and so forth. But these business costs are also the earnings that households receive from firms. By measuring the annual flow of these earnings or incomes, statisticians will again arrive at the GDP.

Hence, a second way to calculate GDP is as the total of factor earnings (wages, interest, rents, and profits) that are the costs of producing society's final products.

Equivalence of the Two Approaches.

Equivalence of the Two Approaches. Now we have calculated GDP by the upper-loop flow-of-product approach and by the lower-loop earnings-flow approach. Which is the better approach? The surprise is that they are *exactly* the same.

We can understand the identity of the two approaches by examining a simple barbershop economy. Say the barbers have no expenses other than labor. If they sell 10 haircuts at $8 each, GDP is $80. But the barbers' earnings (in wages and profits) are also exactly $80. Hence, the GDP here is identical whether measured as flow of products ($80 of haircuts) or as cost and income ($80 of wages and profits).

In fact, the two approaches are identical because we have included "profit" in the lower loop along with other incomes. What exactly is profit? Profit is what remains from the sale of a product after you have paid the other factor costs—wages, interest, and rents. It is the residual that adjusts automatically to make the lower loop's costs or earnings exactly match the upper loop's value of goods.

To sum up:

GDP, or gross domestic product, can be measured in two different ways: (1) as the flow of final products, or (2) as the total costs or earnings of inputs producing output. Because profit is a residual, both approaches will yield exactly the same total GDP.

National Accounts Derived from Business Accounts

You might wonder where on earth economists find all the data for the national accounts. In practice, government economists draw on a wide array of sources, including surveys, income-tax returns, retail-sales statistics, and employment data.

The most important source of data is business accounts. An *account* for a firm or nation is a numerical record of all flows (outputs, costs, etc.) during a

(a) Income Statement of Typical Farm			
Output in farming		**Earnings**	
Sales of goods (corn, apples, etc.)	$1,000	**Costs of production:**	
		Wages	$ 800
		Rents	100
		Interest	25
		Profit (residual)	75
Total	$1,000	Total	$1,000

(b) National Product Account (Millions of Dollars)			
Upper-loop flow of product		**Lower-loop flow of earnings**	
Final output (10 × 1,000)	$10,000	**Costs or earnings:**	
		Wages (10 × 800)	$ 8,000
		Rents (10 × 100)	1,000
		Interest (10 × 25)	250
		Profit (10 × 75)	750
GDP total	$10,000	GDP total	$10,000

TABLE 21-1. Construction of National Product Accounts from Business Accounts

Part (**a**) shows the income statement of a typical farm. The left side shows the value of production, while the right side shows the farm's costs. Part (**b**) then adds up or aggregates the 10 million identical farms to obtain total GDP. Note that GDP from the product side exactly equals GDP from the earnings side.

given period. We can show the relationship between business and national accounts by constructing the accounts for an economy made up only of farms. The top half of Table 21-1 shows the results of a year's farming operations for a single, typical farm. We put sales of final products on the left-hand side and the various costs of production on the right. The bottom half of Table 21-1 shows how to construct the GDP accounts for our simple agrarian economy in which all final products are produced on 10 million identical farms. The national accounts simply add together the outputs and costs of the 10 million identical farms to get the two different measures of GDP.

The Problem of "Double Counting"

We defined GDP as the total production of final goods and services. A *final product* is one that is produced and sold for consumption or investment. GDP excludes *intermediate goods*—goods that are used up to produce other goods. GDP therefore includes bread but not wheat, and cars but not steel.

For the flow-of-product calculation of GDP, excluding intermediate products poses no major complications. We simply include the bread and cars in GDP but avoid including the wheat and dough that went into the bread or the steel and glass that went into the cars. If you look again at the upper loop in Figure 21-1, you will see that bread and cars appear in the flow of products, but you will not find any flour or steel.

What has happened to products like flour and steel? They are intermediate products and are simply cycling around inside the block marked "Business." They are never bought by consumers, and they never show up as final products in GDP.

"Value Added" in the Lower Loop. A new statistician who is being trained to make GDP measurements might be puzzled, saying:

I can see that, if you are careful, your upper-loop product approach to GDP will avoid including intermediate products. But aren't you in some trouble when you use the lower-loop cost or earnings approach?

After all, when we gather income statements from the accounts of firms, won't we pick up what grain merchants pay to wheat farmers, what bakers pay to grain merchants, and what grocers pay to bakers? Won't this result in double counting or even

Bread Receipts, Costs, and Value Added (Cents per Loaf)				
Stage of production	(1) Sales receipts	(2) Cost of intermediate materials or goods		(3) Value added (wages, profit, etc.) (3) = (1) − (2)
Wheat	24	−0	=	24
Flour	33	−24	=	9
Baked dough	60	−33	=	27
Delivered bread	90	−60	=	30
	207	−117		90
				(sum of value added)

TABLE 21-2. GDP Sums Up Value Added at Each Production Stage

To avoid double counting of intermediate products, we carefully calculate value added at each stage, subtracting all the costs of materials and intermediate products not produced in that stage but bought from other businesses. Note that every black intermediate-product item both appears in column (1) and is subtracted, as a negative element, in the next stage of production in column (2). (How much would we overestimate GDP if we counted all receipts, not just value added? The overestimate would be 117 cents per loaf.)

triple counting of items going through several productive stages?

These are good questions, but there is an ingenious answer that will resolve the problem. In making lower-loop earnings measurements, statisticians are very careful to include in GDP only a firm's value added. **Value added** is the difference between a firm's sales and its purchases of materials and services from other firms.

In other words, in calculating the GDP earnings or value added by a firm, the statistician includes all costs that go to factors other than businesses and excludes all payments made to other businesses. Hence business costs in the form of wages, salaries, interest payments, and dividends are included in value added, but purchases of wheat or steel or electricity are excluded from value added. Why are all the purchases from other firms excluded from value added to obtain GDP? Because those purchases will get properly counted in GDP in the values added by other firms.

Table 21-2 uses the stages of bread production to illustrate how careful adherence to the value-added approach enables us to subtract the intermediate expenses that show up in the income statements of farmers, millers, bakers, and grocers. The final calculation shows the desired equality between (1) final

sales of bread and (2) total earnings, calculated as the sum of all values added in all the different stages of bread production.

We can summarize as follows:

Value-added approach: To avoid double counting, we take care to include only final goods in GDP and to exclude the intermediate goods that are used up in making the final goods. By measuring the value added at each stage, taking care to subtract expenditures on the intermediate goods bought from other firms, the lower-loop earnings approach properly avoids all double counting and records wages, interest, rent, and profit exactly one time.

DETAILS OF THE NATIONAL ACCOUNTS

Now that we have an overview of the national income and product accounts, we will proceed, in the rest of this chapter, on a whirlwind tour of the various sectors. Before we start on the journey, look at Table 21-3 to get an idea of where we are going. This table shows a summary set of accounts for both the product and the income sides. If you know the structure of the table and the definitions of the terms in it, you will be well on your way to understanding GDP and its family of components.

Product approach	Earnings approach
Components of gross domestic product:	**Earnings or costs as sources of gross domestic product:**
Consumption (C)	Wages, salaries, and other labor income
+ Gross private domestic investment (I)	+ Interest, rent, and other property income
+ Government (G)	+ Indirect taxes
+ Net exports (X)	+ Depreciation
	+ Profits
Equals: Gross domestic product	**Equals: Gross domestic product**

TABLE 21-3. Overview of the National Income and Product Accounts

This table presents the major components of the two sides of the national accounts. The left side shows the components of the product approach (or upper loop); the symbols C, I, G, and X are often used to represent these four items of GDP. The right side shows the components of the earnings or cost approach (or lower loop). Each approach will ultimately add up to exactly the same GDP.

Real vs. Nominal GDP: "Deflating" GDP by a Price Index

We define GDP as the dollar value of goods and services. In measuring the dollar value, we use the measuring rod of *market prices* for the different goods and services. But prices change over time, as inflation generally sends prices upward year after year. Who would want to measure things with a rubber yardstick—one that stretches in your hands from day to day—rather than a rigid and invariant yardstick?

The problem of changing prices is one of the problems economists have to solve when they use money as their measuring rod. Clearly, we want a measure of the nation's output and income that uses an invariant yardstick. Economists can replace the elastic yardstick with a reliable one by removing the price-increase component so as to create a real or quantity index of national output.

The basic idea is the following: We can measure the GDP for a particular year using the actual market prices of that year; this gives us the **nominal GDP,** or GDP at current prices. But we are usually more interested in determining what has happened to the **real GDP,** which is an index of the volume or quantity of goods and services produced. More precisely, we measure real GDP by multiplying the quantities of goods by an invariant or fixed set of prices. Hence, nominal GDP is calculated using changing prices while real GDP is calculated using constant prices.

When we divide nominal GDP by real GDP, we obtain the **GDP deflator,** which serves as a measure of the overall price level. We can calculate real GDP by dividing nominal GDP by the GDP deflator.

A simple example will illustrate the general idea. Say that a country produces 1000 bushels of corn in year 1 and 1010 bushels in year 2. The price of a bushel is $1 in year 1 and $2 in year 2. We can calculate nominal GDP (PQ) as $1 × 1000 = $1000 in year 1 and $2 × 1010 = $2020 in year 2. Nominal GDP therefore grew by 102 percent between the two years.

But the actual amount of output did not grow anywhere near that rapidly. To find real output, we need to consider what happened to prices. We use year 1 as the base year, or the year in which we measure prices. We set the price index, the GDP deflator, as $P_1 = 1$ in the first, or base, year. From the data in the last paragraph, we see that the GDP deflator is $P_2 = \$2/\$1 = 2$ in year 2. Real GDP (Q) is equal to nominal GDP (PQ) divided by the GDP deflator (P). Hence real GDP was equal to $1000/1 = $1000 in year 1 and $2020/2 = $1010 in year 2. Thus the growth in real GDP, which corrects for the change in prices, is 1 percent and equals the growth in the output of corn, as it should.

A 1929–1933 comparison will illustrate the deflation process for an actual historical episode. Table 21-4 on page 396 gives nominal GDP figures of $104 billion for 1929 and $56 billion for 1933. This represents a 46 percent drop in nominal GDP from 1929 to 1933. But the government estimates that prices on average dropped about 23 percent over this period. If we choose 1929 as our base year, with the GDP deflator of 1 in that year, this means that the 1933

Date	(1) Nominal GDP (current $, billion)	(2) Index number of prices (GDP deflator, 1929 = 1)	(3) Real GDP ($, billion, 1929 prices) $(3) = \dfrac{(1)}{(2)}$
1929	104	1.00	$\dfrac{104}{1.00} = 104$
1933	56	0.77	$\dfrac{56}{0.77} = 73$

TABLE 21-4. Real (or Inflation-Corrected) GDP Is Obtained by Dividing Nominal GDP by the GDP Deflator

Using the price index of column (2), we deflate column (1) to get real GDP, column (3).

(Riddle: Can you show that 1929's real GDP was $80 billion in terms of 1933 prices? *Hint:* With 1933 as a base of 1, 1929's price index is 1.30.)

price index was about 0.77. So our $56 billion 1933 GDP was really worth much more than half the $104 billion GDP of 1929. Table 21-4 shows that real GDP fell to only seven-tenths of the 1929 level: in terms of 1929 prices, or dollars of 1929 purchasing power, real GDP fell to $73 billion. Hence, part of the near-halving shown by the nominal GDP was due to the optical illusion of the shrinking price yardstick.

The black line in Figure 21-2 shows the growth of nominal GDP since 1929, expressed in the actual dollars and prices that were current in each historical year. Then, for comparison, the real GDP, expressed in 1992 dollars, is shown in rust. Clearly, much of the increase in nominal GDP over the last half-century is due to inflation in the price units of our money yardstick.

Table 21-4 shows the simplest way of calculating real GDP and the GDP deflator. Sometimes these calculations give misleading results, particularly when the prices and quantities of important goods are changing rapidly. For example, over the last two decades, computer prices have been falling very sharply while the quantity of computers has risen rapidly (we return below to this issue in our discussion of price indexes).

When relative prices are changing sharply, using prices of a given year (say, computer prices for 1980) will suggest that computer output is rising unrealistically rapidly. To correct for this bias, statisticians use *chain weights.* Instead of keeping the relative weights

on each good fixed, chain weights change each year to reflect the evolving spending patterns in the economy. Today, the official government measures of the U.S. GDP and GDP price index rely upon chain weights. The technical names for these constructs are "real GDP in chained dollars" and the "chain-type price index for GDP."[1] For simplicity, we generally refer to real GDP and the GDP deflator, whose movements track the chain indexes very closely.

To summarize:

Nominal GDP (PQ) represents the total money value of final goods and services produced in a given year, where the values are in terms of the market prices of each year. Real GDP (Q) removes price changes from nominal GDP and calculates GDP in constant prices. The traditional GDP deflator is the "price of GDP" and is defined as follows:

$$Q = \text{real GDP} = \frac{\text{nominal GDP}}{\text{GDP deflator}} = \frac{PQ}{P}$$

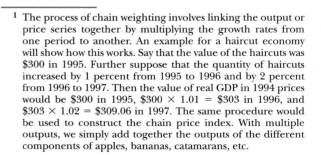

[1] The process of chain weighting involves linking the output or price series together by multiplying the growth rates from one period to another. An example for a haircut economy will show how this works. Say that the value of the haircuts was $300 in 1995. Further suppose that the quantity of haircuts increased by 1 percent from 1995 to 1996 and by 2 percent from 1996 to 1997. Then the value of real GDP in 1995 prices would be $300 in 1995, $300 × 1.01 = $303 in 1996, and $303 × 1.02 = $309.06 in 1997. The same procedure would be used to construct the chain price index. With multiple outputs, we simply add together the outputs of the different components of apples, bananas, catamarans, etc.

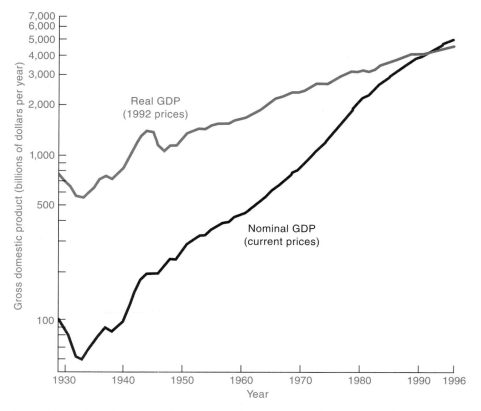

FIGURE 21-2. Nominal GDP Grows Faster than Real GDP Because of Price Inflation

The rise in nominal GDP exaggerates the rise in output. Why? Because growth in nominal GDP includes increases in prices as well as growth in output. To obtain an accurate measure of real output, we must correct GDP for price changes. (Source: U.S. Department of Commerce.)

To correct for rapidly changing relative prices, the U.S. national accounts use chain weights to construct real GDP and price indexes.

Investment and Capital Formation

So far, our analysis has banished all capital goods. In real life, however, nations devote part of their output to production of investment goods. **Investment** consists of the additions to the nation's capital stock of buildings, equipment, and inventories during a year. Investment involves the sacrifice of current consumption to increase future consumption. Instead of eating more pizza now, people build new pizza ovens to make it possible to produce more pizza for future consumption.

 Real investment: Economists define "investment" (or sometimes real investment) as production of durable capital goods. In common usage, "investment" often denotes using money to buy General Motors stock or to open a savings account. For clarity, economists call this *financial investment*. Try not to confuse these two different uses of the word "investment."

If I take $1000 from my safe and put it in the bank or buy a government bond, in economic terms, no investment has taken place. All that has happened is that I have exchanged one financial asset for another. Only when production of a physical capital good takes place is there what the economist calls investment.

How does investment fit into the national accounts? If people are using part of society's production possibilities for capital formation rather than for consumption, economic statisticians recognize that such outputs must be included in the upper-loop flow of GDP. Investments represent additions to the stock of durable capital goods that increase production possibilities in the future. So we must modify our original definition to read:

Gross domestic product is the sum of all final products. Along with consumption goods and services, we must also include gross investment.

Net vs. Gross Investment. Our revised definition includes "gross investment" along with consumption. What does the word "gross" mean in this context? It indicates that investment includes all investment goods produced. Gross investment is not adjusted for **depreciation,** which measures the amount of capital that has been used up in a year. Thus gross investment includes all the machines, factories, and houses built during a year—even though some were bought simply to replace some old capital goods that burned down or were thrown on the scrap heap.

If you want to get a measure of the increase in society's capital, gross investment is not a sensible measure. Because it excludes a necessary allowance for depreciation, it is too large—too gross.

An analogy to population will make clear the importance of considering depreciation. If you want to measure the increase in the size of the population, you cannot simply count the number of births, for this would clearly exaggerate the net change in population. To get population growth, you must also subtract the number of deaths.

The same point holds for capital. To find the net increase in capital, you must start with gross investment and subtract the deaths of capital in the form of depreciation, or the amount of capital used up.

Thus to estimate capital formation we measure *net investment*. Net investment is always births of capital (gross investment) less deaths of capital (capital depreciation):

Net investment equals gross investment minus depreciation.

Figure 21-3 shows net investment and depreciation as a percent of GDP over the last half-century. You can see how depreciation has become increasingly important—largely because short-lived equipment like computers has become an increasingly large fraction of the capital stock. The share of output devoted to *net* investment has declined dramatically—from around $7\frac{1}{2}$ percent of output to about $2\frac{1}{2}$ percent of output in recent years. This low rate of net investment worries economists because investment is the vehicle by which new technologies get introduced into the productive process. As we will see later, nations with high investment rates tend to have high rates of productivity growth.

Government

Up to now we have talked about consumers but ignored the biggest buyer of all—federal, state, and local governments. Somehow GDP must take into account the billions of dollars of product a nation *collectively* consumes or invests. How do we do this?

Measuring government's contribution to national output is complicated because most government services are not sold on the marketplace. Rather, government purchases both consumption-type expenditures (like food for the military) and investment-type items (such as computers or military barracks). In measuring government's contribution to GDP, we simply add all these government purchases to the flow of consumption, investment, and, as we will see later, net exports.

Hence, all the government payroll expenditures on its employees plus the costs of goods (lasers, roads, and airplanes) it buys from private industry are included in this third category of flow of products, called "government consumption expenditures and gross investment." This category equals the contribution of federal, state, and local governments to GDP.

Exclusion of Transfer Payments. Does this mean that every dollar of government expenditure is included in GDP? Definitely not. GDP includes only government purchases of goods and services; it excludes spending on transfer payments.

Government **transfer payments** are government payments to individuals that are not made in exchange for goods or services supplied. Examples of government transfers include unemployment insurance, veterans' benefits, and old-age or disability payments. These payments meet some social purpose. But since they are not payments made to purchase a current good or service, they are omitted from GDP.

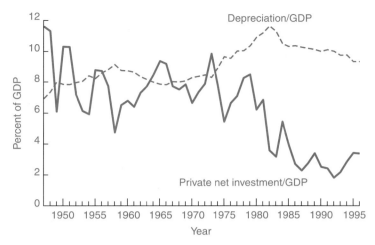

FIGURE 21-3. Investment Share of Output Has Plummeted

Net population change equals gross births minus deaths. Similarly, net investment equals gross investment minus depreciation. The falling line shows how private net investment's share in national output has fallen since the mid-1970s. The upper line shows depreciation as a proportion of GDP. The sum of the two curves is the share of gross private investment in gross domestic product. (Source: U.S. Department of Commerce.)

Thus if you receive a wage from the government because you are a teacher, your wage is a factor payment and would be included in GDP. If you receive a welfare payment because you are poor, that payment is not in return for a service but is a transfer payment and would be excluded from GDP.

One peculiar government transfer payment is the interest on the government debt. Interest is treated as a payment for debt incurred to pay for past wars or government programs and is not considered to be a purchase of a current good or service. Government interest payments are considered transfers and are therefore omitted from GDP.

Finally, do not confuse the way the national income accounts measure government spending on goods and services (*G*) with the official government budget. When the Treasury measures its expenditures, they include expenditures on goods and services (*G*) *plus* transfers.

Taxes. In using the flow-of-product approach to compute GDP, we need not worry about how the government finances its spending. It does not matter whether the government pays for its goods and services by taxing, by printing money, or by borrowing. Wher-

ever the dollars come from, the statistician computes the governmental component of GDP as the actual cost to the government of the goods and services.

It is fine to ignore taxes in the flow-of-product approach. But what about in the earnings or cost approach to GDP? Here we must account for taxes. Consider wages, for example. Part of my wage is turned over to the government through personal income taxes. These direct taxes definitely do get included in the wage component of business expenses, and the same holds for direct taxes (personal or corporate) on interest, rent, and profit.

Or consider the sales tax and other indirect taxes that manufacturers and retailers have to pay on a loaf of bread (or on the wheat, flour, and dough stages). Suppose these indirect taxes total 10 cents per loaf, and suppose wages, profit, and other value-added items cost the bread industry 90 cents. What will the bread sell for in the product approach? For 90 cents? Surely not. The bread will sell for $1, equal to 90 cents of factor costs plus 10 cents of indirect taxes.

Thus the cost approach to GDP includes both indirect and direct taxes as elements of the cost of producing final output.

Net Exports

The United States is an open economy engaged in importing and exporting goods and services. The last component of GDP—and an increasingly important one in recent years—is **net exports,** the difference between exports and imports of goods and services.

How do we draw the line between our GDP and other countries' GDPs? The U.S. GDP represents all goods and services produced within the boundaries of the United States. Production differs from sales in the United States in two respects. First, some of our production (Iowa wheat and Boeing aircraft) is bought by foreigners and shipped abroad, and these items constitute our *exports.* Second, some of what we consume (Mexican oil and Japanese cars) is produced abroad and shipped to the United States, and such items are American *imports.*

For most of the last half-century, exports exceeded imports: net exports were positive. Since 1980, however, U.S. imports grew rapidly and net exports decreased sharply. As a result, the United States incurred a large trade deficit. We will study the sources and implications of the large trade deficit in later chapters.

A Numerical Example. We can use a simple farming economy to understand how the national accounts work. Suppose that Agrovia produces 100 bushels of corn and 7 bushels are imported. Of these, 87 bushels are consumed (in C), 10 go for government purchases to feed the army (as G), and 6 go into domestic investment as increases in inventories (I). In addition, 4 bushels are exported, so net exports (X) are $4 - 7$, or minus 3.

What, then, is the composition of the GDP of Agrovia? It is the following:

$$\text{GDP} = 87 \text{ of } C + 10 \text{ of } G + 6 \text{ of } I - 3 \text{ of } X$$
$$= 100 \text{ bushels}$$

A Simplification. In our survey of macroeconomics, we will sometimes simplify our discussion by combining domestic investment with net exports to get *total national investment,* which we will call I_T. Put differently, we measure total net national investment as net exports plus domestic investment in new capital goods. Let us see why. When a nation exports more than it imports, it is investing the excess (the net exports) abroad. This component is

called *net foreign investment.* This foreign investment should be added to domestic capital formation to obtain the total amount that the nation is setting aside for the future—that is, the total net national investment.

Gross Domestic Product, Net Domestic Product, and Gross National Product

Although GDP is the most widely used measure of national output in the United States, two other concepts are widely cited: net domestic product and gross national product.

Recall that GDP includes *gross* investment, which is net investment plus depreciation. A little thought suggests that including depreciation is rather like including wheat as well as bread. A better measure would include only *net* investment in total output. By subtracting depreciation from GDP we obtain **net domestic product** (NDP). If NDP is a sounder measure of a nation's output than GDP, why do economists and journalists work with GDP? They do so because depreciation is somewhat difficult to estimate, whereas gross investment can be estimated fairly accurately.

An alternative measure of national output, widely used until recently, is **gross national product** (GNP). What is the difference between GNP and GDP? GNP is the total output produced with labor or capital *owned* by U.S. residents, while GDP is the output produced with labor and capital *located inside* the United States. For example, some of the U.S. GDP is produced in Honda plants that are owned by Japanese corporations. The profits from these plants are included in U.S. GDP but not in U.S. GNP because Honda is a Japanese company. Similarly, when an American economist flies to Japan to give a paid lecture on baseball economics, that lecture would be included in Japanese GDP and in American GNP.[2]

---

[2] Until 1991, the United States used GNP rather than GDP as its primary national income and product concept. The United States moved to GDP to conform with the practices of most other countries and because most economic concerns reflect production and employment inside the United States rather than in other countries. The practical difference between GDP and GNP for the United States is negligible, however. In 1996, GDP was only 0.1 percent larger than GNP. In other countries, the two measures can diverge significantly. For example, in Canada, which has considerable earnings on U.S. investment, GNP was 4 percent smaller than GDP in 1990.

1. **GDP from the product side is the sum of four major components:**
   - Personal consumption expenditure on goods and services (C)
   - Gross private domestic investment (I)
   - Government consumption expenditures and gross investment (G)
   - Net exports of goods and services (X), or exports minus imports

2. **GDP from the cost side is the sum of the following major components:**
   - Wages and salaries, interest, rents, and profit (always with the careful exclusion, by the value-added technique, of double counting of intermediate goods bought from other firms)
   - Indirect business taxes that show up as an expense of producing the flow of products
   - Depreciation

3. **The product and cost measures of GDP are identical** (by adherence to the rules of value-added bookkeeping and the definition of profit as a residual).

4. **Net domestic product (NDP) equals GDP minus depreciation.**

TABLE 21-5. Key Concepts of the National Income Accounts

To summarize:

Net domestic product (NDP) equals the total final output produced within a nation during a year, where output includes net investment or gross investment less depreciation:

$$NDP = GDP - depreciation$$

Gross national product (GNP) is the total final output produced with inputs owned by the residents of a country during a year.

Table 21-5 provides a comprehensive definition of important components of GDP.

GDP and NDP: A Look at Numbers

Armed with an understanding of the concepts, we can turn to a look at the actual data in the important Table 21-6.

Flow-of-Product Approach. Look first at the left side of the table. It gives the upper-loop, flow-of-product approach to GDP. Each of the four major components appears there, along with the production in each component for 1996. Of these, C and G and their obvious subclassifications require little discussion.

Gross private domestic investment does require one comment. Its total ($1117 billion) includes all new business fixed investment in plant and equipment, residential construction, and increase in inventory of goods. This gross total excludes subtraction for depreciation of capital. After subtracting

$830 billion of depreciation from gross investment, we obtain $287 billion of net investment.

Finally, note the large negative entry for net exports, −$95 billion. This negative entry represents the fact that in 1996 the United States imported $95 billion more in goods and services than it exported.

Adding up the four components on the left gives the total GDP of $7636 billion. This is the harvest we have been working for: the money measure of the American economy's overall performance for 1996.

Flow-of-Cost Approach. Now turn to the right-hand side of the table, which gives the lower-loop, flow-of-cost approach. Here we have all *net costs of production* plus *taxes* and *depreciation*.

Wages and other employee supplements include all take-home pay, fringe benefits, and taxes on wages. Net interest is a similar item. Remember that interest on government debt is not included as part of G or of GDP but is treated as a transfer.

Rent income of persons includes rents received by landlords. In addition, if you own your own home, you are treated as *paying rent to yourself*. This is one of many "imputations" (or derived data) in the national accounts. It makes sense if we really want to measure the housing services the American people are enjoying and do not want the estimate to change when people decide to own a home rather than rent one.

Gross Domestic Product, 1996 (Billions of Current Dollars)					
Product approach			**Earnings or cost approach**		
1. Personal consumption expenditure		$5,208	1. Wages, salaries, and supplements		$4,427
Durable goods	635		2. Net interest		425
Nondurable goods	1,535		3. Rental income of persons		146
Services	3,038		4. Indirect business taxes, adjustments, and statistical discrepancy		553
2. Gross private domestic investment		1,117	5. Depreciation		830
Residential fixed	309		6. Income of unincorporated enterprises		520
Business fixed	781		7. Corporate profits before taxes		736
Change in inventories	26		Dividends	305	
3. Government consumption and investment purchases		1,407	Undistributed profits	202	
4. Net exports		−95	Corporate profit taxes	229	
Exports	871				
Imports	966				
Gross domestic product		**$7,636**	**Gross domestic product**		**$7,636**

TABLE 21-6. The Two Ways of Looking at the GDP Accounts, in Actual Numbers
The left side measures flow of products (at market prices). The right side measures flow of costs (factor earnings and depreciation plus indirect taxes). (Source: U.S. Department of Commerce.)

Indirect business taxes are included as a separate item along with some small adjustments, including the inevitable "statistical discrepancy," which reflects the fact that the officials never have every bit of needed data.[3]

Depreciation on capital goods that were used up must appear as an expense in GDP, just like other expenses.

Profit comes last because it is the residual—what is left over after all other costs have been subtracted from total sales. There are two kinds of profits: profit of corporations and net earnings of unincorporated enterprises.

Income of unincorporated enterprises consists of earnings of partnerships and single-ownership busi-

nesses. This includes much farm and professional income.

Finally, corporate profits before taxes are shown. This entry's $736 billion in Table 21-6 includes corporate profit *taxes* of $229 billion. The remainder then goes to dividends or to undistributed corporate profits; the latter amount of $202 billion is what you leave or "plow back" into the business and is called *net corporate saving*.

On the right side, the flow-of-cost approach gives us the same $7636 billion of GDP as does the flow-of-product approach. The right and left sides do agree.

From GDP to Disposable Income

The basic GDP accounts are of interest not only for themselves but also because of their importance for understanding how consumers and businesses behave. Some further distinctions will help illuminate the way the nation's books are kept.

National Income. To help us understand the division of total incomes among the different factors of production, we construct data on *national*

---

[3] Statisticians must always work with incomplete reports and fill in data gaps by estimation. Just as measurements in a chemistry lab differ from the ideal, so, in fact, do errors creep into both upper- and lower-loop GDP estimates. These are balanced by an item called the "statistical discrepancy." Along with the civil servants who are heads of units called "Wages," "Interest," and so forth, there actually used to be someone with the title "Head of the Statistical Discrepancy." If data were perfect, that individual would have been out of a job; but because real life is never perfect, that person's task of reconciliation was one of the hardest of all.

income (NI). *NI* represents the total incomes received by labor, capital, and land. It is constructed by subtracting depreciation and indirect taxes from GDP. National income equals total compensation of labor, rental income, net interest, income of proprietors, and corporate profits.

The relationship between GDP and national income is shown in the first two bars of Figure 21-4. The left-hand bar shows GDP, while the second bar shows the subtractions required to obtain *NI*.

Disposable Income. A second important concept asks, How many dollars per year do households actually have available to spend? The concept of disposable personal income (usually called **disposable income** or *DI*) answers this question. To get disposable income, you calculate the market and transfer incomes received by households and subtract personal taxes.

Figure 21-4 shows the calculation of *DI*. We begin with national income in the second bar. We then subtract all direct taxes on households and corporations and further subtract net business saving. (Business saving is depreciation plus profits minus dividends. Net business saving is this total minus depreciation.) Finally, we add back the transfer payments that households receive from governments. This constitutes *DI*, shown as the right-hand bar in Figure 21-4.

FIGURE 21-4. Starting with GDP, We Can Calculate National Income (*NI*) and Disposable Personal Income (*DI*)

Important income concepts are (1) GDP, which is total gross income to all factors; (2) national income, which is the sum of factor incomes and is obtained by subtracting depreciation and indirect taxes from GDP; and (3) disposable personal income, which measures the total incomes, including transfer payments, but minus taxes, of the household sector.

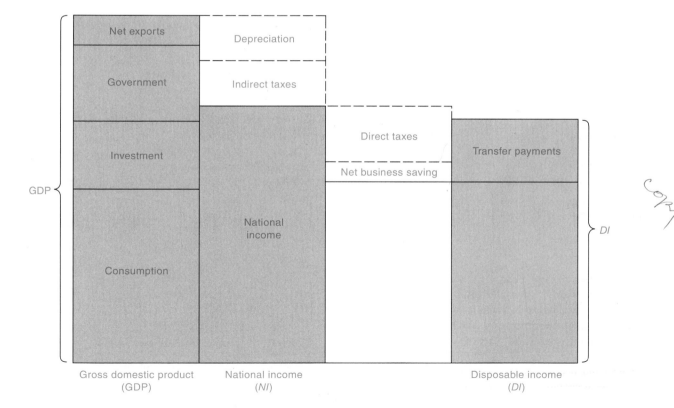

From GDP to National Income to Disposable Income

Disposable income is what actually gets into the public's hands, for consumers to dispose of as they please.

As we will see in the next chapters, *DI* is what people divide between (1) consumption spending and (2) personal saving. For most of the period since World War II, personal saving represented 7 percent of disposable income, with the balance going to consumption and interest payments. In recent years, the personal savings rate has dropped sharply, with the average personal savings rate over the last five years averaging only $4\frac{1}{2}$ percent.

The Identity of Measured Saving and Investment

One of the most important relationships arising from national income accounting is that between saving and investment. To pave the way for the discussion of income determination in Chapter 22, we show here that, under the accounting rules described above, *measured saving is exactly equal to measured investment*. This equality is an identity of national income accounting and holds by definition.

What is investment? Assuming for the moment that there is no government or foreign sector, we know *I* is that part of the upper-loop output that is not *C*. What is saving? Again ignoring government, foreign, and corporate saving, we know *S* is that part of the lower-loop disposable income, or GDP, that is not spent on *C*. To summarize:

$$I = \text{product-approach GDP minus } C$$
$$S = \text{earnings-approach GDP minus } C$$

But the two loops do give the same measure of GDP. Hence, we have

  I = *S:* the identity between measured saving
    and investment

That is the simplest case. Our task will be done when we consider total national investment, for which we need to bring businesses, government, and net exports into the picture. For this discussion, total gross national investment (I_T) will include both gross private domestic investment (*I*) and net foreign investment (*X*). But gross saving (*S*) must be divided into two different categories: (1) private saving (*PS*),

which includes personal saving plus business saving; and (2) the government surplus (*GS*), which represents the excess of government's tax revenues over its total expenditures, both purchases and transfers. Our identity of measured national saving and investment, *S* and I_T, now has to be written in terms of the two components of total *S:*

$$I_T = PS + GS = \text{total saving}$$

Because national investment is the sum of domestic investment (*I*) and net exports (*X*), we can rewrite the equation as:

$$I + X = PS + GS$$

or

  Domestic investment plus net exports equals private saving plus the budget surplus.[4]

National saving always equals national investment. The components of investment are domestic investment in plant, equipment, and inventories and

---

[4] This fundamental identity can be derived by recalling the definitions of GDP and of saving. The fundamental identity for GDP from the product side is

$$GDP = C + I + G + X$$

But gross national investment is defined as $I_T = I + X$, so the product side can be written as

$$GDP = C + I_T + G$$

Next turn to the breakdown of GDP from the earnings or cost side:

$$GDP = Tx - Tr + BS + DI$$

where *Tx* = taxes, *Tr* = transfers, and *BS* is business saving, equal to profits less dividends.

We next define private saving, *PS*, as personal saving (*DI* − *C*) plus business saving. Because *PS* = *DI* − *C* + *BS*, we have

$$GDP = C + PS + (Tx - Tr - G) + G$$
$$= C + I_T + G$$

Because *GS* = *Tx* − *Tr* − *G*, we can cancel *C* and *G* to obtain the saving-investment identity:

$$I_T = PS + GS$$

A final useful identity comes when we recall that $I_T = I + X$, which implies

$$I + X = PS + GS$$

In words, this means that domestic investment plus net exports equals personal saving plus the budget surplus. This calculation omits government investment. If government investment is included in *I*, it must also be excluded from *G* and from the government deficit.

foreign investment or net exports. The sources of saving are private saving (by households and businesses) and government saving (the government budget surplus). This identity must hold whether the economy is in tranquil times, is going into depression, or is in a wartime boom.

BEYOND THE NATIONAL ACCOUNTS

Advocates of the existing economic and social system often argue that market economies have produced a growth in real output never before seen in human history. "Look how GDP has grown because of the genius of free markets," say the admirers of capitalism.

But reliance on these measures has caused a backlash. Critics complain that GDP represents the excessive materialism of a society devoted to endless production of useless goods. As one dissenter said, "Don't speak to me of all your production and your dollars, your gross domestic product. To me, GDP stands for gross domestic pollution!"

What are we to think? Isn't it true that GDP includes government purchases of bombs and missiles, and salaries paid to prison guards? Doesn't an increase in crime boost sales of home alarms, which adds to the GDP? Doesn't cutting our irreplaceable redwoods show up as a positive output in our national accounts? Does modern economics make a fetish of quantity of products at the expense of quality of life?

In recent years, economists have begun developing "augmented national accounts" that correct the major defects of the standard GDP numbers and better reflect the true satisfaction-producing outputs of our economy. The new approaches attempt to extend the boundaries of the traditional accounts by including important nonmarket activities as well as correcting for harmful activities that are omitted from the traditional national accounts. Two interesting examples are the underground economy and environmental pollution.

Pluses: The Underground Economy. In recent years, many writers have argued that there has been an explosive growth in the *underground economy,* which covers a wide variety of activities that are not reported to the government. These include activities like gambling, prostitution, drug dealing, work done by illegal immigrants, bartering of services, padding of expense accounts, smuggling, skimming money from the cash register, and even growing food at home. Some observers have suggested that government regulation and high taxes have driven a substantial part of economic activity underground.

Most underground activity is motivated by the desire to reduce taxes or avoid government control or sanctions. When drug dealers omit sales of cocaine from their tax returns, they do so not only to reduce taxes but also to hide an illegal activity. In contrast, when people hire a full-time nanny to take care of the children and fail to pay social security taxes, they do so only to reduce taxes or avoid the hassle of filling out forms, since the activity itself is perfectly legal.

Not all underground activity is properly part of GDP. In general, national accountants exclude illegal activities from a measure of national output—these are by social consensus "bads" and not "goods." A swelling heroin trade will not enter into GDP. Also, if an art collector sells a Picasso in Zurich and fails to report the capital gains, this is taxable income but does not enter into GDP because the painting was produced several decades ago.

What about legal underground activities: those of carpenters, doctors, nannies, and farmers, for example, who produce valuable goods and services but do not report their incomes to the government? Probably the most reliable estimates come from the Internal Revenue Service (IRS), which has conducted intensive audits of individuals. On the basis of these reviews, the IRS estimates that between 4 and 8 percent of income was unreported in recent years.

Two points should be noted about this estimate of underground activity. First, there is no solid evidence that the size of the underground economy is growing, although some economists detect rapid growth from an increase in the number of $100 bills in circulation. Second, the Commerce Department makes estimates of the size of underreporting based on both surveys and the product side of the circular flow. The unreported income skimmed off by a hot-dog stand will show up in consumer surveys of restaurant expenditures. A careful review of this issue by the Commerce Department concluded that the understatement was unlikely to exceed 1 percent of GDP.

Minuses: Environmental Damage. Sometimes GDP counts the "goods" produced but ignores the "bads." For example, suppose the residents of Suburbia buy 10 million kilowatt-hours of electricity to cool their houses, paying Utility Co. 10 cents per kilowatt-hour. That $1 million covers the labor costs, plant costs, and fuel costs. But suppose the company damages the neighborhood with pollution to produce electricity. It incurs no monetary costs for this externality. Our measure of output should not only add in the value of the electricity (which GDP does) but also subtract the environmental damage caused by the pollution (which GDP does not).[5]

Suppose that in addition to paying 10 cents of direct costs, the surrounding neighborhood suffers 1 cent per kilowatt-hour of environmental damage. This is the cost of pollution (to trees, trout, streams, and people) not paid by Utility Co. Then the total "external" cost is $100,000. To correct for this hidden cost in a set of augmented accounts, we must subtract $100,000 of "pollution bads" from the $1,000,000 flow of "electricity goods."

In 1994, the U.S. Commerce Department unveiled its augmented national accounts with the introduction of *environmental accounts* (sometimes called "green accounts") designed to estimate the contribution of natural and environmental resources to the nation's income. The first step was the development of accounts to measure the contribution of subsoil assets like oil, gas, and coal.

Environmental critics have argued that America's wasteful ways were squandering our precious natural capital. Many were surprised by the results of this first assay into green accounting. The estimates take into account that discovery adds to our proven reserves while extraction subtracts from or depletes these reserves. In fact, these two activities just about canceled each other out: The net effect of both discoveries and depletion from 1958 to 1991 was between minus $2 billion and plus $1 billion, depending on the method, as compared to an average GDP over this period of $4200 billion (all these in 1992 prices).

The next stages of the Commerce Department effort will be to investigate renewable resources like soils and forests and then to move to environmental assets like air, water, and wild animals. Economists and environmentalists are watching this exciting new development carefully.

PRICE INDEXES AND INFLATION

We have concentrated in this chapter on the measurement of output. But people are also concerned with price trends, with movements in the overall price level, with inflation. What do these terms mean?

Let us begin with a careful definition:

A **price index** is a measure of the average level of prices. **Inflation** denotes a rise in the general level of prices. The **rate of inflation** is the rate of change of the general price level and is measured as follows:

Rate of inflation (year t)

$$= \frac{\begin{array}{c}\text{price level} \\ (\text{year } t)\end{array} - \begin{array}{c}\text{price level} \\ (\text{year } t-1)\end{array}}{\text{price level (year } t-1)} \times 100$$

But how do we measure the "price level" that is involved in the definition of inflation? Conceptually, the price level is measured as the weighted average of the prices of the goods and services in an economy. In practice, we measure the overall price level by constructing price indexes, which are averages of prices of goods and services.

As an example, take the year 1996, when consumer prices rose 3.3 percent. In that year, the prices of all major product groups rose: food, beverages, shelter, apparel, transportation, and medical care. It is this general upward trend in prices that we call inflation.

Not all prices rise by the same amount, however. During 1996, for example, the price of clothing fell by 0.2 percent, while the price of gasoline rose by a robust 13 percent; but the increase in the *average price level* was 3.3 percent.

The opposite of inflation is **deflation,** which occurs when the general level of prices is falling. Deflations have been rare in the late twentieth century. In the United States, the last time consumer prices actually fell from one year to the next was

---

[5] Why do the pollution costs not enter GDP? They are omitted because no one buys or sells pollution damage. Recall our discussion of externalities on page 35 in Chapter 2.

1955. Sustained deflations, in which prices fall steadily over a period of several years, are associated with depressions, such as occurred in the 1930s or the 1890s.

Price Indexes

When newspapers tell us "Inflation is rising," they are really reporting the movement of a price index. A price index is a weighted average of the prices of a number of goods and services. In constructing price indexes, economists weight individual prices by the economic importance of each good. The most important price indexes are the consumer price index, the GDP deflator, and the producer price index.

The Consumer Price Index (CPI).

The most widely used measure of inflation is the consumer price index, also known as the CPI. The CPI measures the cost of buying a standard basket of goods at different times. The market basket includes prices of food, clothing, shelter, fuel, transportation, medical care, college tuition, and other goods and services purchased for day-to-day living. Prices on 364 separate classes of goods and services are collected from over 21,000 establishments in 91 areas of the country.

How are the different prices weighted in constructing price indexes? It would clearly be silly merely to add up the different prices or to weight them by their mass or volume. Rather, a price index is constructed by *weighting each price according to the economic importance of the commodity in question.*

In the case of the CPI, each item is assigned a *fixed* weight proportional to its relative importance in consumer expenditure budgets; the weights for each item are proportional to the total spending by consumers on that item as determined by a survey of consumer expenditures in the 1982–1984 period. As of December 1996, housing-related costs were the single biggest category in the CPI, taking up more than 40 percent of consumer spending budgets. By comparison, the cost of new cars and other motor vehicles accounts for only 5 percent of the CPI's consumer expenditure budgets.

We can use a numerical example to illustrate how inflation is measured. Assume that consumers buy three commodities: food, shelter, and medical care. A hypothetical budget survey finds that consumers spend 20 percent of their budgets on food, 50 percent on shelter, and 30 percent on medical care.

Using 1998 as the *base year*, we reset the price of each commodity at 100 so that differences in the units of commodities will not affect the price index. This implies that the CPI is also 100 in the base year $[= (0.20 \times 100) + (0.50 \times 100) + (0.30 \times 100)]$. Next, we calculate the consumer price index and the rate of inflation for 1999. Suppose that in 1999 food prices rise 2 percent to 102, shelter prices rise 6 percent to 106, and medical-care prices are up 10 percent to 110. We recalculate the CPI for 1999 as follows:

$$CPI\ (1999)$$
$$= (0.20 \times 102) + (0.50 \times 106) + (0.30) \times 110)$$
$$= 106.4$$

In other words, if 1998 is the base year in which the CPI is 100, then in 1999 the CPI is 106.4. The rate of inflation in 1999 is then $[(106.4 - 100)/100] \times 100 = 6.4$ percent per year. Note that in a fixed-weight index like the CPI, the *prices* change from year to year but the weights remain the same.

This example captures the essence of how inflation is measured. The only difference between this simplified calculation and the real one is that the CPI in fact contains many more commodities. Otherwise, the procedure is exactly the same.

GDP Deflator.

We met the GDP deflator in our discussion of national income and output accounting earlier in this chapter. Recall that the GDP deflator is the ratio of nominal GDP to real GDP and can thus be interpreted as the price of *all* components of GDP (consumption, investment, government purchases, and net exports) rather than of a single sector. This index also differs from the CPI because it is a variable-weight index that takes into account the changing shares of different goods. In addition, there are deflators for components of GDP, such as for investment goods, personal consumption, and so forth, and these are sometimes used to supplement the CPI. More recently, as we discussed above, the Commerce Department has introduced chain-weighted price indexes that change the commodity weights each period to reflect changes in expenditure shares (see the discussion of chain weights in note 1 on page 396).

The Producer Price Index (PPI). This index, dating from 1890, is the oldest continuous statistical series published by the Labor Department. It measures the level of prices at the wholesale or producer stage. It is based on approximately 3400 commodity prices, including prices of foods, manufactured products, and mining products. The fixed weights used to calculate the PPI are the net sales of each commodity. Because of its great detail, this index is widely used by businesses.

Upward Bias in Prices, Underestimate of Economic Growth

While price indexes like the CPI are enormously useful, they are not without their faults. Some problems are intrinsic to price indexes. One issue is the *index-number problem,* which concerns the choice of an appropriate period for the base year. Recall that the CPI uses a fixed weight for each good. As a result, the cost of living is overestimated compared to the situation where consumers substitute relatively inexpensive for relatively expensive goods.

The case of energy prices can illustrate the problem. When gasoline prices rose sharply in the 1970s, people tended to cut back on their purchases and buy smaller cars or travel less. Yet the CPI assumed that they bought the same quantity of gasoline even though gasoline prices tripled. The overall rise in the cost of living was thereby exaggerated. Statisticians have devised ways of minimizing such index-number problems by using different weighting approaches, such as chain weighting, discussed above, but the consumer price index has not adopted these alternative approaches.

A more important problem arises because of the difficulty of adjusting price indexes to capture the contribution of *new and improved goods and services.* An example will illustrate this problem. In recent years, consumers have benefited from compact fluorescent light bulbs; these light bulbs deliver light at approximately one-fourth the cost of the older, incandescent bulbs. Yet none of the price indexes incorporate the quality improvement. Similarly, as CDs replaced long-playing records, as satellite-dish or cable TV with their hundreds of channels replaced the older technology with a few fuzzy channels, as air travel replaced rail or road travel, and in thousands of other improved goods and services, the price indexes did not reflect the changes.

Recent studies indicate that if quality change had been properly incorporated into price indexes, the CPI would have risen less rapidly in recent years. This problem is especially troubling for medical care. In this sector, reported prices have risen sharply in the 1980s; yet we have no adequate measure of the quality of medical care, and the CPI completely ignores the introduction of new products, such as pharmaceuticals which replace intrusive and expensive surgery.

A panel of distinguished economists led by Stanford's Michael Boskin (chief economist to President George Bush) recently estimated that the upward bias in the CPI was slightly more than 1 percent per year. This is a small number with large implications. It indicates that our real output numbers may have been *overdeflated* by the same amount. If the CPI bias carries through to the GDP deflator, then output per worker-hour in the United States has grown at 2 percent per year over the last two decades rather than the 1 percent per year as measured in the official national accounts.

This finding also implies that cost-of-living adjustments (which are in social security and many labor agreements) have overcompensated people for movements in the cost of living. The Boskin panel estimated that if the government indexes programs according to their bias estimate rather than using the current CPI, this would by 2008 reduce the government deficit by $180 billion and lower the U.S. national debt by more than $1 trillion. These findings indicate that the economics of accounting and of index numbers are no longer just abstruse concepts of interest only to a handful of technicians. Proper construction of price and output indexes affects our government budgets, our retirement programs, and even the way we assess our national economic performance.

ACCOUNTING ASSESSMENT

This chapter has examined the way economists measure national output and the overall price level. Having reviewed the measurement of national output and analyzed the shortcomings of the GDP, what should we conclude about the adequacy of our measures? Do they capture the major trends? Are they adequate measures of economic welfare? The answer was aptly stated in a review by Arthur Okun:

> It should be no surprise that national prosperity does not guarantee a happy society, any more than personal prosperity ensures a happy family. No growth of GDP can counter the tensions arising from an unpopular and unsuccessful war, a long overdue self-confrontation with conscience on racial injustice, a volcanic eruption of sexual mores, and an unprecedented assertion of independence by the young. Still, prosperity . . . is a precondition for success in achieving many of our aspirations.[6]

SUMMARY

1. The gross domestic product (or GDP) is the most comprehensive measure of a nation's production of goods and services. It comprises the dollar value of consumption (C), gross private domestic investment (I), government purchases (G), and net exports (X) produced within a nation during a given year. Recall the formula:

$$GDP = C + I + G + X$$

This will sometimes be simplified by combining private domestic investment and net exports into total gross national investment ($I_T = I + X$):

$$GDP = C + I_T + G$$

2. Because of the way we define residual profit, we can match the upper-loop, flow-of-product measurement of GDP with the lower-loop, flow-of-cost measurement, as shown in Figure 21-1. The flow-of-cost approach uses factor earnings and carefully computes value added to eliminate double counting of intermediate products. And after summing up all (before-tax) wage, interest, rent, depreciation, and profit income, it adds to this total all indirect tax costs of business. GDP does not include transfer items such as interest on government bonds or receipt of welfare payments.

3. By use of a price index, we can "deflate" nominal GDP (GDP in current dollars) to arrive at a more accurate measure of real GDP (GDP expressed in dollars of some base year's purchasing power). Use of such a price index corrects for the "rubber yardstick" implied by changing levels of prices.

4. Net investment is positive when the nation is producing more capital goods than are currently being used up in the form of depreciation. Since depreciation is hard to estimate accurately, statisticians have more confidence in their measures of gross investment than in those of net investment.

5. National income and disposable income are two additional official measurements. Disposable income (DI) is what people actually have left—after all tax payments, corporate saving of undistributed profits, and transfer adjustments have been made—to spend on consumption or to save.

6. Using the rules of the national accounts, measured saving must exactly equal measured investment. This is easily seen in a hypothetical economy with nothing but households. In a complete economy, *private saving and government surplus equal domestic investment plus net foreign investment.* The identity between saving and investment is just that: Saving must equal investment no matter whether the economy is in boom or recession, war or peace. It is a consequence of the definitions of national income accounting.

7. Gross domestic product and even net domestic product are imperfect measures of genuine economic welfare. In recent years, statisticians have started correcting for nonmarket measures such as the underground economy and environmental externalities.

8. Inflation occurs when the general level of prices is rising (and deflation occurs when they are generally falling). Today, we calculate inflation by using price indexes—weighted averages of the prices of thousands of individual products. The most important price concept is the consumer price index (CPI), which measures the cost of a fixed market basket of consumer goods and services relative to the cost of that bundle during a particular base year. Recent studies indicate that the CPI trend has a major upward bias because of index-number problems and omission of new and improved goods.

---

[6] *The Political Economy of Prosperity* (Norton, New York, 1970), p. 124.

CONCEPTS FOR REVIEW

real and nominal GDP
GDP deflator
$GDP = C + I + G + X$
$\quad\quad = C + I_T + G$
$I_T = I + X$
net investment =
$\quad$ gross investment − depreciation

GDP in two equivalent views:
$\quad$ product (upper loop)
$\quad$ earnings (lower loop)
intermediate goods, value added
NDP = GDP − depreciation
government transfers
disposable income (DI)

$I_T = S$
$I + X = PS + GS$
inflation, deflation
price index:
$\quad$ CPI
$\quad$ GDP deflator
$\quad$ PPI

QUESTIONS FOR DISCUSSION

1. Define carefully the following and give an example of each:
   a. Consumption
   b. Gross private domestic investment
   c. Government consumption and investment purchase (in GDP)
   d. Government transfer payment (not in GDP)
   e. Exports
2. Critics of economic accounts argue, "You can't add apples and oranges." Show that by using prices, we do this in constructing GDP.
3. Consider the following data: Nominal GDP for 1993 was $6553 billion, as compared to $6244 for 1992. The GDP deflator for 1993 was 102.6, as compared to 100.0 for 1992.

   Calculate real GDP for 1992 and 1993, in 1992 prices. Calculate the rates of growth of nominal GDP and real GDP for 1993. What was the rate of inflation (as measured by the GDP deflator) for 1993?
4. Robinson Crusoe produces upper-loop product of $1000. He pays $750 in wages, $125 in interest, and $75 in rent. What must his profit be? If three-fourths of Crusoe's output is consumed and the rest invested, calculate Crusoeland's GDP with both the product and the income approaches and show that they must agree exactly.

5. Here are some brain teasers. Can you see why the following are not counted in U.S. GDP?
   a. The home meals produced by a fine chef
   b. Purchase of a plot of land
   c. Purchase of an original Rembrandt painting
   d. The value I get in 1995 from playing a 1990 compact disc
   e. Pollution damage to houses and crops from pollution emitted by electric utilities
   f. Profits earned by IBM on production in a British factory
6. Consider the country of Agrovia, whose GDP is discussed in "A Numerical Example" on page 400. Construct a set of national accounts like that in Table 21-6 assuming that wheat costs $5 per bushel, there is no depreciation, wages are three-fourths of national output, indirect business taxes are used to finance 100 percent of government spending, and the balance of income goes as rent income to farmers.
7. Review the discussion of bias in the CPI. Explain why failure to consider the quality improvement of a new good leads to an upward bias in the trend of the CPI. Pick a good you are familiar with. Explain how its quality has changed and why it might be difficult for a price index to capture the increase in quality.

CHAPTER 22
CONSUMPTION AND INVESTMENT

Annual income twenty pounds, annual expenditure nineteen nineteen six, result happiness. Annual income twenty pounds, annual expenditure twenty pounds ought and six, result misery.

Charles Dickens, **David Copperfield**

Patterns of consumption and investment play a central role in a nation's economy. Nations that consume but a small fraction of their incomes and invest heavily tend to have rapid growth of output, income, and wages; this pattern has characterized particularly the "miracle" economies of East Asia. By contrast, those nations that consume most of their incomes, like the United States or Britain, invest little in new plant and equipment and show more modest rates of growth of productivity and wages. In the language of macroeconomics, high consumption relative to income spells low investment and slow growth, while low consumption relative to income leads to high investment and rapid growth.

The interaction between spending and income plays quite a different role in the short run, during business-cycle expansions and contractions. When economic conditions give rise to rapidly growing consumption and investment, this increases total spending or aggregate demand, raising output and employment in the short run. And when consumption falls because of higher taxes or loss of consumer confidence, this will reduce total spending and may propel the economy into a recession.

Because consumption and investment are such important parts of the macroeconomy, we devote this chapter to them. Figure 22-1 shows how this chapter's analysis fits into the overall structure of the macroeconomy. Once we have surveyed consumption and investment, we can use our knowledge in the next chapter to help understand the determination of aggregate demand in the short run.

A. CONSUMPTION AND SAVING

This section considers consumption and savings behavior, beginning with individual spending patterns and then looking at aggregate consumption behavior. Recall from Chapter 21 that household consumption is spending on final goods and services bought for the satisfaction gained or needs met by their use. Household saving is defined as that part of disposable income not spent on consumption.

Consumption is the largest single component of GDP, constituting 66 percent of total spending over the last decade. What are the major elements of consumption? Among the most important categories are

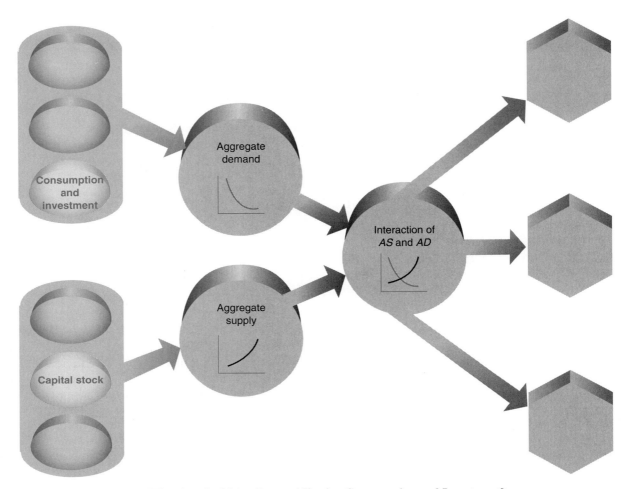

FIGURE 22-1. What Are the Major Forces Affecting Consumption and Investment?

This chapter analyzes two major components of GDP: consumption and investment. In later chapters, we will see that they affect both aggregate supply and aggregate demand.

housing, motor vehicles, food, and medical care. Table 22-1 displays the major elements, broken down into the three categories of durable goods, nondurable goods, and services. The items themselves are familiar, but their relative importance, particularly the increasing importance of services, is worth a moment's study.

Budgetary Expenditure Patterns

How do the patterns of consumption spending differ across different households in the United States? No two families spend their disposable incomes in exactly the same way. Yet statistics show that there is a predictable regularity in the way peo-

ple allocate their expenditures among food, clothing, and other major items. The thousands of budgetary investigations of household spending patterns show remarkable agreement on the general, qualitative patterns of behavior.[1] Figure 22-2 on page 414 tells the story. Poor families must spend their incomes largely on the necessities of life: food and shelter. As income increases, expenditure on many food items

---

[1] The spending patterns shown in Fig. 22-2 are called "Engel's Laws," after the nineteenth-century Prussian statistician Ernst Engel. The average behavior of consumption expenditure does change fairly regularly with income. But averages do not tell the whole story. Within each income class, there is a considerable spread of consumption around the average.

Category of consumption	Value of category, 1996 ($, billion)		Percent of total
Durable goods		632	12
Motor vehicles	253		
Household equipment	254		
Other	125		
Nondurable goods		1,545	30
Food	772		
Clothing and apparel	264		
Energy	133		
Other	375		
Services		2,974	58
Housing	779		
Household operation	310		
Transportation	205		
Medical care	816		
Other	865		
Total, personal consumption expenditures		5,151	100

TABLE 22-1. The Major Components of Consumption

We divide consumption into three categories: durable good, nondurable goods, and services. The size of the service sector is becoming increasingly large as basic needs for food are met and as health, recreation, and education claim a larger part of family budgets. (Source: U.S. Department of Commerce.)

goes up. People eat more and eat better. There are, however, limits to the extra money people will spend on food when their incomes rise. Consequently, the proportion of total spending devoted to food declines as income increases.

Expenditure on clothing, recreation, and automobiles increases more than proportionately to after-tax income, until high incomes are reached. Spending on luxury items increases in greater proportion than income. Finally, as we look across families, note that saving rises very rapidly as income increases. Saving is the greatest luxury of all.

The evolution of consumption in the twentieth century. Continual changes in technology, incomes, and social forces have led to dramatic changes in U.S. consumption patterns over time. In 1918, American households on average spent 41 percent of their incomes on food and drink. By comparison, households now spend only about 19 percent on these items. What lies behind this striking decline? The major factor is that spending on food tends to grow more slowly than incomes. Similarly, spending on apparel has fallen from 18 percent of household income at the beginning of the century to only 6 percent today.

What are the "luxury goods" that Americans are spending more on? One big item is transportation. In 1918, Americans spent only 1 percent of their incomes on vehicles—but of course Henry Ford didn't sell his first Model T until 1908. Today, there are 1.3 cars for every household, so it is not surprising that 23 percent of spending goes for vehicle-related transportation expenses. What about recreation and entertainment? Households now lay out large sums for televisions, cellular phones, and VCRs, items that didn't exist 75 years ago. These new inventions have lifted entertainment expenses to 6 percent of household budgets, up from 3 percent. Housing, too, takes a bigger share of income, 20 percent compared to 14 percent in the earlier period. That reflects, in part, the success of the American Dream: owning a big house in the suburbs is more expensive than renting a small apartment in the city.

Over the last decade, the biggest increase in consumption spending has been for health care, as both con-

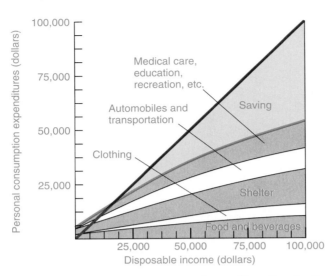

FIGURE 22-2. Family Budget Expenditures Show Regular Patterns

Careful sampling of families and of individuals verifies the importance of disposable income as a determinant of consumption expenditure. Notice the drop in food as a percentage of income as incomes rise. Note also that saving is negative at low incomes but rises to substantial amounts at high incomes. [Source: U.S. Department of Labor, *Consumer Expenditure Survey: Interview Survey 1984* (August 1986), updated to 1997 prices by authors.]

sumer payments for medical care and employer and government contributions for health care have soared. Surprisingly, consumers' out-of-pocket expenses for health care take about the same share of the household budget as they did in the early part of this century. The major increase has come as governments have taken over ever-larger fractions of health-care spending, contributing to the growth in government spending in the United States and other high-income countries.

CONSUMPTION, INCOME, AND SAVING

Income, consumption, and saving are all closely linked. More precisely, **personal saving** is that part of disposable income that is not consumed; saving equals income minus consumption. The relationship between income, consumption, and saving for the United States in 1996 is shown in Table 22-2. Begin with personal income (composed, as Chapter 21 showed, of wages, interest, rents, dividends, transfer

payments, and so forth). In 1996, some $864 billion of personal income, or 13.4 percent, went to personal tax and nontax payments. This left $5586 billion of personal disposable income. Household outlays for consumption (including interest) amounted to 95 percent of disposable income, or $5314 billion, leaving $272 billion as personal saving. The last item in the table shows the important **personal savings rate**. This is equal to personal saving as a percent of disposable income (5 percent in 1996).

Economic studies have shown that income is the primary determinant of consumption and saving. Rich people save more than poor people, both absolutely and as a percent of income. The very poor are unable to save at all. Instead, as long as they can borrow or draw down their wealth, they tend to *dissave*. That is, they tend to spend more than they earn, reducing their accumulated saving or going deeper into debt.

Table 22-3 contains illustrative data on disposable income, saving, and consumption drawn from budget studies on American households. The first column shows seven different levels of disposable

Item	Amount, 1996 ($, billion)
Personal income	**6,450**
Less: Personal tax and nontax payments	864
Equals: Personal disposable income	**5,586**
Less: Personal outlays (consumption and interest)	5,314
Equals: Personal saving	**272**
Memo: Saving as percent of personal disposable income	**4.9**

TABLE 22-2. Saving Equals Disposable Income less Consumption

Source: U.S. Department of Commerce.

income. Column (2) indicates saving at each level of income, and the third column indicates consumption spending at each level of income.

The *break-even point*—where the representative household neither saves nor dissaves but consumes all its income—comes at around $25,000. Below the break-even point, say, at $24,000, the household actually consumes more than its income; it dissaves (see the −$110 item). Above $25,000 it begins to show positive saving [see the +$150 and other positive items in column (2)].

Column (3) shows the consumption spending for each income level. Since each dollar of income is divided between the part consumed and the remaining part saved, columns (3) and (2) are not independent; they must always exactly add up to column (1).

To understand the way consumption affects national output, we need to introduce some new tools. We need to understand how many extra dollars of consumption and saving are induced by each extra dollar of income. This relationship is shown by

• The consumption function, relating consumption and income
• Its twin, the saving function, relating saving and income

The Consumption Function

One of the most important relationships in all macroeconomics is the **consumption function**. The consumption function shows the relationship between the level of consumption expenditures and the level of disposable personal income. This concept, introduced by Keynes, is based on the hypoth-

esis that there is a stable empirical relationship between consumption and income.

We can see the consumption function most vividly in the form of a graph. Figure 22-3 on page 416 plots the seven levels of income listed in Table 22-3. Disposable income [column (1) of Table 22-3] is placed on the horizontal axis, and consumption [column (3)] is on the vertical axis. Each of the income-consumption combinations is represented by a single point, and the points are then connected by a smooth curve.

The relation between consumption and income shown in Figure 22-3 is called the consumption function.

TABLE 22-3. Consumption and Saving Are Primarily Determined by Income

Consumption and saving rise with disposable income. The break-even point at which people have zero saving is shown here at $25,000. How much of each extra dollar do people devote to extra consumption at this income level? How much to extra saving? (Answer: About 85 cents and 15 cents, respectively, when we compare row B and row C.)

	(1) Disposable income ($)	(2) Net saving (+) or dissaving (−) ($)	(3) Consumption ($)
A	24,000	−110	24,110
B	25,000	0	25,000
C	26,000	+150	25,850
D	27,000	+400	26,600
E	28,000	+760	27,240
F	29,000	+1,170	27,830
G	30,000	+1,640	28,360

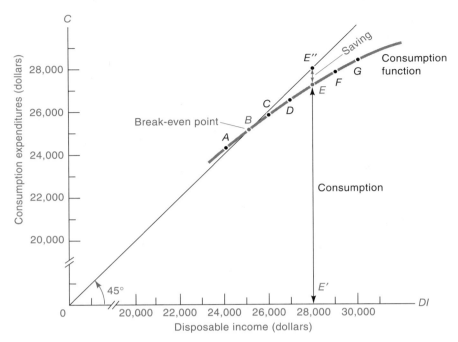

FIGURE 22-3. A Plot of the Consumption Function

The curve through A, B, C, . . . , G is the consumption function. The horizontal axis depicts the level of disposable income (DI). For each level of DI, the consumption function shows the dollar level of consumption (C) for the household. Note that consumption rises with increases in DI. The 45° line helps locate the break-even point and helps our eye measure net saving. (Source: Table 22-3.)

The "Break-Even" Point. To understand the figure, it is helpful to look at the 45° line drawn northeast from the origin. Because the vertical and horizontal axes have exactly the same scale, the 45° line has a very special property. At any point on the 45° line, the distance up from the horizontal axis (consumption) exactly equals the distance across from the vertical axis (disposable income). You can use your eyes or a ruler to verify this fact.

The 45° line tells us immediately whether consumption spending is equal to, greater than, or less than the level of disposable income. The **break-even point** on the consumption schedule that intersects the 45° line represents the level of disposable income at which households just break even.

This break-even point is at B in Figure 22-3. Here, consumption expenditure is exactly equal to disposable income: the household is neither a bor-

rower nor a saver. To the right of point B, the consumption function lies below the 45° line. The relationship between income and consumption can be seen by examining the thin black line from E' to E in Figure 22-3. At an income of $28,000 the level of consumption is $27,240 (see Table 22-3). We can see that consumption is less than income by the fact that the consumption function lies below the 45° line at point E.

What a household is not spending, it must be saving. The 45° line enables us to find how much the household is saving. Net saving is measured by the vertical distance from the consumption function up to the 45° line, as shown by the EE" saving arrow in rust.

The 45° line tells us that to the left of point B the household is spending more than its income. The excess of consumption over income is "dissaving"

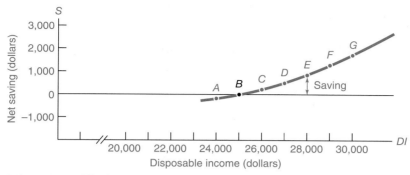

FIGURE 22-4. The Savings Function Is the Mirror Image of the Consumption Function

This savings schedule is derived by subtracting consumption from income. Graphically, the savings function is obtained by subtracting vertically the consumption function from the 45° line in Fig. 22-3. Note that the break-even point *B* is at the same $25,000 income level as in Fig. 22-3.

and is measured by the vertical distance between the consumption function and the 45° line.

To review:

At any point on the 45° line, consumption exactly equals income and the household has zero saving. When the consumption function lies above the 45° line, the household is dissaving. When the consumption function lies below the 45° line, the household has positive saving. The amount of dissaving or saving is always measured by the vertical distance between the consumption function and the 45° line.

The Savings Function

The savings function shows the relationship between the level of saving and income. This is shown graphically in Figure 22-4. Again we show disposable income on the horizontal axis; but now saving, whether negative or positive in amount, is on the vertical axis.

This savings function comes directly from Figure 22-3. It is the vertical distance between the 45° line and the consumption function. For example, at point *A* in Figure 22-3, we see that the household's saving is negative because the consumption function lies above the 45° line. Figure 22-4 shows this dissaving directly—the savings function is below the zero-savings line at point *A*. Similarly, positive saving

occurs to the right of point *B* because the savings function is above the zero-savings line.

The Marginal Propensity to Consume

Modern macroeconomics attaches much importance to the response of consumption to changes in income. This concept is called the marginal propensity to consume, or *MPC*.

The **marginal propensity to consume** is the extra amount that people consume when they receive an extra dollar of disposable income.

The word "marginal" is used throughout economics to mean extra or additional. For example, "marginal cost" means the additional cost of producing an extra unit of output. "Propensity to consume" designates the desired level of consumption. The *MPC* is therefore the additional or extra consumption that results from an extra dollar of disposable income.

Table 22-4 on page 418 rearranges Table 22-3's data in a more convenient form. First, verify its similarity to Table 22-3. Then, look at columns (1) and (2) to see how consumption expenditure goes up with higher levels of income.

Column (3) shows how we compute the marginal propensity to consume. From B to C, income rises by $1000, going from $25,000 to $26,000. How much does consumption rise? Consumption grows from

	(1) Disposable income (after taxes) ($)	(2) Consumption expenditure ($)	(3) Marginal propensity to consume (MPC)	(4) Net saving ($) (4) = (1) − (2)	(5) Marginal propensity to save (MPS)
A	24,000	24,110		−110	
			$\frac{890}{1,000} = 0.89$		$\frac{110}{1,000} = 0.11$
B	25,000	25,000		0	
			$\frac{850}{1,000} = 0.85$		$\frac{150}{1,000} = 0.15$
C	26,000	25,850		+150	
			$\frac{750}{1,000} = 0.75$		$\frac{250}{1,000} = 0.25$
D	27,000	26,600		+400	
			$\frac{640}{1,000} = 0.64$		$\frac{360}{1,000} = 0.36$
E	28,000	27,240		+760	
			$\frac{590}{1,000} = 0.59$		$\frac{410}{1,000} = 0.41$
F	29,000	27,830		+1,170	
			$\frac{530}{1,000} = 0.53$		$\frac{470}{1,000} = 0.47$
G	30,000	28,360		+1,640	

TABLE 22-4. The Marginal Propensities to Consume and to Save

Each dollar of disposable income not consumed is saved. Each extra dollar of disposable income goes either into extra consumption or into extra saving. Combining these facts allows us to calculate the marginal propensity to consume (MPC) and the marginal propensity to save (MPS).

$25,000 to $25,850, an increase of $850. The extra consumption is therefore 0.85 of the extra income. Out of each extra dollar of income, 85 cents goes to consumption and 15 cents goes to saving. As we move from B to C, we see that the marginal propensity to consume, or MPC, is 0.85.

You can compute MPC between other income levels. In Table 22-4, MPC begins at 0.89 for the poor and finally falls to 0.53 at higher incomes.

Marginal Propensity to Consume as Geometrical Slope. We now know how to calculate the MPC from data on income and consumption. Figure 22-5 shows how we can calculate the MPC graphically. Near points B and C a little right triangle is drawn. As income increases by $1000 from point B to point C, the amount of consumption rises by $850. The MPC in this range is therefore $850/$1000 = 0.85. But, as the appendix to Chapter 1 showed, the numerical slope of a line is "the rise

over the run."[2] We can therefore see that the slope of the consumption function is the same as the marginal propensity to consume.

The slope of the consumption function, which measures the change in consumption per dollar change in disposable income, is the marginal propensity to consume.

The Marginal Propensity to Save

Along with the marginal propensity to consume goes its mirror image, the marginal propensity to save, or MPS. The **marginal propensity to save** is defined as the fraction of an extra dollar of disposable income that goes to extra saving.

Why are MPC and MPS related like mirror images? Recall that disposable income equals con-

---

[2] For curved lines, we calculate the slope as the slope of the tangent line at a point.

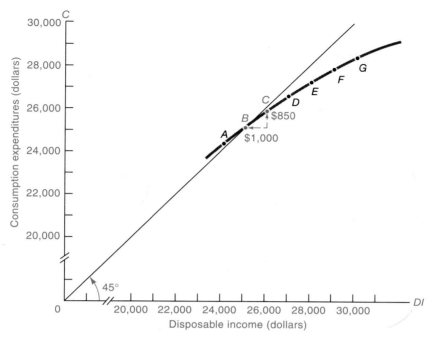

FIGURE 22-5. The Slope of the Consumption Function Is Its *MPC*

To calculate the marginal propensity to consume (*MPC*), we measure the slope of the consumption function by forming a right triangle and relating height to base. From point *B* to point *C*, the increase in consumption is $850 while the change in disposable income is $1000. The slope, equal to the change in *C* divided by the change in *DI*, gives the *MPC*. If the consumption function is everywhere upward-sloping, what does this imply about the *MPC*?

sumption plus saving. This implies that each extra dollar of disposable income must be divided between extra consumption and extra saving. Thus if *MPC* is 0.85, then *MPS* must be 0.15. (What would *MPS* be if *MPC* were 0.6? Or 0.99?) Comparing columns (3) and (5) of Table 22-4 confirms that at any income level, *MPC* and *MPS* must always add up to exactly 1, no more and no less. *Everywhere and always*, MPS ≡ 1 − MPC.

Brief Review of Definitions

Let's review briefly the main definitions we have learned:

1. The consumption function relates the level of consumption to the level of disposable income.
2. The savings function relates saving to disposable income. Because what is saved equals what is not consumed, savings and consumption schedules are mirror images.

3. The marginal propensity to consume (*MPC*) is the amount of extra consumption generated by an extra dollar of disposable income. Graphically, it is given by the slope of the consumption function.
4. The marginal propensity to save (*MPS*) is the extra saving generated by an extra dollar of disposable income. Graphically, this is the slope of the savings schedule.
5. Because the part of each dollar of disposable income that is not consumed is necessarily saved, *MPS* ≡ 1 − *MPC*.

NATIONAL CONSUMPTION BEHAVIOR

Up to now we have examined the budget patterns and consumption behavior of typical families at different incomes. We now turn to a discussion of consumption for the nation as a whole. This transition

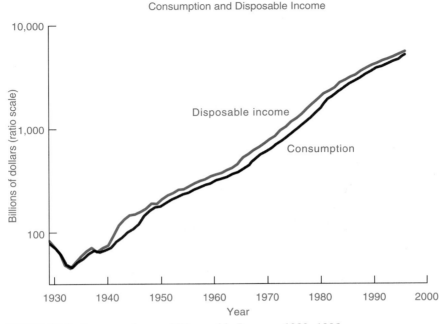

FIGURE 22-6. Consumption and Disposable Income, 1929–1996

U.S. consumption spending has closely tracked the level of personal disposable income over the last six decades. Macroeconomists can make good consumption forecasts based on the historical consumption function. (Source: U.S. Department of Commerce.)

from household behavior to national trends exemplifies the methodology of macroeconomics: We begin by examining economic activity on the individual level and then look at aggregate individuals to study the way the overall economy operates.

Why are we interested in national consumption trends? Consumption behavior is crucial for understanding both short-term business cycles and long-term economic growth. In the short run, consumption is a major component of aggregate spending. When consumption changes sharply, the change is likely to affect output and employment through its impact on aggregate demand. This mechanism will be described in the chapters on Keynesian macroeconomics.

Additionally, consumption behavior is crucial because what is not consumed—that is, what is saved—is available to the nation for investment in new capital goods; capital serves as a driving force

behind long-term economic growth. *Consumption and savings behavior are key to understanding economic growth and business cycles.*

Determinants of Consumption

We begin by analyzing the major forces that affect consumer spending. What factors in a nation's life and livelihood set the pace of its consumption outlays?

Current Disposable Income. Figure 22-6 shows how closely consumption followed current disposable income over the period 1929–1996. The only period when income and consumption did not move in tandem was during World War II, when goods were scarce and rationed and people were urged to save to help the war effort.

Both observation and statistical studies show that the current level of disposable income is the central factor determining a nation's consumption.

Permanent Income and the Life-Cycle Model of Consumption. The simplest theory of consumption uses only the current year's income to predict consumption expenditures. Careful studies have shown that people base their consumption expenditures on long-run income trends as well as on current disposable income.

What are some examples? If bad weather destroys a crop, farmers will draw upon their previous saving. Or consider law students, who can look forward to high professional earnings. They will borrow for consumption purposes while young, confident that their postgraduate incomes will be much higher than their meager student earnings. In both these circumstances, consumers take the long view, asking, "Is this year's income temporarily high or low? Given my current and future income, how much can I consume today without incurring excessive debts?"

Evidence indicates that consumers generally choose their consumption levels with an eye to both current income and long-run income prospects. In order to understand how consumption depends on long-term income trends, economists have developed the permanent-income theory and the life-cycle hypothesis.[3]

Permanent income is the level of income that households would receive when temporary or transient influences—such as the weather, a short business cycle, or a windfall gain or loss—are removed. According to the permanent-income theory, consumption responds primarily to permanent income. This approach implies that consumers do not respond equally to all income shocks. If a change in income appears permanent (such as being promoted to a secure and high-paying job), people are likely to consume a large fraction of the increase in income. On the other hand, if the income change is clearly transitory (for example, if it arises from a one-time bonus or a good harvest), a significant fraction of the additional income may be saved.

The *life-cycle hypothesis* assumes that people save in order to smooth their consumption over their lifetime. One important objective is to have an adequate retirement income. Hence, people tend to save while working so as to build up a nest egg for retirement and then spend out of their accumulated saving in their twilight years. One implication of the life-cycle hypothesis is that a program like social security, which provides a generous income supplement for retirement, will reduce saving by middle-aged workers since they no longer need to save as much for retirement.[4]

Wealth and Other Influences. A further important determinant of the amount of consumption is wealth. Consider two consumers, both earning $25,000 per year. One has $100,000 in the bank, while the other has no saving at all. The first person may consume part of wealth, while the second has no wealth to draw down. The fact that higher wealth leads to higher consumption is called the *wealth effect.*

Normally, wealth does not change rapidly from year to year. Therefore, the wealth effect seldom causes sharp movements in consumption. From time to time, however, exceptions occur. When the stock market tumbled after 1929, fortunes collapsed and paper-rich capitalists became paupers overnight. Some economic historians believe that the sharp decline in wealth after the 1929 stock market crash reduced consumption spending and contributed to the depth of the Great Depression. More recently, the great stock market boom over the 1981–1997 period has increased people's wealth and may have thereby increased consumption. (What would you expect to happen to consumption if the stock market fell sharply from its exalted level of 1997?)

How important are influences other than current income in determining consumption? Few doubt the importance of permanent income, wealth,

---

[3] The pathbreaking studies on longer-term influences were by Milton Friedman (on the permanent-income hypothesis) and Franco Modigliani (for the life-cycle model). Both received the Nobel Prize in economics for their accomplishments in these and other areas.

[4] This has been argued most forcefully by Martin Feldstein, chairman of the Council of Economic Advisers under President Reagan and currently president of the National Bureau of Economic Research and professor at Harvard University. Feldstein's research has emphasized the influence of tax policy and deficit spending on consumption patterns and national investment.

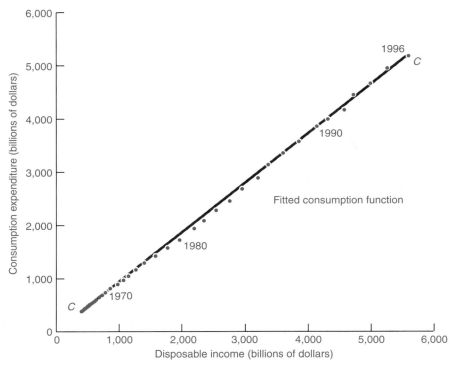

Consumption Relates to Income

FIGURE 22-7. A Consumption Function for the United States, 1966–1996

A straight line has been passed through the scatter of data points. Can you verify that the *MPC* slope of the fitted line is close to 0.93? How can you identify a year in which the personal savings rate was lower than average? (Source: U.S. Department of Commerce.)

social factors, and expectations in affecting savings levels. But from year to year, the major determinant of changes in consumption is actual disposable income.

The National Consumption Function

Having reviewed the determinants of consumption, we may conclude that the level of disposable income is the primary determinant of the level of national consumption. Armed with this result, we can plot recent annual data on consumption and disposable income in Figure 22-7. The scatter diagram shows data for the period 1966–1996, with each point representing the level of consumption and disposable income for a given year.

In addition, through the scatter points we have drawn a gray line—labeled *CC* and marked "Fitted

consumption function." This fitted consumption function shows how closely consumption has followed disposable income over the last quarter-century. In fact, economic historians have found that a close relationship between disposable income and consumption holds back to the nineteenth century.

THE DECLINE IN THRIFT

Although consumption behavior tends to be relatively stable over time, recent years have seen a sharp drop in the personal savings rate in the United States. The rust-colored line in Figure 22-8 shows personal saving as a percent of disposable personal income. Saving was low after World War II as households made up for wartime scarcity. Then the savings

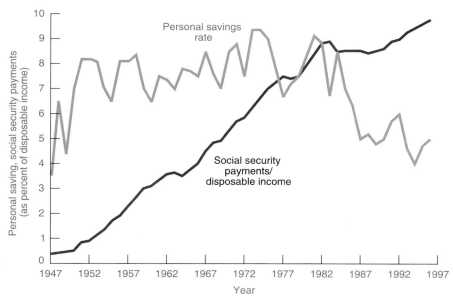

FIGURE 22-8. Personal Savings Rate Has Fallen in the Last Decade

Source: U.S. Department of Commerce.

rate settled into a range of 6 to 8 percent. Since the early 1980s, however, the savings rate has been between 4 and 5 percent.

This drop alarmed many economists because, over the long run, a nation's capital formation is determined by its national savings rate; as we saw in Chapter 21, national saving is the sum of personal, government, and business savings. When a nation saves a great deal, its capital stock increases rapidly and it enjoys rapid growth in its potential output. When a nation's savings rate is low, its equipment and factories become obsolete and its infrastructure begins to rot away.

What are the reasons for the precipitous decline in the personal savings rate? This is a highly controversial question today, but economists point to the following potential causes:

• *Social security system.* Many economists have argued that the social security system has removed some of the need for private saving. In earlier times, as the life-cycle model of consumption suggests, a family would save during working years to build up a nest egg for retirement. Today, the government collects social security taxes and pays out social security benefits,

thereby displacing some of the need for people to save for retirement. Other income-support systems have a similar effect, reducing the need to save for a rainy day: crop insurance for farmers, unemployment insurance for workers, and medical care for the elderly and indigent all alleviate the precautionary motive for people to save. Figure 22-8 shows the ratio of government social security payments to personal disposable income; note how rapidly the share has grown in the last three decades.

• *Capital markets.* Until recently, capital markets had numerous imperfections. People found it hard to borrow funds for worthwhile purposes, whether for buying a house, financing an education, or starting a business. As capital markets developed, often with the help of government, new loan instruments allowed people to borrow more easily. One good example of this is student loans. Decades ago, college educations were financed either out of family saving or by students' working. Today, because the federal government guarantees many student loans, students can borrow to pay for their education and repay the loans from their own earnings later in life. Another example is the proliferation of credit cards, which encourage people to borrow at very high interest rates. All these may reduce the overall savings rate.

- *Slow growth in incomes.* Some economists point out that a decline in the savings rate is quite naturally associated with a slowdown in the economy's growth rate. When income is growing rapidly, the economy will generate considerable net investment just to keep the same ratio of wealth to income. In a stationary economy, by contrast, a given wealth-income ratio requires a *zero* rate of saving and net investment. The most dramatic example of this phenomenon came in Japan after 1973, where GDP growth halved and the personal savings rate fell almost proportionally.
- *Other sources.* Many other culprits have been indicted in the case of the declining personal sav-

ings rate. Some analysts point to weakened incentives to save in recent years because of high tax rates and low posttax returns to saving, although this argument fails to explain why saving did not recover even after tax rates fell and real interest rates rose in the 1980s. Others point to a changing demographic structure, with an increase in the elderly population, which tends to save little or even to dissave.

As this recounting suggests, there is no scarcity of potential reasons for the falling savings rate. While no single answer commands a consensus, most economists agree that this decline in thriftiness has major implications for investment and economic growth.

B. INVESTMENT

The second major component of private spending is investment.[5] Investment plays two roles in macroeconomics. First, because it is a large and volatile component of spending, sharp changes in investment can have a major impact on aggregate demand. These, in turn, affect output and employment in the short run. In addition, investment leads to capital accumulation. Adding to the stock of buildings and equipment increases the nation's potential output and promotes economic growth in the long run.

Thus investment plays a dual role, affecting short-run output through its impact on aggregate

demand and influencing long-run output growth through the impact of capital formation on potential output and aggregate supply.

DETERMINANTS OF INVESTMENT

In this discussion, we focus on gross private domestic investment, or *I*, the domestic investment component of GDP. This is, however, only one component of total social investment, which includes not only *I* but also intangible investments such as ones made in human capital through education and knowledge and increases in technological capital or know-how through research and development.

The major types of gross private domestic investment are purchases of residential structures, investment in business fixed plant and equipment, and additions to inventory. Of the total, about one-quarter is residential housing, one-twentieth is normally change in inventories, and the rest—averaging 70 percent of total investment in recent years—is investment in business plant and equipment.

---

[5] Remember that macroeconomists use the term "investment" or "real investment" to mean additions to the stock of productive assets like capital goods—capital goods being equipment, structures, or inventories. When IBM builds a new factory or when the Smiths build a new house, these actions represent investments. Many people speak of "investing" when buying a piece of land, an old security, or any title to property. In economics, these purchases are really financial transactions or "financial investments," because what one person is buying, someone else is selling. There is investment only when real capital is created.

Why do businesses invest? Ultimately, businesses buy capital goods when they expect that this action will earn them a profit—that is, will bring them revenues greater than the costs of the investment. This simple statement contains the three elements essential to understanding investment: revenues, costs, and expectations.

Revenues

An investment will bring the firm additional revenue if it helps the firm sell more. This suggests that the overall level of output (or GDP) will be an important determinant of investment. When factories are lying idle, firms have relatively little need for new factories, so investment is low. More generally, investment depends upon the revenues that will be generated by the state of overall economic activity. Most studies find that investment is very sensitive to the business cycle. A recent example of a large output effect was seen during the business downturn of 1979–1982, when output fell sharply and investment declined by 22 percent.

One important theory of investment behavior is the **accelerator principle**. This principle holds that the rate of investment will be primarily determined by the rate of change of output. That is, investment will be high when output is growing, while investment will be low when output is falling.

Figure 22-9 shows the sensitivity of investment spending to changes in output. This is a scatter diagram that shows on the horizontal axis the rate of growth of real GDP and on the vertical axis the rate of change of gross private domestic investment. This diagram indicates that there is indeed a close relationship between movements in output and investment. A change in output of 1 percent is associated with a 3 percent change in real investment. The point furthest to the left shows the deep recession of 1982.

Costs

A second important determinant of the level of investment is the costs of investing. Because investment goods last many years, reckoning the costs of

FIGURE 22-9. Investment Responds to Changes in Output

When output rises and capacity utilization is high, investment tends to increase because businesses need more plant and equipment. The point furthest to the left is the deep recession of 1982. (Source: U.S. Department of Commerce.)

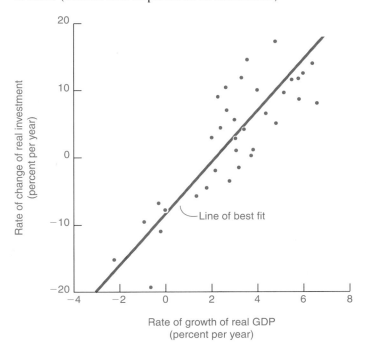

investment is somewhat more complicated than doing so for other commodities like coal or wheat. For durable goods, the cost of capital includes not only the price of the capital good but also the interest rate that borrowers pay to finance the capital as well as the taxes that firms pay on their incomes.

To understand this point, note that investors often raise the funds for buying capital goods by borrowing (say, through a mortgage or in the bond market). What is the cost of borrowing? It is the *interest rate* on borrowed funds. Recall that the interest rate is the price paid for borrowing money for a period of time; for example, you might have to pay 8 percent to borrow $1000 for a year. In the case of a family buying a house, the interest rate is the mortgage interest rate.

Additionally, the federal government sometimes uses fiscal policies to affect investment in specific sectors. In particular, *taxes* imposed by governments affect the cost of investment. The federal corporation income tax takes up to 34 cents of every dollar of corporate profits, thereby discouraging investment in the corporate sector. However, the government gives special tax breaks to oil and gas drilling, increasing activity in that sector. The tax treatment in different sectors, or even in different countries, will have a profound effect upon the investment behavior of profit-seeking companies.

Expectations

The third element in the determination of investment is expectations and business confidence. Investment is, above all, a gamble on the future, a bet that the revenue from an investment will exceed its costs. If businesses are concerned that future economic conditions in Japan will be depressed, they will be reluctant to invest there. Conversely, when businesses see the likelihood of a sharp business recovery in the near future, they begin to plan for plant expansion.

Thus investment decisions hang by a thread on expectations and forecasts about future events. But, as one wit said, predicting is hazardous, especially about the future. Businesses spend much energy analyzing investments and trying to narrow the uncertainties about their investments.

We can sum up our review of the forces lying behind investment decisions as follows:

Businesses invest to earn profits. Because capital goods last many years, investment decisions depend on (1) the demand for the output produced by the new investment, (2) the interest rates and taxes that influence the costs of the investment, and (3) business expectations about the state of the economy.

THE INVESTMENT DEMAND CURVE

In analyzing the determinants of investment, we focus particularly on the relationship between interest rates and investment. This linkage is crucial because interest rates (influenced by central banks) are the major instrument by which governments influence investment. To show the relationship between interest rates and investment, economists use a schedule called the *investment demand curve*.

Consider a simplified economy where firms can invest in different projects: A, B, C, and so forth, up to H. These investments are so durable (like power plants or buildings) that we can ignore the need for replacement. Further, they yield a constant stream of net income each year, and there is no inflation. Table 22-5 shows the financial data on each of the investment projects.

Consider project A. This project costs $1 million. It has a very high return—$1500 per year of revenues per $1000 invested (this is a rate of return of 150 percent per year). Columns (4) and (5) show the cost of investment. For simplicity, assume that the investment is financed purely by borrowing at the market interest rate, here taken alternatively as 10 percent per year in column (4) and 5 percent in column (5).

Thus at a 10 percent annual interest rate, the cost of borrowing $1000 is $100 a year, as is shown in all entries of column (4); at a 5 percent interest rate, the borrowing cost is $50 per $1000 borrowed per year.

Finally, the last two columns show the *annual net profit* from each investment. For lucrative project A, the net annual profit is $1400 a year per $1000 invested at a 10 percent interest rate. Project H loses money.

To review our findings: In deciding among investment projects, firms compare the annual revenues from an investment with the annual cost of capital, which depends upon the interest rate. The difference between annual revenue and annual cost is the annual net profit. When annual net profit is

(1)	(2)	(3)	(4)	(5)	(6)	(7)
			Cost per $1,000 of project at annual interest rate of		Annual net profit per $1,000 invested at annual interest rate of	
	Total investment in project ($, million)	Annual revenues per $1,000 invested ($)	10% ($)	5% ($)	10% ($) (6) = (3) − (4)	5% ($) (7) = (3) − (5)
Project						
A	1	1,500	100	50	1,400	1,450
B	4	220	100	50	120	170
C	10	160	100	50	60	110
D	10	130	100	50	30	80
E	5	110	100	50	10	60
F	15	90	100	50	−10	40
G	10	60	100	50	−40	10
H	20	40	100	50	−60	−10

TABLE 22-5. The Profitability of Investment Depends on the Interest Rate

The economy has eight investment projects, ranked in order of return. Column (2) shows the investment in each project. Column (3) calculates the perpetual return each year per $1000 invested. Columns (4) and (5) then show the cost of the project, assuming all funds are borrowed, at interest rates of 10 and 5 percent; this is shown per $1000 of the project.

The last two columns calculate the annual net profit per $1000 invested in the project. If net profit is positive, profit-maximizing firms will undertake the investment; if negative, the investment project will be rejected.

Note how the cutoff between profitable and unprofitable investments moves as the interest rate rises. (Where would the cutoff be if the interest rate rose to 15 percent per year?)

positive, the investment makes money, while a negative net profit denotes that the investment loses money.[6]

Look again at Table 22-5, and examine the last column, showing annual net profit at a 5 percent interest rate. Note that at this interest rate, investment projects A through G would be profitable. We would thus expect profit-maximizing firms to invest in all seven projects, which [from column (2)] total up to $55 million in investment. Thus at a 5 percent interest rate, investment demand would be $55 million.

However, suppose that the interest rate rises to 10 percent. Then the cost of financing these investments would double. We see from column (6) that investment projects F and G become unprofitable at an interest rate of 10 percent; investment demand would fall to $30 million.

We show the results of this analysis in Figure 22-10. This figure shows the *demand-for-investment schedule*, which is here a downward-sloping step function of the interest rate. This schedule shows the amount of investment that would be undertaken at each

interest rate; it is obtained by adding up all the investments that would be profitable at each level of the interest rate.

Hence, if the market interest rate is 5 percent, the desired level of investment will occur at point *M*, which shows investment of $55 million. At this interest rate, projects A through G are undertaken. If interest rates were to rise to 10 percent, projects F and G would be squeezed out; in this situation, investment demand would lie at point *M'* in Figure 22-10, with total investment of $30 million.[7]

---

[6] This example greatly simplifies the calculations businesses must make in actual investment decisions. Usually, investments involve an uneven stream of returns, depreciation of capital, inflation, taxes, and multiple interest rates on borrowed funds. Discussion of the economics of discounting and present values is found in books on money and finance.

[7] We will later see that when prices are changing, it is appropriate to use a real interest rate, which represents the nominal or money interest rate corrected for inflation.

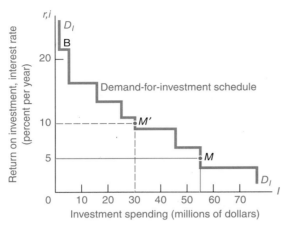

FIGURE 22-10. **Investment Depends upon Interest Rate**

The downward-stepping demand-for-investment schedule plots the amount that businesses would invest at each interest rate, as calculated from the data in Table 22-5. Each step represents a lump of investment: project A has such a high rate that it is off the figure; the highest visible step is project B, shown at the upper left. At each interest rate, all investments that have positive net profit will be undertaken.

Shifts in the Investment Demand Curve

We have seen how interest rates affect the level of investment. Investment is affected by other forces as well. For example, an increase in the GDP will shift the investment demand curve out, as shown in Figure 22-11(*a*).

An increase in business taxation would depress investment. Say that the government taxes away half the net yield in column (3) of Table 22-5, with interest costs in columns (4) and (5) not being deductible. The net profits in columns (6) and (7) would therefore decline. [Verify that at a 10 percent interest rate, a 50 percent tax on column (3) would raise the cutoff to between projects B and C, and the demand for investment would decline to $5 million.] The case of a tax increase on investment income is shown in Figure 22-11(*b*).

Finally, note the importance of expectations. What if investors become pessimistic and think yields will soon halve? Or become optimistic and think yields will double? By working through these cases, you can see how powerful an effect expectations can have on investment. Figure 22-11(*c*) displays how a bout of business pessimism would shift in the investment demand schedule.

After learning about the factors affecting investment, you will not be surprised to discover that investment is the most volatile component of spending. Investment behaves unpredictably because it depends on such uncertain factors as the success or failure of new and untried products, changes in tax rates and interest rates, political attitudes and approaches to stabilizing the economy, and similar changeable events of economic life. *In virtually every business cycle, investment fluctuations have been the driving force behind boom or bust.*

ON TO THE THEORY OF AGGREGATE DEMAND

We have now completed our introduction to the basic concepts of macroeconomics and the major components of national output. We have examined the determinants of consumption and investment and seen how they can fluctuate from year to year, sometimes quite sharply.

But it is not enough to examine the pieces of aggregate demand separately. The essence of macroeconomics is that all of the individual components of aggregate demand interact with each other, and with aggregate supply, to determine national output. The

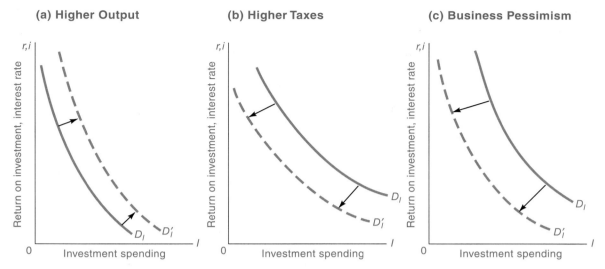

(a) Higher Output   **(b) Higher Taxes**   **(c) Business Pessimism**

FIGURE 22-11. Shifts in Investment Demand Function

In the demand-for-investment (*DI*) schedule, the arrows show the impact of (**a**) a higher level of GDP, (**b**) higher taxes on capital income, and (**c**) a burst of business pessimism such as might accompany the threat of recession or government regulation or nationalization.

next few chapters present the Keynesian theory of short-run output determination. This theory shows how changes in investment, government spending and taxation, foreign trade, and the money supply can be transmitted to the rest of the economy. We will see that actual GDP can diverge from its full-employment potential. We will also see how government fiscal and monetary policies can combat recessions and booms. At the heart of the analysis is the movement of consumption and investment that we explored in this chapter.

SUMMARY

A. Consumption and Saving

1. Disposable income is an important determinant of consumption and saving. The consumption function is the schedule relating total consumption to total disposable income. Because each dollar of disposable income is either saved or consumed, the savings function is the other side or mirror image of the consumption function.

2. Recall the major features of consumption and savings functions:

   a. The consumption (or savings) function relates the level of consumption (or saving) to the level of disposable income.

   b. The marginal propensity to consume (*MPC*) is the amount of extra consumption generated by an extra dollar of disposable income.

   c. The marginal propensity to save (*MPS*) is the extra saving generated by an extra dollar of disposable income.

   d. Graphically, the *MPC* and the *MPS* are the slopes of the consumption and savings schedules, respectively.

   e. $MPS \equiv 1 - MPC$.

3. Adding together individual consumption functions gives us the national consumption function. In simplest form, it shows total consumption expenditures as

a function of disposable income. Other variables, such as permanent income or the life-cycle effect, wealth, and age also have a significant impact on consumption patterns.

4. The personal savings rate has declined sharply in the last decade. This trend concerns economists because personal saving is a major component of national saving and investment. Studies of the causes of the declining savings rate point to diverse possibilities such as the growing importance of social security and government health programs, slower growth in the economy, and changes in capital markets.

B. Investment

5. The second major component of spending is gross private domestic investment in housing, plant, and equipment. Firms invest to earn profits. The major eco-

nomic forces that determine investment are therefore the revenues produced by investment (primarily influenced by the state of the business cycle and seen in the accelerator principle), the cost of investment (determined by interest rates and tax policy), and the state of expectations about the future. Because the determinants of investment depend on highly unpredictable future events, investment is the most volatile component of aggregate spending.

6. An important relationship is the investment demand schedule, which connects the level of investment spending to the interest rate. Because the profitability of investment varies inversely with the interest rate, which affects the cost of capital, we can derive a downward-sloping investment demand curve. As the interest rate declines, more investment projects become profitable, showing why the investment demand schedule slopes downward.

CONCEPTS FOR REVIEW

Consumption and Saving

disposable income, consumption, saving
consumption and savings functions
personal savings rates
marginal propensity to consume (*MPC*)
marginal propensity to save (*MPS*)

$MPC + MPS \equiv 1$
break-even point
45° line
determinants of consumption:
   current disposable income
   permanent income
   age
   wealth

Investment

determinants of investment:
   revenues
   costs
   expectations
role of interest rates in *I*
investment demand function

QUESTIONS FOR DISCUSSION

1. Summarize the budget patterns for food, clothing, luxuries, saving.
2. In working with the consumption function and the investment demand schedule, we need to distinguish between shifts of and movements along these schedules.
   a. Define carefully for both curves changes that would lead to shifts of and those that would produce movements along the schedules.
   b. For the following, explain verbally and show in a diagram whether they are shifts of or movements along the consumption function: increase in disposable income, decrease in wealth, fall in stock prices.
   c. For the following, explain verbally and show in a diagram whether they are shifts of or movements along the investment demand curve: expectation of a decline in output next year, rise of interest rates, increase in taxes on profits.

3. Exactly how were the *MPC* and *MPS* in Table 22-4 computed? Illustrate by calculating *MPC* and *MPS* between points *A* and *B*. Explain why it must always be true that $MPC + MPS \equiv 1$.
4. I consume all my income at every level of income. Draw my consumption and savings functions. What are my *MPC* and *MPS*?
5. Estimate your income, consumption, and saving for last year. If you dissaved (consumed more than your income), how did you finance your dissaving? Estimate the composition of your consumption in terms of each of the major categories listed in Table 22-1.
6. "Along the consumption function, income changes more than consumption." What does this imply for the *MPC* and *MPS*?
7. "Changes in disposable income lead to movements along the consumption function; changes in wealth or other factors lead to a shift of the consumption func-

tion." Explain this statement with an illustration of each case.

8. What would be the effects of the following on the investment demand function illustrated in Table 22-5 and Figure 22-10?

   a. A doubling of the annual revenues per $1000 invested shown in column (3)

   b. A rise in interest rates to 15 percent per year

   c. The addition of a ninth project with data in the first three columns of (J, 10, 70)

   d. A 50 percent tax on *net* profits shown in columns (6) and (7)

9. Using the augmented investment demand schedule from question 8 and assuming that the interest rate is 10 percent, calculate the level of investment for cases **a** through **d** in question 8.

10. **Advanced problem:** According to the life-cycle model, people consume each year an amount that depends upon their *lifetime* income rather than upon their current income. Assume that you expect to receive future income (in constant dollars) according to the schedule in Table 22-6.

    Assume that there is no interest paid on saving. You have no initial saving. Further assume that you want to "smooth" your consumption (enjoying equal consumption each year) because of diminishing extra satisfaction from extra consumption. Derive your best consumption trajectory for the 5 years, and write the figures in column (3). Then calculate your

(1) Year	(2) Income ($)	(3) Consumption ($)	(4) Saving ($)	(5) Cumulative saving (end of year) ($)
1	30,000	_____	_____	_____
2	30,000	_____	_____	_____
3	25,000	_____	_____	_____
4	15,000	_____	_____	_____
5*	0	_____	_____	0

*Retired

TABLE 22-6.

saving and enter the amounts in column (4); put your end-of-period wealth, or cumulative saving, for each year into column (5). What is your average savings rate in the first 4 years?

Next, assume that a government social security program taxes you $2000 in each of your working years and provides you with an $8000 pension in year 5. If you still desire to smooth consumption, calculate your revised savings plan. How has the social security program affected your consumption? What is the effect on your average savings rate in the first 4 years? Can you see why some economists claim that social security can lower saving?

CHAPTER 23
BUSINESS CYCLES AND THE
THEORY OF AGGREGATE DEMAND

The fault, dear Brutus, is not in our stars—but in ourselves.

William Shakespeare, **Julius Caesar**

The history of American capitalism is one of recurrent periods of boom and bust, of recession and expansion. Sometimes business conditions are healthy, with plenty of job vacancies, factories working overtime, rising inflation, and robust profits. The mid-1990s was a period of such economic expansions. At other times, goods are sitting unsold, jobs are hard to find, and profits are low. Sometimes, these downturns are short and mild, as was the case in 1990–1991, while at times like the Great Depression the contraction may be persistent and traumatic. These fluctuations are known as *business cycles,* which are covered in the first part of this chapter.

One of the central problems of macroeconomics is understanding business cycles. We want to understand their salient characteristics, what causes them, and how government policies can reduce their virulence. Economists had little understanding of the causes of business cycles until the 1930s. Then, the revolutionary macroeconomic theories of John Maynard Keynes pointed to the importance of the forces of aggregate demand in determining business fluctuations. The lesson of Keynesian economics is that changes in aggregate demand can have a powerful impact on the overall level of output, employment, and prices in the short run.

There have been many challenges, modifications, and elaborations to the basic framework proposed by Keynes 60 years ago. Still, the theory of aggregate demand remains the best way to understand the business cycle. In the second part of this chapter, therefore, we describe the foundations of aggregate demand analysis and show the basic Keynesian approach to business cycles. In the next chapter, we present the Keynesian multiplier model, which describes the simplest income-determination theory. Figure 23-1 provides a road map for the analysis.

A. BUSINESS CYCLES

Economic history shows that the economy never grows in a smooth and even pattern. A country may enjoy several years of exhilarating economic expansion and prosperity, as the United States did in the 1990s. This might be followed by a recession or even a financial crisis or, on rare occasions, a prolonged

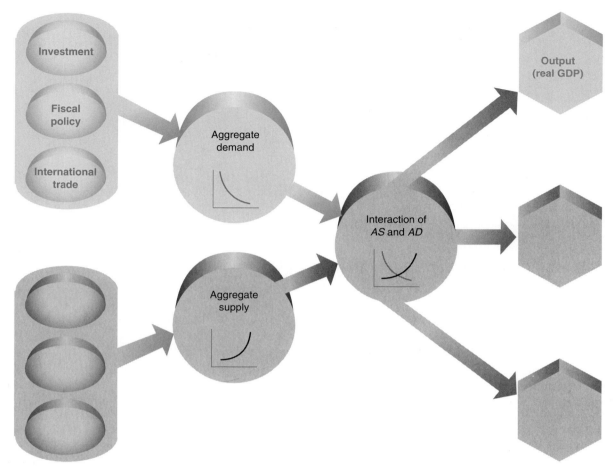

FIGURE 23-1. Business Cycles Have Been a Persistent Feature of Capitalism

We begin with an analysis of the business cycle and then develop the theory of aggregate demand to explain how demand shifts produce business fluctuations.

depression. Then national output falls, profits and real incomes decline, and the unemployment rate jumps to uncomfortably high levels as legions of workers lose their jobs.

Eventually the bottom is reached, and recovery begins. The recovery may be slow or fast. It may be incomplete, or it may be so strong as to lead to a new boom. Prosperity may mean a long, sustained period of brisk demand, plentiful jobs, and rising living standards. Or it may be marked by a quick, inflationary flaring up of prices and speculation, to be followed by another slump.

Upward and downward movements in output, inflation, interest rates, and employment form the business cycle that characterizes all market economies.

FEATURES OF THE BUSINESS CYCLE

What exactly do we mean by "business cycles"?

A **business cycle** is a swing in total national output, income, and employment, usually lasting for a period of 2 to 10 years, marked by widespread expansion or contraction in most sectors of the economy.

Typically economists divide business cycles into two main phases, *recession* and *expansion*. Peaks and troughs mark the turning points of the cycles.

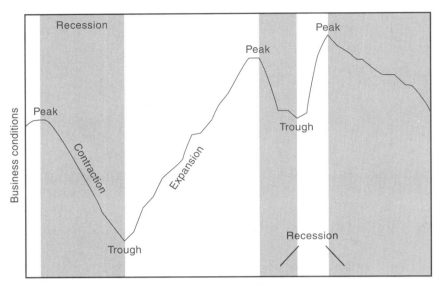

FIGURE 23-2. A Business Cycle, Like the Year, Has Its Seasons

Business cycles are the irregular expansions and contractions in economic activity. (These are the actual monthly data on industrial production for a recent business-cycle period.)

Figure 23-2 shows the successive phases of the business cycle. The downturn of a business cycle is called a **recession**, which is often defined as a period in which real GDP declines for at least two consecutive quarters. The recession begins at a peak and ends at a trough. According to the organization which dates the beginning and end of business cycles, the National Bureau of Economic Research, the last U.S. recession began after the economy peaked in the summer of 1990. This was followed by a brief recession, which ended in March 1991, after which the United States enjoyed one of the longest expansions in its history.

Note that the pattern of cycles is irregular. No two business cycles are quite the same. No exact formula, such as might apply to the revolutions of the planets or of a pendulum, can be used to predict the duration and timing of business cycles. Rather, in their irregularities, business cycles more closely resemble the fluctuations of the weather. Figure 23-3 shows the American business cycle throughout recent history. You can see that cycles are like mountain ranges, with different levels of hills and valleys. Some valleys are very deep and broad, as in the Great Depression; others are shallow and narrow, as in the recession of 1991.

While business cycles are not identical twins, they often have a familial similarity. If a reliable economic forecaster announces that a recession is about to arrive, are there any typical phenomena that you should expect to accompany the recession? The following are a few of the *customary characteristics* of a recession:

- Often, consumer purchases decline sharply, while business inventories of automobiles and other durable goods increase unexpectedly. As businesses react by curbing production, real GDP falls. Shortly afterward, business investment in plant and equipment also falls sharply.
- The demand for labor falls—first seen in a drop in the average workweek, followed by layoffs and higher unemployment.
- As output falls, inflation slows. As demand for crude materials declines, their prices tumble. Wages and prices of services are unlikely to decline, but they tend to rise less rapidly in economic downturns.
- Business profits fall sharply in recessions. In anticipation of this, common-stock prices usually fall as investors sniff the scent of a business downturn. However, because the demand for credit falls, interest rates generally also fall in recessions.

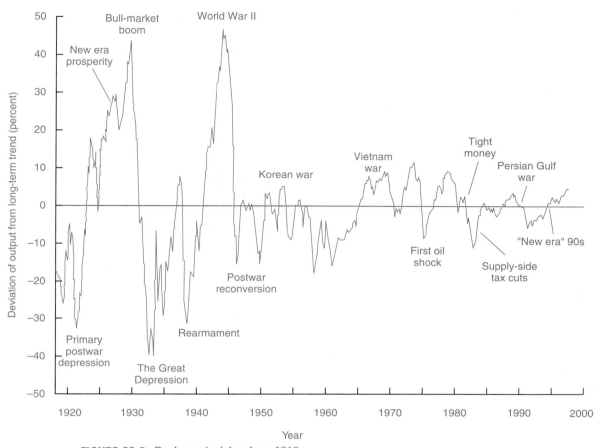

FIGURE 23-3. Business Activity since 1919

Industrial production has fluctuated incessantly around its long-run trend. Can you detect a more stable economy in recent years? (Source: Federal Reserve Board, detrended by authors.)

We have spoken in terms of recessions. Expansions are the mirror images of recessions, with each of the above factors operating in the opposite direction.

BUSINESS-CYCLE THEORIES

External vs. Internal Mechanisms. Over the years macroeconomics has been energized by vigorous debates about the sources of the business cycle. What causes aggregate demand to shift suddenly? Why should market economies blow hot and cold? There is certainly no end of possible explanations, but it is useful to classify the different sources into two categories, external and primarily internal. The *external* theories find the root of the business cycle in

the fluctuations of factors outside the economic system—in wars, revolutions, and elections; in oil prices, gold discoveries, and migrations; in discoveries of new lands and resources; in scientific breakthroughs and technological innovations; even in sunspots or the weather. The 1990–1991 recession, which was triggered by consumer anxieties after the Iraqi invasion of Kuwait, exemplifies the external approach.

By contrast, the *internal* theories look for mechanisms within the economic system itself that give rise to self-generating business cycles. In this approach, every expansion breeds recession and contraction, and every contraction breeds revival and expansion—in a quasi-regular, repeating chain. One important case is the *multiplier-accelerator theory.*

According to the accelerator principle, rapid output growth stimulates investment. High investment in turn stimulates more output growth, and the process continues until the capacity of the economy is reached, at which point the economic growth rate slows. The slower growth in turn reduces investment spending and inventory accumulation, which tends to send the economy into a recession. The process then works in reverse until the trough is reached, and the economy then stabilizes and turns up again. This internal theory of the business cycle shows a mechanism, like the motion of a pendulum, in which an external shock tends to propagate itself throughout the economy in a cyclical fashion.

Demand-Induced Cycles. One important source of business cycles is shocks to aggregate demand. A typical case is illustrated in Figure 23-4, which shows how a decline in aggregate demand lowers output. Say that the economy begins in short-run equilibrium at point *B.* Then, perhaps because of a decline in defense spending or tight money, the aggregate demand curve shifts leftward to *AD'.* If there is no change in aggregate supply, the economy will reach a new equilibrium at point *C.* Note that output declines from *Q* to *Q'.* In addition, prices are lower than they would otherwise be, and the rate of inflation falls.

The case of a boom is, naturally, just the opposite. Here, the *AD* curve shifts to the right, output approaches potential GDP or perhaps even overshoots it, and prices and inflation rise.

Business-cycle fluctuations in output, employment, and prices are often caused by shifts in aggregate demand. These occur as consumers, businesses, or governments change total spending relative to the economy's productive capacity. When these shifts in aggregate demand lead to sharp business downturns, the economy suffers recessions or even depressions. A sharp upturn in economic activity can lead to inflation.

Behind the AS and AD curves

Understanding business cycles requires us to look behind the aggregate supply and demand curves. Here are some of the most important business-cycle theories along with their proponents:

1. *Monetary* theories attribute the business cycle to the expansion and contraction of money and

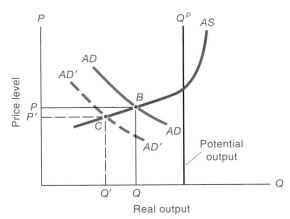

FIGURE 23-4. A Decline in Aggregate Demand Leads to an Economic Downturn

A downward shift in the *AD* curve along a relatively flat and unchanging *AS* curve leads to lower levels of output. Note that as a result of the downward shift in the *AD* curve, actual output declines relative to potential output in a recession.

credit (M. Friedman). Under this approach, monetary factors are the primary source of fluctuations in aggregate demand. For example, the recession of 1981–1982 was triggered when the Federal Reserve raised nominal interest rates to 18 percent to fight inflation.

2. The *multiplier-accelerator model,* described above, proposes that external shocks are propagated by the multiplier mechanism that we examine in the next chapter along with last chapter's accelerator principle (P. Samuelson). This theory shows how the interaction of multiplier and accelerator can lead to regular cycles in aggregate demand; it is one of the few models that generates internal cycles.

3. *Political* theories of business cycles attribute fluctuations to politicians who manipulate fiscal or monetary policies in order to be reelected (W. Nordhaus, E. Tufte). Historically, presidential elections are sensitive to economic conditions in the year preceding the election. As a result, if they have a choice, most presidents would prefer to follow Ronald Reagan's example. Although the U.S. economy went through a deep recession early in his term, by the time he was running for reelection in 1984, the economy was growing rapidly, which contributed to a reelection landslide.

4. *Equilibrium-business-cycle* theories claim that misperceptions about price and wage movements lead people to supply too much or too little labor, which leads to cycles of output and employment (R. Lucas, R. Barro, T. Sargent). In one version of these theories, unemployment rises in recessions because workers are holding out for wages that are too high.

5. *Real-business-cycle* proponents hold that innovations or productivity shocks in one sector can spread to the rest of the economy and cause fluctuations (J. Schumpeter early in this century and E. Prescott, P. Long, C. Plosser in recent years). In this classical approach, cycles are caused primarily by shocks to aggregate supply, and aggregate demand is unimportant for business cycles.

6. *Supply shocks* occur when business cycles are caused by shifts in aggregate supply (R. J. Gordon). The classic examples came during the oil crises of the 1970s, when sharp increases in oil prices contracted aggregate supply, increased inflation, and lowered output and employment. Some economists think that the low inflation and rapid growth of the American economy in the 1994–1997 period is explained by favorable supply shocks. During this period, costs grew slowly because a higher dollar exchange rate lowered import costs while reorganization of the health-care industry reduced businesses' labor costs by reducing the growth of fringe benefits.

These theories are ones that will be explored in greater depth in the chapters that follow, but it will be useful to keep a mental list of the major approaches as we proceed.

Which of these theories best explains the facts of business cycles? Actually, each of the competing theories contains elements of truth, but none is universally valid in all times and places. *The key to macroeconomic wisdom is to combine understanding of the different theories with knowledge of where and when to apply them.*

FORECASTING BUSINESS CYCLES

Economists have developed forecasting tools to help them foresee changes in the economy. Like bright headlights on a car, a good forecast illuminates the economic terrain ahead and helps decision makers adapt their actions to economic conditions.

Econometric Modeling and Forecasting

In an earlier era, economists tried to peer into the future by looking at easily available data on items like money, boxcar loadings, and steel production. For example, a drop in steel production was a sign that businesses had reduced purchases and that the economy would soon slow down. Eventually this process was formalized by combining several different statistics into an "index of leading indicators." While it is not infallible, the index does give an early and mechanical warning on whether the economy is heading up or down.

For a more detailed look into the future, economists turn to computerized econometric forecasting models. An *econometric model* is a set of equations, representing the behavior of the economy, that has been estimated using historical data. Early pioneers in this area were Jan Tinbergen of the Netherlands and Lawrence Klein of the University of Pennsylvania—both winners of the Nobel Prize for their development of empirical macroeconomic models. Today, there is an entire industry of econometricians estimating macroeconomic models and forecasting the future of the economy.

How are computer models of the economy constructed? Generally modelers start with an analytical framework containing equations representing both aggregate demand and aggregate supply. Using the techniques of modern econometrics, each equation is "fitted" to the historical data to obtain parameter estimates (such as the *MPC*, the slope of the investment demand function, etc.). In addition, at each stage modelers use their own experience and judgment to assess whether the results are reasonable.

Finally, the whole model is put together and run as a system of equations. In small models there are one or two dozen equations. Today, large systems forecast from a few hundred to 10,000 variables. Once the exogenous and policy variables are specified (population, government spending and tax rates, monetary policy, etc.), the system of equations can project important economic variables into the future.

Under ordinary circumstances, the forecasts do a fairly good job of illuminating the road ahead. At other times, particularly when there are major policy changes, forecasting is a hazardous profession. Figure 23-5 shows the results of a recent survey of fore-

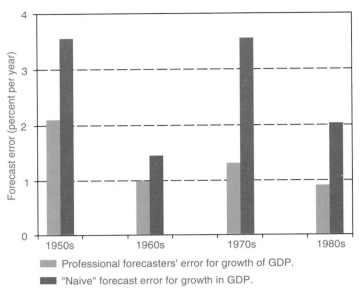

     Professional forecasters' error for growth of GDP.

     "Naive" forecast error for growth in GDP.

FIGURE 23-5. How Have Professional Forecasts Performed?

The record of professional forecasters is compared with that of "naive" forecasts. In every decade since systematic forecasting began, macroeconomic forecasts have improved upon guesswork, and the margin of improvement has grown slightly over time. [Source: Stephen McNees, *New England Economic Review* (July 1992).]

casts of real GDP (or, earlier, real GNP) by the major forecasting groups in the United States. For comparison purposes, the study used as a benchmark a "naive forecast" in which the next year's forecasted output growth was simply equal to the current year's growth rate.

As the figure shows, professional forecasters systematically beat naive forecasts. In the first two decades, the average forecast error among professionals was more than half the error of naive forecasts, while in the 1970s and 1980s, professionals' errors dropped to less than half those of the naive approach. Another interesting feature shown in Figure 23-5 is that instability varies from period to period, with the 1950s and 1970s being relatively volatile while the 1960s and 1980s were tranquil periods. Clearly, forecasting is as much art as science in our uncertain world. Still, the strength of economic forecasting is that, year in and year out, professional forecasters provide more accurate forecasts than do those who use unsystematic or unscientific approaches.

B. FOUNDATIONS OF AGGREGATE DEMAND

The first half of this chapter described the short-term fluctuations in output, employment, and prices that characterize business cycles in market economies. We showed how cyclical movements can occur when there are shifts in aggregate demand.

The time has come to explore in depth the foundations of aggregate demand. What are the major components of aggregate demand? How do they interact with aggregate supply to determine output and prices? What is the Keynesian theory of output determination, and how does it explain short-run fluctuations in GDP? We began to explore these questions in Chapter 20's introduction to macroeconomics. We now look at aggregate demand in more detail in order to get a better understanding of the forces which drive the economy. In the next chapter, we derive the simplest model of aggregate demand—the multiplier model.

Aggregate demand (or *AD*) is the total or aggregate quantity of output that is willingly bought at a given level of prices, other things held constant. *AD* is the desired spending in all product sectors: consumption, private domestic investment, government purchases of goods and services, and net exports. It has four components:

1. *Consumption.* As we saw in the last chapter, consumption (*C*) is primarily determined by disposable income, which is personal income less taxes. Other factors affecting consumption are longer-term trends in income, household wealth, and the aggregate price level. Aggregate demand analysis focuses on the determinants of *real* consumption (that is, nominal or dollar consumption divided by the price index for consumption).

2. *Investment.* Investment (*I*) spending includes private purchases of structures and equipment and accumulation of inventories. Our analysis in Chapter 22 showed that the major determinants of investment are the level of output, the cost of capital (as determined by tax policies along with interest rates and other financial conditions), and expectations about the future. The major channel by which economic policy can affect investment is monetary policy.

3. *Government purchases.* A third component of aggregate demand is government purchases of goods and services (*G*): purchases of goods like tanks or road-building equipment as well as the services of judges and public-school teachers. Unlike private consumption and investment, this component of aggregate demand is determined directly by the government's spending decisions; when the Pentagon buys a new fighter aircraft, this output immediately adds to the GDP.

4. *Net exports.* A final component of aggregate demand is net exports (*X*), which equal the value of exports minus the value of imports. Imports are determined by domestic income and output,

by the ratio of domestic to foreign prices, and by the foreign exchange rate of the dollar. Exports (which are imports of other countries) are the mirror image of imports, determined by foreign incomes and outputs, by relative prices, and by foreign exchange rates. Net exports, then, will be determined by domestic and foreign incomes, relative prices, and exchange rates.

Figure 23-6 shows the *AD* curve and its four major components. At price level *P*, we can read the levels of consumption, investment, government purchases, and net exports, which sum to GDP, or *Q*. The sum of the four spending streams at this price level is aggregate spending, or aggregate demand, at that price level.

FIGURE 23-6. Components of Aggregate Demand

Aggregate demand (*AD*) consists of four streams—consumption (*C*), domestic private investment (*I*), government spending on goods and services (*G*), and net exports (*X*).

Aggregate demand shifts when there are changes in macroeconomic policies (such as monetary changes or changes in government expenditures or tax rates) or shifts in exogenous events affecting spending (as would be the case with changes in foreign output, affecting *X*, or in business confidence, affecting *I*).

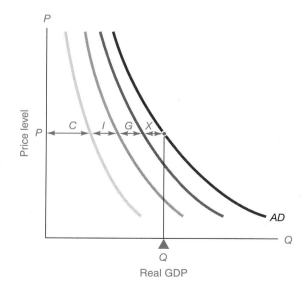

THE DOWNWARD-SLOPING AGGREGATE DEMAND CURVE

You will first notice that the aggregate demand curve in Figure 23-6 slopes downward. This means that, holding other things constant, the level of real spending declines as the overall price level in the economy rises.

The aggregate demand curve slopes downward primarily because of the *money-supply effect*. Remember that when we draw an *AD* curve, we hold other things constant. One important variable held constant is money supply. So when prices rise, the *real money supply* (defined as the nominal money supply divided by the price level) must fall. For example, if the nation's money supply is constant at $600 billion, and the consumer price index rises from 100 to 150, the real money supply falls from $600 billion to $400 (= $600 × 100/150) billion.

As the real money supply contracts, money becomes relatively scarce or "tight." Interest rates and mortgage payments rise, and credit becomes harder to obtain; tight money causes a decline in investment and consumption. In short, a rise in prices with a fixed money supply, holding other things constant, leads to tight money and produces a decline in total real spending.[1] The net effect is a movement along a downward-sloping *AD* curve.

We illustrate the money-supply effect in Figure 23-7(*a*). Say that the economy is in equilibrium at point *B*, with a price level of 100 (in constant prices), a real GDP of $3000 billion, and a money supply of $600 billion. Next assume that as a result of an increase in wages the price level increases to 150. Because the money supply is held constant, the real money supply (in constant prices) declines from $600 billion to $400 billion. The resulting tight money raises interest rates and lowers spending in interest-sensitive sectors like housing, plant and equipment, and automobiles. The net effect is that total real spending declines to $2000 billion, shown as point *C*. The decline in the real money supply will affect aggregate demand through the important monetary mechanism, which is discussed in detail in later chapters.

Other factors also contribute to the relationship between real spending and the price level, although they are today quantitatively less significant than the money-supply effect.

To summarize:

The *AD* curve slopes downward, indicating that the real output demanded declines as the price level rises. The primary reason for the downward-sloping *AD* curve is the money-supply effect, whereby higher prices operating on a fixed nominal money supply produce tight money and lower aggregate spending.

Warning: Microeconomic vs. macroeconomic demand. We pause for an important reminder about the difference between macroeconomic and microeconomic demand curves. Recall from our study of supply and demand that the microeconomic demand curve has the price of an individual commodity on the vertical axis and production of that commodity on the horizontal axis, with all other prices and total consumer incomes held constant.

In the aggregate demand curve, the general price level varies along the vertical axis, while total output and incomes vary along the *AD* curve. By contrast, incomes and output are held constant for the microeconomic demand curve.

Finally, the negative slope of the microeconomic demand curve comes because consumers substitute other goods for the good in question. If the meat price rises, the quantity demanded falls because consumers substitute bread and potatoes for meat, using more of the relatively inexpensive commodities and less of the relatively expensive one. The aggregate demand curve is downward-sloping for quite a different reason: Total spending falls when the overall price level rises primarily because a fixed dollar money supply must be rationed among money demanders by raising interest rates, tightening credit, and reducing total spending.

Macroeconomic *AD* curves differ from their microeconomic cousins because the macro curve depicts changes in prices and output for the entire economy while the micro curve analyzes the behavior of an individual commodity. The *AD* curve slopes downward primarily because of the money-supply effect, while the micro demand curve slopes downward because consumers substitute other goods for the good whose price has risen.

---

[1] We explore the monetary transmission mechanism in more detail in following chapters.

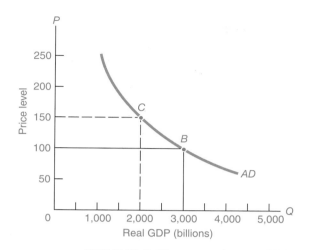

(a) Movements along the Aggregate Demand Curve

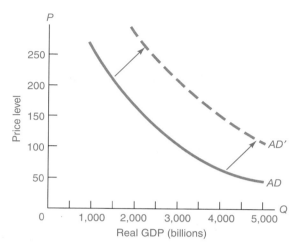

(b) Shifts of Aggregate Demand

FIGURE 23-7. Movement along vs. Shifts of Aggregate Demand

In (**a**), a higher price level with a fixed nominal money supply leads to tight money, higher interest rates, and declining spending on interest-sensitive investment and consumption. We see here a movement along the *AD* curve where other things are held constant.

In (**b**), other things are no longer constant. Changes in variables underlying *AD*—such as money supply, tax policy, technology, or military spending—lead to changes in total spending at a given price level.

Shifts in Aggregate Demand

We have seen that total spending in the economy tends to decline as the price level rises, holding other things constant. But other things tend to change, and these influences produce changes in aggregate demand. What are the key variables that lead to shifts in aggregate demand?

We can separate the determinants of *AD* into two categories, as shown in Table 23-1 on page 442. One set includes the major *policy variables* under government control. These are monetary policy (steps by which the central bank can affect the supply of money and other financial conditions) and fiscal policy (taxes and government expenditures). Table 23-1 illustrates how these government policies can affect different components of aggregate demand.

The second category is *exogenous variables*, or variables that are determined outside the *AS-AD* framework. As Table 23-1 shows, some of these variables (such as wars or revolutions) are outside the scope of macroeconomic analysis proper, some (such as foreign economic activity) are outside the control of

domestic policy, and others (such as the stock market) have significant independent movement.

What would be the effect of changes in the variables lying behind the *AD* curve? Suppose, for example, that the government increased its purchases of tanks, gas masks, and aircraft to fight in the Persian Gulf. The effect of these purchases would be an increase of spending in *G*. Unless some other component of spending offset the increase in *G*, the total *AD* curve would shift out and to the right as *G* increased. Similarly, an increase in the money supply, a radical new innovation that increased the profitability of new investment, or an increase in the value of consumer wealth because of a stock-price increase would lead to an increase in aggregate demand and an outward shift in the *AD* curve.

Figure 23-7(*b*) shows how the changes in the variables listed in Table 23-1 would affect the *AD* curve. To test your understanding, construct a similar table showing forces that would tend to decrease aggregate demand (see question 4 at the chapter's end).

Variable	Impact on aggregate demand
Policy variables	
Monetary policy	Increase in money supply lowers interest rates and improves credit conditions, inducing higher levels of investment and consumption of durable goods.
Fiscal policy	Increases in government purchases of goods and services directly increase spending; tax reductions or increases in transfers raise disposable income and induce higher consumption. Tax incentives like an investment tax credit can induce higher spending in a particular sector.
Exogenous variables	
Foreign output	Output growth abroad leads to an increase in net exports.
Asset values	Stock-price or housing-price rise produces greater household wealth and thereby increases consumption; also, this leads to lower cost of capital and increases business investment.
Advances in technology	Technological advances can open up new opportunities for business investment. Important examples have been the railroad, the automobile, and the computer.
Other	Political events, free-trade agreements, and the end of the cold war promote business and consumer confidence and increase spending on investment and consumer durables.

TABLE 23-1. Many Factors Can Increase Aggregate Demand and Shift Out the *AD* Curve

The aggregate demand curve relates total spending to the price level. But numerous other influences affect aggregate demand—some policy variables, others exogenous factors. The table lists changes that would tend to increase aggregate demand and shift out the *AD* curve.

RELATIVE IMPORTANCE OF FACTORS INFLUENCING DEMAND

While economists generally agree on the factors influencing demand, they differ in the emphasis they place on different forces. For example, some economists concentrate primarily on monetary forces in analyzing movements in aggregate demand, especially stressing the role of the money supply. According to these economists, who are often called *monetarists*, the supply of money is the primary determinant of the total dollar value of spending.

Other economists focus on exogenous factors instead. For example, some have argued that technological progress is one of the key determinants of booms and busts. For instance, railroads first became commercially practical in the 1850s. That innovation opened up two decades of massive investment in railroads all over the world and helped the industrial economies enjoy a sustained economic expansion. More recently, some economists have suggested that the communications revolution of the 1990s may trigger an investment surge, as companies spend tens of billions of dollars developing mobile phone systems and building the infrastructure for the information superhighway.

The mainstream of macroeconomic thinking today is an eclectic approach, which has its roots in the Keynesian tradition but incorporates modern developments as well. This approach, called *Keynesian macroeconomics*, accepts that different policy and exogenous forces move the economy during different periods. For example, fiscal policy would be seen as the leading determinant of aggregate demand during World War II, when military spending was absorbing almost half of GDP. In recent years, however, as the Federal Reserve became more active in combating inflation and unemployment, monetary policy exercised the dominant influence over fluctuations in economic activity.

We now have seen the major elements of the theory of aggregate demand. The next chapter explores the theory in greater depth by analyzing the simplest approach, the multiplier model.

Is the Business Cycle Avoidable?

The history of business cycles in the United States shows a remarkable trend toward stability over the last 150 years (look back at Figure 23-3). The period through 1940 witnessed numerous crises and depressions—prolonged, cumulative slumps like those of the 1870s, 1890s, and 1930s. Since 1945, business cycles have become less frequent and milder. What has changed? Some believe that capitalism is inherently more stable now than it was in earlier times. More important, however, is that a better understanding of macroeconomics now allows governments to take monetary and fiscal steps to prevent shocks from turning into recessions and to keep recessions from snowballing into depressions.

From 1984 to 1996, the American economy enjoyed the most stable period of its macroeconomic history. Inflation was low, and the economy experienced only one mild recession. A large fraction of workers and investors in financial markets had never witnessed a major business crisis during their adult years.

By 1997, some people were wondering whether the business cycle was dead. Perhaps with wise management and free markets, they wrote, we have banished major recessions and inflations from the land. Is such a prognosis warranted? We believe that such pronouncements are premature. A more balanced view was taken by one of the leading analysts of business cycles, Arthur Okun, at the end of another long business expansion:

> Recessions are now generally considered to be fundamentally preventable, like airplane crashes and unlike hurricanes. But we have not banished air crashes from the land, and it is not clear that we have the wisdom or the ability to eliminate recessions. The danger has not disappeared. The forces that produce recurrent recessions are still in the wings, merely waiting for their cue.[2]

Shortly after Okun wrote these words, the United States entered the stormiest period of the postwar era. Contagious optimism cannot prevent business cycles.

SUMMARY

A. Business Cycles

1. Business cycles are swings in total national output, income, and employment, marked by widespread expansion or contraction in many sectors of the economy. They occur in all advanced market economies. We distinguish the phases of expansion, peak, recession, and trough.

2. Many business cycles occur when shifts in aggregate demand cause sharp changes in output, employment, and prices. Aggregate demand shifts when changes in spending by consumers, businesses, or governments change total spending relative to the economy's productive capacity. A decline in aggregate demand leads to recessions or depressions. An upturn in economic activity can lead to inflation.

3. Business-cycle theories differ in their emphasis on external and internal factors. Importance is often attached to fluctuations in such exogenous factors as technology, elections, wars, exchange-rate movements, or oil-price shocks. Most theories emphasize that these exogenous shocks interact with internal mechanisms, such as the multiplier and investment-demand shifts,

to produce cyclical behavior. Just as people suffer from different diseases, so do business-cycle ailments vary in different times and countries.

B. Foundations of Aggregate Demand

4. Ancient societies suffered when harvest failures produced famines. The modern market economy can suffer from poverty amidst plenty when insufficient aggregate demand leads to deteriorating business conditions and soaring unemployment. At other times, excessive reliance on the monetary printing press leads to runaway inflation. Understanding the forces that affect aggregate demand, including government fiscal and monetary policies, can help economists and policymakers design steps to smooth out the cycle of boom and bust.

5. Aggregate demand represents the total quantity of output willingly bought at a given price level, other things held constant. Components of spending include (*a*) consumption, which depends primarily

---

[2] Arthur M. Okun, *The Political Economy of Prosperity* (Norton, New York, 1970), pp. 33 ff.

upon disposable income; (*b*) investment, which depends upon present and expected future output and upon interest rates and taxes; (*c*) government purchases of goods and services; and (*d*) net exports, which depend upon foreign and domestic outputs and prices and upon foreign exchange rates.

6. Aggregate demand curves differ from demand curves used in microeconomic analysis. The *AD* curves relate overall spending on all components of output to the overall price level, with policy and exogenous variables held constant. The aggregate demand curve is downward-sloping primarily because of the money-supply

effect, which occurs when a rise in the price level, with the nominal money supply constant, reduces the real money supply. A lower real money supply raises interest rates, tightens credit, and reduces total real spending. This represents a movement along an unchanged *AD* curve.

7. Factors that change aggregate demand include (*a*) macroeconomic policies, such as monetary and fiscal policies, and (*b*) exogenous variables, such as foreign economic activity, technological advances, and shifts in asset markets. When these variables change, they shift the *AD* curve.

CONCEPTS FOR REVIEW

Business Cycles

business cycle
business-cycle phases:
  peak
  trough
  expansion
  contraction
recession

aggregate demand shifts and business cycles
external and internal cycle theories
macroeconomic models

Aggregate Demand

real variable = nominal variable/price level

aggregate demand, *AD* curve
major components of aggregate demand: *C, I, G, X*
downward-sloping *AD* curve through money-supply effect
factors underlying and shifting the *AD* curve

QUESTIONS FOR DISCUSSION

1. Define carefully what is meant by the aggregate demand curve. Distinguish between movements along the curve and shifts of the curve. What might increase output by moving along the *AD* curve? What could increase output by shifting the *AD* curve?

2. Describe the different phases of the business cycle. In which phase is the U.S. economy now?

3. Some business cycles originate from the demand side, while others arise from supply shocks.
   a. Give examples of each. Explain the observable differences between the two kinds of shocks for output, prices, and unemployment.
   b. State whether each of the following would lead to a supply-side business cycle or a demand-side cycle, and illustrate the impact using an *AS-AD* diagram like Figure 23-4 on page 436: a wartime increase in defense spending; devastation from wartime bombing of factories and power plants; a decrease in net exports from a deep recession in Europe; a sharp increase in innovation and productivity growth.

4. Construct a table parallel to Table 23-1, listing events that would lead to a *decrease* in aggregate demand. (Your table should provide different examples rather than simply change the direction of the factors mentioned in Table 23-1.)

5. In recent years, a new theory of real business cycles (or RBCs) has been proposed. This theory suggests that business cycles are caused by shocks to productivity which then propagate through the economy.
   a. Show the RBC theory in the *AS-AD* framework.
   b. Discuss whether the RBC theory can explain the customary characteristics of business cycles described on pages 434–435.

6. **Advanced problem:** Find two dice and use the following technique to see if you can generate something that looks like a business cycle: Record the numbers from 20 or more rolls of the dice. Take five-period moving averages of the successive numbers. Then plot these. They will look very much like movements in GDP, unemployment, or inflation.

   One sequence thus obtained was 7, 4, 10, 3, 7, 11, 7, 2, 9, 10 . . . . The averages were (7 + 4 + 10 + 3 + 7)/5 = 6.2, (4 + 10 + 3 + 7 + 11)/5 = 7, and so forth.

   Why does this look like a business cycle? [*Hint:* The random numbers generated by the dice are like exogenous shocks of investment or wars. The moving average is like the economic system's (or a rocking chair's) internal multiplier or smoothing mechanism. Taken together, they produce what looks like a cycle.]

7. **Advanced problem:** An eminent macroeconomist, George Perry of Brookings, wrote the following after the Persian Gulf war of 1990–1991:

   Wars have usually been good for the U.S. economy. Traditionally they bring with them rising output, low unemployment, and full use of industrial capacity as military demands add to normal economic activity. This time, for the first time, war and recession occurred together. What does this anomaly tell us about the recession? (*Brookings Review*, Spring 1991)

Use the Internet or go to the library and find data on the major determinants of aggregate demand during the 1990–1991 period as well as during earlier wars (World War II, Korean war, Vietnam war). Examine particularly government spending on goods and services (especially defense spending), taxes, and interest rates. Can you explain the anomaly that Perry describes?

For help with finding data on the Internet, see the discussion on page xxxvi–xxxvii.

CHAPTER 24
THE MULTIPLIER MODEL

The outstanding faults of the economic society in which we live are its failure to provide for full employment and its arbitrary and inequitable distribution of wealth and incomes.

John Maynard Keynes, **The General Theory of Employment, Interest and Money** (*1936*)

All market economies experience swings in business activity when unemployment rises during recessions or when rapid increases in the money supply or spending lead to high and rising inflation. In the present chapter, we develop the *Keynesian multiplier model*, which is the simplest approach to understanding the way that changes in aggregate demand affect national output. According to the simplest multiplier mechanism, outlined in the first part of this chapter, an increase in investment raises the income of consumers and thereby leads to a cascading but ever-decreasing chain of further spending increases.

Investment changes are therefore *multiplied* into larger output increases.

The multiplier mechanism actually applies much more broadly than to investment alone, as we will see in the second half of this chapter. In fact, any change in government purchases, exports, or exogenous spending stream will also be amplified into a larger output change. We show below how government purchases have a multiplied effect upon output in much the same way as does investment; this point led many macroeconomists to recommend using fiscal policy as a tool for stabilizing the economy.

A. THE BASIC MULTIPLIER MODEL

When economists attempt to understand why major increases in wartime military spending lead to rapid increases in GDP, or why the tax cuts of the 1960s or 1980s ushered in long periods of business-cycle expansions, they often turn to the multiplier model for the simplest explanation.

What exactly is the **multiplier model**? This is a macroeconomic theory used to explain how output is determined in the short run. The name "multiplier"

comes from the finding that each dollar change in certain expenditures (such as investment) leads to more than a dollar change (or a multiplied change) in GDP. The multiplier model explains how shocks to investment, foreign trade, and government tax and spending policies can affect output and employment in an economy with unemployed resources.

In this section, we introduce the simplest multiplier model, one which focuses on the impact of

446

changes in private domestic investment in equipment or structures. This of course leaves out all of government fiscal and monetary policy. This important topic is considered in the second half of this chapter and in the two following chapters.

As you study the multiplier, you may be wondering how this approach fits into the *AS-AD* model of Chapter 20. There is no contradiction—they are in no way different theories. Rather, *the multiplier model explains the workings of aggregate demand by showing how consumption, investment, and other variables interact to determine aggregate demand—it is a special case of the aggregate demand-and-supply model.*

The key assumption in the multiplier analysis is that prices and wages are fixed in the short run; because they are fixed, all the adjustments to shocks or economic policies come through output and employment. In other words, we assume the *AS* curve is flat. This helpful assumption of fixed wages and prices is an oversimplification because these variables definitely do react to short-run business conditions. In later chapters we will consider the price and wage reactions that occur as markets respond to supply and demand shocks.

OUTPUT DETERMINATION WITH SAVING AND INVESTMENT

We first show how investment and saving are equilibrated in the multiplier model for a highly simplified economy. Recall Chapter 22's picture of the national consumption and savings functions; these are redrawn in Figure 24-1.[1] Each point on the consumption function shows desired or planned consumption at that level of disposable income. Each point on the savings schedule shows desired or planned saving at that income level. The two schedules are closely related: Since $C + S$ always equals disposable income, the consumption and savings curves are mirror twins that will always add up to the 45° line. We also carry over the *SS* schedule into Figure 24-2 on page 448.

We have seen that saving and investment are dependent on quite different factors: Saving

---

[1] Here we shall initially simplify the picture by leaving out taxes, undistributed corporate profits, foreign trade, depreciation, and government fiscal policy. For the time being, we will assume that income is disposable income and equals GDP.

(a) Consumption Function

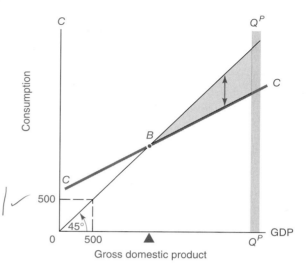

(b) Savings Function

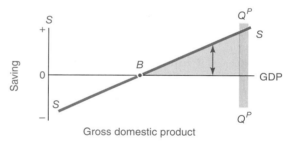

FIGURE 24-1. National Output Determines the Levels of Consumption and Saving

Recall from Chapter 22 the consumption and savings functions, *CC* and *SS*. These are mirror-image curves, so the break-even point at *B* on the upper diagram is the zero-savings point on the lower diagram where *SS* intersects the horizontal axis. The two points in **(a)** marked "500" emphasize the important property of the 45° line: Any point on it depicts a vertical distance exactly equal to the horizontal distance. The gray band marked $Q^P Q^P$ shows the level of potential GDP.

depends primarily on disposable income, while investment depends on factors such as output, interest rates, tax policy, and business confidence. For simplicity here, we treat investment as an *exogenous* variable, one whose level is determined outside the model.

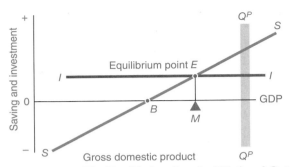

FIGURE 24-2. The Equilibrium Level of National Output Is Determined by Intersection of Savings and Investment Schedules

The horizontal *II* line indicates constant investment. *E* marks the spot where the investment and savings curves intersect. Equilibrium GDP comes at the intersection of the *SS* and *II* curves because this is the only level of GDP at which the desired saving of households exactly matches the desired investment of business.

Say that investment opportunities are such that investment would be exactly $200 billion per year regardless of the level of GDP. This means that if we draw a schedule of investment against GDP, it will have to be a horizontal line. The case of exogenous investment is shown in Figure 24-2, where the investment schedule is labeled *II* to distinguish it from the *SS* savings schedule. (Note that *II* does not mean Roman numeral 2.)

The savings and investment schedules intersect at point *E* in Figure 24-2. This point corresponds to a level of GDP given at point *M* and represents the equilibrium level of output in the multiplier model.

This intersection of the savings and investment schedules is the equilibrium level of GDP toward which national output will gravitate.

The Meaning of Equilibrium

Why do we call point *E* in Figure 24-2 an equilibrium? *The reason is that these levels of saving, investment, and output represent the only levels at which the desired saving of households equals the desired investment of firms.* When desired saving and desired investment are not equal, output will tend to adjust up or down.

The savings and investment schedules shown in Figure 24-2 represent *desired* (or *planned*) levels. Thus

at output level *M,* businesses will want to invest an amount equal to the vertical distance *ME.* Also, at that income level, households desire to save the amount *ME.* But there is no logical necessity for actual saving to equal planned saving (or for actual investment to equal planned investment). People can make mistakes. Or they may forecast events incorrectly. When mistakes happen, saving or investment might deviate from planned levels.

To see how output adjusts until desired saving and desired investment are equated, we consider three cases. In the first case, the system is at *E,* where the schedule of what business firms want to invest intersects the savings schedule of what households want to save. When everyone's plans are satisfied, everyone will be content to go on doing just what he or she has been doing.

At equilibrium, firms will not find inventories piling up on their shelves, nor will their sales be so brisk as to force them to produce more goods. So production, employment, income, and spending will remain the same. In this case GDP stays at point *E,* and we can rightly call it an *equilibrium.*

The second case begins with a GDP higher than at *E;* say, GDP is to the right of *M,* at an income level where the savings schedule is higher than the investment schedule. This is not an equilibrium because at this income level households are saving more than business firms want to invest. Firms will have too few customers and larger inventories of unsold goods than they want. What can businesses do to correct this situation? They can cut back production and lay off workers. This response reduces GDP, moving output leftward in Figure 24-2. The economy returns to equilibrium when it gets back to *E* and has no further tendency to change.

At this point, you should be able to analyze the third case. Show that if GDP were *below* its equilibrium level, strong forces would be set up to move it eastward back to *E.*

All three cases lead to the same conclusion:

The only equilibrium level of GDP occurs at *E,* where planned saving and investment are equal. At any other output, the desired saving of households does not coincide with the desired investment of businesses. This discrepancy will cause businesses to change their production and employment levels, thereby returning the system to the equilibrium GDP.

OUTPUT DETERMINATION BY CONSUMPTION AND INVESTMENT

In addition to the saving-investment balance, there is a second way of showing how output is determined. The equilibrium is exactly the same, but many people find this second approach easier to understand.

This method is called the consumption-plus-investment (or $C + I$) approach. It is illustrated in Figure 24-3, which shows a curve of total spending graphed against total output or income. The black CC line is the consumption function, showing the level of desired consumption corresponding to each level of income. We then add desired investment (which is at fixed level I) to the consumption function. This yields the level of total desired spending, or $C + I$, represented by the rust-colored $C + I$ curve in Figure 24-3.

We next put in a 45° line to help us identify the equilibrium. At any point on the 45° line, the total level of consumption plus investment spending (measured vertically) exactly equals the total level of output (measured horizontally).

We can now calculate the equilibrium level of output in Figure 24-3. Where the desired amount of spending, represented by the $C + I$ curve, equals total output, the economy is in equilibrium.

The total spending (or $C + I$) curve shows the level of desired expenditure by consumers and businesses corresponding to each level of output. The economy is in equilibrium at the point where the $C + I$ curve crosses the 45° line—at point E in Figure 24-3. At point E the economy is in equilibrium because at that level desired spending on consumption and investment exactly equals the level of total output.

The Adjustment Mechanism

It is essential to understand why point E is an equilibrium. *Equilibrium occurs when planned spending (on* C *and* I*) equals planned output.* What would happen if the system were to deviate from equilibrium, say, at output level D in Figure 24-3? At this level of output, the $C + I$ spending line is above the 45° line, so planned $C + I$ spending would be greater than planned output. This means that consumers would be buying more goods than businesses were producing. Auto dealers would find their lots emptying, and shoe stores would be running out of many sizes.

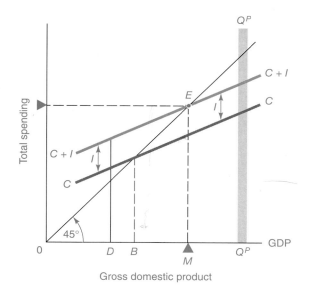

FIGURE 24-3. In the Expenditure Approach, Equilibrium GDP Level Is Found at the Intersection of the $C + I$ Schedule with the 45° Line

Adding II to CC gives the $C + I$ curve of total desired spending. At E, where this curve intersects the 45° line, we get the same equilibrium as in the saving-and-investment diagram. (Note the similarities between this figure and Fig. 24-2: the investment added to CC is the same as II of Fig. 24-2, and so must be the E intersection.)

In this disequilibrium situation, auto dealers and shoe stores would respond by increasing their orders. Automakers and shoe manufacturers would recall workers from layoff and gear up their production lines. Thus, *a discrepancy between output and planned spending leads to a change in output.*

By following this chain of reasoning, we see that only when firms are producing what households and firms plan to spend on C and I, precisely at point E, will the economy be in equilibrium. (You should also work through what happens when output is above equilibrium.)

Planned vs. Actual Amounts. In this section, we repeatedly discuss "planned" or "desired" spending and output. These words call attention to the difference between (1) the amount of planned or desired consumption or investment given by the consumption function or by the investment demand

THE MULTIPLIER MODEL **CHAPTER 24**

450

(1) Levels of GDP and *DI*	(2) Planned consumption	(3) Planned saving (3) = (1) − (2)	(4) Planned investment	(5) Level of GDP (5) = (1)	(6) Total planned consumption and investment (6) = (2) + (4)	(7) Resulting tendency of output
4,200	3,800	400	200	4,200 >	4,000	↓ Contraction
3,900	3,600	300	200	3,900 >	3,800	Contraction
3,600	3,400	200	200	3,600 =	3,600	Equilibrium
3,300	3,200	100	200	3,300 <	3,400	↑ Expansion
3,000	3,000	0	200	3,000 <	3,200	Expansion
2,700	2,800	−100	200	2,700 <	3,000	Expansion

GDP Determination Where Output Equals Planned Spending (Billions of Dollars)

TABLE 24-1. Equilibrium Output Can Be Found Arithmetically at the Level Where Planned Spending Equals GDP

The gray row depicts the equilibrium GDP level, where the $3600 that is being produced is just matched by the $3600 that households plan to consume and that firms plan to invest. In upper rows, firms will be forced into unintended inventory investment and will respond by cutting back production until equilibrium GDP is reached. Interpret the lower rows' tendency toward expansion of GDP toward equilibrium.

schedule and (2) the actual amount of consumption or investment measured after the fact.

This distinction emphasizes that GDP is at equilibrium only when firms and consumers are on their schedules of desired spending and investment. As measured by a national accounts statistician, saving and investment will always be exactly equal, in recession or boom. But *actual* investment will often differ from *planned* investment when actual sales are unequal to planned sales and firms consequently face an involuntary buildup or reduction of inventories. Only when the level of output is such that planned spending on *C* + *I* equals planned output will there be no tendency for output, income, or spending to change.

An Arithmetic Analysis

An arithmetic example may help show why the equilibrium level of output occurs where planned spending and planned output are equal.

Table 24-1 shows a simple example of consumption and savings functions. The break-even level of income, where the nation is too poor to do any net saving on balance, is assumed to be $3000 billion ($3 trillion). Each change of income of $300 billion is assumed to lead to a $100 billion change in saving and a $200 billion change in consumption; in other words, for simplicity *MPC* is assumed to be constant and exactly equal to ⅔. Therefore, *MPS* = ⅓.

Again, we assume that investment is exogenous. Suppose that the only level of investment that will be sustained indefinitely is exactly $200 billion, as shown in column (4) of Table 24-1. That is, at each level of GDP, businesses desire to purchase $200 billion of investment goods, no more and no less.

Columns (5) and (6) are the crucial ones. Column (5) shows the total GDP—this is simply column (1) copied once again into column (5). The figures in column (6) represent what business firms would actually be selling year in and year out; this is the planned consumption spending plus planned investment. It is the *C* + *I* schedule from Figure 24-3 in numbers.

When businesses as a whole are producing too high a level of total product (higher than the sum of what consumers and businesses want to purchase), they will be involuntarily piling up inventories of unsalable goods.

Reading the top row of Table 24-1, we see that if firms are temporarily producing $4200 billion of GDP, planned or desired spending [shown in column (6)] is only $4000 billion. In this situation, excess inventories will be accumulating. Firms will respond by contracting their operations, and GDP will fall. In the opposite case, represented by the bottom row of Table 24-1, total spending is $3000 billion and output is $2700 billion. Inventories are being depleted and firms will expand operations, raising output.

We see, then, that when business firms as a whole are temporarily producing more than they can profitably sell, they will contract their operations, and GDP will fall. When they are selling more than their current production, they will increase their output, and GDP will rise.

Only when the level of output in column (5) exactly equals planned spending in column (6) will business firms be in equilibrium. Their sales will then be just enough to justify continuing their current level of aggregate output. GDP will neither expand nor contract.

THE MULTIPLIER

Where is the multiplier in all this? To answer this question, we need to examine how a change in exogenous investment spending affects GDP. It is logical that an increase in investment will raise the level of output and employment. But by how much? The multiplier model shows that an increase in investment will increase GDP by an amplified or multiplied amount—by an amount greater than itself.

The **multiplier** is the number by which the change in investment must be multiplied in order to determine the resulting change in total output.

For example, suppose investment increases by $100 billion. If this causes an increase in output of $300 billion, the multiplier is 3. If, instead, the resulting increase in output is $400 billion, the multiplier is 4.

Woodsheds and Carpenters. Why is it that the multiplier is greater than 1? Let's suppose that I hire unemployed resources to build a $1000 woodshed. My carpenters and lumber producers will get an extra $1000 of income. But that is not the end of the story. If they all have a marginal propensity to consume of $\frac{2}{3}$, they will now spend $666.67 on new consumption goods. The producers of these goods will now have extra incomes of $666.67. If their *MPC* is also $\frac{2}{3}$, they in turn will spend $444.44, or $\frac{2}{3}$ of $666.67 (or $\frac{2}{3}$ of $\frac{2}{3}$ of $1000). The process will go on, with each new round of spending being $\frac{2}{3}$ of the previous round.

Thus an endless chain of *secondary consumption respending* is set in motion by my *primary* investment of $1000. But, although an endless chain, it is an

ever-diminishing one. Eventually it adds up to a finite amount.

Using straightforward arithmetic, we can find the total increase in spending in the following manner:

$1000.00		$1 \times \$1000$
+		+
666.67		$\frac{2}{3} \times \$1000$
+		+
444.44		$(\frac{2}{3})^2 \times \$1000$
+	=	+
296.30		$(\frac{2}{3})^3 \times \$1000$
+		+
197.53		$(\frac{2}{3})^4 \times \$1000$
+		+
.		.
.		.
.		.
———		———
$3000		$\frac{1}{1 - \frac{2}{3}} \times \$1000$, or $3 \times \$1000$

This shows that, with an *MPC* of $\frac{2}{3}$, the multiplier is 3; it consists of the 1 of primary investment plus 2 extra of secondary consumption respending.

The same arithmetic would give a multiplier of 4 for an *MPC* of $\frac{3}{4}$, because $1 + \frac{3}{4} + (\frac{3}{4})^2 + (\frac{3}{4})^3 + \cdots$ finally adds up to 4. For an *MPC* of $\frac{1}{2}$, the multiplier would be 2.[2]

The size of the multiplier thus depends upon how large the *MPC* is. It can also be expressed in terms of the twin concept, the *MPS*. For an *MPS* of $\frac{1}{4}$, the *MPC* is $\frac{3}{4}$ and the multiplier is 4. For an *MPS* of $\frac{1}{3}$, the multiplier is 3. If the *MPS* were $1/x$, the multiplier would be x.

By this time it should be clear that the simple multiplier is always the inverse, or reciprocal, of the marginal propensity to save. It is thus equal to $1/(1 - MPC)$. Our simple multiplier formula is

$$\text{Change in output} = \frac{1}{MPS} \times \text{change in investment}$$
$$= \frac{1}{1 - MPC} \times \text{change in investment}$$

---

[2] The formula for an infinite geometric progression is

$$1 + r + r^2 + r^3 + \cdots + r^n + \cdots = \frac{1}{1 - r}$$

as long as *MPC* (r) is less than 1 in absolute value.

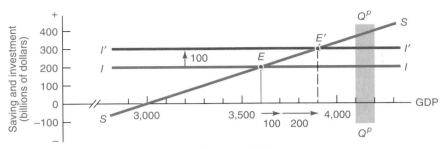

FIGURE 24-4. Each Dollar of Investment Is "Multiplied" into 3 Dollars of Output

New investment shifts II up to $I'I'$. E' gives the new equilibrium output, with output increasing by 3 for each 1 increase in investment. (*Note:* The broken horizontal rust arrow is 3 times the length of the vertical rust-colored arrow of investment shift and is broken to show 2 units of secondary consumption responding for each 1 unit of primary investment.)

In other words, the greater the extra consumption respending, the greater the multiplier.

Up to now, we have discussed the multiplier as relating to the extra consumption and saving. This is only part of the picture. In the next chapter, we will see that the multiplier applies to changes in total spending and changes in total leakages from spending.

Graphical Picture of the Multiplier

Our discussion of the multiplier has relied up to now largely on common sense and arithmetic. Can we get the same result using our graphical analysis of saving and investment? The answer is yes.

Suppose, as in Table 24-1, that the *MPS* is ⅓ and a burst of inventions gives rise to an extra $100 billion of continuing investment. What will be the new equilibrium GDP? If the multiplier is indeed 3, the answer is $3900 billion.

A look at Figure 24-4 can confirm this result. Our old investment schedule II is shifted upward by $100 billion to the new level $I'I'$. The new intersection point is E'; the increase in income is exactly 3 times the increase in investment. As the rust-colored arrows show, the horizontal output distance is 3 times as great as the upward shift in the investment schedule. We know that desired saving must rise to equal the new and higher level of investment. The only way that saving can rise is for national income to rise. With an *MPS* of ⅓ and an increase in investment of $100, income must rise by $300 to bring forth

$100 of additional saving to match the new investment. Hence, at equilibrium, $100 of additional investment induces $300 of additional income, verifying our multiplier arithmetic.[3]

THE MULTIPLIER MODEL IN PERSPECTIVE

The multiplier model has been enormously influential in macroeconomic analysis over the last half-century. At the same time, it leaves many macroeconomic factors out of the picture. As we will see shortly, it neglects the crucial influence of monetary factors on interest rates and, through these, on investment and other interest-sensitive components of output. More importantly, it omits the supply side of the economy as represented by the interaction of spending with aggregate supply and prices.

It will be useful to pause at this point to put all this in perspective and to see how the multiplier model fits into a broader view of the macroeconomy. We are trying to understand what determines the level of national output in a country. In the long run, potential output limits the amount a country

---

[3] Alter Table 24-1, on page 450, to verify this answer. In column (4), we now put $300 billion instead of $200 billion of investment. Show that the new equilibrium output now shifts one row up from the old rust-colored equilibrium row. Can you also show that the multiplier works downward?

can produce. But in the short run, the multiplier model shows how aggregate demand, influenced by investment and consumption spending, determines GDP. This approach will also help us understand why economies sometimes suffer from high unemployment.

While the relationships presented here have been simplified, their essence will remain valid even when extended to situations involving government fiscal policy, monetary policy, and foreign trade. The main point to retain is that the multiplier analysis holds when there are unemployed resources, that is, when output is less than its potential. When there are unemployed resources, an increase in aggregate demand can raise output levels. By contrast, if an economy is producing at its potential, there is little room for expansion when aggregate demand expands. In conditions of full employment, then, demand increases lead to higher prices rather than to output increases.

Putting this in plain English, when investment or other spending increases in an economy with excess capacity and unemployed workers, much of the extra spending will end up in extra real output, with only small increases in the price level. However, as the economy reaches and surpasses potential output, it is not possible to coax out more production at the going price level. Hence, at full employment, higher spending will simply result in higher price levels and little or none of the demand increase will end up in higher real output or employment.

The relationship between the multiplier analysis and the *AS-AD* approach is shown in Figure 24-5. Part (*b*) displays an upward-sloping *AS* curve that becomes relatively steep as output exceeds potential output. In the region where there are unemployed resources, to the left of potential output, output is determined primarily by the strength of aggregate demand. As investment increases, this increases *AD*, and equilibrium output rises.

The same economy can be described by the multiplier diagram in the top panel of Figure 24-5. The multiplier equilibrium gives the same level of output as the *AS-AD* equilibrium—both lead to a real GDP of *Q*. They simply stress different features of output determination.

This discussion again points to a crucial feature of the multiplier model. While it may be a highly useful approach to describe depressions or even reces-

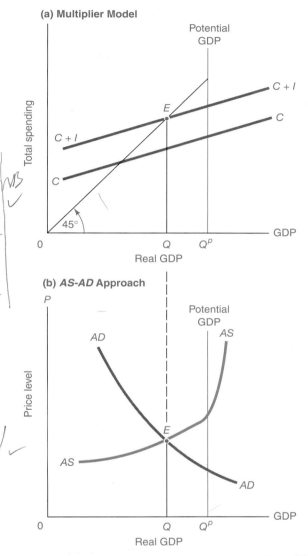

FIGURE 24-5. How the Multiplier Model Fits the *AS-AD* Approach

The multiplier model is a way of understanding the workings of the *AS-AD* equilibrium.

(**a**) The top panel shows the output-expenditure equilibrium in the multiplier model. At point *E*, the spending line just cuts the 45° line, leading to equilibrium output of *Q*.

(**b**) The equilibrium can also be seen in the bottom panel, where the *AD* curve cuts the *AS* curve at point *E*. Both approaches lead to exactly the same equilibrium output, *Q*.

sions, it cannot apply to periods of full employment, when real GDP exceeds potential output. Once factories are operating at full capacity and all the workers are employed, the economy simply cannot produce more output.

We have now completed our presentation of the simple multiplier model. We next move on to extend the analysis of aggregate demand by showing how government fiscal policy enters the picture.

B. FISCAL POLICY IN THE MULTIPLIER MODEL

For centuries, economists have understood the allocational role of fiscal policy (government tax and spending programs). It has long been known that through these programs the government decides how much of the nation's output should be divided between collective and private consumption and how the burden of payment for collective goods should be divided among the population.

Only with the development of modern macroeconomic theory has a further surprising fact been uncovered: Government fiscal powers also have a major impact upon the short-run movements of output, employment, and prices. The knowledge that fiscal policy has powerful effects upon economic activity led to the *Keynesian approach to macroeconomic policy,* which is the active use of government action to moderate business cycles. The approach was described by the eminent Keynesian economist, James Tobin, as follows:

> Keynesian policies are, first, the explicit dedication of macroeconomic policy instruments to real economic goals, in particular full employment and real growth of national income. Second, Keynesian demand management is activist. Third, Keynesians have wished to put both fiscal and monetary policies in consistent and coordinated harness in the pursuit of macroeconomic objectives.

In this section we use the multiplier model to show how government purchases affect output.

HOW GOVERNMENT FISCAL POLICIES AFFECT OUTPUT

To understand the role of government in economic activity, we need to look at government purchases and taxation, along with the effects of those activities on private-sector spending. As you might guess, we now add G to get a $C + I + G$ spending schedule for charting macroeconomic equilibrium when government, with its spending and taxing, is in the picture.

It will simplify our task in the beginning if we analyze the effects of government purchases with total taxes collected held constant (taxes that do not change with income or other economic variables are called *lump-sum taxes*). But even with a fixed dollar value of taxes, we can no longer ignore the distinction between disposable income and gross domestic product. Under simplified conditions (including no foreign trade, transfers, or depreciation), we know from Chapter 21 that GDP equals disposable income plus taxes. But with tax revenues held constant, GDP and DI will always differ by the same amount; thus, after taking account of such taxes, we can still plot the CC consumption schedule against GDP rather than against DI.

An example will clarify how we can depict our consumption function when taxes are present. In Figure 24-6, we have drawn our original consumption function with zero taxes as the black CC line. In this case, GDP = DI. Here, consumption is 3000 at a DI of 3000; consumption is 3400 at a GDP of 3600.

Now introduce taxes of 300. At a DI of 3600, GDP must be equal to 3600 + 300 = 3900. Consumption is thus 3400 at a DI of 3600 or at a GDP of 3900. So we can write consumption as a function of GDP by shifting the consumption function to the right to the rust $C'C'$ curve; the amount of the rightward shift is exactly equal to the amount of taxes, 300.

Alternatively, we can plot the new consumption function as a parallel *downward* shift by 200. As Figure 24-6 shows, 200 is the result of multiplying a decrease in income of 300 times the *MPC* of $\frac{2}{3}$.

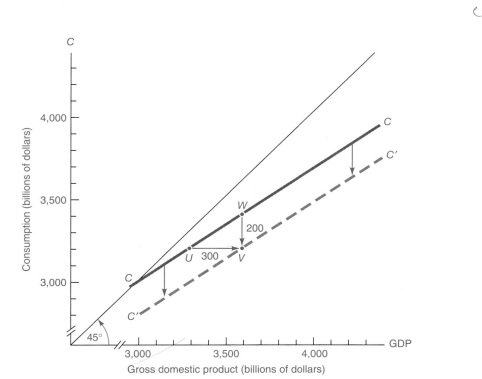

FIGURE 24-6. Taxes Reduce Disposable Income and Shift *CC* Schedule to the Right and Down

Each dollar of tax shifts the *CC* schedule to the right by the amount of the tax. A rightward *CC* shift also means a downward *CC* shift, but the downward *CC* shift is less than the rightward shift. Why? Because the downward shift is equal to the rightward shift times the *MPC*. Thus, if the *MPC* is ⅔, the downward shift is ⅔ times $300 billion = $200 billion. Verify that *WV* = ⅔ *UV*.

Turning next to the different components of aggregate demand, recall from Chapter 21 that GDP consists of four elements:

GDP = consumption expenditure
+ gross private domestic investment
+ government purchases of goods and services
+ net exports
= C + I + G + X

For now, we consider a closed economy with no foreign trade, so our GDP consists of the first three components, C + I + G. (We add the final component of net exports when we consider open-economy macroeconomics.)

Figure 24-7 on page 456 shows the effect of G. This diagram is almost the same as the one used earlier in this chapter (see Figure 24-3). In this diagram,

however, we have added one new variable, G (government purchases of goods and services), on top of the consumption function and the fixed amount of investment. That is, the vertical distance between the C + I line and the C + I + G line is the amount of government purchases of goods and services (police, tanks, roads, etc.).

Why do we simply add G on the top? Because spending on government buildings (G) has the same macroeconomic impact as spending on private buildings (I); the collective expenditure involved in buying a government vehicle (G) has the same effect on jobs as private consumption expenditures on automobiles (C).

We end up with the three-layered cake of C + I + G, calculating the amount of total spending forthcoming at each level of GDP. We now must go to its point of intersection with the 45° line to find the

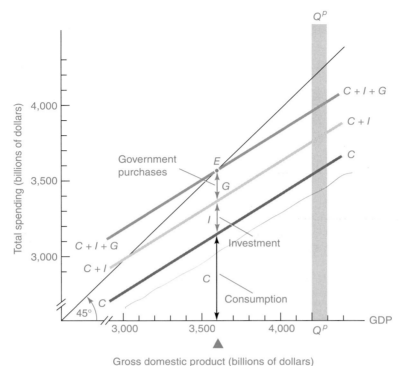

FIGURE 24-7. Government Purchases Add On Just like Investment to Determine Equilibrium GDP

We now add government purchases on top of consumption and investment spending. This gives us the $C + I + G$ schedule. At E, where this schedule intersects the 45° line, we find the equilibrium level of GDP.

equilibrium level of GDP. At this equilibrium GDP level, denoted by point E in Figure 24-7, total planned spending exactly equals total planned output. Point E is thus the equilibrium level of output when we add government purchases to the multiplier model.

Impact of Taxation on Aggregate Demand

How does government taxation tend to reduce aggregate demand and the level of GDP? Extra taxes lower our disposable incomes, and lower disposable incomes tend to reduce our consumption spending. Clearly, if investment and government purchases remain the same, a reduction in consumption spending will then reduce GDP and employment. Thus, in the multiplier model, higher taxes without

increases in government purchases will tend to reduce real GDP.

A look back at Figure 24-6 confirms this reasoning. In this figure, the upper CC curve represents the level of the consumption function with no taxes. But the upper curve cannot be the consumption function because consumers definitely pay taxes on their incomes. Suppose that consumers pay $300 billion in taxes at every level of income; thus, DI is exactly $300 billion less than GDP at every level of output. As shown in Figure 24-6, this level of taxes can be represented by a rightward shift in the consumption function of $300 billion. This rightward shift will also appear as a downward shift; if the MPC is $\frac{2}{3}$, the rightward shift of $300 billion will be seen as a downward shift of $200 billion.

Without a doubt, taxes lower output in our multiplier model, and Figure 24-7 shows why. When

			Output Determination with Government (Billions of Dollars)				
(1) Initial level of GDP	(2) Taxes (T)	(3) Disposable income (DI)	(4) Planned consumption (C)	(5) Planned investment (I)	(6) Government expenditure (G)	(7) Total purchases (C + I + G)	(8) Resulting tendency of economy
4,200	300	3,900	3,600	200	200	4,000 ↓	Contraction
3,900	300	3,600	3,400	200	200	3,800 ↓	Contraction
3,600	300	3,300	3,200	200	200	3,600	Equilibrium
3,300	300	3,000	3,000	200	200	3,400 ↑	Expansion
3,000	300	2,700	2,800	200	200	3,200 ↑	Expansion

TABLE 24-2. Government Purchases, Taxes, and Investment Determine Equilibrium GDP

This table shows how output is determined when government purchases of goods and services are added to the multiplier model. In this example, taxes are "lump-sum" or independent of the level of income. Disposable income is thus GDP minus $300 billion. Total spending is $I + G +$ the consumption determined by the consumption function.

At levels of output less than $3600 billion, spending is greater than output, so output expands. Levels of output greater than $3600 are unsustainable and lead to contraction. Only at output of $3600 is output in equilibrium—that is, planned spending equals output.

taxes rise, $I + G$ does not change, but the increase in taxes will lower disposable income, thereby shifting the CC consumption schedule downward. Hence, the $C + I + G$ schedule shifts downward. You can pencil in a new, lower $C' + I + G$ schedule in Figure 24-7. Confirm that its new intersection with the 45° line must be at a lower equilibrium level of GDP.

Keep in mind that G is government purchases of goods and services. It excludes spending on transfers such as unemployment insurance or social security payments. These transfers are treated as *negative taxes*, so the taxes (T) considered here can best be thought of as taxes less transfers. Therefore, if direct and indirect taxes total $400 billion, while all transfer payments are $100 billion, then net taxes, T, are $400 − $100 = $300 billion. (Can you see why an increase in social security benefits lowers T, raises DI, shifts the $C + I + G$ curve upward, and raises equilibrium GDP?)

A Numerical Example

The points made up to now are illustrated in Table 24-2. This table is very similar to Table 24-1, which illustrated output determination in the simplest multiplier model. The first column shows a reference level of GDP, while the second shows a fixed

level of taxes, $300 billion. Disposable income in column (3) is GDP less taxes. Consumption, taken as a function of DI, is shown in column (4). Column (5) shows the fixed level of investment, while column (6) exhibits the level of government purchases. To find total planned spending in column (7), we add together the $C, I,$ and G in columns (4) through (6).

Finally, we compare total spending in column (7) with the initial level of GDP in column (1). If spending is above GDP, firms raise production to meet the level of spending, and output consequently rises; if spending is below GDP, output falls. This tendency, shown in the last column, assures us that output will tend toward equilibrium at $3600 billion.

FISCAL-POLICY MULTIPLIERS

The multiplier analysis shows that government fiscal policy is high-powered spending much like investment. The parallel suggests that fiscal policy should also have multiplier effects upon output. And this is exactly right.

The **government expenditure multiplier** is the increase in GDP resulting from an increase of $1 in government purchases of goods and services. An initial government purchase of a good or service will set in motion a chain of respending: If the government

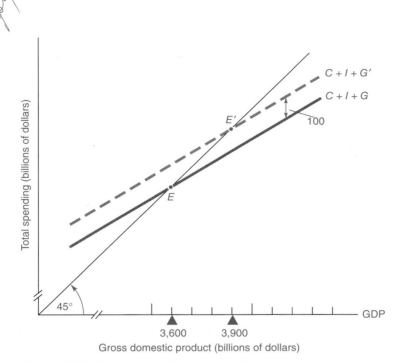

FIGURE 24-8. The Effect of Higher *G* on Output

Suppose that the government raises defense purchases by $100 billion in response to a threat to Mideast oil fields. This shifts upward the *C* + *I* + *G* line by $100 billion to *C* + *I* + *G′*.

The new equilibrium level of GDP is thus read off the 45° line at *E′* rather than at *E*. Because the *MPC* is ⅔, the new level of output is $300 billion higher. That is, the government expenditure multiplier is

$$3 = \frac{1}{1 - \frac{2}{3}}$$

(What would the government expenditure multiplier be if the *MPC* were ¾? ⁹⁄₁₀?)

builds a road, the road-builders will spend some of their incomes on consumption goods, which in turn will generate additional incomes, some of which will be respent. In the simple model examined here, the ultimate effect on GDP of an extra dollar of *G* will be the same as an extra dollar of *I*: The multipliers are equal to $1/(1 - MPC)$. Figure 24-8 shows how a change in *G* will result in a higher level of GDP, with the increase being a multiple of the increase in government purchases.

To show the effects of an extra $100 billion of *G*, the *C* + *I* + *G* curve in Figure 24-8 has been shifted up by $100 billion. The ultimate increase in GDP is equal to the $100 billion of primary spending times the expenditure multiplier. In this case, because the

MPC is ⅔, the multiplier is 3, so the equilibrium level of GDP rises by $300 billion.

This example, as well as common sense, tells us that the government expenditure multiplier is exactly the same number as the investment multiplier. They are both called **expenditure multipliers**.

Also, note that the multiplier horse can be ridden in both directions. If government purchases were to fall, with taxes and other influences held constant, GDP would decline by the change in *G* times the multiplier.

The effect of *G* on output can be seen as well in the numerical example of Table 24-2. You can pencil in a different level of *G*—at $300 billion—and find the equilibrium level of GDP. It should give the same answer as Figure 24-8.

We can sum up:

Government purchases of goods and services (*G*) are an important force in determining output and employment. In the multiplier model, if *G* increases, output will rise by the increase in *G* times the expenditure multiplier. Government purchases therefore have the potential to stabilize or destabilize output over the business cycle.

Defense spending and the economy: The government expenditure multiplier at work is seen in the economic impacts of the U.S. defense budget. In the early 1980s the United States undertook a tremendous expansion of defense spending under President Reagan. The defense budget (in constant dollars) soared from $271 billion in 1979 to $409 billion in 1987, when it reached $7\frac{1}{2}$ percent of GDP. After that peak, defense spending as a share of GDP started drifting down. The cuts in defense spending accelerated beginning in 1990, when it became clear that the cold war was finally over and Soviet communism was no longer a military danger. Presidents Bush and Clinton both proposed budgets calling for further reductions in military spending, and by the mid-1990s defense spending had declined to under 5 percent of GDP.

According to the multiplier theory, the defense buildup of the early 1980s should have exerted a strong stimulative impact on the economy, and that is exactly what happened. As defense spending rose, it helped pull the country out of the recession of 1981–1982 and helped propel the boom of the mid-1980s. To some regions, like southern California, where many aerospace companies were based, the influx of defense dollars brought tremendous prosperity. A newspaper article noted that one well-paid defense position would spin off other jobs, such as "the metal shop supplying some specialized part, the cleaners to keep the jumpsuits white, and the paper company making the pasteboard boxes for the doughnuts that someone picks up on the way to the office."

At the end of the cold war, the multiplier worked in reverse. As defense spending declined, it became an overall drag on the economy. Defense cuts contributed to the sluggish growth in output during the early 1990s. To take one example, from 1990 to 1993 the aircraft manufacturing industry lost 170,000 jobs, mainly because of defense cuts. And southern California, which had benefited from defense spending a decade earlier, ended up being stuck in recession much longer than the rest of the country as defense layoffs slowed growth in that region.

Impact of Taxes

Taxes also have an impact upon equilibrium GDP, although the size of tax multipliers is smaller than that of expenditure multipliers. Consider the following example: Suppose the economy is at its potential GDP and the nation raises defense spending by $200 billion. Such sudden increases have occurred at many points in the history of the United States: in the early 1940s for World War II, in 1951 for the Korean war, in the mid-1960s for the Vietnam war, and in the early 1980s during the Reagan administration's military buildup. Furthermore, say that economic planners wish to raise taxes just enough to offset the effect on GDP of the $200 billion increase in *G*. How much would taxes have to be raised?

We are in for a surprise. To offset the $200 billion increase in *G*, we need to increase tax collections by more than $200 billion. In our numerical example, we can find the exact size of the tax, or *T*, increase from Figure 24-6. That figure shows that a $300 billion increase in *T* reduces disposable income by just enough to produce a consumption decline of $200 billion when the *MPC* is $\frac{2}{3}$. Put differently, a tax increase of $300 billion will shift the *CC* curve down by $200 billion. Hence, while a $1 billion increase in defense spending shifts up the *C* + *I* + *G* line by $1 billion, a $1 billion tax increase shifts down the *C* + *I* + *G* line by only $\frac{2}{3}$ billion (when the *MPC* is $\frac{2}{3}$). Thus offsetting an increase in government purchases requires a larger increase in *T* than the increase in *G*.

Tax changes are a powerful weapon in affecting output. But the tax multiplier is smaller than the expenditure multiplier by a factor equal to the *MPC*:

Tax multiplier = *MPC* × expenditure multiplier

The reason the tax multiplier is smaller than the expenditure multiplier is straightforward. When government spends $1 on *G*, that $1 gets spent directly on GDP. On the other hand, when government cuts taxes by a dollar, only part of that dollar is spent on *C*, while a fraction of that $1 tax cut is saved. The difference in the responses to a dollar of G and to a dollar of T is enough to lower the tax multiplier below the expenditure multiplier.[4]

Fiscal Policy in Practice

In the 1960s, President J. F. Kennedy adopted the principles of Keynesian economics, and fiscal policy became one of the nation's main weapons for fighting recession or inflation. He proposed substantial tax cuts to lift the economy out of a slump; after these were enacted, the economy grew rapidly. However, when the fiscal expansion from the Vietnam war buildup during 1965–1966 was added to the tax cuts, output rose above potential GDP and inflation began to heat up. To fight the rising inflation and offset the increased Vietnam war expenditures, Congress passed a temporary surtax on incomes in 1968, although most economists thought this tax increase was too little and too late.

The 1980s provided another dramatic demonstration of how fiscal policy works. In 1981, Congress passed President Reagan's fiscal package; it contained sharp tax cuts, a large increase in defense spending (described in the example above) and few cuts to civilian expenditure programs. These steps pulled the American economy out of the deep recession of 1981–1982 and into a rapid expansion in 1983–1985.

The mid-1980s ushered in a new fiscal era. The Reagan fiscal policy led to a sharp increase in the government's budget deficit, with the deficit (equal to the difference between spending and revenues) rising from $40 billion (equal to $1\frac{1}{2}$ percent of GDP) in 1979 to over $200 billion (or 6 percent of GDP) in 1983. Congress took steps in 1985 to control the deficit with a deficit-limitation law known as the

Gramm-Rudman Act, and taxes were raised in 1982, 1984, 1990, and 1993. Yet over this period, the ratio of government debt to GDP rose steadily.

Upon entering office, President Clinton faced a painful dilemma. The deficit remained stubbornly high, yet the economy was stagnating and the rate of joblessness was unacceptably high. Should the President tackle the deficit, increasing the level of *public saving* by raising taxes and lowering spending, so that the higher saving might lead to an increase in *national investment*? Or should the President worry that higher taxes and lower G might lower output as the fiscal contraction reduced $C + I + G$ and choked off investment? In the end, the President decided that deficit reduction was the chief priority. The Budget Act of 1993 enacted fiscal measures that lowered the deficit by about $150 billion (or 2 percent of GDP) over the next 5 years.

The analysis in this section has focused primarily on fiscal policy as a tool for stabilizing the economy. But Keynesian economists emphasize that fiscal policy is only one of the potential approaches to business-cycle management. The government has another equally powerful weapon in monetary policy. Although monetary policy works quite differently, as we will see in the next two chapters, it has many advantages as a policy for combating unemployment and inflation.

Like two locomotives on a train—sometimes pulling in one direction and sometimes in different directions—monetary and fiscal policies are powerful engines for affecting output, employment, and prices in the short run.

MULTIPLIERS IN ACTION

A realistic understanding of the size of multipliers is a crucial part of diagnosis and prescription in economic policy. Just as a physician prescribing a painkiller must know the effect of different dosages, so an economist must know the quantitative magnitude of expenditure and tax multipliers. When the economy is growing too rapidly and a dose of fiscal austerity is prescribed, the economic doctor needs to know the actual size of multipliers before deciding how large a dose of tax increases or expenditure reductions to order.

Textbook models give a highly simplified picture of the structure of the macroeconomy. For a

---

[4] The different multipliers can be seen using the device of the "expenditure rounds" shown on page 451. Let the MPC be r. Then if G goes up by 1 unit, the total increase in spending is the sum of secondary respending rounds:

$$1 + r + r^2 + r^3 + \cdots = \frac{1}{1-r}$$

Now, if taxes are reduced by $1, consumers save $(1-r)$ of the increased disposable income and spend r dollars on the first round. With the further rounds, the total spending is thus

$$r + r^2 + r^3 + \cdots = \frac{r}{1-r}$$

Thus the tax multiplier is r times the expenditure multiplier, where r is the MPC.

more realistic picture of the response of output to changes in government purchases, economists estimate large-scale econometric models (see the discussion of this in Chapter 23) and then perform numerical experiments on their models by calculating the impact of a change in government purchases on the economy. Such models can serve as the basis for policy recommendations. These large-scale models include not only the bare-bones factors that we have sketched up to now but also factors that we consider later such as a more realistic treatment of taxes, a complete monetary sector, and the behavior of wages and prices. Including these additional factors tends to reduce the numerical size of multipliers.

A recent comprehensive survey of econometric models of the United States provides a representative sample of multiplier estimates. The models surveyed include equations to predict the behavior of all major sectors of the economy (including both monetary and financial sectors, along with investment demand schedules and consumption functions), and they incorporate a full set of links with the rest of the world. In the estimates, the level of real government purchases of goods and services is permanently increased by $1 billion. The models then calculate the impact on real GDP. The change in real GDP resulting from the increase in government purchases provides an estimate of the size of the government expenditure multiplier.

Figure 24-9 presents the results of this survey. The heavy rust-colored line shows the average government expenditure multiplier estimated by eight models, while the light gray lines show the range of estimates of the individual models. The average multiplier for the first and second years is around 1.4, but after the second year the multiplier tends to decline slightly as monetary forces and international impacts come into play. (The monetary forces represent the impact of higher GDP on interest rates, which leads to a crowding out of investment, as we will explain in later chapters.)

One interesting feature of these estimates is that the different models (represented by the light gray lines in Figure 24-9) show considerable disagreement about the size of multipliers. Why do the esti-

FIGURE 24-9. Expenditure Multipliers in Macroeconomic Models

A careful survey shows the estimated government expenditure multipliers in different macroeconomic models. These experiments show the estimated impact of a permanent $1 billion increase in the real value of government purchases of goods and services on real GDP at different intervals following the spending increase. That is, they show the impact of a $1 billion change in G on Q. The heavy rust-colored line shows the average multiplier for the different models, while the gray lines represent the multipliers for each individual model. [Source: Ralph C. Bryant, Gerald Holtham, and Peter Hooper, "Consensus and Diversity in Model Simulations," in *Empirical Macroeconomics for Interdependent Economies* (Brookings, Washington, D.C., 1988).]

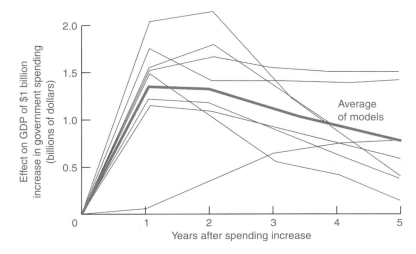

mates differ? To begin with, there is inherent uncertainty about the nature of economic relationships. Uncertainty about the structure of nature or society is of course what makes science so exciting; if everything were perfectly understood, scientists would be out of business. But understanding economic systems poses even greater challenges because economists cannot conduct controlled experiments in a laboratory. Even more vexing is the fact that the economy itself evolves over time, so the "correct" model for 1968 is different from the "correct" model for 1998.

In addition, economists have fundamental disagreements about the underlying nature of the macroeconomy. Some economists believe that a Keynesian approach best explains macroeconomic behavior, while others are convinced that a classical or real-business-cycle or monetarist approach yields better insights. With all these uncertainties and differences in points of view, we can hardly be surprised that economists will provide different estimates of multipliers.

Beyond the Multiplier Model

We have completed our survey of the most important applications of the Keynesian multiplier model. This analysis is an indispensable aid in understanding business fluctuations and the linkage between fiscal policy and national output.

But it would be a mistake to believe you can turn a parrot into a macroeconomist by simply teaching it to say "$C + I + G$" or "Polly has a multiplier." Behind such concepts are important assumptions and qualifications.

Recall that the multiplier model assumes that investment is fixed and ignores the impact of money and credit. Moreover, aggregate supply is left out of the story, so we have no way of analyzing how increases in spending are divided between prices and output. And these are not trifling concerns—rather, they are essential to understanding modern macroeconomics. But before we can incorporate these further realistic elements, we must master monetary theory and policy, as well as the essentials of inflation theory. Once we have incorporated the influence of money and interest rates, along with the behavior of wages and prices, we will see that the impact of fiscal policy on the economy may be quite different from the simplest multiplier model.

We turn next to an analysis of one of the most fascinating parts of all economics, the study of money. Once we understand how the central bank determines the money supply, we will have a fuller appreciation of how governments can tame the business cycles that have run wild through much of the history of capitalism.

SUMMARY

A. The Basic Multiplier Model

1. The multiplier model provides a simple way to understand the impact of aggregate demand on the level of output. In the simplest approach, household consumption is a function of disposable income while investment is fixed. People's desire to consume and the willingness of businesses to invest are brought into balance by adjustments in output. The equilibrium level of national output must be at the intersection of the savings and investment schedules, *SS* and *II*. We can also see this using the expenditure-output approach in which equilibrium output comes at the intersection of the consumption-plus-investment schedule, $C + I$, with the 45° line.

2. If output is temporarily above its equilibrium level, businesses find output higher than sales, with inventories piling up involuntarily and profits plummeting. Firms therefore cut production and employment back toward the equilibrium level. The only sustainable level of output comes when buyers voluntarily purchase exactly as much as businesses desire to produce.

3. Thus, for the simplified Keynesian multiplier model, investment calls the tune and consumption dances to

the music. Investment determines output, while saving responds passively to income changes. Output rises or falls until planned saving has adjusted to the level of planned investment.

4. Investment has a *multiplied effect* on output. When investment changes, output will at first rise by an equal amount. But as the income receivers in the capital-goods industries get more income, they set in motion a whole chain of additional secondary consumption spending and employment.

    If people always spend r of each extra dollar of income on consumption, the total of the multiplier chain will be

$$1 + r + r^2 + \cdots = \frac{1}{1-r} = \frac{1}{1 - MPC} = \frac{1}{MPS}$$

The simplest multiplier is numerically equal to the reciprocal of the *MPS* or, equivalently, to $1/(1 - MPC)$. The multiplier works in either direction, amplifying either increases or decreases in investment. This result occurs because it always takes more than a dollar of increased income to increase saving by a dollar.

5. Key points to remember are (*a*) the basic multiplier model emphasizes the importance of shifts in aggregate demand in affecting output and income and (*b*) it is primarily applicable for situations with unemployed resources.

B. Fiscal Policy in the Multiplier Model

6. The analysis of fiscal policy elaborates the Keynesian multiplier model. It shows that an increase in government purchases—taken by itself, with taxes and investment unchanged—has an expansionary effect on national output much like that of investment. The schedule of $C + I + G$ shifts upward to a higher equilibrium intersection with the 45° line.

7. A decrease in taxes—taken by itself, with investment and government purchases unchanged—raises the equilibrium level of national output. The *CC* schedule of consumption plotted against GDP is shifted upward and leftward by a tax cut. But since extra dollars of disposable income go partly into saving, the dollar increase in consumption will not be quite so great as the dollars of new disposable income. Therefore, the tax multiplier is smaller than the government expenditure multiplier.

8. Using statistical techniques and macroeconomic theory, economists have developed realistic models to estimate expenditure multipliers. For mainstream approaches, these tend to show multipliers of between 1 and $1\frac{1}{2}$ for periods of up to 4 years.

CONCEPTS FOR REVIEW

The Basic Multiplier Model

$C + I$ schedule
two ways of viewing GDP
   determination:
   planned saving = planned investment
   planned C + planned I = planned GDP

investment equals saving: planned vs. actual levels
multiplier effect of investment
multiplier

$$= 1 + MPC + (MPC)^2 + \cdots$$
$$= \frac{1}{1 - MPC} = \frac{1}{MPS}$$

Government Purchases and Taxation

fiscal policy:
   G effect on equilibrium GDP
   T effect on CC and on GDP
multiplier effects of government purchases (G) and taxes (T)
$C + I + G$ curve
estimated multipliers in practice

QUESTIONS FOR DISCUSSION

1. In the simple multiplier model, assume that investment is always zero. Show that equilibrium output in this special case would come at the break-even point of the consumption function. Why would equilibrium output come *above* the break-even point when investment is positive?

2. The saving-and-investment diagram and the 45° line $C + I$ diagram are two different ways of showing how national output is determined in the multiplier model. Describe each. Show their equivalence.

3. Reconstruct Table 24-1 assuming that planned investment is equal to (*a*) $300 billion, (*b*) $400 billion.

What is the resulting difference in GDP? Is this difference greater or smaller than the change in I? Why? When I drops from $200 billion to $100 billion, how much must GDP drop?

4. Give (*a*) the common sense, (*b*) the arithmetic, and (*c*) the geometry of the multiplier. What are the multipliers for *MPC* = 0.9? 0.8? 0.5? For *MPS* = 0.1? 0.8?

5. We have seen that investment responds to output through the accelerator principle (see Chapter 22). We might then define the *marginal propensity to invest* or *MPI*, as the change in investment per unit change in output. Suppose that investment is $I = I + 1.2Q$

(which has an *MPI* of 1.2), while the *MPC* is 0.8. What is the marginal propensity to spend = *MPC* + *MPI*? Work out the explosive (!) chain of spending and responding when the marginal propensity to spend = 2. Try to explain the economics of the divergent infinite geometric series.

6. Explain in words and using the notion of expenditure rounds why the tax multiplier is smaller than the expenditure multiplier.

7. Explain why governments might use fiscal policy to stabilize the economy. Why would fiscal policy be effective in raising output in a Keynesian economy but not in an economy where aggregate supply is vertical?

8. "Even if the government spends billions on wasteful military armaments, this action can create jobs in a recession and will be socially worthwhile." Discuss.

9. **Advanced problem**: The growth of nations depends crucially on saving and investment. And from youth we are taught that thrift is important and that "a penny saved is a penny earned." But will higher saving necessarily benefit the economy? In a striking argument,

Keynes pointed out that when people attempt to save more, this will not necessarily result in more saving for the nation as a whole. Let us analyze this "paradox of thrift."

To see this point, assume that people decide to save more. Illustrate how this shifts up the *SS* curve in the multiplier model of Figure 24-4. Explain why this will *decrease output with no increase in saving*! Provide the intuition here that if people try to increase their saving and lower their consumption for a given level of business investment, sales will fall and businesses will cut back on production. Explain how far output will fall. Here then is the *paradox of thrift:* When the community desires to save more, the effect may actually be a lowering of income and output with no increase of saving.

Explain why this is a good example of the fallacy of composition. Further explain why the paradox might hold in an economy experiencing unemployment, whereas in a "classical" economy with full employment higher saving would indeed raise investment without a decline in output.

CHAPTER 25
MONEY AND COMMERCIAL BANKING

> Over all history, money has oppressed people in one of two ways: either it has been abundant and very unreliable, or reliable and very scarce.
>
> *John Kenneth Galbraith*, The Age of Uncertainty (*1977*)

We are all intimately familiar with money, but we seldom consider what a strange thing money really is. We toil and fret to earn our dollars, yet each bill is just paper, with no intrinsic value. The only utility of money comes when we get rid of it.

From a macroeconomic point of view, we will see that the supply of money has a critical effect on output, employment, and prices. The central bank can use its control over the supply of money to stimulate the economy when growth turns sluggish or to brake the economy when prices rise too quickly. When money is well managed, output can grow smoothly with stable prices. But an unreliable monetary system can lead to inflation or depression. Indeed, many of

the world's most serious macroeconomic problems can be traced to crises in the management of money and finance.

This chapter begins our study of monetary economics. Using our thematic diagram, Figure 25-1 shows the topics covered in this chapter. We start by looking at the essence of money and then analyze interest rates. In the second section of this chapter, we examine the banking system and the supply of money. This will serve as an introduction to the next chapter's analysis of central banking and of the impact of money on overall economic activity. We conclude the chapter by analyzing a crucial part of our financial system—the stock market.

A. MONEY AND INTEREST RATES

THE EVOLUTION OF MONEY

The History of Money

Barter. In an early textbook on money, when Stanley Jevons wanted to illustrate the tremendous leap forward that occurred as societies introduced money, he used the following experience:

Some years since, Mademoiselle Zélie, a singer of the Théâtre Lyrique at Paris, . . . gave a concert in the Society Islands. In exchange for an air from *Norma* and a few other songs, she was to receive a third part of the receipts. When counted, her share was found to consist of three pigs, twenty-three turkeys, forty-four chickens, five thousand cocoa-nuts, besides considerable quantities of bananas, lemons, and

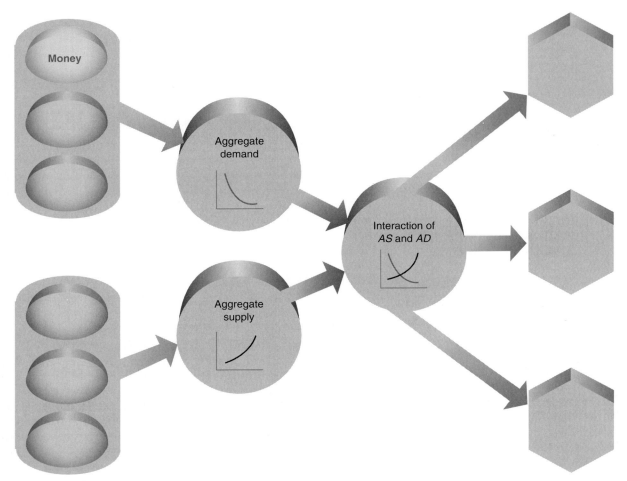

FIGURE 25-1. We Now Turn to Money: Its Demand and the Role of Banks in Its Supply

oranges. . . . [I]n Paris . . . this amount of live stock and vegetables might have brought four thousand francs, which would have been good remuneration for five songs. In the Society Islands, however, pieces of money were scarce; and as Mademoiselle could not consume any considerable portion of the receipts herself, it became necessary in the mean time to feed the pigs and poultry with the fruit.

This example describes **barter**, which consists of the exchange of goods for other goods. Barter contrasts with exchange through the use of **money**, which is anything that serves as a commonly accepted medium of exchange or means of payment. Although barter is better than no trade at all, it operates under grave disadvantages because an

elaborate division of labor would be unthinkable without the introduction of the great social invention of money.

As economies develop, people no longer barter one good for another. Instead, they sell goods for money and then use money to buy other goods they wish to have. At first glance this seems to complicate rather than simplify matters, as it replaces one transaction with two. If you have apples and want nuts, would it not be simpler to trade one for the other rather than to sell the apples for money and then use the money to buy nuts?

Actually, the reverse is true: two monetary transactions are simpler than one barter transaction. For example, some people may want to buy apples, and some may want to sell nuts. But it would be a most unusual circumstance to find a person whose desires exactly complement your own—eager to sell nuts and buy apples. To use a classical economic phrase, instead of there being a "double coincidence of wants," there is likely to be a "want of coincidence." So, unless a hungry tailor happens to find an undraped farmer who has both food and a desire for a pair of pants, under barter neither can make a direct trade.

Societies that traded extensively simply could not overcome the overwhelming handicaps of barter. The use of a commonly accepted medium of exchange, money, permits the farmer to buy pants from the tailor, who buys shoes from the cobbler, who buys leather from the farmer.

Commodity Money. Money as a medium of exchange first came into human history in the form of commodities. A great variety of items have served as money at one time or another: cattle, olive oil, beer or wine, copper, iron, gold, silver, rings, diamonds, and cigarettes.

Each of the above has advantages and disadvantages. Cattle are not divisible into small change. Beer does not improve with keeping, although wine may. Olive oil provides a nice liquid currency that is as minutely divisible as one wishes, but it is a bit messy to handle. And so forth.

By the nineteenth century, commodity money was almost exclusively limited to metals like silver and gold. These forms of money had *intrinsic value,* meaning that they had use value in themselves. Because money had intrinsic value, there was no need for the government to guarantee its value, and the quantity of money was regulated by the market through the supply and demand for gold or silver. But metallic money has shortcomings because scarce resources are required to dig it out of the ground; moreover, it might become abundant simply because of accidental discoveries of ore deposits.

The advent of monetary control by central banks has led to a much more stable currency system. The intrinsic value of money is now the least important thing about it.

Modern Money. The age of commodity money gave way to the age of *paper money.* The essence of money is now laid bare. Money is wanted not for its own sake but for the things it will buy. We do not wish to consume money directly; rather, we use it by getting rid of it. Even when we choose to keep money, it is valuable only because we can spend it later on.

The use of paper currency has become widespread because it is a convenient medium of exchange. Currency is easily carried and stored. The value of money can be protected from counterfeiting by careful engraving. The fact that private individuals cannot legally create money keeps it scarce. Given this limitation in supply, currency has value. It can buy things. As long as people can pay their bills with currency, as long as it is accepted as a means of payment, it serves the function of money.

Most money today is *bank money*—deposits in a bank or other financial institution. Checks are accepted in place of cash payment for many goods and services. In fact, if we calculate the total dollar amount of transactions, nine-tenths take place by bank money, the rest by currency.

Today there is rapid innovation in developing different forms of money. For example, some financial institutions will now link a checking account to a savings account or even to a stock portfolio, allowing customers to write checks on the value of their stock. Traveler's checks can be used for many transactions and are included in the money supply. Many companies are devising "smart cards" that allow people to pay for small items by simply passing the card through an electronic reader.

Components of the Money Supply

Let us now look more carefully at the different kinds of money that Americans use. The major *monetary aggregates* are the quantitative measures of the supply of money. They are known today as M_1 and M_2, and you can read about their week-to-week movements in the newspaper, along with sage commentaries on the significance of the latest wiggle. Here we will provide the exact definitions as of 1997.

Transactions Money. One important and closely watched measure of money is transactions money, or M_1, which consists of items that are actu-

Kinds of money	Billions of dollars		
	1959	1973	1997
Currency (outside of financial institutions)	28.8	61.7	403.7
Demand deposits (excludes government deposits and certain foreign deposits)	110.8	209.7	403.6
Other checkable deposits	0.4	0	257.9
Total transactions money (M_1)	140.0	271.4	1,065.2
Savings accounts, small time deposits, and other	158.8	300.2	2,838.9
Total broad money (M_2)	298.8	572.1	3,904.1

TABLE 25-1. Components of the Money Supply of the United States

Two widely used definitions of the money supply are transactions money (M_1) and broad money (M_2). M_1 consists of currency and checking accounts. M_2 adds to these certain "near-monies" such as savings accounts and time deposits. (Source: Federal Reserve Board, *Federal Reserve Bulletin,* February 1997.)

ally used for transactions. The following are the components of M_1:

- *Coins.* M_1 includes coins not held by banks.
- *Paper currency.* More significant is paper currency. Most of us know little more about a \$1 or \$5 bill than that it is inscribed with the picture of an American statesman, that it bears some official signatures, and that each has a numeral showing its face value.

    Examine a \$10 bill or some other paper bill. You will probably find that it says "Federal Reserve Note." But what "backs" our paper currency? Many years ago, paper money was backed by gold or silver. There is no such pretense today. Today, all U.S. coins and paper currency are *fiat money.* This term signifies something determined to be money by the government even if it has no value. Currency and coins are *legal tender,* which must be accepted for all debts, public and private.

    Coins and paper currency (the sum known as *currency*) add up to about one-third of total transactions money, M_1.

- *Checking accounts.* There is a third component of transactions money—checking deposits or bank money. These are funds, deposited in banks and other financial institutions, that you can write checks on. They are technically known as "demand deposits and other checkable deposits."

    If I have \$1000 in my checking account at the Albuquerque National Bank, that deposit can be

regarded as money. Why? For the simple reason that I can pay for purchases with checks drawn on it. The deposit is like any other medium of exchange. Possessing the essential properties of money, bank checking-account deposits are counted as transactions money, as part of M_1.

Table 25-1 shows the dollar values of the different components of transactions money, M_1.

Broad Money. Although M_1 is, strictly speaking, the most appropriate measure of money as a means of payment, a second closely watched aggregate is *broad money,* or **M_2**. Sometimes called *asset money* or *near-money,* M_2 includes M_1 as well as savings accounts in banks and similar assets that are very close substitutes for transactions money.

Examples of such near-monies in M_2 include deposits in a savings account in your bank, a money market mutual fund account operated by your stockbroker, a deposit in a money market deposit account run by a commercial bank, and so on.

Why are these not transactions money? Because they cannot be used as means of exchange for all purchases; they are forms of near-money, however, because you can convert them into cash very quickly with no loss of value.

There are many other technical definitions of money that are used by specialists in monetary economics. But for our purposes, we need master only the two major definitions of money.

Money is anything that serves as a commonly accepted medium of exchange. The most important concept is **transactions money**, or M_1, which is the sum of coins and paper currency in circulation outside the banks, plus checkable deposits. Another important monetary aggregate is **broad money** (called M_2), which includes assets such as savings accounts in addition to coins, paper currency, and checkable deposits.

INTEREST RATES: THE PRICE OF MONEY

When we examine how money affects economic activity, we will focus on the interest rate, which is often called "the price of money."

Interest is the payment made for the use of money. The **interest rate** is the amount of interest paid per unit of time expressed as a percentage of the amount borrowed. In other words, people must pay for the opportunity to borrow money. The cost of borrowing money, measured in dollars per year per dollar borrowed, is the interest rate.

Some examples will illustrate how interest works:

- When you graduate from college, you have $500 to your name. You decide to keep it in currency. If you spend none of your funds, at the end of a year you still have $500 because currency has a zero interest rate.
- You place $2000 in a savings account in your local bank, where the interest rate on savings accounts is 4 percent per year. At the end of 1 year, the bank will have paid $80 in interest into your account, so the account is now worth $2080.
- You start your first job and decide to buy a small house that costs $100,000. You go to your local bank and find that 30-year, fixed-interest-rate mortgages have an interest rate of 10 percent per year. Each month you make a mortgage payment of $877.58. Note that this payment is a little bit more than the pro-rated monthly interest charge of 10/12 percent per month. Why? Because it includes not only interest but also *amortization*. This is repayment of *principal*, the amount borrowed. By the time you have made your 360 monthly payments, you will have completely paid off the loan.

From these examples we see that interest rates are measured in percent per year. Interest is the price paid to borrow money, which allows the borrower to obtain real resources over the time of the loan.

An Array of Interest Rates

Textbooks often speak of "*the* interest rate," but in fact today's complex financial system has a vast array of interest rates. Interest rates differ mainly in terms of the characteristics of the loan or of the borrower. Let us review the major differences:

Loans differ in their *term* or *maturity*—the length of time until they must be paid off. The shortest loans are overnight. Short-term securities are for periods up to a year. Companies often issue bonds that have maturities of 10 to 30 years, and mortgages are often up to 30 years in maturity. Longer-term securities generally command a higher interest rate than do short-term issues because lenders are willing to sacrifice quick access to their funds only if they can increase their yield.

Loans also vary in terms of *risk*. Some loans are virtually riskless, while others are highly speculative. Investors require that a premium be paid when they invest in risky ventures. The safest assets in the world are the securities of the U.S. government. These bonds and bills are backed by the full faith, credit, and taxing powers of the government. Intermediate in risk are borrowings of creditworthy corporations, states, and localities. Risky investments, which bear a significant chance of default or nonpayment, include those of companies close to bankruptcy, cities with shrinking tax bases, or countries like Russia with large overseas debts and unstable political systems. The U.S. government pays what is called the "riskless" interest rate; over the last two decades this has ranged from 3 to 15 percent per year for short-term loans. Riskier securities might pay 1, 2, or 5 percent per year more than the riskless rate; this premium reflects the amount necessary to compensate the lender for losses in case of default.

Assets vary in their liquidity. An asset is said to be *liquid* if it can be converted into cash quickly and with little loss in value. Most marketable securities, including common stocks and corporate and government bonds, can be turned into cash quickly for close to their current value. Illiquid assets include unique assets for which no well-established market

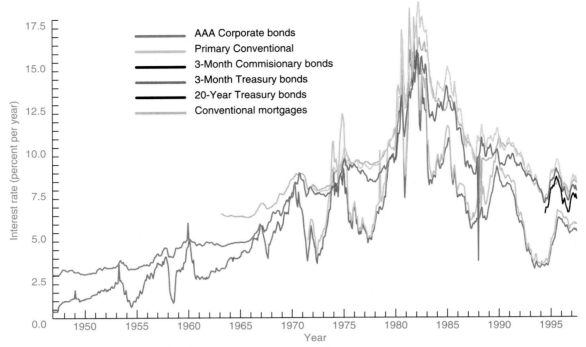

FIGURE 25-2. Most Interest Rates Move Together

This graph shows the major interest rates in the U.S. economy: those on government securities like short-term Treasury bills and long-term Treasury bonds, mortgage rates for homes, and low-grade corporate bonds. (Source: Federal Reserve System.)

exists. For example, if you own a house in a depressed region, you might find it difficult to sell the house quickly or at a price near its replacement cost—your house is an illiquid asset. Because of the higher risk and the difficulty of extracting the borrower's investment, illiquid assets or loans usually command considerably higher interest rates than do liquid, riskless ones.

When these three factors (along with other considerations such as tax status and administrative costs) are considered, it is not surprising that we see so many different financial instruments and so many different interest rates. Figure 25-2 and Table 25-2 show the behavior of a few important interest rates over the last three decades. In the discussion that follows, when we speak of "the interest rate," we are generally referring to the interest rate on short-term government securities, such as the 90-day Treasury-bill rate. As Figure 25-2 shows, most other interest rates rise and fall in step with the 3-month Treasury-bill rate.

Real vs. Nominal Interest Rates

Interest is measured in dollar terms, not in terms of houses or cars or goods in general. The *nominal interest rate* measures the yield in dollars per year per dollar invested. But dollars can become distorted yardsticks. The prices of houses, cars, and goods in general change from year to year—these days prices generally rise due to inflation. Put differently, the interest rate on dollars does not measure what a lender really earns in terms of goods and services. Let us say that you lend $100 today at 5 percent–per-year interest. You would get back $105 at the end of a year. But because prices changed over the year, you would not be able to obtain the same quantity of goods that you could have bought at the beginning of the year with the original $100.

Clearly, we need another concept of interest that measures the return on investments in terms of real goods and services rather than the return in terms of dollars. This alternative concept is the *real interest rate*, which measures the quantity of goods we get

Asset class	Period	Real rate of return (% per year)
United States		
Short-term U.S. government securities (Treasury bills)	1926–1996	0.6
Corporate bonds:		
Safe (Aaa)	1926–1983	0.5
Risky (< Baa)	1926–1983	2.0
Corporate equities	1925–1992	6.5
Consumer loans:		
Mortgages	1975–1988	4.8
Credit cards	1975–1988	6.8
New-car loans	1975–1988	11.2
High-income industrial countries		
Bonds	1960–1984	1.6
Equities	1960–1984	5.4

TABLE 25-2. Real Interest Rates on Major Investments

The real cost of funds depends upon the type of instrument. High-grade corporate bonds have the lowest yield, while consumers pay the highest interest rates. All interest rates are corrected for inflation. [Source: Roger G. Ibbotson and Gary P. Brinson, *Investment Markets* (McGraw-Hill, New York, 1987); *Stocks, Bonds, Bills, and Inflation—1997 Yearbook* (Ibbotson Associates, 1997); Federal Reserve Board; United Nations Development Program; U.S. Bureau of Economic Affairs; data updated by authors.]

tomorrow for goods forgone today. The real interest rate is obtained by correcting nominal or dollar interest rates for the rate of inflation.

The **nominal interest rate** (sometimes also called the *money interest rate*) is the interest rate on money in terms of money. When you read about interest rates in the newspaper, or examine the interest rates in Figure 25-2, you are looking at nominal interest rates; they give the dollar return per dollar of investment.

In contrast, the **real interest rate** is corrected for inflation and is calculated as the nominal interest rate minus the rate of inflation. As an example, suppose the nominal interest rate is 8 percent per year and the inflation rate is 3 percent per year; we can calculate the real interest rate as 8 − 3 = 5 percent per year. In other words, if you lend out 100 market baskets of goods today, you will next year get back only 105 (and not 108) market baskets of goods as principal and real interest payments.

During inflationary periods, we must use real interest rates, not nominal or money interest rates, to calculate the yield on investments in terms of goods earned per year on goods invested. The real

interest rate is the nominal interest rate minus the rate of inflation.

The difference between nominal and real interest rates is illustrated in Figure 25-3 on page 472. It shows that most of the rise in nominal interest rates from 1960 to 1980 was purely illusory, for nominal interest rates were just keeping up with inflation during those years. After 1980, however, real interest rates rose sharply and remained high for a decade.

Inflation-indexed bonds: In 1997, the U.S. government introduced *inflation-indexed bonds*, which are a new financial asset in the United States. These bonds are indexed to the general price level and pay a constant real interest rate over their 10-year maturity. The basic idea is simple. When the bonds were auctioned in January 1997, they had a real interest rate of 3½ percent. This means that the bonds would pay interest of 3½ percent plus the rate of inflation during the past year. Suppose, for example, that the inflation rate in 1997 is 3 percent (as measured by the consumer price index). Then the interest during that year would be 3½ + 3 = 6½

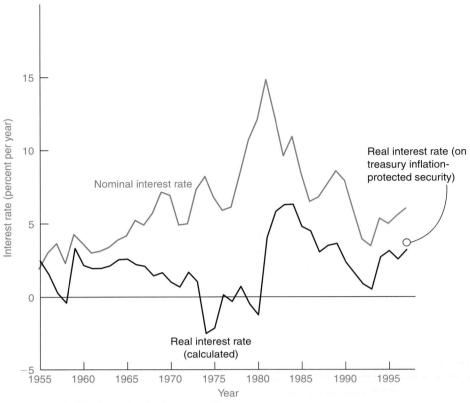

FIGURE 25-3. Real vs. Nominal Interest Rates

The rust line shows the nominal interest rate on safe short-term securities (1-year Treasury notes). The black curve shows the real interest rate, equal to the nominal or money rate less the realized inflation rate over the prior year. Note that real interest rates drifted downward until 1980. After 1980, however, real interest rates moved up sharply. The dot for 1997 shows the real interest rate on inflation-indexed securities. (Source: Federal Reserve Board, U.S. Department of Labor.)

percent. In addition, when the principal is returned at the end of the 10-year loan, it includes any rise in the price level over that period. If inflation were to heat up, people who hold indexed bonds would be protected against loss of income and principal.

Economists have been enthusiasts of indexed bonds for many years. Such bonds can be bought by pensioners who wish to guarantee that their retirement incomes will not be eroded by inflation. Similarly, parents who wish to save for their children's education can sock away some of their investment knowing that it will keep up with the general price level. Even monetary-policy makers find value in indexed bonds, for the difference between conventional bonds and indexed bonds gives an indication of

what is happening to expected inflation. The main puzzle to many economists is why it took so long to introduce this important innovation.

THE DEMAND FOR MONEY

The demand for money is different from the demand for ice cream or movies. Money is not desired for its own sake; you cannot eat nickels, and we seldom hang $100 bills on the wall for the artistic quality of their engraving. Rather, we demand money because it serves us indirectly, as a lubricant to trade and exchange.

Money's Functions

Before we analyze the demand for money, let's note money's functions:

- By far the most important function of money is to serve as a *medium of exchange*. Without money we would be constantly roving around looking for someone to barter with. We are often reminded of money's utility when it does not work properly, as in Russia in the early 1990s, when people spent hours in line waiting for goods and tried to get dollars or other foreign currencies because the ruble ceased functioning as an acceptable means of exchange.

- Money is also used as the *unit of account*, the unit by which we measure the value of things. Just as we measure weight in kilograms, we measure value in money. The use of a common unit of account simplifies economic life enormously.

- Money is sometimes used as a *store of value*; it allows value to be held over time. In comparison with risky assets like stocks or real estate or gold, money is relatively riskless. In earlier days, people held currency as a safe form of wealth. Today, when people seek a safe haven for their wealth, they put it in assets like checking deposits (M_1) and money market mutual funds (M_2). However, the vast preponderance of wealth is held in other assets, such as savings accounts, stocks, bonds, and real estate.

The Costs of Holding Money

These three functions of money are extremely important to people, so important that individuals are willing to incur a cost to hold currency or low-yielding checking accounts. What is the *opportunity cost of holding money*? It is the sacrifice in interest that you must incur by holding money rather than a riskier, less liquid asset or investment.

Say that you put $1000 in a savings account at the beginning of 1996; you would earn about 5 percent interest and would have $1050 at the end of 1996. This represents a 5 percent money or nominal interest rate. By contrast, suppose that you had left your $1000 in currency rather than in the savings account for 1996. You would end up with only $1000, for currency pays no interest. The opportunity cost of holding money as currency in this case would be $50. (Can you see why the opportunity cost of hold-

ing your money in a checking account that paid 2 percent–per-year interest would be $30? Explain why that might be worth the cost.)

Money allows easy and quick transactions, unambiguous determination of price, plus easy storage of value over time. These benefits are not free, however. If wealth were held in stocks, bonds, or savings accounts rather than money, it would yield a higher interest rate.

Two Sources of Money Demand

Transactions Demand. People and firms use money as a medium of exchange: households need money to buy groceries, and firms need money to pay for materials and labor. These needs constitute the *transactions demand for money*.

Figure 25-4 on page 474 illustrates the mechanics of the transactions demand for money. This figure shows the average money holdings of a family that earns $3000 per month, keeps it in money, and spends it during the month. Calculation will show that the family holds $1500 on average in money balances.

This example can help us see how the demand for money responds to different economic influences. If all prices and incomes double, the vertical axis in Figure 25-4 is simply relabeled by doubling all the dollar values. Clearly the nominal demand for M doubles. Thus the transactions demand for money doubles if nominal GDP doubles with no change in real GDP or other real variables.

But how does the demand for money vary with interest rates? Recall that our family is paying an opportunity cost for its checking account—the interest rate on M is less than that on other assets. As interest rates rise, the family might say, "Let's put only half of our money in the checking account at the beginning of the month, and put the other half in a savings account earning 8 percent per annum. Then on day 15, we'll take that $1500 out of the savings account and put it in our checking account to pay the next 2 weeks' bills."

This means that as interest rates rose and the family decided to put half its earnings in a savings account, the average money balance of our family fell from $1500 to $750. This shows how money holdings (or the demand for money) may be sensitive to interest rates: *other things equal, as interest rates rise, the quantity of money demanded declines.*

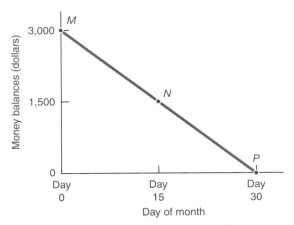

FIGURE 25-4. The Transactions Demand for Money

Assume that the family is paid $3000 at the beginning of the month and spends the whole amount over the course of the month at a constant rate of $100 per day. Moreover, the family does not put any of its money in another asset during the month. Thus the family has $3000 on day 0, $1500 on day 15, and nothing at the end of the month. This is illustrated by the line MNP.

How much money does the family hold on average? Answer: ½ of $3000 = $1500.

To understand the way the demand for money behaves, consider how this figure would change if all prices and incomes doubled, or if real incomes doubled, or if interest rates on savings accounts went to 20 percent.

You might think that the economic gain from a constant reshuffling of portfolios is so trivial that money holdings are not likely to be affected by interest-rate fluctuations. For the household sector, you would be correct: average bank balances change very little when people find they can earn 2 or 4 percent more on their money funds.

In the business sector, however, interest rates have a major impact on the demand for money. Large companies can easily find themselves with bank balances of $100 million one day, $250 million the next day, and so forth. If they do nothing, they could easily lose $20 to $50 million a year in interest payments. Today, large companies engage in "cash management," whereby their funds are constantly invested in high-yield assets

rather than lying fallow in zero-yield checking accounts. And with higher interest rates, corporations work a little harder to keep their cash balances at a minimum.

Asset Demand. In addition to its use for transactions needs, what is money's role as a store of value? This crucial question is addressed by **financial economics,** which analyzes how rational investors should invest their funds to attain their objectives in the best possible manner. We discuss the fundamentals of finance in the last section of this chapter and will only summarize the major point concerning money at this point.

In general, a well-constructed portfolio (or combination of assets) may want to contain low-risk investments as well as riskier ventures. But it is not generally advisable to hold M_1 (currency or checking deposits) as one of these nest eggs. The reason is that other assets (such as government securities or safe money market mutual funds) are just as safe as M_1 and have higher interest rates. In the language of finance, transactions money is a "dominated" asset because other assets are equally safe but have higher yields. However, it might be sensible to hold your assets in M_2 (say, in money market mutual funds) because these are high-yielding safe assets.

We summarize our findings on the demand for money as follows:

The demand for money (M_1) is grounded in the need for a medium of exchange, the transactions demand. We hold currency and checking accounts to buy goods and pay our bills. As our incomes rise, the dollar value of the goods we buy goes up, and we therefore need more money for transactions, raising our demand for money.

The transactions demand for M will be sensitive to the cost of holding money. When interest rates on alternative assets rise relative to the interest rate on money, people and businesses tend to reduce their money holdings.

In addition, people sometimes hold money as an asset or store of value. But modern finance theory shows that transactions money (M_1) should generally not be part of a well-designed portfolio.

B. BANKING AND THE SUPPLY OF MONEY

In most countries currency is issued by central banks, while commercial banks generate the rest of money as checking deposits. Surprisingly, however, the central bank actually controls the total amount of money. This section explains the process of money creation.

BANKING AS A BUSINESS

Bank money and many other financial services are today provided by **financial intermediaries**, which are institutions like commercial banks that take deposits or funds from one group and lend these funds to other groups. For example, financial intermediaries accept checking deposits from households and firms and then lend these funds out to other households and businesses for a variety of purposes.

The largest class of financial intermediaries comprises commercial banks, institutions which contain most of the nation's checking accounts or "checkable deposits." Other important categories are savings banks, life-insurance companies, pension funds, and money market mutual funds. Altogether, in the middle of 1993, all such intermediaries had a total of $11.8 trillion of assets and liabilities.

In what follows we will focus on commercial banks, or "banks" for short. We do so because these institutions are the main source of checking accounts, or the bank-money component of M_1.

Financial institutions transfer funds from lenders to borrowers. In doing this, they create financial assets (like checking and savings accounts). But from a macroeconomic vantage point the most important asset is bank money (or checking accounts), primarily provided by commercial banks.

A Business Venture

Banks and other financial intermediaries are much like other businesses. They are organized to earn profits for their owners. A commercial bank is a relatively simple business concern. It provides certain services for customers and in return receives payments from them.

Table 25-3 shows the consolidated balance sheet of all U.S. commercial banks. A *balance sheet* is a statement of a firm's financial position at a point in time. It lists *assets* (items that a firm owns) and *liabilities* (items the firm owes). The difference between assets and liabilities is called *net worth*. Each entry in a bal-

TABLE 25-3. Reserves and Checking Deposits Are Major Balance Sheet Entries of Commercial Banks

Reserves and checking deposits are key to bank creation of money. Checking accounts are payable on demand and thus can be used quickly when customers write checks. Reserves are held primarily to meet legal requirements, not to provide against possible unexpected withdrawals. (Source: *Federal Reserve Bulletin,* July 1997.)

Balance Sheet of All Commercial Banking Institutions, 1996 (Billions of Dollars)			
Assets		**Liabilities**	
Reserves	$ 231	Checking deposits	$ 713
Loans	2,783	Savings and time deposits	2,119
Investments and securities	989	Other liabilities and net worth	1,588
Other assets	417		
Total	$4,420	Total	$4,420

ance sheet is valued at its actual market value or its historical cost.[1]

Except for minor rearrangements, a bank's balance sheet looks much like the balance sheet of any business. The unique feature of the bank balance sheet is an item called **reserves,** which appears on the asset side; these are assets banks hold in the form of cash on hand or of funds deposited by the bank with the central bank. Some reserves are held for day-to-day business needs, but most serve to meet legal reserve requirements.

How Banks Developed from Goldsmith Establishments

Commercial banking began in England with the goldsmiths, who developed the practice of storing people's gold and valuables for safekeeping. At first, such establishments were simply like baggage checkrooms or warehouses. Depositors left gold for safekeeping and were given a receipt. Later they presented their receipt, paid a small fee for the safekeeping, and got back their gold.

The goldsmiths soon found it more convenient not to worry about returning exactly the same piece of gold that each customer had left. Customers were quite willing to accept any gold as long as it was equivalent in value to what they had deposited. This "anonymity" was important for it freed goldsmiths to relend the gold.

What would balance sheets of a typical goldsmith establishment look like? Perhaps like Table 25-4. We assume that First Goldsmith Bank no longer hammers gold bars but is occupied solely with storing people's money for safekeeping. A total of $1 million

---

[1] Balance sheets, assets, and liabilities are extensively discussed in Chapter 7.

has been deposited in its vaults, and this whole sum is held as a cash asset (this is the item "Reserves" in the balance sheet). To balance this asset, there is a demand deposit of the same amount. Cash reserves are therefore 100 percent of deposits.

If the Goldsmith Bank were here today, its demand deposits would be part of the money supply; they would be "bank money." However, the bank money just offsets the amount of ordinary money (gold or currency) placed in the bank's safe and withdrawn from active circulation. No money creation has taken place. The process would be of no more interest than if the public decided to convert nickels into dimes. *A 100 percent reserve banking system has a neutral effect on money and the macroeconomy because it has no effect on the money supply.*

Modern Fractional-Reserve Banking

Profit maximizing goldsmith-bankers soon recognized that although deposits are payable on demand, they are not all withdrawn together. Reserves equal to total deposits would be necessary if all depositors suddenly had to be paid off in full at the same time, but this almost never occurred. On a given day, some people make withdrawals while others make deposits. The two kinds of transactions generally balanced out.

The bankers did not need to keep 100 percent of deposits as sterile reserves; reserves earn no interest when they are sitting in a vault. So early banks hit upon the idea of using the money entrusted to them to make investments. By putting most of the money deposited with them in earning assets and keeping only fractional cash reserves against deposits, banks maximize their profits.

The transformation into *fractional-reserve banks*— holding fractional rather than 100 percent reserves against deposits—was revolutionary. It enabled banks

---

TABLE 25-4. First Goldsmith Bank Held 100 Percent Cash Reserves against Demand Deposits

In a primitive banking system, with 100 percent backing of deposits, no creation of money out of reserves is possible.

Goldsmith Balance Sheet			
Assets		**Liabilities**	
Reserves	$1,000,000	Demand deposits	$1,000,000
Total	$1,000,000	Total	$1,000,000

THE PROCESS OF DEPOSIT CREATION

Assets		Liabilities	
Reserves	+$1,000	Deposits	+$1,000
Total	+$1,000	Total	+$1,000

TABLE 25-5(a). Bank 1 in Initial Position

Multiple-bank deposit creation is a story with many successive stages. At the start, $1000 of newly created reserves is deposited in the original first-generation bank.

to create money. That is, banks could turn each dollar of reserves into several dollars of deposits. Later in this section we will see how this process works.

Legal Reserve Requirements

In modern banking, bank reserves are held either as cash on hand or as deposits with the central bank. A prudent banker, concerned only with assuring customers that the bank has enough cash for daily transactions, might choose to keep only 5 percent of the bank's checking deposits in reserves. In fact, banks today set aside about 10 percent of their checking deposits in reserves. These are held in cash or in deposits with our central bank, the Federal Reserve System, often called "the Fed."

Reserves are so high because all financial institutions are required by law and Federal Reserve regulations to keep a fraction of their deposits as reserves. Reserve requirements apply to all types of checking and savings deposits, independent of the actual need for cash on hand. (We describe the regulatory system in the next chapter.)

Bank reserves are kept above the prudent commercial level because of legal reserve requirements. The main function of legal reserve requirements is to enable the Federal Reserve to control the amount of checking deposits that banks can create. By imposing high fixed legal reserve requirements, the Fed can better control the money supply.

THE PROCESS OF DEPOSIT CREATION

In our simplified discussion of goldsmith banks, we suggested that banks turn reserves into bank money. There are, in fact, two steps in the process:

- The central bank determines the quantity of reserves of the banking system. The detailed process by which the central bank does this is discussed in the next chapter.

- Using those reserves as an input, the banking system transforms them into a much larger amount of bank money. The currency plus this bank money is the money supply, M_1. This process is called the *multiple expansion of bank deposits*.

How Deposits Are Created: First-Generation Banks

Let us consider what happens when new reserves are injected into the banking system. Assume that the Federal Reserve buys a $1000 government bond from Ms. Bondholder, and she deposits the $1000 in her checking account at Bank 1.

The change in the balance sheet of Bank 1, as far as the new demand deposit is concerned, is shown in Table 25-5(a).[2] When Ms. Bondholder made the deposit, $1000 of bank money, or checking deposits, was created. Now, if the bank were to keep 100 percent of deposits in reserves, as did the old goldsmiths, no extra money would be created from the new deposit of $1000. The depositor's $1000 checking deposit would just match the $1000 of reserves. But modern banks do not keep 100 percent reserves for their deposits. Because banks are assumed to keep a reserve requirement of 10 percent, Bank 1 must set aside as reserves $100 of the $1000 deposit.

But Bank 1 now has $900 more in reserves than it needs to meet the reserve requirement. Because reserves earn no interest, our profit-minded bank will lend or invest the excess $900. The loan might be for a car, or the investment might be a purchase of a Treasury bond. Let's say the bank makes a loan. The person who borrows the money takes the $900

---

[2] For simplicity, our tables will show only the *changes* in balance sheet items, and we use reserve ratios of 10 percent. Note that when bankers refer to their loans and investments, by "investments" they mean their holdings of bonds and other financial assets. They don't mean what economists mean by "investment," which is capital formation.

Assets		Liabilities	
Reserves	+$ 100	Deposits	+$1,000
Loans and investments	+ 900		
Total	+$1,000	Total	+$1,000

TABLE 25-5(b). Bank 1 in Final Position

A profit-maximizing bank will lend or invest any excess reserves. Thus Bank 1 has kept only $100 of the original cash deposit (as required reserves) and has lent or invested the other $900.

Assets		Liabilities	
Reserves	+$900	Deposits	+$900
Total	+$900	Total	+$900

TABLE 25-5(c). Second-Generation Banks in Initial Position

Assets		Liabilities	
Reserves	+$ 90	Deposits	+$900
Loans and investments	+ 810		
Total	+$900	Total	+$900

TABLE 25-5(d). Final Position of Second-Generation Banks

Next, the money lent out by Bank 1 soon goes to new banks, which in turn lend out nine-tenths of it.

(in cash or check) and deposits it in her account in another bank. Very quickly, then, the $900 will be paid out by Bank 1.

After it has lent or invested $900, Bank 1's legal reserves are just enough to meet its legal reserve requirement. The balance sheet of Bank 1, after it has made all possible loans or investments (but still meets its reserve requirement), is shown in Table 25-5(b).

But if we calculate the amount of money, we are in for a big surprise. In addition to the original $1000 of deposits shown on the right of Table 25-5(b), there is $900 of demand deposits in another account (i.e., in the checking account of the person who got the $900). Hence, the total amount of M is now $1900. *Bank 1's activity has created $900 of new money.*

Chain Repercussions on Other Banks

After the $900 created by Bank 1 leaves the bank, it will soon be deposited in another bank, and at that point it starts up a chain of expansion whereby still more bank money is created.

To see what happens to the $900, let's call all the banks that receive the $900 *second-generation banks* (or Bank 2). Their combined balance sheets now appear as shown in Table 25-5(c). To these banks, the dollars deposited function just like our original $1000 deposit. These banks do not care that they are second in a chain of deposits. Their only concern is that they are holding too much nonearning cash, or excess reserves. Only one-tenth of $900, or $90, is legally needed against the $900 deposit. They will use the other nine-tenths to acquire $810 worth of loans and investments. Their balance sheets will soon reach the equilibrium in Table 25-5(d).

At this point, the original $1000 taken out of hand-to-hand circulation has produced a total of $2710 of money. The total of M has increased, and the process continues.

The $810 spent by the second-generation banks in acquiring loans and investments will go to a new

Position of bank	New deposits ($)	New loans and investments ($)	New reserves ($)
Original banks	1,000.00	900.00	100.00
2d-generation banks	900.00	810.00	90.00
3d-generation banks	810.00	729.00	81.00
4th-generation banks	729.00	656.10	72.90
5th-generation banks	656.10	590.49	65.61
6th-generation banks	590.49	531.44	59.05
7th-generation banks	531.44	478.30	53.14
8th-generation banks	478.30	430.47	47.83
9th-generation banks	430.47	387.42	43.05
10th-generation banks	387.42	348.68	38.74
Sum of first 10 generations of banks	6,513.22	5,861.90	651.32
Sum of remaining generations of banks	3,486.78	3,138.10	348.68
Total for banking system as a whole	10,000.00	9,000.00	1,000.00

TABLE 25-6. Finally, Through This Long Chain, All Banks Create New Deposits of 10 Times New Reserves

The actions of all banks together produce the multiple expansion of reserves into *M*. The final equilibrium is reached when every dollar of original new reserves supports $10 of demand deposits. Note that in every generation each bank has "created" new money in the following sense: It ends up with a final bank deposit 10 times the reserve it finally retains. (Make sure you understand why the number is 10 times.)

set of banks called *third-generation banks.* You can create the balance sheets (initial and final) for third-generation banks. Eventually, the third-generation banks will lend out their excess reserves and will thereby create $729 of new money. A fourth generation of banks will clearly end up with nine-tenths of $810 in deposits, or $729, and so on.

Final System Equilibrium

Now let's sum up all the money creation: $1000 + $900 + $810 + $729 + ⋯ ? Table 25-6 shows that the complete effect of the chain of money creation is $10,000. We can get the answer by arithmetic, by common sense, and by elementary algebra.

Common sense tells us that the process of deposit creation must come to an end only when every bank in the system has reserves equal to 10 percent of deposits. In all our examples, no cash reserves ever leaked out of the banking system; the money simply went from one set of banks to another set of banks. The banking system will reach equilibrium when the $1000 of new reserves is all used up as required reserves on new deposits. In other words,

the final equilibrium of the banking system will be the point at which 10 percent of new deposits (*D*) equals the new reserves of $1000. What level of *D* satisfies this condition? The answer is *D* = $10,000.

We can also see the answer intuitively by looking at a consolidated balance sheet for all the generations of banks together. This is shown in Table 25-7 on page 480. If total new deposits were less than $10,000, the 10 percent reserve ratio would not yet have been reached, and full equilibrium would not yet have been attained.[3]

Figure 25-5 on page 480 gives a schematic overview of the process. It shows how $1 of new deposits or reserves, at the upper left, is transformed into $10 of total deposits, or bank money, on the right. Inside the rectangle, which represents the banking system as a

---

[3] The algebraic solution can be shown as follows:

$1000 + $900 + $810 + ⋯

$$= \$1000 \times [1 + \tfrac{9}{10} + (\tfrac{9}{10})^2 + (\tfrac{9}{10})^3 + \cdots]$$

$$= \$1000 \left(\frac{1}{1 - \tfrac{9}{10}}\right) = \$1000 \times \frac{1}{0.1} = \$10,000$$

Assets		Liabilities	
Reserves	+$ 1,000	Deposits	+$10,000
Loans and investments	+ 9,000		
Total	+$10,000	Total	+$10,000

TABLE 25-7. Consolidated Balance Sheet Showing Final Position of All Banks

All banks together ultimately increase deposits and M by a multiple of the original injection of reserves.

whole, Bank 1 receives the initial new deposit. The rust arrows circulating around show how reserves are redistributed, while the black lines show new deposits. Though the chain has many links, each is a dwindling fraction and the whole effect does add up to the 10-to-1 total.

The Money-Supply Multiplier. We see that there is a new kind of multiplier operating on reserves. For every additional dollar in reserves provided to the banking system, banks eventually create $10 of additional deposits or bank money.

We described the expenditure multiplier as the ratio of the change in output to new investment or other spending. The money multiplier is the ratio of the new money created to the change in reserves. Note that the arithmetic of M expansion is similar to that of the expenditure multiplier, *but don't confuse the two because they multiply different things.* The ampli-

fication here is from the stock of reserves to the stock of total M; it has nothing to do with the extra output induced by investment or money.

The ratio of new checking deposits to the increase in reserves is called the **money-supply multiplier**. In the simple case analyzed here, the money-supply multiplier is defined as follows:

$$\text{Money-supply multiplier}$$
$$= \frac{\text{change of money}}{\text{change of reserves}}$$
$$= 10 = \frac{1}{0.1} = \frac{1}{\text{required reserve ratio}}$$

The money-supply multiplier summarizes the logic of how banks create money. The entire banking system can transform an initial increase in reserves into a multiplied amount of new deposits or bank money.

The process of deposit creation can also work in reverse when a drain in reserves reduces bank money. It is useful to reinforce your understanding of money creation by tracing in detail what happens when the Fed permanently destroys $2000 of reserves by selling a government bond to someone who withdraws cash from his checking account to pay for it. In the end, the withdrawal of $2000 of reserves from the banking system kills off $20,000 worth of deposits throughout the whole system.

FIGURE 25-5. Multiple-Bank Expansion of Money

For each dollar of new reserves deposited in a bank, the system as a whole creates about $10 of bank money. The rust arrows in the box show that Bank 1 cannot do it alone. The money supply increases as reserves spread through the banking system.

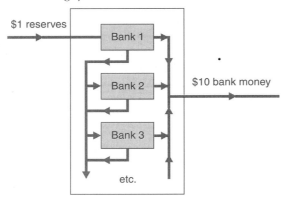

The contagion of bank panics: Fractional-reserve banking has great risks as well as great advantages. The fact that banks cover only a fraction of their deposits opens up the possibility of "bank panics" or "a run on the banks." Remember that under fractional-reserve banking, a bank has on hand only a small portion of the money that it owes to its depositors. Ordinarily, that is no problem, since only a small number of people will want to withdraw their money at any one time.

But what if too many people want their money at once? Then we can have the feeding frenzy known as a *bank run.* As soon as one depositor has trouble getting his or her money immediately, the other depositors get scared that their money is also gone. Driven by fear, depositors descend on the bank like a horde of hungry animals, demanding all of their money right away. Not even healthy banks can withstand this sort of mass demand for deposits. The United States was hit with major bank panics in 1893, 1895, and then in 1907. The bank panics of the 1930s, during the Great Depression, pushed more than 9000 banks into failure.

In the modern financial system, bank runs are rare and less dangerous, for two reasons. One reason is that the federal government ensures that all but the largest depositors will get their money back no matter what happens to the bank. Depositors therefore need not rush down to their bank at the first sign of trouble. In addition, the Federal Reserve takes an active role as the "lender of last resort," providing funds to healthy banks with temporary liquidity problems and making sure sick banks get liquidated in an orderly way.

Still, despite these precautions, bank runs do occasionally happen. In 1985, there were runs at state-chartered banks in Ohio which were not covered by federal deposit insurance. And in 1991, the Bank of New England, one of the largest banks in the country, was hit by a wave of panicky withdrawals which drained perhaps $1 billion from the bank's accounts in only 2 days. The run, which was threatening to spread to other banks in the area, was quickly stopped when the federal government stepped in to take over the bank.

Two Qualifications to Deposit Creation

The actual financial system is more complicated than our simple banking example. We have shown that $1000 of new reserves put into a bank will ultimately result in an increase of $10,000 of bank deposits. This example assumed that all the new money remained as checking accounts in the banking system and that no bank would have excess reserves. Let us see what would happen if some money leaked into circulation or if some banks had excess reserves.

Leakage into Hand-to-Hand Circulation. It is possible that, somewhere along the chain of deposit expansion, an individual who receives a check will not leave the proceeds in a bank checking account. He might put some cash in a cookie jar. Or some of the $1000 might be sent to a cousin in Mexico or used in the underground economy.

The effects of such withdrawals on our analysis are simple. When $1000 stayed in the banking system, $10,000 of new deposits was created. If $100 were to leak into circulation outside the banks and only $900 of new reserves were to remain in the banking system, the new checking deposits created would be $9000 ($900 × 10). Therefore, the 10-to-1 amplification would occur only if no reserves leak from banks.

Possible Excess Reserves. Our analysis proceeded on the assumption that the commercial banks follow their legal reserve requirements to the letter. What would happen if the bank decided to keep rather than lend the new reserves? Then the whole process of multiple deposit creation would stop dead, with no expansion of deposits at all.

This decision would of course make no sense for the bank. Because the bank earns no interest on reserves, it would lose interest payments on the $900. So as long as the interest rate on investments is above the interest rate on reserves (set at zero), banks have a strong incentive to avoid holding any excess reserves.

In certain situations, it might be reasonable to have excess reserves. During the Great Depression, interest rates fell to 0.1 percent per year, so banks during this period often held significant excess reserves. Alternatively, if the Federal Reserve paid market interest rates on bank reserves, banks would have no incentive to invest their excess reserves. In these cases, legal reserve requirements would no longer be binding, and monetary policy would lose its potency as an instrument for control of the economy. For this reason, most economists strenuously oppose paying market interest rates on bank reserves.

With a required reserve ratio of 10 percent, reserves will be multiplied tenfold into new deposits. However, when some of the increased deposits spill into currency or nonmonetary assets, or when banks hold excess reserves, the deposit creation will depart from the ratio of 1/(legal reserve ratio).

We have now surveyed the essentials of the demand for money along with the behavior of commercial banks. We conclude this chapter with an analysis of a fascinating part of our financial system—the stock market. Then in the next chapter we will see how our central bank, the Federal Reserve, can control bank reserves and thereby increase or decrease the total money supply. Armed with our analysis of the supply and demand for money, we can then show how the money supply helps influence output, inflation, and employment.

C. A TOUR OF WALL STREET

A Menu of Financial Assets

This chapter has concentrated on money markets because they are central to understanding the functioning of the macroeconomy. But financial markets come much closer to home when we borrow for a mortgage, invest for our children's education or our own retirement, and set aside funds for a rainy year. In this final section, therefore, we take a tour through the fascinating world of *financial economics*, which studies how rational investors should allocate their funds to attain their objectives in the best possible manner. It is an exciting field—and a crucial one for people who want to invest their funds wisely.

Table 25-8 shows the major financial assets of households. These consist primarily of *dollar-denominated assets* (whose payments are fixed in dollar terms) and *equities* (whose values are set by the market). Here are the major kinds of investments:

- *Money* was defined earlier in this chapter.
- *Savings accounts* are deposits with banks, usually guaranteed by governments, that have a fixed-dollar principal value and interest rates determined by short-term market interest rates.
- *Government securities* are bills and bonds of the federal, state, and local governments. They guarantee repayment of principal on maturity and pay interest along the way. Federal securities are considered the safest of all investments.
- *Equities* are ownership rights to companies. They yield dividends, which are payments drawn from the companies' net profits. Publicly traded equities (or common stocks) are priced on stock markets, where the prices are determined by the market valuation of future dividends. Noncorporate equities are the value of partnerships, farms, and other entities, usually owned by only a few people.
- *Pension funds* represent ownership in the assets that are held by companies or pension plans. Workers and companies contribute to these funds during working years, and the funds are then drawn down to pay pensions during retirement.

Note that these financial assets exclude the single most important assets owned by most people—their houses. In addition, people have implicit assets in their future social security and medical care, but these have no ready market value.

Risk and Return on Different Assets

Recall from our discussion in Section A of this chapter that assets have different characteristics. The most important characteristics are the rate of return (or interest rate) and the risk.

The *rate of return* is the total dollar gain from a security (measured as a percent of the price at the beginning of the period). For savings accounts and short-term bonds, the return would be the interest rate. For example, the return on 1-year Treasury bonds in 1996 was a certain 5.5 percent. For most other assets, the return combines an income (like dividends) with a *capital gain* or *loss*, which represents the increase or decrease in the value of the asset.

We can illustrate the rate of return on stocks using data on stocks. (For this example, we ignore taxes and commissions.) Say that you bought a representative portfolio of $10,000 worth of stocks in U.S. companies in December 1994. During 1995,

Financial Assets of Households		
	Percent of total assets	
Class of asset	1963	1988
Dollar denominated:		
Currency and checking deposits (M_1)	4.6	4.2
Savings accounts	14.3	21.0
Government securities	6.4	8.5
Other	3.3	2.2
Equity in businesses:		
Corporate	31.3	18.4
Noncorporate	25.7	19.8
Pension-fund and life-insurance reserves	13.4	23.9
Other	1.0	1.9
Total	100.0	100.0
Total assets of households ($, billion)	1,641	12,139

TABLE 25-8. Financial Assets of Households

Households own a wide variety of financial assets ranging from money to pension funds. (Source: Federal Reserve Board.)

your fund paid dividends of $256. Moreover, because 1995 was an unusually good year for stocks, your fund rose in value to $13,500 at the end of the year, for a capital gain of 35 percent. Your total return was therefore $(256 + 3500)/10,000 = 37.6$ percent for 1995.

But before you get too excited about these fantastic gains, be warned that you could easily have a big loss. If you bought your stocks in July 1987, you would have had a *minus 12 percent* return over the next year. Or if you bought German bonds in 1922 or Cuban bonds in 1958 or Russian bonds in 1990, you would have lost almost everything to confiscation or inflation.

The fact that some assets have predictable rates of return while others are quite risky leads to the next important characteristic of investments: **Risk** refers to the variability of the returns on an investment. If I buy a 1-year Treasury bond with a 6 percent return, the bond is a riskless investment because I am sure to get my return. On the other hand, if I buy $10,000 of stocks, I am uncertain about their year-end value.

Economists generally measure risk in terms of the standard deviation of returns; this is a measure of dispersion whose range encompasses about two-thirds

of the variation.[4] For example, from 1926 to 1994, common stocks had an annual standard deviation of return of 20 percent and an average annual return of 10 percent. This normally implies that the return was between −10 percent and +30 percent two-thirds of the time. The largest return was 54 percent in 1933, and the largest loss was −43 percent in 1931.

Looking at both return and risk, individuals generally prefer higher return, but they also prefer lower risk because they are *risk-averse*. This means that they must be rewarded by higher returns to induce them to hold investments with higher risks. We would not be surprised, therefore, to learn that over the long run safe investments like bonds have lower returns than risky investments like stocks.

Table 25-2 on page 471 showed the historical returns or interest rates on a number of important investments. We show the most important assets in the *risk-return diagram* in Figure 25-6 on page 484. This diagram shows the average real (or inflation-corrected) return on the vertical axis and the histor-

---

[4] The standard deviation is a measure of variability that can be found in any elementary statistics text. As an example, if a variable takes the values of 1, 3, 1, 3, the mean or expected value is 2 while the standard deviation is 1.

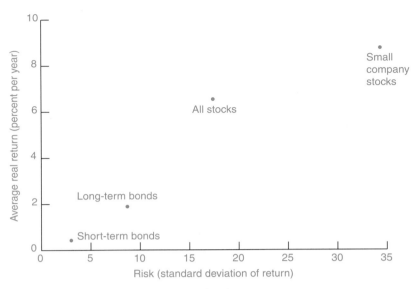

FIGURE 25-6. Risk and Return on Major Investments

Investments vary in their average returns and riskiness. Bonds tend to be safe, while stocks have much higher returns but face higher risks. [Source: Roger G. Ibbotson and Gary P. Brinson, *Investment Markets* (McGraw-Hill, New York, 1987), with updates.]

ical risk (measured as a standard deviation) on the horizontal axis. Note the strong relationship between risk and return.

THE STOCK MARKET

A **stock market** is a place where the shares in publicly owned companies, the titles to business firms, are bought and sold. In 1996, the value of these titles was estimated at $9 trillion in the United States. Sales in a single year might total $3 trillion. The stock market is the hub of our corporate economy.

The New York Stock Exchange is the main stock market, listing more than a thousand securities. Every large financial center has a stock exchange. Major ones are located in Tokyo, London, Frankfurt, Hong Kong, Toronto, Zurich, and, of course, New York. A stock exchange is a critical part of modern market economies. When the countries of Eastern Europe decided to scrap their centrally planned systems and become market economies, one of their first acts was to introduce a stock market to buy and sell ownership rights in companies.

Bubbles and Crashes

The history of finance is one of the most exciting, and sobering, parts of economics. As Burton Malkiel writes in his survey of bubbles, panics, and the madness of crowds, "Greed run amok has been an essential feature of every spectacular boom in history."[5]

Investors are sometimes divided into those who invest on firm foundations and those who try to outguess the market psychology. The firm-foundation approach holds that assets should be valued on the basis of their intrinsic value. For common stocks, the intrinsic value is the expected present value of the dividends. If a stock has a constant dividend of $2 per year and the appropriate interest rate to discount dividends is 5 percent, the intrinsic value would be $2/.05 = $40 per share. The firm-foundation approach is the slow but safe way of getting rich.

---

[5] See Burton Malkiel, *A Random Walk Down Wall Street*, 6th ed. (Norton, New York, 1994), which contains an entertaining and well-informed account of modern financial economics.

Impatient souls might echo Keynes, who argued that investors are more likely to worry about market psychology and to speculate on the future value of assets rather than wait patiently for stocks to prove their intrinsic value. He argued, "It is not sensible to pay 25 for an investment which is worth 30, if you also believe that the market will value it at 20 three months hence." The market psychologist tries to guess what the average investor thinks, which requires considering what the average investor thinks about the average investor, and so on, ad infinitum.

When a psychological frenzy seizes the market, it can result in speculative bubbles and crashes. A *speculative bubble* occurs when prices rise because people think they are going to rise in the future—it is the reverse of Keynes' dictum just cited. A piece of land may be worth only $1000, but if you see a land-price boom driving prices up 50 percent each year, you might buy it for $2000 hoping you can sell it to someone else next year for $3000. A speculative bubble fulfills its own promises. If people buy because they think stocks will rise, their act of buying sends up the price of stocks. This causes people to buy even more and sends the dizzy dance off on another round. But, unlike people who play cards or dice, no one apparently loses what the winners gain. Of course, the prizes are all on paper and would disappear if everyone tried to cash them in. But why should anyone want to sell such lucrative securities? Prices rise because of hopes and dreams, not because the profits and dividends of companies are soaring.

History is marked by bubbles in which speculative prices were driven up far beyond their intrinsic value. In seventeenth-century Holland, a tulip mania drove tulip prices to levels higher than the price of a house. In the eighteenth century, the stock of the South Sea Company rose to fantastic levels on empty promises that the firm would enrich its stockholders. In more recent times, similar bubbles have been found in biotechnology, Japanese land, "emerging markets," and a vacuum-cleaning company called ZZZZ Best, which turned out to have profited from laundering money for the Mafia.

The most famous bubble of them all occurred in the American stock market in the 1920s. The "roaring twenties" saw a fabulous stock market boom, when everyone bought and sold stocks. Most purchases in this wild bull market were on margin. This means a buyer of $10,000 worth of stocks put up only part of the price in cash and borrowed the difference, pledging the newly bought stocks as collateral for the purchase. What did it matter that you had to pay the broker 6, 10, or 15 percent per year on the borrowing when Auburn Motors or Bethlehem Steel might jump 10 percent in value overnight?

The Great Crash. Speculative bubbles always produce crashes and sometimes lead to economic panics. One traumatic event has cast a shadow over stock markets for decades—the 1929 panic and crash. This event ushered in the long and painful Great Depression of the 1930s.

The crash came in "black October" of 1929. Everyone was caught, the big-league professionals as well as the piddling amateurs—Andrew Mellon, John D. Rockefeller, engineer-turned-President Herbert Hoover in the White House, and America's greatest economist, Irving Fisher.

When the bottom fell out of the market in 1929, investors, big and small, who bought on margin could not put up funds to cover their holdings, and the market fell still further. The bull market turned into a bear (or declining) market. By the trough of the Depression in 1933, the market had declined 85 percent.

Trends in the stock market are tracked using *stock-price indexes*, which are weighted averages of the prices of a basket of company stocks. Commonly followed averages include the Dow-Jones Industrial Average (DJIA) of 30 large companies and Standard and Poor's index of 500 companies (the "S&P 500"), which is a weighted average of the stock prices of the 500 largest American corporations.

Figure 25-7 on page 486 shows the history since 1920 of the Standard and Poor's 500. The lower curve shows the nominal stock-price average, which records the actual average during a particular year. The upper line shows the real price of stocks; this equals the nominal price divided by an index of consumer prices that equaled 1 in 1996.

Note the experience of the 1980s, which illustrates both the perils and rewards of "playing the market." Beginning in 1982, the stock market surged steadily upward for 5 years, gaining almost 140 percent. Those who had the luck or vision to put all their assets into stocks made a lot of money. The market peaked in the summer of 1987. On October 19, 1987—"black Monday"—the stock market lost 22

FIGURE 25-7. The Only Guarantee about Stock Prices Is That They Will Fluctuate

Stock prices in nominal terms, shown in the bottom line, tend to rise with inflation. The Standard and Poor's index (the S&P 500) shown here tracks the value-weighted average of the stock prices of the 500 largest American companies.

The top line shows the "real" S&P 500, which is the S&P 500 corrected for movements in the consumer price index.

percent of its value in 6 hours. The shock to securities markets was a vivid reminder of the risks you take when you buy stocks. Nevertheless, 35 million Americans own stocks; 3 million of them are people with incomes under $10,000. Only a small fraction of shares is held by low-income households, but the fact that so many people are willing to invest their wealth this way attests to the lure of prospective gains from stock ownership.

Where will it all end? Is there a crystal ball that will foretell the movement of stock prices? This is the subject of modern finance theory.

Efficient Markets and the Random Walk

Economists and finance professors have long studied prices in speculative markets, like the stock market, and markets for commodities such as corn. Their findings have stirred great controversy and have even angered many financial analysts. Yet this is an area in which the facts have largely corroborated the theories.

Modern economic theories of stock prices are grouped under the heading of **efficient-market theory**.[6] One way of expressing the fundamental theory is: *You can't outguess the market.*

We'll see in a minute why this proposition is plausible. First, let's consider its factual basis. There have

---

[6] "Efficiency" is used differently in finance theory than in other parts of economics. Here, "efficiency" means that information is quickly absorbed, not that resources produce the maximal outputs.

been numerous studies over the years about rules or formulas for making money. Typical rules are "Buy after 2 days of increases" or "Buy on the bad news and sell on the good news." An early study by Alfred Cowles investigated the recommendations of stockbrokers. He examined how well different brokers performed by looking at the return (in dollars of total income per year per dollar invested) on the stocks they selected. He found that, on average, a stockbroker's choices did no better than a random portfolio (or combination) of stocks.

This observation led to the *dartboard theory* of stock selection: you can throw a dart at the *Wall Street Journal* as a way of selecting stocks. Better still, buy a little of everything in the market so that you hold a diversified "index" portfolio of the stock market. This would probably leave you better off than your cousins who follow a broker's advice. Why? Because they would have to pay brokers' commissions while their stocks, on average, would not outperform yours.

This paradoxical view has been generally confirmed in hundreds of studies over the last four decades. Their lesson is not that you will never become rich by following a rule or formula but that, on average, such rules cannot outperform a randomly selected and diversified portfolio of stocks.

Rationale for the Efficient-Market View.
Finance theorists have spent many years analyzing stock and bond markets in order to understand why the dartboard theory might hold. Why do well-functioning financial markets rule out persistent excess profits? The theory of efficient markets explains this.

An **efficient financial market** is one where all new information is quickly understood by market participants and becomes immediately incorporated into market prices. For example, say that Lazy-T Oil Company has just struck oil in the Gulf of Alaska. This event is announced at 11:30 A.M. on Tuesday. When will the price of Lazy-T's shares rise? The efficient-market theory holds that the news will be incorporated into prices immediately. The market participants will react at once, bidding the price of Lazy-T up by the correct amount. In short, at every point in time, markets have already digested and included in stock prices or corn

prices or other speculative prices all the latest available information.

This means that if you read about a heavy frost in Florida over breakfast, you can't enrich yourself by buying frozen-orange-juice futures during your lunch break: the orange-juice price went up the minute the news was reported, or even earlier.

The theory of efficient markets holds that market prices contain all available information. It is not possible to make profits by looking at old information or at patterns of past price changes.

A Random Walk.
The efficient-market view provides an important way of analyzing price movements in organized markets. Under this approach, the price movements of stocks should look highly erratic, like a random walk, when charted over a period of time.

A price follows a *random walk* when its movements over time are completely unpredictable. For example, toss a coin for heads or tails. Call a head "plus 1" and a tail "minus 1." Then keep track of the running score of 100 coin tosses. Draw it on graph paper. This curve is a random walk. Now, for comparison, also graph 100 days' movement of Microsoft stock or of Standard and Poor's 500 index. Note how similar all three figures appear.

Why do speculative prices resemble a random walk? Economists, on reflection, have arrived at the following truths: In an efficient market all predictable things have already been built into the price. It is the arrival of *new* information—a surprisingly large increase in the CPI, a revolution in Saudi Arabia, a report that the Federal Reserve has unexpectedly raised interest rates—that affects stock or commodity prices. Moreover, the news must be random and unpredictable (or else it would be predictable and therefore not truly news).

To summarize:

The efficient-market theory explains why movements in stock prices look so erratic. Prices respond to news, to surprises. But surprises are unpredictable events—like the flip of a coin or next month's rainstorm—that may move in any direction. Because stock prices move in response to erratic events, stock prices themselves move erratically, like a random walk.

Qualifications to the Efficient-Market View. There are four major objections to the efficient-market view of markets:

1. Suppose everybody accepts the efficient-market philosophy and stops trying to digest information quickly. If everyone assumes that stock prices are correctly valued, will those prices *stop* being accurate?

   This is a good question, but it is unlikely that everyone will quit. Indeed, the minute too many people stopped looking ahead, the market would cease being efficient. We could then make profits by acting on old information. So the efficient market is a stable, self-monitoring equilibrium state.

2. Some people are quicker and smarter than others. Some have much money to spend on information to narrow down the odds on the uncertain future. Doesn't it stand to reason that they will make higher profits? There are many such people competing against each other. The Rockefellers can buy the best financial counsel there is. But so can pension funds, university endowments, and many others. Competition provides the checks and balances of efficiency and ensures minimal excess profits. Moreover, the efficient-market theory does suggest that a few people with special flair and skills will permanently earn high returns on their skills—just as great quarterbacks and sopranos do.

3. Economists who look at the historical record ask whether it is plausible that sharp movements in stock prices could actually reflect new information. Consider the sharp drop in the stock market from October 15 to October 19, 1987. The efficient-market view would hold that this drop was caused by economic events that depressed the expected value of future corporate earnings. What were those events? James Tobin, Yale's Nobel Prize–winning economist, commented, "There are no visible factors that could make a 30 percent difference in the value of stock [prices over these four days]." Efficient-market theorists fall silent before this criticism.

4. Finally, the efficient-market view applies to individual stocks but not necessarily to the entire market. Some economists have found evidence of long, self-reversing swings in stock market prices. Others believe that these swings reflect changes in the general mood of the financial community. These long-term swings may lie behind the boom psychology of the 1920s and 1990s or the depression mentality of the 1930s. Let us say that we believed that the whole stock market in 1997 showed an "irrational exuberance" and was overvalued. What could we do? We could not individually buy or sell enough stocks to overcome the entire national mood. So, from a macroeconomic perspective, speculative markets can exhibit waves of pessimism or optimism without powerful economic forces moving in to correct these swings of mood.

PERSONAL FINANCIAL STRATEGIES

In the introductory chapter, we said that studying economics will probably not make you rich. But the careful study of the principles of modern finance can definitely help you invest your nest egg wisely and avoid the worst financial mistakes. In this concluding subsection, we apply the lessons to personal investment decisions.

- *Lesson 1: Know thy investments.* The absolute bedrock of sound investment is to be realistic and prudent in your investment decisions. For important investments, study the materials and get expert advice. What are the lessons of the many studies of the behavior of financial markets and financial advisers? Be skeptical of approaches that claim to have found the quick route to success. You can't get rich by consulting the stars (although, unbelievably, some financial advisers push astrology to their clients). Hunches work out to nothing in the long run. Moreover, the best brains on Wall Street do not, on average, beat the averages (Dow-Jones, Standard & Poor's, etc.). This is not so surprising. Although the big money managers have all the money needed for any kind of research and digging, they are all competing with one another.

- *Lesson 2: Diversify, diversify, that is the law of the prophets of finance.* One of the major lessons of finance is the advantage of diversifying your investments. "Don't put all your eggs in one basket" is one way of expressing this rule. The rationale for diversification is that by putting funds in a number of different investments, you can continue to get a high yield while reducing the risk. For example, suppose that stocks and real estate each have average returns of 10 percent while their risk index (standard deviation) is 30 percent. A portfolio that contains equal shares of each investment would also have an average return of 10 percent. But because a bad year for one is just as likely as not to be balanced by a good year for the other, under simplified conditions (independence of risk and a normal probability distribution), the risk index for the diversified portfolio is only 21.2 percent. Calculations show that by diversifying their wealth among a broad group of investments—different common stocks, conventional and inflation-indexed bonds, perhaps real estate—people can attain a good return on their wealth while minimizing the risk of losing their investments.

- *Lesson 3: Consider common-stock index funds.* Investors who want to invest in the stock market can achieve a good return with the least possible risk by holding a broadly diversified portfolio of common stocks. A good vehicle for this is an *index fund*, which is a portfolio of the stocks of the largest companies that mimics the major indexes like the S&P 500 with minimal management and brokerage fees.
- *Lesson 4: Match your investments to your risk preference.* You can increase your expected return by picking riskier investments (see Figure 25-6). But you must

carefully consider how much risk you can afford, financially and psychologically. As one wit said, investments are a tradeoff between eating well and sleeping well. If you get insomnia worrying about the ups and downs of the market, you can minimize your risks by keeping your assets in inflation-indexed U.S. Treasury bonds. But in the long run, you might be sleeping soundly on a cot! If you want to eat well, you can invest more heavily in stocks, including those in foreign countries and emerging markets, incorporate small companies in your portfolio, and hold little in short-term securities or bonds. Studies indicate that over the long run, you will do much better with your portfolio heavily invested in risky stocks with only a minimal investment in bonds and other fixed-income securities.

If, after reading all this, you still want to try your hand in the stock market, do not be daunted. But take to heart the caution of one of America's great financiers, Bernard Baruch:

> If you are ready to give up everything else—to study the whole history and background of the market and all the principal companies whose stocks are on the board as carefully as a medical student studies anatomy—if you can do all that, and, in addition, you have the cool nerves of a great gambler, the sixth sense of a kind of clairvoyant, and the courage of a lion, you have a ghost of a chance.

SUMMARY

A. Money and Interest Rates

1. Money is anything that serves as a commonly accepted medium of exchange or means of payment. Money also functions as a unit of value and a store of value. Before money came into use, people exchanged goods for goods in a process called barter. Money arose to facilitate trade. Early money consisted of commodities, which were superseded by paper money and then bank money. Unlike other economic goods, money is valued because of social convention. We value money indirectly for what it buys, not for its direct utility.

2. Two definitions of money are commonly used today. The first is transactions money (M_1)—made up of currency and checking deposits. The second important concept is broad money (M_2), which includes M_1 plus highly liquid near-monies like savings accounts. The

definitions of the *M's* have changed over the last two decades as a result of rapid innovation in financial markets.

3. Interest rates are the prices paid for borrowing money; they are measured in dollars per year paid back per dollar borrowed or in percent per year. People willingly pay interest because borrowed funds allow them to buy goods and services to satisfy consumption needs or make profitable investments.

4. We observe a wide variety of interest rates. These rates vary because of many factors such as the term or maturity of loans, the risk and liquidity of investments, and the tax treatment of the interest.

5. Nominal or money interest rates generally rise during inflationary periods, reflecting the fact that the purchasing power of money declines as prices rise. To cal-

culate the interest yield in terms of real goods and services, we use the real interest rate, which equals the nominal or money interest rate minus the rate of inflation. The U.S. government recently issued inflation-indexed bonds, which guarantee a fixed real return on investments.

6. The demand for money differs from that for other commodities. Money is held for its indirect rather than its direct value. But money holdings are limited because keeping funds in money rather than in other assets has an opportunity cost: we sacrifice interest earnings when we hold money.

7. People hold money primarily because they need it to pay bills or buy goods. Such transactions needs are met by M_1 and are chiefly related to the value of transactions or to nominal GDP. Economic theory predicts, and empirical studies confirm, that the demand for money is sensitive to interest rates; higher interest rates lead to a lower demand for M.

B. Banking and the Supply of Money

8. Banks are commercial enterprises that seek to earn profits for their owners. One major function of banks is to provide checking accounts to customers. Modern banks gradually evolved from the old goldsmith establishments in which money and valuables were stored. Eventually it became general practice for goldsmiths to hold less than 100 percent reserves against deposits; this was the beginning of fractional-reserve banking.

9. If banks kept 100 percent cash reserves against all deposits, there would be no creation of money when new reserves were injected by the central bank into the system. There would be only a 1-to-1 exchange of one kind of money for another kind of money.

10. Today, banks are legally required to keep reserves on their checking deposits. These can be in the form of cash on hand or of non-interest-bearing deposits at the Federal Reserve. For illustrative purposes, we examined a required reserve ratio of 10 percent. In this case, the banking system as a whole—together with public or private borrowers and the depositing public—creates bank money 10 to 1 for each new dollar of reserves created by the Fed and deposited somewhere in the banking system.

11. Each small bank is limited in its ability to expand its loans and investments. It cannot lend or invest more than it has received from depositors; it can lend only about nine-tenths as much. Although no bank alone can expand its reserves 10 to 1, the banking system as a whole can. Each bank receiving $1000 of new deposits lends nine-tenths of its newly acquired cash on loans and investments. If we follow through the successive groups of banks in the dwindling, never-ending chain, we find for the system as a whole new deposits of

$$\$1000 + \$900 + \$810 + \$729 + \cdots$$

$$= \$1000 \times [1 + \tfrac{9}{10} + (\tfrac{9}{10})^2 + (\tfrac{9}{10})^3 + \cdots]$$

$$= \$1000 \left(\frac{1}{1 - \tfrac{9}{10}} \right) = \$1000 \left(\frac{1}{0.1} \right)$$

$$= \$10,000$$

More generally:

$$\text{Money-supply multiplier} = \frac{\text{change of money}}{\text{change of reserves}}$$

$$= \frac{1}{\text{required reserve ratio}}$$

12. There may be some leakage of new cash reserves of the banking system into circulation outside the banks and into assets other than checking accounts. When some of the new reserves leak into assets other than checking deposits, the relationship of money creation to new reserves may depart from the 10-to-1 formula given by the money-supply multiplier.

C. A Tour of Wall Street

13. Households own a variety of financial assets. The most important are money, savings accounts, government securities, equities, and pension funds.

14. Assets have different characteristics, the most important being the rate of return (or interest rate) and the risk. The rate of return is the total dollar gain from a security. Risk refers to the variability of the returns on an investment. Because people are risk-averse, they require higher returns to induce them to buy riskier assets.

15. Stock markets, of which the New York Stock Exchange is the most important, are places where titles of ownership to the largest companies are bought and sold. The history of stock prices is filled with violent gyrations, such as the Great Crash of 1929. Trends are tracked by the use of stock-price indexes, such as the Standard and Poor's 500 or the familiar Dow-Jones Industrial Average.

16. Modern economic theories of stock prices generally focus on the role of efficient markets. An efficient market is one in which all information is quickly absorbed by speculators and is immediately built into market prices. In efficient markets, there are no easy profits; looking at yesterday's news or past patterns of prices or elections or business cycles will not help predict future price movements. Thus, in efficient markets, prices respond to surprises. Because surprises are

inherently random, stock prices and other speculative prices move erratically, as in a random walk.

17. Implant the four rules of personal finance firmly in your long-term memory: (*a*) Know thy investments. (*b*) Diversify, diversify, that is the rule of the prophets of finance. (*c*) Consider common-stock index funds. (*d*) Match your investments to your risk preference.

CONCEPTS FOR REVIEW

Money and Interest Rates

commodity *M*, paper *M*, bank *M*, M_1, M_2
interest rate, real and nominal interest rates
interest-rate premiums due to:
  maturity
  risk
  illiquidity
motives for money demand:
  transactions demand
  asset demand

interest as opportunity cost of holding money
inflation-indexed bonds

Banking and Money Supply

banks, financial intermediaries
bank reserves (vault cash and deposits with Fed)
required reserve ratio
fractional-reserve banking
money-supply multiplier

The Stock Market

common stocks (corporate equities)
Standard and Poor's 500
efficient market, random walk of stock prices
index fund
new news, old information, and speculative prices
four rules for personal investing

QUESTIONS FOR DISCUSSION

1. Define M_1 and M_2. What is included in M_1? What is in M_2 but not M_1? Relate each of the components of M_2 to the factors behind the demand for money.

2. Suppose that all banks kept 100 percent reserves. Construct new versions of Tables 25-5(*a*) and 25-6 to reflect $1000 of reserves added to a banking system that keeps 100 percent reserves. What is the net effect of a reserve addition to the money supply in this case? Do banks "create" money?

3. Suppose that banks hold 20 percent of deposits as reserves and that $200 of reserves is *subtracted* from the banking system. Redo Tables 25-5(*a*) through 25-7. What is the money-supply multiplier in this case? Calculate the money-supply multiplier in a second way by using the technique shown in footnote 3.

4. What would be the effect on the demand for money (M_1) of each of the following (with other things held equal)?
   a. An increase in real GDP
   b. An increase in the price level
   c. A rise in the interest rate on savings accounts and Treasury securities
   d. A doubling of all prices, wages, and incomes (Can you calculate exactly the effect on the demand for money?)

5. The opportunity cost of holding money is equal to the yield on safe short-term assets (such as Treasury bills) minus the interest rate on money. What is the impact of the following on the opportunity cost of holding money in checking deposits?
   a. Before 1980 (when checking deposits have zero yield) market interest rates increase from 8 to 9 percent.
   b. In 1984 (when checking accounts have a maximum yield of 5 percent) interest rates increase from (1) 3 to 4 percent and (2) 8 to 9 percent.
   c. In 1991 (when the interest rates on NOW accounts are deregulated), market interest rates increase from (1) 3 to 4 percent and (2) 8 to 9 percent.

   How would you expect the demand for money to respond to the change in market interest rates in each of the above cases if the elasticity of demand for money with respect to the opportunity cost of money is 0.2?

6. Interest-rate problems (which may require a calculator):
   a. You invest $2000 at 13.5 percent per year. What is your total balance after 6 months?
   b. Interest is said to be "compounded" when you earn interest on whatever interest has already been paid; most interest rates quoted today are compounded. If you invest $10,000 for 3 years at a compound annual interest rate of 10 percent, what is the total investment at the end of each year?
   c. Consider the following data: The consumer price index in 1977 was 60.6, and in 1981 it was 90.9.

Interest rates on government securities in 1978 through 1981 (in percent per year) were 7.2, 10.0, 11.5, and 14.0. Calculate the average nominal and real interest rates for the 4-year period 1978–1981.

d. Treasury bills (T-bills) are usually sold on a discounted basis; that is, a 90-day T-bill for $10,000 would sell today at a price such that collecting $10,000 at maturity would produce the market interest rate. If the market interest rate is 6.6 percent per year, what would be the price on a $10,000 90-day T-bill?

e. Consider a 3-year $1000 inflation-indexed bond with a real interest rate of 4 percent. The inflation rates are 3, 6, and 5 percent in the 3 years. Calculate the dollar interest payment at the end of each of the years and the principal repayment at the end of the third year.

7. Explain whether you think that each of the following should be counted as part of the narrow money supply (M_1) for the United States: traveler's checks, savings accounts, subway tokens, postage stamps, credit cards, and $20 bills used by Russians in Moscow.

8. According to the efficient-market theory, what effect would the following events have on the price of GM's stock?

a. A surprise announcement that the government is going to raise corporation taxes on next July 1

b. An increase in tax rates on July 1, which is 6 months after Congress passed the enabling legislation

c. An announcement, unexpected by experts, that the United States is imposing quotas on imports of Japanese cars for the coming year

d. Implementation of (c) by issuing regulations on December 31

9. Suppose reserve requirements were abolished. What would determine the level of reserves in the banking system? What would happen to the money-supply multiplier in this situation?

10. Suppose that one giant bank, the Humongous Bank of America, held all the checking deposits of all the people, subject to a 10 percent legal reserve requirement. If there were an injection of reserves into the economy, could the Humongous Bank lend out more than 90 percent of the deposit addition, knowing that the new deposit must come back to it? Would this change the ultimate money-supply multiplier?

11. **Advanced problem:** Flip a coin 100 times. Count a head as "plus 1" and a tail as "minus 1." Keep a running score of the total. Plot it on graph paper. This is a random walk. (Those with access to a computer can do this using a computer program, a random-number generator, and a plotter.)

Next, keep track of the closing price of the stock of your favorite company for a few weeks (or get it from past issues of the newspaper). Plot the price against time. Can you see any difference in the pattern of changes? Do both look like random walks?

CHAPTER 26
CENTRAL BANKING AND MONETARY POLICY

There have been three great inventions since the beginning of time: fire, the wheel, and central banking.

Will Rogers

Where should you look to find the people who are most responsible for the business cycle? You might be surprised to find that they are not in the White House or Congress but in the Federal Reserve System, which is the central bank of the United States. Through its control of bank reserves the Federal Reserve (or "Fed") sets the level of short-term interest rates and has a major impact on output and employment in the short run. Every modern country has a central bank that is responsible for managing its monetary affairs.

The Federal Reserve's central goal is low and stable inflation. It also seeks to promote steady growth in national output, low unemployment, and orderly financial markets. If aggregate demand is excessive

and prices are being bid up, the Federal Reserve Board may reduce the growth of the money supply. That puts the brakes on the economy and reduces price pressures. If the economy is sluggish and business is languishing, the Fed may consider increasing the money supply. That will usually give a boost to aggregate demand and bring down unemployment. This chapter will help you understand the Federal Reserve's central role in the U.S. economy.

Figure 26-1 shows the role of central banking in the economy and depicts its relationship to the banks, financial markets, and interest rates. In Section A we analyze how the Fed uses its instruments—bank reserves, the discount rate, and other tools—to determine the money supply.

A. CENTRAL BANKING AND THE FEDERAL RESERVE SYSTEM

THE FEDERAL RESERVE SYSTEM

Structure of the Federal Reserve

History. During the nineteenth century, the United States was plagued by banking panics. These

occurred when people suddenly attempted to turn their bank deposits into currency (review the example on bank panics in the last chapter). When they arrived at the banks, they found that the banks had an inadequate supply of currency because the supply of currency was fixed and smaller than the

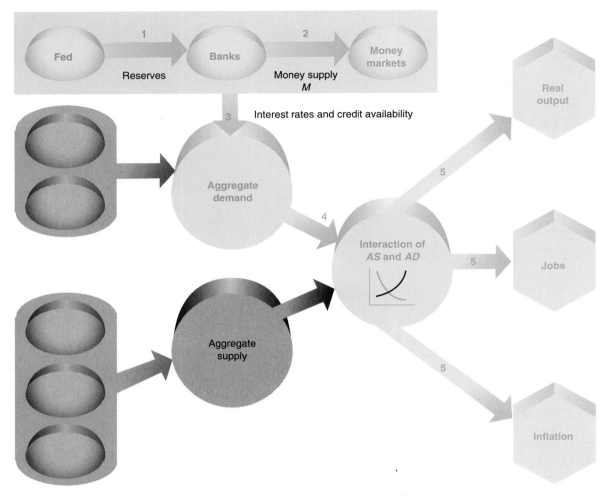

FIGURE 26-1. A Bird's-Eye View of How Monetary Policy Affects Output and Inflation

This diagram shows graphically the steps by which Fed policy affects economic activity. (1) is a change in reserves; leading to (2), a change in *M;* leading to (3), changes in interest rates and credit conditions. In (4), *AD* is changed by a response of investment and other interest-sensitive spending. In (5), changes in output, employment, and inflation follow.

Remember that fiscal policy also feeds into the aggregate demand circle.

amount of bank deposits. Bank failures and economic downturns ensued. After the severe panic of 1907, agitation and discussion led to the <u>Federal Reserve Act of 1913</u> which was to "provide for the establishment of Federal reserve banks [and] to furnish an elastic currency."

As currently constituted, the Federal Reserve System consists of 12 regional Federal Reserve Banks, located in New York, Chicago, Richmond, Dallas, San Francisco, and other major cities. The regional structure was originally designed in a populist age to ensure that different areas would have a voice in banking matters and to avoid too great a concentration of central-banking powers in Washington or in the hands of the eastern bankers. Each Federal Reserve Bank today operates a nationwide payments system, distributes coin and currency, and supervises and regulates banks in its districts.

Who's in Charge? The core of the Federal Reserve is the *Board of Governors* of the Federal Reserve System, which consists of seven members nominated by the President and confirmed by the Senate to serve overlapping terms of 14 years. Members of the board are generally bankers or economists who work full-time at the job.

The key decision-making body in the Federal Reserve System is the *Federal Open Market Committee* (FOMC). The 12 voting members of the FOMC include the seven governors plus five of the presidents of the regional Federal Reserve Banks. This key group controls the single most important and frequently used tool of modern monetary policy—the supply of bank reserves.

At the pinnacle of the entire system is the *Chairman of the Board of Governors,* currently an economist, Alan Greenspan. He chairs the Board of Governors and the FOMC, acts as public spokesman for the Fed, and exercises enormous power over monetary policy. He is often called the "second most powerful individual in America," reflecting the extent to which he can influence the entire economy through his impact on monetary policy.

In spite of the formally dispersed structure of the Fed, close observers think that power is quite centralized. The Federal Reserve Board, joined at meetings by the presidents of the 12 regional Federal Reserve Banks, operates under the Fed Chairman to formulate and carry out monetary policy. The structure of the Federal Reserve System is shown in Figure 26-2.

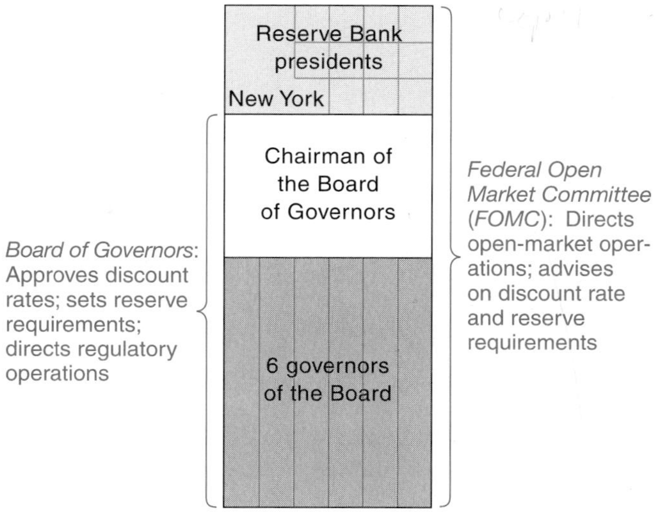

Independence. On examining the structure of the Fed, one might ask, "In which of the three branches of government does the Fed lie?" The answer is, "None. Legally, the 12 regional banks are private. In reality, the Fed as a whole behaves as an independent government agency."

Although nominally a corporation owned by the commercial banks that are members of the Federal Reserve System, the Federal Reserve is in practice a public agency. It is directly responsible to Congress; it listens carefully to the advice of the President; and whenever any conflict arises between its making a profit and promoting the public interest, it acts unswervingly in the public interest. The Fed prints the nation's currency, in return for which it holds interest-bearing government securities. Through this activity, it earns billions of dollars of profits each

FIGURE 26-2. The Major Players in Monetary Policy

The powers of the Federal Reserve are lodged in two bodies. The seven-member Board of Governors approves changes in discount rates and sets reserve requirements. The FOMC directs the setting of bank reserves. The Chairman of the Board of Governors leads both committees. The size of each box indicates that person's or group's relative power; note the size of the Chairman's box.

year. But, to reflect its public mission, all of its profits go to the U.S. government.

Above all, the Federal Reserve is an *independent* agency. While they listen carefully to Congress and the President, and even to the election returns, in the end the members of the Board of Governors and the FOMC decide monetary policy according to their views about the nation's economic interests. As a result, the Fed sometimes comes into conflict with the executive branch. Almost every President has advice, and occasionally some harsh words, for Fed policy. The Fed listens politely but generally chooses the path it thinks best for the country, and its decisions do not have to be approved or ratified by anybody.

From time to time, people argue that the Fed is too independent. "How can a democracy allow a group of private bankers to control monetary policy?" ask critics. Is it democratic to allow a small group of unelected people to run financial markets and even cause recessions? Shouldn't monetary policy be set by elected representatives in Congress or by the executive branch?

The World as Seen from the Fed

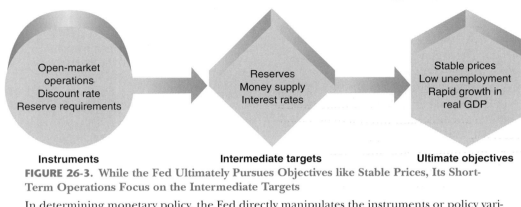

FIGURE 26-3. **While the Fed Ultimately Pursues Objectives like Stable Prices, Its Short-Term Operations Focus on the Intermediate Targets**

In determining monetary policy, the Fed directly manipulates the instruments or policy variables under its control—open-market operations, discount rate, and reserve requirements. These help determine bank reserves, the money supply, and interest rates—the intermediate targets of monetary policy. Ultimately, monetary and fiscal policies are partners in pursuing the major objectives of rapid growth, low unemployment, and stable prices.

There are no right answers to these questions. On the one hand, an independent central bank is the guardian of the value of a nation's currency and the best protection against rampant inflation. Moreover, independence ensures that monetary policy is not subverted for partisan political objectives, as sometimes happens in countries where the executive branch controls the central bank. The Fed's independence allows it the leeway to undertake policies, such as fighting inflation, that have little popular support. The elected branches will not always sacrifice their offices for long-run economic welfare. Historical studies show that countries with independent central banks are usually more successful in keeping down inflation than those whose central banks are under the thumbs of elected officials.

At the same time, critics note that the presidents of Federal Reserve Banks are selected by regional boards populated by bankers and private interests, without any say from the President or Congress. Moreover, because they are so far removed from the political process, monetary managers at the Fed may lose touch with social and economic realities. Members of Congress are routinely forced to confront unemployed autoworkers and bankrupt farmers—groups seldom encountered in the elegant marble Federal Reserve building in Washington.

Policy Objectives. What are the goals of the Federal Reserve System? This is how the Fed sees its role:

> The [Federal Reserve's] objectives include economic growth in line with the economy's potential to expand; a high level of employment; stable prices (that is, stability in the purchasing power of the dollar); and moderate long-term interest rates.[1]

While it is not always easy to understand the exact chain of reasoning that led to a particular monetary-policy step, historians who sift through the decisions usually find that the Fed is ultimately concerned with preserving the integrity of our financial institutions, combating inflation, defending the exchange rate of the dollar, and preventing excessive unemployment.

To summarize:

The Federal Reserve Board in Washington, together with the 12 Federal Reserve Banks, constitutes our American central bank. Every modern

---

[1] *The Federal Reserve System: Purposes and Functions,* Board of Governors of the Federal Reserve System, Washington, D.C., 1994, p. 2. This booklet, available on the Internet, provides a useful description of the operations of the Fed.

country has a central bank. Its primary mission is to control the nation's money supply and credit conditions.

Overview of the Fed's Operations

Figure 26-3 shows the various stages of Federal Reserve operations as seen by the Fed. The Federal Reserve has at its disposal a number of policy instruments. These can affect certain intermediate targets (such as reserves, the money supply, and interest rates). These instruments are intended to help achieve the ultimate objectives of a healthy economy—low inflation, rapid growth in output, and low unemployment. It is important to keep these different groups (policy instruments, intermediate targets, and ultimate objectives) clearly distinct in our analysis.

The three major instruments of monetary policy are:

• *Open-market operations*—buying or selling of U.S. government securities in the open market to influence the level of reserves
• *Discount-rate policy*—setting the interest rate, called the *discount rate*, at which commercial banks and other depository institutions can borrow reserves from a regional Federal Reserve Bank
• *Reserve-requirements policy*—setting and changing the legal reserve ratio requirements on deposits with banks and other financial institutions

In managing money, the Federal Reserve must keep its eye on a set of variables known as *intermediate targets*. These are economic variables that are intermediate in the transmission mechanism between Fed instruments and ultimate policy goals. When the Fed wants to affect its ultimate objectives, it first changes one of its instruments, such as the discount rate. This change affects an intermediate variable like interest rates, credit conditions, or the money supply. Much as a doctor interested in the health of a patient will monitor pulse and blood pressure, so the Federal Reserve keeps a careful watch on its intermediate targets.

Balance Sheet of the Federal Reserve Banks

In analyzing central banking, we need to describe the consolidated balance sheet of the Federal Reserve System, shown in Table 26-1. U.S. government securities (e.g., bonds) make up most of the Fed's assets. The small items, loans and acceptances, are primarily loans or advances to commercial banks. The interest rate the Fed charges banks for such loans, or "discounts," is called the discount rate, which is another of the Fed's tools.

Looking at liabilities, two unique items are currency and reserves. Federal Reserve notes are the Fed's principal liabilities. These are the paper currency we use every day. Of vital importance are the bank reserves, or balances kept on deposit by commercial banks with the Federal Reserve Banks and shown as Fed liabilities. Taken along with the banks' vault

TABLE 26-1. Federal Reserve Notes and Deposits Underlie Our Money Supply

By controlling its earning assets (government securities and loans), the Fed controls its liabilities (deposits and Federal Reserve notes). It determines the economy's money supply (currency and demand deposits, M_1), and thereby affects GDP, unemployment, and inflation. (Source: *Federal Reserve Bulletin*, June 1994.)

Combined Balance Sheet of 12 Federal Reserve Banks, 1994 (Billions of Dollars)			
Assets		**Liabilities and net worth**	
U.S. government securities	$416.9	Federal Reserve notes	$426.5
Loans and acceptances	0.1	Deposits:	
Miscellaneous other assets	60.3	Bank reserves	24.5
		U.S. Treasury	7.7
		Miscellaneous liabilities	18.6
Total	$477.3	Total	$477.3

Federal Reserve Balance Sheet (Billions of Dollars)			
Assets		**Liabilities**	
U.S. securities	−$1	Bank reserves	−$1
Total	**−$1**	**Total**	**−$1**

TABLE 26-2(a). Open-Market Sale by Fed Cuts Reserves Initially

Commercial Banks' Balance Sheet (Billions of Dollars)			
Assets		**Liabilities**	
Reserves	−$ 1	Checking deposits	−$10
Loans and investments	− 9		
Total	**−$10**	**Total**	**−$10**

TABLE 26-2(b). . . . and Ultimately Cuts Deposits 10 to 1

This crucial set of tables shows how open-market operations affect the Fed's balance sheet and the balance sheet of banks.

In (**a**), the Fed has sold $1 billion of securities. The funds used to pay for the securities are deposited in the Fed, reducing bank reserves by $1 billion. Bank reserves thus decline by $1 billion as a result of the open-market operation.

Then, in (**b**), we see the effect on the balance sheet of banks. With a required reserve ratio of 10 percent of deposits, the reserve contraction cascades through the banking system. Thus, deposits must fall by $10 billion for the banking system to be back in equilibrium.

cash, these are the reserves we have been talking about. They provide the basis for multiple deposit creation by the nation's banking system.

By altering its holding of government securities, the Fed can change bank reserves and thereby trigger the sequence of events that ultimately determines the total supply of money.

THE NUTS AND BOLTS OF MONETARY POLICY

Open-Market Operations

The Fed's most useful tool is "open-market operations."

By selling or buying government securities in the open market, the Fed can lower or raise bank reserves. These so-called **open-market operations** are a central bank's most important stabilizing instrument.

In setting policy, the FOMC decides whether to pump more reserves into the banking system by buying Treasury bills (i.e., short-term bonds) and longer-term government bonds or whether to tighten monetary policy by selling government securities.

To see how an open-market operation changes reserves, let us suppose that the Fed thinks the economic winds are blowing up a little inflation, as hap-

pened in early 1994. The FOMC holds its meeting in Washington and hears presentations and projections from its staff of talented economists. The committee decides, "Let's sell $1 billion of Treasury bills from our portfolio to contract reserves and tighten overall money and credit." The motion is unanimously approved by vote of the seven Washington governors and five regional Bank presidents.

To whom are the bonds sold? *To the open market.* This includes dealers in government bonds, who then resell them to commercial banks, big corporations, other financial institutions, and individuals.

The purchasers usually buy the bonds by writing checks to the Fed, drawn from an account in a commercial bank. For example, if the Fed sells $10,000 worth of bonds to Ms. Smith, she writes a check on the Coyote Bank of Santa Fe. The Fed presents the check at the Coyote Bank. When the Coyote Bank pays the check, it will reduce its balance with the Fed by $10,000. At the end of the day, the Coyote Bank, and the entire commercial banking system, will lose $10,000 in reserves at the Federal Reserve System.

Table 26-2(*a*) shows the effect of a $1 billion open-market sale on the Federal Reserve balance sheet. The open-market sale changes the Federal Reserve balance sheet by reducing both assets and liabilities by $1 billion: the Fed has sold $1 billion of government bonds, and its liabilities have declined by exactly the same amount, $1 billion of bank reserves.

Effects on Money. To understand the effect of the reserve change on the money supply, we must consider the banks' response. In this chapter, we continue the algebraic convenience of assuming that banks hold 10 percent of their deposits as reserves with the central bank; the legal reason for this practice is discussed in greater detail later in this chapter.

What happens to the money supply? Reserves go down by $1 billion, and that tends to set off a contraction of deposits. The last chapter showed how a change in bank reserves would lead to a multiplied change in total bank deposits. If the legal reserve requirement is 10 percent, the $1 billion sale of government bonds will result in a $10 billion cut in the community's money supply. Table 26-2(*b*) shows the banks' ultimate position after $1 billion of reserves have been extinguished by the open-market operation. In the end, the Fed's open-market sale has caused a $10 billion contraction in the money supply.

Operating Procedures

The FOMC meets eight times a year to give instructions to its operating arm, the Federal Reserve Bank of New York. The instructions are contained in an "FOMC policy directive." The directive has two parts: a general assessment of economic conditions and a review of the objectives of monetary policy.

The most important part of the procedure is instructing the frontline troops at the New York Fed about how to manage financial markets on a day-to-day basis. The operating procedures have changed over time. Before the 1970s, the FOMC used to give such vague instructions as, "Keep credit conditions and interest rates as tight as they have been." Or, "Loosen credit a little to help expand GDP." Because the Fed acted cautiously, it was sometimes slow to react to changing business-cycle conditions.

In the late 1970s, the Federal Reserve altered its operating procedures to pay closer attention to movements in the money supply. It was accused of helping to reelect President Nixon in 1972; shortly afterward, the Fed was charged with overreacting to the sharp recession of 1974–1975 and with allowing unemployment to rise too sharply. To rein in the

Fed, Congress directed it to set explicit growth-rate targets for the major monetary aggregates.

The most dramatic shift in policy came in 1979, when the Fed undertook its "monetarist experiment" to slow the rapid inflation. This involved targeting reserves and the money supply in a fashion recommended by monetarists. (We will review the monetarist experiment later in this chapter and monetarism in Chapter 32.)

In the decade after 1982, the Fed progressively demoted the role of the monetary aggregates in its operating procedures. It first removed M_1 from its month-to-month directive; then, in 1993, M_2 was also found wanting. The monetary aggregates simply proved to be too unreliable as predictors of movements in aggregate demand.

What replaced these indicators? In the mid-1990s, the Fed tends to look at a wide variety of indicators as well as at economic forecasts. There is no single variable that triggers monetary tightening or loosening. More and more, however, the Fed tends to see price stability as its ultimate objective and to respond when inflation or the threat of inflation looms ahead.

Discount-Rate Policy:
A Second Instrument

When commercial banks are short of reserves, they are allowed to borrow from the Federal Reserve Banks. Their loans were included under the asset heading "Loans and acceptances" in the Fed balance sheet in Table 26-1. These loans are called *borrowed reserves.* When borrowed reserves are growing, the banks are borrowing from the Fed, thereby increasing total bank reserves (borrowed plus unborrowed reserves). Conversely, a drop in borrowed reserves promotes a contraction in total bank reserves.

In the early years, the discount window was the primary vehicle for providing reserves to the banking system. As financial markets developed and the role of monetary policy was better understood, the Fed has turned to open-market operations as the primary tool for adjusting the overall level of reserves. Today, the discount window is used primarily to buffer the day-to-day fluctuations in reserves. Because banks can go to the discount window when there are unanticipated fluctuations in required reserves, the extent of short-term volatility in interest rates is reduced.

Type of deposit	Reserve ratio (%)	Range in which Fed can vary (%)
Checking (transaction) accounts:		
First $49 million	3	No change allowed
Above $49 million	10	8–14
Time and savings deposits:		
Personal	0	
Nonpersonal:		
Up to 1½ years' maturity	0	0–9
More than 1½ years' maturity	0	0–9

TABLE 26-3. Required Reserves for Financial Institutions

Reserve requirements are governed by law and regulation. The reserve-ratio column shows the percent of deposits in each category that must be held in non-interest-bearing deposits at the Fed or in cash on hand. Checking-type accounts in large banks face required reserves of 10 percent, while other major deposits have no reserve requirements. The Fed has power to alter the reserve ratio within a given range but does so only on the rare occasion when economic conditions warrant a sharp change in monetary policy. (Source: *Federal Reserve Bulletin*, August 1997.)

Sometimes, the Fed may raise or lower the **discount rate**, which is the interest rate charged on bank borrowings from the 12 regional Federal Reserve Banks. For many years, the discount rate was the bellwether of monetary policy. For example, in 1965 when the Fed wanted to send a signal to markets that the Vietnam war boom threatened to become inflationary, it raised the discount rate. So powerful was this signal that Fed Chairman Martin was called to the LBJ ranch for a dressing-down by President Johnson, who was afraid the higher discount rate would slow the economy.

Today, the discount rate is a relatively minor instrument of monetary policy. Sometimes, a change in the discount rate is used to signal markets of a major policy change. But mostly, the discount rate simply follows market interest rates to prevent banks from making windfall profits by borrowing at a low discount rate and lending at a higher rate on the open market.

Changing Reserve Requirements

If there were no government rules, banks would probably keep only a small fraction of their deposits in the form of reserves. In fact, American banks are today required to keep substantially more reserves than are necessary for meeting customers' needs.

These legal reserve requirements are a crucial part of the mechanism by which the Fed controls the supply of bank money. This subsection describes the nature of legal reserve requirements and shows how they affect the money supply.

Legal Reserve Requirements. We have mentioned that banks are required to hold a minimum amount as non-interest-bearing reserves. Table 26-3 shows current reserve requirements along with the Fed's discretionary power to change reserve requirements. The key concept is the level of *required reserve ratios*. They range from 10 percent against checkable deposits down to zero for personal savings accounts. For convenience in our numerical examples, we use 10 percent reserve ratios, with the understanding that the actual ratio may differ from 10 percent from time to time.

Legal reserve requirements are set high in order to allow the central bank to control the money supply. Reserve requirements help the Fed conduct its open-market operations by ensuring a stable demand for reserves. By setting reserve requirements above the level that banks desire, the central bank can determine the level of reserves and can thereby control the money supply more precisely. The net effect is an increase in the Federal Reserve's control over short-term interest rates.

Put differently, high reserve requirements ensure that banks will want to hold just that legal minimum. The supply of bank money will then be determined by the supply of bank reserves (determined by the Fed through open-market operations) and by the money-supply multiplier (determined by the required reserve ratio). Because the Fed controls both bank reserves and the required reserve ratio, it has (within a small margin of error) control over the money supply.

Changes in Required Reserves. The Fed can change reserve requirements if it wants to change the money supply quickly. For instance, if the Fed wants to tighten money overnight, it can raise the required reserve ratio for the big banks to the 14 percent statutory limit. It might even raise reserve requirements on time deposits.

Exactly how does an increase in required ratios operate to tighten credit? Suppose the required reserve ratio is 10 percent and banks had built up their reserves to meet this requirement. Now suppose the Fed decides to tighten credit, and Congress allows it to raise the required reserve ratio to 20 percent. (This fantastic figure is for algebraic simplicity. The Fed cannot and would not take such a drastic step today.)

Even if the Fed does nothing by way of open-market operations or discount policy to change bank reserves, banks now have to contract their loans and investments greatly—and their deposits as well. As the last chapter showed, bank deposits can now be only 5 times reserves, not 10 times reserves. So there must be a drop by one-half in all deposits!

This painful cut will start to take place quickly. As soon as the new rule raising the requirement to 20 percent goes into effect, banks will find that they have insufficient reserves. They will have to sell some bonds and call in some loans. The bond buyers and borrowers will drain their checking accounts. The process ends only after banks have brought down their deposits to 5 rather than 10 times their reserves.

Such an enormous change in so short a time would lead to very high interest rates, credit rationing, large declines in investment, and massive reductions in GDP and employment. So this extreme example warns that this powerful tool of changing reserve requirements has to be used with great cau-

tion. *Changes in reserve requirements are made extremely sparingly because they cause too large and abrupt a change in policy. Open-market operations can achieve the same results in a less disruptive way.*

Financial Regulation

In addition to using the three major instruments discussed above, the Federal Reserve (with the help of Congress and other government agencies) has historically regulated financial markets by limiting interest rates. Until the 1980s, most interest rates paid by commercial banks were controlled. Banks were not allowed to pay interest on checking accounts, and there were ceilings on interest rates on savings accounts and time deposits.

Regulated interest rates could not survive in competitive markets. Financial institutions devised new types of instruments which lured funds from low-yield deposits. The high interest rates of the late 1970s and early 1980s put further pressure on the system, because banks (which paid 5 percent per year on their savings accounts) had to compete with money market mutual funds (which paid 10 or 15 percent on their deposits). Eventually the regulatory edifice constructed during the Great Depression began to crumble. Congress reacted with the Banking Acts of 1980 and 1982, which largely deregulated interest rates.

The Banking Acts of 1980 and 1982 created a regulatory structure that has largely decontrolled interest rates in financial markets. The analytical basis of the new approach was to separate transactions accounts from nontransactions accounts. The primary purpose of a *transactions account*, such as a checking account, is to serve as a means of payment. A *nontransactions account* is an asset whose primary purpose is to hold funds for the future, not to pay bills (a savings account is an example of a nontransactions account).

Once this distinction had been made, the 1980 and 1982 acts effectively deregulated nontransactions accounts. This legislation phased out interest-rate ceilings for nontransactions accounts in 1986 and set reserve requirements on these deposits at zero for personal accounts and at minimal levels for business accounts. Today, nontransactions accounts earn market interest rates and are effectively outside the regulatory structure of the Federal Reserve.

Transactions assets like checking accounts have with one major exception also been deregulated. The remaining and critical regulation is, as we see in Table 26-3, that these accounts are subject to substantial reserve requirements. As a result of these sweeping changes, most of the interest-rate controls in financial markets have been removed.

An important remaining set of regulations concerns bank solvency. Since the Great Depression, the federal government has stood behind the banks. To instill confidence in the banking system, the government insures bank deposits, inspects the books of banks, and takes over insolvent banks. One important function of government is the guarantee of bank deposits. The government insures up to $100,000 per deposit at banks that are members of the Federal Deposit Insurance Corporation (FDIC). In addition, the Fed and other regulatory agencies inspect banking practices to ensure that the fraud and abuse of the 1980s savings and loan scandal does not recur.

Monetary Policy in the Open Economy

Central banks are particularly important in open economies, where they manage reserve flows and the exchange rate and monitor international financial developments.

Reserve Flows. The dollar is today used extensively in world trade both as a store of value and as a medium of international exchange. Consequently, dollars are widely held abroad by those who export and import with the United States, by foreign and American investors, by those who finance trade and investments between other countries, by speculators and dealers in foreign financial markets, by foreign governments, by central banks, and by international agencies like the International Monetary Fund. Foreigners own hundreds of billions of dollars in U.S. dollar–denominated assets. Because currency itself yields no interest return, foreigners prefer to hold interest-bearing assets (bonds, stocks, etc.). However, to have a medium for buying and selling such earning assets, foreigners do hold some transactions dollars in M_1.

Why are we concerned about international money holdings at this point? The reason is that deposits by foreigners in the banking system increase the total amount of bank reserves in the same way that deposits by domestic residents do. Thus, changes in foreigners' dollar money holdings can set off a chain of expansion or contraction of the U.S. money supply.

For example, say the Japanese decide to deposit $1000 of U.S. currency in U.S. banks. What happens? There is a $1000 increase in reserves in the domestic banking system, as illustrated in Table 25-5(a) in the last chapter. As a result, the banking system can expand deposits tenfold, in this case to $10,000.

Thus, the Fed's control of the nation's M is modified by international disturbances to bank reserves. But the Fed has the power to offset any change in reserves coming from abroad. It affects this by engaging in what is called sterilization. *Sterilization* refers to actions by a central bank that insulate the domestic money supply from international reserve flows. Sterilization usually is accomplished when the central bank implements an open-market operation that reverses the international reserve movement. In practice, the Fed routinely sterilizes international disturbances to reserves.

To summarize:

The central bank's control over bank reserves is subject to disturbances from abroad. These disturbances can, however, be offset if the central bank sterilizes the international flows.

The Role of the Exchange-Rate System.[2] One important element in a country's financial market is its exchange-rate system. As we will see in later chapters, international trade and finance involve the use of different national currencies, which are linked by relative prices called foreign exchange rates. Important exchange-rate systems include floating exchange rates, in which a country's foreign exchange rate is entirely determined by market forces of supply and demand, and fixed exchange rates, in which countries set and defend certain exchange rates.

The United States and Japan operate floating-exchange-rate systems. These countries can pursue their monetary policies independently of other

---

[2] This section contains materials that will be covered more extensively in Chapter 31 and in Part Seven.

countries. This chapter's analysis concerns mainly the operation of monetary policy under floating exchange rates.

Other countries, including countries like France and Germany, have fixed-exchange-rate systems, pegging their currencies to one or more external currencies. The critical point is that *when a country has a fixed exchange rate, it may be required to align its monetary policy with the policies of other countries.* For example, if Belgium pegs its currency to the German mark, with open capital markets it will have to have the same interest rates as those in Germany.

We return to issues of open economies later. They are particularly crucial for understanding monetary policy outside the United States.

The Foreign Desk. The Federal Reserve acts as the government's operating arm in the international financial system. The Fed buys and sells different currencies on foreign exchange markets on behalf of the Treasury. While this task is generally routine, from time to time foreign exchange markets become disorderly, and the Fed, in cooperation with the Treasury, steps in. Sometimes, the Treasury decides that foreign-exchange-rate *intervention* is necessary—because the exchange rate of the dollar is either significantly higher or considerably lower than seems warranted by underlying fundamentals.

The Fed is the agent of the Treasury in such intervention activities.

In addition, the Federal Reserve often takes the lead in working with foreign countries and with international agencies when international financial crises erupt. The international debt crisis, which erupted in 1981, found many middle-income and poor countries, such as Mexico and Brazil, burdened with extremely high levels of interest payments relative to their export earnings. The Fed understood that the debt crisis could lead to a crisis of confidence in the financial system, because many large American banks had worthless foreign loans that were as large as their net worth. The Fed also played an important role in the Mexican loan package from the United States after the peso crisis in 1994–1995.

We have completed our analysis of the money supply. It can be summarized as follows:

The money supply is ultimately determined by the policies of the Fed. By setting reserve requirements and the discount rate, and especially by undertaking open-market operations, the Fed determines the level of reserves and the money supply. Banks and the public are cooperating partners in this process. Banks create money by multiple expansion of reserves; the public agrees to hold money in depository institutions.

B. THE EFFECTS OF MONEY ON OUTPUT AND PRICES

THE MONETARY TRANSMISSION MECHANISM

Having examined the building blocks of monetary theory, we now describe the **monetary transmission mechanism,** the route by which changes in the supply of money are translated into changes in output, employment, prices, and inflation. For concreteness, assume that the Federal Reserve is concerned about inflation and has decided to slow down the economy. There are five steps in the process:

1. *To start the process, the Fed takes steps to reduce bank reserves.* As we saw in Section A of this chapter,

the Fed reduces bank reserves primarily by selling government securities in the open market. This open-market operation changes the balance sheet of the banking system by reducing total bank reserves.

2. *Each dollar reduction in bank reserves produces a multiple contraction in checking deposits, thereby reducing the money supply.* This step was described in Chapter 25, where we saw that changes in reserves lead to a multiplied change in deposits. Since the money supply equals currency plus checking deposits, the reduction in checking deposits reduces the money supply.

3. *The reduction in the money supply will tend to increase interest rates and tighten credit conditions.* With an unchanged demand for money, a reduced supply of money will raise interest rates. In addition, the amount of credit (loans and borrowing) available to people will decline. Interest rates will rise for mortgage borrowers and for businesses that want to build factories, buy new equipment, or add to inventory. Higher interest rates will also lower the values of people's assets, depressing the prices of bonds, stocks, land, and houses.

4. *With higher interest rates and lower wealth, interest-sensitive spending—especially investment—will tend to fall.* The combination of higher interest rates, tighter credit, and reduced wealth will tend to discourage investment and consumption spending. Businesses will scale down their investment plans, as will state and local governments. When a town finds it cannot float its bonds at any reasonable rate, the new road is not built and the new school is postponed. Similarly, consumers decide to buy a smaller house, or to renovate their existing one, when rising mortgage interest rates make monthly payments high relative to monthly income. And in an economy increasingly open to international trade, higher interest rates may raise the foreign exchange rate of the dollar, depressing net exports. Hence, tight money will raise interest rates and reduce spending on interest-sensitive components of aggregate demand.

5. *Finally, the pressures of tight money, by reducing aggregate demand, will reduce income, output, jobs, and inflation.* The aggregate supply-and-demand (or, equivalently, the multiplier) analysis showed how such a drop in investment and other autonomous spending may depress output and employment sharply. Furthermore, as output and employment fall below the levels that would otherwise occur, prices tend to rise less rapidly or even to fall. Inflationary forces subside. If the Fed's diagnosis of inflationary conditions was on target, the drop in output and the rise in unemployment will help relieve inflationary forces.

We can summarize the steps as follows:

R down → M down → i up → I, C, X down → AD down → real GDP down and inflation down

This five-step sequence—from the Fed's changes in commercial-bank reserves, to a multiple change in total M, to changes in interest rates and credit availability, to changes in investment spending that shift aggregate demand, and finally to the response of output, employment, and inflation—is vital to the determination of output and prices. If you look back at Figure 26-1, you will see how each of the five steps fits into our thematic flowchart. We have already explained the first two steps; the balance of this chapter is devoted to analyzing steps 3 through 5.

THE MONEY MARKET

Step 3 in the transmission mechanism is the response of interest rates and credit conditions to changes in the supply of money. Recall from Chapter 25 that the *demand for money* depends primarily on the need to undertake transactions. Households, businesses, and governments hold money so that they may buy goods, services, and other items. In addition, some part of the demand for M derives from the need for a supersafe and highly liquid asset.

The *supply of money* is jointly determined by the private banking system and the nation's central bank. The central bank, through open-market operations and other instruments, provides reserves to the banking system. Commercial banks then create deposits out of the central-bank reserves. By manipulating reserves, the central bank can determine the money supply within a narrow margin of error.

Supply of and Demand for Money

The supply of and demand for money jointly determine the market interest rates. Figure 26-4 shows the total quantity of money (M) on the horizontal axis and the nominal interest rate (i) on the vertical axis. The supply curve is drawn as a vertical line on the assumption that the Federal Reserve keeps the money supply constant at M^* in Figure 26-4.

In addition, we show the money demand schedule as a downward-sloping curve because the holdings of money decline as interest rates rise. At higher interest rates, people and businesses shift more of their funds to higher-yield assets and away from low-yield or zero-yield money, as described in the last chapter.

The intersection of the supply and demand schedules in Figure 26-4 determines the market

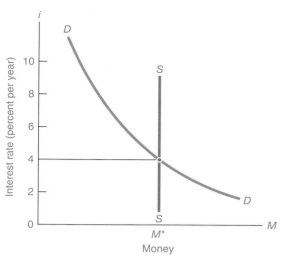

FIGURE 26-4. The Money Market

The interaction of the demand for and supply of money determines the interest rate. The Fed has a money target at M^*. The public has a downward-sloping money demand schedule. Here the money market is in equilibrium with a nominal interest rate of 4 percent per year.

interest rate. Recall that interest rates are the prices paid for the use of money. Interest rates are determined in **money markets**, which are the markets where short-term funds are lent and borrowed. Important interest rates include short-term rates such as the rates on 3-month Treasury bills and on short-term commercial paper (notes issued by large corporations) and the Federal Funds rate that banks pay each other for the overnight use of bank reserves. Longer-term interest rates include 10-year or 20-year government and corporate bonds and mortgages on real estate. (See Figure 25-2 for a graph of recent trends in interest rates.)

In Figure 26-4, the equilibrium interest rate is 4 percent per year. Only at 4 percent is the level of the money supply that the Fed has targeted consistent with the desired money holdings of the public. At a higher interest rate, there would be excessive money balances. People would get rid of their excessive money holdings by buying bonds and other financial instruments, thereby lowering market interest rates toward the equilibrium 4 percent rate. (What would happen at an interest rate of 2 percent?)

Money Market Shifts. To understand the monetary transmission mechanism, we need to see how changes in the money market affect interest rates. Suppose that the Federal Reserve becomes worried about inflation and tightens monetary policy by selling securities and reducing the money supply.

The impact of a monetary tightening is shown in Figure 26-5(*a*) on page 506. The leftward shift of the money supply schedule means that market interest rates must rise to induce people to swap their money for bonds and other nonmonetary assets. The gap between E and N shows the extent of excess demand for money at the old interest rate. Interest rates rise until the new equilibrium is attained, shown in Figure 26-5(*a*) at point E', with a new and higher interest rate of 6 percent per year.

Another disturbance might come from higher prices. Suppose the money supply is held constant by the Fed. However, because of inflation, the money needed to finance transactions increases with no change in real GDP. In this case, shown in Figure 26-5(*b*), the demand for money would increase, shifting the money demand curve to the right from DD to $D'D'$ and leading to an increase in equilibrium interest rates. (To check your understanding, make sure you can answer question 1 at the end of the chapter.)

To summarize our findings about the money market:

The money market is affected by a combination of (1) the public's desire to hold money (represented by the demand-for-money DD curve) and (2) the Fed's monetary policy (which is shown as a fixed money supply, SS). Their interaction determines the market interest rate, i. A tighter monetary policy shifts the SS curve to the left, raising market interest rates. An increase in the nation's output or price level shifts the DD curve to the right and raises interest rates. Monetary easing or a money-demand decline has the opposite effects.

THE MONETARY MECHANISM

Every day, the newspapers and television feature reports on money markets and monetary policy, analyzing how monetary affairs affect interest rates, foreign exchange rates, the trade and budget deficits, output, employment, inflation, and virtually every macroeconomic variable. Newspaper

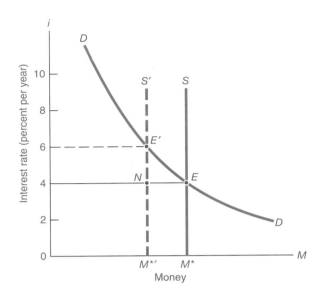

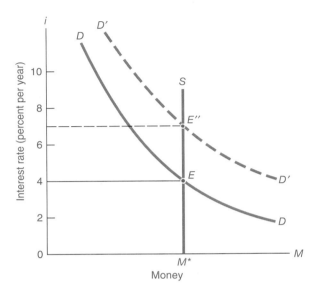

FIGURE 26-5. Changes in Monetary Policy or Prices Affect Interest Rates

In (**a**), the Federal Reserve contracts the money supply in response to fears of rising prices. The lower money supply produces an excess demand for money, shown by the gap *NE*. As the public adjusts its portfolio, interest rates rise to the new equilibrium at *E'*.

In (**b**), the demand for money has increased because of a run-up in the price level with real output held constant. The higher demand for money drives up market interest rates until the quantity of money demanded equals the supply at *M**.

accounts of money markets often contain stories like the following:

> Alan Greenspan has launched yet another monetary missile. Last week, for the fourth time in three months, the central bank hiked short-term interest rates in an effort to blast inflation off his radar screen. But his target, growing price pressure, is barely a blip. (*U.S. News and World Report*)

> Federal Reserve Chairman Greenspan and Senate Banking Committee Democrats clashed today as Senators accused the Fed of putting the skids on economic growth. (*National Journal Congress Daily*)

> JACKSON HOLE, WYOMING. At a gathering here of the Federal Reserve's top officials . . . there was a widespread consensus that inflation has at last been tamed—and that it is time to think about how and whether to exterminate it. (*New York Times*)

Underlying these statements are views about the way the Federal Reserve operates, the way money

affects the economy, and the way political leaders and the populace want to shape monetary policy. Let us look at the impact of changing monetary conditions by using the multiplier model. We then will examine the transmission mechanism by using the aggregate demand-and-supply framework.

Graphical Analysis of Monetary Policy

Figure 26-6 illustrates the effects of a monetary expansion upon economic activity. Part (*a*), in the lower left, shows the money market; (*b*), in the lower right, shows the determination of investment; and (*c*), in the upper right, shows the determination of aggregate demand and GDP by the multiplier mechanism. We can think of the causality as moving counterclockwise from the money market through investment to the determination of aggregate demand and GDP as a whole.

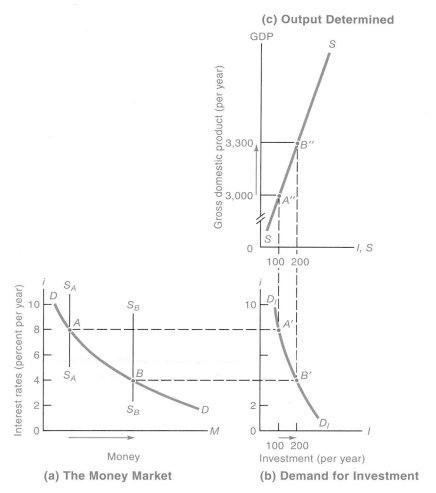

FIGURE 26-6. Central Bank Determines the Money Supply, Changing Interest Rates and Investment, Thereby Affecting GDP

When the Fed raises the money supply, from S_A to S_B, interest rates fall as people increase their money balances, moving down the money demand schedule in (**a**).

Lower interest rates reduce the cost of investment, thus encouraging business purchases of plant and equipment and consumer purchases of houses. The economy moves down the demand-for-investment schedule from A' to B' in (**b**).

By the multiplier mechanism in (**c**), the higher investment raises aggregate demand and GDP from A'' to B''.

Starting at the lower left, in Figure 26-6(a), we see the demand for and supply of money that were depicted in Figures 26-4 and 26-5. For purposes of the present discussion, assume that the money supply schedule was initially S_A and that the interest rate was 8 percent per year. If the Fed was concerned about a looming recession, it might increase the money supply by making open-market purchases, shifting the curve to S_B. In the case shown in Figure 26-6(a), market interest rates would thereby fall to 4 percent per year.

Figure 26-6(b) picks up the story to show how lower interest rates increase spending on interest-sensitive components of aggregate demand. We saw in Chapter 22 that a decline in interest rates would induce businesses to increase their spending on plant, equipment, and inventories. The effects of eased monetary policy are quickly seen in the housing market, where lower interest rates mean lower monthly mortgage payments on the typical house, encouraging households to increase housing purchases.

In addition, consumption spending increases, both because lower interest rates generally increase the value of wealth—as stock, bond, and housing prices tend to rise—and because consumers tend to spend more on automobiles and other big-ticket consumer durables when interest rates are low and credit is plentiful. Moreover, as we will explore in a moment, lower interest rates tend to reduce the foreign exchange rate on the dollar, thereby increasing the level of net exports. We see, then, how lower interest rates lead to increased spending in many different areas of the economy.

These consequences are evident in Figure 26-6(b), where the drop in interest rates (caused by the increase in the money supply) leads to a rise in investment from A' to B'. In this case, we should construe "investment" in the very broad sense sketched a moment ago: it includes not only business investment but also consumer durables and residences, as well as net foreign investment in the form of net exports.

Finally, Figure 26-6(c) shows the impact of changes in investment in the multiplier model. This diagram is really Figure 24-2 turned on its side. Recall from Chapter 24 that, in the simplest multiplier model, equilibrium output is attained when desired saving equals desired investment. In Figure 26-6(c), we have shown this relationship by drawing the savings schedule as the SS schedule; this line represents the desired level of saving (measured along the horizontal axis) as a function of GDP on the vertical axis. Equilibrium GDP is attained at that level where the investment demand from panel (b) equals the desired saving from the SS schedule.

The initial level of investment was 100, as read off at A' in panel (b), producing a level of GDP of 3000. After easier money has lowered the interest rate from 8 to 4 percent, investment rises to 200 at point B'. This higher level of investment raises aggregate spending to the new equilibrium at B'' in panel (c) with a new equilibrium GDP of 3300.

What has occurred? The rise in the money supply from S_A to S_B lowered the interest rate from A to B; this caused investment to rise from A' to B'; and this in turn, acting through the multiplier, led to a rise in GDP from A'' to B''.

Such is the route by which monetary policy acts through intermediate targets like the money supply and interest rates to affect its ultimate targets.

Economic policy in the recession of 1982: As a result of low unemployment and a second oil-price shock, annual inflation in 1979 surged to 13 percent. Subsequently, the Federal Reserve in 1979 undertook a "monetarist experiment," concentrating on the growth of reserves and the money supply rather than on interest rates. It hoped that a clear and decisive strategy of targeting the monetary aggregates would help slow the unacceptable inflation.

The shift to targeting monetary aggregates in 1979 was highly controversial. The immediate result was a sharp reduction in the growth of the money supply and a consequent tightening of monetary policy. This led to an increase of market interest rates to levels not seen since the Civil War. As interest rates rose, investment and other interest-sensitive spending fell sharply, which led to the deepest recession since the 1930s. The policy was definitely successful in reducing inflation to 4 percent by 1982.

As the recession deepened, the Fed worried that its tight monetary policies had gone too far. Unemployment was over 10 percent, and Congress was up in arms. We can use this incident to see how the Fed conducts its monetary policies—tuning in as the Fed decided to relax its monetary policy.

Let's begin with the August 1982 directive. In the midst of the deepest recession of the postwar period, the FOMC began with its review of the economy:[3]

> The information reviewed at this meeting suggests only a little further advance in real GDP in the current quarter, following a relatively small increase in the second quarter, while prices on the average are continuing to rise more slowly than in 1981.

---

[3] The FOMC quotations are from the *Federal Reserve Bulletin*, which contains monthly reports on Federal Reserve activities and other important financial developments.

What objectives did the Fed establish for monetary policy? It stated:

> The Federal Open Market Committee seeks to foster monetary and financial conditions that will help to reduce inflation, promote a resumption of growth in output on a sustainable basis, and contribute to a sustainable pattern of international transactions.

The FOMC then gave the following operational directive to the New York Federal Reserve Bank in August 1982:

> In the short run, the Committee continues to seek behavior of reserve aggregates consistent with growth of M_1 and M_2 from June to September [1982] at annual rates of about 5 percent and about 9 percent respectively.

How should we interpret these words? They are saying that, in light of the sharp recession of 1982, the Fed concluded that its monetary policy had become overly restrictive. Also, the definitions of the monetary aggregates became confused at this time because of the addition of a number of new assets (such as interest-bearing checking accounts) to M_1 and M_2. The ambiguity about the meaning of the M's meant that basing policy only on M movement was unwise.

The Fed therefore abandoned its strict monetary targeting in the fall of 1982. Interest rates fell sharply, with the 3-month Treasury-bill rate falling from 15 percent in the middle of 1981 to 8 percent at the end of 1982. As a result, real spending on housing almost doubled from 1982 to 1984, and the economy began to recover sharply in 1983.

The monetary policies of this period were extremely controversial at that time. In retrospect, many observers believe that they were a good "investment in stable prices."

Monetary Policy in an Open Economy

The monetary transmission mechanism in the United States has evolved over the last two decades as the economy became more open and changes occurred in the exchange-rate system. The relationship between monetary policy and foreign trade has always been a major concern for smaller and more open economies like Canada and Britain. However, after the introduction of flexible exchange rates in 1973 and in the presence of increasing cross-border linkages, international trade and finance have come to play a new and central role in U.S. macroeconomic policy.

Let's review briefly the new route using the historical episode just analyzed. When the Federal Reserve tightened money in the 1979–1982 period, this process drove up interest rates on assets denominated in U.S. dollars. Attracted by higher dollar interest rates, investors bought dollar securities, driving up the floating foreign exchange rate on the dollar. The high exchange rate on the dollar encouraged imports into the United States and hurt U.S. exports. Net exports fell, reducing aggregate demand. This had the impact of both lowering real GDP and lowering the rate of inflation.

We will study the international aspects of macroeconomics in Chapter 31. For now, the main point to grasp is that foreign trade opens up another link in the monetary transmission mechanism. Monetary policy has the same impact on international trade as it has on domestic investment—tight money lowers foreign and domestic investment, thereby depressing output and prices. *The international-trade impact of monetary policy reinforces the domestic-economy impact.*

Monetary Policy in the *AD-AS* Framework

The three-part diagram in Figure 26-6 illustrates how an increase in the money supply would lead to an increase in aggregate demand. We can now show the effect on the overall macroeconomic equilibrium by using aggregate supply and demand curves.

The increase in aggregate demand produced by an increase in the supply of money causes a rightward shift of the *AD* curve as drawn in Figure 26-7 on page 510. This shift illustrates a monetary expansion in the presence of unemployed resources, with a relatively flat *AS* curve. The monetary expansion shifts aggregate demand from *AD* to *AD'*, shifting the equilibrium from *E* to *E'*. This example demonstrates how monetary expansion can increase aggregate demand and have a powerful impact on real output.

The sequence therefore runs as follows:

Monetary expansion bids down market interest rates. This stimulates interest-sensitive spending on business investment, housing, net exports, and the like. Aggregate demand increases via the multiplier mechanism, raising output and prices above the levels they would otherwise attain. Therefore, the basic sequence is

$$M \text{ up} \rightarrow i \text{ down} \rightarrow I,\ C,\ X \text{ up} \rightarrow AD \text{ up} \rightarrow$$
$$GDP \text{ up and } P \text{ up}$$

But never forget the role of unemployed resources. The effect of an AD shift in a fully employed economy can be illustrated in Figure 26-7. Pencil in an AD'' curve going through E'' on the steep segment of the AS curve; then pencil in a monetary expansion as a higher AD'''. Note how the monetary expansion would have little impact on real output. In a fully employed economy, the higher money stock would be chasing the same amount of output and would therefore mainly end up raising prices.

To clinch your understanding of this vital sequence, work through the opposite case of a monetary contraction. Say that the Federal Reserve decides, as it did in 1979–1982 and again in 1994, to raise interest rates, slow the economy, and reduce inflation. You can trace this sequence in Figure 26-6 by reversing the direction of the monetary policy, thereby seeing how money, interest rates, investment, and aggregate demand interact when monetary policy is tightened. Then see how a leftward shift of the AD curve in Figure 26-7 would reduce both output and prices.

Monetary Effects in the Long Run

Many economists believe that changes in the supply of money in the long run will mainly affect the price level with little or no impact upon real output. We can understand this point by analyzing the effects of monetary changes with different-shape AS curves. As shown in Figure 26-7, monetary changes will affect aggregate demand and will tend to change real GDP in the short run when there are unemployed resources and the AS curve is relatively flat.

In our analysis of aggregate supply in the following chapters, we will see that the AS curve tends to be vertical or near-vertical in the long run as wages and prices adjust. Because of the price-wage adjustments and near-vertical AS curve, the output effects of AD shifts will diminish, and the price effects will tend to dominate in the long run. This means that <u>as prices</u> <u>and wages become more flexible in the long run,</u>

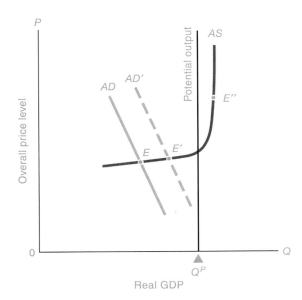

Expansionary Monetary Policy

FIGURE 26-7. An Expansionary Monetary Policy Shifts AD Curve to the Right, Raising Output and Prices

Earlier discussion and Figure 26-6 showed how an increase in the money supply would lead to an increase in investment and net exports and thereby to a multiplied increase in aggregate demand. This results in a rightward shift of the AD curve.

In the Keynesian region where the AS curve is relatively flat, a monetary expansion has its primary effect on real output, with only a small effect on prices. In a fully employed economy, the AS curve is near-vertical (shown at point E''), and a monetary expansion will primarily raise prices and nominal GDP with little effect on real GDP. Can you see why in the long run money may have little impact on real output?

money-supply changes tend to have a larger impact on prices and a smaller impact on output.

What is the intuition behind this difference between the short run and the long run? We can construct a highly simplified example to see the difference. Suppose we start out as in Figure 26-6, with a nominal GDP of 3000 and stable prices; then a monetary expansion that increases the money supply by 10 percent might increase nominal GDP by 10 percent to 3300. Studies by Robert J. Gordon and others indicate that, in the short run, "nominal GDP changes have been divided consistently, with two-thirds taking the form of output change and the remaining one-third the form of price change." Consequently, in the first year, the money-supply expansion might increase real GDP around 7 percent and increase prices around 3 percent. (Or, as is illustrated in Figure 26-7, with a gently sloping *AS* curve we see a large *Q* response and a small *P* response to the *AD* shift.)

As time passes, however, wages and prices begin to adjust more completely to the higher price and output levels. Higher demand in both labor and product markets would raise wages and prices; wages would be adjusted to reflect the higher cost of living; cost-of-living provisions in contracts would raise wages and prices even further. After a second year, prices might rise another 1 or 2 percent, with output then being only 5 or 6 percent above its original level. In the third year, prices might rise again while output falls somewhat. Where would it end? It might continue over a period of years and decades until prices had risen by fully 10 percent and output was back to the original level. Thus, the monetary policy would have raised prices and wages by about 10 percent and real output would be unchanged.

If all adjustments eventually come in prices, all nominal magnitudes are increased by 10 percent while all real magnitudes are unchanged. Nominal magnitudes like the GDP deflator, the CPI, nominal GDP, wages, the money supply, consumption, dollar imports, the dollar value of wealth, and so forth, are 10 percent higher. But real GDP, real consumption, real wages, real incomes, and the real value of wealth are all unchanged by the monetary policy. In such a case, then, we say that *money is neutral.*

A word of caution is in order: The scenario that money changes lead to proportionate changes in all nominal magnitudes but no changes in real variables is intuitively plausible and supported by certain empirical evidence. But it is not a universal law. The long run may be a period of many decades; intervening events may throw the economy off the idealized long-run trajectory; and interest-rate changes along the path might have an irreversible impact upon the ultimate outcome. The long-run neutrality of money is therefore only a tendency and not a universal law.

Note as well that the discussion of the role of monetary policy has taken place without reference to fiscal policy. In reality, whatever the philosophical predilections of the government, every advanced economy simultaneously conducts both fiscal and monetary policies. Each policy has strengths and weaknesses. In the chapters that follow, we return to an integrated consideration of the roles of monetary and fiscal policies both in combating the business cycle and in promoting economic growth.

From Aggregate Demand to Aggregate Supply

We have completed our introductory analysis of the determinants of aggregate demand. To recapitulate our findings: We examined the foundations of aggregate demand and saw that *AD is determined by exogenous or autonomous factors, such as investment and net exports, along with government policies, such as monetary and fiscal policies. In the short run, changes in these factors lead to changes in spending and to changes in both output and prices.*

In today's volatile world, economies are exposed to shocks from both inside and outside their borders. Wars, revolutions, debt crises, oil shocks, and government miscalculations have led to periods of high inflation or high unemployment or both in times of stagflation. Because there is no automatic self-correcting mechanism that quickly eliminates macroeconomic fluctuations, governments today take responsibility for moderating the swings of the business cycle. But even the wisest governments cannot eliminate unemployment and inflation in the face of all the shocks to which an economy is exposed.

We now turn to issues of economic growth, aggregate supply, and economic policy. We begin with an analysis of the process of long-run economic growth, which will deepen our understanding of the determinants of potential output and aggregate supply. We then tackle the interrelated topics of inflation and unemployment and see how modern market economies are severely constrained by the need to maintain stable prices. We broaden our horizon to include the economics of open economies. Finally, we return to the pressing dilemmas of macroeconomic policy today: fiscal policy and the government debt, the interrelation between fiscal policy and monetary policy, and the need to promote long-term economic growth.

SUMMARY

A. Central Banking and the Federal Reserve System

1. The Federal Reserve System is a central bank, a bank for bankers. Its objectives are to allow sustainable economic growth, maintain a high level of employment, ensure orderly financial markets, and above all to preserve reasonable price stability.

2. The Federal Reserve System (or "Fed") was created in 1913 to control the nation's money and credit and to act as the "lender of last resort." It is run by the Board of Governors and the Federal Open Market Committee (FOMC). The Fed acts as an independent government agency and has great discretion in determining monetary policy.

3. The Fed has three major policy instruments: (*a*) open-market operations, (*b*) the discount rate on bank borrowing, and (*c*) legal reserve requirements on depository institutions. Using these instruments, the Fed affects intermediate targets, such as the level of bank reserves, market interest rates, and the money supply. All these operations aim to improve the economy's performance with respect to the ultimate objectives of monetary policy: achieving the best combination of low inflation, low unemployment, rapid GDP growth, and orderly financial markets. In addition, the Fed along with other federal agencies must backstop the domestic and international financial system in times of crisis.

4. The most important instrument of monetary policy is the Fed's open-market operations. Sales by the Fed of government securities in the open market reduce the Fed's assets and liabilities and thereby reduce the reserves of banks. The effect is a decrease in banks' reserve base for deposits. People end up with less *M* and more government bonds. Open-market purchases do the opposite, ultimately expanding *M* by increasing bank reserves.

5. Outflows of international reserves can reduce reserves and *M* unless offset by central-market purchases of bonds. Inflows have the opposite effects unless offset. The process of offsetting international flows is called sterilization. In recent years, the Fed has routinely sterilized international reserve movements. In open economies with fixed exchange rates, monetary policies must be closely aligned with those in other countries.

B. The Effects of Money on Output and Prices

6. If the Fed desires to slow the growth of output, the five-step sequence goes thus:

a. The Fed reduces bank reserves through open-market operations.

b. Each dollar reduction of bank reserves produces a multiple contraction of bank money and the money supply.

c. In the money market, a reduction in the money supply moves along an unchanged money demand schedule, raising interest rates, restricting the amount and terms of credit, and tightening money.

d. Tight money reduces investment and other interest-sensitive items of spending like consumer durables or net exports.

e. The reduction in investment and other spending reduces aggregate demand by the familiar multiplier mechanism. The lower level of aggregate demand lowers output and the price level or inflation.

The sequence is summarized by

$$R \text{ down} \rightarrow M \text{ down} \rightarrow i \text{ up} \rightarrow I, C, X \text{ down} \rightarrow$$
$$AD \text{ down} \rightarrow \text{real GDP down and inflation down}$$

7. Although the monetary mechanism is often explained in terms of money affecting "investment," in fact the monetary mechanism is an extremely rich and complex process whereby changes in interest rates and asset prices influence a wide variety of elements of spending. These sectors include housing, affected by changing mortgage interest rates and housing prices; business investment, affected by changing interest rates and stock prices; spending on consumer durables, influenced by interest rates and credit availability; state and local capital spending, affected by interest rates; and net exports, determined by the effects of interest rates upon foreign exchange rates.

8. In an open economy, the international-trade linkage reinforces the domestic impacts of monetary policy. In a regime of flexible exchange rates, changes in monetary policy affect the exchange rate and net exports, adding yet another facet to the monetary mechanism. The trade link tends to reinforce the impact of monetary policy, operating in the same direction on net exports as it does on domestic investment.

9. Monetary policy may have different effects in the short run and the long run. In the short run, with a relatively flat *AS* curve, most of the change in *AD* will affect output and only a small part will affect prices. In the longer run, as the *AS* curve becomes more nearly

vertical, monetary shifts lead predominantly to changes in the price level and much less to output changes. In the polar case where money-supply changes affect only nominal variables and have no effects on real variables, we say money is neutral. Most real-world monetary shifts have left real economic effects in their wake.

CONCEPTS FOR REVIEW

Central Banking

bank reserves
Federal Reserve balance sheet
open-market purchases and sales
discount rate, borrowings from Fed
legal reserve requirements
FOMC, Board of Governors
policy instruments, intermediate targets, ultimate objectives

The Monetary Transmission Mechanism

demand for and supply of money
five-step monetary transmission mechanism:
  reserve change
  reserves to money
  money to interest rates
  interest rates to investment
  investment to GDP

interest-sensitive components of spending
monetary policy in the *AS-AD* framework
R down $\rightarrow M$ down $\rightarrow i$ up $\rightarrow I$ down $\rightarrow AD$ down $\rightarrow$ GDP down and P down
monetary policy in the short run and the long run
"neutrality" of money

QUESTIONS FOR DISCUSSION

1. Using Figure 26-5, work through each of the following:
   a. The Federal Reserve has decided that unemployment is rising too sharply and wants to reverse this trend by expanding the money supply. What steps must the Fed take to expand money? What will be the impact on the money supply curve? What is the reaction in money markets?
   b. As a result of a rapid economic expansion abroad, exports rise and real GDP increases. What happens to the demand for money? What is the impact upon the market interest rate?
   c. With the spread of automated teller machines (ATMs), people find they need lower "precautionary" balances of currency. The amount of money demanded at each level of interest rate and GDP falls. The Fed is uncertain about the significance of this behavior and therefore keeps the money supply constant. What will be the impact of the asset switch on money supply and demand? On market interest rates?

2. Suppose you are the Chairperson of the Fed's Board of Governors at a time when the economy is beginning to overheat and you are called to testify before a congressional committee. Write an explanation for an interrogating senator outlining how you would proceed to maintain stable prices.

3. Consider the balance sheet of the Fed in Table 26-1. Construct a corresponding balance sheet for banks (like the one in Table 25-3 in the last chapter) assuming that reserve requirements are 10 percent on

checking accounts and zero on everything else.
   a. Construct a new set of balance sheets, assuming the Fed sells $1 billion in government securities by open-market operations.
   b. Construct another set of balance sheets to show what happens when the Fed increases reserve requirements to 20 percent.
   c. Assume banks borrow $1 billion of reserves from the Fed. How will this action change the balance sheets?

4. Study the three newspaper excerpts on page 506. Using the theories developed in the last few chapters, explain the reasoning behind each statement.

5. Using Figure 26-6, explain how the tight-money policies after 1979 lowered GDP. Also, explain each of the steps in words.

6. After the reunification of Germany, payments to rebuild the east led to a major expansion of aggregate demand in Germany. The German central bank responded by slowing money growth and driving German real interest rates extremely high. Trace through why this German monetary tightening would be expected to lead to a depreciation of the dollar. Explain why the depreciation would stimulate economic activity in the United States. Also, explain why European countries that had "pegged" their currencies to the German mark would find themselves plunged into deep recessions as German interest rates rose and pulled other European rates up with them.

PART SIX

ECONOMIC GROWTH AND MACROECONOMIC POLICY

CHAPTER 27
THE PROCESS OF ECONOMIC GROWTH

The Industrial Revolution was not an episode with a beginning and an end. . . . It is still going on.

E. J. Hobsbawm, **The Age of Revolution** *(1962)*

If you read the daily economic or business news, it is dominated by issues such as the hourly movements of the stock market, sage commentary on the actions of the Federal Reserve, the monthly unemployment rate, or the quarterly growth in GDP. But as important as these events are for job hunters or investors, they are only small ripples on the longer wave of economic growth. Year in and year out, advanced economies like the United States accumulate larger quantities of capital equipment, push out the frontiers of technological knowledge, and become steadily more productive. Over the long run of decades and generations, living standards as measured by output per capita or consumption per household are primarily determined by the level of productivity of a country.

Part Five focused primarily on the role of aggregate demand in determining the level of output in the short run. This analysis showed how, in an economy with underutilized resources, governments could tame the business cycle by prudent application of monetary and fiscal measures.

But aggregate demand is not the whole story, and the following chapters will examine the role of aggregate supply. This chapter begins with a survey of the general theory of economic growth and then reviews the historical trends in economic activity with particular application to the United States. The next chapter examines the plight of the developing countries, struggling to reach the levels of affluence in the West. Figure 27-1 presents an overview of the growth chapters, using our familiar flowchart.

The Long-Term Significance of Growth

Look at the inside front cover of this book, where you will see the advance of real (or inflation-corrected) output over the twentieth century. You can see that real GDP has grown *by a factor of almost 18* since 1900. This is perhaps the central economic fact of this century. Continuing rapid economic growth has enabled advanced industrial countries to provide more of everything to their citizens—better food and bigger homes, more resources for medical care and pollution control, universal education for children and comprehensive income support for retirees.

Nations continue to view economic growth as a critical economic and political objective. As countries like Japan grow rapidly, they also rise in the pecking order of nations and serve as role models for other countries seeking the path to affluence. By contrast, countries in economic decline often experience political and social turmoil. The recent revolutions in Eastern Europe and the Soviet Union were sparked by economic stagnation and low economic growth as compared to that of their Western neighbors. Economic growth is the single most important factor in the economic success of nations in the long run.

517

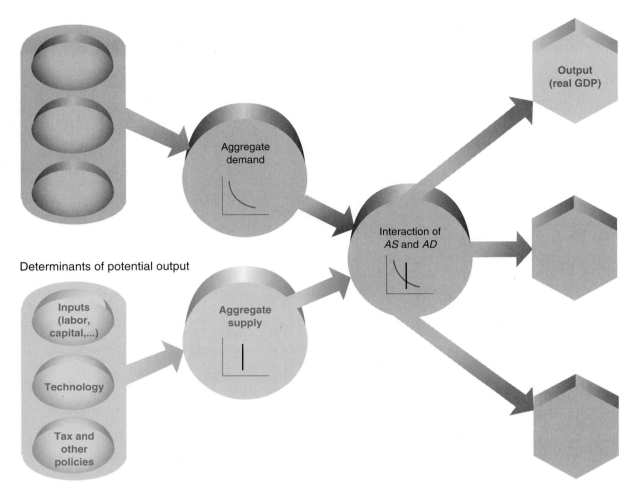

FIGURE 27-1. Economic Growth Is Key to Long-Term Living Standards

In the long run, a nation's economic fortunes depend upon the growth of its potential output. This chapter and the next examine the trends in long-term growth along with the theories that explain the basic trends.

A. THEORIES OF ECONOMIC GROWTH

Let's begin with a careful definition of exactly what we mean by economic growth: ***Economic growth*** *represents the expansion of a country's potential GDP or national output.* Put differently, economic growth occurs when a nation's production-possibility frontier (*PPF*) shifts outward (recall the graphs of the growing *PPF*s in Chapter 1). A closely related concept is the growth rate of output per person. This determines the rate at which the country's standard of living is rising.

Period	GDP	Average annual growth rate in:		
		GDP per person-hour	Labor force	Total hours worked
1870–1913	2.5	1.6	1.2	0.9
1913–1950	1.9	1.8	0.8	0.1
1950–1973	4.9	4.5	1.0	0.3
1973–1990	2.5	2.7	1.1	−0.1

TABLE 27-1. Patterns of Growth in 16 Industrial Countries

Over the last century, major high-income countries like the United States, Germany, France, and Japan have grown sharply. Output has grown faster than inputs of labor, reflecting increases in capital and technological advance. [Source: Angus Maddison, *Phases of Capitalist Development* (Oxford, 1982), updated by authors from data from the World Bank and other publications.]

What are the long-term patterns of economic growth in high-income countries? Table 27-1 shows the history of economic growth since 1870 for 16 high-income countries including the major countries of North America and Western Europe, Japan, and Australia. We see the steady growth of output over this period. Even more important for living standards is the growth in output per hour worked, which moves closely with the increase in living standards. Over the entire period, output per worker grew by an average rate of 2.4 percent annually, which compounds to a growth by a factor of 16 over the 120-year period.

What were the major forces behind this growth? What can nations do to speed up their economic growth rate? And what are the prospects for the twenty-first century, particularly given the declining U.S. savings rate along with the possibility of tighter environmental constraints? These are the issues that must be confronted by economic-growth analysis.

THE FOUR WHEELS OF GROWTH

What is the recipe for economic growth? To begin with, successful countries need not follow the same path. Britain, for example, became the world economic leader in the 1800s by pioneering the Industrial Revolution, inventing steam engines and railroads, and emphasizing free trade. Japan, by contrast, came to the economic-growth race later. It made its mark by first imitating foreign technologies and protecting domestic industries from imports and then by developing tremendous expertise in manufacturing and electronics.

Even though their specific paths may differ, all rapidly growing countries share certain common traits. The same fundamental process of economic growth and development that helped shape Britain and Japan is at work today in developing countries like China and India. Indeed, economists who have studied growth have found that the engine of economic progress must ride on the same four wheels, no matter how rich or poor the country. These four wheels, or factors of growth, are:

- Human resources (labor supply, education, discipline, motivation)
- Natural resources (land, minerals, fuels, environmental quality)
- Capital formation (machines, factories, roads)
- Technology (science, engineering, management, entrepreneurship)

Often, economists write the relationship in terms of an *aggregate production function* (or *APF*), which relates total national output to the inputs and technology. Algebraically, the *APF* is

$$Q = AF(K, L, R)$$

where Q = output, K = productive services of capital, L = labor inputs, R = natural-resource inputs, A represents the level of technology in the economy, and F is the production function. As the inputs of capital, labor, or resources rise, we would expect that output would increase, although output will probably show diminishing returns to additional inputs of production factors. We can think of the role of technology as augmenting the productivity of inputs. **Productivity** denotes the ratio of output to a weighted average of inputs. As technology (*A*) improves through new inventions or the adoption of technologies from abroad, this advance allows a country to produce more output with the same level of inputs.

Let's now see how each of the four factors contributes to growth.

Human Resources

Labor inputs consist of quantities of workers and of the skills of the work force. Many economists believe that the quality of labor inputs—the skills, knowledge, and discipline of the labor force—is the single most important element in economic growth. A country might buy the most modern telecommunications devices, computers, electricity-generating equipment, and fighter aircraft. However, these capital goods can be effectively used and maintained only by skilled and trained workers. Improvements in literacy, health, and discipline, and most recently the ability to use computers, add greatly to the productivity of labor.

Natural Resources

The second classical factor of production is natural resources. The important resources here are arable land, oil and gas, forests, water, and mineral resources. Some high-income countries like Canada and Norway have grown primarily on the basis of their ample resource base, with large output in agriculture, fisheries, and forestry. Similarly, the United States, with its temperate farmlands, is the world's largest producer and exporter of grains.

But the possession of natural resources is not necessary for economic success in the modern world. New York City prospers primarily on its high-density service industries. Many countries that have virtually no natural resources, such as Japan, have thrived by concentrating on sectors that depend more on labor and capital than on indigenous resources. Indeed, tiny Hong Kong, with but a tiny fraction of the land area of resource-rich Russia, actually has a larger volume of international trade than does that giant country.

Capital Formation

Recall that tangible capital includes structures like roads and power plants, equipment like trucks and computers, and stocks of inventories. The most dramatic stories in economic history often involve the accumulation of capital. In the nineteenth century, the transcontinental railroads of North America brought commerce to the American heartland, which had been living in isolation. In this century, waves of investment in automobiles, roads, and power plants increased productivity and provided the infrastructure which created entire new industries. Many believe that computers and the information superhighway will do for the twenty-first century what railroads and highways did in earlier times.

Accumulating capital, as we have seen, requires a sacrifice of current consumption over many years. Countries that grow rapidly tend to invest heavily in new capital goods; in the most rapidly growing countries, 10 to 20 percent of output may go into net capital formation. By contrast, many economists believe that the low national savings rate in the United States—only 4 percent of output in 1996—poses a major economic problem for the country.

When we think of capital, we must not concentrate only on computers and factories. Many investments are undertaken only by governments and lay the framework for a thriving private sector. These investments are called **social overhead capital** and consist of the large-scale projects that precede trade and commerce. Roads, irrigation and water projects, and public-health measures are important examples. All these involve large investments that tend to be "indivisible," or lumpy, and sometimes have increasing returns to scale. These projects generally involve external economies, or spillovers that private firms cannot capture, so the government must step in to ensure that these social overhead or infrastructure investments are effectively undertaken.

Technological Change and Innovation

In addition to the three classical factors discussed above, technological advance has been a vital fourth ingredient in the rapid growth of living standards. Historically, growth has definitely not been a process of simple replication, adding rows of steel mills or power plants next to each other. Rather, a never-ending stream of inventions and technological advances led to a vast improvement in the production possibilities of Europe, North America, and Japan.

Technological change denotes changes in the processes of production or introduction of new

Factor in economic growth	Examples
Human resources	Size of labor force Education, skills, discipline
Natural resources	Oil and gas Soils and climate
Capital formation	Equipment and factories Social overhead capital
Technology and entrepreneurship	Quality of scientific and engineering knowledge Managerial know-how Rewards for innovation

TABLE 27-2. The Four Wheels of Progress

Economic growth inevitably rides on the four wheels of labor, natural resources, capital, and technology. But the wheels may differ greatly among countries, and some countries combine them more effectively than others.

products or services. Process inventions that have greatly increased productivity were the steam engine, the generation of electricity, the internal-combustion engine, the wide-body jet, the photo-copier machine, and the fax machine. Fundamental product inventions include the telephone, the radio, the airplane, the phonograph, the television, and the VCR. The most dramatic technological developments of the modern era are occurring in electronics and computers, where today's tiny notebook computers can outperform the fastest computer of the 1960s. These inventions provide the most spectacular examples of technological change, but technological change is in fact a continuous process of small and large improvements, as witnessed by the fact that the United States issues over 100,000 new patents annually and that there are millions of other small refinements that are part of the routine progress of an economy.

For the most part, technology advances in a quiet, unnoticed fashion as small improvements increase the quality of products or the quantity of output. Occasionally, however, changes in technology create headlines and produce unforgettable visual images. During the war in the Persian Gulf in 1991, the world was stunned by the tremendous advantage that high-technology weapons—stealth aircraft, "smart" bombs, antimissile missiles—gave to the United States and its allies against an opponent armed with a technology that was but a few years behind. Civilian technologi-

cal advances—computers, telecommunications, and other high-technology sectors—are less dramatic but contribute greatly to the increase in living standards of market economies.

Because of its importance in raising living standards, economists have long pondered how to encourage technological progress. Increasingly, it is becoming clear that technological change is not a mechanical procedure of simply finding better products and processes. Instead, rapid innovation requires the fostering of an entrepreneurial spirit. Consider today's U.S. computer industry, where even enthusiasts can hardly keep up with the stream of new hardware configurations and software packages. Why did the entrepreneurial spirit thrive here and not in Russia, home to many of the great scientists, engineers, and mathematicians? One key reason is the combination of an open spirit of inquiry and the lure of free-market profits in Silicon Valley in comparison to the secrecy and deadening atmosphere of central planning in Moscow.

Table 27-2 summarizes the four wheels of economic growth.

THEORIES OF ECONOMIC GROWTH

Virtually everyone is in favor of economic growth. But there are strong disagreements about the best way to accomplish this goal. Some economists and policymakers stress the need to increase capital investment. Others advocate measures to stimulate research and development and technological change. Still a third group emphasizes the role of a better-educated work force.

Economists have long studied the question of the relative importance of different factors in determining growth. In the discussion below, we look at the theories of economic growth, which offer some clues about the driving forces behind growth. Then, in the final part of this section, we see what can be learned about growth from its historical patterns over the last century.

The Classical Dynamics of Smith and Malthus

Unlike growth theorists today, early economists like Adam Smith and T. R. Malthus stressed the critical role of land in economic growth. In *The Wealth of Nations* (1776), Adam Smith provided a handbook of economic development. He began with a hypothetical idyllic age: "that original state of things, which precedes both the appropriation of land and the accumulation of [capital] stock." This was a time when land was freely available to all, and before capital accumulation had begun to matter.

What would be the dynamics of economic growth in such a golden age? Because land is freely available, people simply spread out onto more acres as the population increases, just as the settlers did in the American west. Because there is no capital, national output exactly doubles as population doubles. What about real wages? Wages earn the entire national income because there is no subtraction for land rent or interest on capital. Output expands in step with population, so the real wage per worker is constant over time.

But this golden age cannot continue forever. Eventually, as population growth continues, all the land will be occupied. Once the frontier disappears, balanced growth of land, labor, and output is no longer possible. New laborers begin to crowd onto already-worked soils. Land becomes scarce, and rents rise to ration it among different uses.

Population still grows, and so does the national product. But output must grow more slowly than does population. Why? With new laborers added to fixed land, each worker now has less land to work with, and the law of diminishing returns comes into operation. The increasing labor-land ratio leads to a declining marginal product of labor and hence to declining real wage rates.[1]

How bad could things get? The dour Reverend T. R. Malthus thought that population pressures would drive the economy to a point where workers were at the minimum level of subsistence. Malthus reasoned that whenever wages were above the subsistence level, population would expand; below-subsistence wages would lead to high mortality and population decline. Only at subsistence wages could there be a stable equilibrium of population. He believed the working classes were destined to a life that is brutish, nasty, and short. This gloomy picture led Thomas Carlyle to criticize economics as "the dismal science."

Figure 27-2(a) shows the process of economic growth in Smith's golden age. Here, as population doubles, the production-possibility frontier (*PPF*) shifts out by a factor of 2 in each direction, showing that there are no constraints on growth from land or resources. Figure 27-2(b) shows the pessimistic Malthusian case, where a doubling of population leads to a less-than-doubling of food and clothing, lowering per capita output, as more people crowd onto limited land and diminishing returns drive down output per person.

Are There Limits to Growth?

Often, earlier ideas reemerge in light of new social trends or scientific findings. In the last two decades, Malthusian ideas have surfaced as many antigrowth advocates and environmentalists have argued that economic growth is limited by the finiteness of our natural resources and by environmental constraints.

Economic growth involves a rapid increase in the use of land and mineral resources and (if not controlled) in the emissions of air and water pollution. For example, energy consumption from fuels totaled 220 trillion Btu (British thermal units) in 1850. By

---

[1] The theory in this chapter relies on an important finding from microeconomics. In analysis of the determination of wages under simplified conditions, including perfect competition, it is shown that the wage rate of labor will be equal to the extra or marginal product of the last worker hired. For example, if the last worker contributes goods worth $12.50 per hour to the firm's output, then under competitive conditions the firm will be willing to pay up to $12.50 per hour in wages to that worker. Similarly, the rent on land is the marginal product of the last unit of land, and the real interest rate will be determined by the marginal product of the least productive piece of capital.

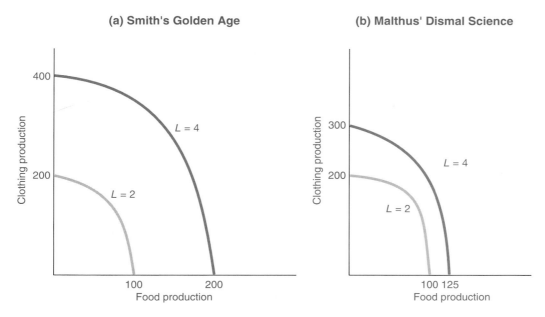

(a) Smith's Golden Age

(b) Malthus' Dismal Science

FIGURE 27-2. The Classical Dynamics of Smith and Malthus

In (**a**), unlimited land on the frontier means that when population doubles, labor can simply spread out and produce twice the quantity of any food and clothing combination. In (**b**), limited land means that increasing population from 2 million to 4 million triggers diminishing returns. Note that potential food production rises by only 25 percent with a doubling of labor inputs.

1900, the total reached 7600 trillion Btu, and in 1995 energy use was 66,000 trillion Btu. At the same time, the emissions of sulfur dioxide grew from around 0.2 million tons annually in 1850, peaked at 31 million tons in 1970, and declined to 22 million tons in 1993. This important example shows why people are concerned that rapid economic growth may lead to resource exhaustion and environmental degradation.

Worries about the viability of growth surfaced prominently with a series of studies by the ominous-sounding "Club of Rome" in the early 1970s. Growth critics found a receptive audience because of mounting alarm about rapid population growth in developing countries and, after 1973, the upward spiral in oil prices and the sharp decline in the growth of productivity and living standards in the major industrial countries. This first wave of anxiety subsided with declines in natural-resource prices after 1980 and slowing population growth in developing countries.

A second wave of growth pessimism emerged in the last decade. It involves not the depletion of min-

eral resources like oil and gas but the presence of environmental constraints on long-term economic growth. The possibility of global environmental constraints arises because of mounting scientific evidence that industrial activity is significantly changing the earth's climate and ecosystems. Among today's concerns are global warming, in which use of fossil fuels is warming the climate; widespread evidence of acid rain; the appearance of the Antarctic "ozone hole" along with ozone depletion in temperate regions; deforestation, especially in the tropical rain forests, which may upset the global ecological balance; soil erosion, which threatens the long-term viability of agriculture; and species extinction, which threatens to limit potential future medical and other technologies.

Global environmental constraints are closely linked to the Malthusian constraints of an earlier age. Whereas Malthus held that production would be limited by finite land, today's growth pessimists argue that growth will be limited by the finite absorptive capacity of our environment. We can, some say,

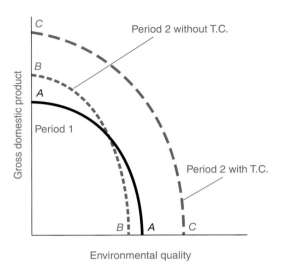

FIGURE 27-3. Environmental Constraints Can Be Overcome with New Technologies

Economic growth with resource and environmental constraints can increase GDP from period 1 to period 2. This may result in a deterioration in environmental quality when old, polluting technologies continue to be employed and there are no environmental regulations. The pessimistic case is shown by the *BB* curve labeled "Period 2 without T.C." (i.e., without technological change). However, application of prudent environmental policies along with development of environmentally sound new technologies may push the *PPF* outward to *CC* so that a society can have its environmental cake and eat a full measure of GDP as well.

burn only a limited amount of fossil fuel before we face the threat of dangerous climate change. The need to reduce the use of fossil fuels might well slow our long-term economic growth.

The dilemma is illustrated in Figure 27-3. An economy begins in period 1 with the illustrated *PPF* between environmental quality and output labeled as *AA*. Economic growth without technological change moves the *PPF* to *BB*. In this new situation, society might experience higher output at the expense of deteriorating environmental quality. A happier state occurs when technological change—introducing equipment to mine and burn low-sulfur coal, requiring pollution-control devices on automobiles, or developing safe and economical nuclear or solar power—pushes out the *PPF* to *CC* so that society can have both more output and a cleaner environment.

What is the empirical evidence on the effect of resource exhaustion and environmental limits on economic growth? There has been clear evidence

that the quality of land and mineral resources has deteriorated over the last century and that we are required to drill deeper for oil, use more marginal lands, and mine lower-grade mineral ores. But until now technological advance has largely outweighed these trends, so the prices of oil, gas, most minerals, and land have actually declined relative to the price of labor. Moreover, new environmentally friendly technologies have become increasingly important, and many of the worst environmental abuses have been alleviated in the last two decades. Nonetheless, environmental constraints have become more costly, and some economists believe that the United States has experienced a significant slowdown in measured productivity growth because of the costs of environmental regulations.

Economic Growth with Capital Accumulation: The Neoclassical Model

Malthus' forecast was dramatically wide of the mark because he did not recognize that technological innovation and capital investment could overcome the law of diminishing returns. Land did not become the limiting factor in production. Instead, the Industrial Revolution brought forth power-driven machinery that increased production, factories that gathered teams of workers into giant firms, railroads and steamships that linked together the far points of the world, and iron and steel that made possible stronger machines and faster locomotives. As market economies entered the twentieth century, important new industries grew up around the telephone, the automobile, and electric power. Capital accumulation and new technologies became the dominant force affecting economic development. Moreover, if the growth pessimists of today prove wrong, it will be largely because new environmentally friendly and resource-saving capital replaces today's resource-intensive, polluting technologies.

To understand how capital accumulation and technological change affect the economy, we must understand the **neoclassical model of economic growth**. This approach was pioneered by Robert Solow of MIT, who was awarded the 1987 Nobel Prize for this and other contributions to economic-growth theory. The neoclassical growth model serves as the basic tool for understanding the growth process in advanced countries and has been applied in empirical studies of the sources of economic growth.

Apostle of economic growth: Robert M. Solow was born in Brooklyn and educated at Harvard and then moved to MIT in 1950. In the next few years he developed the neoclassical growth model and applied it in a number of studies using the growth-accounting framework discussed later in this chapter. According to the committee that awards the Nobel Prize, "The increased interest of government to expand education and research and development was inspired by these studies. Every long-term report . . . for any country has used a Solow-type analysis."

Solow is known for his enthusiasm for economics as well as for his humor. He worries that the hunger for publicity has led some economists to exaggerate their knowledge. He criticized economists for "an apparently irresistible urge to push their science further than it will go, to answer questions more delicate than our limited understanding of a complicated question will allow. Nobody likes to say 'I don't know.' "

A lively writer, Solow worries that economics is terrifically difficult to explain to the public. At his news conference after winning the Nobel Prize, Solow quipped, "The attention span of the people you write for is shorter than the length of one true sentence." Nonetheless, Solow continues to labor for his brand of economics, and the world increasingly listens to the apostle of economic growth at MIT.

Basic Assumptions. The neoclassical growth model describes an economy in which a single homogeneous output is produced by two types of inputs, capital and labor. In contrast to the Malthusian analysis, labor growth is determined by forces outside the economy and is unaffected by economic variables. In addition, we assume that the economy is competitive and always operates at full employment, so we can analyze the growth of potential output.

The major new ingredients in the neoclassical growth model are capital and technological change. For the moment, assume that technology remains constant and focus on the role of capital in the growth process. Capital consists of durable produced goods that are used to make other goods. Capital goods include structures like factories and houses, equipment like computers and machine tools, and inventories of finished goods and goods in process.

For convenience, we will assume that there is a single kind of capital good (call it K). We then measure the aggregate stock of capital as the total quantity of capital goods. In our real-world calculations, we approximate the universal capital good as the total dollar value of capital goods (i.e., the constant-dollar value of equipment, structures, and inventories). If L is the number of workers, then (K/L) is equal to the quantity of capital per worker, or the *capital-labor ratio*. We can write our aggregate production function for the neoclassical growth model without technological change as $Q = F(K, L)$.

Turning now to the economic-growth process, economists stress the need for **capital deepening**, which is the process by which the quantity of capital per worker increases over time. Examples of capital deepening include the multiplication of farm machinery and irrigation systems in farming, of railroads and highways in transportation, and of computers and communication systems in banking. In each of these industries, societies have invested heavily in capital goods, increasing the amount of capital per worker. As a result, the output per worker has grown enormously in farming, transportation, and banking.

What happens to the return on capital in the process of capital deepening? For a given state of technology, a rapid rate of investment in plant and equipment tends to depress the rate of return on capital.[2] This occurs because the most worthwhile investment projects get constructed first, after which later investments become less and less valuable. Once a full railroad network or telephone system has been constructed, new investments will branch into more sparsely populated regions or duplicate existing lines. The rates of return on these later investments will be lower than the high returns on the first lines between densely populated regions.

In addition, the wage rate paid to workers will tend to rise as capital deepening takes place. Why? Each worker has more capital to work with and his or her marginal product therefore rises. As a result, the competitive wage rate rises along with the marginal product of labor. Hence, the wage rates rise for farm laborers, transport workers, or bank tellers as increases in capital per worker raise labor's marginal products in those sectors.

We can summarize the impact of capital deepening in the neoclassical growth model as follows:

Capital deepening occurs when the stock of capital grows more rapidly than the labor force. In the absence of technological change, capital deepening will produce a growth of output per worker, of the marginal product of labor, and of wages; it also will lead to diminishing returns on capital and a consequent decline in the rate of return on capital.

Geometrical Analysis of the Neoclassical Model

We can analyze the effects of capital accumulation by using Figure 27-4. This figure shows the aggregate production function graphically by depicting output per worker on the vertical axis and capital per worker on the horizontal axis. In the background, *and held constant for the moment,* are all the other variables that were discussed at the start of this section—the amount of land, the endowment of natural resources, and, most important of all, the technology used by the economy.

What happens as the society accumulates capital? As each worker has more and more capital to work with, the economy moves up and to the right on the aggregate production function. Say that the capital-labor ratio increases, from $(K/L)_0$ to $(K/L)_1$. Then the amount of output per worker increases, from $(Q/L)_0$ to $(Q/L)_1$.

What happens to the factor prices of labor and capital? As capital deepens, diminishing returns to capital set in, so the rate of return on capital and the real interest rate fall. (The slope of the curve in Figure 27-4 is the marginal product of capital, which is seen to fall as capital deepening occurs.) Also, because each worker can work with more capital, workers' marginal productivities rise and the real wage rate consequently also rises. The reverse would happen if the amount of capital per worker were to fall for some reason. For example, wars tend to reduce much of a nation's capital to rubble and lower the capital-labor ratio; after wars, therefore, we see a scarcity of capital and high returns on capital. Hence, our earlier verbal summary of the impact of capital deepening is verified by the analysis in Figure 27-4.

Long-Run Steady State. What is the long-run equilibrium in the neoclassical growth model without technological change? Eventually, the capital-labor ratio will stop rising. *In the long-run, the economy will enter a steady state in which capital deepening ceases, real wages stop growing, and capital returns and real interest rates are constant.*

We can show how the economy moves toward the steady state in Figure 27-4. As capital continues to accumulate, the capital-labor ratio increases as shown by the arrows from E' to E'' to E''' until finally the capital-labor ratio stops growing at V. At that point, output per worker (Q/L) is constant, and real wages stop growing.

Without technological change, incomes and wages end up stagnating. This is certainly a far better outcome than the world of subsistence wages predicted by Malthus. But the long-run equilibrium of the neoclassical growth model makes it clear that if economic growth consists only of accumulating cap-

---

[2] Under perfect competition and without risk or inflation, the rate of return on capital is equal to the real interest rate on bonds and other financial assets.

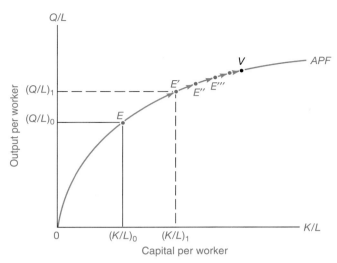

FIGURE 27-4. Economic Growth through Capital Deepening

As the amount of capital per worker increases, output per worker also increases. This graph shows the importance of "capital deepening," or increasing the amount of capital each worker has on hand. Remember, however, that other factors are held constant, such as technology, quality of the labor force, and natural resources.

ital through replicating factories with existing methods of production, then the standard of living will eventually stop rising.

The Importance of Technological Change

While the capital-accumulation model is a good first step down the road to understanding economic growth, it leaves some major questions unanswered. To begin with, the model with an unchanging technology predicts that real wages will gradually stagnate. But real wages have certainly not stagnated in the twentieth century. Additionally, it cannot explain the tremendous growth in productivity over time, nor does it account for the tremendous differences in per capita income among countries.

What is missing is technological change—advances in the processes of production and introduction of new and improved goods and services. We can depict technological change in our growth diagram as an upward shift in the aggregate production function, as illustrated in Figure 27-5 on page 528. In this diagram, we have shown the aggregate production function for both 1950 and 1995. Because of

technological change, the aggregate production function has shifted upward from APF_{1950} to APF_{1995}. This upward shift shows the advances in productivity that are generated by the vast array of new processes and products like electronics, computers, advances in metallurgy, improved service technologies, and so forth.

Therefore, in addition to considering the capital deepening described above, we must also take into account the advances in technology. The sum of capital deepening and technological change is the arrow in Figure 27-5, which produces an increase in output per worker from $(Q/L)_{1950}$ to $(Q/L)_{1995}$. Instead of settling into a steady state, the economy enjoys rising output per worker, rising wages, and increasing living standards.

Of particular interest is the impact of changing technologies on rates of profits and real interest rates. As a result of technological progress, the real interest rate need not fall. Invention increases the productivity of capital and offsets the tendency for a falling rate of profit.

Bias of Invention. Not all inventions are evenhanded. Some inventions favor capital; others,

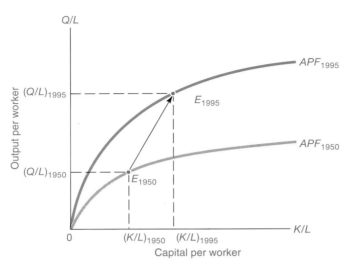

FIGURE 27-5. Technological Advance Shifts Up the Production Function

As a result of improvements in technology, the aggregate production function shifts *upward over time.* Hence improvements in technology combine with capital deepening to raise output per worker and real wages.

labor. For example, machines and tractors reduce the need for labor and increase the demand for capital. These are thus called *labor-saving inventions,* and they increase profits relative to wages. An invention that reduces the capital requirement more than the labor requirement (such as the introduction of multiple-shift workdays) is *capital-saving* and raises wages relative to profits. Between the two are *neutral inventions,* which have no major effect on the relative demands of or returns to different factors. Since the Industrial Revolution, inventions appear to have been labor-saving on balance.

Technological Change as an Economic Output

Up to now we have treated technological change as something that floats mysteriously down from scientists and inventors like manna from heaven. Recent research on economic growth has begun to focus on the *sources of technological change.* This research, sometimes called the "new growth theory" or the "theory of endogenous technological change," seeks to uncover the processes by which private market forces, public-policy decisions, and alternative institutions lead to different patterns of technological change.

One important point is that technological change is an output of the economic system. Edison's lightbulb was the result of years of research into different lightbulb designs; the transistor resulted from the efforts of scientists in Bell Labs to find a process that would improve telephone switching devices; pharmaceutical companies spend hundreds of millions of dollars doing research on and testing new drugs. Those who are talented and lucky may earn supernormal profits, or even become billionaires like Bill Gates of Microsoft, but many are the disappointed inventors or companies who end up with empty pockets.

The other unusual feature of technologies is that they are public goods, or "nonrival" goods in technical language. This means that they can be used by many people at the same time without being used up. A new piece of software, a new miracle drug, a design for a new steelmaking process—I can use each of these without reducing its productivity for you and the British and the Japanese and everyone else. In addition, inventions are expensive to produce but inexpensive to reproduce. These features of technological change can produce severe market failures—they mean that inventors sometimes have great difficulty profiting from their inventions because other people can copy them. The market failures are largest for the most basic and fundamental forms of research. Furthermore, governments must pay careful attention to ensuring that inventors have adequate incentives to engage in research and development. Governments increasingly pay attention to *intellectual property rights*, such as patents and copyrights, to provide adequate market rewards for creative activities.

What is the major contribution of the new growth theory? It has changed the way we think about the growth process and public policies. If technological differences are the major reason for differences in living standards among nations, and if technology is a produced factor, then economic-growth policy will have to focus much more sharply on how nations can improve their technological performance. This is just the lesson drawn by Stanford's Paul Romer, one of the leaders of new growth theory:

> Economists can once again make progress toward a complete understanding of the determinants of long-run economic success. Ultimately, this will put us in position to offer policymakers something more in-

sightful than the standard neoclassical prescription—more saving and more schooling. We will be able to rejoin the ongoing policy debates about tax subsidies for private research, antitrust exemptions for research joint ventures, the activities of multinational firms, the effects of government procurement, the feedback between trade policy and innovation, the scope of protection for intellectual property rights, the links between private firms and universities, the mechanisms for selecting the research areas that receive public support, and the costs and benefits of an explicit government-led technology policy.[3]

To summarize:

Technological change—which increases output produced for a given bundle of inputs—is a crucial ingredient in the growth of nations. The new growth theory seeks to uncover the processes which generate technological change. This approach emphasizes that technological change is an output that is subject to severe market failures because technology is a public good that is expensive to produce but cheap to reproduce. Governments increasingly seek to provide strong intellectual property rights for those who develop new technologies.

B. THE PATTERNS OF GROWTH IN THE UNITED STATES

The Facts of Economic Growth

Modern economics has moved beyond qualitative discussion to an empirical science thanks to the painstaking gathering of data and construction and analysis of national accounts by Simon Kuznets, Edward Denison, Dale Jorgenson, and many others. Figure 27-6 on page 530 depicts the key trends of economic development for the United States in this century. Similar patterns have been found in most of the major industrial countries.

Figure 27-6(*a*) shows the trends in real GDP, the capital stock, and population. Population and employment have more than tripled since 1900. At

the same time, the stock of physical capital has risen more than tenfold. Thus the amount of capital per worker (the *K/L* ratio) has increased by a factor of almost 3. Clearly, capital deepening has been an important feature of twentieth-century American capitalism.

What about the growth in output? Has output grown less rapidly than capital, as would occur in a model that ignored technological change? No. The

---

[3] Paul Romer, "The Origins of Endogenous Growth," *Journal of Economic Perspectives* (Winter 1994), pp. 3–22.

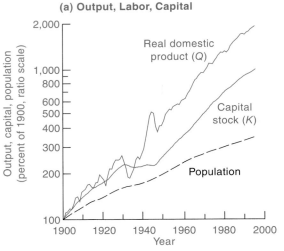

(a) Output, Labor, Capital

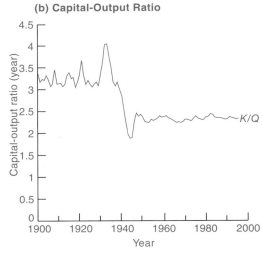

(b) Capital-Output Ratio

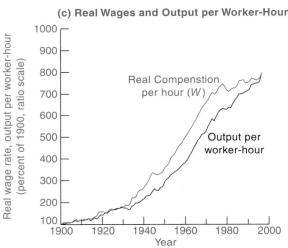

(c) Real Wages and Output per Worker-Hour

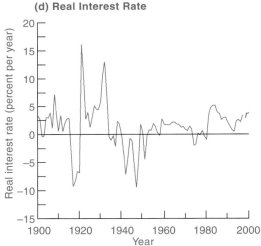

(d) Real Interest Rate

FIGURE 27-6. Economic Growth Displays Striking Regularities

(**a**) Capital stock has grown faster than population and labor supply. Nonetheless, total output has grown even more rapidly than capital. (**b**) The capital-output ratio declined sharply during the first half of the twentieth century, but it has remained steady over the last four decades. (**c**) Real wages have grown steadily and somewhat faster than average product per worker-hour. Note the slowdown of growth in output, real wages, and productivity since 1973. Does the productivity slowdown auger the end of the Industrial Revolution? (**d**) Real interest rate has been trendless over this century, suggesting that technological change has offset diminishing returns to capital accumulation. (Source: U.S. Departments of Commerce and Labor, Federal Reserve Board, Bureau of the Census, and historical studies by John Kendrick.)

fact that the output curve in Figure 27-6(*a*) is not in between the two factor curves, but actually lies above the capital curve, demonstrates that technological progress must have increased the productivity of cap-

ital and labor. Indeed, the capital-output ratio—shown in Figure 27-6(*b*)—has fallen over time, rather than rising as would be expected in the capital-accumulation model without technological progress.

For most people, an economy's performance is measured by earnings, shown in Figure 27-6(c) in terms of real wages (or money wages corrected for inflation). Wages have shown an impressive growth for most of this century, as we would expect from the growth in the capital-labor ratio and from steady technological advance.

The real interest rate (i.e., the money interest rate minus the rate of inflation) is shown in Figure 27-6(d). Interest rates and profit rates fluctuate greatly in business cycles and wars but display no strong trend upward or downward for the whole period. Either by coincidence or because of an economic mechanism inducing this pattern, technological change has largely offset diminishing returns to capital.

Output per worker-hour is the solid black curve in Figure 27-6(c). As could be expected from the deepening of capital and from technological advance, output per worker has risen steadily.

The fact that wages rise at the same rate as output per worker does not mean that labor has captured all the fruits of productivity advance. Rather, it means that labor has kept about the same share of total product, with capital also earning about the same relative share throughout the period. Actually, a close look at Figure 27-6(c) shows that real wages have grown slightly faster than has output per worker-hour over the last nine decades, although labor's share has changed little in the last few years. When labor's share increases, its rise implies a corresponding decline in the share of capital, land, and other property income in national income.

Seven Basic Trends of Economic Development

The economic history of the advanced nations can be summarized approximately by the following trends:

- *Trend 1.* The capital stock has grown more rapidly than population and employment, resulting in capital deepening.
- *Trend 2.* For most of this century, there has been a strong upward trend in real wage rates.
- *Trend 3.* The share of wages and salaries in national income has edged up very slightly over the long run but has been virtually constant over the last two decades.

- *Trend 4.* There have been major oscillations in real interest rates and the rate of profit, particularly during business cycles, but there has been no strong upward or downward trend in this century.
- *Trend 5.* Instead of steadily rising, which would be predicted by the law of diminishing returns with unchanging technology, the capital-output ratio has actually declined since 1900.
- *Trend 6.* For most of the twentieth century, the ratios of national saving and of investment to GDP have been stable. Since 1980, the national savings rate has declined sharply in the United States.
- *Trend 7.* After effects of the business cycle are removed, national product has grown at an average rate of close to 3 percent per year. Output growth has been much higher than a weighted average of the growth of capital, labor, and resource inputs, suggesting that technological innovation must have played a key role in economic growth.

Warning: The historical trends are not inevitable. The persistence of these trends in economic growth might suggest that they have taken on a certain inevitability—that we can forever expect our economy to generate rapid growth in output per worker, real wages, and real output.

But this view of constant growth should be resisted, for it misreads the lessons of history and economic theory. While trends have been persistent, a closer examination shows major waves or deviations during periods of a decade or more. Moreover, there is no theoretical reason why technological innovation should remain high, forever raising living standards. Eventually, diminishing returns may become more significant, or perhaps the need to combat pollution or global environmental threats may overwhelm technological change. The period since 1973—with a marked slowdown in growth of output, real wages, and output per worker—is a reminder that no law of economics ensures that the future must continue to provide the robust growth of incomes experienced over the last century.

While the seven trends of economic history are not like the immutable laws of physics, they do portray fundamental facts about growth in the modern era. How do they fit into our economic-growth theories?

Trends 2 and 1—higher wage rates when capital deepens—fit nicely into our neoclassical growth model shown in Figure 27-4. Trend 3—that the wage share has grown only very slowly—is an interesting coincidence that is consistent with a wide variety of production functions relating Q to L and K.

Trends 4 and 5, however, warn us that technological change must be playing a role here, so Figure 27-5, with its picture of advancing technology, is more realistic than the steady state depicted in Figure 27-4. A steady profit rate and a declining, or steady, capital-output ratio cannot hold if the K/L ratio rises in a world with unchanging technology; taken together, they contradict the basic law of diminishing returns under deepening of capital. We must therefore recognize the key role of technological progress in explaining the seven trends of modern economic growth. Our models confirm what our intuition suggests.

The Sources of Economic Growth

We have seen that advanced market economies grow through increases in labor and capital and by technological change as well. But what are the relative contributions of labor, capital, and technology? To answer this question, we turn to an analysis of the quantitative aspects of growth and of the useful approach known as growth accounting. This approach is the first step in the quantitative analysis of economic growth for any country.

The Growth-Accounting Approach. Detailed studies of economic growth rely on what is called **growth accounting**. This technique is not a balance sheet or national product account of the kind we met in earlier chapters. Rather, it is a way of separating out the contributions of the different ingredients driving observed growth trends.

Growth accounting usually begins with the aggregate production function we met earlier in this chapter, $Q = AF(K, L, R)$. Often resources are omitted because land is constant. Using elementary calculus and some simplifying assumptions, we can express the growth of output in terms of the growth of the inputs plus the contribution of technological change. Growth in output (Q) can be decomposed into three separate terms: growth in labor (L), times

its weight, growth in capital (K) times its weight, and technological innovation itself (T.C.).

Momentarily ignoring technological change, an assumption of constant returns to scale means that a 1 percent growth in L together with a 1 percent growth in K will lead to a 1 percent growth in output. But suppose L grows at 1 percent and K at 5 percent. It is tempting, but wrong, to guess that Q will then grow at 3 percent, the simple average of 1 and 5. Why wrong? Because the two factors do not necessarily contribute equally to output. Rather, the fact that three-fourths of national income goes to labor while only one-fourth goes to capital suggests that labor growth will contribute more to output than will capital growth.

If labor's growth rate gets 3 times the weight of K's, we can calculate the answer as follows: Q will grow at 2 percent per year (= ¾ of 1 percent + ¼ of 5 percent). To growth of inputs, we add technological change and thereby obtain all the sources of growth.

Hence, output growth per year follows the *fundamental equation of growth accounting:*

$$\% \; Q \text{ growth} \qquad\qquad\qquad (1)$$
$$= \tfrac{3}{4} \, (\% \; L \text{ growth}) + \tfrac{1}{4} \, (\% \; K \text{ growth}) + \text{T.C.}$$

where "T.C." represents technological change (or total factor productivity) that raises productivity and where ¾ and ¼ are the relative contributions of each input to economic growth. Under conditions of perfect competition, these fractions are equal to the shares of national income of the two factors; naturally, these fractions would be replaced by new fractions if the relative shares of the factors were to change or if other factors were added.

To explain per capita growth, we can eliminate L as a separate growth source. Now, using the fact that capital gets one-fourth of output, we have from equation (1)

$$\% \, \frac{Q}{L} \text{ growth} = \% \; Q \text{ growth} - \% \; L \text{ growth}$$
$$= \tfrac{1}{4} \left(\% \, \frac{K}{L} \text{ growth} \right) + \text{T.C.} \qquad (2)$$

This relation shows clearly how capital deepening would affect per capita output if technological advance were zero. Output per worker would grow only one-fourth as fast as capital per worker, reflecting diminishing returns.

Contribution of Different Elements to Growth in Real GDP, United States, 1948–1994	In percent per year	As percent of total
Real GDP growth (private business sector)	3.4	100
Contribution of inputs	2.1	62
Capital	1.1	32
Labor	1.0	29
Hours	0.8	24
Composition	0.2	6
Total factor productivity growth	1.3	38
Education	0.4	12
Research and development	0.2	6
Advances in knowledge and other sources	0.7	21

TABLE 27-3. Education and Advances in Knowledge Outweigh Capital in Contributing to Economic Growth

Studies using the techniques of growth accounting break down the growth of GDP in the private business sector into contributing factors. Recent comprehensive studies find that capital growth accounted for 32 percent of output growth. Education, research and development, and other advances in knowledge made up 38 percent of total output growth and more than half of the growth of output per worker. [Source: Edward F. Denison, *Trends in American Economic Growth, 1929–1982* (Brookings, Washington, D.C., 1985), for estimates of the contribution of education; U.S. Department of Labor, "Multifactor Productivity Measures, 1994," January 1996, for other estimates.]

One final point remains: We can measure Q growth, K growth, and L growth, as well as the shares of K and L. But how can we measure T.C. (technological change)? We cannot. Rather, we must *infer* T.C. as the residual or leftover after the other components of output and inputs are calculated. Thus if we examine the equation above, T.C. is calculated by subtraction from equation (1) as

$$\text{T.C.} = \% \; Q \text{ growth} - \tfrac{3}{4} \, (\% \; L \text{ growth}) - \tfrac{1}{4} \, (\% \; K \text{ growth}) \qquad (3)$$

This equation allows us to answer critically important questions about economic growth. What part of per capita output growth is due to capital deepening, and what part is due to technological advance? Does society progress chiefly by dint of thrift and the forgoing of current consumption? Or is our rising living standard the reward for the ingenuity of inventors and the daring of innovator-entrepreneurs?

Numerical Example. To determine the contributions of labor, capital, and other factors in output growth, we substitute representative numbers for

the period 1900–1996 into equation (2) for the growth of Q/L. Since 1900, worker hours have grown 1.3 percent per year, and K has grown 2.5 percent per year, while Q has grown 3.1 percent per year. Thus, by arithmetic, we find that

$$\% \, \frac{Q}{L} \text{ growth} = \tfrac{1}{4} \left(\% \frac{K}{L} \text{ growth} \right) + \text{T.C.}$$

becomes

$$1.8 = \tfrac{1}{4} \, (1.2) + \text{T.C.} = 0.3 + 1.5$$

Thus of the 1.8 percent–per-year increase in output per worker, about 0.3 percentage point is due to capital deepening, while the largest portion, 1.5 percent per year, stems from T.C. (technological change).

Detailed Studies. More thorough studies refine the simple calculation but show quite similar conclusions. Table 27-3 presents the results of studies by the Department of Labor and private studies analyzing the sources of growth over the 1948–1994 period. During this time, output (measured as gross output of the private business sector) grew at an

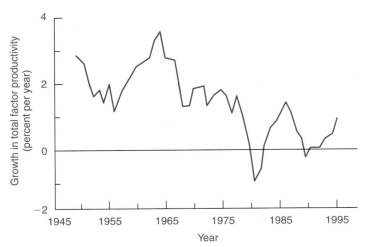

FIGURE 27-7. Economywide Productivity Growth Has Slowed in Last Two Decades

The figure shows the growth in total factor productivity, or output per composite unit of labor and capital, in the private business sector. Productivity slowed from around $1\frac{1}{2}$ percent in the 1948–1973 period to half that rate after 1973. Spurred by tremendous gains in computers and electronics, productivity in manufacturing has grown rapidly in recent years. (Source: U.S. Department of Labor; figures are 5-year averages.)

average rate of 3.4 percent per year, while input growth (of capital, labor, and land) contributed 2.1 percentage points per year. Hence **total factor productivity**—the growth of output less the growth of the weighted sum of all inputs, or what we have called T.C—averaged 1.3 percent annually.

Somewhat more than one-half of the growth in output in the United States can be accounted for by the growth in labor and capital. The remaining growth is a residual factor that can be attributed to education, research and development, innovation, economies of scale, scientific advances, and other factors.

Other countries show different patterns of growth. For example, scholars have used growth accounting to study the Soviet Union, which grew rapidly during the period from 1930 until the mid-1960s. It appears, however, that the high growth rate came primarily from forced-draft increases in capital and labor inputs. For the last few years of the U.S.S.R.'s existence, productivity actually *declined* as the central-planning apparatus became more dysfunctional, as corruption deepened, and as incentives worsened. On the whole, the estimated pace of

growth in total factor productivity for the Soviet Union over the half-century before its collapse was slower than that for the United States and other major market economies. Only the ability of the central government forcibly to divert output into investment (and away from consumption) offset the system's inefficiency.

THE PRODUCTIVITY SLOWDOWN

Given the importance of productivity to living standards, economists viewed with alarm the sharp decline in U.S. productivity growth that occurred around 1973. This break in the trend, which is called the **productivity slowdown**, can be seen in Figure 27-7. This graph shows estimates of the growth in total factor productivity in the private business economy. It is calculated in the way we described in the section on growth accounting, above. Productivity began to slow down in the early 1970s. A careful look at the data indicates that labor productivity actually slowed in virtually all sectors of the economy. Among the areas with the biggest deterioration in productivity were mining, construction, and services. Similar pat-

Productivity and Real Wages*		
Period	Average annual percentage growth in:	
	Labor productivity	Real wages
1948–1973	3.0	3.1
1973–1996	1.0	0.7

*Productivity is for the U.S. business sector; nominal compensation is deflated using the consumption deflator for personal consumption expenditures.

TABLE 27-4. Real Wages Mirror Productivity Growth

Over the long run, real wages tend to move with trends in labor productivity. After the productivity slowdown in 1973, real wages stagnated. (Source: U.S. Department of Labor.)

terns, with a slowdown of productivity growth in the aggregate and in most sectors after 1973, characterize all major industrial countries.

Productivity is particularly important because of its association with growth in living standards. Table 27-4 shows the effect of the productivity decline on real wages. Some elementary arithmetic shows that if labor's share of national income is constant, this implies that real wages will grow at the rate of growth of labor productivity.[4] The slowdown in productivity in the last two decades is therefore largely responsible for the stagnation in living standards over that period. Those who entered the labor force after World War II experienced healthy growth in real wages, while the average worker over the last two decades experienced very slow growth in living standards.

Explaining the Slowdown. Studies of productivity point to a number of unfavorable factors converging on the American economy at about the same time, including the following:

- Beginning in the 1970s, environmental regulations required firms to spend money on plant and operations to improve health and safety, yet these improvements did not show up as measured output increases. One of the most dramatic cases was productivity in nuclear power plants, in which regulations increased costs so

sharply that they became uneconomical to build and even sometimes to run.

- The increase in energy prices in the 1970s led firms to substitute other inputs (labor and capital) for energy. As a result, the productivity of labor and capital declined relative to earlier periods.

- Some economists believe that a deterioration in labor quality (or perhaps a slowdown in the increase in quality) may be an important contributor to the productivity-growth slowdown. The important indicators here include a deterioration in test scores of American students and a sharp increase in the share of low-skilled immigrants in the work force.

- A final suspect in the mystery of the productivity slowdown is the nature of research and development (R&D). Compared to most other high-income countries, the United States spends a large share of its research dollars on defense and space. While Japan and Germany are investing in new electronics or automotive technologies, about one-third of U.S. R&D is on defense and space applications. While these efforts may produce spectacular displays of military prowess, few demonstrable benefits to civilian technology can be found.

In later chapters, we will consider economic policies that can reverse recent productivity trends.

This concludes our introduction to economic growth. In the chapters that follow we apply this theory to the developing world and then derive the basic elements of aggregate supply. This framework will allow us to better understand many of the policy issues that face nations hoping to increase their economic-growth rates and improve their living standards.

---

[4] To see this, write labor's share as $W \times L = $ constant $\times P \times Q$, where W = money wage rate, L = hours of work, P = price index, and Q = output. Dividing both sides by L and P yields $(W/P) = $ constant $\times (Q/L)$. Hence as long as the share of labor in national income is constant (and ignoring complications in measuring the indexes), real compensation will grow at the same rate as labor productivity.

SUMMARY

A. Theories of Economic Growth

1. The analysis of economic growth examines the factors that lead to the growth of potential output over the long run. Reviewing the experience of nations over space and time, we see that the economy rides on the four wheels of economic growth: (*a*) the quantity and quality of its labor force; (*b*) the abundance of its land and other natural resources; (*c*) the stock of accumulated capital; and, perhaps most important, (*d*) the technological change and innovation that allow greater output to be produced with the same inputs. There is no unique combination of these four ingredients, however; the United States, Europe, and Asian countries have followed different paths to economic success.

2. The classical models of Smith and Malthus describe economic development in terms of land and population. In the absence of technological change, increasing population ultimately exhausts the supply of free land. The resulting increase in population density triggers the law of diminishing returns, so growth produces higher land rents with lower competitive wages. The Malthusian equilibrium is attained when the wage has fallen to the subsistence level, below which population cannot sustain itself. In reality, however, technological change has kept economic development progressing in industrial countries by continually shifting the productivity curve of labor upward.

3. Concerns about the finiteness of natural resources and increasing environmental spillovers from economic activity have led many to question whether economic growth at present rates can long continue. One set of worries based on limited supplies of land, energy, and mineral resources has receded with continuing new discoveries and resource-saving technological change. Global environmental constraints may lead to costly environmental damages or the need for expensive preventive measures.

4. Capital accumulation with complementary labor forms the core of modern growth theory in the neoclassical growth model. This approach uses a tool known as the aggregate production function, which relates inputs and technology to total potential GDP. In the absence of technological change and innovation, an increase in capital per worker (capital deepening) would not be matched by a proportional increase in output per worker because of diminishing returns to capital. Hence, capital deepening would lower the rate of return on capital (equal to the real interest rate under risk-free competition) while raising real wages.

5. Technological change increases the output producible with a given bundle of inputs. This pushes upward the aggregate production function, making more output available with the same inputs of labor and capital. Recent analysis in the "new growth theory" seeks to uncover the processes which generate technological change. This approach emphasizes (*a*) that technological change is an output of the economic system, (*b*) that technology is a public or nonrival good that can be used simultaneously by many people, and (*c*) that new inventions are expensive to produce but inexpensive to reproduce. These features mean that governments must pay careful attention to ensuring that inventors have adequate incentives, through strong intellectual property rights, to engage in research and development.

B. The Patterns of Growth in the United States

6. Numerous trends of economic growth are seen in data for this century. Among the key findings are that real wages and output per hour worked have risen steadily, although there has been a marked slowdown since the 1970s; that the real interest rate has shown no major trend; and that the capital-output ratio has declined. The major trends are consistent with the neoclassical growth model augmented by technological advance. Thus economic theory confirms what economic history tells us—that technological advance increases the productivity of inputs and improves wages and living standards.

7. The last trend, continual growth in potential output over the twentieth century, raises the important question of the sources of economic growth. Applying quantitative techniques, economists have used growth accounting to determine that "residual" sources—such as technological change and education—outweigh capital deepening in their impact on GDP growth or labor productivity.

CONCEPTS FOR REVIEW

four wheels of growth:
  labor
  resources
  capital
  technology
aggregate production function
Smith's golden age
capital-labor ratio

Malthus' limited land
modern Malthusianism: limited
  resources and environmental
  constraints
neoclassical growth model
K/L rise as capital deepens
new growth theory
technology as a produced good

productivity-growth slowdown
seven trends of economic growth
growth accounting:

$$\% \ Q \text{ growth} = \tfrac{3}{4} \ (\% \ L \text{ growth})$$
$$+ \tfrac{1}{4} \ (\% \ K \text{ growth})$$
$$+ \text{ T.C.}$$
$$\% \ Q/L \text{ growth} = \tfrac{1}{4} \ (\% \ K/L$$
$$\text{growth}) + \text{ T.C.}$$

QUESTIONS FOR DISCUSSION

1. According to economic data, the living standards of a family in 1996 were about $5\tfrac{1}{2}$ times that of a family in 1900. What does this mean in terms of actual consumption patterns? Discuss with your parents or older relatives how your living standards today compare with those of their parents; make a comparison of the difference.

2. "If the government strengthens intellectual property rights, subsidizes basic science, and controls business cycles, we will see economic growth that would astound the classical economists." Explain what the writer meant by this statement.

3. "With zero population growth and no technological change, persistent capital accumulation would ultimately destroy the capitalist class." Explain why such a scenario might lead to a zero real interest rate and to a disappearance of profits.

4. Recall the growth-accounting equation [Equation (1) on page 532]. Calculate the growth of output if labor grows at 1 percent per year, capital grows at 4 percent per year, and technological change is $1\tfrac{1}{2}$ percent per year.

    How would your answer change if:
  a. Labor growth slowed to 0 percent per year.

  b. Capital growth increased to 5 percent per year.
  c. Labor and capital had equal shares in GDP.
    Also, calculate for each of these conditions the rate of growth of output per worker.

5. Reinterpret Figure 27-3 to explain why Malthus' predictions were faulty.

6. A brooding pessimist might argue that 1973 marked the end of the great expansion that began with the Industrial Revolution. Assume that all the features of the earlier era were still present today *except* that technological change and innovation were to cease. What would the new seven trends look like for coming decades? What would happen to the important real wage? What steps could be taken to counteract the new trends and put the economy back on the earlier path?

7. **Advanced problem:** Many fear that computers will do to humans what tractors and cars did to horses—the horse population declined precipitously early in this century after technological change made horses obsolete. If we treat computers as a particularly productive kind of K, what would their introduction do to the capital-labor ratio in Figure 27-4? Can total output go down with a fixed labor force? Under what conditions would the real wage decline? Can you see why the horse analogy might not apply?

CHAPTER 28
THE CHALLENGE OF ECONOMIC DEVELOPMENT

> I believe in materialism. I believe in all the proceeds of a healthy materialism—good cooking, dry houses, dry feet, sewers, drain pipes, hot water, baths, electric lights, automobiles, good roads, bright streets, long vacations away from the village pump, new ideas, fast horses, swift conversation, theaters, operas, orchestras, bands—I believe in them all for everybody. The man who dies without knowing these things may be as exquisite as a saint, and as rich as a poet; but it is in spite of, not because of, his deprivation.
>
> *Francis Hackett*

Of the 5 billion people on this planet, perhaps 1 billion live in absolute poverty—barely able to survive from day to day. What causes the great differences in the wealth of nations? Can the world peacefully survive with poverty in the midst of plenty, with agricultural surpluses in America alongside starvation and environmental degradation in Africa? What steps can poorer nations take to improve their living standards? What are the responsibilities of affluent countries?

These questions, concerning the obstacles facing less developed countries, are among the greatest challenges facing modern economics. It is here that the tools of macroeconomics, particularly economic-growth theory, can make the greatest difference to people's daily lives. We begin by describing the characteristics of developing countries and reviewing some of the key ingredients in the process of economic development. The second part of this chapter examines alternative approaches to economic growth in developing countries, particularly the more successful models in Asia along with the failed communist experiment in Russia.

A. ECONOMIC GROWTH IN POOR COUNTRIES

ASPECTS OF A DEVELOPING COUNTRY

What is meant by a developing country, or a less developed country (LDC)? The most important characteristic of a **developing country** is that it has low per capita income. In addition, people in developing countries usually have poor health and short life expectancy, have low levels of literacy, and suffer from malnutrition.

Table 28-1 is a key source of data for understanding the major players in the world economy, as well as important indicators of underdevelopment. Countries are grouped into the categories of low-income, lower-middle-income, upper-middle-income, and high-income economies.

A number of interesting features emerge from the table. Clearly, low-income countries are much poorer than advanced countries like the United

		Gross domestic product				
			Per capita			
Country group	Population, 1995 (million)	Total, 1995 ($, billion)	Level, 1995 ($)	Growth, 1985–1995 (% per year)	Adult illiteracy, 1995 (%)	Life expectancy at birth (years)
Low-income economies						
China and India	2,130	1,035	499	6.1	32	66
Other	1,050	317	290	−1.4	46	56
Lower-middle-income economies (e.g., Peru, Philippines, Thailand)	1,153	2,026	1,670	−1.3	20	67
Upper-middle-income economies (e.g., Brazil, Malaysia, Mexico)	438	1,982	4,260	0.2	14	69
High-income economies (e.g., United States, Japan, France)	902	22,486	32,039	1.9	<5	77

TABLE 28-1. Important Indicators for Different Country Groups

Countries are grouped by the World Bank into four major categories depending upon their per capita incomes. In each, a number of important indicators of economic development are shown. Note that low-income countries tend to have high illiteracy and low life expectancy. [Source: World Bank, *World Development Report, 1997* (World Bank, Washington, 1997).]

States. People in countries with the lowest average incomes earn only about one-twentieth as much as people in high-income countries. (For the table's data, *purchasing-power parity* calculations were used to measure relative incomes. Market exchange rates tend to understate the incomes of low-wage countries.)

In addition, many social and health indicators show the effects of poverty in low-income nations. Life expectancy is low, and educational attainment and literacy are modest, reflecting low levels of investment in human capital.

Table 28-1 also shows that there is a great diversity among developing countries. Some remain at the ragged edge of starvation—these are the poorest countries like Chad, Bangladesh, or Somalia. Other countries that were in that category two or three decades ago have graduated to the rank of middle-income countries. The more successful ones—Hong Kong, South Korea, and Taiwan—are called *newly industrializing countries*, or NICs. The most successful of these have per capita incomes that have reached the top ranks of high-income countries. Yesterday's successful developing countries will be tomorrow's high-income countries.

Life in Low-Income Countries

To bring out the contrasts between advanced and developing economies, imagine that you are a typical 21-year-old in a low-income country such as Mali, India, or Bangladesh. You are poor. Even after making generous allowance for the goods that you produce and consume, your annual income barely averages $300. Your counterpart in North America might have more than $20,000 in average earnings. Perhaps you can find cold comfort in the thought that only 1 person in 4 in the world averages more than $3000 in annual income.

For each of your fellow citizens who can read, there is one like you who is illiterate. Your life expectancy is four-fifths that of the average person in an advanced country; already two of your brothers and sisters have died before reaching adulthood. Birth rates are high, particularly for families where women receive no education, but mortality rates are also much higher here than in countries with good health-care systems.

Most people in your country work on farms. Few can be spared from food production to work in factories. You work with but one-sixtieth the horsepower of a prosperous North American worker. You know little about science, but much about your village traditions.

You and your fellow citizens in the 40 poorest countries constitute 55 percent of the world population but must divide among each other only 4 percent of world income. You are often hungry, and the food you eat is mainly roughage or rice. While you were among those who got some primary schooling, like most of your friends you did not go on to high school, and only the wealthiest go to a university. You work long hours in the fields without the benefit of machinery. At night you sleep on a mat. You have little household furniture, perhaps a table and a radio. Your only mode of transportation is an old pair of boots.

Human Development

This review of life in the poorest countries of the world reminds us of the importance of adequate incomes in meeting basic needs as well as of the fact that life involves more than market incomes. An interesting new approach that combines economic indicators with social indicators is the *Human Development Index,* or HDI, developed by the United Nations Development Program with the assistance of economists Amartya Sen and Gustav Ranis. The HDI includes four different indexes: per capita real GDP, life expectancy at birth, school enrollment, and adult literacy. The idea is that economic growth should enrich people's health and education as well as their purses.

Figure 28-1 shows a plot of the HDI and per capita output. The correlation is strong, but there are exceptions to the general positive relationship. Some countries, such as Algeria, Gabon, and Singapore, score poorly on the HDI scale for their income levels. Others—Costa Rica, Canada, and Sri Lanka—emphasize human development and score high relative to other countries with their income levels. This interesting new approach is a reminder that we should not neglect the human dimensions of economic growth.

THE FOUR ELEMENTS IN DEVELOPMENT

Having seen what it means to be a developing country, we now turn to an analysis of the process by which low-income countries improve their living standards. We saw in the last chapter that economic growth in the United States—growth in its potential output—rides on four wheels. These are (1) human resources, (2) natural resources, (3) capital formation, and (4) technology. The sources of growth are no different in other countries, no matter how rich or poor. Let's see how each of the four wheels operates in developing countries and consider how public policy can steer the growth process in favorable directions.

Human Resources

Population Explosion: The Legacy of Malthus. Many poor countries are forever running hard just to stay in place. Even as a poor nation's GDP rises, so does its population. Recall our discussion in the last chapter of the Malthusian population trap where population grows to keep incomes at subsistence levels. While the high-income countries left Malthus behind long ago, Africa is still caught in the Malthusian bind of high birth rates and stagnant incomes. And the population expansion has not stopped—demographers project that the poor countries will add about 1.5 billion people over the next 25 years, while the high-income countries will add perhaps 50 million.

It's hard for poor countries to overcome poverty with birth rates so high. But there are escape routes from overpopulation. One strategy is to take an active role in curbing population growth, even when such actions run against prevailing religious norms. Many countries have introduced educational campaigns and subsidized birth control. China has been particularly forceful in curbing population growth among its more than 1 billion inhabitants, putting tight quotas on the number of births and imposing economic penalties and mandatory sterilization on those who violate their "baby quota."

And for countries which manage to boost their per capita incomes, there is the prospect of making the *demographic transition,* which occurs when a population stabilizes with low birth rates and low death rates. Once countries get rich enough, and infant mortality drops, people voluntarily reduce their birth rates. When women are educated and emerge from sub-

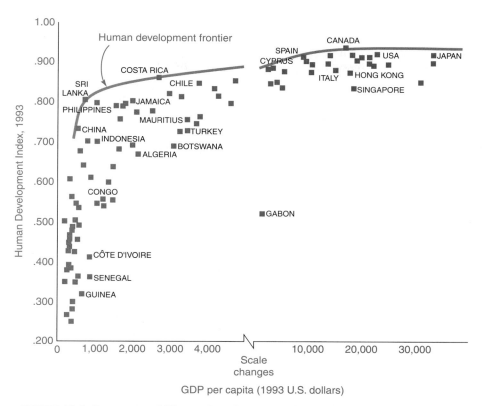

FIGURE 28-1. Incomes and Human Development Are Linked, but Some Countries Do Better for Their Income Levels

A new Human Development Index (HDI) includes schooling, literacy, and life expectancy along with income. Most poor countries fare poorly on the HDI, but an emphasis on the human side of economic growth can reduce inequality and improve the quality of life. [Source: United Nations Development Program, *Human Development Report 1996* (Oxford, New York, 1996), p. 67.]

servience, they may decide to spend less of their lives in childbearing. Families decide to focus resources on providing a good education for fewer children. Mexico, Korea, and Taiwan have all seen their birth rates drop sharply as their incomes have risen and their populations have received more education.

Slowly the results of economic development and birth control are being felt. The birth rate in poor countries has declined from 42 per 1000 in 1965 to 30 per 1000 in 1990, but that's still far higher than the birth rate of 13 per 1000 in the high-income countries. The struggle against poverty induced by excessive population growth continues.

Human Capital. In addition to dealing with excessive population growth, developing countries must also be concerned with the quality of their human resources. Economic planners in developing countries emphasize the following specific programs: (1) *Control disease and improve health and nutrition.* Raising the population's health standards not only makes people happier but also makes them more productive workers. Health-care clinics and provision of safe drinking water are vitally useful social capital. (2) *Improve education, reduce illiteracy, and train workers.* Educated people are more productive workers because they can use capital more effectively, adopt new technologies, and learn from their mistakes. For advanced learning in science, engineering, medicine, and management, countries will benefit by sending their best minds abroad to bring back the newest advances. But countries must beware of the *brain drain,* in which the most able people get drawn off to high-wage countries. (3) *Above all, do not underestimate the importance of human resources.* Most other factors can be bought in the international marketplace. Most labor is home-grown, although labor can sometimes be augmented through immigration. The crucial role of skilled labor has been shown again and again when sophisticated mining, defense, or manufacturing machinery fell into disrepair and disuse because the labor force of developing countries had not acquired the necessary skills for operation and maintenance.

Natural Resources

Some poor countries of Africa and Asia have meager endowments of natural resources, and such land and minerals as they do possess must be divided among dense populations. Perhaps the most valuable natural resource of developing countries is arable land. Much of the labor force in developing countries is employed in farming. Hence, the productive use of land—with appropriate conservation, fertilizers, and tillage—will go far in increasing a poor nation's output.

Moreover, landownership patterns are a key to providing farmers with strong incentives to invest in capital and technologies that will increase their land's yield. When farmers own their own land, they have better incentives to make improvements, such as in irrigation systems, and undertake appropriate conservation practices.

Economists suspect that natural wealth from oil or minerals is not an unalloyed blessing. Some countries—like the United States, Canada, and Norway—have used their natural wealth to form the solid base of industrial expansion. In other countries, the wealth has been like loot subject to plunder and *rent seeking* by corrupt leaders and military cliques. Countries like Nigeria and Congo (formerly Zaire), which are fabulously wealthy in terms of mineral resources, failed to convert their underground assets into productive human or tangible capital because of venal

rulers who drained that wealth into their own bank accounts and conspicuous consumption.

Capital Formation

A modern economy requires a vast array of capital goods. Countries must abstain from current consumption to engage in fruitful roundabout production. But there's the rub, for the poorest countries are near a subsistence standard of living. When you are poor to begin with, reducing current consumption to provide for future consumption seems impossible.

The leaders in the growth race invest at least 20 percent of output in capital formation. By contrast, the poorest agrarian countries are often able to save only 5 percent of national income. Moreover, much of the low level of saving goes to provide the growing population with housing and simple tools. Little is left over for development.

But let's say a country has succeeded in hiking up its rate of saving. Even so, it takes many decades to accumulate the highways, telecommunications systems, computers, electricity-generating plants, and other capital goods that underpin a productive economic structure.

Even before acquiring the most sophisticated computers, however, developing countries must first build up their *infrastructure,* or social overhead capital, which consists of the large-scale projects upon which a market economy depends. For example, a regional agricultural adviser helps farmers in an area learn of new seeds or crops; a road system links up the different markets; a public-health program inoculates people against typhoid or diphtheria and protects the population beyond those inoculated. In each of these cases it would be impossible for an enterprising firm to capture the social benefits involved, because the firm cannot collect fees from the thousands or even millions of beneficiaries. Because of the large indivisibilities and external effects of infrastructure, the government must step in to make or ensure the necessary investments.

In many developing countries, the single most pressing problem is too little saving. Particularly in the poorest regions, urgent current consumption competes with investment for scarce resources. The result is too little investment in the productive capital so indispensable for rapid economic progress.

Foreign Borrowing and Periodic Debt Crises. If there are so many obstacles to finding domestic savings for capital formation, why not borrow abroad? Does not economic theory tell us that a rich country, which has tapped its own high-yield investment projects, can benefit both itself and the recipient by investing in high-yield projects abroad?

The history of lending from rich to poor regions shows a cycle of opportunity, lending, profits, overexpansion, speculation, crisis, and drying-up of funds, followed by a new round of lending by yet another group of starry-eyed investors. In the nineteenth century, America experienced periodic bursts of investment and financial crisis in canals and railroads.

The latest example of this syndrome was the debt crisis of the 1980s. The figures on foreign investment in middle-income countries showed an impressive record of capital transfer. Investors in wealthy countries sent their funds abroad in search of higher returns; poor countries, hungry for funds, welcomed this flow of foreign capital.

By the early 1980s, however, the extent of foreign borrowing by developing countries had become unsustainably large. Total outstanding debt grew almost 20 percent per year and increased by almost $500 billion from 1973 to 1982. Some of the loans were put to good use in investments in oil drilling, textile factories, and coal-mining equipment, but others simply raised consumption levels.

As long as the exports of these countries grew at the same rate as borrowings, all seemed well. But with the rise in world interest rates and the slowdown in the world economy after 1980, many countries found that their borrow-and-invest strategy had led them into a financial crisis. Some countries (such as Bolivia and Peru) needed all their export earnings simply to pay the interest on their foreign debt. Others found themselves unable to meet debt-repayment schedules. Almost all indebted developing countries were staggering under heavy debt-service burdens (i.e., the need to repay the interest and principal on their loans). As a result, country after country, particularly in Latin America, failed to make interest payments and had their debts "rescheduled," or postponed.

By the mid-1990s, a decade of *adjustment* in the heavily indebted countries—slow output growth, declining real wages, debt reschedulings, and even trade surpluses—had put most countries in a more sustainable debt position. Private investment was once again flowing into poor regions, spurred in part by the privatizations and free-market strategies in these countries. The world had learned to live with the large unpaid debts of many developing countries. The debt-crisis virus was lying dormant, waiting for the next herd of exuberant speculators to emerge.

Technological Change and Innovations

The final and most important wheel is technological advance. Here developing countries have one potential advantage: They can hope to benefit by relying on the technological progress of more advanced nations.

Imitating Technology. Poor countries do not need to find modern Newtons to discover the law of gravity; they can read about it in any physics book. They don't have to repeat the slow, meandering inventions of the Industrial Revolution; they can buy tractors, computers, and power looms undreamed of by the great merchants of the past.

Japan and the United States clearly illustrate this in their historical developments. Japan joined the industrial race late, and only at the end of the nineteenth century did it send students abroad to study Western technology. The Japanese government took an active role in stimulating the pace of development and in building railroads and utilities. By adopting productive foreign technologies, Japan moved into its position today as the world's second-largest industrial economy.

The case of the United States provides a hopeful example to the rest of the world. The key inventions involved in the automobile originated almost exclusively abroad. Nevertheless, Ford and General Motors applied foreign inventions and rapidly became the world leaders in the automotive industry. The examples of the United States and Japan show how countries can thrive by adapting foreign science and technology to local market conditions.

Entrepreneurship and Innovation. From the histories of Japan and the United States, it might appear that adaptation of foreign technology is an easy recipe for development. You might say: "Just go abroad; copy more efficient methods; put them into effect at home; then sit back and wait for the extra output to roll in."

Alas, technological change is not that simple. You can send a textbook on chemical engineering to Poorovia, but without skilled scientists, engineers, entrepreneurs, and adequate capital, Poorovia couldn't even think about building a working petrochemical plant. Remember, the advanced technology was itself developed to meet the special conditions of the advanced countries—including ample skilled engineers and workers, reliable electrical service, and quickly available spare parts and repair services. These conditions do not prevail in poor countries.

One of the key tasks of economic development is the fostering of an entrepreneurial spirit. A country cannot thrive without a group of owners or managers willing to undertake risks, open new plants, adopt new technologies, confront strife, and import new ways of doing business. Government can help entrepreneurship by setting up extension services for farmers, educating and training the work force, and establishing management schools, while making sure that government itself maintains a healthy respect for profits and the role of private initiative.

Vicious Cycles to Virtuous Circles

We have emphasized that poor countries face great obstacles in combining the four elements of progress—labor, capital, resources, and innovation. In addition, countries find that the difficulties reinforce each other in a *vicious cycle of poverty*.

Figure 28-2 illustrates how one hurdle raises yet other hurdles. Low incomes lead to low saving; low saving retards the growth of capital; inadequate capital prevents introduction of new machinery and rapid growth in productivity; low productivity leads to low incomes. Other elements in poverty are also self-reinforcing. Poverty is accompanied by low levels of education, literacy, and skill; these in turn prevent the adoption of new and improved technologies and lead to rapid population growth, which eats away at improvements in output and food production.

Overcoming the barriers of poverty often requires a concerted effort on many fronts, and some development economists recommend a "big push" forward to break the vicious cycle. If a country is fortunate, simultaneous steps to invest more,

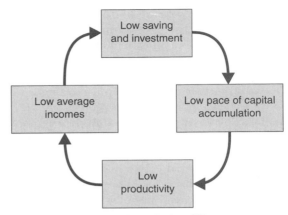

FIGURE 28-2. The Vicious Cycle of Poverty

Many obstacles to development are reinforcing. Low levels of income prevent saving, retard capital growth, hinder productivity growth, and keep income low. Successful development may require taking steps to break the chain at many points.

improve health and education, develop skills, and curb population growth can break the vicious cycle of poverty and stimulate a virtuous circle of rapid economic development.

STRATEGIES OF ECONOMIC DEVELOPMENT

We see how countries must combine labor, resources, capital, and technology in order to grow rapidly. But this is no real formula; it is the equivalent of saying that an Olympic sprinter must run like the wind. Why do some countries succeed in running faster than others? How do poor countries ever get started down the road of economic development?

Historians and social scientists have long been fascinated by the differences in the pace of economic growth among nations. Some early theories stressed climate, noting that all advanced countries lie in the earth's temperate zone. Others have pointed to custom, culture, or religion as a key factor. Max Weber emphasized the "Protestant ethic" as a driving force behind capitalism. More recently, Mancur Olson has argued that nations begin to decline when their decision structure becomes brittle and interest groups or oligarchies prevent social and economic change.

No doubt each of these theories has some validity for a particular time and place. But they do not hold up as universal explanations of economic development. Weber's theory leaves unexplained why the cradle of civilization appeared in the Near East and Greece while the later-dominant Europeans lived in caves, worshiped trolls, and wore bearskins. Where do we find the Protestant ethic in bustling Hong Kong? How can we explain that a country like Japan, with a rigid social structure and powerful lobbies, has become one of the world's most productive economies?

Even in the modern era, people become attached to simple, holistic explanations of economic development. Two decades ago, people considered import substitution (the replacement of imports with domestically produced goods) to be the most secure development strategy. Then, in the 1970s, reliance on labor-intensive techniques was thought advantageous. Today, as we will see, economists tend to emphasize reliance on market forces with an outward orientation. This history should serve as a warning to be wary of oversimplified approaches to complex processes.

Nonetheless, historians and development economists have learned much from the study of the varieties of economic growth. What are some of the lessons? The following account represents a montage of important ideas developed in recent years. Each approach describes how countries might break out of the vicious cycle of poverty and begin to mobilize the four wheels of economic development.

The Backwardness Hypothesis

One view emphasizes the international context of development. We saw above that poorer countries have important advantages that the first pioneers along the path of industrialization did not. Developing nations can now draw upon the capital, skills, and technology of more advanced countries. A hypothesis advanced by Alexander Gerschenkron of Harvard suggests that *relative backwardness* itself may aid development. Countries can buy modern textile machinery, efficient pumps, miracle seeds, chemical fertilizers, and medical supplies. Because they can lean on the technologies of advanced countries, today's developing countries can grow more rapidly than did Britain or Western Europe in the period 1780–1850. As low-income countries draw upon the more productive technologies of the leaders, we would expect to see *convergence* of countries toward the technological frontier. Convergence occurs when those countries or regions that have initially low incomes tend to grow more rapidly than ones with high incomes.

Industrialization vs. Agriculture

In most countries, incomes in urban areas are almost double those in rural agriculture. And in affluent nations, much of the economy is in industry and services. Hence, many nations jump to the conclusion that industrialization is the cause rather than the effect of affluence.

We must be wary of such inferences, which confuse the association of two characteristics with causality. Some people say, "Rich people drive BMWs, but driving a BMW will not make you a rich person." Similarly, there is no economic justification for a poor country to insist upon having its own national airline and large steel mill. These are not the fundamental necessities of economic growth.

The lesson of decades of attempts to accelerate industrialization at the expense of agriculture has led many analysts to rethink the role of farming. Industrialization is capital-intensive, attracts workers into crowded cities, and often produces high levels of unemployment. Raising productivity on farms may require less capital, while providing productive employment for surplus labor. Indeed, if Bangladesh could increase the productivity of its farming by 20 percent, that advance would do more to release resources for the production of comforts than would trying to construct a domestic steel industry to displace imports.

State vs. Market

The cultures of many developing countries are hostile to the operation of markets. Often, competition among firms or profit-seeking behavior is contrary to traditional practices, religious beliefs, or vested interests. Yet decades of experience suggest that extensive reliance on markets provides the most effective way of managing an economy and promoting rapid economic growth.

What are the important elements of a market-oriented policy? The important elements include an outward orientation in trade policy, low tariffs and few quantitative trade restrictions, the promotion of small business, and the fostering of competition. Moreover, markets work best in a stable macroeconomic environment—one in which taxes are predictable and inflation is low.

Growth and Openness

A fundamental issue of economic development concerns a country's stance toward international trade. Should developing countries attempt to be self-sufficient, replacing most imports with domestic production? (This is known as a strategy of *import substitution*.) Or should a country strive to pay for the imports it needs by improving efficiency and competitiveness, developing foreign markets, and keeping trade barriers low? (This is called a strategy of *openness* or *outward orientation*.)

Policies of import substitution were often popular in Latin America until the 1980s. The policy most frequently used toward this end was to build high tariff walls around manufacturing industries so that local firms could produce and sell goods that would otherwise be imported.

A policy of openness keeps trade barriers as low as practical, relying primarily on tariffs rather than quotas and other nontariff barriers. It minimizes the interference with capital flows and allows supply and demand to operate in financial markets. It avoids a state monopoly on exports and imports. It keeps government regulation to bare necessities for an orderly market economy. Above all, it relies primarily on a private market system of profits and losses to guide production, rather than depending on public ownership and control or the commands of a government planning system.

The success of outward-expansion policies is best illustrated by the East Asian NICs. A generation ago, countries like Taiwan, South Korea, and Singapore had per capita incomes one-quarter to one-third of those in the wealthiest Latin American countries. Yet, by saving large fractions of their national incomes and channeling these to high-return export industries, the East Asian NICs overtook every Latin American country by the late 1980s. The secret to success was not a doctrinaire laissez-faire policy, for the governments in fact engaged in selective planning and intervention. Rather, the openness and outward orientation allowed the countries to reap economies of scale and the benefits of international specialization and thus to increase employment, use

domestic resources effectively, enjoy rapid productivity growth, and provide enormous gains in living standards.

The fruits of openness were demonstrated in a recent study by Jeffrey Sachs and Andrew Warner.[1] They examined the relationship between openness and economic growth. An *open economy* is defined as one characterized by low trade barriers, open financial markets, and private markets. A *closed economy* is the opposite.

They find that openness is strongly associated with rapid economic growth. The basic story is shown in Figure 28-3. The left panel shows the performance of closed economies. The closed economies had an average growth rate of per capita income of only 0.9 percent annually over the 1970–1989 period. There was no convergence of these countries—many with low incomes—toward the high-income countries. Figure 28-3(*b*) shows the growth of open economies. These grew at an average rate of 4.5 percent annually over the same period; moreover, low-income open economies showed strong convergence toward rich countries. The importance of openness could hardly be more emphatically shown than by these trends.

Summary Judgment

Decades of experience in dozens of countries have led many development economists to the following summary view of the way government can best promote rapid economic development.

The government has a vital role in establishing and maintaining a healthy economic environment. It must ensure respect for the rule of law, enforce contracts, and orient its regulations toward competition and innovation. Government often plays a leading role in investment in human capital through education, health, and transportation, but it should minimize its intervention in sectors where it has no comparative advantage. Government should focus its efforts on areas where there are clear signs of market failures and should dismantle regulatory impediments to the private sector in areas where government has comparative disadvantage.

---

[1] "Economic Reform and the Process of Global Integration," *Brookings Papers on Economic Activity*, no. 1, 1995, pp. 1–118.

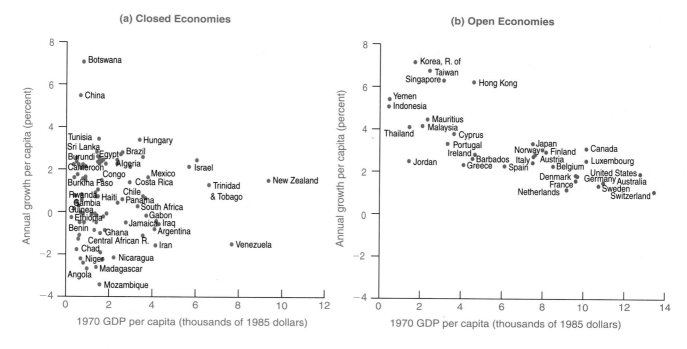

FIGURE 28-3. Openness and Economic Growth, 1970–1989

What is the impact of openness on economic growth? Panel (**a**) shows that closed economies grow slowly and do not converge to high-income countries. Panel (**b**) shows the open economies—nonsocialist economies with relatively low barriers to trade and financial flows. They grow much more rapidly and tend to converge to the highest-income regions. (Source: Jeffrey Sachs and Andrew Warner, "Economic Reform and the Process of Global Integration," *Brookings Papers on Economic Activity*, no. 1, 1995, pp. 42–43.)

B. ALTERNATIVE MODELS FOR DEVELOPMENT

Humanity has not managed to create anything more efficient than a market economy. . . . Its self-adjustment and self-regulation are geared to promote the best possible coordination of economic activity, rational use of labor, material, and financial resources, and balance in the national economy.

The 500 Day Plan: Transition to the Market,
report of a group of Russian economic experts
to Presidents M. Gorbachev and B. Yeltsin (1990)

People continually look for ways to improve their living standards. Economic betterment is particularly compelling for poor countries seeking a path to the riches they see around them. This textbook has surveyed in depth the mixed market economy of the United States, which combines fundamentally free markets with a sizable government sector. What other alternatives are available?

A BOUQUET OF "ISMS"

At one extreme is *free-market absolutism*, which holds that the best government is the least government. At the other extreme is complete *communism*, with the government operating a collectivized economic order in which the first-person singular hardly exists. Between the extremes of complete laissez-faire and communism lie mixed capitalism, managed markets, socialism, and many combinations of these models. In this section, we describe briefly some of the influential alternative strategies for growth and development:

1. *The Asian managed-market approach.* South Korea, Taiwan, Singapore, and other countries of East Asia have devised their own brands of economics that combine strong government oversight with powerful market forces.
2. *Socialism.* Socialist thinking encompasses a wide variety of different approaches. In Western Europe after World War II, socialist governments operating in a democratic framework expanded the welfare state, nationalized industries, and planned their economies. In recent years, however, these countries moved back toward a free-market framework with extensive deregulation and privatization.
3. *Soviet-style communism.* For many years, the clearest alternative to the market economy existed in the Soviet Union. Under the Soviet model, the state owns all the land and most of the capital, sets wages and most prices, and directs the microeconomic operation of the economy.

The Central Dilemma: Market vs. Command

A survey of alternative economic systems may seem like a bewildering array of economic "isms." And indeed, there is a great variety in the way countries organize their economies.

But one central issue runs through all the debates about alternative economic systems: Should economic decisions be taken primarily in the private market or by government commands?

At one end of the spectrum is the *market economy.* In a market system, people act voluntarily and primarily for financial gain or personal satisfaction. Firms buy factors and produce outputs, selecting inputs and outputs in a way that will maximize their profits. Consumers supply factors and buy consumer goods to maximize their satisfactions. Agreements on production and consumption are made voluntarily and with the use of money, at prices determined in free markets, and on the basis of arrangements between buyers and sellers. Although individuals differ greatly in terms of economic power, the relations between individuals and firms are horizontal in nature, essentially voluntary, and nonhierarchical.

At the other end of the spectrum is the *command economy,* where decisions are made by government bureaucracy. In this approach, people are linked by a vertical relationship, and control is exercised by a multilevel hierarchy. The planning bureaucracy determines *what* goods are produced, *how* they are produced, and *for whom* output is produced. The highest level of the pyramid makes the major decisions and develops the elements of the plan for the economy. The plan is subdivided and transmitted down the bureaucratic ladder, with the lower levels of the hierarchy executing the plan with increasing attention to detail. Individuals are motivated by coercion and legal sanctions; organizations compel individuals to accept orders from above. Transactions and commands may or may not use money; trades may or may not take place at established prices.

In between are the socialist and the managed-market economies. In both cases government plays an important role in guiding and directing the economy, though much less so than in a command economy. The tension between markets and command runs through all discussions about alternative economic systems. Let us look in more detail at some of the alternatives to the mixed market economies.

THE ASIAN MODELS

Dragons and Laggards

The most impressive growth performance in the last half-century has occurred in East Asia. Everyone knows about the Japanese miracle, but South Korea, Singapore, Hong Kong, and Taiwan have also shown remarkable economic progress. Table 28-2 compares

Regions	Average growth of per capita GDP, 1965–1990	Investment as percent of GDP, 1990
High-performing Asian economies*	5.6	35
South Asia	1.9	19
Latin America	1.8	17
Sub-Saharan Africa	0.2	9

*Japan, South Korea, Singapore, Hong Kong, Indonesia, Malaysia, and Taiwan

TABLE 28-2. Attention to Fundamentals Spurred Growth for the Asian Dragons

Source: World Bank, *The East Asia Miracle: Economic Growth and Government Policies* (World Bank, Washington, D.C., 1993).

the performance of the Asian dragons to that of the Latin laggards and the stagnant economies of sub-Saharan Africa.

A recent World Bank study analyzed the economic policies of different regions to see whether any patterns emerged.[2] The results confirmed common views but also found a few surprises. Here are the high points:

- *Investment rates.* The Asian dragons followed the classical recipe of high investment rates to ensure that their economies benefited from the latest technology and could build up the necessary infrastructure. As Table 28-2 shows, investment rates among the Asian dragons were almost 20 percentage points higher than those of other regions.

- *Macroeconomic fundamentals.* Successful countries had a steady hand on macroeconomic policies, keeping inflation low and investment rates high. They invested heavily in human capital as well as in physical capital and did more to promote education than any other developing region. The financial systems were managed to ensure monetary stability and a sound currency.

- *Outward orientation.* The Asian dragons were outward-oriented, often keeping their exchange rates undervalued to promote exports, encouraging exports with fiscal incentives, and pursuing technological advance by adopting best-practice techniques of high-income countries.

- *Government-sponsored competition.* In a controversial break from pure market-oriented

approaches, successful countries were often effective in using "nonmarket contests" to allocate resources. These governments would sometimes identify strategic areas and then set up a race among domestic firms to stimulate competition. The report contends that a well-run contest can generate even better results than unregulated markets by providing a focus for competition and inducing the participants to cooperate as they compete (one business strategist calls this "coopetition"). This strategy depends upon the caliber and integrity of the civil service, however, so it cannot work in countries where public employees are corrupt and incompetent.

This study is a useful reminder of the importance of simple virtues like thrift and honesty, which are often omitted in the fancier economic theories. At the same time, it is not yet clear whether the East Asian growth formula can be applied in other parts of the world.

The Chinese Giant: Market Leninism

One of the major surprises in economic development during the last decade was the rapid growth in the Chinese economy. After the Chinese revolution of 1949, China initially adopted a Soviet-style central-planning system. The high-water mark of centralization came with the Cultural Revolution of 1966–1969, which led to an economic slowdown in China. After the death of the revolutionary leader Mao Tse-tung, a new generation concluded that economic reform was necessary if the Communist party was to survive. Under Deng Xiaoping (1977–1997),

---

[2] World Bank, *The East Asia Miracle: Economic Growth and Government Policies* (World Bank, Washington, D.C., 1993).

China decentralized a great deal of economic power and allowed competition. Economic reform was, however, not accompanied by political reform; the democracy movement was ruthlessly repressed in Tiananmen Square in 1989, and the Communist party has continued to monopolize the political process.

To spur economic growth, the Chinese leadership has taken dramatic steps such as setting up "special economic zones" and allowing alternative forms of ownership. The most rapidly growing parts of China have been the coastal regions, such as the southern region near Hong Kong. This area has become closely integrated with countries outside China and has attracted considerable foreign investment. In addition, China has allowed collective, private, and foreign firms, free from central planning or control, to operate alongside state-owned firms. These more innovative forms of ownership have grown rapidly and by the mid-1990s were producing more than half of China's GDP.

The robust performance of the Chinese economy has surprised observers almost as much as did the collapse of the Soviet economy. For the last decade, according to official statistics, China's real GDP growth averaged almost 10 percent per year. Exports grew seven-fold during the 1980–1995 period. By 1995 China had an export surplus of more than $30 billion with the United States and had accumulated almost $75 billion in foreign exchange reserves at a time when Russia was essentially bankrupt. Many countries are watching carefully to see if China can stay on its fast-growth track.

SOCIALISM

As a doctrine, socialism developed from the ideas of Marx and other radical thinkers of the nineteenth century. Socialism is a middle ground between laissez-faire capitalism and the central-planning model, which we discuss in the next subsection. A few common elements characterize most socialist philosophies:

- *Government ownership of productive resources.* Socialists traditionally believed that the role of private property should be reduced. Key industries such as railroads and banking should be nationalized (that is, owned and operated by the state). In recent years, because of the poor performance of

many state-owned enterprises, enthusiasm for nationalization has ebbed in most advanced democracies.
- *Planning.* Socialists are suspicious of the "chaos" of the marketplace and question the allocational efficiency of the invisible hand. They insist that a planning mechanism is needed to coordinate different sectors. In recent years, planners have emphasized subsidies to promote the rapid development of high-technology industries, such as microelectronics, aircraft manufacture, and biotechnology; these policies are sometimes called "industrial policies."
- *Redistribution of income.* Inherited wealth and the highest incomes are to be reduced by the militant use of government taxing powers; in some West European countries, marginal tax rates have reached 98 percent. Social security benefits, free medical care, and cradle-to-grave welfare services collectively provided out of progressive-tax sources increase the well-being of the less privileged and guarantee minimum standards of living.
- *Peaceful and democratic evolution.* Socialists often advocate the peaceful and gradual extension of government ownership—evolution by ballot rather than revolution by bullet.

Over the last decades, socialist approaches have waned with the fall of communism, the stagnation in Europe, and the success of market-oriented economies. Thoughtful socialists are combing through the wreckage to find a future role for this branch of economic thought.

THE FAILED MODEL: SOVIET COMMUNISM

For many years, developing countries looked to the Soviet Union and other communist countries as role models on how to industrialize. Communism offered both a theoretical critique of Western capitalism and a seemingly workable strategy for economic development. We begin by reviewing the theoretical underpinnings of Marxism and communism and then examine how the Soviet-style command economy worked in practice. Finally, we will look at the problems that the ex-communist countries are experiencing in making the transition to a market-based economy.

![Karl Marx icon]

Karl Marx: Economist as revolutionary:
On the surface, Karl Marx (1818–1883) lived an uneventful life, studiously poring through books in the British Museum, writing newspaper articles, and working on his scholarly studies of capitalism. Although originally attracted to German universities, his atheism, pro-constitutionalism, and radical ideas led him to journalism. He was eventually exiled to Paris and London, where he wrote his massive critique of capitalism, *Capital* (1867, 1885, 1894).

The centerpiece of Marx's work is an incisive analysis of the strengths and weaknesses of capitalism. Marx argued that all commodity value is determined by labor content—both the direct labor and the indirect labor embodied in capital equipment. For example, the value of a shirt comes from the efforts of the textile workers who put it together, plus the efforts of the workers who made the looms. By imputing all the value of output to labor, Marx attempted to show that profits—the part of output that is produced by workers but received by capitalists—amount to "unearned income."

In Marx's view, the injustice of capitalists' receiving unearned income justifies transferring the ownership of factories and other means of production from capitalists to workers. He trumpeted his message in *The Communist Manifesto* (1848): "Let the ruling classes tremble at a Communist revolution. The proletarians have nothing to lose but their chains." And the ruling capitalist classes did tremble at Marxism for more than a century!

Like many great economists, but with more passion than most, Marx was greatly moved by the struggle of working people and hoped to improve their lives. He penned the words that appear on his gravestone: "Up 'til now philosophers have only interpreted the world in various ways. The point, though, is to change it!" Our epitaph for Marx might echo the appraisal of the distinguished intellectual historian, Sir Isaiah Berlin: "No thinker in the nineteenth century has had so direct, deliberate, and powerful an influence on mankind as Karl Marx."

increasing accumulation of capital has two contradictory consequences. As the supply of available capital increases, the rate of profit on capital falls. At the same time, with fewer jobs, the unemployment rate rises, and wages fall. In Marx's terms, the "reserve army of the unemployed" would grow, and the working class would become increasingly "immiserized"—by which he meant that working conditions would deteriorate and workers would grow progressively alienated from their jobs.

As profits decline and investment opportunities at home become exhausted, the ruling capitalist classes resort to imperialism. Capital tends to seek higher rates of profit abroad. And, according to this theory (particularly as later expanded by Lenin), the foreign policies of imperialist nations increasingly attempt to win colonies and then mercilessly milk surplus value from them.

Marx believed that the capitalist system could not continue this unbalanced growth forever. Marx predicted increasing inequality under capitalism, along with a gradual emergence of class consciousness among the downtrodden proletariat. Business cycles would become ever more violent as mass poverty resulted in macroeconomic underconsumption. Finally, a cataclysmic depression would sound the death knell of capitalism. Like feudalism before it, capitalism would contain the seeds of its own destruction.

The *economic interpretation of history* is one of Marx's lasting contributions to Western thought. Marx argued that economic interests lie behind and determine our values. Why do business executives vote for conservative candidates, while labor leaders support those who advocate raising the minimum wage or increasing unemployment benefits? The reason, Marx held, is that people's beliefs and ideologies reflect the material interests of their social and economic class. In fact, Marx's approach is hardly foreign to mainstream economics. It generalizes Adam Smith's analysis of self-interest from the dollar votes of the marketplace to the ballot votes of elections and the bullet votes of the barricades.

Baleful Prophesies

Marx saw capitalism as inevitably leading to socialism. In Marx's world, technological advances enable capitalists to replace workers with machinery as a means of earning greater profits. But this

From Textbooks to Tactics: Soviet-Style Command Economy

Marx wrote extensively about the faults of capitalism, but he left no design for the promised socialist land. His arguments suggested that communism would arise in the most highly developed industrial countries. Instead, it was feudal Russia that adopted the Marxist vision. Let's examine this fascinating and horrifying chapter of economic history.

Historical Roots. An analysis of the Russian Revolution and its aftermath is of the utmost importance for economics because the Soviet Union served as a laboratory for theories about the functioning of a command economy. Some economists claimed that socialism simply could not work; the Soviet experience proved them wrong. Its advocates argued that communism would overtake capitalism; Soviet history also refutes this thesis.

Although czarist Russia grew rapidly from 1880 to 1914, it was considerably less developed than industrialized countries like the United States or Britain. World War I brought great hardship to Russia and allowed the communists to seize power. From 1917 to 1933, the Soviet Union experimented with different socialist models before settling on central planning. But dissatisfaction with the pace of industrialization led Stalin to undertake a radical new venture around 1928—collectivization of agriculture, forced-draft industrialization, and central planning of the economy.[3]

Under the collectivization of Soviet agriculture between 1929 and 1935, 94 percent of Soviet peasants were forced to join collective farms. In the process, many wealthy peasants were deported, and conditions deteriorated so much that millions perished. The other part of the Soviet "great leap forward" came through the introduction of economic planning for rapid industrialization. The planners created the first 5-year plan to cover the period 1928–1933. The first plan established the priorities of Soviet planning: heavy industry was to be favored over light industry, and consumer goods were to be the residual sector after all the other priorities had been met. Although there were many reforms and changes in emphasis, the Stalinist model of a command economy applied in the Soviet Union, and after World War II in Eastern Europe, until the fall of Soviet communism at the end of the 1980s.

How the Command Economy Functioned.
In the Soviet-style command economy, the broad categories of output were determined by political decisions. Military spending in the Soviet Union was always allocated a substantial part of output and scientific resources, while the other major priority was investment. Consumption claimed the residual output after the quotas of higher-priority sectors were filled.

In large part, decisions about how goods were to be produced were made by the planning authorities. Planners first decided on the quantities of final outputs (the *what*). Then they worked backward from outputs to the required inputs and the flows among different firms. Investment decisions were specified in great detail by the planners, while firms had considerable flexibility in deciding upon their mix of labor inputs.

What motivated managers to fulfill the plans? Clearly no planning system could specify all the activities of all the firms—this would have required trillions of commands every year. Many details were left to the managers of individual factories, but *faulty managerial incentives* were a recurrent problem for the command economy.

The managerial-incentive system produced significant distortions in the command economy. One notable example came in book production. In a market economy, commercial decisions about books are made primarily on the basis of profit and loss. In the Soviet Union, because profits were taboo, planners instead used quantitative targets. A first managerial incentive was to reward firms according to the number of books produced, so publishers printed thousands of thin unread volumes. Faced with a clear incentive problem, the planners shifted to the number of pages, so the publishers turned to fat books with onion-skin paper and large type. The planners then changed to the number of words as a criterion—to which the publishers responded by printing huge volumes with tiny type. In all these schemes, the ultimate beneficiary of the book—the reader—was nowhere in sight.

The problem of faulty incentives crops up in organizations in all countries, but the Soviet model had few mechanisms (like bankruptcy in markets and elections for public goods) to provide an ultimate check on waste.

---

[3] A highly readable account of developments in Soviet economic history is contained in Alec Nove, *An Economic History of the U.S.S.R.*, 3d ed. (Penguin, Baltimore, 1986). A careful study of the Soviet economic system is provided by Paul R. Gregory and Robert C. Stuart, *Soviet Economic Structure and Performance*, 4th ed. (Harper & Row, New York, 1990).

Comparative Economic Performance. From World War II until the mid-1980s, the United States and the Soviet Union engaged in a super-power competition for public opinion, military superiority, and economic dominance. How well did the command economies perform in the economic growth race? Any attempt at answering this question is bedeviled by the absence of reliable statistics. Most economists believed until recently that the Soviet Union grew rapidly from 1928 until the mid-1960s, with growth rates perhaps surpassing those in North America and Western Europe. After the mid-1960s, growth in the Soviet Union stagnated and output actually began to decline. Estimates of living standards today are treacherous, but per capita income in Russia in the early 1990s appears to be less than one-quarter of that in the United States.

A revealing comparison of the performance of market and command economies can be made by contrasting the experience of East Germany and West Germany. These countries started out with roughly equal levels of productivity and similar industrial structures at the end of World War II. After four decades of capitalism in the West and Soviet-style socialism in the East, productivity in East Germany had fallen to a level estimated between one-fourth and one-third of that in West Germany. Moreover, the East German growth tended to emphasize production of intermediate goods and commodities of little value to consumers. Quantity, not quality, was the goal.

Finally, what of the scourges of capitalism—unemployment and inflation? Unemployment was traditionally low in Soviet-style economies because labor was generally in short supply as a result of the ambitious economic plans. Furthermore, controlled prices tended to be quite stable, so measured inflation was absent. In the late 1980s and early 1990s, however, open inflation erupted. In addition, prices were well below market-clearing levels, and acute shortages arose in what is called *repressed inflation.*

Is there a final balance sheet on the Soviet experience? The Soviet model has demonstrated that a command economy is capable of mobilizing resources for rapid economic growth. But it did so in an atmosphere of great human sacrifice and political repression. Moreover, in the modern world of open borders and high-quality goods and services, the blunt control of the command economy could not match the finely tuned incentives and innovation of a market economy. But whatever economic merits a command economy might have, the repressive political system was unacceptable to the people of the Soviet Union and Eastern Europe and was universally rejected beginning in 1989.

From Marx to Market

A cruel joke heard in Eastern Europe is "Question: What is communism? Answer: The longest road from capitalism to capitalism." Having decided to take the road back to a market economy, a command economy has an arduous path to follow. Among the major obstacles on the road to reform are the following:

- *Price reform and free-market pricing.* Prices of both inputs and outputs are often far from market-determined prices. Food, housing, and energy are generally heavily subsidized, while automobiles and consumer durables sell at levels far above the world price levels. Sooner or later, prices must be freely determined by supply and demand.
- *Hard budget constraints.* Enterprises in command economies operate with "soft budget constraints," a term signifying that operating losses are covered by subsidies and do not lead to bankruptcy. In a market economy, firms must be fiscally responsible—enterprises must know that unprofitability ultimately means economic bankruptcy for the firm and economic ruin for the managers.
- *Privatization.* In market economies, output is primarily produced in private firms; in the United States, for example, only 3 percent of GDP is produced by the federal government. In Soviet-style communist countries, by contrast, between 80 and 90 percent of output was produced by the state. Moving to the market requires that the actual decisions about buying, selling, pricing, producing, borrowing, and lending must be made by private agents.
- *Other reforms.* In addition, transition to the market requires setting up the legal framework for a market, establishing a modern banking system, breaking up the pervasive monopolies, tightening monetary and fiscal policy in order to prevent runaway inflation, and opening up the economy to international competition.

- *Sequencing of the transition.* One of the most difficult issues is to know where to begin. The reform debate usually divides between a radical (or "shock-therapy") approach and a gradual (or "step-by-step") approach. When gradual approaches accomplished little, Western economists generally advocated making a rapid transition. One influential economist was Harvard's Jeffrey Sachs, a brilliant young economist who has nursed many ailing countries back to health. He persuaded the Polish government to adopt the shock-therapy approach in January 1990. This was the model that Russia followed in 1991–92 under President Yeltsin and a government led by economist Yegor Gaidar. The radical reformers freed prices and international trade, dismantled the planning apparatus, and attempted to keep money tight. The next few years saw pitched battle between the reformers, bureaucrats from the old regime, and wistful romantics who yearned for the "good old days" under communism. "Two steps forward and one step backward" has characterized the reform movement in Russia and many formerly socialist countries.

Clearly, reformers in the Soviet-style economies face a Herculean task. But this checklist of reforms applies more universally to countries in Latin America or Africa who have traveled some distance down the road to a centrally planned economy and want a more market-oriented economy.

Reform's Progress. Reforms in communist countries are in their infancy, and it will be many years before we can evaluate the results. But the initial returns are sobering. First, virtually all countries suffered deep depressions as they shucked off their socialist structures. The sources of the decline in output are unclear, but a major reason is undoubtedly that the delicate web of buyer-seller relationships was completely disrupted by the transition. Second, many countries experienced rapid inflation, and some (like Ukraine) suffered from hyperinflation. The major reasons were that the freeing of prices and wages triggered an initial inflation, and this was followed by a classic wage-price spiral. An additional impetus to inflation came in those countries where a weak government was unable to contain the budget deficit and government consequently relied upon the monetary printing press to finance its expenditures.

The most successful countries were those who had the shortest history of central planning, those which made the most rapid transition, and those which moved most quickly to integrate themselves into the larger world economy. The Czech Republic exemplified a successful transition. The greatest difficulties in the transition came in the remnants of the former Soviet Union, particularly in those countries where the transition was slow and reluctant.

A CAUTIONARY FINAL NOTE

This chapter has described the problems and prospects of poor countries struggling to improve the living conditions of their population—providing the dry houses, education, electric lights, fast horses, automobiles, and long vacations that we wrote of at the beginning of the chapter. What are the prospects of attaining these goals? We close with a hopeful note and sober warning from Sachs and Warner:

> The world economy at the end of the twentieth century looks much like the world economy at the end of the nineteenth century. A global capitalist system is taking shape, drawing almost all regions of the world into arrangements of open trade and harmonized economic institutions. As in the nineteenth century, this new round of globalization promises to lead to economic convergence for the countries that join the system. . . .
>
> And yet there are also profound risks for the consolidation of market reforms in Russia, China, and Africa, as well as for the maintenance of international agreements among the leading countries. . . . The spread of capitalism in the [last] twenty-five years is an historic event of great promise and significance, but whether we will be celebrating the consolidation of a democratic and market-based world system [twenty-five years hence] will depend on our own foresight and good judgments in the years to come.[4]

---

[4] "Economic Reform and the Process of Global Integration," *Brookings Papers on Economic Activity*, no. 1, 1995, pp. 63–64.

SUMMARY

A. Economic Growth in Poor Countries

1. Most of the world consists of developing countries, which have relatively low per capita incomes. Such countries often exhibit rapid population growth and low literacy and have a high proportion of their population living and working on farms. Within the group of developing countries, some are middle-income newly industrializing countries, or NICs. This group has been successful in breaking the vicious cycle of underdevelopment.

2. The key to development lies in four fundamental factors: human resources, natural resources, capital formation, and technology. Population causes problems of explosive growth as the Malthusian prediction of diminishing returns haunts less developed countries. On the constructive agenda, improving the population's health, education, and technical training has high priority.

3. Investment and savings rates in poor countries are low because incomes are so depressed that little can be saved for the future. International finance of investment in poor countries has witnessed many crises over the last two centuries. The most recent cycle came when many middle-income countries borrowed heavily in the 1970s to finance ambitious development programs. The economic slowdown of the early 1980s led to swollen debts, which left these countries unable to export enough to cover their debt service and customary import levels.

4. Technological change is often associated with investment and new machinery. It offers much hope to the developing nations because they can adopt the more productive technologies of advanced nations. This requires entrepreneurship. One task of development is to spur internal growth of the scarce entrepreneurial spirit.

5. Numerous theories of economic development help explain why the four fundamental factors are present or absent at a particular time. Geography and climate, custom, religious and business attitudes, class conflicts and political systems—each affects economic development. But none does so in a simple and invariable way. Development economists today emphasize the growth advantage of relative backwardness, the need to respect the role of agriculture, and the art of finding the proper boundary between state and market. The most recent consensus is on the advantages of openness.

B. Alternative Models for Development

6. Other approaches have competed with the mixed market economy as models for economic development. Alternative strategies include the managed-market approach of the East Asian countries, socialism, and the Soviet-style command economy.

7. The managed-market approach of Japan and the Asian dragons, such as South Korea, Hong Kong, Taiwan, and Singapore, have proved remarkably successful over the last quarter-century. Among the key ingredients are macroeconomic stability, high investment rates, a sound financial system, rapid improvements in education, and an outward orientation in trade and technology policies.

8. Socialism is a middle ground between capitalism and communism, stressing government ownership of the means of production, planning by the state, income redistribution, and peaceful transition to a more egalitarian world.

9. Historically, Marxism took its deepest roots in semifeudal Russia. A study of resource allocation in the Soviet-style command economy shows great central planning of broad elements of resource allocation, particularly the emphasis on heavy industry. The Soviet economy grew rapidly in its early decades, but stagnation and collapse have today put Russia and other formerly communist countries at income levels far below those of North America, Japan, and Western Europe.

10. Faced with slowing economic growth and the desire for economic reform, Russia and other formerly communist countries are making the difficult transition to market economies. Transition raises many obstacles, such as soft budget constraints, frozen and distorted prices, and an inadequate legal framework. Two major transition strategies are the shock-therapy approach of multiple simultaneous measures and the more cautious step-by-step approach, in which reforms are sequenced to prevent disruption. The lessons of the transition are broadly applicable to countries hoping to cast off government controls for a market-oriented system.

CONCEPTS FOR REVIEW

Economic Development

developing country, LDC
indicators of development
Human Development Index
four elements in development
vicious cycles, virtuous circles

backwardness hypothesis
openness and convergence

Alternative Models for Development

the central dilemma of markets vs.
command

socialism, communism
Soviet-style command economy
transition to the market

QUESTIONS FOR DISCUSSION

1. Do you agree with the celebration of material well-being expressed in the chapter's opening quotation? What would you add to the list of the benefits of economic development?

2. Delineate each of the four important factors driving economic development. With respect to these, how was it that the high-income oil-exporting countries became rich? What hope is there for a country like Mali, which has very low per capita resources of capital, land, and technology?

3. Some fear the "vicious cycle of underdevelopment." In a poor country, rapid population growth eats into whatever improvements in technology occur and lowers living standards. With a low per capita income, the country cannot save and invest and mainly engages in subsistence farming. With most of the population on the farm, there is little hope for education, decline in fertility, or industrialization. If you were to advise such a country, how would you break through the vicious cycle?

4. Compare the situation a developing country faces today with the one it might have faced (at an equivalent level of per capita income) 200 years ago. Considering the four wheels of economic development, explain the advantages and disadvantages that today's developing country might experience.

5. Analyze the way that *what, how,* and *for whom* are solved in a Soviet-style command economy, and compare your analysis with the solution of the three central questions in a market economy.

6. **Advanced problem** (relying upon the growth accounting of Chapter 27): We can extend our growth-accounting equation to include three factors and write the following equation:

$$g_Q = s_L \, g_L + s_K \, g_K + s_R \, g_R + \text{T.C.}$$

where g_Q = the growth rate of output, g_i = the growth rate of inputs (i = inputs to production: L for labor, K for capital, and R for land and other natural resources), and s_i = the contribution of each input to output growth as measured by its share of national income ($0 \leq s_i \leq 1$ and $s_L + s_K + s_R = 1$). T.C. measures technological change.

a. In the poorest developing countries, the share of capital is close to zero, the main resource is agricultural land (which is constant), and there is little technological change. Can you use this to explain the Malthusian hypothesis in which per capita output is likely to be stagnant or even to decline (i.e., $g_Q < g_L$)?

b. In advanced industrial economies, the share of land resources drops to virtually zero. Why does this lead to the growth-accounting equation studied in the last chapter? Can you use this to explain how countries can avoid the Malthusian trap of stagnant incomes?

c. According to economists who are pessimistic about future prospects (including a group of *neo-Malthusians* from the Club of Rome, which was discussed in the last chapter), T.C. is close to zero, the available supply of natural resources is declining, and the share of resources is large and rising. Does this explain why the future of industrial societies might be bleak? What assumptions of the neo-Malthusians might you question?

CHAPTER 29
UNEMPLOYMENT AND THE FOUNDATIONS OF AGGREGATE SUPPLY

Be nice to people on your way up because you'll meet them on your way down.

Wilson Mizner

The last two chapters examined the process of economic growth, looking at the trends for industrial economies like the United States and the pressing needs of developing countries. We now show how our economic-growth theory dovetails with our analytical framework of aggregate supply. After deriving the *AS* curve, we then take up one of the most difficult social issues of market economies—the plague

of unemployment. We will see that unemployment shifts over the business cycle are best understood as changes in aggregate demand relative to aggregate supply. Although better understanding of the nature of unemployment has allowed most countries to avoid the worst depressions, even today many market economies have undesirably high levels of unemployment.

A. THE FOUNDATIONS OF AGGREGATE SUPPLY

The chapters of Part Five described how output, employment, and prices in the economy are determined by the interaction between aggregate supply and demand, focusing primarily on aggregate demand and its determinants. But we must not give aggregate supply a short shrift. Aggregate supply—which describes the quantity of goods and services that will be produced at a given price level—is critical for understanding the evolution of the economy. In the short run, the nature of the inflationary process and the effectiveness of government countercyclical policies depend on aggregate supply. In the long run of a decade or more, economic growth and

rising living standards are closely linked with increases in aggregate supply.

This distinction between short-run and long-run aggregate supply is crucial to modern macroeconomics. In the short run, it is the interaction of aggregate supply and demand that determines business-cycle fluctuations, inflation, unemployment, recessions, and booms. But in the long run, it is the growth of potential output working through aggregate supply which explains the trend in output and living standards.

Let's start with a few definitions. Recall that **aggregate supply** describes the behavior of the production side of the economy. We can construct the **aggregate supply curve**, or *AS* curve, as the schedule showing the level of total national output that will be produced at each possible price level, other things being equal.

In analyzing aggregate supply, it is crucial to distinguish *AS* curves according to the period. The short run of a year or so involves the **short-run aggregate supply schedule**. This relationship is depicted as an *upward-sloping AS* curve—one along which higher prices are associated with increases in the production of goods and services.

For the long run (several years or a decade or more), we look at the **long-run aggregate supply schedule**. This relationship is shown as a *vertical AS* schedule, one in which increases in the price level are not associated with an increase in total output supplied.

This section is devoted to explaining these central points.

DETERMINANTS OF AGGREGATE SUPPLY

Aggregate supply depends fundamentally upon two distinct sets of forces: potential output and input costs. Let us examine each of these influences.

Potential Output

The underlying foundation of aggregate supply is the productive capability of the economy, or its *potential output*. Recall that potential output represents the maximum output that the economy can produce without triggering rising inflationary pressures. That is, a country's potential output is the maximum sustainable production given the technology, managerial skills, capital, labor, and resources that are available.

Over the long run, aggregate supply depends primarily upon potential output. Hence, long-run *AS* is determined by the same factors which influence long-run growth: the amount and quality of available labor, the quantity of machines and other capital goods used by workers, the level of technology, and so on. The analysis of long-run growth trends therefore concerns both the growth of potential output and the determination of aggregate supply.

For quantitative purposes, macroeconomists generally use the following definition of potential output:

Potential GDP is the highest sustainable level of national output. We measure potential GDP as the output that would be produced at a benchmark level of the unemployment rate called the *lowest sustainable unemployment rate* (LSUR). For the United States in the mid-1990s, most estimates of the lowest sustainable unemployment rate are in the range of 5 to 6 percent of the labor force.

In times of recession, businesses produce less than potential output. In such periods, workers are frequently laid off and have trouble finding good jobs, companies are downsized, and profits are depressed. In high-pressure periods such as wartime, actual output may exceed potential output for short periods. If the economy produces more than its potential output, price inflation will heat up as unemployment falls, factories are worked intensively, and workers and businesses try to extract higher wages and profits. Between these extremes of high and low utilization of capacity is the sustainable level of output that we designate as potential output.

Potential output is obviously a moving target. As the economy grows, potential output increases as well, and the aggregate supply curve shifts to the right. Table 29-1 shows the key determinants of aggregate supply, broken down into factors affecting potential output and production costs. From our analysis of economic growth, we know that the prime factors determining the growth in potential output are the growth in inputs and technological progress.

Input Costs

The aggregate supply curve is affected not only by potential output but also by changes in the costs of production. As production costs rise, businesses are willing to supply a given level of output only at a higher price. For example, if input costs rose so much that production costs exactly doubled, the price at which businesses would supply each level of output would also double. The *AS* curve would shift upward so that each output *AS* pair (P, Q) would be replaced by $(2P, Q)$.

Table 29-1 shows some of the cost factors affecting aggregate supply. By far the most important cost is labor earnings, which constitute about three-quarters of the overall cost of production for a country like the United States. For the small open economies

Variable	Impact on aggregate supply
Potential output	
Inputs	Supplies of capital, labor, and land determine inputs into productive process. Unemployment of labor and that of other resources are at lowest sustainable levels. Growth of inputs increases potential output and aggregate supply.
Technology and efficiency	Potential output is affected by level of efficiency and technologies used by businesses. Innovation and technological improvement increase the level of potential output.
Production costs	
Wages	Lower wages lead to lower production costs (other things equal). Lower costs for a given potential output mean that quantity supplied will be higher at every price level.
Import prices	With a decline in foreign prices or an appreciation in the exchange rate, import prices fall. This leads to lower production costs and raises aggregate supply.
Other input costs	Lower oil prices or less burdensome environmental regulation lowers production costs and thereby raises aggregate supply.

TABLE 29-1. Aggregate Supply Depends upon Potential Output and Production Costs

Aggregate supply relates total output supplied to the price level. Behind the *AS* curve lie fundamental factors of productivity as represented by potential output as well as the cost structure. Listed factors would increase aggregate supply, shifting the *AS* curve down or to the right.

like the Netherlands or Hong Kong, import costs play an even greater role than wages in determining aggregate supply.

How can we graph the relationship between potential output, costs, and aggregate supply? Figure 29-1 on page 560 illustrates the effect of changes in potential output and in costs on aggregate supply. The left-hand panel shows that an increase in potential output with no change in production costs would shift the aggregate supply curve outward from *AS* to *AS'*. If production costs were to increase with no change in potential output, the curve would shift straight up from *AS* to *AS''*, as shown in Figure 29-1(*b*).

The real-world shifting of *AS* is displayed in Figure 29-2 on page 560. The curves are realistic empirical estimates for two different years, 1982 and 1995. The vertical lines, marked Q^p and $Q^{p'}$, indicate the levels of potential output in the two years. According to studies, real potential output grew about 37 percent over this period.

The figure shows how the *AS* curve shifted outward and upward over the period. The *outward* shift

was caused by the increase in potential output that came from growth in the labor force and capital as well as from improvements in technology. The *upward* shift was caused by increases in the cost of production, as wages, import prices, and other production costs rose. Putting together the cost increases and the potential-output growth gives the aggregate supply shift shown in Figure 29-2.

AGGREGATE SUPPLY IN THE SHORT RUN AND LONG RUN

Do shifts in aggregate demand have an impact on output and employment? And if so, for how long will the impact last? These questions engage one of the major controversies about modern macroeconomics—the determination of aggregate supply.

The major bone of contention is whether the aggregate supply curve is flat, or steep, or even vertical. Many economists of the **Keynesian school** hold that the *AS* curve is relatively flat in the short run. This implies that changes in aggregate demand have a significant and lasting effect on output. Another

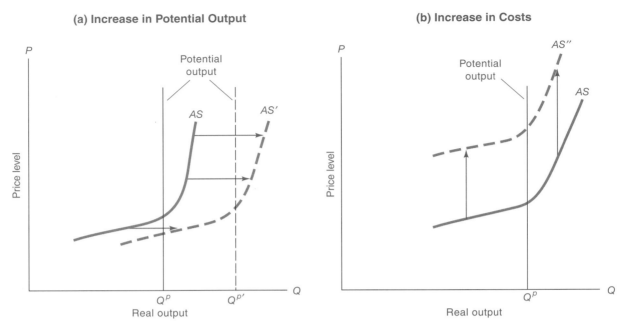

FIGURE 29-1. How Do Growth in Potential Output and Cost Increases Affect Aggregate Supply?

In (**a**), growth in potential output with unchanged production costs shifts the *AS* curve rightward from *AS* to *AS'*. When production costs increase, say, because of higher wages or import costs, but with unchanged potential output, the *AS* curve shifts vertically upward, as from *AS* to *AS''* in (**b**).

view is represented by the **classical approach** to macroeconomics. This school emphasizes the strength of self-correcting forces that operate through the price mechanism. According to the classical view, there is little or no involuntary unemployment or waste from business cycles, and policies to manage aggregate demand have little or no impact upon output or employment. In terms of the *AS* function, the classical approach holds that the *AS* curve is very steep or even vertical; changes in aggregate demand therefore have little lasting effect on output.

Actually, each view has merit in certain circumstances, as shown in Figure 29-3. The short-run *AS* curve on the left is upward-sloping or Keynesian. It indicates that firms are willing to increase their output levels in response to higher prices, particularly at low levels of output. In other words, as the level of aggregate demand rises, firms produce more output at the higher price level.

Note, however, that the expansion of output cannot go on forever even in the short run. As output

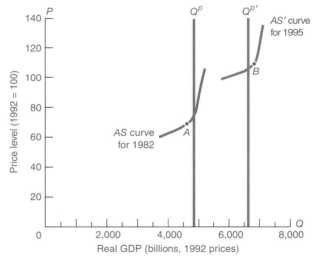

FIGURE 29-2. In Reality, Aggregate Supply Shifts Combine Cost Increases and Increased Potential Output

Between 1982 and 1995, potential output grew due to increases in capital and labor inputs along with technological improvements. At the same time, increases in wages and other costs meant that the price level at which businesses would produce the economy's potential output increased.

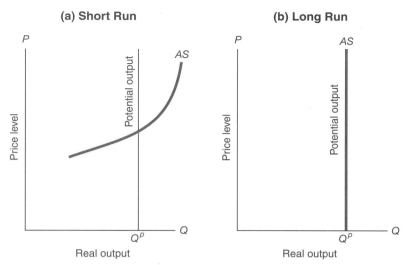

FIGURE 29-3. *AS* **Is Relatively Flat in the Short Run but Turns Vertical in the Long Run**

The short-run *AS* curve in (**a**) slopes upward because many costs are inflexible in the short run. But inflexible prices and wages become unstuck as time passes, so the long-run *AS* curve in (**b**) is vertical and output is determined by potential output. Can you see why a Keynesian economist in (**a**) might desire to stabilize the economy through demand-management policies while a classical economist in (**b**) would concentrate primarily on increasing potential output?

increases, labor shortages appear and factories operate close to capacity. Firms cannot raise prices without losing customers to rivals. Therefore, as production rises above potential output, a larger fraction of the response to demand increases comes in the form of price increases and a smaller fraction comes in output increases. This means that the short-run *AS* curve will be relatively flat where output is less than potential output (that is, to the left of the potential-output line). However, *AS* will become steeper and steeper as output increases beyond potential output.

Figure 29-3(*b*) illustrates the long-run classical-type response of aggregate supply to different price levels. This panel shows that the long-run *AS* curve is vertical or classical, with the output corresponding to potential output. In a classical case, the level of output supplied is independent of the price level.

Why Do Short-Run *AS* and Long-Run *AS* Differ?

Why does aggregate supply behave differently in the long and short runs? Why do firms raise both prices and output in the short run as aggregate demand increases? Why, by contrast, do increases in demand lead to price changes with little output change in the long run?

The key to these puzzles lies in the behavior of wages and prices in a modern market economy. Some elements of business costs are *inflexible* or *sticky* in the short run. As a result of this inflexibility, businesses can profit from higher levels of aggregate demand by producing more output.

Suppose that concerns over national security lead to an increase in defense spending. Firms know that in the short run many of their production costs are fixed in dollar terms—workers are paid $15 per hour, rent is $1500 per month, and so forth. In response to the higher demand, firms will generally raise their output prices and increase production. This positive association between prices and output is seen in the upward-sloping *AS* curve in Figure 29-3(*a*).

We have spoken repeatedly of "sticky" or "inflexible" costs. What are some examples? The most significant is wages. For a variety of reasons, wages adjust slowly when economic conditions change. Take unionized workers as an example. They are usually paid according to a long-term union contract which specifies a dollar wage rate. For the life of the labor agreement, the wage rate faced by the firm will be largely fixed in dollar terms. It is quite rare for wages to be raised more than once a year even for nonunion workers. It is even more uncommon for money wages or salaries actually to be cut, except when a company is visibly facing the threat of bankruptcy.

Other prices and costs are similarly sticky in the short run. When a firm rents a building, the lease will often last for a year or more and the rental is generally set in dollar terms. In addition, firms often sign contracts with their suppliers specifying the prices to be paid for materials or components. Some prices are fixed by government regulation, particularly those for utilities like electricity, water, and local telephone service.

Putting all these cases together, you can see how a certain short-run stickiness of wages and prices exists in a modern market economy.

What happens in the long run? Eventually, the inflexible or sticky elements of cost—wage contracts, rent agreements, regulated prices, and so forth—become unstuck and negotiable. Firms cannot take advantage of fixed-money wage rates in their labor agreements forever; labor will soon recognize that prices have risen and insist on compensating increases in wages. Ultimately, all costs will adjust to the higher output prices. If the general price level rises by x percent because of the higher demand, then money wages, rents, regulated prices, and other costs will in the end respond by moving up around x percent as well.

Once costs have adjusted upward as much as prices, firms will be unable to profit from the higher level of aggregate demand. In the long run, after all elements of cost have fully adjusted, firms will face the same ratio of price to costs as they did before the change in demand. There will be no incentive for firms to increase their output. The long-run AS curve therefore tends to be vertical, which means that output supplied is independent of the level of prices and costs.

The aggregate supply for an economy will differ from potential output in the short run because of inflexible elements of costs. In the short run, firms will respond to higher demand by raising both production and prices. In the longer run, as costs respond to the higher level of prices, most or all of the response to increased demand takes the form of higher prices and little or none the form of higher output. Whereas the short-run AS curve is upward-sloping, the long-run AS curve is vertical because, given sufficient time, all costs adjust.

B. UNEMPLOYMENT

Although the deepest depressions no longer appear to be a major threat to advanced market economies, massive unemployment continues to plague the modern mixed economy. Indeed, across the industrialized world the number of unemployed workers reached a record level of 35 million in 1996. How can millions of people be unemployed when there is so much work to be done? What flaw in a modern mixed economy forces so many who want work to remain idle? Should nations take steps to alleviate the hardships of joblessness? To what extent is high unemployment primarily due to flawed unemployment insurance and other government programs that reduce the incentive to work? These questions come up again and again, every time the unemployment rate rises.

This section provides a whirlwind tour of the meaning and measurement of unemployment.

MEASURING UNEMPLOYMENT

Changes in the unemployment rate make monthly headlines. What lies behind the numbers? Statistics on unemployment and the labor force are among the most carefully designed and comprehensive economic data the nation collects. The data are gathered monthly in a procedure known as *random sampling*

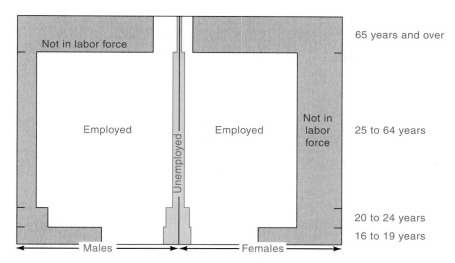

FIGURE 29-4. Labor-Force Status of the Population, 1996

How do Americans spend their time? This figure shows how males and females of different ages are divided among employed, unemployed, and not in the labor force. The size of each block indicates the relative proportion of the population in the designated category. Note the continuing difference in labor-force behavior of men and women. (Source: U.S. Department of Labor, *Employment and Earnings.*)

of the population.[1] Each month about 60,000 households are interviewed about their recent work history.

The survey divides the population 16 years and older into four groups:

- **Employed.** These are people who perform any paid work, as well as those who have jobs but are absent from work because of illness, strikes, or vacations.
- **Unemployed.** This group includes people who are not employed but are actively looking for work or waiting to return to work. More precisely, a person is unemployed if he or she is not working and (1) has made specific efforts to find a job during the last 4 weeks, (2) has been laid off from a job and is waiting to be recalled, or (3) is waiting to report to a job in the next month. To

be counted as unemployed, a person must do more than simply think about work—say, through contemplating the possibility of making a movie or being a rock star. A person must report specific efforts to find a job (such as having a job interview or sending out resumes).

- **Not in the labor force.** This includes the 34 percent of the adult population that is keeping house, retired, too ill to work, or simply not looking for work.
- **Labor force.** This includes all those who are either employed or unemployed.

Figure 29-4 shows how the male and female populations in the United States are divided among the categories of employed, unemployed, and not in the labor force. (The status of students is examined in question 6 at the end of this chapter.)

The official definition of labor-force status is the following:

People with jobs are employed; people without jobs but looking for work are unemployed; people without jobs who are not looking for work are outside the labor force. The **unemployment rate** is the number of unemployed divided by the total labor force.

---

[1] Random sampling is an essential technique for estimating the behavior or characteristics of an entire population. It consists of choosing a subgroup of the population at random (say, by selecting telephone digits through a computer-generated series of random numbers) and then surveying the selected group. Random sampling is used in many social sciences, as well as in market research.

	Lost output		
	Average unemployment rate (%)	GDP loss ($, billion, 1996 prices)	As percent of GDP during the period
Great Depression (1930–1939)	18.2	4,400	38.5
Oil and inflation crises (1975–1984)	7.7	1,250	2.5
Recent tranquility (1985–1996)	6.3	500	0.6

TABLE 29-2. Economic Costs from Periods of High Unemployment

The two major periods of high unemployment since 1929 occurred during the Great Depression and during the oil shocks and high inflation from 1975 to 1984. The lost output is calculated as the cumulative difference between potential GDP and actual GDP. Note that during the Great Depression losses relative to GDP were more than 10 times those of recent periods of slow growth. (Source: Authors' estimates on the basis of official GDP and unemployment data.)

IMPACT OF UNEMPLOYMENT

High unemployment is both an economic and a social problem. Unemployment is an economic problem because it represents waste of a valuable resource. Unemployment is a major social problem because it causes enormous suffering as unemployed workers struggle with reduced incomes. During periods of high unemployment, economic distress spills over to affect people's emotions and family lives.

Economic Impact

When the unemployment rate goes up, the economy is in effect throwing away the goods and services that the unemployed workers could have produced. During recessions, it is as if vast quantities of automobiles, housing, clothing, and other commodities were simply dumped into the ocean.

How much waste results from high unemployment? What is the opportunity cost of recessions? Table 29-2 provides a calculation of how far output fell short of potential GDP during the major periods of high unemployment over the last half-century. The largest economic loss occurred during the Great Depression, but the oil and inflation crises of the 1970s and 1980s also generated more than a trillion dollars of lost output. The last decade has been one of unprecedented stability in the United States, with very small business cycle losses.

The economic losses during periods of high unemployment are the greatest documented wastes in a modern economy. They are many times larger than the estimated inefficiencies from microeconomic waste due to monopoly or than the waste induced by tariffs and quotas.

Social Impact

The economic cost of unemployment is certainly large, but no dollar figure can adequately convey the human and psychological toll of long periods of persistent involuntary unemployment. The personal tragedy of unemployment has been proved again and again. We can read of the futility of a job search in San Francisco during the Great Depression:

> I'd get up at five in the morning and head for the waterfront. Outside the Spreckles Sugar Refinery, outside the gates, there would be a thousand men. You know dang well there's only three or four jobs. The guy would come out with two little Pinkerton cops: "I need two guys for the bull gang. Two guys to go into the hole." A thousand men would fight like a pack of Alaskan dogs to get through. Only four of us would get through.[2]

Or we can listen to the recollection of an unemployed construction worker:

> I called the roofing outfits and they didn't need me because they already had men that had been working for them five or six years. There wasn't that many openings. You had to have a college education for most of them. And I was looking for anything, from car wash to anything else.

---

[2] Studs Terkel, *Hard Times: An Oral History of the Great Depression in America* (Pantheon, New York, 1970).

So what do you do all day? You go home and you sit. And you begin to get frustrated sitting home. Everybody in the household starts getting on edge. They start arguing with each other over stupid things 'cause they're all cramped in that space all the time. The whole family kind of got crushed by it.[3]

It would be surprising if such experiences did not leave scars. Psychological studies indicate that being fired from a job is generally as traumatic as the death of a close friend or failure in school. In the late 1980s and early 1990s, many people who lost their jobs were well-paid managers, professionals, and similar white-collar workers who had never expected to be out of work. For them, the shock of being unemployed hit hard. Listen to the story of one middle-aged corporate manager who lost his job in 1988 and was still without permanent work in 1992:

> I have lost the fight to stay ahead in today's economy. . . . I was determined to find work, but as the months and years wore on, depression set in. You can only be rejected so many times; then you start questioning your self-worth.[4]

Perhaps the most dramatic evidence of the social impact of economic downturns came in Russia after the shock therapy of market reforms (see last chapter's discussion). By 1995, one in five workers was out of work, and real output had dropped sharply. Health status deteriorated catastrophically, with life expectancy of men dropping from 64 in 1990 to 57 in 1995. Outside of war, no industrial country has ever experienced such a sharp decline in health status as that associated with the current economic depression in Russia.

Economist as policymaker: Arthur Okun (1929–1979) was one of the most creative American economic policymakers of the postwar era. Educated at Columbia, he taught at Yale until he joined the staff of President Kennedy's Council of Economic Advisers in 1961. He became a CEA member in 1964 and President Johnson's chairman in 1968. After he left the CEA, Okun stayed in Washington at the Brookings Institution.

Okun first derived the concept of potential output and then went on to uncover the relation between output and unemployment that is now known as Okun's Law. One of Okun's central concerns was to find ways of containing inflation without throwing millions of people out of work. He espoused a novel approach to anti-inflation policies called *tax-based incomes policies* (TIP), which we will discuss in Chapter 30.

In addition, Okun was renowned for his use of simple homilies to illustrate economic points. He compared arguments against the 1968 tax increase to his 7-year-old's arguments against taking medicine: "He is perfectly well; he is so sick that nothing can possibly help him; he will take it later in the day if his throat doesn't get better; it isn't fair unless his brothers take it too." Okun proved time and again that a well-told tale is often worth more than 1000 equations.

OKUN'S LAW

The most distressing consequence of any recession is a rise in the unemployment rate. As output falls, firms need fewer labor inputs, so new workers are not hired and current workers are laid off. The impact can be dramatic: By the end of the recession of 1981–1982, about 1 out of every 10 American workers was unemployed. Conditions in Europe were equally depressed in the mid-1990s, when unemployment reached over 10 percent of the work force.

It turns out that unemployment usually moves in tandem with output over the business cycle. The remarkable comovement of output and unemployment, along with the numerical relationship, was first identified by Arthur Okun and is known as Okun's Law.

Okun's Law states that for every 2 percent that GDP falls relative to potential GDP, the unemployment rate rises about 1 percentage point.

This means that if GDP begins at 100 percent of its potential and falls to 98 percent of potential, the unemployment rate rises by 1 percentage point, say, from 6 to 7 percent. Figure 29-5 shows how output and unemployment have moved together over time.

We can use a historical example, involving the 3 years of economic stagnation from 1979 to 1982, to illustrate Okun's Law. During the 1979–1982 period, actual real GDP didn't grow at all. By contrast, poten-

---

[3] Harry Maurer, *Not Working: An Oral History of the Unemployed* (Holt, New York, 1979).
[4] *Business Week*, Mar. 23, 1992.

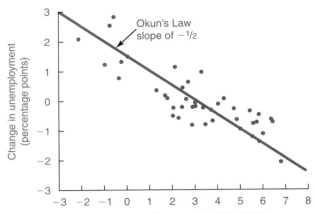

FIGURE 29-5. Okun's Law Illustrated, 1955–1996

According to Okun's Law, whenever output grows 2 percent faster than potential GDP, the unemployment rate declines 1 percentage point. This graph shows that unemployment changes are well predicted by the rate of GDP growth. What output growth would lead to no change in unemployment according to the line? (Source: U.S. Departments of Commerce and Labor.)

tial GDP grew at 3 percent per year, increasing a total of 9 percent over the 3-year period. What would Okun's Law predict about the movement of the unemployment rate from 1979 to 1982? Okun's Law holds that each 2 percent shortfall of GDP relative to potential adds 1 percentage point to the unemployment rate; therefore, a 9 percent shortfall in GDP should have led to a rise of 4.5 percentage points in the unemployment rate. Starting with an unemployment rate of 5.8 percent in 1979, then, Okun's Law would predict a 10.3 percent unemployment rate in 1982. According to official statistics, the actual unemployment rate was 9.7 percent for 1982. This example shows how Okun's Law can be used to track unemployment over the business cycle.

Unemployment and politics: Voters tend to penalize presidents when unemployment is high during election years. During depressions and recessions, as in 1932, 1960, 1980, and 1992, incumbent parties lost the White House. By contrast, in boom years with low unemployment (like 1964, 1972, 1984, and 1996), incumbents were reelected.

Suppose that you are elected President in 2000, when the unemployment rate is 8 percent, and you

would like to lower the rate to 6 percent by the time you run for reelection 4 years later. Question: How fast must the economy grow over the 4 years from 2000 to 2004? Answer: It must grow at the growth rate of potential GDP (about 2½ percent annually for the United States today), plus enough to reduce the unemployment rate about ½ percentage point each year. The average annual growth rate for GDP must then be 2½ percent for trend plus 1 percent to reduce unemployment. This sum equals 3½ percent annually over the 4-year period.

One important consequence of Okun's Law is that actual GDP must grow as rapidly as potential GDP just to keep the unemployment rate from rising. In a sense, GDP has to keep running just to keep unemployment in the same place. Moreover, if you want to bring the unemployment rate down, actual GDP must be growing faster than potential GDP.

Okun's Law provides the vital link between the output market and the labor market. It describes the association between short-run movements in real GDP and changes in unemployment.

ECONOMIC INTERPRETATION OF UNEMPLOYMENT

Let's turn now to the economic analysis of unemployment. Some of the important questions we address are: What are the reasons for being unemployed? What is the distinction between "voluntary" and "involuntary" unemployment? What is the relationship between different kinds of unemployment and the business cycle?

Three Kinds of Unemployment

In sorting out the structure of labor markets, economists identify three different kinds of unemployment: frictional, structural, and cyclical.

Frictional unemployment arises because of the incessant movement of people between regions and jobs or through different stages of the life cycle. Even if an economy were at full employment, there would always be some turnover as students search for jobs when they graduate from school or parents reenter the labor force after having children. Because frictionally unemployed workers are often moving between jobs, or looking for better jobs, it is often thought that they are *voluntarily unemployed*.

Structural unemployment signifies a mismatch between the supply of and the demand for workers. Mismatches can occur because the demand for one kind of labor is rising while the demand for another kind is falling, and supplies do not quickly adjust. We often see structural imbalances across occupations or regions as certain sectors grow while others decline. For example, an acute shortage of nurses arose in the mid-1980s as the number of nurses grew slowly while the demand for nursing care grew rapidly because of an aging population and other forces. Not until nurses' salaries rose rapidly and the supply adjusted did the structural shortage of nurses decline. By contrast, the demand for coal miners has been depressed for decades because of the lack of geographical mobility of labor and capital; unemployment rates in coal-mining communities remain high today. In European countries, high real wages, welfare benefits, and taxes have created high levels of structural unemployment for entire economies over the last decade.

Cyclical unemployment exists when the overall demand for labor is low. As total spending and output fall, unemployment rises virtually everywhere. In the recession year 1982, the unemployment rate rose in 48 of the 50 states. This simultaneous rise in unemployment in many markets signaled that the increased unemployment was largely cyclical.

The distinction between cyclical, frictional, and structural unemployment helps economists diagnose the general health of the labor market. High levels of frictional or structural unemployment can occur even though the overall labor market is in balance, for example, when turnover is high or when high minimum wages price certain groups out of the labor force. Cyclical unemployment occurs during recessions, when employment falls as a result of an imbalance between aggregate supply and demand.

Microeconomic Foundations

On the face of it, the cause of unemployment seems clear: too many workers chasing too few jobs. Yet this simple phenomenon has presented a tremendous puzzle for economists for 60 years. Experience shows that prices rise or fall to clear competitive markets. At the market-clearing price, buyers willingly buy what sellers willingly sell. But something is gumming up the workings of the labor market when many hospitals are searching for nurses but cannot find them while thousands of coal miners want to work at the going wage but cannot find a job. Similar symptoms of labor market failures are found in all market economies.

Economists look to the microeconomics of labor markets to help understand the existence of unemployment. Although no universally accepted theory has emerged, many analysts believe that unemployment arises because wages are not flexible enough to clear markets. We explore below why wages are inflexible and why inflexible wages lead to involuntary unemployment.

Voluntary and Involuntary Unemployment

Let us first start by examining the causes of *voluntary unemployment* in a typical labor market. A group of workers has a labor supply schedule shown as *SS* in Figure 29-6 on page 568. The supply curve becomes completely inelastic at labor quantity L^* when wage levels are high. We will call L^* the labor force.

The left-hand panel of Figure 29-6 shows the usual picture of competitive supply and demand, with a market equilibrium at point *E* and a wage of W^*. At the competitive, market-clearing equilibrium, firms willingly hire all qualified workers who desire to work at the market wage. The number of employed is represented by the line from *A* to *E*. Some members of the labor force would like to work, but only at a higher wage rate. These unemployed workers, represented by the segment *EF,* are voluntarily unemployed in the sense that they choose not to work at the market wage rate.

The existence of voluntary unemployment implies an often misunderstood point. *Unemployment may be an efficient outcome in a situation where heterogeneous workers are searching for and testing different kinds of jobs.* The voluntarily unemployed workers might prefer leisure or other activities to jobs at the going wage rate. Or they may be frictionally unemployed, perhaps searching for their first job. Or they might be low-productivity workers who prefer welfare or unemployment insurance to low-paid work. There are countless reasons why people might voluntarily choose not to work at the going wage rate, and yet these people might be counted as unemployed in the official statistics.

But now go back to reread the quotations from unemployed workers on pages 564–65. Who would seriously argue that these workers are voluntarily

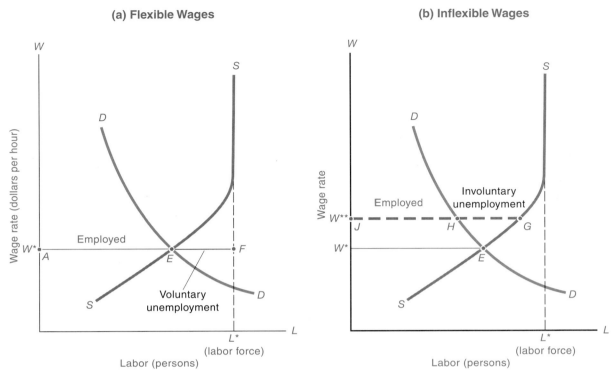

FIGURE 29-6. Inflexible Wages Can Lead to Involuntary Unemployment

We can depict different kinds of unemployment by using the microeconomic supply-and-demand framework. In (**a**), wages move to W^* to clear the labor market. All unemployment is voluntary. Part (**b**) shows what happens if wages do not adjust to clear the labor market. At the too high wage at W^{**}, JH workers are employed, but HG workers are involuntarily unemployed. Many believe that (**a**) resembles the flexible labor market of the United States while (**b**) shows the impact of high labor taxes, comprehensive minimum wages, and generous social-welfare legislation in Europe.

unemployed? They surely do not sound like people carefully balancing the value of work against the value of leisure. Nor do they resemble people choosing unemployment as they search for a better job. We simply cannot reconcile the experience of many unemployed workers with an elegant classical theory of voluntary unemployment. One of Keynes' great breakthroughs was to let the facts oust this beautiful but irrelevant theory. He explained why we see occasional bouts of involuntary unemployment, periods in which qualified workers are unable to get jobs at the going wage rates.

The key to his approach was to note that wages do not adjust to clear labor markets. Instead, wages tend to respond sluggishly to economic shocks. If wages do not move to clear markets, a mismatch between job seekers and job vacancies can arise. This mismatch may lead to the patterns of unemployment that we see today.

We can understand how inflexible wages lead to involuntary unemployment with an analysis of a *non-clearing labor market*, shown in Figure 29-6(*b*). Here, an economic disturbance leaves the labor market with too high a wage rate. Labor's wage is at W^{**} rather than at the equilibrium or market-clearing wage of W^*.

At the too high wage rate, there are more qualified workers looking for work than there are vacancies looking for workers. The number of workers willing to work at wage W^{**} is at point G on the supply curve, but firms want to hire only *H* workers, as shown by the demand curve. Because the wage exceeds the market-clearing level, there is a surplus of workers. The unemployed workers represented by the dashed line segment *HG* are said to be **involuntarily unemployed**, signifying that they are qualified workers who want to work at the prevailing wage but cannot find jobs. When there is a surplus of workers, firms will ration out the jobs by setting more stringent skill requirements and hiring the most qualified or most experienced workers.

The opposite case occurs when the wage is below the market-clearing rate. Here, in a labor-shortage economy, employers cannot find enough workers to fill the existing vacancies. Firms put help-wanted signs in their windows, advertise in newspapers, and even recruit people from other towns.

Sources of Wage Inflexibility

The theory of involuntary unemployment assumes that wages are inflexible. But this raises a further question: Why do wages not move up or down to clear markets? Why are labor markets not like the auction markets for grain, corn, and common stocks?

These questions are among the deepest unresolved mysteries of modern economics. Few economists today would argue that wages move quickly to erase labor shortages and surpluses. Yet no one completely understands the reasons for the sluggish behavior of wages and salaries. We can therefore provide no more than a tentative assessment of the sources of wage inflexibility.

A helpful distinction is that between auction markets and administered markets. An *auction market* is a highly organized and competitive market where the price floats up or down to balance supply and demand. At the Chicago Board of Trade, for example, the price of "number 2 stiff red wheat delivered in St. Louis" or "dressed 'A' broiler chickens delivered in New York" changes every minute to reflect market conditions—market conditions that are seen in frantic buy and sell orders of farmers, millers, packers, merchants, and speculators.

Most goods and all labor are sold in administered markets and not in competitive auction markets. Nobody grades labor into "number 2 subcompact-automobile tire assembler" or "class AAA

assistant professor of economics." No specialist burns the midnight oil trying to make sure that steelworkers' wages or professors' salaries are set at just the market-clearing level where all qualified workers are placed into jobs.

Rather, most firms *administer* their wages and salaries, setting pay scales and hiring people at an entry-level wage or salary. These wage scales are generally fixed for a year or so, and when they are adjusted, the pay goes up for all categories. For example, a bank might have 15 different categories of staff: three grades of secretaries, two grades of tellers, and so forth. Each year, the bank managers will decide how much to increase wages and salaries—say, 3 percent in 1999 on average. Sometimes, the compensation in each category will move up by that percentage; sometimes, the firm might decide to move one category up or down more than the average. Given the procedure by which wages and salaries are determined, there is little room for major adjustments when the firm finds shortages or gluts in a particular area. Except in extreme cases, the firm will tend to adjust the minimum qualifications required for a job rather than its wages when it finds labor market disequilibrium.[5]

For unionized labor markets, the wage patterns are even more rigid. Wage scales are typically set for a 3-year contract period; during that period, wages are not adjusted for excess supply or demand in particular areas. Moreover, unionized workers seldom accept wage cuts even when many of the union's workers are unemployed.

To summarize:

Wages in America and other market economies are administered by firms or contracts. Wages and salaries are set infrequently and adjust to meet shortages or surpluses only over an extended period of time.

Let's go a step further and ask, What is the economic reason for the sluggishness of wages and

---

[5] The example of college admissions illustrates the kind of adjustment that takes place when shortages or gluts occur. Many colleges found that applications for places soared in the 1990s. How did they react? Did they raise their tuition enough to choke off the excess demand? No. Instead, they raised their admission standards, requiring better grades in high schools and higher average SAT scores. Upgrading the requirements rather than changing wages and prices is exactly what happens in the short run when firms experience excess supply of labor.

Labor market group	Unemployment rate of different groups (% of labor force)		Distribution of total unemployment across different groups (% of total unemployed)	
	Recession (1982)	Boom (1989)	Recession (1982)	Boom (1989)
By age:				
16–19 years	23.2	14.7	18.5	17.7
20 years and older	8.6	4.6	81.5	82.3
By race:				
White	8.6	4.6	77.2	74.5
Black and other	17.3	9.4	22.8	25.5
By sex (adults only):				
Male	8.8	4.3	58.5	51.1
Female	8.3	5.0	41.5	48.9
All workers	**9.7**	**5.3**	**100.0**	**100.0**

TABLE 29-3. Unemployment by Demographic Group

This table shows how unemployment varies across different demographic groups in boom and recession years. The first set of figures shows the unemployment rate for each group in 1982 and 1989. The last two columns show the percent of the total pool of unemployed that is in each group. (Source: U.S. Department of Labor, *Employment and Earnings.*)

salaries? Many economists believe that the inflexibility arises because of the costs of administering compensation (such costs are called "menu costs"). To take the example of union wages, negotiating a contract is a long process that requires much worker and management time and produces no output. It is because collective bargaining is so costly that such agreements are generally negotiated only once every 3 years.

Setting compensation for nonunion workers is less costly, but it nevertheless requires scarce management time and has important effects on worker morale. Every time wages or salaries are set, every time fringe benefits are changed, earlier compensation agreements are changed as well. Some workers will feel the changes are unfair, others will complain about unjust procedures, and grievances may be triggered.

Personnel managers therefore prefer a system in which wages are adjusted infrequently and most workers in a firm get the same pay increase, regardless of the market conditions for different skills or categories. This system may appear inefficient to economists, because it does not allow for a perfect adjustment of wages to reflect market supply and demand. But it does economize on scarce managerial time and helps promote a sense of fair play and equity in the firm. In the end, it may be cheaper to recruit workers more actively or to change the required qualifications than to upset the entire wage structure of a firm simply to hire a few new workers.

The theory of sticky wages and involuntary unemployment holds that the slow adjustment of wages produces surpluses and shortages in individual labor markets. Labor markets are nonclearing markets in the short run. But labor markets do eventually respond to market conditions as wages of high-demand occupations move up relative to those of low-demand occupations. In the long run, major pockets of unemployment and job vacancies tend to disappear as wages and employment adjust to market conditions. But the long run may be many years, and periods of unemployment can therefore persist for many years.

LABOR MARKET ISSUES

Having analyzed the causes of unemployment, we turn next to major labor market issues for today. Which groups are most likely to be unemployed?

How long are they unemployed? Why has unemployment in Europe skyrocketed in the last decade?

Who Are the Unemployed?

We can diagnose labor market conditions by comparing years in which output is above its potential (of which 1989 was a recent year) with those of deep recessions (such as was seen in 1982). Differences between these years show how business cycles affect the amount, sources, duration, and distribution of unemployment.

Table 29-3 shows unemployment statistics for boom and recession years. The first two columns of numbers are the unemployment rates by age, race, and sex. These data show that the unemployment rate of every group tends to rise during recession. The last two columns show how the total pool of unemployment is distributed among different groups; observe that the distribution of unemployment across groups changes relatively little throughout the business cycle.

Note also that nonwhite workers tend to experience unemployment rates more than twice those of whites in both recession and boom periods. Until the 1980s, women tended to have higher unemployment rates than men, but in recent years unemployment rates differed little by gender. Teenagers, with high frictional unemployment, have generally had unemployment rates much higher than adults.

Duration of Unemployment

Another key question concerns duration. How much of the unemployment experience is long-term and of major social concern, and how much is short-term as people move quickly between jobs?

Figure 29-7 shows the duration of unemployment in the full-employment year of 1996. A surprising feature of American labor markets is that a very large fraction of unemployment is of short duration. In 1996, more than two-fifths of unemployed workers were jobless for less than 5 weeks, and long-term unemployment was rare.

In Europe, with lower mobility and greater legal obstacles to economic change, long-term unemployment in the mid-1990s reached 50 percent of the unemployed. Long-term unemployment poses a serious social problem because the resources that families have available—their savings, unemployment

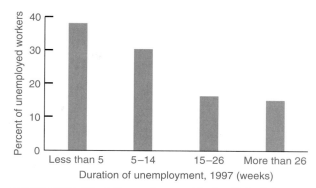

FIGURE 29-7. Most Unemployment in the United States Is Short-Term

How long have workers been unemployed? The duration figures show the distribution of length of unemployment. In the full-employment year 1997, only 15 percent of the unemployed were unemployed for more than 26 weeks, while almost 40 percent were unemployed for less than 5 weeks. In recessions, the duration of unemployment increases. European countries with stagnant labor markets find that more than half of their unemployed have been without jobs for more than a year. (Source: U.S. Department of Labor, *Employment and Earnings,* June 1997.)

insurance, and goodwill toward one another—begin to run out after a few months.

Sources of Joblessness

Why are people unemployed? Figure 29-8 on page 572 shows how people responded when asked the source of their unemployment, looking at the recession year of 1982 and the high-employment year of 1989.

There is always some unemployment that results from changes in people's residence or from the life cycle—moving, entering the labor force for the first time, and so forth. The major changes in the unemployment rate over the business cycle arise from the increase in job losers. This source swells enormously in recession for two reasons: First, the number of people who lose their jobs increases, and then it takes longer to find a new job.

Unemployment by Age

How does unemployment vary over the life cycle? Teenagers generally have the highest unemployment rate of any demographic group, and nonwhite teenagers in recent years have experienced unemployment rates between 30 and 50 percent. Is this unemployment frictional, structural, or cyclical?

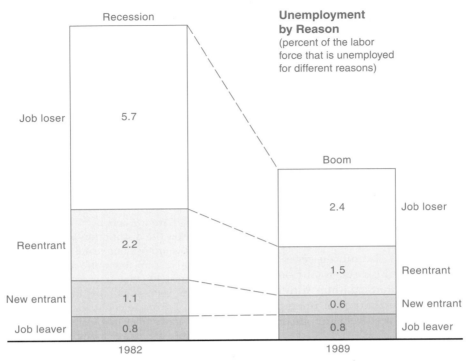

FIGURE 29-8. Distribution of Unemployment by Reason

Why do people become unemployed? Less than 1 percent of those in the labor force are unemployed because they left their jobs, and another 2 to 3 percent are new entrants into the labor force (say, because they just graduated from college) or reentrants (people who earlier left the labor force and are back looking for a job). The major change in unemployment from boom to recession, however, is found in the number of job losers. From 1982 to 1989 the fraction of workers who became unemployed because they lost their jobs fell from 5.7 to 2.4 percent. (Source: U.S. Department of Labor, *Employment and Earnings.*)

Recent evidence indicates that, particularly for whites, teenage unemployment has a large frictional component. Teenagers move in and out of the labor force very frequently. They get jobs quickly and change jobs often. The average duration of teenage unemployment is only half that of adult unemployment; by contrast, the average length of a typical job is 12 times greater for adults than teenagers. In most years, half the unemployed teenagers are "new entrants" who have never had a paying job before. All these factors suggest that teenage unemployment is largely frictional; that is, it represents the job search and turnover necessary for young people to discover their personal skills and to learn what working is all about.

But teenagers do eventually learn the skills and work habits of experienced workers. Table 29-4 shows the unemployment rates at different ages for blacks and whites in 1996. The acquisition of experience and training, along with a greater desire and need for full-time work, is the reason middle-aged workers have much lower unemployment rates than teenagers.

Teenage Unemployment of Minority Groups. While most evidence suggests that unemployment is largely frictional for white teenagers, the labor market for young African-American workers has behaved quite differently. After World War II, the labor market data for black teenagers were virtually identical to those for white teenagers; the labor-force participation rates and unemployment rates of black and white teenagers were virtually identical until 1955. Since that time, however, unemployment rates for black teenagers have risen relative to those of other groups while their labor-force participation rates have fallen. By 1997, 35 percent of black teenagers (16 to 19 years of age) were unemployed, compared to 14 percent of white teenagers. The employment rate (equal to the ratio of total employment to total population) was only 24 percent for black teenagers as opposed to 47 percent for white teenagers.

What accounts for this extraordinary divergence in the experience of the two groups? One explanation might be that labor market forces (such as the composition or location of jobs) have worked against black workers in general. This explanation does not tell the whole story. While adult black workers have always suffered higher unemployment rates than adult white workers—because of lower education attainment, fewer contacts with people who can provide jobs, less on-the-job training, and racial discrimination—the ratio of black to white adult unemployment rates has not increased since World War II.

Numerous studies of the sources of the rising black teenage unemployment rate have turned up no clear explanations for the trend. One possible source is discrimination, but a rise in the black-white unemployment differential would require an increase in racial discrimination—even in the face of increased legal protection for minority workers.

Another theory holds that a high minimum wage tends to drive low-productivity black teenagers into unemployment. The change in the relation of the minimum wage to average wages allows a test of this hypothesis. From 1981 to 1989, the ratio of the minimum wage to average wages in nonfarm establishments fell from 46 to 34 percent, yet no improvement in the relative unemployment situation of black teenagers occurred. That no improvement took place casts doubt on the minimum wage as the prime suspect. Some conservative critics of the modern welfare state blame high unemployment of blacks on the culture of dependency that is nurtured by government aid to the poor, although there is little firm data to support this proposition.

Does high teenage unemployment lead to long-lasting labor market damage, with permanently

Age	Unemployment rate (% of labor force)	
	White	Black
16–17	17.3	39.2
18–19	11.6	32.6
20–24	6.3	20.1
25–34	3.5	10.1
35–44	3.0	5.9
45–54	2.4	5.1
55–64	2.6	3.4
65 and over	3.0	3.8

TABLE 29-4. Unemployment Rates at Different Ages, May 1997

As workers search for jobs and gain training, they settle on a particular occupation; they tend to stay in the labor force; and they find a preferred employer. As a result, the unemployment rates of older people fall to a fraction of those of teenagers. (Source: U.S. Department of Labor, *Employment and Earnings*, June 1997.)

lower levels of skills and wage rates? This question is a topic of intensive ongoing research, and the tentative answer is yes, particularly for minority teenagers. It appears that when youths are unable to develop on-the-job skills and work attitudes, they earn lower wages and experience higher unemployment when they are older. This finding suggests that public policy has an important stake in devising programs to reduce teenage unemployment among minority groups.

Unemployment Rising in Europe, Falling in America

While unemployment in the United States has remained relatively stable in recent years, European unemployment has risen sharply and persistently over the last three decades. Figure 29-9 on page 574 shows the unemployment history in the two regions.

How can we explain the divergent labor markets of these two regions? Part of the reason probably lies in differences in macroeconomic policies. The United States has a single central bank, the Federal Reserve, that keeps careful watch over the American economy. When unemployment begins to rise, as it did in 1982 and again in 1991, the Fed loosens monetary policy to stimulate aggregate demand, increase output, and stem the unemployment increase.

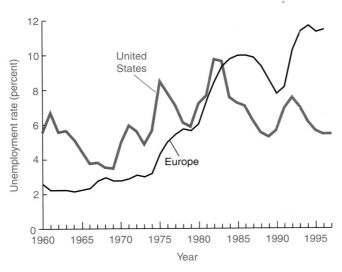

FIGURE 29-9. Unemployment in the United States and Europe

While unemployment has cycled without a marked trend in the United States, European unemployment has risen sharply over the last three decades. Some of the increase in European unemployment stems from the demand side, but the general trend stems from European labor market rigidities and social-welfare legislation. (Source: U.S. Department of Labor and OECD.)

No such institution exists today in Europe. Europe is a confederation of countries whose monetary policies are dominated by the German central bank, the Bundesbank. The Bundesbank is fiercely independent and aims primarily at maintaining price stability *in Germany.* When unemployment rises in the rest of Europe and inflation rises in Germany—as happened after the reunification of Germany in 1990—the Bundesbank raises interest rates. This tends to depress output and raise unemployment in countries whose monetary policies are tied to Germany's. You can see this feature in the rise in unemployment in Europe after 1990.

A second feature of European unemployment relates to rising structural unemployment. Europe was the birthplace of the welfare state, and countries like Sweden, France, and the Netherlands have legislated generous welfare benefits, unemployment insurance, minimum wages, and job protection for workers. These policies tend to increase real wages because workers possess greater bargaining power and have more attractive alternative uses for their time. Persons who are collecting welfare or unem-

ployment benefits might be voluntarily unemployed, but they are generally counted as unemployed in the actual statistics. The United States has been less generous in its unemployment and welfare benefits, and recent changes in welfare laws will make welfare even less attractive relative to work in the coming years.

We can understand the divergent economies in terms of our labor market supply-and-demand diagrams in Figure 29-6. American labor market institutions resemble the flexible-wage economy shown in part (*a*). A decline in the demand for labor will lead to an equilibrium at *E.* By contrast, the more rigid labor market institutions in Europe resemble Figure 29-6(*b*). In Europe, real wages have not declined as much as in the United States, but the number of the employed has grown slowly while unemployment has grown sharply.

What is the remedy for European unemployment? Some economists believe that a unified European central bank would maintain a better balance of aggregate supply and demand in that large region. Demand-management policies will do little to cure Europe's structural unemployment. Many experts believe that it will also be necessary to improve European labor market institutions by reducing the generosity of welfare and unemployment insurance, removing restrictions on hiring and firing practices of firms, and reducing the burden of taxes on labor. These labor market reforms are likely to prove extremely unpopular, however, so no quick solution is in sight.

SUMMARY

A. The Foundations of Aggregate Supply

1. Aggregate supply describes the relationship between the output that businesses willingly produce and the overall price level, other things being constant. The factors underlying aggregate supply are (*a*) potential output, determined by the inputs of labor, capital, and natural resources available to an economy, along with the technology or efficiency with which these inputs are used, and (*b*) input costs, such as wages, oil and other energy prices, and import prices. Changes in these underlying factors will shift the *AS* curve.

2. Two major approaches to output determination are the classical and Keynesian views. The classical view holds that prices and wages are flexible; any excess supply or demand is quickly extinguished and full employment is established after *AD* or *AS* shocks. The classical view is represented by a vertical *AS* curve. The Keynesian view holds that prices and wages are sticky in the short run due to contractual rigidities such as labor-union agreements. In this kind of economy, output responds positively to higher levels of aggregate demand because the *AS* curve is relatively flat, particularly at low levels of output. In a Keynesian variant, the economy can experience long periods of persistent unemployment because wages and prices adjust slowly to shocks and equilibration toward full employment is slow.

3. A synthesis of classical and Keynesian views distinguishes the long run from the short run. In the short term, because wages and prices do not have time to adjust fully, the *AS* curve is upward-sloping, showing that businesses will supply more output at a higher price level. By contrast, in the long run, wages and prices have time to adjust fully to shocks, so we treat the long-run *AS* curve as vertical or classical. Hence, in the long run, output will be determined by a nation's potential output, and the evolution of aggregate demand will affect prices rather than output.

B. Unemployment

4. The government gathers monthly statistics on unemployment, employment, and the labor force in a sample survey of the population. People with jobs are categorized as employed; people without jobs who are looking for work are said to be unemployed; people without jobs who are not looking for work are considered outside the labor force. Over the last decade, 66 percent of the population over 16 was in the labor force, while 6 percent of the labor force was unemployed.

5. There is a clear connection between movements in output and the unemployment rate over the business cycle. According to Okun's Law, for every 2 percent that actual GDP declines relative to potential GDP, the unemployment rate rises 1 percentage point. This rule is useful in translating cyclical movements of GDP into their effects on unemployment.

6. Recessions and the associated high unemployment are extremely costly to the economy. Major periods of slack like the 1970s and early 1980s cost the nation hundreds of billions of dollars and have great social costs as well. Yet, even though unemployment has plagued capitalism since the Industrial Revolution, understanding its causes and costs has been possible only with the rise of modern macroeconomic theory.

7. Economists divide unemployment into three groups: (*a*) frictional unemployment, in which workers are between jobs or moving in and out of the labor force; (*b*) structural unemployment, consisting of workers who are in regions or industries that are in a persistent slump because of labor market imbalances or high real wages; and (*c*) cyclical unemployment, pertaining to workers laid off when the overall economy suffers a downturn.

8. Understanding the causes of unemployment has proved to be one of the major challenges of modern macroeconomics. Some unemployment (often called voluntary) would occur in a flexible-wage, perfectly competitive economy when qualified people chose not to work at the going wage rate. Voluntary unemployment might be the efficient outcome of competitive markets.

9. The theory of sticky wages and involuntary unemployment holds that the slow adjustment of wages

produces surpluses and shortages in individual labor markets. This theory holds that the high cyclical unemployment or the numerous job losses that occur during recessions do not reflect voluntary decisions of qualified workers not to work. Rather, cyclical unemployment occurs because wages are inflexible, failing to adjust quickly to labor surpluses or shortages. If a wage is above the market-clearing level, some workers are employed but other qualified workers cannot find jobs. Such unemployment is involuntary and also inefficient in that both workers and firms could benefit from an appropriate use of monetary and fiscal policies.

10. Labor markets do not "clear" fully in the short run. Wage inflexibility arises partly because of costs involved in administering the compensation system. Frequent adjustment of compensation for market conditions would command too large a share of management time, would upset workers' perceptions of fairness, and would undermine worker morale and productivity. Eventually, however, wages do adjust, eroding abnormal levels of unemployment or job vacancies. But the slow pace of wage adjustment means that societies may suffer prolonged periods of unemployment.

11. A careful look at the unemployment statistics reveals several regularities:

    a. Recessions hit all groups in roughly proportional fashion—that is, all groups see their unemployment rates go up and down in proportion to the overall unemployment rate.

    b. A very substantial part of U.S. unemployment is short-term. In low-unemployment years (such as 1997) about 85 percent of unemployed workers are unemployed less than 26 weeks. The average duration of unemployment rises sharply in deep and prolonged recessions.

    c. In most years, a substantial amount of unemployment is due to simple turnover, or frictional causes, as people enter the labor force for the first time or reenter it. Only during recessions is the pool of unemployed composed primarily of job losers.

    d. The persistent unemployment in Europe appears to arise from a combination of weak aggregate demand and inflexible labor market institutions.

CONCEPTS FOR REVIEW

Foundations of Aggregate Supply

aggregate supply, *AS* curve
factors underlying and shifting aggregate supply
aggregate supply: role of potential output and production costs
short-run vs. long-run *AS*
classical vs. Keynesian view of aggregate supply

flexible vs. sticky wages and prices

Unemployment

population status:
    unemployed
    employed
    labor force
    not in labor force
unemployment rate

frictional, structural, and cyclical unemployment
Okun's Law
flexible-wage (market-clearing) unemployment vs. inflexible-wage (non-market-clearing) unemployment
voluntary vs. involuntary unemployment

QUESTIONS FOR DISCUSSION

1. Explain carefully what is meant by the aggregate supply curve. Distinguish between movements along the curve and shifts of the curve. What might increase output by moving along the *AS* curve? What could increase output by shifting the *AS* curve?

2. Construct a table parallel to Table 29-1, illustrating events that would lead to a decrease in aggregate supply. (Be imaginative rather than simply using the same examples.)

3. What, if anything, would be the effect of each of the following on the *AS* curve in both the short run and the long run, other things being constant?

    a. Potential output increases by 25 percent.

    b. The threat of war leads the government to raise defense spending, and the central bank offsets the expansionary impact of this through tight money.

    c. A war in the Mideast leads to a doubling of world oil prices.

    d. Environmentalists persuade governments to impose costly regulations on all new investments and energy use and to curb output in natural-resource sectors.

4. Assume that the unemployment rate is 8 percent and GDP is $4000 billion. What is a rough estimate of

potential GDP if the lowest sustainable unemployment rate is 6 percent? Assume that potential GDP is growing at 3 percent annually. What will potential GDP be in 2 years? How fast will GDP have to grow to reach potential GDP in 2 years?

5. What is the labor-force status of each of the following?
   a. A teenager who is searching for a first job
   b. An autoworker who has been dismissed and would like to work but has given up hope of finding work
   c. A retired person who moved to Florida and answers advertisements for part-time positions
   d. A parent who works part-time, wants a full-time job, but doesn't have time to look
   e. A teacher who has a job but is too ill to work

6. In explaining its procedures, the Department of Labor gives the following examples:
   a. "Joan Howard told the interviewer that she has filed applications with three companies for summer jobs. However, it is only April and she doesn't wish to start work until at least June 15, because she is attending school. Although she has taken specific steps to find a job, Joan is classified as not in the labor force because she is not currently available for work."
   b. "James Kelly and Elyse Martin attend Jefferson High School. James works after school at the North Star Cafe, and Elyse is seeking a part-time job at the same establishment (also after school). James' job takes precedence over his non–labor

force activity of going to school, as does Elyse's search for work; therefore, James is counted as employed and Elyse is counted as unemployed."

Take a survey of your classmates. Using the examples above, have people classify themselves in terms of their labor-force status into employed, unemployed, and not in the labor force.

7. Assume that Congress is considering a minimum-wage law that sets the minimum wage above the market-clearing wage for teenagers but below that for adult workers. Using supply-and-demand diagrams, show the impact of the minimum wage on the employment, unemployment, and incomes of both sets of workers. Is the unemployment voluntary or involuntary? What would you recommend to Congress if you were called to testify about the wisdom of this measure?

8. Do you think that the economic costs and personal stress of a teenager unemployed for 1 month of the summer might be less or more than those of a head-of-household unemployed for 1 year? Do you think that this suggests that public policy should have a different stance with respect to these two groups?

9. Make a list of reasons why unemployment looks so different in the United States as compared to Europe. Using the framework in Figure 29-6, show how a decrease in the demand for labor would lead to higher employment but lower wages in flexible-wage America, shown in (a), but to lower employment, higher unemployment, and higher wages in rigid-wage Europe, in (b).

CHAPTER 30
ENSURING PRICE STABILITY

Lenin is said to have declared that the best way to destroy the capitalist system was to debauch the currency. By a continuing process of inflation, governments can confiscate, secretly and unobserved, an important part of the wealth of their citizens.

J. M. Keynes

A. NATURE AND IMPACTS OF INFLATION

We have seen that unemployment and recessions impose great costs on societies. Yet countries do not today employ their monetary and fiscal powers to reduce unemployment to minimal frictional levels. While countries proclaim the importance of work over welfare, they tolerate high levels of unemployment. Moreover, when output approaches its potential, as occurred in the United States in 1994 and again in 1997, central banks often begin to raise interest rates and slow the expansion. If unemployment is so costly, why do countries not use demand policies to get rid of it? Why do central banks take the punch bowl away just when the macroeconomic party gets bubbly?

The reason is simple. Extremely high levels of capacity utilization and low levels of unemployment create shortages in a market economy. As a result, inflation soon rises to intolerable levels. No one has described this dilemma more clearly than Arthur Okun:

The task of combining prosperity with price stability stands as the major unsolved problem of aggregative

economic performance. We must find a satisfactory compromise that yields growth and unemployment rates that we can be proud of, on the one hand, and a price performance that we can be comfortable with, on the other.[1]

In fact, high inflation has been contained in high-income countries over the last decade. But lower inflation in Europe was accompanied by steadily rising unemployment, as we saw in the last chapter. Moreover, soaring prices have plagued many developing countries that relied too heavily on the printing press to finance government spending. Recently, as formerly centrally planned countries like Poland, Ukraine, and Russia took steps to free prices and make the transition to the market, they found their price levels increasing rapidly.

It is time to analyze questions of aggregate price behavior and inflation. Figure 30-1 provides an overview of this chapter.

---

[1] Arthur M. Okun, *The Political Economy of Prosperity* (Norton, New York, 1970), p. 130.

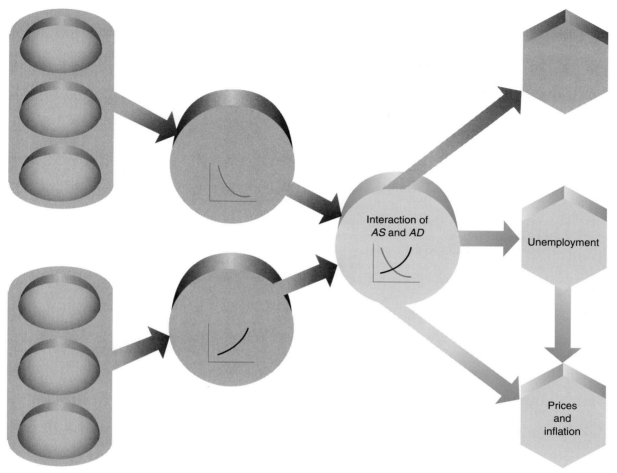

FIGURE 30-1. Inflation Is a Fundamental Constraint on Economic Policy

What are inflation's economic impacts? What forces lead to persistent inflation? How can governments slow inflation? These questions are central to macroeconomic theory and policy today.

WHAT IS INFLATION?

We described the major price indexes and defined inflation in Chapter 21, but it will be useful to reiterate the basic definitions here:

Inflation occurs when the general level of prices is rising. Today, we calculate inflation by using price indexes—weighted averages of the prices of thousands of individual products. The consumer price index (CPI) measures the cost of a market basket of consumer goods and services relative to the cost of

that bundle during a particular base year. The GDP deflator is the price of GDP. The rate of inflation is the percentage change in the price level:

Rate of inflation (year t)

$$= \frac{\begin{array}{c} \text{price level} \\ (\text{year } t) \end{array} - \begin{array}{c} \text{price level} \\ (\text{year } t-1) \end{array}}{\text{price level (year } t-1)} \times 100$$

If you are unclear on the definitions, refresh your memory by reviewing Chapter 21.

The Long History of Inflation

Inflation is as old as market economies. Figure 30-2 depicts the history of prices in England since the thirteenth century. Over the long haul, prices have generally risen, as the rust-colored line reveals. But examine also the black line, which plots the path of *real wages* (the wage rate divided by consumer prices). Real wages meandered along until the Industrial Revolution. Comparing the two lines shows that inflation is not necessarily accompanied by a decline in real income. You can see, too, that real wages have climbed steadily since around 1800, rising more than tenfold.

Figure 30-3 focuses on the behavior of consumer prices in the United States since the Civil War. Until 1945, the pattern was regular: Prices would soar during wartime and then fall back during the postwar slump. But the pattern changed

FIGURE 30-2. English Price Level and Real Wage, 1270–1996 (1270 = 1)

The graph shows England's history of prices and real wages since the Middle Ages. Note that the price of a market basket of goods has risen almost 400-fold since 1270. In early years, price increases were associated with increases in the money supply, such as from discoveries of New World treasure and the printing of money during the Napoleonic Wars. Note the meandering of the real wage prior to the Industrial Revolution. Since then, real wages have risen sharply and steadily. (Source: E. H. Phelps Brown and S. V. Hopkins, *Economica*, 1956, updated by the authors.)

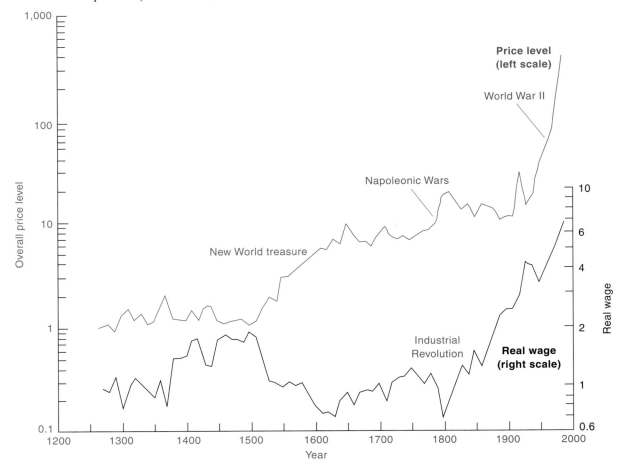

dramatically after World War II. Prices and wages now travel on a one-way street upward. They rise rapidly in periods of economic expansion; in recessions they do not fall but merely rise less rapidly. In other words, prices and wages are no longer flexible downward.

Three Strains of Inflation

Like diseases, inflations exhibit different levels of severity. It is useful to classify them into three categories: low inflation, galloping inflation, and hyperinflation.

Low Inflation. Low inflation is characterized by prices that rise slowly and predictably. We might define this as single-digit annual inflation rates. When prices are relatively stable, *people trust money.* They are willing to hold on to money because it will be almost as valuable in a month or a year as it is today. People are willing to write long-term contracts in money terms because they are confident that the relative prices of goods they buy and sell will not get too far out of line. Most indus-

trial countries have experienced low inflation over the last decade.

Galloping Inflation. Inflation in the double- or triple-digit range of 20, 100, or 200 percent a year is called "galloping inflation." From time to time advanced industrial countries like Italy or Japan suffer from this syndrome. Many Latin American countries, such as Argentina and Brazil, had inflation rates of 50 to 700 percent per year in the 1970s and 1980s.

Once galloping inflation becomes entrenched, serious economic distortions arise. Generally, most contracts get indexed to a price index or to a foreign currency, like the dollar. In these conditions, money loses its value very quickly, so people hold only the bare-minimum amount of money needed for daily transactions. Financial markets wither away, as capital flees abroad. People hoard goods, buy houses, and never, never lend money at low nominal interest rates. A surprising finding is that economies with galloping inflation often manage to grow rapidly even though the price system is behaving so badly.

FIGURE 30-3. U.S. Prices since the Civil War

Until World War II, prices shot up with each war and then drifted down afterward. But since 1940, the trend has been upward, both here and abroad. The only changes today are in the *rate* of inflation, not in the *fact* of inflation. (Source: U.S. Department of Labor, Bureau of Labor Statistics.)

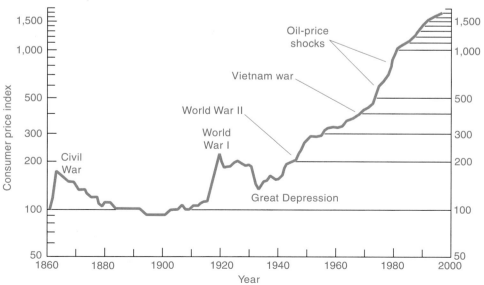

Hyperinflation. While economies seem to survive under galloping inflation, a third and deadly strain takes hold when the cancer of hyperinflation strikes. Nothing good can be said about a market economy in which prices are rising a million or even a trillion percent per year.

Hyperinflations are particularly interesting to students of inflation because they highlight its disastrous impacts. Consider this description of hyperinflation in the Confederacy during the Civil War:

> We used to go to the stores with money in our pockets and come back with food in our baskets. Now we go with money in baskets and return with food in our pockets. Everything is scarce except money! Prices are chaotic and production disorganized. A meal that used to cost the same amount as an opera ticket now costs twenty times as much. Everybody tends to hoard "things" and to try to get rid of the "bad" paper money, which drives the "good" metal money out of circulation. A partial return to barter inconvenience is the result.

The most thoroughly documented case of hyperinflation took place in the Weimar Republic of Germany in the 1920s. Figure 30-4 shows how the government unleashed the monetary printing presses, driving both money and prices to astronomical levels. From January 1922 to November 1923, the price index rose from 1 to 10,000,000,000. If a person had owned 300 million marks worth of German bonds in early 1922, this amount would not have bought a piece of candy 2 years later.

Studies have found several common features in hyperinflations. First, the real demand for money (measured by the money stock divided by the price level) falls drastically. By the end of the German hyperinflation, real money demand was only one-thirtieth of its level 2 years earlier. People are in effect rushing around, dumping their money like hot potatoes before they get burned by money's loss of value. Second, relative prices become highly unstable. Under normal conditions, a person's real wages move only a percent or less from month to month. During 1923, German real wages changed on average one-third (up or down) each month. This huge variation in relative prices and real wages—and the inequities and distortions caused by these fluctuations—took an enormous toll on workers and businesses, highlighting one of the major costs of inflation.

The German Hyperinflation

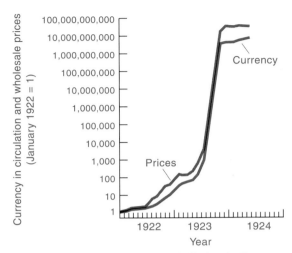

FIGURE 30-4. Money and Hyperinflation in Germany, **1922–1924**

In the early 1920s, the young Weimar Republic of Germany was struggling to meet harsh reparations payments and satisfy creditors. It could not borrow or raise enough taxes to pay for government spending, so it used the printing press to pay the government's bills. The stock of currency rose astronomically from early 1922 to December 1923, and prices spiraled upward as people frantically tried to dump their money before it lost all value. If you held a billion marks in January 1922, what would be left of your riches at the end of this hyperinflation?

The impact of inflation was beautifully expressed by J. M. Keynes:

> As inflation proceeds and the real value of the currency fluctuates wildly from month to month, all permanent relations between debtors and creditors, which form the ultimate foundation of capitalism, become so utterly disordered as to be almost meaningless; and the process of wealth-getting degenerates into a game and a lottery.

Anticipated vs. Unanticipated Inflation

An important distinction in the analysis of inflation is whether the price increases are anticipated or unanticipated. Suppose that all prices are rising at 3 percent each year and everyone expects this trend to continue. Would there be any reason to get excited about inflation? Would it make any difference if both the actual and the expected inflation rates were 1 or 3 or 5 percent each year? Economists generally believe that anticipated inflation at modest rates has little effect on economic efficiency or on the distribution of income and wealth. Prices would simply be a changing yardstick to which people adjust their behavior.

But the reality is that inflation is usually unanticipated. For example, the Russian people had become accustomed to stable prices for many decades. When prices were liberalized in 1992, no one, not even the professional economists, guessed that prices would rise by 1000-fold over the next 5 years. People who were unlucky enough to hold their wealth in rubles (whether in currency or savings accounts) saw their savings become worthless.

In more stable countries like the United States, the impact of unanticipated inflation is less dramatic, but the same general point applies. An unexpected jump in prices will impoverish some and enrich others. How costly is this redistribution? Perhaps "cost" does not describe the problem. The effects may be more social than economic. An epidemic of burglaries may not lower GDP, but it causes great distress. Similarly, randomly redistributing wealth by inflation is like forcing people to play a lottery they would prefer to avoid.

THE ECONOMIC IMPACTS OF INFLATION

Central bankers are united in their determination to contain inflation. During periods of high inflation, opinion polls often find that inflation is economic enemy number one. What is so dangerous and costly about inflation? We noted above that during periods of inflation all prices and wages do not move at the same rate; that is, changes in *relative prices* occur. As a result of the diverging relative prices, two definite effects of inflation are

- A *redistribution* of income and wealth among different groups
- *Distortions* in the relative prices and outputs of different goods, or sometimes in output and employment for the economy as a whole

Impacts on Income and Wealth Distribution

The major distributional impact of inflation arises from differences in the kinds of assets and liabilities that people hold.[2] When people owe money, a sharp rise in prices is a windfall gain for them. Suppose you borrow $100,000 to buy a house and your annual fixed-interest-rate mortgage payments are $10,000. Suddenly, a great inflation doubles all wages and incomes. Your *nominal* mortgage payment is still $10,000 per year, but its *real* cost is halved. You will need to work only half as long as before to make your mortgage payment. The great inflation has increased your wealth by cutting in half the real value of your mortgage debt.

This kind of thinking is a common feature of speculative real-estate bubbles. For example, when land prices rose sharply in the 1920s and 1970s, people borrowed heavily to buy houses or farmland. Then, when inflation slowed and the economy turned sour, the mortgage payments were so burdensome that thousands of people went bankrupt.

If you are a lender and have assets in fixed-interest-rate mortgages or long-term bonds, the shoe is on the other foot. An unexpected rise in prices will leave you the poorer because the dollars repaid to you are worth much less than the dollars you lent.

If an inflation persists for a long time, people come to anticipate it and markets begin to adapt. An allowance for inflation will gradually be built into the market interest rate. Say the economy starts out with interest rates of 3 percent and stable prices. Once people expect prices to rise at 9 percent per year, bonds and mortgages will tend to pay 12 percent rather than 3 percent. The 12 percent nominal interest rate reflects a 3 percent real interest rate plus a 9 percent inflation premium. There are no further major redistributions of income and wealth once interest rates have adapted to the new inflation rate. The adjustment of interest rates to chronic inflation has been observed in all countries with a long history of rising prices.[3]

---

[2] The important elements of balance sheets were described in Chapters 7 and 25.

[3] Fig. 25-3 shows movements in nominal and real interest rates for the United States in recent years.

Because of institutional changes, some old myths no longer apply. It used to be thought that common stocks were also a good inflation hedge, but stocks have proved to move inversely with inflation in recent years. A common saying was that widows and orphans were hurt by inflation; today, they receive social security pensions that are indexed to consumer prices, so they are insulated from inflation because benefits automatically increase as the CPI increases. Also, many kinds of debt (like "floating-rate" mortgages) have interest rates that move up and down with market interest rates, so unanticipated inflation benefits debtors and hurts lenders less than before.

There have been volumes of research on the redistributive impacts of inflation. The summary wisdom of these studies indicates that the overall impact is highly unpredictable. Those who live on capital income tend to lose from inflation, while wage earners tend to gain.

The major redistributive impact of inflation occurs through its effect on the real value of people's wealth. In general, unanticipated inflation redistributes wealth from creditors to debtors, helping borrowers and hurting lenders. An unanticipated decline in inflation has the opposite effect. But inflation mostly churns income and assets, randomly redistributing wealth among the population with little significant impact on any single group.

Impacts on Economic Efficiency

In addition to redistributing incomes, inflation affects the real economy in two specific areas: It affects total output, and it influences economic efficiency. Let's begin with the efficiency impacts.

Inflation impairs economic efficiency because it distorts price signals. In a low-inflation economy, if the market price of a good rises, both buyers and sellers know that there has been an actual change in the supply and/or demand conditions for that good, and they can react appropriately. For example, if the neighborhood supermarkets all boost their beef prices by 50 percent, perceptive consumers know that it's time to start eating more chicken. Similarly, if the prices of new computers fall by 90 percent, you may decide it's time to turn in your old model.

By contrast, in a high-inflation economy it's much harder to distinguish between changes in rela-

tive prices and changes in the overall price level. If inflation is running at 20 or 30 percent per month, stores change their prices so often that changes in relative prices get missed in the confusion.

Inflation also distorts the use of money. Currency is money that bears a zero nominal interest rate. If the inflation rate rises from 0 to 10 percent annually, the real interest rate on currency falls from 0 to -10 percent per year. There is no way to correct this distortion.

As a result of the negative real interest rate on money, people devote real resources to reducing their money holdings during inflationary times. They go to the bank more often—using up "shoe leather" and valuable time. Corporations set up elaborate cash-management schemes. Real resources are thereby consumed simply to adapt to a changing monetary yardstick rather than in making productive investments.

Many economists point to the distortion of inflation on taxes. Certain parts of the tax code are written in dollar terms. When prices rise, the real value of those provisions tend to decline. For example, you might be able to subtract a fixed-dollar "standard deduction" from your income in calculating your taxable income. With inflation, the real value of that standard deduction would decline and the real value of your taxes would rise. Such "taxation without legislation" has led many countries to index their tax laws to prevent inflation-induced tax increases. Parts of the U.S. tax code were indexed during the 1980s.

Indexing of tax brackets alone will not purge the tax system of the impacts of inflation because inflation distorts the measurement of income. For example, if you earned an interest rate of 6 percent on your funds in 1996, half of this return simply replaced your loss in the purchasing power of your funds from a 3 percent inflation rate. Yet the tax code does not distinguish between real return and the interest that just compensates for inflation. Many similar distortions of income and taxes are present in the tax code today.

But these are not the only costs; some economists point to *menu costs* of inflation. The idea is that when prices are changed, firms must spend real resources adjusting their prices. For instance, restaurants reprint their menus, mail-order firms reprint their catalogs, taxi companies remeter their cabs, cities adjust parking meters, and stores change the price tags of goods. Sometimes, the costs are intangible, such as those involved in gathering people to make new pricing decisions.

The impact of inflation turns up in unexpected corners. Often governments let the real value of their programs erode as prices rise. A recent study shows that government welfare payments to poor people have declined in real terms as governments chose not to increase their budgets in line with the rising cost of living. Regulated industries sometimes find that their requests for price increases are trimmed or rejected during inflationary periods. Most company pension plans provide benefits that are fixed in nominal terms, so the real benefits decline in inflationary periods. These are among the many examples of how inflation can affect people's incomes in unexpected ways.

Macroeconomic Impacts on Efficiency and Growth

In addition to the microeconomic and distributional impacts, are there effects of inflation on overall economic activity? This question is addressed in the next section, so we merely highlight the major points here. Until the 1970s, high inflation usually went hand in hand with high employment and output. In the United States, inflation tended to increase when investment was brisk and jobs were plentiful. Periods of deflation or declining inflation—the 1890s, the 1930s, 1954, 1958, 1982, and 1991—were times of high unemployment of labor and capital.

But a more careful examination of the historical record has revealed an interesting fact: The positive association between output and inflation appears to be only a temporary relationship. Over the longer run, there seems to be an inverse-U-shaped relationship between inflation and output growth. Table 30-1 shows the results of a recent multicountry study of the association between inflation and growth. It indicates that economic growth is strongest in countries with low inflation, while countries with high inflation or deflation tend to grow more slowly. (But beware the *ex post* fallacy here, as explored in question 7 at the end of the chapter.)

Whatever the short-run or long-run impact of inflation on output and efficiency, there is no doubt about the reaction of the Federal Reserve when inflation threatens. Whenever inflation threatens to

Inflation rate (% per year)	Growth of per capita GDP (% per year)
−20–0	0.7
0–10	2.4
10–20	1.8
20–40	0.4
100–200	−1.7
1,000 +	−6.5

TABLE 30-1. Inflation and Economic Growth
The pooled experience of 127 countries shows that the most rapid growth is associated with low inflation rates. Deflation and moderate inflation accompany slow growth, while hyperinflations are associated with sharp downturns. (Source: Michael Bruno and William Easterly, "Inflation Crises and Long-Run Growth," World Bank Policy Research Working Paper 1517, September 1995.)

rise, the Fed today takes forceful steps to stop inflation in its tracks—by reducing money growth, raising interest rates, and thereby restraining the growth of real output and raising unemployment. Indeed, the decision by central banks to contain inflation was the prime cause of the long and deep recession in North America that followed the 1979 oil-price increase as well as the profound downturn that has persisted in Western Europe in the first half of the 1990s.

Thus, whatever economists may conclude about the menu costs or other microeconomic costs of inflation, the reaction of policymakers must be counted as one of the costs of inflation. And that reaction has generally been to contain inflation by high unemployment and low GDP growth. As Section C shows, the amount of output and the number of jobs that are lost to curb inflation are very large.

What Is the Optimal Rate of Inflation?

Most nations seek rapid economic growth, full employment, and price stability. But just what is meant by "price stability"? What is a desirable long-term trend for prices? Most macroeconomists point to the advantage of relatively low and stable inflation. In the 1991–1996 period in the United States, for example, consumer price inflation was stable at about 3 percent per year. During this period, output and price growth were relatively predictable, leading to a stable macroeconomic environment in the United States.

Some today argue that policy should go further and aim for absolutely stable prices or zero inflation. Stanford economist Robert Hall and Fed governor W. Lee Hoskins point to the value of having a predictable level of future prices when people make their investment decisions. A bill recently introduced by Senator Connie Mack, chairman of the Joint Economic Committee, directs the Federal Reserve to pursue stable prices because "price stability maintains the highest possible levels of productivity, real incomes, living standards, employment, and global competitiveness."

Many macroeconomists demur. They point out that, while a zero-inflation target might be sensible in an ideal economy, we do not live in a frictionless system. Perhaps the most important friction is the resistance of workers to declines in money wages. If the average wage level were stable, this would be the average of some wages that are rising and some that are falling. But workers and firms are extremely reluctant to cut money wages. Evidence for the downward rigidity of wages is found in a comprehensive government survey of wage changes in manufacturing over the period 1958–1978. During this period, on average less than 0.1 percent of workers received wage cuts, even in years when inflation was extremely low.

From a macroeconomic point of view, this suggests that stable prices and wages would be associ-ated with a higher sustainable level of unemployment and a lower level of output than would be the case at an inflation rate of 2 to 4 percent. A recent study estimates that targeting stable prices would cost the United States between 1 and 3 percent lower output and employment *permanently* as compared with an inflation target of around 3 percent. The authors conclude:

> Downward rigidity [of wages] interferes with the ability of some firms to make adjustments in real wages, leading to inefficient reductions in employment. . . . The main implication for policymakers is that targeting zero inflation will lead to a large inefficiency in the allocation of resources, as reflected in a sustainable rate of unemployment that is unnecessarily high.[4]

We can summarize our discussion in the following way:

> While economists may disagree on the exact target for inflation, it appears that a predictable and gently rising price level provides the best climate for healthy economic growth. A careful sifting of the evidence suggests that low inflation like that seen recently in the United States has little impact on productivity or real output. By contrast, galloping inflation or hyperinflation can cause serious harm to productivity and to individuals through the redistribution of income and wealth. Finally, even though the costs of inflation appear modest, central bankers will not long tolerate high inflation; they take measures to curb inflation by slowing output growth and raising unemployment.

B. MODERN INFLATION THEORY

Can market economies simultaneously enjoy the blessings of full employment and price stability? Is there no way to control inflation other than by economic slowdowns that keep unemployment undesirably high? If recessions are too high a price to pay for the control of inflation, do we need "incomes policies" that can lower inflation without raising unemployment?

Questions, questions, questions. Yet answers to these are critical to the economic health of modern mixed economies. In the balance of this chapter we

---
[4] See George A. Akerlof, William T. Dickens, and George L. Perry, "The Macroeconomics of Low Inflation," *Brookings Papers on Economic Activity*, no. 1, 1996, pp. 1–59.

explore modern inflation theory and analyze the costs of lowering inflation.

PRICES IN THE *AS-AD* FRAMEWORK

There is no single source of inflation. Like illnesses, inflations occur for many reasons. Some inflations come from the demand side; others, from the supply side. But one key fact about modern inflations is that they develop an internal momentum and are costly to stop once under way.

Inertial Inflation

In modern industrial economies like the United States, inflation is highly *inertial*. That is, it will persist at the same rate until economic events cause it to change. We can compare inertial inflation to a lazy old dog. If the dog is not "shocked" by the push of a foot or the pull of a cat, it will stay where it is. Once disturbed, the dog may chase the cat, but then it eventually lies down in a new spot where it stays until the next shock.

During the 1990s, prices in the United States rose steadily at around 3 percent annually, and most people came to expect that inflation rate. This expected rate of inflation was built into the economy's institutions. Wage agreements between labor and management were designed around a 3 percent inflation rate; government monetary and fiscal plans assumed a 3 percent rate. During this period, the *inertial rate of inflation* was 3 percent per year. Other names sometimes heard for this concept are the *core*, *underlying*, or *expected* inflation rate.

The rate of inflation that is expected and built into contracts and informal arrangements is the **inertial rate of inflation**.

Inertial inflation can persist for a long time—as long as most people expect the inflation rate to remain the same. Under this condition, inflation is built into the system. But history shows that inflation does not remain undisturbed for long. Frequent shocks from changes in aggregate demand, sharp oil-price changes, poor harvests, movements in the foreign exchange rate, productivity changes, and countless other economic events move inflation above or below its inertial rate. The major kinds of shocks are demand-pull and cost-push.

At a given time, the economy has an ongoing rate of inflation to which people's expectations have adapted. This built-in inertial inflation rate tends to persist until a shock causes it to move up or down.

Demand-Pull Inflation

One of the major shocks to inflation is a change in aggregate demand. In earlier chapters we saw that changes in investment, government spending, or net exports can change aggregate demand and propel output beyond its potential. We also saw how a nation's central bank can affect economic activity. Whatever the reason, **demand-pull inflation** occurs when aggregate demand rises more rapidly than the economy's productive potential, pulling prices up to equilibrate aggregate supply and demand. In effect, demand dollars are competing for the limited supply of commodities and bid up their prices. As unemployment falls and workers become scarce, wages are bid up and the inflationary process accelerates.

We often see demand inflation at work when nations rely on money to finance their spending. Rapid money-supply growth increases aggregate demand, which in turn increases the price level. In this example, the direction of causation is clear-cut. It proceeds from the money supply through aggregate demand to inflation. Thus, when the German central bank printed billions and billions of paper marks in 1922–1923 and they came into the marketplace in search of bread or housing, it was no wonder that the German price level rose a billionfold, making the currency worthless. This was demand-pull inflation with a vengeance. This scene was replayed when the Russian government financed its budget deficit by printing rubles in the early 1990s. The result was an inflation rate that averaged 25 percent *per month* [or $100 \times (1.25^{12} - 1) = 1355$ percent per year].

Figure 30-5 on page 588 illustrates the process of demand-pull inflation in terms of aggregate supply and demand. Starting from an initial equilibrium at point E, suppose there is an expansion of spending that pushes the AD curve up and to the right. The economy's equilibrium moves from E to E'. At this higher level of demand, prices have risen from P to P'. Demand-pull inflation has taken place.

Cost-Push Inflation

The rudiments of demand-pull inflation were understood by the classical economists and used by them to explain historical price movements. But during the last half-century, the inflation process changed, as a glance back at the history of prices on page 580 reminds us. Prices today travel a one-way street—up in recessions, up faster in booms. And this is true for all the market economies of the world. What differentiates modern inflation from the simple demand-pull variety is that prices and wages begin to rise before full employment is reached. They rise even when 30 percent of factory capacity lies idle and 10 percent of the labor force is unemployed. This phenomenon is known as *cost-push* or *supply-shock* inflation.

Inflation resulting from rising costs during periods of high unemployment and slack resource utilization is called **cost-push inflation**.

Cost-push inflation does not appear to have been present in the early stages of market economies. It first appeared during the 1930s and 1940s, leading to the dramatic change in the pattern of price behavior after World War II shown in Figure 30-3 on page 581.

In looking for explanations of cost-push inflation, economists often start with wages, which are clearly an important part of businesses' costs. In 1982, for example, when the unemployment rate was almost 10 percent, wages rose 5 percent. Wages tend to rise even in recession because they are administered prices and because of the strong resistence to wage cuts.

Since the 1970s, cost-push shocks have often come from sharp changes in the prices of oil and food and from exchange-rate movements. In 1973, in 1978, and again briefly in 1990, countries were minding their own macroeconomic business when severe shortages in oil markets occurred. Oil prices rose sharply, and business costs of production increased. The outcomes were not identical for the three cases, but in each period a sharp burst of cost-push inflation followed the oil-price increase. Sometimes, cost shocks are favorable. For example, the favorable trends in health costs and the dollar's foreign exchange rate in the United States in the mid-1990s slowed the rise in *AS*.

Expectations and Inertial Inflation

Why, you might ask, does inflation have such strong inertia or momentum? The answer is that most prices and wages are set with an eye to future economic conditions. When prices and wages are rising rapidly and are expected to continue doing so,

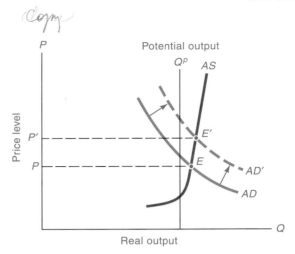

FIGURE 30-5. Demand-Pull Inflation Occurs When Too Much Spending Chases Too Few Goods

At high output levels, when aggregate demand increases, the rising spending is competing for limited goods. With a steep *AS* curve, much of the higher aggregate spending ends up in higher prices. Prices rise from *P* to *P′*. This is demand-pull inflation. How would cost-push inflation be analyzed in this framework?

businesses and workers tend to build the rapid rate of inflation into their price and wage decisions. High or low inflation expectations tend to be self-fulfilling prophecies.

We can use a hypothetical example to illustrate the role of expectations in inertial inflation. Say that in 1997, Brass Mills Inc., a nonunionized light-manufacturing firm, was contemplating its annual wage and salary decisions for 1998. Its sales were growing well, and it was experiencing no major supply or demand shocks. Brass Mills' chief economist reported that no major inflationary or deflationary shocks were foreseen, and the major forecasting services were expecting national wage growth of 4 percent in 1998. Brass Mills had conducted a survey of local companies and found that most employers were planning on increases in compensation of 3 to 5 percent during the next year. All the signals, then, pointed to wage increases of around 4 percent for 1998 over 1997.

In examining its own internal labor market, Brass Mills determined that its wages were in line with the local labor market. Because the managers did not want to fall behind local wages, Brass Mills decided that it would try to match local wage increases. It therefore set wage increases at the

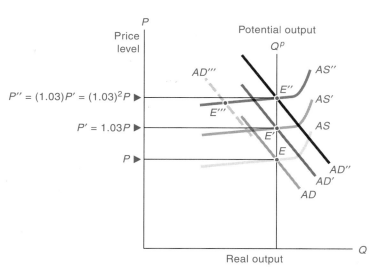

FIGURE 30-6. An Upward Spiral of Prices and Wages Occurs When Aggregate Supply and Demand Shift Up Together

Suppose that production costs are rising by 3 percent each year. Thus, for every level of output, the *AS* curve will be 3 percent higher next year, another 3 percent higher the year after, and so on. If *AD* moves up at the same pace, output will stay close to potential and prices will also rise by 3 percent. As the macro equilibrium moves from *E* to *E'* to *E''*, prices march up steadily because of inertial inflation. Using this framework, can you depict an inertial rate of inflation of 1 or 5 percent per year?

expected market increase, an average 4 percent wage increase for 1998.

The process of setting wages and salaries with an eye to expected future economic conditions can be extended to virtually all employers. This kind of reasoning also applies to many product prices—such as college tuitions, automobile-model prices, and long-distance telephone rates—that cannot be easily changed after they have been set. Because of the length of time involved in modifying inflation expectations and in adjusting most wages and many prices, inertial inflation will yield only to major shocks or changes in economic policy.

Figure 30-6 illustrates the process of inertial inflation. Suppose that potential output is constant and that there are no supply or demand shocks. If everyone expects average costs and prices to rise at 3 percent each year, the *AS* curve will shift upward at 3 percent per year. If there are no demand shocks, the *AD* curve will also shift up at that rate. The intersection of the *AD* and *AS* curves will be 3 percent higher each year. Hence, the macroeconomic equilibrium

moves from *E* to *E'* to *E''*. Prices are rising 3 percent from one year to the next: Inertial inflation has set in at 3 percent.

Inertial inflation occurs when the *AS* and *AD* curves are moving steadily upward at the same rate.

Price Levels vs. Inflation

Using Figure 30-6, we can make the useful distinction between movements in the price level and movements in inflation. In general, an increase in aggregate demand will raise prices, other things being equal. Similarly, an upward shift in the *AS* curve resulting from an increase in wages and other costs will raise prices, other things being equal.

But of course other things always change; in particular, *AD* and *AS* curves never sit still. Figure 30-6 shows, for example, the *AS* and *AD* curves marching up together.

What if there were an unexpected shift in the *AS* or *AD* curve during the third period? How would prices and inflation be affected? Suppose, for example, that the third period's *AD''* curve shifted to the left to AD''' because of a monetary contraction. This might cause a recession, with a new equilibrium at E''' on the AS'' curve. At this point, output would have fallen below potential; prices and the inflation rate would be lower than at E'', but the economy would still be experiencing inflation because the price level at E''' is still above the previous period's equilibrium E' with price P'.

Economic forces may reduce the price level below the level it would otherwise have attained. Nonetheless, because of the momentum of cost and price increases, the economy may continue to experience inflation even in the face of these contractionary shocks.

THE PHILLIPS CURVE

A useful way of representing the process of inflation was developed by the economist A. W. Phillips, who quantified the determinants of wage inflation. After careful study of more than a century's worth of data on unemployment and money wages in the United Kingdom, Phillips found an inverse relationship between unemployment and the changes in money wages. He found that wages tended to rise when unemployment was low and vice versa. Why might high unemployment lower the growth in money wages? The reason is that workers would press less strongly for wage increases when fewer alternative jobs were available, and, in addition, firms would resist wage demands more firmly when profits were low.

The Phillips curve is useful for analyzing short-run movements of unemployment and inflation. The simplest version is shown in Figure 30-7. On the diagram's horizontal axis is the unemployment rate. On the black left-hand vertical scale is the annual rate of price inflation. The rust right-hand vertical scale shows the rate of money-wage inflation. As you move leftward on the Phillips curve by reducing unemployment, the rate of price and wage increase indicated by the curve becomes higher.

An important piece of inflation arithmetic underlies this curve. Say that labor productivity (output per worker) rises at a steady rate of 1 percent each year. Further, assume that firms set prices on the basis of average labor costs, so prices always change just as much as average labor costs per unit

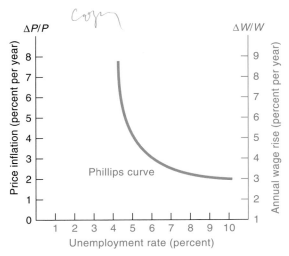

FIGURE 30-7. The Short-Run Phillips Curve Depicts the Tradeoff between Inflation and Unemployment

A short-run Phillips curve shows the inverse relationship between inflation and unemployment. The rust-colored wage-change scale on the right-hand vertical axis is higher than the black left-hand inflation scale by the assumed 1 percent rate of growth of average labor productivity.

of output. If wages are rising at 4 percent, and productivity is rising at 1 percent, then average labor costs will rise at 3 percent. Consequently, prices will also rise at 3 percent.

 Economics at work: Wage-price arithmetic: This relationship between prices, wages, and productivity can be formalized as follows: The fact that prices are based on average labor costs per unit of output implies that P is always proportional to WL/Q, where P is the price level, W is the wage rate, L is labor-hours, and Q is output. Further assume that average labor productivity (Q/L) is growing smoothly at 1 percent per year. Hence, if wages are growing at 4 percent annually, prices will grow at 3 percent annually (= 4 growth in wages −1 growth in productivity). More generally,

$$\begin{pmatrix} \text{rate} \\ \text{of} \\ \text{inflation} \end{pmatrix} = \begin{pmatrix} \text{rate of} \\ \text{wage} \\ \text{growth} \end{pmatrix} - \begin{pmatrix} \text{rate of} \\ \text{productivity} \\ \text{growth} \end{pmatrix}$$

This shows the relationship between price inflation and wage inflation.

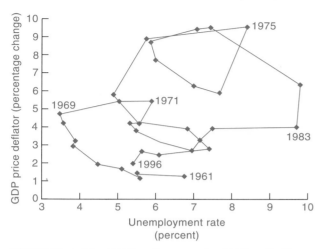

FIGURE 30-8. The Phillips Curve or the Phillips Curl?

Data on unemployment and inflation over the last three decades show a complicated relationship. Modern sustainable-unemployment-rate theories explain the Phillips curl and the inward and outward drift by changes in the expected rate of inflation. (Source: *Economic Report of the President*, 1997; the price index here is the chain-weighted price index for GDP.)

Using this inflation arithmetic, we can see the relation between wage and price increases in Figure 30-7. These two scales in the figure differ only by the assumed rate of productivity growth (so the price change of 4 percent per year would correspond to a wage change of 5 percent per year if productivity grew by 1 percent per year and if prices always rose as fast as average labor costs).

Interpretation

How does the Phillips curve fit into our model of aggregate supply and demand? The best way to think of the Phillips curve shown in Figure 30-7 is as a *short-run relationship between inflation and unemployment when aggregate demand shifts but aggregate supply continues to change at its inertial rate.* This can be understood by comparing Figures 30-6 and 30-7.

Assume that a 6 percent unemployment rate corresponds to potential output. Then, as long as output stays at its potential, unemployment stays at 6 percent and inflation continues to rise at 3 percent per year. Suppose, however, that a shift in aggregate demand occurs in the third period, so the equilibrium is at point E''' rather than E'' in Figure 30-6.

Then output will be below potential, unemployment will rise above 6 percent, and inflation will fall. To cement your understanding of this point, pencil into Figure 30-7 the unemployment and inflation rates that correspond to points E'' and E''' in Figure 30-6.

It is important to note that the Phillips curve is not a fixed tradeoff. When the inertial rate of inflation changes, the Phillips curve will also shift. Figure 30-8 shows the plot of inflation and unemployment over the period 1961–1996. The points circle clockwise, with some movement outward and inward. One of the major issues in modern macroeconomics has revolved around the interpretation of the clockwise movements in the Phillips curve.

THE LOWEST SUSTAINABLE UNEMPLOYMENT RATE

To explain the strange looking "Phillips curl" in Figure 30-8, economists modified the original Phillips approach. Growing out of theoretical work of Edmund Phelps and Milton Friedman, and tested by scores of econometricians, the modified theory distinguishes between the long-run Phillips curve and the short-run Phillips curve. It asserts that the downward-sloping Phillips curve of Figure 30-7 holds only in the short run. In the long run, there is a minimum unemployment rate that is consistent with steady inflation. This is the *lowest sustainable unemployment rate,* or *LSUR* (pronounced to rhyme with "me-burr").[5] Most macroeconomists believe that the long-run Phillips curve is vertical.

Begin with a careful definition:

The **lowest sustainable unemployment rate** (*LSUR*) is that rate at which upward and downward forces on price and wage inflation are in balance. At the *LSUR*, inflation is stable, with no tendency to show either accelerating or declining inflation. The *LSUR* is the lowest level of unemployment that can be sustained for long without upward pressure on inflation.

---

[5] Other terms will sometimes be encountered. The original name for the *LSUR* was the "natural rate of unemployment." This term is unsatisfactory because there is nothing natural about the *LSUR*. Critics of the early theories coined another commonly used term, the "nonaccelerating inflation rate of unemployment" or *NAIRU*. This term hardly rolls off the tongue and is slightly misleading because it is prices rather than inflation that accelerate at low unemployment rates.

We can understand this theory in the following way: At any point in time, the economy has inherited a given inertial or expected rate of inflation. If (1) there is no excess demand and if (2) there are no supply shocks, actual inflation will continue at the inertial rate. What do these conditions signify? Condition (1) means that unemployment is at that sustainable level at which the upward pressure on wages from vacancies just matches the downward wage pressure from unemployment. Condition (2) denotes the absence of unusual changes in the costs of production from wages or materials like oil and imports, so the aggregate supply curve is rising at the inertial rate of inflation. Putting conditions (1) and (2) together leads to a state in which inflation can continue to rise at its inertial or expected rate.

What would happen in the presence of demand or cost shocks? At very low unemployment, such as occurred during the Vietnam war, inflation is pushed above its inertial rate as we move up along the short-run Phillips curve. By contrast, if unemployment rises far above the sustainable rate, as in the early 1980s, inflation will decline as the economy moves down the short-run Phillips curve.

But the story does not end here. Once actual inflation rises above its inertial level, people begin to adapt to the new level of inflation. They begin to expect higher inflation. The inertial rate of inflation then adjusts to the new reality, and the short-run Phillips curve shifts.

This brief narrative makes a crucial point about inflation: The tradeoff between inflation and unemployment remains stable only as long as the inertial or expected inflation rate remains unchanged. But when the inertial inflation rate changes, the short-run Phillips curve will shift.

The Shifting Phillips Curve

This important idea—of a shifting Phillips curve—can be understood as a sequence of steps, illustrated by a "boom cycle" here and in Figure 30-9.

• *Period 1.* In the first period, unemployment is at the sustainable rate. There are no demand or supply surprises, and the economy is at point *A* on the lower short-run Phillips curve (*SRPC*) in Figure 30-9.
• *Period 2.* A rapid increase in output during an economic expansion lowers the unemployment

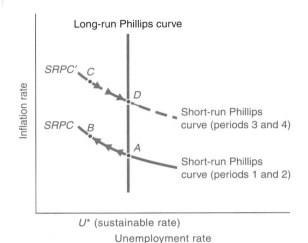

FIGURE 30-9. How Shocks Move the Phillips Curve

This figure shows how a period of low unemployment shifts the short-run Phillips curve. The economy starts at point *A*. The economy then expands, with unemployment falling below the sustainable rate at point *B* in period 2. As a result, inflation rises above the inertial rate.

As time passes, however, the higher inflation becomes anticipated and gets built into the new short-run Phillips curve, *SRPC'*. When the economy comes back to the lowest sustainable rate at point *D* in period 4, it is now saddled with higher inertial and actual inflation rates.

Note that if points *A*, *B*, *C*, and *D* represent different years, you can connect the dots. The shifting curve has produced a clockwise loop like that seen in Fig. 30-8.

rate. As unemployment declines, firms tend to recruit workers more vigorously, giving larger wage increases than formerly. As output exceeds its potential, capacity utilization rises and price markups increase. Wages and prices begin to accelerate. In terms of our Phillips curve, the economy moves up and to the left to point *B* on its short-run Phillips curve (along *SRPC* in Figure 30-9). Inflation expectations have not yet changed, but the lower unemployment rate raises inflation during the second period.
• *Period 3.* With higher inflation, firms and workers begin to expect higher inflation. The higher expected rate of inflation is incorporated into wage and price decisions. The expected rate of inflation thus increases. The higher expected inflation shows up in the Phillips-curve framework when the short-run Phillips curve shifts

upward and the new equilibrium is at point *C*. The new short-run Phillips curve (labeled *SRPC'* in Figure 30-9) lies above the original Phillips curve, reflecting the higher expected rate of inflation.

- *Period 4.* In the final period, as the economy slows, the contraction in economic activity brings output back to its potential, and the unemployment rate returns to the sustainable level at point *D*. Inflation declines because of the higher unemployment, but once the *LSUR* is reached, the new expected rate of inflation is higher.

Note the surprising outcome. Because the expected or inertial inflation rate has increased, the rate of inflation is higher in period 4 than during period 1 even though the unemployment rate is the same. The economy will experience the same *real* GDP and unemployment levels as it did in period 1, even though the *nominal* magnitudes (prices and nominal GDP) are now growing more rapidly than they did before the expansion raised the expected rate of inflation.

We sometimes also track an "austerity cycle" that occurs when unemployment rises and the actual inflation rate falls below the inertial rate. The inertial rate of inflation declines in recessions, and the economy enjoys a lower inflation rate when it returns to the sustainable unemployment rate. This painful cycle of austerity occurred during the Carter-Volcker-Reagan wars against inflation during 1979–1984.

The Vertical Long-Run Phillips Curve

When the unemployment rate departs from the lowest sustainable unemployment rate, the inflation rate will tend to change. What happens if the gap between the actual unemployment rate and the *LSUR* persists? For example, say that the *LSUR* is 6 percent while the actual unemployment rate is 4 percent. Because of the gap, inflation will tend to rise from year to year. Inflation might be 3 percent in the first year, 4 percent in the second year, 5 percent in the third year—and might continue to move upward thereafter.

When would this upward spiral stop? It stops only when unemployment moves back to the *LSUR*. Put differently, as long as unemployment is below the sustainable rate, wage inflation will tend to increase.

The opposite behavior will be seen at high unemployment. In that case, inflation will tend to fall as long as unemployment is above the sustainable rate.

Only when unemployment is *at* the sustainable rate will inflation stabilize; only then will the shifts of supply and demand in different labor markets be in balance; only then will inflation—at whatever is its inertial rate—tend neither to increase nor to decrease.

According to the sustainable-unemployment-rate theory, the only level of unemployment consistent with a stable inflation rate is the lowest sustainable unemployment rate. The long-run Phillips curve must, in this theory, be drawn as a vertical line, rising straight up at the *LSUR* as shown by the vertical *DA* line in Figure 30-9.

The sustainable-unemployment-rate theory of inflation has two important implications for economic policy. First, it implies that there is a minimum level of unemployment that an economy can sustain in the long run. According to this view, a nation cannot push unemployment below the sustainable rate for long without igniting an upward spiral of wage and price inflation.

Second, a nation may be able to ride the short-run Phillips curve. A government might use monetary and fiscal policies to drive the unemployment rate below the sustainable rate, and the nation can temporarily enjoy low unemployment. But this prosperity comes at the price of rising inflation. Conversely, when a nation thinks that its inertial inflation rate is too high, as was the case in 1979–1982, it can steel itself for a period of austerity, tighten money, induce a recession, and thereby reduce inflation.

Quantitative Estimates

Although the sustainable unemployment rate is a crucial macroeconomic concept, precise numerical estimates of the sustainable rate have proved elusive. Many macroeconomists, such as Robert J. Gordon, James Stock, and Mark Watson, have used their judgment along with advanced techniques to estimate the *LSUR*. For this text, we have adopted the consensus estimates prepared by the Congressional Budget Office (CBO), which estimates the *LSUR* on the basis of scholarly studies. According to the CBO, the *LSUR* rose gradually from the 1950s and peaked at 6.3 percent of the labor force around 1980. Since

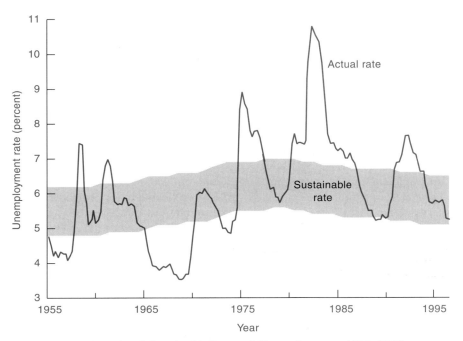

FIGURE 30-10. Actual and Sustainable Rates of Unemployment, 1955–1996
The lowest sustainable unemployment rate comes where forces acting on inflation are in balance. Below that rate, inflation generally tends to rise; above it, inflation tends to subside.
The sustainable rate appears to have risen in the 1970s and 1980s and then declined over the
last decade. The sustainable rate is shown as a wide band to reflect the fact that it is difficult
to estimate the *LSUR* precisely. (Source: Actual unemployment rate from U.S. Department
of Labor, *Employment and Earnings*; sustainable unemployment rate from the Congressional
Budget Office and research of private scholars.)

then, the CBO estimates that the *LSUR* has declined
to 5.8 percent in 1996. CBO estimates, along with
the actual unemployment rate through the end of
1996, are shown in Figure 30-10.

Academic economists have produced a range of
numbers, with informed opinion putting the sustainable rate between 5 and 6½ percent of the labor
force for the mid-1990s. Most economists hold that,
given today's price- and wage-setting institutions, the
United States could not maintain an unemployment
rate below 5 percent without risking rising inflation.

Many people are discouraged that the sustainable rate is so high. Why is it not possible to guarantee good jobs to all without accelerating inflation?
One reason lies in the high level of frictional unemployment in the United States. For example, in 1997,
a year in which the economy was near its sustainable
rate, over one-third of the unemployed workers were

young (under 25 years of age); only 2.1 percent of
those in the labor force were unemployed job losers;
and of the 136 million adults in the labor force, only
990,000 had been unemployed for longer than 26
weeks.

Besides the frictional component of unemployment, there is normally a great deal of structural and
involuntary unemployment. Even when the unemployment rate is low, a substantial fraction of the
unemployed consists of job losers and the long-term
unemployed. Labor markets do not quickly match
up job vacancies and unemployed workers.

In summary:

The lowest sustainable unemployment rate is
high in the United States in part because the mobility of workers is so great and in part because the
labor market is unable to quickly match up job
vacancies and unemployed workers.

The Declining Sustainable Rate

The best evidence suggests that—after having risen in the 1970s and 1980s—the sustainable rate in the United States has declined by between ½ and 1 percentage point over the last decade. One reason for the decline has been the decrease in the power of labor unions. Labor unions controlled almost one-quarter of the labor force at their peak, but by 1996 that fraction had shrunk to about one-eighth of the work force, with particularly sharp declines in the private sector. This weakening of labor's monopoly power means that labor market conditions, particularly high unemployment, are more quickly transmitted into wage changes.

Another important structural feature lowering the *LSUR* is the strengthening of competition in the American economy. Over the last two decades, many industries have been deregulated, and foreign firms have invaded many previously sheltered domestic markets. In automobiles, telecommunications, and energy markets, stronger competition in the product market in effect increases competition in the labor market as well. With pressure from other, often foreign or nonunion firms, wages tend to rise less during periods of strong demand, reducing the *LSUR*. Some analysts believe that the pressure on labor markets from increased immigration reinforces the competitiveness of labor markets.

Evidence of a decline in the sustainable rate is seen in several labor market statistics. For example, the level of vacancies in 1996 was far below that in 1989 even though the unemployment rate was identical. With fewer vacancies, upward wage pressures tend to moderate. In addition, the fraction of workers who were "job leavers" was one-third lower in 1996 than in 1989 (see the discussion of this component of unemployment in Chapter 29). This indicates that fewer people are leaving their jobs to chase higher wages elsewhere. Economists will be sifting through the data carefully to see whether the apparent decline in the sustainable unemployment rate is a durable feature of the American economy.

Doubts about the Sustainable Rate

The concept of the lowest sustainable unemployment rate, along with its output twin, potential GDP, is crucial for understanding inflation and the connection between the short run and the long run in macroeconomics. But the mainstream view sketched here is not universally held by macroeconomists.

One issue is whether the sustainable rate is a stable magnitude. Some believe that an extended period of high unemployment will lead to a deterioration of job skills, to loss of on-the-job training and experience, and thereby to a higher sustainable unemployment rate. Might not slow growth of real GDP reduce investment and leave the country with a diminished capital stock? Might not that capacity shortage produce rising inflation even with unemployment rates above the sustainable rate?

Experience in Europe over the last two decades confirms some of these worries (recall our discussion of the European unemployment puzzle at the end of the last chapter). In the early 1960s, labor markets in Germany, France, and Britain appeared to be in equilibrium with unemployment rates between 1 and 2 percent. By the early 1990s, after a decade of stagnation and slow job growth, labor market equilibrium seemed to be in balance with unemployment rates in the 6 to 12 percent range. On the basis of recent European experience, many macroeconomists are looking for ways to explain the instability of the sustainable rate and its dependence upon actual unemployment as well as labor market institutions.

Review

The major points to understand are the following:

- Inflation has great momentum and is highly inertial. It tends to persist until shocked either by demand or by costs.
- In the short run, an increase in aggregate demand which lowers the unemployment rate below the sustainable rate will tend to increase the inflation rate. A demand decrease will tend to lower inflation. In the short run, while the Phillips curve is stable, there is a tradeoff between inflation and unemployment.
- The Phillips curve tends to adapt to the ongoing rate of inflation. A period of low unemployment and increasing inflation will lead people to expect higher inflation and will tend to shift up the short-run Phillips curve.
- According to the sustainable-unemployment-rate theory, the long-run Phillips curve is vertical at the lowest sustainable unemployment rate (*LSUR*); as long as the unemployment rate is below the sustainable rate, inflation will tend to rise continually.

C. DILEMMAS OF ANTI-INFLATION POLICY

The economy evolves in response to political forces and technological change. Our economic theories, designed to explain issues like inflation and unemployment, must also adapt. In this final section on inflation theory, we discuss the pressing issues that arise in combating inflation.

How Long Is the Long Run?

The sustainable-unemployment-rate theory holds that the Phillips curve is vertical in the long run. Just how long is the long run for this purpose? The length of time that it takes the economy to adjust fully to a shock is not known with precision. Recent studies suggest that full adjustment takes at least 5 years or perhaps even a decade. The reason for the long delay is that it takes years for expectations to adjust, for labor and other long-term contracts to be renegotiated, and for all these effects to percolate through the economy. In the long run, a market economy adjusts to shocks to aggregate supply or demand and tends to restore full employment, but the adjustment process is slow.

How Much Does It Cost to Reduce Inflation?

Our analysis suggests that a nation can reduce the inertial rate of inflation by temporarily reducing output and raising unemployment. But in weighing anti-inflation policies, policymakers may want to know just how much it costs to squeeze inflation out of the economy. How costly is *disinflation,* which denotes the policy of lowering the rate of inflation? This is equivalent to asking about the shape of the short-run Phillips curve. If the Phillips curve is relatively flat, reducing inflation will require much unemployment and loss in output; if the Phillips curve is steep, a small rise in unemployment will bring down inflation quickly and relatively painlessly.

Studies of this subject find that the cost of reducing inflation varies depending upon the country, the initial inflation rate, and the policy used. Analyses for the United States give a reasonably consistent answer: Lowering the inertial inflation rate by 1 percentage point costs the nation about 4 percent of 1 year's GDP. In terms of the current level of GDP, this amounts to an output loss of about $300 billion (in 1996 prices) to reduce the inflation rate by 1 percentage point.

We can explain this estimate using the Phillips curve. Statistical analyses indicate that when the unemployment rate rises 1 percentage point above the lowest sustainable unemployment rate for 1 year and then returns to the sustainable rate, the inflation rate will decline about $\frac{1}{2}$ percentage point. Therefore, to reduce inflation by 1 full percentage point, unemployment must be held 2 percentage points above the sustainable unemployment rate for 1 year.

Recall that Okun's Law (discussed in Chapter 29) holds that when the unemployment rate is 2 percentage points above the sustainable rate, actual GDP is 4 percent below potential GDP. In 1996 terms, with a potential GDP (in 1996 prices) of $7600 billion, reducing inflation by 1 percentage point would require about a 2-percentage-point increase in the unemployment rate (U) for 1 year. In dollars, then, a disinflation of 1 percentage point would cost 2 U points × 2 percent of GDP per U point × $7600 billion of GDP = $304 billion. Other estimates of the cost range from $140 to $400 billion per point of inflation reduction.

This statistical estimate of the cost of reducing inflation can be compared to the American experience during the deep recession in the early 1980s. Table 30-2 shows a calculation of the estimated output loss from the recession (compared to producing at potential output), along with the estimated decline in the inertial inflation rate. This calculation indicates that the disinflation of the 1980–1984 period cost the nation approximately $300 billion of lost output (in 1996 prices) per percentage-point reduction in inflation. This episode corroborates statistical estimates of the cost of disinflation.

The Cost of Disinflation, 1980–1984	
Inertial rate of inflation:	
1979	9%
1984	4%
Change:	−5 percentage points
Difference between potential and	
actual GDP (1996 prices):	
1980	$150 billion
1981	210
1982	470
1983	470
1984	200
Total: $1,500 billion	
Cost of disinflation = $1,500 billion/5 percentage points	
= $300 billion per percentage point	

TABLE 30-2. Illustration of the Cost of Disinflation
This table illustrates the cost of reducing the inertial rate of inflation from around 9 percent in 1979 to around 4 percent in 1984. Over that period the inertial rate declined 5 percentage points, while the economy produced $1500 billion less than its potential GDP. Dividing these two figures provides an estimate of $300 billion of output lost per percentage-point reduction in inflation. This figure has been confirmed by numerous statistical studies of the American economy. (Source: Authors' estimates.)

Credibility and Inflation

One of the most important questions in anti-inflation policy concerns the role of credibility of policy. Many economists argue that the Phillips-curve approach is too pessimistic. The dissenters hold that *credible* and publicly announced policies—for example, adopting fixed monetary rules or targeting nominal GDP—would allow anti-inflation policies to reduce inflation with lower output and unemployment costs.

The idea relies on the fact that inflation is an inertial process that depends on people's expectations of future inflation. A credible monetary policy—such as one that relentlessly targets a fixed, low inflation rate—would lead people to believe that shocks would not lead to inflation, and this belief would in some measure be a self-fulfilling prophecy. Those emphasizing credibility backed their theories by citing "regime changes," such as monetary and fiscal reforms that ended Austrian and Bolivian hyperinflations at relatively low cost in terms of unemployment or lost GDP.

Many economists were skeptical about claims that credibility would lower the output costs of disinflation. They countered that—while such policies might work in countries torn by hyperinflation, war, or revolution—a Draconian anti-inflation policy would be less credible in the United States. Congress and the President often lose heart when unemployment rises sharply to fight inflation, and farmers or construction workers storm the Capitol and circle the White House.

The bold experiment of 1980–1984 provided a good laboratory to test the credibility critique. During this period, monetary policy was tightened in a clear and forceful manner. Yet the price tag was extremely high, as Table 30-2 shows. Using tough, preannounced policies to enhance credibility does not appear to have lowered the cost of disinflation in the United States.

Can We Lower the Lowest Sustainable Unemployment Rate?

The finding that it costs the nation $140 to $400 billion per point of inflation reduction provokes different responses from people. Some people want to reduce the *LSUR*. Others ask whether the costs are worth the benefits of lower inflation or if there are not cheaper ways to lower inflation. These are questions that arise in the design of anti-inflation policies, to which we turn next.

Given the costs of high unemployment, we might ask: Is the sustainable rate the optimal level of unemployment? If not, what can we do to lower it toward a more desirable level? Economists of a classical persuasion often argue that the sustainable rate (or what they call the "natural rate") represents the economy's efficient unemployment level. They hold that it is the outcome of supply and demand grinding out an efficient pattern of jobs, job vacancies, and job search. It would make no more sense to lower the sustainable unemployment rate than to lower the vacancy rate for apartments.

Other economists strongly disagree, holding that the *LSUR* is likely to be above the optimal unemployment rate or the unemployment rate at which an economy's net economic welfare is maximized. This group argues that there are many spillovers or externalities in the labor market. For example, workers who have been laid off suffer from a variety of social and economic hardships. Yet employers do not pay the costs of unemployment; most of the costs (unemployment insurance, health costs, family distress, etc.) spill over as external costs and are absorbed by the worker or by the government. To the extent that unemployment has "external" costs, the sustainable unemployment rate is likely to be higher than the optimal rate. Lowering the unemployment rate would raise the nation's net economic welfare.

If the *LSUR* is neither natural nor optimal, why not simply aim for a lower level of unemployment? The reason is, as we have stressed above, that such a step would lead to rising and unacceptable inflation. An enormous social dividend, therefore, would reward the society that discovers how to reduce the sustainable unemployment rate significantly.

What measures might lower the sustainable rate? Some important suggestions include the following:

- *Improve labor market services.* Some unemployment occurs because job vacancies are not matched up with unemployed workers. Through better information, such as computerized job lists, the amount of frictional and structural unemployment can be reduced.
- *Bolster training programs.* If you read the help-wanted section of your Sunday newspaper, you will find that most of the job vacancies call for skills held by few people. Conversely, most of the unemployed are unskilled or semiskilled workers or find themselves in the wrong job or in a depressed industry. Many believe that government or private training programs can help unemployed workers retool for better jobs in growing sectors. If successful, such programs provide the double bonus of allowing people to lead productive lives and of reducing the burden on government transfer programs.
- *Remove government obstacles.* We noted above that, in protecting people from the hardships of unemployment and poverty, the government has at the same time removed the sting of unemployment and reduced incentives to seek work. Some economists call for reforming the unemployment-insurance system; reducing the disincentives for work in health, disability, and social security programs; and strengthening work requirements in welfare programs. The United States has significantly reduced the generosity of

its income-support programs in the last two decades, including a radical restructuring of welfare in 1996. While these reforms are likely to increase the labor-force participation of low-income households, the impact on the *LSUR* is unclear. If welfare cuts bring into the work force unskilled and inexperienced workers who tend to have higher unemployment rates, these measures may well raise the *LSUR*.

Having reviewed the options for reducing the *LSUR*, we must add a cautionary note. Intensive research and labor market experiments on this subject have led objective analysts to be extremely modest in their claims. The *LSUR* in the United States has been remarkably stable in the face of enormous social and economic changes over the last four decades, and few responsible scholars believe that realistic reforms would change the *LSUR* by more than a few tenths of a percentage point. On the other hand, even such a change would have a major impact on the potential output of the economy.

Eliminate or Adapt to Inflation?

Given the costs of eliminating inflation and the difficulty of reducing the sustainable unemployment rate, people often ask whether it is really desirable to eliminate inflation through recession and high unemployment. Wouldn't it be better to learn to live with inflation as the lesser evil, as has been done by many countries in Latin America and elsewhere?

One technique for adaptation is to "index" the economy. **Indexing** is a mechanism by which wages, prices, and contracts are partially or wholly compensated for changes in the general price level. Examples of partial indexation are found in many labor contracts which guarantee workers cost-of-living adjustments (or COLAs). A typical example would run as follows: Next year a firm will give a worker a 2 percent wage increase if there is no inflation. However, if prices rise 10 percent over the next 12 months, the firm will add another 4 percent as a cost-of-living adjustment. Other sectors that are sometimes indexed include the tax system, rents, and long-term industrial contracts.

Why not completely index the entire economy? In such a world, inflation would not matter for anything "real," and we could ignore inflation and concentrate on reducing unemployment. This sounds like a good idea, but in practice it has serious drawbacks. Full indexation is impossible because it guarantees a certain level of *real* incomes that may simply not be producible.

Moreover, the greater the indexation, the more an inflationary shock will rage through the economy like an epidemic. A high rate of indexation is like a big multiplier—it amplifies outside price shocks. Full indexation is an invitation to galloping inflation. Adaptation to inflation thus contains a paradox: The more a society insulates its members from inflation, the more unstable inflation is likely to become. Countries that have thoroughly indexed their economies (such as Brazil) found it extremely costly to eradicate inflation even through harsh measures.

Wanted: A Low-Cost Anti-inflation Policy

Orthodox inflation theory holds that we can prevent rising inflation only by keeping unemployment from falling below the sustainable rate. Moreover, we indicated above that society must pay a high price in terms of lost output and employment to maintain price stability. Some economists find this conclusion too pessimistic and seek to find less costly ways of containing inflation. One set of policies is called **incomes policies**, which are government actions that attempt to moderate inflation by direct steps, whether by verbal persuasion, legal controls, or other incentives. In essence, these unorthodox policies attempt to shift the Phillips curve inward.

What are some approaches to anti-inflation policies? How successful have they been? Here are some examples:

- *Wage-price controls* or *voluntary wage-price guidelines* have been used in Scandinavia, Britain, the United States, and elsewhere. Unfortunately, mandatory price controls tend to become ineffective because people evade them. Moreover, they are unlikely to slow price and wage increases unless they are accompanied by restrictive fiscal and monetary policies. There are today very few advocates of using wage-price controls to check inflation.
- A *market strategy* has been urged by many economists. This approach would rely on the discipline of markets to restrain price and wage increases.

Advocates emphasize strengthening market forces by deregulation of regulated industries; removing market impediments to competition in perverse antitrust laws and in retail-price maintenance; repealing government laws that inhibit competition such as foreign-trade quotas and minimum-wage laws; banning labor-union monopolies; and, above all, encouraging international competition. Policies that strengthen market forces may increase the resistance to price and wage increases, particularly in imperfectly competitive labor and product markets.

- *Tax-based incomes policies* (sometimes dubbed "TIP") have been proposed as a way of using the market mechanism to attain macroeconomic objectives. TIP would use fiscal carrots and sticks to encourage anti-inflationary actions by taxing those whose wages and prices are rising rapidly and subsidizing those whose wages and prices are rising slowly. The TIP approach has been used in former socialist countries such as Hungary and Poland with some success, and has sometimes been proposed for the United States. Even the enthusiasts of TIP stress, however, that it is a complement and not a substitute for the discipline of the market mechanism and for the tight fiscal and monetary policies necessary to contain inflation.
- *Profit-sharing policies* have been proposed by Harvard's Martin Weitzman and Cambridge University's James Meade. The idea here is to devise new kinds of labor contracts that give workers a share of the profits or revenues rather than a straight wage. Under such an approach, the marginal cost of a worker would be less than the average compensation, so it would be less profitable for firms to lay off workers in recessions. The layoff "externality" we discussed above would be reduced, and, if successful, the *LSUR* would consequently be reduced.

Clearly, economists have not found the Holy Grail in their search for an effective and durable incomes policy. Many economists are skeptical of these radical approaches because they are seen as unwarranted government interference in the marketplace. Advocates counter that the payoff to such interferences measures in the hundreds of billions of dollars each year—surely worth serious consideration.

The Cruel Dilemma

Many economists today think that there is a lowest sustainable rate of unemployment below which our economies can operate only at the risk of spiraling inflation. Moreover, the sustainable rate is often thought to be inefficiently high. Critics of capitalism find the high unemployment that prevails in North America and Europe to be the central flaw in modern capitalism. The search for a way to resolve the cruel dilemma of needing high unemployment to contain inflation continues to be one of the most pressing concerns of modern macroeconomics.

SUMMARY

A. Nature and Impacts of Inflation

1. Recall that inflation occurs when the general level of prices is rising. The rate of inflation is the percentage change in a price index from one period to the next. The major price indexes are the consumer price index (CPI) and the GDP deflator.

2. Like diseases, inflations come in different strains. We generally see low inflation in the United States (a few percentage points annually). Sometimes, galloping inflation produces price rises of 50 or 100 or 200 percent each year. Hyperinflation takes over when the printing presses spew out currency and prices start rising many times each month. Historically, hyperinflations have almost always been associated with war and revolution.

3. Inflation affects the economy by redistributing income and wealth and by impairing efficiency. Unanticipated inflation usually favors debtors, profit seekers, and risk-taking speculators. It hurts creditors, fixed-income classes, and timid investors. Inflation leads to distortions in relative prices, tax rates, and real interest rates. People take more trips to the bank, taxes may creep up, and measured income may become distorted. And when central banks take steps to lower inflation, the real costs of such steps in terms of lower output and employment can be painful.

B. Modern Inflation Theory

4. At any time, an economy has a given inertial or expected inflation rate. This is the rate that people have come to anticipate and that is built into labor contracts and other agreements. The inertial rate of inflation is a short-run equilibrium and persists until the economy is shocked.

5. In reality, the economy receives incessant price shocks. The major kinds of shocks that propel inflation away from its inertial rate are demand-pull and cost-push. Demand-pull inflation results from too much spending chasing too few goods, causing the aggregate demand curve to shift up and to the right. Wages and prices are then bid up in markets. Cost-push inflation is a new phenomenon of modern industrial economies and occurs when the costs of production rise even in periods of high unemployment and idle capacity.

6. The Phillips curve shows the relationship between inflation and unemployment. In the short run, lowering one rate means raising the other. But the short-run Phillips curve tends to shift over time as expected inflation and other factors change. If policymakers attempt to hold unemployment below the sustainable rate for long periods, inflation will tend to spiral upward.

7. Modern inflation theory relies on the concept of the lowest sustainable rate of unemployment, or *LSUR*, which is the lowest sustainable rate that the nation can enjoy without risking an upward spiral of inflation. It represents the level of unemployment of resources at which labor and product markets are in inflationary balance. Under the sustainable-unemployment-rate theory, there is no permanent tradeoff between unemployment and inflation, and the long-run Phillips curve is vertical.

C. Dilemmas of Anti-inflation Policy

8. A central concern for policymakers is the cost of reducing inertial inflation. Current estimates indicate that a substantial recession is necessary to slow inertial inflation.

9. Economists have put forth many proposals for lowering the sustainable unemployment rate; notable proposals include improving labor market information, improving education and training programs, and refashioning government programs so that workers have greater incentives to work. Sober analysis of politically viable proposals leads most economists to expect only small improvements from such labor market reforms.

10. Because of the high costs of reducing inflation through recessions, nations have often looked for other approaches. These are incomes policies such as wage-price controls and voluntary guidelines, tax-based approaches, and market-strengthening strategies.

CONCEPTS FOR REVIEW

History and Theories of Inflation

$$\text{Inflation}(t) = \frac{P(t) - P(t-1)}{P(t-1)} \times 100$$

strains of inflation:
  low
  galloping
  hyperinflation
impacts of inflation (redistributive, on output and employment)
anticipated and unanticipated inflation

costs of inflation:
  "shoe leather"
  menu costs
  income and tax distortions
  loss of information
inertial, demand-pull, and cost-push inflation
short-run and long-run Phillips curves
lowest sustainable rate of unemployment (*LSUR*) and the long-run Phillips curve

sustainable vs. optimal rate of unemployment

Anti-inflation Policy

costs of disinflation
measures to lower the *LSUR*
incomes policies:
  wage-price controls and guidelines
  competition
  TIP
  profit sharing

QUESTIONS FOR DISCUSSION

1. Consider the following impacts of inflation: tax distortions, income and wealth redistribution, shoe-leather costs, menu costs. For each, define the cost and provide an example.

2. "During periods of inflation, people use real resources to reduce their holdings of fiat money. Such activities produce a private benefit with no corresponding social gain, which illustrates the social cost of inflation." Explain this quotation and give an example.

3. Unanticipated deflation also produces serious social costs. For each of the following, describe the deflation and analyze the associated costs:
   a. During the Great Depression, prices of major crops fell along with the prices of other commodities. What would happen to farmers who had large mortgages?
   b. Many students have borrowed more than $20,000 to pay for their college education, hoping that inflation would allow them to pay off their loans in depreciated dollars. What would happen to these students if wages and prices began to *fall* at 5 percent per year?

4. The data in Table 30-3 describe inflation and unemployment in the United States from 1979 to 1996. Note that the economy started out near the lowest sustainable unemployment rate in 1979 and ended near the sustainable rate in 1990. Can you explain the decline of inflation over the intervening years? Do so by drawing the short-run and long-run Phillips curves for each of the years from 1979 to 1996.

5. Many economists argue as follows: "Because there is no long-run tradeoff between unemployment and inflation, there is no point in trying to shave the peaks and troughs from the business cycle." This view suggests that we should not care whether the economy is stable or fluctuating widely as long as the average level of unemployment is the same. Discuss critically.

6. A leading economist has written: "If you think of the social costs of inflation, at least of moderate inflation, it is hard to avoid coming away with the impression that they are minor compared with the costs of unemployment and depressed production." Write a short essay describing your views on this issue.

TABLE 30-3. Recent Unemployment and Inflation Data for the United States
Source: *Economic Report of the President*, 1997.

Year	Unemployment rate (%)	Inflation rate, CPI (% per year)
1979	5.9	11.3
1980	7.2	13.5
1981	7.6	10.4
1982	9.7	6.2
1983	9.6	3.2
1984	7.5	4.4
1985	7.2	3.5
1986	7.0	1.9
1987	6.2	3.7
1988	5.5	4.1
1989	5.3	4.8
1990	5.6	5.4
1991	6.9	4.2
1992	7.5	3.0
1993	6.9	3.0
1994	6.1	2.6
1995	5.6	2.8
1996	5.4	2.9

7. Consider the data on annual inflation rates and growth of per capita GDP shown in Table 30-1. Can you see that low inflation is associated with the highest growth rates? What are the economic reasons why growth might be lower for deflation and for hyperinflation. Explain why the *ex post* fallacy might apply here (see the discussion in Chapter 1).

8. The following policies and phenomena affected labor markets over the last decade. Explain the likely effect of each on the lowest sustainable unemployment rate:

   a. The minimum wage fell 25 percent relative to the average wage rate.

   b. Unemployment insurance became subject to taxation.

   c. Funds for training programs for unemployed workers were cut sharply by the federal government.

   d. Because of high cyclical unemployment, many minority-group teenagers received little on-the-job training.

   e. The fraction of the work force in labor unions fell sharply.

9. Consider the following anti-inflation policies: high unemployment, wage and price controls, and tax-based incomes policies. For each, list the advantages and disadvantages in terms of inflation control and other economic objectives. Which would you choose if the President asked for your recommendation?

10. Review the ideas discussed in the section on the optimal rate of inflation. The study of Akerlof, Dickens, and Perry suggests that the sustainable unemployment rate rises as the inflation rate approaches zero. Assuming that the *LSUR* is 6 percent at moderate inflation rates, draw a long-run Phillips curve consistent with their theory. How does their study and your new diagram fit in with the data in Table 30-1?

CHAPTER 31
OPEN-ECONOMY MACROECONOMICS

> Trade is the natural enemy of all violent passions. Trade makes men independent of one another and gives them a high idea of their personal importance: it leads them to want to manage their own affairs and teaches them to succeed therein. Hence it makes them inclined to liberty but disinclined to revolution.
>
> *Alexis de Tocqueville*, Democracy in America *(1840)*

In an earlier era, foreign trade exerted only a modest influence on the overall economic activity of the United States. Americans could afford to ignore the economic linkages between nations, leaving that topic to specialists who toiled in universities or in the State Department. But revolutionary developments in communication, transportation, and trade policy have increasingly linked together the economic fortunes of nations. Trading ties among Japan, Mexico, Canada, and the United States are closer today than were those between New York and California a century ago. The international business cycle exerts a powerful effect on every nation of the globe; monetary-policy actions in Washington can produce depressions, poverty, and revolutions in South America; political disturbances in the Middle East can set off a spiral in oil prices that sends the

world into recessions; revolutions in Russia disturb stock markets around the world. To ignore international trade is to miss half the economic ball game.

It is now time to complete our macroeconomic analysis by recognizing the linkages among nations. We begin this chapter by highlighting the major elements of international trade and finance and then show how macroeconomic shocks in one country have ripple effects on the output and employment of others. Foreign exchange rates—the prices of one country's currency in terms of other country's monies—will play an important part in the transmission mechanism of economic policies. We conclude the chapter by considering longer-run questions involving saving and investment and economic growth in open economies.

A. FOREIGN TRADE AND ECONOMIC ACTIVITY

Net Exports: Concepts and Trends

Open-economy macroeconomics involves the interactions of trade, output, spending, employment, and price levels among different nations. Foreign trade involves imports and exports. A country's imports are its purchases of goods and services from other nations. Although the United States produces most of what it consumes, it nonetheless has a large

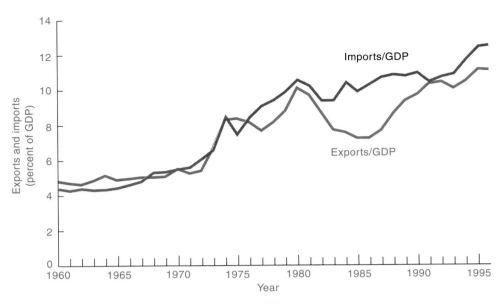

FIGURE 31-1. Imports Outstripped Exports in 1980s

U.S. foreign trade grew rapidly over the last four decades. In the period after World War II, the United States had a net-export surplus. After 1980, however, imports grew rapidly while exports shrank as a percent of GDP. Net exports have been negative since 1980 reflecting the excess of U.S. spending over U.S. production. (Source: U.S. Department of Commerce.)

quantity of **imports**, which are goods and services produced abroad and consumed domestically. U.S. imports for 1996 totaled $966 billion. Of this, $803 billion was merchandise trade, including $35 billion of foodstuffs, $205 billion of industrial supplies, $229 billion of capital goods, $129 billion of automotive products, and $171 billion of other consumer goods. Other items included services as well as $204 billion of income from foreign assets in the United States.

Exports are goods and services produced domestically and purchased by foreigners. For the United States during 1996, exports of goods and services totaled $871 billion. The major components of exports were merchandise exports of $612 billion, which included $55 billion of foodstuffs, $148 billion of industrial products, $253 billion of capital goods, and $65 billion of automotive goods. Other exports included $206 billion of income earned on U.S. assets abroad.

Net exports are defined as exports of goods and services minus imports of goods and services. For 1996, net exports were *minus* $95 billion, or $871 billion of exports minus $966 billion of imports. An

important component of trade involves **merchandise trade**, which is trade in goods like foodstuffs and manufacturing. The U.S. has had a **merchandise trade deficit** in recent years, and in 1996 the deficit on goods totaled $191 billion, representing the difference between $612 billion of exported goods and $803 billion of imports of goods. When a country has positive net exports, it is accumulating foreign assets. The counterpart of net exports is therefore **net foreign investment**, which denotes net saving or investment abroad and is approximately equal to the value of net exports.

Figure 31-1 shows the trends in U.S. exports and imports as a share of GDP since 1960. Over most of the twentieth century, the United States has had a positive balance on its net exports. A dramatic deterioration in the U.S. trade position occurred in the mid-1980s, and by 1987 imports exceeded exports by $142 billion. The huge trade deficit has become one of the major political and economic issues of the United States and its trading partners.

Once we acknowledge the possibility of exports and imports, we must also recognize that a nation's expenditures may differ from its production. Total *domestic expenditures* (sometimes called *domestic demand*) are equal to consumption plus domestic investment plus government purchases. This measure differs from total *domestic product* (or GDP) for two reasons. First, some part of domestic expenditures will be on goods produced abroad, these items being imports (denoted by *Im*) like Mexican oil and Japanese automobiles. In addition, some part of America's domestic production will be sold abroad as exports (denoted by *Ex*)—items like wheat and Boeing aircraft. The difference between national output and domestic expenditures is $Ex - Im$ = net exports = X.

To calculate the *total* production of American goods and services, we need to include not only domestic demand but also trade. That is, we need to know the total production for American residents as well as the net production for foreigners. This total must include domestic expenditures ($C + I + G$) plus sales to foreigners (Ex) less domestic purchases from foreigners (Im). Total output, or GDP, equals consumption plus domestic investment plus government purchases plus net exports:

$$\text{Total domestic output} = \text{GDP}$$
$$= C + I + G + X$$

Foreign Exchange Rates

Foreign trade involves the use of different national currencies. The relative price of two currencies is called the **foreign exchange rate**, which measures the price of 1 unit of domestic currency in terms of foreign currency. The foreign exchange rate is determined in the foreign exchange market, which is the market where different currencies are traded. For example, if the French franc sells at 5 francs to the U.S. dollar, we say that the foreign exchange rate is 5 francs per dollar.[1]

The foreign exchange rate is an important determinant of international trade because it has a large effect on the relative prices of the goods of different countries. To see how the foreign exchange rate affects foreign trade, take wine as an example. The relative prices of U.S. wine and French wine will depend upon the domestic prices of the wines and upon the foreign exchange rate. Say that California Chardonnay wines sell for $6 per bottle, while the equivalent French Chardonnay sells for 40 French francs. Then at the 1984 exchange rate of 10 French francs to the dollar, French wine sells at $4 per bottle while California wine sells at $6, giving an advantage to the imported variety.

Say that by 1996 the foreign exchange rate of the dollar fell (or *depreciated*) to 5 francs. Then with unchanged domestic prices, the French wine would sell for $8 as compared to $6 for the California wine. Note that when the dollar was expensive, in 1984, French wine sold for only two-thirds the price of the California variety, while the fall in the value of the dollar over the next decade left French wine selling at a one-third premium over California wines. The fall in the exchange rate on the dollar had the effect of making imports less "competitive" by turning relative prices against imports and in favor of domestic products. If the dollar's price had risen (or *appreciated*), relative prices would have moved in favor of imports and against domestic production.

Foreign trade involves a new factor—a nation's exchange rate, or the price of the nation's currency relative to other currencies. When a nation's exchange rate rises or "appreciates," the prices of imported goods fall while exports become more expensive in world markets. The result is that the nation becomes less competitive in world markets and its net exports decline. Changes in exchange rates can have major effects on output, employment, and inflation. All these impacts make the exchange rate increasingly important for all nations.

Flexible and Fixed Exchange Rates. There are two major exchange-rate systems, and they have an important impact on macroeconomic policy. One basic system occurs when exchange rates move purely under the influence of market supply and demand. This system, known as **flexible exchange rates**, is one where governments neither announce an exchange rate nor take steps to enforce one. That is, in a flexible-exchange-rate system, the relative prices of currencies are determined in the marketplace through the buying and selling of households and businesses. The United States, Canada, and Japan currently operate flexible-exchange-rate systems.

---

[1] Part Seven of this text explores the economics of exchange rates in depth, but the basic elements are presented in this chapter.

The other major system is **fixed exchange rates**, where governments specify the rate at which their currency will be converted into other currencies. Historically, the most important fixed-exchange-rate system was the gold standard, which was used off and on from 1717 until 1933. Today, many small countries operate fixed-exchange-rate systems, and most European countries have had their own system of fixed exchange rates since 1979.

Determinants of Trade and Net Exports

What determines the movements of exports and imports and therefore net exports? It is best to think of the import and export components of net exports separately.

Begin with imports. Imports into the United States are positively related to U.S. income and output. When U.S. GDP rises, U.S. imports increase because some of the increased $C + I + G$ purchases (such as cars and shoes) come from foreign production and also because America uses foreign-made inputs (like oil or steel) in producing its own goods. In addition, the choice between foreign and domestic goods responds to their relative prices. If the price of domestic cars rises relative to the price of Japanese cars, say, because the exchange rate appreciates, Americans will buy more Japanese cars and fewer American ones. Hence the volume and value of imports will be affected by the relative prices of domestic and foreign goods.

Exports are the mirror image of imports: U.S. exports are other countries' imports. Exports therefore depend primarily upon the incomes and outputs of America's trading partners, as well as upon the prices of U.S. exports relative to the goods with which they compete. As foreign output rises, or as the foreign exchange rate of the dollar falls, or depreciates, the volume and value of American exports tend to grow.

What caused the major changes in the U.S. trade patterns shown in Figure 31-1? From 1960 to 1969, the American economy grew rapidly and the nation's prices rose relative to those of its trading partners; consequently, imports tended to grow faster than exports. After 1972, the value of the dollar fell relative to other major currencies. Consequently, U.S. goods became relatively cheaper, the growth of imports slowed, and exports boomed. The 1970s were a period in which the U.S. economy opened up to the global marketplace, and the share of both exports and imports grew rapidly.

The early 1980s dealt a sharp blow to the U.S. trade surplus. The value of the dollar rose or appreciated sharply from 1980 to 1985, so imports into the United States became increasingly competitive. Also, foreign economies grew less rapidly than the home economy, depressing exports. The ensuing effect was a massive turn toward a deficit in net exports.

After 1985, however, exports began to recover. The exchange rate of the dollar fell, the U.S. economy grew more slowly, and many foreign economies recovered from the worldwide recession and debt crisis of the early 1980s. By 1996, the net-export deficit was down to one-half of its peak in 1986.

SHORT-RUN IMPACT OF TRADE ON GDP

How do changes in a nation's trade flows affect its GDP and employment? We first analyze this question in the context of our short-run model of output determination, the multiplier model of Chapter 24. The multiplier model shows how, in the short run when there are unemployed resources, changes in trade will affect aggregate demand, output, and employment.

The major new elements of the analysis in the presence of international trade are two: First, we have a fourth component of spending, net exports, which adds to aggregate demand. Second, an open economy has different multipliers for private investment and government domestic spending because some of spending leaks out to the rest of the world.

Table 31-1 shows how introducing net exports affects output determination. This table begins with the same components as those for a closed economy (look back to Table 24-2 to refresh your memory about the major components and the way they sum to total spending). Total domestic demand in column (2) is composed of the consumption, investment, and government purchases we analyzed earlier. Column (3) then adds the exports of goods and services. As described above, these depend upon foreign incomes and outputs and upon prices and exchange rates, all of which are also taken as given

	Output Determination with Foreign Trade (Billions of Dollars)					
(1) Initial level of GDP	(2) Domestic demand $(C + I + G)$	(3) Exports (Ex)	(4) Imports (Im)	(5) Net exports $(X = Ex - Im)$	(6) Total spending $(C + I + G + X)$	(7) Resulting tendency of economy
4,100	4,000	250	410	−160	3,840	Contraction
3,800	3,800	250	380	−130	3,670	Contraction
3,500	3,600	250	350	−100	3,500	Equilibrium
3,200	3,400	250	320	− 70	3,330	Expansion
2,900	3,200	250	290	− 40	3,160	Expansion

TABLE 31-1. **Net Exports Add to Aggregate Demand of Economy**

To the domestic demand of $C + I + G$, we must add net exports of $X = Ex - Im$ to obtain total aggregate demand for a country's output. Note that higher net exports have the same multiplier as do investment and government purchases.

for this analysis. Exports are assumed to be a constant level of $250 billion of foreign spending on domestic goods and services.

The interesting new element arises from imports, shown in column (4). Like exports, imports depend upon exogenous variables such as prices and exchange rates. But, in addition, imports depend upon domestic incomes and output, which clearly change in the different rows of Table 31-1. For simplicity, we assume that the country always imports 10 percent of its total output, so imports in column (4) are 10 percent of column (1).

Subtracting column (4) from column (3) gives net exports in column (5). Net exports are a negative number when imports exceed exports and a positive number when exports are greater than imports. Net exports in column (5) are the net addition to the spending stream contributed by foreign trade. Total spending on domestic output in column (6) equals domestic demand in column (2) plus net exports in column (5). Equilibrium output in an open economy comes at the point where total net domestic and foreign spending in column (6) exactly equals total domestic output in column (1). In this case, equilibrium comes with net exports of −100, indicating that the country is importing more than it is exporting. At this equilibrium, note as well that domestic demand is greater than output. (Make sure that you can explain why the economy is not in equilibrium when spending does not equal output.)

Figure 31-2 on page 608 shows the open-economy equilibrium graphically. The upward-sloping

black line marked $C + I + G$ is the same curve used in Figure 24-7. To this line we must add the level of net exports that is forthcoming at each level of GDP. Net exports from column (5) of Table 31-1 are added to get the rust-colored line of total aggregate demand or total spending. When the rust-colored line lies below the black curve, imports exceed exports and net exports are negative. When the rust-colored line is above the black line, the country has a net-export or trade surplus and output is greater than domestic demand.

Equilibrium GDP occurs where the rust-colored line of total spending intersects the 45° line. This intersection comes at exactly the same point, at $3500 billion, that is shown as equilibrium GDP in Table 31-1. Only at $3500 billion does GDP exactly equal what consumers, businesses, governments, and foreigners want to spend on goods and services produced in the United States.

The Marginal Propensity to Import and the Spending Line

Note that the aggregate demand curve, the rust-colored $C + I + G + X$ curve in Figure 31-2, has a slightly smaller slope than the black curve of domestic demand. The explanation of this is that *there is an additional leakage from spending into imports.* This new leakage arises from our assumption that 10 cents of every dollar of income is spent on imports. To handle this requires introducing a new term, the marginal propensity to import. The **marginal propensity to import**, which we will denote *MPm*, is

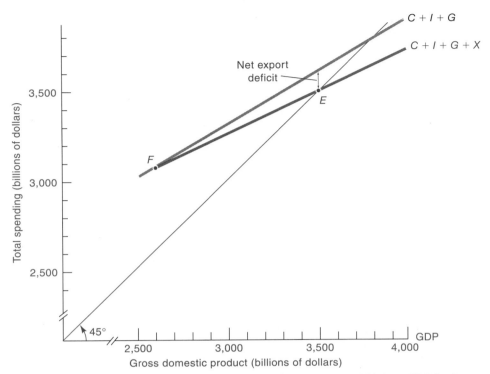

FIGURE 31-2. Adding Net Exports to Domestic Demand Gives Equilibrium GDP in the Open Economy

The black line represents domestic demand ($C + I + G$), purchases by domestic consumers, businesses, and governments. To this must be added net foreign spending. Net exports plus domestic demand give the rust-colored line of total spending. Equilibrium comes at point E, where total GDP equals total spending on goods and services produced in the United States. Note that the slope of the rust-colored total demand curve is less than that of domestic demand to reflect the leakage from spending into imports.

the increase in the dollar value of imports for each $1 increase in GDP.

Recall that we labeled the increase in consumption per unit increase of income the "marginal propensity to consume." The marginal propensity to import is closely related. It tells how much is imported for each dollar increase in total GDP. In our example, the MPm is 0.10 because every $300 billion of increased income leads to $30 billion of increased imports. (What is the marginal propensity to import in an economy with no foreign trade? Zero.)

Returning to Figure 31-2, let us examine the slope of the total spending line (that is, the line showing total spending on $C + I + G + X$). Note that the slope of the total spending line is less than the slope of the domestic demand line of $C + I + G$.

As GDP and total incomes rise by $300, spending on consumption rises by the income change times the MPC (assumed to be two-thirds), or by $200. At the same time, spending on imports, or foreign goods, also rises by $30. Hence spending on domestic goods rises by only $170 (= $200 − $30), and the slope of the total spending line falls from 0.667 in our closed economy to $170/$300 = 0.567 in our open economy.

The Open-Economy Multiplier

The leakage of spending outside the economy into imports has the surprising effect of changing the multiplier in an open economy. Let us see why.

One way of understanding the expenditure multiplier in an open economy is to calculate the rounds of spending and respending generated by an additional dollar of government spending, investment, or exports. For example, say that Germany needs to buy American computers to modernize antiquated facilities in what used to be East Germany. Each extra dollar of U.S. computers will generate $1 of income in the United States, of which $⅔ = \$0.667$ will be spent by Americans on consumption. However, because the marginal propensity to import is 0.10, one-tenth of the extra dollar of income, or \$0.10, will be spent on foreign goods and services, leaving only \$0.567 of spending on domestically produced goods. That \$0.567 of domestic spending will generate \$0.567 of U.S. income, from which $0.567 \times \$0.567 = \$0.321$ will be spent on consumption of domestic goods and services in the next round. Hence the total increase in output, or the open-economy multiplier, will be

$$\begin{array}{ll}\text{Open-economy} \\ \text{multiplier}\end{array} = 1 + 0.567 + (0.567)^2 + \cdots$$

$$= 1 + (\tfrac{2}{3} - \tfrac{1}{10}) + (\tfrac{2}{3} - \tfrac{1}{10})^2 + \cdots$$

$$= \frac{1}{1 - \tfrac{2}{3} + \tfrac{1}{10}} = \frac{1}{^{13}\!/_{30}} = 2.3$$

This compares with a closed-economy multiplier of $1/(1 - 0.667) = 3$.

Another way of calculating the multiplier is as follows: Recall that the multiplier in our simplest model was $1/MPS$, where MPS = the marginal propensity to save or the "leakage" of spending into nonconsumption items (saving). This result can be extended by noting that the analog to the MPS in an open economy is the total leakage per dollar of extra income—the dollars leaking into saving (the MPS) plus the dollars leaking into imports (the MPm). Hence, the open-economy multiplier should be $1/(MPS + MPm) = 1/(0.333 + 0.1) = 1/0.433 = 2.3$. Note that both the leakage analysis and the rounds analysis provide exactly the same answer.

To summarize:

Because a fraction of any income increase leaks into imports in an open economy, the open-economy multiplier is smaller than that of a closed economy. The exact relationship is

$$\text{Open-economy multiplier} = \frac{1}{MPS + MPm}$$

where MPS = marginal propensity to save and MPm = marginal propensity to import.

The U.S. Trade Deficit and Economic Activity

In a world where nations are increasingly linked by trade and finance, countries must pay close attention to events abroad. If a country's policies are out of step with those of its trading partners, the roof can fall in, with recession, inflation, or major trade imbalances.

A good example of the influence of trade on economic activity is shown in Figure 31-3 on page 610, which depicts one of the major economic events of the last decade—the deterioration of the U.S. net-export position during the early 1980s. To get a rough measure of the size of the shift, we can compare 1980 and 1986, years in which the overall utilization of resources was approximately the same. From 1980 to 1986, real net exports in 1992 prices moved from a surplus of \$10 billion to a deficit of \$164 billion. This decline of \$174 billion in real net exports represented *4 percent of the average real GDP for this period.* This is an astounding amount, with much of the pain being felt by manufacturing workers who were losing their jobs as imports replaced domestic production.

Taken by itself, this sharp decline in net exports would be contractionary. It is as if government purchases declined by an equivalent amount. The overall impact on the economy would depend upon whether or not other forces were moving in step with the shift in net exports. In fact, from 1980 to 1982, the decline in net exports was reinforced by monetary policy. A sharp tightening of monetary policy in 1979 led to a decline in domestic investment. The overall result was a steep decline in U.S. aggregate demand and the deepest recession in 50 years. However, after 1982, the decrease in net exports was countered by a shift in the federal budget in an *expansionary* direction. The fiscal expansion, along with a loosening of monetary policy, more than offset the decline in net exports, and the economy grew steadily after 1982.

MACROECONOMIC POLICY AND THE EXCHANGE-RATE SYSTEM

Our analysis of business cycles and economic growth has generally focused on policies in a closed economy. We analyzed the way that monetary and fiscal policies can help stabilize the business cycle, shaving the peaks off inflation and the troughs off output.

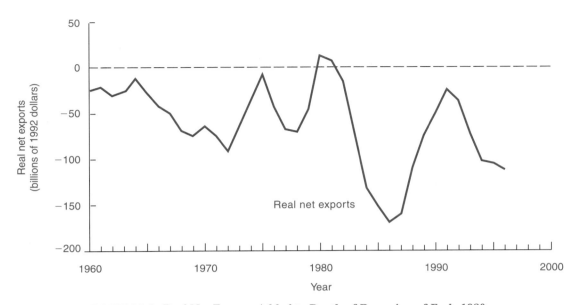

FIGURE 31-3. Real Net Exports Added to Depth of Recession of Early 1980s

With strong rise (or "appreciation") of the U.S. dollar and weak economic growth abroad, U.S. real net exports turned sharply negative in the early 1980s. This shift produced a massive drag on aggregate spending in the $C + I + G + X$ equation and helped produce the deepest recession of the last half-century. (Source: U.S. Department of Commerce.)

How do macroeconomic policies change in an open economy? Surprisingly, the answer to this question depends crucially on whether the country has a fixed or flexible exchange rate.

In our discussion, we concentrate on high-income countries whose financial markets are closely linked together. Countries like the United States, Canada, Britain, and Germany are open to financial flows from each other. When financial capital can flow easily among countries and the regulatory barriers to financial investment are low, we say that these countries have *high capital mobility*.

Fixed Exchange Rates. The key feature of countries with fixed exchange rates and high capital mobility is that their interest rates must be very closely aligned. For example, if France and Germany have a fixed exchange rate and investors can easily move funds between French francs and German marks, the interest rates of the two countries must move together. Any interest-rate divergence will attract speculators who will sell one currency and buy the other until the interest rates are at the same level.

Consider a small country which pegs its exchange rate to a larger country. It could be Holland pegging to Germany or Hong Kong pegging to the United States. *Because the small country's interest rates are determined by the monetary policy of the large country, the small country no longer has an independent monetary policy.* The small country's monetary policy must be devoted to ensuring that its interest rates are aligned with its partner's.

Macroeconomic policy in such a situation is therefore exactly the case described in our multiplier model above. From the small country's point of view, investment is exogenous, because it is determined by world interest rates. Fiscal policy will be highly effective because there will be no monetary reaction to changes in G or T.

Flexible Exchange Rates. Surprisingly, macroeconomic policy with flexible exchange rates operates in quite a different way from the fixed-exchange-rate case. Monetary policy becomes highly effective with a flexible exchange rate.

Let's consider the case of the United States. The monetary transmission mechanism in the United States has evolved over the last two decades as the economy has become more open and changes have occurred in the exchange-rate system. After the introduction of flexible exchange rates in 1973 and in the presence of increasingly closely linked financial markets, international trade and finance have come to play a new and central role in U.S. macroeconomic policy.

One of the best examples of the operation of macroeconomic policy with flexible exchange rates occurred when the Federal Reserve tightened money in the 1979–1982 period. The monetary tightening raised U.S. interest rates, which attracted funds into dollar securities. This increase in demand for dollars drove up the foreign exchange rate on the dollar. At this point, the multiplier mechanism swung into action. The high dollar exchange rate decreased net exports and contributed to the deep U.S. recession of 1981–1983 in the way we described earlier. This had the impact of both lowering real GDP and lowering the rate of inflation.

Another example occurred in 1994–1997. During this period, the U.S. economy grew rapidly while Europe and Japan stagnated. Monetary policy in the United States was relatively tight, while Japanese short-term interest rates approached zero. As a result, the dollar appreciated sharply against European and Japanese currencies. This was what the macroeconomic doctor ordered, however, for the appreciation of the dollar retarded growth in the United States just as it was pushing against productive capacity while giving a boost to the depressed output in the other regions.

We see, then, that foreign trade actually opens up another link in the monetary transmission mechanism. Monetary policy affects net foreign investment (equal to net exports) as well as domestic investment. It is important to note that the foreign-investment impact reinforces the domestic investment: tight money lowers output and prices.

Realistic Complications. International trade opens new investment and consumption opportunities for a country, but it also complicates the life of economic policymakers. One complication occurs because the quantitative relationships between monetary policy, the exchange rate, foreign trade, and output and prices are extremely complex, particularly at the very first link. Current economic models cannot accurately predict the impact of monetary-policy changes on exchange rates. Further, even if we knew the exact money–exchange-rate relationship,

the impact of exchange rates on net exports is complicated and difficult to predict. Moreover, exchange rates and trade flows will be simultaneously affected by the fiscal and monetary policies of other countries, so we cannot always disentangle the causes and effects of changes in trade flows. And the capital account may add further layers of complexity and unpredictability. When political conditions, tax laws, or the inflation outlook change, this may attract or repel investors' funds, change the demand for a nation's assets, and affect exchange rates. On balance, confidence in our ability to determine the best timing and likely effects of monetary policies has diminished in recent years as our economy has become more open to trading and financial flows.

Foreign economic relations add another dimension to economic policy. Domestic policymakers must concern themselves with foreign repercussions of domestic policies. Rising interest rates at home change interest rates, exchange rates, and trade balances abroad, and these changes may be unwelcome. Higher interest rates increase debt-service burdens in heavily indebted countries, such as Brazil and Mexico. In the 1980s, skyrocketing interest rates caused severe hardships for these countries. In addition, these countries owe billions of dollars to American banks, and loan defaults could cause untold damage to the U.S. financial system. When Mexico teetered on the edge of bankruptcy in 1994 and 1995, the United States had to proceed cautiously in its monetary policies lest interest-rate increases cause Mexico, and indirectly the United States, greater financial difficulties. Finally, the nation cares not only about the total of its GDP; the composition of output matters as well. When the exchange rate appreciates through tight money, the situation tends to hurt "tradeable" sectors (manufactures, mining, and agriculture), which become less competitive with foreign producers.

With a flexible exchange rate, monetary policy can operate independently from other countries; under flexible rates, the international link of monetary policy with net exports and foreign investment reinforces the monetary impact on domestic investment. By contrast, when countries with a high degree of capital mobility adopt fixed exchange rates, they lose control of monetary policy and must rely on fiscal policy for macroeconomic policy adjustments.

B. INTERDEPENDENCE IN THE GLOBAL ECONOMY

ECONOMIC GROWTH IN THE OPEN ECONOMY

The first section described the short-run impact of international trade and policy changes in the open economy. These issues are crucial for open economies combating unemployment and inflation. But countries must always keep their eye on the implications of their policies for long-run economic growth. Particularly for small countries, the concerns about economic-growth policies are paramount. Sometimes, it is useful to think of an individual region within the United States (such as a state or metropolitan area) as a small open economy with fixed exchange rates.

Economic growth involves a wide variety of issues, as we saw in Chapters 27 and 28. Perhaps the single most important approach for promoting rapid economic growth is to ensure high levels of saving and investment. Figure 31-4 shows the association of national investment rates with rates of growth of per capita GDP. We begin by examining the determinants of saving and investment in the open economy.

But economic growth involves more than just capital. It requires moving toward the technological frontier by adopting the best technological practices. It requires developing institutions that nurture investment and the spirit of enterprise. Other issues—trade policies, intellectual property rights, policies toward direct investment, and the overall macroeconomic climate—are essential ingredients in the growth of open economies.

SAVING AND INVESTMENT IN THE OPEN ECONOMY

In a closed economy, total investment equals domestic saving. When an economy engages in international trade and finance, another source of investment funds and another outlet for domestic saving open up. Countries that are hungry for funds because of high domestic investment opportunities can go to world capital markets to finance their investments. Traditionally, middle-income countries

in Latin America or Asia have borrowed from abroad to finance domestic capital, and the United States has been a magnet for foreign saving in recent years.

The other side of the coin comes in countries that have high savings rates but lack sufficient high-yield domestic investment opportunities. Countries like England in the last century or Japan in recent years have provided substantial funds to capital-short countries.

Recall our saving-investment identity from Chapter 21:

$$I_T = I + X = S + (T - G)$$

This states that total national investment (I_T) consists of investment in domestic capital (I) plus net foreign investment or net exports (X). This must equal total private saving (S) by households and businesses plus total public saving, which is given by

---

FIGURE 31-4. National Investment and Economic Growth

Countries that have high savings and investment rates also have above-average rates of per capita economic growth. Promoting high saving and investment is in the long run one of the most secure routes to increasing growth. (Source: OECD.)

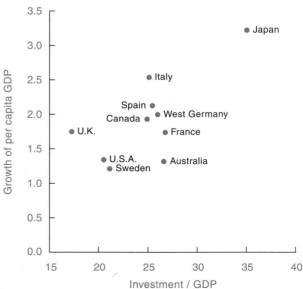

Saving and Investment as Percent of GDP					
Period	I_T	I	X	S	$(T - G)$
1946–1950	17	16	1	15	3
1951–1980	16	16	0	16	−1
1981–1996	13	15	−2	15	−3

TABLE 31-2. National Saving and Investment, United States

National investment (I_T) consists of domestic and net foreign investment. The sources are private and public saving. The United States was a high-saving country when it financed European reconstruction after World War II. Since 1980, the United States has reduced both public and private saving, resulting in decreased investment and negative net foreign investment. (Source: Bureau of Economic Analysis. For 1946–1958, government investment is estimated by the perpetual inventory method. National identities may not hold due to statistical discrepancy and rounding error.)

the government surplus $(T - G)$. The components of total U.S. national investment for recent decades are shown in Table 31-2.

Determination of Saving and Investment at Full Employment

We need to go beyond the identities to understand the mechanism by which saving and investment are equalized in the open economy. The equilibration of saving and investment in the short run is just the mirror image of the multiplier mechanism shown in Figure 31-2.

Additionally, we want to understand the long-run determination of saving and investment in a full-employment situation where prices and wages are flexible. For this purpose, we consider full-employment situations when actual output equals potential output and look at the equilibration of saving and investment in the capital market.

The capital market is the market where the supply of saving is equilibrated with the demand for investment. In a simplified world without inflation or uncertainty, the interest rate is the price that balances saving and investment. Let's begin with a closed economy and then extend the analysis to an open economy.

Closed Economy. In an open economy, we know that investment must equal private saving plus the government surplus. The government surplus depends upon taxes and spending programs, but it does not depend upon the interest rate. Moreover, historical experience indicates that private saving is

also relatively independent of interest rates. In our analysis we assume that total domestic saving responds positively but only slightly to higher real interest rates.

Investment, as we learned in Chapter 22, is heavily dependent upon the interest rate. Higher interest rates reduce spending on housing and other structures. We therefore write our investment schedule as $I(r)$ to indicate that investment depends upon the real interest rate, r.

Figure 31-5 on page 614 shows how national saving and investment are equilibrated in a full-employment closed economy. The original schedules determine an interest rate at $r*$ with a healthy level of saving and investment. Suppose that the government increases purchases, however, increasing the government deficit. Then total national saving declines, shifting the savings schedule to the left to $S + T - G'$. As a result, the real interest rate increases and the level of investment falls. We see, then, how a government deficit lowers saving and investment in the closed economy with full employment.

Open-Economy Saving. An open economy has alternative sources of investment and alternative outlets for saving. We show this situation in Figure 31-6 on page 615 for a small open economy with a high degree of capital mobility. A small open economy must equate its domestic interest rate with the world real interest rate, r^W. It is too small to affect the world interest rate, and because capital mobility is high, financial capital will move to equilibrate interest rates at home and abroad.

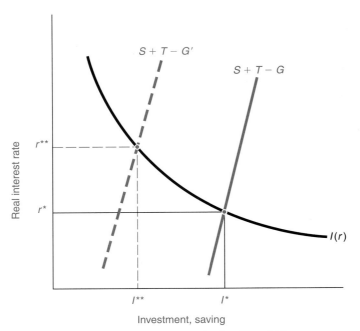

FIGURE 31-5. Saving and Investment in the Closed Economy

Investment is inversely related to the real interest rate, while private saving and public saving are relatively unresponsive to the interest rate. Equilibrium saving and investment comes at r^*. Suppose that government purchases increase. This increases the government deficit and therefore reduces public saving. The result is a shift in the national savings curve to the left to $S + T - G'$, raising the market interest rate to r^{**} and reducing national saving and investment to I^{**}.

Figure 31-6 helps explain the determination of saving, investment, and net exports in the open economy. At the prevailing world interest rate, total investment is shown at point *A*, which is the intersection of the investment schedule and the interest rate. Total national saving is given at point *B* on the total savings schedule, $S + T - G$. The difference between them—given by the line segment *AB*—is shown by the saving-investment identity to be net exports.

Hence net exports or the country's international trade position is determined by the balance between national saving and investment as determined by domestic factors plus the world interest rate.

This discussion pushes into the background the mechanism by which a country adjusts its trade, saving, and investment. It is here that the exchange rate plays the crucial equilibrating role. *Changes in exchange rates are the mechanism by which saving and*

investment adjust. That is, exchange rates move to ensure that the level of net exports balances the difference between domestic saving and investment.[2]

This analysis can help explain the trends in savings, investment, and trade patterns in major countries in recent years. Figure 31-6 describes well the role of Japan in the world economy. Japan has traditionally had a high domestic savings rate. Yet in recent years—because of high production costs at

---

[2] More generally, the adjustment occurs through changes in the relative prices of domestic and foreign goods. The relative price of domestic to foreign goods is determined by both the foreign exchange rate and the domestic and foreign price levels. Under a flexible exchange rate, the adjustment would occur quickly through changes in the exchange rate itself. With a fixed exchange rate, the price levels of the two countries would do the adjustment. The required end result—a change in the relative prices—is the same in either case.

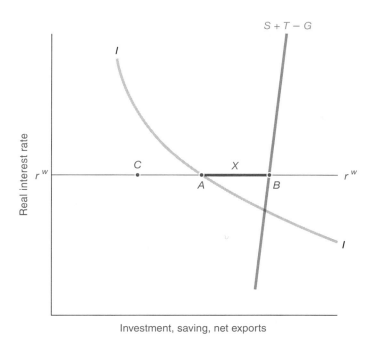

FIGURE 31-6. Saving and Investment in a Small Open Economy

Domestic investment and domestic saving are determined by income, interest rates, and government fiscal policy, as in Figure 31-5. But the small open economy with mobile capital has its real interest rates determined in world capital markets. At the relatively high real interest rate at r^W, domestic saving exceeds domestic investment and the excess saving flows to more lucrative investment opportunities abroad. The difference is net exports or net foreign investment, X, which is the difference between national saving and domestic investment at the prevailing interest rate. A trade surplus such as has been seen in Japan and Germany for most of the last two decades is caused by the interaction of high domestic saving and depleted domestic investment. Modify this diagram to explain why the United States has had a large net-export deficit over the last two decades.

home and competitive conditions in neighboring newly industrialized countries—the return on Japanese capital has been depressed. Japanese saving therefore seeks outlets abroad, with the consequence that Japan has had a large trade surplus and high net exports. Similar trends were seen in Germany until German reunification in 1990.

The United States has seen an interesting twist in its savings and investment position, as was shown in Table 31-2. Until 1980, the United States had a modest positive net-export position. But in the early 1980s the U.S. government's fiscal position shifted sharply toward deficit. You can depict this by drawing a new $S + T' - G'$ line in Figure 31-6 that intersects the real-interest-rate line at point C. What would be

the level of national saving with the large government deficit? Why would domestic investment be unchanged? Why would net exports be negative and given by the line segment CA?

We can also use this analysis to explain the mechanism by which net exports adjust to provide the necessary investment when the government runs a budget deficit. Suppose that the country initially has a net-export surplus as shown in Figure 31-6; say that the government then begins to run a large budget deficit. This change will lead to an imbalance in the saving-investment market, pushing up domestic interest rates relative to world interest rates. The rise in domestic interest rates will attract funds from abroad and will lead to an appreciation in the foreign exchange rate of the country running the budget deficit. The appreciation will lead to falling exports and rising imports, or a decrease in net exports. This trend will continue until net exports have fallen sufficiently to close the saving-investment gap.

Other important examples of the open-economy saving-investment theory in the small open economy are the following:

- An increase in private saving or lower government spending in a country will lead to a rightward shift in the national savings schedule in Figure 31-6. This will lead to a depreciation of the exchange rate until net exports have increased enough to balance the increase in domestic saving.
- An increase in domestic investment, say, because of an improved business climate or a burst of innovations, will lead to a shift in the investment schedule. This will lead to an appreciation of the exchange rate until net exports decline enough to balance saving and investment. In this case, domestic investment crowds out foreign investment.
- An increase in world interest rates will reduce the level of investment. This will lead to an increase in net domestic saving, to a depreciation in the foreign exchange rate, and to an increase in net exports and foreign investment.

Diagram each of these cases. Also make sure you can work through the cases of decreases in the government's fiscal deficit, in private saving, in investment, and in world interest rates.

Integration of a country into the world financial system adds an important new dimension to economic performance and economic policy. The foreign sector provides another source for domestic investment and another outlet for domestic saving. Higher saving at home—whether in the form of higher private saving or a lower government deficit—will lead to a combination of higher investment at home and higher net exports. A country's trade balance is primarily a reflection of its national saving and investment rather than of its productivity or inventiveness. Adjustments in a country's trade accounts require a change in domestic saving or investment, and in the long run the adjustments will be brought about by movements in the country's relative prices, often through exchange-rate changes.

PROMOTING GROWTH IN THE OPEN ECONOMY

Increasing the growth of output in open economies involves more than just waving a magic wand that will attract investors or savers. The saving and investing climate involves a wide array of policies, including a stable macroeconomic environment, secure property rights, and, above all, a predictable and attractive climate for investment. We review in this section some of the ways that open economies can improve their growth rates by using the global marketplace to their best advantage.

Over the long run, the single most important way of increasing per capita output and living standards is to ensure that the country *adopts best-practice techniques* in its production processes. It does little good to have a high investment rate if the investments are in the wrong technology. This point was abundantly shown in the last years of Soviet central planning, when the investment rate was extremely high but much investment was poorly designed, left unfinished, or made in unproductive sectors. Moreover, individual small countries do not need to start from scratch in designing their own turbines, machinery, computers, and management systems. Often, reaching the technological frontier will involve engaging in joint ventures with foreign firms, which in turn requires that the institutional framework be hospitable to foreign capital.

Another important set of policies is *trade policies*. Evidence suggests that an open trading system promotes competitiveness and adoption of best-practice technologies. (Recall the discussion of outward orientation in Chapter 28.) By keeping tariffs and other barriers to trade low, countries can ensure that domestic firms feel the spur of competition and that foreign firms are permitted to enter domestic markets when domestic producers sell at inefficiently high prices or tend to monopolize particular sectors.

When countries consider their saving and investment, they must not concentrate entirely on physical capital. *Intangible capital* is just as important. Studies show that countries that invest in human capital tend to perform well and be resilient in the face of shocks. Many countries have valuable stocks of natural

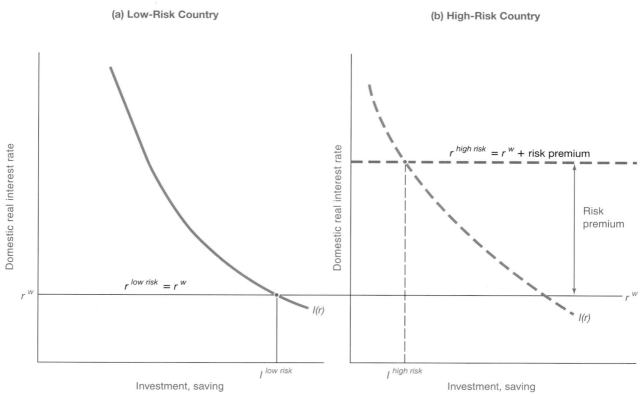

(a) Low-Risk Country

(b) High-Risk Country

FIGURE 31-7. Business Climate Affects Interest Rate and Investment Level

In the low-risk country in (**a**), a stable economic climate leads to a low domestic interest rate at r^W and a high level of investment at $I^{low\ risk}$. In the high-risk country, racked by political turmoil, corruption, and economic uncertainty, investors require a large risk premium on their investments, so the domestic interest rate is far above the world interest rate. The result is a depressed level of investment as foreign investors seek safer terrain.

resources—forests, minerals, oil and gas, fisheries, and arable land—that must be managed carefully to ensure that they provide the highest yield for the country.

One of the most complex factors in a country's growth involves *immigration* and *emigration*. Historically, the United States has attracted large flows of immigrants that not only have increased the size of its labor forces but also have enhanced the quality of its cultures and scientific research. More recently, however, the immigrants have possessed less education and lower skills than the domestic labor force. As a result, according to some studies, immigration has depressed the relative wages of low-wage workers in the United States. Countries that "export" work-

ers, such as Mexico, often have a steady stream of earnings that are sent home by citizens to their relatives, and this can provide a nice supplement to export earnings.

One of the most important and subtle influences concerns the *institutions of the market*. The most successful open economies—like the Netherlands and Luxembourg in Europe or Korea and Hong Kong (through 1997) in Asia—provided a secure environment for investment and entrepreneurship. This involved establishing a secure set of property rights, guided by the rule of law. Increasingly important is the development of intellectual property rights so that inventors and creative artists are assured that they will be able to profit from their activities. Countries must fight corruption, which is a kind of private taxation system that preys on the most profitable enterprises, creates uncertainty about property rights, raises costs, and has a chilling effect on investment.

A stable macroeconomic framework means that taxes are reasonable and predictable, and inflation is low so that lenders need not worry about inflation confiscating their investments. It is crucial that exchange rates be relatively stable, with a *convertibility* that allows easy and inexpensive entry into and exit out of the domestic currency. Countries that provide a favorable institutional structure attract large flows of foreign capital, while countries that have unstable institutions, like Russia or Iraq, attract relatively little foreign funds and suffer capital flight.

Figure 31-7 on page 617 illustrates the impact of the investment climate on national investment. The left-hand panel depicts a country that has a favorable investment climate, so the domestic interest rate is equal to the world interest rate. The overall level of investment there is high, and the country can attract foreign funds to finance domestic investment. Panel (*b*) shows a high-risk country—plagued by revolu-

tion, high inflation, unpredictable taxes, nationalizations, corruption, an unstable foreign exchange rate, and so on. In the high-risk country, domestic interest rates have a high "risk premium" over world interest rates, so the real cost of capital might be 10 or 20 or 30 percent per year compared to 5 percent in the low-risk country. The risky country will have trouble attracting domestic *or* foreign investment, and the resulting level of investment will be low.

Promoting economic growth in an open economy involves ensuring that business is attractive for foreign and domestic investors who have a wide array of investment opportunities in the world economy. The ultimate goals of policy are to have high rates of saving and investment in productive channels and to ensure that businesses use the best-practice techniques. Achieving these goals involves setting a stable macroeconomic climate, guaranteeing dependable property rights for both tangible investments and intellectual property, providing exchange-rate convertibility that allows investors to take home their profits, and maintaining confidence in the political and economic stability of the country.

SUMMARY

A. Foreign Trade and Economic Activity

1. An open economy is one that engages in international exchange of goods, services, and investments. Exports are goods and services sold to buyers outside the country, while imports are those purchased from foreigners. The difference between exports and imports of goods and services is called net exports. For most of the twentieth century, the United States had balanced trade, but after 1980 net exports moved sharply into deficit.

2. When foreign trade is introduced, domestic demand can differ from national output. Domestic demand comprises consumption, investment, and government purchases ($C + I + G$). To obtain GDP, exports (Ex) must be added and imports (Im) subtracted, so

$$GDP = C + I + G + X$$

where X = net exports = $Ex - Im$. Imports are determined by domestic income and output along with the prices of domestic goods relative to those of foreign goods; exports are the mirror image, determined by foreign income and output along with relative prices.

The dollar increase of imports for each dollar increase in GDP is called the marginal propensity to import (MPm).

3. A new element at work with international trade is the foreign exchange rate, which is the price at which one country's currency exchanges for the currency of another country. When a nation's exchange rate rises (or appreciates), import prices fall, export prices rise abroad, and the nation becomes less competitive in world markets. The net result is a decline in net exports.

4. Foreign trade has an effect on GDP similar to that of investment or government purchases. As net exports rise, there is an increase in aggregate demand for domestic output. Net exports hence have a multiplier effect on output. But the expenditure multiplier in an open economy will be smaller than that in a closed economy because of leakages from spending into imports. The multiplier is

$$\text{Open-economy multiplier} = \frac{1}{MPS + MPm}$$

Clearly, other things equal, the open-economy multiplier is smaller than the closed-economy multiplier, where $MPm = 0$.

5. The operation of monetary policy has new implications in an open economy. An important example involves the operation of monetary policy in a small open economy that has a high degree of capital mobility. Such a country must align its interest rates with those in the countries to whom it pegs its exchange rate. This means that countries operating on a fixed exchange rate essentially lose monetary policy as an independent instrument of macroeconomic policy. Fiscal policy, by contrast, becomes a powerful instrument of policy because fiscal stimulus is not offset by changes in interest rates.

6. An open economy operating with flexible exchange rates can use monetary policy for macroeconomic stabilization which operates independently of other countries. In this case, the international link adds another powerful channel to the domestic monetary mechanism. A monetary tightening leads to higher interest rates, attracting foreign financial capital and leading to a rise (or appreciation) of the exchange rate. The exchange-rate appreciation tends to depress net exports, so this impact reinforces the contractionary impact of higher interest rates on domestic investment.

7. The international monetary mechanism was an important factor in changing the U.S. investment pattern in the 1980s. Loose fiscal policy and tight money reduced net exports and shifted the composition of GDP away from tradeable goods to nontradeable goods. Open-economy considerations complicate the life of central banks both because the links between money and net exports are imprecise and because additional political and economic concerns are raised by the impact of domestic policies on the composition of GDP, on foreign economies, and on developing-country debt.

B. Interdependence in the Global Economy

8. In the longer run, operating in the global marketplace provides new constraints and opportunities for countries to improve their economic growth. Perhaps the most important element concerns saving and investment, which are highly mobile and respond to incentives and the investment climate in different countries.

9. The foreign sector provides another source for saving and another outlet for investment. Higher domestic saving—whether through private saving or government fiscal surpluses—will increase the sum of domestic investment and net exports. In the long run, a country's trade position primarily reflects its national savings and investment rates. Reducing a trade deficit requires changing domestic saving and investment. One important mechanism for bringing trade flows in line with domestic saving and investment is through the exchange rate.

10. Besides promoting high saving and investment, countries increase their growth through a wide array of policies and institutions. Important considerations are a stable macroeconomic climate, strong property rights for both tangible investments and intellectual property, a convertible currency with few restrictions on capital flows, and political and economic stability.

CONCEPTS FOR REVIEW

$C + I + G + X$ curve for open economy
net exports $= X = Ex - Im$
domestic demand vs. spending on
    GDP
marginal propensity to import (MPm)
foreign exchange rate

multiplier:
    in closed economy $= 1/MPS$
    in open economy $= 1/(MPS + MPm)$
impact of trade flows, exchange rates
    on GDP

saving-investment identity in closed
    and open economies
equilibration in saving-investment
    market in closed and open
    economies
growth policies in the open economy

QUESTIONS FOR DISCUSSION

1. Assume that an expansionary monetary policy leads to a decline or depreciation of the U.S. dollar relative to the currencies of America's trading partners in the short run with unemployed resources. Explain the mechanism by which this will produce an economic expansion in the United States. Explain how the trade impact reinforces the impact on domestic investment.

2. Explain the impact upon net exports and GDP of the following in the multiplier model, using Table 31-1 where possible:
    a. An increase in investment (I) of $100 billion

b. A decrease in government purchases (G) of $50 billion
c. An increase of foreign output which increased exports by $10 billion
d. A depreciation of the exchange rate that raised exports by $30 billion and lowered imports by $20 billion at every level of GDP

3. What would the expenditure multiplier be in an economy without government spending or taxes where the *MPC* is 0.8 and the *MPm* is 0? Where the *MPm* is 0.1? Where the *MPm* is 0.9? Explain why the multiplier might even be less than 1.

4. Consider the city of New Heaven, which is a very open economy. The city exports reliquaries and has no investment or taxes. The city's residents consume 50 percent of their disposable incomes, and 90 percent of all purchases are imports from the rest of the country. The mayor proposes levying a tax of $100 million to spend on a public-works program. Mayor Cains argues that output and incomes in the city will rise nicely because of something called "the multiplier." Estimate the impact of the public-works program on the incomes and output of New Heaven. Do you agree with the mayor's assessment?

5. After the reunification of Germany, payments to rebuild the east led to a major expansion of aggregate demand in Germany. The German central bank responded by slowing money growth and driving up German real interest rates. Trace through why this German monetary tightening would be expected to lead to a depreciation of the dollar. Explain why the depreciation would stimulate economic activity in the United States. Also, explain why European countries with fixed exchange rates that had pegged their currencies to the German mark would find themselves plunged into deep recessions as German interest rates rose and pulled other European rates up with them.

6. Review the bulleted list of the three interactions of saving, investment, and trade on page 616. Make a graph like that of Figure 31-6 to illustrate each of the impacts. Make sure that you can also explain the reverse cases mentioned in the sentence that follows the bulleted list.

7. Politicians often decry the large trade deficit of the United States. Economists reply that if the trade deficit were smaller, domestic investment would have to be reduced. Explain this point using the analysis of the saving-investment balance in Figure 31-6.

8. Consider a country like Russia, which is trying to make a transition to the market. It has had high inflation, many changes in its tax treatment of foreign investment, political instability (including a near-victory by the communists in the presidential election of 1996), and highly uncertain and variable property rights. Explain why each of these factors would reduce the attractiveness of investment in Russia, and use your discussion to explain the risk premium on investment in Figure 31-7.

9. Consider the example of small open economies like Belgium and the Netherlands that have highly mobile capital and fixed exchange rates but also have high government budget deficits. Suppose that these countries find themselves in a depressed economic condition, with low output and high unemployment. Explain why they cannot use monetary policy to stimulate their economies. Why would fiscal expansion be effective if they could tolerate higher budget deficits? Why would a depreciation of the exchange rate produce both higher output and a lower government deficit?

CHAPTER 32
THE WARRING SCHOOLS OF MACROECONOMICS

[Now] is a time in which macroeconomists are again entertaining new hypotheses about the mechanisms governing the economy and reaching out for a new paradigm. . . . Pluralism is best, and recurrent outbreaks of pluralism are inevitable.

Edmund S. Phelps, Seven Schools
of Macroeconomic Thought *(1990)*

If you listen to the debates about key macroeconomic issues such as the budget deficit, monetary policy, or inflation, you will hear spirited arguments on almost everything except the definition of GDP. Some economists propose raising taxes to cut the deficit, while others argue for lower taxes to spur long-term growth. Some want the government to take a more active role in managing the economy, while others believe that the best thing to do is to make the government as small and unobtrusive as possible. It's easy to see why G. B. Shaw said, "If you lay all the economists end to end, they still won't reach a conclusion."

But if you look behind the contesting arguments, you will see that there are a few recurring issues that separate the different schools. One has to do with different views about how aggregate demand is determined; another concerns the role of price flexibility; yet another revolves around the extent of rationality in human decisions.

Our philosophy in this textbook is to consider all the important schools of thought. We tend to emphasize the modern mainstream Keynesian approach as the best way to explain the business cycle in market economies. But the forces behind long-run economic growth are best understood by using the neoclassical model. And to these basic

tools we must increasingly add the open-economy issues discussed in Chapter 31.

Along the way, we have mentioned some of the particular schools of macroeconomic thought. Our experience has convinced us of the importance of keeping minds open to alternative points of view. Time and again in science, the orthodoxies of one period are overturned by new discoveries. Schools, like people, are subject to hardening of the arteries. Students learn the embalmed truth from their teachers and sacred textbooks, and the imperfections in the orthodox doctrines are ignored or glossed over as unimportant. For example, John Stuart Mill, one of the greatest economists and philosophers of all time, wrote in his 1848 classic, *Principles of Political Economy:* "Happily, there is nothing in the laws of Value which remains for the present and any future writer to clear up." And this was written before supply-and-demand analysis was even discovered!

Historians of science observe that the progress of science is discontinuous. New schools of thought rise, spread their influence, and convince skeptics. Perhaps somewhere in the warring schools of macroeconomics that we review in this chapter lie the seeds of the new theory that will resolve the painful dilemmas of the mixed market economy.

621

A. CLASSICAL STIRRINGS AND KEYNESIAN REVOLUTION

THE CLASSICAL TRADITION

Since the dawn of economics two centuries ago, economists have wondered whether or not a market economy has a tendency to move spontaneously toward a long-run, full-employment equilibrium without the need for government intervention. Using modern language, we label as **classical** those approaches that emphasize the self-correcting forces in an economy; classical macroeconomic thinking has its roots in the writings of Adam Smith (1776), J. B. Say (1803), and John Stuart Mill (1848). The classical approach holds that prices and wages are flexible and the economy is stable, so the economy moves automatically and quickly to its full-employment equilibrium. In the discussion that follows, we will use aggregate supply-and-demand analysis to explain the scientific foundations and the policy implications of the classical approach to macroeconomics.

Say's Law of Markets

Before Keynes developed his macroeconomic theories, the major economic thinkers generally adhered to the classical view of the economy, at least in good times. Early economists were fascinated by the Industrial Revolution, with its division of labor, accumulation of capital, and growing international trade. These economists knew about business cycles, but they viewed them as temporary and self-correcting aberrations. Their analysis revolved around **Say's Law of Markets**. This theory, propounded in 1803 by the French economist J. B. Say, states that overproduction is impossible by its very nature. This is sometimes expressed today as "supply creates its own demand." What is the rationale for Say's Law? It rests on a view that there is no essential difference between a monetary economy and a barter economy—that whatever factories can produce, workers can afford to buy.

A long line of the most distinguished economists, including David Ricardo (1817), John Stuart Mill (1848), and Alfred Marshall (1890), subscribed to the classical macroeconomic view that overproduction is impossible. Even during the Great Depres-

sion, when one-quarter of the American labor force was unemployed, the eminent economist A. C. Pigou wrote, "With perfectly free competition there will always be a strong tendency toward full employment. Such unemployment as exists at any time is due wholly to the frictional resistances [that] prevent the appropriate wage and price adjustments being made instantaneously."[1]

As the quote from Pigou suggests, the rationale behind the classical view is that wages and prices are flexible so that markets will "clear," or return to equilibrium, very quickly. If prices and wages adjust rapidly, the short run in which prices are sticky will be so short that it can be neglected for all practical purposes. Classical macroeconomists conclude that the economy operates at full employment or at its potential output.

The durable and valid core of Say's Law and of the classical approach is shown in Figure 32-1. This shows an economy where prices and real wages are determined in competitive markets, moving flexibly up and down to eliminate any excess demand or supply. In terms of our *AS-AD* analysis, it can be described by a standard, downward-sloping aggregate demand curve along with a vertical aggregate supply curve.

Suppose that aggregate demand falls due to tight money, falling exports, or other exogenous forces. As a result, the *AD* curve shifts leftward to *AD'* in Figure 32-1. Initially, at the original price level of *P*, total spending falls to point *B*, and there might be a very brief period of falling output. But the demand shift is followed by a rapid adjustment of wages and prices, with the overall price level falling from *P* to *P'*. As the price level falls, total output returns to potential output, and full employment is reestablished at point *C*.

In the classical view, changes in aggregate demand affect the price level but have no lasting impact upon output and employment. Price and wage flexibility ensures that the real level of spending is sufficient to maintain full employment.

---

[1] *The Theory of Unemployment* (1933).

Policy Consequences

The classical view has two conclusions that are vitally important for economic policy. To begin with, under the classical view the economy has only brief and temporary lapses from full employment and full utilization of capacity. There will be no long and sustained recessions or depressions, and qualified workers can quickly find work at the going market wage.

The classical analysis does not hold that there is no frictional unemployment, and market power may produce *microeconomic* waste, distortions, and inefficiencies. We may, for example, observe unemployment of people who are moving between jobs or of unionized workers who have bargained for above-equilibrium wage rates. But in the classical view, an economy has no pervasive and persistent *macroeconomic* waste in the sense of underutilized resources due to insufficient aggregate demand.

FIGURE 32-1. According to Say's Law, Supply Creates Its Own Demand as Prices Move to Balance Demand with Aggregate Supply

Classical economists thought that persistent periods of glut could not occur. If *AS* or *AD* shifted, prices would react flexibly to ensure that full-employment output was sold. Here we see how flexible prices move down enough to match real expenditures with full-employment output after a decline in aggregate demand. (What would happen if *AD* were unchanged but potential output increased to E''? What forces would move the economy to E''?)

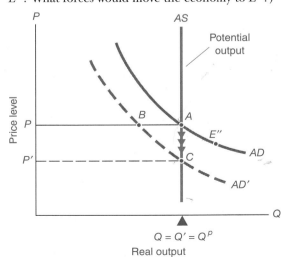

The second surprising element of the classical view is that aggregate demand policies cannot influence the level of unemployment and real output. Rather, monetary and fiscal policies can affect only the economy's price level, along with the composition of real GDP. This second classical proposition is easily seen in Figure 32-1. Consider an economy in equilibrium at point *A*, the intersection of the *AD* and the vertical *AS* curves. Suppose that the central bank decides to contract the money supply to reduce inflation. For a brief instant, at the initial price level *P*, there is excess supply. However, as prices and wages quickly begin to fall under the pressure of excess supply, the economy moves to the new equilibrium at point *C*. The contractionary economic policy has reduced the overall price level. But output and employment are essentially unchanged because price and wage flexibility has ensured a smooth transition between the old equilibrium and the new one.

At the heart of the classical view is the belief that prices and wages are flexible and that wage-price flexibility provides a self-correcting mechanism that quickly restores full employment and always maintains potential output. This approach is very much alive in the writings of today's new classical school, which we review later in this chapter. New classical economists move beyond the simplest classical approaches by allowing for imperfect information, the existence of technological shocks, and frictions from shifts of resources among industries. Although dressed in modern clothing, their policy conclusions are closely linked to those of the classical economists of an earlier age.

THE KEYNESIAN REVOLUTION

While classical economists were preaching the impossibility of persistent unemployment, economists of the 1930s could hardly ignore the vast army of unemployed workers begging for work and selling pencils on street corners. How could economics explain such massive and persistent idleness?

Keynes' *The General Theory of Employment, Interest and Money* (1936) offered an alternative macroeconomic theory, a new set of theoretical spectacles for looking at the impact of economic policies as well as external shocks. In fact, the Keynesian revolution combined two different elements. First, Keynes presented the concept of aggregate demand that was explored in depth in earlier chapters. A second and equally revolutionary feature was the Keynesian theory of aggregate supply. Whereas the classical approach assumed flexible prices and wages with the implication of a vertical classical *AS* curve, the Keynesian approach insisted on price and wage inflexibility and the flat or upward-sloping *AS* curve. In Keynes' approach, supply definitely does not create its own demand; output can deviate from its potential for indefinitely long periods.

The Surprising Consequences

By combining these two new elements, Keynes brought a veritable revolution to macroeconomics. The essence of Keynes' argument is shown in Figure 32-2. This now familiar diagram combines an aggregate demand curve with a Keynesian, upward-sloping aggregate supply curve.

The first observation is that a modern market economy can get trapped in an underemployment equilibrium—a balance of aggregate supply and demand in which output is far below potential and a substantial fraction of the work force is involuntarily unemployed. For example, if the *AD* curve intersects the *AS* curve far to the left, as illustrated at point *A*, equilibrium output may lie far below potential output. Keynes and his followers emphasized that, because wages and prices are inflexible, there is no economic mechanism that will quickly restore full employment and ensure that the economy produces at full capacity. A nation could remain in its low-output, high-misery condition for a long time because there is no self-correcting mechanism or invisible hand to guide the economy back to full employment.

Keynes' second observation follows from the first. Through monetary and fiscal policies, the government can stimulate the economy and help maintain high levels of output and employment. For example, if the government were to increase its purchases, aggregate demand would increase, say, from *AD* to *AD'* in Figure 32-2. The impact would be an increase in output from *Q* to *Q'*, which reduces the gap between actual GDP and potential GDP. In short, with appropriate use of economic policy, government can take steps to ensure high levels of national output and employment.

Keynes' analysis created a revolution in macroeconomics, particularly among young economists

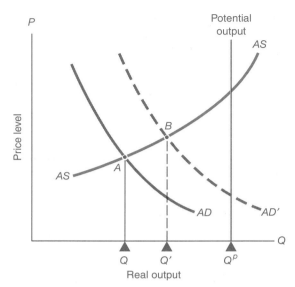

FIGURE 32-2. Aggregate Demand Helps Determine Output in the Keynesian Approach

According to Keynesian economics, aggregate supply slopes upward, implying that output will increase with higher aggregate demand as long as there are unused resources. When *AD* is depressed, output will be in equilibrium at point *A*, with high unemployment.

If aggregate demand increases from *AD* to *AD'*, the level of real output increases from *A* to *B*, with prices increasing as well. In the Keynesian approach, economic policies that increase aggregate demand succeed in increasing output and employment.

who were living through the Great Depression of the 1930s and sensed something was terribly wrong with the classical model. Of course, the Great Depression was not the first event to reveal the incredibility of the classical synthesis. Anyone with common sense could see the massive involuntary unemployment during depressions. But for the first time, the classical approach was confronted by a competing analysis. The Keynesian approach presented a new synthesis that swept through economics and fundamentally changed the way that economists and governments think about business cycles and economic policy.

THEORIES AND POLICY

In economics, what people see depends upon the

theoretical spectacles they wear. Does a President, senator, or macroeconomist lean toward a classical or a Keynesian view? The answer to this question will often explain that person's view on many of the major economic-policy debates of the day.

Examples are legion. Economists who tend toward the classical view will often be skeptical about the need for government to stabilize business cycles. They argue that a government policy designed to increase aggregate demand will instead lead to escalating inflation. Even worse, Keynesian remedies will, in their view, slow long-run economic growth. Classical-type economists tend to worry about the long-run consequences of government actions on potential output and therefore on aggregate supply. For example, in the classical view, government deficits may crowd out private investment. More public spending on highways or the environment will divert resources from private investment in factories and machinery.

Keynesian economists take a different tack. They think that the macroeconomy is prone to prolonged business cycles, with alternating periods of high unemployment followed by speculation and inflation. If the classical economist sees the economy as a temperate fellow who has the requisite glass of mineral water and vitamins every day, the Keynesian might picture the economy as a manic-depressive who periodically has a binge of irrational exuberance and shortly thereafter falls into a depressed

hangover. Indeed, one Fed chairman said that the role of the Federal Reserve was to take the punch bowl away just when the party was getting lively.

Keynesians believe that the government can affect real economic activity by taking monetary or fiscal steps to change aggregate demand. A modern Keynesian economist would approve of steps to reduce aggregate demand when inflation threatens to rise sharply or to increase aggregate demand in recessions. Such economists in the United States increasingly lean toward using monetary policy to stabilize business cycles. But they also maintain the importance of fiscal automatic stabilizers that reduce the multiplier effect of unforeseen shocks, and they argue vehemently against policies, such as a constitutional amendment requiring a balanced budget, that would have fiscal policy exacerbate business fluctuations.

The debate between Keynesian and classical economists revolves fundamentally around whether the economy has strong self-correcting forces in flexible wages and prices that help maintain full employment. Classical approaches generally emphasize long-run economic growth and forgo business-cycle stabilization policies. Keynesian economists desire to supplement growth policies with appropriate monetary and fiscal policies to curb business-cycle excesses.

B. THE MONETARIST APPROACH

Inflation is always and everywhere a monetary phenomenon in the sense that it is and can be produced only by a more rapid increase in the quantity of money than in output.

Milton Friedman, **The New Palgrave Dictionary of Economics** *(1987)*

Money cannot manage itself. Central bankers must decide on the supply of money and the degree of tightness of money and credit. Today, there are many different philosophies about the best way to manage monetary affairs. Some believe in an active

policy that "leans against the wind" by slowing money growth when inflation threatens, and vice versa. Others are skeptical about the ability of policymakers to use monetary policy to "fine-tune" inflation and unemployment and would limit monetary policy to containing inflation. At the far end of the spectrum are the monetarists, who believe that discretionary monetary policy should be replaced by a fixed rule.

We can best understand monetarism if we first trace its history in the older quantity theory of money and prices (usually called the quantity theory of money). Then we can see that it has close linkages to both classical and Keynesian approaches.

THE ROOTS OF MONETARISM

Monetarism holds that the money supply is the major determinant of short-run movements in nominal GDP and of long-run movements in prices. Of course, Keynesian macroeconomics also recognizes the key role of money in determining aggregate demand. The main difference between monetarists and Keynesians lies in their approaches to the determination of aggregate demand. While Keynesian theories hold that many forces other than money affect aggregate demand, monetarists argue that changes in the money supply are the primary factor that determines output and price movements.

In order to understand monetarism, we need to introduce a new concept—the *velocity of money*—and describe a new relationship—the *quantity theory of money*.

The Velocity of Money

Sometimes money turns over very slowly; it sits in cookie jars or in bank accounts for long periods between transactions. At other times, particularly during rapid inflation, people get rid of money quickly and money circulates rapidly from hand to hand. The speed of turnover of money is described by the concept of the velocity of money, introduced at the turn of this century by Cambridge University's Alfred Marshall and Yale's Irving Fisher. It measures the speed at which money is changing hands or circulating through the economy. When the quantity of money is large relative to the flow of expenditures, the velocity of circulation is low; when money turns over rapidly, money's velocity is high.

More precisely, the **income velocity of money** is the ratio of nominal GDP to the stock of money.

Velocity measures the rate at which the stock of money turns over relative to the total income or output of a nation. Formally:[2]

$$V \equiv \frac{\text{GDP}}{M} \equiv \frac{p_1 q_1 + p_2 q_2 + \cdots}{M} \equiv \frac{PQ}{M}$$

Here P stands for the average price level and Q stands for real GDP. Velocity (V) is defined as nominal GDP each year divided by the money stock.

We can think of the income velocity of money intuitively as the speed at which money changes hands in the economy. As a simple example, assume that the economy produces only bread and that GDP consists of 48 million loaves of bread, each selling at a price of $1, so GDP = PQ = $48 million per year. If the money supply is $4 million, then by definition V = $48/$4 = 12 per year. This means that money turns over once a month as earnings are used to buy monthly bread.[3]

Figure 32-3 shows the recent history of the income velocity of transactions money (M_1). Note that nominal GDP has been rising faster than the money supply over the last four decades. We can thus conclude that the income velocity of money has been rising over time. The question of the stability and predictability of the velocity of money is central to macroeconomic policy.

The Quantity Theory of Prices

Having defined an interesting new variable called velocity, we now describe how early monetary specialists used the concept of velocity to explain movements in the overall price level. The key assumption is that *the velocity of money is relatively stable and predictable*. The reason for stability, according to these economists, is that velocity mainly reflects underlying patterns in the timing of income and spending. If

---

[2] The definitional equations have been written with the three-bar identity symbol rather than with the more common two-bar equality symbol. This usage emphasizes that they are "identities"—statements which tell us nothing about reality but which hold true by definition even if the United States experienced a hyperinflation or were in a deep depression.

[3] The velocity of money is closely related to the demand for money. If we rewrite the velocity equation, we have $M/PQ \equiv 1/V$. The left-hand side is the demand for money per unit of GDP. Our earlier discussion of money demand applies equally well to an analysis of velocity.

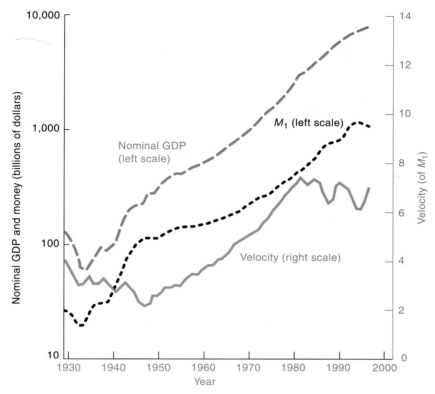

FIGURE 32-3. Velocity and Its Components, 1929–1995
Income velocity for transactions money is the ratio of nominal GDP to M_1. One of the tenets of monetarism is that V is relatively stable and predictable. How stable does V appear? Can you think of some reasons why V has grown over time? *Hint:* How do interest rates affect velocity? (Source: V constructed by the authors from data from the Federal Reserve Board and the Department of Commerce.)

people get paid once a month and tend to spend all their incomes evenly over the course of the month, income velocity will be 12 per year. Incomes could double, prices might rise 20 percent, and total GDP may be up many times—yet with unchanged spending patterns the income velocity of money would remain unchanged. Only as people or businesses modify their spending patterns or the way they pay their bills does the velocity of income change.

On the basis of this insight about the relative stability of velocity, some early writers, particularly the classical economists, used velocity to explain changes in the price level. This approach, called the **quantity theory of money and prices**, rewrites the definition of velocity as follows:

$$P \equiv \frac{MV}{Q} \equiv \left(\frac{V}{Q}\right) M \equiv kM$$

This equation is obtained from the earlier definition of velocity by substituting the variable k as a shorthand for V/Q and solving for P. We write the equation this way because many classical economists believed that if transactions patterns were stable, k would be constant or relatively stable. In addition, they generally assumed full employment, which meant real output would grow smoothly and would equal potential GDP. Putting these two assumptions together, k $(= V/Q)$ would be near-constant in the short run and a smoothly growing trend in the long run.

What are the implications of the quantity theory? As we can see from the equation, if k were constant, the price level would then move proportionally with the supply of money. A stable money supply would produce stable prices; if the money supply grew rapidly, so would prices. Similarly, if the money supply was multiplied by 10 or 100, the economy would experience galloping inflation or hyperinflation. Indeed, the most vivid demonstrations of the quantity theory of money can be seen in hyperinflations. Turning back to Figure 30-4 (page 582), note how prices rose a billionfold in Weimar Germany after the central bank unleashed the monetary printing presses. This is the quantity theory with a vengeance.

To understand the quantity theory of money, it is essential to recall that money differs fundamentally from ordinary goods like bread or cars. We want bread to eat and cars to drive. But we want money only because it buys us bread or cars. If prices in Russia today are 1000 times what they were a few years ago, it is natural that people will need about 1000 times as much money to buy things as they did before. Here lies the core of the quantity theory of money: the demand for money rises proportionally with the price level.

The quantity theory of money and prices holds that prices move proportionally with the supply of money. Although the quantity theory of money and prices is only a rough approximation, it does help explain why countries with low money growth have moderate inflation while others with rapid money growth find their prices galloping along.

MODERN MONETARISM

Modern monetary economics was developed after World War II by Chicago's Milton Friedman and his numerous colleagues and followers. Under Friedman's leadership, monetarists challenged the Keynesian approach to macroeconomics and emphasized the importance of monetary policy in macroeconomic stabilization. About two decades ago, the monetarist approach branched. One fork continued the older tradition, which we will now describe. The younger offshoot became the influential new classical school, which is analyzed later in this chapter.

The monetarist approach postulates that the growth of money determines nominal GDP in the short run and prices in the long run. This analysis operates in the framework of the quantity theory of money and prices and relies on the analysis of trends in velocity. Monetarists argue that the velocity of money is stable (or in extreme cases constant). If correct, this is an important insight, for the quantity equation shows that if V is constant, movements in M will affect PQ (or nominal GDP) proportionally.

The Essence of Monetarism

Like all serious schools of thought, monetarism has differing emphases and degrees. The following points are central to monetarist thinking:

1. *Money-supply growth is the prime systematic determinant of nominal GDP growth.* Monetarism is basically a theory of the determinants of aggregate demand. It holds that nominal aggregate demand is affected primarily by changes in the money supply. Fiscal policy is important for some things (like the fraction of GDP devoted to defense or private consumption), but the major macroeconomic variables (aggregate output, employment, and prices) are affected mainly by money. This was put neatly in the following oversimplified way: "Only money matters."

What is the basis for the monetarist belief in the primacy of money? It is based on two central propositions. First, as Friedman has stated, "There is an extraordinary empirical stability and regularity to such magnitudes as income velocity that cannot but impress anyone who works extensively with monetary data." Second, many monetarists used to argue that the demand for money is completely insensitive to interest rates.[4]

Why do these two assumptions lead to the monetarist view? From the quantity equation of exchange, if velocity V is stable, M will determine $PQ \equiv$ nominal GDP. Similarly, fiscal policy is irrelevant according to the monetarists because if V is stable, the only force that can affect PQ is M. With constant V, there is simply no door by

---

[4] If velocity is constant, then it is invariant to the interest rate. On the other hand, if velocity responds to the interest rate, this allows fiscal policy and other nonmonetary forces to affect output by changing velocity. The proposition that the demand for money is insensitive to the interest rate has been discredited and has generally fallen out of favor in recent years.

which taxes or government expenditures can enter the stage.

2. *Prices and wages are relatively flexible.* Recall that one of the precepts of Keynesian economics is that prices and wages are "sticky." While generally accepting the view that there is some inertia in wage-price setting, monetarists argue that the Phillips curve is relatively steep even in the short run and insist that the long-run Phillips curve is vertical. In the *AS-AD* framework, monetarists hold that the short-run *AS* curve is quite steep.

The monetarists put points 1 and 2 together. Because (1) money is the prime determinant of nominal GDP and (2) prices and wages are fairly flexible around potential output, the implication is that money-supply changes have only small and temporary effects on real output. *M* mainly affects *P*.

Accordingly, money can affect both output and prices in the short run. But within a few years, because the economy tends to operate near full employment, money's main impact is on the price level. Fiscal policy affects output and prices negligibly in both the short run and the long run. This is the essence of monetarist doctrine.

3. *The private sector is stable.* Finally, monetarists believe that the private economy, left to its own devices, is not prone to instability. Instead, most fluctuations in nominal GDP result from government action—in particular, changes in the money supply, which depend on the policies followed by the central bank.

Comparison of Monetarist and Keynesian Approaches

How do monetarist views compare with modern Keynesian approaches? In fact, there has been considerable convergence in views between these schools over the last three decades, and the disputes today are ones of emphasis rather than of fundamental beliefs.

We depict the major differences between monetarists and modern Keynesians in Figure 32-4. This

Copy

FIGURE 32-4. Comparison of Monetarist and Keynesian Views
In essence, monetarists say, "Only money matters for aggregate demand." Mainstream macroeconomists reply, "Money matters, but so does fiscal policy." A second difference revolves around aggregate supply, where Keynesian economists stress that the *AS* curve is relatively flat. If prices and wages are relatively flexible, as monetarists believe, then output will generally be close to its potential.

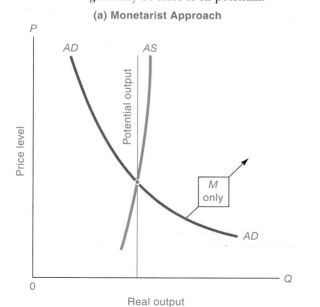

(a) Monetarist Approach

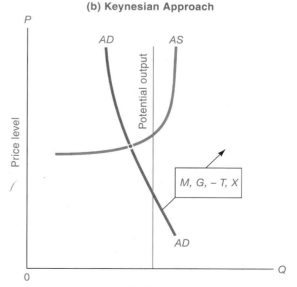

(b) Keynesian Approach

figure shows both views in terms of the behavior of aggregate supply and demand. Two major differences stand out.

First, the two schools disagree about the forces that operate on aggregate demand. Monetarists believe that aggregate demand is affected solely (or primarily) by the money supply and that the impact of money on aggregate demand is stable and reliable. They also believe that fiscal policy or autonomous changes in spending, unless accompanied by monetary changes, will have negligible effects upon output and prices.[5]

Keynesian economists, by contrast, hold that the world is more complex. While agreeing that money has an important effect upon aggregate demand, output, and prices, they argue that other factors also matter. In other words, Keynesian economists hold that money enters into output determination *along with* spending variables like fiscal policy and net exports. Moreover, they point to conclusive evidence that *V* rises systematically with interest rates, so keeping *M* constant is not enough to keep nominal or real GDP constant. In one of the most interesting examples of convergence, both monetarists and Keynesians today tend to believe that stabilization policy in the United States should be conducted primarily through monetary policy.

The second major difference between monetarist and Keynesian economists concerns the behavior of aggregate supply. Keynesian economists emphasize the inertia in prices and wages. Monetarists think that Keynesian economists exaggerate the economy's wage-price stickiness and that the short-run *AS* curve is quite steep—not vertical, perhaps, but much steeper than a Keynesian economist would allow.

Because they hold differing views about the slope of the *AS* curve, Keynesian economists and monetarists disagree on the short-run impact of changes in aggregate demand. Keynesian economists believe that a change in (nominal) demand will significantly change output with little effect on

prices in the short run. Monetarists hold that a shift in demand will primarily end up changing prices rather than quantities.

> The essence of monetarism in macroeconomic thinking centers on the importance of money in determining aggregate demand and on the relative flexibility of wages and prices.

The Monetarist Platform: Constant Money Growth

Over the last three decades, monetarism has played a significant role in shaping economic policy. Monetarist economists often espouse free markets and laissez-faire microeconomic policies. But the foremost contribution to macroeconomic policy has been their advocacy of fixed monetary rules in preference to discretionary fiscal and monetary policies.

In principle, a monetarist might recommend using monetary policy to fine-tune the economy. But monetarists have taken a different tack, arguing that the private economy is stable and that the government tends to destabilize the economy. Moreover, monetarists believe that money affects output only after long and variable lags, so the design of effective stabilization policies is a formidable task.

Thus a cardinal part of the monetarist economic philosophy is a **monetary rule:** Optimal monetary policy sets the growth of the money supply at a fixed rate and holds to that rate through all economic conditions.

What is the rationale for this view? Monetarists believe that a fixed growth rate of money (at 3 to 5 percent annually) would eliminate the major source of instability in a modern economy—the capricious and unreliable shifts of monetary policy. If we replaced the Federal Reserve with a computer program that always produces a fixed *M*-growth rate, there would be no bursts in *M* growth. With stable velocity, money GDP would grow at a stable rate. And if *M* grew at about the growth rate of potential GDP, the economy would soon attain price stability.

The Monetarist Experiment

Monetarist views gained widespread influence in the late 1970s. In the United States, many thought

---

[5] Note as well that the *AD* curve is drawn as a "rectangular hyperbola" under the monetarist assumptions. Recall that an equation *xy* = *constant* describes a rectangular hyperbola in a graph of *x* and *y*. For given *M* and *V*, the aggregate demand curve is described by *PQ* = *constant*, so the *AD* curve is a rectangular hyperbola.

that Keynesian stabilization policies had failed to contain inflation. When inflation moved up into the double-digit range in 1979, many economists and policymakers believed that monetary policy was the only hope for an effective anti-inflation policy.

In October 1979, the new Chairman of the Federal Reserve, Paul Volcker, launched a fierce counterattack against inflation in what has been called a *monetarist experiment.* In a dramatic change of its operating procedures, the Fed decided to stop focusing on interest rates and instead endeavored to keep bank reserves and the money supply on predetermined growth paths.[6]

The Fed hoped that a strict quantitative approach to monetary management would accomplish two things. First, it would allow interest rates to rise sharply enough to reduce aggregate demand, raise unemployment, and slow wage and price growth through the Phillips-curve mechanism. In addition, some believed that a tough and credible monetary policy would deflate inflationary expectations, particularly in labor contracts, and demonstrate that the high-inflation period was over. Once people's expectations were deflated, the economy could experience a relatively painless reduction in the underlying rate of inflation.

The experiment was clearly successful in slowing the economy and reducing inflation. As a result of the high interest rates induced by slow money growth, interest-sensitive spending slowed. Consequently, real GDP stagnated from 1979 to 1982, and the unemployment rate rose from under 6 percent to a peak of 10 percent in late 1982. Inflation fell sharply. Any lingering doubts about the effectiveness of monetary policy were killed. Money works. Money matters. But of course this is not the same thing as proving that *only* money matters!

But what of the monetarist claim that a tough and credible monetary policy was a low-cost anti-inflation strategy? Numerous economic studies of this question over the last decade suggest that the tough monetarist policy worked but at a cost. In terms of unemployment and output losses, the economic sacrifices of the monetarist disinflation policy were about as large, per point of disinflation, as those of anti-inflation policies in earlier periods.

Money works, but it does not work miracles. There is no free lunch on the monetarist menu.

The Decline of Monetarism

Paradoxically, just as the monetarist experiment succeeded in rooting inflation out of the American economy—perhaps because of the success—changes in financial markets led to shifts in behavior that undermined the monetarist approach. The major shift during and after the monetarist experiment lay in the behavior of velocity. Recall that monetarists hold that velocity is relatively stable and predictable. Given stable velocity, changes in the money supply would get smoothly translated into changes in nominal GDP.

But just as the monetarist doctrine was adopted, velocity became extremely unstable. Indeed, M_1 velocity changed more in 1982 than it had in several decades (see Figure 32-3). The high interest rates of this period spurred financial innovations and the spread of interest-bearing checking accounts. As a result, velocity became increasingly unstable after 1980. Some believe that the instability in velocity was actually produced by the heavy reliance placed upon monetary policy during this period.

The instability of M_1 velocity led the Federal Reserve to stop using it as a guide for policy and focus instead on M_2 velocity (which is simply PQ/M_2). Then in 1992, M_2 velocity also began to deviate from its historical trend, and the Federal Reserve stopped using M_2 as a key guide to policy. The dilemma for the Fed is sketched in the following observation by the Federal Reserve Bank of Cleveland:

> The demise of M_2 as a policy guide has created the need for a better understanding of the relationship between the . . . management of . . . interest rates and the long-term trend in the price level. . . . The hard part is determining whether the [interest] rate is too high or too low without waiting to see what happens to prices.[7]

The inability to use the monetary aggregates as beacons for monetary policy has indeed complicated the decisions of central bankers. In Chapter 33, we address the question of substitutes for a fixed-money rule in the postmonetarist age.

---

[6] Recall the discussion of the monetarist experiment in Chapter 26, p. 508.

[7] Federal Reserve Bank of Cleveland, *Economic Trends* (September 1993).

C. NEW CLASSICAL MACROECONOMICS

> **Existing Keynesian macroeconomic models cannot provide reliable guidance in the formulation of monetary, fiscal, or other types of policy. . . . [T]here is no hope that minor or even major modifications of these models will lead to significant improvements in their reliability.**
>
> *Robert E. Lucas Jr. and Thomas J. Sargent,*
> **"After Keynesian Macroeconomics"**

Although most macroeconomists agree that monetary policy can affect unemployment and output, at least in the short run, a new branch of the classical school challenges the standard approach. This theory, called **new classical macroeconomics**, was developed by Robert Lucas (Chicago), Thomas Sargent (Stanford), and Robert Barro (Harvard). This approach is much in the spirit of the classical approach, discussed above, in emphasizing the role of flexible wages and prices, but it adds a new feature, called rational expectations, to explain observations such as the Phillips curve. For his contributions to developing the new classical approach, and particularly the modern view of rational expectations, Robert Lucas was awarded the Nobel Prize in economics in 1996.

FOUNDATIONS

New classical macroeconomics holds that (1) prices and wages are flexible and (2) people use all available information. These two postulates are the essence of the new classical approach to macroeconomics.

The first part of the new classical approach draws on the classical assumption of price and wage flexibility. This familiar assumption simply means that prices and wages adjust rapidly to balance supply and demand.

The second assumption is brand new, drawing upon modern developments in areas such as statistics and behavior under uncertainty. This hypothesis holds that people form their expectations on the basis of all available information. Under this assumption, the government cannot "fool" the people, for people are well informed and have access to the same information as the government.

We discussed the significance of price and wage flexibility for macroeconomics earlier in this chapter. We now turn to the rational-expectations hypothesis.

Rational Expectations

Expectations are important in economic life. They influence how much investors will spend on investment goods and whether consumers spend or save for the future. But what is a sensible way to treat expectations in economics? New classical macroeconomists answer this question with the **rational-expectations hypothesis**. According to rational expectations, forecasts are unbiased and are based on all available information.

To begin with, the rational-expectations hypothesis holds that people make unbiased forecasts.[8] A more controversial assumption is that people use all available information and economic theory. This implies that people understand how the economy works and what the government is doing. Thus, suppose that Congress always boosts spending in election years. Rational-expectations theory assumes that people will anticipate this kind of behavior and act accordingly.

The key new assumption in new classical macroeconomics is that because of rational expectations the government cannot fool the people with systematic economic policies.

---

[8] A forecast is "unbiased" if it contains no systematic forecasting errors. Clearly a forecast cannot always be perfectly accurate—you cannot foresee how a coin flip will come up on a single toss. But you should not commit the statistical sin of *bias* by predicting that a fair coin would come up tails 10 or 90 percent of the time. You would be making an *unbiased* forecast if you predicted that the coin would come up tails 50 percent of the time or that one of the numbers on a die would, on average, come up one-sixth of the time.

Penrec?

IMPLICATIONS FOR MACROECONOMICS

The approach of new classical macroeconomics can be fruitfully applied in many areas of economics. Here we concentrate on two implications: the nature of the labor market and the Phillips curve.

Unemployment

Is unemployment voluntary or involuntary? In our discussion in Chapter 29, we defined involuntary unemployment as a situation where qualified workers are unable to find jobs at the going wage. Refresh your memory with a glance back at Figure 29-6, which illustrates both voluntary and involuntary unemployment. Also recall that Keynesian economists think that in recessions a sizable fraction of unemployment is involuntary.

By contrast, new classical economists think that most unemployment is voluntary. In their view, labor markets adjust quickly after shocks as wages change to rebalance supply and demand. Unemployment, in this view, increases because more people are hunting for better jobs during recessions, not because they cannot find jobs. People are unemployed because they have quit their jobs to look for higher-paying ones rather than because wages are too high, as in the case of sticky-wage unemployment.

The Illusory Phillips Curve

One of the major challenges for any macroeconomic theory is to explain the business cycle in a way that is internally consistent and that conforms to the regularities of economic behavior. The classical approach to macroeconomics is attractive because it conforms well to most of the microeconomics of supply and demand. But the challenge is to explain important features of business cycles, such as the Phillips curve or Okun's Law. If unemployment is high in recessions, it simply won't do to say that people have decided that it is a good year for longer vacations. How would such theories explain the long global depression of the 1930s or the more recent downturns in European economies?

Misperceptions Theories. The cyclical movements of unemployment are the greatest challenge for the new classical macroeconomics. One early approach (developed by Robert Lucas) pointed to *misperceptions* as the key to business cycles. Under this approach, high unemployment arises because workers are confused about economic conditions; workers voluntarily quit their jobs in the hope of getting better ones but are surprised to find themselves in the unemployment office. In the expansion phase of the business cycle, high output and low unemployment occur when people are fooled into working harder because they overestimate real wages.

The analysis can be illustrated using the Phillips curve of inflation theory. A classical economic approach would hold that the short-run Phillips curve is vertical at the equilibrium or natural unemployment rate. This conclusion is the Phillips-curve counterpart of the vertical classical aggregate supply curve in which output is unaffected by aggregate demand.

Where then do the actual downward-sloping Phillips curves come from? They come from a dynamic process in which people are temporarily confused about real wages. This line of reasoning leads to the *new classical Phillips curve,* shown in Figure 32-5 on page 634. Denote the expected rate of change of money wages as W^e, and assume prices rise as fast as wages. If the actual rate of increase of wages (W) is equal to the expected rate (so $W = W^e$), nobody is surprised or fooled, and unemployment is equal to the natural rate. Thus point A represents the no-surprise, natural-rate outcome.

The challenge is to generate points B and C. Each case arises from some kind of economic shock. To generate point B, assume that the Federal Reserve has unexpectedly increased the money supply, leading to an unexpected increase in wages and prices. Workers misperceive economic events, not knowing that prices are rising as rapidly as wages. They supply more labor, unemployment falls, and the economy goes to point B. You should trace through how we can generate point C by an unexpected cut in wages and prices.

Surprisingly, if we connect points B and C, they trace out a downward-sloping line that resembles the Phillips curve. Thus, in new classical macroeconomics, the downward-sloping *apparent* or *illusory short-run Phillips curve* arises from misperceptions of real wages or relative prices.

Real Business Cycles

A closely related approach that has increasingly attracted classical macroeconomists, also relying on

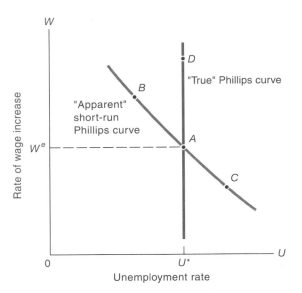

FIGURE 32-5. The New Classical Phillips Curve

According to new classical macroeconomics, the true Phillips curve is vertical. But we may observe an illusory or apparent downward-sloping short-run Phillips curve, drawn through points *B, A,* and *C.* Point *B* arises when an inflationary shock raises money wages above their expected levels. Confused workers, thinking that their real wages have increased, work more, and unemployment falls. Thus the economy moves from point *A* to point *B.* (Trace through the opposite case where workers quit their jobs and produce point *C.*) This produces what looks like a downward-sloping short-run Phillips curve.

rational expectations and competitive markets but emphasizing different mechanisms, is **real-business-cycle (RBC) theory.** This approach explains business cycles purely as shifts in aggregate supply, without any reference to monetary or other demand-side forces.

In the RBC approach, shocks to technology, investment, or labor supply shift the vertical *AS* curve. These shocks then get transmitted into actual output by the fluctuations of aggregate supply and are completely independent of *AD.* Similarly, movements in the unemployment rate are the result of movements in the lowest sustainable unemployment rate (*LSUR*) due to microeconomic forces such as the intensity of sectoral shocks or to tax and regulatory policies.

Efficiency Wages

Another important recent development, fusing elements of both classical and Keynesian economics,

is called **efficiency-wage theory.** This approach was developed by Columbia's Edmund Phelps, Joseph Stiglitz (chair of President Clinton's Council of Economic Advisers in 1995–1997), Janet Yellen (a governor of the Fed and chair of the Council of Economic Advisers in President Clinton's second term), and others. It explains the rigidity of real wages and the existence of involuntary unemployment in terms of firms' attempts to keep wages above the market-clearing level to increase productivity. According to this theory, higher wages lead to higher productivity because workers are healthier (particularly in poor countries), because workers will have higher morale or be less likely to goof off, because good workers are then less likely to quit and look for new jobs, or because higher wages may attract better workers.

As firms raise their wages to increase productivity, job seekers may be willing to stand in line for these high-paying jobs, thereby producing involuntary wait unemployment. *The startling feature of this theory is that the involuntary unemployment is an equilibrium feature and will not disappear over time.*

This approach was summarized in a thorough analysis by Columbia's Edmund Phelps. Phelps argued that much of the rise in unemployment in industrial countries came because efficiency-wage elements worsened, increasing the lowest sustainable unemployment rate. He presented statistical estimates showing that higher payroll taxes, increases in real interest rates, and energy-price shocks were responsible for the rising unemployment of the last two decades. The remedy for the future, according to Phelps, would be to reverse these trends, especially by reducing labor taxes and moving from labor taxes to consumption and value-added taxes. This path-breaking tome will be studied carefully by economists and policymakers in the years ahead.[9]

POLICY IMPLICATIONS

Policy Ineffectiveness

New classical macroeconomics has important policy implications. The most important is the ineffectiveness of systematic fiscal and monetary policies in

---

[9] *Structural Slumps: The Modern Equilibrium Theory of Unemployment, Interest, and Assets* (Harvard University Press, Cambridge, Mass., 1994).

combating unemployment. Say that the government tended to stimulate the economy whenever elections approached. After a couple of episodes of politically motivated fiscal policy, people would rationally come to expect that behavior. They would say to themselves, "Yes, elections are coming. From past experience, I know that the government always pumps up spending before elections. They can't fool *me* and get me to work any harder." In terms of the Phillips curve of Figure 32-5, the government tries to stimulate the economy and move it from point *A* to point *B*. But as people anticipate the government's economic stimulation, the economy ends up at point *D*, with unemployment equal to the sustainable rate, but with higher inflation.

This is the **policy ineffectiveness theorem** of classical macroeconomics. With rational expectations and flexible prices and wages, anticipated government policy cannot affect real output or unemployment.

The policy ineffectiveness theorem depends on both rational expectations and flexible prices. The assumption of flexible prices implies that the only way that economic policy can affect output and unemployment is by surprising people and causing misperceptions. But you can hardly surprise people if your policies are predictable. Hence predictable policies cannot affect output and unemployment.

The Desirability of Fixed Rules

Earlier, we described the monetarist case for fixed rules. New classical macroeconomics puts this argument on a much firmer footing. An economic policy can be divided into two parts, a predictable part (the "rule") and an unpredictable part ("discretion").

New classical macroeconomists argue that discretion is a snare and a delusion. Policymakers, they contend, cannot forecast the economy any better than the private sector can. Therefore, by the time policymakers act on the news, flexibly moving prices in markets populated by well-informed buyers and sellers have already adapted to the news and reached their efficient supply-and-demand equilibria. There are no further *discretionary* steps the government can take to improve the outcome or prevent the unemployment that is caused by transient misperceptions or real-business-cycle shocks.

Although they cannot make things better, government policies can definitely make things worse.

They can generate unpredictable discretionary policies that give misleading economic signals, confuse people, distort their economic behavior, and cause waste. According to new classical macroeconomists, governments should completely avoid any discretionary macroeconomic policies rather than risk such confusing "noise."

Monetarist Rules and the Lucas Critique

Although the new classical school has shown some pitfalls that face policy-making, it has also levied a devastating argument against a key monetarist assumption. Monetarists believe that the velocity of money has shown a remarkable stability. Thus, they conclude, we can stabilize $MV \equiv PQ \equiv$ nominal GDP by imposing a fixed-money rule.

But the *Lucas critique,* named after Chicago's Robert Lucas, argues that people may change their behavior when policy changes. Just as the apparent short-run Phillips curve might shift when Keynesian governments attempt to manipulate it, so might the apparently constant velocity change if the central bank adopts a fixed-money-growth rule.

This insight was borne out in the period from 1979 to 1982, when the United States conducted the monetarist experiment described in the previous section. Velocity became extremely unstable, and eventually the Fed had to abandon the use of monetary aggregates in managing monetary policy.

The Lucas critique is a stern warning that economic behavior can change when policymakers rely too heavily upon past regularities.

STATE OF THE DEBATE

The new classical macroeconomics is quite controversial among macroeconomists. In one sense, the debate is a replay of the earlier arguments between Keynes and the classical economists. As in earlier debates, one of the key issues revolves around the extent of price and wage flexibility. Keynesian economists point to much evidence suggesting that prices and particularly wages move slowly in response to shocks, and few economists believe that labor markets are in constant supply-demand equilibrium. When the assumption of perfectly flexible wages and prices is abandoned, policy will regain its power to affect the real economy in the short run.

In addition, many economists take issue with the rational-expectations assumption that humans behave like supercomputers and incorporate the latest forecast or data into their behavior. Empirical studies of behavior have uncovered significant elements of non-rational expectations, even among the most sophisticated professional economic forecasters.

Finally, critics point to some of the counterfactual implications of new classical macroeconomics. The theory forecasts that misperceptions lie behind business-cycle fluctuations. But can misperceptions about wages and prices really explain deep depressions and persistent bouts of unemployment? Did it really take people a full decade to learn how hard times were in the Great Depression? And can Europeans be unaware of the depressed job markets that have persisted in their countries since 1990?

Moreover, how can we reconcile the theoretical prediction that cyclical unemployment is produced when workers quit to look for better jobs with the evidence showing that the fraction of job losers rises sharply in recessions (see Figure 29-8, page 572)? Because most classical theories have similar implausible implications, many mainstream economists are skeptical of the usefulness of new classical approaches for understanding short-term movements in output, employment, and goods prices.

A New Synthesis?

After two decades of digesting the new classical approach to macroeconomics, elements of a synthesis of old and new theories are beginning to appear. Economists now realize they must pay careful attention to expectations. A useful distinction is between the adaptive (or "backward-looking") approach and the rational (or "forward-looking") approach. The adaptive assumption holds that people form their expectations simply and mechanically on the basis of past information; the forward-looking or rational approach was described above. The importance of forward-looking expectations is crucial to understanding behavior, particularly in competitive auction markets like those in the financial sector.

Some macroeconomists have begun to fuse the new classical view of expectations with the Keynesian view of product and labor markets. This synthesis is embodied in macroeconomic models that assume (1) labor and goods markets display inflexible wages and prices, (2) the prices and quantities in financial

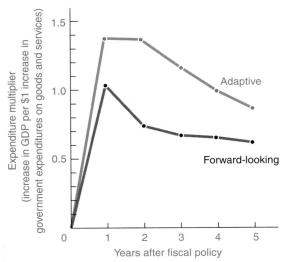

FIGURE 32-6. Comparison of Multipliers in Forward-Looking and Adaptive Models

What is the difference in the expenditure multipliers of models that are adaptive (or backward-looking) and forward-looking (or rational)? Because interest rates crowd out domestic investment and exchange rates affect net exports, adjustment takes place more rapidly in forward-looking models. Forward-looking expenditure multipliers are considerably smaller than those in adaptive models. [Source: Ralph C. Bryant, Gerald Holtham, and Peter Hooper, "Consensus and Diversity in the Model Simulations," in Ralph C. Bryant et al., eds., *Empirical Macroeconomics for Interdependent Economies* (Brookings, Washington, D.C., 1988), fig. 3-33.]

auction markets adjust rapidly to economic shocks and expectations, and (3) the expectations in auction markets are formed in a forward-looking way.

A recent survey compares the behavior of macroeconomic models that incorporate different approaches to new classical macroeconomics, focusing particularly on expectations. One salient feature is that forward-looking models tend to have large "jumps" or discontinuous changes in interest rates, stock prices, or exchange rates when major changes in policy or external events occur. For example, an election of an expansionist President or prime minister might lead people to think that inflation is on the horizon. This perception could result in a sharp jump in interest rates along with a fall in the stock market and exchange rates. Or, when the central bank unexpectedly changes its stance on inflation, as occurred in the United States in February 1994, markets may get jittery and drive up long-term interest rates in anticipation of further interest-rate increases that may follow. The prediction of "jumpy" prices replicates one realistic feature of auction markets and thus suggests where forward-looking expectations might be important in the real world.

Figure 32-6 compares another difference, the expenditure multipliers of four forward-looking models and of seven adaptive-expectations models. Note that the multipliers of the forward-looking models are significantly smaller than those of the adaptive models.

The smaller multipliers in the forward-looking models arise because of faster reactions in financial markets. One reason is that, after a fiscal expansion, interest rates generally rise more rapidly in forward-looking models because forward-looking market participants predict a future expansion of output after an increase in government spending. This higher expected future output tends to increase interest rates *today,* and investment therefore tends to decline rapidly in forward-looking models. In addition, as interest rates rise quickly in response to a fiscal stimulus in forward-looking models, the flexible exchange rate of the dollar tends to jump upward. A rise in the exchange rate of the dollar leads to a reduction in net exports and tends to reduce the size of the fiscal stimulus.

The new classical approach to macroeconomics has brought many fruitful insights. Most important, it reminds us that the economy is populated by intelligent information processors who react to and sometimes anticipate policy. This reaction and counterreaction can actually change the way the economy behaves.

D. ULTRA-CLASSICISM: SUPPLY-SIDE ECONOMICS

During most of the period from World War II until 1980, economic policy focused on the need to counter the evils of inflation and unemployment. Whenever unemployment rose, liberals would call for tax cuts or monetary ease; whenever inflation threatened, conservatives would prescribe the unpleasant medicine of tight monetary policies or expenditure cuts.

Toward the end of the 1970s, critics of the conventional approach to macroeconomics argued that economic policy had become too oriented toward the short-run management of aggregate demand. Monetarists called for a fixed-money-growth rule, while new classical economists saw governments destabilizing the economy whenever they tried to use discretionary stabilization policy. Some critics, including orthodox conservative economists, pressed for a return to more traditional policies of balancing the budget and squeezing inflation out of the economy.

In the early 1980s, yet another group joined the debate. This school, known as **supply-side economics**, emphasized incentives for people to work and to save and proposed large tax cuts to reverse slow economic growth and slumping productivity growth. Supply-side economics was espoused forcefully by President Reagan in the United States (1981–1989) and by Prime Minister Thatcher in Great Britain (1979–1990). Republican presidential candidate Bob Dole introduced a supply-side tax cut as the centerpiece of his economic policy in 1996.

MACROECONOMIC POLICIES

Although supply-side economists and political leaders have embraced a wide variety of positions, two central features of supply-side economics emerge: emphasis on incentives and advocacy of large tax cuts.

A New Emphasis on Incentives

A first theme of supply-side economics is the key role played by *incentives,* which denote adequate returns to working, saving, and entrepreneurship. Supply siders point to the miracles performed by unfettered free markets and seek to avoid the disincentives due to high tax rates; moreover, they argue

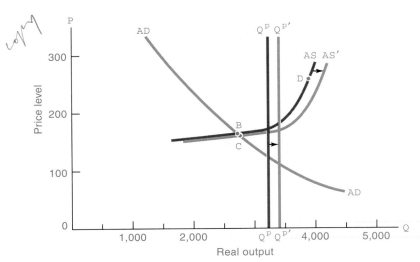

FIGURE 32-7. Impact of a Pure Supply-Side Policy
Potential output increases from $Q^P = 3200$ to $Q^{P'} = 3400$. If the *AS* curve is flat, the change in actual GDP will be small for unchanged *AD*. If *AD* cuts the *AS* curve in its classical section, such as at point *D*, almost all the increase in potential output would show up in actual output.

that Keynesians, in their excessive concern with demand management, have ignored the impact of tax rates and incentives on aggregate supply. The following discussion by a supply-side advocate explains the essential features:

> Supply-side economics emphasizes the role of fiscal policy in the determination of economic growth and aggregate supply. Our analysis relies upon straight classical price theory. According to supply-side economics, tax changes affect the economy through their effect on post-tax factor rewards rather than on dollar flows of incomes and spending; tax rates affect the relative prices of goods and thereby affect supplies of labor and capital. We seek to raise the after-tax rewards to growth activities such as labor, saving, and investment relative to leisure and consumption.
>
> It is far more important to analyze the impact of a tax change on the rate of return to labor or saving or investment than to look at the dollar amount of the tax change on disposable income. By lowering tax rates on labor or interest or dividends, we can increase saving, investment, and economic growth.[10]

What is the hypothesized relationship between tax policy and overall economic activity? In the con-

text of aggregate supply-and-demand analysis, lowering tax rates would raise the posttax return to capital and labor; higher posttax returns would induce greater labor and capital supply, along with higher rates of innovation and productivity growth; and the increase of inputs and innovation would increase the growth of potential output and thereby shift aggregate supply to the right.

Figure 32-7 illustrates the effects of a hypothetical supply-side program. Suppose that the supply-side program has the net effect of increasing the total supply of inputs like labor and capital. This increase of inputs increases potential output and shifts the *AS* curve outward as shown in the figure.

The macroeconomic impact of this supply-side measure depends upon the shape of the aggregate supply curve. If the economy is in a recession with the relatively flat *AS* curve shown at point *B* in Figure 32-7, the impact of the supply shift on actual output will be relatively modest. In the hypothetical case, the equilibrium moves from point *B* to point *C*, with a small increase of output and a tiny decrease in the overall price level.

Quite a different impact will occur if the economy behaves in a classical mode, as shown at point *D* on the *AS* curve in Figure 32-7. In this case, the

---

[10] This excerpt is a paraphrase of Stephen J. Entin, "Comments on the Critics," *Treasury News* (December 1985).

increase in potential output from Q^P to $Q^{P'}$ will translate into a substantial increase in actual output, with each unit increase in potential output producing almost a unit increase in actual output. This result shows the classical nature of supply-side economies and emphasizes that supply-side policies are likely to be most effective when the economy behaves in a classical fashion.

How large an impact are supply-side policies likely to have in reality? At the beginning of the Reagan administration, supply-side enthusiasts predicted that the program would lead to rapid economic recovery, with an anticipated growth in real GDP of 20 percent over the next 4 years. In fact, the actual growth rate fell far short of the forecast, achieving growth of only 10 percent over that period. Given the difficulty of increasing the growth of potential output, we should not be surprised to learn that the supply-side policies had little impact on potential-output growth in the 1980s. The wheels of supply-side policies grind exceedingly slowly.

Tax Cuts

The other strand of supply-side thinking emerges in its advocacy of large tax cuts. We saw in our analysis of the multiplier model how taxes could affect aggregate demand and output. Supply-side economists believe that the role of taxes in affecting aggregate demand has been overemphasized. They argue that government has too often used taxes to raise revenues or stimulate demand while ignoring the impacts of the rising tax burden on incentives. High taxes, in their view, lead people to reduce their labor and capital supply. Indeed, some supply-side economists, particularly Arthur Laffer, have suggested that high tax rates might actually lower tax revenues. This "Laffer-curve" proposition holds that high tax rates shrink the tax base because they reduce economic activity.[11] Mainstream economists across the political spectrum, and even some supply-side economists, have scoffed at the Laffer proposition that cutting tax rates today would increase tax revenues.

---

[11] Say that R = total tax revenues, t = tax rate, and B = the tax base. The Laffer proposition holds that, after a point, higher t shrinks B so rapidly that revenue ($R = tB$) actually declines.

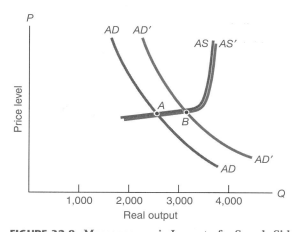

FIGURE 32-8. Macroeconomic Impact of a Supply-Side Tax Cut

Supply-side economists recommend tax cuts to promote economic growth. Tax cuts have two effects: They shift out the AD curve by multiplier analysis, and they increase potential output. Statistical studies indicate that most of the impact is on aggregate demand.

To fix what they view as a defective tax system, supply-side economists propose a radical restructuring of the tax system, through an approach sometimes called "supply-side tax cuts." The philosophy underlying supply-side tax cuts is that the reforms should improve incentives by lowering tax rates on the last dollar of income (or marginal tax rates); that the tax system should be less progressive (that is, it should lower the tax burden on high-income individuals); and that the system should be designed to encourage productivity and supply rather than to manipulate aggregate demand.

Figure 32-8 uses *AS-AD* analysis to illustrate the impact of a supply-side tax cut from a mainstream perspective. We know from our multiplier analysis that, other things being equal, tax cuts will increase consumption and increase aggregate demand. A large permanent tax cut—such as the 25 percent cut in personal taxes enacted in 1981—produces a large shift in *AD*, as shown in Figure 32-8. In addition, such a tax cut might increase potential output if labor or capital supply increased. However, economic studies indicate that the size of the potential-output increase would be modest in the short run. We therefore show the tax cut as shifting the *AS* curve only slightly to the right.

Just as the supply siders predict, the net effect of a massive supply-side tax cut is a significant increase in output. This change is shown by the movement from point *A* to point *B* in Figure 32-8. In the short run, economic expansion from supply-side tax cuts stems mainly from their impact on aggregate demand rather than the effect on potential output and aggregate supply. Some economists have argued that the Reagan economic expansion of the mid-1980s was simply a demand-side recovery dressed up in supply-side clothing.

RETROSPECTIVE

After occupying center stage during the 1980s, the supply-side approach to economics disappeared when Ronald Reagan left office. What, it can be asked, is the preliminary verdict on this experiment? While numerous questions remain, economists generally have found that many of the supply-side propositions were not supported by economic experience in the 1980s. Among the key findings are the following:

- The supply siders predicted that the major cuts in tax rates would stimulate economic activity and that incomes would rise so much that tax revenues would hardly fall and might even rise. In fact, tax revenues fell sharply relative to trend after the tax cuts, leading to an increase in the federal budget deficit that has persisted into the 1990s.
- Inflation was brought down sharply in the early 1980s. But the decline was, as Keynesian economists had predicted, bought at a high price in terms of unemployment during the deep recession of 1981–1982.
- Supply-side economists predicted that the lower tax rates, by increasing incentives for saving and investing, would increase national saving. All the supply-side encouragement of saving appears to have had no net positive effect on the national savings rate. Indeed, the national savings rate fell sharply over the 1980s and reached its lowest level since World War II in 1987.
- The fundamental goal of supply-side policies was to increase the rate of growth of potential output. The average rate of growth of potential output is estimated to have fallen from 3.6 percent

per year in 1960–1970 to 3.1 percent per year in 1970–1980 to 2.3 percent per year in 1980–1996. While the fall in potential growth in the 1980s cannot be entirely attributed to macroeconomic policies, the decline does suggest that there was no sea change in economic performance in the supply-side years.

AN INTERIM APPRAISAL

This chapter has reviewed the debates that have divided macroeconomists in recent years. How might a jury of impartial economists conclude after hearing the evidence? If it did not end up a hung jury, a few cautious and preliminary conclusions would probably emerge:

1. *Long-run economic growth.* Most macroeconomists agree that in the long run it is the potential output or capacity growth that determines the trend in living standards, real wages, and real incomes. Furthermore, potential output depends upon the quality and quantity of inputs like labor and capital as well as on the technology, entrepreneurship, and management skills in an economy. To improve long-run economic growth, economic policy must affect the growth of inputs or lead to improvements in efficiency and technology.

2. *Short-run output and employment.* In the short run, the picture is more controversial. Output and employment in the short run are determined by the interaction of aggregate supply and demand. The weight of evidence is that, at least for a few years, movements in aggregate demand (whether influenced by fiscal and monetary policies or by exogenous factors) can definitely influence the cyclical movements in output and employment. This implies that monetary and fiscal policies have the potential to stabilize business cycles. Most economists today would call upon the Federal Reserve to take the lead in stabilization policy.

3. *Unemployment and inflation.* The preponderance of the evidence indicates that inflation can be affected by the pressure of demand in labor and product markets. If unemployment is pushed above the lowest sustainable unemployment rate, inflation tends to moderate, while high output and employment tend to lead to rising

inflation. But the inflation-unemployment trade-off appears to be unstable over time and space, so managing inflation is a complicated process. Moreover, there does not appear to be a permanent tradeoff, so countries cannot buy permanently lower unemployment by allowing high inflation to persist.

Beyond these three major conclusions that emerge from our review of the warring factions in macroeconomics, there are many fine points and continuing controversies that must be left to advanced treatises. In the next chapter, we put these conclusions to work so that we can understand the major policy issues of today.

SUMMARY

A. Classical Stirrings and Keynesian Revolution

1. Classical economists relied upon Say's Law of Markets, which holds that "supply creates its own demand." In modern language, the classical approach means that flexible wages and prices quickly erase any excess supply or demand and quickly reestablish full employment and full utilization of capacity. In a classical system, macroeconomic policy has no role to play in stabilizing the real economy, although it will still determine the path of prices.

2. The Keynesian revolution postulated inflexibility of prices and wages, so output and unemployment are determined by the interaction of supply and demand forces. The Keynesian *AS* curve is upward-sloping rather than classically vertical, and monetary or fiscal policies therefore affect both prices and real output. There is no automatic self-correcting price mechanism, and the economy can therefore experience prolonged periods of depression or inflation.

3. In the modern Keynesian view, monetary and fiscal policies can substitute for flexible wages and prices, stimulating the economy during recessions and slowing aggregate demand during booms to forestall inflationary tendencies.

B. The Monetarist Approach

4. Monetarism holds that the money supply is the primary determinant of short-run movements in both real and nominal GDP as well as of long-run movements in nominal GDP.

5. Monetarism relies upon the analysis of trends in the velocity of money to understand the impact of money on the economy. The income velocity of circulation of money (V) is defined as the ratio of the dollar GDP flow to the stock of *M:*

$$V \equiv \frac{\text{GDP}}{M} \equiv \frac{PQ}{M}$$

While V is definitely not a constant—if only because it rises with interest rates—monetarists count on its movements being regular and predictable.

6. From velocity's definition comes the quantity theory of prices:

$$P \equiv kM \quad \text{where } k \equiv \frac{V}{Q}$$

The quantity theory of prices regards P as almost strictly proportional to M. This view is useful for understanding hyperinflations and certain long-term trends, but it should not be taken literally.

7. The monetarist school holds to three major propositions: (*a*) The growth of the money supply is the major systematic determinant of nominal GDP growth; (*b*) prices and wages are relatively flexible; and (*c*) the private economy is stable. These propositions suggest that macroeconomic fluctuations arise primarily from erratic money-supply growth.

8. Monetarism is generally associated with a laissez-faire and anti-big-government political philosophy. Because of a desire to avoid active government and a belief in the inherent stability of the private sector, monetarists often propose that the money supply grow at a fixed rate of 3 or 5 percent annually. Some monetarists believe that this will produce steady growth with stable prices in the long run.

9. The Federal Reserve conducted a full-scale monetarist experiment from 1979 to 1982. The experience from this period convinced remaining skeptics that money is a powerful determinant of aggregate demand and that most of the short-run effects of money changes are on output rather than on prices. However, as suggested by the Lucas critique, velocity may become quite unstable when a monetarist approach is followed.

C. New Classical Macroeconomics

10. New classical macroeconomics rests on two fundamental hypotheses: People's expectations are formed efficiently and rationally, and prices and wages are flexible. It follows from these assumptions in a new classical economy that unemployment is voluntary. Further, the Phillips curve is vertical in the short run, even though it may appear otherwise. The theory of

the real business cycle points to supply-side techno-logical disturbances and labor market shifts as the clue to business-cycle fluctuations.

11. The policy ineffectiveness theorem holds that pre-dictable government policies cannot affect real out-put and unemployment. The new classical theory states that, while we may *observe* a downward-sloping short-run Phillips curve, we cannot *exploit* the slope for the purposes of lowering unemployment. If eco-nomic policymakers systematically attempt to increase output and decrease unemployment, people will soon come to understand and to anticipate the policy. Fixed policy rules will produce better economic out-comes.

12. Critics of new classical macroeconomics argue that prices and wages are inflexible in the short run. And the predictions—particularly that business cycles are caused by misperceptions and that cyclical unemploy-ment comes when confused people quit their jobs—seem farfetched as an explanation of serious down-turns, like those of the 1930s or early 1980s in the United States and of the 1990s in Europe.

D. Ultra-Classicism: Supply-Side Economics

13. In the 1980s, supply-side economists proposed a new approach to macroeconomic policy-making: (*a*) a non-Keynesian approach to fiscal policy, focusing on the medium run, avoiding fine-tuning of the economy, and downplaying the importance of changes in aggre-gate demand; (*b*) a new emphasis on economic incen-tives—paying particular attention to the impact of tax policy on posttax returns to labor and capital, as this impact was seen as determining saving, investment, and labor supply; and (*c*) advocacy of large tax cuts, sometimes holding that these might actually pay for themselves by generating larger revenues.

14. The historical record of the 1980s suggests that supply-side policies were not successful in improving the per-formance of the U.S. economy. The legacy of this period was stubborn federal budget deficits, slow growth in potential output, and a low national savings rate.

15. Study the interim appraisal for the current main-stream synthesis of the warring schools of macroeco-nomics.

CONCEPTS FOR REVIEW

Keynes vs. the Classical Economists

flexible vs. sticky wages and prices
Say's Law of Markets
alternative views of aggregate supply

Velocity and Monetarism

velocity of circulation of money:
$$MV \equiv PQ$$
1979–1982 monetarist experiment

quantity theory of money and prices:
$$P \equiv kM$$

New Classical Macroeconomics

rational (forward-looking) expecta-tions, adaptive (backward-looking) expectations
policy ineffectiveness theorem
real business cycle, efficiency wages

key assumptions: rational expecta-tions and flexible prices and wages
Lucas critique

Supply-Side Economics

tenets of supply-side economics
impact of policies on economic per-formance

QUESTIONS FOR DISCUSSION

1. Monetarists say, "Only money matters." Keynesians answer, "Money matters, but other things, like fiscal policy, matter too." Explain and evaluate each posi-tion. Could you disagree with monetarists and still believe that monetary policy should be used to counter recessions? Explain.

2. Assume that nominal GDP was $1000 billion in year 0 while the GDP deflator was 1 in year 0. Furthermore, the money supply in years 0, 1, 2, 3, and 4 was (in bil-lions) $50, $52, $55, $58, and $60.
   a. Give the level of nominal output in years 1, 2, 3, and 4 according to the strict quantity theory of money.

   b. If there was no growth in potential output and the level of the money supply was following a pre-announced path, what would the level of real GDP be according to the new classical macroeco-nomics?

3. If, in boom times, we printed and spent $100 trillion in new greenbacks, what would happen to prices? Is there some truth, then, to the quantity theory? What might happen to prices if *M* were increased 1 percent in a depression? Compare the two cases.

4. A supply-side economist might recommend a large tax cut to revive the economy. How might such a measure affect the *AS* curve? The *AD* curve? The resulting

levels of price and real output? Does this point to a limitation of the quantity theory?

5. Define income velocity (V). For the data in Table 32-1, calculate the annual growth rate of the money supply and the level and rate of change of velocity. Also draw or plot on a computer graphs of the variables.

6. The *Economic Report of the President*, 1994, contains the following analysis of the impact of taxes on economic behavior: "Evidence from postwar experience strongly suggests that personal income tax revenues rise when marginal tax rates are increased, and fall when marginal rates are reduced" (p. 89). How does this conclusion relate to the beliefs of supply-side economists? What implication does it have for the role of taxes in reducing government deficits and stabilizing the economy?

7. What would monetarists, Keynesians, supply siders, and new classical macroeconomists predict to be the impacts of each of the following on the course of prices, output, and employment (in each case, hold tax rates and the money supply constant unless specifically mentioned):

   a. A large tax cut
   b. A large increase in the money supply
   c. A wave of innovations that increase potential output by 10 percent
   d. A burst of exports

8. In the discussion of the demand for money, and in the demand-for-money schedule in Figure 26-4 (page 505), it was shown that the demand for money would be sensitive to interest rates. What would be the impact of higher interest rates on velocity for a given level of nominal GDP? What are the implications of interest-sensitive demand for money on monetarist arguments that rely upon constant velocity of money?

9. State and explain Say's Law of Markets. Starting from a macroeconomic equilibrium, assume that potential output increases but aggregate demand is unchanged. Using a graphical extension of Figure 32-1, show how supply creates its own demand. Describe the process in words.

10. **Advanced problem** (on rational expectations): Consider the effect of rational expectations on consumption behavior. Say the government proposes a temporary tax cut of $20 billion, lasting for a year. Consumers with adaptive expectations might assume that their disposable incomes would be $20 billion higher every year. What would be the impact on consumption spending and GDP in the simple multiplier model of Chapter 24?

   Next suppose that consumers have rational expectations. They rationally forecast that the tax cut is for only 1 year. Being "life-cycle" consumers, they recognize that their average lifetime incomes will increase (say) only $2 billion per year, not $20 billion per year. What would be the reaction of such consumers? Analyze, then, the impact of rational expectations on the effectiveness of temporary tax cuts.

TABLE 32-1.

Year	Nominal GDP ($, billion)	Money supply, M_1 ($, billion, lagged 12 months)
1981	3,053	408.9
1982	3,166	436.5
1983	3,406	474.5
1984	3,772	521.2
1985	4,015	522.1
1986	4,232	620.1
1987	4,516	724.7
1988	4,874	750.4
1989	5,201	787.5
1990	5,463	794.8

CHAPTER 33
POLICIES FOR GROWTH AND STABILITY

> The task of economic stabilization requires keeping the economy from straying too far above or below the path of steady high employment. One way lies inflation, and the other lies recession. Flexible and vigilant fiscal and monetary policy will allow us to hold the narrow middle course.
>
> *President John F. Kennedy (1962)*
>
> Productivity isn't everything, but in the long run it is almost everything.
>
> *Paul Krugman (1990)*

The U.S. economy has changed enormously over the last 50 years. A much smaller share of the population works in factories, and many more people work behind desks and in stores and hospitals. Taxes are higher, and big government has become a permanent part of the economic landscape. Technology has revolutionized daily life: advanced telecommunications systems enable businesses to spread their operations across the country and around the world, and ever-more-powerful computers have eliminated many of the repetitive tasks which used to employ so many people. Goods and money flow much more easily across national boundaries, and, after dominating the world economy in the years following World War II, the United States now faces competition from countries large and small.

Yet, after a half-century of change, the central goals of good macroeconomic policy are unchanged: good jobs, low unemployment, rising productivity and real incomes, and low and stable inflation. The challenge is to find a set of policies which can achieve these objectives in the economy of the 1990s and beyond.

This chapter uses the tools of macroeconomics that we have developed to examine some of today's major policy issues. We begin with an assessment of the consequences of government deficits and debt on economic activity. We then analyze controversies involving short-run economic stabilization, including current questions on the merits of monetary policy and fiscal policy. Should the government stop trying to smooth out business cycles and, instead, rely on fixed rules rather than discretion? We conclude with an analysis of the nagging worries posed by the slowdown in productivity and real wage growth over the last two decades and inquire into the policies that countries can pursue to improve their productivity and growth performance.

A. THE ECONOMIC CONSEQUENCES OF THE DEBT

Like a monster rising from the deep, the budget deficit seemed to swallow up the nation's fiscal resources and terrify the populace in the 1980s and early 1990s. From $40 billion in 1979, the budget deficit grew to a peak of $290 billion in 1992. Although the deficit has declined since then, preventing large deficits remains one of the nation's top economic priorities. Politicians routinely take the floor in the Senate or the House to denounce the deficit or to defend a constitutional amendment requiring a balanced budget.

How did the budget deficit get so high when people so regularly denounce it? We will see that the popular concern with deficits has a firm economic foundation. A high deficit and government debt during periods of full employment carry serious consequences, including reduced national saving and investment and slower long-run economic growth.

Trends and Definitions

For the first two centuries after the American Revolution, the federal government of the United States generally balanced its fiscal budget. Heavy military spending during wartime was financed by borrowing, so the government debt—the total amount owed by the government—tended to soar in wartime. In peacetime, the government would pay off some of its debt, and the debt burden would shrink.

This pattern changed during the 1980s, when the Reagan administration's supply-side policies produced a major tax cut and defense buildup without an offsetting decrease in civilian spending. With less revenue and more spending, the government had to borrow to fill the gap. The federal budget deficit grew to over $200 billion a year by the mid-1980s, and the government debt during the Reagan-Bush years (1981–1992) increased from $660 billion to $3 trillion. The persistent deficit has dramatically changed the ground rules for fiscal policy.

Governments use budgets to plan and control their fiscal affairs. A **budget** shows, for a given year, the planned expenditures of government programs and the expected revenues from tax systems. The budget typically contains a list of specific programs (education, welfare, defense, etc.), as well as tax sources (individual income tax, social-insurance taxes, etc.).

A **budget surplus** occurs when all taxes and other revenues exceed government expenditures for a year. A **budget deficit** is incurred when expenditures exceed taxes. When revenues and expenditures are equal during a given period—a rare event on the federal level—the government has a **balanced budget**.

When the government incurs a budget deficit, it must borrow from the public to pay its bills. To borrow, the government issues bonds, which are IOUs that promise to pay money in the future. The **government debt** (sometimes called the *public debt*) consists of the total or accumulated borrowings by the government; it is the total dollar value of government bonds owned by the public (households, banks, businesses, foreigners, and other nonfederal entities).

One key point to remember about debt and deficits is the following: The government debt is the stock of liabilities of the government. The deficit is a flow of new debt incurred when the government spends more than it raises in taxes. Never confuse the stock of debt with the flow of deficits.

GOVERNMENT BUDGET POLICY

The government budget serves two major economic functions. First, it is a device by which the government can set national priorities, allocating national output among private and public consumption and investment and providing incentives to increase or reduce output in particular sectors. From a macroeconomic point of view, it is through fiscal policy that the budget affects the key macroeconomic goals. More precisely, by **fiscal policy** we mean the setting of taxes and public expenditures to help dampen the swings of the business cycle and contribute to the maintenance of a growing, high-employment economy, free from high or volatile inflation.

Some early enthusiasts of the Keynesian approach believed that fiscal policy was like a knob they could turn to control or "fine-tune" the pace of the economy. A bigger budget deficit meant more stimulus for aggregate demand, which could lower unemployment and pull the economy out of recession. A smaller budget deficit or a budget surplus could slow down an overheated economy and dampen the threat of inflation.

Today, few believe that the business cycle can be quite so easily eliminated. Some 60 years after Keynes, recessions and inflations are still with us, and fiscal policy works better in theory than in practice. Moreover, monetary policy has become the preferred tool for moderating economic swings. Still, whenever unemployment rises, there is usually strong public

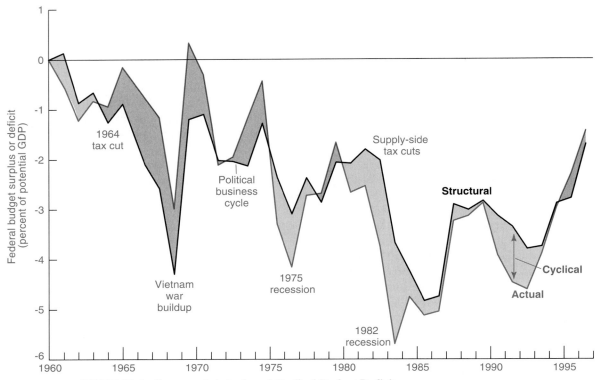

FIGURE 33-1. Structural, Actual, and Cyclical Budget Deficits

The rust line shows the actual budget deficit or surplus (as a percentage of potential GDP). The black curve depicts the structural component. The difference between the actual and structural deficits or surpluses is the cyclical deficit or surplus. (Source: Congressional Budget Office.)

pressure for the government to boost spending. In this section, we will review the major ways in which government can employ fiscal policy, and we will examine the practical shortcomings that have become apparent.

Cyclical, Structural, and Actual Budgets

Modern public finance distinguishes between structural and cyclical deficits. The idea is simple. The *structural* part of the budget is active—determined by discretionary policies such as those covering tax rates, public-works or education spending, or the size of defense purchases. In contrast, the *cyclical* part of the budget is determined passively by the state of the business cycle, that is, by the extent to which national income and output are high or low. The precise definitions follow:

The **actual budget** records the actual dollar expenditures, revenues, and deficits in a given period.

The **structural budget** calculates what government revenues, expenditures, and deficits would be if the economy were operating at potential output.

The **cyclical budget** is the difference between the actual budget and the structural budget. It measures the impact of the business cycle on the budget, taking into account the effect of the cycle on revenues, expenditures, and the deficit.

The actual, structural, and cyclical budget deficits as a share of GDP are shown in Figure 33-1. The distinction between the actual and the structural budgets is important for policymakers who want to distinguish between long-term or trend budget changes and short-term changes that are primarily driven by the business cycle. Structural spending and revenues consist of the discretionary programs

Budget component	Percent of GDP		
	1979	1990	1997
Expenditures	**20.7**	**21.9**	**20.3**
Social security	4.3	4.6	4.6
General operating budget	16.4	17.3	15.7
Health care	1.7	2.7	3.8
Net interest	1.8	3.4	3.1
Subtotal, health and interest	3.4	6.1	6.9
All other	13.0	11.2	8.8
Defense	4.8	5.5	3.4
Civilian	8.2	5.8	5.4
Revenues	**19.1**	**18.9**	**19.8**
Social security	4.0	5.2	5.6
General operating budget	15.1	13.7	14.2
Surplus or deficit (−)	**−1.7**	**−3.0**	**−0.4**

TABLE 33-1. Federal Budget Trends, 1979–1997
The federal budget deficit is the difference between spending and revenues. From 1979 to 1990, the share of revenues was stable while those of interest and health-care costs grew rapidly. The deficit-reduction packages of 1990 and 1993 reduced the deficit share, but rising health-care costs are still a wild card. [Source: Charles L. Schultze, "Paying the Bills," in Henry J. Aaron and Charles L. Schultze, eds., *Setting Domestic Priorities: What Can Government Do?* (Brookings, Washington, D.C., 1992), updated by authors using data from the Congressional Budget Office.]

enacted by the legislature; cyclical spending and deficits consist of the taxes and spending that react automatically to the state of the economy.

The experience from 1992 through 1996 is an interesting application of these concepts. From 1992 to 1996, the federal deficit declined from $290 to $107 billion. President Clinton proclaimed that his policies had been successful in reducing the budget deficit by more than half. Critics replied that it was mainly the improved business cycle that was responsible, rather than his policies. This argument is resolved by examining the movement of the structural budget deficit over this period. According to the Congressional Budget Office (CBO), the structural deficit over this period declined from $224 billion in 1992 to $125 billion in 1996. Therefore, of the $183 billion in deficit reduction, $99 billion was due to a reduction in the structural deficit. About half the deficit reduction was due to policies and the other half was due to improved economic conditions.

The nation's savings and investment balance is primarily affected by the structural budget. Efforts to reduce the deficit should focus on the structural budget because no durable deficit reduction comes simply from a reduction due to an economic boom.

The Roaring Eighties

Since the early 1980s, the most perplexing macroeconomic controversies have revolved around the mounting federal budget deficit. Even though Congress passed laws attempting to stop the rising tide of red ink, the deficit climbed throughout this period. Deficits were not new to the American economy, but a deficit of such a magnitude during peacetime was unique, unusual, and disturbing.

Why did the deficit get so large? Republicans blamed the growing deficit on 50 years of Democratic "tax-and-spend" policies. Democrats counterattacked that Republican presidents were responsible and pointed to supply-side policies as the culprit in the mounting government debt.

What are the facts? No simple analysis can resolve this complex question, but Table 33-1 can help illuminate the major trends. This table lists the major federal budget categories and their shares in GDP for 1979, 1990, and 1997. These years were chosen

	Ratio of debt to gross domestic product (%)			
Country	1974	1979	1989	1993
Italy	45	56	96	113
Canada	5	12	40	60
United States	22	19	30	39
United Kingdom	60	48	30	42
France	8	14	25	36
Germany	−5	12	23	28
Japan	−5	15	15	6

TABLE 33-2. Budget Trends in Major Industrial Countries

The United States was not alone in its rising debt-GDP ratio. Only the United Kingdom under Margaret Thatcher succeeded in lowering the debt burden in the 1980s. [Source: *OECD Economic Outlook* (December 1993).]

because they were full-employment years, so the actual budgets were close to the structural budgets. The data show that during the 1980s the structural deficit increased from 1.7 to 3.0 percent of GDP. The key features behind this change were the following:

- The share of federal revenues in GDP declined over this period. And this was true even though the share of social security taxes on payrolls increased. The income-tax reductions of the early 1980s clearly contributed to the growing deficit.
- Expenditures rose over the period, but by only 1.2 percent of GDP. This increase was less than the average decadal rise over the prior half-century.
- The major unplanned increases in the budget were in interest payments and in health care, which together rose by 2.7 percent of GDP. Each of these poses stubborn long-term problems of control: Interest payments are nondiscretionary and can be reduced only by lowering either interest rates or the size of the government debt. Health-care expenditures are insulated from the normal play of supply and demand in the marketplace.
- Public concern over the high deficits led to a series of controversial deficit-reduction measures, the most important being the 1990 and 1993 budget acts of the Bush and Clinton administrations. These put tight caps on expenditure growth and raised taxes, especially on high-income households. The result—as shown in Table 33-1—was that by 1997 the federal budget was approaching balance.

ECONOMIC IMPACT OF DEFICITS AND DEBT

What are the various economic problems created by large deficits? What is the relationship between private saving and public saving? Answering these questions is an important task for macroeconomics. At one extreme, we must avoid the customary practice of assuming that public deficits are bad because private debtors are punished. On the other hand, we must recognize the genuine problems associated with excessive government deficits.

Historical Trends

Long-run data for the United States appear in the figure on the front endpaper of this text, which shows the ratio of federal debt to GDP since 1789. Notice how wars drove up the ratio of debt to GDP, while rapid output growth with roughly balanced budgets in peacetime normally reduced the ratio of debt to GDP. After 1980, the historical pattern changed and government deficits climbed in a way not seen in earlier periods of peace and prosperity.

Most other industrialized countries today find themselves in a similar quandary. Table 33-2 compares the United States with six other large industrial countries. Only Japan has kept its debt-GDP ratio down to a relatively low level.

To understand how government debt and deficits affect the economy, it is useful to analyze the short-run and the long-run outcomes separately. In the short run, the stock of government debt is given, and the deficit may affect the business cycle and the saving-investment balance. The short-run impact of budget deficits upon the economy is known as "crowding out," which we address first. In the long run, which is usefully analyzed as a full-employment economy, the government debt affects current capital formation and the consumption of future generations. This issue, known as the "burden of the debt," is considered at the end of this section.

THE CROWDING-OUT CONTROVERSY

Politicians and business leaders often argue that government spending undermines the economy, saying in effect, "Government spending saps our nation's vitality. When the government spends people's money on entitlement programs, these funds simply crowd out private investment."

This argument—that government spending reduces private investment—invokes the **crowding-out hypothesis**. In its extreme form, this hypothesis suggests that when the government purchases $100 in goods and services, private investment and other interest-sensitive spending falls by $100.

Crowding Out and the Money Market

What is the crowding-out mechanism? Suppose that the government spends money on school lunches or fuel for its ships. Our multiplier model says that in the short run, with no change in interest or exchange rates, GDP will rise by 2 or 3 times the increase in G. The same argument applies (with a smaller multiplier) to reductions in taxes.

This analysis is oversimplified because it must take into account the reaction of financial markets. As output and inflation rise, their increase is likely to provoke a monetary tightening, increasing interest rates and leading to an appreciation of the foreign exchange rate if the country has a floating exchange rate. The rising interest rates and appreciated currency will tend to choke off or "crowd out" domestic and foreign investment.[1] We showed the

---

[1] Recall that tight money leads to reduced spending in interest-sensitive sectors such as business investment, housing, consumption spending on consumer durables, net exports, and capital items of state and local governments. In the discussion that follows, we will examine the impact on investment, but keep in mind that the other components of spending are just as important.

way a fiscal deficit would lead to lower domestic and foreign investment in Chapter 31's analysis of savings and investment (see particularly Figures 31-5 and 31-6).

An increase in the *structural* deficit, coming through tax cuts or higher government spending, will tend to raise interest rates and reduce or crowd out investment.

But be warned: Crowding out applies only to structural deficits. If the cyclical deficit rises because of a recession, the logic of crowding out simply does not apply. A recession causes a *decline* in the demand for money and leads to *lower* interest rates; the monetary authority tends to *loosen* monetary policy in a recession. The fact that crowding out does not apply in recessions is a reminder that there is no automatic link between deficits and investment.

Empirical Evidence

Does actual experience corroborate crowding-out theories? It depends on which period you are looking at. During the 1960s, fiscal expansions appear to have encouraged investment, partly because there were ample unutilized resources and partly because the Federal Reserve allowed the economy to expand without raising interest rates.

In the 1980s, by contrast, higher government deficits definitely did appear to discourage investment. The actual pattern of saving and investment for three periods before, during, and after the supply-side experiment of the 1980s is given in Table 33-3 on page 650. We conclude from this, first, that households and businesses actually reduced their saving as a share of GDP in the 1980s and early 1990s. This reduction was surprising because they were faced with lower tax rates and higher posttax real returns on saving.

Second, private domestic investment in housing and business plant and equipment fell as a share of GDP in the late 1980s and early 1990s. To some degree this occurred because of a glut in the real-estate market following the earlier building boom. But it seems clear that business investment was also being crowded out by the higher interest rates of that period.

Third, a significant part of the impact came in a decline in net foreign investment. As we emphasized in our survey of open-economy macroeconomics, countries with flexible exchange rates and mobile

Sector	National Saving and Investment (Percent of GDP)		
	Pre-supply-side years (1977–1980)	Supply-side years (1981–1988)	Post-supply-side years (1989–1996)
Average gross saving:			
Personal	4.0	4.3	3.4
Business	12.4	12.3	11.5
Government	0.6	−2.9	−2.6
Average gross investment:			
Private domestic investment (includes residential and business)	18.0	16.4	14.0
Net foreign investment	−1.2	−2.6	−1.5

TABLE 33-3. Higher Government Deficit Produced Surprising Results

The increase in deficits of the 1980s provided a laboratory for different macroeconomic theories. During the supply-side years, the government deficits (or dissaving) grew sharply. Public dissaving was reinforced by lower personal and business saving. The impact was seen on both domestic and foreign investment. (Source: U.S. Department of Commerce. Note that gross investment does not sum to gross saving because of statistical discrepancies.)

capital will see some of their savings changes spill over into world financial markets. Without this inflow of foreign capital, the budget deficits would have crowded out even more private investment.

The events of the last decade—particularly the decline in investment—lend support to the argument that structural government budget deficits do indeed crowd out private investment. But this link is not an absolute law which holds for all situations. The connection between deficit spending and investment depends on so many factors—including savings behavior, expectations, foreign exchange rates and foreign trade, financial markets, and monetary policy—that the exact impact of fiscal-policy changes is difficult to predict.

GOVERNMENT DEBT AND ECONOMIC GROWTH

We turn now from the short-run impact of government deficits to ask how the government debt affects living standards over the long run. To answer this, we need to analyze the difficulties of servicing a large external debt, the inefficiencies of levying taxes to pay interest on the debt, and the impact of the debt on capital accumulation.

External vs. Internal Debt

The first distinction to be made is between an internal debt and an external debt. An *internal debt* is owed by a nation to its own citizens. Many argue that an internal debt poses no burden because "we owe it all to ourselves." While this statement is oversimplified, it does represent a genuine insight. If each citizen owned $10,000 of government bonds and were liable for the taxes to service just that debt, it would make no sense to think of debt as a heavy load of rocks that each citizen must carry. People simply owe the debt to themselves.

An *external debt* is owed by a nation to foreigners. This debt does involve a net subtraction from the resources available to people in the debtor nation. In the 1980s, many nations experienced severe economic hardships after they incurred large external debts. They were forced to export more than they imported—to run trade surpluses—in order to service their external debts, that is, to pay the interest and principal on their past borrowings. Countries like Brazil and Mexico need to set aside one-fourth to one-third of their export earnings to service their external debts. The debt-service burden on an external debt represents a reduction in the consumption possibilities of a nation.

In the late 1980s, the United States joined the list of debtor countries when large external deficits transformed America from a creditor nation into a debtor nation. By 1996, the United States owed close to $1000 billion to foreigners. While that seems like a large sum, it pales next to an annual output of $7500 billion. Still, the United States will need to export many billions of dollars more in aircraft, food, and other goods and services than it imports to pay the interest on its foreign loans.

Efficiency Losses from Taxation

An internal debt requires payments of interest to bondholders, and taxes must be levied for this purpose. But even if the same people were taxed to pay the same amounts they receive in interest, there would still be the *distorting effects on incentives* that are inescapably present in the case of any taxes. Taxing Paula's interest income or wages to pay Paula interest would introduce microeconomic distortions. Paula might work less and save less; either of these outcomes must be reckoned as a distortion of efficiency and well-being.

Displacement of Capital

Perhaps the most serious consequence of a large public debt is that it displaces capital from the nation's stock of private wealth. As a result, the pace of economic growth slows and future living standards will decline.

What is the mechanism by which debt affects capital? Recall from our earlier discussion that people accumulate wealth for a variety of purposes, such as retirement, education, and housing. We can separate the assets people hold into two groups: (1) government debt and (2) capital like houses and financial assets like corporate stocks that represent ownership of the stock of private capital.

The effect of government debt is that people will accumulate government debt instead of private capital, and the nation's private capital stock will be displaced by public debt.

To illustrate this point, suppose that people desire to hold exactly 1000 units of wealth for retirement and other purposes. As the government debt increases, people's holdings of other assets will be reduced dollar for dollar. This occurs because as the government sells its bonds, other assets must be reduced, since total desired wealth holdings are fixed. But these other assets ultimately represent the stock of private capital; stocks, bonds, and mortgages are the counterparts of factories, equipment, and houses. In this example, if the government debt goes up 100 units, we would see that people's holdings of capital and other private assets fall by 100 units. This is the case of 100 percent displacement (which is the long-run analog of 100 percent crowding out).

Full displacement is unlikely to hold in practice. The higher debt may increase interest rates and stimulate domestic saving. In addition, the country may borrow abroad rather than reduce its domestic capital stock (as America did in the 1980s). The exact amount of capital displacement will depend on the conditions of production and on the savings behavior of domestic households and foreigners.

A Geometric Analysis. The process by which the stock of capital is displaced in the long run is illustrated in Figure 33-2 on page 652. The left panel shows the supply and demand for capital as a function of the real interest rate or return on capital. As interest rates rise, firms demand less capital, while individuals may want to supply more. The equilibrium shown is for a capital stock of 4000 units with a real interest rate of 4 percent.

Now say that the government debt rises from 0 to 1000—because of war, recession, supply-side fiscal policies, or some other reason. The impact of the increase in debt can be seen in the right-hand diagram of Figure 33-2. This figure shows the 1000-unit increase in debt as a shift in the supply-of-capital (or SS) curve. As depicted, the households' supply-of-capital schedule shifts 1000 units to the left, to $S'S'$.

We represent an increase in government debt as a leftward shift in the households' supply-of-capital schedule. Note that, because the SS curve represents the amount of private capital that people willingly hold at each interest rate, the capital holdings are equal to the total wealth holdings minus the holdings of government debt. Since the amount of government debt (or assets other than capital) rises by 1000, the amount of private capital that people can buy after they own the 1000 units of government debt is 1000 less than total wealth at each interest rate. Therefore, if SS represents the total wealth held by people, $S'S'$ (equal to SS less 1000) represents the total amount of capital held by people. In short, after

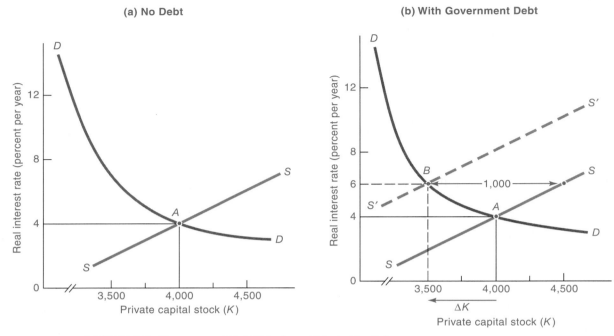

(a) No Debt   **(b) With Government Debt**

FIGURE 33-2. Government Debt Displaces Private Capital

Firms demand capital, while households supply capital by saving in private and public assets. The demand curve is the downward-sloping business demand for *K*, while the supply curve is the upward-sloping household supply of *K*.

Before-debt case in (**a**) shows the equilibrium without government debt: *K* is 4000 and the real interest rate is 4 percent.

After-debt case in (**b**) shows the impact of 1000 units of government debt. Debt shifts the net supply of *K* to the left by the 1000 units of the government debt. The new equilibrium arises northwest along the demand-for-*K* curve, moving from point *A* to point *B*. The interest rate is higher, firms are discouraged from holding *K*, and the capital stock falls.

1000 units of government debt are sold, the new supply-of-capital schedule is *S'S'*.

As the supply of capital dries up—with national saving going into government bonds rather than into housing or into companies' stocks and bonds—the market equilibrium moves northwest along the demand-for-*K* curve. Interest rates rise. Firms slow their purchases of new factories, trucks, and computers.

In the illustrative new long-run equilibrium, the capital stock falls from 4000 to 3500. Thus, in this example, 1000 units of government debt have displaced 500 units of private capital. Such a reduction has significant economic effects, of course. With less

capital, potential output, wages, and the nation's income are lower than they would otherwise be.

The diagrams in Figure 33-2 are illustrative. Economists do not have a firm estimate of the magnitude of the displacement effect. Looking at historical trends, the best evidence suggests that domestic capital is partially displaced by government debt but that some of the impact comes in higher foreign debt.

Debt and Growth

Considering all the effects of government debt on the economy, a large public debt is likely to reduce long-run economic growth. Figure 33-3 illustrates this connection. Say that an economy were to operate over time with no debt. According to the principles of economic growth outlined in Chapter 28, the capital stock and potential output would follow the hypothetical paths indicated by the solid black lines in Figure 33-3.

Next consider a situation with a growing national debt. As the debt accumulates over time, more and more capital is displaced, as shown by the dashed rust line for the capital stock in the bottom of Figure 33-3. As taxes are raised to pay interest on the debt, inefficiencies further lower output. Also, an increase in external debt lowers national income and raises the fraction of national output that has to be set aside for servicing the external debt. Taking all the effects together, output and consumption will grow more slowly than they would have had there been no large government debt and deficit, as can be seen by comparing the top lines in Figure 33-3.

This is the major point about the long-run impact of a large government debt on economic growth: A large government debt tends to reduce a nation's growth in potential output because it displaces private capital, increases the inefficiency from taxation, and forces a nation to reduce consumption to service its foreign borrowing.

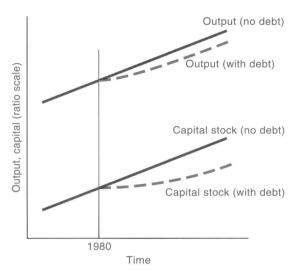

FIGURE 33-3. Impact of Government Debt on Economic Growth

The solid lines show the paths of capital and output if the government balances its books and has no debt. When the government incurs a debt, private capital is reduced. The dashed lines illustrate the impact on capital and output of the higher government debt.

Concluding Thoughts on Deficits and Debt

As we end our discussion of the government debt and its impact on economic growth, it is useful to pause to reflect upon the fiscal experience of the last two decades. Following a set of controversial policy measures—the supply-side tax cuts—of the early 1980s, the United States entered a period of large deficits and rapidly growing government debt. For more than a decade, the Congress, President, and public struggled to right the fiscal ship and move toward a balanced budget. During this time, as Charles Schultze noted, "the large deficits made it virtually impossible for [the federal government] to seriously consider major new programs or substantial additions to existing ones."[2] Faced with the large deficits, the federal government radically changed its approach to budgeting, enacted several major tax increases, and curbed some of its growing entitlement programs.

By 1997, as a result, the budget outlook was dramatically improved. The deficit had declined to less than 1 percent of GDP—the smallest of any major industrial country. Most budget analysts believed that the federal government might even run budget surpluses unless bad luck or bad judgment intervened. This episode shows the great difficulties posed by the need to change deeply entrenched fiscal problems, but it also demonstrates that concerted application of standard fiscal tools will do the job.

---

[2] Charles L. Schultze, "Paying the Bills," in Henry J. Aaron and Charles L. Schultze, eds., *Setting Domestic Priorities: What Can Government Do?* (Brookings, Washington, D.C., 1992), p. 295.

B. STABILIZING THE ECONOMY

Events of the last few years show that no country, no matter how well managed, is immune from recession. In the early 1990s the United States, Germany, and Japan—the three strongest economies in the world—all slipped into lingering downturns in which job growth stopped and incomes fell. While inflation has been stilled in most countries, few can forget the runaway price increases of the 1970s and early 1980s.

That means it is still critical to find policies which strike the proper balance between growth and inflation. We have seen that the path of output and prices is determined by the interaction of aggregate supply and demand. But *policies* to stabilize the business cycle must operate primarily through their impact on aggregate demand. In other words, the primary way that government can counter recessions or slow inflation is by using its monetary and fiscal levers to affect the growth in aggregate demand. For example, government can take steps to stimulate aggregate demand. More rapid growth in aggregate demand will then lead to higher levels of real output; it will also increase the pressure on wages and prices and tend to increase the rate of inflation.

But these observations leave open two crucial questions: To stabilize the economy, what is the best division of labor between monetary and fiscal policies? And having answered that question, we would then ask, Is it possible that monetary and fiscal policymakers do more harm than good by actively trying to stabilize the economy?

THE INTERACTION OF MONETARY AND FISCAL POLICIES

For a large economy like the United States, the best combination of monetary and fiscal policies will depend upon two factors: the need for demand management and the desired fiscal-monetary mix.

Demand Management

The top consideration for any economic policymaker—whether the President or the Federal Reserve Chairman—is the overall state of the economy and the need to adjust aggregate demand. When the economy is stagnating, fiscal and monetary policies can be used to stimulate the economy and promote economic recovery. When inflation threatens, monetary and fiscal policies can help slow the economy and dampen inflationary fires. These are examples of *demand management,* which refers to the active use of monetary and fiscal policies to affect the level of aggregate demand.

Suppose, for example, that the economy is entering a severe recession. Aggregate demand is depressed relative to potential output. What can the government do to revive the lagging economy? It can manage aggregate demand by raising money growth or increasing the structural budget deficit or both. After the economy has responded to the monetary and fiscal stimulus, output growth and employment will increase and unemployment will fall. (What steps could the government take during inflationary periods?)

Let's review the relative strengths and weaknesses of monetary policy and fiscal policy.

Does Fiscal Policy Matter? Over the last three decades, fiscal policy has lost much of its attractiveness to policymakers and macroeconomists as a stabilization tool. In the early stages of the Keynesian revolution, macroeconomists emphasized fiscal policy as the most powerful and balanced remedy for demand management. Gradually, shortcomings of fiscal policy became apparent. The shortcomings stem from timing, politics, macroeconomic theory, and the fiscal deficit itself.

One concern is that the time span between cyclical shock and effective response is long and growing longer. To begin with, it takes time before economists can recognize that a cyclical turning point has been reached. Then, in addition to the recognition lag, there is a response lag while the President decides what to do and Congress debates and passes the measure. Finally, even when taxation or spending is changed, there is an effectiveness lag before the economy responds.

While recognition, response, and effectiveness lags are present for both monetary policy and fiscal policy, the response lag for fiscal policy can be so long that it becomes useless for stabilization. The response lag has lengthened over the last few years as congressional budget procedures have become more complex, with almost a year's delay between presidential recommendations and final congressional action.

Another difficulty is that it is easier to cut taxes than to raise them, and easier to raise spending than to cut it. During the 1960s, Congress was enthusiastic about passing the Kennedy-Johnson tax cuts. Two years later, when the Vietnam war expansion ignited inflationary pressures, contractionary policies were called for. But President Johnson and Congress delayed acting until inflation had already risen. Similarly, President Bush had to struggle mightily to get a relatively small tax increase through Congress as part of the 1990 deficit-reduction package, and even that small step badly damaged his standing within the Republican party and helped contribute to his defeat in 1992.

In addition, even when put into action speedily, fiscal policy may not work as well as macroeconomists once thought. For example, many economists used to advocate temporary tax cuts during recessions and temporary tax increases when the economy becomes overheated and inflation looms. However, studies indicate that consumers realize that the tax changes are temporary and do not change their spending patterns very much, since the temporary tax changes have little effect upon their permanent or lifetime incomes.

But the biggest impediment of all to fiscal policy today is simply the enormous size of the federal deficit. With such a large structural deficit, lawmakers are reluctant to boost spending and cut taxes even when unemployment is high. And the natural reluctance to increase the deficit is reinforced by the congressional budget constraints we discuss below.

Fiscal policy is no longer a major tool of stabilization policy in the United States. Over the foreseeable future, stabilization policy will be primarily handled by Federal Reserve monetary policy.

Effectiveness of Monetary Policy. Compared to fiscal policy, monetary policy operates much more indirectly on the economy. Whereas an expansive fiscal policy puts more money right into the hands of consumers and businesses, monetary policy affects spending by altering interest rates, credit conditions, exchange rates, and asset prices. In the early years of the Keynesian revolution, some macroeconomists were skeptical about the effectiveness of monetary policy, just as they were enthusiastic about the newfound tool of fiscal policy. But over the last two decades the Federal Reserve has adopted a more active role and shown itself quite capable of slowing, or speeding up, the economy.

The Federal Reserve is much better placed to conduct stabilization policy than are the fiscal-policy makers. Its staff of professional economists can recognize cyclical movements as well as anyone. And it can move quickly when the need arises. For example, on January 28, 1994, the Commerce Department announced that the economy was growing surprisingly rapidly at year-end 1993; only a week later, the Fed moved to slow the expansion by raising interest rates for the first time in half a decade. This episode stands in stark comparison to the delay of 2 years in tightening fiscal policy during the Vietnam war. A key ingredient in Fed policy is its independence, and the Fed has proved that it can stand the heat of making politically unpopular decisions when they are necessary to slow inflation. Most important, as we noted above, is that from the point of view of demand management, monetary policy can do, or undo, anything that fiscal policy can accomplish.

Of course, to stabilize the economy, the central bank has to apply the right amount of monetary stimulus or restraint. Recent estimates of the quantitative impacts of monetary policy on the economy in different macroeconomic models are shown in Table 33-4 on page 656. This study estimated the impact on the U.S. economy of increasing the money supply by 4 percent above the money supply of a baseline projection, with the money supply remaining 4 percent higher than the baseline for the indefinite future.

The results show a substantial initial response of real GDP to an increase in the money supply. By contrast, the increase in the price level builds up slowly over time, with less than one-fifth of the increase in nominal GDP in year 1 coming in prices. At the end of 5 years, according to the model simulations, most of the increase in nominal GDP shows up in prices rather than in real output. The models confirm the Keynesian prediction of a sluggish reaction of wages

Money, Output, and Prices					
	Response of affected variable to 4 percent change in money supply (% change in affected variable from baseline path)				
Affected variable	Year 1	Year 2	Year 3	Year 4	Year 5
Real GDP	0.9	1.1	1.2	1.1	0.8
Consumer prices	0.2	0.7	1.1	1.5	1.8
Nominal GDP	1.1	1.8	2.3	2.5	2.7

TABLE 33-4. Estimated Effect of Monetary Policy on Output and Prices

A survey studied the impact of a change in monetary policy in eight different econometric models. In each case, a baseline run of the model was "shocked" by adding 4 percent to the money supply in year 1 and holding the money supply 4 percent above the baseline in all years thereafter. Estimates in the table show the average calculated response of the models.

Note the strong initial response of real output to a monetary-policy shift, with the peak response coming in year 3. The impact upon the price level builds up gradually because of the inertial response of price and wage behavior. Note that the impact on nominal GDP is less than proportional to the money growth even after 5 years. [Source: Ralph C. Bryant, Peter Hooper, and Gerald Holtham, "Consensus and Diversity in the Model Simulations," in Ralph Bryant et al., eds., *Empirical Macroeconomics for Interdependent Economies* (Brookings, Washington, D.C., 1988).]

and prices to changes in the money supply but also indicate that the economy behaves increasingly like a classical economy in the long run.

How might the monetary authorities use these statistical results? Suppose, for example, that the Federal Reserve forecasts that real GDP will grow by 4 percent in the coming year; further, the Fed believes that a growth rate of 3 percent is the most that the economy can sustain without the risk of an unacceptable inflation. What change in the money supply would be needed to slow the rate of growth of real GDP by 1 percentage point? The answer is that the money-supply growth would have to be slowed by somewhat more than 4 percent to produce a 1-percentage-point decrease in real GDP.

Of course, the usefulness of such calculations depends on whether the statistical correlations which held in the past will still be true in the future. Monetary economists stress that the impacts of monetary policy are uncertain and may even change over time as the economy evolves. For example, as the economy becomes increasingly exposed to foreign trade, the impact of monetary policy on net exports becomes more important at the same time that the impact upon housing and other domestic sectors is mitigated by financial deregulation.

In terms of stabilization policy, monetary policy is today the only game in town. Few doubt the effectiveness of monetary policy in determining aggregate demand, but the impacts have long and variable lags.

The Fiscal-Monetary Mix

The second factor affecting fiscal and monetary policy is the desired **fiscal-monetary mix**, which refers to the relative strength of fiscal and monetary policies and their effect on different sectors of the economy. The basic idea is that fiscal policy and monetary policy are substitutes in demand management. But while alternative combinations of monetary and fiscal policies can be used to stabilize the economy, they have different impacts upon the *composition* of output. By varying the mix of taxes, government spending, and monetary policy, the government can change the fraction of GDP devoted to business investment, consumption, net exports, and government purchases of goods and services. This can be easily seen in the following examples:

• *Example 1.* Let's say that the President decides that it is necessary to increase defense spending greatly and that this should come at the expense

Sector		Change in output ($, billion, 1996 prices)
Investment sectors		**$132**
Gross private domestic investment	$48	
Housing	18	
Business fixed investment	30	
Net exports	83	
Consumption sectors		**−106**
Government purchases of goods and services	−68	
Personal consumption expenditures	−38	
Memoranda:		
Change in real GDP		26
Change in federal deficit		−100

TABLE 33-5. Changing the Fiscal-Monetary Mix

What would be the impact of a change in the fiscal-monetary mix for the United States? This simulation assumes that the federal deficit is cut by $100 billion through higher personal taxes and lower federal nondefense expenditures while the Federal Reserve uses monetary policy to keep unemployment on an unchanged trajectory. The simulation takes the average of the changes from the baseline path over the period 1990–1999. (Source: Simulation using the DRI model of the U.S. economy.)

of domestic investment and net exports. What could be done? The country could increase defense spending, leave taxes alone or even cut taxes, and tighten money, thereby raising interest rates enough to squeeze investment and net exports to make room for the added government purchases. This policy would also lead to an increase in the structural budget deficit and higher real interest rates. The United States followed this path under President Reagan in the early 1980s.

• *Example 2.* Suppose that a country becomes concerned about a low national savings rate and desires to raise investment so as to increase the capital stock and boost the growth rate of potential output. To implement this approach, the country could raise consumption taxes and squeeze transfer payments so as to reduce disposable income and thereby lower consumption; slow the growth in government purchases; and undertake an expansionary monetary policy to lower interest rates and raise investment, lower the exchange rate, and expand net exports. This course would encourage private investment by increasing public saving. This was the economic philosophy of President Clinton and was embodied in the 1993 Budget Act.

Effect of Changing the Mix of Monetary and Fiscal Policies. To understand the impact of changing the fiscal-monetary mix, let's examine a specific set of policies. Suppose that the federal government reduces the federal budget deficit by $100 billion and that higher monetary growth exactly offsets the contractionary impact of the fiscal steps. This package is similar to Clinton's deficit-cutting package enacted in 1993 along with a monetary policy that offset the drag from higher taxes and lower government spending.

We can estimate the impact using a quantitative economic model, such as the sophisticated DRI long-term model of the United States.[3] Table 33-5 shows the results of this experiment. Two interesting features emerge: First, the simulation indicates that a change in the fiscal-monetary mix would indeed change the composition of real GDP. While the deficit declines by $100 billion, business investment goes up by $30 billion. Investment in housing, too,

---

[3] This model was designed by the eminent Harvard macroeconomist Otto Eckstein. It contains a standard Keynesian structure for determining aggregate demand, and monetary and fiscal policies are both effective. Aggregate supply has endogenous potential output (determined by capital, labor, R&D, and energy), while prices and wages follow a Phillips-curve-type reaction to unemployment.

increases as interest rates fall. At the same time, personal consumption declines, freeing up resources for investment. This simulation shows how a change in the fiscal-monetary mix might change the composition of output.

The simulation contains one particularly interesting result: Net exports rise far more than either housing or business fixed investment. This occurs because of the strong depreciation of the dollar which results from the lower interest rates. While this result is clearly sensitive to the reaction of financial markets and exchange rates to the deficit-reduction package, it suggests that some of the popular analyses of the impact of such a package may be misleading. Many analysts have argued that a deficit-reduction package would have a significant impact upon domestic business investment and upon productivity. However, to the extent that lower deficits mainly help net exports and housing, the nation is likely to experience relatively little increase in productivity growth. According to the DRI model, cutting the budget deficit by $100 billion will raise the growth rate of potential output from 2.3 percent per year to 2.6 percent per year over a 10-year period. Perhaps the small size of the payoff explains why it is so hard to muster the political will to cut the deficit.

RULES VS. DISCRETION

We have seen that fiscal and monetary policy can *in principle* stabilize the economy. Many economists believe that countries should *in practice* take steps to shave the peaks and troughs off the business cycle. Other economists are skeptical of our ability to forecast cycles and take the right steps at the right time for the right reasons; this second group concludes that government cannot be trusted to make good economic policy, so its freedom to act should be strictly limited.

For example, fiscal conservatives worry that it's easier for Congress to increase spending and cut taxes than to do the reverse. That means it's easy to increase the budget deficit during recessions but much harder to turn around and shrink the deficit again during booms, as a countercyclical fiscal policy would require. For that reason, conservatives have made several attempts to limit the ability of Congress to appropriate new funds or increase the deficit.

At the same time, monetary conservatives would like to tie the hands of the central bank through a monetary-growth or output-targeting rule. For example, instead of having the Federal Reserve increase or decrease the money supply in response to economic conditions—to lean against the winds as measured by the Fed—monetarists propose that the Fed follow a policy of increasing the money supply at a steady rate. This would have the advantage of eliminating uncertainty in the financial markets and enhancing the credibility of the central bank as an inflation fighter.

At the most general level, the debate about "rules versus discretion" boils down to whether the advantages of flexibility in decision making are outweighed by the uncertainties and potential abuse in unconstrained decisions. Those who believe that the economy is inherently unstable and complex and that governments generally make wise decisions are comfortable with giving policymakers wide discretion to react aggressively to stabilize the economy. Those who believe that the government is the major destabilizing force in the economy and that policymakers are prone to misjudgments or venality favor tying the hands of the fiscal and monetary authorities.

Budget Constraints on Legislatures?

As deficits began to grow during the 1980s, many people argued that Congress lacks the self-control to curb excessive spending and a burgeoning government debt. In response, Congress passed the *Gramm-Rudman Act* in 1985, which required that the deficit be reduced by a specified dollar amount each year and balanced by 1991. If Congress was unable to meet the quantitative Gramm-Rudman target, expenditures would be automatically cut across the board.

The results fell far short of the congressional mandate. The Gramm-Rudman bill went into effect in late 1985, but the ambitious deficit targets were not met. The bill was amended in 1987, but the controls on the deficits proved unworkable and ineffective. In 1990 the targets were replaced by a set of spending limitations. These limitations were incorporated in the 1993 Budget Act and impose stringent restrictions on the growth of discretionary programs (which include defense and nonentitlement civilian programs like education, science, and general government). The 1993 and 1997 Budget Acts require that discretionary programs decline by almost one-quarter in real terms over the 1993–1998 period.

The other important change introduced in the 1990 amendments and included in the 1993 and 1997 acts is a *pay-as-you-go budget rule*. This requires that Congress find the revenues to pay for any new spending program. Otherwise, automatic spending cuts will be imposed to offset the increased deficit.

The pay-as-you-go provision imposes a budget constraint on Congress, requiring that the costs of new programs be explicitly recognized either through higher taxes or lower expenditures in other areas.

What has been the impact of the budget constraints on Congress? The set of budget rules has helped whittle down the size of the structural deficit over the last decade. But any rule legislated by Congress can be changed by Congress. Moreover, the budget rules have great difficulty dealing with entitlement programs, such as social security and health care, so the future of this self-imposed discipline is uncertain.

Many conservatives have over the last decade campaigned for a constitutional amendment requiring a balanced budget. This measure was contained in the *Contract with America* that formed the core of the Republicans' winning congressional platform in 1994. Such an amendment, if passed by Congress and approved by enough states, would make it difficult to use fiscal policy to fight recessions. To date, none of the proposed constitutional amendments has passed Congress.

Monetary Rules for the Fed?

In our discussions of monetarism, we laid out the case for fixed policy rules. The traditional argument for fixed rules is that the private economy is relatively stable and active policy-making is likely to destabilize rather than stabilize the economy. Moreover, to the extent that the central bank may be tempted to expand the economy before elections and to create a political business cycle, fixed rules will tie its hands. In addition, modern macroeconomists point to the value of being able to commit to action in advance. If the central bank can commit to follow a noninflationary rule, people's expectations will adapt to this rule and inflationary expectations may be damped.

Until recently, advocates of fixed monetary rules (particularly monetarists) recommended a fixed nominal growth of, say, 4 percent per year in the money supply. With a constant velocity and output growing at 3 percent a year, this would lead to steady annual inflation of 1 percent. But as the data on velocity show (see particularly Figure 32-3 in the last chapter), velocity was never terribly stable and it has become much more unstable in the last decade. Given the apparent instability of velocity, it would be hard to claim that a fixed monetary rule could have actually stabilized output during this period.

Targeting Inflation. Central banks have adopted many different approaches to monetary policy in recent decades. These range from highly discretionary approaches which coordinate monetary and fiscal policies under the direction of the government to highly mechanized approaches with fixed targets for the money supply or bank reserves.

One of the most important new developments in the last decade has been the trend toward inflation targeting in many countries. **Inflation targeting** is the announcement of official target ranges for the inflation rate along with an explicit statement that low and stable inflation is the overriding goal of monetary policy. Inflation targeting in hard or soft varieties has been adopted in recent years by many industrialized countries, including Canada, Britain, Australia, and New Zealand, and is pursued in an indirect form by Germany. The treaty underlying the new European monetary unit, the Euro, mandates price stability as the primary objective of the European central bank.[4] A number of economists and legislators are advocating this approach for the United States as well.

Inflation targeting involves the following:

- The government or central bank announces that monetary policy will strive to keep inflation near a numerically specified target.
- The target usually involves a range, such as 1 to 3 percent per year, rather than literal price stability. Generally, the government targets an inertial or core inflation rate such as the CPI excluding volatile food and energy prices and excluding price-raising taxes.
- Inflation is the primary or overriding target of policy in the medium run and long run. However, countries always make room for short-run

---

[4] European monetary union is discussed in Chapter 36.

stabilization objectives, particularly with respect to output, unemployment, financial stability, and the foreign exchange rate. These short-run objectives recognize that supply shocks can affect output and unemployment and that it may be desirable to have temporary departures from the inflation target to avoid excessive unemployment or output losses.

Those who defend inflation targeting point to many advantages. If we accept that there is no long-run tradeoff between unemployment and inflation, it is sensible to set an inflation target at the level that maximizes the efficiency of the price system. Our analysis of inflation in Chapter 30 suggested that a low and stable (but positive) rate of inflation would promote efficiency and minimize unnecessary redistribution of income and wealth. In addition, some economists believe that a strong and credible commitment to low and stable inflation will improve the short-run inflation-unemployment tradeoff.

Inflation targeting is a compromise between rule-based approaches and purely discretionary policies. The main disadvantage would come if the central bank began to rely too rigidly on the inflation rule and thereby allowed excessive unemployment in periods of severe supply shocks. Critics recall the difficulties with rigid rules that came with the 1979–1982 monetarist experiment. That period triggered the deepest recession since the Great Depression, and after 1983 the rigid operating procedures were consequently abandoned. Skeptics worry that the economy is too complex to be governed by fixed rules. Arguing by analogy, they ask whether one would advocate a fixed speed limit for cars or an automatic pilot for aircraft in all kinds of weather and emergencies.

The debate over rules versus discretion is one of the oldest debates of political economy. There is no single best approach for all times and places. Indeed, the dilemma reflects the difficulty that democratic societies have in making tradeoffs between short-run policies intended to attract political support and long-run policies designed to enhance the general welfare. What is needed is not rigid adherence to rules but farsighted dedication to the public welfare. Ironically, one of the most acclaimed economic policymakers of the postwar period was Federal Reserve Chairman Paul Volcker, whose tenure (1979–1987) was marked by sharp, discretionary policy changes aimed at balancing the competing goals of reducing inflation, maintaining high employment and output, and protecting the nation's financial system. His successes testify to the power of wise and disinterested discretionary policies.

C. INCREASING LONG-TERM GROWTH

The importance of productivity and economic growth in the long-run fortunes of nations was well captured by MIT's Paul Krugman:

> Productivity isn't everything, but in the long run it is almost everything. A country's ability to improve its living standards over time depends almost entirely on its ability to raise its output per worker.[5]

This statement reflects the finding from Chapter 27 that the pace of real wages and per capita income tracks closely the growth of labor productivity. See Figure 27-6 for the history of these variables over this century.

HIGH STAKES

Promoting a high and growing standard of living for the nation's residents is one of the fundamental goals of macroeconomic policy. Because the current *level* of real income reflects the history of the *growth* of productivity, we can measure the relative success of past growth by examining the per capita GDPs of different countries. A brief list is presented in Table 33-6. This

---

[5] Paul Krugman, *The Age of Diminished Expectations* (MIT Press, Cambridge, Mass., 1990), p. 9.

Country	Per capita GDP, 1995
United States	$27,000
Switzerland	25,900
Japan	22,100
France	21,000
Germany	20,100
Russia	4,500
China	2,900
India	1,400

TABLE 33-6. Current Incomes Represent Effects of Past Growth

Those countries that have grown most rapidly in the past have reached the highest levels of per capita GDP. (Source: World Bank, *World Development Report, 1997*, Washington, D.C., 1997; data adjusted using purchasing-power parity exchange rates.)

table compares incomes by using *purchasing-power parity* exchange rates that measure the purchasing power of (or quantity of goods and services that can be bought by) different national currencies. Evidently, the United States has been successful in its past growth performance. But current trends are worrisome because America's growth rate is low, and living standards for many Americans have stagnated in recent years.

In discussing growth rates, the numbers often seem tiny. A successful pro-investment and pro-innovation policy might increase a country's growth rate by only 1 percentage point per year (recall the estimated impact of the deficit-reduction package in the last section). But over long periods, this makes a big difference. Table 33-7 shows how tiny acorns grow into mighty oaks as small growth-rate differences cumulate and compound over time. A 4 percent–per-year growth difference leads to a 50-fold difference in income levels over a century.

How can public policy boost economic growth? Our analysis of economic growth in Chapters 27 and 28 showed that the major ingredients are capital deepening and technological change. Capital deepening refers to an increase in the capital per worker; it should be broadly interpreted from a policy perspective to include increases in the quantity and quality of plant and equipment, education and training, as well as natural and environmental capital. Technological change should also be broadly construed to include not only new products and processes but also improvements in management as well as entrepreneurship and the spirit of enterprise.

THE CAPITAL CONNECTION

Where Has All the Saving Gone?

Over the long run, a nation's capital stock is primarily determined by its national savings rate. When a nation saves a great deal, its capital stock grows rapidly and it enjoys rapid growth in its potential output. When a nation's savings rate is low, its equipment and factories become obsolete and its infrastructure begins to rot away. This close relationship between saving, investment, and economic growth is the major reason why economists focus on a nation's savings rate.

Table 33-8 on page 662 lists the net private savings rates of major countries between 1960 and 1989. During this period, Japan led the league in private saving as a percent of national income, while the United States lagged behind other major countries. Figure 33-4 on page 662 shows trends in both the national savings rate and the personal component of national saving (which excludes business saving). The **national savings rate** is equal to total saving, private and public, divided by net domestic product.

TABLE 33-7. Small Differences in Growth Rates Compound into Large Income Differentials over the Decades

Growth rate (% per year)	Real income per capita (1996 prices)		
	1996	2046	2096
0	$24,000	$ 24,000	$ 24,000
1	24,000	39,471	64,916
2	24,000	64,598	173,872
4	24,000	170,560	1,212,118

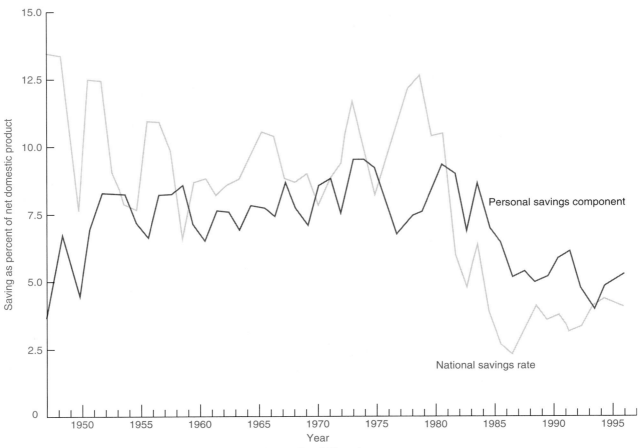

FIGURE 33-4. U.S. Savings Rate Has Declined Sharply
The national savings rate equals total saving (domestic and foreign) divided by net domestic product. By definition, national saving equals national investment. The declining U.S. savings rate in the 1980s led to slower growth at home and a large foreign debt. (Source: U.S. Department of Commerce.)

TABLE 33-8. U.S. Savings Rate Trails That of Other Major Industrial Countries

The table shows net private saving (equal to net saving of households and businesses at home and abroad) divided by GDP. [Source: OECD, *National Accounts, 1960–89* (Paris, 1991); U.S. Department of Commerce.]

Country	Private savings rate, 1960–1989 (net private saving as % of GDP)
Japan	20.7
West Germany	14.0
France	13.6
Canada	9.9
United Kingdom	7.4
United States	7.2

The national savings rate is the sum of the personal, government, and business components. As can be seen in the figure, much of the decline in national saving has come from developments outside the personal sector, primarily from the decrease in government saving caused by growing budget deficits. The net effect is that the national savings rate declined from around 8 percent for the 1948–1979 period to around 3 percent in the 1980s. As the deficit was reduced in the 1990s, however, the national savings rate improved slightly.

What were the reasons for the precipitous decline in the national savings rate? This is a highly controversial question today, but economists point to the following contributing factors:

- *Federal budget deficits.* Having generally balanced its books during peacetime, the government began to run a large deficit in the early 1980s. By the early 1990s, the total government sector was running a deficit of around 4 percent of output. (Recall our discussion of the sources of the growing federal deficit in the first part of this chapter.) There does not appear to have been an increase in private saving to offset the increase in government dissaving, so the net effect of the deficit has been a lower national savings rate.

- *Personal saving.* The second contributor to the shrinking national savings rate has been the declining share of personal saving in total output. We discussed the sources of the decrease in personal saving in Chapter 22. That discussion pointed to such factors as an increase in the generosity of government transfer programs, particularly social security and Medicare, which reduce the need to save for old age; growing access to capital markets, which allows people to borrow more easily; the slowdown in the growth of incomes, which leads to a decline in the steady-state savings rate for a given wealth-income ratio; and the aging of the population, with a larger fraction of the population in the older age groups in which saving is relatively low.

While we can find a few clues here, the case of the declining national savings rate remains a puzzling phenomenon, testing the ingenuity of macroeconomists. Although no one has demonstrated conclusively why the U.S. national savings rate has dropped so sharply in recent years, virtually all believe that the savings rate is too low to guarantee a vital and healthy rate of investment in the 1990s.

Increasing National Saving

How can the nation increase its savings rate? This requires both reducing the full-employment level of consumption and ensuring that the increased desired saving actually gets channeled into investment. In other words, monetary and fiscal policies must be changed so as to increase the savings rate while ensuring that aggregate demand does not decline.

While few people question the wisdom of increasing national saving, economists today debate whether to use income-oriented or price-oriented approaches. *Income-oriented* approaches include changing the monetary-fiscal mix by lowering government dissaving and private consumption while stimulating investment through lower interest rates. Those macroeconomists who believe that the large federal deficit lay behind the decline in national saving in the 1980s see a reduction of the deficit as the major goal of policy today.

Other economists emphasize *price-oriented* measures, or economic incentives to increase saving and investment. Such measures include raising the rate of return to investment or saving by lowering taxes on capital income or capital gains, and raising the reward to investment by offering investment tax credits or faster depreciation allowances. The 1980s provided a laboratory for price-oriented measures since real after-tax interest rates rose sharply during this period. The fact that the private savings rate declined suggests that price-oriented measures may on their own be insufficient to boost national saving.

The 1993 Budget Act

On entering office in 1993, President Bill Clinton submitted a major economic plan, which was enacted by Congress as the Budget Act of 1993. This measure was aimed at decreasing the federal budget deficit primarily through an income-oriented approach of higher taxes and lower government spending; it contained no major price-oriented incentives. The main features of the 1993 act are the following:

- *Tax increases.* The measure contains a number of tax increases, primarily falling on high-income individuals. These include an increase of the top marginal tax rate to 39.6 percent, an increase in social security taxes on top earners, and a small increase in the gasoline tax.
- *Expenditure reductions.* The 1993 package continued to wind down the cold war with major reductions in defense spending. Decisions on other mandated spending cuts were left for the future.
- *Debt service.* As the debt rises, a vicious cycle of debt, debt service, larger deficits, and more debt ensues. Deficit-reduction programs set off a virtuous cycle. Because of the shrinking deficit,

interest has entered a virtuous cycle and is now a declining share of the federal budget.

- *Deficit reduction.* The effect of these steps has been a significant reduction in the structural federal deficit, with the structural deficit declining from $242 billion in 1993 to $91 billion in 1997. This reduction—representing a reduction in the structural deficit of 2.5 percent of GDP—was due in approximately equal measures to tax increases and expenditure reductions.

The 1993 Budget Act made a significant step on the road to restoring fiscal balance for the United States. But a number of issues are still unresolved, particularly the continued growth of entitlement programs in health.

The 1997 Budget Act

During the 1996 presidential campaign, President Clinton adopted many of the Republican fiscal-policy prescriptions, including the proposal for a balanced budget and the desirability of targeted tax cuts. These promises were met in the 1997 Budget Act. Unlike the 1990 and 1993 acts, this measure contained few programmatic cuts. Instead, the balanced budget was to be attained by reducing future medical-care payments to doctors and hospitals and by lowering the overall caps on discretionary spending. In addition, the 1997 act contained cuts in capital-gains and inheritance taxes as well as new tax credits for educational expenditures. Economists had few words of praise for the tax measures, but the overall effect on the economy was relatively modest.

Nonbusiness Investment

What is included in a nation's capital stock? Table 33-9 shows the major components. Discussion of the need to increase investment often focuses on the narrow slice of the nation's capital consisting of business plant and equipment. Many economists are primarily concerned with business equipment because technological advances (such as those arising from the electronic revolution in computer hardware and software and in communications) are embodied in new equipment, so increasing investment in this area will promote rapid productivity change. But national wealth is a much broader concept, so we must not focus only on business investment.

The wealth of a nation: We must not lose sight of the fact that much of the nation's wealth lies outside the corporate sector. A nation's wealth includes the human capital of education and skills embodied in its labor force; the health capital that makes for productive workers; the technological know-how developed in laboratories and on the factory floors; the informational capital stored in libraries; as well as land, subsoil assets, and environmental resources. A comprehensive list of a nation's wealth would therefore be as follows:

Total National Wealth

Reproducible capital:
    Private business
    Residential
    Government
Human capital:
    Education
    Skills and training
    Health
Technological capital:
    Management
    Scientific and engineering base
    Colleges, universities, and libraries
Land
Resources:
    Subsoil assets
    Environmental resources

When we take into account the breadth of the concept of capital, we can understand why countries like Germany and Japan, which had much of their visible capital destroyed during World War II, were able to recover so rapidly: much of their human and technological capital was not touched by bombing.

What can governments do to promote capital deepening outside the area of business investment? The most important point is that changing fiscal and monetary policies toward a tight-fiscal–easy-money mix will automatically stimulate private investment in all areas because this approach lowers real interest rates and makes future income flows more attractive. *Whether the investment is in equipment, medical technologies, a college education, or reforestation, if real interest rates are lower, more investment will be stimulated.*

	Value ($, billion)	Percent of total
Private business:		
Equipment	$ 3,051	13.5
Structures	4,903	21.7
Residential:		
Structures	7,733	34.2
Consumer durables	2,339	10.3
Goverment:		
Military	873	3.9
Nonmilitary	3,711	16.4
Total	$22,608	100.0

TABLE 33-9. Capital Stock of the United States, 1995

Only a fraction of the nation's net stock of structures and equipment is in the business sector. (Source: U.S. Department of Commerce, *Survey of Current Business,* May 1997.)

In some investment areas, particularly education and health, governments have major responsibilities. Most precollege education in the United States is funded and operated by state and local governments. Improvements in human capital will come about primarily by improving the efficiency of public schools rather than simply pouring more dollars into them. College education is an interesting case. Studies suggest that investments in human capital involved in going to college have a return of about 10 percent per year. Stimulating private investment or using public funds to increase the amount of college education is an intangible way to improve productivity and increase economic growth, and it benefits individuals directly.

Some economists have argued that government has a special role to play in other areas of the economy as well, notably spending on public infrastructure. Over the last 10 years there has been a vigorous debate as to whether U.S. productivity could be enhanced by more spending in traditional areas like highways, bridges, airports, and other aspects of public infrastructure, as well as in new areas such as the "information superhighway." The conclusion seems to be that under some limited circumstances, more money for infrastructure can have a positive impact on productivity.

Increasing investment to speed up growth must be a broad-based policy that touches not only business investment but also human, technological, and other forms of tangible and intangible wealth.

THE SPIRIT OF ENTERPRISE

This brings us to the second major determinant of a country's long-run economic performance, the pace of its technological advance. We often measure the state of technology by **total factor productivity,** which measures total output per unit of all inputs. Technological advance is complementary to capital deepening but is perhaps even more important. If we took workers in 1895 and doubled or tripled their capital in mules, saddles, cow paths, and single-furrow plows, their productivity still could not come close to that of today's workers using huge tractors, superhighways, and supercomputers.

Fostering Technological Advance

While it is easy to see how technological advance promotes growth in productivity and living standards, governments cannot simply command people to think longer or be smarter. Centrally planned socialist countries used "sticks" to promote science, technology, and innovation, but their efforts failed because neither the institutions nor the "carrots" were present to encourage both innovation and introduction of new technologies. Governments often promote rapid technological change best when they set a sound economic and legal framework with strong intellectual property rights and then allow great economic freedom within that framework. *Free markets in labor, capital, products, and ideas have proved to be the most fertile soil for innovation and technological change.*

Within the framework of free markets, governments can foster rapid technological change both by encouraging new ideas and by ensuring that technologies are effectively used. Policies can focus on both the supply side and the demand side.

Promoting Demand for Better Technologies.

The world is full of superior technologies that have not been adopted; otherwise, how could we explain the vast differences in productivity shown in Table 33-6? Before considering how to supply new technologies, therefore, governments must help ensure that firms and industries are at the *technological frontier*, which is the best-practice technology anywhere.

The major lesson here is that "necessity is the mother of invention." In other words, vigorous competition among firms and industries is the ultimate discipline that ensures innovation. Just as athletes perform better when they are trying to outrun their competitors, so are firms spurred to improve their products and processes when the victors are given fame and fortune while the laggards may go bankrupt.

Vigorous competition involves both domestic and foreign competitors. For large countries on the technological frontier, domestic competition is necessary to promote innovation. The movement to deregulation over the last two decades has brought competition to airlines, energy, telecommunications, and finance, and the positive impact on innovation has been dramatic. For small or technologically backward countries, import competition is crucial to adopting advanced technologies and ensuring product market competition.

Promoting Supply of New Technologies.

Rapid economic growth requires pushing out the technological frontier by increasing the supply of inventions as well as ensuring that there is adequate demand for existing advanced technologies. There are three ways by which governments can encourage the supply of new technologies.

First, governments can ensure that the basic science, engineering, and technology are appropriately supported. In this respect, the world leader in the last half-century has been the United States, which combines company support for applied research with top-notch university basic research generously supported by government funding. Particularly outstanding have been the impressive improvements in biomedical technology in the form of new drugs and equipment that benefit consumers directly in daily life. Today, American commercial, for-profit research and development (R&D) is increasingly challenged by Japanese and European enterprises. The government's role in supporting for-profit research is accomplished by a strong patent system, predictable and cost-effective regulations, and fiscal incentives such as the current R&D tax credit.

Second, governments can advance technologies at home through encouraging investment by foreign firms. As foreign countries increasingly reach and pass the American technological frontier, they can also increasingly contribute to American know-how by establishing operations in the United States. The last decade has brought a number of Japanese automakers to the United States, and Japanese-owned plants have introduced new technologies and managerial practices to the benefit of both the profits of Japanese shareholders and the productivity of American workers.

Third, governments can promote new technologies by pursuing sound macroeconomic policies. These include low and stable taxes on capital income and a low cost of capital to firms. Indeed, the importance of the cost of capital brings us back full circle to the issue of the low savings rate and high real interest rate. It is often said that American firms are myopic while Japanese firms are farsighted. At least part of this difference comes from differences in real interest rates: high real interest rates in the United States *force* rational American firms to look for quick payoffs in their investments, while low real interest rates in Japan *allow* Japanese firms to undertake investments with long time horizons. Therefore, a change in economic policy that lowered real interest rates would change the "economic spectacles" through which firms look when considering their technological policies. If real interest rates were lower, firms would view long-term, high-risk projects like innovation more favorably, and the increased investment in knowledge would lead to more rapid improvements in technology and productivity.

Valediction

Following the Keynesian revolution, the capitalist democracies believed that they could flourish and grow rapidly while moderating the extremes of unemployment and inflation, poverty and wealth, privilege and deprivation. Many of these goals were met as the market economies experienced a period of output expansion and employment growth never before seen, and the last 15 years have been a period of unprecedented stability and low inflation in the United States. All the time, Marxists carped that capitalism was doomed to crash in a cataclysmic depression; ecologists fretted that market economies would choke in their own fumes and wastes; and libertarians worried that the government-sponsored remedies were worse than the diseases. But the pessimists overlooked the spirit of enterprise which was unleashed by the free market and which led to a continuous stream of technological improvements.

A valediction from John Maynard Keynes, as timely today as it was in an earlier age, provides a fitting conclusion to our study of macroeconomics:

> It is Enterprise which builds and improves the world's possessions. If Enterprise is afoot, wealth accumulates whatever happens to Thrift; and if Enterprise is asleep, wealth decays whatever Thrift may be doing.

SUMMARY

A. The Economic Consequences of the Debt

1. Budgets are systems used by governments and organizations to plan and control expenditures and revenues. Budgets are in surplus (or deficit) when the government has revenues greater (or less) than its expenditures. Macroeconomic policy depends upon fiscal policy, comprised of the overall stance of spending and taxes.

2. Economists separate the actual budget into its structural and cyclical components. The structural budget calculates how much the government would collect and spend if the economy were operating at potential output. The cyclical budget accounts for the impact of the business cycle on tax revenues, expenditures, and the deficit. To assess fiscal policy, we should pay close attention to the structural deficit; changes in the cyclical deficit are a *result* of changes in the economy, while structural deficits are a *cause* of changes in the economy.

3. The government debt represents the accumulated borrowings from the public. It is the sum of past deficits. A useful measure of the size of the debt is the debt-GDP ratio, which for the United States has tended to rise during wartime and fall during peacetime. The 1980s were an exception, for the debt-GDP ratio rose sharply during this period.

4. In the short run, economists worry that structural government deficits crowd out investment. The extent of crowding out depends upon financial markets and international linkages, the determinants of investment, and how deficits are financed. The best bet today is that, outside of deep recessions, national investment (both domestic and foreign) will be significantly crowded out by government spending.

5. To the degree that we borrow from abroad for consumption and pledge posterity to pay back the interest and principal on such external debt, our descendants will indeed find themselves sacrificing consumption to service this debt. If we leave future generations an internal debt but no change in capital stock, there are various internal effects. The process of taxing Peter to pay Paula, or taxing Paula to pay Paula, can involve various distortions of productivity and efficiency but should not be confused with owing money to another country.

6. Economic growth may slow if the public debt displaces capital. This syndrome occurs when people substitute public debt for capital or private assets, thereby reducing the economy's private capital stock. In the long run, a larger government debt may slow the growth of potential output and consumption because of the costs of servicing an external debt, the inefficiencies that arise from taxing to pay the interest on the debt, and the diminished capital accumulation that comes from capital displacement.

B. Stabilizing the Economy

7. Nations face two considerations in setting monetary and fiscal policies: the appropriate level of aggregate demand and the best monetary-fiscal mix. The mix of fiscal and monetary policies helps determine the composition of GDP. A high-investment strategy would call for a budget surplus along with low real interest rates. The mix in practice in the United States has evolved toward loose fiscal and tight monetary policies—a sure recipe for a low ratio of investment to GDP and for slow growth of potential output.

8. After the Keynesian revolution, many economists had high hopes for countercyclical stabilization policy. In practice, fiscal policy has proved a cumbersome policy, particularly because of the difficulty of raising taxes and cutting expenditures during inflationary periods. Consequently, the United States today relies almost entirely upon monetary policy to stabilize the economy. Econometric models, which use statistical techniques to estimate the impact of monetary-policy changes on the macroeconomy, generally find that money-supply changes have their primary impact upon output in the short run, with a larger and larger share of the impact coming in inertial prices and wages as time proceeds.

9. Should governments follow fixed rules or discretion? The answer involves both positive economics and normative values. Conservatives often espouse rules, while liberals often advocate active fine-tuning of monetary policy to attain economic goals. More basic is the question of whether active and discretionary policies stabilize or destabilize the economy. Increasingly, economists stress the need for *credible* policies, whether credibility is generated by rigid rules or by wise leadership. A recent trend among countries is inflation targeting, which is a flexible rule-based system that sets a medium-term inflation target while allowing short-run flexibility when economic shocks make attaining a rigid inflation target too costly.

C. Increasing Long-Term Growth

10. Remember the dictum: "Productivity isn't everything, but in the long run it is almost everything." A country's ability to improve its living standards over time depends almost entirely on its ability to improve the technologies and capital used by the work force.

11. The U.S. national savings rate has declined sharply in the last decade. Studies point to the growing fiscal deficit of the federal government as one of the major culprits. Most economists believe that a lower federal deficit is the best single way to increase the national savings rate today. This requires both reducing the full-employment level of consumption and ensuring that the savings are channeled to high-productivity uses.

12. Policies aimed at increasing investment should take into account the fact that a nation's wealth extends far beyond business investment to other forms of tangible and intangible wealth, especially human capital.

13. Promoting economic growth also entails improving the pace of total factor productivity, which measures total output per unit of all inputs. The major role of government is to ensure free markets, protect strong intellectual property rights, promote vigorous competition, and support basic science and technology.

CONCEPTS FOR REVIEW

The Economics of Debt and Deficits

government budget
budget deficit, surplus, and balance
budget:
   actual
   structural
   cyclical
short-run impact: crowding out vs.
   investment encouragement
ratio of debt to GDP

long-run impacts on economic
   growth:
   internal vs. external debt
   distortions from taxation
   displacement of capital

Stabilization

demand management
fiscal-monetary mix
fixed rules vs. discretion

inflation targeting

Long-Run Growth and Productivity

the declining national savings rate:
   sources
   policies to reverse
different forms of wealth
reaching the technological frontier
   vs. moving it outward
the spirit of enterprise

QUESTIONS FOR DISCUSSION

1. A common confusion is that between the debt and the deficit. Explain each of the following:
   a. A budget deficit leads to a growing government debt.
   b. Reducing the deficit does not reduce the government debt.
   c. Reducing the government debt requires running a budget surplus.
   d. Even though the deficit fell by more than half in the first term of the Clinton administration, the government debt still rose significantly.

2. Is it possible that government *promises* might have a displacement effect along with government debt? Thus, if the government were to promise large future social security benefits to workers, would workers feel richer? Might they reduce saving as a result? Could the capital stock end up smaller? Illustrate using Figure 33-2.

3. Trace the impact upon the government debt, the nation's capital stock, and real output of a government program that borrows abroad and spends the money on the following:
   a. Capital to drill for oil, which is exported (as did Mexico in the 1970s)
   b. Grain to feed its population (as did the Soviet Union in the 1980s)

4. Construct a graph like that in Figure 33-3 showing the path of consumption and net exports with and without a large government debt.

5. Explain how a change in the mix of monetary and fiscal policies toward loose fiscal policy and tight money would increase the budget deficit, decrease domestic investment, and increase the trade or net-export deficit.

6. What are the various arguments for and against rigid inflation targeting in which the inflation target is required each year? Specifically, consider the difficulties of attaining a rigid inflation target after a sharp supply shock which shifted the Phillips curve up. Compare a rigid inflation target with a flexible inflation target in which the target would be attained on average over a 5-year period.

7. Political candidates have proposed the policies listed below to speed economic growth for the 1990s. For each, explain qualitatively the impact upon the growth of potential output and of per capita potential output. If possible, give a quantitative estimate of the increase in the growth of potential output and per capita potential output over the next decade.
   a. Cut the federal budget deficit by 2 percent of GDP, increasing the ratio of investment to GDP by the same amount.
   b. Increase the federal subsidy to R&D by $\frac{1}{4}$ percent of GDP, assuming that this subsidy will increase private R&D by the same amount and that R&D has a social rate of return that is 4 times that of private investment.
   c. Decrease defense spending by 1 percent of GDP, with a multiplier of 2.
   d. Increase the labor-force participation rate of females so that total labor inputs increase by 1 percent.
   e. Increase investments in human capital (or education and on-the-job training) by 1 percent of GDP.

8. J. M. Keynes wrote, "If the Treasury were to fill old bottles with banknotes, bury them in disused coal mines, and leave it to private enterprise to dig the notes up again, there need be no more unemployment and the real income of the community would probably become a good deal greater than it actually is" (*The General Theory,* p. 129). Explain why Keynes' analysis of the utility of a discretionary public-works program might be correct during a depression. How could well-designed fiscal or monetary policies have the same impact on employment while producing a larger quantity of useful goods and services?

PART SEVEN

INTERNATIONAL TRADE AND THE WORLD ECONOMY

CHAPTER 34
INTERNATIONAL TRADE AND EXCHANGE RATES

The benefit of international trade—a more efficient employment of the productive forces of the world.

John Stuart Mill

As we go about our daily lives, it is easy to overlook the importance of international exchange. America ships enormous volumes of food, airplanes, computers, and construction machinery to other countries; and in return we get vast quantities of oil, VCRs, cars, kiwi fruits, and other goods and services. Even more important for most countries are the new products and services that have over the years derived from other regions. While we may produce most of our national output, it is sobering to reflect how much our consumption—including clocks, railroads, accounting, penicillin, radar, and the Beatles—originates in the ingenuity of long-forgotten people in faraway places.

What are the economic forces that lie behind international trade? Simply put, trade promotes specialization, and specialization increases productivity. Over the long run, increased trade and higher productivity raise living standards for all nations. Gradually, countries have realized that opening up their economies to the global trading system is the most secure road to prosperity.

In this final part, we survey the principles governing *international trade and finance*, which is the system by which nations export and import goods, services, and financial capital. International economics involves many of the most controversial questions of the day: Why does the United States benefit from importing almost one-quarter of its automobiles and half of its petroleum? What are the advantages to the

United States, Canada, and Mexico of a free-trade region? Is there wisdom in the European countries' adopting a common currency? And why has the United States become the world's largest debtor country in the last decade? The economic stakes are high in finding wise answers to these questions.

International vs. Domestic Trade

How does the analysis of international trade differ from that of domestic markets? There are three differences:

1. *Expanded trading opportunities.* The major advantage of international trade is that it expands trading horizons. If people were forced to consume only what they produced at home, the world would be poorer on both the material and the spiritual planes. Canadians could drink no wine, Americans could eat no bananas, and most of the world would be without jazz and Hollywood movies.

2. *Sovereign nations.* Trading across frontiers involves people and firms living in different nations. Each nation is a sovereign entity which regulates the flow of people, goods, and finance crossing its borders. This contrasts with domestic trade, where there is a single currency, trade and money flow freely within the borders, and people

673

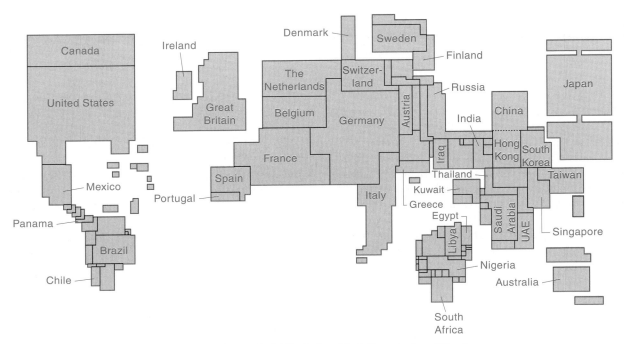

FIGURE 34-1. Countries of the World Scaled to Their International Trade

In this map, the area of each country is drawn proportional to its share of total world trade in 1991. Compare the size of the advanced industrial countries with that of Africa and Asia. [Adapted from Michael Kidron and Ronald Segal, *The New State of the World Atlas* (Simon and Schuster, New York, 1991), updated by authors.]

can migrate easily to seek new opportunities. Sometimes, political barriers to trade are erected when affected groups object to foreign trade and nations impose tariffs or quotas. This practice, called protectionism, is analyzed in the next chapter.

3. *Exchange rates.* Most nations have their own currencies. I want to pay for a Japanese car in dollars, while Toyota wants to be paid in Japanese yen. The international financial system must ensure a smooth flow of dollars, yen, and other currencies—or else risk a breakdown in trade.

A. ECONOMIC BASIS FOR INTERNATIONAL TRADE

TRENDS IN FOREIGN TRADE

We begin by examining the patterns of international trade. Figure 34-1 is a trade map, showing how the world would look if each country's geographical size were proportional to its share of world trade. Notice how large the United States, Western Europe, and Japan loom, while tiny Hong Kong appears larger than India.

An economy that engages in international trade is called an **open economy**. A useful measure of openness is the ratio of a country's exports or imports to its GDP. Figure 34-2 shows the trend in the shares of imports and exports for the United States. It shows the dip in the trade share during the trade wars of the 1930s, followed by the steady expansion of trade with lower trade barriers over the last three decades. Still, the United States is a relatively self-sufficient economy. Many nations, particularly in Western Europe and East Asia, are highly open economies and export and import more than 50 percent of their GDP.

The degree of openness is much higher in many U.S. industries, such as steel, textiles, consumer electronics, and autos, than it is for the U.S. economy as a whole. Table 34-1 on page 676 shows the commodity composition of U.S. foreign trade for 1996. These data reveal that despite being an advanced industrial economy, the United States exports surprisingly large amounts of primary commodities (such as food) and imports large quantities of sophisticated, capital-intensive manufactured goods (like automobiles and telecommunications equipment). Moreover, we find a great deal of two-way, or intraindustry, trade. Within a particular industry, the United States both exports and imports at the same time because a high degree of product differentiation means that different countries tend to have niches in different parts of a market.

THE SOURCES OF INTERNATIONAL TRADE IN GOODS AND SERVICES

What are the economic factors that lie behind the patterns of international trade? Nations find it beneficial to participate in international trade for several reasons: because of diversity in the conditions of production, because of decreasing costs of production, and because of differences in tastes among nations.

FIGURE 34-2. Growing U.S. Openness

Like all major market economies, the United States has increasingly opened its borders to foreign trade over the last half-century. The result is a growing share of output and consumption involved in international trade. In the late 1980s, imports far outdistanced exports, causing the United States to become the world's largest debtor nation. (Source: U.S. Department of Commerce.)

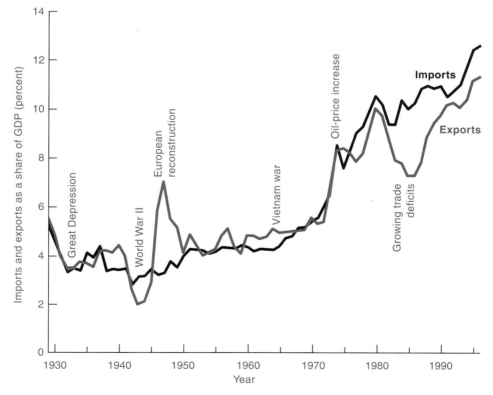

U.S. Merchandise Trade, 1996		
	Share of each commodity as percent of total	
Commodity classification	Exports	Imports
Industrial supplies:		
Food and beverages	9	4
Petroleum and petroleum products	1	8
Other	22	15
Manufactures:		
Capital goods		
Computers and related equipment	7	7
Civilian aircraft and related equipment	5	1
Other capital goods	27	19
Automotive vehicles and parts	10	16
Consumer goods	11	21
Other	5	5
Total	100	100

TABLE 34-1. The United States Exports Surprising Amounts of Primary Goods and Imports Many Manufactures

The United States exports a large volume of primary commodities, especially food and coal, mainly because of its ample natural resources. At the same time, it imports many manufactured goods, like cars and cameras, because other countries specialize in different market niches and enjoy economies of scale. (Source: U.S. Department of Commerce.)

Diversity in Natural Resources

Trade may take place because of the diversity in productive possibilities among countries. In part, these differences reflect endowments of natural resources. One country may be blessed with a supply of petroleum, while another may have a large amount of fertile land. Or a mountainous country may generate large amounts of hydroelectric power which it sells to its neighbors, while a country with deep-water harbors may become a shipping center.

Differences in Tastes

A second cause of trade lies in preferences. Even if the conditions of production were identical in all regions, countries might engage in trade if their tastes for goods were different.

For example, suppose that Norway and Sweden produce fish from the sea and meat from the land in about the same amounts, but the Swedes have a great fondness for meat while the Norwegians are partial to fish. A mutually beneficial export of meat from Norway and fish from Sweden would take place. Both countries would gain from this trade; the sum of human happiness is increased, just as when Jack Sprat trades fat meat for his wife's lean.

Decreasing Costs

Perhaps the most important reason for trade is differences among countries in production costs. For example, manufacturing processes enjoy economies of scale; that is, they tend to have lower average costs of production as the volume of output expands. So when a particular country gets a head start in a particular product, it can become the high-volume, low-cost producer. The economies of scale give it a significant cost and technological advantage over other countries, which find it cheaper to buy from the leading producer than to make the product themselves.

Take consumer electronics as an example. No doubt a company such as GE or IBM could make a videocassette recorder (VCR) in the United States if it wanted to. But it could not make one cheap enough to compete with Japanese manufacturers like Sony, which have the advantages of enormous volumes and long experience in making consumer electronics. As a result, the United States imports almost all of its VCRs.

The shoe is on the other foot when it comes to civilian aircraft, where the United States dominates the world market. Boeing, the leading exporter in the United States, has two important advantages. First, Boeing has a long track record in building reliable and safe passenger jets. This is not an easy task for a competitor to match. Because modern planes are complicated and technologically sophisticated, it takes time and practice to learn how to build reliable planes at an affordable price.

Large scale is often an important advantage in industries with large research and development expenses. As the leading aircraft maker in the world, Boeing can spread the enormous cost of designing, developing, and testing a new plane over a large sales volume. That means it can sell planes at a lower price than competitors with a smaller volume. Boe-

ing's only real competitor, Airbus, got off the ground through large subsidies from several European countries to cover its research and development costs.

The example of decreasing cost helps explain the important phenomenon of extensive intra-industry trade shown in Table 34-1. Why is it that the United States both imports and exports computers and related equipment? The reason is that the United States has exploited the economies of scale in microprocessors and is specialized in that area, while Japan enjoys a cost advantage in memory chips and video screens for notebook computers and tends to specialize and export in that part of the market. Similar patterns of intraindustry specialization are seen with cars, steel, textiles, and many other manufactured products.

The next chapter synthesizes the different reasons for trade in the theory of comparative advantage.

B. THE DETERMINATION OF FOREIGN EXCHANGE RATES

FOREIGN EXCHANGE RATES

We are all familiar with domestic trade. When I buy Florida oranges or California shirts, I naturally want to pay in dollars. Luckily, the orange grower and the shirt manufacturer want payment in U.S. currency, so all trade can be carried out in dollars. Economic transactions within a country are simple.

But if I am interested in importing Japanese bicycles, the transaction becomes more complicated. The bicycle manufacturer needs to be paid in Japanese currency rather than in U.S. dollars. Therefore, in order to import the Japanese bicycles, I must first buy Japanese yen (¥) and use those yen to pay the Japanese manufacturer. Similarly, if the Japanese want to buy U.S. merchandise, they must first obtain U.S. dollars. This new complication involves foreign exchange.

Foreign trade involves the use of different national currencies. The **foreign exchange rate** is the price of one currency in terms of another currency. The foreign exchange rate is determined in the foreign exchange market, which is the market where different currencies are traded.

That little paragraph contains much information that will be explained in this section. To begin with, recall that all major countries have their own currencies—the U.S. dollar, the British pound, the Japanese yen, the German mark, the Mexican peso, and so forth. *We follow the convention of measuring exchange rates as the amount of foreign currency that can be bought with 1 unit of the domestic currency.* For example, the foreign exchange rate of the dollar might be 100 yen per U.S. dollar (¥100/$).

When we want to exchange one national money for another, we do so at a foreign exchange rate. For example, if you traveled to Canada in 1997, you would get about 1.4 Canadian dollars for 1 U.S. dollar. There is a foreign exchange rate between U.S. dollars and the currency of each and every other country. In mid-1997, the foreign exchange rate per U.S. dollar was 0.62 British pound, 1.8 German marks, 118 Japanese yen, and 7.97 Mexican pesos.

With foreign exchange, it is possible for me to buy a Japanese bicycle. Suppose its quoted price is 20,000 yen. I can look in the newspaper for the foreign exchange rate for yen. Suppose the rate is ¥100/$. I could go to the bank to convert my $200 into ¥20,000. With my Japanese money, I then can pay the exporter in the currency it needs for my bicycle.

You should be able to show what Japanese importers of American trucks have to do if they want to buy, say, a $36,000 shipment from an American exporter. Here yen must be converted into dollars. You will see that, when the foreign exchange rate is 100 yen per dollar, the truck shipment costs them ¥3,600,000.

Businesses and tourists do not have to know anything more than this for their import or export transactions. But the economics of foreign exchange rates cannot be grasped until we analyze the forces underlying the supply and demand for foreign currencies and the functioning of the foreign exchange market.

THE FOREIGN EXCHANGE MARKET

Foreign exchange rates, for the most part, are not fixed over time. Instead, like other prices, they vary from week to week and month to month according to the forces of supply and demand. The **foreign exchange market** is the market in which currencies of different countries are traded and foreign exchange rates are determined. Foreign currencies are traded at the retail level in many banks and firms specializing in that business. Organized markets in New York, Tokyo, London, and Zurich trade hundreds of billions of dollars worth of currencies each day.

We can use our familiar supply and demand curves to illustrate how markets determine the price of foreign currencies. Figure 34-3 shows the supply and demand for U.S. dollars in U.S. dealings with Japan.[1] The *supply* of U.S. dollars comes from people in the United States who need yen to purchase Japanese goods, services, or financial instruments. The *demand* for dollars comes from people in Japan who buy U.S. goods, services, or investments and who, accordingly, need to pay for these items in dollars. The price of foreign exchange—the foreign exchange rate—settles at that price where supply and demand are in balance.

Let us first consider the supply side. The supply of U.S. dollars to the foreign exchange market originates when Americans need yen to buy Japanese automobiles, cameras, and other commodities, to vacation in Tokyo, and so forth. In addition, foreign exchange is required if Americans want to purchase Japanese investments, such as shares in Japanese companies. In short, *Americans supply dollars when they purchase foreign goods, services, and assets.*

In Figure 34-3, the vertical axis is the crucial *foreign exchange rate*, e, *measured in units of foreign currency per unit of domestic currency*—that is, in yen per dollar, in Mexican pesos per dollar, and so forth. Make sure you understand the units here. The horizontal axis

FIGURE 34-3. **Exchange-Rate Determination**

Behind the supplies and demands for foreign exchange lie purchases of goods, services, and financial flows. Behind the demand for dollars is the Japanese desire for American goods and investments. The supply of dollars comes from Americans desiring Japanese goods and assets. Equilibrium comes at *E*. If the foreign exchange rate were above *E*, there would be an excess supply of dollars. Unless the government bought this excess supply for official reserves, market forces would push the foreign exchange rate back down to balance supply and demand at *E*.

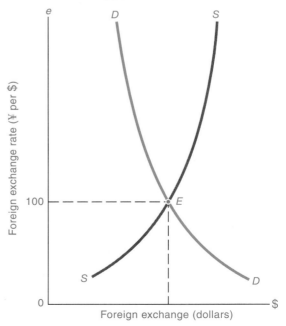

shows the quantity of dollars transacted in the foreign exchange market.

The supply of U.S. dollars is represented by the upward-sloping *SS* curve. The central point here is that as the foreign exchange rate rises, the number of yen that can be bought per dollar increases. This means, other things being equal, that the prices of Japanese goods fall relative to those of American goods. Hence, Americans will tend to buy more Japanese goods, and the supply of U.S. dollars therefore increases. This shows why the supply curve slopes upward. Let's take the example of bicycles. If the foreign exchange rate were to rise from ¥100/$ to ¥200/$, the bicycle which cost ¥20,000 would fall in price from $200 to $100. If other things were unchanged, Japanese bicycles would be more attractive, and Americans would require more dollar foreign exchange to buy a larger quantity of bicycles. Hence, the quantity supplied of dollars would be higher at a higher exchange rate.

What lies behind the demand for dollars (represented in Figure 34-3 by the *DD* demand curve for dollar foreign exchange)? Foreigners demand U.S. dollars when they buy American goods, services, and assets. For example, suppose a Japanese student buys an American economics textbook or takes a trip to the United States. She will require U.S. dollars to pay for these items. Or when JAL buys a Boeing 767 for its fleet, this transaction increases the demand for U.S. dollars. In short, *foreigners demand U.S. dollars to pay for their purchases of American goods, services, and assets.*

The demand curve in Figure 34-3 slopes downward to indicate that as the dollar's value falls (and the yen therefore becomes more expensive), Japanese residents will want to buy more foreign goods, services, and investments. They will therefore demand more U.S. dollars in the foreign exchange market. Consider what happens when the foreign exchange rate on the dollar falls from ¥100/$ to ¥50/$. American computers, which had sold at $2000 × (¥100/$) = ¥200,000 now sell for only $2000 × (¥50/$) = ¥100,000. Japanese purchasers will therefore tend to buy more American computers, and the quantity demanded of U.S. foreign exchange will increase.

The purpose of the foreign exchange market is to equilibrate supply and demand. Market forces move the foreign exchange rate up or down to balance the supply and demand. The price will settle at the *equilibrium foreign exchange rate,* which is the rate at which the dollars willingly bought just equal the dollars willingly sold.

The balance of supply and demand for foreign exchange determines the foreign exchange rate of a currency. At the market exchange rate of 100 yen per dollar shown at point *E* in Figure 34-3, the exchange rate is in equilibrium and has no tendency to rise or fall.

We have discussed the foreign exchange market in terms of the supply and demand for dollars. But in this market, there are two currencies involved, so we could just as easily analyze the supply and demand for Japanese yen. To see this, you should sketch a supply-and-demand diagram with yen foreign exchange on the horizontal axis and the yen rate ($ per ¥) on the vertical axis. If ¥100/$ is the equilibrium looking from the point of view of the dollar, then $0.01/¥ is the *reciprocal exchange rate.* As an exercise, go through the analysis in this section for the reciprocal market. You will see that in this simple bilateral world, for every dollar statement there is an exact yen counterpart: supply of dollars is demand for yen; demand for dollars is supply of yen.

There is just one further extension necessary to get to actual foreign exchange markets. In reality, each country has its own currency. We therefore need to find the supplies and demands for each and every currency. And in a world of many nations, it is the many-sided exchange and trade, with demands and supplies coming from all parts of the globe, that determines the entire array of foreign exchange rates.

Exchange-Rate Systems

While this chapter is primarily devoted to laying out the basic tools for international economics, it is important to recognize that there are different approaches to managing a nation's exchange rates. The two systems most widely used today are flexible and fixed exchange rates. One system occurs when exchange rates are completely flexible and move purely under the influence of supply and demand. With this system, known as *flexible exchange rates* (or sometimes "floating" exchange rates), governments take a hands-off policy toward their exchange rate and do not try to set a particular rate. That is, in a flexible-exchange-rate system, the relative prices of currencies are determined in the marketplace through the buying and selling of households and businesses. The United States currently relies upon a flexible exchange rate.

The other major system is *fixed exchange rates*, where governments specify the rate at which their currency will be converted into other currencies. The gold standard was a fixed-exchange-rate system, as was the Bretton Woods system used by most countries after World War II. Over the last decade, many European countries have operated a fixed-exchange-rate system.

We will review the economic advantages and disadvantages of different exchange-rate systems in the last chapter of this book.

Terminology for Exchange-Rate Changes

Foreign exchange markets have a special vocabulary. By definition, a fall in the price of one currency in terms of one or all others is called a *depreciation*. A rise in the price of a currency in terms of another currency is called an *appreciation*. In our example above, when the price of the dollar rose from ¥100/$ to ¥200/$, the dollar appreciated. We also know that the yen depreciated.

In the supply-and-demand diagram for U.S. dollars, a fall in the foreign exchange rate (*e*) is a depreciation of the U.S. dollar, and a rise in *e* represents an appreciation.

The term "devaluation" is often confused with the term "depreciation." *Devaluation* is confined to situations in which a country has officially set or "pegged" its exchange rate relative to one or more other currencies. In this case, a devaluation occurs when the pegged rate or parity is changed by lowering the price of the currency. A *revaluation* occurs when the official price is raised.

For example, in December 1994 Mexico devalued its currency when it lowered the official price at which it was defending the peso from 3.5 pesos per dollar to 3.8 pesos per dollar. Mexico soon found it could not defend the new parity and "floated" its exchange rate. At that point, the peso fell, or depreciated, even further.

When a country's currency falls in value relative to that of another country, we say that the domestic currency has undergone a **depreciation** while the foreign currency has undergone an **appreciation**.

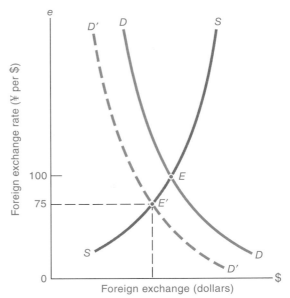

FIGURE 34-4. A Decrease in Demand for Dollars Leads to Dollar Depreciation

Suppose that a recession or deflation in Japan reduces the Japanese demand for dollars. This would shift the demand for dollars to the left from *DD* to *D'D'*. The exchange rate of the dollar depreciates, while the yen appreciates. Why would the new exchange rate discourage American purchases of Japanese goods?

When a country's official foreign exchange rate is lowered, we say that the currency has undergone a **devaluation**. An increase in the official foreign exchange rate is called a **revaluation**.

Effects of Changes in Trade

What would happen if there were changes in demand? For example, there might be a deep recession in Japan, or Japan might take protectionist measures by putting a quota on American goods.

In each of these cases, the demand for American dollars would decrease. The result is shown in Figure 34-4. The decline in purchases of American goods, services, and investments decreases the demand for dollars in the market. This change is represented by a leftward shift in the demand curve. The result will be a lower foreign exchange rate—that is, the dollar will depreciate and the yen will appreciate. At the lower exchange rate, the quantity of dollars supplied by Americans to the market will decrease because

Japanese goods are now more expensive. Moreover, the quantity of dollars demanded by the Japanese will decline because of the recession and protectionist measures. How much will exchange rates change? Just enough so that the supply and demand are again in balance. In the example shown in Figure 34-4, the dollar has depreciated from ¥100/$ to ¥75/$.

Purchasing-Power Parity and Exchange Rates

In the short run, market-determined exchange rates are highly volatile in response to monetary policy, political events, and changes in expectations. But over the longer run, economists believe, exchange rates are determined primarily by the relative prices of goods in different countries. An important implication is the *purchasing-power parity (PPP) theory of exchange rates.* Under this theory, a nation's exchange rate will tend to equalize the cost of buying traded goods at home with the cost of buying those goods abroad.

A special case is the *law of one price,* which states that (in the absence of transportation costs and trade barriers) identical goods must sell at the same price in all markets. The PPP theory can then be illustrated with a simple example. Suppose the price of a market basket of goods (automobiles, jewelry, oil, foods, and so forth) costs $1000 in the United States and 10,000 pesos in Mexico. At an exchange rate of 100 pesos to a dollar, this bundle would cost $100 in Mexico. Given these relative prices and the free trade between the two countries, we would expect to see American firms and consumers streaming across the border to buy at the lower Mexican prices. The result will be higher imports from Mexico, and an increased demand for Mexican pesos. That will cause the exchange rate of the Mexican peso to appreciate relative to the U.S. dollar, so you will need more dollars to buy the same number of pesos. As a result, the prices of the Mexican goods *in dollar terms* rise even though the prices in pesos have not changed.

Where would this process end? If the law of one price holds, with unchanged prices in the two countries the peso's exchange rate must fall to 10 pesos to the dollar. Only at this exchange rate would the price of the market basket of goods be equal in the two markets. At 10 pesos to the dollar, we say that the currencies have equal purchasing power in terms of the traded goods.

The PPP doctrine also holds that countries with high inflation rates will tend to have depreciating currencies. For example, if Country A's inflation rate is 10 percent while inflation in Country B is 2 percent, the currency of Country A will tend to depreciate relative to that of Country B by the difference in the inflation rates, that is, 8 percent annually. Alternatively, let's say that runaway inflation leads to a 100-fold rise of prices in Russia over the course of a year, while prices in the United States are unchanged. According to the PPP theory, the Russian ruble should depreciate by 99 percent in order to bring the prices of American and Russian goods back into equilibrium.

We should caution that the PPP theory is only an approximation and cannot predict the precise movement of exchange rates. The leeway in the PPP theory is seen in the relationship between the U.S. dollar and the Japanese yen over the last decade; this exchange rate has been as high as 168 yen to a dollar and as low as 85 yen to a dollar, even though most economists calculate the PPP level as being around 120 yen to a dollar. Trade barriers, transportation costs, and the presence of nontraded services allow prices to diverge significantly across countries. In addition, financial flows can overwhelm trade flows in the short run. So while the PPP theory is a useful guide to exchange rates in the long run, exchange rates can diverge from their PPP level for many years.

PPP and the size of nations: By any measure, the United States still has the largest economy in the world. But which country has the second largest? Is it Japan, Germany, Russia, or some other country? You'd think this would be an easy question to answer, like measuring height or weight. The problem, though, is that Japan totes up its national output in yen, while Germany's national output is given in marks, and America's is in dollars. To be compared, they all need to be converted into the same currency.

The customary approach is to use the market exchange rate to convert each currency into dollars, and by that yardstick Japan has the second-largest economy. However, there are two difficulties with using the market rate. First, because market rates can rise and fall sharply, the size of countries could easily change by 10 or 20 percent in a year. More-

	GDP using market exchange rates ($, billion)	GDP using PPP exchange rates ($, billion)
United States	6,648	6,648
Japan	4,591	2,802
China	522	2,473
Germany	2,046	1,558
India	294	1,174
France	1,330	1,117
United Kingdom	1,017	997
Indonesia	175	714
Russia	377	655
Mexico	377	635
Philippines	64	185
Malaysia	71	171
Nigeria	35	150
Hong Kong	132	128

TABLE 34-2. PPP Calculations Change the Relative Size of Nations, 1994

Using PPP exchange rates changes the economic ranking of nations. After correcting for the purchasing power of incomes, China moves from a middle-ranking country to an economic superpower. (Source: World Bank.)

over, using market exchange rates, many poor countries appear to have a very small national output.

Today, economists generally prefer to use PPP exchange rates to compare the living standards in different countries. The difference can be dramatic, as Table 34-2 shows. When market exchange rates are used, the outputs of low-income countries like China and India tend to be understated. This understatement occurs because a substantial part of their output comes in labor-intensive services, which are usually extremely inexpen-

sive in low-wage countries. Hence, when we calculate PPP exchange rates including the prices of nontraded goods, the GDPs of low-income countries rise relative to those of high-wage countries. For example, when PPP exchange rates are used, China's GDP is 5 times the level calculated with market exchange rates. Furthermore, on the basis of PPP exchange rates, China leaps ahead of Germany to become the third-largest economy in the world.

C. THE BALANCE OF INTERNATIONAL PAYMENTS

BALANCE-OF-PAYMENTS ACCOUNTS

Economists keep score by looking at income statements and balance sheets. In the area of international economics, the key accounts are a nation's balance of payments. A country's **balance of international payments** is a systematic statement of all economic transactions between that country and the rest of the world. Its major components are the cur-

rent account and the capital account. The basic structure of the balance of payments is shown in Table 34-3, and each element is discussed below.

Debits and Credits

Like other accounts, the balance of payments records each transaction as either a plus or a minus. The general rule in balance-of-payments accounting is the following:

I.	Current account
	Merchandise (or "trade balance")
	Services
	Investment income
	Unilateral transfers
II.	Capital account
	Private
	Government
	Official reserve changes
	Other

TABLE 34-3. Basic Elements of the Balance of Payments

The balance of payments has two fundamental parts. The current account represents the spending and receipts on goods and services along with transfers. The capital account includes asset purchases and sales. An important principle is that the two must always sum to zero.

If a transaction earns foreign currency for the nation, it is called a *credit* and is recorded as a plus item. If a transaction involves spending foreign currency, it is a *debit* and is recorded as a negative item. In general, exports are credits and imports are debits.

Exports earn foreign currency, so they are credits. Imports require spending foreign currency, so they are debits. How is the U.S. import of a Japanese camera recorded? Since we ultimately pay for it in Japanese yen, it is clearly a debit. How shall we treat interest and dividend income on investments received by Americans from abroad? Clearly, they are credit items like exports because they provide us with foreign currencies.

Details of the Balance of Payments

Balance on Current Account. The totality of items under section I in Table 34-3 is the **balance on current account**. This includes all items of income and outlay—imports and exports of goods and services, investment income, and transfer payments. The current-account balance is akin to the net income of a nation. It is conceptually similar to net exports in the national output accounts.

In the past, many writers concentrated on the **trade balance**, which consists of merchandise imports or exports. The composition of merchandise imports and exports was shown in Table 34-1; it consists mainly of primary commodities (like food and fuels) and manufactured goods. In an earlier era,

the mercantilists strove for a trade surplus (an excess of exports over imports), calling this a "favorable balance of trade." They hoped to avoid an "unfavorable trade balance," by which they meant a trade deficit (an excess of imports over exports). This point of view has carried over to today as many nations seek trade surpluses.

Today, economists avoid this language because a trade deficit is not necessarily harmful. Sometimes, a nation may have a trade deficit because the domestic productivity of capital is extremely high and borrowing to import capital equipment will in the long run raise national income.

In addition, *services* are increasingly important in international trade. Services consist of such items as shipping, financial services, and foreign travel. A third item in the current account is *investment income,* which includes the earnings on foreign investments (that is, earnings on U.S. assets abroad). One of the major developments of the last two decades has been the growth in services and investment income. A final element is transfers, which represent payments not in return for goods and services.

Table 34-4 on page 684 presents a summary of the U.S. balance of international payments for 1996. Note its two main divisions: current account and capital account. Each item is listed by name in column (a). Credits are listed in column (b), while column (c) shows the debits. Column (d) then lists the net credits or debits; it shows a credit if on balance the item added to our stock of foreign currencies or a debit if the total subtracted from our foreign-currency supply.

In 1996 our merchandise exports gave us credits of $612 billion. But our merchandise imports gave us debits of $803 billion. The *net* difference between credits and debits was a debit of $191 billion. This trade deficit is listed in column (d), on the first row. (Be sure you know why the algebraic sign is shown as − rather than as +.) From the table we see that services provided a surplus, while net investment income was close to zero. Our current-account deficit was thus $148 billion for 1996.

Capital Account. We have now completed analysis of the current account. But how did the United States "finance" its $148 billion current-account deficit in 1996? It must have either borrowed or reduced its foreign assets, for by definition that which you buy you must either pay for or owe for. This means that *the balance of international*

U.S. Balance of Payments, 1996 (Billions of Dollars)				
Section	(a) Items	(b) Credits (+)	(c) Debits (−)	(d) Net credits (+) or debits (−)
I.	Current account			−148
	a. Merchandise trade balance	612	−803	−191
	b. Services	237	−157	80
	c. Investment income	206	−204	3
	d. Unilateral transfers			−40
II.	Capital account [lending (−) or borrowing (+)]			148
	a. Private (including statistical discrepancy)			20
	b. Government			
	Official U.S. reserve changes			7
	Other foreign government changes			121
Sum of Current and Capital Account				0

TABLE 34-4. Basic Elements fo Balance of Payments

Source: U.S. Department of Commerce, *Survey of Current Business,* September 1997.

payments as a whole must by definition show a final zero balance.

Capital-account transactions are asset transactions between Americans and foreigners. They occur, for example, when a Japanese pension fund buys U.S. government securities or when an American buys stock in a Japanese firm.

It is easy to decide which items are credits and which are debits in the capital account if you use the following rule: Always think of the United States as exporting and importing stocks, bonds, or other securities—or, for short, exporting and importing IOUs in return for foreign currencies. *Then you can treat these exports and imports of securities like other exports and imports.* When we borrow abroad to finance a current-account deficit, we are sending IOUs (in the form of Treasury bills) abroad and gaining foreign currencies. Is this a credit or a debit? Clearly this is a credit because it brought foreign currencies into the United States.

Similarly, if U.S. banks lend abroad to finance a computer assembly plant in Mexico, the U.S. banks are importing IOUs from the Mexicans and the United States is losing foreign currencies; this is clearly a debit item in the U.S. balance of payments.

Line II shows that in 1996 the United States was a net *borrower:* we borrowed abroad more than we lent to foreigners. The United States was a net exporter of IOUs (a net borrower) in the amount of $148 billion.[2]

Official Reserves. One part of the capital account is a special feature—the line showing the official-reserve changes. When all countries have purely market-determined exchange rates, the entry on line II(c) of Table 34-4 must be zero. When countries "intervene" in foreign exchange markets, they attempt to affect the exchange rate by buying and selling foreign currencies. This shows up in the balance of payments as changes in *official reserves.*

We will see that official reserves play a crucial role when countries have fixed exchange rates and defend the official exchange rates. When a country defends its official exchange rate, it does so by buying and selling foreign currencies. This leads to changes in official reserves. By contrast, when countries have market-determined (or flexible) exchange rates, there is little intervention and changes in official reserves are relatively small. In today's increas-

---

[2] As in all economic statistics, there are statistical errors (called the "statistical discrepancy" in the balance-of-payments accounts). These reflect the fact that many flows of goods and finance (from small currency transactions to the drug trade) are not recorded. We include the statistical discrepancy in the private capital account in line II(a) of Table 34-4.

ingly integrated capital markets, capital flows are dominated by private asset transactions.

Exchange Rates and the Balance of Payments

We can now see the connection between exchange rates and adjustments in the balance of payments. In the simplest case, assume that exchange rates are determined by supply and demand. Consider what happened after German unification when the German central bank decided to raise interest rates to curb inflation. After the monetary tightening, foreigners moved some of their assets into German marks to benefit from high German interest rates. This produced an excess demand for the German mark at the old exchange rate. In other words, at the old foreign exchange rate, people were, on balance, buying German marks and selling other currencies.

Here is where the exchange rate plays its role as equilibrator. As the demand for German marks increased, it led to an appreciation of the German mark and a depreciation of other currencies, like the U.S. dollar. The movement in the exchange rate continued until the capital and current accounts were back in balance. The equilibration for the current account is easiest to understand. Here, the appreciation of the mark made German goods more expensive and led to a decline in German exports and an increase in German imports. Both of these factors tended to reduce the German current-account surplus.

Exchange-rate movements serve as a balance wheel to remove disequilibria in the balance of payments.

LIFE CYCLE OF THE BALANCE OF PAYMENTS

A review of the economic history of industrialized countries reveals that they go through similar life cycles in their balance of payments as they grow from young debtor to mature creditor. This sequence is found, with variations related to their particular histories, in the advanced economies of North America, Europe, and Southeast Asia. We can illustrate the stages by recounting briefly the history of the balance of payments of the United States:

1. *Young and growing debtor nation.* From the Revolutionary War until after the Civil War, the United States imported on current account more than it exported. Europe lent the difference, which allowed the country to build up its capital stock. The United States was a typical young and growing debtor nation.

2. *Mature debtor nation.* From about 1873 to 1914, the U.S. balance of trade moved into surplus. But growth of the dividends and interest that were owed abroad on past borrowing kept the current account more or less in balance. Capital movements were also nearly in balance as lending just offset borrowing.

3. *New creditor nation.* During World War I, the United States expanded its exports tremendously. American citizens and the government lent money to allies England and France for war equipment and postwar relief needs. The United States emerged from the war a creditor nation.

4. *Mature creditor nation.* In the fourth stage, earnings on foreign capital and investments provided a large surplus on invisibles that was matched by a deficit on merchandise trade. This pattern was followed by the United States until the early 1980s. Countries like Japan today play the role of mature creditor nation as they enjoy large current-account surpluses which they in turn invest abroad.

The United States has entered an interesting new position in the last two decades. In this stage, the nation is again borrowing from abroad to finance its domestic investment. In part, the foreign borrowing is caused by low levels of U.S. domestic saving. In addition, capital is attracted to the United States because of the country's political stability, low inflation, and robust inventiveness. The counterpart of American dissaving is that foreigners, particularly Japanese investors, are purchasing substantial amounts of American assets.

Is this new stage of the U.S. balance of payments a transient period? Or does it mark the beginning of a long period of "structural" current-account deficits that will last for decades to come? No one can answer this question with certainty. Corrective forces in the 1990s appear to be shifting the U.S. current account back toward balance, but with a heavy foreign debt to service. When balance occurs, the United States will once again be a mature debtor nation, going back to stage 2, above.

SUMMARY

A. Economic Basis for International Trade

1. Specialization, division of labor, and trade increase productivity and consumption possibilities. The gains from trade hold among nations as well as within a nation. Engaging in international exchange is more efficient than relying only on domestic production.

2. Diversity is the fundamental reason that nations engage in international trade. Within this general principle, we see that trade occurs (*a*) because of differences in the conditions of production, (*b*) because of decreasing costs (or economies of scale), and (*c*) because of diversity in tastes.

B. The Determination of Foreign Exchange Rates

3. International trade involves the new element of different national currencies, which are linked by relative prices called foreign exchange rates. When Americans import Japanese goods, they ultimately need to pay in Japanese yen. In the foreign exchange market, Japanese yen might trade at ¥100/$ (or reciprocally, ¥1 would trade for $0.01). This price is called the foreign exchange rate.

4. In a foreign exchange market involving only two countries, the supply of U.S. dollars comes from Americans who want to purchase goods, services, and investments from Japan; the demand for U.S. dollars comes from Japanese who want to import commodities or financial assets from America. The interaction of these supplies and demands determines the foreign exchange rate. More generally, foreign exchange rates are determined by the complex interplay of many countries buying and selling among themselves. When trade or capital flows change, supply and demand shift and the equilibrium exchange rate changes.

5. A fall in the market price of a currency is a depreciation; a rise in a currency's value is called an appreciation. In a system where governments announce official foreign exchange rates, a decrease in the official exchange rate is called a devaluation, while an increase is a revaluation.

6. According to the purchasing-power parity (PPP) theory of exchange rates, exchange rates tend to move with changes in relative price levels of different countries. The PPP theory applies better to the long run than the short run. When this theory is applied to measure the purchasing power of incomes in different countries, it raises the per capita outputs of low-income countries.

C. The Balance of International Payments

7. The balance of international payments is the set of accounts that measures all the economic transactions between a nation and the rest of the world. It includes exports and imports of goods, services, and financial capital. Exports are credit items, while imports are debits. More generally, a country's credit items are transactions that make foreign currencies available to it; debit items are ones that reduce its holdings of foreign currencies.

8. The major components of the balance of payments are:
   I. Current account (merchandise trade, services, investment income, transfers)
   II. Capital account (private, government, and official-reserve changes)
   The fundamental rule of balance-of-payments accounting is that the sum of all items must equal zero: I + II = 0.

9. Historically, countries tend to go through stages of the balance of payments: from the young debtor borrowing for economic development, through mature debtor and young creditor, to mature creditor nation living off earnings from past investments. In the 1980s, the United States moved to a different stage where low domestic saving and attractive investment opportunities again led it to borrow heavily abroad and become a debtor nation.

CONCEPTS FOR REVIEW

Principles of International Trade

open economy
sources of trade:
   cost differences
   decreasing costs
   differences in tastes

Foreign Exchange Rates

foreign exchange rate, foreign
   exchange market
supply of and demand for foreign
   exchange
exchange rate terminology:
   appreciation and depreciation
   revaluation and devaluation

Balance of Payments

balance of payments (current
   account, capital account)
official-reserve changes
balance of payments components:
   I + II = 0
debits and credits
stages of balance of payments

QUESTIONS FOR DISCUSSION

1. Table 34-5 shows some foreign exchange rates (in units of foreign currency per dollar) as of early 1997. Fill in the last column of the table with the reciprocal price of the dollar in terms of each foreign currency, being especially careful to write down the relevant units in the parentheses.

2. Figure 34-3 shows the demand and supply for U.S. dollars in an example in which Japan and the United States trade only with each other.

   a. Describe and draw the reciprocal supply and demand schedules for Japanese yen. Explain why the supply of yen is equivalent to the demand for dollars. Also explain and draw the schedule that corresponds to the supply of dollars. Find the equilibrium price of yen in this new diagram and relate it to the equilibrium in Figure 34-3.

   b. Assume that Americans develop a taste for Japanese goods. Show what would happen to the supply and demand for yen. Would the yen appreciate or depreciate relative to the dollar? Explain.

3. Draw up a list of items that belong on the credit side of the balance of international payments and another list of items that belong on the debit side. What is meant by a trade surplus? By the balance on current account?

4. Construct hypothetical balance-of-payments accounts for a young debtor country, a mature debtor country, a new creditor country, and a mature creditor country.

5. Consider the situation for Germany described on page 685. Using a figure like Figure 34-3, show the supply and demand for German marks before and after the shock. Identify on your figure the excess demand for marks *before* the appreciation of the mark. Then show how an appreciation of the mark would wipe out the excess demand.

6. A Middle East nation suddenly discovers huge oil resources. Show how its balance of trade and current account suddenly turn to surplus. Show how it can acquire assets in New York as a capital account offset. Later, when it uses the assets for internal development, show how its current and capital items reverse their roles.

7. Consider the following quotation from the 1984 *Economic Report of the President*:

   > In the long run, the exchange rate tends to follow the differential trend in the domestic and foreign price level. If one country's price level gets too far out of line with prices in other countries, there will eventually be a fall in demand for its goods, which will lead to a real depreciation of its currency.

   Explain how the first sentence relates to the PPP theory of exchange rates. Explain the reasoning behind the PPP theory. In addition, using a supply-and-demand diagram like that of Figure 34-3, explain the sequence of events, described in the second sentence of the quotation, whereby a country whose price level is relatively high will find that its exchange rate depreciates.

8. A nation records the following data for 1994: exports of automobiles ($100) and corn ($150); imports of oil ($150) and steel ($75); tourist expenditures abroad ($25); private lending to foreign countries ($50); private borrowing from foreign countries ($40); official-reserve changes ($30 of foreign exchange bought by domestic central bank). Calculate the statistical discrepancy and include it in private lending to foreign countries. Create a balance-of-payments table like Table 34-4.

TABLE 34-5.

| | Price | |
Currency	Units of foreign currency per dollar	Dollars per unit of foreign currency
Zloty (Poland)	3.09 (zloty/$)	_____ ($/zloty)
Real (Brazil)	1.06	_____ (_____)
Renminbi (China)	8.33	_____ (_____)
Peso (Mexico)	7.97	_____ (_____)
Drachma (Greece)	268	_____ (_____)

CHAPTER 35
COMPARATIVE ADVANTAGE AND PROTECTIONISM

> To the Chamber of Deputies: We are subject to the intolerable competition of a foreign rival, who enjoys such superior facilities for the production of light that he can inundate our national market at reduced price. This rival is no other than the sun. Our petition is to pass a law shutting up all windows, openings, and fissures through which the light of the sun is used to penetrate our dwellings, to the prejudice of the profitable manufacture we have been enabled to bestow on the country.
> Signed: The Candle Makers
>
> *F. Bastiat*

In his "Petition of the Candle Makers," the French economist Frederic Bastiat was satirizing the many solemn proposals to block out foreign goods that compete with domestic suppliers. Today, people often regard foreign competition with suspicion, and campaigns to "Buy American" sound patriotic.

Yet economists since the time of Adam Smith have marched to a different drummer. Economics teaches that international trade is beneficial to a nation. It encourages specialization and expands a nation's consumption possibilities. Japan sells America cameras; America sells computers to Australia; Australia closes the circle by selling coal to Japan. By specializing in its areas of greatest relative productivity, each nation can consume more than it could produce alone. This is the simple yet elusive essence of foreign trade which will be presented in this chapter.

A. COMPARATIVE ADVANTAGE AMONG NATIONS

THE PRINCIPLE OF COMPARATIVE ADVANTAGE

It is only common sense that countries will produce and export goods for which they are uniquely qualified. But there is a deeper principle underlying *all* trade—in a family, within a nation, and among nations—that goes beyond common sense. The *principle of comparative advantage* holds that a country can benefit from trade even if it is absolutely more efficient (or absolutely less efficient) than other countries in the production of every good. Indeed, trade according to comparative advantage provides mutual benefits to all countries.

Uncommon Sense

Say that the United States has higher output per worker (or per unit of input) than the rest of the world in making both computers and grain. But suppose the United States is relatively more efficient in computers than it is in grain. For example, it might be 50 percent more productive in computers and 10 percent more productive in grain. In this case, it would benefit the United States to export that good in which it is relatively more efficient (computers) and import that good in which it is relatively less efficient (grain).

Or consider a poor country like Mali. How could impoverished Mali, whose workers use handlooms and have productivity that is only a fraction of that of industrialized countries, hope to export any of its textiles? Surprisingly, according to the principle of comparative advantage, Mali can benefit by exporting the goods in which it is *relatively* more efficient (like textiles) and importing those goods which it produces *relatively* less efficiently (like turbines and automobiles).

The principle of **comparative advantage** holds that each country will benefit if it specializes in the production and export of those goods that it can produce at relatively low cost. Conversely, each country will benefit if it imports those goods which it produces at relatively high cost.

This simple principle provides the unshakable basis for international trade.

The Logic of Comparative Advantage

To explain the principle of comparative advantage, we begin with a simple example of specialization among people and then move to the more general case of comparative advantage among nations.

Consider the case of the best lawyer in town who is also the best typist in town. How should the lawyer spend her time? Should she write and type her own legal briefs? Or should she leave the typing to her secretary? Clearly, the lawyer should concentrate on legal activities, where her *relative* or *comparative* skills are most effectively used, even though she has *absolutely* greater skills in both typing and legal work.

Or look at it from the secretary's point of view. He is a fine typist, but his legal briefs are likely to lack sound legal reasoning and be full of errors. He is *absolutely* less efficient than the lawyer both in writing and in typing, but he is *relatively* or *comparatively* more efficient in typing.

In this scenario, the greatest efficiency will occur when the lawyer specializes in legal work and the secretary concentrates on typing. The most efficient and productive pattern of specialization occurs when people or nations concentrate on activities in which they are relatively or comparatively more efficient

than others; this implies that some people or nations may specialize in areas in which they are absolutely less efficient than others. But even though individual people or countries may differ in absolute efficiency from all other people and countries, each and every person or country will have a definite comparative advantage in some goods and a definite comparative disadvantage in other goods.

Ricardo's Analysis of Comparative Advantage

Let us illustrate the fundamental principles of international trade by considering America and Europe of a century ago. If labor (or resources, more generally) is absolutely more productive in America than in Europe, does this mean that America will import nothing? And is it economically wise for Europe to "protect" its markets with tariffs or quotas?

These questions were first answered in 1817 by the English economist David Ricardo, who showed that international specialization benefits a nation. He called this result the law of comparative advantage.

For simplicity, Ricardo worked with only two regions and only two goods, and he chose to measure all production costs in terms of labor-hours. We will follow his lead here, analyzing food and clothing for Europe and America.[1]

Table 35-1 on page 690 shows the illustrative data. In America, it takes 1 hour of labor to produce a unit of food, while a unit of clothing requires 2 hours of labor. In Europe the cost is 3 hours of labor for food and 4 hours of labor for clothing. We see that America has *absolute advantage* in both goods, for it can produce them with greater absolute efficiency than can Europe. However, America has *comparative advantage* in food, while Europe has comparative advantage in clothing, because food is relatively inexpensive in America while clothing is relatively less expensive in Europe.

From these facts, Ricardo proved that both regions will benefit if they specialize in their areas of comparative advantage—that is, if America specializes in the production of food while Europe specializes in the production of clothing. In this situation,

---

[1] An analysis of comparative advantage with many countries and many commodities is presented later in this chapter.

American and European Labor Requirements for Production		
	Necessary labor for production (labor-hours)	
Product	In America	In Europe
1 unit of food	1	3
1 unit of clothing	2	4

TABLE 35-1. Comparative Advantage Depends Only on Relative Costs

In a hypothetical example, America has lower labor costs in both food and clothing. American labor productivity is between 2 and 3 times Europe's (twice in clothing, thrice in food).

America will export food to pay for European clothing, while Europe will export clothing to pay for American food.

To analyze the effects of trade, we must measure the amounts of food and clothing that can be produced and consumed in each region (1) if there is no international trade and (2) if there is free trade with each region specializing in its area of comparative advantage.

Before Trade. Start by examining what occurs in the absence of any international trade, say, because all trade is illegal or because of a prohibitive tariff. Table 35-1 shows the real wage of the American worker for an hour's work as 1 unit of food or ½ unit of clothing. The European worker earns only ⅓ unit of food or ¼ unit of clothing per hour of work.

Clearly, if perfect competition prevails in each isolated region, the prices of food and clothing will be different in the two places because of the difference in production costs. In America, clothing will be 2 times as expensive as food because it takes twice as much labor to produce a unit of clothing as it does to produce a unit of food. In Europe, clothing will be only ⅓ as expensive as food.

After Trade. Now suppose that all tariffs are repealed and free trade is allowed. For simplicity, further assume that there are no transportation costs. What is the flow of goods when trade is opened up? Clothing is relatively more expensive in America, and food is relatively more expensive in Europe. Given these relative prices, and with no tariffs or transportation costs, food will soon be shipped from America to Europe and clothing from Europe to America.

As European clothing penetrates the American market, American clothiers will find prices falling

and profits shrinking, and they will begin to shut down their factories. By contrast, European farmers will find that the prices of foodstuffs begin to fall when American products hit the European markets; they will suffer losses, some will go bankrupt, and resources will be withdrawn from farming.

After all the adjustments to international trade have taken place, the prices of clothing and food must be equalized in Europe and America (just as the water in two connecting pipes must come to a common level once you remove the barrier between them). Without further knowledge about the exact supplies and demands, we cannot know the exact level to which prices will move. But we do know that the relative prices of food and clothing must lie somewhere between the European price ratio (which is ¾ for the ratio of food to clothing prices) and the American price ratio (which is ½). Let us say that the final ratio is ⅔, so 2 units of clothing trade for 3 units of food. For simplicity, we measure prices in American dollars and assume that the free-trade price of food is $2 per unit, which means that the free-trade price of clothing is $3 per unit.

With free trade, the regions have shifted their productive activities. America has withdrawn resources from clothing and produces food, while Europe has contracted its farm sector and expanded its clothing manufacture. *Under free trade, countries shift production toward their areas of comparative advantage.*

The Economic Gains from Trade

What are the economic effects of opening up the two regions to international trade? America as a whole benefits from the fact that imported clothing costs less than clothing produced at home. Likewise, Europe benefits by specializing in clothing and consuming food that is less expensive than domestically produced food.

We can most easily reckon the gains from trade by calculating the effect of trade upon the real wages of workers. Real wages are measured by the quantity of goods that a worker can buy with an hour's pay. Using Table 35-1, we can see that the real wages after trade will be greater than the real wages before trade for workers in both Europe *and* America. For simplicity, assume that each worker buys 1 unit of clothing and 1 unit of food. Before trade, this bundle of goods costs an American worker 3 hours of work and a European worker 7 hours of work.

After trade has opened up, as we found, the price of clothing is $3 per unit while the price of food is $2 per unit. An American worker must still work 1 hour to buy a unit of food; but at the price ratio of 2 to 3, the American worker need work only $1\frac{1}{2}$ hours to produce enough to buy 1 unit of European clothing. Therefore the bundle of goods costs the American worker $2\frac{1}{2}$ hours of work when trade is allowed—this represents an increase of 20 percent in the real wage of the American worker.

For European workers, a unit of clothing will still cost 4 hours of labor in a free-trade situation, for clothing is domestically produced. To obtain a unit of food, however, the European worker need produce only $\frac{2}{3}$ of a unit of clothing (which requires $\frac{2}{3} \times 4$ hours of labor) and then trade that $\frac{2}{3}$ clothing unit for 1 unit of American food. The total European labor needed to obtain the bundle of consumption is then $4 + 2\frac{2}{3} = 6\frac{2}{3}$, which represents an increase in real wages of about 5 percent over the no-trade situation.

When countries concentrate on their areas of comparative advantage under free trade, each country is better off. Compared to a no-trade situation, workers in each region can obtain a larger quantity of consumer goods for the same amount of work when they specialize in the areas of comparative advantage and trade their own production for goods in which they have a relative disadvantage.

GRAPHICAL ANALYSIS OF COMPARATIVE ADVANTAGE

We can use the production-possibility frontier (*PPF*) to expand our analysis of comparative advantage. We will continue the numerical example based upon

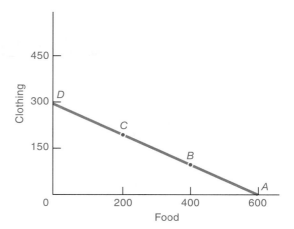

America's production-possibility schedule
(1-to-2 constant-cost ratio)

Possibilities	Food (units)	Clothing (units)
A	600	0
B	400	100
C	200	200
D	0	300

FIGURE 35-1. American Production Data

The constant-cost line *DA* represents America's domestic production-possibility frontier. America will produce and consume at *B* in the absence of trade.

labor costs, but the theory is equally valid in a competitive world with many different inputs.

America without Trade

Chapter 1 introduced the *PPF*, which shows the combinations of commodities that can be produced with a society's given resources and technology. Using the production data shown in Table 35-1, and assuming that both Europe and America have 600 units of labor, we can easily derive each region's *PPF*. The table that accompanies Figure 35-1 shows the possible levels of food and clothing that America can produce with its inputs and technology. Figure 35-1 plots the production possibilities; the rust line *DA* shows America's *PPF*. The *PPF* has a slope of $-\frac{1}{2}$, for this represents the terms on which food and clothing can be substituted in production; in competitive markets with no international trade, the price ratio of food to clothing will also be one-half.

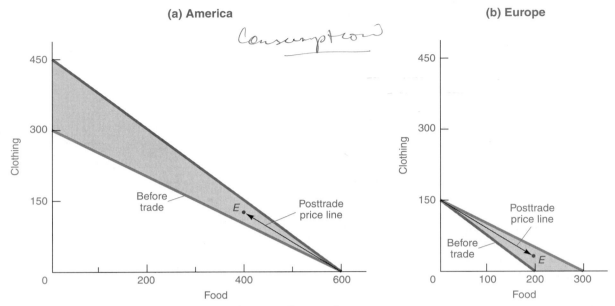

FIGURE 35-2. Comparative Advantage Illustrated

Through trade, both Europe and America improve their available consumption. If no trade is allowed, each region must be satisfied with its own production. It is therefore limited to its production-possibility curve, shown for each region as the line marked "Before trade." After borders are opened and competition equalizes the relative prices of the two goods, the relative-price line will be as shown by the arrow. If each region is faced with prices given by the arrows, can you see why its consumption possibilities must improve?

So far we have concentrated on production and ignored consumption. Note that if America is isolated from all international trade, it can consume only what it produces. Say that, for the incomes and demands in the marketplace, point *B* in Figure 35-1 marks America's production and consumption in the absence of trade. Without trade, America produces and consumes 400 units of food and 100 units of clothing.

We can do exactly the same thing for Europe. But Europe's *PPF* will look different from America's because Europe has different efficiencies in producing food and clothing. Europe's price ratio is ³⁄₄, reflecting Europe's relative productivity in food and clothing.

Opening Up to Trade

Now allow trade between the two regions. Food can be exchanged for clothing at some price ratio. We call the ratio of export prices to import prices

the **terms of trade**. To indicate the trading possibilities, we put the two *PPF*s together in Figure 35-2. America's rust *PPF* shows its domestic production possibilities, while Europe's black *PPF* shows the terms on which it can domestically substitute food and clothing. Note that Europe's *PPF* is drawn closer to the origin than America's because Europe has lower productivities in both industries; it has an absolute disadvantage in the production of both food and clothing.

Europe need not be discouraged by its absolute disadvantage, however, for it is the difference in *relative* productivities or *comparative* advantage that makes trade beneficial. The gains from trade are illustrated by the outer lines in Figure 35-2. If America could trade at Europe's relative prices, it could produce 600 units of food and move northwest along the outer black line in Figure 35-2(*a*)—where the black line represents the price ratio or terms of trade that are generated by Europe's *PPF*. Similarly, if

Europe could trade at America's prices, Europe could specialize in clothing and move southeast along the rust line in Figure 35-2(*b*)—where the rust line is America's pretrade price ratio.

This leads to an important and surprising conclusion: Small countries have the most to gain from international trade. They affect world prices the least and therefore can trade at world prices that are very different from domestic prices. From this, you can see why countries that are different from other countries gain much while large countries have the least to gain. (These points are raised in question 3 at the end of this chapter.)

Equilibrium Price Ratio. Once trade opens up, some set of prices must hold in the world marketplace depending upon the overall market supplies and demands. Without further information we cannot specify the exact price ratio, but we can determine what the price range will be. The prices must lie somewhere between the prices of the two regions. That is, we know that the relative price of food and clothing must lie somewhere in the range between $\frac{1}{2}$ and $\frac{3}{4}$.

The final price ratio will depend upon the relative demands for food and clothing. If food is very much in demand, the food price would be relatively high. If food demand were so high that Europe produced food as well as clothing, the price ratio would be at Europe's relative prices, or $\frac{3}{4}$. On the other hand, if clothing demand were so strong that America produced clothing as well as food, the terms of trade would equal America's price ratio of $\frac{1}{2}$. If each region specializes completely in the area of its comparative advantage, with Europe producing only clothing and America producing only food, the price ratio will lie somewhere between $\frac{1}{2}$ and $\frac{3}{4}$. The exact ratio will depend on the strength of demand.

Assume now that the demands are such that the final price ratio is $\frac{2}{3}$, with 3 units of food selling for 2 units of clothing. With this price ratio, each region will then specialize—America in food and Europe in clothing—and export some of its production to pay for imports at the world price ratio of $\frac{2}{3}$.

Figure 35-2 illustrates how trade will take place. Each region will face a consumption-possibility curve according to which it can produce, trade, and consume. *The consumption-possibility curve begins at the region's point of complete specialization and then runs out*

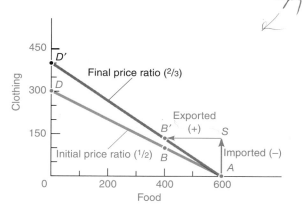

FIGURE 35-3. America Before and After Trade

Free trade expands the consumption options of America. The rust-colored line *DA* represents America's production-possibility curve when America is able to trade freely at the price ratio $\frac{2}{3}$ and, in consequence, to specialize completely in the production of food (at *A*). The rust arrows from *S* to *B'* and *A* to *S* show the amounts exported (+) and imported (−) by America. As a result of free trade, America ends up at *B'*, with more of both goods available than if it produced what it consumed along *DA*.

at the world price ratio of $\frac{2}{3}$. Figure 35-2(*a*) shows America's consumption possibilities as a thin black arrow with slope of $-\frac{2}{3}$ coming out of its complete-specialization point at 600 units of food and no clothing. Similarly, Europe's posttrade consumption possibilities are shown in Figure 35-2(*b*) by the black arrow running southeast from its point of complete specialization with a slope of $-\frac{2}{3}$.

The final outcome is shown by the points *E* in Figure 35-2. At this free-trade equilibrium, Europe specializes in producing clothing and America specializes in producing food. Europe exports $133\frac{1}{3}$ units of clothing for 200 units of America's food. Both regions are able to consume more than they would produce alone; both regions have benefited from international trade.

Figure 35-3 illustrates the benefits of trade for America. The rust inner line shows the *PPF*, while the black outer line shows the consumption possibilities at the world price ratio of $\frac{2}{3}$. The rust arrows show the amounts exported and imported. America ends up at point *B'*. Through trade it moves along the black line *D'A* just as if a fruitful new invention had pushed out its *PPF*.

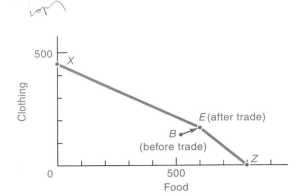

FIGURE 35-4. Free Trade Allows the World to Move to Its Production-Possibility Frontier

We show here the effect of free trade from the viewpoint of the world as a whole. Before trade is allowed, each region is on its own national *PPF*. Because the no-trade equilibrium is inefficient, the world is inside its *PPF*.

Free trade allows each region to specialize in the goods in which it has comparative advantage. As a result of efficient specialization, the world moves out to the efficiency frontier.

The lessons of this analysis are summarized in Figure 35-4. This figure shows the *world* production-possibility frontier. The world *PPF* represents the maximum output that can be obtained from the world's resources when goods are produced in the most efficient manner—that is, with the most efficient division of labor and regional specialization.

The world *PPF* is built up from the two regional *PPF*s in Figure 35-2 by determining the maximum level of world output that can be obtained from the individual regional *PPF*s. For example, the maximum quantity of food that can be produced (with no clothing production) is seen in Figure 35-2 to be 600 units in America and 200 units in Europe, for a world maximum of 800 units. This same point (800 food, 0 clothing) is then plotted in the world *PPF* in Figure 35-4. Additionally, we can plot the point (0 food, 450 clothing) in the world *PPF* by inspection of the regional *PPF*s. All the individual points in between can be constructed by a careful calculation of the maximum world outputs that can be produced if the two regions are efficiently specializing in the two goods.

Before opening up borders to trade, the world is at point *B*. This is an inefficient point—inside the world *PPF*—because regions have different levels of *relative* efficiency in different goods. After opening

the borders to trade, the world moves to the free-trade equilibrium at *E*, where countries are specializing in their areas of comparative advantage.

Free trade in competitive markets allows the world to move to the frontier of its production-possibility curve.

EXTENSIONS TO MANY COMMODITIES AND COUNTRIES

The world of international trade consists of more than two regions and two commodities. However, the principles we explained above are essentially unchanged in more realistic situations.

Many Commodities

When two regions or countries produce many commodities at constant costs, the goods can be arranged in order according to the comparative advantage or cost of each. For example, the commodities might be aircraft, computers, wheat, automobiles, wine, and shoes—all arranged in the comparative-advantage sequence shown in Figure 35-5. As you can see from the figure, of all the commodities, aircraft is least expensive in America relative to the costs in Europe. Europe has its greatest comparative advantage in shoes, while its advantage in wine is somewhat less than that in shoes.

We can be virtually certain that the introduction of trade will cause America to produce and export aircraft, while Europe will produce and export shoes. But where will the dividing line fall? Between wheat and automobiles? Or wine and shoes? Or will the dividing line fall on one of the commodities rather than between them—perhaps automobiles will be produced in both places.

You will not be surprised to find that the answer depends upon the demands and supplies of the different goods. We can think of the commodities as beads arranged on a string according to their comparative advantage; the strength of supply and demand will determine where the dividing line between American and European production will fall. An increased demand for aircraft and computers, for example, would tend to shift prices in the direction of American goods. The shift might lead America to specialize so much more in areas of its comparative advantage that it would no longer be profitable to produce in areas of comparative disadvantage, like automobiles.

*Consents / Jated
on B. Trade
Imbalance*

America's comparative advantage ◄———•—•—•—•—•—► Europe's comparative advantage

Aircraft Computers Wheat   Automobiles Wine Shoes

FIGURE 35-5. With Many Commodities, There Is a Spectrum of Comparative Advantages

Many Countries

What about the case of many countries? Introducing many countries need not change our analysis. As far as a single country is concerned, all the other nations can be lumped together into one group as "the rest of the world." The advantages of trade have no special relationship to national boundaries. The principles already developed apply between groups of countries and, indeed, between regions within the same country. In fact, they are just as applicable to trade between our northern and southern states as to trade between the United States and Canada.

Triangular and Multilateral Trade

With many countries brought into the picture, it will generally be beneficial to engage in *triangular* or *multilateral trade* with many other countries. *Bilateral* trade between two countries is generally unbalanced.

Consider the simple example of triangular trade flows presented in Figure 35-6, where the arrows show the direction of exports. America buys consumer electronics from Japan, Japan buys oil and primary commodities from developing countries, and developing countries buy machinery from America. In reality, trade patterns are even more complex than this triangular example.

The multilateral nature of trade shows the fallacy in arguments that focus on the bilateral balance between particular countries. In recent years, the large bilateral trade imbalance between the United States and Japan has fueled protectionist sentiment. On many occasions over the last two decades, the United States has threatened to impose trade sanctions on Japan. But the bilateral balance by itself has no economic significance. Even countries that have a zero current-account balance will run surpluses with some countries and deficits with others. What would happen if all nations signed bilateral trade agreements that balanced trade between each pair of countries? Trade would be sharply curbed;

imports would balance exports, but at the level of whichever was the smaller. The gains from trade would be severely reduced.

QUALIFICATIONS AND CONCLUSIONS

We have now completed our look at the elegant theory of comparative advantage. Its conclusions apply for any number of countries and commodities. Moreover, it can be generalized to handle many inputs, changing factor proportions, and diminishing returns. But we cannot conclude without noting two important qualifications of this elegant theory.

1. *Classical assumptions.* From a theoretical point of view, the major defect lies in its classical assumptions. The theory assumes a smoothly working competitive economy with flexible prices and wages and no involuntary unemployment. Would the theory still hold if autoworkers, laid off when the share of Japanese cars sold in the American market rises rapidly, cannot easily find new jobs? What if an overvalued foreign exchange rate

FIGURE 35-6. Triangular Trade Benefits All

Advantages of multilateral trade would be much reduced if bilateral balancing were required.

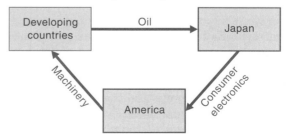

reduces the demand for manufacturing workers and these workers cannot find comparable jobs in other sectors? In such cases, trade might well push a nation *inside* its *PPF* as unemployment rises and GDP falls. When the economy is in depression or the price system malfunctions, we cannot be sure that countries will gain from trade or that the theory of comparative advantage will hold in every case.

Given this reservation, there can be little wonder that the theory of comparative advantage sells at a big discount during business downturns. In the Great Depression of the 1930s, as unemployment soared and real outputs fell, nations built high tariff walls at their borders and the volume of foreign trade shrank sharply. In every recession, underutilized labor and capital lobby to protect their markets from foreign competition. These periods of history remind us that the classical theory of comparative advantage is strictly valid only when exchange rates, prices, and wages are at appropriate levels and when macroeconomic policies banish major business cycles and trade dislocations from the economic scene.

2. *Income distribution.* A second proviso concerns the impact on particular people, sectors, or factors of production. We showed above that opening a country to trade will raise a country's national income. The country can consume more of all goods and services than would be possible if the borders were sealed to trade.

But this does not mean that every individual, firm, sector, or factor of production will benefit from trade. If free trade increases the supply of goods that are produced by particular factors of production or in particular regions, those factors or regions may end up with lower incomes than under restricted trade. Suppose that free trade increases the supply of cheap cotton shirts in the United States. We would not be surprised to learn that textile firms suffered losses and bankruptcies. Recent studies indicate that unskilled labor in high-income countries has in the last two decades suffered reductions in real wages because of the increased imports of goods in related industries from low-wage developing countries. Wage losses occurred because imports are produced by factors that are close substitutes for the unskilled labor in high-income countries.

The theory of comparative advantage shows that other sectors will gain more than the injured sectors will lose. Moreover, over long periods of time, those displaced from low-wage sectors eventually gravitate to higher-wage jobs. But those who are temporarily injured by international trade are genuinely harmed and are vocal advocates for protection and trade barriers.

Notwithstanding its limitations, the theory of comparative advantage is one of the deepest truths in all of economics. Nations that disregard comparative advantage pay a heavy price in terms of their living standards and economic growth.

B. PROTECTIONISM

The theory of comparative advantage shows how countries can benefit from specialization and international division of labor. Notwithstanding this established economic finding, legislatures are continuously besieged by groups lobbying for "protective" measures in the form of tariffs or import quotas. In the United States, Congress and the President struggle every year over whether to enact measures to protect domestic industries from inexpensive imports.

Is protectionism sound economic policy? Economists generally agree that it is not. They believe that free trade promotes a mutually beneficial division of labor among nations and that free and open trade allows *each* nation to expand its production and consumption possibilities, raising the world's living standard.

But many people disagree with this assessment. Just as Alexander Hamilton wanted to build tariff

copy

copy

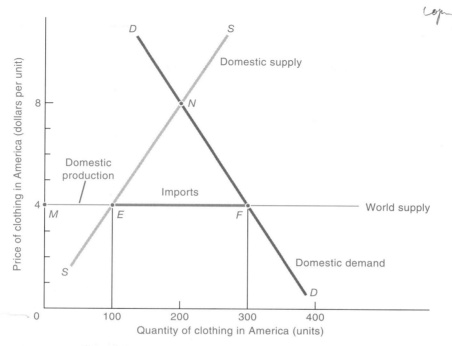

FIGURE 35-7. American Production, Imports, and Consumption with Free Trade

We see here the free-trade equilibrium in the market for clothing. America has a comparative disadvantage in clothing. Therefore, at the no-trade equilibrium at *N*, America's price would be $8, while the world price is $4.

Assuming that American demand does not affect the world price of $4 per unit, the free-trade equilibrium comes when America produces *ME* (100 units) and imports the difference between demand and domestic supply, shown as *EF* (or 200 units).

walls around our manufacturing industries in 1789, so today people argue that we need to protect our industries against foreign competition. This section reviews the economic impact of protectionism.

SUPPLY-AND-DEMAND ANALYSIS OF TRADE AND TARIFFS

Free Trade vs. No Trade

The theory of comparative advantage can be illuminated through the analysis of supply and demand for goods in foreign trade. Consider the clothing market in America. Assume, for simplicity, that America is a small part of the market and therefore cannot affect the world price of clothing. (This assumption will allow us to analyze supply and demand very easily; the more realistic case in which

a country can affect world prices will be considered later in this chapter.)

Figure 35-7 shows the supply and demand curves for clothing in America. The demand curve of American consumers is drawn as *DD* and the domestic supply curve of American firms as *SS*. We assume that the price of clothing is determined in the world market and is equal to $4 per unit. Although transactions in international trade are carried out in different currencies, for now we can simplify by converting the foreign supply schedule into a dollar supply curve by using the current exchange rate.

No-Trade Equilibrium. Suppose that transportation costs or tariffs for clothing were prohibitive (say, $100 per unit of clothing). Where would the no-trade equilibrium lie? In this case, the American market for clothing would be at the intersection

Commodity class	Average tariff rate, 1994 (%)	
	United States	Japan
Food	6.3	12.3
Beverages and tobacco	2.9	16.1
Crude materials, except fuels	0.3	1.3
Fuels	0.5	0.8
Chemicals	4.0	3.7
Manufactured goods	3.3	5.1
Machinery and transport equipment	1.9	0.1

TABLE 35-2. Average Tariff Rates for the United States and Japan

Tariff rates for industrial countries like the United States and Japan are generally low today. High tariffs or import quotas are found in politically sensitive sectors like agriculture in Japan and clothing in the United States. [Source: U.S. Department of Commerce and World Trade Organization.]

of *domestic* supply and demand, shown at point *N* in Figure 35-7. At this no-trade point, prices would be relatively high at $8 per unit, and domestic producers would be meeting all the demand.

Free Trade. Next, open up trade in clothing. In the absence of transport costs, tariffs, and quotas, the price in America must be equal to the world price. Why? Because if the American price were above the European price, sharp-eyed entrepreneurs would buy where clothing was cheap (Europe) and sell where clothing was expensive (America); Europe would therefore export clothing to America. Once trade flows fully adjust to supplies and demands, the price in America would equal the world price level. (In a world with transportation and tariff costs, the price in America would equal the world price adjusted for these costs.)

Figure 35-7 illustrates how prices, quantities, and trade flows will be determined under free trade in our clothing example. The horizontal line at $4 represents the supply curve for imports; it is horizontal, or perfectly price-elastic, because American demand is assumed to be too small to affect the world price of clothing.

Once trade opens up, imports flow into America, lowering the price of clothing to the world price of $4 per unit. At that level, domestic producers will supply the amount *ME,* or 100 units, while at that price consumers will want to buy 300 units. The difference, shown by the heavy line *EF,* is the amount of imports. Who decided that we would import just this amount of clothing and that domestic producers would supply only 100 units? A European planning agency? A cartel of clothing firms? No, the amount of trade was determined by supply and demand.

Moreover, the level of prices in the no-trade equilibrium determined the direction of the trade flows. America's no-trade prices were higher than Europe's, so goods flowed into America. Remember this rule: *Under free trade, indeed in markets generally, goods flow uphill from low-price regions to high-price regions.* When markets are opened to free trade, clothing flows uphill from the low-price European market to the higher-price American market until the price levels are equalized.

Trade Barriers

For centuries, governments have used tariffs and quotas to raise revenues and influence the development of individual industries. Since the eighteenth century—when the British Parliament attempted to impose tariffs on tea, sugar, and other commodities on its American colonies—tariff policy has proved fertile soil for revolution and political struggle.

We can use supply-and-demand analysis to understand the economic effects of tariffs and quotas. To begin with, note that a **tariff** is a tax levied on imports. Table 35-2 lists tariff rates for major categories for the United States and Japan in 1994. To take an example, the United States has a 1.9 percent tariff on automobiles. If a foreign car costs $20,000, the domestic price including the tariff will be $20,380. A **quota** is a limit on the quantity of imports.

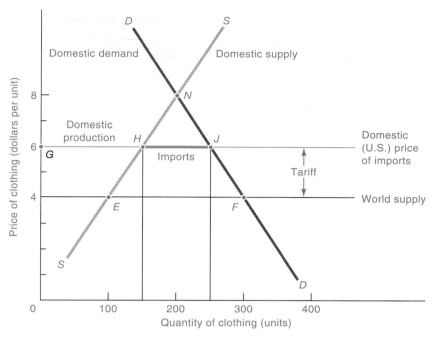

FIGURE 35-8. Effect of a Tariff

A tariff lowers imports and consumption, raises domestic production and price. Starting from the free-trade equilibrium in Fig. 35-7, America now puts a $2 tariff on clothing imports. The price of European clothing imports rises to $6 (including the tariff).

The market price rises from $4 to $6, so the total amount demanded falls. Imports shrink from 200 to 100 units, while domestic production rises from 100 to 150 units.

The United States has quotas on many products, including peanuts, textiles, and beef.

Prohibitive Tariff. The easiest case to analyze is a *prohibitive tariff*—one that is so high that it chokes off all imports. Looking back at Figure 35-7, what would happen if the tariff on clothing were more than $4 per unit (that is, more than the difference between America's no-trade price of $8 and the world price of $4)? This would be a prohibitive tariff, shutting off all clothing trade. Any importer who buys clothing at the world price of $4 would sell it in America at above the no-trade price of $8. But this price would not cover the cost of the good plus the tariff. Prohibitive tariffs thus kill off all trade.

Nonprohibitive Tariff. Lower tariffs (less than $4 per unit of clothing) would injure but not kill off trade. Figure 35-8 shows the equilibrium in the clothing market with a $2 tariff. Again assuming no transportation costs, a $2 tariff means that for-

eign clothing will sell in America for $6 per unit (equal to the $4 world price plus the $2 tariff).

The equilibrium result of a $2 tariff is that domestic consumption (or quantity demanded) is lowered from 300 units in the free-trade equilibrium to 250 units after the tariff is imposed, the amount of domestic production is raised by 50 units, and the quantity of imports is lowered by 100 units. This example summarizes the economic impact of tariffs:

A tariff will tend to raise price, lower the amounts consumed and imported, and raise domestic production.

Quotas. Quotas have the same qualitative effect as tariffs. A prohibitive quota (one that prevents all imports) is equivalent to a prohibitive tariff. The price and quantity would move back to the no-trade equilibrium at *N* in Figure 35-8. A less stringent quota might limit imports to 100 clothing units; this quota would equal the heavy line *HJ* in Figure 35-8.

A quota of 100 units would lead to the same equilibrium price and output as did the $2 tariff.

Although there is no essential difference between tariffs and quotas, some subtle differences do exist. A tariff gives revenue to the government, perhaps allowing other taxes to be reduced and thereby offsetting some of the harm done to consumers in the importing country. A quota, on the other hand, puts the profit from the resulting price difference into the pocket of the importers or exporters lucky enough to get a permit or import license. They can afford to use the proceeds to wine, dine, or even bribe the officials who give out import licenses.

Because of these differences, economists generally regard tariffs as the lesser evil. However, if a government is determined to impose quotas, it should auction off the scarce import-quota licenses. An auction will ensure that the government rather than the importer or the exporter gets the revenue from the scarce right to import; in addition, the bureaucracy will not be tempted to allocate quota rights by bribery, friendship, or nepotism.

Transportation Costs. What of transportation costs? The cost of moving bulky and perishable goods has the same effect as tariffs, reducing the extent of beneficial regional specialization. For example, if it costs $2 per unit to transport clothing from Europe to the United States, the supply-and-demand equilibrium would look just like Figure 35-8, with the American price $2 above the European price.

But there is one difference between protection and transportation costs: Transport costs are imposed by nature—by oceans, mountains, and rivers—whereas restrictive tariffs are squarely the responsibility of nations. Indeed, one economist called tariffs "negative railroads." Imposing a tariff has the same economic impact as throwing sand in the engines of vessels that transport goods to our shores from other lands.

The Economic Costs of Tariffs

What happens when America puts a tariff on clothing, such as the $2 tariff shown in Figure 35-8? There are three effects: (1) The domestic producers, operating under a price umbrella provided by the tariff, can expand production; (2) consumers are faced with higher prices and therefore reduce their consumption; and (3) the government gains tariff revenue.

Tariffs create economic inefficiency. When tariffs are imposed, the economic loss to consumers exceeds the revenue gained by the government plus the extra profits earned by producers.

Diagrammatic Analysis. Figure 35-9 shows the economic cost of a tariff. The supply and demand curves are identical to those in Figure 35-8, but three areas are highlighted. (1) Area *B* is the tariff revenue collected by the government. It is equal to the amount of the tariff times the units of imports and totals $200. (2) The tariff raises the price in domestic markets from $4 to $6, and producers increase their output to 150. Hence total profits rise by $250, shown by the area *LEHM* and equal to $200 on old units and an additional $50 on the 50 new units. (3) Finally, note that a tariff imposes a heavy cost on consumers. The total consumer-surplus loss is given by the area *LMJF* and is equal to $550.

The overall social impact is then a gain to producers of $250, a gain to the government of $200, and a loss to consumers of $550. The net social cost (counting each of these dollars equally) is therefore $100. We can reckon this as equal to areas *A* and *C*. The interpretation of these areas is important:

- Area *A* is the net loss that comes because domestic production is more costly than foreign production. When the domestic price rises, businesses are thereby induced to increase the use of relatively costly domestic capacity. They produce output up to the point where the marginal cost is $6 per unit instead of up to $4 per unit under free trade. Firms reopen inefficient old factories or work existing factories extra shifts. From an economic point of view, these plants have a comparative disadvantage because the new clothing produced by these factories could be produced more cheaply abroad. The new social cost of this inefficient production is area *A,* equal to $50.

- In addition, there is a net loss to the country from the higher price, shown by area *C*. This is the loss in consumer surplus that cannot be offset by business profits or tariff revenue. This area represents the economic cost incurred when

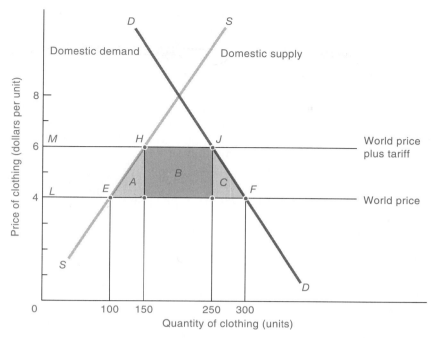

FIGURE 35-9. Economic Cost of a Tariff

Imposing a tariff raises revenues and leads to inefficiency. We see the impact of the tariff as three effects. Rectangle *B* is the tariff revenue gained by the government. Triangle *A* is the cost of the inefficiency in production induced by a higher domestic price. Triangle *C* is the net loss in consumer surplus from the inefficiently high price after subtracting both the tariff revenue and business profits from the lost consumer surplus. Areas *A* and *C* are the irreducible inefficiencies caused by the tariff.

consumers shift their purchases from low-cost imports to high-cost domestic goods. This area is also equal to $50.

Hence, the total social loss from the tariff is $100, calculated either way.

Figure 35-9 illustrates one feature that is important in understanding the politics and history of tariffs. When a tariff is imposed, part of the economic impact comes because tariffs redistribute income from consumers to the protected domestic producers and workers. In the example shown in Figure 35-9, areas *A* and *C* represent efficiency losses from inefficiently high domestic production and inefficiently low consumption, respectively. Under the simplifying assumptions used above, the efficiency losses sum up to $100. The redistribution involved is much larger, however, equaling $200 raised in tariff revenues levied upon consumers of the commodity plus

$250 in higher profits. Consumers will be unhappy about the higher product cost, while domestic producers and workers in those firms will benefit. We can see why battles over import restrictions generally center more on the redistributive gains and losses than on the issues of economic efficiency.

Imposing a tariff has three effects: It encourages inefficient domestic production; it induces consumers to reduce their purchases of the tariffed good below efficient levels; and it raises revenues for the government. Only the first two of these necessarily impose efficiency costs on the economy.

The cost of textile protection: Let's flesh out this analysis by examining the effects of a particular tariff, one on clothing. Today, tariffs on imported textiles and apparel are among the highest levied by the United States. How do these high tariffs affect consumers and producers?

To begin with, the tariff raises domestic clothing prices. Because of the higher prices, many factories, which would otherwise be bankrupt in the face of a declining comparative advantage in textiles, remain open. They are just barely profitable, but they manage to eke out enough sales to continue domestic production. Employment in textiles exceeds the free-trade situation, although—because of pressure from foreign competition—textile wages are among the lowest of any manufacturing industry.

From a national point of view, we are wasting resources in textiles. These workers, materials, and capital would be more productively used in other sectors—perhaps in producing computers or aircraft or financial services. The nation's productive potential is lower because it keeps factors of production in an industry in which it has lost its comparative advantage.

Consumers, of course, pay for this protection of the textile industry with higher prices. They get less satisfaction from their incomes than they would if they could buy textiles from Korea, China, or Indonesia at prices that exclude the high tariffs. Consumers are induced to cut back on their clothing purchases, channeling funds into food, transportation, and recreation, whose relative prices are lowered by the tariff.

Finally, the government gets revenues from tariffs on textiles. These revenues can be used to buy public goods or to reduce other taxes, so (unlike the consumer loss or the productive inefficiency) this effect is not a real social burden.

THE ECONOMICS OF PROTECTIONISM

Having examined the impact of tariffs on prices and quantities, we now turn to an analysis of the arguments for and against protectionism. The arguments for tariff or quota protection against the competition of foreign imports take many different forms. Here are the main categories: (1) noneconomic arguments that suggest it is desirable to sacrifice economic welfare in order to subsidize other national objectives, (2) arguments that are based on a misunderstanding of economic logic, and (3) analyses that rely on market power or macroeconomic imperfections. Many of these arguments are a century old;

others have been developed by a school known as "new international economics."[2]

Noneconomic Goals

If you are ever on a debating team given the assignment of defending free trade, you will strengthen your case at the beginning by conceding that there is more to life than economic welfare. A nation surely should not sacrifice its liberty, culture, and human rights for a few dollars of extra income.

The U.S. semiconductor industry provides a useful example here. In the 1980s, the Defense Department claimed that without an independent semiconductor industry, the military would become excessively dependent on Japanese and other foreign suppliers for chips to use in high-technology weaponry. This led to an agreement to protect the industry. Economists were skeptical about the value of this approach. Their argument did not question the goal of national security. Rather, it focused on the efficiency of the means of achieving the desired result. They thought that protection was more expensive than a policy targeted on the industry, perhaps a program to buy a minimum number of high-quality chips.

National security is not the only noneconomic goal in trade policy. Countries may desire to preserve their cultural traditions or environmental conditions. France recently has argued that its citizens need to be protected from "uncivilized" American movies. The fear is that the French film industry could be drowned by the new wave of stunt-filled, high-budget Hollywood thrillers. As a result, France has maintained strict quotas on the number of U.S. movies and television shows that can be imported, upholding its stance even in the face of strong pressure from the United States in the latest round of trade negotiations. In another example, the Swiss government chose to ban trucks passing through Switzerland in an effort to pre-

---

[2] An official statement on trade policy is contained in the *Economic Report of the President*, 1991 (U.S. Government Printing Office, Washington, D.C., 1991). For a nontechnical account of the sources of the trade deficit and an account of new international economics as told by one of its leading practitioners, see Paul Krugman, *The Age of Diminished Expectations: U.S. Economic Policy in the 1990s* (MIT Press, Cambridge, Mass., 1990).

serve the tranquility and clean air of its mountain valleys.

Unsound Grounds for Tariffs

Mercantilism. To Abraham Lincoln has been attributed the remark, "I don't know much about the tariff. I do know that when I buy a coat from England, I have the coat and England has the money. But when I buy a coat in America, I have the coat and America has the money."

This reasoning represents an age-old fallacy typical of the so-called mercantilist writers of the seventeenth and eighteenth centuries. They considered a country fortunate which sold more goods than it bought, because such a "favorable" balance of trade meant that gold would flow into the country to pay for its export surplus.

The mercantilist argument confuses means and ends. Accumulating gold or other monies will not improve a country's living standard. Money is worthwhile not for its own sake but for what it will buy from other countries. Most economists today therefore reject the idea that raising tariffs to run a trade surplus will improve a country's economic welfare.

Tariffs for Special-Interest Groups. The single most important source of pressure for protective tariffs is powerful special-interest groups. Firms and workers know very well that a tariff on their particular products will help *them,* whatever its effect on some abstract goal like total economic welfare. Adam Smith understood this point well when he wrote:

> To expect freedom of trade is as absurd as to expect Utopia. Not only the prejudices of the public, but what is much more unconquerable, the private interests of many individuals, irresistibly oppose it.

If free trade is so beneficial to the nation as a whole, why do the proponents of protectionism continue to wield such a disproportionate influence in Congress? The few who benefit gain much from specific protection and therefore devote large sums to lobbying politicians. By contrast, individual consumers are only slightly affected by the tariff on one product; because losses are small and widespread, individuals have little incentive to spend resources expressing an opinion on every tariff case. A century ago, outright bribery was used to get the votes necessary to pass tariff legislation. Today, powerful political action committees (PACs), financed by labor or business, round up lawyers and drum up support for tariffs or quotas on textiles, lumber, autos, steel, sugar, and other goods.

If political votes were cast in proportion to total economic benefit, nations would legislate most tariffs out of existence. But all dollars of economic interests do not always get proportional representation. It is much harder to organize the masses of consumers and producers to agitate for the benefits of free trade than it is to organize a few companies or labor unions to argue against "cheap Chinese labor" or "unfair Japanese competition." In every country, the tireless enemies of free trade are the special interests of protected firms and workers.

A dramatic case is the U.S. quota on sugar, which benefits a few producers while costing American consumers over $1 billion a year. The average consumer is probably unaware that the sugar quota costs $1\frac{1}{2}$ cents a day per person, so there is little incentive to lobby for free trade.

Competition from Cheap Foreign Labor. Of all the arguments for protection, the most persistent is that free trade exposes U.S. workers to competition from low-wage foreign labor. The only way to preserve high U.S. wages, so the argument goes, is to protect domestic workers by keeping out or putting high tariffs on goods produced in low-wage countries. An extreme version of this contention is that under free trade U.S. wages would converge to the low foreign wages. This point was trumpeted by presidential candidate Ross Perot during the debates over the North American Free Trade Agreement (NAFTA) when he argued:

> Philosophically, [NAFTA] is wonderful, but realistically it will be bad for our country. That thing is going to create a giant sucking sound in the United States at a time when we need jobs coming in, not jobs going out. Mexican wages will come up to $7\frac{1}{2}$ an hour and our wages will come down to $7\frac{1}{2}$ an hour.

This argument is superficially appealing, but it has a big flaw because it ignores the principle of comparative advantage. The reason American workers have higher wages is that they are on average more productive. If our equilibrium wage is 3 times that in Mexico, it is because we are on average roughly 5 times more productive in the production of tradable goods and services. Trade flows according to comparative advantage, not wage rates or absolute advantage.

Having shown that the nation gains from importing the goods produced by "cheap foreign labor" in which it has a comparative disadvantage, we should not ignore the costs that this strategy may temporarily impose on the affected workers and firms. If plants in a particular locality are unexpectedly shut down because production moves overseas, the local labor market may be inundated with job seekers. Older workers with outdated job skills may have trouble finding attractive jobs and will suffer a decline in their real incomes. The difficulties of displaced workers will be greater when the overall economy is depressed or when the local labor markets have high unemployment. Over the long run, labor markets will reallocate workers from declining to advancing industries, but the transition may be painful for many people.

In summary:

The economic answer to the cheap-foreign-labor argument rests on the comparative-advantage analysis. This shows that a country will benefit from trade even though its wages are far above those of its trading partners. High wages come from high efficiency, not from tariff protection.

Retaliatory Tariffs. While many people would agree that a world of free trade would be the best of all possible worlds, they note that this is not the world we live in. They reason, "As long as other countries impose import restrictions or otherwise discriminate against our products, we have no choice but to play the protection game in self-defense. We'll go along with free trade only as long as it is fair trade. But we insist on a level playing field." On several occasions in the 1990s, the United States went to the brink of trade wars with Japan and China, threatening high tariffs if the other country did not stop some objectionable trade practice.

While this argument seems sensible, it is not well grounded in economic analysis or history. As we have seen, when another country increases its tariffs, doing so is akin to increasing its transportation costs. But if France decided to slow down trade by putting mines in its harbors, should we mine ours? Few would think so. Similarly, if China violated trade

agreements by pirating American CDs, how would the United States gain by putting 100 percent tariffs on Chinese silks and other textiles?

Those who advocate this approach argue that retaliation may help reform other countries' trade practices. This rationale was described in a 1982 analysis of protection in the *Economic Report of the President:*

> Intervention in international trade . . . , even though costly to the U.S. economy in the short run, may, however, be justified if it serves the strategic purpose of increasing the cost of interventionist policies by foreign governments. Thus, there is a potential role for carefully targeted measures . . . aimed at convincing other countries to reduce their trade distortions.

While potentially valid, this argument should be used with great caution. Just as building missiles leads to an arms race as often as to arms control, protectionist bluffs may end up hurting the bluffer as well as the opponent. Historical studies show that retaliatory tariffs usually lead other nations to raise their tariffs still higher and are rarely an effective bargaining chip for multilateral tariff reduction.

Import Relief. In the United States and other countries, firms and workers who are injured by foreign competition attempt to get protection in the form of tariffs or quotas. Today, relatively little direct tariff business is conducted on the floor of Congress. Congress realized that tariff politics was too hot to handle and has set up specialized agencies to decide on complaints. Generally, a petition for relief is analyzed by the U.S. Department of Commerce and the U.S. International Trade Commission. Relief measures include the following actions:

- The *escape clause* was popular in earlier periods. It allows temporary import relief (tariffs, quotas, or export quotas negotiated with other countries) when an industry has been "injured" by imports. Injury occurs when the output, employment, and profits in a domestic industry have fallen while imports have risen.
- *Antidumping tariffs* are levied when foreign countries sell in the United States at prices below their average costs or at prices lower than those in the home market. When dumping is found, a "dumping duty" is placed on the imported good.

- *Countervailing duties* are imposed when foreigners subsidize exports to the United States. They became the most popular form of import relief and were pursued in hundreds of cases.

What is the justification for enacting such retaliatory measures or for protecting an industry threatened by imports? Import relief may sound reasonable, but it actually runs completely counter to the economic theory of comparative advantage. That theory says that an industry which cannot compete with foreign firms ought to be injured by imports. *Looking at this from an economic vantage point, less productive industries are actually being killed off by the competition of more productive domestic industries.*

This sounds ruthless indeed. No industry willingly dies. No region gladly undergoes conversion to new industries. Often the shift from old to new industries involves considerable unemployment and hardship. The weak industry and region feel they are being singled out to carry the burden of progress.

Potentially Valid Arguments for Protection

Finally, we can consider three arguments for protection that may have true economic merit:

- Tariffs may move the terms of trade in favor of a country.
- Temporary tariff protection for an "infant industry" with growth potential may be efficient in the long run.
- A tariff may under certain conditions help reduce unemployment.

The Terms-of-Trade or Optimal-Tariff Argument.

One valid argument for imposing tariffs is that doing so will shift the terms of trade in a country's favor and against foreign countries. (Recall that the *terms of trade* are the ratio of export prices to import prices.) The idea is that when a large country levies tariffs on its imports, the tariffs will reduce the world price of its imports while increasing the prices of its exports. Such a change will be an improvement in the terms of trade. By shifting the terms of trade in its favor, the United States can export less wheat and fewer aircraft in order to pay for imports of oil and cars. The set of tariffs that maximizes our domestic real incomes is called the *optimal tariff.*

The terms-of-trade argument goes back 150 years to the free-trade proponent John Stuart Mill. It is the only argument for tariffs that would be valid under conditions of full employment and perfect competition. We can understand it by considering the simple case of an optimal tariff on oil. The optimal tariff on oil will raise the domestic price above the foreign price. But because our demand is curtailed as a result of the tariff, and because we are a significant part of the world demand for oil, the world market price of oil will be bid down. So part of the tariff really falls on the oil producer. (We can see that a very small country could not use this argument, since it cannot affect world prices.)

Have we not therefore found a theoretically secure argument for tariffs? The answer would be yes if we could forget that this is a "beggar-thy-neighbor" policy and could ignore the reactions of other countries. But other countries are likely to react. After all, if the United States were to impose an optimal tariff of 30 percent on its imports, why should the European Union and Japan not put 30 or 40 percent tariffs on their imports? In the end, as every country calculated and imposed its own domestic optimal tariff, the overall level of tariffs might spiral upward in the tariff version of an arms race.

Ultimately, such a situation would surely not represent an improvement of either world or individual economic welfare. When all countries impose optimal tariffs, it is likely that *everyone's* economic welfare will decline as the impediments to free trade become great. All countries are likely to benefit if all countries abolish trade barriers.

Tariffs for Infant Industries.

In his famous *Report on Manufactures* (1791), Alexander Hamilton proposed to encourage the growth of manufacturing by protecting "infant industries" from foreign competition. According to this doctrine, which received the cautious support of free-trade economists like John Stuart Mill and Alfred Marshall, there are lines of production in which a country could have a comparative advantage if only they could get started.

Such infant industries would not be able to survive the rough treatment by larger bullies in the global marketplace. With some temporary nurturing, however, they might grow up to enjoy economies of mass production, a pool of skilled labor, inventions well adapted to the local economy, and the technological efficiency typical of many mature industries. Although protection will raise prices to the consumer at first, the mature industry would become so efficient that cost and price would actually fall. A tariff is justified if the benefit to consumers at that later date would be more than enough to make up for the higher prices during the period of protection.

This argument must be weighed cautiously. Historical studies have turned up some genuine cases of protected infant industries that grew up to stand on their own feet. And studies of successful newly industrialized countries (such as Singapore and South Korea) show that they have often protected their manufacturing industries from imports during the early stages of industrialization. But the history of tariffs reveals even more contrary cases like steel, sugar, and textiles in which perpetually protected infants have not shed their diapers after lo these many years.

Brazil's tragic protection of its computer industry: Brazil offers a striking example of the pitfalls of protectionism. In 1984, Brazil passed a law actually banning most foreign computers. The idea was to provide a protected environment in which Brazil's own infant computer industry could develop. The law was vigorously enforced by special "computer police" who would search corporate offices and classrooms looking for illegal imported computers.

The results were startling. Technologically, Brazilian-made computers were years behind the fast-moving world market, and consumers paid 2 or 3 times the world price when they could get them. By one estimate, the law cost Brazilian consumers about $900 million each year. At the same time, because Brazilian computers were so expensive, they could not compete on the world market, so Brazilian computer companies could not take advantage of economies of scale by selling to other countries. The high price of computers hurt competitiveness in the rest of the economy as well. "We are effectively very backward because of this senseless nationalism," said Zelia Cardoso de Mello, Brazil's economy minister in 1990. "The computer problem effectively blocked Brazilian industry from modernizing."

The combination of pressure from Brazilian consumers and businesses and U.S. demands for open markets forced Brazil to drop the ban on imported comput-

ers in 1992. Within a year, electronics stores in São Paulo and Rio de Janeiro were filled with imported laptop computers, laser printers, and cellular telephones, and Brazilian companies could begin to exploit the computer revolution. Each country and each generation learns anew the lessons of comparative advantage.

Tariffs and Unemployment. Historically, a powerful motive for protection has been the desire to increase employment during a period of recession or stagnation. Protection creates jobs by raising the price of imports and diverting demand toward domestic production; Figure 35-8 demonstrates this effect. As domestic demand increases, firms will hire more workers and unemployment will fall.[3] This too is a beggar-thy-neighbor policy, for it raises domestic demand at the expense of output and employment in other countries.

However, while economic protection may raise employment, it does not constitute an effective program to pursue high employment, efficiency, and stable prices. Macroeconomic analysis shows that there are better ways of reducing unemployment than by imposing import protection. By the appropriate use of monetary and fiscal policy, a country can increase output and lower unemployment. Moreover, the use of general macroeconomic policies will allow workers displaced from low-productivity jobs in industries losing their comparative advantage to move to high-productivity jobs in industries enjoying a comparative advantage.

This lesson was amply demonstrated during the 1980s. From 1982 to 1987, the United States created 15 million net new jobs while maintaining open markets and low tariffs and sharply increasing its trade deficit; by contrast, the countries of Europe created virtually no new jobs while moving toward a position of trade surpluses.

---

[3] Those who have studied the chapters on macroeconomics can understand the mechanism by which tariffs increase employment in the short run. Recall that higher investment or government spending increases aggregate demand, output, and employment. By similar reasoning, greater protection or higher tariffs increase spending on domestic production and thereby increase aggregate demand. This expenditure switch will have multiplier effects in the short run much like those of investment or government spending on goods and services.

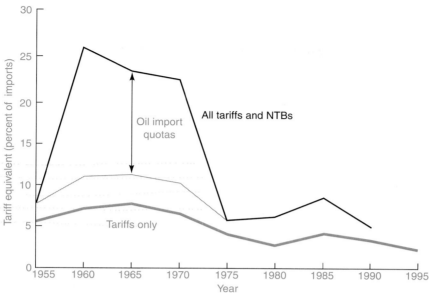

FIGURE 35-10. The Importance of NTBs Has Declined since the 1960s

Non-tariff barriers (NTBs) play a significant role in U.S. trade. The biggest trade barrier in the last four decades was a quota on imported oil. Even with NTBs included, however, barriers to trade have declined sharply and are far below those before World War II.

Tariffs and import protection are an inefficient way to create jobs or to lower unemployment. A more effective way to increase productive employment is through domestic monetary and fiscal policy.

Other Barriers to Trade

While this chapter has mainly spoken of tariffs, most points apply equally well to any other impediments to trade. Quotas have much the same effects as tariffs, for they prevent the comparative advantages of different countries from determining prices and outputs in the marketplace. In recent years, countries have negotiated quotas with other countries. The United States, for example, forced Japan to put "voluntary" export quotas on automobiles and negotiated similar export quotas on televisions, shoes, and steel.

We should also mention the so-called nontariff barriers (or NTBs). These consist of informal restrictions or regulations that make it difficult for countries to sell their goods in foreign markets. For example, American firms complained that Japanese regulations shut them out of the telecommunications, tobacco, and construction industries.

How important are the nontariff barriers relative to tariffs? Figure 35-10 shows estimates of the tariff equivalent of the most important nontariff barriers for the United States from 1955 through 1990. Nontariff barriers were actually more important than tariffs during the 1960s because of a quota on oil imports; in recent years, they have effectively doubled the protection found in the tariff codes.

MULTILATERAL TRADE NEGOTIATIONS

Given the tug-of-war between the economic benefits of free trade and the political appeal of protection, which force has prevailed? The history of U.S. tariffs, shown in Figure 35-11 on page 708, has been bumpy. For most of American history, the United States has been a high-tariff nation. The pinnacle came after the infamous Smoot-Hawley tariff of 1930, which was opposed by virtually every American economist, yet sailed through Congress.

The trade barriers erected during the Depression helped raise prices and exacerbated economic distress. In the trade wars of the 1930s, countries

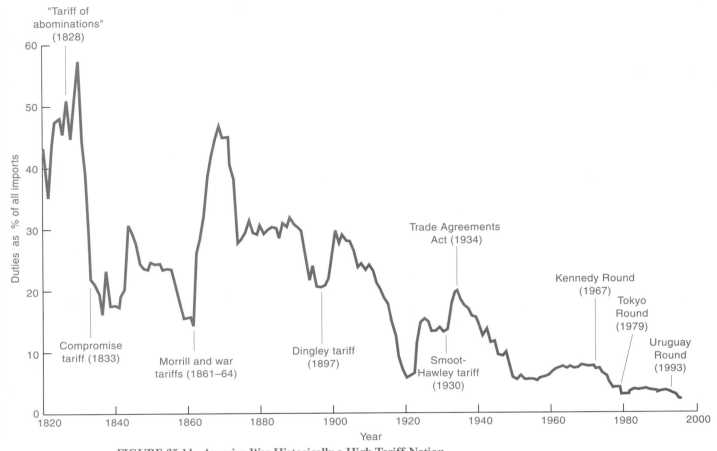

FIGURE 35-11. America Was Historically a High-Tariff Nation

Duties were high for most of our nation's history, but trade negotiations since the 1930s have lowered tariffs significantly.

attempted to raise employment and output by raising trade barriers at the expense of their neighbors. Nations soon learned that at the end of the tariff-retaliation game, all were losers.

Negotiating Free Trade

At the end of World War II, the international community established a number of institutions to promote peace and economic prosperity through cooperative policies. One of the most successful of these was the General Agreement on Tariffs and Trade (GATT), which became the World Trade Organization (WTO) at the beginning of 1995. Their charters speak of raising living standards through "substantial reduction of tariffs and other barriers to trade and the elimination of discrimina-

tory treatment in international commerce." The WTO currently has 130 member countries, which account for 90 percent of international trade.

Among the principles underlying the WTO are (1) countries should work to lower trade barriers; (2) all trade barriers should be applied on a nondiscriminatory basis across nations (i.e., all nations should enjoy "most-favored-nation" status); (3) when a country increases its tariffs above agreed-upon levels, it must compensate its trading partners for the economic injury; and (4) trade conflicts should be settled by consultations and arbitration.

The history of trade negotiations has proved to be one of the major successes in international economic cooperation. Every few years, representatives of major industrialized countries meet together to identify major trade barriers and negotiate their removal. In 1993 nations completed the "Uruguay Round." In addition to pursuing the traditional goal of reducing tariff and quota barriers, the new round undertook the ambitious goals of lowering trade barriers and subsidies in agriculture and removing quotas on textiles, and it has extended free trade to services and intellectual property. In addition, the WTO has substantially increased powers to enforce international-trade agreements.

Recent Steps. Over the last few years, governments have taken a number of steps to promote free trade or to broaden markets. Among the most important were the following:

- In 1987, the United States and Canada negotiated a set of principles for free trade between the two countries. This agreement was particularly significant because Canada is the largest trading partner of the United States, with total trade flows between the two of $276 billion in 1995. Canada's tariff rates were among the highest of the major industrial countries, and Canada curtailed foreign investment on nationalist grounds. Economists have estimated that the free-trade agreement will raise real incomes in Canada by 5 percent and those in the United States by 1 percent.

- The most controversial proposal for lowering trade barriers was the North American Free Trade Agreement (NAFTA), which was hotly debated and passed by Congress by a close vote in 1993. Mexico is the third-largest trading partner of the United States, and most U.S.-Mexico trade is in manufactured goods. NAFTA not only allows goods to pass tariff-free across the borders but also liberalizes regulations on investments by the United States and Canada in Mexico. Proponents of the plan argued that it would allow a more efficient pattern of specialization and would enable U.S. firms to compete more effectively against firms in other countries; opponents, par-

ticularly labor groups, argued that it would increase the supply of goods produced by low-skilled labor and thereby depress the wages of workers in the affected industries. Economists caution, however, that regional trading agreements like NAFTA can cause inefficiency if they exclude potential trading countries. They point to the stagnation in the Caribbean countries that followed the passage of NAFTA as a cautionary example of the dangers of the regional approach.

- The most far-reaching trade accord has been the movement toward a single market among the major European countries. The nations of the European Union (EU) are developing a common market with no or few barriers to international trade or movement of factors of production in the European area. The first step involved eliminating all internal tariff and regulatory barriers to trade and labor and capital flows. The second and more difficult step is to introduce a common currency for the core members of the European Union. The issues involving European monetary union (EMU) are analyzed in Chapter 36.

Appraisal

After World War II, policymakers around the world believed firmly that free trade was essential for world prosperity. These convictions translated into several successful agreements to lower tariffs, as Figure 35-11 shows. The free-trade conviction among economists and market-oriented policymakers has been severely tested by periods of high unemployment and exchange-rate disturbances. Nevertheless, most countries have continued the trend toward increased openness and outward orientation.

By most accounts, countries have benefited from more open trade in increased trade flows and higher living standards. But the struggle to preserve open markets is constantly tested as interest groups use new weapons and arguments in their tireless attempt to fell the mighty theory of comparative advantage.

SUMMARY

A. Comparative Advantage among Nations

1. Recall that trade occurs because of differences in the conditions of production or diversity in tastes. The foundation of international trade is the Ricardian principle of comparative advantage. The principle of comparative advantage holds that each country will benefit if it specializes in the production and export of those goods that it can produce at relatively low cost.

Conversely, each country will benefit if it imports those goods which it produces at relatively high cost. This principle holds even if one region is absolutely more or less productive than another in all commodities. As long as there are differences in *relative* or *comparative* efficiencies among countries, every country must enjoy a comparative advantage or a comparative disadvantage in some goods.

2. The law of comparative advantage predicts more than just the geographical pattern of specialization and direction of trade. It also demonstrates that countries are made better off and that real wages (or, more generally, total national income) are improved by trade and the resulting enlarged world production. Prohibitive quotas and tariffs, designed to "protect" workers or industries, will lower a nation's total income and consumption possibilities.

3. Even with many goods or many countries, the same principles of comparative advantage apply. With many commodities, we can arrange products along a continuum of comparative advantage, from relatively more efficient to relatively less efficient. With many countries, trade may be triangular or multilateral, with countries having large bilateral (or two-sided) surpluses or deficits with other individual countries.

B. Protectionism

4. Completely free trade equalizes prices of tradeable goods at home with those in world markets. Under trade, goods flow uphill from low-price to high-price markets.

5. A tariff raises the domestic prices of imported goods, leading to a decline in consumption and imports along with an increase in domestic production. Quotas have very similar effects and may, in addition, lower government revenues.

6. A tariff causes economic waste. The economy suffers losses from decreased home consumption and from wasting resources on goods lacking comparative advantage. The losses generally exceed government revenues from the tariff.

7. Most arguments for tariffs simply rationalize special benefits to particular pressure groups and cannot withstand economic analysis. Three arguments that can stand up to careful scrutiny are the following: (*a*) The terms-of-trade or optimal tariff can in principle raise the real income of a large country at the expense of its trading partners. (*b*) In a situation of less-than-full employment, tariffs might push an economy toward fuller employment, but monetary or fiscal policies could attain the same employment goal with fewer inefficiencies than this beggar-thy-neighbor policy. (*c*) Sometimes, infant industries may need temporary protection in order to realize their true long-run comparative advantages.

8. The principle of comparative advantage must be qualified if markets malfunction because of unemployment or exchange market disturbances. Moreover, individual sectors or factors may be injured by trade if imports lower their returns.

CONCEPTS FOR REVIEW

Principles of International Trade

absolute and comparative advantage (or disadvantage)
principle of comparative advantage
economic gains from trade
triangular and multilateral trade
world vs. national *PPFs*

consumption vs. production possibilities with trade

Economics of Protectionism

price equilibrium with and without trade
tariff, quota

effects of tariffs on price, imports, and domestic production
mercantilist, cheap-foreign-labor, and retaliatory arguments
the optimal tariff, unemployment, and infant-industry exceptions
WTO and trade negotiations

QUESTIONS FOR DISCUSSION

1. State whether or not each of the following is correct and explain your reasoning. If the quotation is incorrect, provide a corrected statement.
   a. "We Mexicans can never compete profitably with the Northern colossus. Her factories are too efficient, she has too many computers and ma-

chine tools, and her engineering skills are too advanced. We need tariffs, or we can export nothing!"
   b. "If American workers are subjected to the unbridled competition of cheap Mexican labor, our real wages must necessarily fall drastically."

c. "The current account for a country need not balance bilaterally (i.e., with each country), but it must balance multilaterally (i.e., with all countries)."

d. "The principle of comparative advantage applies equally well to families, cities, and states as it does to nations and continents."

e. The quotation from Ross Perot on page 703.

2. Reconstruct Figure 35-1 and its accompanying table to show the production data for Europe; assume that Europe has 600 units of labor and that labor productivities are those given in Table 35-1.

3. What if the data in Table 35-1 changed from (1, 2; 3, 4) to (1, 2; 2, 4)? Show that all trade is killed off. Use this to explain the adage, *"Vive la différence!"* (freely translated as "Let diversity thrive!"). Why do the largest gains in trade flow to small countries whose pretrade prices are very different from prevailing world prices?

4. *Follow-up to question 3:* Suppose that the data in Table 35-1 pertain to a newly industrialized country (NIC) and America. What are the gains from trade between the two countries? Now suppose that NIC adopts American technology and has production possibilities identical to that in the American column of Table 35-1. What will happen to international trade? What will happen to NIC's living standards and real wages? What will happen to America's living standards? Is there a lesson here for the impact of converging economies on trade and welfare?

5. A U.S. senator wrote the following: "Trade is supposed to raise the incomes of all nations involved—or at least that is what Adam Smith and David Ricardo taught us. If our economic decline has been caused by the economic growth of our competitors, then these philosophers—and the entire discipline of economics they founded—have been taking us on a 200-year ride."

Explain why the first sentence is correct. Also explain why the second sentence does not follow from the first. Can you give an example of how economic growth of Country J could lower the standard of living in Country A? (*Hint:* The answer to question 4 will help uncover the fallacy in the quotation.)

6. New international economics developed theories that might support the following arguments for protecting domestic industries against foreign competition:

a. In some situations, a country could improve its standard of living by imposing protection if no one else retaliated.

b. If the marketplace is not working well and there is excessive unemployment, tariffs might lower the unemployment rate.

c. A country might be willing to accept a small drop in its living standard to preserve certain industries that it deems necessary for national security, such as supercomputers or oil, by protecting them from foreign competition.

d. Wages in Korea are but one-tenth of those in the United States. Unless we limit the imports of Korean manufactures, we face a future in which our trade deficit continues to deteriorate under the onslaught of competition from low-wage East Asian workers.

In each case, relate the argument to one of the traditional defenses of protectionism. State the conditions under which it is valid, and decide whether you agree with it.

7. The United States has had quotas on steel, shipping, automobiles, textiles, and many other products. Economists estimate that by auctioning off the quota rights, the Treasury would gain at least $10 billion annually. Use Figure 35-9 to analyze the economics of quotas as follows: Assume that the government imposes a quota of 100 on imports, allocating the quota rights to importing countries on the basis of last year's imports. What would be the equilibrium price and quantity of clothing? What would be the efficiency losses from quotas? Who would get revenue rectangle *C*? What would be the effect of auctioning off the quota rights?

CHAPTER 36
MANAGING THE GLOBAL ECONOMY

Before I built a wall I'd ask to know
What I was walling in or walling out . . .

Robert Frost

A history of the twentieth century shows two distinct periods. The period from 1914 to 1945 was characterized by destructive competition, hot and cold military and trade wars, despotism, and depression. From 1945 to the present, the world has enjoyed cooperation, widening trade linkages, an expansion of democracy, and rapid economic growth.

The stark contrast between the first and second halves of this century is a reminder of the high stakes in the wise management of our national and global economies. Economically, no nation is an island unto itself. When the bell tolls depressions or financial crisis, the sounds reverberate around the world.

What are the economic links among nations? The last two chapters surveyed the major economic mechanisms. We saw that international exchange takes place not by barter but through the medium of money. Trade occurs through the buying or selling of commodities for dollars or pesos or other currencies. Further, we saw that international trade allows nations to raise their standards of living by specializing in areas of comparative advantage, exporting goods in which they are relatively efficient and importing those in which they are relatively inefficient.

Yet the forces of comparative advantage are not the whole story. Some countries have managed their economies well, opening their economies, adapting to the evolving technologies and markets in the world economy, growing, and prospering. Others have fallen behind, either because they are trapped in the vicious cycle of poverty or because war, corruption, and the heavy hand of government regulation have snuffed out the flames of entrepreneurship and wrecked the best-laid plans.

Trade among nations sometimes seems a brutal Darwinian conflict for market shares, profits, and vital resources. But humans have in the second half of this century evolved beyond the red-in-tooth-and-claw struggle—they have built institutions that serve the common cause of growth and fairness in the international arena. These institutions include a system for managing international finance mechanisms, a system for coordinating monetary policies, and agreements for curbing trade restrictions. In this final chapter, we examine the major international economic problems and some of the cooperative institutions that have grown up to make international markets operate more smoothly.

◆ A. THE INTERNATIONAL MONETARY SYSTEM ◆

We start with an analysis of the **international monetary system**. This term denotes the institutions under which payments are made for transactions that reach across national boundaries. In particular, the international monetary system determines how foreign exchange rates are set and how governments can affect exchange rates.

 Reminder: The essence of foreign exchange. Chapter 34 explained that international trade involves the use of different national currencies, which are linked by relative prices called foreign exchange rates. In the foreign exchange market, the demand for American dollars comes from foreigners who want to purchase goods, services, and investments from America; the supply of American dollars comes from Americans who want to purchase foreign commodities or financial assets. The interaction of these supplies and demands determines the foreign exchange rate.

A fall in the market price of a currency is a depreciation; a rise in a currency's value is called an appreciation. In a system where governments have official foreign exchange rates, a decrease in the official exchange rate is called a devaluation while an increase is a revaluation.

The importance of the international monetary system was well described by economist Robert Solomon:

> Like the traffic lights in a city, the international monetary system is taken for granted until it begins to malfunction and to disrupt people's lives. . . . A well-functioning monetary system will facilitate international trade and investment and smooth adaptation to change. A monetary system that functions poorly may not only discourage the development of trade and investment among nations but subject their economies to disruptive shocks when necessary adjustments to change are prevented or delayed.[1]

---
[1] Robert Solomon, *The International Monetary System, 1945–1976: An Insider's View* (Harper & Row, New York, 1977), pp. 1, 7.

The central element of the international monetary system involves the arrangements by which exchange rates are set. In recent years, nations have used one of three major exchange-rate systems:

- A system of flexible or floating exchange rates, where exchange rates are entirely determined by market forces
- A system of fixed exchange rates
- A hybrid system of "managed" exchange rates, which involves some currencies whose values float freely, some currencies whose values are determined by a combination of government intervention and the market, and some that are pegged or fixed to one currency or a group of currencies

PURE FLEXIBLE EXCHANGE RATES

At one extreme is an international monetary system in which exchange rates are completely flexible and move purely under the influence of supply and demand. This system, known as **flexible exchange rates**, is one where governments neither announce an exchange rate nor take steps to enforce one. (Another term often used is "floating" exchange rates, which means the same thing.) In a flexible-exchange-rate system, the relative prices of currencies are determined by buying and selling among households and businesses.

Let us see how exchange rates are determined under flexible rates. In 1994, the peso was under attack in foreign exchange markets, and the Mexicans allowed the peso to float. At the original exchange rate of approximately 4 pesos per U.S. dollar, there was an excess supply of pesos. This meant that at that exchange rate, the supply of pesos by Mexicans to buy American and other foreign goods and assets outweighed the demand for pesos by Americans and others who wanted to purchase Mexican goods and assets.

What was the outcome? As a result of the excess supply, the peso depreciated relative to the dollar.

How far did the exchange rates move? Just far enough so that—at the depreciated exchange rate of about 6 pesos to the dollar—the quantities supplied and demanded were balanced.

What lies behind the equilibration of supply and demand? Two main forces are involved: (1) With the dollar more expensive, it costs more for Mexicans to buy American goods, services, and investments, causing the supply of pesos to fall off in the usual fashion. (2) With the depreciation of the peso, Mexican goods and assets become less expensive for foreigners. This increases the demand for pesos in the marketplace. (Note that this simplified discussion assumes that all transactions occur only between the two countries; a more complete discussion would involve the demands and supplies of currencies from all countries.)

Where is the government? In a freely flexible exchange-rate system, the government is on the sidelines. It allows the foreign exchange market to determine the value of the dollar, just as it allows markets to determine the value of lettuce, machinery, GM stock, or copper. Consequently, it is possible to get enormous swings in flexible exchange rates over relatively short periods.

FIXED EXCHANGE RATES: THE CLASSICAL GOLD STANDARD

At the other extreme is a system of **fixed exchange rates**, where governments specify the exact rate at which dollars will be converted into pesos, yen, and other currencies. Historically, the most important fixed-exchange-rate system was the **gold standard**, which was used off and on from 1717 until 1933. In this system, each country defined the value of its currency in terms of a fixed amount of gold, thereby establishing fixed exchange rates among the countries on the gold standard.[2]

The functioning of the gold standard can be seen easily in a simplified example. Suppose people

---

[2] Why was gold used as the standard of exchange and means of payment, rather than some other commodity? Certainly other materials could have been used, but gold had the advantages of being in limited supply, being relatively indestructible, and having few industrial uses. Can you see why wine, wheat, or cattle would not be a useful means of payment among countries?

everywhere insisted on being paid in bits of pure gold metal. Then buying a bicycle in Britain would merely require payment in gold at a price expressed in ounces of gold. By definition there would be no foreign-exchange-rate problem. Gold would be the common world currency.

This example captures the essence of the gold standard. Once gold became the medium of exchange or money, foreign trade was no different from domestic trade; everything could be paid for in gold. The only difference between countries was that they could choose different *units* for their gold coins. Thus, Queen Victoria chose to make British coins about $\frac{1}{4}$ ounce of gold (the pound) and President McKinley chose to make the U.S. unit $\frac{1}{20}$ ounce of gold (the dollar). In that case, the British pound, being 5 times as heavy as the dollar, had an exchange rate of $5/£1.

This was the essence of the gold standard. In practice, countries tended to use their own coins. But anyone was free to melt down coins and sell them at the going price of gold. So exchange rates were fixed for all countries on the gold standard. *The exchange rates (also called par values or parities) for different currencies were determined by the gold content of their monetary units.*

Hume's Adjustment Mechanism

The purpose of an exchange-rate system is to promote international trade while facilitating adjustment to shocks and disequilibria. Key to understanding international economics is to see how the *international adjustment mechanism* functions. What happens if a country's wages and prices rise so sharply that its goods are no longer competitive in the world market? Under flexible exchange rates, the country's exchange rate could depreciate to offset the domestic inflation. But under fixed exchange rates, equilibrium must be restored by deflation at home or inflation abroad.

Let's examine the international adjustment mechanism under a fixed-exchange-rate system with two countries, America and Britain. Suppose that American inflation has made American goods uncompetitive. Consequently, America's imports rise and its exports fall. It therefore runs a trade deficit with Britain. To pay for its deficit, America would have to ship gold to Britain. Eventually—if there were no adjustments in either America or Britain—America would run out of gold.

In fact, an automatic adjustment mechanism does exist, as was demonstrated by the British philosopher David Hume in 1752. He showed that the outflow of gold was part of a mechanism that tended to keep international payments in balance. His argument, though nearly 250 years old, offers important insights for understanding how trade flows get balanced in today's economy.

Hume's explanation rested in part upon the quantity theory of prices, which is a theory of the overall price level that is analyzed in macroeconomics. This doctrine holds that the overall price level in an economy is proportional to the supply of money. Under the gold standard, gold was an important part of the money supply—either directly, in the form of gold coins, or indirectly, when governments used gold as backing for paper money.

What would be the impact of a country's losing gold? First, the country's money supply would decline either because gold coins would be exported or because some of the gold backing for the currency would leave the country. Putting both these consequences together, a loss of gold leads to a reduction in the money supply. According to the quantity theory, the next step is that prices and costs would change proportionally to the change in the money supply. If the United States loses 10 percent of its gold to pay for a trade deficit, the quantity theory predicts that U.S. prices, costs, and incomes would fall 10 percent. In other words, the economy would experience a deflation. If gold discoveries in California increase America's gold supplies, we would expect to see a major increase in the price level in the United States.

Copy

The Four-Pronged Mechanism.
Now consider Hume's theory of international payments equilibrium. Suppose that America runs a large trade deficit and begins to lose gold. According to the quantity theory of prices, this loss of gold reduces America's money supply, driving down America's prices and costs. As a result, (1) America decreases its imports of British and other foreign goods, which have become relatively expensive; and (2) because America's domestically produced goods have

become relatively inexpensive on world markets, America's exports increase.

The opposite effect occurs in Britain and other foreign countries. Because Britain's exports are growing rapidly, it receives gold in return. Britain's money supply therefore increases, driving up British prices and costs according to the quantity theory. At this point, two more prongs of the Hume mechanism come into play: (3) British and other foreign exports have become more expensive, so the volume of goods exported to America and elsewhere declines; and (4) British citizens, faced with a higher domestic price level, now import more of America's low-priced goods.

Figure 36-1 on page 716 illustrates the logic in Hume's mechanism. Make sure you can follow the logical chain from the original deficit at the top through the adjustment to the new equilibrium at the bottom.

The result of Hume's four-pronged gold-flow mechanism is an improvement in the balance of payments of the country losing gold and a worsening in that of the country gaining the gold. In the end, an equilibrium of international trade and finance is reestablished at new relative prices, which keep trade and international lending in balance with no net gold flow. This equilibrium is a stable one and requires no tariffs or other government intervention.

Adjustment with Fixed Exchange Rates.
Understanding the gold standard is important not only because of its historical role but also because it is a pure example of a fixed-exchange-rate system. The same analysis applies to all fixed-exchange-rate systems: If exchange rates are not free to move when the prices or incomes among countries get out of line, *domestic* prices and incomes must adjust to restore equilibrium. If Europe decides to adopt a common currency, the mechanism by which adjustments will occur is similar to that under a gold standard.

In Hume's mechanism, it is gold flows that move prices and wages and ensure equilibrium. In modern macroeconomic thinking, output and employment are also part of the international adjustment mechanism. We will see later in this chapter that *the necessity of having real output and employment adjust to ensure relative-price equilibrium among countries on a fixed exchange rate is a crucial dilemma faced by countries*

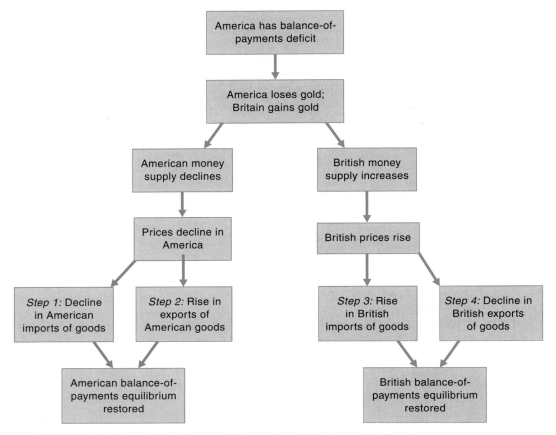

FIGURE 36-1. Hume's Four-Pronged International Adjustment Mechanism

Hume explained how a balance-of-payments disequilibrium would automatically produce equilibrating adjustment under a gold standard. Trace the lines from the original disequilibrium at the top through the changes in prices to the restored equilibrium at the bottom. This mechanism works in modified form under any fixed-exchange-rate system. Modern economics augments the mechanism in the fourth row of boxes by replacing the fourth row with "Prices, output, and employment decline in Amercia" and "Prices, output, and employment rise in Britain."

considering a fixed exchange rate. The same question arises in Europe's decision on whether to adopt a common currency.

MANAGED EXCHANGE RATES

Few countries today adopt either the extreme of absolutely fixed exchange rates or that of pure flexible exchange rates. Rather, the norm is the middle ground of **managed exchange rates**, meaning that exchange rates are basically determined by market forces but governments buy or sell currencies or change their money supplies to affect their exchange rates. Sometimes governments lean against the winds of private markets. At other times governments have "target zones" which guide their policy actions.

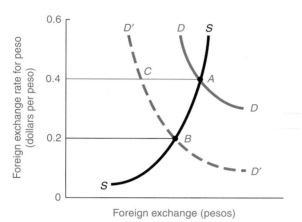

FIGURE 36-2. Governments Intervene to Defend Fixed Exchange Rate

Say the Mexican government announces a fixed exchange rate of 0.4 dollars per peso (2½ pesos per dollar). Initial equilibrium is at A. Deteriorating economic conditions—perhaps inflation or concerns over Mexico's political stability—lead to a decline in the demand for pesos. In a flexible-exchange-rate system, the new equilibrium would be at B, with an exchange rate of 0.2 dollars to the peso (or 5 pesos to the dollar). Central banks can reestablish official parity by buying CA worth of pesos, in effect shifting the demand back to the original demand curve, D. Alternatively, by raising Mexican interest rates, the governments can induce private investors to increase their demand for pesos by CA.

Intervention

Managing the exchange rate requires that governments intervene in foreign exchange markets. Government exchange-rate **intervention** occurs when the government buys or sells its own or foreign currencies to affect exchange rates. For example, the Japanese government on a given day might buy $1 billion worth of Japanese yen with U.S. dollars. This would cause a rise in value, or an appreciation, of the yen. In general, a government intervenes when it believes its foreign exchange rate is out of line with its currency's fundamental value.

Figure 36-2 illustrates the operation of a fixed-exchange-rate system. Suppose that Mexico decides to peg its exchange rate at $0.40 per peso (or 2½ pesos per dollar). The initial equilibrium is shown as

point A in Figure 36-2. At an exchange rate of $0.40 per peso, the quantities of Mexican pesos supplied and demanded are equal.

Suppose that the demand for pesos falls, perhaps because inflation in Mexico is higher than in the United States. This produces a downward shift in the demand for pesos from D to D'. In a world of flexible exchange rates, the peso would depreciate and reach a new equilibrium at B in Figure 36-2.

Here is where the new wrinkle appears: Recall that Mexico is committed to maintaining the parity of $0.40 per peso. What can it do?

- One approach is to intervene by *buying the depreciating currency (pesos) and selling the appreciating currency (dollars)*. In this example, if the Mexican central bank buys the amount shown by the segment CA, this will increase the demand for pesos and maintain the official parity.
- An alternative would be to use monetary policy. The Mexican central bank could *induce the private sector to increase its demand for pesos* by raising Mexican interest rates. Say that Mexican interest rates rise relative to U.S. rates; this would lead investors to move funds into pesos and increase the private demand for pesos, in effect moving the private demand curve back toward the original D demand curve.

These two operations are not really so different as they sound. In effect, both involve monetary policies in Mexico. In fact, one of the complications of managing the open economy, as we will shortly see, is that the need to use monetary policies to manage the exchange rate can collide with the need to use monetary policy to stabilize the domestic business cycle.

To summarize:

A *freely flexible* exchange rate is one determined purely by supply and demand without any government intervention. A *fixed-exchange-rate* system is one where governments state official exchange rates, which they defend through intervention and monetary policies. A *managed-exchange-rate* system is a hybrid of fixed and flexible rates in which governments attempt to affect their exchange rates *directly* by buying or selling foreign currencies or *indirectly*, through monetary policy, by raising or lowering interest rates.

B. INTERNATIONAL INSTITUTIONS

In the early part of the twentieth century, even nations which were ostensibly at peace engaged in debilitating trade wars and competitive devaluations. After World War II, international institutions were developed to foster economic cooperation among nations. These institutions continue to be the means by which nations coordinate their policies and seek solutions to common problems. This section surveys the major international institutions and examines the issues raised by interdependencies among nations.

The United States emerged from World War II with its economy intact—able and willing to help rebuild the countries of friends and foes alike. The postwar international political system responded to the needs of war-torn nations by establishing durable institutions that facilitated the quick recovery of the international economy. The major international economic institutions of the postwar period were the General Agreement on Tariffs and Trade (rechartered as the World Trade Organization in 1995), the Bretton Woods exchange-rate system, the International Monetary Fund, and the World Bank. These four institutions stand as monuments to wise and far-sighted statecraft.

The Bretton Woods System

The major economists of the 1940s, particularly John Maynard Keynes, were greatly affected by the economic crisis of the prewar period. They were determined to avoid the economic chaos and competitive devaluations that had occured during the Great Depression.

Under the intellectual leadership of Keynes, nations gathered in 1944 at Bretton Woods, New Hampshire, and hammered out an agreement that led to the formation of the major economic institutions. For the first time, nations agreed upon a system for regulating international financial transactions. Even though some of the rules have changed since 1944, the institutions established at Bretton Woods continue to play a vital role today.

Those who attended the Bretton Woods conference remembered well how the gold standard was too inflexible and served to deepen economic crises. To replace the gold standard, the **Bretton Woods system** established a parity for each currency in terms of both the U.S. dollar and gold. Currencies were defined in terms of both gold and the dollar, and exchange rates among currencies were determined in much the same way as they had been under the gold standard. For example, the parity of the British pound was set at £12.5 per ounce of gold. Given that the gold price of the dollar was $35 per ounce, this implied an official exchange rate between the dollar and the pound of $35/£12.5 = $2.80 per £1, which was thereby set as the official parity on the pound.

The revolutionary innovation of the Bretton Woods system was that exchange rates were *fixed but adjustable.* When one currency got too far out of line with its appropriate or "fundamental" value, the parity could be adjusted. The ability to adjust exchange rates when fundamental disequilibrium arose was the central distinction between the Bretton Woods system and the gold standard. Ideally, exchange-rate changes would be worked out among countries in a cooperative way.

By creating a fixed but adjustable system, the designers of Bretton Woods hoped to have the best of two worlds. They could maintain the *stability* of the gold standard, a world in which exchange rates would be predictable from one month to the next, thereby encouraging trade and capital flows. At the same time, they would simulate the *adjustment* of flexible exchange rates, under which persistent relative-price differences among countries could be adjusted to by exchange-rate changes rather than by the painful deflation and unemployment necessary under the gold standard.

The International Monetary Fund (IMF)

An integral part of the Bretton Woods system was the establishment of the International Monetary Fund (or IMF), which still administers the international monetary system and operates as a central bank for central banks. Member nations subscribe by lending their currencies to the IMF; the IMF then relends these funds to help countries in balance-of-payments difficulties. In recent years, the IMF has played a key role in organizing a cooperative response to the international debt crisis and in helping formerly communist countries make the transition to the market.

How would the IMF accomplish this objective? Suppose, for example, that Russia's transition to the market is in trouble because of a rapid inflation and an inability to raise funds in private markets. The country is having trouble paying interest and principal on its foreign loans. The IMF might send a team of specialists to pore over the country's books. The IMF team would come up with an austerity plan for Russia, generally involving reducing the budget deficit and tightening credit; these measures would slow inflation and increase confidence in the Russian ruble. When Russia and the IMF agree on the plan, the IMF would lend money to Russia, perhaps $5 billion, to "bridge" the country over until its balance of payments improved. In addition, there would probably be a debt restructuring, wherein banks would lend more funds and stretch out payments on existing loans.

If the IMF program was successful, Russia's balance of payments would begin to improve, and the country would resume economic growth.

The World Bank

Another international financial institution created after World War II was the World Bank. The Bank is capitalized by rich nations that subscribe in proportion to their economic importance in terms of GDP and other factors. The Bank makes low-interest loans to countries for projects which are economically sound but which cannot get private-sector financing. As a result of such long-term loans, goods and services flow from advanced nations to developing countries. In 1996, the World Bank made new loans of $21 billion.

If the projects are selected wisely, production in the borrowing lands will rise by more than enough to pay interest on the loans; wages and living standards generally will be higher, not lower, because the foreign capital has raised GDP in the borrowing countries. In addition, as the loans are being paid back, the advanced nations will gain by enjoying somewhat higher imports of useful goods.

Demise of the Bretton Woods System

For the first three decades after World War II, under the Bretton Woods arrangements, the U.S. dollar was the key currency. Most international trade and finance were carried out in dollars, and payments were most often made in dollars. Exchange-rate parities were quoted in dollar terms, and private and government reserves were kept invested in dollar securities. This was a period of unprecedented growth and prosperity. The industrial nations began to lower trade barriers and to make all their currencies freely convertible. The economies of Western Europe and East Asia recovered from war damage and grew at spectacular rates. During this period, the world was on a dollar standard. In essence, the U.S. dollar was the world currency because of its stability, convertibility, and widespread acceptability.

But recovery contained the seeds of its own destruction. U.S. trade deficits were fueled by an overvalued currency, budget deficits to finance the Vietnam war, and growing overseas investment by American firms. Dollars consequently began to pile up abroad as Germany and Japan developed trade surpluses. Dollar holdings abroad grew from next to nothing in 1945 to $50 billion in the early 1970s.

By 1971, the stock of liquid dollar balances had become so large that governments had difficulty defending the official parities. People began to lose confidence in the "almighty dollar." And the lower barriers to financial flows meant that billions of dollars could cross the Atlantic in minutes and threaten to overwhelm existing parities. On August 15, 1971, President Nixon formally severed the link between the dollar and gold, bringing the Bretton Woods era to an end. No longer would the United States automatically convert dollars into other currencies or into gold at $35 per ounce; no longer would the United States set an official parity of the dollar and then defend this exchange rate at all costs. As the United States abandoned the Bretton Woods system, the world moved into the modern era.

Today's Hybrid System

Unlike the earlier uniform system under either the gold standard or Bretton Woods, today's exchange-rate system fits into no tidy mold. Without anyone's having planned it, the world has moved to a hybrid exchange-rate system. The major features are as follows:

Today's Hybrid System

- A few countries allow their currencies to *float freely,* as the United States has for some periods in the last two decades. In this approach, a country allows markets to determine its currency's value and it rarely intervenes.
- Some major countries have *managed but flexible* exchange rates. Today, this group includes Canada, Japan, and more recently Britain. Under this system, a country will buy or sell its currency to reduce the day-to-day volatility of currency fluctuations. In addition, a country will sometimes engage in systematic intervention to move its currency toward what it believes to be a more appropriate level.
- Many countries, particularly small ones, *peg* their currencies to a major currency or to a "basket" of currencies. Sometimes, the peg is allowed to glide smoothly upward or downward in a system known as a *gliding* or *crawling peg.*
- Some countries join together in a *currency bloc* in order to stabilize exchange rates among themselves while allowing their currencies to move flexibly relative to those of the rest of the world. The most important of these blocs is the European Monetary System (discussed below).
- In addition, almost all countries tend to intervene either when markets become "disorderly" or when exchange rates seem far out of line with the "fundamentals," that is, with exchange rates that are appropriate for existing price levels and trade flows.

MACROECONOMIC INTERACTIONS

For much of the nation's history, economic policies in the United States have concentrated on domestic affairs, influenced largely by domestic inflation, unemployment, and elections. During the turbulent 1980s, the United States came of age as a mature leader in world economic affairs. It saw its domestic monetary and fiscal policies spill over to affect exchange rates and trade flows, and American unemployment and inflation were buffeted by trends in the world economy.

The central lesson of the last decade is clear: In a world where economies are increasingly linked by trade and finance, interdependence is unavoidable. No walls can insulate a country from global economic forces. Isolationism is today no more feasible in economic affairs than it is in political or military affairs. We devote the remainder of this section to describing the major economic linkages among nations.

Economic Interaction

Domestic economic welfare depends upon the health of the entire international economy. This fact is captured in the old saying, "When America sneezes, Europe catches cold." To see why economic ailments can be contagious, let's examine the principal links in the interaction of nations' economic policies.

Multiplier Link: Net Exports and Multiplier Effects. The first link relates to the spillovers from business cycles in different regions. Suppose that income and output in America fall, perhaps because America decides to contract the economy to slow inflation or maybe simply because demand in the private sector is weak. We know that lower income in America will lead to lower imports from other countries. But American imports are other countries' exports, so Europe may find its exports declining, and the decrease tends to reduce Europe's aggregate demand, output, and employment. Therefore, any factor that reduces America's national output also tends to reduce output and employment abroad. The causation is summarized as

$$Y_A \downarrow \rightarrow Im_A \downarrow \rightarrow Ex_E \downarrow \rightarrow Y_E \downarrow$$

Here Y_A and Y_E are output in America and Europe, Im_A is America's imports, while Ex_E is Europe's exports.

This multiplier link is what governments have in mind when they try to persuade their trading partners to expand their economies. For example, in 1993, Lawrence Summers, an eminent Harvard economist serving as the U.S. undersecretary of the Treasury, pointed out to Japanese business leaders that if the Japanese government increased its fiscal outlays, boosting Japanese national income and imports from abroad, then jobs would be created abroad too:

> The extra demand that would be created by a return of the Japanese current account surplus to its historically average level of one and a half percent of GDP would be enough to create more than $60 billion in

additional exports from the rest of the world, which translates into an extra one to two million jobs.[3]

A Japanese fiscal expansion would stimulate production (and employment) in other nations; Summers' argument is an example of the multiplier link.

Monetary Link: Financial Markets and Interest-Rate Effects.

While the multiplier link works through the current account, the monetary link operates through financial markets. Under flexible exchange rates, large countries have room to change their monetary policies. When central banks raise interest rates through a monetary tightening, the higher interest rates attract funds and the country's foreign exchange rate tends to appreciate. This in turn reduces exports, raises imports, lowers output, and slows inflation. Empirical studies on the United States have found that the international transmission mechanism for monetary policy (whereby interest rates affect exchange rates and net exports) is just as powerful as the domestic mechanism (whereby higher interest rates reduce domestic investment).

But here again we find that the domestic policy spills over to other nations. Consider what happens in Europe when America raises its interest rates. As America's interest rate (r_A) rises, investors sell European financial assets and buy American financial assets. This leads to an appreciation of the dollar ($e_\$\uparrow$) and a depreciation of European currencies. It also tends to raise European interest rates (r_E).

There are a number of effects on America's trading partners. The higher interest rates tend to depress domestic investment in Europe and thereby to lower Europe's output and employment. However, the depreciated value of Europe's currency will tend to stimulate Europe's economy, as the increase in exports to America increases Europe's net exports. The overall effect for Europe is depressed domestic investment and increased exports, with an uncertain impact on total output and employment. This then is the monetary link among nations:

$$r_A \uparrow \rightarrow \begin{cases} e_\$ \uparrow \rightarrow Ex_E \uparrow \rightarrow Y_E \uparrow \\ r_E \uparrow \rightarrow I_E \downarrow \rightarrow Y_E \downarrow \end{cases}$$

---

[3] *Treasury News,* June 25, 1993, p. 4.

where I_E is Europe's domestic investment (other variables were defined under the equation in the multiplier link discussion).

In addition, note that the multiplier link comes into play here, as the economic contraction in America will also lower output in Europe through the direct effect on Europe's exports.

Savings and Investment Link.

The first two linkages show how business-cycle shocks ripple through the world economy. We also want to understand the impact of changes in domestic saving and investment upon other countries. What would happen, for example, if the United States decides to balance its budget? Or if Japan has more saving than it can productively use at home?

Let's take the example of a U.S. fiscal tightening. Higher taxes and lower government spending increase public saving. The savings and investment mechanism is as follows:

$$(T-G)_A \uparrow \rightarrow \begin{cases} r_A \downarrow, e_\$ \downarrow \rightarrow X_A \uparrow \rightarrow I_A \uparrow \\ r_E \downarrow, e_\$ \downarrow \rightarrow X_E \uparrow \rightarrow I_E \uparrow \end{cases}$$

This equation shows the effect of a decrease in the U.S. budget deficit—an increase in $(T-G)_A$. The top line after the bracket states that the fiscal tightening will lower U.S. interest rates and lead to a depreciation of the dollar. This will increase both America's domestic investment (I_A) and American net exports or net foreign investment (X_A). The lower line shows how the American fiscal policy affects Europe. The lower U.S. interest rates also lower European interest rates. This will tend to increase European domestic investment in equipment and structures. Europe's net foreign investment is likely to decline, however, as its net exports to the United States decline as the counterpart of the higher U.S. net exports. Note that American net savings and national investment will increase because both components of investment rise. For Europe, the impact is uncertain because the two components of investment go in opposite directions. But we can see that the composition of Europe's saving and investment definitely changes as a result of American fiscal policy.

We can easily understand this policy looking from the point of view of the world as a whole. Because the world is a closed economy, a lower budget deficit in the United States increases world sav-

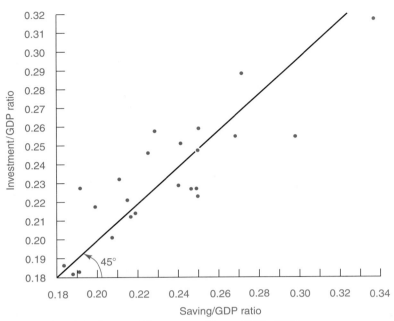

FIGURE 36-3. National Savings and Investment Rates, 1960–1986

Each point shows the average savings and investment rate of one of the 23 advanced industrial countries. For example, the point furthest out is Japan, with a ratio of saving to GDP of 34 percent and an investment-GDP ratio of 32 percent over the 1960–1986 period. Over the long run, higher savings rates tend to increase domestic investment rather than foreign investment. [Source: Adapted from Rudiger Dornbusch, "Comment," in B. Douglas Bernheim and John B. Shoven, *National Saving and Economic Performance* (University of Chicago Press, 1991).]

ing. This tends to lower world interest rates and raise total world investment.

Because of the complexity of the underlying relationships, economists have examined the actual pattern of investment and saving. It turns out that a nation's domestic savings rate tends to be highly correlated with its domestic investment rate. In other words, increases in a nation's savings rate are associated with almost equal increases in its investment rate. Figure 36-3 portrays this correlation for 23 industrialized nations over the 1960–1986 period.

This result is surprising because, if capital is highly mobile, saving would flow to the country with the highest productivity. A low savings rate in Canada would mean that Canada would borrow abroad whatever it needed to equate the cost of capital with capital's marginal productivity. If the investment rate in Canada is entirely determined by the productivity of capital in Canada, and foreign saving fills any

remaining gap left after domestic saving has done its job, the scatter of points in Figure 36-3 would be flat, with a slope of zero.

But the scatter in Figure 36-3 definitely has a positive slope, suggesting that there are substantial barriers to the free flow of capital. The reasons for this lack of capital mobility have puzzled economists. One possible reason is that deficit countries have trouble raising funds in international markets because foreign investors worry about getting back their investments. Another factor is that investors are averse to the risks of investing in other countries, so they tend to keep their funds at home. In addition, if corporations tend to finance their investments out of retained earnings rather than from the world capital market, this practice would directly link domestic saving and investment. All these factors may moderate in the future as countries become more integrated, and evidence suggests that the correlation between domestic saving and investment has declined in the last decade.

The limited mobility of capital has important implications for policy. The most important is that changes in domestic saving will primarily affect the domestic capital stock and the productivity of domestic workers. If budget deficits or other factors reduce domestic saving, in this view, nations cannot look to the saving of other nations to make up the shortfall.

In summary:

Three important factors link countries together: (1) The multiplier link means that output changes in one country are transmitted abroad. (2) The monetary link means that one country's monetary policy affects exchange rates and interest rates abroad. (3) The savings and investment link determines how changes in domestic saving differentially affect investment at home and abroad.

The Need for Coordination

Just because nations have economic problems does not necessarily mean that an international conclave of finance ministers is always a useful remedy. Some problems are largely domestic and must be addressed domestically. But other problems arise from the interaction among nations—because of spillovers, or a large oil-price increase, or a breakdown of the international monetary system. Such systemic problems generally require active or tacit cooperation among nations. Coordination can be fruitful when market failures, external constraints, or conflicting objectives produce counterproductive economic policies. Here are some specific examples:

- *Market failures.* A pervasive market failure comes from the lack of price and wage flexibility, which leads to business cycles and alternating periods of unemployment and inflation. A single economy cannot attain full employment with price stability; nor can all nations together. Nations will find it in their interests to cooperate in their pursuit of macroeconomic stability so that they do not export their unemployment or inflation.

- *External constraints.* Problems arise when governments lose credibility in financial markets. Private investors may believe that a nation will not

FIGURE 36-4. Cooperation Can Replace Beggar-Thy-Neighbor Policies

Nations may decide to improve their incomes through trade restrictions or macroeconomic policies that export inflation or unemployment. Such noncooperative policies move America from U to N_A and Europe from U to N_E. International cooperation looks for "win-win" policies, such as ones that move nations from U to C, making all countries better off.

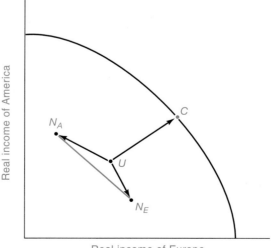

pay back its debts (as was the case for many Latin American countries in the 1980s and Mexico in 1994–1995) or that a nation is trying to defend an unrealistic exchange rate (as happened for country after country in Europe during the early 1990s). In these cases, a country may find that its currency is under speculative attack or, sometimes, that capital markets completely dry up. In effect, interest rates are sky-high and no longer reflect the true cost of funds or productivity of capital. In such cases, more liquid governments can step in and provide temporary loans until capital markets open up for the affected country. The United States did so for Mexico after the 1994 peso crisis, reducing the risk of a spiraling crisis of insolvencies and exchange-rate disruptions in other countries.

• *Conflicting objectives.* Sometimes, individual countries may act in their own national interests, adopting policies that increase domestic incomes and outputs at the expense of other countries. Nations may be tempted to depreciate their currencies to export their unemployment. Sometimes, nations engage in antisocial trade policies, giving valuable preferences to domestic over foreign production. A final facet of international coordination, therefore, is to bring nations together to agree on rules and standards that minimize the amount of antisocial economic activity.

The benefits of cooperation can be seen in the income-possibility curve in Figure 36-4 on page 723. Say that because of policy or exogenous shocks Europe and America find themselves stuck at point U with high unemployment and low incomes due to high interest rates, stubborn government deficits, and strong protectionist lobbies for domestic industries. America considers taking a *noncooperative policy,* perhaps introducing trade barriers, moving to its noncooperative optimum at point N_A. Europe might be weighing the same kind of noncooperative policy, restricting trade, depreciating its currency, or increasing purchases from within its borders—in effect moving to its noncooperative point at N_E. In pursuing these noncooperative policies along the rust $N_A N_E$ line, nations would not only beggar their neighbors but beggar themselves as well.

The alternative would be to find a cooperative approach that had positive rather than negative spillovers. This might involve lowering trade barriers, having a joint policy of monetary expansion, and tightening fiscal policies to increase saving and investment. If successfully designed and implemented, such a policy might move both America and Europe out to point C on the income-possibility curve in Figure 36-4.

International cooperation is designed to overcome the failures that prevent full utilization of resources as well as to promote the free and efficient flow of capital among nations.

C. INTERNATIONAL ECONOMIC ISSUES AT CENTURY'S END

In this final section, we apply the tools of international economics to examine three of the central issues that have concerned nations in recent years. We begin by examining the turbulent dollar "bubble" of the 1980s, showing the forces that led to the dollar overvaluation as well as the impacts of the overvaluation. One of the effects of the dollar's rise was a sharp deterioration in output in the U.S. tradeable sectors such as manufacturing, leading to the diagnosis that America was "deindustrializing." We will see that this raises the broader issue of the fundamental difference between competitiveness and

productivity. Finally, we will turn to one of the major issues of the late 1990s, the dilemma facing Europe as it moves toward monetary union.

THE RISE AND FALL OF THE DOLLAR

We have reviewed the rapid evolution of the international monetary system governing foreign exchange rates over the last half-century. Figure 36-5 shows the average exchange value of the dollar against major currencies. The dollar's exchange rate was quite stable until the Bretton Woods system broke down in

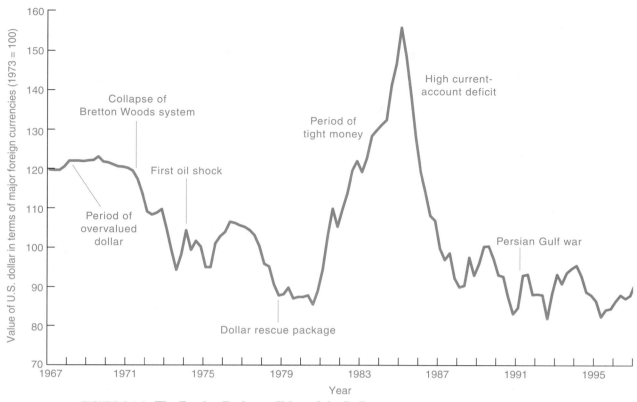

FIGURE 36-5. The Foreign Exchange Value of the Dollar

Before the collapse of the Bretton Woods system, the dollar's value was stable in exchange markets. Then, as the United States pursued its tight-money policies in the early 1980s, the high interest rates pulled up the dollar, decreased net exports, and led to large foreign debt. (Source: Federal Reserve System.)

1971. The dollar then depreciated sharply from 1971 to 1980.

The decade of the 1980s witnessed a dramatic cycle of dollar rise and fall—appreciation and depreciation. The rise of the dollar began in 1980 after a tight monetary policy and loose fiscal policy in the United States drove interest rates up sharply. This period witnessed high dollar interest rates, a conservative administration in the United States, a cut in U.S. tax rates, economic difficulties in continental Europe, socialism in France, and political unrest and a debt crisis in many Latin American countries. All these forces combined to attract mobile funds from other currencies to U.S. dollars.

Figure 36-5 shows the result: from 1979 to early 1985, the exchange rate on the dollar rose 80 percent. Many economists and policymakers became convinced that the dollar was overvalued by 1985, and a swift decline soon followed. Over the next 6 years, the dollar fell more than it had risen in the early 1980s. This sequence has been called a speculative bubble by many.

The Overvalued Dollar

Many economists believed that the dollar was overvalued in the mid-1980s. An *overvalued currency* is one whose value is high relative to its long-run or sustainable level. The consequences of overvaluation were profound not only for the United States but for the entire world economy.

We examined the way tight monetary policies spill across national borders in our discussion of the monetary link earlier in this section. In this case, the first results came as the high interest rates

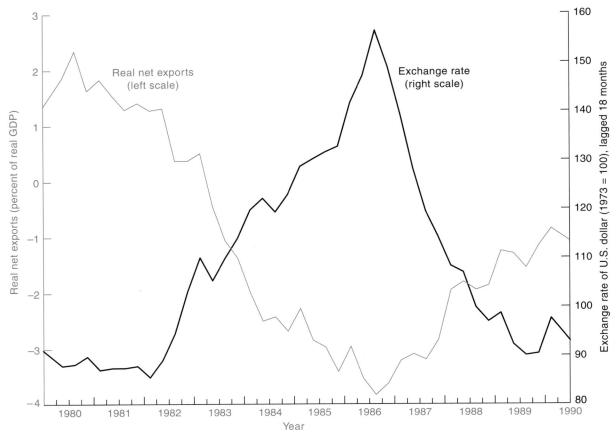

FIGURE 36-6. Trade and Exchange Rates

Real net exports react to exchange-rate changes, but with a time lag. The rising real exchange rate of the dollar during the early 1980s increased U.S. export prices and reduced prices of goods imported into the United States. As a result, real net exports (that is, exports minus imports, both measured in constant prices) fell sharply. When the dollar started to fall in 1985, real net exports began to react only after a considerable time lag. (Source: Real exchange rate is trade-weighted exchange rate corrected for differences in national price levels, from Federal Reserve Board; real net exports from U.S. Department of Commerce.)

in the United States reduced business and residential investment, thereby decreasing aggregate spending, slowing economic activity, and raising unemployment.

In addition, the high U.S. interest rates pulled up the interest rates of other major countries. These high interest rates reduced investment in other industrial economies and triggered a sharp slowdown in overall economic activity in the industrial world. This slowdown began in 1981 and continued through much of the 1980s. In addition, the high interest rates increased debt-service burdens in poor and middle-income countries and contributed to the international debt crisis.

The next effect came as a result of changing exchange rates. As the dollar rose, American export prices increased and the prices of goods imported into the United States fell. As a result, America's exports declined while its imports mounted sharply. From 1980 to 1985, the prices of imported goods and services fell by 6 percent, while the prices of our exports in foreign currencies rose over 80 percent. In response, the volume of imports rose 51 percent while export volumes rose only 2 percent.

The impact on the overall economy is measured by the changes in *real net exports,* which measure the trade balance in quantity terms; more precisely, real net exports are the quantity of exports minus the quantity of imports, where both are measured in constant prices. Figure 36-6 illustrates the dramatic effect of the rising exchange rate of the dollar on real net exports. From the peak in 1980 to the trough in 1986, real net exports declined by $158 billion, or 3 percent of 1983 GDP (all these figures are in 1992 prices).

Overall, the drop in real net exports had a contractionary effect upon domestic output and employment. When foreigners spent less here and Americans spent more abroad, the demand for American goods and services declined, real GDP fell, and unemployment rose. Economic studies indicate that the fall in real net exports was a major contributor to the deep recession in the early 1980s and tended to retard the growth of real GDP during much of the first half of the 1980s.

Dollar Correction and Economic Recovery

In economics, what goes up unsustainably sometimes comes crashing down. In the dollar's case, the dollar peaked in 1985 and began a sharp decline. The reversal was caused in part when governments intervened by selling dollars and buying other currencies, in part by speculators who believed that the dollar was overvalued, and in part by lower relative dollar interest rates. As can be seen in Figure 36-5, the dollar declined steadily for the next 6 years, and by 1991 it had lost all the ground gained between 1980 and 1985.

As the dollar depreciated, the recovery in U.S. net exports after 1985 was slow but steady. Figure 36-6 shows how U.S. real net exports gradually rose after the dollar bubble burst. The recovery in net exports contributed to the long expansion in economic activity from 1982 through 1990.

COMPETITIVENESS AND PRODUCTIVITY

"The Deindustrialization of America"

The roller-coaster ride of the dollar in the 1980s raised alarms about the fundamental performance of the American economy. The overvalued dollar produced severe economic hardships in many U.S. sectors exposed to international trade. Industries like automobiles, steel, textiles, and agriculture found the demand for their products shrinking as their prices rose relative to the prices of foreign competitors. Unemployment in the manufacturing heartland increased sharply as factories were closed, and the midwest became known as the "rust belt."

Many noneconomists interpreted U.S. trade problems as indicative of "America in decline." They fretted that America's technological leadership was eroding because of all sorts of factors, from lack of innovation to managerial sloth. They sometimes advocated economic protection against Japan and Western Europe; often, they argued for "industrial policies" for beleaguered industries to help stem the "deindustrialization of America." It was argued that Americans would be condemned to serving potato chips while others were manufacturing our computer chips.

Economists saw a different syndrome at work—the classic disease of an overvalued exchange rate. To understand the fundamentals, we must distinguish a nation's competitiveness from its productivity. *Competitiveness* refers to the extent to which a nation's goods can compete in the marketplace; this depends primarily upon the relative prices of domestic and foreign products. Competitiveness is, however, quite distinct from a nation's *productivity,* which is measured by the output per unit of input. Productivity is fundamental to the growth in living standards in a nation: it is roughly correct to state that the real income of a nation grows in step with its productivity growth.

It is true that U.S. competitiveness fell sharply during the 1980s. But the cause was not a deterioration in productivity growth. Rather, deteriorating competitiveness during the 1980s arose because the appreciation of the dollar raised American prices relative to those of its trading partners. In fact, there was no major change in the overall trend in productivity growth during the 1980s, and if anything, productivity probably grew more rapidly during that period than in the prior decade.

Make sure you understand this fundamental point about competitiveness: As the theory of comparative advantage demonstrates, nations are not inherently uncompetitive. Rather, they become uncompetitive when their prices move out of line with those of their trading partners because of an overvalued exchange rate. This point is indeed just a restatement of the law of comparative advantage, which shows that all nations can fruitfully engage in trade on the basis of their comparative advantage.

Trends in Productivity

The real story about U.S. real income is not about competitiveness—it concerns productivity. Recall that productivity measures the output per worker or per bundle of inputs. If American real incomes have stagnated over the last two decades, it is because productivity growth has slowed and not because America has become uncompetitive.

Competitiveness is important for trade but has no intrinsic relationship to the level or growth of real incomes. China has enjoyed a massive trade surplus in recent years at the same time that the United States ran a large trade deficit. But surely that does not mean that Americans would trade their living standards for those in China. Loss of competitiveness in international markets results from a nation's *prices* being out of line from those of its trading partners; it has no necessary connection with how a nation's *productivity* compares with other countries' productivity.

What are the recent trends in productivity? Despite the popular rhetoric, the growth of U.S. output, productivity, and consumption has changed little over the last quarter-century. Indeed, U.S. GDP per capita and output per hour worked still far exceed those of its major trading partners, Germany and Japan.

A particularly revealing study by the McKinsey Global Institute found that in 1990 manufacturing productivity in Japan was 17 percent below that in the United States while German productivity was 21 percent below U.S. levels.[4] Furthermore, the United States maintained a productivity lead in four of the nine manufacturing industries studied: computers, soaps and detergents, beer, and food. Japanese workers had higher productivity than U.S. workers in automobiles, auto parts, metalworking, steel, and consumer electronics production. In none of the industries surveyed were German workers the most productive, and indeed German productivity had declined relative to that in the United States during the 1980s.

The McKinsey study investigated the sources of productivity differences among the major countries in the nine industries studied. What emerged was surprising:

- Economies of scale and manufacturing technologies had a small role in some industries.
- Surprisingly, workers' skill levels and education were of little importance, being essentially the same in all three nations.
- Large differences in productivity exist within firms in the same industry. Managers could significantly improve productivity in *all* industries by adopting best-practice technologies.

One of the most striking findings of the McKinsey study was the importance of *globalization,* which denotes exposure to competition with the world leader in a particular industry. The study found that foreign direct investment by the most productive country (such as the Japanese auto transplants on American soil) has contributed to dramatic productivity improvements both through introducing leading-edge technologies and in stimulating competition.

This study provides further evidence that the surest route to high productivity and therefore to high living standards is to open markets to trade, capital, and ideas from the most advanced countries and to allow vigorous competition with companies that have adopted the most advanced technologies.

PARADISE LOST: THE SEARCH FOR STABLE EXCHANGE RATES

Fixed Exchange Rates and Monetary Policy

An ideal exchange-rate system is one that allows high levels of predictability of relative prices while ensuring smooth adjustment to economic shocks. In a well-functioning system, people can trade and invest in other countries without worrying that exchange rates will suddenly change and make their ventures unprofitable. This ideal seemed to be attained during most of the Bretton Woods era, when exchange-rate changes were infrequent yet output and trade grew rapidly. Outside of that period, the experience has been less satisfactory. The flexible-exchange-rate regime since 1973 has been one of great volatility as well as prolonged overvaluation and undervaluation. Fixed-exchange-

---

[4] McKinsey Global Institute, *Manufacturing Productivity* (Washington, D.C., 1993).

rate systems have sometimes been the subject of intense speculative attack, as occurred in Europe in 1992 and Mexico in 1994.

The difficulty in all fixed-exchange-rate systems is that they may impede economic adjustment if prices and trade among countries get too far out of line. The most ambitious attempt to curb exchange market fluctuations came in Europe with the creation in 1978 of a currency bloc known as the European Monetary System (or EMS). A group of West European countries, primarily Germany and France, designed this system along the lines of the Bretton Woods regime. As members of the EMS, nations commit to keeping their exchange rates within prescribed and narrow bands. These bands can be realigned periodically, but in between realignments each nation must take steps to ensure that member-country exchange rates remain inside the band.

Unfortunately, exchange-rate systems cannot operate in isolation from other macroeconomic policies. As we explained earlier in this chapter, keeping a currency at some prescribed level requires engaging in monetary policies through intervention or interest rates. In other words, adopting a fixed-exchange-rate system requires giving up control over domestic interest rates. If France has an exchange rate that is tightly tied to the German mark, free-market French interest rates cannot diverge significantly from those in Germany. A major divergence would lead to an avalanche of capital flows that would either overturn the exchange-rate system or drive interest rates together. (To see this, ask yourself if there can be major differences in the risk-free interest rates between Connecticut and California in the fixed-exchange-rate system of the United States.)

The exchange-rate system is an integral part of monetary policy. Nations which opt for open financial markets and a fixed exchange rate must devote their monetary policies to maintaining the exchange rate. In such a system, it is not possible to have independent monetary policies.

The Crisis of the European Monetary System

The loss of control over monetary policy by a bloc of countries operating a fixed exchange rate system would not be fatal during normal times, when the bloc's interest rates are close to those that would be desirable for the individual countries. But in times of crisis, the actual and desired monetary policies may diverge too much. That is exactly what happened in 1989–1993, and this divergence almost destroyed the European Monetary System.

The first key factor in the crisis of the EMS was the reunification of Germany in 1990. Following reunification, Germany's fiscal policy turned sharply expansionary as it subsidized East German industry. The expansion in western Germany led to an uptick in the German inflation rate. The German central bank (the Bundesbank) responded by raising German interest rates to dampen domestic demand. Here monetary policy was being used for domestic macroeconomic management, and the effects of the measures on Germany's trading partners were subordinated to domestic economic concerns.

Faced with rising German interest rates, other nations in the EMS had to raise their interest rates to prevent their currencies from depreciating against the German mark and moving outside the prescribed range. These interest-rate increases, along with a worldwide recession and a sharp decline in output from the collapsing communist bloc, pushed Europe, outside of Germany, into ever-deeper recession.

Speculative Attack! Eventually, the EMS was brought down by speculators who believed that countries would not tolerate unrealistic exchange rates and interest rates indefinitely. One by one, currencies came under attack—the Finnish mark, the Swedish crown, the Italian lira, the British pound, the Spanish peseta. In the end, only the inner sanctum of France and Germany withstood the speculative attacks.

If we sift through the rubble, we discover an important point: *A fixed exchange rate system is prone to devastating speculative attack if financial capital flows freely among countries.* The reason is the following: A fixed but adjustable exchange rate is susceptible to attack whenever speculators believe that changes are imminent. If a currency is likely to be devalued, speculators will quickly start selling that currency. The supply of the currency increases while demand drops.

At this point, central banks step in to defend the currency (recall Figure 36-2, above). But given the private resources available for speculative attacks—easily tens of billions of dollars in a few hours—the defender of a weak currency quickly runs out of reserves. Unless "hard-currency" countries are willing to provide unlimited lines of credit, the defending central bank will sooner or later give up and either devalue or allow the currency to float.

Toward a Common Currency: The Euro

The lesson of the 1992 crisis was, according to thoughtful scholars, that a country cannot simultaneously have (1) a fixed but adjustable exchange rate, (2) open capital markets, and (3) an independent domestic monetary policy. After three decades of integration, the major European countries have decided to resolve this dilemma by moving to a common currency. Under the Maastricht Treaty of 1991, European countries have decided to adopt a common currency (named the "Euro"). This process is called **monetary union**.

The basic philosophy behind monetary union is that it is necessary to complete European integration and that the full benefits of a single market require that countries adopt a common currency. This general belief is buttressed by the emerging view—sketched in the previous paragraph—that the fixed-exchange-rate system of multiple currencies would become increasingly unstable as the financial markets of European countries became increasingly open and integrated.

The monetary structure under a European monetary union would resemble that of countries like the United States. Monetary policy would be lodged in a European central bank (ECB), which would conduct monetary policy for countries in the European Union who adopt the common currency. The ECB would undertake open-market operations and determine interest rates of the Euro. As currently envisioned, the ECB would have price stability as its primary objective.

Those who endorse monetary union see important *benefits*. Under a common currency, exchange-rate volatility within Europe would be reduced to zero, so trade and finance would no longer have to contend with the uncertainties about prices induced by changing exchange rates. The primary result would be a reduction in transactions costs among countries. To the extent that national capital markets are segmented (recall the savings and investment link discussed above), moving to a common currency may allow a more efficient allocation of capital.

Many economists are skeptical and point to significant *costs* of monetary union. The dominant concern is the loss of the exchange rate as a tool for macroeconomic adjustment. The idea, going back to Robert Mundell, concerns the optimal currency area for Europe. An *optimal currency area* is one in which the differential shocks among nations are small or where labor mobility is sufficiently high to ensure rapid adjustment. Many economists worry that all of Europe is not an optimal currency area because of the rigidity of wage structures and the low degree of labor mobility among the different countries.

The fundamental problem arises because of inflexible wages and prices. When a shock occurs—such as the reunification of Germany, discussed above—inflexible wages and prices lead to rising inflation in the region with a demand increase and rising unemployment in the depressed region. In the United States, evidence suggests that differential regional shocks quickly lead to labor migration, so after a few years unemployment rates move back to preshock levels. Europe, by contrast, has much lower labor mobility, and unemployment differentials among nations tend to persist for many years. Monetary union will, in this view, condemn some regions and countries to persistent low growth and high unemployment.

Notwithstanding these reservations, Europeans are intent on moving to a single currency. Countries must satisfy certain *convergence criteria* before they will be allowed in the club. These include inflation and interest rates that are close to the lowest among the countries, along with severe limitations on government deficits and debts. The current timetable envisions that a core group of countries, including at least Germany and France, will irrevocably adopt the Euro on January 1, 1999—a prospect with a slightly millennial ring.

Monetary union in Europe is one of the great experiments of the twentieth century. Never before has such a large and powerful group of countries turned its economic fortunes over to a multinational body. Never before has a central bank been charged with containing the inflation and unemployment of a dozen nations with 300 million people producing $7 trillion of goods and services. Many economists worry that this experiment may lead to persistent stagnation and unemployment in large parts of Europe because of the lack of price and wage flexibility and insufficient labor mobility among countries.

FINAL ASSESSMENT

This survey of international economics must acknowledge a mixed picture, with some successes and some failures. But if we step back from the individual issues, an impartial jury of historians would surely rate the last half-century as one of unparalleled success for the countries of North America, Western Europe, and East Asia. The jury would point to the following:

- *Robust economic performance.* The period has seen the most rapid and sustained economic growth in recorded history. It is the only half-century since the Industrial Revolution that has avoided a deep depression, and none of the major industrial countries suffered from the cancer of hyperinflation.
- *The growth of trade.* Having learned the dangers of protectionism in the 1930s, nations have joined together in multinational trade treaties and agreements to desist from imposing trade restrictions. The latest of these was the Uruguay Round, completed in late 1993, which extended the principles of free and open trade to new sectors and new nations. The proof of the pudding in this area has been that international trade has grown faster than output for every major country.
- *The reemergence of free markets.* You often hear that imitation is the sincerest form of flattery. In economics, imitation occurs when a nation adopts another nation's system of organization in the hope that it will produce growth and stability. In the 1980s and 1990s, country after country threw off the shackles of communism and stifling central planning—not because the textbooks convinced them to do so but because they used their own eyes to see how the market-oriented countries of the West prospered while the command economies of the East collapsed. *For the first time, an empire collapsed simply because it could not produce sufficient butter along with its guns.*

Maintaining and strengthening the current international economic system is a worthy challenge for all.

SUMMARY

A. The International Monetary System

1. International trade and finance involve the use of different national currencies, which are linked by relative prices called foreign exchange rates. A well-functioning international economy requires a smoothly operating exchange-rate system, which denotes the institutions that govern financial transactions among nations. Three important exchange-rate systems are (*a*) the pure flexible-exchange-rate system, in which a country's foreign exchange rate is entirely determined by market forces of supply and demand; (*b*) the fixed-exchange-rate system (such as the gold standard or the Bretton Woods system), in which countries set and defend a given structure of exchange rates; and (*c*) the managed-exchange-rate system, in which government interventions and market forces interact to determine the level of exchange rates.

2. Classical economists like David Hume explained international adjustments to trade imbalances by the gold-flow mechanism. Under this process, gold movements would change the money supply and the price level. For example, a trade deficit would lead to a gold outflow and a decline in domestic prices that would (*a*) raise exports and (*b*) curb imports of the gold-losing country while (*c*) reducing exports and (*d*) raising imports of the gold-gaining country. This mecha-

nism shows that under fixed exchange rates, countries which have balance-of-payments problems must adjust through changes in domestic price and output levels.

B. International Institutions

3. After World War II, countries created a group of international economic institutions to organize international trade and finance. These included the International Monetary Fund (IMF), which oversees exchange-rate systems and helps countries with balance of payment difficulties; the World Bank, which lends money to low-income countries; and the Bretton Woods exchange-rate system. Under the Bretton Woods system, countries "pegged" their currencies to the dollar and to gold, providing fixed but adjustable exchange rates. When official parities deviated too far from fundamentals, countries could adjust parities and achieve a new equilibrium without incurring the hardships of inflation or recession.

4. When the Bretton Woods system broke down in 1971, it was replaced by today's hybrid system. Some large countries or regions allow their currencies to float independently; most small countries peg their currencies to the dollar or to other currencies; and many European countries adhere to the European Monetary System (EMS), which is a close cousin of the Bretton Woods system. Governments often intervene when their currencies get too far out of line from fundamentals or when exchange markets become disorderly.

5. Nations are interdependent through the multiplier and monetary links, wherein changes in output or monetary policy spill over to the output and investment of other countries. Countries are also linked through saving and investment. Sometimes, however, the uncoordinated activities of individual nations lead to inefficient outcomes—macroeconomic outcomes with high unemployment, or trade wars, or governments' loss of credibility in financial markets. International cooperation is designed to overcome the failures that prevent full utilization of resources and free and efficient flow of capital among nations.

6. Because of the increasing interdependence of national economies, countries often attempt to coordinate their economic policies. Important policy issues are the following:

   a. National trade policies affect the output and employment of other countries. A policy of protecting one's own industries by trade barriers is a beggar-thy-neighbor approach, in essence exporting unemployment and trade deficits.

   b. Foreign exchange rates can affect relative prices and net exports. A rise in a nation's foreign exchange rate will depress that nation's net exports and output, while a fall in a nation's foreign exchange rate will increase net exports and output. Because of the significant impact of exchange rates on national economies, countries have entered into agreements on international monetary arrangements.

   c. In recent years, countries have often coordinated their macroeconomic policies, trying to increase their national outputs or to lower their national inflation rates. By cooperating on fiscal or monetary policies, countries can take advantage of the expansionary or contractionary impacts that inevitably spill over the borders when output changes.

C. International Economic Issues at Century's End

7. When exchange rates get too far out of line, adverse consequences can occur. The United States experienced an overvalued currency in the mid-1980s as a result of tight money, loose fiscal policy, and speculative forces. The result was a severe contraction of those sectors exposed to international trade—particularly manufacturing—and this contraction deepened an already serious recession.

8. Popular analysis saw "deindustrialization" in the dollar overvaluation in the 1980s. But these discussions overlook the important distinction between productivity and competitiveness. Competitiveness refers to how well a nation's goods can compete in the global marketplace and is determined primarily by relative prices. Productivity denotes the level of output per unit of input. Real incomes and living standards depend primarily upon productivity, whereas the trade and current-account positions depend upon competitiveness. There is no close linkage between competitiveness and productivity.

9. European countries are moving toward monetary union, which involves a common currency and a unitary central bank. A common currency is appropriate when a region forms an optimal currency area. Those who favor European monetary union point to the improved predictability, lower transactions costs, and potential for better capital allocation. Skeptics worry that a common currency—like any irrevocably fixed-exchange-rate system—will require flexible wages and prices to promote adjustment to macroeconomic shocks. In an area with relatively low labor mobility, monetary union may doom major regions or countries to long periods of slow growth and high unemployment.

CONCEPTS FOR REVIEW

international monetary system
exchange-rate systems:
   flexible
   fixed rates
   managed flexible
managing exchange rates (intervention, monetary policy)

gold standard
international adjustment mechanism
Hume's four-pronged gold-flow
   mechanism
World Bank and IMF
Bretton Woods system, European
   Monetary System

international linkages:
   multiplier link
   monetary link
   savings and investment link
competitiveness vs. productivity
monetary union

QUESTIONS FOR DISCUSSION

1. James Tobin has written, "A great teacher of mine, Joseph Schumpeter, used to find puzzling irony in the fact that liberal devotees of the free market were unwilling to let the market determine the prices of foreign currencies." For what reasons might economists allow the foreign exchange market to be an exception to a general inclination toward free markets?

2. In the Louvre accord in 1987, major countries agreed to keep their currencies within "reference zones." Say that the United States and Germany agree to keep the German mark in the range of 1.60 to 1.80 marks to the dollar. Show with the help of a supply-and-demand diagram how the governments could implement this policy.

3. Consider two situations:
   a. Real incomes in America and Japan are growing at 1 percent per annum.
   b. Real incomes in America are growing at 2 percent, while real incomes in Japan are growing at 4 percent.

   Would you as an American prefer **a** or **b**? Defend your answer. Relate the question to the difference between absolute and relative incomes.

4. Consider the following three exchange-rate systems: the classical gold standard, freely flexible exchange rates, and the Bretton Woods system. Compare and contrast the three systems with respect to the following characteristics:
   a. Role of government vs. that of market in determining exchange rates
   b. Degree of exchange-rate volatility
   c. Method of adjustment of relative prices across countries
   d. Need for international cooperation and consultation in determining exchange rates
   e. Potential for establishment and maintenance of severe exchange-rate misalignment

5. The text states that a country cannot simultaneously have (*a*) a fixed but adjustable exchange rate, (*b*) open capital markets, and (*c*) an independent domestic monetary policy. Explain this statement. Apply it to the European monetary crisis of 1992. Why is there not a problem for the fixed-exchange-rate system between "California dollars" and "Texas dollars."

6. Consider the proposed European monetary union. List the pros and cons. How do you come down on the question of the advisability of monetary union? Would your answer change if the question concerned the United States?

VALEDICTION

We have now finished our tour of the exciting world of introductory economics. For us, the authors, this marks the fiftieth anniversary of our pilgrimage. Through sixteen editions, we have seen economics transformed into one of the most exciting and innovative of all the sciences.

For you, the introductory student, this marks the end of your first serious study of economics and the beginning of your life as a practicing economist. In this tour through the wonders of the world of economics you have discovered the realm of the qualified invisible hand, the promises and pitfalls of macroeconomic policy, and the opportunities to use market tools to preserve our precious environment. The market economy has been our major focus. We have seen that markets can be mighty engines of prosperity, but that they can also dish out great inequalities.

One of the extraordinary results of a careful study of economic principles is that you view the world through different eyes. You see the pattern in economic life—instead of the raw data of the upticks of the stock market and the downsizings of the labor market.

This golden anniversary provides the occasion for us to pause to reflect upon the evolution of economics and the economy. In designing this book, we try to be mindful of the fact that the principles learned here must serve the reader for the *next* five decades. We continually ask ourselves: What will the American and the global economies look like once we have crossed into the twenty-first century? What vital problems and cruel dilemmas will arise when today's students are running tomorrow's businesses, governments, and central banks?

One surprise about economics is how little the maladies change from decade to decade. As one old alum complained, "In economics, it's not the questions that change—it's the answers." The core problems of the 1990s differ little from those of the 1960s or the 1930s. We worry today as we did then about growth, stability, and distribution. Is our economic growth satisfactory? Are inflation and unemployment under control? Are the fruits of economic growth distributed fairly among the populace?

Central to all these questions is the perennial issue of how we should use our material gains to improve our personal and civic life. A striking analysis of this question was given by this century's greatest economist, John Maynard Keynes, in 1930. Keynes mused about the long-run prospects of the capitalist system and had these startling reflections:

> Suppose that a hundred years hence we are eight times better off than today. Assuming no important wars and no important increase in population, the *economic problem* may be solved. This means that the eco-

nomic problem is not—if we look into the future—*the permanent problem of the human race.*

Why, you may ask, is this so startling? It is startling because the economic problem, the struggle for subsistence, always has been hitherto the primary, most pressing problem of the human race—not only of the human race, but of the whole of the biological kingdom from the beginnings of life in its most primitive forms.

Thus we have been expressly evolved by nature—with all our impulses and deepest instincts—for the purpose of solving the economic problem. If the economic problem is solved, mankind will be deprived of its traditional purpose. I think with dread of the readjustment of the habits and instincts of the ordinary man, bred into him for countless generations, which he may be asked to discard within a few decades.

Must we not expect a general "nervous breakdown"? Thus for the first time since his creation man will be faced with his real, his permanent problem—how to use his freedom from pressing economic cares, how to occupy the leisure, which science and compound interest will have won for him, to live wisely and agreeably and well.

There are changes in other spheres too which we must expect to come. When the accumulation of wealth is no longer of high social importance, there will be great changes in the code of morals. The love of money as a possession—as distinguished from the love of money as a means to the enjoyments and realities of life—will be recognized for what it is, a somewhat disgusting morbidity, one of those semi-criminal, semi-pathological propensities which one hands over with a shudder to the specialists in mental disease. . . .

But beware! The time for all this is not yet. For at least another hundred years we must pretend to ourselves and to everyone that fair is foul and foul is fair; for foul is useful and fair is not. Avarice and usury and precaution must be our gods for a little longer still.[1]

We close with these fascinating thoughts because they remind us that great affluence has indeed not brought about a slackening of economic ambition in America. Even though our average real incomes are more than 4 times their levels at the beginning of this century, our society has become more competitive in the struggle for profits and jobs and markets. Markets are more pervasive, more intrusive. The growing orientation toward the market has accompanied widespread desire for smaller government, less regulation, and lower taxes.

Ours is the "ruthless economy." People are increasingly judged on their current productivities rather than past contributions. Old-fashioned loyalty to firm or community counts for little. Suppose a firm finds it profitable to lay off 1000 workers, or moves from New England to the Sunbelt, or moves from the United States to Mexico. It is likely to move in the relentless pursuit of profits . . . and as a protection against another firm gaining a competitive advantage.

Market-oriented economists will tell you that inequality is the price we pay for invention—that you can't make an omelette without breaking eggs. This hardheaded focus on efficiency pays no mind to the incomes of laid-off workers, of bankrupt firms, of crumbling cities, or of nations or regions which lose their comparative advantage.

But a closer look finds a silver lining behind this ruthlessness. With increased foreign competition, deregulation of many industries, and labor unions at their weakest since the Great Depression, labor and product markets have nowadays become increasingly competitive. With more vigorous competition, America's macroeconomic performance has perceptibly improved. Compared to a decade ago, the United States produces $1.5 trillion more output and has provided 17 million net new jobs. Money wage growth and price inflation have remained low and stable even as the unemployment rate fell below what most economists thought was its lowest sustainable rate. The labor force in our ruthless economy may feel cowed and anxious. But, from a macroeconomic point of view, meekness is a virtue because it keeps inflation low, allows a lower overall unemployment rate, and, most significantly, shields the least skilled workers from being frozen out of any employment at all.

Europe—the cradle of the welfare state—models itself as the "compassionate economy" and is a stark contrast. European workers of the 1990s are "protected" by strong unions, generous income-support systems, high minimum wages, and many restraints on hiring and firing. But weakening of market forces has led to hardening of the economic arteries as microeconomic generosity led to macroeconomic inefficiency. With growing inflexibility of its welfare

---

[1] John Maynard Keynes, "Economic Possibilities for Our Grandchildren," reprinted in his *Essays in Persuasion* (Macmillan, London, 1933), with minor editing.

and labor market institutions, the lowest sustainable unemployment rate in Europe has climbed steadily over the last three decades. By 1997, the European unemployment rate was twice that in the United States. Many European politicians are asking themselves whether they should in some degree emulate the ruthless competitiveness of the American model.

But before applauding the American successes too loudly, recall that competitive markets not only giveth much but also taketh away. Not everybody can be the "master of the universe" in the competitive Darwinian economy. The growing inequality of income in America—and the large numbers of people who are locked into dead-end jobs and living in run-down neighborhoods—is a sober reminder of the harsh inequalities possible in a market economy.

In the end, we render two cheers for the market, but not three. The last cheer is reserved for that day when everyone has the opportunity for a good job, an adequate income, and a safe environment. These are worthy goals for economics and for economists in the next 50 years!

GLOSSARY OF TERMS[1]

A

Ability-to-pay principle (of taxation). The principle that one's tax burden should depend upon the ability to pay as measured by income or wealth. This principle does not specify *how much* more those who are better off should pay.

Absolute advantage (in international trade). The ability of Country A to produce a commodity more efficiently (i.e., with greater output per unit of input) than Country B. Possession of such an absolute advantage does not necessarily mean that A can export this commodity to B successfully. Country B may still have the comparative advantage.

Accelerator principle. The theory that a change in the rate of output induces a change in the demand for investment in the same direction.

Actual, cyclical, and structural budget. The **actual budget** deficit or surplus is the amount recorded in a given year. This is composed of the **structural budget**, which calculates what government revenues, expenditures, and deficits would be if the economy were operating at potential output, and the **cyclical budget**, which measures the effect of the business cycle on the budget.

Adaptive expectations. See **expectations**.

Adjustable peg. An exchange-rate system in which countries maintain a fixed or "pegged" exchange rate with respect to other currencies. This exchange rate is subject to periodic adjustment, however, when it becomes too far out of line with fundamental forces. This system was used for major currencies during the Bretton Woods period from 1944 to 1971 and is called the **Bretton Woods system**.

Administered (or **inflexible**) **prices.** A term referring to prices which are set and kept constant for a period of time and over a series of transactions. (In contrast, refer to **price flexibility**.)

Adverse selection. A type of market failure in which those people with the highest risk are most likely to buy insurance. More broadly, adverse selection encompasses situations in which sellers and buyers have different information about a product, such as in the market for used cars.

Aggregate demand. Total planned or desired spending in the economy during a given period. It is determined by the aggregate price level and influenced by domestic investment, net exports, government spending, the consumption function, and the money supply.

Aggregate demand (*AD*) **curve.** The curve showing the relationship between the quantity of goods and services that people are willing to buy and the aggregate price level, other things equal. As with any demand curve, important variables lie behind the aggregate demand

[1] Words in bold type within definitions appear as separate entries in the glossary. For a more detailed discussion of particular terms, the text will provide a useful starting point. More complete discussions are contained in Douglas Greenwald, ed., *The McGraw-Hill Encyclopedia of Economics* (McGraw-Hill, New York, 1994); David W. Pearce, *Macmillan Dictionary of Modern Economics,* rev. ed. (Macmillan, London, 1992); *International Encyclopedia of the Social Sciences* (Collier and Macmillan, New York, 1968); and John Eatwell, Murray Milgate, and Peter Newman, *The New Palgrave: A Dictionary of Economics* (Macmillan, London, 1987), four volumes.

curve, e.g., government spending, exports, and the money supply.

Aggregate supply. The total value of goods and services that firms would willingly produce in a given time period. Aggregate supply is a function of available inputs, technology, and the price level.

Aggregate supply (AS) curve. The curve showing the relationship between the output firms would willingly supply and the aggregate price level, other things equal. The AS curve tends to be vertical at potential output in the very long run but may be relatively flat in the short run.

Allocative efficiency. A situation in which no reorganization or trade could raise the utility or satisfaction of one individual without lowering the utility or satisfaction of another individual. Under certain limited conditions, perfect competition leads to allocative efficiency. Also called **Pareto efficiency**.

Antitrust legislation. Laws prohibiting monopolization, restraints of trade, and collusion among firms to raise prices or inhibit competition.

Appreciation (of a currency). See **depreciation** (of a currency).

Appropriable. Describes a resource for which the owner can capture the full economic value. In a well-functioning competitive market, appropriable resources are usually priced and allocated efficiently. Also refer to **inappropriable**.

Arbitrage. The purchase of a good or asset in one market for immediate resale in another market in order to profit from a price discrepancy. Arbitrage is an important force in eliminating price discrepancies, thereby making markets function more efficiently.

Asset. A physical property or intangible right that has economic value. Important examples are plant, equipment, land, patents,

copyrights, and financial instruments such as money or bonds.

Asset demand for money. See **demand for money**.

Automatic (or built-in) **stabilizers.** The property of a government tax and spending system that cushions income changes in the private sector. Examples include unemployment compensation and progressive income taxes.

Average cost. Refer to **cost, average**.

Average cost curve, long-run (*LRAC*, or *LAC*). The graph of the minimum average cost of producing a commodity for each level of output, assuming that technology and input prices are given but that the producer is free to choose the optimal size of plants.

Average cost curve, short-run (*SRAC*, or *SAC*). The graph of the minimum average cost of producing a commodity, for each level of output, using the given state of technology, input prices, and existing plant.

Average fixed cost. Refer to **cost, average fixed**.

Average product. Total product or output divided by the quantity of one of the inputs. Hence, the average product of labor is defined as total product divided by the amount of labor input, and similarly for other inputs.

Average propensity to consume. See **marginal propensity to consume**.

Average revenue. Total revenue divided by total number of units sold—i.e., revenue per unit. Average revenue is generally equal to price.

Average variable cost. Refer to **cost, average variable**.

B

Balance of international payments. A statement showing all of a nation's transactions with the rest of the world for a given period. It includes purchases and sales of goods and

services, gifts, government transactions, and capital movements.

Balance of trade. The part of a nation's balance of payments that deals with merchandise (or visible) imports or exports, including such items as foodstuffs, capital goods, and automobiles. When services and other current items are included, this measures the **balance on current account**.

Balance on current account. See **balance of trade**.

Balance sheet. A statement of a firm's financial position as of a given date, listing **assets** in one column, **liabilities** plus **net worth** in the other. Each item is listed at its actual or estimated money value. Totals of the two columns must balance because net worth is defined as assets minus liabilities.

Balanced budget. Refer to **budget, balanced**.

Bank, commercial. A financial intermediary whose prime distinguishing feature until recently was that it accepts checkable deposits. All financial institutions that hold savings and checkable deposits are called depository institutions.

Bank money. Money created by banks, particularly the checking accounts (part of M_1) that are generated by a multiple expansion of bank reserves.

Bank reserves. Refer to **reserves, bank**.

Barriers to entry. Factors that impede entry into a market and thereby reduce the amount of competition or the number of producers in an industry. Important examples are legal barriers, regulation, and product differentiation.

Barter. The direct exchange of one good for another without using anything as money or as a medium of exchange.

Benefit principle (of taxation). The principle that people should be taxed in proportion to the benefits they receive from government programs.

Bond. An interest-bearing certificate issued by a government or corporation, promising to repay a sum of money (the principal) plus interest at specified dates in the future.

Break-even point (in macroeconomics). For an individual, family, or community, that level of income at which 100 percent is spent on consumption (i.e., the point where there is neither saving nor dissaving). Positive saving begins at higher income levels.

Bretton Woods system. See **adjustable peg**.

Broad money. A measure of the money supply (also known as M_2) that includes transactions money (or M_1) as well as savings accounts in banks and similar assets that are very close substitutes for transactions money.

Budget. An account, usually for a year, of the planned expenditures and the expected receipts. For a government, the receipts are tax revenues.

Budget, balanced. A budget in which total expenditures just equal total receipts (excluding any receipts from borrowing).

Budget constraint. See **budget line**.

Budget deficit. For a government, the excess of total expenditures over total receipts, with borrowing not included among receipts. This difference (the deficit) is ordinarily financed by borrowing.

Budget, government. A statement showing, for the government in question, planned expenditures and revenues for some period (typically 1 year).

Budget line. A line indicating the combination of commodities that a consumer can buy with a given income at a given set of prices. Also sometimes called the **budget constraint**.

Budget surplus. Excess of government revenues over government spending; the opposite of budget deficit.

Built-in stabilizers. See **automatic stabilizers**.

Business cycles. Fluctuations in total national output, income, and employment, usually lasting for a period of 2 to 10 years, marked by widespread and simultaneous expansion or contraction in many sectors of the economy. In modern macroeconomics, business cycles are said to occur when actual GDP rises relative to potential GDP (expansion) or falls relative to potential GDP (contraction or recession).

C

$C + I$, $C + I + G$, or $C + I + G + X$ **schedule.** A schedule showing the planned or desired levels of aggregate demand for each level of GDP, or the graph on which this schedule is depicted. The schedule includes consumption (C), investment (I), government spending on goods and services (G), and net exports (X).

Capital (capital goods, capital equipment). (1) In economic theory, one of the triad of productive inputs (land, labor, and capital). Capital consists of durable produced goods that are in turn used in production. (2) In accounting and finance, "capital" means the total amount of money subscribed by the shareholder-owners of a corporation, in return for which they receive shares of the company's stock.

Capital consumption allowance. See **depreciation** (of an asset).

Capital deepening. In economic-growth theory, an increase in the capital-labor ratio. (Contrast with **capital widening**.)

Capital gains. The rise in value of a capital asset, such as land or common stocks, the gain being the difference between the sales price and the purchase price of the asset.

Capital markets. Markets in which financial resources (money, bonds, stocks) are traded. These, along with **financial intermediaries**, are institutions through which saving in the economy is transferred to investors.

Capital-output ratio. In economic-growth theory, the ratio of the total capital stock to annual GDP.

Capital widening. A rate of growth in real capital stock just equal to the growth of the labor force (or of population), so that the ratio between total capital and total labor remains unchanged. (Contrast with **capital deepening**.)

Capitalism. An economic system in which most property (land and capital) is privately owned. In such an economy, private markets are the primary vehicles used to allocate resources and generate incomes.

Cardinal utility. See **ordinal utility**.

Cartel. An organization of independent firms producing similar products that work together to raise prices and restrict output. Cartels are illegal under U.S. antitrust laws.

Central bank. A government-established agency (in the United States, the Federal Reserve System) responsible for controlling the nation's money supply and credit conditions and for supervising the financial system, especially commercial banks and other depository institutions.

Change in demand vs. change in quantity demanded. A change in the quantity buyers want to purchase, prompted by any reason other than a change in price (e.g., increase in income, change in tastes, etc.), is a "change in demand." In graphical terms, it is a shift of the demand curve. If, in contrast, the decision to buy more or less is prompted by a change in the good's price, then it is a "change in quantity demanded." In graphical terms, a change in quantity demanded is a movement along an unchanging demand curve.

Change in supply vs. change in quantity supplied. This distinction is the same for supply as for demand, so see **change in demand vs. change in quantity demanded**.

Checking accounts (or **bank money**). A deposit in a commercial bank or other financial intermediary upon which checks can be written and which is therefore transactions money (or M_1), also called "checkable deposits." Checkable deposits are the largest component of M_1.

Chicago School of Economics. A group of economists (among whom Henry Simons, F. A. von Hayek, and Milton Friedman have been the most prominent) who believe that competitive markets free of government intervention will lead to the most efficient operation of the economy.

Classical approach. See **classical economics**.

Classical economics. The predominant school of economic thought prior to the appearance of Keynes' work; founded by Adam Smith in 1776. Other major figures who followed him include David Ricardo, Thomas Malthus, and John Stuart Mill. By and large, this school believed that economic laws (particularly individual self-interest and competition) determine prices and factor rewards and that the price system is the best possible device for resource allocation.

Classical theories (in macroeconomics). Theories emphasizing the self-correcting forces in the economy. In the classical approach, there is generally full employment and policies to stimulate aggregate demand have no impact upon output.

Clearing market. A market in which prices are sufficiently flexible to equilibrate supply and demand very quickly. In markets that clear, there is no rationing, unemployed resources, or excess demand or supply. In practice, this is thought to apply to many commodity and financial markets but not to labor or many product markets.

Closed economy. See **open economy**.

Coase theorem. A view (not actually a theorem) put forth by Ronald Coase that externalities or economic inefficiencies will under certain conditions be corrected by bargaining between the affected parties.

Collective bargaining. The process of negotiations between a group of workers (usually a union) and their employer. Such bargaining leads to an agreement about wages, fringe benefits, and working conditions.

Collusion. Agreement between different firms to cooperate by raising prices, dividing markets, or otherwise restraining competition.

Collusive oligopoly. A market structure in which a small number of firms (i.e., a few oligopolists) collude and jointly make their decisions. When they succeed in maximizing their joint profits, the price and quantity in the market closely approach those prevailing under monopoly.

Command economy. A mode of economic organization in which the key economic functions—*what, how,* and *for whom*—are principally determined by government directive. Sometimes called a "centrally planned economy."

Commodity money. Money with **intrinsic value**; also, the use of some commodity (cattle, beads, etc.) as money.

Common stock. The financial instrument representing ownership and, generally, voting rights in a corporation. A certain share of a company's stock gives the owner title to that fraction of the votes, net earnings, and assets of the corporation.

Communism. A communist economic system (also called Soviet-style central planning) is one in which the state owns and controls the means of production, particularly industrial capital. These economies are also characterized by extensive central planning, with the state setting many prices, output levels, and other important economic variables.

Comparative advantage (in international trade). The law of comparative advantage says that a nation should specialize in producing and exporting those commodities which it can produce at *relatively* lower cost, and that it should import those goods for which it is a *relatively* high-cost producer. Thus it is a comparative advantage, not an absolute advantage, that should dictate trade patterns.

Compensating differentials. Differences in wage rates among jobs that serve to offset or compensate for the nonmonetary differences of the jobs. For example, unpleasant jobs that require isolation for many months in Alaska pay wages much higher than those for similar jobs nearer to civilization.

Competition, imperfect. Refers to markets in which perfect competition does not hold because at least one seller (or buyer) is large enough to affect the market price and therefore faces a downward-sloping demand (or supply) curve. Imperfect competition refers to any kind of imperfection—pure **monopoly, oligopoly,** or **monopolistic competition**.

Competition, perfect. Refers to markets in which no firm or consumer is large enough to affect the market price. This situation arises where (1) the number of sellers and buyers is very large and (2) the products offered by sellers are homogeneous (or indistinguishable). Under such conditions, each firm faces a horizontal (or perfectly elastic) demand curve.

Competitive equilibrium. The balancing of supply and demand in a market or economy characterized by **perfect competition**. Because perfectly competitive sellers and buyers individually have no power to influence the market, price will move to the point at which it equals both marginal cost and marginal utility.

Competitive market. See **competition, perfect**.

Complements. Two goods which "go together" in the eyes of consumers (e.g., left shoes and right shoes). Goods are **substitutes** when they compete with each other (as do gloves and mittens).

Compound interest. Interest computed on the sum of all past interest earned as well as on the principal. For example, suppose $100 (the principal) is deposited in an account earning 10 percent interest compounded annually. At the end of year 1, interest of $10 is earned. At the end of year 2, the interest payment is $11, $10 on the original principal and $1 on the interest—and so on in future years.

Concentration ratio. The percentage of an industry's total output accounted for by the largest firms. A typical measure is the **four-firm concentration ratio**, which is the fraction of output accounted for by the four largest firms.

Conglomerate. A large corporation producing and selling a variety of unrelated goods (e.g., some cigarette companies have expanded into such unrelated areas as liquor, car rental, and movie production).

Conglomerate merger. See **merger**.

Constant returns to scale. See **returns to scale**.

Consumer price index (CPI). A price index that measures the cost of a fixed basket of consumer goods in which the weight assigned to each commodity is the share of expenditures on that commodity by urban consumers in 1982–1984.

Consumer surplus. The difference between the amount that a consumer would be willing to pay for a commodity and the amount actually paid. This difference arises because the marginal utilities (in dollar terms) of all but the last unit exceed the price. Under certain conditions, the money value of consumer surplus can be measured (using a demand-curve diagram) as the area under the demand curve but above the price line.

Consumption. In macroeconomics, the total spending, by individuals or a nation, on consumer goods during a given period. Strictly speaking, consumption should apply only to those goods totally used, enjoyed, or "eaten up" within that period. In practice, consumption expenditures include all consumer goods bought, many of which last well beyond the period in question—e.g., furniture, clothing, and automobiles.

Consumption function. A schedule relating total consumption to personal disposable income (DI). Total wealth and other variables are also frequently assumed to influence consumption.

Consumption-possibility line. See **budget line**.

Cooperative equilibrium. In game theory, an outcome in which the parties act in unison to find strategies that will optimize their joint payoffs.

Corporate income tax. A tax levied on the annual net income of a corporation.

Corporation. The dominant form of business organization in modern capitalist economies. A corporation is a firm owned by individuals or other corporations. It has the same rights to buy, sell, and make contracts as a person would have. It is legally separate from those who own it and has "limited liability."

Correlation. The degree to which two variables are systematically associated with each other.

Cost, average. Total cost (refer to **cost, total**) divided by the number of units produced.

Cost, average fixed. Fixed cost divided by the number of units produced.

Cost, average variable. Variable cost (refer to **cost, variable**) divided by the number of units produced.

Cost, fixed. The cost a firm would incur even if its output for the period in question were zero. Total fixed cost is made up of such individual contractual costs as interest payments, mortgage payments, and directors' fees.

Cost, marginal. The extra cost (or the increase in total cost) required to produce 1 extra unit of output (or the reduction in total cost from producing 1 unit less).

Cost, minimum. The lowest attainable cost per unit (whether average, variable, or marginal). Every point on an average cost curve is a minimum in the sense that it is the best the firm can do with respect to cost for the output which that point represents. Minimum average cost is the lowest point, or points, on that curve.

Cost-push inflation. Inflation originating on the supply side of markets from a sharp increase in costs. In the aggregate supply-and-demand framework, cost-push is illustrated as an upward shift of the AS curve. Also called **supply-shock** inflation.

Cost, total. The minimum attainable total cost, given a particular level of technology and set of input prices. Short-run total cost takes existing plant and other fixed costs as given. Long-run total cost is the cost that would be incurred if the firm had complete flexibility with respect to all inputs and decisions.

Cost, variable. A cost that varies with the level of output, such as raw materials, labor, and fuel costs. Variable costs equal total cost minus fixed cost.

Crawling (or sliding) peg. A technique for managing a nation's exchange rate that allows the exchange rate (or the bands around the rate) to "crawl" up or down by a small amount each day or week (say, 0.25 percent per week).

Credit. (1) In monetary theory, the use of someone else's funds in exchange for a promise to pay (usually with interest) at a later date. The major examples are short-term loans from a bank, credit extended by suppliers, and commercial paper. (2) In balance-of-payments accounting, an item such as exports that earns a country foreign currency.

Cross elasticity of demand. A measure of the influence of a change in one good's price on the demand for another good. More precisely, the cross elasticity of demand equals the percentage change in demand for good A when the price of good B changes by 1 percent, assuming other variables are held constant.

Crowding-out hypothesis. The proposition that government spending or government deficits reduce the amount of business investment.

Currency. Coins and paper money.

Currency appreciation (or depreciation). See **depreciation** (of a currency).

Current account. See **balance of trade**.

Cyclical budget. See **actual, cyclical,** and **structural budget**.

Cyclical unemployment. See **frictional unemployment**.

D

Deadweight loss. The loss in real income or consumer and producer surplus that arises because of monopoly, tariffs and quotas, taxes, or other distortions. For example, when a monopolist raises its price, the loss in consumer satisfaction is more than the gain in the monopolist's revenue—the difference being the deadweight loss to society due to monopoly.

Debit. (1) An accounting term signifying an increase in assets or decrease in liabilities. (2) In balance-of-payments accounting, a debit is an item such as imports that reduces a country's stock of foreign currencies.

Decreasing returns to scale. See **returns to scale**.

Deficit spending. Government expenditures on goods and services and transfer payments in excess of its receipts from taxation and other revenue sources. The difference must be financed by borrowing from the public.

Deflating (of economic data). The process of converting "nominal" or current-dollar variables into "real" terms. This is accomplished by dividing current-dollar variables by a **price index**.

Deflation. A fall in the general level of prices.

Demand curve (or demand schedule). A schedule or curve showing the quantity of a good that buyers would purchase at each price, other things equal. Normally a demand curve has price on the vertical or Y axis and quantity demanded on the horizontal or X axis. Also see **change in demand vs. change in quantity demanded**.

Demand for money. A summary term used by economists to ex-plain why individuals and businesses hold money balances. The major motivations for holding money are (1) **transactions demand**, signifying that people need money to purchase things, and (2) **asset demand**, relating to the desire to hold a very liquid, risk-free asset.

Demand-pull inflation. Price inflation caused by an excess demand for goods in general, caused, for example, by a major increase in aggregate demand. Often contrasted with **cost-push inflation**.

Demography. The study of the behavior of a population.

Depreciation (of an asset). A decline in the value of an asset. In both business and national accounts, depreciation is the dollar estimate of the extent to which capital has been "used up" or worn out over the period in question. Also termed **capital consumption allowance** in national-income accounting.

Depreciation (of a currency). A nation's currency is said to depreciate when it declines relative to other currencies. For example, if the foreign exchange rate of the dollar falls from 6 to 4 French francs per U.S. dollar, the dollar's value has fallen, and the dollar has undergone a depreciation. The opposite of a depreciation is an **appreciation**, which occurs when the foreign exchange rate of a currency rises.

Depression. A prolonged period characterized by high unemployment, low output and investment, depressed business confidence, falling prices, and widespread business failures. A milder form of business downturn is a **recession**, which has many of the features of a depression to a lesser extent; the precise definition of a recession today is a period in which real GNP declines for at least two consecutive calendar quarters.

Derived demand. The demand for a factor of production that results (is "derived") from the demand for the final good to which it contributes. Thus the demand for tires is derived from the demand for automobile transportation.

Devaluation. A decrease in the official price of a nation's currency, as expressed in the currencies of other nations or in terms of gold. Thus, when the official price of the dollar was lowered with respect to gold in 1971, the dollar was devalued. The opposite of devaluation is **revaluation**, which occurs when a nation raises its official foreign exchange rate relative to gold or other currencies.

Developing country. Same as **less-developed country**.

Differentiated products. Products which compete with each other and are close substitutes but are not identical. Differences may be manifest in the product's function, appearance, location, quality, or other attributes.

Diminishing marginal utility, law of. The law which says that, as more and more of any one commodity is consumed, its marginal utility declines.

Diminishing returns, law of. A law stating that the additional output from successive increases of one input will eventually diminish when other inputs are held constant. Technically, the law is equivalent to saying that the marginal product of the varying input declines after a point.

Direct taxes. Those levied directly on individuals or firms, including taxes on income, labor earnings, and profits. Direct taxes contrast with **indirect taxes**, which are those levied on goods and services and thus only indirectly on people, and which include sales taxes and taxes on property, alcohol, imports, and gasoline.

Discount rate. (1) The interest rate charged by a Federal Reserve Bank (the central bank) on a loan that it makes to a commercial bank. (2) The rate used to calculate the present value of some asset.

Discounting (of future income). The process of converting future income into an equivalent present value. This process takes a future dollar amount and reduces it by a discount factor that reflects the appropriate interest rate. For example, if someone promises you $121 in 2 years, and the appropriate interest rate or discount rate is 10 percent per year, then we can calculate the present value by discounting the $121 by a discount factor of $(1.10)^2$. The rate at which future incomes are discounted is called the **discount rate**.

Discrimination. Differences in earnings that arise because of personal characteristics that are unrelated to job performance, especially those related to gender, race, ethnicity, sexual orientation, or religion.

Disequilibrium. The state in which an economy is not in **equilibrium**. This may arise when shocks (to income or prices) have shifted demand or supply schedules but the market price (or quantity) has not yet adjusted fully. In macroeconomics, unemployment is often thought to stem from market disequilibria.

Disinflation. The process of reducing a high inflation rate. For example, the deep recession of 1980–1983 led to a sharp disinflation over that period.

Disposable income (*DI*). Roughly, take-home pay, or that part of the total national income that is available to households for consumption or saving. More precisely, it is equal to GNP less all taxes, business saving, and depreciation plus government and other transfer payments and government interest payments.

Disposable personal income. Same as **disposable income**.

Dissaving. Negative saving; spending more on consumption goods during a period than the disposable income available for that period (the difference being financed by borrowing or drawing on past saving).

Distribution. In economics, the manner in which total output and income is distributed among individuals or factors (e.g., the distribution of income between labor and capital).

Division of labor. A method of organizing production whereby each worker specializes in part of the productive process. Specialization of labor yields higher total output because labor can become more skilled at a particular task and because specialized machinery can be introduced to perform more carefully defined subtasks.

Dominant equilibrium. See **dominant strategy**.

Dominant strategy. In game theory, a situation where one player has a best strategy no matter what strategy the other player follows. When all players have a dominant strategy, we say that the outcome is a **dominant equilibrium**.

Downward-sloping demand, law of. The rule that says that when the price of some commodity falls, consumers will purchase more of that good when other things are held equal.

Duopoly. A market structure in which there are only two sellers. (Compare with **oligopoly**.)

Duopoly price war. A situation where the market is supplied by two firms which are engaged in an economic warfare of continual undercutting of each other's price.

E

Easy-money policy. The central-bank policy of increasing the money supply to reduce interest rates. The purpose of such a policy is to increase investment, thereby raising GDP. (Contrast with **tight-money policy**.)

Econometrics. The branch of economics that uses the methods of statistics to measure and estimate quantitative economic relationships.

Economic good. A good that is scarce relative to the total amount of it that is desired. It must therefore be rationed, usually by charging a positive price.

Economic growth. An increase in the total output of a nation over time. Economic growth is usually measured as the annual rate of increase in a nation's real GDP (or real potential GDP).

Economic regulation. See **regulation**.

Economic rent. Refer to **rent, economic**.

Economic surplus. A term denoting the excess in total satisfaction or utility over the costs of production. Equals the sum of consumer surplus (the excess of consumer satisfaction over total value of purchases) and producer surplus (the excess of producer revenues over costs).

Economics of information. Analysis of economic situations that involve information as a commodity. Because information is costly to produce but cheap to reproduce, market failures are common in markets for informational goods and services such as invention, publishing, and software.

Economies of scale. Increases in productivity, or decreases in average cost of production, that arise from increasing all the factors of production in the same proportion.

Economies of scope. Economies of producing multiple goods or services. Thus economies of scope exist if it is cheaper to produce good X and good Y together rather than separately.

Effective tax rate. Total taxes paid as a percentage of the total income or other tax base.

Efficiency. Absence of waste, or the use of economic resources that produces the maximum level of satisfaction possible with the given inputs and technology. A shorthand expression for **allocative efficiency**.

Efficiency-wage theory. According to this theory, higher wages lead to higher productivity. This occurs because with higher wages workers are healthier, have higher morale, or have lower turnover.

Efficient market. A market where all new information is quickly understood by market participants and becomes immediately incorporated into market prices. In economics, efficient-market theory holds that all currently available information is already incorporated into the price of common stocks (or other assets).

Elasticity. A term widely used in economics to denote the responsiveness of one variable to changes in another. Thus the elasticity of X with respect to Y means the percentage change in X for every 1 percent change in Y. For especially important examples, see **price elasticity of demand** and **price elasticity of supply**.

Employed. According to official U.S. definitions, persons are employed if they perform any paid work, or if they hold jobs but are absent because of illness, strike, or vacations. Also see **unemployment**.

Equal-cost line. A line in a graph showing the various possible combinations of factor inputs that can be purchased with a given quantity of money.

Equal-product curve (or **isoquant**). A line in a graph showing the various possible combinations of factor inputs which will yield a given quantity of output.

Equilibrium. The state in which an economic entity is at rest or in which the forces operating on the entity are in balance so that there is no tendency for change.

Equilibrium (for a business firm). That position or level of output in which the firm is maximizing its profit, subject to any constraints it may face, and therefore has no incentive to change its output or price level. In the standard theory of the firm, this means that the firm has chosen an output at which marginal revenue is just equal to marginal cost.

Equilibrium (for the individual consumer). That position in which the consumer is maximizing utility, i.e., has chosen the bundle of goods which, given income and prices, best satisfies the consumer's wants.

Equilibrium, competitive. Refer to **competitive equilibrium**.

Equilibrium, general. Refer to **general-equilibrium analysis**.

Equilibrium, macroeconomic. A GDP level at which intended aggregate demand equals intended aggregate supply. At the equilibrium, desired consumption (C), government expenditures (G), investment (I), and net exports (X) just equal the quantity that businesses wish to sell at the going price level.

Equimarginal principle. Principle for deciding the allocation of income among different consumption goods. Under this principle, a consumer's utility is maximized by choosing the consumption bundle such that the marginal utility per dollar spent is equal for all goods.

Exchange rate. See **foreign exchange rate**.

Exchange-rate system. The set of rules, arrangements, and institutions under which payments are made among nations. Historically, the most important exchange-rate systems have been the gold exchange standard, the Bretton Woods system, and today's flexible-exchange-rate system.

Excise tax vs. sales tax. An **excise tax** is one levied on the purchase of a specific commodity or group of commodities (e.g., alcohol or tobacco). A **sales tax** is one levied on all commodities with only a few specific exclusions (e.g., all purchases except food).

Exclusion principle. A criterion by which public goods are distinguished from private goods. When a producer sells a commodity to person A and can easily exclude B, C, D, etc., from enjoying the benefits of the commodity, the exclusion principle holds and the good is a private good. If, as in public health or national defense, people cannot easily be excluded from enjoying the benefits of the good's production, then the good has public-good characteristics.

Exogenous vs. induced variables. Exogenous variables are those determined by conditions outside the economy. They are contrasted with **induced variables**, which are determined by the internal workings of the economic system. Changes in the weather are exogenous; changes in consumption are often induced by changes in income.

Expectations. Views or beliefs about uncertain variables (such as future interest rates, prices, or tax rates). Expectations are said to be **rational** if they are not systematically wrong (or "biased") and use all available information. Expectations are said to be **adaptive** if people form their expectations on the basis of past behavior.

Expenditure multiplier. See **multiplier**.

Exports. Goods or services that are produced in the home country and sold to another country. These include merchandise trade (like cars), services (like transportation), and interest on loans and investments. **Imports** are simply flows in the opposite direction—into the home country from another country.

External diseconomies. Situations in which production or consumption imposes uncompensated costs on other parties. Steel factories that emit smoke and sulfurous fumes harm local property and public health, yet the injured parties are not paid for the damage. The pollution is an external diseconomy.

External economies. Situations in which production or consumption yields positive benefits to others without those others paying. A firm that hires a security guard scares thieves from the neighborhood, thus providing external security services. Together with external diseconomies, these are often referred to as **externalities**.

External variables. Same as **exogenous variables**.

Externalities. Activities that affect others for better or worse, without those others paying or being compensated for the activity. Externalities exist when private costs or benefits do not equal social costs or benefits. The two major species are **external economies** and **external diseconomies**.

F

Factors of production. Productive inputs, such as labor, land, and capital; the resources needed to produce goods and services. Also called **inputs**.

Fallacy of composition. The fallacy of assuming that what holds for individuals also holds for the group or the entire system.

Federal Reserve System. The **central bank** of the United States.

Fiat money. Money, like today's paper currency, without **intrinsic value** but decreed (by fiat) to be legal tender by the government. Fiat money is accepted only as long as people have confidence that it will be accepted.

Final good. A good that is produced for final use and not for resale or further manufacture. (Compare with **intermediate goods**.)

Financial economics. That branch of economics which analyzes how rational investors should invest their funds to attain their objectives in the best possible manner.

Financial intermediary. An institution that receives funds from savers and lends them to borrowers. These include depository institutions (such as commercial or savings banks) and nondepository institutions (such as money market mutual funds, brokerage houses, insurance companies, or pension funds).

Firm (business firm). The basic, private producing unit in an economy. It hires labor and buys other inputs in order to make and sell commodities.

Fiscal-monetary mix. Refers to the combination of fiscal and monetary policies used to influence macroeconomic activity. A tight-monetary–loose-fiscal policy will tend to encourage consumption and retard investment, while an easy-monetary–tight-fiscal policy will have the opposite effect.

Fiscal policy. A government's program with respect to (1) the purchase of goods and services and spending on transfer payments, and (2) the amount and type of taxes.

Fixed cost. Refer to **cost, fixed**.

Fixed exchange rate. See **foreign exchange rate**.

Flexible exchange rates. A system of foreign exchange rates among countries wherein the exchange rates are predominantly determined by private market forces (i.e., by supply and demand) without governments' setting and maintaining a particular pattern of exchange rates. Also sometimes called **floating exchange rates**. When the government refrains from any intervention in exchange markets, the system is called a pure flexible-exchange-rate system.

Floating exchange rates. See **flexible exchange rates**.

Flow vs. stock. A flow variable is one that has a time dimension or flows over time (like the flow through a stream). A stock variable is one that measures a quantity at a point of time (like the water in a lake). Income represents dollars per year and is thus a flow. Wealth as of December 1998 is a stock.

Foreign exchange. Currency (or other financial instruments) of different countries that allow one country to settle amounts owed to other countries.

Foreign exchange market. The market in which currencies of different countries are traded.

Foreign exchange rate. The rate, or price, at which one country's currency is exchanged for the currency of another country. For example, if you can buy 1.9 German marks for one U.S. dollar, then the exchange rate for the mark is 1.9. A country has a **fixed exchange rate** if it pegs its currency at a given exchange rate and stands ready to defend that rate. Exchange rates which are determined by market supply and demand are called **flexible exchange rates**.

Four-firm concentration ratio. See **concentration ratio**.

Fractional-reserve banking. A regulation in modern banking systems whereby financial institutions are legally required to keep a specified fraction of their deposits in the form of deposits with the central bank (or in vault cash).

Free goods. Those goods that are not **economic goods**. Like air or seawater, they exist in such large quantities that they need not be rationed out among those wishing to use them. Thus, their market price is zero.

Free trade. A policy whereby the government does not intervene in trading between nations by tariffs, quotas, or other means.

Frictional unemployment. Temporary unemployment caused by changes in individual markets. It takes time, for example, for new workers to search among different job possibilities; even experienced workers often spend a minimum period of unemployed time moving from one job to another. Frictional is thus distinct from **cyclical unemployment**, which results from a low level of aggregate demand in the context of sticky wages and prices.

Full employment. A term that is used in many senses. Historically, it was taken to be that level of employment at which no (or minimal) involuntary unemployment exists. Today, economists rely upon the concept of the **lowest sustainable rate of unemployment** (*LSUR*) to indicate the highest sustainable level of employment over the long run.

G

Gains from trade. Refers to the aggregate increase in welfare accruing from voluntary exchange. Equal to the sum of consumer surplus and gains in producer profits.

Galloping inflation. See **inflation**.

Game theory. An analysis of situations involving two or more decision makers with at least partially conflicting interests. It can be applied to the interaction of oligopolistic markets as well as to bargaining situations such as strikes or to conflicts such as games and war.

General-equilibrium analysis. Analysis of the equilibrium state for the economy as a whole in which the markets for all goods and services are simultaneously in equilibrium. By contrast, **partial-equilibrium analysis** concerns the equilibrium in a single market.

GDP deflator. The "price" of GDP, that is, the price index that measures the average price of the components in GDP relative to a base year.

GDP gap. The difference or gap between potential GDP and actual GDP.

GNP. See **gross national product**.

Gold standard. A system under which a nation (1) declares its currency unit to be equivalent to some fixed weight of gold, (2) holds gold reserves and will buy or sell gold freely at the price so proclaimed, and (3) puts no restriction on the export or import of gold.

Government debt. The total of government obligations in the form of bonds and shorter-term borrowings. Government debt held by the public excludes bonds held by quasi-governmental agencies such as the central bank.

Government expenditure multiplier. The increase in GDP resulting from an increase of $1 in government purchases.

Graduated income tax. See **income tax, personal**.

Gresham's Law. A law first attributed to Sir Thomas Gresham, adviser to Queen Elizabeth I of England, who stated in 1558 that "bad money drives out good"—i.e., if the public is suspicious of one component of the money supply, it will hoard the "good money" and try to pass off the "bad money" to someone else.

Gross domestic product, nominal (or **nominal GDP**). The value, at current market prices, of the total final output produced inside a country during a given year.

Gross domestic product, real (or **real GDP**). Nominal GDP corrected for inflation, i.e., real GDP = nominal GDP divided by the GDP deflator.

Gross national product, nominal (or nominal GNP). The value, at current market prices, of all final goods and services produced during a year by the factors owned by a nation.

Gross national product, real (or real GNP). Nominal GNP corrected for inflation, i.e., real GNP = nominal GNP divided by the GNP deflator.

Growth accounting. A technique for estimating the contribution of different factors to economic growth. Using marginal productivity theory, growth accounting decomposes the growth of output into the growth in labor, land, capital, education, technical knowledge, and other miscellaneous sources.

H

Hedging. A technique for avoiding a risk by making a counteracting transaction. For example, if a farmer produces wheat that will be harvested in the fall, the risk of price fluctuations can be offset, or hedged, by selling in the spring or summer the quantity of wheat that will be produced.

High-powered money. Same as **monetary base**.

Horizontal equity vs. vertical equity. **Horizontal equity** refers to the fairness or equity in treatment of persons in similar situations; the principle of horizontal equity states that those who are essentially equal should receive equal treatment. **Vertical equity** refers to the equitable treatment of those who are in different circumstances.

Horizontal integration. See **integration, vertical vs. horizontal**.

Horizontal merger. See **merger**.

Human capital. The stock of technical knowledge and skill embodied in a nation's work force, resulting from investments in formal education and on-the-job training.

Hyperinflation. See **inflation**.

I

Imperfect competition. Refer to **competition, imperfect**.

Imperfect competitor. Any firm that buys or sells a good in large enough quantities to be able to affect the price of that good.

Implicit-cost elements. Costs that do not show up as explicit money costs but nevertheless should be counted as such (such as the labor cost of the owner of a small store). Sometimes called **opportunity cost**, although "opportunity cost" has a broader meaning.

Imports. See **exports**.

Inappropriability. See **inappropriable**.

Inappropriable. Describes resources for which the individual cost of use is free, or less than the full social costs. These resources are characterized by the presence of externalities, and thus markets will allocate their use inefficiently from a social point of view.

Incidence (or tax incidence). The ultimate economic burden of a tax (as opposed to the legal requirement for payment). Thus a sales tax may be paid by a retailer, but it is likely that the incidence falls upon the consumer. The exact incidence of a tax depends on the price elasticities of supply and demand.

Income. The flow of wages, interest payments, dividends, and other receipts accruing to an individual or nation during a period of time (usually a year).

Income effect (of a price change). Change in the quantity demanded of a commodity because the change in its price has the effect of changing a consumer's real income. Thus it supplements the **substitution effect** of a price change.

Income elasticity of demand. The demand for any given good is influenced not only by the good's price but by buyers' incomes. Income elasticity measures this responsiveness. Its precise definition is percentage change in quantity demanded divided by percentage change in income. (Compare with **price elasticity of demand**.)

Income statement. A company's statement, covering a specified time period (usually a year), showing sales or revenue earned during that period, all costs properly charged against the goods sold, and the profit (net income) remaining after deduction of such costs. Also called a **profit-and-loss statement**.

Income tax, negative. Refer to **negative income tax**.

Income tax, personal. Tax levied on the income received by individuals in the form either of wages and salaries or income from property, such as rents, dividends, or interest. In the United States, personal income tax is **graduated,** meaning that people with higher incomes pay taxes at a higher average rate than people with lower incomes.

Income velocity of money. See **velocity of money**.

Incomes policy. A government policy that attempts directly to restrict wage and price changes in an effort to slow inflation. Such policies range from voluntary wage-price guidelines to outright legal control over wages, salaries, and prices.

Increasing returns to scale. See **returns to scale**.

Independent goods. Goods whose demands are relatively separate from each other. More precisely, goods A and B are independent when a change in the price of good A has no effect on the quantity demanded of good B, other things equal.

Indexing (or indexation). A mechanism by which wages, prices, and contracts are partially or wholly adjusted to compensate for changes in the general price level.

Indifference curve. A curve drawn on a graph whose two axes measure amounts of different goods consumed. Each point on one curve (indicating different combinations of the two goods) yields exactly the same level of satisfaction for a given consumer.

Indifference map. A graph showing a family of indifference curves for a consumer. In general, curves that lie farther northeast from the graph's origin represent higher levels of satisfaction.

Indirect taxes. See **direct taxes**.

Induced variables. See exogenous vs. induced variables.

Industry. A group of firms producing similar or identical products.

Inertial rate of inflation. A process of steady inflation that occurs when inflation is expected to persist and the ongoing rate of inflation is built into contracts and people's expectations.

Infant industry. In foreign-trade theory, an industry that has not had sufficient time to develop the experience or expertise to exploit the economies of scale needed to compete successfully with more mature industries producing the same commodity in other countries. Infant industries are often thought to need tariffs or quotas to protect them while they develop.

Inferior good. A good whose consumption goes down as income rises.

Inflation (or **inflation rate**). The inflation rate is the percentage of annual increase in a general price level. **Hyperinflation** is inflation at extremely high rates (say, 1000, 1 million, or even 1 billion percent a year). **Galloping inflation** is a rate of 50 or 100 or 200 percent annually. **Moderate inflation** is a price-level rise that does not dis-

tort relative prices or incomes severely.

Inflation targeting. The announcement of official target ranges for the inflation rate along with an explicit statement that low and stable inflation is the overriding goal of monetary policy. Inflation targeting in hard or soft varieties has been adopted in recent years by many industrial countries.

Innovation. A term particularly associated with Joseph Schumpeter, who meant by it (1) the bringing to market of a new and significantly different product, (2) the introduction of a new production technique, or (3) the opening up of a new market. (Contrast with **invention**.)

Inputs. Inputs (or **factors of production**) are commodities or services used by firms in their production processes.

Insurance. A system by which individuals can reduce their exposure to risk of large losses by spreading the risks among a large number of persons.

Integration, vertical vs. horizontal. The production process is one of stages—e.g., iron ore into steel ingots, steel ingots into rolled steel sheets, rolled steel sheets into an automobile body. **Vertical integration** is the combination in a single firm of two or more different stages of this process (e.g., iron ore with steel ingots). **Horizontal integration** is the combination in a single firm of different units that operate at the same stage of production.

Intellectual property rights. Laws governing patents, copyrights, trade secrets, electronic media, and other commodities comprised primarily of information. These laws generally provide the original creator the right to control and be compensated for reproduction of the work.

Interest. The return paid to those who lend money.

Interest rate. The price paid for borrowing money for a period of time, usually expressed as a percentage of the principal per year. Thus, if the interest rate is 10 percent per year, then $100 would be paid for a loan of $1000 for 1 year.

Intermediate goods. Goods that have undergone some manufacturing or processing but have not yet reached the stage of becoming final products. For example, steel and cotton yarn are intermediate goods.

International monetary system (also **international financial system**). The institutions under which payments are made for transactions that reach across national boundaries. A central policy issue concerns the arrangement for determining how foreign exchange rates are set and how governments can affect exchange rates.

Intervention. An activity in which a government buys or sells its currency in the foreign exchange market in order to affect its currency's exchange rate.

Intrinsic value (of money). The commodity value of a piece of money (e.g., the market value of the weight of copper in a copper coin).

Invention. The creation of a new product or discovery of a new production technique. (Distinguish from **innovation**.)

Investment. (1) Economic activity that forgoes consumption today with an eye to increasing output in the future. It includes tangible capital such as houses and intangible investments such as education. Net investment is the value of total investment after an allowance has been made for depreciation. Gross investment is investment without allowance for depreciation. (2) In finance terms, investment has an altogether different meaning and denotes the purchase of a security, such as a stock or a bond.

Investment demand (or **investment demand curve**). The schedule showing the relationship between the level of investment and the cost of capital (or, more specifically, the real interest rate); also, the graph of that relationship.

Invisible hand. A concept introduced by Adam Smith in 1776 to describe the paradox of a laissez-faire market economy. The invisible-hand doctrine holds that, with each participant pursuing his or her own private interest, a market system nevertheless works to the benefit of all as though a benevolent invisible hand were directing the whole process.

Involuntarily unemployed. See **unemployment**.

Iron law of wages. In the economic theories of Malthus and Marx, the theory that there is an inevitable tendency in capitalism for wages to be driven down to a subsistence level.

Isoquant. See **equal product curve**.

K

Keynesian economics. The body of thought developed by John Maynard Keynes holding that a capitalist system does not automatically tend toward a full-employment equilibrium. According to Keynes, the resulting underemployment equilibrium could be cured by fiscal or monetary policies to raise aggregate demand.

Keynesian school. See **Keynesian economics**.

L

Labor force. In official U.S. statistics, that group of people 16 years of age and older who are either employed or unemployed.

Labor-force participation rate. Ratio of those in the labor force to the entire population 16 years of age or older.

Labor productivity. See **productivity**.

Labor supply. The number of workers (or, more generally, the number of labor-hours) available to an economy. The principal determinants of labor supply are population, real wages, and social traditions.

Labor theory of value. The view, often associated with Karl Marx, that every commodity should be valued solely according to the quantity of labor required for its production.

Laissez-faire ("Leave us alone"). The view that government should interfere as little as possible in economic activity and leave decisions to the marketplace. As expressed by classical economists like Adam Smith, this view held that the role of government should be limited to maintenance of law and order, national defense, and provision of certain public goods that private business would not undertake (e.g., public health and sanitation).

Land. In classical and neoclassical economics, one of the three basic factors of production (along with labor and capital). More generally, land is taken to include land used for agricultural or industrial purposes as well as natural resources taken from above or below the soil.

Least-cost rule (of production). The rule that the cost of producing a specific level of output is minimized when the ratio of the marginal revenue product of each input to the price of that input is the same for all inputs.

Legal tender. Money that by law must be accepted as payment for debts. All U.S. coins and currency are legal tender, but checks are not.

Less-developed country (LDC). A country with a per capita income far below that of "developed" nations (the latter usually includes most nations of North America and Western Europe).

Liabilities. In accounting, debts or financial obligations owed to other firms or persons.

Libertarianism. An economic philosophy that emphasizes the importance of personal freedom in economic and political affairs; also sometimes called "liberalism." Libertarian writers, including Adam Smith in an earlier age and Milton Friedman and James Buchanan today, hold that people should be able to follow their own interests and desires and that government activities should be limited to guaranteeing contracts and to providing police and national defense, thereby allowing maximum personal freedom.

Limited liability. The restriction of an owner's loss in a business to the amount of capital that the owner has contributed to the company. Limited liability was an important factor in the rise of large corporations. By contrast, owners in partnerships and individual proprietorships generally have **unlimited liability** for the debts of those firms.

Long run. A term used to denote a period over which full adjustment to changes can take place. In microeconomics, it denotes the time over which firms can enter or leave an industry and the capital stock can be replaced. In macroeconomics, it is often used to mean the period over which all prices, wage contracts, tax rates, and expectations can fully adjust.

Long-run aggregate supply schedule. A schedule showing the relationship between output and the price level after all price and wage adjustments have taken place, and the *AS* curve is therefore vertical.

Lorenz curve. A graph used to show the extent of inequality of income or wealth.

Lowest sustainable rate of unemployment (or *LSUR*). The lowest sustainable unemployment rate (*LSUR*) is that rate at which upward and downward forces on price and wage inflation are in balance. At the *LSUR,* inflation is stable, with no tendency to show either accelerating or declining inflation. The *LSUR* is the lowest level of unemployment that can be attained for long without upward pressure on inflation. Equivalently, it is the unemployment rate at which the long-run **Phillips curve** is vertical.

Lump-of-labor fallacy. The mistaken idea that the total amount of work to be done in a society is fixed. It is false because labor markets can adjust through wage changes or migration to accommodate changes in the supply and demand for labor.

M

M_1, M_2. See **money supply**.

Macroeconomics. Analysis dealing with the behavior of the economy as a whole with respect to output, income, the price level, foreign trade, unemployment, and other aggregate economic variables. (Contrast with **microeconomics**.)

Malthusian theory of population growth. The hypothesis, first expressed by Thomas Malthus, that the "natural" tendency of population is to grow more rapidly than the food supply. Per capita food production would thus decline over time, thereby putting a check on population. In general, a view that population tends to grow more rapidly as incomes or living standards of the population rise.

Managed exchange rate. The most prevalent exchange-rate system today. In this system, a country occasionally intervenes to stabilize its currency but there is no fixed or announced parity.

Marginal cost. Refer to **cost, marginal**.

Marginal principle. The fundamental notion that people will maximize their income or profits when the marginal costs and marginal benefits of their actions are equal.

Marginal product (*MP*). The extra output resulting from 1 extra unit of a specified input when all other inputs are held constant. Sometimes called marginal physical product.

Marginal product theory of distribution. A theory of the distribution of income proposed by John B. Clark, according to which each productive input is paid according to its **marginal product**.

Marginal propensity to consume (*MPC*). The extra amount that people consume when they receive an extra dollar of disposable income. To be distinguished from the **average propensity to consume**, which is the ratio of total consumption to total disposable income.

Marginal propensity to import (*MPm*). In macroeconomics, the increase in the dollar value of imports resulting from each dollar increase in the value of GDP.

Marginal propensity to save (*MPS*). That fraction of an additional dollar of disposable income that is saved. Note that, by definition, $MPC + MPS = 1$.

Marginal revenue (*MR*). The additional revenue a firm would earn if it sold 1 extra unit of output. In perfect competition, *MR* equals price. Under imperfect competition, *MR* is less than price because, in order to sell the extra unit, the price must be reduced on all prior units sold.

Marginal revenue product (*MRP*) (of an input). Marginal revenue multiplied by marginal product. It is the extra revenue that would be brought in if a firm were to buy 1 extra unit of an input, put it to work, and sell the extra product it produced.

Marginal tax rate. For an income tax, the percentage of the last dollar of income paid in taxes. If a tax system is progressive, the marginal tax rate is higher than the average tax rate.

Marginal utility (*MU*). The additional or extra satisfaction yielded from consuming 1 additional unit of a commodity, with amounts of all other goods consumed held constant.

Market. An arrangement whereby buyers and sellers interact to determine the prices and quantities of a commodity. Some markets (such as the stock market or a flea market) take place in physical locations; other markets are conducted over the telephone or are organized by computers, and some markets now are organized on the Internet.

Market economy. An economy in which the *what, how,* and *for whom* questions concerning resource allocation are primarily determined by supply and demand in markets. In this form of economic organization, firms, motivated by the desire to maximize profits, buy inputs and produce and sell outputs. Households, armed with their factor incomes, go to markets and determine the demand for commodities. The interaction of firms' supply and households' demand then determines the prices and quantities of goods.

Market equilibrium. Same as **competitive equilibrium**.

Market failure. An imperfection in a price system that prevents an efficient allocation of resources. Important examples are **externalities** and **imperfect competition**.

Market power. The degree of control that a firm or group of firms has over the price and production decisions in an industry. In a monopoly, the firm has a high degree of market power; firms in perfectly competitive industries have no market power. **Concentration ratios** are the most widely used measures of market power.

Market share. That fraction of an industry's output accounted for by an individual firm or group of firms.

Markup pricing. The pricing method used by many firms in situations of imperfect competition; under this method they estimate average cost and then add some fixed percentage to that cost in order to reach the price they charge.

Marxism. The set of social, political, and economic doctrines developed by Karl Marx in the nineteenth century. As an economic theory, Marxism predicted that capitalism would collapse as a result of its own internal contradictions, especially its tendency to exploit the working classes. The conviction that workers would inevitably be oppressed under capitalism was based on the **iron law of wages**, which holds that wages would decline to subsistence levels.

Mean. In statistics, the same thing as "average." Thus for the numbers 1, 3, 6, 10, 20, the mean is 8.

Median. In statistics, the figure exactly in the middle of a series of numbers ordered or ranked from lowest to highest (e.g., incomes or examination grades). Thus for the numbers 1, 3, 6, 10, 20, the median is 6.

Mercantilism. A political doctrine emphasizing the importance of balance-of-payments surpluses as a device to accumulate gold. Proponents therefore advocated tight government control of economic policies, believing that laissez-faire policies might lead to a loss of gold.

Merchandise trade balance. See **trade balance**.

Merger. The acquisition of one corporation by another, which usually occurs when one firm buys the stock of another. Important examples are (1) **vertical mergers**, which occur when the two firms are at different stages of a production process (e.g., iron ore and steel), (2) **horizontal mergers**, which occur when the two firms produce in the same market (e.g., two automobile manufacturers), and (3) **conglomerate mergers**, which occur when the two firms operate in unrelated markets (e.g., shoelaces and oil refining).

Microeconomics. Analysis dealing with the behavior of individual elements in an economy—such as the determination of the price of a single product or the behavior of a single consumer or business firm. (Contrast with **macroeconomics**.)

Minimum cost. Refer to **cost, minimum**.

Mixed economy. The dominant form of economic organization in noncommunist countries. Mixed economies rely primarily on the price system for their economic organization but use a variety of government interventions (such as taxes, spending, and regulation) to handle macroeconomic instability and market failures.

Model. A formal framework for representing the basic features of a complex system by a few central relationships. Models take the form of graphs, mathematical equations, and computer programs.

Moderate inflation. See **inflation**.

Momentary run. A period of time that is so short that production is fixed.

Monetarism. A school of thought holding that changes in the money supply are the major cause of macroeconomic fluctuations. For the short run, this view holds that changes in the money supply are the primary determinant of changes in both real output and the price level. For the longer run, this holds that prices tend to move proportionally with the money supply. Monetarists often conclude that the best macroeconomic policy is one with a stable growth in the money supply.

Monetary base. The net monetary liabilities of the government that are held by the public. In the United States, the monetary base is equal to currency and bank reserves. Sometimes called **high-powered money**.

Monetary economy. An economy in which the trade takes place through a commonly accepted medium of exchange.

Monetary policy. The objectives of the central bank in exercising its control over money, interest rates, and credit conditions. The instruments of monetary policy are primarily open-market operations, reserve requirements, and the discount rate.

Monetary rule. The cardinal tenet of monetarist economic philosophy is the monetary rule which asserts that optimal monetary policy sets the growth of money supply at a fixed rate and holds to that rate through thick and thin.

Monetary transmission mechanism. In macroeconomics, the route by which changes in the supply of money are translated into changes in output, employment, prices, and inflation.

Monetary union. An arrangement by which several nations adopt a common currency as a unit of account and medium of exchange. The European Monetary Union is scheduled to adopt the "Euro" as the common currency in 1999.

Money. The means of payment or medium of exchange. For the items constituting money, see **money supply**.

Money demand schedule. The relationship between holdings of money and interest rates. As interest rates rise, bonds and other securities become more attractive, lowering the quantity of money demanded. See also **demand for money**.

Money funds. Shorthand expression for very liquid short-term financial instruments whose interest rates are not regulated. The major examples are money market mutual funds and commercial bank money market deposit accounts.

Money market. A term denoting the set of institutions that handle the purchase or sale of short-term credit instruments like Treasury bills and commercial paper.

Money supply. The narrowly defined money supply (M_1) consists of coins, paper currency, plus all demand or checking deposits; this is narrow, or transactions, money. The broadly defined supply (M_2) includes all items in M_1 plus certain liquid assets or near-monies— savings deposits, money market funds, and the like.

Money-supply effect. The relationship whereby a price rise operating on a fixed nominal money supply produces tight money and lowers aggregate spending.

Money-supply multiplier. The ratio of the increase in the money supply (or in deposits) to the increase in bank reserves. Generally, the money-supply multiplier is equal to the inverse of the required reserve ratio. For example, if the required reserve ratio is 0.125, then the money-supply multiplier is 8.

Money, velocity of. Refer to **velocity of money**.

Monopolistic competition. A market structure in which there are many sellers who are supplying goods that are close, but not perfect, substitutes. In such a market, each firm can exercise some effect on its product's price.

Monopoly. A market structure in which a commodity is supplied by a single firm. Also see **natural monopoly**.

Monopsony. The mirror image of monopoly: a market in which there is a single buyer; a "buyer's monopoly."

Moral hazard. A type of market failure in which the presence of in-

surance against an insured risk increases the likelihood of the risky event occurring. For example, a car owner insured against auto theft may be careless about locking the car because the presence of insurance reduces the incentive to prevent the theft.

MPC. See **marginal propensity to consume**.

MPS. See **marginal propensity to save**.

Multiplier. A term in macroeconomics denoting the change in an induced variable (such as GDP or money supply) per unit of change in an external variable (such as government spending or bank reserves). The **expenditure multiplier** refers to the increase in GDP that would result from a $1 increase in expenditure (say, on investment).

Multiplier model. In macroeconomics, a theory developed by J. M. Keynes that emphasizes the importance of changes in autonomous expenditures (especially investment, government spending, and net exports) in determining changes in output and employment. Also see **multiplier**.

N

Nash equilibrium. In game theory, a set of strategies for the players where no player can improve his or her payoff given the other player's strategy. That is, given player A's strategy, player B can do no better, and given B's strategy, A can do no better. The Nash equilibrium is also sometimes called the **noncooperative equilibrium**.

National debt. Same as **government debt**.

National income and product accounts (NIPA). A set of accounts that measures the spending, income, and output of the entire nation for a quarter or a year.

National savings rate. Total saving, private and public, divided by net domestic product.

Natural monopoly. A firm or industry whose average cost per unit of production falls sharply over the entire range of its output, as for example in local electricity distribution. Thus a single firm, a monopoly, can supply the industry output more efficiently than can multiple firms.

"Near-money." Financial assets that are risk-free and so readily convertible into money that they are close to actually being money. Examples are money funds and Treasury bills.

Negative income tax. A plan for replacing current income-support programs (welfare, food stamps, etc.) with a unified program. Under such a plan, poor families would receive an income supplement and would have benefits reduced as their earnings increase.

Neoclassical model of growth. A theory or model used to explain long-term trends in economic growth of industrial economies. This model emphasizes the importance of capital deepening (i.e., a growing capital-labor ratio) and technological change in explaining the growth of potential real GDP.

Net domestic product (NDP). GDP less an allowance for depreciation of capital goods.

Net economic welfare (NEW). A measure of national output that corrects several limitations of the GDP measure.

Net exports. In the national product accounts, the value of exports of goods and services minus the value of imports of goods and services.

Net foreign investment. Net savings by a country abroad, also approximately equal to net exports.

Net investment. Gross investment minus depreciation of capital goods.

Net national product (NNP). GNP less an allowance for depreciation of capital goods.

Net worth. In accounting, total assets minus total liabilities.

New classical macroeconomics. This theory holds that (1) prices and wages are flexible and (2) people make forecasts in accordance with the rational expectations hypothesis. The main implication of this theory is the policy ineffectiveness theorem. See **rational expectations hypothesis** and **policy ineffectiveness theorem.**

NNP. See **net national product.**

Nominal GDP. See **gross domestic product, nominal.**

Nominal GNP. See **gross national product, nominal.**

Nominal (or money) interest rate. The **interest rate** paid on different assets. This represents a dollar return per year per dollar invested. Compare with the **real interest rate**, which represents the return per year in goods per unit of goods invested.

Noncooperative equilibrium. See **Nash equilibrium.**

Nonrenewable resources. Those natural resources, like oil and gas, that are essentially fixed in supply and whose regeneration is not quick enough to be economically relevant.

Normative vs. positive economics. Normative economics considers "what ought to be"—value judgments, or goals, of public policy. Positive economics, by contrast, is the analysis of facts and behavior in an economy, or "the way things are."

Not in the labor force. That part of the adult population that is neither working nor looking for work.

NOW (negotiable order of withdrawal) account. An interest-bearing checking account. See also **checking accounts.**

O

Okun's Law. The empirical relationship, discovered by Arthur Okun, between cyclical movements in GDP and unemployment. The law states that when actual GDP declines 2 percent relative to potential GDP, the unemployment rate increases by about 1 percentage point. (Earlier estimates placed the ratio at 3 to 1.)

Oligopoly. A situation of imperfect competition in which an industry is dominated by a small number of suppliers.

Open economy. An economy that engages in international trade (i.e., imports and exports) of goods and capital with other countries. A **closed economy** is one that has no imports or exports.

Open-economy multiplier. In an open economy, income leaks into imports as well as into savings. Therefore, the open-economy multiplier for investment or government expenditure is given by

$$\frac{\text{Open-economy}}{\text{multiplier}} = \frac{1}{MPS + MPm}$$

where MPS = marginal propensity to save and MPm = marginal propensity to import.

Open-market operations. The activity of a central bank in buying or selling government bonds to influence bank reserves, the money supply, and interest rates. If securities are bought, the money paid out by the central bank increases commercial-bank reserves, and the money supply increases. If securities are sold, the money supply contracts.

Opportunity cost. The value of the next best use (or opportunity) for an economic good, or the value of the sacrificed alternative. Thus, say that the best alternative use of the inputs employed to mine a ton of coal was to grow 10 bushels of wheat. The opportunity cost of a ton of coal is thus the 10 bushels of wheat that *could* have been produced but were not. Opportunity cost is particularly useful for valuing nonmarketed goods such as environmental health or safety.

Ordinal utility. A dimensionless utility measure used in demand theory. Ordinal utility enables one to state that A is preferred to B, but we cannot say by how much. That is, any two bundles of goods can be ranked relative to each other, but the absolute difference between bundles cannot be measured. This contrasts with **cardinal utility,** or dimensional utility, which is sometimes used in the analysis of behavior toward risk. An example of a cardinal measure comes when we say that a substance at 100 K (kelvin) is twice as hot as one at 50 K.

Other things constant. A phrase (sometimes stated "ceteris paribus") that signifies that a factor under consideration is changed while all other factors are held constant or unchanged. For example, a downward-sloping demand curve shows that the quantity demanded will decline as the price rises, as long as other things (such as incomes) are held constant.

Outputs. These are the various useful goods or services that are either consumed or used in further production.

P

Paradox of thrift. The principle, first proposed by John Maynard Keynes, that an attempt by a society to increase its saving may result in a reduction in the amount which it actually saves.

Paradox of value. The paradox that many necessities of life (e.g., water) have a low "market" value, while many luxuries (e.g., diamonds) with little "use" value have a high market price. It is explained by the fact that a price reflects not the total utility of a commodity but its marginal utility.

Pareto efficiency (or **Pareto optimality**).   See **allocative efficiency**.

Partial-equilibrium analysis. Analysis concentrating on the effect of changes in an individual market, holding other things equal (e.g., disregarding changes in income).

Partnership. An association of two or more persons to conduct a business which is not in corporate form and does not enjoy limited liability.

Patent. An exclusive right granted to an inventor to control the use of an invention for, in the United States, a period of 20 years. Patents create temporary monopolies as a way of rewarding inventive activity and, like other intellectual property rights, are a tool for promoting invention among individuals or small firms.

Payoff table. In game theory, a table used to describe the strategies and payoffs of a game with two or more players. The profits or utilities of the different players are the **payoffs**.

Payoffs.   See **payoff table**.

Perfect competition.   Refer to **competition, perfect**.

Personal income. A measure of income before taxes have been deducted. More precisely, it equals disposable personal income plus net taxes.

Personal saving. That part of income which is not consumed; in other words, the difference between disposable income and consumption.

Personal savings rate. The ratio of personal saving to personal disposable income, in percent.

Phillips curve. A graph first devised by A. W. Phillips, showing the tradeoff between unemployment and inflation. In modern mainstream macroeconomics, the downward-sloping "tradeoff" Phillips curve is generally held to be valid only in the short run; in the long run, the Phillips curve is usually thought to be vertical at the lowest sustainable rate of unemployment.

Policy ineffectiveness theorem. A theorem which asserts that, with rational expectations and flexible prices and wages, anticipated government monetary or fiscal policy cannot affect real output or unemployment.

Portfolio theory. An economic theory that describes how rational investors allocate their wealth among different financial asset— that is, how they put their wealth into a "portfolio."

Positive economics.   See **normative vs. positive economics**.

Post hoc **fallacy.** From the Latin, *post hoc, ergo propter hoc*, which translates as "after this, therefore because of this." This fallacy arises when it is assumed that because event A precedes event B, it follows that A *causes* B.

Potential GDP. High-employment GDP; more precisely, the maximum level of GDP that can be sustained with a given state of technology and population size without accelerating inflation. Today, it is generally taken to be equivalent to the level of output corresponding to the **lowest sustainable rate of unemployment**.

Potential output.   Same as **potential GDP**.

Poverty. Today, the U.S. government defines the "poverty line" to be the minimum adequate standard of living.

PPF.   See **production-possibility frontier**.

Present value (of an asset). Today's value for an asset that yields a stream of income over time. Valuation of such time streams of returns requires calculating the present worth of each component of the income, which is done by applying a discount rate (or interest rate) to future incomes.

Price-elastic demand (or elastic demand). The situation in which price elasticity of demand exceeds 1 in absolute value. This signifies that the percentage change in quantity demanded is greater than the percentage change in price. In addition, elastic demand implies that total revenue (price times quantity) rises when price falls because the increase in quantity demanded is so large. (Contrast with **price-inelastic demand**.)

Price elasticity of demand. A measure of the extent to which quantity demanded responds to a price change. The elasticity coefficient (price elasticity of demand E_P) is percentage change in quantity demanded divided by percentage change in price. In figuring percentages, use the averages of old and new quantities in the numerator and of old and new prices in the denominator; disregard the minus sign. Refer also to **price-elastic demand, price-inelastic demand, unit-elastic demand**.

Price elasticity of supply.   Conceptually similar to **price elasticity of demand**, except that it measures the supply responsiveness to a price change. More precisely, the price elasticity of supply measures the percentage change in quantity supplied divided by the percentage change in price. Supply elasticities are most useful in perfect competition.

Price flexibility.   Price behavior in "auction" markets (e.g., for many raw commodities or the stock market), in which prices immediately respond to changes in demand or in supply. (In contrast, refer to **administered prices**.)

Price index.   An index number that shows how the average price of a bundle of goods has changed over a period of time. In computing the average, the prices of the different goods are generally weighted by their economic importance (e.g., by each commodity's share of total consumer expenditures in the **consumer price index**).

Price-inelastic demand (or **inelastic demand**). The situation in which price elasticity of demand is below 1 in absolute value. In this case, when price declines, total revenue declines, and when price is increased, total revenue goes up. Perfectly inelastic demand means that there is no change at all in quantity demanded when price goes up or down. (Contrast with **price-elastic demand** and **unit-elastic demand**.)

Private good. See **public good**.

Producer price index. The **price index** of goods sold at the wholesale level (such as steel, wheat, oil).

Product, average. Refer to **average product**.

Product differentiation. The existence of characteristics that make similar goods less-than-perfect substitutes. Thus locational differences make similar types of gasoline sold at separate points imperfect substitutes. Firms enjoying product differentiation face a downward-sloping demand curve instead of the horizontal demand curve of the perfect competitor.

Product, marginal. Refer to **marginal product**.

Production function. A relation (or mathematical function) specifying the maximum output that can be produced with given inputs for a given level of technology. Applies to a firm or, as an aggregate production function, to the economy as a whole.

Production-possibility frontier (*PPF*). A graph showing the menu of goods that can be produced by an economy. In a frequently cited case, the choice is reduced to two goods, guns and butter. Points outside the *PPF* (to the northeast of it) are unattainable. Points inside it are inefficient since resources are not being fully employed, resources are not being used properly, or outdated production techniques are being utilized.

Productivity. A term referring to the ratio of output to inputs (total output divided by labor inputs is **labor productivity**). Productivity increases if the same quantity of inputs produces more output. Labor productivity increases because of improved technology, improvements in labor skills, or capital deepening.

Productivity growth. The rate of increase in **productivity** from one period to another. For example, if an index of labor productivity is 100 in 1990 and 101.7 in 1991, the rate of productivity growth is 1.7 percent per year for 1991 over 1990.

Productivity of capital, net. See **rate of return**.

Productivity slowdown. The sharp decline in U.S. productivity growth that occurred around 1973.

Profit. (1) In accounting terms, total revenue minus costs properly chargeable against the goods sold (see **income statement**). (2) In economic theory, the difference between sales revenue and the full opportunity cost of resources involved in producing the goods.

Profit-and-loss statement. See **income statement**.

Progressive, proportional, and regressive taxes. A progressive tax weighs more heavily upon the rich; a regressive tax does the opposite. More precisely, a tax is progressive if the average tax rate (i.e., taxes divided by income) is higher for those with higher incomes; it is a regressive tax if the average tax rate declines with higher incomes; it is a proportional tax if the average tax rate is equal at all income levels.

Property rights. Property rights define the ability of individuals or firms to own, buy, sell, and use the capital goods and other property in a market economy.

Proportional tax. See **progressive, proportional**, and **regressive taxes**.

Proprietorship, individual. A business firm owned and operated by one person.

Protectionism. Any policy adopted by a country to protect domestic industries against competition from imports (most commonly, a tariff or quota imposed on such imports).

Public choice (also **public-choice theory**). Branch of economics and political science dealing with the way that governments make choices and direct the economy. This theory differs from the theory of markets in emphasizing the influence of vote maximizing for politicians, which contrasts to profit maximizing by firms.

Public debt. See **government debt**.

Public good. A commodity whose benefits are indivisibly spread among the entire community, whether or not particular individuals desire to consume the public good. For example, a public-health measure that eradicates smallpox protects all, not just those paying for the vaccinations. To be contrasted with **private goods**, such as bread, which, if consumed by one person, cannot be consumed by another person.

Pure economic rent. See **rent, economic**.

Q

Quantity demanded. See **change in demand vs. change in quantity demanded**.

Quantity equation of exchange. A tautology, $MV \equiv PQ$, where M is the money supply, V is the income velocity of money, and PQ (price times quantity) is the money value of total output (nominal GDP). The equation must always hold exactly since V is defined as PQ/M.

Quantity supplied. See **change in supply vs. change in quantity supplied**.

Quantity theory of money. A theory of the determination of output and the overall price level holding that prices move proportionately with the money supply. A more cautious approach put forth by monetarists holds that the money supply is the most important determinant of changes in nominal GDP (see **monetarism**).

Quota. A form of import protectionism in which the total quantity of imports of a particular commodity (e.g., sugar or cars) during a given period is limited.

R

Random-walk theory (of stock market prices). See the **efficient-market theory**.

Rate of inflation. See **inflation**.

Rate of return (or return) on capital. The yield on an investment or on a capital good. Thus, an investment costing $100 and yielding $12 annually has a rate of return of 12 percent per year.

Rational-expectations hypothesis. This hypothesis holds that people make unbiased forecasts and further that people use all available information and economic theory to make these forecasts.

Rational-expectations macroeconomics. A school, led by Robert Lucas, Robert Barro, and Thomas Sargent, holding that markets clear quickly and that expectations are rational. Under these and other conditions it can be shown that predictable macroeconomic policies have no effect on real output or unemployment. Sometimes called **new classical macroeconomics**.

Real-business-cycle theory. A theory that explains business cycles purely as shifts in aggregate supply, primarily due to technological disturbances, without any reference to monetary or other demand-side forces.

Real GDP. See **gross domestic product, real**.

Real interest rate. The interest rate measured in terms of goods rather than money. It is thus equal to the money (or nominal) interest rate less the rate of inflation.

Real wages. The purchasing power of a worker's wages in terms of goods and services. It is measured by the ratio of the money wage rate to the consumer price index.

Recession. A downturn in real GDP for two or more successive quarters. See also **depression**.

Regressive tax. See **progressive, proportional**, and **regressive taxes**.

Regulation. Government laws or rules designed to control the behavior of firms. The major kinds are **economic regulation** (which affects the prices, entry, or service of a single industry, such as telephone service) and **social regulation** (which attempts to correct externalities that prevail across a number of industries, such as air or water pollution).

Renewable resources. Natural resources (like agricultural land) whose services replenish regularly and which, if properly managed, can yield useful services indefinitely.

Rent, economic (or **pure economic rent**). This term was applied to income earned from land. The total supply of land available is (with minor qualifications) fixed, and the return paid to the landowner is rent. The term is often extended to the return paid to any factor in fixed supply—i.e., to any input having a perfectly inelastic or vertical supply curve.

Required reserves. See **reserves, bank**.

Reserves, bank. That portion of deposits that a bank sets aside in the form of vault cash or non-interest-earning deposits with Federal Reserve Banks. In the United States, banks are required to hold 12 percent of checking deposits (or transactions accounts) in the form of reserves.

Reserves, international. Every nation holds at least some reserves, in such forms as gold, currencies of other nations, and special drawing rights. International reserves serve as "international money," to be used when a country encounters balance-of-payments difficulties. If a nation were prepared to allow its exchange rate to float freely, it would need minimal reserves.

Resource allocation. The manner in which an economy distributes its resources (its factors of production) among the potential uses so as to produce a particular set of final goods.

Returns to scale. The rate at which output increases when all inputs are increased proportionately. For example, if all the inputs double and output is exactly doubled, that process is said to exhibit **constant returns to scale**. If, however, output grows by less than 100 percent when all inputs are doubled, the process shows **decreasing returns to scale**; if output more than doubles, the process demonstrates **increasing returns to scale**.

Revaluation. An increase in the official foreign exchange rate of a currency. See also **devaluation**.

Risk. In financial economics, refers to the variability of the returns on an investment.

Risk averse. A person is risk averse when, faced with an uncertain situation, the displeasure from losing a given amount of income is greater than the pleasure from gaining the same amount of income.

Risk spreading. The process of taking large risks and spreading them around so that they are but small risks for a large number of people. The major form of risk spreading is **insurance**, which is a kind of gambling in reverse.

Rule of 70. A useful shortcut for approximating compound interest. A quantity that grows at r percent per year will double in about $70/r$ years.

S

Sales tax. See **excise tax vs. sales tax**.

Savings function. The schedule showing the amount of saving that households or a nation will undertake at each level of income.

Say's Law of Markets. The theory that "supply creates its own demand." J. B. Say argued in 1803 that, because total purchasing power is exactly equal to total incomes and outputs, excess demand or supply is impossible. Keynes attacked Say's Law, pointing out that an extra dollar of income need not be spent entirely (i.e., the marginal propensity to spend is not necessarily unity).

Scarcity. Scarcity is the distinguishing characteristic of an economic good. That an economic good is scarce does not mean that it is rare, but only that it is not freely available for the taking. To obtain such a good, one must either produce it or offer other economic goods in exchange.

Scarcity, law of. The principle that most things that people want are available only in limited supply (the exception being **free goods**). Thus goods are generally scarce and must somehow be rationed, whether by price or some other means.

Securities. A term used to designate a wide variety of financial assets, such as stocks, bonds, options, and notes; more precisely, the documents used to establish ownership of these assets.

Short run. A period in which not all factors can adjust fully. In microeconomics, the capital stock and other "fixed" inputs cannot be adjusted and entry is not free in the short run. In macroeconomics, prices, wage contracts, tax rates, and expectations may not fully adjust in the short run.

Short-run aggregate supply schedule. The schedule showing the relationship between output and prices in the short run wherein changes in aggregate demand can affect output. Also represented by an upward-sloping or horizontal *AS* curve.

Shutdown price (or **point**, or **rule**). In the theory of the firm, the shutdown point comes at that point where the market price is just sufficient to cover average variable cost and no more. Hence, the firm's losses per period just equal its fixed costs; it might as well shut down.

Single-tax movement. A nineteenth-century movement, originated by Henry George, holding that continued poverty in the midst of steady economic progress was attributable to the scarcity of land and the large rents flowing to landowners. The "single tax" was to be a tax on economic rent earned from landownership.

Slope. In a graph, the change in the variable on the vertical axis per unit of change in the variable on the horizontal axis. Upward-sloping lines have positive slopes, downward-sloping curves (like demand curves) have negative slopes, and horizontal lines have slopes of zero.

Social insurance. Mandatory insurance provided by government to improve social welfare by preventing the losses created by market failures such as moral hazard or adverse selection.

Social overhead capital. The essential investments on which economic development depends, particularly for sanitation and drinking water, transportation, and communications. Sometimes called "infrastructure."

Social regulation. See **regulation**.

Socialism. A political theory that holds that all (or almost all) the means of production, other than labor, should be owned by the community. This allows the return on capital to be shared more equally than under capitalism.

Speculator. Someone engaged in speculation, i.e., someone who buys (or sells) a commodity or financial asset with the aim of profiting from later selling (or buying) the item at a higher (or lower) price.

Spillovers. Same as **externalities**.

Stagflation. A term, coined in the early 1970s, describing the coexistence of high unemployment, or *stag*nation, with persistent in*flation*. Its explanation lies primarily in the inertial nature of the inflationary process.

Statistical discrimination. Treatment of individuals on the basis of the average behavior or characteristics of members of the group to which they belong. Statistical discrimination can be self-fulfilling by reducing incentives for individuals to overcome the stereotype.

Stock, common. Refer to **common stock**.

Stock market. An organized marketplace in which common stocks are traded. In the United States, the largest stock market is the New York Stock Exchange, on which are traded the stocks of the largest U.S. companies.

Stock vs. flow. See **flow vs. stock**.

Strategic interaction. A situation in oligopolistic markets in which each firm's business strategies depend upon its rivals' plans. A formal analysis of strategic interaction is given in **game theory**.

Structural budget. See **actual, cyclical**, and **structural budget**.

Structural unemployment. Unemployment resulting because the regional or occupational pattern of job vacancies does not match the pattern of worker availability. There may be jobs available, but unemployed workers may not have the required skill; or the jobs may be in different regions from where the unemployed workers live.

Subsidy. A payment by a government to a firm or household that provides or consumes a commodity. For example, governments often subsidize food by paying for part of the food expenditures of low-income households.

Substitutes. Goods that compete with each other (as with gloves and mittens). By contrast, goods that go together in the eyes of consumers (such as left shoes and right shoes) are **complements**.

Substitution effect (of a price change). The tendency of consumers is to consume more of a good when its relative price falls (to "substitute" in favor of that good) and to consume less of the good when its relative price increases (to "substitute" away from that good). This substitution effect of a price change leads to a downward-sloping demand curve. (Compare with **income effect**.)

Substitution rule. This asserts that if the price of one factor falls while all other factor prices remain the same, firms will profit by substituting the now-cheaper factor for all the other factors. The rule is a corollary of the **least-cost rule**.

Supply curve (or **supply schedule**). A schedule showing the quantity of a good that suppliers in a given market desire to sell at each price, holding other things equal.

Supply shock. In macroeconomics, a sudden change in production costs or productivity that has a large and unexpected impact upon aggregate supply. As a result of a supply shock, real GNP and the price level change unexpectedly.

Supply-side economics. A view emphasizing policy measures to affect aggregate supply or potential output. This approach holds that high marginal tax rates on labor and capital incomes reduce work effort and saving.

T

Tariff. A levy or tax imposed upon each unit of a commodity imported into a country.

Tax incidence. See **incidence**.

Technological change. A change in the process of production or introduction of new products such that more or improved output can be obtained from the same bundle of inputs. It results in an outward shift in the production-possibility curve.

Technological progress. See **technological change**.

Terms of trade (in international trade). The "real" terms at which a nation sells its export products and buys its import products. It equals the ratio of an index of export prices to an index of import prices.

Theory of income distribution. A theory explaining the manner in which personal income and wealth are distributed in a society.

Tight-money policy. A central-bank policy of restraining or reducing the money supply and of raising interest rates. This policy has the effect of slowing the growth of real GDP, reducing the rate of inflation, or raising the nation's foreign exchange rate. (Contrast with **easy-money policy**.)

Time deposit. Funds, held in a bank, that have a minimum "time of withdrawal." Included in broad money (M_2) but not in M_1 because they are not accepted as a means of payment.

Token money. Money with little or no intrinsic value.

Total cost. Refer to **cost, total**.

Total factor productivity. An index of productivity that measures total output per unit of total input. The numerator of the index is total output (say, GDP), while the denominator is a weighted average of inputs of capital, labor, and resources. The growth of total factor productivity is often taken as an index of the rate of technological progress.

Total product (or **output**). The total amount of a commodity pro-

duced, measured in physical units such as bushels of wheat, tons of steel, or number of haircuts.

Total revenue. Price times quantity, or total sales.

Trade balance or **merchandise trade balance.** See **balance of trade**.

Trade barrier. Any of a number of protectionist devices by which nations discourage imports. Tariffs and quotas are the most visible barriers, but in recent years nontariff barriers (or NTBs), such as burdensome regulatory proceedings, have replaced more traditional measures.

Transactions demand for money. See **demand for money**.

Transactions money. A measure of money supply (also known as M_1) which consists of items that are actually for transactions, namely, currency and checking accounts.

Transfer payments, government. Payments made by a government to individuals, for which the individual performs no current service in return. Examples are social security payments and unemployment insurance.

Treasury bills (T-bills). Short-term bonds or securities issued by the federal government.

U

Underground economy. Unreported economic activity. The underground economy includes otherwise legal activities not reported to the taxing authorities (such as garage sales or services "bartered" among friends) and illegal activities (such as the drug trade, gambling, and prostitution).

Unemployed. People who are not employed but are actively looking for work or waiting to return to work.

Unemployment. (1) In economic terms, **involuntary unemployment** occurs if there are qualified workers who would be willing to work at prevailing wages but cannot find jobs. (2) In the official (U.S. Bureau of Labor Statistics) definition, a worker is unemployed if he or she (*a*) is not working and (*b*) either is waiting for recall from layoff or has actively looked for work in the last 4 weeks.

Unemployment, frictional. Refer to **frictional unemployment**.

Unemployment rate. The percentage of the labor force that is unemployed.

Unit-elastic demand. The situation, between **price-elastic demand** and **price-inelastic demand**, in which price elasticity is just equal to 1 in absolute value. See also **price elasticity of demand**.

Unlimited liability. See **limited liability**.

Usury. The charging of an interest rate above a legal maximum on borrowed money.

Utility (also **total utility**). The total satisfaction derived from the consumption of goods or services. To be contrasted with **marginal utility**, which is the additional utility arising from consumption of an additional unit of the commodity.

Utility-possibility frontier. Analogous to the **production-possibility frontier**; a graph showing the utility or satisfaction of two consumers (or groups), one on each axis. It is downward-sloping to indicate that redistributing income from A to B will lower the utility of A and raise that of B. Points on the utility-possibility frontier display **allocative** (or **Pareto**) **efficiency**. For Pareto- efficient allocations, it is impossible to find feasible outcomes that would make one person better off without making someone else worse off.

V

Value added. The difference between the value of goods produced and the cost of materials and supplies used in producing them. In a $1 loaf of bread embodying $0.60 worth of wheat and other materials, the value added is $0.40. Value added consists of the wages, interest, and profit components added to the output by a firm or industry.

Value-added tax (or **VAT**). A tax levied upon a firm as a percentage of its value added.

Value, paradox of. Refer to **paradox of value**.

Variable. A magnitude of interest that can be defined and measured. Important variables in economics include prices, quantities, interest rates, exchange rates, dollars of wealth, and so forth.

Variable cost. Refer to **cost, variable**.

Velocity of money. In serving its function as a medium of exchange, money moves from buyer to seller to new buyer and so on. Its "velocity" refers to the "speed" of this movement. The **income velocity of money** is defined as nominal GNP divided by the total money supply $V \equiv P \times Q/M \equiv GNP/M$.

Vertical equity. See **horizontal equity vs. vertical equity**.

Vertical integration. See **integration, vertical vs. horizontal**.

Vertical merger. See **merger**.

Voluntarily unemployed. Describes an individual who is unemployed because she perceives the value of wages to be less than the opportunity use of time, say in leisure.

W

Wealth. The net value of tangible and financial items owned by a nation or person at a point of time. It equals all assets less all liabilities.

Welfare economics. The normative analysis of economic systems, i.e., the study of what is "wrong" or "right" about the economy's functioning.

Welfare state. A concept of the mixed economy arising in Europe in the late nineteenth century and introduced in the United States in the 1930s. In the modern conception of the welfare state, markets direct the detailed activities of day to day economic life while governments regulate social conditions and provide pensions, health care, and other aspects of the social safety net.

What, how, and *for whom*. The three fundamental problems of economic organization. *What* is the problem of how much of each possible good and service will be produced with the society's limited stock of resources or inputs. *How* is the choice of the particular technique by which each good of the what shall be produced. *For whom* refers to the distribution of consumption goods among the members of that society.

Winner-take-all games. Situations in which payoffs are determined by merit relative to other competitors/players rather than by absolute merit. These contests generally are characterized by rewards heavily or entirely concentrated among the very best competitors.

Y

Yield. Same as the **interest rate** or **rate of return** on an asset.

Z

Zero-profit point. For a business firm, that level of price at which the firm breaks even, covering all costs but earning zero profit.

INDEX

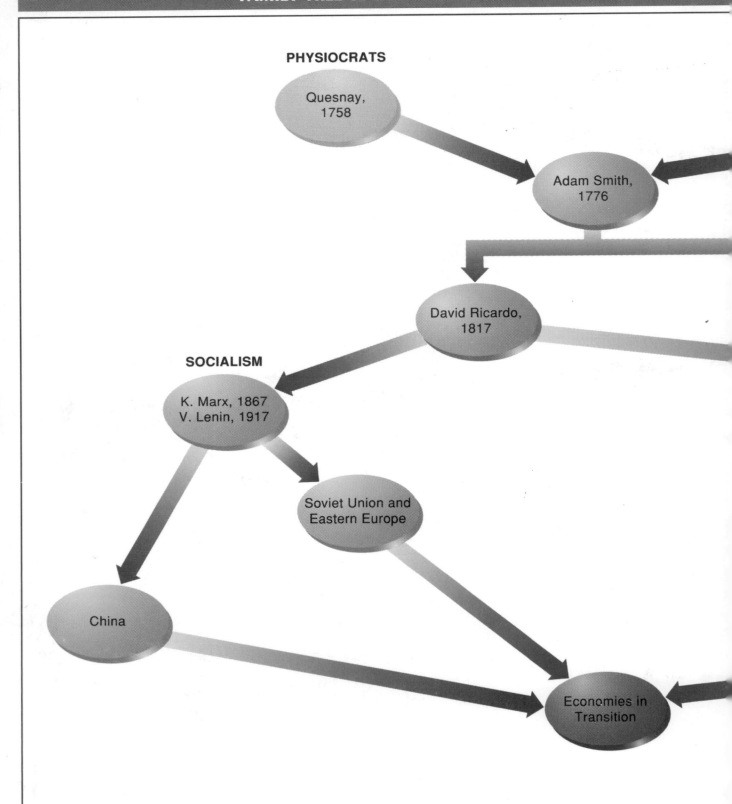